THE STORYTELLER'S THESAURUS

FANTASY, HISTORY, AND HORROR

Printed in the United States by Chenault & Gray Publishing.

First Unabridged Edition
Edited by Tim Burns

Cover Design by Peter Bradley
Cover Art by Peter Bradley

Library of Congress Cataloging-in-Publication Data

Ward, James M., 1951-
Brown, Anne, 1962-

Storyteller's Thesaurus

ISBN 978-1-936822-35-5

Library of Congress Control Number: 2014956060

THE STORYTELLER'S THESAURUS

FANTASY, HISTORY, AND HORROR

JAMES M. WARD AND ANNE K. BROWN

Cover by: Peter Bradley

Chenault & Gray Publishing
1818 North Taylor, #143
Little Rock, AR 72207
www.chenaultandgraypublishing.com
Email:troll@trolllord.com

Printed in U.S.A

TABLE OF CONTENTS

INTRODUCTION 11
WHAT MAKES THIS BOOK DIFFERENT 11
THE STORYTELLER'S RESPONSIBILITY: RESEARCH 12
WHAT THIS BOOK DOES NOT CONTAIN 12
A WHISPER OF ENCOURAGEMENT 13
CHAPTER 1: CHARACTER BUILDING 14
GENDER 14
AGE 14
PHYSICAL ATTRIBUTES 14
SIZE AND BODY TYPE 14
FACIAL FEATURES 15
HAIR 16
SPECIES 16
PERSONALITY 17
PHOBIAS 18
OCCUPATIONS 20
ADVENTURERS 20
CIVILIANS 21
ORGANIZATIONS 24
CHAPTER 2: CLOTHING 25
STYLES OF DRESS 25
CLOTHING PIECES 25
CLOTHING CONSTRUCTION 27
CHAPTER 3: ARCHITECTURE AND PROPERTY 28
ARCHITECTURAL STYLES AND ELEMENTS 28
BUILDING MATERIALS 29
PROPERTY TYPES 29
SPECIALTY ANATOMY 32
CHAPTER 4: FURNISHINGS 33
CHAPTER 5: EQUIPMENT AND TOOLS 34
ADVENTURER'S GEAR 34
GENERAL EQUIPMENT AND TOOLS 34
KITCHEN EQUIPMENT 38
LINENS 39
MUSICAL INSTRUMENTS 40

TOOLS 40
FARM EQUIPMENT 41
CHAPTER 6: FOOD 42
BAKERY 42
BREAD 42
SWEET BAKERY 42
CANDY 43
DAIRY 43
DRY GOODS/PANTRY 44
EGGS 45
FISH/SEAFOOD 45
FRUIT 45
MEAT 46
POULTRY 47
SALAD, SANDWICH, SOUP, SNACKS 47
VEGETABLES 47
BEVERAGES 48
ALCOHOLIC 48
NONALCHOHOLIC 48
CHAPTER 7: COMBAT, ARMOR, AND WEAPONS 49
COMBAT VOCABULARY 49
FENCING 50
PRE-1900 GEAR AND WEAPONS 50
ARMOR 50
SHIELDS 50
WEAPONS 50
POST-1900 GEAR AND WEAPONS 52
WEAPONS 53
SPECIAL WEAPONS AND TACTICS 53
HANDGUNS/PISTOLS 53
REVOLVERS 53
RIFLES 54
Centerfire Rifles 54
Rimfire Rifles 54
Sniper Rifles 54
SHOTGUNS 54

CHAPTER 8: MILITARY 55
RANKS 55
AIR AND WATER CRAFT 56
GROUND VEHICLES 57
WEAPONS 60
U.S. ARMY 60
U.S. AIR FORCE 60
CHAPTER 9: TRANSPORTATION 61
GENERAL VOCABULARY 61
INFRASTRUCTURE 61
GROUND TRANSPORTATION 62
AIR TRANSPORTATION 62
WATER TRANSPORTATION 62
TRANSPORTATION 63
CHAPTER 10: GEOLOGY, GEOGRAPHY, METEOROLOGY, AND BOTANY 64
GEOLOGY 64
ROCKS AND MINERALS 65
GEOLOGIC TIME 67
SOIL 69
GEOGRAPHY 70
LANDFORMS 71
MAN-MADE BOUNDARIES 71
METEOROLOGY 71
BOTANY 73
FUNGUS 73
HERBACEOUS PLANTS 73
WOODY PLANTS 77
TREES 77
CHAPTER 11: ASTRONOMY AND CHEMISTRY 80
ASTRONOMY 80
STAR NAMES 82
PLANETS AND MOONS 84
CHEMISTRY 85
ELEMENTS 86
POISONS 86
CHAPTER 12: ANATOMY AND PHYSIOLOGY 88
ANATOMY 88

AILMENTS 88
ANATOMY AND PHYSIOLOGY 89
CHAPTER 13: THE ARTS 90
DANCE 90
MUSIC 91
THEATER 91
THE ARTS 91
VISUAL ART 92
CHAPTER 14: PHILOSOPHY AND RELIGION 93
PHILOSOPHY 93
RELIGION 93
MAJOR RELIGIOUS BOOKS 95
BOOKS OF THE BIBLE 95
GODS AND PANTHEONS 95
CHAPTER 15: ANIMALS AND CREATURES 97
ANIMAL HOMES 97
AMPHIBIANS 97
BIRDS 97
FISH 98
MAMMALS 99
INSECTS, BUGS, AND SPIDERS 102
REPTILES 104
SNAKES 105
CHAPTER 16: MONSTERS 106
MONSTER LAIRS AND LOCATIONS 108
CHAPTER 17: MAGIC 110
MAGIC VOCABULARY 110
MAGICAL TRANSPORTATION 110
MAGICAL OBJECTS AND SPELLS 110
CLASSIC MAGICAL OBJECTS 111
DESIGNING MAGICAL OBJECTS 111
DESIGNING SPELLS 111
LIST OF POSSIBLE MAGICAL EFFECTS 112
WITCHCRAFT 117
CHAPTER 18: LEGENDARY, MYSTERIOUS, AND MYTHICAL ITEMS AND LOCATIONS 118

LEGENDARY/MYTHICAL LOCATIONS 118
LEGENDARY CHARACTERS 119
ARTHURIAN LEGEND 119
LEGENDARY/MYTHICAL OBJECTS 120
SECRET/MYSTICAL ORGANIZATIONS 122
NOTEWORTHY EVENTS 122
CHAPTER 19 — SYMBOLOGY & SYMBOLIC OBJECTS AND PLACES 123
CLASSIC HERALDRY 123
POSTURE 123
SYMBOLIC ITEMS 124
HOLIDAYS 125
COLLECTIVE SYMBOLS 126
DIVINATION AND FORTUNE TELLING 127
PALM READING 127
TAROT CARDS 127
SUPERSTITIONS 127
CHAPTER 20: DESCRIPTIVE TERMS 130
ADJECTIVES 130
COLORS 132
EXPLETIVES 132
EMOTIONS 133
NOUNS 134
VERBS 134
CHAPTER 21 — STORY ELEMENTS AND TREASURE 136
PARANORMAL THEMES AND CONCEPTS 136
WESTERN THEMES 136
TREASURE 137
STORY ELEMENTS AND TREASURE 137
GEMS AND JEWELRY 138
CHAPTER 22 — SCIENCE FICTION 139
LITERARY CLASSIFICATIONS 139
GEAR AND VEHICLES 140
SPACESHIPS 140
CHAPTER 23: HORROR 141
LITERARY CLASSIFICATIONS 141

GENERAL CONCEPTS 143
CHAPTER 24: FANTASY 144
LITERARY CLASSIFICATIONS 144
GENERAL CONCEPTS 144
APPENDIX A: COMMONLY CONFUSED WORDS 145
APPENDIX B: PROVERBS 147
ALPHABETICAL INDEX 152
– NUMERIC – 152
–A– 153
–B– 178
–C– 210
–D– 252
–E– 271
–F– 284
–G– 304
–H– 321
–I– 338
–J– 346
–K– 350
–L– 356
–M– 371
–N– 396
–O– 404
–P– 413
–Q– 441
–R– 443
–S– 459
–T– 504
–U– 526
–V– 531
–W– 536
–X– 549
–Y– 550
–Z– 552

INTRODUCTION

According to some sources, the word thesaurus is synonymous with treasury. That definition is especially fitting for this book, which departs from the typical alphabetical thesaurus with its closely-linked synonyms, and instead provides groups of words for storytellers who are groping for just the right idea. This book is less about technical accuracy and etymology and more about helping authors to craft a setting, envision a character, or unfold a scene.

Every author reaches a point in a writing project (usually at about 66,000 words of a 100,000 word manuscript) at which she'd like to conjure up an out-of-control city bus to careen down a forest path, flatten her group of fantasy heroes, describe their gelatinous remains, and gleefully write the words "The End." This book is for moments like that.

This book is also for those moments when everything sounds like a cliché, when every fantasy story contains a hooded stranger in a tavern, and when all the villains and monsters in all types of fiction suddenly sound like two-dimensional cardboard rip-offs of the mustached bad guys tying young damsels to railroad tracks in black-and-white melodramas. This book is for those moments when nothing appearing on the computer screen sounds any good. This book is about inspiration.

We rarely know where inspiration comes from, so without a roadmap or a clearly defined formula, this book might be the next best thing. It is designed to trigger ideas, to link concepts not normally linked, and to familiarize authors with places and things outside their daily lives. It is also meant to remind us of interesting things we don't think about very often. This book might remind an author of Grandma's rhubarb pie and inspire a character with a passion for rhubarb; it might help an author in a warm climate write about snow; and it might suggest an unusual hobby or phobia that subtly motivates an emerging hero. By using a mix-and-match selection throughout this book, endless combinations are possible for settings and characters, such as the nephew of an archbishop who works as a gymnastics coach, wears suspenders, and collects antique hat pins. This book is designed to offer a multitude of choices to solve a multitude of writing problems.

WHAT MAKES THIS BOOK DIFFERENT

The first thing to notice about this thesaurus is that it is arranged by subject, not alphabet. It is designed by storytellers for storytellers. When trying to picture a rural scene, it isn't helpful to see the entries for forest followed by the entries forget, fork, and formal. It's much more useful to find entries for terrain features, rocks, trees, plants, and weather all in one chapter. While browsing for forest features, other woodland details will become apparent to add depth to the scene.

The next thing to notice is that this book isn't about exact synonyms, but about groups of words that make sense together. Sometimes authors envision a scene but their minds just can't fill in the details. Maybe it's one of those days when we have to fight for every word, or maybe the topic is something that just isn't familiar. Imagine writing a scene about a character who is a seamstress, for example. For anyone who has never taken a sewing class, it's foreign territory. Even for an author with a fairly good working knowledge of sewing, this can be a challenge. What types of fabrics and doodads and implements will surround the seamstress? A visit to the section about clothing construction in Chapter 2 will provide several pages of terms that might be useful in describing the work of our seamstress. In a standard thesaurus, a visit to the word seamstress will likely turn up only similar occupations such as tailor, and offer little in the way of sewing terminology. Thus, this book is designed to offer numerous choices to authors so they can effectively design a character or location.

Another goal of this book is to function as a reverse dictionary. Perhaps an author just can't recall a particular word and doesn't know where to start in a standard dictionary. By turning to the section on Garment Pieces, for example, he might be nudged into recalling that the name of the odd stand-up collar popular on jackets during the 1970s was the Nehru collar. Likewise, he might wonder what a French cuff looks like and research it to discover that it is the type of cuff that requires cuff links—just the thing for the spoiled dilettante he is creating.

THE STORYTELLER'S RESPONSIBILITY: RESEARCH

Like any treasury, some things will be familiar and some will not. For unfamiliar items, research is essential in order to incorporate new objects and ideas correctly. A fiction story from a slush pile many years ago comes to mind that illustrates the pitfalls of research. This story was filled with details of a Persian setting, and the author did a nice job of establishing the flavor of the environment. But the scene fell apart when a character took a bite from a pomegranate. The author had researched his setting well enough to understand that pomegranates were native to the region he was describing, but he had not gone far enough to understand that no one would take a bite from a pomegranate. The leathery skin and thick pith surrounding the juicy, edible seeds would make that almost impossible, not to mention messy. (This was in the days before the internet and before the pomegranate health-food craze.) Authors owe it to their work to make their word choices carefully and select words that fit well.

Research goes beyond understanding what an item looks like, feels like, and tastes like. It also means researching the way an item fits into society, the time period, and the geography. It means being mindful of a number of circumstances.

SOCIETY: We all know that social norms dictate a great deal about language, dress, manners, and customs. When considering unfamiliar terms, bear in mind that different occasions require different conventions, and some words vary in acceptability in different regions or countries. The word fanny, for example, is acceptable in polite company in the United States, but in parts of England, it refers not to the back of a girl, but the front of a girl, and its mention in certain situations may raise eyebrows. A few extra minutes of research can help avoid such stickiness.

TIME PERIODS: Characters in the late 1970s did not spend an evening at home with a movie rental (video stores did not exist yet), and doctors treating patients sick with the plague in the middle ages did not wash their hands (the communication of diseases was not understood). All kinds of styles and fads come and go, and in order to be authentic, authors need to immerse themselves in their time periods. Likewise, language changes over time as phrases gain and lose popularity, and can effectively enhance a setting or show a reader that the author has not done his homework.

GEOGRAPHY AND CLIMATE: We all know that trees don't grow in Antarctica, and most people probably know that palm trees don't grow in Wisconsin. But it's less obvious that very few azalea bushes grow in Wisconsin, armadillos do not live in Minnesota, and grass lawns are not the norm in Arizona. Likewise, the peaks of the Rocky Mountains are not covered in trees due to the high altitude. Some research is needed to put things in their proper places and make a setting realistic. And while it might be tempting to fill a garden scene with crocuses, clematis, and chrysanthemums, it will show that the author didn't do her research. Crocuses bloom in early spring, clematis blooms in summer, and chrysanthemums bloom in autumn. Even in a fantasy setting, readers expect a certain consistency that makes sense.

FORM AND FUNCTION: Just like the pomegranate example, it's important to understand concepts that are unfamiliar. An author who selects a halberd as a character's weapon first needs to realize that a halberd is a broad blade on a long pole. The author had better not write about a character slipping a halberd into his boot, and such a weapon will influence the character's fighting style. Because a halberd is difficult to conceal, it may pose problems in tight quarters or draw attention. Authors need to consider the long-term big picture when selecting armor, weapons, equipment, occupations, character traits, and so on.

NUANCE OF LANGUAGE: Because the categories in this book are broad, many words listed for a category are not exact synonyms and are instead cousins, stepchildren, or friends of the family of those words. The entry for easy, for example, contains the words painless and tranquil. A chemistry exam might be described as painless or a fisherman's mood might be described as tranquil, but the words are not interchangeable. It's important for authors to understand the words they choose and ensure that they convey the proper intent.

WHAT THIS BOOK DOES NOT CONTAIN

INTELLECTUAL PROPERTY: Storytellers must always be mindful of the property of other storytellers. Writing about a school of magic might be okay, but it's not okay to use terms from movies, television,

fiction, or other copyrighted sources. Those concepts are owned by their authors, publishers, producers, and movie studios. In this thesaurus, every effort was made to omit ideas that are intellectual property; to do otherwise could give the impression that use of those ideas is freely accessible.

Public domain material, however, is incorporated throughout this book. Public domain works are those publications whose copyrights have expired (or never existed), making them fair game for storytellers. The concept of a basilisk, for example, originates in classical mythology; it is not owned by anyone and it is free to use. In general, works printed in the United States prior to 1923 are considered public domain, but for works more recent than 1923, the rules vary greatly. Copyright law varies from country to country as well, and exceptions do exist, so careful research is recommended before incorporating material that might be under copyright.

CURSE WORDS AND INAPPROPRIATE LANGUAGE: Vulgarities and curse words are not included in this thesaurus. Such words should be chosen carefully and with purpose, and they were not included in this book so as not to give the illusion of an endorsement.

Likewise, gender and racial slurs are also omitted. These words need to be selected with a purpose in mind and with consideration of the time period in which they are used. Such terms should be incorporated only after serious and thoughtful deliberation, and should serve a purpose, make social commentary, or illustrate certain traits about a character.

A WHISPER OF ENCOURAGEMENT

As storytellers, we face many pitfalls—writer's block, stale prose, clichés, cardboard characters, repetition, and our own personal writing flaws. Our hope is that during those times when the muses of legend are not whispering brilliant prose into our ears, this book will serve as a dependable substitute for those fickle muses. We hope it provides inspiration and motivation in order to reduce the storyteller's perspiration.

CHAPTER 1: CHARACTER BUILDING

GENDER

MALE: bachelor, boy, boy child, boyfriend, brother, brother-in-law, chap, dad, dada, daddy, dude, father, father-in-law, fellow, fiancé, gent, gentleman, granddad, grandfather, grandpa, grandson, great grandfather, great grandson, great uncle, guy, half-brother, hubby, husband, lad, man, master, mister, nephew, pa, papa, patriarch, pop, son, son-in-law, stepbrother, stepfather, stepson, stripling, uncle, widower, Y chromosome, young man

FEMALE: aunt, babe, bachelorette, black widow, chick, consort, dame, damsel, daughter, daughter-in-law, doll, fiancée, girl, girlfriend, granddaughter, grandma, grandmother, great aunt, great granddaughter, great grandmother, half-sister, lady, lady love, lass, lassie, little lady, ma, maid, maiden, mama, matriarch, matron, minx, miss, missy, mistress, mom, mommy, mother, mother-in-law, Mrs., nana, niece, paramour, schoolgirl, sister, sister-in-law, stepdaughter, stepmother, stepsister, wench, widow, wife, woman, X chromosome, young lady

RELATIONAL: affianced, ancestor, betrothed, child, cousin, cousin once removed, cousin twice removed, descendant, forebear, friend, grandchild, grandparent, kin, kinsman, kith, offspring, parent, predecessor, progeny, relative, scion, second cousin, sibling, significant other, spouse, successor, third cousin

TERMS OF ENDEARMENT: adore, beloved, better half, cherished, darling, dear, dearest, fancy, favorite, honey, love, lover, pet, precious, prized, sweet, sweetheart, sweetie, sweetie pie, treasure

AGE

CHILD: adolescent, babe, babe-in-arms, baby, foundling, infant, junior, juvenile, kid, kindergartener, minor, munchkin, newborn, nipper, orphan, preschooler, prodigy, ragamuffin, rug rat, shaver, sophomoric, teen, teenager, toddler, tot, tyke, underage, urchin, waif, wunderkind, youngster, youth

ADULT: grown, grown-up, middle-aged, mature

ELDERLY: advanced, aged, ancient, antiquarian, archaic, biddy, blue-haired, centenarian, chronologically advanced, codger, crone, doddering, dotage, dowager, elder, experienced, geriatric, hoary, long in the tooth, Methuselah, nonagenarian, octogenarian, old, old as the hills, old coot, older than dirt, old fart, oldster, old-timer, one foot in the grave, revered, senior, senior citizen, septuagenarian, silver-haired, venerable, vintage, wizened; See also Old in the chapter Descriptive Terms

PHYSICAL ATTRIBUTES

SIZE AND BODY TYPE

LARGE/HEAVY: abundant, Amazon, ample, beefy, big, blubbery, bulky, burly, brawny, broad, chubby, chunky, colossal, corpulent, curvaceous, curvy, doughy, dumpy, endomorph, enormous, fat, fleshy, gargantuan, giant, giantlike, gigantic, gigantism, great, heavy set, hefty, heroic, heroic proportions, huge, hulky, husky, immense, imposing, long-limbed, lumpy, massive, mesomorph, mighty, monstrous, muscular, muscle-bound, obese, overweight, paunchy, plump, ponderous, portly, pot bellied, powerful, pudgy, rangy, robust, rotund, significant, sizeable, solid, stout, strapping, strong, substantial, tall, thickset, towering, vast, vital, well fed, well padded, wide; See also the chapter Descriptive Terms

SMALL/THIN: angular, anorexic, bare-boned, beanpole, bony, cadaverous, childlike, delicate, diminutive, dwarfish, dwarfism, ectomorph, elfin, emaciated, fine, fine spun, flimsy, fragile, frail, gangling, gangly, gaunt, gawky, half-pint, insubstantial, insufficient, lanky, lean, little, midget, mini, miniature, narrow, petite, pixie, pygmy, scrawny, short, shrimp, shrimpy, skeletal, skin and bones, skinny, slender, slight, slim, spare, spindly, squat, stringbean, stubby, thin, tiny, teensy, trim, undernourished, undersize, underweight, weak, weakling, wimp; See also the chapter Descriptive Terms

MOBILITY: active, agile, alert, alive, animated, athletic, awkward, brisk, busy, clumsy, dexterous, dynamic, efficient, energetic, exegetic, expeditious, fleet, flexible, graceful, hasty, heavy, hurried, inactive, indefatigable, indolent, labored, lethargic, limber, limping, lissome, lithe, lively, nimble, on-the-go, ponderous, plodding, quick, rapid, sedentary, shuffling, slow, sluggish, speedy, sprightly, spry, stiff, supple, swift, torpid, vigorous

FACIAL FEATURES

CHEEKS: apple-cheeked, chubby, fat, full, high cheekbones, hollow, round, rounded, sunken

CHIN: bearded, chinless, cleft, double, lantern, pointed, prognathous, prominent, rounded, smooth, square, strong, triple, uneven

EARS: attached lobes, detached lobes, elongated, deep, flabby, flappy, flat, large, long, pierced, plugged, pointed, round, short, small

EYEBROWS: abundant, arched, bushy, curving, narrow, penciled, plucked, pointed, shaggy, slanted, sparse, straight, thick, thin, unibrow, unkempt, wild

EYE COLOR: amber, blue, black, brown, gold-flecked, gray, green, hazel, lavender, pink, violet

EYE TYPE: beady, bleary-eyed, blind, blinking, bloodshot, cataracts, close-set, color blind, cyclopean, dark circles, deep-set, farsighted, legally blind, multiple-eyed, nearsighted, one-eyed, shifty, slanted, sleepy, squinty, two-eyed, watery

FACE: diamond, heart-shaped, inverted triangle, large, oblong, oval, rectangular, round, small, square, triangle

FACIAL HAIR, BEARD: Amish, balbo, beaver, bewhiskered, bristly, bushy, chin curtain, chin fuzz, chinstrap, chin strip, clean shaven, dundrearies, extended goatee, five o'clock shadow, friendly muttonchops, full, goatee, imperial, lemmy, long, muttonchops, neckbeard, peach fuzz, royale, Santa Claus, scraggly, Shenandoah, short, sideburns, sideboards, smooth shaven, soul patch, stashburns, stubble, thin, unshaven, van dyke, Verdi, whiskers, Wild Bill Hickok

FACIAL HAIR, MUSTACHE: bushy, Charlie Chaplan, chevron, cowboy, Dali, devil, Einstein, English, Errol Flynn, Fu Manchu, handlebar, Hitler, horseshoe, imperial, lampshade, painter's brush, pencil, petit handlebar, prospector, pyramid, toothbrush, walrus

FOREHEAD: bulging, five-finger, high, low, Neanderthal, prominent, receding hairline, widow's peak

LIPS: cracked, cupid's bow, dry, full, luscious, moist, narrow, pursed, ruby red, scaly, smooth, thin, thin-lipped, tight-lipped, voluptuous

MOUTH: chops, ear-to-ear smile, jaws, maw, narrow, pie hole, round, small, trap, wide, yap

NOSE: aquiline, beak, bent, broken, button, cauliflower, crooked, flat, hooked, hooter, muzzle, pointy, prominent, pug, Roman, round, schnoz, schnozzle, short, snoot, snout, stubby

SKIN TYPES AND FEATURES: albino, ashy, bald, birthmark, black, brown, caramel, cracked, creamy, dry, flushed, freckles, fuzzy, hairless, hairy, ivory, mole, mottled, pockmarked, porcelain, peach, peaches-and-cream, port wine stain, psoriasis, ruddy, sallow, sanguine, scaly, scarred, scarified, smooth, warty, white

TEETH: adult, baby, broken, brown, buck-toothed, chipped, choppers, clean, cracked, crooked, decayed, deciduous, discolored, even, fangs, horsey, large, long, milk teeth, missing, pearly, pearly whites, permanent, pointy, rotten, shiny, small, stained, white, yellowed

TEETH, DENTAL WORK: bands, braces, bridge, bridgework, crown, dental implants, dentures, extraction, false teeth, filling, head gear, implants, partial plate, plate, retainer, root canal, rubber bands, spacers, veneers, wire

VOCAL/SPEECH QUALITY: accented, affected, anxious, artificial, authoritative, bleating, booming, breathy, bright, brittle, broad, caterwauling, childlike, cold, computer generated, creaky, croaky, dark, dead, deep, disembodied, dramatic, drawl, dulcet, dull, dynamic, edgy, falsetto, feminine, flat, fruity, grating, gravelly, gruff, guttural, hard, harsh, high-pitched, hoarse, honeyed, husky, jittery, light, like a foghorn, like fingernails on a chalkboard, lisp, loud, low, masculine, matter-of-fact, mellow, melodramatic, modulated, monotone, monotonous, nasal, off-key, operatic, orotund, out of tune, penetrating, pitchy, plummy, projected, quavering, quiet, raspy, raucous, reedy, resonant, rich, ringing, robotic, rough, round, screaming, sexy, shaky, sharp, shouting, shrill, silvery, singing, singsong, slack, small, smoky, smooth, soft, soft-spoken, soothing, sotto, squeaky, stentorian, stiff, strangled, strident, taut, tense, thick, thin, throaty, tight, toneless, tremor, tremulous, twang, undertone, velvety, vibrant, vibrato, warm, weak, wheezy, whining, whispery, wobbly, yawning

HAIR

COLOR: ash blond, auburn, black, blond, blue-black, brown, brunette, caramel, champagne blond, chestnut, coal-black, copper, dishwater blond, ginger, golden blond, golden brown, gray, jet-black, platinum, red, reddish brown, salt-and-pepper, silver, straw, strawberry blond, white, titian, towheaded

STYLE: Afro, bald, beehive, bob, bouffant, bowl cut, braid (Dutch, fishtail, French, herringbone, ribbon, rope), bun, buzz cut, Caesar cut, chignon, chonmage, combover, cornrows, crew cut, crop, crown braid, curtained, devilock, dreadlocks, ducktail, extensions, fauxhawk, feathered, feelers, finger curls, finger wave, flat top, flip, flipthrough, fontange, French twist, fringe, high and tight, hime cut, jarhead, knot, layered, Liberty spikes, long, Mohawk, mop, mullet, odango, pageboy, parted, pigtails, pin curls, pixie, plait, Pollyanna, pompadour, ponytail, pullback, rag curls, rattail, razor cut, ringlets, rolled, shag, shaved, Shirley Temple, shoulder length, slicked, spiked, tail, teased, tonsured, top knot, twist, undercut, updo, weave, wedge, widow's peak, wings

TREATED: colored, crimped, curled, dyed, flatironed, frosted, highlighted, ironed, ombre, permed, permanent, permanent wave, straightened, tinted

TYPE: bushy, coarse, curly, damaged, dry, dull, fine, kinky, oily, shiny, smooth, split ends, straight, thick, thin, wavy, wild, wispy

SPECIES

> USAGE NOTE: All humans belong to the same species. Dwarves, elves, gnomes, giants, and others would be considered separate species in most settings. Dwarves, elves, gnomes, and certain others are commonly considered to be on equal footing with humans as far as characteristics and abilities.

The term humanoid does not describe a single species, but describes creatures with humanlike shape but which exhibit certain degrees of animalistic or untamed qualities in physical characteristics, intelligence, or other attributes. Each type of humanoid may be an individual species depending upon the setting.

Authors must determine the parameters of each species in their setting, the evolutionary relationships between the species, and any subspecies.

DWARF: cave, cavern, hill, dark, duergar, mountain, shadow

ELF: aquatic, arboreal, dark, desert, gray, forest, half, high, jungle, primitive, shadow, star, tree, wild, wood

GNOME: forest, hill, jungle, lost, meadow, mountain, river, vale

HUMAN RACES, FICTIONAL: Abarimon, Abatwa, Atlantean, Blemmyes, changeling, Cyclops, Leprechaun, Mermaid/Merfolk, Nephilim, Selkie, Tellem

HUMANLIKE GROUPS: giant (cloud, fire, frost, hill, mountain, sky, stone, storm), goblin, hobgoblin, orc, ogre, merfolk, rakshasa, troll

HUMAN GROUPS

USAGE NOTE: At one time, humans were described in terms of three races: black (Negroid), yellow (Mongoloid), and white (Caucasoid). This classification was replaced by narrower categories comprising Black (Sub-Saharan Africa), Brown (South Asians), Red (Native American), Yellow (East Asian), and White (European). In modern times, however, DNA studies have revealed no scientific racial distinctions among humans, and the term "race" is becoming obsolete. Scientists no longer divide the human species into races since no clear biological borders exist between groups. Current trends divide humans based upon ethnicity or populations, and ethnic groups are often subdivided by nationality, tribe, or location.

Authors need to be diligent about research in describing human groups and should take care to use terminology that is correct in historical contexts. Hundreds of ethnic groups have been documented; this number increases exponentially when mixed-ethnicity individuals are included. The list that follows is a sampling of some of the more prominent groups.

HUMAN ETHNIC GROUPS: Aboriginal Australian, Acadian, Acelmese, Adyghe, Afar, African-American, Afrikaner, Aimaq, Akuapem, Akyem, Albanian, Amish, Andalusian, Ansar, Arab, Asian, Aymaras, Azeris, Bahrani, Badui, Baka, Balinese, Bakongo, Balkars, Baltic German, Bamar, Bamileke, Banat Swabians, Bantu, Bashkirs, Basque, Batswana, Bavarian, Bedouin, Belarusian, Berber, Bhotia, Bosniak, Brahmin, Breton, Briton, Cajun, Cantonese, Castilian, Celt, Cornish, Cossack, Créole, Cuman, Czech, Danish, Dorian, Dutch, Egyptian, English, Eskimo, European, Fars, Fir Bolg, Finn, Flemish, Frank, French, French Canadian, Frisian, Gael, Galacian, Georgian, German, Greek, Haitian Creole, Han, Hausa, Hawaiian, Hindi, Hispanic, Hmong, Hui Chinese, Hungarian, Hun, Hutterite, Hutu, Icelander, Inca, Indian, Irani, Iranian, Irish, Italian, Jakaltek, Jamaican, Japanese, Jassic, Javanese, Jewish, Karelian, Ket, Khufi, Kongo, Korean, Kurd, Latvian, Lebanese, Leonese, Liechtenstein, Lithuanian, Luhya, Massai, Macedonian, Madeiran, Magyar, Maltese, Manchu, Manx, Maori, Mbochi, Memon, Mennonite, Mestizo, Mexican, Mon, Mongol, Montenegrin, Moor, Moravian, Moriori, Moro, Naga, Negrito, Ni-Vanuatu, Norwegian, Nubian, Okinawan, Pacific Islander, Palestinian, Pashtun, Parsi, Pennsylvania Dutch, Pennsylvania German, Persian, Phoenician, Pict, Polish, Polynesian, Portuguese, Puerto Rican, Punjabi, Quechuas, Roma, Romanian, Russian, Sami, Samoan, Sardinian, Saxon, Scottish, Selkup, Senegalese, Serb, Sherpa, Sicilian, Sinti, Slav, Slovak, Slovene, Somali, Spanish, Sudanese, Swahili, Swazi, Swede, Swiss, Tagalog, Taiwan, Tamil, Thai, Tibetan, Toltec, Tonga, Tongans, Transylvanian, Turk, Tutsi, Ukrainian, Valencian, Vandal, Venda, Venetian, Vietnamese, Visayan, Volga German, Welsh, Wu, Yakuts, Yanomami, Yugoslav, Zambo, Zapotec

NATIVE AMERICAN PEOPLES: Abenaki, Accohannock, Achomawi, Acoma, Ahtna, Ak Chin, Alabama, Aleut, Algonquian, Alutiiq, Apache, Ashiwi, Aztec, Beaver, Blackfoot, Caddo, Catawba, Cayuse, Chemehuevi, Cherokee, Cheynne, Chickasaw, Chicora, Chilcotin, Chimakum, Chinookan, Chippewa, Chitimacha, Choctaw, Chontal, Cheyenne, Cochiti, Coeur d'Alene, Comanche, Cree, Creek, Crow, Cupik, Esaw, Eskimo, Fox, Haidi, Ho-Chunk, Hopi, Huron, Hupa, Inokinki, Inuit, Iroquois, Kickapoo, Kiowa, Kuna, Laguna, Lakota, Lenape, Lumbee, Lummi, Maya, Mohican, Menominee, Modoc, Mohave, Mohawk, Muckleshoot, Narragansett, Naskapi, Navajo, Nez Percé, Oglala, Ojibwa, Onondaga, Oneida, Osage, Otie, Passamaquoddy, Pawnee, Penobscot, Pima, Potawatomi, Powhatan, Pueblo, Sauk, Seminole, Seneca, Shawnee, Shoshone, Sioux, Tohono, Washo, Wea, Wendat, Winto, Yaqui, Yuma, Yupik, Zuni

PERSONALITY

ANGRY: annoyed, antagonistic, cross, contemptuous, enraged, fuming, furious, hostile, incensed, infuriated, irate, heated, livid, mad, outraged, peeved, pissed off, seeing red, ticked off

GROUCHY: bitchy, bitter, cantankerous, crabby, cranky, grumpy, ornery, witchy

INTELLIGENT: bookish, brainiac, brainy, bright, clever, genius, intellectual, sharp, smart

POSITIVE: calm, caring, cheerful, compassionate, concerned, considerate, friendly, generous, gentle, good, good-natured, happy, helpful, hopeful, kind, loving, splendid, thoughtful, warm, welcoming

NEGATIVE: abusive, acrimonious, argumentative, arrogant, bad, belligerent, boring, bully, conceited, condescending, controlling, cruel, cynical, derisive, destructive, difficult, disapproving, disdainful, disgusting, disparaging, disrespectful, distrustful, downer, dull, embittered, evil, greedy, indignant, irritable, irritated, lazy, long-suffering, mad, mean, melancholy, mocking, nasty, obnoxious, pessimistic, poisonous, pushy, repellent, reproachful, resentful, rude, sad, scornful, self-centered, selfish, sneering, sour, spiteful, sulky, surly, tetchy, unreasonable, uncaring, venomous, vicious, wicked, womanizer

STUBBORN: adamant, bull-headed, determined, fixed, headstrong, inflexible, insistent, mulish, obstinate, persistent, pigheaded, uncompromising, unmoving, unmovable

UNINTELLIGENT: bird-brain, brainless, common, daft, dense, dim, dim-witted, dull, dull-witted, dumb, moron, moronic, slow, stupid, thick, unwise

OTHER: advanced, aggressive, ambitious, apathetic, aristocratic, assertive, audacious, authoritative, brash, brave, bold, bored, celebrated, charming, chic, coarse, committed, confident, courageous, cowardly, cultured, dandy, daring, decent, dedicated, developed, determined, detracting, devoted, dignified, dilettante, disillusioned, disorganized, distinguished, drama queen, dramatic, driven, droopy, economical, elegant, eminent, energetic, enthusiastic, experienced, extroverted, fair, faithful, false, famed, famous, fanatical, fearless, fickle, fine, firm, forceful, forthright, fop, foppish, gallant, garrulous, genuine, graceful, gracious, great, gullible, heroic, honest, hopeful, horrible, hyper, illustrious, indifferent, infamous, intrepid, introverted, keen, known, laid-back, late, lazy, lethargic, lighthearted, legendary, listless, loquacious, lovely, loud, low class, lowly, loyal, lunatic, lusty, malicious, malevolent, mellow, mentally ill, militant, misleading, motivated, mousy, naïve, neat, nervous, nervy, noble, notable, notorious, obsessed, optimistic, organized, outgoing, patrician, pessimistic, phony, plucky, polished, Pollyanna, prideful, prominent, proven, proud, polished, poised, punctual, pushy, quiet, recognized, refined, regal, renowned, reprehensible, respectful, responsible, reverent, righteous, salesman, sarcastic, sardonic, self-assured, self-sacrificing, serious, shy, single-minded, skeptical, smarmy, snobbish, stalwart, sophisticated, sporting, strong, stylish, superior, suspicious, talkative, timid, titled, unafraid, uncommitted, unconcerned, undistinguished, uninterested, unknown, upper class, valiant, wasteful, weary, well-bred, well-known, willful, withering

PHOBIAS

USAGE NOTE: The possible types of phobias are endless, and may be as specific as a certain color of small dog or as broad as all species of animals. The causes, reactions, and severity of phobias are also widely varied. Examples of phobias follow; authors may invent new phobias to suit their characters or setting. Phobias provide a wealth of opportunities for character development and plot devices.

A number of phobias have multiple names or variant spellings. For the purposes of this list, preferred or more conventional spellings were chosen. In the case of multiple names, the simpler or more easily pronounced names were selected.

achluophobia: darkness

acousticophobia: noise

acrophobia: heights

agateophobia: insanity

hadephobia: hell

hagiophobia: saints or holy things

heliophobia: the sun

hemophobia: blood

agliophobia: pain

agoraphobia: open spaces or crowded, public places

agrizoophobia: wild animals

ailurophobia: cats

alektorophobia: chickens

algophobia: pain

androphobia: men

anthophobia: flowers

anthropophobia: people or society

apiphobia: bees

aquaphobia: water

arachnophobia: spiders

arithmophobia: numbers

arsonphobia: fire

astraphobia: thunder and lightning

ataxophobia: disorder or untidiness

atelophobia: imperfection

atychiphobia: failure

autophobia: being alone

aviophobia: flying

bacteriophobia: bacteria

barophobia: gravity

batrachophobia: amphibians

bibliophobia: books

botanophobia: plants

bufonophobia: toads

carcinophobia: cancer

catoptrophobia: mirrors

cenophobia: new things or ideas

chaetophobia: hair

chiraptophobia: being touched

chiroptophobia: bats

chrometophobia: money

chromophobia: colors

chronophobia: time

herpetophobia: reptiles

hippopotomonstrosesquipedaliophobia: long words

homichlophobia: fog

hylophobia: forests

hypsiphobia: height

katsaridaphobia: cockroaches

kenophobia: voids or empty spaces

lachanophobia: vegetables

lilapsophobia: tornadoes and hurricanes

logophobia: words

mastigophobia: punishment

melophobia: music

methyphobia: alcohol

metrophobia: poetry

mysophobia: dirt or contamination

mycophobia: mushrooms

necrophobia: death or dead things

neophobia: anything new

nyctophobia: darkness

oenophobia: wines

ombrophobia: rain or being rained on

oneirophobia: dreams

ornithophobia: birds

panthophobia: suffering and disease

panphobia: everything

parasitophobia: parasites

paraskavedekatriaphobia: Friday the 13th

pediophobia: dolls

peniaphobia: poverty

phasmophobia: ghosts

phobophobia: phobias

placophobia: tombstones

plutophobia: wealth

pharmacophobia: drugs

ranidaphobia: frogs

claustrophobia: confined spaces

cleithrophobia: being locked in an enclosed place

coimetrophobia: cemeteries

coulrophobia: clowns

cremnophobia: precipices

cryophobia: extreme cold, ice, or frost

cynophobia: dogs

decidophobia: making decisions

dementophobia: insanity

demonophobia: demons

dentophobia: dentists

doraphobia: fur or animal skins

ecclesiophobia: church

ecophobia: home

electrophobia: electricity

entomophobia: insects

eosophobia: dawn or daylight

eremophobia: loneliness

gamophobia: marriage

geliophobia: laughter

gerontophobia: old people or growing old

glossophobia: speaking in public

gymnophobia: nudity

gynophobia: women

samhainophobia: Halloween

satanophobia: Satan

sciaphobia: shadows

scoleciphobia: worms

selenophobia: the moon

somniphobia: sleep

staurophobia: crosses or the crucifix

tachophobia: speed

taphophobia: cemeteries or being buried alive

thalassophobia: the sea

theophobia: gods or religion

thermophobia: heat

topophobia: certain places or situations, such as stage fright

triskaidekaphobia: the number 13

tropophobia: moving or making changes

urophobia: urine or urinating

vaccinophobia: vaccination

verbophobia: words

verminophobia: germs

vestiphobia: clothing

wiccaphobia: witches and witchcraft

xenophobia: strangers or foreigners

zelophobia: jealousy

zoophobia: animals

OCCUPATIONS

ADVENTURERS

ASSASSIN: attacker, bodyguard, contract killer, death-dealer, demolisher, destroyer, eradicator, executioner, Gurkha, killer, hired gun, hit man, hitter, mercenary, murderer, ninja, predator, slaughterer, slayer, sniper, special ops operative

BARBARIAN: adventurer, backpacker, buccaneer, desert dweller, drifter, explorer, guide, fortune hunter, Indian, itinerant, migrant, mountain man, native, nomad, opportunist, pioneer, planes rider, rambler, rover, savage, scout, swashbuckler, trailblazer, traveler, trekker, tribesman, vagrant, voyager, wanderer, wayfarer

BARD: artist, artiste, chronicler, clown, comedian, comic, composer, crooner, diva, entertainer, fool, humorist, jester, joker, jokester, lore master, lyricist, minstrel, musician, poet, skald, troubadour, orator, poet, sage, satirist, schemer, singer, songstress, stand-up comedian, wag, wit

CLERIC: acolyte, advocate, apostle, archbishop, archdeacon, astrologer, augur, bishop, bodhisattva, brother, canon, cantor, cardinal, celebrant, chief priest, clairvoyant, clergyman, counselor, deacon, disciple, ecclesiastic, father, follower, fortune teller, friar, high priest, holy man, holy woman, imam, lama, maharishi, matriarch, metropolitan, minister, missionary, monk, mother, mufti, nun, oracle, parson, pastor, patriarch, preacher, priest, prophet, oracle, rector, rabbi, reverend, sadhu, sangha, seminarian, shaman, sister, soothsayer, spiritualist, taper-bearer, vicar, wise man, yogi

FIGHTER: adversary, aggressor, Amazon, antagonist, archer, artillerist, assailant, assassin, attacker, barbarian, blade master, bodyguard, boxer, brigand, brute, bully, cavalry, challenger, combatant, competitor, contender, crossbowman, crusader, curator, custodian, death dealer, defender, demolisher, destroyer, enemy, executioner, fencer, foe, foot soldier, gangster, general, gladiator, goon, guard, guardian, guerrilla, henchman, hired gun, hood, hooligan, infantry, insurrectionary, insurgent, intimidator, invader, killer, knight, leader, lieutenant, lookout, man-at-arms, marauder, mercenary, mobster, mugger, murderer, musketeer, mutineer, ninja, officer, opponent, paladin, persecutor, picket, pirate, pistoleer, protector, provoker, pugilist, raider, ranger, rapist, rebel, ronin, ruffian, samurai, sentinel, sentry, serial killer, shield bearer, shield maiden, sootiest, slayer, soldier, sniper, special ops, squire, steward, templar, terrorist, thug, trooper, tough, tough guy, tyrant, Viking, warden, warrior, watch, watchman, wrestler

ILLUSIONIST: augur, dreamer, hypnotist, magician, master of illusion, mesmerist, mystic, prestidigitator

KNIGHT: bondsman, cavalier, cavalry man, chivalrous knight, courtier, crusader, elite warrior, green knight, heavy cavalry man, horseman, knight, knight-errant, knight grand commander, knights of Bath, knights hospitaller, mounted warrior, noble, order knight, Ritter, squire, templar, Teutonic knight, white knight

MARTIAL ARTIST/MONK: grandmaster, ninja, sensei, kung fu master

RELATED, BELT RANKS: black, blue, brown, green, orange, purple, red, white, yellow

NATURE: archdruid, communer, diviner, druid, forager, forester, herbalist, lore master, naturalist, oak-knower, oak-prophet, oak-seer, pagan, ranger, seer, shapechanger, skinchanger, sorcerer, tree hugger, wise man

PALADIN: crusader, holy knight, holy warrior, monastic warrior, knight of the cross, templar

THIEF: bandit, beggar, brigand, buccaneer, burglar, button man, cad, card sharper, card shark, charlatan, confidence man, copycat, criminal, crook, cutpurse, drifter, faker, falsifier, felon, fence, flimflam man, footpad, forger, fraud, fraudster, gambler, gatecrasher, gokudo, grifter, gypsy, highwayman, hobo, housebreaker, huckster, hypocrite, imitator, imposter, impressionist, intruder, interloper, liar, looter, made man, marauder, mechanic, mobster, mole, moocher, offender, plant, pickpocket, pilferer, pirate, prowler, rake, raider, rapscallion, robber, rogue, roué, scam artist, scion, scoundrel, sharper, shoplifter, slippery customer, snake oil salesman, stalker, stealer, taker, thief, thug, tramp, trespasser, trickster, vagabond, yakuza

WIZARD: academic, archmage, assessor, astrologer, augur, authoritarian, autocrat, canvasser, conjurer, counselor, crone, despot, diviner, dreamer, enchanter, examiner, executer, fakir, fantasist, forecaster, fortune teller, futurist, guru, hag, invoker, leading-light, logician, magician, maharishi, medium, mind reader, mystic, necromancer, oppressor, oracle, parapsychologist, performer, philosopher, practitioner, predictor, persecutor, prestidigitator, prophet, psychic, researcher, sage, scholar, seer, shaman, soothsayer, sorcerer, spellcaster, spiritual guide, spiritualist, sibyl, telepath, telepathist, theorist, thinker, tormenter, trendsetter, truth-seeker, tyrant, visionary, warlock, wide-man, witch

CIVILIANS

ACADEMIC: admissions clerk, advisor, archivist, assistant principal, counselor, dean, instructor, headmaster, headmistress, intellectual, librarian, narrator, nurse, principal, professor, psychologist, researcher, scholar, school board member, scribe, secretary, special education teacher, specialist, storyteller, student, superintendant, teacher, translator, treasurer, undergraduate

AGRICULTURAL: apiarist, agronomist, beekeeper, breeder, caretaker, cultivator, farmer, farm hand, grower, horticulturalist, plantation owner, planter, rancher, ranch hand, rose grower, trapper

> **USAGE NOTE:** Almost any type of farm or ranch is conceivable. Choose any product suitable to the setting; the result might be anything from rhubarb farmer to rabbit rancher to pecan grower.

ANIMAL/EQUESTRIAN: chiropractor, farrier, groom, instructor, jockey, massage therapist, nutritionist, rider, show judge, stable boy, stable manager, stable master, trainer, veterinarian, veterinary assistant

ARTISTS AND CRAFTSPEOPLE: artist, artiste, basket maker, blacksmith, bookbinder, boot maker, bottle maker, bowl turner, bowyer, broom maker, brush maker, candle maker, carpenter, cartwright, cobbler, conservator, costumer, cooper, engraver, etcher, florist, flower arranger, gemologist, glassblower, haberdasher, jeweler, metal crafter, pewtersmith, potter, seamstress, silversmith, tailor, tinsmith, wainwright, weaponsmith, weaver, wheelwright

CASTLE INHABITANTS AND PERSONNEL: archer, armorer, arrowsmith, artist, bard, blacksmith, bowyer, brick layer, butcher, butler, carpenter, chef, cleric, concubine, cook, courtesan, courtier, crossbowman, dungeon guard, engineer, falconer, farrier, fletcher, florist, food taster, footman, gardener, groundskeeper, guard, houndmaster, huntmaster, jailor, jester, juggler, knight, lady in waiting, maid, major domo, mason, merchant, minstrel, page, poet, priest, scribe, scullery maid, sculptor, seamstress, serf, shepherd, shepherdess, sommelier, spy, squire, stablehand, tailor, tanner, tax collector, tinker, trooper, vintner, weaponsmith

> **USAGE NOTE:** The possible occupations within a castle or palace are endless. Buckingham Palace, for example, employs approximately 1,200 staffers, including one individual whose sole duty is to keep all of the clocks cleaned and in good working order.

CONSTRUCTION: architect, boilermaker, bricklayer, carpenter, carpet layer, contractor, crane operator, drywall installer, electrician, interior decorator, interior designer, mason, painter, plasterer, plumber, rigger, roofer, steel worker, tile setter

FINANCE: accountant, actuary, analyst, appraiser, auditor, banker, bill collector, bookkeeper, chief financial officer, evaluator, financial advisor, money changer, money lender, stock broker, tax collector, underwriter

FOOD SERVICE: baker, banquet captain, barkeep, barrista, bartender, bar wench, brewer, busboy/girl, butcher, chef, cook, executive chef, head chef, host/hostess, ice man, lunch lady, maitre d', maitre d'hotel, pastry chef, salad girl, server, serving girl, sommelier, sous chef, vintner, waiter/waitress, winemaker

FORTUNE TELLER: astrologer, card reader, clairvoyant, crystal reader, gypsy, medium, mystic, numerologist, palm reader, phrenologist, psychic, scryer, spiritualist

GENERAL: agent, antique dealer, apprentice, assembler, attendant, auctioneer, babysitter, bagger, beggar, boss, bum, cashier, clerk, consultant, coordinator, custodian, director, dog catcher, exterminator, foreman, funeral director, garbage man, grave digger, greeter, guide, housewife, janitor, laborer, lifeguard, machine operator, maintenance worker, manager, mechanic, mentor, merchant, researcher, repairman, sales girl/lady/man/woman, sanitation worker, secret agent, shopkeeper, spy, steward, stool pigeon, technician, ticket seller, ticket taker, tour guide, trash collector, technician, village idiot, volunteer, wastrel

GOVERNMENT: alderman, alderperson, alderwoman, burgermeister, cabinet member, congress, congressman, congresswoman, county executive, first lady, founding fathers, governor, mayor, poll worker, president, representative, senator, vice president, village administrator

HOSPITALITY: baggage attendant, bellhop, bouncer, concierge, desk clerk, doorman, hotel manager, porter; See also Food Service, Housekeeping

HOUSEKEEPING: cleaning lady, cleaning woman, domestic, handmaid, handmaiden, housekeeper, maid (downstairs, lady's, scullery, upstairs), maid-of-all-work, maid-servant, servant, washerwoman, window washer

ILLICIT: blackmailer, bookie, conman, convict, criminal, crook, delinquent, drug dealer, drug dealer, drug mule, embezzler, escort, felon, grifter, identity thief, inmate, jailbird, john, lady of the evening, lawbreaker, loan shark, mob boss, mugger, murderer, offender, outlaw, pedophile, pickpocket, pimp, prisoner, prostitute, rapist, serial killer, shoplifter, thug, torturer, whore, working girl, villain; See also Assassin, Fighter, Thief

LAW ENFORCEMENT: agent, beat cop, bobby, border guard, capitol police, Coast Guard, commissioner, constable, cop, crime scene investigator, deputy, desk clerk, detective, double agent, federal agent, harbor patrol, lawman, liaison, mall cop, Mountie, night watchman, police officer, prison guard, prison matron, profiler, security guard, sheriff, sketch artist, secret agent, secret service, sharpshooter, sniper, special agent, SWAT team, Texas Ranger, warden, watch, watchman

LEGAL: adjudicator, adjuster, advocate, arbitrator, attorney, bail bondsman, bailiff, barrister, chief justice, esquire, guardian ad litem, judge, justice, lawyer, legal aide, legal assistant, legal secretary, lobbyist, magistrate, supreme court justice

MARITIME: admiral, barge operator, boat builder, boatswain, bo'sun, captain, commander, crew, diver, ensign, first mate, fleet admiral, frigate admiral, frigate captain, lieutenant, lookout, mariner, midshipman, oar maker, pirate, privateer, rear admiral, sail maker, sailor, seadog, seaman, submariner, vice admiral

MEDIA: anchor, announcer, camera operator, commentator, emcee, engineer, field reporter, host/hostess, investigative reporter, master/mistress of ceremonies, meteorologist, moderator, sportscaster, traffic reporter, weather girl/man

MEDICAL: acupressurist, acupuncturist, ambulance attendant/driver, anatomist, anesthesiologist, attending physician, audiologist, cardiologist, chiropractor, dermatologist, diagnostician, doctor, druggist, emergency room doctor/nurse, EMT, endocrinologist, gastroenterologist, general practitioner, gynecologist, healer, homeopath, intern, medic, medical assistant, midwife, nurse, paramedic, pharmacist, physician's assistant, preceptor, mortician, mortuary worker, obstetrician, optician, optometrist, ophthalmologist, osteopath, pediatrician, podiatrist, psychiatrist, psychologist, psychotherapist, resident, shrink, surgeon, therapist (art, music, physical, occupational), thoracic surgeon

MILITARY: See the chapter Military

MUSICAL: band leader, bassist, cellist, choir director, concertmaster, conductor, director, flutist, front man, front woman, kapellmeister, konzertmeister, leader, maestro, minstrel, musical director, musician, organist, percussionist, pianist, player, violist, violinist, voice coach

OPERATIONS: analyst, buyer, logistics, purchasing manager, receptionist, secretary

PERFORMING ARTS: acrobat, actor, actress, aerialist, ballerina, belly dancer, casting director, choreographer, costume designer, dancer, director, fight choreographer, gymnast, jester, lighting designer, mime, musical director, principal dancer, puppeteer, scenic designer, sound designer, stage manager, theater technician, tight rope walker, tumbler, ventriloquist; See also the chapter The Arts

PERSONAL SERVICES: aesthetician, barber, beautician, cosmetologist, hair stylist, makeup artist, manicurist, tattoo artist

PUBLISHING: advertising agent, agent, artist, author, bibliographer, biographer, chronicler, columnist, critic, cub reporter, editor (assistant, associate, copy, development, executive, managing), editor-in-chief, food critic, graphic designer, illustrator, journalist, keyliner, movie critic, newspaperman, novelist, obituary writer, photographer, playwright, poet, proofreader, publisher, reporter (entertainment, fashion, feature, food, news, sports, technology), reviewer, technical writer, typesetter, writer

RELIGIOUS: abbot, acolyte, administrator, archdeacon, archpriest, altar boy/girl, archbishop, bishop, cardinal, chancellor, chaplain, cleric, deacon, monk, monsignor, pastor, pastoral associate, patriarch, pope, preacher, prelate, priest, rabbi, reverend, shaman, vicar, vicar general

ROYAL/NOBLE: archduke, archduchess, baron, baroness, baronet, Caesar, court, courtier, crown prince, crown princess, count, countess, dame, duke, duchess, earl, emperor, empress, food taster, grand prince, grand princess, grand duke, grand duchess, jester, king, knight, lady, lady-in-waiting, marchioness, margrave, margravine, marquess, marquis, prince, princess, queen, shah, viceroy, vicereine, viscount, viscountess

RURAL: explorer, forager, forester, hermit, logger, miner, ranger, woodcutter, trapper

SCIENTIST: aeronautical engineer, anthropologist, archeologist, astronaut, astronomer, bacteriologist, biochemist, biologist, biomedical engineer, botanist, chemist, engineer, geologist, geomancer, mineralogist, physicist, seismologist; See also Geologic Fields of Study

SINGER: bard, crooner, diva, minstrel, opera singer, pop singer, rock 'n' roll star, soloist, songstress, torch singer, troubadour

USAGE NOTE: A singer might specialize in any type of music; See also Bard and Musical in this chapter.

SOCIAL DISTINCTION: blue collar, bon vivant, bumpkin, caste, commoner, debutante, dilettante, elite, hayseed, high class, high society, hoi polloi, homeless, lower class, middle class, rabble, redneck, riff-raff, social climber, society girl, trailer trash, white collar, white trash, unemployed, upper class, upper echelon, village idiot, working class, working poor

SPECIAL OCCASION: bride, bridesmaid, event planner, flower girl, graduate, groom, groomsman, guest of honor, host, hostess, maid/matron of honor, retiree, ring bearer, usher, wedding planner

SPORTS: athletic director, cheerleader, coach, equipment manager, manager, mascot, player, team doctor, trainer

TRANSPORTATION: bus driver, cabbie, cab driver, chauffer, co-pilot, driver, drover, flight attendant, jockey, navigator, pilot, stewardess

UNIQUE: voodoo priest, voodoo priestess

WANDERER: gypsy, hobo, itinerant, rover, tramp, vagabond, vagrant

ORGANIZATIONS

GUILDS: assassins, blacksmiths, construction workers, farmers, grave diggers, mariners, merchants, money changers, plumbers, thieves, sewermen, tailors, traders

RELATED: chamber of commerce, neighborhood association, trade union

USAGE NOTE: A guild is an association of persons of a similar profession or pursuit. They are often created to protect pricing, eliminate outside competition, or create a level playing field for their operations within a city or region. Guilds are not always altruistic and are highly susceptible to corruption. The occupations and activities listed here are only a sample; a guild might be created for almost any group. Guilds are somewhat different from trade unions, which are designed to safeguard workers and provide a unified voice in negotiations with management.

POLITICAL PARTIES: Democrat, Federalist, Green, Libertarian Republican, Whig

SOCIAL CLUBS: association, auxiliary, benevolent order, club, fraternity, guild, hermetic order, men's club, service club, sodality, sorority, women's club

CHAPTER 2: CLOTHING

STYLES OF DRESS

African, ancient Greek, ancient Roman, androgynous, Arabian, artsy, athletic, Asian, battle, beach wear, Bedouin, black tie, blue collar, Bohemian, Boho, Bollywood, bridal, Bronze Age, burn-out, business casual, Byzantine, camouflage, career, Carribean, casual, caveman, Chinese, Civil War, classic, Colonial, come hither, commando, construction worker, costume, courtier, dance, dervish, dowdy, dressy, dressed up, eclectic, Edwardian, effeminate, Egyptian, elegant, Emo, empire, European, Euro-trash, fashion forward, fashion model, feminine, flapper, flight attendant, folk, formal, French Revolution, frumpy, funereal, gang, gangster, gay, geeky, ghetto, girly-girl, Goth, greaser, grunge, gypsy, Halloween, Harajuku, harem girl, haute couture, hippie, hobo, holiday, Hollywood, hoochie mama, hunting, Japanese, jock, Las Vegas, loungewear, martial arts, masculine, masque, masquerade, medical personnel, medieval, Middle Eastern, military uniform, monk, mourning, native, nerdy, night club, noble, nun, old-fashioned, out of style, patrician, peasant, pioneer, preppie, pimp, pinup girl, pirate, primitive, Prom, punk, rebel, red carpet, redneck, Renaissance, retro, rock star, romantic, royalty, school uniform, school marm, semi-formal, sexy, Shakespearean, showgirl, ska, skater, sleepwear, slutty, southern belle, southwestern, sportswear, sporty, streetwalker, Stone Age, student, Sunday best, sweat clothes, tailored, Templar, Texan, thrift shop, tomboy, trailer trash, tramp, travel, tribal, unconstructed, uniform, unisex, vacation wear, Victorian, vintage, Western, white collar, white tie, white trash

CLOTHING PIECES

ACCESSORIES: backpack, bag, baguette bag, balaclava, barrel bag, beach bag, belt, boa, bowling bag purse, box purse, briefcase, bucket purse, cane, carpetbag, chatelaine bag, clutch, compact, cosmetic bag, dog collar, drawstring bag, duffel purse, evening bag, fan, fingerless gloves, handkerchief, half-moon purse, hobo bag, hosiery, leg warmers, makeup bag, messenger bag, mittens, muff, muffler, parasol, pocketbook, pocket protector, pocket square, pompadour bag, pouch, purse, reticule handbag, rucksack, saddlebag, satchel, scarf, shades, shoe lace, shoe string, shopping bag, shopping tote, shoulder bag, sunglasses, suspenders, sword cane, texting gloves, top handle purse, tote, umbrella, walking stick, wallet, wristband, wristlet

ATHLETIC SHOES: baseball, basketball, bowling, cleats, climbing, cross-trainer, football, golf, gym, jogging, running, soccer, tennis, track, walking, wrestling

BOOTS: chukka, cowboy, dominatrix, galoshes, granny, gum, hiking, hip, low, mukluks, overboots, overshoes, rain, riding, rubbers, slouch, ski, snow, thigh-high, waders, Wellies, Wellington, work

FOOTWEAR/SHOES: ankle straps, ballet flats, camel toes, clogs, deck, dress, espadrilles, flats, flip flops, garden clogs, heels (curved, French, Louis, pompadour), huaraches, ice skates (figure, hockey, speed), kiltie loafers, kitten heel, lace-ups, loafers, Mary Janes, moccasins, mules, ombre, oxford, penny loafers, platforms, pumps (d'Orsay, peep toe, platform, spectator), roller skates, saddle, sandals, scuffs, slingback, skis (cross country, downhill), slides, slip-on, slippers, sneakers, snow shoes, spats, stacked heels, stilettos, stilts, swim fins, thongs, T-straps, water shoes, wedge, wingtips; see also Dance Shoes in the chapter The Arts

SOCKS: ankle, athletic, bobbie cotton, dress, gym, hiking, knee, knee-highs, over-the-knee, sweat, trouser, tube, winter, wool

HAIR ACCESSORIES: barrette, bobby pin, clamp, clip, comb, hair net, ponytail holder, roller, roller pin, scarf, scrunchie, slumber cap, sponge roller

LADIES' WEAR: baby doll top, baby doll nightgown, bikini, blouse, body stocking, body suit, bolero coat, bolero pants, booty shorts, bra (bullet, convertible, demi, full coverage, full figure, halter, long-line, maternity, minimizer, nursing, padded, peek-a-boo, push-up, racerback, shelf, sports, strapless, underwire), bralet, brassiere, bridal gown, bridesmaid gown, bustier, cami, camisole, capris, capri pants, catsuit, chemise, corset, cowl neck, crinoline, crop top, culottes, Daisy Dukes, dress (cocktail, formal, hanbok, pageant, sheath, sun, sweater), evening gown, falsies, fishnets, full slip, fur stole, garter belt, gauchos, girdle, gown, half-slip,

halter top, hoop skirt, hot pants, jeggings, kimono, leggings, leotard, lingerie, maternity, merry widow, mom jeans, negligee, nightgown, nylons, opera gloves, panties (bikini, brief, French cut, granny, high-cut, hipster, maternity, thong), pant suit, pantyhose, peignoir, peignoir set, petticoat, pinafore, Prom dress, sari, shell, shimmy, short shorts, skirt (A-line, balloon hem, ballerina length, dirndl, full, full-length, hoop, long, maxi, midi, mini, pencil, sarong, shawl, short, straight, tea length, tiered), skort, slip, stockings, swim cover-up, sweater coat, sweater set, tanga, tankini, tank top, tap pants, teddy, thigh-high stockings, tights, top, tube top, tummy shaper, tutu, twin set, waist cincher, wedding gown, yoga pants

MEN'S WEAR: armhole shirt, ascot, board shorts, boxers, boxer shorts, braces, briefs, cravat, dhoti, doublet, drawers, dress shirt, frock coat, grand boubou, hanbok, knickers, Madras plaid shorts, morning coat, muscle shirt, smoking jacket, spats, sport coat, stays, suit (casual, church, dinner, disco, double-breasted, evening, funeral, leisure, luxury, one-button, sack, sharkskin, three-piece, two-button, two-piece, three-button, zoot), swim trunks, tailcoat, tie (bola, bow, neck), tighty-whiteys, trousers, trunks, tuxedo, tuxedo shirt, undershirt, waistcoat, wife beater

UNISEX: apron, Bermuda shorts, bathing suit, bath robe, blazer, caftan, coat (over, pea, rain, trench, winter), coveralls, dickie, dressing gown, formal wear, garters, gloves (cotton, dress, driving, leather, long, short, work), G-string, Hawaiian shirt, henley, jacket, jeans (bell bottom, blue, boot cut, elephant leg, flare, hip hugger, low rise, skinny, trouser leg), khakis, kilt, long johns, long underwear, lounge pants, mackintosh, nightshirt, nightwear, overalls, pajamas, pants, parka, pjs, polo shirt, robe, shirt, shorts, slacks, suit, sweater (cardigan, pullover), sweater vest, sweat pants, sweatshirt, swim suit, tank top, thermal underwear, t-shirt (long sleeve, short sleeve, V-neck), turtleneck, union suit, vest

HEADGEAR: akubra, aviator cap, balaclava, balmoral, bandana, barretina, batting helmet, beanie, bearskin, beret, bongrace, bonnet (archer's, baby, capote, Glengarry, feather, gypsy, leghorn, mourning, poke, sun), bowler, burka, busby, bycoket, cap (baseball, bunnet, cloth, cricket, coonskin, cyclist's, driver, fisherman's, garrison, golf, Juliet, knit, muir, newsboy, night, nurse's, patrol, policeman's, sailor, ski, slouch, smoking, sock, stocking, toboggan, watch, watchman's, Windsor), capotain, capuchin, caubeen, chilote cap, chupalla, circlet, coif, coronet, crown, diadem, do-rag, ear muffs, fascinator, fedora, fez, hairpiece, hat (artist's, bandeau, basher, beaver, Beefeater's, beehive, bicorne, bird cage, boater, bongrace, boonie, bucket, capeline, cartwheel, cavalier, carriage, chef's, chip, cloche, cockle, cocktail, coolie, Cossack, cowboy, deerstalker, demicastor, derby, fan-tail, fruit, Gainsborough, Garbo, Garibaldi, grebe, gypsy, halo-brim, hard, hunting, jerry, kevenhuller, kiss-me-quick, knit, mandarin, marquis, matinee, merry widow, military, moab, mourning, muff-box, mushroom, oke, pillbox, porkpie, skimmer, Stetson, stovepipe, straw, sugar loaf, sun, ten-gallon, top, tricorn, veiled), headband, headdress, homburg, hood (chaperon, Flemish, French, gable, medieval, mourning, riding), karakul, kepi, kippah, kofia, kufi, liripipe, mantilla, mortarboard, pakol, pith helmet, plume, rogatywka, salakot, Santa Claus cap, scarf, skullcap, skully, shower cap, snood, sombrero, sweatband, swim cap, tam, tam o'shanter, taqiya, tiara, topi, toupee, trilby, tubeteika, tuque, turban, ushanka, veil, visor, wedding veil, wig, wiglet, wimple, wreath, yarmulke, zucchetto

JEWELRY: anklet, bracelet (bangle, charm, cuff), brooch, cameo, chain, crown, cuff link, earring (dangle, hoop, post, stud), necklace, pendant, pin, scatter pin, signet ring, tiara, tie bar, tie pin, watch (pocket, wrist), watch chain, watch fob; For more jewelry types and gem stones, see also the chapter Story Elements and Treasure

MASKS: ancestral, animal, carnival, Cherokee, death, dragon, drama, face shield, funeral, grotesque, half-mask, harlequin, hockey, jester, Halloween, Kachina, Mardi Gras, masquerade, Navajo, nightmare, pharaoh, persona, shaman, silver, ski, specter, thief's, trick or treat

OUTERWEAR: cape, cloak, coat (car, over, pea, rain, trench), fur coat, jacket (ski, winter), mackintosh, mantle, parka, raincoat, ski vest, snowmobile suit, snow pants

RELIGIOUS: chasuble, miter, robe, Roman collar, scapular, skullcap, stole, vestment

SPECIAL PURPOSE: chaps, conn, costume, graduation gown, hospital gown, judge's robe, lab coat, safety vest, school uniform, singlet, straight jacket, surgical scrubs, tabard

UNDERGARMENTS: bloomers, foundations, foundation garment, intimate apparel, intimates, knickers, novelty, smalls, smallclothes, shorts, skivvies, unmentionables, underclothes, underpants, underwear

CLOTHING CONSTRUCTION

FABRIC: angora, bamboo, barathea, barkcloth, basket weave, batiste, batting, bengaline, berber fleece, boiled wool, boucle, broadcloth, brocade, buckram, bunting, burlap, canvas, cashmere, challis, chambray, chamois, Chantilly lace, charmeuse, cheesecloth, chiffon, chintz, cloque, coating, corduroy, cotton, cotton/polyester blend, coutil, crash, crepe, crepe de chine, crinkle, crinoline, crushed velvet, damask, denim, dobby weave, doeskin, double knit, double weave, drill, duchess satin, duck, dupioni, end-on-end, eyelet, faille, faux fur, faux leather, faux suede, felt, fishnet, flannel, flannelette, fleece, flocked, foil, foulard, French terry, fringe, fun fur, gabardine, gauze, gazar, georgette, gossamer, habutai, hemp, hopsack, ikat, illusion, Jacquard, jersey, knit, lace, lamé, lawn, leather, linen, lining, linsey-woolsey, loden, marabou, marocain, matelassé, matka, matte jersey, melton, mercerized cotton, merino wool, mesh, microfiber, moiré, monk's cloth, moss crepe, mousseline, muslin, net, netting, noil, oil cloth, organdy, organza, osnaburg, ottoman, oxford, panné, parachute, percale, piqué, plissé, plush, point d'esprit, pointelle, polished cotton, polyester, pongee, ponte di roma, poplin, quilted, rayon, raschel, rib knit, reversible, sailcloth, sateen, satin, saxony, seersucker, serge, shantung, sharkskin, sheer, sheeting, sherpa, shetland, silk, silk-knit, stretch, suede cloth, surah, taffeta, tapestry, tartan, terry cloth, terry velour, thermal, ticking, tricot, tulle, tussah, tweed, twill, union cloth, velour, velvet, velveteen, voile, waffle, whipcord, wool, worsted

FABRIC PATTERNS: batik, calico, camouflage, checked, checkerboard, dotted Swiss, floral, gingham, herringbone, houndstooth, paisley, pinstripe, plaid (buffalo, Madras, windowpane), polka dot, printed, stripe

FUR: chinchilla, coyote, ermine, faux, fox, leopard, mink, sealskin

EMBELLISHMENTS: appliqué, beading, beadwork, blackwork, bow, braiding, broderie anglaise, button, couching, crewel, drawstring, embossing, embroidery, feather, gathering, hardanger, lettuce edge, marabou, monogram, orphrey, piping, quilting, rickrack, rhinestone, ring, rivet, scallop, sequin, shirring, smocking, stud, tie-dye, topstitching, trapunto

EMBROIDERY STITCHES: basting, blanket, buttonhole, buttonhole wheel, chain, closed buttonhole, cloud-filling, Cretan, cross, double blanket, double chain, double cross, double darning, double featherstitch, featherstitch, fishbone, fly, French knot, hem, herringbone, Holbein, interlaced running, Japanese darning, knotted blanket, lazy daisy, outline, quilting, running, satin, square chain, threaded chain, threaded herringbone, twisted chain, Vandyke, wave, weaving, whipped running, whipped web, woven web, zigzag chain

GARMENT PIECES: back, belt, bodice, buttonhole, casing, collar (Nehru, Peter Pan, pointed, standup), cuff, dart, drawstring, epaulet, facing, fly, French cuff, front, gore, gusset, hem, hood, interfacing, interlining, lapel, lining, neckline, peplum, placket, pocket (inset, patch), pocket flap, ruffle, sash, seam allowance, sleeve (cap, dolman, juliette, leg o'mutton, long, puffy, raglan, short, set in, three-quarter length), strap, tie back, waistband

NOTIONS: bias tape, button, elastic, frog, hook and eye, hook and loop fastener, seam binding, snap, thread, yarn, zipper

SEWING EQUIPMENT: bobbin, bodkin, curve square, cutting board, dressmaker's form, embroidery hoop, iron, ironing board, mannequin, needle (crewel, darning, quilting, sewing, weaving), pattern, pin cushion, pins, quilter's quarter, ruler, scissors, seam gauge, seam ripper, sewing basket, sewing kit, sewing machine, shears, steamer, tailor's chalk, tambour, tape measure, tracing paper

SEWING TECHNIQUES: baste, block, boning, clip, crochet, cut, embroider, French seam, grazed seam allowance, hem, iron, knit, lay out, line, miter, paint, pleat, press, purl, rip, serge, sew, steam, tack, trim, tuck, weave, zigzag

SEWING TERMS: bias, burn-out, button hole, dart, décolletage, grazed seam allowance, heather, keyhole, nap, ombre, pile, pucker, seam allowance, selvage, sewing line, wale, warp

CHAPTER 3: ARCHITECTURE AND PROPERTY

ARCHITECTURAL STYLES AND ELEMENTS

STYLES: Adirondack, A-Frame, African Vernacular, Anglo-Saxon, American Colonial, American Craftsman, American Empire, American Foursquare, Amsterdam, Ancient Egyptian, Ancient Greek, Ancient Roman, Antebellum, Arcachon Villa, Arcology, Art Deco, Art Nouveau, Arts and Crafts, Baroque, Bauhaus, Bay and Gable, Bay Area Regional, Biedermeier, Blobitechture, Brick Gothic, Bristol Byzantine, Broch, Brutalist, Buddhist, Bungalow, Byzantine, Cape Cod, Carolingian, Carpenter Gothic, Castle, Chalet, Chicago School, Chilota, Churrigueresque, City Beautiful, Classical, Colonial, Colonial Revival, Conch, Constructivist, Contemporary, Corporate Modern, Cottage, Creole Cottage, Danish Functionalism, Deconstructivist Modern, Decorated Period, Dragestil, Dutch Colonial, Early English, Early Georgian, Early Modern, Eastlake, Egyptian Revival, Elizabethan, Empire, English Baroque, Expressionist Modern, Farmhouse, Federal, Florida Cracker, Florida Modern, Four Square, French Colonial, French Provincial, Functionalism, Futurist, Georgian, Googie, Gothic, Gothic Revival, Greek Revival, Heliopolis, Hindu, Interactive, International, Isabelline, Islamic, Italianate, Jacobean, Jeffersonian, Jengki, Jugendstil, Manueline, Medieval, Mediterranean Revival, Merovingian, Mid-Century Modern, Mission, Modern, Modern American, Nazi, Neoclassical, Neo-Greek, Neolithic, Neo-Vernacular, New England, Norman, Ottonian, Palladian, Perpendicular, Polish Cathedral, Polite, Postmodern, Prairie, Pueblo, Queen Anne, Queenslander, Ranch, Regency, Renaissance, Richardsonian, Rococo, Roman, Romanesque, Romantic, Russian Revival, Rustic, Saltbox, Shotgun, Sicilian Baroque, Southern Colonial, Spanish Colonial Revival, Split Level, Stick, Storybook, Structuralism, Sumerian, Swiss Chalet, Sumerian, Tidewater, Town House, Traditional Japanese, Tudor, Tudor Revival, Vernacular, Victorian, Villa

ROOMS: antechamber, anteroom, arcade, assembly, attic, atrium, audience chamber, auditorium, balcony, ballroom, barroom, basement, bathroom, bedroom, billiards room, board, boudoir, breakfast nook, break room, catacomb, cellar, chamber, chapel, cloister, cold room, conservatory, cookery, corridor, court, craft, crypt, cubicle, dance studio, deck, den, dining, dressing room, entry, entrance hall, entry hall, family, foyer, front room, fruit cellar, gallery, garret, great hall, great room, hall, hallway, hearth, inglenook, kitchen (summer, winter), lab, laboratory, laundry, lavatory, library, lobby, loft, living room, media, meeting, music room, office, pantry, passage, passageway, play, porch, privy, quarters, rec room, reception area, recreation room, rehearsal room, rest room, root cellar, safe room, salon, sauna, scullery, secret room, security, sewing, showroom, spa, stall, stockroom, studio, study, theater, throne, toilet, tomb, vault, veranda, vestibule, waiting, walk-in closet, wine cellar, work, workshop, workspace

BATHROOMS: bath, chemical toilet, facilities, garderobe, head, john, ladies' room, latrine, lavatory, little boys' room, little girls' room, loo, men's room, necessary room, outhouse, pit toilet, potty, privy, rest room, toilet, water closet

BATHROOM FEATURES AND FIXTURES: bathtub, bidet, cabinet, clawfoot tub, closet, counter, double sink, exhaust fan, faucet, medicine cabinet, mirror, pedestal sink, sink, shower, shower doors, shower over tub, shower stall, soaking tub, toilet, toilet paper holder, towel bar, towel rack, vanity

BUILDING ELEMENTS AND FEATURES: aisle, arch, archway, baseboard, bones, booth, built-in safe, buttress, cabinet, cantilever, ceiling, ceiling tile, chimney, closet, clothes chute, coal chute, compartment, counter, crown molding, cupboard, divider, doorbell, door chime, door jamb, doorway, downspout, fireplace, fireside, floor, flying buttress, frame, gable, gate, gutter, hearth, I-beam, joist, keystone, leaded glass, ledge, lintel, mailbox, mail slot, mantle, milk chute, mirror, newel, paneling, partition, platform, plinth, post, roof, roof vent, rostrum, shelf, shutter, soffit, soldier course brick, stage, stained glass, staircase, stairway, stairwell, steps, stovepipe, sunken room, threshold, tile, tower, trim, turret, vault, wall, workstation

BUILDING SYSTEMS: air conditioner, air filtration, alarm system, baseboard heater, boiler, cable television, ceiling fan, central air, central vacuum, coal bin, coal chute, cold air return, computer network, dimmer switch, ductwork, electrical box, electrical outlet, electric heating, exhaust fan, furnace, fuse box, gas furnace, heating duct, humidifier, HVAC, keypad, light fixture, light switch, motion detector, motion sensor, oil tank, pipes, plumbing, radiant floor heating, radiator, recessed lighting, security system, sump pump, swamp heater, telephone lines, telephone wiring, thermostat, vent, ventilation, whole house fan, wireless internet, wireless telephone, wiring

DOORS: attic dropdown, automatic, back, barn, double, Dutch, entrance, entry, front, garage, overhead, patio, pocket, portico, portal, prison bars, rear, screen, security, side, sliding, storm, swinging, swivel, threshold

DOORS, ATYPICAL: access tunnel, airlock, cave mouth, dimensional portal, dog door, flap, gate, gateway, hatch, hatchway, hole in the wall, iris, secret entrance, waterfall

DOOR MATERIALS: bamboo, blanket, bookcase, bullet proof, cane, curtain of beads, fiberglass, glass, hide, leather, paper, planks, rattan, steel, stone, thatch, timber, wicker, wood

WINDOWS: basement, bay, bow, casement, circle head, double hung, corner picture, fixed bay, fixed bow, French picture, garden, glass block, intermediate combination, jalousie, manual awning, octagonal, picture, projected intermediate, round, sidelight, sliding, stained glass, transom, traverse

RELATED: counterweights, frame, lock, pane, screen, shutter, sill, storm

ROOF STYLES: butterfly, double pitch, Dutch, flat, gable, gambrel, hip, lean-to, mansard, M-style, parapet, pyramid, sawtooth, semi-circular, single pitch, traditional, Victorian

PROPERTY FEATURES: barbecue, basketball court, boathouse, bocce ball court, cache, carport, cistern, dog house, doughboy, driveway, driving range, fence, fire pit, fountain, furnace, garage, gate, gazebo, golf course, greenhouse, hot tub, maze, patio, pit, pool, potting shed, putting green, shed, sidewalk, stable, swimming pool, tennis court, terrace, walkway, well, woodshed

LANDSCAPING: arbor, bird bath, bird feeder, border, fence, gate, hedge, lawn, garden, pergola, pond, rose garden, stepping stones, water feature, waterfall

TRAPS: acid, ambush, arrow, bait, ballista, bear, bottle, bungee sticks, bursting bladder, cannon net, choking gas, closing walls, collecting cage, contact poison, cursed scroll, cursed magic item, darts, deadfall, deadly spider, door, engineered secret door, falling stone, false floor, floor, foothold, gas, giant spider webs, illusion, leghold, lightning, lock, loop, magical, maze, mouse, net, pit, pivoting floor, poison coated spike, poison needle, poison thorns, quick sand, rock fall, sand, sliding stone, snare, sound, spear, spike, spring-blade, spring-loaded, staircase, steam blast, steel-jawed, sticky, teleportation, toxic pool, trap door, trip wire, water, wire

BUILDING MATERIALS

EXTERIOR: adobe, aluminum siding, block, brick, clapboard, half-timber, log, mud, reed, sod, stone, stucco, vinyl siding, wood

INTERIOR: carpet, chip board, drywall, engineered lumber, gypsum board, hardwood, lumber, particle board, plaster, plywood, slate, stone, tile, veneer, wood

ROOFING: asphalt shingle, cedar shake, cedar shingle, clay tile, glass, grass, green, metal, rubber, shingle, slate, tar and gravel, thatch, tile

PROPERTY TYPES

ADMINISTRATIVE: capitol, city hall, consulate, county seat, court, courthouse, embassy, federal building, Parliament

AMUSEMENT PARK/CARNIVAL/CIRCUS/FAIR: animal barns, barker's stand, booth, bumper cars, carousel, circus ring, Ferris wheel, fun house, gates, giant slide, grandstand, grounds, huckster booth, merry-go-round, roller coaster, sideshow, stage, tent, ticket booth, tilt-a-whirl, tunnel of love

RELATED, FOOD: corn dog, cotton candy, cream puff, elephant ear, French fries, fried cheese, fried chicken, funnel cake, hamburger, hot dog, lemonade, roasted corn

RELATED, GAMES: balloon pop, basketball toss, coin toss, dart throwing, guess-your-weight, pingpong ball toss, ring toss, shooting gallery, water pistol

ACADEMIC: academy, amphitheater, archive, art school, auditorium, campanile, campus, classroom, college, concert hall, conservatory, gymnasium, lab, laboratory, lecture hall, lecture room, library, military academy, military school, museum, preschool, school (elementary, grade, high, junior high), seminary, student union, theater, university

BUSINESS: accounting office, antique store, apothecary, bakery, bank, bazaar, bookstore, bowyer, bottling plant, brewery, carpet store, courthouse, day care center, department store, depository, depot, dry cleaner, factory, fletcher, florist, forge, foundry, funeral chapel, funeral home, funeral parlor, furniture store, gallery, gas station, glassblower, greenhouse, grocery store, guild, hypermarket, insurance agency, kiln, laboratory, lumber yard, mill, office, office equipment store, office furniture store, office park, pharmacy, market, medical office, mini mall, nursery, office building, plant, police station, recording studio, resale shop, retail store, shop, shopping mall, smithy, stockroom, stockyard, store, storehouse, storeroom, studio, storehouse, strip mall, supermarket, superstore, variety store, warehouse, wedding chapel, workplace, workshop

CEMETERY: burial chamber, burial ground, caretaker's home, catacomb, cellar, cenotaph, chapel, crypt, coffin, crematorium, churchyard, fence, grave, graveyard, haunt, mausoleum, memorial, memorial park, monument, necropolis, office, pyramid, resting place, sarcophagus, sepulcher, subterranean vault, tomb, vault

CRIMINAL: den, hangout, haunt, hideaway, hideout, hole, lair, refuge, safehouse

ENTERTAINMENT: amphitheater, arena, art gallery, auditorium, baseball diamond, basketball court, beer garden, bowling alley, brothel, carnival, club, casino, cinema, comedy club, concert hall, dance hall, dance studio, disco, discotheque, festhall, football field, forum, gambling hall, gentleman's club, gymnasium, massage parlor, movie theater, museum, night club, opera house, pitch, playing field, show house, soccer field, skating rink, sports center, sports club, stadium, strip club, tennis court, theater

FANTASY: druid's circle, druid's grove, wizard's tower

FARM/OUTBUILDING: animal pen, arable land, barn, chicken coop, chicken house, coop, corn crib, corral, fallow land, field, farmhouse, farmstead, fence, garage, granary, grazing land, greenhouse, hayloft, hothouse, machine shop, milking house, milking parlor, orchard, outhouse, paddock, pasture, plantation, pen, pig pen, poke, ranch, ring, root cellar, shack, shed, silo, stable, storage shed, storm cellar, stall, sty, watermill, well house, wind mill

RELATED, CROPS AND LIVESTOCK: alfalfa, canola, cattle, chicken, cotton, dairy, duck, eggs, field corn, field pea, fish, fonio, hay, hemp, hog, hops, grain, pigeon pea, rapeseed, soybeans, sheep, shrimp, sugar cane, tobacco, veal

USAGE NOTE: Every food substance must be farmed, grown, or raised; refer to the section on foods for more possible types of farms. The products listed here are not generally considered table foods or must be processed to be usable.

FOOD/DRINK ESTABLISHMENT: banquet hall, bar, bar and grill, bistro, buffet, café, cafeteria, canteen, cantina, cigar bar, coffee bar, coffee house, coffee shop, diner, dining hall, drinking hole, drive-in, eatery, family restaurant, fast food restaurant, food court, inn, joint, pizzeria, pub, public house, refectory, restaurant, tavern, saloon, supper club, tap, watering hole

FORTIFICATION: armory, arsenal, barbican, barricade, barracks, barrier, base, bastion, battery, battlement, berm, billet, bivalate, blockade, blockhouse, bulwark, bunker, burg, burh, camp, castle, citadel, compound, cordon, crannog, crenellation, dike, ditch, donjon, earthwork, embankment, fastness, fire support base, fort, foxhole, fortress, garrison, gatehouse, guardhouse, keep, kill zone, magazine, marine camp, military (base, college, institute, outpost, station), mine field, missile silo, moat, motte-and-bailey, munitions storage, outpost, palisade, parade ground, parapet, peel, picket, pillbox, post, practice yard, rampart, redoubt,

ringwork, shelter, sickbay, star fortification, stockade, stronghold, strongpoint, tower, trench, turret, wall, watch tower, weapons storage

GENERAL BUILDINGS: administrative center, animal shelter, community center, community hall, complex, compound, concourse, courtyard, depository, depot, enclave, enclosure, guild, haven, headquarters, home office, labyrinth, repository, retreat, sanctuary, sanctum, skyscraper, warren

GENERAL PROPERTY: aqueduct, commune, fair grounds, festival grounds, industrial park, market (farm, flea, fruit, green, mini, open, public, stall, wet), marketplace, park, parking lot, parking structure, playground, plaza, public pool, zoo

HEALTH CARE: asylum, birthing center, clinic, consultation room, dental office, detox clinic, doctor's office, drugstore, emergency room, health center, health resort, health spa, hospital, hospice, infirmary, orthodontic office, pharmacy, private clinic, operating theater, rehab, rehabilitation hospital, rest home, sanitarium, sickbay, sickroom, surgical center, urgent care center, waiting room

HOSPITALITY: barracks, bed and breakfast, cottage, dude ranch, inn, hostel, hostelry, hotel, lodge, motel, public house, resort

MARINA: anchorage, beach, berth, buoy, break wall, canal basin, channel marker, dock, dockside, dockyard, ferry slip, harbor, jetty, landing, launch, lighthouse, pier, port, quay, quayside, riverside, seaport, slip, tie-up, waterfront, waterside, wharf, yacht club

MILITARY: administrative, ammunition storage, armory, barracks, base exchange (BX), blockhouse, bunker, citadel, commissary, correctional facility, fort, fortification, hospital, housing, infirmary, mess hall, motor pool, museum, military intelligence facility, parade grounds, post exchange (PX), recreation center, research facility, storage, training facility, watch tower, water tower

OUTDOOR: base camp, bath house, cabin, camp, campground, colliery, deck, encampment, excavation, fair grounds, gazebo, labor camp, lean-to, gravel pit, lodge, market (farm, flea, fruit, green, open, public, stall), marketplace, mine, mine shaft, oil rig, pavilion, piazza, plaza, porch, public pool, quarry, shelter, souk, square (market, town, village), tent, terrace, tunnel, veranda

PRISON: cage, cell, detention center, concentration camp, cell block, death row, dungeon, gulag, isolation cell, jail, jailhouse, labor camp, lockup, penal colony, penal complex, penitentiary, poky, prison ship, reformatory, slammer, solitary confinement, stockade, supermax, top-security center, up the river

PUBLIC SERVICES: bottled water delivery, cell phone provider, cable television provider, carpet cleaner, coal yard, diaper service, electrical plant, electrical tower, fire house, fire station, gas company, heating oil delivery, linen service, police station, post office, power plant, telephone company, uniform service, water treatment plant, water works

RESIDENTIAL: apartment, apartment block, apartment house, abode, bachelor pad, bi-level, bungalow, cabana, cabin, castle, chalet, chateau, Colonial, condominium, cottage, domicile, dormitory, dump, duplex, dwelling, estate, flat, flophouse, gated community, habitat, habitation, hideout, high-rise, hold, holding, home, homestead, house, hovel, hut, igloo, lean-to, lodge, log cabin, manor, mansion, nursing home, old folks' home, outhouse, palace, ranch, residence, shack, shanty, subdivision, tent, tree house, tri-level, Victorian, villa

RESIDENTIAL, SLANG: bachelor pad, castle, cave, condo, coop, crash pad, crib, digs, hangout, hole, hole in the wall, joint, pad

RELIGIOUS: ashurkhana, basilica, cathedral, cattedrale, chapel, church, duomo, fire temple, gurdwara, house of worship, hussainia, imambargah, martyrium, mithraeum, monastery, mosque, oratory, pagoda, pyramid, religious institution, seminary, shrine, stupa, synagogue, temple

SPECIAL PURPOSE: dojo, convention center, industrial complex, mill, National Guard Post, Pentagon, refinery, reservoir, stock exchange, tide mill, triumphal arch, wind turbine

UNIQUE: Acropolis of Athens, Alcatraz, Calat Alhambra, Angkor Wat, Channel Tunnel (Chunnel), Chichen Itza, City of Petra, CN Tower, Coliseum of Rome, Christ the Redeemer Statue, Easter Island Moai, Eerie Canal, Eiffel Tower, Empire State Building, Golden Gate Bridge, Great Pyramid at Giza, Great Wall of China, Hagia Sophia, Hoover Dam, Kiyomizu-dera, Leaning Tower of Pisa, London Eye, Machu Picchu, Mount Rushmore, Neuschwanstein, Panama Canal, Red Square, Space Needle, Sears Tower, Sphinx, Statue of Liberty, Stonehenge, Sydney Opera House, Taj Mahal, Vatican, Wailing Wall, Windsor Castle

UNIQUE, DESTROYED: Colossus of Rhodes, Hanging Gardens of Babylon, Library of Alexandria, Lighthouse of Alexandria, Mausoleum of Halicarnassus, Porcelain Tower of Nanjing, Statue of Zeus at Olympia, Temple of Artemis, World Trade Center

SPECIALTY ANATOMY

CASTLE ANATOMY: aisle, allure, apse, arcade, arch (corbelled, depressed, drop, lancet, ogee, pointed, rounded, two-centered), arrow loop, arrow slit, aumbry, bailey, baluster, balustrade, barbican, bastion, battlement, bay, berm, blockhouse, breastwork, buttery, buttress, casemate, catacomb, cesspit, column, cornice, counterguard, creasing, crenel, crenellation, cross and orb, crosswall, crownwork, cupola, curtain wall, dead ground, dormer, drawbridge, drum tower, dungeon, enceinte, forebuilding, fosse, fresco, gable, gallery, garderobe, gate house, glacis, great chamber, great hall, guard tower, half-timber, hall, hallway, hillfort, hoarding, inner curtain, inner ward, joist, keystone, lancet, lantern, lintel, loophole, louvre, machicolations, mantlet, merlon, meurtriere, moat, motte, murder hole, newel, oilette, oratory, oriel, oubliette, outer curtain, outer ward, palisade, parados, parapet, pediment, pier, pilaster, pinnacle, piscina, pitching, plinth, portcullis, postern gate, putlog, putlog hole, quadrangle, quoin, rampart, rear arch, refectory, revetment, ringwork, roofridge, rubble, sally-port, scaffolding, scarp, shaft, shell keep, sill, soffit, solar, squint, stepped, steyned, stockade, tower, transom, treasury, truss, turning bridge, turret, vault, wall stair, wall walk, wattle, weathering, wicket, wing wall, yett

CHURCH ANATOMY: aisle, altar (bye, side), apse, belfry, chancel, cloister, crossing, crypt, narthex, nave, niche, sacristy, sanctuary, sepulcher, side chapel, steeple, transept, vestibule, yard

RELATED: catacombs, cemetery, community hall, memorial, parish center, rectory, school

RELATED: mihrab

CHAPTER 4: FURNISHINGS

BEDS: air, bassinet, box spring, brass, bunk, bunk bed, California king, canopy, cot, cradle, crib, day, double, feather, four-poster, full, futon, hammock, heart-shaped, hideaway, Hollywood, hospital, iron, Jenny Lind, junior, king, loft, marriage, mattress, Murphy, pallet, pencil post, pillowtop mattress, platform, queen, rollaway, rope, single, sleeper sofa, sleeping mat, sleigh, sofa bed, toddler, trundle, twin, youth, vibrating, water

CHAIRS AND STOOLS: arm chair, back chair, bar stool, beach, bean bag, bentwood rocker, bow-back, butterfly, caned seat, Chippendale, club, comb-back, easy chair, Empire, ergonomic, firehouse, folding, footstool, hearth stool, Hepplewhite, high chair, Hitchcock, kneeling, kitchen stool, ice cream parlor, ladderback, leather, lounge chair, lyre-back, massage, milking stool, occasional, office, platform rocker, overstuffed, pod, potty, pressed back, Queen Anne, recliner, ribbon-back, rocker, rocking chair, rod-back, rush seat, Shaker, Sheraton, side, slat-back, swivel-base, three-legged stool, throne, thumb-back, tripod stool, Victorian, wicker, Windsor, wing

DESKS: fall-front, lady's, lap, partners, reception, rolltop, secretary, school, schoolmaster's, Wooton, writing

DECORATIVE OBJECTS: art print, artwork, bric-a-brac, framed art, framed photograph, knickknack, memento, oil painting, painting, photograph, picture, portrait, print, souvenir, statue, statuette

ELECTRONICS: 8-track tape player, 33-1/3 rpm record player, 45 rpm record player, 78 rpm record player, amplifier, Beta player, Beta recorder, boombox, Blu-ray player, cassette player, cassette recorder, CD boombox, CD player, DVD player, DVR, equalizer, gramophone, graphic equalizer, HD DVD, hi-fi, magnetic tape recorder, minidisc player, personal music player, phonograph, phonograph cylinder, portable CD player, quadraphonic stereo, radio, radio cabinet, receiver, record player, reel-to-reel tape recorder, speaker, stereo, surround sound system, television (big screen, black and white, color, console, flat screen, plasma, portable, projector), transistor radio, transmitter, turntable, VHS player, VHS recorder, video cassette recorder, VCR, Victrola

FLOOR COVERINGS: bathroom rug, bearskin, braided rug, carpet (berber, flatweave, floor mat, hooked, knotted, needlefelt, pile, plush, sculpted, shag, tapestry weave, tufted, woven), carpeting, needlepoint carpet, Oriental rug, Persian rug, prayer rug, rag rug, rug, runner, throw rug, wall-to-wall carpet, welcome mat

> **RELATED—IMPORTED CARPETS:** Afghan, Armenian, Azerbaijani, Bulgarian, Chinese, English, French, Indian, Oriental, Pakistani, Persian, Spanish, Turkish, Turkmen

MAJOR APPLIANCES: built-in dishwasher, chest freezer, dishwasher, double oven, dryer, garbage disposal, ice box, oven, microwave oven, portable dishwasher, range, refrigerated drawer, refrigerator (bottom freezer, side by side, top freezer), refrigerator/freezer, stove, trash compactor, upright freezer, wall oven, washer, washing machine (front load, top load), wine refrigerator

MISCELLANEOUS: apparatus, bar, cart, contraption, device, drying rack, engine, equipment, fireplace screen, folding screen, hall tree, instrument, machine, magazine rack, mechanism, mirror (cheval, girandole, full length, ogee frame, transitional, wall), playpen, quilt rack, tea cart, umbrella stand

SEATING: backless bench, bench, chaise longue, canapé, chesterfield, cobbler's bench, couch, cricket bench, davenport, divan, fainting couch, Grecian couch, hassock, loveseat, ottoman, pew, seat, settee, sociable couch, sofa, S-shaped, vis-à-vis

SPECIAL PURPOSE: dais, dictionary stand, lectern, pedestal, podium, pulpit, stand

STORAGE: baker's rack, blanket chest, bonnet-top highboy, bookcase, bowfront chest, breakfront china cabinet, buffet, bureau, cabinet, cedar chest, cellarette, chest of drawers, chest on chest, chest on frame, chifforobe, china cabinet, corner cupboard, credenza, cupboard, dresser, etagere, file cabinet, floating shelf, footlocker, highboy, high chest, Hoosier, hope chest, hutch, jelly cabinet, lateral file cabinet, locker, lowboy, low chest, open-top cupboard, pewter cupboard, pie safe, Pilgrim chest, sewing cabinet, sideboard, six-board chest, standing cupboard, steamer trunk, swellfront chest, toy chest, traveling chest, trunk, wall shelf, wardrobe

TABLES: butcher block, candle stand, card, cast iron, cocktail, coffee, commode, corner, dining room, drop-leaf, embalming, end, examining, farmhouse, folding, game, gate-leg, harvest, kitchen, laboratory, lamp, marble top, massage, night stand, occasional, patio, pedestal-base, picnic, planter, plant stand, potting bench, refectory, sawbuck, side, smoking stand, snake-foot, spool-turned, swing-leg, surgical, tavern, tea, telephone, tilt-top, TV table, TV tray, vanity, washstand, wicker, work, writing

CHAPTER 5: EQUIPMENT AND TOOLS

ADVENTURER'S GEAR

GENERAL SURVIVAL GEAR: animal trap, backpack, batteries, bedroll, blanket, camp stove, candle, canteen, carabiner, compass, cooking gear, crampons, first aid kit, flashlight, flint and steel, food, grappling hook, ground cloth, jackknife, lantern, lantern oil, map, mess kit, oil cloth, piton, propane, rope (cable, cord, heavy, leather, light, nylon, plastic, silk, twine), spikes, tarp, tarpaulin, tent (cabin, pavilion, pup), tinder, toilet paper, torch, walking stick, water container, weapon, writing materials

See also: Equipment lists throughout this chapter, also the chapters Clothing; Food; Animals and Creatures; Transportation; Magic; Story Elements and Treasure

SPECIALTY SURVIVAL GEAR: acid, barrel of sand, black clothing, costume, disguise kit, face paint, flammable oil, gold pan, juggling balls, juggling clubs, lock picks, lodestone, magnet, makeup kit, money belt, musical instrument, poison, scroll tube, sealing wax, thief's tools, wax, weapon black, weapon oil

WIZARD'S GOODS: acid, alcohol, amber, ambergris, amulet, animal organs, animal fur, animal skin, aromatic plant, ashes, balm, balsam, beeswax, bell, berries, bird's foot, bird's nest, black lotus pollen, bones, book, brazier, broken glass, broom, broom straw, candle, cauldron, chain, chalk, charm, chicory, claw, coal, coke, copper shot, cording, crystal ball, crystals, dragon scales, dried leaves, dung, dust, egg, eyeball, eyelashes, eye of newt, fang, feathers, filament, filings, fingernail clippings, firecracker, firewood, flash powder, flour, flower petals, frankincense, fungus, fur, garlic, gas, gastric juice, gems, glycerin, grave dust, graveyard earth, ground glass, gum arabic, hair, herbs, incense, ingot, ink, insects, jelly, key, lens, lint, lock, lodestone, looking glass, magic wand, magnifying glass, marbles, metal dust, milk, minion, mirror, molasses, mold, mummy powder, mummy wrapping, mushroom, myrrh, needle, oil, parchment, paste, pentacle, petroleum, pine cone, pine needles, poison, potion, quill, ribbon, ring, roots, rubber, sand, sap, scroll, seashells, seeds, shavings, snakeskin, soot, spellbook, spices, spider, spider web, string, sugar, sulfur, swamp water, tablet, tacks, tea leaves, teeth, thread, toadstool, unguent, vellum, venom, vial, water, wax, wicking, wing of bat, wolfsbane, wood chips

> **USAGE NOTE:** The items on this list might serve as components to cast a spell, to imbue an object with a spell effect, to concoct a potion, or to be useful in any number of experiments. For more materials, cross reference Body Parts, Bones, Organs, and so on in the chapter Anatomy and Physiology with an animal, creature, or monster in the chapters Animals and Creatures and Monsters to obtain results such as cobra's spleen, troll's claw, or dragon's scale.

GENERAL EQUIPMENT AND TOOLS

ART MATERIALS: adhesive, beads (ceramic, glass, metal, plastic), blotting paper, carbon dust, cardstock, carving materials (granite, ice, ivory, marble, plaster, stone, wax, wood), casting materials (cement, metal, plaster, plastic, synthetic resin, wax), chalk, charcoal, clay, crayon, corrugated fiberboard, drawing base (architecture, canvas, card, cloth, glass, metal, paper, plaster, wall, wood), edible materials, eraser, found objects, glass, gem stones, glue, glue stick, gold leaf, graphite, ink, marker, metal, modeling materials (clay, papier-mâché, plaster, polymer clay, sand), paint (acrylic, aerosol, black light, fresco, gesso, glaze, gouache, ink, latex, magna, oil, primer, sumi, tempera, vinyl, vitreous enamel, watercolor), paper, paperboard, parchment, pastels, pencil, plastic, sand, scratch board, sketch pad, synthetic resin, textiles, tile, tracing paper, varnish, vellum, wire, wood

ART TOOLS: airbrush, brayer, bristled brush, brush, chisel, clamp, cutting torch, easel, foam brush, hammer, kiln, knife, mallet, palette, palette knife, pen, pen holder, pliers, potter's wheel, power tool, quill pen, saw, scraper, snips, stencil, stylus, wire cutter

BOOKS/PUBLICATIONS: anthology, atlas, block book, board book, chapbook, chapter book, chart, clay tablet, codex, coloring book, cookbook, diagram, diary, dictionary (pocket, foreign language, un-

abridged), digest, document, E-book, encyclopedia, ethnodrama, field guide, hardbound, hardcover, hornbook, how-to book, journal, magazine, manuscript, map, newspaper, novel, paperback, parchment, phrase book, picture book, poetry, reference, reference guide, schematic, scroll, softcover, storybook, textbook, thesaurus, tome, trilogy, work of fiction

RELATED: book cover, book light, bookmark, bookplate, dust jacket, end papers, map case

RELATED, LITERARY STYLES: allegory, autobiography, biography, diet, drama, fable, fairy tale, fiction, legend, medical, mythology, narrative, nonfiction, parable, psychology, saga, science fiction, self-help, yarn

CANDLES: bayberry, birthday, candelabrum, candleholder, candle lamp, candle lantern, candle stand, candlestick, chamber stick, dipped, Easter candle, emergency, fire-starter, hog scraper, jar, candle mold, pillar, push-up candlestick, reflector, rolled beeswax, scented, sconce, snuffer, taper, tealight, vigil, votive; See also Illumination/Light Sources

CLEANING SUPPLIES/GADGETS: broom (hearth, push, whisk), brush, buffer, buffing cloth, buffing pad, chemicals, dust cloth, dust mop, dust pan, feather duster, floor buffer, floor wax, furniture polish, janitor caddy, lint brush, metal polish, mop, mop bucket, pail, pipe cleaners, pressure washer, rag, scrub brush, silver polish, squeegee, sponge, steam cleaner, toilet brush, toilet cleaner, trash bags, vacuum cleaner, wax, wax applicator, window cleaner, wringer

COMPUTER EQUIPMENT: 3-1/2 inch floppy disk, 5-1/4 inch floppy disk, cable, central processing unit, CPU, database, desktop PC, docking station, external hard drive, external speakers, flash drive, floppy disk, internet connection, keyboard, laptop, mainframe, microphone, modem, monitor, mouse, mouse pad, notebook computer, PC, personal computer, platform, power cord, processor, printer, router, scanner, server, supercomputer, tablet, terminal, thumb drive, USB connector, wire, zip drive

CONTAINERS AND VESSELS: ampule, attaché case, backpack, bag (canvas, cloth, paper, plastic, school, shopping, zipper), barrel (large, oak, small, wine), basin, basket, belt pouch, bin, birdcage, bottle (clay, glass, metal, plastic), bowl (cereal, mixing, salad, sugar), box, briefcase, bucket, bud vase, cage, can, canteen, carafe, carrier, carton, case, cashbox, cask, casket, chest (banded, large, small, tool, toy, treasure), cigar case, cigarette case, coffer, coffin, crate, crock, decanter, document box, drum, envelope, ewer, flagon, flask, folder, garbage can, hipflask, holder, humidor, jar, jewel case, jug, knapsack, luggage, pack, package, packet, pail, pallet, pan, pet carrier, pitcher, pocket, portfolio, pot, pouch, quiver, receptacle, rucksack, sachet, sack (burlap, large, leather, medium, plastic, silk, small), saddlebag, safe, sarcophagus, satchel, shoulder bag, snuffbox, spice chest, strongbox, suitcase, tea chest, trash can, traveling case, trunk, tub, tun, vase, urn, wash basin, waste basket, water gourd, waterskin, wineskin, vat, vial, vacuum bottle; See also Accessories in the chapter Clothing

FASTENERS: cable, chain (heavy, light, medium), cord, cuffs, dowel, fetter, handcuffs, irons, line, manacles, rope, shackles, spike, string (heavy, kitchen, light, silk, waxed), tape (cellophane, duct, masking, painters'), thread, twine

FISHING GEAR: bait, bead, bite indicator, blade, bobber, cast net, clevise, creel basket, float, gaff, harpoon, hook, landing net, line, lure, net, pole, reel, rod, sinker, sling, snap, spear, speargun, spinner, split ring and wire, spoon, swivel, tackle, tackle box, terminal tackle, trap, trident, waders

GAMES: action, arcade, backgammon, ball, bingo, board, card, carnival, checkers, chess, children's, Chinese checkers, computer, dice, electronic, math, playground, role-playing, online, skill, word

RELATED, CARD GAMES: 52 pick-up, agram, alcalde, alkort, all fives, all fours, aluette, Arizona 29-card pitch, baccarat, back alley, back street bridge, badugi, barbu, bartok, basra, beggar my neighbor, belote, between the sheets, big three, big two, bingo, biritch, blackjack, black Maria, blind Don, boonaken, brag, bridge, brouc, buck euchre, bura, burraco, busca, bust, butthead, calabresella, calypso, canasta, cancellation hearts, cap-it, carioca, carousel, casino, challenge, chase the ace, chase the pig, cheat, Chicago bridge, chicken foot, Chinese ten, clabber, concentration, conquian, contract bridge, contract

rummy, couillon, court piece, crash, crates, crazy eights, cribbage, cricket, cuckoo, cucumber, cuttle, doppelkopf, double sir, draw and discard bridge, drawbridge, durak, Egyptian ratscrew, eighty-three, Eleusis, etori, euchre, fan tan, fapfap, farmers' rummy, faro, fast track, fifty-five, fifty-six, finagle, fipsen, fish pitch, five hundred, five hundred rummy, five card brag, flush, forty-one, Texas 42, four of a kind, four-card brag, frog, game-flip-flop, garbage, German solo, German whist, gin rummy, ging, gleek, go fish, go stop, golf, guts, hand and foot, hearts, high card pool, hokm, hola, Hollywood garbage, honeymoon bridge, hoola, hoskin, humbug, hundred and ten, I doubt it, in between, kaiser, kalookie, kalter schlag, king, king's corners, knaves, knock-out whist, kozel, kraken, last one, laugh and lie down, laus, let it ride, Leyden, literature, Liverpool rummy, loba, loo, losing lodam, manipulation rummy, manni, marriage rummy, memory bridge, mendikot, Michigan, Michigan rummy, mighty, mille, minibridge, nap, napalm, new canasta, nine card Don, nine five two, nine-card brag, ninety-eight, ninety-nine, noddy, oh hell!, Oklahoma 10-point pitch, old maid, omi, one-arm Joe, one hundred, page one, palace, pan, pandoeren, paskahousu, paston, Pedro, pegs and jokers, pelmanism, penneech, pennies from heaven, phat, pig, pilotta, pinochle, pip-pip, piquet, pishe pasha, pisti, pitch, pitch with fives, pitty pat, plus-minus, poch, polignac, Polish red dog, pontoon, Pope Joan, preferans, preference, president, quadrille, race horse, racing demon, railroad canasta, ramchi, razz, red dog, red frog black frog, remi, reversis, ride the bus, robbers' rummy, ronda, royal casino, rubber bridge, ruff and honours, rummy, rummy 500, Russian bank, samba, scat, schnapsen, schwimmen, screw your neighbor, Sebastapol, seep, sergeant major, seven and a half, seven bridge, seven rocks, Shanghai, sheepshead, shoot, single dummy bridge, six-card brag, slippery Sam, sixty-three, skitgubbe, slapjack, slosh, smear, solo, solo whist, South African casino, spades, spar, speculation, speed, spit, spite and malice, spitzer, spoons, spot hearts, steal war, stitch, swazi casino, Swiss jass, stops, tarok, tausendeins, taxes, teen pathi, telefunken, telesina, three card brag, three-card Monte, tiddly-wink, twenty-one, tournament blackjack, tractor, trains, Tripoli, trumps, two hundred, ugly, Vatikan, war, whist, Yukon

RELATED, POKER CARD GAMES: Abyssinia, ace-to-five lowball, ace-to-six lowball, all for one and one for all, auction, baseball, bitch, black Mariah, blind man's buff, Buddha's folly, California draw, California lowball, California stud, Caribbean, Casino hold 'em, Chicago, Chinese, church, Cincinnati, cowpie, crazy pineapple, criss cross, Dakota, dealer's choice, dirty Schultz, do ya, double draw, draw, eight game mix, elevator, English stud, five card draw, five card draw with a bug, five card stud, five card stud high-low, follow the queen, football, grocery store dots, have a heart, henway, high Chicago, high-low, HORSE, HOSE, iron cross, Italian, jack the shifter, jacks back, jacks or better, Kansas City lowball, lame brain Pete, London lowball, low Chicago, lowball, low, Mexican stud, Mexican sweat, midnight baseball, Mississippi mud, night baseball, no peek, Omaha, Omaha high, pass the trash, pick a partner, pineapple, poker bull, poker menteur, Polish poker, psycho, push, pyramid, ROE, roll your own, round the world, San Francisco, second hand high, selection/rejection, sequence, seven card stud, spit in the ocean, strip, stud, substitution, ten-card regrets, Texas hold'em, the good the bad and the ugly, three card, three five seven, tic-tac-toe, trees, triple draw, trips to win, Turkish, Wall Street, whisky, Woolworth, Yukon hold'em

RELATED, SOLITAIRE CARD GAMES: accordion, aces up, baker's dozen, beleaguered castle, blind alleys, Canfield, clock, demon patience, double, eight off, fascination, flower garden, four seasons, gaps, golf, good measure, Klondike, La Belle Lucie, memory, Monte Carlo, penguin, pile of 28, poker, pyramid, scorpion, solitaire 13, spider, Yukon, zodiac

HARDWARE: anchor, ball bearings, bolt, bracket, brad, C-clamp, clamp, deadbolt, flange, hinge, nail, nut, peg, pin, pipe, screw (drywall, masonry, wood), spike, sweeping compound, tack, tackcloth, washer

ILLUMINATION/LIGHT SOURCES: Aladdin lamp, Argand lamp, barn lamp, Betty lamp, camphene lamp, can light, ceiling light, chandelier, cruise lamp, fat lamp, flashlight, flint and steel, glowstick, lamp (accent, bedside, candlestick, counter, desk, electric, floor, ginger jar, hurricane, kerosene, lava, library, oil, overhead, reading, storm, table, Tiffany), lantern (beacon, bull's eye, hurricane, hooded, oil, Paul Revere, propane, railroad), lighter, light fixture, lighting magnifier, limelight, matchbox, matches, match safe, night light, oil (kerosene, Greek fire, paraffin, tallow, whale), parade torch, rush light, tinderbox, torch, whale oil; See also Candles

ILLUMINATION, BULB AND TUBE TYPES: carbon arc, compact fluorescent, electric arc, deuterium arc, fluorescent, germicidal, grow light, halogen, incandescent, iodide, LED, mercury vapor, metal halide, neon, parabolic reflector, sodium vapor, sulfur, tanning lamp, UV lamp

LABORATORY EQUIPMENT: agar plate, alembic, analytical balance, apron, aspirator, autoclave, beaker, biosafety cabinet, Boston round bottle, Büchner funnel, Bunsen burner, burette, burner, calorimeter, carafe, centrifuge, chemical spoon, chemostat, clamp, cold finger, colony counter, condenser, conical measure, cover slip, crucible, crucible cover, crucible tongs, cup, cuvette, Dean-Stark apparatus, desiccator, dissecting pins, dropper, dropping funnel, dry erase board, eudiometer, evaporating dish, eyewash, file, filter, filter funnel, filter paper, fire blanket, flask (Büchner, Erlenmeyer, Fernbach, fleaker, Florence, retort, round-bottom, Schlenk, volumetric), fume hood, funnel, gas burner, gas syringe, glove box, gloves, graduated cylinder, glass rod, hand lens, homogenizer, hose clamp, hot air oven, hot plate, incubator, keys, laminar flow cabinet, lancet, loupe, magnetic stirrer, magnifying glass, Meker-Fisher burner, microscope, microtiter plate, mortar and pestle, pipette, Petri dish, picotiter plate, plate reader, pycnometer, retort stand, safety goggles, safety shower, scale, scalpel, scoopula, separatory funnel, slide, Soxhlet extractor, spatula, specific gravity bottle, spectrophotometer, static mixer, stir bar, stirring rod, stopper, striker, support ring, Teclu burner, test tube, test tube holder, test tube rack, thermometer, tongs, tube (boiling, capillary, ignition, NMR, test, Thiele, thistle), tubing, Tesla coil, van de Graff generator, vacuum dry box, vortex mixer, wash bottle, watch glass, wire gauze; See also Computer Equipment

LABORATORY SUPPLIES: acids, agenda, catalog, chart, chronicle, diagram, directory, first aid kit, graph, index, inventory, list, litmus paper, log, logbook, record, register, schedule, schema, spreadsheet, timetable

LOCKS: bolt, catch, bicycle, combination, deadbolt, door, hook, padlock with key, security system, skeleton key

MAKEUP: blush, blusher, compact, concealer, contouring, eye liner, eye shadow, eyebrow pencil, eyelash curler, fake fingernails, false eyelashes, foundation, French manicure, highlight, lip gloss, lip liner, lipstick, loose powder, makeup brush, makeup remover, manicure, manicure set, mascara, nail polish, pedicure, pressed powder, rouge

OFFICE/SCHOOL/WRITING SUPPLIES: address book, assignment book, backpack, batteries, binder, binder clip, blotter, book cover, book strap, brass fastener, bulletin board, calculator, card catalog, cellophane tape, chalk, chalkboard, clipboard, colored pencils, compass, composition book, cork board, crayon, dictionary, ditto master, dry erase board, duplicating fluid, envelope (business, interoffice, kraft, window) extension cord, file box, file folder, filler paper, folder, flip chart, glue, glue stick, hanging folder, highlighter, hole punch, index card, ink, ink bottle, ink cartridge, legal pad, lock, locker, loose leaf paper, manila folder, marker (dry erase, permanent, washable, wet erase), masking tape, neon message board, notebook, notepad, paper clip, paper cutter, paper folding tool, paper (carbon, colored, construction, copier), papyrus, parchment, pen (ballpoint, fountain), pencil case, pencil grip, pencil pouch, pencil sharpener, pointer, poster board, power strip, protractor, push pins, quill, report cover, ring binder, rotary card storage, rubber cement, ruler, school bag, school glue, self-stick notes, sheet protector, slate, slate pencil, spiral notebook, staple puller, stapler, staples, stationery, stencils, steno pad, stenographer pad, sticky notes, storage box, strip binding supplies, stylus, tag board, tape, tape gun, thesaurus, three-hole punch, thumb tacks, ticker tape, toner, toner cartridge, T-square, vellum, white board, yard stick

OFFICE/SCHOOL MACHINES: adding machine, answering machine, binding machine, cash register, check protector, comb binding machine, bursting machinte, comptometer, conference call speaker, copier, dictophone machine, ditto machine, document feeder, document shredder, duplicating machine, electric hole punch, electric stapler, fax machine, intercom, laminator, laser pointer, key punch machine, mimeograph machine, movie screen, pencil sharpener, postage meter, postage scale, printer, printing press, projector (filmstrip, movie, opaque, overhead, slide, video), record player, scanner, smart board, speaker phone, speakers, stencil machine, stenotype, stock ticker, switchboard, telephone, teletype, typesetting machine, typewriter (daisy wheel, electric, manual)

OPTICS: binoculars, contact lenses (disposable, extended wear, gas permeable, hard, soft), electron microscope, eyeglasses, glasses, kaleidoscope, magnifying glass, microscope, monocle, monoscope, opera glasses, spectacles, stereoscope, spyglass, telescope

PERSONAL CARE: after shave, after shave lotion, antiperspirant, bar soap, bath oil, body splash, body spray, body wash, bubble bath, cologne, comb, conditioner, dental floss, deodorant, depilatory, disposable razor, eau de toilette, emery board, eye cream, hair brush, hair gel, hair mousse, hair pick,

hair spray, mirror (glass, metal, pocket, silver, unbreakable), mouthwash, nail clipper, nail file, night cream, perfume, powder, razor, razor blade, shampoo, shaver, shaving brush, shaving cream, shaving mug, shaving soap, soap, straight razor, toilet water, toothbrush, toothpaste, tooth powder, tweezers; See also Hair Accessories in the chapter Clothing

RELIGIOUS ITEMS: altar, book, candle, chalice, collection basket, collection plate, cross, crucifix, holy book, holy symbol (ceramic, clay, crystal, glass, gold, silver, stone, wooden), holy water, hymnal, monstrance, prayer beads, prayer book, prayer rug, prayer shawl, scroll, Star of David, tithing plate, vestment

SIGNAL DEVICES: bell, drum, flag, flare, fog horn, lantern, lighthouse, mirror, Morse code, signal fire, smoke, telegraph, whistle

SPORTING GOODS, BALLS: baseball, basketball, croquet, football, pingpong, polo, rugby, soccer, softball, table tennis, tennis

SPORTING GOODS, OTHER: badminton racquet, baseball bat, baseball glove, baseball mitt, birdie, bobsled, boogie board, catcher's mitt, croquet mallet, fielder's mitt, hockey pads, hockey puck, hockey stick, ice skates (figure, hockey, speed), inline skates, pads, parallel bars, polo mallet, pommel horse, roller skates, shin guards, shuttlecock, skateboard, sled, snowboard, snow saucer, snow skiis (cross country, downhill), tennis racquet, uneven parallel bars, water skiis; See also Footwear in the chapter Clothing

SPY GEAR: acid vial, accomplice, attaché case, binoculars, body armor, brief case, camera pen, car phone, changeable license plates, climbing rope and grappling hook, cloaking device, code, code book, computer, computer hacker, dark glasses, diamonds, disguise kit, dossier, evening gown, explosive item (cigar, golf ball, gum, jewelry, pen, ring), facial recognition software, fax machine, false beard, false document, false fingerprints, false identification, false mustache, fencing gear, fingerprint/palmprint recognition system, floppy disk, foreign currency, garrote, getaway car, gloves (climbing, evening, insulated, latex), GPS, grenade, gun (derringer, golf club rifle, pistol, rifle), hat, knock-out drops, laptop computer, laser beam, listening device, lock picks, micro camera, microchip, microfilm, microphone, miniature explosive, miniature submarine, mobile phone, motorcycle, newspaper with hole cut out, parachute, passport, perfume, personal jet pack, plastic explosives, poisoned lipstick, poison powder, poison ring, portable radar unit, retina scanner, rope, safecracking tools, safehouse, satellite linkup, scuba gear, scuba rebreather, secret identity, shoe device, sleep gas, smoke bomb, space suit, specialized suit (bullet proof, flying, heat proof, telemetry, water proof) sports car, spy camera, sword cane, tracking device, trench coat, tuxedo, two-way radio, video camera, voice recorder, walkie-talkie, weapon (atomic bomb, briefcase bomb, grenade launcher, industrial laser, rocket launcher, sniper rifle, surface-to-air missile), underwater car, wire cutter, x-ray glasses

TIMEKEEPING: alarm clock, anniversary clock, carriage clock, chronometer, cuckoo clock, egg timer, grandfather clock, grandmother clock, hourglass, pocket watch, stopwatch, sundial, timer, travel clock, watch, water clock, wristwatch

TOYS: action figure, ant farm, baby doll, ball, balloon, barrel of monkeys, BB gun, bean bag, bean bag toss, blocks, board game, building bricks, building logs, button on a string, cap pistol, car, cards, cash register, cat's cradle, chemistry set, cowboy hat, cowboy pistols, dice, dinosaurs, dishes, doll, doll bed, doll buggy, doll clothes, doll stroller, dominoes, easel, electronic game, fashion doll, finger puppet, flying disk, glider, gyroscope, gun holster, jacks, jigsaw puzzle, juggling balls, jump rope, kitchen set, marbles, model airplane, model car, model rocket, paper dolls, pedal car, pickup sticks, pinball game, pinwheel, plastic animals, plastic army men, pop gun, pogo stick, punching ball, puppet, race track, radio controlled car, ragdoll, scooter, shadow puppet, sled, slingshot, slot cars, soapbox racer, sock monkey, stuffed animal, tea set, teddy bear, top, train set, truck, wagon, walkie-talkie, yoyo; See also Sporting Goods

KITCHEN EQUIPMENT

APPLIANCES: 30-cup coffee maker, air popper, Belgian waffle iron, blender, bread maker, can opener, cappuccino machine, coffee grinder, coffee maker, coffee pot, deep fryer, electric frying pan, electric roaster,

electric tea pot, food processor, griddle, grill, hand mixer, hot dog roller, hot plate, hot pot, juicer, microwave oven, milkshake machine, percolator, pizza oven, popcorn popper, rice steamer, stand mixer, slow cooker, spice grinder, toaster, toaster oven, waffle iron

DRINKWARE: bottle, canteen, chalice, cup (coffee, demitasse, foam, paper, plastic, punch, tea, tin), glass (balloon, beer, champagne, claret, cocktail, cordial, flute, highball, iced tea, juice, martini, margarita, red wine, rocks, schooner, sherbet, shot, tea, water, white wine), goblet, mug, saki cup, saki server, snifter, tankard, tea bowl, tumbler, water bottle

EATING UTENSILS: crab cracker, fork (dessert, dinner, fondue, lobster, salad), knife (butter, dinner, fish, steak), lobster pick, spoon (caviar, dessert, grapefruit, iced tea spoon, serving, soup, sugar, tea, teaspoon), spork, straw

EQUIPMENT: babka mold, bain marie, bamboo steamer, banneton, boti, bowl, breadbox, bread board, bundt pan, butcher block, broiler pan, cabbage slicer, cake tin, canisters, canister set, canning kettle, casserole, cauldron, chafing dish, cheesecloth, chinoise, coffee filters, coffee mill, colander, cookie jar, cookie mold, cookie press, copper bowl, crock, crockery, custard cup, cutting board, decorating tips, double boiler, egg piercer, food mill, gelatin mold, griddle, gridiron, jelly sieve, kettle, knife sharpener, mandolin, mated colander pot, measuring cups, meat board, meat saw, mixing bowl, muffin tin, oil spritzer, oven mitt, pan (angel food cake, bread, cupcake, deep dish pie, frying, grill, jelly roll, muffin, pie, pizza, round cake, sauté, sheet, square cake, tart, tube), pepper mill, pizza peel, plastic containers, potholder, pot watcher, puree sieve, roulade needle, salad crisper, scale, scoop, spoon rest, sieve, skillet, soup pot, spice grinder, spider, stone jug, strainer, stockpot, string, tami, tea kettle

TABLEWARE: ash tray, asparagus server, berry bowl, bonbon dish, butter dish, cake basket, cake plate, cake stand, candy dish, celery server, cereal bowl, charger, cheese dome, cheese stand, coaster, coffee pot, comport, compote, console, cracker plate, creamer, cream soup bowl, deviled egg plate, divided bowl, egg cup, epergne, escargot plate, finger bowl, grill plate, gooseneck, gravy boat, hot chocolate pot, ice bucket, liner plate, marmalade jar, mayonnaise server, nappy dish, olive dish, oyster plate, parfait glass, pitcher, plate (bread and butter, dessert, dinner, luncheon, salad), platter, punch bowl, ramekin, relish tray, salt cellar, salt and pepper shakers, salad bowl, salver, samovar, sandwich server, sauce boat, saucer, serving bowl, sherbet dish, snack plate, soup cup, soup plate, sugar bowl, tea pot, tidbit plate, tiered server, tray, trencher, trifle bowl, tureen, vase, vegetable bowl

KITCHEN UTENSILS: baster, basting brush, basting syringe, bench scraper, boning scissors, cake server, cake tester, can opener, cheese slicer, chopsticks, citrus squeezer, cleaver, coconut grater, cookie cutter, crab cracker, cutlery, donut cutter, drum sieve, egg beater, egg slicer, egg timer, funnel, garlic press, grater (cheese, microplane, nutmeg, tower), honey server, ice cream scoop, ice pick, ladle, lame, kitchen scissors, knife (angel food cake, bread, butcher, butter, carving, chef, fillet, grapefruit, paring, steak, tomato, utility, vegetable), meat tenderizer, melon baller, mortar and pestle, nutcracker, nut grinder, offset spatuala, pancake turner, pastry bag, pastry blender, pastry brush, peeler, pie bird, pizza cutter, potato masher, reamer, ricer, roasting rack, rolling pin, rolling pin sock, rubber scraper, salt shaker, scraper, sifter, skimmer, spatula, spoon (measuring, mixing, serving, slotted, wooden), spreader, thermometer (candy, instant-read, meat), timer, tongs, whisk, zester

LINENS

BED: bed curtains, bed spread, blanket (cotton, electric, fur, winter, wool), chenille bedspread, comforter, covers, coverlet, draw sheet, dust ruffle, duvet, duvet cover, eiderdown comforter, fitted sheet, flat sheet, mattress pad, pillow case, pillow protector, pillow slip, quilt, throw

MISCELLANEOUS: doily, dresser scarf, mantle scarf

PILLOWS: accent, bed, bolster, cushion, neck support, throw

TABLE: napkin, placemat, runner, tablecloth

TOWEL: bar mop, bath, bath sheet, beach, dish, dish cloth, dish rag, face cloth, fingertip, flour sack, hand, kitchen, tea, Turkish towel, wash cloth, wash rag

WINDOW TREATMENTS: blinds, café curtains, curtains, draperies, drapes, holdbacks, kitchen curtains, mini blinds, Roman shade, shade, sheers, shutters, tiebacks, tiers, valance, Venetian blinds, wooden blinds

MUSICAL INSTRUMENTS

ELECTRONIC: etherophone, organ, piano, synthesizer, theremin

PERCUSSION: celesta, chime, clapper, clavichord, concussion club, cymbal, drum (bass, bongo, conga, kettle, side, slit, snare), fortepiano, glockenspiel, gong, jaw harp, marimba, metallophone, mouth harp, piano, pianoforte, rattle, tambourine, tam-tam, timpani, triangle, tubular bells, vibraphone, xylophone

STRING: banjo, bass (guitar, string), cello, cembalo, double bass, dulcimer, fiddle, guitar (acoustic, classical, electric, steel, steel-string, twelve-string), harp, harpsichord, lute, lyre, mandolin, spinet, viol, viola, viola d'amore, viole da gamba, violin, violone, virginal, zither

WIND/WOODWIND AND BRASS: accordion, bagpipe, baritone, bassoon (also fagott, fagotto), bass clarinet, bullroarer, clarinet, clarino, cor anglais, cornet, cornetto, dijerido, double bassoon, flute, harmonica, harmonium, horn (alp, English, French, flugel, ivory, steel, wood), kazoo, oboe, pan pipes, piccolo, post horn, recorder, rhombus, sackbut, saxophone (alto, baritone, bass, tenor, soprano), shell trumpet, sheng, Sousaphone, transverse flute, trombone, trumpet, tuba, turndun

ACCESSORIES: baton, bow, brush, capo, capotasto, case, chord finder, cleaner, cleaning cloth, cleaning kit, cover, drumsticks, electronic bow for guitar, fret marker, gig bag, guitar pick (felt, finger, flat, metal, plastic, rubber, thumb), instrument stand, metronome, music stand, mute, pickup, pick holder, pitch pipe, slide, strap, throat spray, tuner, tuning fork, whammy bar

PARTS: body, bridge, bridge pin, fret, hammer, key, keyboard, mouthpiece, neck, reed, rosette, string, tuning peg

TOOLS

ARCHITECTURAL/ENGINEERING: architect's scale, beam compass, caliper, chalk box, compass, engineer's scale, flexible curve, jig, laser level, laser line level, laser measuring tool, micrometer, plumb-bob, protractor, ruler, scale, sliding T-bevel, spirit level, square, straightedge, tape measure, template, triangle

HAND: adze, anvil, ax, baling hook, block & tackle, bolt cutter, box cutter, bradawl, breaker bar, broach, caulk gun, chisel, clamp, C-clamp, countersink, crimping pliers, crowbar, draw knife, drill, drill bit, emery cloth, file, glass cutter, grease gun, hammer (ball peen, rock, sledge, tack, upholstery), hatchet, knife, lathe, locking pliers, mallet, miter box, nut driver, paint brush, paint roller, pipe cutter, plane, pliers, plumber's snake, plunger, pocket knife, pry bar, pulley, punch, putty knife, rasp, ratchet, razor blade, reamer, rock pick, sandpaper, saw (bow, coping, fret, hand, masonry, metal, wood), scissors, scraper, scratch awl, screwdriver (flat head, Phillips), sharpening stone, spike, spike maul, skinning knife, splitting maul, splitting wedge, staple gun, staples, steel wool, tile nipper, tire iron, tongs, tongue and groove pliers, utility knife, wedge, whetstone, wire brush, wire cutter, wire stripper, wrench (allen, lug, monkey, pipe, sink, socket, torque,)

GARDEN: bulb planter, cultivator, dibble, edging tool, fertilizer spreader, fork, grass shears, hand shears, hand truck, hoe, hose, Korean hand plow, lopping shears, machete, pick, pickaxe, pitchfork, poacher's spade, posthole digger, pruning shears, rake, scythe, shovel, sickle, sod cutter, spade, sprinkler, tomato cage, trowel, wagon, watering can

LARGE: electric generator, garden cart, grindstone, jackhammer, ladder (extension, metal, step, wooden), merchant's scale, miter box, pressure washer, lawn roller, lawn sweeper, router table, sharpening wheel, wheelbarrow

POWER: angle grinder, auger, band saw, belt sander, blow torch, broaching machine, chain saw, chop saw, circular saw, concrete saw, cutting torch, diamond saw blade, die grinder, drill press, endmill, finishing sander, gear shaper, glue gun, grinding machine, grinding wheel, hammer drill, heat gun, hedge trimmer, hobbing machine, hydraulic torque wrench, impact driver, impact wrench, jack hammer, jig borer, jig saw, jointer, jointer planer, lawn aerator, lawn edger, lawn mower, leaf blower, metalworking lathe, milling cutter, miter saw, nail gun, orbital sander, planer, plasma cutter, pneumatic torque wrench, power drill, power lathe, power trowel, radial arm saw, random orbital sander, reciprocating saw, rivet gun, rotary tool, rototiller, router, sander, screw gun, screw machine, scroll saw, shaper, snow blower, snow plow, soldering iron, steam box, string trimmer, table saw, tap and die, thread restorer, tile cutter, thickness planer, tool bit, torque wrench, turret lathe, wall chaser, welder, wet/dry vacuum, wood shaper

FARM EQUIPMENT

GENERAL: air seeder, Allen scythe, backhoe loader, bale lifter, bale mover, bale spike, bale splitter, bale trailer, bale wrapper, baler, beet cleaner/loader, bed tiller, broadcast seeder, buck rake, bulk tank, center pivot irrigation, chaser bin, conditioner, conveyor analyzer, conveyor belt, cotton picker, cultivator, cultipacker, chisel plow, destoner, diet feeder, drip irrigation, fanning mill, feed grinder, fertilizer spreader, flail mower, gleaner, grain auger, grain cart, grain cleaner, grain dryer, gravity wagon, haulm topper, haulout transporter, harrow (disk, drag, spike), harvester, hay rake, hay tedder, hydroponics, liquid manure spreader, loader (front end, skid-steer, wagon), milking machine, milking pipeline, mower, mulch tiller, planter, plow, post driver, potato planter, potato spinner, power link box, power tiller, precision drill, produce sorter, rice huller, ridger, rock windrower, roller, rotary tiller, seed drill, self-loading wagon, shear grab, sickle, slurry agitator, spading machine, sprayer, stone picker, subsoiler, swather, terragator, topper, tractor mounted forklift, transplanter, transport box, tree trimmer, yard scraper; See also Tools

HORSE DRAWN: cart, corn planter, cultivator, forecart, grain seeder, hay chopper, hay tedder, mower, potato plow, potato spinner, reaper, reaper-binder, rotary side delivery rake, scraper, seed drill, sickle mower, skidder, three-point plow, spring tine harrow, threshing machine, wagon plow, walking plow

STEAM POWERED: agricultural engine, drag harrow, flail, hog oiler, plowing engine, portable engine, reaper, reaper-binder, stationary steam engine, steam tractor, winnowing fan, threshing machine, winnowing machine

CHAPTER 6: FOOD

BAKERY

BREAD

USAGE NOTE: Nearly every culture on earth has some form of bread, ranging from a grilled flour and water mixture to complex braided or fruit-studded creations. Bread can be as fancy or as simple as a setting requires. Thousands of different types of bread are known around the world.

GENERAL VARIETIES: anadama, artisan, babka, bagel, baguette, bannock, bara brith, barmbrack, batter, batter bread, beer, biscuit, bizcochos, black, bocadillo, bolillo, balloon, Boston brown, boule, bran, broa, brioche, brown, bun, bush bread, challah, chapati, ciabatta, cheese, cinnamon, cinnamon roll, cocktail rye, corn, corn fritter, cottage loaf, cracked wheat, crepe, crisp bread, croissant, crumpet, damper, dampfnudel, dinkelbrot, dinner roll, egg twist, English muffin, flatbread, focaccia, fougasse, French, fry bread, granary, griddle cake, grissini, hallulla, hardtack, hoecake, hushpuppy, Indian, injera, Italian, Johnny cake, journey cake, lavash, lefse, mantou, matzo (ball, cracker, meal), monkey, naan, oatmeal, oplatek (Christmas wafer), packaged, pain au levain, pan bread, pancake, pan de piso, pandesal, pandoro, pan dulce, panettone, pan serrano, paratha, parker house roll, pizza crust, pita, popover, pogacha, potato, pretzel, proja, pull-apart, pumpernickel, puri, raisin, rghifa, rice, roti, rumali roti, rye (dark, German, Jewish, light, marbled), scali, scone, seed cake, ship's biscuit, soda bread, sopaipilla, sourdough, spoonbread, stollen, sweet roll, taco shell, tiger, tortilla (flour, corn, whole wheat), unleavened, Vienna, wafer, waffle, wheat, whole wheat, wonton, wonton wrapper, zopf, zwieback

RELATED: batter, bread bowl, bread pudding, bread stick (garlic, hard, soft), brewis, bruschetta, cheesy garlic bread, crouton, crumb, crust, dough, dressing, dumpling, garlic bread, heel, loaf, Melba toast, sippet, sop, spaetzel, stuffing, Texas toast, toast, toast point, tortilla chip

QUICK BREAD: apple, banana, beer, blueberry, cinnamon, cranberry, pumpkin, raisin, zucchini

USAGE NOTE: A quick bread is distinguished by its technique; liquid ingredients are combined in one bowl while dry ingredients are combined in another. The two are then mixed together, resulting in the quick bread batter. This is in contrast to yeast bread, which requires time for dough to rise alternated with kneading and shaping.

RELIGIOUS: communion, Eucharist, holy communion, host, sacramental bread, wafer

SWEET BAKERY

CAKE: angel, angel food, apple, applesauce, bakewell tart, banana, banana chocolate chip, birthday, Black Forest, blitz, buccellato, buche de noel, bundt, butter, butterfly, butter brickle, carrot, cheesecake, chiffon, chocolate, chocolate chip, Christmas, coffee cake, coconut, confetti, cupcake, date, date nut, devils food, flourless chocolate, fruitcake (light, dark), fruit cocktail, genoise, German chocolate, ginger bread, gold, graham cracker, groom's, half-sheet, hot milk, ice cream, ice cream roll, jelly roll, lady finger, lava, layer, lemon, madeira, marble, molten chocolate, moon, Napolean, nut, oatmeal, orange, orange coconut, pavlova, petits fours, pineapple, pineapple upside-down, poppyseed, pound, queen's, raisin, red velvet, rhubarb, ring, round, rum, sacher torte, sheet, simnel, soufflé, spice, sponge, square, stack, streusel, sun, Swiss roll, teacake, tiered, tiramisu, tomato soup, tres leches, upside-down, wedding, Welsh, white, yellow, zucchini

COOKIE: apple, apricot, bar, blond brownie, blondie, boiled, bourbon ball, brownie, butter, butterscotch, chocolate, chocolate chip, chocolate chunk, cinnamon, coconut, cornflake, cowboy, cut-out, drop, ginger bread, ginger snap, graham cracker, lace, macaroon, madeline, Mexican wedding cake, molasses, oatmeal (chocolate chip, date, iced, raisin), peanut butter, pecan finger, petticoat tail, pinwheel, pizelle, potato chip, pumpkin, pumpkin bar, ranger, refrigerator, rolled, sandwich, thumbprint, snickerdoodle, snow ball, sugar, tart, whoopie pie

DONUT/DOUGHNUT: bear claw, beaver tail, beignet, Berliner, bismark, Boston cream, chocolate, chocolate cream filled, chocolate frosted, churro, cider, cinnamon roll, cinnamon twist, coconut, comfit, cream

filled, custard filled, cruller, danish, donut hole, elephant ear, fritter, frosted, fudge covered, glazed, jelly filled, kolache, long John, mini, paczki, pershing, plain, potato, powdered sugar, sopaipilla, sour cream, sugar

MUFFIN: apple, bacon, banana, blueberry, bran, butter, cheese, cherry, chocolate, chocolate chip, cinnamon, cranberry, cream cheese, lemon poppyseed, peach, pumpkin, raspberry, streusel

PIE: apple (Dutch, sour cream, streusel), apple cranberry, banana cream, blueberry, brownie, butter, chess, chocolate (chip, cream, sundae), coconut, cream, custard, date, double crust, funeral, grasshopper, key lime, lemon cream, lemon meringue, lattice, meringue, mincemeat, nectarine, peach, pear, pecan, plum, prune, pumpkin, raspberry, rhubarb, shoo-fly, sour cream raisin, strawberry, streusel, toffee,

MISCELLANEOUS DESSERT: baked Alaska, bread pudding, buckle, cannoli, cheesecake, chocolate éclair, cobbler, cream puff, crème brulee, dumpling, fool, fruit pizza, plum pudding, pudding, rice pudding, schaum torte, slump, strawberry shortcake, tapioca pudding, tart, trifle; See also Dairy

CANDY

GENERAL: after dinner mint, all-day sucker, anise, anise bears, bark, boiled sweet, bon bon, Boston baked beans, brittle, bubblegum, bubblegum cigar, butter mint, butterscotch, butterscotch disk, candied fruit, candy bar, candy buttons, candy cane, candy cigarette, candy corn, candy floss, candy necklace, candy raisin, candy stick, caramel, cherry sour, chewing gum, cinnamon bear, cinnamon gum, cinnamon drops, circus peanuts, coconut haystacks, coffee, confection, conversation hearts, cotton candy, cream, divinity, fairy floss, fairy food, French burnt peanuts, fruit slices, glazed nuts, gumball, gumdrop, gummi bears, gummi fish, gummi worms, Halloween, hard, hazelnut, jawbreaker, jelly bean, jelly nougat, licorice, licorice pastel, licorice wheel, lipstick, lollipop, maple, marshmallow, marshmallow ice cream cone, marzipan, mint, nougat, nut bark, nut brittle, orange slices, party mint, pastel mint, peanut brittle, peanut butter fudge, peppermint, peppermint bark, peppermint disk, peppermint stick, popcorn ball, praline, red hots, red licorice, ribbon, rock candy, root beel barrel, safety sucker, salt water taffy, seafoam, shoelace licorice, sour, spearmint leaves, sucker, sugar-free, Swedish fish, taffy, tart, toffee, Turkish delight, Turkish taffy, wafer, wax bottles, wax lips

CHOCOLATE: assorted, baking, bridge mix, chips, chocolate-covered caramel, chocolate-covered cherry, chocolate-covered peanuts, chocolate-covered raisins, Christmas, chunk, coin, dark, Easter (bunny, egg, rabbit), fountain, fudge, hearts, heart-shaped box, light, milk, mint meltaway, nonpareil, nut cluster, peanut butter cup

DAIRY

CHEESE, COMMON VARIETIES: acapella, American, asiago, baby Swiss, bakers, bathtub, beer, bleu, blue vein, breakfast, brick, brie, camembert, cheddar (longhorn, marbled, mild, medium, processed, sharp, extra sharp), cheddar clothbound, cheese ball, cheese spread, Cojack, Colby, Colby-Jack, cold pack, Cougar Gold, crowley, Cypress Grove chevre, curds, dry Jack, edam, English cheddar, farmer, feta, fontina, fresh Jack, fresh mozzarella, gorgonzola, gouda, gruyere, havarti, Hubbardston blue cow, Jarlsberg, monastery, Monterey Jack, Monterey Jack dry, mozzarella, Muenster, parmesan, pasteurized processed, pecorino, pepper jack, Pinconning, Plymouth, provel, provolone, queso, romano, roquefort, smoked, Sonoma jack, spray cheese in a can, stilton, string, Swiss, Texas goat cheese, Tillamook cheddar

RELATED, CHEESE DISHES: cheese pizza, cheese quesadilla, macaroni and cheese

CHEESE, MOIST: cottage (low fat, fat free), cream, crème fraiche, flavored cream cheese, mascarpone, Neufchatel, ricotta

CHEESE, INTERNATIONAL VARIETIES: abertam, akkawi, allgauer, anari, anthotyros, areesh, arseniko naxou, ayib, aura, bachensteiner, bandel, basket, batzos, Bavaria blue, beast, bergkase, bokmakiri, bonifaz, brinsen, Brussels, byaslang, cambozola, caravane, chevre metsovou, cherni vit green, chhena, chhurpi, chimay, chura kampo, chura loenpa, danbo, Danish blue, Danish port-salut, Danish tilsit, dimsi, dunavia, esrom, flower of rajya, formaela, froumaela, fynbo, galotyri, gelundener kase, gbejna, gouda, graviera, grevenbroeker, grilled halloumi, handkase, harzer, hellim, herve, hirtenkase, hofoingi, imsil, kalathaki, kalathotos, kefalotyri, kesong, khoa,

komyati, kwaito, jameed, jibneh arabieh, karikeftos, kaseri, kashkaval, kashkawan, kashta, katiki, kefalograviera, kefalotyri, korozott, kopanisti, krasotyri, krema, labneh, ladenios, ladotyri, latvijas, le wavreumont, lappi, leipajuusto, lighvan, limburger, liptauer, livno, lori, luneberg, maish krej, majdoule, malaka, manouri, mastelo, maredsous, mekkerbek, melichlora, mesh, metsovella, metsovone, milbenkase, molbo, mondseer, montafoner sauerkase, mqundu, myzithra, nabulsi, naxos, nguri, oazis, orda, olomoucke syrecky, oltermanni, palpusztai, paneer, parmigiano reggiano, paski sir, passendale, petroti, pichtogalo chanion, quesong puti, raejuusto, rauchkase, remoudou, rodoric, romadur, roomy, rubing, rushan, saga, sakura, samso, san michali, selles-sur-cher, sfela, shanklish, sirene, sirenje, skripavac, skyr, staazer, stamatini, steirerkase, suluguni, syrian, tilsit, tiroler graukase, touloumisio, tounjski sir, trappista, tybo, Tyrolean grey, urda, xygalo, xynomizithra, xynotyro, wara, weisslacker

ICE CREAM: hand packed, lowfat, scoop, soft serve, sugar-free

RELATED: frappe, gelato, granita, frozen custard, frozen yogurt, frozen fudge pop, ice pop, Italian ice, malt, milkshake, sherbet, sorbet

RELATED, ICE CREAM FLAVORS: amaretto, apple, apricot, banana, banana split, birthday cake, blackberry, black cherry, black forest, black walnut, blueberry, blue moon, brownie, butter brickle, butter pecan, cappuccino, caramel, caramel cashew, caramel turtle, cheesecake, cherry, cherry amaretto, chocolate, chocolate chip, cinnamon, coconut, coffee, cookie dough, cookies and cream, cotton candy, espresso, French vanilla, German chocolate, key lime, lemon, maple, marshmallow, mint, mint chocolate chip, mocha, neopolitan, orange, peach, peanut butter, piña colada, pistachio, praline, pumpkin, raspberry, rocky road, rum, strawberry, toffee, tutti frutti, vanilla, vanilla bean, watermelon

RELATED, ICE CREAM CONES: cookie bowl, flat-bottom, sugar cone, wafer cone, waffle bowl, waffle cone

RELATED, ICE CREAM MIX-INS: brownie, cookie, cheesecake, chocolate chip, chocolate chunk, chocolate flake, crumb, crunch, marshmallow, pie crust, ribbon, ripple, streusel; See also Fruit, Nuts

RELATED, ICE CREAM TOPPINGS: banana, brownie, caramel, chocolate sauce, hot fudge, maraschino cherry, marshmallow, nuts, strawberries, raspberries, whipped cream

RELATED, ICE CREAM DESSERTS: banana split, ice cream cake, ice cream cake roll, ice cream sandwich, parfait, sundae

MILK: 1%, 2%, chocolate, evaporated, fat free, goat's, low fat, sheep's, skim, whole

MILK, NONDAIRY: almond milk, soy milk

OTHER: cream, coffee creamer, light cream, Greek yogurt, half and half, heavy cream, light yogurt, sour cream (low fat, fat free), whipped cream, whipping cream, yogurt

> **USAGE NOTE:** Whipping cream is liquid and is identical to heavy cream. Whipped cream is a liquid cream that has been whipped to a semisolid state.

DRY GOODS/PANTRY

CONDIMENTS: barbecue sauce, catsup, chutney, cocktail sauce, horseradish, ketchup, mayonnaise, mustard (brown, Dijon, honey, yellow), cranberry relish, pickle relish, tartar sauce

GRAIN: amaranth, barley, buckwheat, corn, emmer, oat, maize, millet (finger, foxtail, Japanese, kodo, pearl, proso), polenta, quinoa, rice (basmati, brown, instant, jasmine, white, wild), rye, spelt, teff, triticale, wheat

JAM/JELLY/PRESERVES: apple butter, apricot, blackberry, blueberry, cherry, grape, orange marmalade, peach, pear, pineapple, plum, raspberry, rhubarb, strawberry

LEGUMES: adzuki bean, black bean, black-eyed pea, black soybean, broad bean, butter bean, calico bean, cannellini bean, chickpea, edamame, fava bean, garbanzo bean, great northern bean, Italian bean, kidney bean (dark red, light red), lentil, lima bean, mung bean, navy bean, peanut, pink bean, pinto bean, red bean, soy bean, split pea (green, yellow), white bean

NUTS: almond, brazil, cashew, filbert, hazelnut, macadamia, peanut (dry roasted, beer, honey roasted), pecan, pistachio, walnut

OILS: almond, beech nut, canola, cashew, coconut, corn, cottonseed, flaxseed, grapeseed, hazelnut, lemon, macadamia, olive, orange, palm, peanut, pecan, pine nut, pistachio, rapeseed, safflower, sesame, soybean, sunflower, truffle, vegetable, walnut,

PASTA: alphabet, angel hair, bowtie, bucatini, campanelle, cannelloni, capellini, cavatelli, couscous, farfalle, fettuccini, fusilli, gemelli, lasagna, linguine, macaroni, manicotti, mostaccioli, orzo, penne, penne rigate, radiator, ravioli, rigatoni, rotelle, rotini, shell, spaghetti, spiral, tagliatelle, thin spaghetti, tortellini, vermicelli, wagon wheel

PICKLED/RELISH: beet, bread & butter, cantaloupe pickle, corn relish, cranberry, cranberry orange, cucumbers (dill, garlic, kosher, midget, refrigerator, relish, sweet), mushroom, onion, pepper, pepperoncini, pepper relish, spiced apples, sweet-sour, three bean, watermelon pickle

SALAD DRESSING: cole slaw, French, fruit, green goddess, hot bacon, Italian (creamy, oil and vinegar), mayonnaise, oil and vinegar, ranch, sour cream, thousand island, vinaigrette,

SEEDS: flax, mustard, poppy, safflower, sesame, sunflower

SPICES: allspice, basil, bay leaf, cardamom, cinnamon, chervil, chili powder, chives, cilantro, cloves, coriander, cumin, curry powder, dill weed, garlic powder, ginger, mace, marjoram, mustard, nutmeg, oregano, paprika, parsley, pepper (black, red, white), poppyseed, poultry seasoning, rosemary, sage, saffron, savory, star anise, thyme, turmeric

STAPLES: baking ammonia, baking powder, baking soda, corn meal, corn syrup (dark, light), cream of tartar, flour (bread, cake, pastry, rice, unbleached, white, whole wheat), honey, molasses, peanut butter (chunky, smooth), sorghum, sugar (10x, brown, confectioner's, dark brown, granulated, light brown, powdered, superfine, white), yeast (cake, dry, quick-rise)

EGGS

SIZES: extra large, jumbo, large, medium, small

STYLES: boiled, frittata, hard boiled, omelet, over easy, over medium, over hard, poached, quiche, scrambled, shirred, soft boiled, sunny side up

FISH/SEAFOOD

TYPES: abalone, anchovy, baby scallop, calamari, catfish, clam, cod, coho salmon, crab, grouper, haddock, herring, king salmon, lake perch, lake trout, lobster, mahi mahi, northern pike, ocean perch, octopus, oyster, pike, pollack, prawn, rainbow trout, salmon, sea scallop, shark, shrimp (tiny, small, medium, large, jumbo), smelt, tilapia, tuna, walleye pike, whitefish

MEALS: bouillabaisse, casserole, crab cake, croquette, en coquille, en croute, fillet, fish and chips, fish burger, fish sandwich, fish sticks, hot dish, kabob, Newburg, pie, planked fish, tuna patty, scampi-style, seafood newburg, sushi

FRUIT

APPLES: Braeburn, Cortland, crab, Fuji, gala, Granny Smith, Ida red, Jonagold, mackintosh, red delicious, Rome beauty, royal gala, yellow delicious

BERRIES: blackberry, black currant, black raspberry, blueberry, boysenberry, cranberry, elderberry, gooseberry, huckleberry, kiwiberry, lingonberry, loganberry, mulberry, red currant, strawberry, white currant

CITRUS: blood orange, citron, clementine, key lime, kumquat, lemon, lime, mandarin orange, naval orange, orange, pink grapefruit, red grapefruit, sour orange, tangelo, tangerine, uglifruit, white grapefruit

GRAPES: black, green, raisin, red

MELONS: cantaloupe, casaba, honeydew, musk, Santa Claus, watermelon

PEARS: Anjou, D'anjou, Bartlett, Bosc, green, yellow

PIT FRUITS: apricot, avocado, cherry (bing, black, red, sour, tart), nectarine, peach (cling, donut, white flesh), plum (beach, black, Italian, red, prune), pluot

TROPICAL/EXOTIC: banana, carambola, coconut, date, fig, guava, kiwi, mango, papaya, passion fruit, persimmon, pineapple, plantain, pomegranate, star fruit

UNUSUAL EDIBLE: abiu, acai, acerola, ackee, African cherry orange, ambarella, araza, arhat, atemoya, babaco, bacupari, bacuri, bael, barbadine, batuan, bearberry, betel nut, bignay, bilberry, bilimbi, biribi, bitter melon, black apple, black sapote, blue tongue, bolwarra, boquila, breadnut, broad-leaf bramble, Buddha's hand, buffaloberry, butterfruit, button mangosteen, caimito, calamansi, calamondin, camucamu, canistel, cardon, carob, cashew apple, cassabanana, cawesh, ceriman, charichuelo, chayote, chempedak, chenet, cherimoya, chokeberry, chupa-chupa, cloudberry, cluster fig, cobrafruit, cocky apple, conkerberry, crowberry, cudrang, cupuacu, custard apple, date, dead man's fingers, desert banana, desert fig, dewberry, doubah, double coconut, dragonfruit, duku, durian, eggfruit, elephant apple, emu apple, emu berry, feijoa, five fingers fruit, gac, galia melon, gambooge, genip, giant granadilla, goumi, granadilla, greengage, grumichama, guanabana, guavaberry, hackberry, horned melon, huito, imbe, jabuticaba, jackfruit, jambul, jatoba, jelly palm, jocote, jujube, juniper berry, kabosu, kahikatea, kapok, karkalla, karonda, kei apple, keule, key apple, kitembilla, kiwano, korlan, kutjera, kwai muk, lady apple, langsat, lanzones, lapsi, lardizabala, lillypilly, limeberry, limequat, longan, longevity fruit, longkong, loquat, lychee, mabolo, madrono, mamey, mammee apple, mamoncillo, manoao, ma-praang, maqui, marang, marula, mayhaw, medlar, melinjo, melon pear, midyim, miracle fruit, mombin, morinda, mortino, mundu, muntries, muscadine, naartjie, nageia, nance, nangka, nannyberry, naranjilla, neem, noni, nungu, olallieberry, papaya, pawpaw, peumo, phalsa, pitanga, pitaya, pitomba, pomcite, pomelo, pommerac, pond-apple, prickly pear, pulasan, pummelo, pupunha, purple apple-berry, quince, rambutan, rattan fruit, riberry, rimu, rollinia, rose hip, rowan, rumberry, safou, sageretia, saguaro, salak, salal, salmonberry, santol, saskatoonberry, scuppernong, serviceberry, shipova, snakefruit, snow berry, soncoya, sorb, soursop, southern crabapple, spanish tamarind, spiny monkey-orange, star apple, strawberry pear, sugar apple, sultana, sweet apple-berry, sweet granadilla, sweet lemon, sweet pepper, sweetsop, Sycamore fig, Tahitian apple, tamarillo, tamarind, tanjong, tayberry, thimbleberry, toyon, ugni, vanilla, wampee, water apple, whortleberry, wineberry, wolfberry, wongi, wood apple, yantok, yellow mombin, yellow sapote, youngberry, zig zag vine

MEAT

BEEF: brain, chuck roast, chuck steak, filet mignon, ground (beef, chuck, sirloin), hamburger, heart, liver, New York strip, porterhouse, prime rib, ribs, rump roast, roast, short rib, sirloin, sirloin tip roast, standing rib roast, steamship round, sweetbread, tongue, steak

PORK: crown roast of pork, ground pork, ham, hocks, loin chop, loin roast, pig roast, rib chop, sausage, shredded pork, tenderloin

MEALS: bangers and mash, bourguinon, casserole, cheeseburger, chili, corned beef, croquette, cube steak, cutlet, goulash, hamburger, hash, head cheese, lasagna, meatball, meatloaf, paprikash, pasta sauce, patty (ham, hamburger) pizza, porcupine meatball, pot pie, pot roast, pulled pork, rouladen, sarma, sauerbraten, schnitzel, stew, stroganoff, stuffed pepper, stuffed pork chop, sulz, Swiss steak

MEAT PIES: bacon and egg, corned beef, cottage, curry, homity, mince, pizza, pot pie, pork, scotch, shell, shepherd's, stargazy, steak and kidney, tourtière, wild game

OTHER: frog leg, lamb, lamb chops, mutton, venison

SAUSAGE: andoulli, blood, bratwurst, chorizo, corn dog, frankfurter, hot dog, Hungarian, Italian, kielbasa, Polish, ring bologna, wiener

WILD GAME: bear, chipmunk, deer, hare, opossum, rabbit, squirrel

POULTRY

TYPES: chicken, Cornish hen, duck, goose, grouse, partridge, pheasant, quail, squab, turkey

MEALS: ala king, cacciatore, casserole, chicken pot pie, coq au vin, croquette, hot dish

SALAD, SANDWICH, SOUP, SNACKS

SALADS: antipasto, Caesar, caprese, chef, chicken, cobb, dinner, garden, gelatin, green, layered, pasta, seafood, shrimp, side, spinach, tossed, tuna, vegetable

SANDWICHES: bacon-lettuce-and-tomato, barbecue, barbecued chicken, calzone, cheese, cheeseburger, chicken, chicken salad, club, crabmeat, Cuban, Dagwood, egg salad, finger, grilled cheese, gyro, ham, hamburger, ham salad, Monte Cristo, muffuletta, panini, pasty, peanut butter and banana, peanut butter and jelly, pulled pork, reuben, roast beef, salami, sandwich loaf, sloppy joe, submarine, tuna salad, turkey, watercress

SOUP: barley, bean, beef, borscht, chicken, chicken noodle, chicken rice, chowder, cream (asparagus, broccoli, carrot, celery, chicken, mushroom), egg drop, gazpacho. gumbo, hot and sour, lentil, minestrone, mulligatawny, oxtail, tomato, ramen noodle, vegetable, vichysoisse

SNACKS: beef jerky, cheese ball, cheese curls, corn chip, corn curls, nuts & bolts, popcorn (air popped, caramel, cheddar, cheese, kettle corn, microwave, movie, pizza, popcorn ball, white, yellow), pretzel (Bavarian, nugget, rod, soft, stick, tiny twist, twist), potato chip (barbecue, cheese, deli, kettle cooked, plain, sour cream & onion), snack mix, tortilla chip, turkey jerky

VEGETABLES

VARIETIES: alfalfa sprout, artichoke, arugula, asparagus (green, white), avocado, bamboo shoot, bean (bush, green, pole, runner, wax, yellow), beet, beet green, bell pepper (green, orange, red, yellow), bok choy, broccoli, broccoli rabe, Brussels sprouts, cabbage (Chinese, green, kimchee, napa, purple, red, sauerkraut, Savoy), carrot, cassava, cauliflower, celeriac, celery, chard (Swiss, red, white, yellow), chickweed, chicory, collard greens, corn (baby, bicolor, sweet, white, yellow), cress, cucumber, daikon, eggplant (purple, white), elephant garlic, ginger, gobo, endive, fennel, fiddlehead, horseradish, garlic, Jerusalem artichoke, jicama, kale, kohlrabi, lettuce (asparagus, bibb, Boston, butter, butterhead, crisphead, cos, green leaf, head, iceberg, leaf, red leaf, romaine, stem) leek, mushroom (baby bella, button, morel, portabella, shitake), mustard greens, okra, olive (black, green, ripe) onion (green, red, Spanish, Vidalia, white, yellow), parsnip, peas (baby, English, le seur, tiny, medium, mixed, snap, snow, sugar snap), pimiento, potato (fingerling, new, red, russet, salad, white, Yukon gold), pumpkin, purslane, radicchio, radish, ramp, rhubarb, rutabaga, salsify, scallion, shallot, spinach, sorrel, summer squash (yellow, zucchini), squash blossom, sweet potato, taro, tomatillo, tomato (cherry, grape, red, yellow), turnip, turnip green, water chestnut, winter squash (also called hard squash: acorn, butternut, hubbard), yam

VEGETABLES, COOKED: baked beans, green bean casserole, potatoes (au gratin, American fries, baked, boiled, broiled, cottage fries, duchess, escalloped, French fries, hash brown, mashed, pancake, riced, shoestring, suzette, twice-baked, waffle fries), spinach soufflé

BEVERAGES

ALCOHOLIC

Beer: ale, black and tan, bock, dark, ginger, half and half, hard cider, hard lemonade, lager, light, limbic, malt liquor, microbrew, mybock, near, Oktoberfest, pilsner, porter, stout, weiss, wheat

COCKTAILS: boilermaker, bloody Mary, blue lagoon, blue Hawaiian, dacquiri, godfather, godmother, mai tai, manhattan, martini, old fashioned, piña colada, sidecar, Singapore sling, stinger, swamp water, Tom Collins, whisky sour, zombie

USAGE NOTE: An unlimited number of cocktails, generally called rail drinks, can be formed by mixing a liquor with a soda, such as rum and cola, scotch and soda, or gin and tonic.

GARNISHES: celery salt, celery stick, coffee bean, lemon twist, lemon wheel, lime wedge, lime wheel, maraschino cherry, nutmeg, olive, orange slice, paper umbrella, pickle, pickled onion, pineapple wedge

HARD LIQUOR: anisette, bourbon, brandy, cognac, crème de cacao, crème de menthe, gin, rum (dark, light), rye, schnapps (peach, peppermint, root beer), scotch, sloe gin, vermouth (dry, sweet), vodka, whisky

HOT DRINKS: flaming rum punch, hot buttered rum, Irish coffee, schnapps and hot chocolate

ICE CREAM DRINKS: brandy alexander, grasshopper, pink squirrel

MIXERS (NONALCOHOLIC): bitters, cream, grenadine, ice cream, lime juice, simple syrup, sugar, Worcestershire sauce

WINE, RED: beaujolais, burgundy, cabernet sauvignon, carminere, chianti, marsala (dry, sweet), merlot, pinot noir, sangiovese, sangria, sherry, shiraz, syrah, zinfandel

WINE, WHITE: auslese, beerenauslese, chablis, champagne, chardonnay, gewürztraminer, Johannesberg riesling, kabinett, late harvest riesling, liebfraumilch, mead, pinot grigio, rhine, riesling, sauterne, sauvignon blanc, sparkling wine, white merlot, white zinfandel

NONALCHOHOLIC

COFFEE DRINKS: café au lait, café mocha, cappuccino, decaf, espresso, frappuccino, half-caf, iced, latte, regular, Turkish coffee, Vienna coffee

COFFEE VARIETIES: Arabica, Barako, Liberica, Robusto

RELATED, COFFEE BEAN ROASTS: American, cinnamon, city, continental, French, full city, half-city, Italian, New England, Spanish, Vienna

DAIRY: eggnog, frappe, malted milk, milk (1%, 2%, butter, chocolate, fat free, low fat, skim, whole), milk shake, Tom & Jerry

FRUIT DRINKS: hot cider, lemonade, limeade, orangeade, punch, slush, slushie, smoothie

FRUIT JUICE: apple, apple cider, cherry, cranberry, grape, grapefruit, mango, orange, passionfruit, pomegranate

TEA: assam, black, bohea, Chinese gunpowder, darjeeling, dianhong, Earl Grey, English breakfast, Formosa oolong, Golden Monkey, green, herbal, Irish breakfast, keemun, lapsang souchong, Nepal, nilgiri, oolong, orange pekoe, pekoe, peppermint, rize, rooibos, rose hip, Silver Needle, Tibeti, Vietnamese, white, yerba mate, Yingdehong

SOFT DRINKS: club soda, cola, ginger ale, root beer, pop, seltzer, soda (black cherry, blue raspberry, cherry, grape, lemon-lime, peach, white), soda water, sparkling water, tonic water

VEGETABLE JUICE: beet, carrot, cucumber, celery, dandelion green, fennel, kale, parsley, pumpkin, tomato, turnip

CHAPTER 7: COMBAT, ARMOR, AND WEAPONS

This chapter details many forms of combat, armor, and weapons from a variety of cultures and across many centuries. A few notes are in order to help guide users through this section.

HISTORICAL CONTEXT: In any writing, research is needed to select proper weapons and armor for the time period and culture. In the sections that follow, weapons and armor are divided into Pre-1900 and Post-1900 lists. This helps to divide objects into approximate modern and antique categories.

RESOURCES: In fiction, some liberties may be taken with armor and weapons as long as those liberties are plausible. The invention of entirely new weapons is reasonable depending upon available resources. Consider the climate and setting when inventing objects. In a desert setting in which trees are scarce, such as ancient Egypt, weapons are likely to be made of metal or stone rather than wood. In an arctic climate, inhabitants are not likely to have access to metal deposits, so bone tools and weapons might be common.

TECHNOLOGY LEVEL: Weapons and armor changed dramatically over time depending upon technological advances. The earliest weapons were rocks and sticks. Weapons then evolved as sticks were sharpened and hardened in fire, and stones were chipped or split to form axes and arrow points.

A culture's technology level will impact its objects. Even in the presence of great iron, copper, or other metal deposits, a culture will need the means to excavate those metals and work them into tools and weapons. This implies some level of competence in smelting, smithing, and forging.

COMBAT VOCABULARY

GENERAL: absent without leave, adversaries, ambush, armistice, assail, assault, army, atrocities, AWOL, attack, battalion, battle, beachhead, beset, blitz, blitzkrieg, blockade, bluff, bombard, bombardier, bombardment, breakout, calculated risk, campaign, capitulate, casualty, ceasefire, charge, civilian, Civil War, clash, collateral damage, column, combat, combined arms maneuver, conflict, confrontation, conquest, cordon, cover, cover fire, cower, crusade, damage, defeat, defend, defense, defense in depth, deserter, desertion, deterrence, dispute, enchant, encircle, enfilade, engulf, enmesh, ensnare, entrap, envelop, eradicate, espionage, ethnic cleansing, explosion, exterminate, extraction, extricate, fire (cover, masking), flank, fog of war, foothold, foray, fortification, fracas, fray, genocide, give ground, goal (operational, strategic, tactical), guard, harass, holy war, incursion, impasse, infiltration, inquisition, insertion, insurgency, invasion, invade, invader, jihad, joint operations, joist, lightning strike, line of defense, logistics, looting, melee, MIA, military-industrial complex, missing in action, mutiny, no-fly zone, neutralize, objective, occupation, offense (air, ground, naval), offensive, onslaught, operation, oppose, overthrow, overwhelm, peace keeping force, penetration, picket, pillage, pillaging, pinned down, plunder, police action, post traumatic stress, POW, pre-dawn, preemptive strike, prisoner, prisoner of war, prone, pursue, raid, ranged combat, ransack, rebellion, recoil, resistance, retreat, retreat in force, revolt, revolution, rout, sabotage, salvo, saturation bombing, security, seize, sharpshooter, skirmish, slash and burn, sniper, sniping, sortie, spy, spying, squad, squadron, stalemate, stalk, strategic offensive, submit, surprise attack, strike, surgical strike, superiority (air, ground, naval), supremacy, support (air, ground, naval), surrender, surround, surprise, surveillance, tactics, target, targeting, terrain warfare (air, arctic, desert, house-to-house, jungle, littoral, naval, trench, urban), theater of war, trap, treaty, troop, truce, upheaval, uprising, volley fire, war (asymmetric, biological, chemical, guerrilla, mountain, nuclear, space, unconventional), war council, warfare, war of attrition, war tribunal, waylay, weapons of mass destruction, withdraw, withdrawal, yield

ATTACK: annihilate, assassinate, bash, batter, beat, bespell, blast, butcher, charge, clobber, clout, counterattack, crush, cuff, destroy, devastate, discharge, dispatch, eliminate, eradicate, execute, explode, force, gouge, gun down, hammer, hit, initiate, injure, instigate, jab, kill, launch, lunge, massacre, murder, obliterate, overcome, overwhelm, paralyze, plunge, poke, pounce, pound, prod, pummel, punch, purge, ravage, shoot, slap, slaughter, slay, smack, stab, strike, stun, subdue, surprise, swing, swipe, thrash, thrust, thump, trap, trigger, trounce, unleash, wallop, whack, wrestle, wound

MOVES: absorb, blind, block, charge, concealed, cowering, defense, defenseless, disarm, disengage, dodge, evade, flank, invisible, melee, prone, stun, ranged combat, rear, stable footing, storm, rout, surrender, unstable footing, war cry

TACTICS: blockade, embargo, flank, guerilla, hit-and-run, pike line, pincer maneuver, scorched earth, siege, smokescreen, surround

FENCING

EQUIPMENT: bayonet, blade (forte, middle, foible), broadsword, button, épée, fencing jacket, fencing vest, foil (anatomical, French, Italian), French grip, guard, glove (cotton, fencing, leather), hilt, lamé, Italian grip, maraging (steel), marker points, martingale, mask (foil, saber, three-weapon), pistol grip, plastron, pommel, rapier, saber, small sword, three-prong, two-prong, whites (clothing)

VOCABULARY: absence of blade, advance, arm position (high, inside, low, outside), assault, attack, balestra, beat, bind, bout, bouting, broken time, change of engagement, compound, concentration, contre-temp, contre de quarte, contre de sixte, coule, counter parry, counterattack, coupe, cross, cut, deception, direct attack, disengage, displacement, double attack, engage, engagement, en garde, envelopement, false attack, feint, fencing strip, fleche, flick, footwork, glide, grip (left-handed, right-handed), guard position, interception, invitation, lateral parry, line, low line attack, low line counterattack, low line parry, lunge, match, measure, muscle memory, on guard, opposition, out of distance, parry (prime, seconde, tierce, quatre, quinte, sixte, septime, octave), pass, passé, piste, plaqué, point, point in line, preparation, presentation, press, recovery, redoublement, remise, reprised attack, retreat, right-of-way, riposte, running attack, saber cut, saber parry, saber thrust, salle, salute, stop thrust, sword arm, sword fighting, sword hand, taking the blade, thrust, timed thrust, timing, touch, touché, USFA-sanctioned

PRE-1900 GEAR AND WEAPONS

ARMOR

HEAD GEAR: bacinet, benin, casquetel, chainmail coif, leather cap, leather coif, great helm, helm, helmet, kettle hat, plume, war bonnet, war hat

ARMOR PIECES: bracer, breastplate, bullet-proof vest, cuirass, doublet, gauntlet, gorget, greave, hauberk, lance rest, leather coat, loin guard, mail hauberk, mail shirt, pauldron, plate harness, rondel, vambrace

ARMOR TYPES: banded mail, boiled leather, brigandine, chain mail, coat of plates, cuir bouillie, ensemble Greek, ensemble Roman, full chain suit, full plate, hide, laminar leather, leather, padded, plate mail, Polish Hussar, ring mail, scale mail, splint mail, studded leather

HORSE BARDING MATERIALS: chain mail, leather, padded, plate, scale, studded leather

HORSE BARDING PIECES: chanfron, crinet, crupper, cuello, flanchard, poitrel

SHIELDS

TYPES: buckler, figure-eight, flatiron, heater, kite, large, oval, pavis, rectangular, round, scalloped, small, spiked buckler, square, steel, targ, tower, triangular, wooden

WEAPONS

AKLYS: The aklys deserves special mention; it is identified as a Roman javelin, small club, dart, throwing stick, or boomerang depending upon the origin of the item.

AXES: adze, axe-knife, bardiche, battleaxe, bearded, Bhuj, billibong, broad, Dane, double-headed, English long, francisca, gandasa, hand, hatchet, head, hurlbat, masakari, miner's, ono, pick, piercing, pole, shepherd's, sparth, stone, tabarzin, throwing, tomahawk, two-handed, Viking

> **USAGE NOTE:** Some axes are designed primarily as tools but are effective when wielded as weapons. Certain other axes are designed for combat; a number of these are engineered to be thrown rather than swung. Consider the style of axe and its potential use in combat, especially when choosing a primary weapon for a fictional character.

BLACK POWDER: arquebus, blunderbuss, breechloader, brown Bess rifle, cannon, coach gun, dueling pistol, flintlock, fowling pistol, grenade, hunt gun, Kentucky long rifle, musket, pistol, wall gun, wheel lock

> **USAGE NOTE:** Black powder firearms require gunpowder technology.

BLUDGEONS: ball and chain, baton, baton Francais, belaying pin, bō, cambuk, chui, club, clubbing boomerang, cudgel, eku, eskrima stick, flail, gurz, hammer, hanbō, holy water sprinkler, jo, jutte, kanab□, knobkierrie, kurunthadi, la canne, lathi, Lucerne hammer, macana, mace, maul, mere, morning star, nightstick, nunchaku, ōtsuchi, patu, plançon a picot, quarterstaff, rod, roundhead, rungu, sam jeet kwun, sap, scepter, shareeravadi, shepherd's crook, shillelagh, spiked club, spiked mace, staff, taiaha, tambo, three-section staff, tonfa, truncheon, two-handed hammer, waddy, war hammer, yawara

CANNON: artillery, autocannon, basilisk, breechloader, bombard, culverin, demi-cannon, demi-culvern, falconet, field artillery, field gun, hand cannon, handgun, minon, howitzer, mortar, muzzle loader, organ gun, saker

CHAIN: chigiriki, double-ended flail, flying claws, meteor hammer, slungshot

> **USAGE NOTE:** A slungshot is not to be confused with a slingshot. The slungshot is a long cord with a weight or monkey's paw attached to one end. Its purpose is to cast a line from one place to another, especially a mooring line.

DAGGERS AND KNIVES: athame, baupmet, blade, Bowie knife, Celtic, chilanum, cinquedea, cleaver, deer horn, dirk, glaive, haladie, katara, kidney, knife, kris knife, leaf-shaped, left-hand dagger, main gauche, obsidian, parrying, poniard, stiletto, switchblade, throwing knife

> **USAGE NOTE:** Daggers and knives are discerned by their sharpened edges. A knife traditionally has one sharpened edge, whereas a dagger typically has both edges sharpened.

FLEXIBLE: bullwhip, cat o' nine tails, chain whip, crop, garrote, knout, lasso, meteor hammer, net, rope dart, small whip, whip

HAND WEAPONS: bakh-nakh, bayonet, bich'hwa, brass knuckles, buckhorn parrying stick, cestus, fist, gaff, gauntlet, hora, Korean fan, Larim wrist knife, Roman scissor, sap, scourge, spiked gauntlet, tessen, war fan

IMPROVISED WEAPONS: aerosol can, bar stool, baseball bat, brick, broom, butcher knife, chair, dinner fork, dirt, fireplace poker, flower pot, frying pan, garden shovel, golf club, hot beverage, iron, ironing board, lead pipe, log, nail gun, pitcher, pool balls, pool cue, power tool, rake, riding crop, rocks, sand, sledgehammer, snow shovel, soda bottle, steak knife, tire iron, trash can lid, vase, wine bottle

MAN-TRAPS: catch-pole, man-catcher

MISSILE: arbalest, atlatl, blow gun, blow pipe, bola, bow (composite, English, horse, long, short), boomerang, chakram, chu ko nu, crossbow (bullet, English bullet, German stone, pistol, repeating), dart, hand crossbow, harpoon, hoeroa bone, javelin, pilum, throwing blade, sling, spear thrower, staff sling, throwing hachet, shuriken, throwing star

> **USAGE NOTE:** A number of other weapons can become missile weapons when thrown, such as axes, blades, improvised, and pole weapons.

MISSILE LOADS: aclis, arrow, bolt, bullet, cannon ball, canister shot, crossbow bolt, quarrel, rock, sling stone, stone, war dart

RELATED: arrowhead, bowstring, case, fletching, pouch, quiver

POINTED WEAPONS: bungee stick, caltrop, horseman's pick, pick, pike, spike

POLE WEAPONS: atgeir, bardiche, bec de corbin, bill-guisarme, billhook, boarding pike, chauves souris, crowbill, fauchard, fauchard-fork, flamberge, fork, glaive, glaive-guisarme, guisarme, guisarme-voulge, halberd, hammer, half moon, hook-fauchard, lance (footman's, horseman's, jousting), leading staff, Lucerne hammer, mail piercer, naginata, partisan, pick, poleaxe, voulge

SIEGE EQUIPMENT: battering ram, boiling oil, boiling water, boulder, catapult load, field artillery, fire pot, flaming catapult load, grenade, Greek fire, hot pitch, ladder, petard, sea fire, siphon

SIEGE ENGINES: ballista, bolt thrower, bombard, cannon, catapult, corvus, espringal, fire archer, fire lance barrel, fire ship, gastrophetes, mangonel, mons meg, onager, scorpion, siege crossbow, siege tower, sulfur thrower, tortoise, trebuchet

USAGE NOTE: Siege weapons require trained crew to haul, position, and fire the weapon.

RELATED, CREW: artillerist, gun crew, siege crew, weapon master

SPEARS: ahlspiess, assegai, awl pike, bear, boar, brandistock, dangpa-chang, dory, feather staff, half pike, harpoon, hasta, hoko yari, jukjangchangbo, lance, menaulion, military fork, pike, ranseur, saintie, sarissa, sibat, spetum, spontoon, swordstaff, trident, trishula, winged, wolf, yari

SWORDS, ONE-HANDED: aikuchi, arming, back, barong, baselard, basket-hilted, bastard, bilbo, broad, Caucasian shashka, chokutō, cinquedea, colichemarde, Cossack shashka, claymore, cutlass, dao, dha, dussack, épée, espada ropera, estoc, falchion, firangi, flyssa, foil, gladius, heavy cavalry blade, hook, hunting, hwandudaedo, ida, jian, kampilan, karabela, kaskara, katar, katzbalger, khanda, khopesh, kilij, klewang, kodachi, krabi, kukri, liuyedao, long, machete, malibar, mameluke, messer, misericorde, nimcha, nine ring, ninjato, piandao, pulwar, pinuti, quama, rapier, saber, samurai, schweitersäbel, scimitar, shamshir, shikomizue, short, sica, sickle-sword, side, small, spadrone, spadroon, spatha, sword cane, sword stick, szabla, takoba, talwar, voulge, wakizashi, xiphos, yanmaodao

SWORDS, TWO-HANDED: assamese dao, boar sword, changdao, claymore, dadao, dōtanuki, espadon, executioner's, flame-bladed, great, hand-and-a-half, heading, highland, katana, lowland, miao dao, nandao, panabas, tachi, uchigatana, zweihänder

USAGE NOTE: Two-handed swords are distinguished by several characteristics. They can measure up to 6 feet long and may weigh 4 to 7 pounds, with ceremonial blades weighing as much as 16 pounds. Their hilts are long enough for two large, gloved hands to grip, and the quillons (crossguard) are enlarged. Two-handed swords were typically carried not in a sheath, but strapped across the back or shoulders. One of their uses was to break an enemy's pike or pole arm before assaulting the wielder.

USAGE NOTE: A flame-bladed sword or flambard is not on fire; rather, it refers to a blade that is wavy or undulating. Historically, they are true two-handed swords.

TOOLS: hay fork, hammer, hoe, machete, pitch fork, rake, scythe, sickle, sledgehammer, trident

POST-1900 GEAR AND WEAPONS

USAGE NOTE: This book avoids the use of brand names. In the case of weapons, however, the listing of brand names allows for a sampling of various weapons. No product endorsement is implied. Readers are advised to observe correct copyright and intellectual property treatment.

BODY ARMOR: ballistic face mask, barrier vest, bomb suit, bullet proof vest, bullet resistant face mask, bullet resistant vest, chicken plates (silicon carbide), dragon skin, Kevlar vest, modular tactical vest, outer tactical vest, PASGT helmet, PASGT vest, quilted nylon vest, ranger body armor

SHIELDS: ballistic, bullet resistant, riot, tactical

FIELD EQUIPMENT: flame thrower, land mine

WEAPONS

SPECIAL WEAPONS AND TACTICS

SWAT EQUIPMENT: armored vehicle, ballistic shield, bean bag munitions, entry tools, grenade (flash bang, stinger, stun, tear gas), heavy body armor, K9 unit, motion detector, night vision optics, pepper spray, riot control agent

SWAT WEAPONS: assault rifle, carbine (Colt CAR-15, Heckler & Koch G36, HK416, M4), pepperball pistol, semi-automatic pistol (Beretta 92, Glock, H&K, M1911, Sig Sauer), shotgun (Benelli M1, Benelli M4, Mossberg 500, Remington 870,), sniper rifle (M14, Remington 700P), submachine gun (Heckler & Koch MP5, Heckler & Koch UMP), taser

HANDGUNS/PISTOLS

USAGE NOTE: The historical definition of a pistol is a gun that can be held in the hand. The category has shifted in modern times and is currently considered a semi-automatic handgun. According to traditional usage, a dueling pistol, two-shot derringer, and a revolver could all correctly be called pistols. The choice of terminology will depend upon the time period of the setting.

DERRINGER: ladies' gun, muff pistol, Philadelphia Deringer, purse gun, stocking gun

USAGE NOTE: Derringers hold one to four bullets depending upon the model. The spelling of Deringer with one "r" is a brand name produced from 1852 to 1868. The spelling derringer is genericized and was adopted by competitors; currently, it refers to small-scale handguns.

PISTOL, SEMIAUTOMATIC: Arcus 98DA, Armalite AR-25, Auto-ordnance 1911A1, Les Baer H.C. 40, Beretta 92FS Type M9A1, Beretta 21 bobcat, Ed Brown Classic custom, Browning Buck Mark Standard URX, Browning Buck Mark Camper, Colt New Agent Series, C 75 Series, EAA Witness Steel, EAA Witness Elite Gold, FN Five-Seven USG, Glock 17, HK Mark 23, KAHR K9, Let-Tec PF9, Kimber Crimson Carry, MRI Desert Eagle Series, Nighthawk Custom 10-8 Dominator, North American Arms Guardian, Olympic Arms Cohort, Para PXT 1911, Remington 1911 R1, Ruger Mark III, Ruger LCP, Shooters Arms Military Pistol, Sig Sauer P250, Smith & Wesson, Springfield 1911A-1, STI Spartan Lawman, Stoeger Cougar 8000, Tarus 738 TCP, Walther P22, Walther PPS, Dan Wesson Bobtail, Wilson Comp, Wilson Professional, Wilson Protector, Wilson Sentinel, Wilson Tactical Elite

PISTOL, SINGLE SHOT: Thompson Center Encore, Thompson Center G2 Contender, Thompson Pro Hunter

REVOLVERS

USAGE NOTE: All revolvers are pistols, but not all pistols are revolvers. A revolver has a rotating cylinder into which bullets are loaded, one at a time. Handguns that use a magazine or in which bullets are breech loaded are not revolvers.

SINGLE ACTION: Beretta Stampede, Charter Arms Dixie Derringer, Cimarron Bisley SAA, Cimarron Lightning, Colt Single Action Army, Colt SAA Frontier Six Shooter, EAA Bounty Hunter, EMF 1873 Great Western Series, EMF 1875 Remington, Freedom Arms Model 83, Heritage Rough Rider Smallbore, Heritage Rough rider Large Bore, MRI BFR, Navy Arms 1873, Ruger New Bearcat, Ruger New Model Blackhawk Bisley, Ruger New Vaquero, STI Texican, Taylor's & CO. 1873, Taylor's & CO. 1873 Cattleman Bird's Head, Uberti Model 1873 Buntline, Uberti Top-Break Schofield, U.S. Fire Arms Bisley, U.S. Fire Arms Gunslinger, U.S. Fire Arms .22 Plinker, U.S. Fire Arms Rodeo, U.S. Fire Arms Double Eagle

DOUBLE ACTION: Charter Arms Bulldog, Charter Arms Patriot, EAA Windicator, Rossi model 351, Ruger LCR, Ruger Redhawk, Smith & Wesson model 10, Smith & Wesson Hunter, Smith & Wesson Night Guard, Smith & Wesson Bodyguard, Taurus 4510, Taurus Judge Public Defender Polymer, Taurus Model 85 Protector Polymer, Taurus Raging Bull Series, Taurus Tracker

RIFLES

Centerfire Rifles

BOLT ACTION: Anschutz 1730, Armalite AR30, Browning A-Bolt Stalker, Browning A-Bolt Medallion, CZ 550 American, Ed Brown Damara, Ed Brown Express, Ed Brown Marine Sniper, Kimber 84M, Kimber Montana, Lee-Enfield SMLE, Legacy Howa, Marlin XL7, Mauser K98k carbine, Mossberg 4X4, MRI Magnum Lite Eagle, Remington model 700, Ruger Hawkeye, Ruger model 77 Target, Sako 85, Smith & Wesson I-bolt, Springfield 1903, Winchester Ultimate Shadow

LEVER ACTION AND PUMP: Browning BLR Lightweight, Cimarron 1860 Henry, Cimarron Spencer Repeater, Dixie Henry, Legacy Puma M92, Marlin model 336, Mossberg 464, Navy Arms Henry, Remington synthetic, Rossi Rio Grande, Taylor's Lightning, Uberti Lightning, Winchester Extra Light Grade, Winchester Safari

SEMIAUTOMATIC: AK-47, Armalite AR-10, Auto-Ordnance M1 Carbine, FN FAL, FN SCAR, Les Baer Custom Police Special, Les Baer Custom Ultimate AR, Benelli R1, Beretta CX4 Storm, Browning BAR, Bushmaster ACR Combat, Bushmaster Predator, Bushmaster Varminter, Century International Bullpup, Doublestar Marksman, DPMS Panther, DSA SA58 Carbine, Knight SR-15, LMT Defender, M1 Garand, M14, M16, Olympic Arms K4B, Para Tactical Target, Remington R-15, Rock River Government Model, Ruger Mini-14, Ruger Ranch, SIG 556, Smith & Wesson M&P15, Springfield M1A, Steyr AUG, Sturmgewehr 44, Thompson 1927A1

SINGLE SHOT: Browning B78, Cimarron 1874 Sharps, H&R Buffalo Classic, H&R CR Carbine, H&R Hunter, Navy Arms 1873, Navy Arms 1885 High Wall, Ruger Light Sporter, Shiloh Sharps, Shiloh Sharps Long Range Express, Thompson Center Encore, Traditions 1874 Sharps, Winchester Black Powder

Rimfire Rifles

BOLT ACTION: Anschutz model 64, Browning T-Bolt, Henry ACU-Bolt, Marlin model 915Y, Mossberg model 802 Plinkster, Sako Quad Hunter, Savage Cub, Savage Mark I, Stevens Cadet, Weatherby Model XXII, Winchester Wildcat

LEVER ACTION AND PUMP: Browning BL-22, Henry lever action, Henry pump action, Marlin 39A, Mossberg 464, Remington model 572

SEMIAUTOMATIC: Browning Semiauto Grade I, Browning Buck Mark Sporter, Bushmaster Carbon 15, Marlin model 60, Smith & Wesson M&P 15-22, Thompson Center R55, Walther G22

SINGLE SHOT: Cimarron 1885 Low Wall, Cimarron High Wall, H&R Ultra Varmint, Rossi model 17, Stevens model 30, Taylor's model 1885, Uberti Rolling Block

Sniper Rifles

BOLT ACTION: British Whitworth, Bur, M24, M40, M82A1 SASR, Mosin-Nagant

SHOTGUNS

GENERAL: 12-gauge, 20-gauge, Atchisson assault shotgun, auto-assault gun, backpacker, bolt action, Browning automatic, double-barreled, lever action, pepper gun, pump action, repeating action, riding, riot gun, sawed-off, scatter gun

OVER/UNDER: Beretta Onyx, Browning Lightning, CZ Mallard, Ruger Red Label, Smith & Wesson Elite Silver, Stevens model 512, Winchester model 101

PUMP: Benelli Supernova, Browning BPS, FN tactical police, Mossberg model 500, Remington Marine Magnum, Weatherby PA-08, Wilson Combat standard

SEMIAUTOMATIC: Benelli M2, Benelli Vinci, Beretta Xtrema2, Browning Maxus, Legacy Escort, Mossberg Magnum, Remington model SP-10, Smith & Wesson model 2000, Winchester Super X3

SIDE-BY-SIDE: Century Arms Coach, DZ Durango, Mossberg Silver Reserve, Smith & Wesson Elite Gold, Stoeger Coach, Weatherby Orion

SINGLE SHOT: Browning BT-99, H&R Tamer, H&R ultra slug, Rossi slug, Thompson Contender

CHAPTER 8: MILITARY

General Equipment: armored vest, batteries, bayonet, camp stove, canteen, combat boots, communications system, dog tag silencers, dog tags, ear plugs, eating utensils, elbow pads, entrenching tool, first aid kit, flashlight, flotation device, gas mask, gloves, goggles, helmet, knee pads, knife, lifeline, matches, meals-ready-to-eat, MRE, night vision system, notepad, optical sight, pack, parachute, pencil, personal communications radio, poncho, rations, robot system, seabag, sleeping bag, sunglasses, sweatband, tactical vest, tarpaulin, tent, thermal imaging system, toilet paper, vision system, water bottle, water purification system

RANKS

USAGE NOTE: The lists of ranks below are organized in descending order. The navy uses the term rate, not rank.

U.S. AIR FORCE, ENLISTED: chief master sergeant of the Air Force, command chief master sergeant, chief master sergeant, senior master sergeant, master sergeant, technical sergeant, staff sergeant, senior airman, airman first class, airman, airman basic

U.S. AIR FORCE, OFFICER: general of the Air Force, general Air Force chief of staff, lieutenant general, major general, brigadier general, colonel, lieutenant colonel, major, captain, first lieutenant, second lieutenant

U.S. ARMY, ENLISTED: sergeant major of the army, command sergeant major, sergeant major, first sergeant, master sergeant, sergeant first class, staff sergeant, sergeant, corporal, specialist, private first class, private 2, private

U.S. ARMY, OFFICER: general of the Army, general, lieutenant general, major general, brigadier general, colonel, lieutenant colonel, major, captain, first lieutenant, second lieutenant

U.S. ARMY, WARRANT OFFICER: chief warrant officer 5, chief warrant officer 4, chief warrant officer 3, chief warrant officer 2, warrant officer

U.S. MARINES, ENLISTED: sergeant major of the Marine Corps, sergeant major, master gunnery sergeant, first sergeant, master sergeant, gunner sergeant, staff sergeant, sergeant, corporal, lance corporal, private first class, private

U.S. MARINES, OFFICER: general, lieutenant general, major general, brigadier general, colonel, lieutenant colonel, major, captain, first lieutenant, second lieutenant

U.S. MARINES, WARRANT OFFICER: chief warrant officer 5, chief warrant officer 4, chief warrant officer 3, chief warrant officer 2, warrant officer

U.S. NAVY, ENLISTED: master chief petty officer of the navy, master chief petty officer, senior chief petty officer, chief petty officer, petty officer (1st class, 2nd class, 3rd class), seaman, seaman apprentice, seaman recruit

U.S. NAVY, OFFICER: fleet admiral, admiral, vice admiral, rear admiral (upper), rear admiral (lower), captain, commander, lieutenant commander, lieutenant, lieutenant junior grade, ensign

USAGE NOTE: The rate of fleet admiral is used only in war time.

U.S. NAVY, WARRANT OFFICER: chief warrant officer 5, chief warrant officer 4, chief warrant officer 3, chief warrant officer 2, warrant officer

USAGE NOTE: The title of warrant officer is obsolete in the United States Navy.

ARMED FORCES, OTHER COMMON TITLES (POSSIBLY OBSOLETE OR FOREIGN): cadet, commodore, field marshal, flight leader, flying officer, group captain, marshal, officer cadet, pilot officer, soldier, squadron leader, troop, wing commander

NAVY, OTHER COMMON TITLES (POSSIBLY OBSOLETE OR FOREIGN): boatswain, commodore, first mate, mate, midshipman, leading seaman, sailor, second mate, sublieutenant

AIR AND WATER CRAFT

AIRCRAFT: airborne command and control, air superiority fighter, attack, attack VTOL, bomber, cargo, electronic warfare, fighter, fighter VSTOL, gunship, maritime patrol, multi-mission, multi-mission VTOL, observation, passenger, search and rescue, stealth bomber, stealth fighter, surveillance, tanker, trainer, training VTOL, unmanned aerial vehicle, utility, VIP transport, VIP/passenger transport, weather reconnaissance

AIRCRAFT, PRE-1962: airborne early warning, ambulance, anti-submarine, anti-submarine drone, assault drone, attack, bomber, bomber fighter, bomber drone, bomber torpedo, bomb glider, drone, fighter, glider, hospital, marine expeditionary, observation, observation scout, patrol, patrol bomber, patrol torpedo bomber, pursuit, racer, research, rotorcycle, scout, scout bomber, scout observation, scout trainer, tanker, target drone, torpedo, torpedo bomber, torpedo scout, trainer, trainer glider, transport, transport glider, transport single engine, unpiloted drone, unified sequence drone, utility, utility transport

AIRSHIPS, PRE-1962: airborne early warning, patrol, scout, training

USAGE NOTE: Airships are commonly referred to as zeppelins; the military term is airship.

HELICOPTERS, GENERAL: anti-submarine warfare, attack, cargo, electronic warfare, multi-mission, observation, search and rescue, training, utility

ROTARY WING AIRCRAFT: HH-60 Search and Rescue, MH-53 Sea Dragon, MH-60, SH-60 anti-submarine, TH-57 Training

U.S. AIR FORCE AIRCRAFT: A-10 Thunderbolt II, AC-130 Spectre, B-1 Lancer bomber, B-2 Spirit, B-52 Stratofortress, Boeing C-32 passenger aircraft, Boeing RC-135 Reconnaissance, C-12 Huron cargo, C-130 Hercules, C-130J Super Hercules, C-17 Globemaster III, C-20 Gulfstream passenger, C-21 Learjet, C-22 Boeing, C-26 Metroliner cargo, C-27J Spartan, C-37 Gulfstream, C-38 Gulfstream, C-40 Clipper, C-5 Galaxy cargo, E-22 Raptor, E-3 Sentry airborne and command, E-35 Lightning II, E-4 Boeing , E-8 Joint STARS, E9A Widget surveillance, EC-130 Commando Solo electronic warfare, EC-130J Commando Solo, F-15 Eagle fighter, F-15E Strike Eagle, F-16 Fighting Falcon, HC-30 search and rescue, IC-135 Open Skies observation system, KC-10 Extender tanker, KC-135 Stratotanker, MC-130 Combat Talon, MQ-1 Predator unmanned system, MQ-9 Reaper, RQ-170 Sentinel, RQ-4 Global Hawk, T-1 Jayhawk trainer, T-38 Talon, T-41 Mescalero, T-51 Cessna, T-6 Texan II

U. S. ARMY AIRCRAFT: Alenia C27J, C-12 Huron, C-23 Sherpa, C-26 Metroliner, Cessna UC-35, Dash 7, RC-12 Huron

U. S. ARMY HELICOPTER: AH-6 Littlebird, AH-64 Apache, CH-47 Chinook, EH-60 Black Hawk, MH-47 Chinook, MH-60 Black Hawk, OH-58 Kiowa, TH-67 Creek, UH-1 Iroquois, UH-60 Black Hawk, UH-72 Lakota, MQ-1C Warrior

U. S. NAVY AIRCRAFT: C-2 cargo transport, E-2 electronic warfare, EA-18 growler electronic warfare, EA-6 electronic warfare, F-5 trainer, FA-18 fighter, MQ-1C Grey Eagle unmanned, P-3 maritime patrol, RQ-11 Raven unmanned, RQ-5 Hunter unmanned, RQ-7 Shadow unmanned, T-34 trainer, T-44 trainer, T-45 trainer, T-6 trainer

U. S. NAVY VESSELS: Arleigh Burke class destroyer, Austin class, Avenger class, Blue Ridge command ship, Cyclone class patrol boat, Freedom class combat ship, Harpers Ferry class, Independence class combat ship, Los Angeles class attack submarine, minesweeper , Nimitz class aircraft carrier, Ohio class missile submarine, Oliver Hazard Perry class frigate, San Antonio class, Seawolf class attack submarine, Spruance class, Tarawa class amphibious assault ship, Ticonderoga class cruiser, Virginia class attack submarine, Wasp class, Whidbey Island class

WATER CRAFT, GENERAL MILITARY: aircraft carrier (airborne aircraft, anti-submarine, aviation, CATOBAR, colossus class, commando, diesel, escort, fleet, light fleet, merchant, nuclear, seacraft, STOBAR, STOVL), amphibious assault, balloon carrier, balloon tender, battle cruiser, battleship, beach transport, capital ship, coastal defense ship, corvette, cruiser (armed merchant, armored, battle, guided missile, heavy, light, missile, nuclear, protected), cruiser killer, destroyer (area air defense, guided missile, light, tender, torpedo boat, troop transport), dreadnought, fast attack craft, flight deck cruiser, frigate (anti-air, anti-submarine, guided missile, nuclear powered, ocean escort, sail, steam), gunboat, heavy battleship, helicopter carrier, ironclad warship, light battleship, light capital ship, merchantman, monitor, nuclear submarine, off-shore patrol vessel, pocket battleship, post ship, privateer, seaplane carrier, seaplane tender, ship of the line, sloop, submarine, supercarrier, superdreadnought, torpedo boat, torpedo boat destroyer, transport, warship

GROUND VEHICLES

USAGE NOTE: The lists that follow are a sampling of military vehicle types used around the world. The lists are intended to give the flavor and feel of the terminology. Research is required to determine the correct vehicles in any given time period or setting.

GENERAL: ambulance, anti-tank vehicle, armored car, armored fighting vehicle, armored personnel carrier, armored security vehicle, armored vehicle, articulated tractor and trailer, battle tank, bridging vehicle, infantry fighting vehicle, light reconnaissance vehicle, light tank, main battle tank, maintenance vehicle, self-propelled rocket launcher, radio and command utility vehicle, reconnaissance vehicle, tracked tank destroyer, transport truck

ARMORED VEHICLES: AFV, armored car, armored fighting vehicle, infantry fighting vehicle, personnel carrier, train car, self-propelled artillery, tank

TANKS, AMERICAN: M1 Abrams, M2 Bradley, M3 Grant, M3A1 Stuart III, M26 Pershing, M46 Patton, M60 MBT, M551 Sheridan

TANKS, BRITISH: Centurion, Challenger 2, Chieftain MK1, Churchill, Crusader

TANKS, GERMAN: Elephant, Hummel, Jagdpanther, Leopard, PzKw Tiger, PzKw V Panther G

TANKS, RUSSIAN: T-34, T-64, T-80

AUSTRALIA: ASLAV 8×8 infantry fighting vehicle, Cruiser Mk 1 tank, Bushmaster 4×4 mine protected armored personnel carrier, Dingo 4×4 armored car

CANADA: ASLAV 8×8 infantry fighting vehicle, AVGP Cougar wheeled fire support vehicle, AVGP Grizzly wheeled armored personnel carrier, AVGP Husky wheeled maintenance and recovery vehicle, Bison 8×8 armored personnel carrier, C8 4×4 8-cwt truck, C15 4×2 and 4×4 15-cwt truck, C30 4×4 30-cwt

truck, C60 4×4 and 6×6 60-cwt truck, Coyote reconnaissance vehicle, F15 4×2 and 4×4 15-cwt truck series, F30 4×4 30-cwt truck series, F60 4×4 and 6×4 60-cwt truck series, M152 4×4 radio and command utility vehicle

CHINA: A531 armored personnel carrier, Al-Khalid 2000 main battle tank, B-531 armored personnel carrier, BJ2020 4×4 utility vehicle, BJ2022 Brave Warrior 4×4 utility vehicle, BJ212 Beijing Jeep 4×4 utility vehicle, CA1091 4x25 ton truck, CQ261 wheeled truck, D421 cable carrier, EQ1108 4×2 5 ton truck, EQ1141 4×2 8 ton truck, EQ2050 Mengshi 4×4 utility vehicle, EQ2058 up-armored 4×4 utility vehicle, EQ2081 6×6 2.5 ton truck, EQ2100 6×6 3.5 ton truck, HY472 6×6 truck tractor and trailer, WZ91 4×4 self-propelled HJ-8 anti-tank missile carrier, WZ302 self-propelled 122mm mortar/gun, WZ501 infantry fighting vehicle, WZ504 self-propelled anti-tank vehicle

FRANCE: A4 AVL 4x4 armored utility vehicle, ACG-1 light tank, ACG-2 self propelled anti-tank 75mm gun, AMC 34 light tank, AML 20 4×4 armored car, AML 60 4×4 armored car, AML 90 4×4 armored car, AMR 33 light tank, AMX-10P armored personnel carrier, AMX-10RC 6×6 armored fighting vehicle, AMX-13 light tank, AMX 30 main battle tank, AMX 40 main battle tank, AMX 56 main battle tank, AMX VCI infantry fighting vehicle, Buffalo wheeled armored personnel carrier, CA1 light tank, Char 2C Alsace super-heavy tank, Char B1 medium tank, Char Leger Hotchkiss H-35 tank, EBR 8×8 reconnaissance vehicle, ERC-20 Kriss 6×6 armored car, ERC-60 Sagaie 6×6 armored car, ERC-90 F1 Lynx 6×6 armored car, ERC-90 Sagaie 2 6×6 armored car, FCM 2C Alsace heavy tank, FCM 36 light tank, FT-17 light tank, FT-31 light tank, GCT self-propelled 155mm artillery, H35 light tank

GERMANY: A7V Sturmpanzerwagen heavy tank, AHSVS 8×8 armored truck, Condor 4×4 armored personnel carrier, Fuchs Transportpanzer 1, Jagdpanzer Jaguar 1 self-propelled HOT missile vehicle, Jagdpanzer Jaguar 2 self-propelled TOW missile vehicle, Jagdpanzer Kanone tank destroyer, Jagdpanzer Rakete self-propelled SS.11 missile vehicle, Jaguar main battle tank, Kleiner Panzerbefehlwagen I command Panzer I tank, Kubelwagen 4-wheeler, Leopard I tank, Marder II self-propelled 75mm antitank gun, Panzer VI Tiger heavy tank, Type 86 Kubelwagen 4×4 utility vehicle, Type 87 Kommandeurwagen 4×4 command vehicle

ISRAEL: Achzarit armored personnel carrier, M1 Isherman medium tank, M240 Storm 4×4 utility vehicle, V-242 Storm Mark III 4×4 utility vehicle, Magach main battle tank, MAR 290 self-propelled multiple rocket launcher, Plazan Sand Cat light armored vehicle, Sabra main battle tank

ITALY: AB40 4x4 armored car, AB41 4x4 armored car, ACTL transport vehicle, LSVW 4x4 utility vehicle, B1 Centauro 8×8 tank destroyer, C1 Ariete main battle tank, C13 Dardo infantry fighting vehicle, Carro Leggero tank, Carro Pesante tank, Carro Veloce fast tank, Centauro 8×8 tank destroyer, CV-33 light tank, Dardo C13 infantry fighting vehicle, Fiat 2000 light tank, Fiat 3000 light tank, Fiat 6614 wheeled armored personnel carrier, Fiat 6616 heavy armored car, Freccia VBM 8×8 infantry fighting vehicle, L3/35 Carro Veloce light tank, OF-40 main battle tank, OF-120 main battle tank, Semovente 47 self-propelled 47mm gun

NORTH KOREA: BM-11 6×6 self-propelled multiple rocket launcher, Ch'omna-ho main battle tank, K1 main battle tank, K2 Black Panther main battle tank

POLAND: 7TP light tank, BLG-60 bridging vehicle, BWP-40 infantry fighting vehicle, BWP-2000 infantry fighting vehicle, Dzik armored car, PRP-4 Deyterij artillery reconnaissance vehicle

RUSSIA: ASU-57 self-propelled 57mm gun, ASU-85 self-propelled 85mm gun, AT-P tracked prime mover and artillery crew transporter, 2S1 Gvozdika self-propelled 122mm howitzer, 2S3 Akatsiya self-propelled 152mm howitzer, 2S4 Tyulpan self-propelled 240mm mortar, 2S5, 2S7 Pion self-propelled 203mm gun, 2S9 Anona self-propelled 120mm mortar, 2S30 Iset self-propelled 155mm howitzer, 9A51 Prima 6x6 self-propelled multiple rocket launcher, 9P117 8x8 scud short-range ballistic missile launcher, 9P157 self-propelled anti-tank vehicle, 9S482 8x8 air defense command vehicle, ATS 56 G artillery tractor, BA-3 6×4 armored car, BA-10 6×4 armored car, BA-64 4×4 armored car, Black Eagle main battle tank, BM-21 Grad 4×4 and 6×6 self-propelled multiple rocket launcher, BMD-1 infantry fighting vehicle, BMD-3 infantry fighting vehicle, BMM-2 8×8 ambulance, BMM-80 8×8 ambulance, BMP-1 infantry fighting vehicle, BMP-3 infantry fighting vehicle, BMR mine clearing vehicle, BRDM-1 4×4 reconnaissance vehicle, BRDM-3 wheeled anti-tank vehicle, BREM-2 armored recovery vehicle, BT-2 light tank, BT-5 light tank, BTR-40 4×4 armored

personnel carrier, BTR-50 tracked armored personnel carrier, BTR-60 8×8 armored personnel carrier, BTR-90 8×8 armored personnel carrier, BTR-140 6×6 armored personnel carrier, BTR-152 6×6 armored personnel carrier, BTR-T infantry fighting vehicle, BTS-1 armored recovery vehicle, BTS-3 armored recovery vehicle, DPM convoy escort vehicle, GAZ 46 4×4 utility vehicle, GAZ-5903 8×8 armored personnel carrier, Josef Stalin heavy tank, Kilment Voroshilov heavy tank, T-55 main battle tank, 2S1 Gvozdika self-propelled anti-aircraft 23mm gun, 2S3 Akatsiya self-propelled 152mm howitzer, 2S4 Tyulpan self-propelled 240mm mortar, MTK-2 mine clearing vehicle, Tunguska-M1 self-propelled twin 30mm anti-aircraft guns and missiles, P-240 8×8 switchboard vehicle, PRP-4 Deyterij artillery reconnaissance vehicle, PRP-4 Deyterij artillery reconnaissance vehicle, SPR-2 8×8 electronic warfare vehicle, Tunguska-M1 2S9M air-defense vehicle

SOUTH AFRICA: Bateleur 4×4 self-propelled multiple rocket launcher, Buffel 4×4 mine protected armored personnel carrier, Casspir mine proof wheeled APC, Eland 4×4 armored car

SPAIN: ASCOD series armored vehicles, BLR 4×4 armored personnel carrier, BMR-600 6×6 armored personnel carrier, Cazador tracked TOW missile carrier

TURKEY: ACV 300 infantry fighting vehicle, ACV-S armored vehicle, AMV self-propelled 81mm or 120mm mortar, Arma amphibious tactical wheeled armored vehicle, ATV self-propelled TOW anti-tank missile, EJDER 6x6 armored wheeled vehicle

UNITED KINGDOM: A9 Cruiser Mark I medium tank, A13 Cruiser Mark III medium tank, Covenanter Cruiser Mark V medium tank, A27 Cromwell cruiser Mark VIII medium tank, A30 Challenger cruiser Mark VIII medium tank, A34 Comet cruiser medium tank, A39 Tortoise anti-tank vehicle, A43 Black Prince infantry medium tank, A45 Caernarvon heavy tank, Archer tank destroyer, Armadillo wood and gravel AFV, AT105 Saxon wheeled armored personnel carrier, Bison concrete armored lorry, Buffalo amphibious vehicle, C8 Quad 4x4 Tractor, Carden Loyd Tankette, Crusader tank Mark VI model A15, Cultivator No. 6 trench forming machine, Dingo 4×4 armored car, Ferret FV711 armored car, Fox armored car, FV101 Scorpion light tank, FV104 Samaritan armored ambulance, FV105 Sultan command vehicle, FV106 Samson armored recovery vehicle, FV107 Scimitar light tank, FV120 Spartan self-propelled anti-tank vehicle, FV214 Conqueror main battle tank, FV219 armored recovery vehicle, FV222 Conqueror armored recovery vehicle, FV401 Cambridge armored personnel carrier, FV421 armored cargo carrier, FV424 armored engineering vehicle, FV426 anti-tank vehicle, FV435 Wavell communications vehicle, FV437 Pathfinder vehicle with snorkel gear, FV438 Wavell self-propelled anti-tank vehicle, FV439 signals vehicle, FV510 Warrior infantry fighting vehicle, FV511 Warrior command vehicle, FV512 Warrior armored repair vehicle, FV513 Warrior armored recovery vehicle, FV514 Warrior reconnaissance vehicle, FV515 Warrior artillery command vehicle, FV603 Saracen 6×6 armored personnel carrier, FV621 Stalwart amphibious 6×6 5 ton truck, FV624 Stalwart amphibious 6×6 5 ton recovery vehicle, FV711 Ferret 4×4 armored car, FV721 Fox 4×4 armored car, FV1601 Humber 1 ton 4×4 truck, FV1606 Humber 1 ton 4×4 wrecker/tow truck, FV1609 Humber 1 ton 4×4 armored vehicle, FV1620 Humber 1 ton 4×4 anti-tank vehicle, FV3804 ammunition supply vehicle, FV3901 bridge layer, FV3904 armored personnel carrier, FV4001 Centurion main battle tank, FV4002 Centurion AVLB bridging vehicle, FV4003 Centurion AVRE combat engineer vehicle, FV4005 self-propelled anti-tank gun, FV4010 anti-tank vehicle, FV4019 bulldozer, FV4101 self-propelled anti-tank gun, FV4333 Stormer armored personnel carrier, Sherman Firefly medium tank, Whippet Mk A medium tank

UNITED STATES: A7SC 4x2 armored car, AAPC armored personnel carrier, AAV-7 amphibious armored vehicle, AAVC-7 amphibious command vehicle, AAVC-7 amphibious armored personnel carrier, AAVR-7 amphibious recovery vehicle, AIFV infantry fighting vehicle, Blitz 4x4 truck, M1 Abrams main battle tank, ATV self-propelled TOW anti-tank missile, Avenger air defense vehicle, Black Knight unmanned combat vehicle, Buffalo 6×6 anti-mine vehicle, Bushmaster LVT-3 amphibious vehicle, CTLS light tank, Dragoon 300 wheeled armored fighting vehicle, DUKW 6×6 amphibious utility vehicle, EIFV infantry fighting vehicle, LVTE-5 amphibious mine clearing vehicle, M1 6×4 armored vehicle, M2 Bradley infantry fighting vehicle, M3 Lee medium tank, M3 Bradley armored reconnaissance vehicle, M4 mortar halftrack carrier, M6 Linebacker self-propelled anti-aircraft vehicle, M6 4×4

1.5 ton bomb disposal truck, M7 snow tractor, M10 Wolverine tank destroyer, M16 MGMC anti-aircraft vehicle, M18 Hellcat self-propelled 76mm anti-tank gun, M24 Chaffee light tank, M26 Pershing tank, M25 Dragon Wagon tank transporter, M29 Weasel cargo carrier, M31 Honest John rocket carrier, M35 6x6 armored truck, M36 self-propelled 90mm anti-tank gun, M36 Nike-Hercules launcher-loader, M41 Walker Bulldog light tank, M45 armored serving and refueling vehicle, M46 Patton medium tank, M47 6x6 dump truck, M48 Chaparral tracked surface-to-air missile carrier, M50 super Sherman medium tank, M50 6x6 water tanker, M56 anti-tank vehicle, M58 smoke generator vehicle, M60 Patton main battle tank, M67 medium flamethrower tank, M113 armored personnel carrier, M133 armored flame-thrower, M133 6x6 canteen vehicle, M139 6x6 bridge layer, M162 Vulcan air defense system, M268 6×6 propellant tanker, M289 wheeled missile launcher truck, M561 Gama 6×6 articulated truck, M601 4x4 power generator carrier, M624 6x6 dump truck, M656 8×8 5 ton air-transportable and floatable truck, M756 6x6 pipeline maintenance vehicle, M763 6x6 telephone maintenance vehicle, M764 6x6 earth boring maintenance vehicle, M901 ITV self-propelled TOW missile launcher, M992 FAASV ammunition vehicle, M1015 electronic warfare systems carrier, M1042 HMMWV 4x4 shelter carrier, M117 Guardian 4x4 armored security vehicle, M901 ITV self-propelled TOW missile launcher

WEAPONS

GENERAL: anti-structure weapon system, anti-tank weapon system, grenade, grenade machine gun, heavy rifle, light support weapon, machine gun, mortar, pistol, rifle, semi-automatic rifle, shotgun, smoke grenade, sniper rifle, under slung grenade launcher

U.S. ARMY

ANTI-TANK: AT4

ASSAULT RIFLE: M16, M4 carbine, FN SCAR, M231 FPW, M14, M22, anti-material

HOWITZER: M109, M119, M198, M777

MACHINE GUN: M249, M60 belt-fed, M24 medium belt-fed, M2 heavy, MK19 belt fed grenade machine gun

MISSILE: FGM-148 Javelin, BGM-71TOE wire guided, FIM-92 Stinger, patriot

MORTAR: 18-inch railway howitzer, big bertha, blacker bombard, coast defense mortar, heavy mortar, hedgehog, light mortar, little David, M120, M224, M252, monster mortar, siege mortar, spigot mortar

MULTIPLE ROCKET LAUNCHER: HIMARS, M270

RIFLE ATTACHMENT: M9 bayonet, M203 grenade launcher

SEMIAUTOMATIC PISTOL: M9

SNIPER RIFLE: M24, XM2010 Enhanced, M110 semiautomatic

VEHICLE-MOUNTED WEAPON SYSTEM: M240, MK 19, M2, M230 autocannon, M242 autocannon

U.S. AIR FORCE

BOMB: air blast, cluster, general purpose, laser guided, thermonuclear

MISSILE: air-to-air, air-to-surface, anti-aircraft intercontinental ballistic, surface-to-air

SATELLITE: defense communication system, defense support system, global positioning system

SMALL ARMS: M2 machine gun, M4 rifle, MP5 submachine gun, M9 pistol, M11 pistol, M16 rifle

CHAPTER 9: TRANSPORTATION

GENERAL VOCABULARY

EXPLORATION: cave-diving, climbing, divining, geocaching, hiking, prospecting, rock climbing, mountain climbing, mountaineering, spelunking

LOCOMOTION: advance, amble, ascend, bounce, bound, burrow, caper, cavort, charge, clamber, climb, crash, crawl, creep, cruise, coast, dance, dart, dash, dawdle, delve, depart, descend, dive, drag, drift, drive, drop, exit, exodus, explore, fall, flee, flight, float, flutter, fly, freefall, frolic, gambol, glide, go, gyrate, hike, hop, hover, hurdle, hurtle, jaunt, journey, jump, launch, leap, leave, levitate, lunge, lurch, march, meander, mosey, move, pace, parade, pass, plod, plummet, plunge, pounce, prance, proceed, promenade, ram, ramble, rebound, recoil, reel, retreat, ride, rise, roam, rocket, romp, rout, rove, run, rush, sail, sally forth, sashay, saunter, scale, scramble, scurry, scuttle, shuffle, sink, skid, skip, skulk, slink, slither, slog, sneak, soar, spin, spring, sprint, stagger, stampede, step, stride, stroll, strut, stumble, submerge, swagger, sway, swim, tiptoe, toddle, topple, tour, tramp, traipse, travel, trek, trudge, tumble, turn, vault, venture, voyage, walk, wander, whirl, withdraw

SWIMMING STROKES: American crawl, arm tow, Australian crawl, back float, backstroke, breaststroke, butterfly, catch-up stroke, combat sidestroke, corkscrew, dead man's float, dog paddle, dolphin crawl, dolphin kick, double trudgeon, double trudgeon crawl, eggbeater kick, elementary backstroke, extended arm tow, finning, flutter back finning, flutter kick, frog kick, front crawl, freestyle, gliding, human stroke, inverted breaststroke, inverted butterfly, jellyfish float, lifesaving stroke, medley, moth stroke, oarstroke, pulling rescue stroke, relay, scissors kick, sculling, side stroke, slow butterfly, snorkeling, survival float, survival travel stroke, synchronized swimming, treading water, trudgeon, trudgeon crawl, turtle float, turtle stroke, underwater, water polo stroke, winging

TRAVEL HAZARDS: aliens, angry large animal, animal stampede, bad food, bad weather, bathroom dirty, bathroom inoperative, bedbugs, belligerent drunkard, biting insects, bridge out, broken engine belt, broken engine hose, bug swarms, car collision, car collision with animal, clueless travelers, cockroaches, con man, contaminated water, criminal, dead battery, dehydration, dirty hotel room, drug dealer, drug trafficker, engine trouble, flat tire, flies, foodborne illness, foreign language, gangs, getting lost, grouchy hotel employee, grouchy officials, grouchy waiter/waitress, heat exhaustion/stroke, hostile hippies, hostile locals, lack of cell phone service, lack of radio/TV reception, lack of toilet paper, liquid leaks in luggage, lost luggage, lost reservations, medical emergency, money/supplies stolen, Montezuma's revenge, motion sickness, no air conditioning , no heat, obnoxious travelers, out of gas, outhouse, poison ivy/oak/sumac, poisonous insects, poisonous plants, pollen, poor road conditions, prostitute, road rage, road washed out, roadblock, skunks, snakes, spiders, spoiled food, stolen luggage, sunburn, terrorists, thorns, tourists, trap, traveler's diarrhea, uncomfortable bed, unexpected death, waterborne illness

INFRASTRUCTURE

BUILDINGS: airdrome, airfield, airport, airport terminal, airstrip, bus shelter, bus station, bus stop, bus terminal, cab stand, concourse, control tower, depot, ferry dock, ferry slip, hangar, landing field, passenger terminal, rail station, rail terminal, rail yard, runway, taxi stand, train station, terminal, terminus, ticket booth, train station

BRIDGES: aqueduct, arch, beam, bending, cable-stayed, compression, cantilever, clapper, covered, double-deck, draw, foot, girder, log, moon, moveable, railroad, rope, pontoon, shear, skywalk, suspension, tension, torsion, trestle, truss, viaduct

ROADS: access road, alley, alleyway, artery, arterial highway, asphalt road, avenue, blind alley, boardwalk, boulevard, bridle path, bridleway, catwalk, causeway, channel, cobblestone road, conduit, corridor, course, cul-de-sac, dead end, deer trail, divided highway, drive, expressway, fast lane, footpath, freeway, highway, horse trail, interstate, lane, limited-access highway, line, main line, main road, major road, narrow road, narrows, overpass, parkway, passage, passageway, passing lane, path, pathway, pavement, public way, roadway, route, side road, skywalk, street, strip, super highway, thoroughfare, thruway, toll road, track, trail, traffic lane, through street, tunnel, viaduct, walk, walkway, way

GROUND TRANSPORTATION

ANIMALS: alpaca, ass, bullock, camel, donkey, elephant, horse, llama, mule, pack mule, pony, ox, reindeer, yak, water buffalo

RELATED: bit, blanket, blinders, bridle, brush, comb, curry, jockey, harness, horseshoe, horseshoe nail, racetrack, saddle, saddlebag, saddle blanket, shoe, tack, trainer

ANIMAL-POWERED: buckboard, bullock cart, carriage, cart, chaise, chariot, coach, dog cart, dog sled, hansom cab, horsecar, horse-drawn barge/boat, horse-drawn tram, howdah, litter, sled, sledge, stage coach, streetcar, surrey, tram, travois, trolley, wagon, wagon train

HUMAN-POWERED: baby buggy, baby stroller, bicycle, bicycle built for two, cart, coaster wagon, dolly, handcar, hand truck, inline skates, jogging stroller, kick scooter, kick sled, litter, longboard, pallet jack, perambulator, pram, rickshaw, roller skates, scooter, sedan chair, shopping cart, skateboard, stretcher, tandem bicycle, tricycle, unicycle, wheelbarrow, wheelchair

FARM: combine, hay wagon, horse trailer, livestock trailer, milk tanker, silage trailer, tiller, tractor, trailer, two-wheel tractor, wagon

MASS TRANSIT: bus (coach, double decker, school, sightseeing), commuter train, elevated train, ferry, high speed rail, intercity rail, metro, monorail, motor coach, rail, shuttle, subway, train, tram

MILITARY: See the chapter Military

MOTORIZED: all-terrain vehicle, ambulance, automobile, camper, car, cargo van, carpool, clown car, compact, convertible, coupe, drag racer, dragster, elevator, family car, forklift, four-door, jeep, hatchback, hearse, hot rod, limousine, luxury, mini, minibike, minivan, motorcycle, motor vehicle, muscle car, race, ragtop, recreational vehicle, RV, sedan, sidecar, sports car, station wagon, subcompact, SUV, taxi, van, vintage, woody

MOTORIZED TRUCK: car carrier, delivery, eighteen wheeler, flatbed, garbage, ice cream, milk, monster, paddy wagon, panel, pickup, plumber's, refrigerated, semi, snow plow, tanker, tractor trailer, tow

RAILROAD: car (auto, club, dining, food, freight, hopper, passenger, Pullman, refrigerator, sleeper, tanker), engine (electric, diesel, steam), locomotive, monorail, rail, rolling stock, track, train

AIR TRANSPORTATION

VEHICLES: air bus, aircraft, airliner, airplane, airship, balloon, blimp, cargo plane, dirigible, fixed wing, flying saucer, glider, hang glider, helicopter, jet (fighter, jumbo, passenger), jet pack, parachute, rocket, rocket ship, sea plane, space ship, space shuttle, war plane, zeppelin; See also the chapter Military

WATER TRANSPORTATION

WATER TERMS: anchorage, apparent wind, aquatic, arroyo, bay, bayou, bog, breaker, breakwall, brook, canal, cay, channel, chop, coast, coral reef, cove, creek, current, dock, ebb tide, everglade, fen, fenland, fjord, fog, gulf, harbor, haven, inland waterway, inlet, jet stream, jetty, lock, marina, maritime, marsh, marshland, ocean, oceanic, pier, port, port-of-call, quagmire, quay, reef, rip tide, river, riverbank, riverside, rivulet, sandbar, sea, seashore, seaside, shoal, shore, shoreline, slip, sound, stream, squall, surf, swamp, swell, tide, trade wind, tributary, true wind, undercurrent, watercourse, water spout, waterfront, waterway, wave, waypoint, westerly, wetland, wharf, whitecap

WATERCRAFT, HUMAN-POWERED: boat, canoe, craft, dinghy, gondola, inflatable raft, kayak, life boat, life raft, longship, outrigger, paddle boat, punt, raft, rowboat, rubber raft, sailboard, sea kayak, skiff, surfboard

WATERCRAFT, SMALL: airfoil, bareboat, bathysphere, boat, catamaran, catboat, cigarette, corvette, craft, cutter, dinghy, ferry, fire boat, fishing, glass bottom, houseboat, iceboat, keelboat, ketch, passenger liner, picnic boat, pontoon boat, sailboat, ship, shrimp boat, skiff, speed, swamp boat, tramaran, vessel, water bus, yacht water craft, water taxi, yacht, yawl

WATERCRAFT, LARGE: cargo, carrack, coal boat, clipper, cog, cruise liner, cruise ship, cutter, gambling, galleon, galley, junk, liner, merchantman, ocean liner, paddlewheel, pirate ship, schooner, showboat, slave ship, sloop, tanker

USAGE NOTE: The distinction between small and large watercraft is relative. A ferry, for example, might range from a raft designed to carry a few passengers to a double-deck affair capable of holding dozens of cars. The lists above are sorted based on general conception and common sense. The sizes of individual boats and ships will vary widely.

BOAT/SHIP ANATOMY: anchor, anchor chain, astrolabe, ballast, barometer, belaying pin, bell, bilge, binnacle, block, boathook, boom, bosun's chair, bowsprit, bridge, bucket, bulkhead, bunk, buoy, cable, cabin, capstan, centerboard, chart, chain locker, cleat, cockpit, companionway, compass, course sail, crane, crew, crow's nest, deck, figurehead, flagstaff, float coat, fog horn, forecastle, foremast, foresail, galley, global positioning system, grapnel, GPS, gunwale, halyard, hammock, hatch, head, helm, helmsman, hold, holystone, horn, hull, jib, keel, ladder, life jacket, life line, line, locker, log, knot, mainsail, map, mast, mizzen, mizzen mast, moonraker, mooring, oar, oarlock, personal floatation device, piling, prop, poop deck, pulley, quarterdeck, rail, railing, rig, rigging, rope, royal sail, rudder, sail, sextant, sheet, shroud, skysail, spar, spinnaker, standing rigging, stern castle, tack, tackle, tiller, topgallant, topsail, yard, wardroom, weather gauge, wheel, winch

BOAT/SHIP TERMINOLOGY: abeam, adrift, aft, aground, astern, beam, bearing, bearing away, buoyancy, bow, capsize, cardinal points, careen, casting off, close-hauled, Coast Guard, compass course, course, course-plotting, dead reckoning, deviation, downwind, draft, drifting, drop anchor, ebb, ebb tide, embark, fathom, floating, fully battened sails, harbor patrol, heavy air, hoist, hoisting sail, in harm's way, jibe, jibing, jury-rig, keelhaul, keeling, latitude, launch, leeward, leeway, longitude, luff, magnetic (east, north, south, west), mooring-under-sail, navigation, no-sail-zone, outgoing tide, overboard, port, port tack, ramming speed, reefing, regatta, sail zone, seasick, seaworthy, starboard, steer, steering, St. Elmo's fire, stern, swamping, tacking, to windward, towing, underway, wake, weigh anchor

SAILING KNOTS: anchor bend, backup knot, bowline, buntline, butterfly, carrack bend, cleat hitch, clove hitch, constrictor, cow hitch, defined, double fisherman's, figure eight, fisherman's bend, girth hitch, granny, half hitch, heaving line, mooring hitch, monkey's fist, monkey's paw, pile hitch, Prusik, reef, rolling hitch, running bowline, sheepshank, sheet bend, slip knot, slipped buntline, stopper knot, square knot, tautline hitch, Turk's head, trucker's hitch, two half hitches, water knot, whistle knot

CHAPTER 10: GEOLOGY, GEOGRAPHY, METEOROLOGY, AND BOTANY

GEOLOGY

CAVE ANATOMY: active cave, anthodite, aragonite, arch, bedrock, blind valley, block, boulder choke, box-work, breccias, calcite, cave coral, cave pearls, cave pool, cave system, chamber, chimney, choke, cleft, clint, cobble, column, crust, crystal, crystal pool, current marking, curtain, dark zone, daylight hole, dead cave, decoration, diagen-esis, dike, dip, dome, dormant cave, drapery, dripline, dripstone, duck-under, escarpment, false floor, fault, fault cave, fissure, fissure cave, flattener, flowstone, formation, fossil, foul air, frostwork, glacial cave, gour, grade, gravel, grike, grot-hole, grotto, ground-trog, groundwater, gypsum, gypsum flower, half blind valley, hall, ice cave, inflow cave, joint, karren, keyhole, labyrinth, lava cave, ledge, leg, limestone, limestone cave, live cave, marble, maze, moonmilk, natu-ral arch, natural bridge, outflow cave, overhang, passage, pebble, pendant, percolation, permeable, phosphorescence, phreatic development, pillar, pipe, pisolite, pit, pitch, plunge pool, pothole, rift, rill, rimstone, rimstone dam, rock pile, rock shelter, roof crust, rootsicle, sand, saturated, sea cave, sediment, seepage water, shaft, shawl, shield, silt, sinkhole, siphon, soda straw, solution flute, speleotherm, splash cup, spongework, spring, squeeze, stalactite, stalagmite, straw, stream sink, streambed, strike, sump, supersaturated, swirl hole, terrace, through cave, towerkarst, trap, tube, tufa, tunnel, vadose development, walk-through, water sink, weathering, wet cave, window

GEOLOGIC CONCEPTS: law of superposition, principle of original horizontality, principle of lateral con-tinuity, ordering rock strata, volcanism, uniformitarianism, plate tectonic theory, principle of intrusive relation-ships, principle of cross-cutting relationships, principle of inclusions and components, principle of superposition, principle of faunal succession

GEOLOGIC FIELDS OF STUDY: biogeochemistry, biostratigraphy, chronostratigraphy, dendrochronol-ogy, earth science, economic geology, engineering geology, environmental geology, geoarchaeology, geochemistry, geochronology, geodetics, geological modeling, geometallurgy, geomicrobiology, geomorphology, geomythology, geo-physics, geotechnical engineering, glaciology, historical geology, hydrogeology, isotope geochemistry, isotope geology, lithostratigraphy, marine geology, metamorphic petrology, micropaleontology, mineralogy, mining geology, paleocli-matology, paleontology, pedology, petro physics, petroleum geology, petrology, planetary geology, plate tectonics, sedi-mentology, seismology, soil mechanics, soil science, speleology, stratigraphy, structural geology, volcanology

GEOLOGICAL NATURAL HAZARDS: aftershock, avalanche, avulsion, cave-in, cliff, earthquake, falling stalactite, flood, foreshock, geyser eruption, jutting stalactite, landslide, lava, liquefaction, loose rock, mudslide, quicksand, river channel migration, rock fall, sinkhole, slippery rock, tides, tsunami, confusing cave passage, volcanic eruption, waterfall

GEOLOGICAL VOCABULARY: absolute dating, abyssal plain, accretion, aftershock, alkaline, alloch-thonous, alluvial fan, alluvium, angular unconformity, anticline, aquifer, aragonite sea, archean eon, archi-pelago, asphalt, asthenosphere, autochthonous, banded iron formation, basement rock, basin, basin and range province, batholith, bedrock, bioerosion, biostratigraphy, biostratinomy, bioturbation, boudin, Bowen's reac-tion series, brackish, buckling, calcareous, calcite sea, caldera, carbon film, carbonate, carbonate hardgrounds, casting, cenozoic era, clast, cleavage, coccolith, coccolithophore, compaction, compression, concretion, con-glomerate, continental crust, continental margin, continental shelf, convergent boundary, copal, coprolite, core, craton, cross-bedding, crude oil, crust, daughter product, delta, dendrite, deposition, detachment fault, diagenesis, diapir, dike, dip slope, disconformity, divergent plate boundary, drill core, drumlin, earthquake, eon, epicenter, epoch, erosion, erratic, escarpment, esker, estuary, evaporate, exfoliation, extension, extrusive, fan-ning, fault, fault zone, felsic, ferromagnesian mineral, fold, fold buckling, foliation, fossil, fracture, freezing, gas-trolith, geode, geologic map, glass, Gondwanaland, half-life, hinge, hinge line, hot spring, hydrothermal vent, hypersaline, ichnology, igneous rock, interbedded, intrusion, island arc, isotope, joint, kame, karst, kettle, kink, kink band, klastos, lava, liquefaction, loess, lowland, mafic, magma, mantle, marine terrace, mélange, meta-morphic rock, metamorphism, micropaleontology, mid-oceanic ridge, mineral, mineralization, Mohs scale of hardness, molding, moraine, mullion, normal fault, oolitic, orogenesis, Pangea, pelite, plate tectonics, plumose, porphyry, psammite, quaternary, reverse fault, rock, sediment strap, sedimentary rock, shear zone, slickenside, soil liquefaction, stylolite, Tethys ocean, upheaval, urchin, Urgonian, Variscan orogeny, vein, verging, vitrinite, vug, wiggle trace, x-ray diffraction, x-ray fluorescence, Young's modulus, zeolite

GEOLOGICAL FIELD WORK METHODS: biogeochemistry, electrical resistivity tomography, geological mapping, geomicrobiology, glaciology, ground-penetrating radar, groundwater detection, high-resolution stratigraphy, hydrocarbon exploration, paleontology, sample collection, shallow seismic surveys, stratigraphic mapping, structural mapping, surficial mapping, surveying of topographic features

ROCKS AND MINERALS

FORMS: aggregate, boulder, crystal, erratic, gravel, mineral, pebble, river rock, scree

MINERALS: acerila, achroite, acmite, adamine, adularia, African amethyst, African jade, agaric mineral, agate, agate geode, agate jasper, agate opal, agatized wood, agua nueva agate, alabaster, alabaster, alacranite, alamandine, albite-anorthite series, alexandrite, allemontite, allemontite I, allemontite II, allemontite III, almandine spinel, almandite, alpha quartz, alurgite, amatite, Amazon stone, amazonite, Amazonstone, amber opal, amesite, amethyst, amethyst quartz, ametrine, amianthus, analbite, Andamooka opal, angelite, annite, anorthose, antigorite, antimonite, antimony glance, antozonite, aphrite, apricotine, aqua aura, aquamarine, argentiferous galena, argentite, Arizona ruby, arkansite, arsenical pyrites, arsenolamprite, asbestos, asbestos amphibole, aventurine, awaruite, azure copper ore, azure-malachite, balas ruby, ballas, banded opal, bandfire opal, baryte, basanite, bastite, bayerite, bazzite, biggs jasper, binghamite, bitter salt, bixbite, black jack, black lead, black opal, blanchardite, blende, blister copper, blood jasper, bloodstone, blue cap tourmaline, blue jasper, blue john, blue lace agate, blue vitriol, blushing copper, bog iron, bog iron ore, Bohemian garnet, bohmite, Bolivian amethyst, bologna stone, bonamite, bone opal, bone turquoise, bort, Botswana agate, boulder opal, bowenite, brass ore, Brazilian amethyst, brecciated agate, brecciated jasper, breunnerite, brimstone, bronzite, brown iron ore, Bruneau jasper, buergerite, bustamite, byssolite, cabrerite, cachalong opal, cactus amethyst, cactus citrine, cactus quartz, cadmium smithsonite, cairngorm, calamine, calcareous sinter, calcareous tufa, calciocelsian, calciotherite, calcspar, calderite, californite, campylite, Canadian amethyst, Cape May diamond, capillitite, carbonado, carbonate apatite, carbonate fluorapatite, carbonate hydroxylapatite, carbonatecyanotrichite, carbonate-rich apatite, carbonate-rich fluorapatite, carbonate-rich hydroxylapatite, carnelian, carnelian onyx, cathedral pyrite, cat's eye, cave creek jasper, celestite, ceylonite, chalcedon, chalcedonite, chalcedony, chalcedonyx, chalcotrichite, chalk, chalybite, chaoite, cherry opal, chert, chessylite, chlorapatite, chloropal, chlorophane, chlorospinel, chromdravite, chrome diaspore, chrome garnet, chrome tourmaline, chrome vesuvianite, chrome-diopside, chrome-enstatite, chrome-magnetite, chrome-spinel, chrome-tremolite, chromohercynite, chrysolite, chrysomelane, chrysopal, chrysoprase, chrysotile, chrysotile asbestos, cinnabarite, cinnamon stone, citrine, citrine, claro opal, clay ironstone, cleavelandite, cleiophane, cleiophane, cleveite, clinocervantite, clinochrysotile, clinoenstatite, clinoferrosillite, clinomimetite, clinothulite, clinozoisite, cloud agate, cobalt bloom, cobalt calcite, cobaltian adamite, cobaltian calcite, cobaltian dolomite, cobaltian loellingite, cobaltoadamite, cobaltocalcite, collophane, Colombian emerald, Colorado ruby, common garnet, common mica, common opal, common salt, condor agate, contra luz opal, Coober Pedy opal, copper adamite, copper pyrites, copper smithsonite, copper sulfate, copper vitriol, corn spar, cornelian, cornflower sapphire, Coyamito agate, crazy lace agate, cromfordite, cromite, cronstedtite, crystal opal, crystalline quartz, cuproadamite, cupropyrite, cymatolite, cymophane, cyprine, cyrtolite, danaite, dark opal, dauphinite, dekalbite, demantoid, dendritic agate, Deschutes jasper, desert rose, deweylite, diasporite, diatomacious opal, diatomite, dogtooth calcite, dogtooth spar, dollar, dolomite rock, dolostone, doyleite, dravite, dry bone ore, dryhead agate, ducktownite, dunite, eastonite, Eden Valley wood, Egyptian jasper, Eilat stone, elbaite, electrum, Elie ruby, emerald, emery, endlichite, enhydritic agate, enhydro agate, epidote, epsom, epsom salt, erubescite, essonite, evening stone, eye agate, faden quartz, Fairburn agate, falcon's eye, fancy, fassaite, fayalite, ferro-actinolite, ferro-magnesite, ferrosillite, ferrotitanite, ferrous chromite, ferrowollastonite, ferruginous quartz, fire agate, fire opal, flame opal, flame spinel, flash opal, flashfire opal, flint, flos ferri, flowstone, fluor, fluorannite, fluorapatite, fluor-dravite, fluorophlogopite, fluorspar, fool's gold, forsterite, fortification agate, fossil agate, fossil opal, fossil turquoise, fowlerite, fraipontite, frazil, freshwater, frost, fuschite, gahnite, gahnospinel, galaxite, galenite, garnet jade, garnierite, gelite, genthite, geyserite, geyserite, girasol, glacier, glass opal, glaze, gold opal, golden beryl, golden citrine, goshenite, goslarite, grafito, green beryl, green jasper, green lead ore, green onyx, grossularite, gudmundite, gymnite, gypsite, gypsum flower, gypsum rock, hackmanite, hafnium zircon, hailstone, halfbreed, hancockite, harlequin opal, hawk's eye, haytorite, heavy spar, heliodor, heliodorite, heliotrope, hercynite, Herkimer diamond, hessonite, hexagonite, hibschite, hiddenite, hog-toothed spar, holly blue, honey opal, horn lead, hornstone, hungarian opal, hyacinth, hyacinth opal, hyalite, hyalophane, hydrargillite, hydrargyllite, hydrargy-

rum, hydrogarnet, hydrogen dioxide, hydrogrossular, hydrohalite, hydrophane opal, hydroxyl-apatite, hypercinnabar, hypersthene, iceberg, Iceland spar, Iceland spar magnesite, icicle, idocrase, ilmenorutile, imperial topaz, Inca rose, indicolite, iridot, iris agate, iris quartz, iron, iron mica, iron rose, iserine, isinglass, isopyre, jacinth, jade, jargon, jargoon, jasp agate, jaspe, jasper, jasper opal, jasponyx, jeffersonite, jelly opal, josephinite, kaemmererite, kamacite, kammererite, kasoite, katoite, kidney ore, kimberlite, king topaz, kinradite, kittlite, kunzite, kutnohorite, Laguna agate, Lake Superior agate, landscape agate, lapis, lapis lazuli, larimar, lavender amethyst, lead glance, lead spar, lechosos opal, lemon opal, lemon quartz, leopard jasper, leopard stone, lepidomelane, lettsomite, leuco-garnet, leucoxene, levin opal, liddicoatite, light opal, lightning ridge opal, lime-soda feldspar, limestone, limestone onyx, liquid silver, lithium mica, lithoxyl opal, liver opal, lizardite, lodestone, löllingite, lonsdaleite, lussatine, lussatite, mackintoshite, Madeira citrine, magnesiochromite, malacolite, malaia garnet, malaya garnet, Mali garnet, mangan diaspore, manganapatite, manganbabingtonite, manganophyllite, manganowollastonite, mangansiderite, manganvesuvianite, marble, mariposite, marmatite, marmolite, martite, matrix opal, melanite, menaccanite, menilite, metacinnabarite, meteoric iron, Mexican fire opal, Mexican lace agate, Mexican onyx, mica, microcline and sanidine, microcrystalline quartz, milk opal, milky quartz, mineral salt, mispickel, Moctezuma agate, Mojave blue agate, moonstone, Moor's Head tourmaline, morenosite, Morgan Hill jasper, morganite, morion, morrisonite, moss agate, moss jasper, moss opal, mossottite, mother of opal, mother of pearl opal, mountain cork, mountain leather, mountain opal, mullicite, mushroom tourmaline, myrickite, myrmekite, nail head spar, native antimony, native arsenic, native bismuth, native copper, native gold, native iron, native lead, native mercury, native nickel, native platinum, native silver, native sulfur, native tellurium, natural salt, nealite, needle tin, nephrite, nepouite, neslite, Nevada opal, niccolo, nicholsonite, nickel, nickel bloom, nickelian loellingite, nickel-iron, niigataite, Nipomo agate, noble orthoclase, nostrandite, occidental turquoise, ocean jasper, octahedrite, odontolite, odontolite, odontolite, oisanite, oligonite, olivinoid, onegite, onice, onofrite, onyx, onyx marble, onyx opal, opal jasper, opal matrix, opaline, opalite, opalized bone, opalized fossil, opalized shell, opalized wood, ophiolite, optical calcite, orangite, orbicular jasper, orbiculated jasper, Oregon snakeskin agate, oriental alabaster, oriental garnet, orthoantigorite, orthochamosite, orthochrysotile, Owyhee jasper, padparadschah, paint ore, painted boulder, pajsbergite, pallasite, Palmeria citrine, paracelsian, parachrysotile, Paraiba tourmaline, peach beryl, peacock copper, peacock ore, pearl opal, pearl spar, pencil ore, pennine, penninite, pericline, peridot, peristerite, perthite, petrified wood, pezzottaite, phantom quartz, piconite, picotite, picrochromite, picroilmenite, picrolite, picture jasper, picture rock, pineapple opal, pinfire opal, pinpoint opal, pipe opal, pistacite, pitch opal, pitchblende, plagioclase feldspar, plasma, pleonast, pleonaste, plumbago, plume agate, poppy jasper, potash mica, potassium feldspar, potch, prase, prase opal, praseme, prasiolite, praziolite, precious beryl, precious cat's eye, precious fire opal, precious opal, purple copper ore, pycnite, pyralspite, pyrite cube, pyrite sun, pyritohedron, pyrophane, Queensland agate, Queensland opal, quicksilver, quinzite opal, radiolite opal, rainbow agate, rainbow aura quartz, rainbow garnet, rainbow hematite, rainbow opal, rainbow quartz, rasorite, raspberry beryl, raspberry garnet, raspberry spar, raspberyl, red beryl, red cobalt, red flash opal, red iron ore, red lead ore, retinalite, rhodochrosite onyx, rhodolite, rhyacolite, riband jasper, rice grain spar, ringwoodite, ripidolite, rock crystal, rock salt, rogueite, rose quartz, rosickyite, rosinca, rosolite, rubellite, rubicelle, ruby, ruby fuschite, ruby jack, ruby spinel, ruby sulfur, ruby zoisite, rumanite, Russian jasper, rutilated quartz, sagenite, sagenite agate, salaite, salite, salmon calcite, salt, saltwater, sammite, sand calcite, sand celestine, sand gypsum, sapphire, sapphire quartz, sard, sardonyx, satin spar, scenic agate, scepter quartz, schalenblende, schefferite, scherbencobalt, schernikite, schorl, schorlomite, seam opal, seawater, Seiland zircon, selenite, semiopal, seraphinite, sericite, serpentine marble, serpentine rock, serpentinite, shell opal, sherry topaz, shirozulite, Siberian amethyst blue quartz, siberite, siderophyllite, sideroplesite, silica, silicafied wood, silver glance, smoky quartz, snakeskin agate, snow, snowflake, soaprock, soapstone, soda feldspar, sodaclase, soda-lime feldspar, souesite, South African jade, spectrolite, specularite, spessartite, sphaerosiderite, spherocobaltite, spinel, staffelite, stalactite, stalagmite, star muscovite, star quartz, star ruby, star sapphire, starlite, steatite, Stone Canyon jasper, stream tin, strontian, strüverite, suisan marble, sulfur, sun opal, sunstone, sweetwater agate, Syrian garnet, tabasheer, taenite, tanzanite, tarnowitzite, television rock, television stone, terrestrial iron, tetraferriannite, tetraferriphlogopite, tetrataenite, thorogummite, thulite, thunder egg, thuringite, tiger's eye, tin stone, tincal, tirodite, titanoferrite, titano-hematite, titano-magnetite, topazolite, torite, tourmalinated quartz, Transvaal jade, trapiche emerald, travertine, triphane, tsavorite, tube agate, tufa, turgite, turkey fat ore, turquoise odontolite, tv stone, ugrandite, ultralite, umbalite, unakite, uralite, uranothorite, utahite, uvite, vanadiumdravite, variegated copper, velvet copper ore, velvet tourmaline, Venus hair quartz, Venus hair stone, Veracruz amethyst, verde antique, verdelite, vermarine, violane, Virgin Valley opal, Volga blue, wadsleyite, wascoite, wash opal, washingtonite,

water opal, watermelon tourmaline, wax opal, White Cliffs opal, white feldspar, white lead ore, white opal, white topaz, williamsite, wiluite, wood opal, wood tin, xanthitane, xanthite, yellow citrine, yellow copper, Yowah nut, yttrocerite, yttrofluorite, zebra jasper, zinc blende, zultanite

IGNEOUS ROCKS: adakite, andesite, anorthosite, aplite, basalt, basaltic trachyandesite, basanite, benmoreite, boninite, carbonatite, charnockite, comendite, dacite, diabase, diorite, dunite, enderbite, essexite, foidolite, gabbro, granite, granodiorite, granophyre, harzburgite, hawaiite, hornblendite, hyaloclastite, icelandite, ignimbrite, ijolite, kimberlite, komatiite, lamproite, lamprophyre, latite, lherzolite, monzogranite, monzonite, mugearite, nepheline syenite, nephelinite, norite , obsidian, pantellerite, pegmatite, peridotite, phonolite, picrite, porphyry, pumice, pyroxenite, quartz diorite, quartz monzonite, rhyodacite , rhyolite, scoria, shoshonite, sovite, syenite, tachylyte, tephrite, tonalite, trachyandesite, trachyte, trondhjemite, tuff, websterite, wehrlite

METAMORPHIC ROCKS: amphibolite, anthracite coal, blueschist, cataclasite, eclogite, gneiss, gossan, granulite, greenschist, hornfels, marble, migmatite, mylonite, pelite, phyllite, psammite, pseudotachylite, quartzite, schist, serpentinite, skarn, slate, soapstone, suevite, talc carbonate, whiteschist

SEDIMENTARY ROCKS: argillite, arkose, banded iron formation, breccia, chalk, chert, claystone, coal, conglomerate, coquina, diamictite, diatomite, dolomite, dolostone, evaporite, flint, greywacke, gritstone, itacolumite, jaspillite, laterite, lignite, limestone, marl, mudstone, oil shale, oolite, sandstone, shale, siltstone, travertine, turbidite, wackestone

GEOLOGIC TIME

USAGE NOTE: The timeline is arranged from oldest to most recent.

- Precambrian Eon (4,600 to 542 million years ago)
  - Hadean Era
  - Archean Era
    - Eoarchean Period
    - Paleoarchean Period
    - Mesoarchean Period
    - Neoarchean Period
  - Proterozoic Era
    - Paleoproterozoic Period
    - Mesoproterozoic Period
    - Neoproterozoic Period
- Phanerozoic Eon (542 million years ago to present)
  - Paleozoic Era
    - Cambrian Period
      - Terreneuvian Age
      - Series 2 Age
      - Series 3 Age
      - Furongian Age
    - Ordovician Period
      - Lower Age
      - Middle Age

- Upper Age
- Silurian Period
  - Llandovery Age
  - Wenlock Age
  - Ludlow Age
  - Pridoli Age
- Devonian Period
  - Lower Age
  - Middle Age
  - Upper Age
- Carboniferous Period
  - Mississippian Age
    - Lower
    - Middle
    - Upper
  - Pennsylvanian Age
    - Lower
    - Middle
    - Upper
- Permian Period
  - Cisuralian Age
  - Guadalupian Age
  - Lopingian Age

Mesozoic Era
- Triassic Period
  - Lower Age
  - Middle Age
  - Upper Age
- Jurassic Period
  - Lower Age
  - Middle Age
  - Upper Age
- Cretaceous Period
  - Lower Age
  - Upper Age

Cenozoic Era
- Paleogene Period
  - Paleocene Age
  - Eocene Age
  - Oligocene Age

Neogene Period

Miocene Age

Pliocene Age

Quaternary Period

Pleistocene Age

Holocene Age

SOIL

GENERAL VOCABULARY: acid sulfate soil, acrisol, active layer, akadama, albeluvisols, alfisol, alkali soil, andisol, angle of repose, Antigo soil, aridisol, atriplex, Baer's law, Bama soil, barren vegetation, base-richness, bay mud, bearing capacity, Berkshire soil, bevameter, biochar, biogeology, Blandford soil, bog, brickearth, brown earth, brown podzolic, calcareous grassland, calciorthid, calcisol, cambisol, capacitance probe, carbon cycle rebalancing, Casa Grande soil, Cecil soil, cellular confinement, characterization of pore space in soil, Charlottetown soil series, chernozem, clay, claypan, cob material, cohesion, compressed earth block, consolidation, contour plowing, critical state soil mechanics, Darcy, Darcy's law, dark earth, dispersion, Downer soil, downhill creep, drainage research, drilosphere, Drucker Prager yield criterion, Drummer soil, dry quicksand, dryland salinity, duricrust, durisol, dynamic compaction, ecological land classification, ecosystem ecology, edaphic, edaphology, effective stress, eluvium, entisol, erosion, European soil bureau network, European soil database, expansive clay, fech fech, fen, ferrallitization, fill dirt, flatwood, flownet, fractal in soil mechanics, frequency domain sensor, Fresno scraper, frost heaving, frost line, Fuller's earth, gelisol, geosmin, geotechnical investigation, gley soil, gleysols, gravitational erosion, groundwater-related subsidence, guelph soil, gypcrust, gypsisol, hardpan, headland, HESCO bastion, Hilo soil, histosol, Houdek soil, Hume soil, humin, humus, hydraulic conductivity, hydric soil, hydro axe mulching, hydrological transport model, hydropedology, hydrophobic soil, immobilization, inceptisol, International Humic Substances Society, International Soil Reference and Information Center, International Union of Soil Sciences, jory soil, kalkaska sand, kerogen, lahar, laimosphere, land improvement, lateral earth pressure, leaching, leaching model, leptosol, lessivage, Liming soil, linear aeration, lixisol, loam, loess, lunar soil, Miami soil, mineralization, mollisol, Muck soil, mud, Multiscale European Soil Information System, Multiscale Soil Information Systems, muskeg, Myakka soil, Narragansett soil, Natchez silt loam, National Society of Consulting Soil Scientists, natural organic matter, Newmark's influence chart, no-till method, on-grade mat foundation for expansive soils, OPAL Soil Center, Orovada soil, orthent, overburden pressure, oxisol, paleosol, particle size, Paxton soil, peat, pedalfer, pedocal, pedodiversity, pedology, permeability, petrichor, plaggen soil, planosol, podsol, pore water pressure, porosity, port silt loam, prime farmland, psamment, pygmy forest, quick clay, quicksand, rankers, red Mediterranean soil, regosol, rendzina, Reynolds dilatancy, rill, rock flour, SahysMod, saline seep, salt marsh, salting the earth, SaltMod, San Joaquin soil, sand, sand boil, sandbag, Scobey soil, Seitz soil, serpentine soil, shear strength, shear strength test, shrub swamp, silt, slope stability, slump, soil, soil alkalinity, soil amendment, soil and water assessment tool, Soil Association, soil biodiversity, soil biology, soil carbon, soil cement, soil chemistry, soil classification, soil compaction, soil conditioner, soil conservation, Soil Conservation and Domestic Allotment Act, soil contamination, soil crust, soil depletion, soil ecology, soil erosion, soil fertility, soil food web, soil functions, soil gradation, soil guideline value, soil health, soil horizon, soil inoculant, soil life, soil liquefaction, soil management, soil mechanics, soil moisture, soil moisture sensors, soil nailing, soil organic matter, soil pH, soil physics, soil policy, soil profile, soil resilience, soil respiration, soil salinity, soil salinity control, soil science, Soil Science Society of America, soil series, soil solarization, soil steam sterilization, soil structure, soil survey, soil test, soil texture, soil type, soil water retention, soils retrogression and degradation, solonchak, solonetz, specific storage, specific weight, spodic soil, stagnosol, strip farming, Stuttgart soil, subaqueous soil, subsidence, subsoil, suckiaug, talik, Tanana soil, technosol, tepetate, terra preta, Terra rosa soil, terrace farming, terracette, terramechanics, Terzaghi's Principle, thaw depth, thixotropy, Threebear soil, throughflow, Tifton soil, tillage, topsoil, tropical peat, ultisol, umbric horizon, umbrisol, Unified Soil Classification System, USDA soil taxonomy, ustochrept, vegetation and slope stability, vertisol, vibro stone column, void ratio, water content, weathering, Windsor soil, World Congress Of Soil Science, yedoma

GEOGRAPHY

GENERAL VOCABULARY: absolute humidity, absolute location, accessibility, acid rain, aerosol, air mass, altitude, atmosphere, biological diversity, biosphere, biota, boundary, carrying capacity, cartographer, central business district, climate, climax vegetation, continent, continental climate, continental divide, continentality, contour lines, conurbation, core area, crop-lien system, crust, cryosphere, culture, culture hearth, de facto segregation, de jure segregation, degree, degree day, demography, dry farming, economy of agglomeration, economy of scale, elevation, emergent coastline, enclave, equator, evapotranspiration, extended family, exurb, fall line, fallow, fault, fault, fault zone, fault-block mountain, federation, focality, functional diversity, geomorphology, geosphere, ghetto, glacial till, glaciation, glacier, globe, great circle route, grid, growing season, harmonic tremor, hazardous waste, hearth, heavy industry, hemisphere, hinterland, horizon, hot spot, humus, hydroponics, hydrosphere, ice age, indentured labor, insular, international date line, intervening opportunity, intracoastal waterway, isohyet, jurisdiction, karst, lacustrine plain, latitude, lava, leaching, leeward, legend, life cycle, light industry, lithosphere, longitude, magma, mantle, map, maritime climate, Mediterranean climate, metes and bounds, nodal region, open range, orographic rainfall, outwash, overburden, palisade, panhandle, permafrost, physiographic region, piedmont, platted land, plural society, populated place, post-industrial, prevailing winds, Prime Meridian, rainshadow, region, resource, riparian rights, scale, sea level, sharecropping, sinkhole, site, situation, snowline, spreading ridges, staple product, sustainable yield, tectonic plates, territory, threshold, time distance, topographic map, topography, township and range, transhumance, tree line, Tropic of Cancer, Tropic of Capricorn, tropics, vent, water table, windward, zoning

BOG TYPES: blanket, peat, raised, string

BOGS OF NORTH AMERICA: Strangmoor Bog Michigan, Rhine Center Bog Wisconsin, Burns Bog British Columbia, Spruce Hole Bog New Hampshire, Tannersville Cranberry Bog Pennsylvania, Tom S. Cooperrider-Kent Bog Ohio, Pinhook Bog Indiana, Volo Bog Illinois, Saco Heath Bog Maine, Joseph Pines Bog Virginia, Mer Bleue Bog Ontario , Alfred Bog Ontario, Johnville Bog Quebec

CLIMATIC ZONES: arctic, arid, desert, jungle, Mediterranean, mountain, polar, subarctic, subtropical, temperate, tropical

CLIMATIC ZONES BASED ON KOEPPEN SYSTEM: arid, cool summer, highlands, humid subtropical, ice, marine west coast, Mediterranaean, semiarid, subarctic, tropical dry, tropical wet, tundra, uplands, warm summer

> **USAGE NOTE:** Several different systems of classification exist for global climate zones. If accuracy is important, consult several sources and choose the system that works for an individual project.

ECOSYSTEMS: aquatic, badland, coral reef, desert, estuary, forest, glade, grassland, grove, heath, intertidal, jungle, lentic freshwater, lotic freshwater, marine, meadow, moor, mountain, oceanic, prairie, rainforest, salt marsh, savannah, taiga, temperate deciduous, temperate evergreen, tropical deciduous, tropical evergreen, tundra, veldt, wasteland, wetland, woods

GEOGRAPHICAL ZONES (BASED ON LATITUDE): north frigid zone, north temperate zone, torrid zone, south temperate zone, south frigid zone

GRADE/SLOPE: decline, gentle, incline, steep, switchback, terraced

TERRAIN FEATURES: abyss, area, brush, burrow, crag, cavern, catacomb, chasm, cleft, copse, coppice, coulee, countryside, cove, crater, crevasse, crevice, dell, depression, desert, ditch, everglade, fastness, fen, fenland, field, fissure, foothill, ford, forest, glacier, glade, glen, gorge, grassland, grotto, grove, gulf, headland, hillock, hollow, hummock, ice, iceberg, jungle, kane, Karst topography, kettle, knob, knoll, labyrinth, lair, lowland, maze, meadow, mire, morass, mound, mount, mountaintop, outcropping, overhang, pampas, patch, peak, plain, pinnacle, pit, point, prairie, precipice, promontory, prominence, quagmire, quicksand, rain forest, rift, rock face, sandbank, sand pit, sinkhole, slough, summit, tangle, tarn, thicket, timberland, tropical forest, tropical rain forest, underground, undergrowth, warren, wilderness, wood, woods, woodland, wasteland

WATER FEATURES: bayou, bog, brook, coral (island, isle, reef), creek, delta, fish pond, flowage, lake, marsh, marshland, mill pond, oasis, oxbow lake, pond, puddle, river, riverbank, rivulet, stream, streamlet, swamp, swampland, tributary, watercourse

LANDFORMS

AEOLIAN: barchan, blowout, desert pavement, desert varnish, dreikanter, dry lake, dune, erg, loess, sandhill, ventifact, yardang

COASTAL AND OCEANIC: abyssal fan, abyssal plain, arch, archipelago, atoll, ayre, barrier bar, barrier island, bay, beach, beach cusps, beach ridge, bight, blowhole, calanque, cape, channel, cliff, coast, continental shelf, coral reef, cove, cuspate foreland, dune system, estuary, firth, fjord, geo, gulf, headland, inlet, island, islet, isthmus, lagoon, machair, marine terrace, mid-ocean ridge, ocean, oceanic basin, oceanic plateau, oceanic trench, peninsula, raised beach, ria, river delta, salt marsh, sea, sea cave, seamount, shoal, shore, sound, spit, stack, strait, stump, submarine canyon, surge channel, tombolo, volcanic arc, wave cut platform

EROSION: butte, canyon, cave, cliff, cuesta, dissected plateau, erg, exhumed river channel, gulch, gully, hogback, hoodoo, inverted relief, lavaka, limestone pavement, malpais, mesa, monadnock, natural arch, pediment, pediplain, peneplain, potrero, ridge, roche moutonnée, rock formations, structural bench, structural terrace, tea table, tepui, tor, valley

FLUVIAL: ait, alluvial fan, anabranch, arroyo, bar, basin, bayou, bench, braided channel, cave, cliff, confluence, crevasse splay, cutbank, delta, drainage basin, endorheic basin, esker, exhumed river channel, floodplain, fluvial island, fluvial terrace, gorge and canyon, gully, marsh, meander, natural levee, natural pool, oxbow lake, plunge pool, point bar, rapid, riffle, river, river island, rock-cut basin, shoal, shut-in, spring, stream, stream pool, swamp, thalweg, towhead, vale, valley, wadi, wash, waterfall, watershed

GLACIAL AND MOUNTAIN: arête, cirque, col, corrie, crevasse, cwm, dirt cone, drumlin, drumlin field, esker, fjord, fluvial terrace, glacial horn, glacier, glacier cave, glacier foreland, hanging valley, hill, kame, kame delta, kettle, monadnock, moraine, moulin, mountain, mountain cove, mountain pass, mountain range, nunatak, outwash fan, outwash plain, pingo, proglacial lake, ribbed moraine, rift valley, roche moutonnée, sandur, side valley, summit, trim line, tunnel valley, u-shaped valley, valley

SLOPE: alas, bluff, butte, cliff, cuesta, dale, defile, dell, draw, escarpment, glen, gully, hill, interfluve, knoll, mesa, mountain pass, plain, plateau, ravine, ridge, rock shelter, scree, strath, summit, terrace, terracettes, vale, valley, valley shoulder

VOLCANIC: caldera, complex volcano, crater lake, cryovolcano, geyser, guyot, lava dome, lava flow, lava lake, lava plain, lava spine, lava tube, maar, malpais, mamelon, mid-ocean ridge, mud volcano, oceanic trench, pit crater, pseudocrater, sand volcano, shield volcano, stratovolcano, subglacial mound, submarine volcano, supervolcano, tuya, vent, volcanic cone, volcanic craters, volcanic dam, volcanic field, volcanic group, volcanic island, volcanic plateau, volcanic plug, volcano

MAN-MADE BOUNDARIES

POLITICAL DIVISIONS: associated state, bailiwick, canton, chiefdom, colony, commonwealth, community council, constituency, county, country, country subdivision, department, dependency, district, division, duchy, emirate, federacy, federal state, federated state, federation, island council, municipal district, municipality, nation-state, possession, prefecture, province, region, republic, rural district, section, settlement, sovereign state, state, sultanate, territory, viceroyalty, voivodeship, ward

CITY: barrio, borough, civic center, colony, commune, community, downtown, ghetto, hamlet, metropolis, municipality, neighborhood, parish, settlement, shire, suburbs, town, township, unincorporated, village

METEOROLOGY

GENERAL VOCABULARY: accumulation, advisory, air, air mass, air pollution, air pressure, anemometer, atmosphere, atmospheric pressure, aurora, autumn, balmy, barometer, barometric pressure, Beaufort wind scale, biosphere, calm, cell, climate, climatology, cloud, cloud bank, cloudburst, cloudy, cold, cold front, cold snap, cold wave, condensation, contrail, convergence, current, cyclonic flow, degree, depression, dew point, disturbance, doldrums, downburst, downdraft, downwind, drift, drifting snow, drought, dust storm, earthlight, easterlies, eddy, EF-scale, El Niño, emergency radio, evaporation, eye, eye wall, fair, fall,

feeder bands, firewhirl, flash flood, flood stage, forecast, freeze, front, Fujita scale, global warming, graupel, greenhouse effect, gully washer, haboob, halo, haze, heat, heat index, heat wave, high, humid, humidity, hurricane season, hydrologic cycle, hydrology, hydrometer, hydrosphere, hygrometer, ice crystals, icicle, inversion, isobar, isotherm, jet stream, Kelvin, knot, lake effect, landfall, landspout, leeward, low, low clouds, low pressure system, macroburst, meteorologist, meteorology, microburst, National Hurricane Center (NHC), National Weather Service (NWC), NEXRAD, nor'easter, normal, outflow, outlook, overcast, ozone, parhelion, partly cloudy, permafrost, polar, polar front, pollutant, precipitation, pressure, prevailing wind, radar, radiation, rain gauge, rain shadow, relative humidity, ridge, rope tornado, sandstorm, scattered, sky, smog, smoke, snow level, snow line, spring, squall line, St. Elmo's fire, stationary front, storm tracks, stratosphere, subtropical, summer, sun dog, sun pillar, sunrise, sunset, supercell, surge, swell, temperate, temperature, thaw, thermal, thermometer, tornado alley, trace, triple point, tropical, tropical depression, tropical disturbance, tropical wave, troposphere, trough, turbulence, twilight, unstable, updraft, upwelling, upwind, vapor, vapor trail, visibility, vortex, wall cloud, warm, warning, watch, water, water cycle, wave, weather, weather balloon, weather map, weather satellite, weathering, weathervane, wedge, westerly, whiteout, wind chill, wind chill factor, wind shear, wind vane, windsock, winter, zone

COLD: arctic, chilly, freezing, frigid, frosty, icy, nip in the air, nippy, wind chill, wintry

WARM: baked, desertlike, hot, sultry, summery, tropical

DRY: arid, dehydrated, desiccated, mummified

WET: damp, dew, fog, fog bank, ground fog, humid, moist, moisture, muggy, steam, steamy

CLOUDS: altocumulus, altostratus, cirriform, cirrostratus, cirrus, cumuliform, cumulonimbus, cumulus, mammatus cloud, nimbostratus, nimbus, orographic cloud, pileus cloud, stratocumulus, stratus

PRECIPITATION: barrage, cascade, cloudburst, deluge, downpour, drenching, dribble, drip, driving rain, drizzle, drop, freezing rain, glaze, heavy rain, inundation, light rain, mist, mizzle, monsoon, peppering, pouring, pouring pitchforks, rain, rain bands, rainbow, raindrop, raining cats and dogs, raining frogs, rainfall, rain shower, rainwater, saturate, shower, sleet, snow, soaking, spitting, spray, streaming, torrent, torrential rain, trickle

SEVERE WEATHER: blizzard, cyclone, flood, funnel, funnel cloud, hail, hurricane, ice storm, lightning, snowstorm, squall, storm, storm surge, thunder, thunderhead, thunderstorm, tornado, tropical storm, twister, typhoon, waterspout, whirlwind

SNOW EVENTS: black ice, blizzard, falling snow, flurries, frost, frostiness, frozen snow, glaciated snow, hoar frost, ice, ice pack, iciness, lake-effect precipitation, lake-effect snow, rime, snow angel, snow band, snowball, snow belt, snowboarding, snow cave, snow cover, snow day, snow drift, snowfall, snowflake, snow fort, snowman, snowmelt, snowmobile, snow pack, snow plow, snow shoeing, snow shower, snow skiing, snow slab, snow sledding, snow squall, snowstorm, thundersnow, whiteness, whiteout

SNOWSTORMS: Alberta clipper, Colorado low, Gulf low, nor'easter, panhandle hook

SNOW TYPES: crystal aggregates, crystal facets, crystal pellets, crystalline water ice, dendritic crystals, dry snow, fluffy flakes, freezing snow, granular ice material, granular snow, graupel, hail stones, ice aggregate, ice lattice, ice nucleus, ice particles, ice pellets, ice snow, planar crystals, plate crystals, powder, sleet, slush, snow aggregate, snow crystals, snow grains, snow ice, snow pellets, snowflakes, supercooled cloud droplets, wet snow

WIND: air current, air stream, blowing, blustery, breeze, calm, Chinook wind, draft, dust devil, flow of air, gale, gust, hurricane force, jet stream, land breeze, light wind, mistral wind, prevailing wind, puff, puff of air, Santa Ana wind, sea breeze, squall, tempest, waft, wind advisory, windstorm, zephyr

WINDS OF THE MEDITERRANEAN: Gregale, Levante, Libeccio, Mistral, Ostro, Ponente, Sirocco, Tramontane

BOTANY

FUNGUS

USAGE NOTE: Mushrooms and fungus can be deadly and difficult to identify. Use caution when referencing mushrooms so as not to overlook or conceal a potential danger.

COMMON NAMES: aborted entoloma, agaricus (bleeding, crocodile, spring), alcohol inky cap, American matsutake, angels' wings, aniseed toadstool, anise-scented, apricot jelly mushroom, aspen scaber stalk, bear's head, beechwood sickener, belly-button mushroom, black forest mushroom , black fungus, black kame, black saddle mushroom, blackening waxcap, bleeding milky cap, blewit, blue milky cap, blusher, blushing bracket, bolete (admirable, barrow, bay, butter, king, regal, two-colored, Zellers), bracelet cortinarius, brown hay cap, brown kame, butter mushroom, button mushroom, candle-snuff fungus, candy cap, cauliflower fungus, cauliflower mushroom, chanterelle (black, cinnabar-red, clustered blue, golden, smooth, trumpet, white), charcoal burner, chicken of the woods, click beetle, cloud ear mushroom, comb tooth mushroom, commercial mushroom, common store mushroom, coral fungus, coral hericium, crimson waxcap, death cap, delicious milky cap, destroying angel, dotted-stalk suillus, drumstick mushroom, earth balls, edulis, egg mushroom, enoki, fairies' bonnet, fairy club, fairy ring, fairy-ring mushroom, fawn mushroom, field mushroom, fragrant clitocybe, garlic marasmius, golden needle, green-spored parasol, gypsy mushroom, hairy stereum, hedgehog mushroom, hen of the woods, honey fungus bootlace, honey mushroom, hoof fungus, horn of plenty, horse mushroom, inky cap, jelly baby, Judas's ear, lethal webcaps, lawyer's wig, man on horseback, Manzanita scaber stalk, matsutake, meadow mushroom, mica cap, milkcap (saffron, ugly, watery, wooly), monkey head, morel, nameko, oak mushroom, old man of the woods, orange jelly, orange-capped scaber stalk, oyster mushroom, paddy straw mushroom, painted suillus, parasol mushroom, phallus, pig's ear, pine mushroom, poison pie, pom-pom, porcini, puffball, red-tipped coral mushroom, russula (bare-toothed, birch, blackening, shellfish-scented, short-stem, tacky green), russula-like waxy cap, scaber stalk, scarlet hood, shaggy mane, shaggy parasol mushroom, shiitake, short-stalked slippery cap, silver ear mushroom, snow mushroom, snowbank false morel, sponge, stink horn with face fly, straw mushroom, stump puffball, sweet tooth, sweetbread mushroom, the prince, tree ear, truffle (French black, Italian white, Oregon white, summer, Texas white), trumpet of death, umbrella polypore , velvet foot, white jelly fungus, willow fomes, wine-cap stropharia, winter mushroom, witches butter, wolf's milk, wood ear mushroom, yellow brain fungus

HERBACEOUS PLANTS

USAGE NOTE: Herbaceous plants have stems and leaves that die down to the ground in the fall. They may be annuals (living only one season), perennials (returning each spring for an indefinite number of seasons), or biennials (living for two seasons, in which the plant remains low and leafy in the first season and becomes taller and flowering in the second season).

USAGE NOTE: The distinction between an annual plant and a perennial plant is sometimes a matter of geography; some plants are considered perennials in warm climates but are grown as annuals in cold climates since they are unlikely to survive the winter.

GARDEN ANNUALS: ageratum, alpine wallflower, alyssum, baby blue eyes, bachelor button, balsam, begonia, bells of Ireland, bishop's week, blanket flower, carnation, celosia, cockscomb, coleus, cosmos, dianthus, dusty miller, firecracker plant, forget-me-not, fuchsia, geranium, Gerbera daisy, globe amaranth, heliotrope, hibiscus, impatiens, ivy geranium, Johnny jump-up, lantana, larkspur, leadwort, lobelia, love in a mist, mallow, marigold, Mexican heather, milkweed, million bells, money plant, moonflower, morning glory, moss rose, nasturtium, New Guinea impatiens, nicotiana, nigella, ornamental kale, ornamental Swiss chard, pansy, pentas, petunia, phlox, pincushion flower, pinks, polka dot, purple fountain grass, purslane, sage, salvia, snapdragon, snow on the mountain, spike, statice, strawflower, sunflower, sweet pea, sweet William,

thistle, toadflax, torenia, treasure flower, tree mallow, true daisy, trumpet flower, tuberous begonia, twinspur, verbena, vinca, vinca vine, viola, wallflower, wax begonia, zinnia

GARDEN BULBS: allium, alstromeria, amaryllis, anemone, blackberry lily, caladium, calla, camassia, canna, Chinese ground orchid, colchicum, corydalis, crinum lily, crocosmia, crocus, daffodil, dahlia, dog's tooth violet, double daffodil, double tulip, elephant ear, four o'clock, freesia, fringed tulip, fritillaria, gladiolus, gloriosa lily, glory of the snow, grape hyacinth, hyacinth, iris, jack in the pulpit, jonquil, lily, lily of the valley, oxalis, parrot tulip, peacock flower, pineapple lily, rain lily, snowdrop, society garlic, Spanish bluebell, spider lily, squill, summer snowflake, taro, tuberous begonia, tulip, waterlily tulip, wind flower, winter aconite

GARDEN PERENNIALS: adder's tongue, ageratum, Alexander, alkanet, Allegheny spurge, alpine violet, alumroot, American dream, American feverfew, American pokeweed, American spikenard, anise mint, Apache plume, apple blossom grass, arctic willow, arrow broom, avens, Aztec Indian berry, baby's breath, bachelor button, ball cactus, balloon flower, baneberry, barren strawberry, basket of gold, bear's breech, beardtongue, beautyberry, bee balm, bellflower, bellwort, betony, big ears, birch double, bird's foot trefoil, bird-foot violet, birthwort, bishop's weed, bitter root, black cohosh, black mondo grass, blackberry lily, black-eyed Susan, bladder pod, blanket flower, blazing star, bleeding heart, bloodroot, bloody crane's bill, blue cohosh, blue indigo, blue mist spirea, blue pickerel plant, bluebell, bluestar , Boston ivy, bouncing bet, bowman's root, boxwood, bright star, broom, bugleweed, bugloss, bush clover, bush morning glory, bush palmetto, bush pea, butter bur, buttercup, butterfly bush, butterfly milkweed, button bush, button snakeroot, button willow, California fuchsia, campion, Canadian milkvetch, candylily, candytuft, Canterbury bells, cardinal flower, cardoon, carnation, Carolina moonseed, carpenter plant, catchfly, catmint, celandine, chamomile, checkerbloom, cheddar pink, Chinese foxglove, Chinese lantern, Chinese yam, chocolate flower, chocolate vine, cinnamon vine, cinquefoil, clove pink, clover, cohosh, Colorado rubber plant, columbine, comfrey, compass plant, coneflower, coral beads, coral bells, cowslip, crane's bill, creeping phlox, crimson glory vine, cross vine, crown of snow, crown vetch, crowsfoot, Culver's physic, cup and saucer, cup plant, Cupid's dart, curly onion, dame's rocket, daylily, dead nettle, dense gentian, devil's paintbrush, dittany of Crete, dog-toothed violet, doll's eyes, dong dang gui, double bird's foot trefoil, double bubble mint, double gloriosa, double robin white breast, dragonhead, drumstick primrose, dunce caps, dusty miller, Dutchman's pipe, dwarf blue rabbit brush, dwarf golden, dwarf palmetto, dwarf red, echinacea, Edelweiss, elder, Englemann daisy, English daisy, European elder, evening primrose, evergreen bittersweet, everlasting, Faassen's catnip, fairy candles, fairy lily, false chamomile, false dragonhead, false indigo, false lupine, false mallow, false miterwort, false salvia, false Solomon's seal, false strawberry, fern-leaf, feverfew, fire pink, fireball, firecracker, five finger, five-leaf aralia, flax, fleabane, fleece flower, fleur-de-lis, foamflower, forget-me-not, four-winged saltbush, foxglove, fraxinella, Fremont's crowfoot, French honeysuckle, fringed finger poppy mallow, fringed sage, garden heliotrope, garden phlox, garden sorrel, gas plant, gayfeather, gentian, German garlic, German statice , germander, giant burnet, giant flowered salvia, ginger , globe mallow, globe thistle, globeflower, Gloriosa daisy, goatsbeard, gold crown, gold dust, gold net, goldball, golden Alexander, golden bells, golden poppy, golden star, golden strawberry, goldenrod, gooseberry leafed globe mallow, gooseneck loosestrife, goutweed, grape, great merrybells, greater celandine, Greek valerian, green-and-gold, greenthreads, ground elder, ground plum, gumbo lily, Hall's honeysuckle, hardy ice plant, harebell, hawkweed, heartleaf Alexander, Helen's flower, heliotrope, helmet flower, hen and chicks, heron's-bill, hoary skullcap, hollyhock, honey bells, honeysuckle, hopflower oregano, hops, horehound, horsemint, hosta, hummingbird, hyssop, hyssop skullcap, Indian physic, Indian strawberry, Indian turnip, indigo, Irish moss, ironweed, Italian bugloss, ivy, jack in the pulpit, Jacob's ladder, Japanese parsley, Joe-Pye weed, joint fir, knapweed, Korean boxwood, lacy veil, ladies' tresses, lady's leek, lady's mantle, ladybells, lamb's ear, Lambert's locoweed, lantern plant, lavender cotton, lavender monkey flower, lead plant, leadwort, lemon lace vine, lemon lily, Lenten rose, leopard plant, leopard's bane, lily, lily of the valley, lilyturf, little pickles, littleleaf mock orange, liverleaf, lizard tail, loosestrife, Low's Japanese creeper, lungwort, lupine, magnolia vine, mahogany plant, maidenhair tree, mallow, Maltese cross, malva, man of the earth, marsh marigold, Martha Washington's plume, masterwort, matricaria, mayapple, meadow parsley, meadow rue, meadowsweet, Mexican hat, mile-a-minute, milfoil, milkvetch, milkweed, miniature hen and chicks, mint shrub, Missouri primrose, mist flower, mock orange, mondo grass, moneywort, monk's hood vine, monkey flower, monkshood, moon carrot, moss campion, mother of thyme, mountain bluet, mountain fringe, mountain gold, mountain lady's mantle, mountain mint, Mt. Atlas daisy, mullein, myrtle, Naples onion, nettle , New Jersey tea, nightshade, Nordic dragonhead, northern crepe myrtle, obedience plant, October daphne, old fashioned bleeding heart, old man of the mountain, old man of the prairie, old woman, onion, orris root, ostrich plume, our lady's bedstraw, oxeye daisy, pansy, pasque flower, peach bells, pearlwort, pearly everlasting, pennywort, peony , periwinkle, Persian stonecrest, Persian violet, pie

plant, pincushion cactus, pincushion flower, pink fleece flower, pink prairie onion, pinks, plumbago, plume poppy, poker plant, poppy, poppy mallow, porcelain vine, prairie baptisia, prairie clover, prairie coneflower , prairie groundsel, prairie mallow, prairie smoke, prairie spiderwort , primrose, prince's plume, purple coneflower, purple leaf Japanese parsley, purple rockcress, purple-leaf wintercreeper, quarter vine, Queen Anne's lace, queen of the meadow, rain lily, rainbow, rattlesnake master, red false mallow, red hot poker, red puccoon, red valerian, rhubarb, Riddell's goldenrod, robin white breast, rock cress, rock garden statice, rock rose, rockfoil, rose mallow, rose of Sharon, rose of the rockery, rose sage, rue, rue anemone, rupturewort, Russian hibiscus, Russian hibiscus, Russian sage, sage, sandwort, scarlet rocket, Scotch bluebells, sea holly, sea lavender, sea pink, seaside daisy, self heal, seven son flower, Shasta daisy, shining bluestar, shooting star, shrub ice plant, silkweed, silver butterfly bush, silver lace vine, silver vine, silver-leafed nettle, silvervein creeper, skullcap, smoke bush, snail-seed, snakehead, snakeroot, snapdragon, sneezeweed, snowdrop, snow-in-summer, snowy tansy, soapweed, soapwort, society garlic, Solomon's seal, Spanish snapdragon, speedwell, spiderwort, spirea, spurge, St. John's wort, standing wine cups, starburst ice plant, statice, Stoke's aster, stonecrop sedum, stork's bill, strawberry, sulphur flower, summer solstice, sun daisy, sun rose, sundrop, sunflower, sunray flower, sunset hyssop, swamp milkweed, sweet autumn clematis, sweet coneflower, sweet flag, sweet pea, sweet William, sweet woodruff, Texas rose, threadleaf bluestar, thrift, thriller, thyme, tickseed, tiger's jaws, toad lily, toadflax, torch lily, tree mallow, tritoma, trout lily, trumpet creeper, tufted ice plant, Turk's cap, turtlehead, twinspur, valerian, variegated ground ivy, variegated sweet marjoram, variegated yellow rocket, veil of lace, Venetian sumac, vervain, vesper iris, violet, virgin's bower, Virginia creeper, wand bloom, white bouquet, wild ginger, wild oats, wild onion, wild petunia, wild snowball, willow, Wils quinine, wine cup, winter fat, wintercreeper, wood poppy, wood sunflower, woodbine, woodwaxen, wooly thyme, wormwood, woundwort, yarrow, yellow archangel, yellow flag, yellow horned poppy, yellow storksbill

POISONOUS PLANTS: aconite, Adam and Eve, African sumac, akar saga, angel's trumpet, angel wings, asparagus berry, autumn crocus, azalea, bad-man's oatmeal, beaver poison, belladonna, betel nut palm, bittersweet nightshade, black hellebore, black locust, black nightshade, black snakeroot, bleeding heart, blind-your-eye mangrove, blister bush, bloodroot, blue-green algae, blue passion flower, bobbins, bracken, broom, calabar bean, castor oil plant, children's bane, Christmas rose, cocklebur, columbine, common ivy, corn cockle, corn lily, cows and bulls, cowbane, crab's eye, cuckoo-pint, daffodil, daphne, darnel, datura, deadly nightshade, death-of-man, deathcamas, desert-rose, devils and angels, devil's cherry, doll's eyes, dumbcane, Dutchman's breeches, elderberry, elephant ear, european spindle, false parsley, foxglove, frangipani, giant hogweed, giddee giddee, gifblaar, graveyard tree, greater celandine, heart of Jesus, hemlock, henbane, holly, horse chestnut, hyacinth, Indian licorice, jack in the pulpit, Jamestown weed, jequirity, Jerusalem cherry, jimson weed, John Crow bead, jumbie bead, kudu, larkspur, lily of the valley, lords and ladies, Madiera winter cherry, manchineel tree, manchineel, mayapple, meadow saffron, mistletoe, monkshood, moonseed, mother of millions, mountain laurel, oleander, ongaonga, ordeal beans, palma Christi, pinyang, poinsettia, poison ivy, poison oak, poison ryegrass, poison sumac, pokeweed, precatory bean, privet, ragwort, redoul, rhubarb, river poison tree, rosary pea, ruti, sabi star, snakeweed, spotted parsley, starch-root, stinkweed, strychnine tree, suicide tree, thorn apple, tomato, wake robin, water-dropwort, water hemlock, weather plant, white baneberry, white snakeroot, wild arum, wild carrot, wild parsnip, wolfsbane, yellow Jessamine

USAGE NOTE: The plants listed above are considered poisonous for a variety of reasons. Some are poisonous only in part; for example, in some plants, only the bulb, flower, or fruit is dangerous. Some species are dangerous only at certain times in their growth cycle.

A distinction should also be made between plants that are poisonous and those that are toxic. Poisonous plants cause illness or death through ingestion. Toxic plants are those that cause a rash or other reaction through touch. When including any of these plants in a fictional setting, research is required to describe their effects properly.

WEEDS: air potato, American willow herb, Armenian blackberry, Asiatic blue dayflower, Asiatic tearthumb, Asiatic witchweed, Australian pine, Australian swamp stonecrop, Australian wattles, autumnal crocus, baby rose, bead tree, Bermuda buttercup, Bermuda grass, bindweed, black locust, bramble, Brazilian pepper, Brazilian waterweed, broadleaf plantain, broad-leaved paper bark, bugweed, burdock, camphor laurel, camphor tree, Canadian pondweed, castor oil plant, Ceylon cedar, chinaberry, Chinese privet, Chinese

tallow tree, Chinese tearthumb, Christmasberry, climbing maidenhair, cogon grass, common broom, common field speedwell, common ivy, common lambsquarters, common reed, common water hyacinth, coral bush, coralberry, cotton thistle, creeping Charlie, creeping Jenny, curled dock, curly dock, curly-leaf pondweed, dandelion, desert false indigo, devil shield, devil's tail tearthumb, diffuse knapweed, dog-strangling vine, downy brome, drooping brome, English ivy, Esthwaite waterweed, eucalyptus, Eurasian water milfoil, European privet, evening primrose, Filao tree, fleece flower, floating pennywort, Florida aspen, Florida holly, flowering rush, fox and cubs, garlic mustard, giant cow parsley, giant hogweed, giant reed, giant salvinia, goldenrod, grape caulerpa, grass rush, gray popcorn tree, green spurge, Guernsey fleabane, gum tree, hedge garlic, heraldic thistle, herb twopence, Himalayan balsam, Himalayan blackberry, honey locust, Hottentot fig, humble plant, Japanese barberry, Japanese climbing fern, Japanese honeysuckle, Japanese knotweed, Japanese stiltgrass, Japanese wineberry, jewelweed, kariba weed, "killer algae", kudzu, large-flowered waterweed, leafy spurge, least duckweed, Mauritius thorn, mesquite, Mexican poppy, mile-a-minute weed, milk thistle, moneywort, Morrow's honeysuckle, multiflora rose, musk thistle, narrow dock, natal grass, natal redtop, Nepalese browntop, nodding thistle, old man's beard, Old World climbing fern, orange hawkweed, Oxford ragwort, pampas grass, paper bark tea tree, parrot feather, parsnip, Persian lilac, Persian silk tree, Pigmy weed, pink lady's thumb, pink siris, poison hemlock, poison ivy, prickly pear, princess tree, purple dewplant, purple loosestrife, purple lythrum, purple pitcher, queen of the night cactus, ragweed, rambler rose, rhododendron, rose natal grass, rose pepper, Russian knapweed, Russian vine, saltcedar, saltmarsh cordgrass, Scotch broom, Scots thistle, Scottish thistle, sensitive plant, shameful plant, skunk vine, sleeping grass, smooth cordgrass, sorrel, sour dock, southern blue gum, Spanish cane, spiked loosestrife, spiked water milfoil, spotted knapweed, St John's wort, sulfur cosmos, sumac, swallowwort, tamarisk, Tartarian honeysuckle, Tasmanian blue gum, tawny hawkweed, Thunberg's barberry, torpedo grass, touch-me-not, tree of heaven, triffid weed, tropical soda apple, two penny grass, water caltrop, water chestnut, water fern, water hyacinth, white cedar, white clover, white knapweed, whorled water milfoil, wild carrot, wild privet, wild taro, wine raspberry, wineberry, winter creeper vine, wood sorrel, woolly thistle, yellow cockspur, yellow cosmos, yellow dock, yellow nutsedge, yellow starthistle

USAGE NOTE: Beauty is in the eye of the beholder. So are weeds. One gardener's weed is another gardener's treasure. A lawn might look pretty in the spring sprinkled with bright yellow dandelions, but to a golf course groundskeeper, a dandelion is an intruder. The list above includes plants that are frequently regarded as weeds—but they might not be weeds to everyone. Even useful plants can be considered weeds in the wrong setting—in the Midwest, for example, war is being waged against garlic mustard, an edible salad green that has become an invasive species and crowds out native plants. Climate also drives the determination of a weed; in cold climates, certain plants are kept in check, but in warmer zones, those same plants might grow uncontrolled. When referencing weeds, consider the climate and placement of these plants.

WILDFLOWERS: Adam and Eve, African daisy, American hogpeanut, aniseroot, arroyo lupine, baby blue eyes, baby's breath, bachelor button, baneberry, beebalm, bird's eyes, bird's foot trefoil, bishop's flower, black-eyed Susan, blanket flower, blue cohosh, blue flax, bluebonnet, blue-eyed grass, bull thistle, butterfly weed, California bluebell, California poppy, calliopsis, candytuft, catchfly, chamomile, chicory, cinnamon fern, clasping coneflower, columbine, corn poppy, cornflower, cosmos, crane's bill, crimson clover, cucumber root, dame's rocket, daylily, dense blazing star, Drummond phlox, Dutchman's breeches, dwarf red plains coreopsis, evening primrose, farewell-to-spring, field clover, fire wheel, five spot, Flanders poppy, flannel plant, fleabane, fluxweed, foxglove, goatsbeard, gold yarrow, goldenseal, ground cedar, hepatica, Iceland poppy, Indian blanket, ironweed, Johnny jump-up, lacy phacelia, lance-leaved coreopsis, leadplant, lemon mint, marsh marigold, Maximilian sunflower, mayapple, mealy blue sage, Mexican hat, Missouri primrose, moss verbena, mouse ears, mullein, nettle, New England aster, northern maidenhair fern, oxeye daisy, partridge pea, perennial lupine, pink ladyslipper, plains coreopsis, prairie aster, purple coneflower, purple horse mint, purple prairie clover, purple tansy, Queen Anne's lace, red corn poppy, rocket larkspur, Rocky Mountain penstemon, rose angel, rose mallow, rue anemone, scarlet flax, scarlet lobelia, scarlet sage, Shasta daisy, Shirley poppy, showy primrose, sleeping plant, smooth horsetail, smooth scouring rush, sneezeweed, speedwell, spurred snapdragon, standing cypress, stiff vervain, succulent lupine, sweet Alyssum, sweet William, Tahoka daisy, Texas bluebonnet, Texas paintbrush, thimbleberry, tickseed, tidy tips, toadflax, tuber vervain, Venus

slipper, Virginia bluebells, wallflower, water lily, whorled milkweed, widow's frill, wild bergamot, wild comfrey, wild garlic, wild geranium, wild ginger, wild lettuce, wild oats, wild strawberry, wine cup, wood betony, wood violet, yarrow, yellow cosmos

USAGE NOTE: The term wildflower is rather vague. Wildflowers have been incorporated into gardens, and garden flowers have escaped into the wild. Expect a high level of crossover between garden plants and wildflowers.

WOODY PLANTS

SHRUBS: abelia, actinidia, Alexandrian laurel, aloe, angelica tree, angel's trumpet, antelope bush, Apache plume, aralia, arborvitae, artemisia, aucuba, azalea, barberry, bayberry, bearberry, beautyberry, beauty bush, bilberry, bladder senna, bladdernut, blue spiraea, blueberry, bottlebrush, bougainvillea, boxthorn, boxwood, bramble, broom bush, buckthorn, bush clover, bush honeysuckle, butterfly bush, camellia,carpenteria, ceanothus, cherry, chilean firebush, chokeberry, clerodendrum, cliff bush, cliff rose, colletia, corkwood, cotoneaster, cranberry, crape myrtle, cream bush, crinodendron, crowberry, currant, daisy bush, daphne, decaisnea, desfontainea, deutzia, dipelta, doghobble, dogwood, dragon tree, elaeagnus, elder, ephedra, escallonia, eucryphia, fabiana, fatsia, fernbush, firethorn, flannel bush, forsythia, fothergilla, franklinia, fringe tree, fuchsia, glory pea, gorse, grevillea, griselinia, hakea, hardy plumbago, hawthorn, heath, heather, hebe, Hercules' club, hibiscus, holly, honeysuckle, huckleberry, hudsonia, hydrangea, hyssop, indigo, ivy, Japanese quince, jasmine, Jerusalem sage, jojoba, Joshua tree, juniper, kerria, kowhai, lacebark, lantana, lavender, lavender cotton, leadwort, leatherleaf, leatherwood, ledum, leycesteria, lilac, loblolly bay, loquat, magnolia, mahonia, manuka, manzanita, menziesia, mescal bean, Mexican buckeye, Mexican orange blossom, microcachrys, milkwort, mistletoe, mock orange, moonseed, moss heather, mountain avens, mountain mahogany, mountain laurel, myricaria, myrtle, neillia, ninebark, oak, oleander, osmanthus, pachysandra, pagoda bush, paper bush, pearl bush, pea tree, pepperbush, periwinkle, photinia, pieris, pistachio, pittosporum, privet, quassia, quillay, rhododendron, rockrose, rose, rose of Sharon, rosemary, rue, Russian sage, sabia, sage, sagebrush, salal, sea buckthorn, senecio, shrubby cinquefoil, silk tassel, silverbell, skimmia, smilax, smoketree, snowberry, soapberry, sorbaria, Spanish broom, spicebush, spindle, spiraea, staff vine, star anise, stephanandra, styrax, sumac, sweetfern, sweetshrub, sweetspire, tamarix, thyme, trailing arbutus, tree lupin, tree mallow, tree poppy, tree peony, trochodendron, twinflower, verbena, vervain, viburnum, vinca, waratah, weigela, willow, winter hazel, winter's bark, wintersweet, witch hazel, wonder hedge, xanthoceras, xylosma, yellowroot, yew, yucca, zanthoxylum, zauschneria, zenobia, ziziphus

TREES

USAGE NOTE: Many trees are known by multiple names that are dependent upon location and source. The same tree might be known by different names in different regions; research is essential to determine the correct name in a given setting. Likewise, spellings (especially hyphenation) vary by source. Users need to determine the appropriate spelling for their situation and remain consistent.

DECIDUOUS: Allegheny chinkapin, almond willow, almondleaf willow, American basswood, American beech, American elm, American green alder, American hackberry, American hop hornbeam, American hornbeam, American mountain ash, American plum, American sycamore, American walnut, Angelica tree, Arce, Arizona black walnut, Arizona madrone, Arizona madrono, Arizona oak, Arizona walnut, Arizona white oak, ashleaf maple, aspen, balsam poplar, barren oak, basket oak, basswood, bay, bay laurel, bay tree, beak willow, beaked willow, bearberry, beaverwood, Bebb willow, beech, bellota, big drunk bean, big laurel, big leaf maple, bigtooth aspen, bigtree, Biltmore ash, Biltmore white ash, bitter cherry, bitternut, bitternut hickory, black birch, black cherry, black jack oak, black locust, black myrtle, black oak, black tupelo, black walnut, black willow, blackgum, blackjack oak, blue beech, blue oak, blue paloverde, blue poplar, blue gum, blue gum eucalyptus, bluejack oak, Bois D'arc, bottomland post oak, bottomland red oak, box elder, Boynton post oak, broadleaf

maple, broom hickory, buckeye, bull bay, bullnut, bur oak, butternut, buttonball tree, cabbage palmetto, California bay, California black walnut, California blue oak, California box elder, California buckeye, California fan palm, California filbert, California hazelnut, California laurel, California nutmeg, California palm, California redwood, California walnut, California Washington palm, California white oak, cane ash, canoe birch, canoe cedar, canyon live oak, Carolina beech, cat spruce, caudate willow, cedar pine, cedro, cedro blanco, Cedro De La Sierra, cherioni, cherrion, cherrybark oak, chestnut oak, chinaberry, chinkapin, chinkapin oak, chinquapin, chinquapin oak, cinnamon bush, cinnamon oak, cinnamon wood, cipres, ciruela, coast redwood, coastal laurel oak, Colorado blue spruce, Colorado spruce, Columbian spruce, common hackberry, common honey locust, common larch, common persimmon, common red oak, common sassafras, Coos bay laurel, coral bean, Corsican pine, Coulter pine, cow oak, Crimean pine, cross oak, Cuban pine, Curtiss possumhaw, custard apple, Darlington oak, deciduous holly, Delta post oak, desert palm, devil's walking stick, diamond willow, diamond-leaf oak, dogberry, downy serviceberry, Drummond post oak, Drummond soapberry, duck oak, Dudley willow, dwarf canyon live oak, dwarf interior live oak, dwarf post oak, dwarf walnut, eastern black walnut, eastern hop hornbeam, eastern larch, eastern persimmon, eastern red oak, eastern redbud, Elliott oak, Emory oak, European larch, European speckled alder, evergreen coral bean, evergreen magnolia, false acacia, false banana, false elm, false shagbark, fetid shrub, Fijolito, fire birch, Florida elm, Florida persimmon, forked-leaf white oak, Frijolillo, giant chinkapin, giant chinquapin, giant evergreen chinquapin, giant sequoia, glaucous willow, golden chinkapin, golden willow, goldenleaf chestnut, Goodding willow, goosefoot maple, gray alder, gray beech, gray birch, gray dogwood, gray elm, gray oak, gray willow, grayleaf willow, gray-leaved willow, gray-stemmed dogwood, green alder, green locust, grey birch, grey dogwood, grey oak, grey she-oak, gulf black willow, gumbo file, gumwood, hackberry, hackmatack, hard maple, hazel alder, hedge apple, Hercules' club, highland live oak, Hill's oak, hoary alder, hognut, hojalito, honey locust, honey shucks locust, hop hornbeam, horse chestnut, Illinois nut, Indian banana, Indian soap plant, inland box elder, interior live oak, iron oak, ironwood, jaboncillo, jack oak, Judas tree, juneberry, knobcone pine, Knowlton hop hornbeam, lady's leg , larch, large-flower magnolia, large-tooth aspen, laurel, laurel leaf oak, laurel magnolia, laurel oak, lily-of-the-valley tree, linden, little walnut, live oak, loblolly bay, locust, long-beaked willow, lowland hackberry, Lyall's larch, madroña, madrone, madroño, Manitoba maple, maul oak, Mexican blue oak, Mexican persimmon, Mexican soapberry, Mexican walnut, missey-mossey, Mississippi valley oak, mockernut, mockernut hickory, moosewood, mossycup oak, mossy overcup oak, mountain alder, mountain ash, mountain birch, mountain black cherry, mountain laurel, mountain mahogany, mountain oak, mountain red oak, mountain white oak, mulberry, musclewood, myrtle, myrtlewood, Naked Indian, namboca, netleaf hackberry, nettletree, New Mexico locust, nogal, nogalillo, nogalito, northern hackberry, northern pin oak, northern red oak, nuzu-ndu, obtusa oak, oilnut, Oldfield birch, opossum tree, orange oak, Oregon alder, Oregon maple, Oregon myrtle, Osage orange, overcup oak, Ozark chinkapin, Pacific Coast alder, Pacific madrone, Pacific myrtle, Pacific willow, Palo blanco, panicled dogwood, paper birch, pawpaw, pawpaw apple, peach oak, peach willow, peachleaf willow, pecan, pecan hickory, pepperidge, pepperwood, persimmon (sometimes 'simmon), pignut, pignut hickory, pin oak, plane tree, possum oak, possumhaw, possumwood, post locust, post oak, Potawatomi plum, prickly ash, prickly elder, punk oak, quaking aspen, quercitron, quercitron oak, red alder, red bean, red beech, red birch, red elm, red hickory, red maple, red mulberry, red oak, red plum, red willow, redbay, redbud, redgum, redwood, ridge beech, ridge white oak, river alder, river birch, river oak, river plum, river she-oak, river walnut, roble, rock chestnut oak, rock maple, rock oak, Rocky Mountain birch, roundwood, rowan, rum cherry, rune tree, runner oak, Sabal palmetto, saloop, sand post oak, sandhill post oak, sandjack oak, sandpaper oak, sapgum, sassafras, satin walnut, savin, scalybark hickory, scarlet maple, scarlet oak, Schneck oak, scrub bay, scrub interior live oak, scrub live oak, scrub oak, scrubby post oak, scythe-leaved willow, shadblow, shadbush, shagbark hickory, shellbark hickory, she-oak, shin oak, shipmast locust, shore bay, shotbush, Shumard oak, Shumard red oak, Sierra alder, Sierra live oak, silk bay, silver birch, silver maple, Sitka alder, slippery elm, small-fruited mountain ash, small-seed white ash, smelling stick, smooth bark hickory, smooth bark oak, smooth bebb willow, soapberry, soft elm, soft maple, soft-shelled hickory, sorrel tree, sourgum, sourwood, Southern California black walnut, Southern California walnut, southern hackberry, southern magnolia, southern red oak, southern sweetbay, southwestern black willow, southwestern locust, southwestern peach willow, Spanish oak, speckled alder, spice tree, spotted oak, spring birch, staghorn sumac, starleaf gum, stave oak, stinking nutmeg, striped maple, striped oak, subalpine larch, sugar hackberry, sugar maple, sugarberry, sugarplum, swamp bay, swamp birch, swamp blackgum, swamp chestnut oak, swamp hickory, swamp laurel oak, swamp magnolia, swamp oak, swamp post oak, swamp red oak, swamp Spanish oak, swamp tupelo, swamp white oak, swamp willow, swamp willow oak, sweet bay, sweet bean locust, sweet gum, sweet magnolia, sweet pecan, sweet pignut hickory, sycamore, tag alder, tamarack, tamarack larch, tan oak, tanbark oak, tanoak, Tasmanian blue gum, Texas arbutus, Texas black walnut,

Texas madrone, Texas madroño, Texas mountain laurel, Texas oak, Texas persimmon, Texas red oak, Texas sugarberry, Texas walnut, Texate, thinleaf alder, timberline larch, toothache tree, trembling aspen, tulip poplar, tulip tree, tupelo, tupelo gum, Una de Gato, upland willow oak, valley oak, valley white oak, valley willow, Vasey shin oak, velvet mesquite, velvet sumac, vinegar tree, Virginia live oak, walnut, Washington palm, water beech, water birch, water elm, water oak, water white oak, wavyleaf alder, weeping oak, West Texas live oak, western alder, western black willow, western box elder, western chinkapin, western hackberry, western hop hornbeam, western soapberry, whiplash willow, whistlewood, white alder, white ash, white bay, white beech, white birch, white elm, white gum, white hickory, white laurel, white locust, white myrtle, white oak, white sassafras, white walnut, white willow, whiteheart hickory, wild black cherry, wild cherry, wild china tree, wild chinaberry, wild plum, willow oak, winterberry, wire birch, witch hazel, wolf hop hornbeam, woolly hop hornbeam, woolly larch, Wright willow, yellow birch, yellow butt oak, yellow chestnut oak, yellow gum, yellow locust, yellow myrtle, yellow oak, yellow plum, yellow poplar, yellow willow, yellow-bark oak, yellowwood

EVERGREEN: ague tree, ahuehuete, Alaska cedar, Alaska cypress, Alaska yellow cedar, Alaskan larch, Alberta spruce, Alberta white spruce, alligator-tree, alpine fir, alpine hemlock, alpine larch, amabilis fir, American holly, American larch, Apache pine, arborvitae, Arizona cypress, Arizona fir, Arizona longleaf pine, Arizona rough cypress, Arkansas pine, Arkansas soft pine, ashe juniper, Atlantic white cedar, Australian pine, Austrian pine, Baker cypress, bald cypress, balsam, balsam fir, balsam Fraser fir, Banks pine, Banksian pine, beach pine, big cone Douglas fir, big cone Douglas spruce, big cone pine, big cone spruce, Bishop pine, Bishop's pine, black hemlock, Black Hills spruce, black pine, blister fir, blue spruce, border limber pine, border pinyon, border white pine, bottom white pine, bracted balsam fir, break cedar, brewer spruce, bristlecone fir, bull pine, California coulter pine, California juniper, California red fir, California swamp pine, California torreya, Cambria pine, Canada balsam, Canada hemlock, Canadian spruce, Carolina hemlock, Cascades fir, Cedros Island pine, Chihuahua pine, coast Douglas fir, coast pignut hickory, coast pine, coast spruce, copalm balsam, corkbark fir, cypress, Dade County pine, Dade County slash pine, Del Mar pine, desert fir, desert white cedar, Douglas fir, dune holly, eastern arborvitae, eastern fir, eastern hemlock, eastern red pine, eastern spruce, eastern white cedar, eastern white pine, enebro, Engelmann spruce, European black pine, European spruce, evergreen , false cedar, false cypress, false hemlock, Florida torreya, Florida yew, foothills pine, Forbes cypress, four-needle pinyon, Fraser fir, giant arborvitae, giant red cedar, ginger pine, golden fir, gopherwood, gordonia, Gowen cypress, gray pine, Guadalupe Island pine, gulf cypress, he-balsam, hemlock, hemlock spruce, hickory pine, holly bay, horsetail Casuarina, Hudson bay pine, hummock holly, Idaho white pine, incense cedar, Insignis pine, jack pine, Jeffrey pine, Jersey pine, juniper, Lawson cypress, Lawson false cypress, loblolly pine, lodgepole pine, longleaf Casuarina, lovely fir, Macnab cypress, manzanita, Menzies' spruce, mescal bean, mescal bean sophora, Mexican juniper, Mexican pinyon, Mexican white pine, Modoc cypress, Monterey cypress, Monterey pine, Montezuma bald cypress, mountain cedar, mountain cypress, mountain hemlock, mountain pine, mountain spruce, mountain white pine, noble fir, Nootka cypress, Nootka false cypress, North Carolina pine, northern pine, northern scrub pine, northern white cedar, northern white pine, Norway pine, Norway spruce, nut pine, Oldfield pine, Oregon cedar, Oregon Douglas fir, Ozark white cedar, Pacific hemlock, Pacific Ponderosa pine, Pacific red cedar, Pacific silver fir, Pacific yew, papershell pinyon, Parry pinyon, pin blanc, pinabete, pitch pine, polecat wood, pond cypress, Ponderosa pine, porsild spruce, Port Orford cedar, Port Orford white cedar, possum pine, post cedar, poverty pine, prickle-cone pine, prickly pine, princess pine, Pyrenees pine, radiata pine, red cypress, red fir, red pine, red spruce, redberry juniper, rock cedar, Rocky Mountain fir, rose-fruited juniper, rough bark cypress, sabino, sand pine, Santa Lucia fir, Santa Rosa Island torrey pine, Sargent cypress, Scots pine, scrub holly, scrub pine, Shasta fir, Shasta red fir, she-balsam, shinglewood, shore pine, short straw pine, shortleaf pine, shortleaf yellow pine, Sierra lodgepole pine, Sierra-Cascade lodgepole pine, silver fir, silver pine, silver spruce, silvertip fir, Siskiyou cypress, Sitka cypress, Sitka spruce, skunk spruce, slash pine, smooth bark cypress, soft pine, Soledad pine, South Florida slash pine, southern balsam fir, southern cypress, southern fir, southern white cedar, southern yellow pine, southwestern white pine, spruce pine, stinking cedar, stinking yew, subalpine fir, sugar pine, swamp cedar, swamp cypress, swamp holly, swamp pine, table mountain pine, tamarack pine, tascate, Tecate cypress, Texas cedar, tideland spruce, torrey pine, Virginia pine, Walter's pine, Washoe pine, weeping spruce, West Coast hemlock, West Virginia spruce, western balsam fir, western hemlock, western red cedar, western spruce, western white pine, western white spruce, western yellow pine, western yew, Weymouth pine, whistling pine, white balsam, white cedar, white cedar, white cypress, white fir, white pine, white spruce, yellow cedar, yellow cypress, yellow pine, yellow slash pine, yellow spruce, yew, yew brush

CHAPTER 11: ASTRONOMY AND CHEMISTRY

ASTRONOMY

GENERAL VOCABULARY: absolute magnitude, absolute zero, albedo, altitude, antimatter, antipodal point, aphelion, apogee, apparent magnitude, asteroid, astronomical unit, atmosphere, aurora, aurora australis, aurora borealis, axis, azimuth, big bang, binary, black hole, blueshift, bolide, celestial equator, celestial poles, celestial sphere, cepheid variable, chaos, chasma, chondrite, chondrule, chromosphere, circumpolar star, circumstellar disk, comet, conjunction, constellation, corona, cosmic ray, cosmogony, cosmology, crater, dark matter, density, disk, Doppler effect, double star, dwarf planet, eccentricity, eclipse, ecliptic, ejecta, electromagnetic radiation, electromagnetic spectrum, ellipse, elliptical galaxy, elongation, equinox, escape velocity, event horizon, extinction, extragalactic, extraterrestrial, eyepiece, faculae, filament, finder, fireball, flare star, galactic halo, galactic nucleus, galaxy, gamma ray, geosynchronous orbit, globular cluster, granulation, gravitational lens, gravity, greenhouse effect, heliopause, heliosphere, hydrogen, Hubble's law, hydrostatic equilibrium, hypergalaxy, ice, inclination, inferior conjunction, inferior planet, international astronomical union, interplanetary magnetic field, interstellar medium, ionosphere, iron meteorite, irregular galaxy, irregular satellite, jansky, jet, Kelvin, Kepler's first law, Kepler's second law, Kepler's third law, kiloparsec, Kirkwood gap, Kuiper belt, Lagrange point, lenticular galaxy, libration, light year, limb, luminosity, lunar eclipse, lunar month, lunation, Magellanic clouds, magnetic field, magnetic pole, magnetosphere, magnitude, main belt, major planet, mare, mass, matter, meridian, metal, meteor, meteor shower, meteorite, meteoroid, millibar, minor planet, molecular cloud, nadir, nebula, neutrino, neutron star, Newton's first law of motion, Newton's second law of motion, Newton's third law of motion, nova, nuclear fusion, obliquity, oblateness, occultation, Oort cloud, open cluster, opposition, orbit, parallax, parsec, patera, penumbra, perigee, perihelion, perturb, phase, photon, photosphere, planemo, planet, planetary mass object, planetary nebula, planetesimal, planitia, planum, plasma, precession, prominence, prograde orbit, proper motion, protoplanetary disk, protostar, pulsar, quadrature, quasar, quasi-stellar object, radial velocity, radiant, radiation, radiation belt, red giant, redshift, regular satellite, resonance, retrograde motion, retrograde orbit, right ascension, ring galaxy, Roche limit, rotation, satellite, scarp, Seyfert galaxy, shell star, shepherd satellite, sidereal, sidereal month, sidereal period, singularity, small solar system body, solar cycle, solar eclipse, solar flare, solar nebula, solar wind, solstice, spectrometer, spectroscopy, spectrum, spicules, spiral galaxy, star, star cluster, steady state theory, stellar wind, stone meteorite, sunspot, supergiant, superior conjunction, superior planet, supernova, supernova remnant, synchronous rotation, synodic period, tektite, telescope, terminator, terrestrial, terrestrial planet, tidal force, tidal heating, transit, trans-neptunian object, trojan, ultraviolet, umbra, universal time, Van Allen belts, variable star, visible light, Virgo cluster, visual magnitude, wavelength, white dwarf, X-ray, X-ray astronomy, X-ray star, yellow dwarf, zenith, zodiac, zodiacal light

ASTEROIDS: Aaltje, Aase, Abnoba, Abundantia, Academia, Achilles, Ada, Adalberta, Adelaide, Adele, Adelgunde, Adelheid, Adelinda, Adeona, Admete, Adolfine, Adorea, Adrastea, Adria, Adriana, Aegina, Aegle, Aemilia, Aeolia, Aeria, Aeternitas, Aethra, Agamemnon, Agathe, Aglaja, Agnes, Agnia, Agrippina, Aguntina, Ahrensa, Aida, Aidamina, Alagasta, Alauda, Albert, Alekto, Alemannia, Aletheia, Alexandra, Algunde, Alice, Alinda, Aline, Alkeste, Alkmene, Alleghenia, Alma, Alphonsina, Alsatia, Alstede, Althaea, Altona, Amalasuntha, Amalia, Amalthea, Amanda, Ambrosia, Amelia, America, Amherstia, Amicitia, Amneris, Ampella, Amphitrite, Anacostia, Anahita, Anastasia, Andromache, Angelica, Angelina, Ani, Anna, Anneliese, Annika, Antigone, Antikleia, Antiope, Antonia, Apollonia, Appella, Aquitania, Ara, Arabella, Arachne, Aralia, Arduina, Arequipa, Arete, Arethusa, Argentina, Ariadne, Arizona, Armenia, Armida, Armor, Arne, Arsinoe, Artemis, Aschera, Asia, Aslog, Aspasia, Asplinda, Asporina, Astarte, Asteria, Asterope, Astraea, Atala, Atalante, Ate, Athalia, Athamantis, Athanasia, Athene, Athor, Atossa, Atropos, Augusta, Auravictrix, Aurelia, Aurora, Ausonia, Austria

ASTEROIDS WITH UNUSUAL NAMES: Annefrank, Asimov, Benfranklin, Bilbo, Bradbury, Bratfest, Conandoyle, Dahl, Elvis, Gershwin, Hitchcock, Isaac Newton, James Bond, Jabberwock, Jack London, Misterrogers, Mr. Spock, Pink Floyd, Pocahontas, Roddenberry, Tolkien

USAGE NOTE: Official names of all celestial bodies are approved and maintained by the International Astronomical Union (IAU). It administers several naming systems for various astronomical objects.

USAGE NOTE: More than 9,000 asteroids have been named. Asteroids receive a sequential designation number and are then eligible for an assigned name. The alphabetical list of asteroid names above is a short sample of typical names. Naming rules are fairly broad and thus result in whimsical or honorary names such as those seen in the preceding list (a sample from approximately 1,000 asteroids named for individuals). Names from mythology dominate the overall list.

COMETS: Arend, Arend-Roland, Biela, Bennett, Borrelly, Brorsen, Bus, Caesar's, Comas Sola, d'Arrest, Daniel, Donati's, Encke, Faye, Finlay, Forbes, Gale, Gunn, Hale-Bopp, Halley, Holmes, Hyakutake, Ikeya-Seki, Kojime, Kopff, Lovejoy, McNaught, Olbers, Oterma, Perron-Mrkos, Pons-Brooks, Pons-Winnecke, Seki-Lines, Shoemaker-Levy, Skjellerup-Maristany, Spitaler, Taylor, Tempel, Tuttle, West, Westfall, Whipple, Wild, Wirtanen, Wolf

USAGE NOTE: More than 4,100 comets are currently known. This list is a sample of some better-known comets.

CONSTELLATIONS: Andromeda, Antlia, Aquarius, Aquila, Apus, Ara, Aries, Auriga, Bootes, Camelopardalis, Caelum, Chamealeon, Cancer, Canes Venatiki, Canis Major, Canis Minor, Capricornus, Carina, Cassiopeia, Centaurus, Cepheus, Cetus, Circinus, Columbia, Coma Berenices, Corona Australis, Corona Borealis, Corvus, Crater, Crux, Cygnus, Delphinus, Dorado, Draco, Eridanus, Equuleus, Fornax, Gemini, Grus, Hercules, Horologium, Hydra, Hydrus, Indus, Lacerta, Leo, Leo Minor, Lepus, Libra, Lupus, Lynx, Lyra, Mensa, Microscopium, Monoceros, Musca, Norma, Octans, Ophiuchus, Orion, Pavo, Pegasus, Perseus, Phoenix, Pictor, Pisces, Pisces Austrinus, Puppis, Pyxis, Reticulum, Sagitta, Sagittarius, Scorpius, Sculptor, Scutum, Serpens, Sextans, Taurus, Telescopium, Triangulum, Triangulum Austraulis, Tucana, Ursa Major, Ursa Minor, Vela, Virgo, Volans, Vulpecula

HYPOTHETICAL SOLAR SYSTEM BODIES: Chiron (moon of Saturn), additional Earth moons, fifth planet, Mercury moon, Neith, Nemesis, Planet V, Planet X, S/2000 J 11, Theia, Themis, Tyche, Vulcan, Vulcanoids

PLANETARY SYSTEMS: accretion disc, brown dwarf, Earth's solar system, exoplanetary, extrasolar, main sequence, multiplanetary, multi-star, pulsar, red dwarf, transiting

RELATED: habitable zone

STAR SYSTEMS: binary, galaxy, multiple, quadruple, quintuple, septuple, sextuple, star cluster, triple

RELATED: common envelope, contact binary

USAGE NOTE: A planetary system is a group of astronomical objects that orbit a star. A star system (also called stellar system) is a pair or group of stars that orbit each other and are bound by gravity.

STAR TYPES AND RELATIVES: blue straggler, blue variable, bok globule, boson, circumpolar, compact, dark matter star, degenerate, dwarf (black, blue, brown, red, white), exotic, giant (blue, red), helium planet, hypergiant, hypernova, iron star, magnetar, Mira variable, molecular cloud, neutron, planetary nebula, quasistar, red nova, pole star, pulsar, stellar black hole, stellar nursery, subdwarf, subgiant, supergiant (blue, red, yellow), supernova, variable, young stellar object

STAR NAMES

USAGE NOTE: The spelling of star names can be inconsistent due to the variety of languages in which they were originially named and the translations of those names. In addition, stars sometimes have more than one popular name. For purposes of this list, simpler and more easily spelled options were selected.

Popular	Scientific
Acamar	Theta Eridani
Achernar	Alpha Eridani
Acrab	Beta Scorpii
Acrux	Alpha Crucis
Acubens	Alpha Cancri
Adhara	Epsilon Canis Majoris
Agena	Beta Centauri
Albireo	Beta Cygni
Alcor	80 Ursae Majoris
Alcyone	Eta Tauri
Aldebaran	Alpha Tauri
Alderamin	Alpha Cephei
Alfirk	Beta Cephei
Algedi	Alpha Capricorni
Algenib	Gamma Pegasi
Algieba	Gamma Leonis
Algol	Beta Persei
Alhena	Gamma Geminorum
Alioth	Epsilon Ursae Majoris
Alkaid	Eta Ursae Majoris
Alkalurops	Mu Boötis
Almaak	Gamma Andromedae
Alnair	Alpha Gruis
Alnasl	Gamma Sagittarii
Alnath	Beta Tauri
Alnilam	Epsilon Orionis
Alnitak	Zeta Orionis
Alphard	Alpha Hydrae
Alphecca	Alpha Coronae Borealis
Alpheratz	Alpha Andromedae
Alrami	Alpha Sagittarii
Alrescha	Alpha Piscium
Alshain	Beta Aquilae
Altair	Alpha Aquilae
Izar	Epsilon Boötis
Kaus Australis	Epsilon Sagittarii
Kitalpha	Alpha Equulei
Kocab	Beta Ursae Minoris
Kornephoros	Beta Herculis
Lesath	Upsilon Scorpii
Maia	20 Tauri
Markab	Alpha Pegasi
Megrez	Delta Ursae Majoris
Menkalinan	Beta Aurigae
Menkar	Alpha Ceti
Menkent	Theta Centauri
Merak	Beta Ursae Majoris
Merope	23 Tauri
Mesarthim	Gamma Arietis
Miaplacidus	Beta Carinae
Mimosa	Beta Crucis
Mintaka	Delta Orionis
Mira	Omicron Ceti
Mirach	Beta Andromedae
Mirfak	Alpha Persei
Mirzam	Beta Canis Majoris
Mizar	Zeta Ursae Majoris
Mothallah	Alpha Trianguli
Muhlifain	Gamma Centauri
Muliphein	Gamma Canis Majoris
Naos	Zeta Puppis
Nashira	Gamma Capricorni
Nekkar	Beta Boötis
Nihal	Beta Leporis
Nunki	Sigma Sagittarii
Peacock	Alpha Pavonis
Phact	Alpha Columbae
Phad	Gamma Ursae Majoris

Alya	Theta Serpentis
Ankaa	Alpha Phoenicis
Antares	Alpha Scorpii
Arcturus	Alpha Boötis
Arkab	Beta Sagittarii
Arneb	Alpha Leporis
Asellus Australis	Delta Cancri
Asellus Borealis	Gamma Cancri
Asterope	21 Tauri
Atlas	27 Tauri
Atria	Alpha Trianguli Australis
Avior	Epsilon Carinae
Becrux	Beta Crucis
Bellatrix	Gamma Orionis
Benetnasch	Eta Ursae Majoris
Betelgeuse	Alpha Orionis
Canopus	Alpha Carinae
Capella	Alpha Aurigae
Caph	Beta Cassiopeiae
Castor	Alpha Geminorum
Cebalrai	Beta Ophiuchi
Celaeno	16 Tauri
Chara	Beta Canum Venaticorum
Cor Caroli	Alpha Canum Venaticorum
Cursa	Beta Eridani
Dabih	Beta Capricorni
Deneb Algedi	Delta Capricorni
Deneb Kaitos	Beta Ceti
Deneb	Alpha Cygni
Denebola	Beta Leonis
Diphda	Beta Ceti
Dschubba	Delta Scorpii
Dubhe	Alpha Ursae Majoris
Electra	17 Tauri
Elnath	Beta Tauri
Eltanin	Gamma Draconis
Enif	Epsilon Pegasi
Errai	Gamma Cephei
Etamin	Gamma Draconis
Fomalhaut	Alpha Piscis Austrini
Pherkad	Gamma Ursae Minoris
Pleione	28 Tauri
Polaris	Alpha Ursae Minoris
Pollux	Beta Geminorum
Porrima	Gamma Virginis
Procyon	Alpha Canis Minoris
Propus	Eta Geminorum
Pulcherrima	Epsilon Boötis
Rasalgethi	Alpha Herculis
Rasalhague	Alpha Ophiuchi
Rastaban	Beta Draconis
Regulus	Alpha Leonis
Rigel	Beta Orionis
Rigil Kent	Alpha Centauri
Ruchbah	Delta Cassiopeiae
Rukbat	Alpha Sagittarii
Sabik	Eta Ophiuchi
Sadachbia	Gamma Aquarii
Sadalmelik	Alpha Aquarii
Sadalsuud	Beta Aquarii
Sadr	Gamma Cygni
Saiph	Kappa Orionis
Scheat	Beta Pegasi
Schedar	Alpha Cassiopeiae
Seginus	Gamma Boötis
Shaula	Lambda Scorpii
Sheliak	Beta Lyrae
Sheratan	Beta Arietis
Sirius	Alpha Canis Majoris
Sirrah	Alpha Andromedae
Spica	Alpha Virginis
Suhail	Lambda Velorum
Tarazed	Gamma Aquilae
Taygeta	19 Tauri
Thuban	Alpha Draconis
Toliman	Alpha Centauri
Unukalhai	Alpha Serpentis
Vega	Alpha Lyrae
Vindemiatrix	Epsilon Virginis
Wasat	Delta Geminorum

Gacrux	Gamma Crucis
Gemma	Alpha Coronae Borealis
Giedi	Alpha Capricorni
Gienah	Gamma Corvi
Girtab	Theta Scorpii
Gomeisa	Beta Canis Minoris
Graffias	Beta Scorpii
Hadar	Beta Centauri
Hamal	Alpha Arietis
Homam	Zeta Pegasi
Wezen	Delta Canis Majoris
Yed Posterior	Epsilon Ophiuchi
Yed Prior	Delta Ophiuchi
Yildun	Delta Ursae Minoris
Zaurak	Gamma Eridani
Zavijava	Beta Virginis
Zosma	Delta Leonis
Zubenelgenubi	Alpha Librae
Zubeneschamali	Beta Librae

PLANETS AND MOONS

MERCURY: no moons

VENUS: Neith (discredited)

USAGE NOTE: Neith was observed as a moon of Venus in 1672. Debate about its presence ensued until 1887, when it was declared nonexistent and attributed to optical illusions.

EARTH: Moon

MARS: Deimos, Phobos

CERES (DWARF PLANET IN ASTEROID BELT): no moons

JUPITER: Adrastea, Aitne, Amalthea, Ananke, Aoede, Arche, Autonoe, Callirrhoe, Callisto, Carme, Carpo, Chaldene, Cyllene, Elara, Erinome, Euanthe, Eukelade, Euporie, Europa, Eurydome, Ganymede, Harpalyke, Helike, Hegemone, Hermippe, Herse, Himalia, Isonoe, Kale, Kallichore, Kalyke, Kore, Leda, Lysithea, Io, Iocaste, Megaclite, Mneme, Metis, Orthosie, Pasiphae, Pasithee, Praxidike, Sinope, Sponde, Taygete, Thebe, Thelxinoe, Themisto, Thyone

SATURN: Aegaeon, Aegir, Albiorix, Anthe, Atlas, Bebhionn, Bergelmir, Bestia, Calypso, Daphnis, Dione, Enceladus, Epimetheus, Erriapus, Farbauti, Fenrir, Fornjot, Greip, Hati, Helene, Hyperion, Hyrrokkin, Iapetus, Ijiraq, Janus, Jarnsaxa, Kari, Kiviuq, Loge, Methone, Mimas, Mundilfari, Narvi, Paaliaq, Pan, Pandora, Pellene, Phoebe, Polydeuces, Prometheus, Rhea, Siarnaq, Skathi, Skoll, Surtur, Suttungr, Tarqeq, Tarvos, Telesto, Tethys, Thrymr, Titan, Ymir

URANUS: Ariel, Belinda, Bianca, Caliban, Cordel, Cressida, Cupid, Desdemona, Ferdinand, Francisco, Juliet, Mab, Margaret, Miranda, Oberon, Ophelia, Perdita, Portia, Prospero, Puck, Rosalind, Setebos, Stephano, Sycorax, Titania, Trinculo, Umbriel

NEPTUNE: Despina, Galatea, Halimede, Larissa, Laomedeia, Naiad, Nereid, Neso, Proteus, Psamathe, Sao, Thalassa, Triton

PLUTO: Charon, Nix, P4, Hydra

USAGE NOTE: Pluto is listed here as a planet even though it was demoted to a dwarf planet in 2006. Usage will depend upon the time frame and whether a scientific or mystical classification is desired.

MAKEMAKE (DWARF PLANET, PLUTOID): no moons

HAUMEA (DWARF PLANET, PLUTOID): Namaka, Hi'iaka

ERIS (DWARF PLANET, PLUTOID): Dysnomia

CHEMISTRY

GENERAL VOCABULARY: absolute entropy, absolute zero, absorption spectrum, acid, acidic salt, activation energy, active metal, actual yield, addition reaction, adhesive forces, adsorption, alcohol, aldehyde, alkali metals, alkaline battery, alkaline earth metals, alkyl group, allotropes, alloying, amino acid, amorphous solid, ampere, amphiprotism, amphoterism, aromatic hydrocarbons, artificial transmutation, atmosphere, atom, atomic mass unit, atomic number, atomic orbital, atomic radius, atomic weight, Avogadro's law, Avogadro's number, background radiation, band, band of stability, band theory of metals, barometer, base, basic anhydride, basic salt, beta particle, biodegradability, binary acid, binary compound, binding energy, boiling point, bond energy, bond order, bonding pair, boron hydrides, Born-Haber cycle, Boyle's law, breeder reactor, Bronsted-Lowry acid, buffer solution, buret, calorie, calorimeter, canal ray, capillary, capillary action, carbanion, carbonium ion, carcinogen, catalyst, catenation, cathode, cathodic protection, cathode ray tube, cation, chain reaction, chain termination step, Charles's law, chemical bonds, chemical change, chemical equation, chemical equilibrium, chemical hygiene officer, chemical hygiene plan, chemical kinetics, chemical periodicity, cloud chamber, coefficient of expansion, cohesive forces, coke, colligative properties, collision theory, colloid, combination reaction, combustible, common ion effect, complex ions, composition stoichiometry, compound, compressed gas, concentration, condensation, condensed phases, condensed states, conduction band, conjugate acid-base pair, conformations, continuous spectrum, control rods, conjugated double bonds, contact process, coordinate covalent bond, coordinate covalent bond, coordination compound, coordination isomers, coordination number, coordination sphere, corrosion, coulomb, coulometry, covalent bond, covalent compounds, critical mass, critical point, critical pressure, critical temperature, crystal field stabilization energy, crystal field theory, crystal lattice, crystal lattice energy, crystalline solid, Curie, cyclotron, daughter nuclide, debye, degenerate, delocalization, denaturation, denatured, density, deposition, derivative, dermal toxicity, designated area, detergent, deuterium, dextrorotatory, diagonal similarities, diamagnetism, differential scanning calorimetry, differential thermal analysis, differential thermometer, dilution, dimer, dipole, dipole-dipole interactions, dipole moment, dispersing medium, dispersed phase, displacement reactions, disproportionation reactions, dissociation, dissociation constant, distilland, distillate, distillation, domain, donor atom, D-orbitals, dosimeter, double bond, double salt, doublet, Downs cell, DP number, dry cells, dynamic equilibrium, effective collisons, effective molality, effective nuclear charge, electrical conductivity, electrochemistry, electrodes, electrode potentials, electrolysis, electrolyte, electrolytic cells, electrolytic conduction, electromagnetic radiation, electromotive series, electron, electron affinity, electron configuration, electron deficient compounds, electronic transition, electronegativity, electronic geometry, electrophile, electrophoresis, electroplating, element, emission spectrum, emulsifying agent, emulsion, endothermic, endothermicity, energy, enthalpy, entropy, enzyme, equilibrium constant, equivalent weight, essential oil, ether, evaporization, excited state, exothermic, exothermicity, explosive, extrapolate, Faraday constant, Faraday's law of electrolysis, fast neutron, ferromagnetism, flammable, flash point, fluorescence, fossil fuels, first law of thermodynamics, flotation, fluids, flux, foam, forbidden zone, formal charge, formula, fractional distillation, free radical, freezing point depression, frequency, fuel cells, gamma ray, galvanizing, gangue, Geiger counter, gel, geometrical isomers, Graham's law, greenhouse effect, Haber process, half-cell, half-life, half-reaction, halogens, hard water, heat, heat capacity, heat of condensation, heat of crystallization, heat of fusion, heat of solution, heat of vaporization, heavy water, Heisenberg uncertainty principle, heterogeneous catalyst, heterogeneous equilibria, homogeneous catalyst, homogeneous equilibria, homogeneous mixture, homologous series, homonuclear, Hund's rule, hybridization, hydrate, hydrate isomers, hydration, hydration energy, hydride, hydrocarbons, hydrogen bond, hydrogenation, hydrogen-oxygen fuel cell, hydrolysis, hydrolysis constant, hydrometer, hydrophilic colloids, inner orbital complex, isomers, ionization isomers, inert S-pair effect, insoluble compound, indicators, ionization constant, ion product for water, inhibitory catalyst, integrated rate equation, ionization, ideal solution, insulator, intermolecular forces, ideal gas, ideal gas law, ionization, ionic bonding, ionic compunds, ionic geometry, isoelectric, ionization energy, isotopes, ion, joule, K capture, ketone, kinetic energy, kinetic-molecular theory, Lanthanides, Lanthanide contraction, law of combining volumes, law of conservation of energy, law of conservation of matter, law of

conservation of matter and energy, law of definite proportions, law of partial pressures, lead storage battery, Leclanché cell, leveling effect, linear accelerator, low spin complex, magnetic quantum number, manometer, mass, mass action expression, mass deficiency, mass number, mass spectrometer, matter, mechanism, melting point, meniscus, metal, metallic bonding, metallurgy, miscibility, mixture, molality, molecular equation, molecular formula, molecular weight, molecule, mole fraction, mother nuclide, native state, natural radioactivity, Nernst Equation, neutralization, neutron, nickel-cadmium cell, nitrogen cycle, Noble gases, nonbonding orbital, nonelectrolyte, nonpolar bond, nuclear binding energy, nuclear fission, nuclear reaction, nuclear reactor, nucleons, nucleus, nuclides, octahedral, octane number, oil, open sextet, optical activity, ore, organic chemistry, osmosis, osmotic pressure, Ostwald process, outer orbital complex, oxidation, oxidation numbers, oxidation-reduction reactions, oxide, oxidizing agent, pairing, pairing energy, paramagnetism, partial pressure, particulate matter, percentage ionization, percent by mass, percent composition, percent purity, period, periodicity, periodic law, periodic table, peroxide, phase diagram, phenol, photoelectric effect, photon, plasma, polar bond, polarimeter, polarization, polydentate, polyene, polymerization, polymer, polymorphous, polyprotic acid, positron, potential energy, precipitate, primary standard, primary voltaic cells, proton, pseudobinary ionic compounds, quantum mechanics, quantum numbers, radiation, radical, radioactive dating, radioactive tracer, radioactivity, Raoult's law, rate-determining step, rate-law expression, rate of reaction, reactants, reaction quotient, reaction ratio, reaction stoichiometry, reducing agent, resonance, reverse osmosis, reversible reaction, salt bridge, saponification, saturated hydrocarbons, saturated solution, second law of thermodynamics, semiconductor, semipermeable membrane, shielding effect, sigma bonds, sigma orbital, silicones, single bond, solubility product constant, solubility product principle, solute, solution, solvation, solvent, solvolysis, S orbital, specific gravity, specific heat, specific rate constant, spectator ions, spectrum, standard electrodes, standard electrode potential, standard entropy, standard molar enthalphy of formation, standard reaction, strong electrolyte, structural isomers, sublimation, substance, supercooled liquids, supercritical fluid, suspension, temperature, ternary acid, tetrahedral, theoretical yield, thermal cracking, thermodynamics, thermonuclear energy, third law of thermodynamics, titration, total ionic equation, transition state theory, Tyndall effect, unsaturated hydrocarbons, valence bond theory, valence electrons, valence shell electron pair repulsion theory, vapor, vapor pressure, voltage, voltaic cells, water equivalent, weak electrolyte, weak field ligand, zone refining

ELEMENTS

Actinium, Aluminum, Americium, Antimony, Argon, Arsenic, Astatine, Barium, Berkelium, Beryllium, Bismuth, Bohrium, Boron, Bromine, Cadmium, Calcium, Californium, Carbon, Cerium, Cesium, Chlorine, Chromium, Cobalt, Copernicium, Copper, Curium, Darmstadtium, Dubnium, Dysprosium, Einsteinium, Erbium, Europium, Fermium, Fluorine, Francium, Gadolinium, Gallium, Germanium, Gold, Hafnium, Hassium, Helium, Holmium, Hydrogen, Indium, Iodine, Iridium, Iron, Krypton, Lanthanum, Lawrencium, Lead, Lithium, Lutetium, Magnesium, Manganese, Meitnerium, Mendelevium, Mercury, Molybdenum, Neodymium, Neon, Neptunium, Nickel, Niobium, Nitrogen, Nobelium, Osmium, Oxygen, Palladium, Phosphorus, Platinum, Plutonium, Polonium, Potassium, Praseodymium, Promethium, Protactinium, Radium, Radon, Rhenium, Rhodium, Roentgenium, Rubidium, Ruthenium, Rutherfordium, Samarium, Scandium, Seaborgium, Selenium, Silicon, Silver, Sodium, Strontium, Sulfur, Tantalum, Technetium, Tellurium, Terbium, Thallium, Thorium, Thulium, Tin, Titanium, Tungsten, Ununnilium, Uranium, Vanadium, Xenon, Ytterbium, Yttrium, Zinc, Zirconium

POISONS

USAGE NOTE AND DISCLAIMER: The list that follows includes chemical substances with dangerous, possibly deadly, potential. All household and industrial chemicals should be handled, stored, and disposed of properly. All medications should be taken only under the advice of a licensed physician and should be taken according to directions. These items should be bought, sold, transported, and used only according to state and federal laws. The nature and degree of danger of these chemicals varies. Many of the pharmaceuticals in this list are safe in proper quantities but become unsafe at higher doses. Authors should incorporate these substances into their works only after thorough research and with appropriate cautions. Authors are advised to avoid any descriptions that might advise or enable readers to try dangerous experimentation at home.

DANGEROUS CHEMICALS: acetone cyanohydrin, acetone thiosemicarbazide, acrolein, acrylamide, acrylonitrile, acryloyl chloride, adiponitrile, aldicarb, aldrin, allyl alcohol, allylamine, aluminum phosphide, aminopterin, amiton, amiton oxalate, ammonia, amphetamine, aniline, aniline, antimony pentafluoride, antimycin, arsenic, arsenous oxide, arsenous trichloride, arsine, azinphos-ethyl, azinphos-methyl, benzenamine, benzenearsonic acid, benzimidazole, benzotrichloride, benzyl chloride, benzyl cyanide, bitoscanate, boron trichloride, boron trifluoride, boron trifluoride compound with methyl ether, bromadiolone, bromine, cadmium oxide, cadmium stearate, calcium arsenate, camphechlor, cantharidin, carbachol chloride, carbamic acid, carbofuran, carbon disulfide, carbophenothion, chlordane, chlorfenvinfos, chlorine, chlormephos, chlormequat chloride, chloroacetic acid, chloroform, chloromethyl ether, chloromethyl methyl ether, chlorophacinone, chloroxuron, chlorthiophos, chromic chloride, cobalt carbonyl, cobalt, colchicine, coumaphos, cresol, crimidine, crotonaldehyde, crotonaldehyde, cyanogen bromide, cyanogen iodide, cyanophos, cyanuric fluoride, cycloheximide, cyclohexylamine, decaborane, demeton, demeton-s-methyl, dialifor, diborane, dichloroethyl, ether, dichlorvos, dicrotophos, diepoxybutane, diethyl chlorophosphate, digitoxin, diglycidyl ether, digoxin, dimefox, dimethoate, dimethyl phosphorochloridothioate, dimethyl-p-phenylenediamine, dimethyldichlorosilane, dimethylhydrazine, dimetilan, dinitrocresol, dinoseb, dinoterb, dioxathion, diphacinone, disulfoton, dithiazanine iodide, dithiobiuret, endosulfan, endothion, endrin, epichlorohydrin, ergocalciferol, ergotamine tartrate, ethanesulfonyl chloride, ethanol, ethion, ethoprophos, ethylene fluorohydrin, ethylene oxide, ethylenediamine, ethyleneimine, ethylthiocyanate, fenamiphos, fenitrothion, fensulfothion, fluenetil, fluorine, fluoroacetamide, fluoroacetic acid, fluoroacetyl chloride, fluorouracil, fonofos, formaldehyde, formaldehyde cyanohydrin, formetanate hydrochloride, formothion, formparanate, fosthietan, fuberidazole, furan, gallium trichloride, hexamethylenediamine, hydrazine, hydrocyanic acid, hydrogen chloride, hydrogen fluoride, hydrogen peroxide, hydrogen selenide, hydrogen sulfide, hydroquinone, iron, pentacarbonyl, isobenzan, isocyanic acid, isodrin, isophorone diisocyanate, isopropylmethylpyrazolyl dimethylcarbamate, lactonitrile, leptophos, lewisite, lindane, lithium hydride, malononitrile, manganese, tricarbonyl methylcyclopentadienyl, mechlorethamine, mercuric acetate, mercuric chloride, mercuric oxide, methacrolein diacetate, methacrylic anhydride, methacrylonitrile, methacryloyl chloride, methacryloyloxyethyl isocyanate, methamidophos, methanesulfonyl fluoride, methidathion, methiocarb, methomyl, methyl bromide, methyl chloroformate, methyl hydrazine, methyl isocyanate, methyl isothiocyanate, methyl phenkapton, methyl phosphonic dichloride, methyl thiocyanate, methyl vinyl ketone, methylmercuric dicyanamide, metolcarb, mevinphos, mexacarbate, mitomycin c, monocrotophos, muscimol, mustard gas, nickel carbonyl, nicotine, nicotine sulfate, nitric oxide, nitrobenzene, nitrocyclohexane, nitrogen dioxide, nitrosodimethylamine, norbormide, organorhodium complex, ouabain, oxamyl, oxetane, oxydisulfoton, paraquat, paraquat methosulfate, parathion, parathion-methyl, Paris green, pentaborane, pentadecylamine, peracetic acid, phenol, phenoxarsine, phenyl dichloroarsine, phenylhydrazine hydrochloride, phenylmercury acetate, phenylsilatrane, phenylthiourea, phosacetim, phosfolan, phosgene, phosmet, phosphamidon, phosphine, phosphonothioic acid, methyl, phosphoric acid, phosphorothioic acid, phosphorus, phosphorus oxychloride, phosphorus pentachloride, phosphorus pentoxide, phosphorus trichloride, physostigmine, picrotoxin, piperidine pirimifos-ethyl, plutonium, polonium-210, potassium arsenite, potassium cyanide, potassium silver cyanide, promecarb, propargyl bromide, propionitrile, propionitrile, propiophenone, propyleneimine, prothoate, pyridine, pyriminil, ricin, salcomine, sarin, selenious acid, semicarbazide hydrochloride, silane, sodium arsenate, sodium azide, sodium cacodylate, sodium cyanide, sodium fluoroacetate, sodium pentachlorophenate, sodium selenate, sodium selenite, stannane, strychnine, strychnine sulfate, sulfotep, sulfoxide, sulfur dioxide, sulfur tetrafluoride, sulfur trioxide, sulfuric acid, tabun, tellurium, tellurium hexafluoride, TEPP, terbufos, tetraethyllead, tetraethyltin, tetranitromethane, thallium sulfate, thallous carbonate, thallous chloride, thallous malonate, thallous sulfate, thiocarbazide, thiofanox, thionazin, thiophenol, thiosemicarbazide, thiourea, thiourea, titanium tetrachloride, toluene 2, trans-1, triamiphos, triazofos, trichloroacetyl chloride, trichloroethylsilane, trichloronate, trichlorophenylsilane, triethoxysilane, trimethylchlorosilane, trimethyltin chloride, triphenyltin chloride, valinomycin, vinyl acetate monomer, warfarin, xylylene dichloride, zinc phosphide

POISONOUS CHEMICALS IN PLANTS: abrus precatorius, aconitum, actaea pachypoda, alkaloid tomatine, amygdalin, atropine, cyanide, cyanogenic glycoside, diaminopropionic acid, glycoalkaloid, hydrogen cyanide, linamarase, linamarin, lotaustralin, lupinine, myristicin, neurotoxic amino acid, oxalic acid, phytohaemagglutinin, sparteine, tropane alkaloids

CHAPTER 12: ANATOMY AND PHYSIOLOGY

ANATOMY

BLOOD: albumin, antibody, antigen, antiserum, bilirubin, bone marrow, coagulation, crenation, cross match, electrolyte, erythrocyte, fibrinogen, glucose, granulocyte, hematocrit, hematologic, hematologist, hemoglobin, hemolysis, hemostasis, leukocyte, lymphocyte, macrocyte, phlebotomy, plasma, platelet, purpura, red cell, Rh factor, Rh negative, Rh positive, sepsis, serum, transfusion, white cell, whole blood

BODY PARTS: abdomen, adam's apple, ankle, arch, arm, armpit, back, bread basket, belly, breast, butt, buttock, calf, cheek, cheekbone, chest, chin, clitoris, ear, earlobe, elbow, eye, eyeball, eyebrow, eyelash, finger, fingernail, fist, foot, forearm, forehead, funny bone, groin, gut, hair, hand, head, heel, hip, instep, jaw, knee, labia, leg, limb, lip, mouth, nape, navel, neck, nose, nostril, offal, palate, palm, pelvis, penis, shoulder, temple, thigh, thorax, throat, thumb, thumbnail, tongue, toe, toenail, tonsil, tooth, torso, uvula, scalp, scrotum, shin, shoulder, sole, spine, testicle, underarm, upper arm, vagina, vulva, waist, wrist

BONES: anvil/incus, atlas, calcaneous, capitate bone, carpal, clavicle, coccyx, cranium, cuboid bone, distal phalange, ethmoid bone, femur, fibula, frontal bone, hamate bone, hammer/malleus, humerus, hyoid bone, inferior nasal conchae, ilium, intermediate cuneiform bone, intermediate phalange, ischium, kneecap (patella), lacrimal bone, lateral cuneiform bone, lunate bone, mandible, manubrium, maxilla, medial cuneiform bone, metacarpal, metatarsal, nasal bone, navicular bone, occipital bone, os coxae, parietal bone, patella, pelvic girdle, palatine bone, phalange, pisiform bone, proximal phalange, pubis, radius, rib, sacrum, scaphoid bone, scapula, sphenoid bone, sternum, stirrup/stapes, talus, tarsal, temporal bone, tibia, trapezium, trapezoid bone, triquestrum bone, ulna, vertebra, vomer, zygomatic bone, xiphoid process

EXCREMENT: bowel movement, crap, defecation, diarrhea, doo-doo, droppings, dung, excreta, fecal matter, feces, manure, meconium, poo, poop, scat, sewage, stool, turd, urine, waste

ORGANS/MAJOR STRUCTURES: adenoid, adrenal gland, amygdala, anterior thalamic nuclei, anus, aorta, appendix, artery, ascending colon, basal ganglia, bladder, brain, brain stem, bronchus, capillary, cecum, cerebellum, cerebral cortex, descending colon, diaphragm, duodenum, esophagus, eye, fallopian tube, fornix, gall bladder, heart, hippocampus, hypothalamus, ileum, jejunum, kidney, large intestine, larynx, ligament, limbic cortex, liver, lung, mammary gland, medulla, midbrain, nerves, ovary, pancreas, parathyroid gland, penis, pharynx, pineal gland, pituitary gland, pleura, pons, prostate, rectum, salivary gland, seminal vesicle, septum, skin, small intestine, spinal cord, spleen, stomach, tendon, testicle, thalamus, thymus gland, thyroid gland, tonsil, trachea, transverse colon, ureter, urethra, uterus, vagina, vas deferens, vein

BODY SYSTEMS: circulatory, digestive, endocannabinoid, endocrine, immune, integumentary, limbic, lymphatic, musculoskeletal, nervous, reproductive, respiratory, urinary, vestibular

TEETH: baby, bicuspid, canine, central incisor, cuspid, first molar, incisor, lateral incisor, milk, molar, permanent, precanine, premolar, second molar, third molar, wisdom

AILMENTS

ALLERGIES: animals, apple, artificial color, cat, chicken, cut grass, dander, dog, dust, egg, fish, food, fur, gluten, grass pollen, latex, medication, melon, milk, mold, peanut, pollen, preservatives, ragweed, seeds, shellfish, soy, spice (specific variety), tree, tree nut, wheat

BLOOD-RELATED AILMENTS: anemia, aneurysm, bacteremia, clot, deep venous thrombosis, disseminated intravascular coagulation, hematoma, hemochromatosis, hemophilia, hemorrhage, leukemia, lymphoma, malaria, multiple myeloma, myocardial infarction, polycythemia, sickle cell disease

DISEASES: African sleeping sickness, AIDS, anthrax, athlete's foot, bocavirus, body lice, Bolivian hemorrhagic fever, botulism, cancer, cat-scratch disease, cellulitis, Chagas disease, chicken pox, chlamydia, cholera, Colorado tick fever, common cold, consumption, crab lice, dengue fever, diabetes, diphtheria, ebola hemor-

rhagic fever, enterovirus infection, epidemic typhus, fatal familial insomnia, food poisoning, gangrene, gonorrhea, hand foot and mouth disease, hantavirus pulmonary syndrome, head lice, hepatitis, herpes simplex, histoplasmosis, hookworm, human papillomavirus (HPV), influenza, jock itch, Kawasaki disease, keratitis, kuru, lassa fever, Legionnaires' disease, leprosy, listeriosis, Lyme disease, malaria, measles, meningitis, mononucleosis, mumps, pelvic inflammatory disease (PIV), plague, pneumococcal infection, pneumonia, polio, pubic lice, rabies, ringworm, Rocky mountain spotted fever, rotavirus, rubella, SARS, scabies, schistosomiasis, sepsis, shingles, smallpox, streptococcal infection, syphilis, tetanus, toxic shock syndrome, toxoplasmosis, trichinellosis, tuberculosis, vapors, West Nile fever, whooping cough (pertussis)

USAGE NOTE: Thousands of diseases exist around the world. This list contains some of the more common, well known, or interesting diseases, and they are listed by common names. When referencing diseases, research is essential to understand symptoms, onset, degree of contagion, and cures.

HANGOVER: black dog, crapulence, morning fog, one-day flu

INJURIES/MEDICAL EMERGENCIES: allergic reaction, anaphylactic shock, aneurysm, animal bite, bedsores, bee sting, black eye, bleeding, blood clot, blood sugar drop, blow to the head, boil, broken bone, broken nose, bruise, bump, burns, car accident, chest pain, choking on object, compound fracture, concussion, contusion, cut requiring stitches, deep or multiple cuts, dehydration, drowning, ear/eye injury, embedded object, fainting, fall from height, fat lip, fingers slammed in car door, food poisoning, fracture (compound, greenstick, simple), frostbite, heart attack, heat exhaustion/stroke, hyperthermia, hypothermia, impaled object, insect bites, motion sickness, muscle cramps, muscle pull, nosebleed, not breathing, poisoning, radiation burns, scrape, shiner, shock, slip and fall, sliver/splinter, snake bite, sprain, stinger, stroke, struck by falling object, sunburn, sunstroke, ticks, traveler's diarrhea, twisted ankle, upset stomach, upset stomach, windburn

FICTIONAL DISEASES: chalk-dust flu, cooties, lycanthropy, walking dead

CHAPTER 13: THE ARTS

DANCE

BALLET TERMS: à la Seconde, à Terre, Adagio, Agrippina Vaganova, Allégro, Arabesque, Assemblé, Attitude, Balancé, ballerina, ballet, ballet master, ballet mistress, Balletomane, Ballon, Ballotté, Barre, Battement, Battement dégagé, Battement fondu développé, Battement frappé, Battement tendu, Battu, Bras, Bras bas, Brisé, Brisé volé, Cabriole, Cavalier, Cecchetti method, Centre practice, Chaînés, Changement, Chassé, choreographer, choreography, Cinq, cinq positions des Pieds, Cinquiéme, Classical ballet, Coda, Corps, Corps de ballet, Cou-de-pied position, Coupé jeté en tournant, Couru, Croisé/croisée, Danse, Danse de caractère, de Côté, Demi-plié, Derrière, Dessous, Dessus, Deux, Deuxième, Devant, Développé, Divertissement, double, double Cabriole, Écarté, Échappé, Échappé sur les pointes, Effacé/effacée, Élévation, en Arriére, en Avant, en Cloche, en Croix, en Dedans, en Dehors, en Diagonale, en Face, en l'Air, en Tournant, Enrico Cecchetti, Entrechat, Entrechat six, Épaulement, Exercises à la barre, extension, fish dive, five positions of the feet, Fondu/fondue, Fouetté, Fouetté en tourant, Fouetté rond de jambe en tournant, French School, Gateway, Glissade, grand Assemblé en tournant, grand Battement, grand Battement en cloche, grand in attitude Jeté, grand Jeté, grand Pas de deux, grand Sissonne ouverte, Grand/grande, grande Pirouette à la second, Italian School, Jambe, Jeté, Jeté battu, Jeté entrelacé, Jeté entrelacé, Labanotation, Leçon, Ligne, Manèges, Mazurka/mazurek, methods, mime, Neuf, notation, Ouvert/ouverte, Pas, pas Ballonné, Pas de bourrée, Pas de bourrée couru, Pas de chat, Pas de deux, Pas de quatre, Pas de trois, Pas de valse, Pas marché, Penché/penchée, petit Battement sur le cou-de-pied, petit Jeté, Petit/petite, Piqué, pirouette, pirouette piquée, plié, pointe shoes, Poisson, polonaise, Port de bras, Porté/portée, positions des Bras, Premier/première, Quatre, Quatrième, Relevé, Retiré, rise, rolling, romantic ballet, Rond de jambe, Rond de jambe à terre, Rond de jambe en l'air, Royale, Russian School, Saut de basque, Sauté/sautée, Sept, Sickling, Sissonne, Sissonne fermée, Six, supporting leg, sur les Demi-pointes, sur les Pointes, Temps lié sur les pointes, Tour de force, tour de Promenade, Tour en l'air, Tour jeté, Trois, Troisiéme, turn-out, tutu, variation, virtuoso, working leg

DANCE CLOTHING: booty short, bustle tutu, camisole leotard, cargo pants, chiffon skirt, circle skirt, costume, fishnet tights, flamenco skirt, fringe skirt, halter leotard, jazz pants, leggings, leg warmers, leotard, long sleeve leotard, rehearsal skirt, Russian tutu, tank leotard, tank top, tights, tulip skirt, tutu, unitard, wrap skirt

DANCE EQUIPMENT: barre, dance mat, garment bag, gym mat, mirror, rosin box, sprung floor

DANCE SHOES: ballet slipper, ballroom shoes, clogging shoes, dance sneaker, folklorical, hiphop, Irish stepdance, jazz, lyrical, pointe, split sole jazz, tap, toe

SHOE ACCESSORIES: bunion pad, elastic, fitting kit, glue, heel gripper, lambs wool, pillow, pointe shoe cover, ribbon, stitch kit, tape, toe pad, toe spacer, toe wrap

DANCE MOVES: arabesque, attitude, balloon, battement, batterie, bourrée, brisé, capriole, chasse, ciseaux, corps de ballet, coryphée, divertissement, écarté, élevation, entrechat, fish dive, fouetté, glissade, jeté, pas de deux, pas de seul, pirouette, plié, pointe, régisseur, répétiteur, splits, stulchak

DANCE STYLES: bachata, ballet, belly, big apple, black bottom, bolero, Bollywood, boogie-woogie, breakdance, bunny hop, cakewalk, calypso, cha cha cha, Charleston, contemporary, disco, electric boogaloo, flamenco, flash mob, folk, foxtrot, grinding, hand jive, hiphop, jazz, jazz ballet, jitterbug, jive, jump up, krumping, lindy hop, line dancing, lyrical, mambo, maxixe, merengue, modern, one-step, paso doble, pogo, popping, robot, rumba, salsa, samba, shag, skanking, soca, soft shoe, stepping, swing, tango, tap, two-step, vogue, waltz

ETHNIC/FOLK DANCES: allemande (Germany), attan (Afghanistan), bhangra (Punjab), bolero (Spain), bourrée (France), cajun (United States), chaconne (Spain), clog (England), Cossack (Ukraine), courante (France), dragon (China), English country (England), fandango (Galicia), flamenco (Spain), German dance, habanera (Cuba), havanaise (Cuba), hora (Israel), hornpipe (England), hula (United States), Irish (Ireland), jota (Spain), kalinka (Russia), landler (Austria), lion (China), long sword (England), loure (France), malagueña (Spain), maypole (England), mazurka (Polish), minuet (France), morris (Britain), polonaise (Polish), rigaudon (France), saltarello (Italian), schuhplattler (Austria, Germany), seguidilla (Spain), square dance (United States), tarantella (Italy), zydeco (United States)

HISTORICAL DANCES: farandole, five-step waltz, galliard, galop, gigue, jig, minuet, pavan, polka, quadrille, reel, sarabande, schottische, trotto, two-step, waltz

MUSIC

GENERAL MUSIC VOCABULARY: a cappella, acciaccatura, accidental, accompaniment, ad lib, ad libitum, appoggiatura, atonal, beat, cadence, cadenza, canon, cantabile, cantata, cappella, chord, chromatic, chromatic scale, coloratura, continuo, counterpoint, da capo, descant, diatonic scale, dissonance, flat, fundamental, grace note, ground bass, harmony, improvisation, instrumentation, interval, intonation, leitmotif, lied, ligature, melisma, metamorphosis, mezzo, mode, motif, movement, orchestration, natural, obbligato, octave, opus, ostinato, pantomime, part, pentatonic, performance practice, phrase, pitch, più, poco, polacca, portamento, quarter-tone, register, reprise, rhythm, ritornello, scale, sempre, senza, serialism, sharp, sostenuto, sotto voce, stretto, subject, temperament, ternary form, theme, time, tone, transcription, transposition, trill, turca, tutti, twelve-note composition, unison, variation, verismo, vibrato

VOICES: alto (first, second), baritone, bass, bass-baritone, contralto, countertenor, falsetto, heldentenor, mezzosoprano, tenor (first, second), treble, soprano (first, second)

GROUPS: chamber orchestra, chapel, choir, chorus, concertino, consort, ensemble, orchestra, philharmonia, philharmonic, piano quartet, piano quintet, piano trio, quartet, quintet, septet, sextet, trio

MUSICAL PERIOD: baroque (early, middle, late), classical, modern, romantic

COMPOSITION TYPES: air, anthem, aria, aubade, badinerie, bagatelle, ballad, barcarolle, berceuse, canticle, caprice, cassation, chanson, chant, chorale, chorale prelude, concerto, cycle, divertimento, duet, duo, elegy, entr'acte, etude, exposition, fanfare, fantasy, la follia, fugue, Gregorian chant, harmoniemusik, hornpipe, humoresque, hymn, impromptu, interlude, intermezzo, lament, lamentations, madrigal, magnificat, mass (also missa), mélodie, monody, monophony, motet, nachtmusik, nocturne, nonet, octet, oratorio, overture, partita, passion, pastorale, plainchant, polophony, programme music, postlude, prelude, psalm, quodlibet, recitative, requiem mass, rhapsody, rondo, scherzo, semi-opera, serenade, siciliana, sinfonia, sinfonia concertante, sinfonietta, singspiel, sonata, sonata-form, sonatina, study, suite, symphonic poem, symphony, tafelmusik, te deum, toccata, tombeau, tone poem, trio sonata, vespers, vocalise, voluntary

MUSICAL STYLES: bluegrass, blues, Broadway, chamber music, classical, country, country & western, easy listening, gospel, impressionism, jazz, neoclassical, new wave, opera (bouffa, bouffe, comique, seria), operetta, pop, polka, rhythm & blues (R&B), rock 'n' roll (acid, hard, heavy metal, soft), ska

PRINTED MUSIC: hymnal, libretto, score, sheet, songbook

NOTATION: alto clef, arco, bar, bar line, bass clef, brace, bird's eye, clef, coda, double bar line, double flat, double sharp, fermata, flat, interval, key, key signature, major, minor, measure, natural, note (eighth, half, quarter, sixteenth, thirty-second, whole), rest (crotchet, demisemiquaver, minim, quaver, semibreve, semiquaver), sharp, staff, treble clef, time signature

DYNAMICS: crescendo, decrescendo, diminuendo, forte, metzo forte, fortissimo, piano, pianissimo

TEMPO/MOOD: accelerando, adagietto, adagio, affettuoso, agitato, allargando, allegretto, allegro, amoroso, andante, andantino, animato, appassionato, assai, bewegt, brio, capriccioso, con brio, con sordino, con spirito, giocoso, giusto, grave, grazioso, grave, istesso, l'istesso, larghetto, largo, legato, leggero, lento, maestoso, mesto, moderato, molto, mosso, moto, prestissimo, presto, rallentando, ritardando, ritenuto, rubato, stringendo, tempo rubato, tanto, troppo, vigoroso, vivace

INSTRUMENT TECHNIQUE: arco, arpeggio, double stop, glissando, legno, pizzicato, sul ponticello, tremolo

THEATER

PERFORMANCE GENRES: biography, blackface minstrels, burlesque, children's, comedy, courtroom drama, dinner theater, docudrama, drama, ethnotheater, experimental, fantasy, farce, fringe, folk, Greek drama, grotesque, historical, horror, melodrama, morality play, musical, mystery, opera, operetta, pantomime, passion play, performance art, psychological drama, puppetry, radio drama, restoration comedy, sat-

ire, science fiction, Shakespeare, social commentary, suspense, theater of the absurd, tragedy, variety show, vaudeville, ventriloquism, western

PARTS OF THE THEATER: aisle, apron, backstage, balcony, box office, box seats, catwalk, control booth, cyclorama, dressing room, front of house, fly loft, house, lobby, loge, orchestra pit, orchestra seating, proscenium, quick change room, scrim, seats, stage, wings

STAGE DIRECTIONS: camera left, camera right, downstage, house left, house right, stage left, stage right, upstage

STAGE TERMS: ad lib, blocking, break a leg, casting, crossover, cue, dress rehearsal, dry run, follow-on cue, marking out, offstage, onstage, pitch, projection, publicity, read-through, repertoire, reveal, segue, sightline, stand-by, technical rehearsal, turn, visual cue

TECHNICAL TERMS: acoustics, backlight, baffle, blackout, boom, cable, cheat sheet, clearance, counterweight, dimmer, dolly, downlight, drape, dubbing, echo, ellipsoidal, fade, feed, feedback, fill light, flat, focus, focus spot, follow spot, footlight, forestage, fresnel, ghostlight, greasepaint, headset, key light, kill, kit, ladder, lavalier microphone, legs, lighting plan, limelight, makeup, memory board, microphone, mirror ball, mixer, monitor, pit, playback, prompt book, properties, props, public address system, rigging, safety curtain, sandbag, script, secondary lighting, sequencing, smoke machine, sound check, spotlight, transom, trap, truck, truss

VISUAL ART

ART GENRES: album cover, animal, anime, avant-garde, botanical, cartoon, character sketch, cityscape, cloudscape, commercial, conceptual, courtroom, decorative, diorama, dream, environmental, erotic, fan, fantasy, fetish, figurative, folk, found, glass, graffiti, grotesque, historical, horse, hybrid, landscape, marine, military, miniature painting, naïve, narrative, national, nude, old master, paleoart, pastoral, perceptual, political, portrait, primitive, propaganda, protest, psychedelic, public, punk, religious, rosemaling, scenic painting, self-portrait, self-taught, skyscape, space, still life, street, street painting, street poster, studio, surveillance, textile, tribal, underground, urban, velvet, war, wearable, western, wildlife

ART MEDIA: acid, acrylic paint, architectural structure, blacklight paint, brush texture, canvas texture, card, cement, chalk, charcoal, cloth, conté, crayon, digital, electronic, film, finger, fresco, gesso, glass, glaze, gouache, graphite, human body, ink, latex paint, letterpress, light, magna paint, marker, metal, nib/pen, oil paint, paint, paper, pastel, pen and ink, pencil, photography, plaster, primer, quill and ink, stone, sumi-e, tapestry, tempera, vinyl, vitreous enamel, wall, watercolor, wood; See also the chapter Equipment and Tools

ART MOVEMENTS: Abstract, Abstract expressionism, Academic, Aestheticism, American realism, Anti-realism, Art Deco, Art Nouveau, Arts and Crafts, Baroque, Bauhaus, Byzantine, Chinese, Classical realism, Constructivism, Cubism, Dada, De Stijl, Deconstructivism, Early Renaissance, Egyptian, Expressionism, Fantastic realism, Fauvism, Futurism, Greek, Harlem Renaissance, Hellenistic, High Renaissance, Hudson River school, Hypermodernism, Hyperrealism, Impressionism, Indian, International gothic, Islamic, Japanese, Letterism, Lowbrow, Lyrical abstraction, Magic realism, Mannerism, Massurrealism, Mesopotamian, Metaphysical painting, Middle Ages, Minimalism, Modernism, Neoclassical, Neoism, Northern Renaissance, Orphism, Photorealism, Pixel art, Plein Air, Pointillism, Pop art, Post-impressionism, Postmodernism, Primitivism, Process art, Purism, Realism, Remodernism, Rococo, Roman, Romanesque, Romanticism, Shock Art, Socialist realism, Stone Age, Supremativism, Surrealism, Symbolism, Toyism, Transgressive art, Venetian Renaissance, Vorticism

ART PRINCIPLES: balance, contrast, harmony, movement, pattern/rhythm, proportion, references, unity, variety

ART TECHNIQUES: airbrush, batik, blend, burnish, caricature, carpentry, cartooning, carve, collage, conservation, crop, cut, digital painting, drawing, fire, form, glaze, marbleize, mosaic, paint, printmaking, rub, sand, sculpt, shade, shape, slide projection, solder, superimpose, texturize, wash, weld, whittle, wood cut, wood working

VISUAL ELEMENTS: color, form, line, shape, space, texture, tone, value, volume

CHAPTER 14: PHILOSOPHY AND RELIGION

PHILOSOPHY

BASIC CONCEPTS: absolute, abstract object, accident, actuality, aesthetics, all men are created equal, analytic, analysis, apperception, a priori, a posteriori, atheism, attribute, beauty, being, belief, boredom, capitalism, category, causality, cause, chaos, choice, civic virtue, class, common good, common sense, communism, concept, conscience, consciousness, consent, construct, contingency, courage, creativity, cuteness, darkness, deduction, death, definition, determinism, dialectic, disgust, distrust, dogma, doubt, duty, ecstasy, elegance, emergence, emotion, empiric generalization, empiricism, entertainment, entity, epistemology, eroticism, essence, eternity, ethics, evil, evolutionalism, excellence, existence, existentialism, experience, extension, fallacy, fact, fasting of the mind, feeling, fidelity, finite, form, freedom, free will, God, good, half-truth, happiness, harmony, hedonism, hermeneutics, humanism, human rights, idea, idealism, identity, ideology, ignorance, induction, infallibility, inference, infinite, injustice, innocence, intellect, intellectual intuition, intention, intuition, intentionality, judgment, justice, knowledge, life imitating art, light, linguistics, logic, logos, love, loyalty, magnificence, matter, meaning, meaning of life, mental, mercy, metaphysics, method, methodology, mind, minority, motion, myth, mythos, name, nation, natural selection, nature, necessity, nihilism, nominalism, norm, nothingness, notion, noumenon, object, objectivity, obligation, ontology, ought, pantheism, paradox, particular, passion, pattern, peace, perception, phenomenon, phenomenological reduction, phenomenology, philosophy, physical body, political consciousness, potency, possibility, principle, progress, property, proposition, quality, quantity, rationality, realism, reality, reason, reciprocity, reform, representation, right, right to exist, science, self, semantics, sensation, sense, sensory, social contract, socialism, society, soul, space, speculative, spirit, spiritualism, statement, stoicism, style, subject, sublime, substance, substitution, suffering, symbol, syntax, synthetic, taste, temperance, the Golden Rule, thing in itself, thinking, thought, time, transcendental, trust, truth, type, understanding, unity, universal, universality, unobservable, unity, validity, value, void, virtual, virtue, will, wisdom, wonder, work of art

Seven Blunders of the World by Mohandas Ghandi

Wealth without work

Pleasure without conscience

Knowledge without character

Commerce without morality

Science without humanity

Worship without sacrifice

Politics without principle

RELIGION

ANGELS, COMMON TERMS: angel of death, angel of leadership, archangel, bene elohim, cherub, cherubim, dominion, grigori, guardian angel, hamalat al-arsh, host, messenger, messenger of God, potentate, power, principality, seraph, seraphim, shining one, spirit of motion, throne, virtue, warrior angel

USAGE NOTE: Very few angels are actually named in the Bible. Some versions list only Gabriel, Michael, and Lucifer (a fallen angel who was cast out of heaven).

Angels of Good: Adriel, Ambriel, Amesha Spenta, Arariel, Ariel, Azrael, Barachiel, Cassiel, Darda'il, Dumah, Eremiel, Gabriel, Gagiel, Hadraniel, Haniel, Harut, Hesediel, Israfel, Jegudiel, Jehoel, Jequn, Jerahmeel, Jophiel, Kasdeja, Kiraman Katibin, Kushiel, Leliel, Maalik, Malik, Marut, Metatron, Michael, Munkar, Muriel, Mu'aqqibat, Nakir, Nuriel, Ophan, Orifiel, Pahaliah, Penemue, Puriel, Qaphsiel, Raguel, Raphael, Raqib, Raziel, Remiel, Ridwan, Sachiel, Sandalphon, Sariel, Selaphiel, Seraphiel, Simiel, Tennin, Tzaphqiel, Uriel, Uzziel, Zabaniyah, Zachariel, Zadkiel, Zephon, Zophiel

FALLEN ANGELS: Abbadon, Ahriman, Azazel, Camael, Gadreel, Mephistopheles, Samael, Satan, Shamsiel

USAGE NOTE: Lore surrounding angels varies widely and is often contradictory. Because many angels derive from many different religions and are written in many languages, spellings also vary widely. Sometimes a single letter distinguishes one angel from another, and sometimes a variant spelling can create confusion between a good angel and a fallen angel. Careful research from reputable sources is needed to identify angels correctly.

FOLLOWERS: congregation, faithful, flock, follower, member, parishioner, souk, sycophant, worshiper

GROUPINGS: archdiocese, cluster, diocese, parish, synod

CATHOLIC HOLY DAYS OF OBLIGATION: Acension, All Saints, Assumption, Christmas, Epiphany, Holy Body and Blood of Christ, Immaculate Conception, Mary—Mother of God

USAGE NOTE: This list applies to the United States. The list varies in different countries around the world. Some of these are celebrated on the Sunday nearest to their actual date.

CHRISTIAN RELICS: Ark of the Covenant, Staff of Moses, Tablets of the Ten Commandments

RELICS OF JESUS: Bridle of Constantine, burial shroud, Chalice of the Last Supper, Church of the Holy Sepulchre, Column of the Flagellation, crown of thorns, crucifixion nails, Gifts of the Magi, Holy Coat, Holy Lance/Spear of Destiny/Spear of Longinus, Holy Sponge, Image of Edessa, Iron Crown of Lombardy, Mandylion, manger, Mount Calvary, Shroud of Turin, Sudarium of Oviedo, swaddling clothes, Veil of Veronica, wood of the True Cross

RITUALS: abstinence, Advent candles, Advent wreath, anoint, ashes, blessing, bread, bread and wine, breaking bread, candle, chant, Easter candle, Eucharistic adoration, fasting, genuflect, grace, holy water, immersion, incense, kiss, kneel, laying on of hands, litany, meal prayer, petition, prayer, praying hands, meditation, menorah, offering, offertory, palms, poverty, procession, rosary, shroud, sign of the Cross, silence, singing, Stations of the Cross, tithe, veneration of the Cross, vespers, visitation, water, wine

SACRAMENTS: Anointing of the Sick, Baptism, Christening, Confession, Confirmation, First Communion, First Eucharist, First Holy Communion, Holy Orders, Last Rites, Marriage, Penance, Reconciliation

USAGE NOTE: Sacraments differ by religion. Terminology has changed throughout history; research the time period to select the appropriate term.

TEN PLAGUES ON EGYPT: blood, boils, darkness, death of firstborn, flies or animals, frogs, fleas or gnats or lice, hail, locusts, pestilence

USAGE NOTE: The ambiguity of fleas or gnats or lice and flies or animals is a result of variations in translation.

TWELVE APOSTLES: Andrew, Bartholomew, James the Greater, James the Lesser, John, Judas, Jude, Matthew, Matthias, Peter, Philip, Simon, Thomas

USAGE NOTE: After Judas betrayed Jesus and hanged himself, the remaining apostles selected Matthias as his successor.

MAJOR RELIGIOUS BOOKS

Baha'i Texts, Bhagavad Gita, Bible, Book of Enoch, Book of Mormon, Book of Moses, Books of Jeu, Buddhist Texts, Confucian Texts, Corpus Hermeticum, Dead Sea Scrolls, Egyptian Book of the Dead, Enuma Elish, Ethiopian Texts, Gnostic Texts, Hindu Texts, Islamic Texts, Jain Texts, Koran, Midrash, Mormon Texts, Nag Hammadi Texts, New Testament, New Testament Apocrypha, Old Testament, Old Testament Apocrypha, Old Testament Pseudepigrapha, Pistis Sophia, Sepher Yetzirah, Shinto Texts, Sikh Texts, Talmud, Taoist Texts, Tibetan Book of the Dead, Torah, Urantia Book, Zen Texts, Zoroastrian Texts

BOOKS OF THE BIBLE

Old Testament (in order)

Genesis	1 Chronicles	Ecclesiastes	Amos
Exodus	2 Chronicles	The Song of Songs	Obadiah
Leviticus	Ezra	Wisdom	Jonah
Numbers	Nehemiah	Ecclesiasticus/Sirach	Micah
Deuteronomy	Tobit	Isaiah	Nahum
Joshua	Judith	Jeremiah	Habakkuk
Judges	Esther	Lamentations	Zephaniah
Ruth	1 Maccabees	Baruch	Haggai
1 Samuel	2 Maccabees	Ezekiel	Zechariah
2 Samuel	Job	Daniel	Malachi
1 Kings	Psalms	Hosea	
2 Kings	The Proverbs	Joel	

New Testament (in order)

Matthew	2 Corinthians	1 Timothy	2 Peter
Mark	Galatians	2 Timothy	1 John
Luke	Ephesians	Titus	2 John
John	Philippians	Philemon	3 John
Acts of Apostles	Colossians	Hebrews	Jude
Romans	1 Thessalonians	James	Revelation
1 Corinthians	2 Thessalonians	1 Peter	

GODS AND PANTHEONS

USAGE NOTE: In the lists that follow, names refer to gods unless otherwise noted; females are identified as goddess.

USAGE NOTE: The lists that follow are not meant to be comprehensive, but are a sampling of deities from major religions. Research is necessary to select appropriate deities for a setting and a situation.

AZTEC PANTHEON: Chalchiuhtlicue (lake goddess), Chantico (hearth goddess), Coyolxauhqui (moon goddess), Huehueteotl (war), Huitzilopochtli (father of all gods), Ixtlilton (healing and gaming), Mictlantecuhtle (the dead), Tecciztecatl (oceans), Tepeyollotl (mountains), Tezcatlipoca (illusion and war)

BABYLONIAN PANTHEON: Anshar (darkness), Anu (leader of the gods), Druaga (evil), Girru (fire), Ishtar (goddess of love and war), Marduk (the city), Nergal (the dead), Ramman (storms)

CELTIC PANTHEON: Anoghus (love), Arawn (the dead), Brigit (goddess of fire and poetry), Cernunnus (nature), Dagda (leader of the gods), Danu (goddess of fertility), Diancecht (healing), Dunatis (mountains), Goibhne (blacksmiths), Lugh (generalities), Manannan mac lir (the sea), Morrigan (goddess of war), Nuada (war), Oghma (knowledge), Silvanus (nature)

CENTRAL AMERICAN PANTHEON: Camazotz (bat god), Chalchiuhtlicue (goddess of love), Huhueteotl (fire), Huitzilopochtli (war), Itzamna (medicine), Mictlantecuhtli (death), Quetzalcoatl (leader of the gods), Tezcatlipoca (sun), Tlaloc (rain god), Tlazolteotl (goddess of vice), Zochipilli (gambling)

CHINESE PANTHEON: Chao Kung Ming (demigod of war), Chih-Chiang Fyu-Ya (archers), Chih Sung-Tzu (storms), Chung Kuel (truth), Huan-Ti (war), Kuan Yin (goddess of mercy), Lu Yueh (epidemics), No Cha (demigod of thieves), Shan Hai Ching (the sea), Shang-Ti (leader of the gods), Tou Mu (goddess of the north star)

EGYPTIAN PANTHEON: Anhur (war), Anubis (the dead), Apshai (insects), Bastet (goddess of felines), Bes (luck), Geb (the earth), Hathor (dancing), Horus (demigod of revenge), Isis (goddess of magic), Nephthys (goddess of wealth), Osiris (nature), Ptah (the stars), Ra (leader of the gods), Seker (light), Sekhmet (goddess of destruction), Set (evil), Shu (the sky), Tefnut (goddess of storms), Thoth (knowledge)

FINNISH PANTHEON: Ahto (water), Hiisi (evil), Ilmatar (goddess of mothers), Kiputytto (goddess of sickness), Loviatar (goddess of pain), Mielikki (goddess of nature), Surma (demigod of death), Tuonetar (goddess of the underworld), Tuoni (underworld), Ukko (leader of the gods), Untamo (dreams)

GREEK PANTHEON: Aphrodite (goddess of love), Apollo (the sun, truth, music, poetry, healing), Ares (war), Artemis (goddess of the hunt, archery, childbirth), Athena (goddess of wisdom and combat), Demeter (goddess of fertility and agriculture), Dionysus (wine), Hades (underworld), Hecate (goddess of magic), Hephaestus (blacksmiths, fire), Hera (goddess of marriage and family), Heracles (demigod of strength), Hermes (travel, business, sports, messenger of the gods), Hestia (goddess of the hearth), Nike (goddess of victory), Pan (nature), Poseidon (the seas), Tyche (goddess of good fortune), Zeus (weather, leader of the gods)

INDIAN PANTHEON: Agni (fire), Brahma (creation god), Durga (mother of the universe, supreme power), Ganesha (education, knowledge, wisdom), Indra (leader of the gods), Kali (goddess of death), Karttikeya (demigod of war), Lakshmi (goddess of fortune), Ratri (goddess of thieves and the night), Rudra (goddess of dead), Shiva (destruction), Surya (sun), Tvashtri (demigod of science), Ushas (goddess of the dawn), Varuna (law and order), Vayu (sky), Vishnu (mercy), Yama (demigod of death)

JAPANESE PANTHEON: Amaterasu Omikami (goddess of the sun), Ama-tsu-mara (blacksmiths), Benzaiten (goddess of the flow), Bishamonten (war), Daikoku (luck), Fujin (the winds), Hachiman (divine protection), Kishijoten (goddess of luck), Omoikane (thought), Raijin (storms), Ryujin (the sea), Susanoo-no-mikoto (water), Tsukiyomi (moon)

NATIVE AMERICAN PANTHEON: Atira (mother goddess), Breathmaker (river), Coyote (nature), Hastselts (red lord), Hastsezini (black lord), Heng (thunder spirit), Hino (storm), Hotoru (wind), Ocasta (magic), Raven (nature), Shakak (winter spirit), Snake man (war), Tobadzistsini (war spirit), Wakan-tanka (sun and wind), Weywot (sky)

NORSE PANTHEON: Aegir (storms), Asa-thor (thunder), Baldur (light), Bragi (song), Brynhild (goddess of battle), Freya (goddess of fertility), Frigga (goddess of the air), Forseti (justice), Heimdall (the white god), Hel (goddess of death), Idun (goddess of the spring), Loki (god of evil), Magni (strength), Odin (ruler of all gods), Sif (goddess of battle skill), Tyr (victory), Uller (magic)

ROMAN PANTHEON: Apollo (healing, light, music, prophecy), Aurora (goddess of dawn), Bacchus (wine), Ceres (goddess of agriculture), Cupid (love), Diana (goddess of the hunt, moon), Janus (gates), Juno (goddess of women, marriage), Jupiter (leader of the gods), Justitia (goddess of law), Mars (war), Mercury (messenger of the gods), Minerva (goddess of magic), Neptune (oceans), Pluto (underworld), Saturn (harvest), Uranus (sky), Venus (goddess of love), Vesta (goddess of hearth), Vulcan (craftsmanship)

SUMERIAN PANTHEON: Enki (oceans), Enlil (war), Inanna (goddess of war), Ki (goddess of nature), Nanna-Sin (moon), Nin-Hursag (goddess of the earth), Utu (sun)

CHAPTER 15: ANIMALS AND CREATURES

ANIMAL HOMES

MAN-MADE: aquarium, barn, bat house, birdhouse, cage, coop, corral, crate, dog house, enclosure, exhibit, farm, habitat, kennel, stable, sty, terrarium, zoo

NATURAL: aerie, anthill, burrow, cave, cavern, den, drey, form, henhouse, hive, hole, hollow log, hollow tree, holt, lair, lodge, mound, nest, riverbank, sett, shell, tide pool, tree, tunnel, warren, web

AMPHIBIANS

CAECILIANS: Aleku, Battersby's, Boulenger's, Brazilian, Columbian, common, Congo, Cooper's, Daniel's, forest, Frigate Island, Gaboon, Guinae, Makumuno Assumbo, Mexican, ringed, Sao Paulo, Seychelles, South American, tiny, West African, wet forest, worm patterned

FROGS: African dwarf, Australian corroboree, bullfrog, Darwin, fire-bellied, Goliath, green tree, poison dart, rainbow, rainforest rocket, South African ghost, Titicaca water

NEWTS: alpine, banded, crested, crocodile, eastern, firebelly, Pacific, paddle-tail, ribbed, small bodied, Spanish brook, spiny, spotted, wart

SALAMANDERS: alpine, Asiatic, Chinese giant, Congo, Dunn's, giant, greater siren, hellbender, marbled, mole, plethodontid, Mexican, olm, red black, spotted

TOADS: Amargosa, Arizona, arroyo, Betic midwife, black, boreal, California, cane, common Indian, East Texas, Eastern American, fire bellied, golden, Great Plains, Gulf Coast, Houston, narrow-mouthed, red-spotted, Rocky Mountain, Sonoran green, southern, southwestern Woodhouse's, Surinam, Texas, western green, Yosemite

BIRDS

BACKYARD: bluebird, blue jay, cardinal, cedar waxwing, chickadee, cowbird, crow, finch (gold, house), grackle, hummingbird, junco, martin, mockingbird, mourning dove, nighthawk, oriole, pigeon, red-winged blackbird, robin, sapsucker, sparrow, swallow, swift, woodpecker

BIRD OF PREY: buzzard, caracara, condor, eagle, falcon, harrier, hawk, kestrel, kite, osprey, owl, raptor, secretary bird

CHICKENS: Ameraucana, American game, buckeye, blue hen of Delaware, California gray, Cornish game, Delaware, Derbyshire redcap, Dominique, Dorking, Holland, Iowa blue, Ixworth, Java, Jersey giant, Lamona, Marsh daisy, modern game, muffed old English game, New Hampshire, Norfold grey, Old English game, Old English pheasant fowl, Orpington, Plymouth Rock, Rhode Island red, Rhode Island white, rosecomb, Scots dumpy, Scots grey, Sebright, Sussex, Winnebago, Wyandotte

DOMESTICATED FARM: duck, goose, guinea hen, turkey

DOMESTICATED PET: African gray, budgerigar, canary, chattering lory, cockatiel, cockatoo, conure, cordon bleu, lorikeet, lovebird, macaw, Meyers parrot, mynah, nightingale, parakeet, parrot, parrotlet, pigeon, rosella, Senegal, toucan, waxbill, zebra finch

OWLS: ashy-faced, band-bellied, bare-legged, barking, barred jungle owlet, barred, black and white, black-banded, boreal, buff-fronted, burrowing, chestnut-winged owlet, common barn, common grass, crested, cuckoo owlet, eagle, eastern grass, elf, fearful, fish, fishing, forest owlet, fulvous, great gray, great hawk, great horned, greater sooty, hoot, Hume's, laughing, lesser masked, lesser sooty, little, long-eared, long-whiskered owlet, maned, masked, mottled, northern hawk, owlet, Palau, powerful, pygmy, red-chested owlet, rufous, rufous-banded, rufous-legged, saw-whet, scops, screech, short-browed, short-eared, snowy, spadiced owlet, spectacled, spotted little, spotted, spotted owlet, striped, stygian, tawny, tawny-browed, white-chinned, white-faced, winking, wood

WILD, OTHER: albatross, cormorant, crane, cuckoo, curlew, dove, duck, emu, grebe, flamingo, fowl, godwit, goose, gull, heron, hoatzin, kingfisher, kiwi, loon, mousebird, nightjar, ostrich, passerine, pelican, penguin, petrel, phoebe, plover, ptarmigan, puffin, raven, rook, sandgrouse, stork, sunbittern, swan, trogon, turaco, turkey, turkey vulture, vulture, warbler, waterfowl, weaver

FISH

AQUARIUM FRESHWATER: African jewelfish, angelfish, arowana, bala shark, barb, betta, black molly, black tetra, bleeding heart tetra, blind cave tetra, blue gourami, bronze cory, Buenos Aires tetra, cardinal tetra, catfish, cherry barb, cichlid, clown barb, clown loach, convict cichlid, cory, danio, diamond tetra, discus, dwarf gourami, firemouth, glass catfish, glowlight tetra, goldfish, gourami, guppy, hatchetfish, head and taillight tetra, Jack Dempsey, jewelfish, kissing gourami, kribensis, kuhli loach, lemon tetra, livebearer, loach, long-fin swordtail, marbled hatchetfish, molly, Montezuma swordtail, neon tetra, orange-finned loach, oscar, otocinclus, paradisefish, pearl gourami, peppered cory, platy, plecostomus, rainbowfish, ram, red-tailed shark, redtail botia, rosy barb, rummynose tetra, sailfin molly, serpae tetra, Siamese fighting fish, silver arowana, silver dollar, skunk cory, sun catfish, swordtail, tetra, three-spot gourami, tiger barb, tiger-banded peckoltia, tropheus moorii, upside-down catfish, white cloud, zebra danio

AQUARIUM SALTWATER: achilles tang, angelfish, anthias, azure damsel, banggai cardinal, bay pipefish, black and gold chromis, blacktip grouper, black cap gramma, blenny (bicolor, black combtooth, black sailfin, blackline fang, blue and gold, bundoon, canary fang, diamond, ember), blue assessor, blue devil, blue gudgeon dartfish, bluespotted boxfish, bluestreak cardinalfish, boxfish, butterflyfish, cardinalfish, chalk bass, cinnamon anemonefish, clownfish, copperbanded butterflyfish, damselfish, domino damsel, eel, firefish, frogfish, goby, golden puffer, golden stripe soapfish, green chromis, grouper, hawkfish, hippo tang, jawfish, lionfish, longhorned cowfish, lyretail anthias, marine comet, maroon clown, naso tang, orbiculate batfish, painted comber, pajama cardinal, peach anthias, percula clown, porcupine puffer, powder blue tang, pufferfish, rabbitfish, royal gramma, scribbled boxfish, seahorse, sergeant major, soldierfish, spotted mandarin, squarespot anthias, squirrelfish, striped burrfish, surgeonfish, tang, threadfin anthias, triggerfish, wrasse, yellow tang, yellowtail damsel

WILD FRESHWATER: alewife, balaos, bass (black, rock, yellow), bluegill, bullhead, candlefish, crappie, croaker, flier, minnow, perch, pike (northern, walleye), pumpkinseed, red ear sunfish, salmon (coho, king,), sand launces, sand roller, tench, three-spined stickleback, trout (lake, rainbow), whitefish, warmouth, yellow perch

WILD SALTWATER: albacore tuna, amberjack, American eel, American shad, anchovy, arrow tooth flounder, Atlantic cod, Atlantic croaker, Atlantic flounder, Atlantic moonfish, Atlantic salmon, Atlantic spade, Atlantic thread tuna, ballyhoo, banded rudderfish, bar jack, barracuda, bat ray, Bermuda chub, big eye, big eyes cad, big head sea robin, bigeye tuna, black drum, black fish, black margate, black marlin, blackfin tuna, blue angel, blue fish, blue marlin, blue parrot, blue runner, bluefin tuna, bonefish, bonito tuna, butterfish, canary, chilipepper, chinook salmon, cobia, coho salmon, copper, cowcod, cub mackerel, cusk, cutlass fish, Dover sole, eelpout, English sole, French angel, French grunt, goose head, gray king fish, gray sole, gray triggerfish, green moray, green spotted, green sturgeon, grouper, gulf flounder, gulf toad fish, haddock, hard head catfish, hatchet marlin swordfish, herring, hog fish, horse eye jack, hound fish, inshore lizard, John dory, killie, ladyfish, leather jack, ling cod, liza, lizard fish, longbill spearfish, mackerel, margate, minnow, mullet, needle fish, northern king fish, ocean trigger, oil fish, olive, orange roughy, Pacific halibut, Pacific moonfish, palometa, peanut bunker, petrale sole, pigfish, pilot fish jack, pink salmon, pollock, pompano, porgy, pork fish, pudding wife, queen angel, queen parrot, queen trigger, rainbow parrot, rainbow runner, red drum, red hake, red tails cad, rex sole, round ray, rudder fish, sailfish, sand dab, sand perch, sand seatrout, sandtile, saw fish, scaled sardine, scorpion rockfish, scrawled cowfish, sculpin, sea bass, sea robin, silver perch, silver seatrout, skate, skipjack tuna, smooth puffer, snapper, snook, southern king fish, southern puffer, southern sting ray, spot fish, spotfin croaker, spotted moray, spotted scorpion, spotted seatrout, squire fish, squirl, stargazer, starry, starry flounder, striped bass, striped marlin, striped minnow, sun dial fish, swordfish, tarpon, tile fish, triggerfish, triple tail, tuna, vermilion, wahoo, wall eye pollock, weakfish, white croaker, white grunt, white marlin, white sturgeon, whiting, widow, winter flounder, wolf fish, yellow fin, yellow jack, yellow stripe shad, yellow tail flounder, yellowfin tuna, yellowtail

JELLYFISH: box, cannonball, flower hat, hydromedusa, irukandji, lion's mane, moon, purple-striped, sea nettle, white-spotted

OCTOPI: benthic, blanket, California two-spot, deep sea, gelatinous, giant Pacific, glass, greater blue-ringed, mimic, seven-armed, telescope

SHARKS: angle, basking, blue, bramble, bullhead, carpet, cat, cow, dogfish, frilled, goblin, great white, ground, hammerhead, hand, nurse, horn, hound, longfin, mackerel, megamouth, requiem, reef (blacktail, caribbean, gray, whitetip), rough, prickly, sawshark, shortfin, thresher, tiger, whale, wobbegong, zebra

SQUID: armhook, bigfin, bobtail, bush-club, comb-finned, cuttlefish, European, fire, flying, giant, giant axon, glacial, grass, Grimaldi scaled, hooked, Humboldt, jewel, Patagonian, ram's horn, rhomboid, vampire, whiplash

MAMMALS

APES: bonobo, chimpanzee (central, eastern, Nigerian, western), gibbon, gorilla (cross river, eastern lowland, mountain, western lowland), human, orangutan (Bornean, Sumatran), siamang

BATS: bamboo, banana, big brown, big free-tailed, big-eared, big-eyed, blossom, bonneted, broad-nosed, buffy flower, bulldog, butterfly, canyon, cave myotis, chocolate, disk-winged, dusky doglike, eastern red, epauletted, evening, false vampire, fig-eating, flat-headed, flower-faced, flying fox, free-tailed, fringed myotis, fringe-lipped, fruit, fruit-eating, funnel-eared, ghost-faced, giant wooly, gray myotis, groove-toothed, hairy-footed, hairy-nosed, harlequin, heart-nosed, hoary, hog-nosed, horn-skinned, horseshoe, house, Ipanema, large forest, leaf-chinned, leaf-nosed, little, little fruit, long-eared myotis, long-legged, long-nosed, long-snouted, long-tailed, long-tongued, mastiff, monkey-faced, mouse-tailed, mustached, myotis, naked-backed, nectar, noctule, northern, northern yellow, nosed, pallid, pipistrelle, pocketed free-tailed, pond, pouched, round leaf, round-eared, rousette, sac-winged, Seminole, serotine, shaggy, sheath-tailed, short-headed, short-nosed, short-tailed, silvered, silver-haired, single leaf, slit-faced, small-footed myotis, smoky, southern yellow, spear-nosed, spotted, strange big-eared brown, striped, stripe-faced, sucker-footed, sword-nosed, tailed tailless, tailless, tailless leaf-nosed, tent-making, thick-eared, thick-thumbed, thumbless, tomb, tree, tri-colored, trident, tropical, trumpet-eared, tube-nosed, tufted, vampire, vesper, visored, wattled, western red, western yellow, whiskered, white, white-shouldered, white-winged dog, Woermann's, wrinkle-faced, yellow, yellow-eared, yellow-lipped, yellow-throated big, Yuma

BEARS: Alaskan brown, American black, ape man, Asiatic black, Asiatic brown, Aswail, bai bao, Baloo, black, black and white, black beast, brown, bruang, bruin, cat, cave, cinnamon, dog, European brown, fiery fox, Florida black, formosa, giant cat, giant panda, glacier, grizzly, Himalayan snow, honey, ice, Jungle joker, Kermode, Kodiak, lip, Maylay, Nanook, polar, sea, shining cat, shi ti shou, short-faced, sloth, spectacled, sun, Syrian, walking, white

CATS, BIG: bobcat, cheetah, cougar, jaguar, leopard (black, clouded, snow), lion, lioness, lynx, mountain lion, puma, tiger

CATS, DOMESTIC: Abyssinian, American bobtail, American curl, American ringtail, American shorthair, American wirehair, Anatolian, Australian Mist, Balinese, Bengal, Birman, Bombay, British shorthair, Burmese, Burmilla, California spangled cat, Chantilly/Tiffany, Chartreux, Chausie, Colorpoint shorthair, Cornish Rex, Devonshire Rex, domestic long hair, domestic medium hair, domestic shorthair, Don hairless, Egyptian Mau, European Burmese, European shorthair, exotic shorthair, Gato, Havana Brown, Highlander, Himalayan, Japanese bobtail, Javanese, Khao Manee, Korat, LaPerm, Maine coon, manx, Minskin, Munchkin, Nebelung, Norwegian forest cat, Ocicat, Oriental, Persian, Peterbald, Pixie-Bob, Ragamuffin, Ragdoll, Russian Blue, Savannah, Scottish Fold, Selkirk Rex, Siamese, Siberian, Singapura, Snowshoe, Sokoke, Somali, Sphynx, Thai, Tiffanie, Tonkinese, Toyger, Turkish Angora, Turkish Van

COWS, NORTH AMERICAN DAIRY: Ayrshire, Brown Swiss, Canadienne, Dutch Belted, Guernsey, Holstein, Jersey, Kerry, Milking Devon, Milking Shorthorn, Norwegian red

COWS, OTHER: Africander, Albères, Alentejana, Allmogekor, American, American White Park, Amerifax, Amrit Mahal, Anatolian Black, Andalusian Black, Andalusian Grey, Angeln, Angus, Ankole, Ankole-Watusi, Argentine Criollo, Asturian Mountain, Asturian Valley, Aubrac, Aulie-Ata, Australian Braford, Australian Friesian Sahiwal, Australian Lowline, Australian Milking Zebu, Azaouak, Bachaur, Baladi, Baltana

Romaneasca, Barka, Barzona, Bazadais, Béarnais, Beefalo, Beefmaker, Beefmaster, Belarus Red, Belgian Blue, Belgian Red, Belmont Adaptaur, Belmont Red, Belted Galloway, Bengali, Berrendas, Bhagnari, Blacksided Trondheim and Norland, Blanca Cacereña, Blanco Orejinegro, Blonde d'Aquitaine, Bonsmara, Boran, Bordelais, Braford, Brahman, Brahmousin, Brangus, Braunvieh, British White, Busa, Cachena, Canary Island, Canchim, Carinthian Blond, Caucasian, Channi, Charbray, Charolais, Chianina, Chinampo, Chinese Black-and-White, Cholistani, Corriente, Costeño con Cuernos, Dajal, Damascus, Damietta, Dangi, Danish Jersey, Danish Red, Deoni, Devon, Dexter, Dhanni, Dølafe, Droughtmaster, Dulong, Dutch Friesian, East Anatolian Red, Enderby Island, English Longhorn, Estonian Red, Evolène, Fighting Bull, Finnish, Fjall, Florida Cracker/Pineywoods, Fulani Sudanese, Galician Blond, Galloway, Gaolao, Gascon, Gelbray, Gelbvieh, German Angus, German Red Pied, Gir, Glan, Gloucester, Gobra, Greek Shorthorn, Greek Steppe, Groningen Whiteheaded, Gudali, Guzerat, Hallikar, Hariana, Hartón, Hays Converter, Hereford, Herens, Highland, Hinterwald, Holando-Argentino, Horro, Hungarian Grey, Icelandic, Illawarra, Indo-Brazilian, Irish Moiled, Israeli Holstein, Israeli Red, Istoben, Jamaica Black, Jamaica Hope, Jamaica Red, Jaulan, Kangayam, Kankrej, Karan Fries, Karan Swiss, Kazakh, Kenwariya, Kherigarh, Khillari, Kholmogory, Kilis, Krishna Valley, Kurdi, Kuri, Latvian Brown, Limousin, Limpurger, Lincoln Red, Lithuanian Red, Lohani, Lourdais, Luing, Madagascar Zebu, Maine Anjou, Malvi, Mandalong, Marchigiana, Maremmana, Masai, Mashona, Maure, Mazandarani, Meuse-Rhine-Yssel, Mewati, Mirandesa, Modicana, Mongolian, Montbéliard, Morucha, Murboden, Murray Grey, Muturu, Nagori, Nanyang, N'dama, Nelore, Nguni, Nimari, Normande, Ongole, Orma Boran, Oropa, Ovambo, Parthenais, Philippine native, Piedmontese, Pinzgauer, Polish Red, Polled Hereford, Ponwar, Qinchuan, Rath, Rathi, Rätien Gray, Red Angus, Red Brangus, Red Fulani, Red Pied Friesian, Red Poll, Red Polled Østland, Red Sindhi, Red Steppe, Reggiana, Retinta, Rojhan, Romagnola, Romosinuano, Russian Black Pied, Sahiwal, Salers, Salorn, San Martinero, Sanhe, Santa Cruz, Santa Gertrudis, Sarabi, Senepol, Sharabi, Shetland, Shorthorn, Siboney, Simbrah, Simmental, Siri, Slovenian Cika, South Devon, Sussex, Swedish Friesian, Swedish Red Polled, Swedish Red-and-White, Tarentaise, Telemark, Texas Longhorn, Texon, Tharparkar, Tswana, Tuli, Turkish Grey Steppe, Ukrainian Beef, Ukrainian Grey, Ukrainian Whitehead, Umblachery, Ural Black Pied, Vestland Fjord, Vestland Red Polled, Vosges, Wagyu, Welsh Black, White Cáceres, White Park, Xinjiang Brown, Yanbian

DOGS/CANINE: American jackal, bitch, companion animal, coyote, Heinz 57, litter, man's best friend, mutt, pup, puppy, purebred, seeing eye dog, sire, prairie wolf

DOG GROUPS: herding, hound, miscellaneous, nonsporting, retriever, sporting, terrier, toy, working

DOG BREEDS: Affenpinscher, Afghan Hound, Airedale Terrier, Akita, Alaskan Malamute, American Bulldog, American English Coonhound, American Eskimo, American Foxhound, American Pit Bull Terrier, American Staffordshire Terrier, American Water Spaniel, Anatolian Shepherd, Argentine Dogo, Australian Cattle Dog, Australian Shepherd, Australian Terrier, Basenji, Basset Hound, Beagle, Bearded Collie, Beauceron, Bedlington Terrier, Belgian Malinois, Belgian Sheepdog, Belgian Tervuren, Bernese Mountain Dog, Bichon Frise, Black Russian Terrier, Black and Tan Coonhound, Bloodhound, Bluetick Coonhound, Border Collie, Border Terrier, Borzoi, Boston Terrier, Bouvier des Flandres, Boxer, Boykin Spaniel, Briard, Brittany, Brussels Griffon, Bull Terrier, Bulldog, Bullmastiff, Cairn Terrier, Canaan Dog, Cane Corso, Cardigan Welsh Corgi, Cavalier King Charles Spaniel, Cesky Terrier, Chesapeake Bay Retriever, Chihuahua, Chinese Crested Dog, Chinese Shar-Pei, Chinook, Chow Chow, Clumber Spaniel, Cocker Spaniel, Collie (rough, smooth), Curly-Coated Retriever, Dachshund, Dalmatian, Dandie Dinmont Terrier, Doberman Pinscher, Dogue de Bordeaux, English Cocker Spaniel, English Foxhound, English Setter, English Springer Spaniel, English Toy Spaniel, Entlebucher Mountain, Field Spaniel, Finnish Lapphund, Finnish Spitz, Flat-Coated Retriever, Fox Terrier (smooth, wire), French Bulldog, German Pinscher, German Shepherd, German Shorthaired Pointer, German Wirehaired Pointer, Giant Schnauzer, Glen of Imaal Terrier, Golden Retriever, Gordon Setter, Great Dane, Great Pyrennes, Greater Swiss Mountain Dog, Greyhound, Harrier, Havanese, Hovawart, Ibizan Hound, Icelandic Sheepdog, Irish Red & White Setter, Irish Setter, Irish Terrier, Irish Water Spaniel, Irish Wolfhound, Italian Greyhound, Japanese Chin, Keeshond, Kerry Blue Terrier, Komondor, Kuvasz, Labrador Retriever, Lakeland Terrier, Leonberger, Lhasa Apso, Löwchen, Maltese, Manchester Terrier, Mastiff, Miniature Bull Terrier, Miniature Pinscher, Miniature Poodle, Miniature Schnauzer, Neapolitan Mastiff, Newfoundland, Norfolk Terrier, Norwegian Buhund, Norwegian Elkhound, Norwegian Lundehund, Norwich Terrier, Nova Scotia Duck Tolling Retriever, Old English Sheepdog, Otterhound, Papillon, Parson Russell Terrier, Pekingese, Pembroke Welsh Corgi, Petit Basset Griffon Vendeen, Pharaoh Hound, Plott, Pointer, Polish Lowland Sheepdog, Pomeranian, Portuguese Water Dog, Pug, Puli, Pyrenean Shepherd, Rat Ter-

rier, Redbone Coonhound, Rhodesian Ridgeback, Rottweiler, Russell Terrier, Saint Bernard, Saluki, Samoyed, Schipperke, Schnauzer (Standard), Scottish Deerhound, Scottish Terrier, Sealyham Terrier, Shetland Sheepdog, Shiba Inu, Shih Tzu, Siberian Husky, Silky Terrier, Skye Terrier, Soft Coated Wheaten Terrier, Spinone Italiano, Staffordshire Bull Terrier, Standard Poodle, Sussex Spaniel, Swedish Vallhund, Tibetan Mastiff, Tibetan Spaniel, Tibetan Terrier, Tosa, Toy Fox Terrier, Toy Manchester Terrier, Toy Poodle, Treeing Walker Coonhound, Vizsla, Weimaraner, Welsh Springer Spaniel, Welsh Terrier, West Highland White Terrier, Whippet, Wirehaired Pointing Griffon, Xoloitzcuintli, Yorkshire Terrier

> **USAGE NOTE:** A spelling discrepancy exists between dog breeds and a mythological creature. The dog breed is spelled griffon; the creature is spelled griffin.

DOLPHINS: bottlenosed, burrunan, Chinese white, dusky, Hector's, hourglass, long-beaked, melon-headed, northern rightwhale, southern rightwhale, oceanic, pilot, rough-toothed, short-beaked, spinner, spotted, striped, white-sided

FOXES: arctic, Azara's zorro, bat-eared, Bengal, Blanford's, cape, corsac, crab-eating, culpeo, Darwin's, fennec, gray, grey zorro, hoary zorro, island gray, kit, pale, Pampas, red, Ruppell's, Sechuran zorro, small-eared zorro, swift, Tibetan

GLIDING: cobego, colugo, flying lemur, flying squirrel, gliding possum, sugar glider

HORSES: foal, gelding, mare, miniature, pony, stallion

RELATED: African wild ass, ass, burro, donkey, feral donkey, jack, jenny, kiang, mule, onager, paramo donkey, Poitou donkey, zebra

HORSE BREEDS: Abyssinian, Akhal Teke, Albanian, Altai, American Cream Draft, American Creme and White, American Walking Pony, Andalusian, Andravida, Anglo-Kabarda, Appaloosa, AraAppaloosa, Arabian, Ardennes, Argentine Criollo, Asturian, Australian Brumby, Australian Stock Horse, Azteca, Balearic, Baluchi, Banker, Ban-ei, Barb, Bashkir, Bashkir Curly, Basotho Pony, Belgian, Bhirum Pony, Bhotia Pony, Black Forest, Boer, Breton, Buckskin, Budyonny, Byelorussian Harness, Camargue, Campolina, Canadian, Carthusian, Caspian, Cayuse, Cheju, Chilean Corralero, Chincoteague Pony, Cleveland Bay, Clydesdale, Colorado Ranger Horse, Connemara Pony, Crioulo, Dales Pony, Danube, Dartmoor Pony, Deliboz, Djerma, Døle, Dongola, Dülmen Pony, Dutch Draft, Dutch Warmblood, East Bulgarian, Egyptian, Eriskay Pony, Estonian Native, Exmoor Pony, Faeroes Pony, Falabella, Fell Pony, Finnhorse, Fleuve, Fouta, Frederiksborg, French Saddlebred, French Trotter, Friesian, Galiceño, Galician Pony, Gelderlander, Gidran, Golden American Saddlebred, Gotland, Groningen, Guangxi, Hackney, Haflinger, Hanoverian, Hequ, Highland Pony, Hokkaido, Holsteiner, Hucul, Hungarian Warmblood, Icelandic, Iomud, Irish Draught, Jinzhou, Jutland, Kabarda, Karabair, Karabakh, Kazakh, Kerry Bog Pony, Kiger Mustang, Kirdi Pony, Kisber Felver, Kiso, Kladruby, Knabstrup, Kushum, Kustanai, Latvian, Lithuanian Heavy Draft, Lipizzan, Lokai, Losino, Lusitano, Malopolski, Mangalarga, Marwari, M'Bayar, Mérens Pony, Messara, Miniature, Misaki, Missouri Fox Trotting Horse, Miyako, Mongolian, Morab, Morgan, Moyle, Mustang, Murgese, National Show Horse, New Forest Pony, New Kirgiz, Newfoundland Pony, Noma, Nooitgedacht Pony, Noric, Nordland, Northeastern, North Swedish Horse, Norwegian Fjord, Ob, Oldenburg, Orlov Trotter, Paint, Palomino, Pantaneiro, Paso Fino, Percheron, Peruvian Paso, Pindos Pony, Pinia, Pintabian, Pinto, Polish Konik, Pony of the Americas, Pottok, Przewalski, Pyrenean Tarpan, Qatgani, Quarab, Quarter Horse, Quarter Pony, Racking Horse, Rocky Mountain Horse, Russian Don, Russian Heavy Draft, Russian Trotter, Saddlebred, Sanhe, Schleswiger Heavy Draft, Schwarzwälder Fuchs, Selle Francais, Shagya, Shetland Pony, Shire, Single-Footing Horse, Skyros Pony, Somali Pony, Sorraia, Soviet Heavy Draft, Spanish Mustang, Spanish-Barb, Spanish-Norman, Standardbred, Sudan Country-Bred, Suffolk, Swedish Warmblood, Taishuh, Tarpan, Tawleed, Tennessee Walking Horse, Tersk, Thessalian, Thoroughbred, Tokara, Tori, Trakehner, Ukrainian Saddle, Vlaamperd, Vladimir Heavy Draft, Vyatka, Welara Pony, Welsh Cob, Welsh Pony, West African Barb, Western Sudan Pony, Wielkopolski, Xilingol, Yakut, Yanqi, Yili, Yonaguni, Zaniskari Pony, Zhemaichu

LIONS: American cave, Asiatic, Barbary, Cape, Eurasian cave, European cave, Indian, Katanga, Massai, Northeast Congo, Persian, Southeast African, Southwest African, Transvaal, Tsavo, West African

MONKEYS, NEW WORLD: Amazonian marmoset, Atlantic marmoset, black howler, black tamarin, black-capped capuchin, black-headed spider, black-mantled tamarin, brown howler, brown-mantled tamarin, capuchin, Central American squirrel, Coiba Island howler, douroucouli, dwarf marmoset, Emperor tamarin, Geoffrey's spider, Geoffrey's tamarin, golden-headed lion tamarin, golden-mantled tamarin, Guatemalan black howler, howler, lion tamarin, mantled howler, marmoset, Midas tamarin, muriqui, night monkey, owl monkey, Panamanian night monkey, pygmy marmoset, saki monkey, spider, squirrel, tamarin, three-striped night monkey, titi monkey, uakari monkey, white-fronted capuchin, white-headed capuchin, white-mantled tamarin, wooly monkey, wooly spider

MONKEYS, OLD WORLD: African, baboon, colobus, douc, drill, gelada, gray langur, grivet, guenon, guereza, kipunji, langur, leaf monkey, lutung, macaque, malbrouck, mandrill, mangabey, mona monkey, odd-nosed, papionini, pig-tailed monkey, proboscis monkey, red-tailed monkey, snub-nosed monkey, spot-nosed monkey, surili, talapoin, vervet

PIGS: Aksai black pied, American landrace, American Yorkshire, Angeln saddleback, Appalachian English, Arapawa Island, Auckland Island, Australian Yorkshire, Babi Kampung, Ba Xuyen, Bantu, Bazna, Beijing black, Belarus black pied, Belgian landrace, Bengali brown Shannaj, Bentheim black pied, Berkshire, black Slavonian, black Canarian, Breitovo, British landrace, British lop, British saddleback, Bulgarian white, Cantonese, Chato Murciano, Chester white, Choctaw hog, Creole, Cumberland, Czech, improved white, Danish landrace, Danish protest, Dermantsi pied, Dorset gold tip, Duroc, Dutch landrace, East Balkan, Essex, Estonian bacon, Fengjing, Finnish landrace, forest mountain, French landrace, Gasçon, German landrace, Gloucestershire old spots, Grice, Guinea hog, Hampshire, Hante, Hereford, Hezuo, Iberian, Italian landrace, Japanese landrace, Jeju black, Jersey red, Jinhua, Kakhetian, Kele, Kemerovo, Korean native, Krskopolje, Kunekune. Lacombe, large black, large black-white, large white, Latvian white, Leicoma, Lithuanian native, Lithuanian white, Lincolnshire curly-coated, Livny, Mangalitsa, Meishan, Middle white, miniature, Minzhu, Minokawa Buta, Mong Cai, Mora Romagnola, Moura, Mukota, Mulefoot, Myrhorod, Neijiang, Ningxiang, north caucasian, north Siberian, Norwegian landrace, Norwegian Yorkshire, Ossabaw Island, Oxford sandy and black, Philippine native, Piétrain, Poland China, red wattle, Semirechye, Siberian black pied, small black, small white, spots, Surabaya Babi, Swabian-Hall, Swedish landrace, Taihu, Tamworth, Thuoc Nhieu, Tibetan, Tokyo-X, Tsivilsk, Turopolje, Ukrainian spotted steppe, Ukrainian white steppe, Urzhum, Vietnamese potbelly, Welsh, Wessex saddleback, West French white, Windsnyer, Wuzishan, Yanan, Yorkshire blue and white

POCKET PETS: gerbil, guinea pig, hamster, rat

TIGERS: Bali, Bengal, Caspian, Corbett's, golden tabby, Indochinese, Javan, liger, Malayan, saber-toothed, Siberian, South China, Sumatran, white

WHALES: baleen, beaked, beluga, blue, bowhead, fin, humpback, killer, minke, pilot, pygmy, sperm

WOODLAND: badger, beaver, chipmunk, field mouse, gopher, gray squirrel, hare, hedgehog, mole, mouse, opossum, pika, porcupine, red squirrel, rabbit, raccoon, shrew, skunk, weasel, wolverine, vole

WILD MAMMALS, OTHER: aardvark, African elephant, alpaca, anteater, antechinus, antelope, armadillo, Asian elephant, Asiatic linsang, bandicoot, bettong, bilby, bison, boar, brushtail possum, bush baby, camel, caribou, chevrotain, chinchilla, civet, colugo, coyote, cuscus, deer, dunnart, echidna, elephant shrew, ermine, falanouc, fossa, giant panda, giraffe, goat, hippopotamus, hyena, hyrax, jackal, kangaroo, koala, lemur, llama, mammoth, manatee, marsupial, marsupial mole, mastodon, mink, mongoose, monitor del monte, moose, mountain goat, musk deer, musk ox, numbat, okapi, otter, ox, pachyderm, pangolin, peccary, platypus, potoroo, pronghorn, quoll, rat, rat kangaroo, red panda, rhinoceros, rodent, sea lion, seal, sheep, shrew opossum, tamandua, tapir, tarsier, Tasmanian devil, Tasmanian tiger, Tasmanian wolf, three-toed sloth, tree shrew, two-toed sloth, wallaby, walpurti, walrus, water buffalo, wildebeest, wolf, wombat, yak

INSECTS, BUGS, AND SPIDERS

ANT: Amazon, army, black, bull, bulldog, carpenter, colony, driver, drone, egg, larva, lemon, leafcutter, Jerdon's jumping, fire, meat, pavement, pharaoh, queen, red, Sahara desert, sugar, weaver, warrior, worker

USAGE NOTE: More than 12,000 species of ants have been classified around the world.

ARACHNIDS, NONVENOMOUS: camel, cellar, common house, corn, crab, daddy longlegs, garden, ghost, golden silk, green lynx, ground, jumping

ARACHNIDS, VENOMOUS: bird, black house, black widow, Brazilian wandering, broad-faced sac, brown recluse, brown widow, funnelweb, grass, hobo, huntsman, mouse, orb weaver, redback, St. Andrew's Cross, tarantula, trap-door, white-tail, wolf, yellow sac

USAGE NOTE: The strength of spider venom varies widely. A few venoms are capable of killing a human in a few minutes, while others cause only mild irritation in humans or are capable of killing small birds or rodents. Note also that the fangs of some spiders are too weak to penetrate human skin.

BEE: Africanized, allodapine, bumblebee, carpenter, cuckoo, digger, drone, honey, hornfaced, killer, leafcutting, mason, orchid, queen, sweat, vulture, worker

RELATED: dance, hive, honey, honeycomb

BEETLE: Asian lady, boll weevil, bombardier, carpet, clerid, cowboy, dogbane, forest dung, golden-bloomed, golden stag, grooved diving, ground, Hawthorn jewel, Japanese, June, lady bug, larch ladybird, marsh click, minotaur, museum, musk, pea, powderpost, red apion weevil, red-brown skipjack, rhinoceros, rose, rove, soldier, sun, strawberry blossom weevil, tanbark, tiger, tortoise, two-spot ladybird, water, western grape, wood dor

BUTTERFLY: admiral, alpine, arctic, azure, birdwing, brown, brushfooted, buckeye, checkerspot, clearwing, cloudywing, comma, copper, cracker, crescent, daggerwing, elfin, emperor, duke of burgundy, duskywing, flasher, fritillary, gossamer wing, greenstreak, groundstreak, hairstreak, jezebel, karner blue, longtail, leafwing, leopard, lime, metalmark, monarch, mourning cloak, nymphalidae, orangetip, peacock, painted lady, papilionidae, Parnassian, pearly-eye, purplewing, red pierrot, ringlet, satyr, scallopwing, sicklewing, skipper, skipperling, small white, sootywing, sulphur, swallowtail (black, blue, citrus, yellow, zebra), tortoiseshell, viceroy, wood-nymph, xerces blue

DRAGONFLY: emperor, skimmer, common whitetail, hawker, darter, chaser, darner, downy emerald, great pondhawk, banded pennant, Texas emerald

FLIES: awl, bee fly, black fly, blow, blue bottle fly, crane, deer, drain, flesh, fruit fly, gnat, horse, house, hunchback, long-legged, midge, mosquito, moth fly, robber, sand, small-headed, snipe fly, soldier, stable, stiletto, thick-headed, water snipe fly, window, wood soldier

MOTH: antler, atlas moth, black witch, blotched emerald, bogong, bordered white, cabbage, cecropia, clouded border, codling, comet, corn earworm, cotton bollworm, dark dagger, death's-head hawkmoth, elephant hawk, emperor gum, frosted orange, gothic, grease, gypsy, hummingbird hawkmoth, imperial, Indianmeal, lesser yellow underwing, light brown apple, luna, Madagascan sunset, marbled beauty, May highflyer, nutmeg, pale beauty, peppered, polyphemus, poplar gray, scalloped oak, silkworm, silver, turnip, wax, white witch, willow beauty, winter, yellowtail

ORTHOPTERA: cricket, grasshopper, katydid, locust, weta

PHASMID: Lord Howe Island stick, leaf insect, titan stick, two-striped walking stick, walking stick

SCORPION: albino, black, blue, burrowing, deathstalker, lesser brown, red, red claw, rock-loving, sand, sand-loving, tailless whip, wandering, whip

WASP: Cicada killer, cuckoo, digger, fig, flower, gall, German, hornet, mud, mud daubers, paper, pollen, potter, sand, scoliid, yellow jacket

REPTILES

CROCODILIANS: African dwarf crocodile, American alligator, American crocodile, Australian freshwater crocodile, black caiman, broad-snouted caiman, Chinese alligator, Cuban crocodile, Cuvier's dwarf caiman, Estuarine crocodile, false gharial, Indian gharial, Jacare caiman, Morelet's crocodile, mugger, New Guinea crocodile, Nile crocodile, Orinoco crocodile, Philippine crocodile, Schneider's dwarf caiman, Siamese crocodile, slender-snouted crocodile, spectacled caiman

DINOSAUR TYPES: ankylosaur, ceratopsian, dino-bird, hadrosaur, ornithomimid, ornithopod, pachycephalosaur, prosauopod, raptor, sauropod, stegosaur, therizinosaur, theropod, titanosaur, tyrannosaur

DINOSAURS, COMMONLY KNOWN: allosaurus, ankylosaurus, apatosaurus, brachiosaurus, brachylophosaurus, carcharodontosaurus, deinonychus, diplodocus, dromaeosaur, giganotosaurus, iguanodon, maiasaura peeblesorum, oviraptor philoceratops, protoceratops andrewsi, spinosaurus, stegosaurus, triceratops, troodon formosus, tyrannosaurus, velociraptor mongoliensis

SCALED REPTILES: agama, agamid lizard, American arboreal lizard, American legless lizard, anole, blind lizard, casquehead lizard, central bearded dragon, chameleon, clubtail lizard, collared lizard, chuckwalla, dwarf lizard, earless monitor lizard, flap-footed lizard, frilled lizard, gecko, Gila monster, glass lizard, helmet lizard, horned lizard, iguanas, iguanid, knob-scaled lizard, komodo dragon, lacertid, legless lizard, leopard lizard, Madagascar iguanid, Malagasy iguana, monitor lizard, neotropical ground lizard, night lizard, plated lizard, shorthead worm lizard, skinks, spectacled lizard, spinytail lizard, tegu, thorny devil, tropidurid lizard, two-legged worm lizard, whiptail, wood lizard, worm lizard

TORTOISES: Abingdon Island giant, African spurred, African tent, Aldabra giant, angulated, Argentine, Bell's hinge-back, Bolson, bowsprit, brown, Burmese star, Cape, Cape Berkeley giant, Chaco, Chatham Island giant, desert, Egyptian, elongated, Forsten's, Galapagos giant, geometric, gopher, Greek, Herman's, Home's hinge-back, impressed, Indefatigable Island giant, Indian star, Isabela Island giant, James Island giant, leopard, Lobatse hinge-back, Madagascan flat-tailed, Madagascan spider, marginated, Narborough Island giant, Natal hinge-back, pancake, Pinta Island giant, radiated, red-footed, Russian, serrated hinge-back, serrated star, Sonoran desert, Speke's hinge-back, Texas, Travancore, Volcan wolf giant, yellow-footed

TURTLES, FRESHWATER: African helmeted, African keeled mud, African sideneck, alligator snapping, American sideneck, American sideneck river, Asian box, Asian giant river terrapin, Asian leaf, Asian wood, Baja California slider, Barbour's map, Beal's-eyed, Belize slider, Big Bend slider, big-headed, black knob sawback, black marsh, black wood, black-bellied mud, black-breasted leaf, Blanding's, bog, Borneo painted, box, brown roofed, Cagle's map, Caspian pond, Central American wood, Chiapas giant musk, chicken, Chinese golden box, Chinese golden thread, Chinese pond, Chinese stripe-necked, clown red-eared slider, Colombian slider, common map, common musk, common toad-headed, Cumberland slider, desert box, diamondback terrapin, East Coast diamondback terrapin, Eastern Australian snakeneck, eastern box, eastern chicken, eastern mud, eastern painted, eastern snapping, eastern spiny softshell, Escambia map, European pond, Florida box, Florida chicken, Florida cooter, Florida mud, Florida red-bellied, Florida snapping, Florida softshell, fly river, Gabon sideneck, golden thread, Guadalupe spiny softshell, Gulf coast box, Hieroglyphic river cooter, Honduran wood, Japanese wood, Liberian black mud, MacLeay river, Madagascar big-headed sideneck, Malayan flat-shelled, Mexican giant musk, Mexican ornate slider, Midland painted, Mississippi mid, mud, Murray river, New Guinea snapping, Nicaraguan slider, Nigerian black mud, North African helmeted, North American spotted, North American wood, northern black-knobbed map, northern red-bellied, northern red-faced, northern snakeneck, ornate box, ornate wood, Pacific pond, painted river terrapin, painted wood, peninsula cooter, pig-nosed, pink belly, pink belly snapper, pond, red-cheeked mud, red-eared slider, red-eared slider, Reeves turtle, river , saw-shelled snapping, scorpion mud, Senegal flapshell, snapping, softshell, Sonoran mud, spiny, spotted pond, stinkpot musk, Texas cooter, Texas map, Texas spiny softshell, western painted, western pond, yellow mud, yellow-bellied slider

TURTLES, SEA: black, flatback, green, hawksbill, Kemp's ridley, leatherback, loggerhead, olive ridley

SNAKES

ADDER: Berg, common, deaf, death, desert death, horned, long-nosed, many-horned, mountain, mud, Namaqua dwarf, night, Peringuey's, puff, rhombic night, water

BOA: Abaco Island, Amazon tree, constrictor, Cuban, Dumeril's, dwarf, emerald tree, Hogg Island, Jamaican, Madagascar ground, Madagascar tree, Puerto Rican, rainbow, red-tailed, rosy, rubber, sand, tree

COBRA: black-necked, Cape, Chinese, cobra de capello, common, eastern water, Egyptian, false, false water, forest, Gold's tree, Indian, king, monocled, Mozambique spitting, Philippine, red spitting, Rinkhals, shield-nosed, spectacled, spitting, white-lipped, yellow

GENERAL FAMILIES: anaconda, asp, beaked, bird, black-headed, black rat, black, blind, boiga, boomslang, brown, bull, bushmaster, canebrake, cantil, cat-eyed, cat, chicken, coachwhip, Collett's, Congo, copperhead, coral, corn, cottonmouth, crowned, Cuban wood, diamondback, dice, dugite, carpet, egg-eater, fer-de-lance, fishing, flying, fox, garter, glossy, gopher, grass, green, ground, Habu, harlequin, hognose, hoop, hundred pacer, indigo, king brown, king, large shield, lancehead, lora, lyre, mamba, mangrove, milk, moccasin, Montpellier, mud, night, parrot, patchnose, pine, pipe, queen, racer, rat, ribbon, river jack, shield-tailed, sidewinder, small-eyed, smooth, Sonoran, stiletto, sunbeam, taipan, tentacled, tic polonga, tiger, tree, twig, Urutu, vine, wart, water moccasin, water, whip, wolf, worm, wutu, yarara

KEELBACK: Andrea's, Asian, Assam, black-striped, buff-striped, Burmese, common, hill, Himalayan, Khasi Hills, modest, Nicobar Island, Nilgiri, orange-collared, red-necked, Sikkim, speckle-bellied, tiger, Wall's, white-lipped, Wynaad, Yunnan

KRAIT: banded, black, blue, Burmese, Ceylon, Indian, lesser black, Malayan, many-banded, northeastern hill, red-headed, Sind, South Andaman

PIT VIPER: banded, bamboo, Barbour's, black-tailed horned, Bornean, Brongersma's, brown spotted, Cantor's, elegant, eyelash, Fan-Si-Pan horned, flat-nosed, Godman's, green tree, Habu, Hagen's, horseshoe, Jerdon's, Kanburian, Kaulback's lance-headed, Kham Plateau, large-eyed, Malabar rock, Malayan, mangrove, Mangshan, Motuo bamboo, Nicobar bamboo, Philippine, red-tailed bamboo, Schultze's, Stejneger's bamboo, Sri Lankan, temple, Tibetan bamboo, tiger, undulated, Wagler's, Wirot's

PYTHON: African rock, amethystine, Angolan, Australian scrub, ball, Bismarck ringed, black-headed, blood, Boelen, Borneo short-tailed, Bredl's, brown water, Burmese, Calabar, carpet, children's, Dauan Island water, desert woma, diamond, Flinders, green tree, Halmahera, Indian, Indonesian water, Macklot's, Mollucan, Oenpelli, olive, Papuan, pygmy, red blood, reticulated, rough-scaled, royal, Savu, spotted, Stimson's, Sumatran short-tailed, Tanimbar, Timor, Wetar Island, white-lipped, woma

RATTLESNAKE: Arizona black, Aruba, Chihuahuan ridge-nosed, Coronado Island, Durango rock, dusky pigmy, eastern diamondback, Grand Canyon, Great Basin, Hopi, lance-headed, long-tailed, Massasauga, Mexican green, Mexican west coast, midget faded, Mojave, northern black-tailed, Oaxacan small-headed, rattler, red diamond, Southern Pacific, southwestern speckled, Tancitaran dusky, tiger, timber, tropical, twin-spotted, Uracoan, western diamondback

SEA: anomalous, beaked, bighead, Grey's, Hediger's, horned, Jerdon's, mangrove, mudsnake, olive, Port Darwin, Shaw's, spine-bellied, spiny-headed, Stokes's, turtlehead, yellow bellied

VIPER: asp, bamboo, blunt-nosed, Brazilian mud, burrowing, bush , carpet, crossed, Cyclades blunt-nosed, eyelash, Fea's, fifty pacer, Gaboon, hog-nosed, horned desert, horned, jumping, Kaznakov's, leaf-nosed, leaf, levant, long-nosed, McMahon's, mole, nose-horned, Palestinian, Pallas', palm , pit , Portuguese, rhinoceros, river jack, Russell's, sand, saw-scaled, Schlegel's, sedge, sharp-nosed, snorkel, temple, tree, Ursini's, western hog-nosed

WORLD'S TEN MOST VENOMOUS: inland taipan, eastern brown, coastal taipan, many-banded krait, peninsula tiger, saw-scaled viper, black mamba, western tiger, eastern coral, Philippine cobra

CHAPTER 16: MONSTERS

The monsters listed in this chapter are collected from myths, stories, and legends from all around the world. Every effort has been made to include only creatures that are public domain and to avoid monsters from copyrighted sources.

MONSTER CATEGORIES/TERMS: aberration, alien, brute, colossus, creature, enchanted, extra-terrestrial, feral, fiend, horror, hybrid, creature of legend, mutant, paranormal, reptile, sea creature, space invader, swarm; See also category names that follow

> **USAGE NOTE:** Animals frequently serve as monsters in fiction and games. Mundane animals are listed in the chapter Animals and Creatures and are available to be used as monsters depending upon the desires of the author. Any animal could potentially become a monster, especially in giant form, depending upon the situation.

ANIMATED: Refer to clothing, furniture, tools, and weapons; almost any object might be magically animated for any number of reasons and for any purpose.

AQUATIC: aboleth, bahamut, bunyip, ceffyl dwr, encantado, hippocampus, kappa, kelpie, kraken, merfolk, leviathan, merman/mermaid, naiad, nixie, ogopogo, selkie, swamp monster

BEAST: achaierai, ahool, ankheg, arrowhawk, axebeak, bai ze, bakeneko, barghest, basilisk, behir, bulette, Camazotz, catoplepas, centaur, Cerberus, Ceryneian hind, chimera, Chiron, cockatrice, crocotta, cu sith, dark naga, darkmantle, dragonne, dryad, ettercap, fenrir, fleshcrawler, frost worm, gilled antelope, goldhorn, gorgon, griffin, grim reaper, guardian naga, hellhound, hippocamp, hippogriff, hydra, jaculus, kelpie, kirin, lamassu, lamia, manticore, minotaur, naga, nightmare, nuckelavee, owlbear, pegasus, phase spider, pooka, purple worm, pyro-hydra, quasit, remorhaz, roper, sahuagin, sphinx, sphinx-andro, sphinx-crio, sphinx-gyno, sphinx-hiera, spirit naga, stirge, unicorn, vampire bat, vulkodlak, wendigo, white antelope, white stag, will-o'-wisp, winter wolf, worg, wyvern, yuan-ti

CONSTRUCT: automaton, bronze bull, cabeirian horses, celedones, clay guardian, galatea, golden maidens, golem (clay, flesh, glass, iron, stone), metallic dog, robot, Talos, ushabti

FAE CREATURES

GENERAL FAE: banshee, bean-nighe, boggart, bogie, bogles, brownie, buttery spirit, coblynau, dwarf, duergar, fachan, faerie, fir darrig, goblin, grig, hag, kelpie, knocker, kobold, leprechaun, nixie, nymph, pixie, phooka, redcap, satyr, spriggan, trow, wee folk, wichtlein, will o' the wisp

FAE RELATED: daoine sidhe, faerie islands, faerie glamour, faerie ring, faun, midsummer's eve, satyr, seelie court, theena shee, unseelie court, Tuatha-de-danann

WATER FAERIE: asrai, glastig, lorelei, mermaid, merrow, naiad, nixie, selkie, undine, Welsh water faerie

DEMON: aatxe, abatwa, ahpuch, aini, akvan, aldinach, ammit, asag, asura, azi-dahaka, babi, bali, bdud, bolla, bori, bunyip, changing bear maiden, cherufe, daevas, dasyus, demon of the lotus cave, djinn, dodo, domovoi, drug, duergar, eloko, fair lady, fox fairy, fujin, galla, gandarewa, gandharva, ganesha, ghoula, gong gong, guta, gwyllion, herensugue, hiranyakashipu, ho'ok, huwawa, ifrit, imdugud, incubus, isitwalangcengce, iya, jata, kaia, kalevanpojat, kappa, karina, kayeri, ke'lets, kelpie, dewanambo, khabhanda, kiliakai, kingu, kishi, kitchen fairies, kitsune, kitsune-tsuki, koschei, kulshedra, kumbhakarna, kuru-pira, lamia, leyak, liderc, lioumere, madame white, mahisha-asura, mahr, mamu, manuane, mara, mare, maruta, mbulu, merrow, mimi, mountain fairy, namarrgon, ngarara, night witch, ninimini, nisse, nixie, nuckelavee, oni, ox-demon, palis, patupairehe, pazuzu, pey, pishacha, ponaturi, psezpolnica, puck, rahu, rakshasa, ravana, red child, sebettu, shetan, skoggra, strigae, succubus, surem, tawiskaron, tengu, tiamat, tommy-knockers, udu, vodyanoi, vucub-caquix, white monkey, windigo, wood wives, yakirai, yaksas, yamantaka, yezerha-ra, yunwi-djunsti

DEVIL: abaddon, abigor, abraxus, adramelech, agares, ahriman, al, alastor, anarazel, asmodeus, astaroth, azazel,

baal, balam, beelzebub, belial, bune, croucher, devalpa, div, dybbuk, flauros, forneus, gamygn, gerasene, huldrefolk, iblis, kosk, leshii, Lilith, Lucifer, malphas, mammon, marchocias, rusalka, samael, satanchia, shaitan, shedim

> **USAGE NOTE:** The names, legends, and spellings of demons and devils vary widely depending upon the source. Research is required to understand the body of material about any particular demon or devil.

DRAGON: amber, ancient, Argonautica fleece guardian, Bibliotheca (classical Greek), black, blue, brass, bronze, copper, egg, emerald, emerald serpent, Euflamm, Fafnir Hreidmarsson, gold, gray, green, hatchling, hydra, jabberwock, Lydian, Melusine, miniature, pseudodragon, purple, red, reluctant dragon, ring dragon, ruby, sapphire, shadow, silver, skeleton, Theban, Tiamat, undead, violet, Völsunga Saga, white, young, zombie

> **USAGE NOTE:** "Jabberwocky" is the name of the poem that appears in Louis Carroll's book Through the Looking-Glass and What Alice Found There. The creature that is the subject of that poem is the Jabberwock, which has dragonlike characteristics.

ELEMENTAL: air, belker, earth, fire, lava, mud, salamander, steam, stone, water

EXTRAPLANAR: barghest, couatl, devourer, djinni, genie, night hag, imp, ghost naga, nightmare, salamander, shadow mastiff, tavis wyrm

GIANTS

> **USAGE NOTES:** Virtually any creature can be designed in giant form, from an amoeba to a great blue whale. A plausible rationale for their existence is not always needed; nature is capable of some impressive extremes.

GIANT CREATURES: ant, eagle, frog, leech, lizard, lynx, octopus, otter, rat, spider, squid, tick, toad

GIANTS OF LEGEND: Aloadae, Antaeus, Argus Panoptes, Cacus, Echidnades, elder cyclopes, Gegenees, Geryon, Hekatonkheires, Laestrygonians, Orion, Typhon

GIANT HUMANOIDS: cloud, fire, ettin, frost, hill, hundred-handed-ones, minotaur, mountain, ogre, ogre mage, roc, stone, storm, titan, troll

FLYING CREATURES: alkonost, bennu, berunda, birds of Ares, caladrius, Caucasian eagle, cetan, chamrosh, cinnamon bird, devil bird, Ethiopian pegasoi, feng huang, gamayun, griffin, harpy, hippalektryon, Odin's raven, owlman, phoenix, roc, Stymphalian birds, tengu, thunderbird, vermilion bird, Zeus's eagle

HUMANOID: bugbear, gargoyle, genie, goblin, gorgon, green hag, hag, harpy, kobold, lizardman, lizard folk, locathah, Medusa, orc, rakshasa, troglodyte, troll, wolfman

> **USAGE NOTE:** In Greek mythology, Medusa was the name of the female creature with snakes for hair who was capable of turning victims to stone. The term gorgon describes her race.

INSECTOID: Anansi, Arachne, Khepri, myrmecoleon, myrmidon, scorpion man

LYCANTHROPE: loup garou, werebear, wereboar, werepanther, werepython, wererat, wereraven, weretiger, werewolf

USAGE NOTE: Lycanthropy is generally considered to be a fictitious disease transmitted through the bite of an infected individual. The victim suffers an unwilling transformation into an animal form, usually triggered by the full moon. The most common forms of lycanthropy in fiction and movies are canines and felines, but other creatures have also been adapted to lycanthropy, including pigs, pythons, rats, and ravens. The nature of lycanthropy varies widely in literature; in some cases, transformation can occur on demand, and in some lore, the individual retains memory and thought processes while transformed.

MYTHICAL CREATURES AND MONSTERS: abominable snowman, amphisbaena snake, Beast of Bray Road, Bigfoot, Cadmus snake, Calydonian boar, Charybdis, Chiron centaur, crommyonian sow, el chupacabra, Frankenstein monster, Gamera, gill-man, Godzilla, jackalope, Jersey Devil, kraken, Loch Ness monster, Mothra, mummy, Nagraj King of Snakes, Nessie, Questing Beast, Sasquatch, satyr, Scylla, siren, sphinx, ogopogo, Telchines, yeti

USAGE NOTE: The study of creatures that have not yet been proven to exist is cryptozoology.

FROM THE TWELVE LABORS OF HERCULES: Cereberus hound, Ceryneian hind, Cretan bull, Erymanthian boar, Geryon, Hesperides, Lernaean hydra, Mares of Diomedes, Nemean lion, Stymphalian birds

PLANT: assassin vine, shambling mound, strangling vine, treant, Venus fly trap

OOZE: acidic ooze, blob, cave pudding, jelly, slime

SHAPECHANGER: changeling, doppelganger, lamia, nagual, shen, skinwalker, spriggan, tanuki, tengu

UNDEAD: apparition, banshee, bodak, ghast, ghost, ghoul, lich, mummy, phantasm, phasma, phantom, shade, shadow, skeleton, specter, spirit, vampire, wight, wraith, zombie

MONSTER LAIRS AND LOCATIONS

USAGE NOTE: The list that follows offers suggested encounter locations or habitats for a variety of creatures and antagonists. Many of these suggestions are appropriate for numerous creatures. A "mix and match" approach is advised to custom tailor an appropriate setting; for example, an abandoned mine is listed for devil, but dozens of other creatures might inhabit an abandoned mine. Likewise, a devil could dwell almost anywhere. This list is not intended to limit, but to serve as an idea generator for habitat or encounter design.

AIR ELEMENTAL: cliff top, cloud castle, cumulus tower, sky hut, summoning circle

ANKYLOSAURIA: grassland, moor, oil bog, scrubland, swamp

BANSHEE: blighted forest, cliff spire, deserted mansion, orchard, ruined coach

BLACK DRAGON: cavern network, mountain cleft, overlook, swamp, valley

CENTAUR: badlands, farm field, hidden valley, oasis, thicket

DEITY, DEMIGOD: afterlife bridge, death's door, glitter caves, heaven, hell, lovers' leap, mirror lake, valley of doom, waterfall

DEVIL: abandoned mine, deserted island, fjord, glacier, volcano

DEMON: bog, dunes, summoning pentagram, ruin, stronghold

DWARF: citadel, crag, inn, shrine, smithy

ELF: bazaar, bower, forest, glen, hollow

EARTH ELEMENTAL: burial mound, coal mine, monolith, summoning circle, wizard's tower

FEY: castle garden, glade, grotto, mountaintop, ring

FIRE ELEMENTAL: lava stream, magma pool, temple of flame, volcanic vent, wizard's keep

GHOST: cursed locket, dungeon dead end, hero's grave, mystic mirror, necromancer's lab

GREEN DRAGON: creek, flooded caves, forest hatchery, hidden vale, oasis

GOBLIN: armor smithy, catacombs, combat practice field, hidden cove, mountain rift

GHOUL: cave network, crypt, sewers, swamp, tunnels

GNOME: fort, jewel mines, laboratory, labyrinth, temple

GOLD DRAGON: caravan route, cloud maze, diamond mine, fortification, mountain peak

HAG: bayou shanty, ice cave, jungle, maze complex, ruins

HALFLING: bakery, corn crib, farm field, hamlet, inn

HALF-ELF: caravan route, garden, glade, library, tower

HALF-ORC: arroyo, blockade, ravine, sepulcher, tor

KOBOLD: inlet, knob, timberland, rain forest, warren

LICH: crypt, enchanted portal, gulch, mortuary, ruined mosque

LIZARDMAN: bayou, coliseum, gully, market, tarn

MASTIFF: dales, hills, hunting grounds, moors, wasteland

NIGHT HAG: bayou, bog, boondocks, marsh, slum

OGRE: boggy glen, dark forest, quagmire, ruined villa, shaman hut

ORC: forge, moor, temple, tower, warren

PALADIN: castle, encampment, hunting party, temple, war room

PEGASUS: atoll, flying fortress, meadow, paddock, vale

RANGER: barn, bower, camp, tangle, waterway

RED DRAGON: bloodstone excavation, magma fountain, molten lair, mountain reach, volcano

SHADOW: alley, cavern, cell, haunt, rift

SHAMAN: den, hut, grotto, tree house, yurt

SILVER DRAGON: canyon, cloister, glacier, great salt marsh, waterfall

SKELETON: bayou, cove, drawbridge, steeple, shrine

SORCERER: gazebo, hillock, island, keep, mansion

STIRGE: crevasse, haunted hollow, ocean grotto, redwood nest, temple belfry

TITAN: badlands, hot springs, jungle, mountain peak, veldt

TREANT: brook, brushland, grove, raspberry patch, mountain valley

TROLL: abandoned barn, gulch, mountain pass, ruined bridge, watch tower

TROLL LORD: burial crypt, royal labyrinth, ruined castle, treasure vault, warren

TYRANNOSAURUS REX: fen, isle, peninsula, plains, swamp

UNICORN: glade, grassland, orchard, stream, waterfall

VAMPIRE: bell tower, crypt, necropolis, plantation, sarcophagus

VELOCIRAPTOR: briar patch, jungle, lakeshore, nesting grounds, pyramid of the raptor

WATER ELEMENTAL: emerald pool, enchanted fountain, lake of the sword, tide pool, village well

WEREWOLF: abandoned farm, cliff cave, hidden glade, oak grove, warlock's lair

WITCH: abyss, cliff, gorge, hut, maze

WIZARD: dungeon, fortress, haven, portal, vineyard

ZOMBIE: barracks, churchyard, loft, shed, throne room

CHAPTER 17: MAGIC

For general supplies, see Wizards's Good in the chapter Equipment and Tools.

MAGIC VOCABULARY

EFFECTS, TYPES, AND SYNONYMS: absorb, absorbed, allure, alluring, amaze, amazing, amazement, arcane, artifice, apparition, astonishing, astounding, awe, awed, awestruck, bizarre, baffle, baffling, bamboozle, beckon, beckoning, befuddle, beguile, bemuse, bespell, bewilder, bewildering, bewilderment, bizarre, blight, brainteaser, captivate, captivated, clairvoyance, clairvoyant, charm, charmed, charming, chimera, clandestine, command, confound, confuse, conjure, control, controlling, conundrum, covert, craft, creepy, cryptic, curse, daydream, delusion, divine, disenchant, disenchanted, disillusion, dominate, dream, dreaming, eerie, enigmatic, enamored, enamored, enchant, enchanted, enchantment, engross, engrossed, enigma, enmesh, enrapture, enraptured, ensnare, enthrall, enthralled, entrance, entice, enticing, entranced, entrap, entrapped, envisioning, esoteric, extrasensory, fabulous, fancy, fantasize, fantasizing, fantastic, fantasy, farsighted, fascinate, foresight, foreboding, glamour, grip, gripped, hallucination, held, hex, hidden, hiding, hoax, hypnotize, illusion, illusionary, incredible, inducement, inexplicable, influence, immerse, impenetrable, inscrutable, invoke, lure, magic, magical, manipulate, mesmerize, mesmerized, mindreading, miracle, miracles, miraculous, mirage, mysteries, mysterious, mystery, mystic, mystical, myth, mythic, mythical, necromancy, numinous, obscure, obscurity, odd, oppress, paranormal, perceptive, persuasion, phantasm, poser, prediction, prophecy, psychic, puzzle, puzzlement, puzzling, rapt, rivet, riveted, riddle, riddling, ruse, sacred, second-sighted, secret, seize, sequester, shadowy, spell, spellbound, sphinxlike, spiritual, stupefy, summon, supernatural, surreptitious, tangle, telepathic, telekinetic, tempt, temptation, trance, trick, trickery, uncanny, unexplained, unfathomable, unknowable, unknown, unnatural, unusual, unworldly, veiled, veiling, vision, weird, whimsy, wild, wish, wonder, wonderful

MAGICAL TRANSPORTATION

CREATURES: dragon, giant creatures (select a creature from the chapters Animals and Creatures or Monsters), griffin, hippogriff, mammoth, pegasus, roc, sphinx, unicorn, wyvern

DEVICES: bubble, broom, enchanted boots/shoes, enchanted cloud, flying boat, flying carpet, magical gate, magical hole, magical map, mirror, pocket ship, portal, waxed wings, wings

EFFECTS: astral travel, dancing, dimensional travel, fast movement, giant steps, flight, levitation, mist, planar travel, smoke, teleportation, tornado

USAGE NOTE: Almost any object might be imbued with the ability to provide magical transportation, from a feather or ring to a cloak or footwear. Such objects should be designed with the resources available to the creator in mind. Similarly, creatures or characters might possess an innate or magical ability such as teleportation, flight, or the ability to change into smoke. Elemental travel is the ability to travel great distances via clouds, earth, fire, lava, trees, or water (or similar objects) by stepping into a substance, such as a campfire or pool of water, and exiting via another source of fire or water.

MAGICAL OBJECTS AND SPELLS

Many genres of fiction incorporate enchanted objects. Tailoring a magical object to a specific setting requires some time and thought. Choose an object that makes sense in the setting and for the purposes of the creator. Then determine an enchantment for the object. Effects might be broad, such as repelling flying insects, or they might be specific, such as causing a tingling when a specific enemy is near. Carefully consider the intentions, capabilities, and resources of the creator when designing a magical item. A magnificent jeweled steel sword is not likely to be created by a primitive jungle tribe.

Spontaneous magical items are also possible. These might occur when an object is struck by lightning, held by a dying king, or passed down through many generations. The effects might manifest instantaneously or might develop gradually and strengthen over time.

In addition to helpful or beneficial effects, magical objects might also be imbued with curses. When designing magical objects, remember that these items might carry beneficial as well as harmful (cursed) effects, and might even carry both.

CLASSIC MAGICAL OBJECTS

TYPICAL MAGICAL OBJECTS: amulet, armor, bracer crystal ball, book, bowl, brazier, candle, cloak, dancing weapon, doll, drum, figurine, flying broom, flying carpet, genie bottle, grimoire, intelligent item, jewelry, musical instrument, pentacle, pentagram, phylactery, potion, ring, rod, scroll, singing item, staff, talking item, tome, vorpal blade, wand, weapon; See also the chapters Equipment and Tools; Combat, Armor, and Weapons; Clothing; and Legendary, Mysterious, and Mythical Items and Locations

ANIMATED ITEMS: These objects have the power to act on their own and can be designed to attack, defend, guard, spy, dance, sing, entrap, communicate, or perform any other specific purpose. They tend to be extremely rare and are sometimes imbued with intelligence. Select an appropriate item and define the specific parameters of its animation, including when and how the item is activated or deactivated.

DESIGNING MAGICAL OBJECTS

Select a weapon, item of clothing, piece of jewelry, or other object from the lists elsewhere in this book. Relate the magical effect to the object; for example, to create an item intended to confer enhanced speed, consider boots, shoes, a ring, a pin, or another small item that can be worn constantly and activated upon demand. A cloak, helmet, or shield is not a logical choice, but an argument can be made in the case of an insane wizard who created the object. As long as a plausible explanation can be made for the character designing the item, anything is possible.

DESIGNING SPELLS

Spell design is similar to object design. In theory, any spellcaster is capable of inventing a new spell. The power of the spell should relate to the ability of the caster. An apprentice wizard might be able to invent a spell to blow leaves away or repel mosquitoes, but likely isn't skilled enough to generate a tornado or block a raging dragon. Similarly, a wizard might work to build a new spell from one she already knows; a spellcaster who can repel mosquitoes might try to invent a new spell to repel bees, birds, rats, or eventually, a stampede of bison or antelope.

Spellcasters often learn spells from other casters, such a a mentor, or from a spellbook or scroll. The individual fantasy world will determine the parameters for learning and using spells; in some worlds, magic is scarce and hard-won, while in others, spellcasting is a common talent. When designing a new fantasy setting, authors must decide how prevalent and powerful magic will be.

Another idea to keep in mind is that accidents happen. A wizard who is at work designing a spell to create fireballs that rain down like hailstones is likely to have some mishaps, and should take precautions not to burn down his tower or corner of the forest. Likewise, many fictional characters have started trouble by attempting a spell beyond their power or reading from a spellbook without understanding the text. The possible plot devices are endless.

Magic doesn't have to make sense scientifically. If a wizard summons a griffin for a ride, most readers aren't worried about where the griffin comes from. Magic does need to be plausible within the confines of the setting. In a high fantasy setting, a wizard won't be able to summon a racecar. Similarly, magic needs to be balanced. Magic becomes boring if a character can perform any action with a snap of the fingers. When designing magic, limits upon the frequency and power of magic use are essential.

LIST OF POSSIBLE MAGICAL EFFECTS

A long list of possible magical effects is provided here for consideration in spells or magical items.

abjure
absorb energy
adapt to climate
adapt to surroundings
agility
aid companion
alarm
animate dead
animate object
animate statue
athletics
attraction
balance
bash
batter
befriend animal
befriend monster
befriend person
befriend undead
bind
blend into surroundings
blessing
blindness
blink to another place
blurry form
blur vision
break oath
breathe in a vacuum
breathe in poisonous environment
breathe underwater
build
call a familiar
call upon a deity
call upon spirits
call upon the fates
camouflage
cancel magic
imbue symbol
imbue with power
immunity to acid
immunity to cold
immunity to disease
immunity to electricity
immunity to heat or fire
immunity to magic
immunity to poison
implant thought
influence action
influence opinion
influence thought
inspiration
intelligence
interpret languages
intuition
invulnerability
invisibility
judgment
jumping
leadership
levitation
lightning
literacy
long life
luck (good or bad)
magic absorption
magic reading
magic resistance
magic turning
memory
mental acuity
mimic behavior
mimic individual
mind shield
miniature animal

cause coma
cause fear
cause feebleness
cause panic
cause terror
cauterize wound
chameleon color change
change appearance
change clothing
change smell
change voice
charisma
charity
charm animal
charm individual
charm monster
charm plant
charm undead
clairaudience
clairvoyance
clean
climbing
clone animal
clone object
clone person
coldness
cold resistance
cold touch
color confusion
common sense
communicate with animals
communicate with fae creatures
communicate with monsters
confusion
conjure
contingent action
control animals
control demons and devils
control dragon
control elementals
miniature item
move creature
move earth
move object
move water
move weather
necromancy
negate magic
open doors and windows
open lock
persuasion
pick pocket
piety
pilfer
poison resistance
polymorph into creature
polymorph into object
powerful punch
prayer
protection from attacks
protection from death
protection from demons and devils
protection from detection
protection from dragons
protection from elements
protection from energy
protection from evil
protection from fae creatures
protection from falling
protection from fire
protection from good
protection from insects
protection from magic
protection from mental attacks
protection from missiles
protection from monsters (usually one type)
protection from poison
protection from scrying
protection from undead
protection from weather

control fire
control lightning
control shadows
control water
control water creature
control weather
copy object
copy magical item
copy person
copy spell
corruption
counter spell
create fire
create food
create light
create mount
create object
create sound
create trap
create water
cure blindness
cure deafness
cure disease
cure evil
cure illness
cure group
cure paralysis
cure poison
cure rash
cure wound
dance
dazzling light
deafness
death
defend
deflect missiles
delayed reaction
destroy building
destroy door
destroy item
protection from wounds
pull
puncture
push
quickness
reaction time
read languages
reasoning
reduced size
regenerate limb
regenerate organ
regeneration
reflect gaze
reflect magic
reflect missile
reflect sound
remove curse
repair object
repel insects
repel monsters
repel undead
resist cold
resist dragon fear
resist fire
resist hypnosis
resist lightning
resist magic
restoration
restore limb
resurrection
secret pocket
seduce
shape change
sharpen weapon
shatter object
shield
shimmering color
silence
silent movement
siren singing

destroy lock
destroy wall
detect animal
detect demons and devils
detect elementals
detect dragon
detect evil
detect good
detect invisibility
detect magic
detect object
detect poison
detect secret
detect trap
detect treasure
detect undead
dexterity
dig
disguise
disintegration
dispel curse
dispel magic
dispel vapor
disrupt spellcasting
divination
drain life force
efficiency
elemental command
elemental communication
elemental control
elemental trap
enchant armor
enchant object
enchant missiles
enchant weapon
endurance
enhanced hearing
enhanced intelligence
enhanced vision
enlarged size

slam
slipperiness
slowness
smell
smoke form
smooth talk
snake charm
speak languages
speak with animals
speak with dead
speak with monster
speak with plants
speed
speed for creature or mount
spell storing
spider walk
spider web
stabilize victim
stamina
store knowledge
store memory
strength
stop time
suggest action
suggest thought
summon animal
summon dragon
summon elemental
summon insect swarm
summon monster
summon object
swimming
tease
telekinesis
telepathy
teleportation
teleport with accuracy
tickle
time travel
toughen skin and nails

escape
ESP
ethereal transformation
evasion
evoke
extract oath
extradimensional space
faithfulness
fake coma
fake death
find answer
find fae creatures
find path
fire hurling
fire resistance
fire summoning
flaming garment
flawless fencing
flash
flight/flying
flirt
freeze
force field
free movement
gate to astral plane
gate to elemental plane
gate to other location
gate to other time
gate to sanctuary
generate building
generate darkness
generate fog
generate food
generate fortress
generate illusion
generate maze
generate noise
generate object
generate shadows
generate smoke
transform
transform into gas
transport via clouds
transport via earth
transport via plants and trees
transport via water
trap
trap life force
trap soul
travel over ice and snow
turn curse
turn evil
turn lightning
turn missile
turn monster
turn undead
turn water
undead command
undead communication
undead trap
understanding
unhindered movement
unhindered movement in water
untrackable travel
vanish creature
vanish object
ventriloquism
vision at a distance
vision in the dark
walk on air
walk on walls and ceilings
walk on water
walk long distance
walk to other plane
wall of darkness
wall of energy
wall of fire
wall of fog
wall of ice
wall of illusion

generate snow or rain
generate storm
generate thunder or lightning
generate undead
generate wall
generate water
generate wind
genie bottle
gentle fall
glow in the dark
hand-eye coordination
healing
health (improve or worsen)
hearing
heat resistance
hidden items
hypnosis
identify object
identify magic
identify magical item
identify provenance
imbue object
wall of iron
wall of light
wall of lightning
wall of plants
wall of stone
wall of thorns
wall of weapons
wall of wind
wall of wood
war cry
war trumpets
warding
water breathing
well being
willpower
wisdom
wither creature
wither plant
wither limb
wishes
woodland travel
X-ray vision

WITCHCRAFT

USAGE NOTE: The concept of whether witchcraft is real has been debated down through the centuries. The topic of witchcraft, however, provides a broad, deep, and rich source of plot devices, behaviors, groups, and activities. The reality of whether witchcraft is real is not debated in this book; in any given story or setting, it can be as real as an author wishes to make it. The task is then to make it plausible for the situation.

WITCHCRAFT VOCABULARY: abracadabra, All Hallows' Eve, amulet, backfire, bad luck, bargain, bat, beguile, bewitch, black cat, black magic, blight, blood oath, boil, brew, broom, broomstick, cackle, candle, cape, captivate, cauldron, chant, charlatan, charm, concoct, coven, craft, crossroads, crystal ball, curse, dance, death, devil, devil's carriage, distill, divining rod, dragon, dung, enchant, enchantment, enthrall, entice, evil, evil eye, familiar, fascinate, ferment, fire, fly, forget, frog, full moon, gallows, good, good luck charm, hanging, Halloween, hell, hex, hocus pocus, hourglass, kettle, incantation, infuse, ley line, libram, lucky charm, magic circle, magician, midnight, midsummer's eve, minion, moon, moonlight, nature magic, oath, pact, pentacle, pentagram, pet, pointed hat, pointed shoes, potion, power, pox, red-hot test, relic, ring, shapeshift, sleep, solstice (summer, winter), sorcerer, sorceress, sorcery, spell, spellbook, spellcasting, talisman, toad, three witches (from Macbeth), wand, warlock, wart, water test, white magic, Wicca, Wiccan, witches' sabbath

CHAPTER 18: LEGENDARY, MYSTERIOUS, AND MYTHICAL ITEMS AND LOCATIONS

LEGENDARY/MYTHICAL LOCATIONS

AFTERLIFE/UNDERWORLD: abyss, Annwn, Arcadia, Elysium, Hades, Happy Hunting Grounds, heaven, Hel, hell, inferno, Islands of the Blessed, limbo, Mag Mell, netherworld, paradise, purgatory, Tartarus, Tir na Nog, Valhalla

FICTIONAL/MYTHOLOGICAL LOCATIONS: Agartha, Alfheim, Asgard, Biarmaland, bifrost bridge, Cockaigne, El Dorado, Garden of the Hesperides, Hyperborea, Jotunheim, Kvenland, labyrinth of Daedalus, Lemuria, Mars colony, moon colony, Mount Olympus, Mu, Muspelheim, Nysa, over the rainbow, rainbow bridge, Shambhala, Shangri-la, Utopia, Yggdrasil

REAL PLACES STEEPED IN LEGEND OR MYSTERY: Area 51, Baalbeck in Lebanon, band of holes at Pisco Valley in Chile, Bermuda Triangle, Bosnian Pyramid of the Sun, Chichen Itza, City of Cuzco, crop circles, Ed Leedskalnin's Coral Castle, Fatima, Georgia Guidestones, Göbekli Tepe, Great Pyramid at Giza, Easter Island, Kailasa Temple in India, Khajuraho Monuments in India, Kryptos sculpture at the CIA in Langley Virginia, Loch Ness, Machu Picchu, Medjugorje in Bosnia-Herzegovina, Megaliths of Carnac, Ollantaytambo in Peru, Poveglia Island in Italy, Puma Punku in Bolivia, Red Pyramid at Dashur, Sphinx, Stonehenge, Timbuktu, Tiwanaku, Ulama ball court at Nahuatl, Xanadu

SITES LOST OR UNPROVEN TO EXIST: Atlantis, Flying Dutchman, Ghenna, King Solomon's mines, Santa's village at the North Pole, sargasso sea, Tower of Babel, Ur

SEVEN WONDERS OF THE ANCIENT WORLD: Colossus of Rhodes, Great Pyramid at Giza, Hanging Gardens of Babylon, Lighthouse at Alexandria, Mausoleum of Halicarnassus, Statue of Zeus at Olympia, Temple of Artemis at Ephesus

SEVEN WONDERS OF THE INDUSTRIAL WORLD: Bell Rock Lighthouse, Brooklyn Bridge, First Transcontinental Railroad, Hoover Dam, London Sewerage System, Panama Canal, S.S. Great Eastern

SEVEN WONDERS OF THE MIDDLE AGES: Catacombs of Korn el Shoqafa, Colosseum, Great Wall of China, Hagia Sophia, Leaning Tower of Pisa, Porcelain Tower of Nanjing, Stonehenge

USAGE NOTE: Depending upon the source, the Seven Wonders of the Middle Ages sometimes substitute the Cairo Citadel, Cluny Abbey, Ely Cathedral, or the Taj Mahal.

SEVEN WONDERS OF THE MODERN WORLD: Channel Tunnel, CN Tower, Empire State Building, Golden Gate Bridge, Itaipu Dam, Delta Works/Zuidersee Works, Panama Canal

SEVEN WONDERS OF THE NATURAL WORD: Aurora (Borealis and Australis), Grand Canyon, Great Barrier Reef, Harbor of Rio de Janeiro, Mount Everest, Paricutin volcano, Victoria Falls

SEVEN WONDERS OF THE UNDERWATER WORLD: Belize Barrier Reef, Deep Sea Vents, Galapagos Islands, Great Barrier Reef, Lake Baikal, Northern Red Sea, Palau

USAGE NOTE: Some of these lists are based on popular opinion or tradition while others are based on systematic vote. Research is necessary when referencing these sites as wonders in order to understand their origins.

LEGENDARY CHARACTERS

FICTIONAL: Beowulf, Captain Ahab, Count Dracula, Dr. Frankenstein, Goldilocks, Grendl, Headless Horseman, Hester Prynne, Hansel and Gretel, Hiawatha, Icabod Crane, Jack the Giant Killer, Jane Eyre, Little Bo Peep, Little Red Riding Hood, Oliver Twist

FOLKLORE: Baba Yaga, bogey man, Blackbeard the Pirate, Bluebeard the Pirate, Green Man, Mother Nature, Mothman, Sandman, Tommy Knockers

SIR ARTHUR CONAN DOYLE: Dr. John Watson, Inspector LeStrade, Irene Adler, Mrs. Hudson, Mycroft Holmes, Professor James Moriarty, Sherlock Holmes

LEGENDARY PEOPLE PRESUMED TO BE FICTIONAL: Cúchulainn, Fionn mac Cumhaill, Hua Mulan, John Henry, Juan Bautista Cabral, Molly Pitcher, Robin Hood, Siegfried, Till Eulenspiegel, William Tell

REAL PEOPLE WITH LEGENDARY STATUS: Abraham Lincoln, Annie Oakley, Arminius, Betsy Ross, Billy the Kid, Black Hawk, Boudica, Bonnie and Clyde, Brian Boru, Caesar Augustus, Calamity Jane, Casey Jones, Che Guevara, Christopher Columbus, Cleopatra, Daniel Boone, Daniel Shays, Davy Crockett, D. B. Cooper, Dick Turpin, Doc Holliday, Florence Nightingale, Geronimo, Ghengis Khan, Gregorio Cortez, Guy Fawkes, Ishikawa Goemon, Jack the Ripper, Jesse James, Joan of Arc, John Brown, Johnny Appleseed, Joseph Cinqué, Juan Santamaria, Julius Caesar, King Herod, Kublai Khan, Lady Godiva, Mohandas Gandhi, Mike Fink, Marco Polo, Nathan Hale, Nat Turner, Ned Kelly, Nostradamus, Paul Revere, Rasputin, Rob Roy, Saint Nicholas, Samuel Steele, Sitting Bull, Spartacus, The Smith of Kochel, Tomoe Gozen, Tutankhamun, Ustym Karmaliuk, Vercingetorix, Vlad the Impaler, Wild Bill Hickok, William Wallace, Wyatt Earp

> **USAGE NOTE:** Betsy Ross is legendary, but no historical evidence exists to prove that she sewed the first American flag.

TALL TALES: Alfred Bulltop Stormalong, Babe the Blue Ox, Brer Fox, Brer Rabbit, Davy Crockett, Febold Feboldson, Joe Magarac, Koba, Paul Bunyan, Pecos Bill, Sally Ann Thunder Ann Whirlwind Crockett

TWELVE PEERS OF CHARLEMAGNE (ACCORDING TO SONG OF ROLAND): Anseis, Berengier, Engelier, Gerier, Gerin, Girard, Ivoire, Ivon, Oliver, Otton, Roland, Samson

TWELVE PEERS OF CHARLEMAGNE (ACCORDING TO THE WORKS OF BOIARDO AND ARIOSTO): Astolpho, Ferumbras, Florismart, Guy de Bourgogne, Ganelon, Malagigi, Namo, Ogier the Dane, Oliver, Orlando, Otuel, Rinaldo

> **USAGE NOTE:** The Twelve Peers were the most prominent warriors of Charlemagne's court, and the model for the archetype known as the paladin, or holy warrior. The names of the twelve differ depending upon the source text.

ARTHURIAN LEGEND

ARTHUR'S HORSES: Hengroen, Llamrei, Passelande

ARTHURIAN CHARACTERS: Bran, Camelot, Egraine, Excalibur, Green Knight, Guinevere, Huail, King Arthur, Knights of the Round Table, Lady of the Lake, Lady of Shalot, Merlin, Mordred, Morgana, Morganeuse, Morgan LeFay, Pendragon family, Uther Pendragon, Vivien

KNIGHTS OF THE ROUND TABLE: Agravain, Bagdemagus, Balan, Balin, Ban, Bedivere, Bellinore, Bors, Breunor, Cador, Calogrenant, Caradoc, Clegis, Culwych, Dagonet, Dinadan, Dodinas le Savage, Donard, Ector de Maris, Ector Ector, Elyan the White, Gaheris, Galahad, Gareth, Gawain, Geraint, Griflet le Fise de Dieu, Harry le Fise Lake, Hector de Maris, Hervis de Revel, Heylan, Kay, la Cote Mal Taile, Lamorak de Gales, Lancelot, Leodegrance, Lionel, Lohot, Lucan, Meleagant, Marhuas, Ozanna le Cure Hardy, Palamedes/Palomides, Pelleas, Pelinore Pellinor, Percival, Safir, Sagramore, Segwarides, Tor, Tristan, Uriens, Valadon, Ywain (also Yvain, Owain, Owen), Ywain the Bastard

USAGE NOTE: The spelling of many Arthurian names is inconsistent due to centuries of lore, the source language of various works of literature, and the translations of those works. Alternate spellings are feasible and worthy of consideration. The name of Arthur's horse also varies depending upon the source. Historical literary sources place the number of Knights of the Round Table anywhere from 50 to 1,600. Many more names are buried in various sources.

ARTHURIAN LOCATIONS: Camelot, Camlann, Excalibur Lake, Isle of Avalon, Lyonesse

ARTHURIAN OBJECTS: Arthur's Round Table, Goosewhite (helmet), Merlin's spellbook, Pridwen (Arthur's shield or ship, depending upon the source), sword in the stone, Wigar (Arthur's armor)

ARTHURIAN WEAPONS: Arondight (Lancelot's sword), Carnwennan (Arthur's dagger), Clarent (sword in the stone), Excalibur (bestowed by the Lady of the Lake), Fail-not (Tristan's bow), Galatine, Grail Sword, Rhongomiant/Ron (King Arthur's spear or lance)

LEGENDARY/MYTHICAL OBJECTS

ARMOR OF LEGEND: armor of Achilles, armor of Beowulf, armor of Karna, armor of Thor (girdle of might, magic belt, and iron gloves)

WEAPONS OF LEGEND: Almace (Turpin), Asi, Balisarda, Beagalltach (the Little Fury), Colada (El Cid's sword), Courtain, Crocea Mors (sword of Julius Caesar), Cronus's sickle, Death's scythe, Durandal (Roland's sword), Hauteclaire, Heaven's Will (sword of Thuan Thien), Hrunting (Beowulf), Joyeuse (Charlemagne's sword), Kladenets (Russian magic sword), Kongō (trident), Kris Empu Gadring (kris of Ken Arok), Kusanagi-no-tsurugi (sword of Susanoo), Lobera, Mimung (Wudga), Murgleis, Naegling (Beowulf), Nagelring, Nothung (Siegfried), Poseidon's Trident, Precieuse, Ruyi Jingu Bang staff, Sauvagine, Shamshir-e-Zomorrodnegar (King Solomon's emerald-studded sword), Sudarshana Chakra, sword of Atilla, sword of Peleus, Taming Sari (kriss of Hang Tuah), Tizona (El Cid's sword), Totsuka no Tsurugi (sword of Yamata no Orochi), Trishula (trident of Shiva), Vajra (staff of Indra), Zeus's thunderbolts, Zulfiqar (sword of Ali)

BOOKS OF LEGEND: black books, Black Pullet, blessed book, book of necromancy, book of shadows, book of summoning, Book of Thoth, Daoist Jade Books in Heaven, demonology, Egyptian Book of the Dead, Dragon Rouge, Golden Plates, Grand Grimoire, Grand Oracle of Heaven, Grimoirium Verum, Key of Solomon, Lesser Key of Solomon, Magia Naturalus, Mesopotamian Tablets of Destiny, Necronomicon, Of the Supreme Mysteries of Nature, Of Occult Philosophy or Of Magical Ceremonies:The Fourth Book, Petit Albert, Pseudomonarchia Daemonum, Secret Grimoire of Turiel, Sibylline Books, Sworn Book of Honorius, Testament of Solomon, The Art of Divine Magic, The Fourth Book of Occult Philosophy, The Magus, The Philosophical Merlin, The Picatrix, The Sixth and Seventh Books of Moses, Three Tomes of Occult Philosophy

USAGE NOTE: Names in italics are actual titles of published books.

USAGE NOTE: The Necronomicon is a fictitious book invented by H. P. Lovecraft and is mentioned in a number of his stories. By strict standards, it is the intellectual property of Lovecraft, but the Necronomicon has become the subject of much folklore. Research and/or permission is recommended if considering the use of this item in a work of fiction.

LEGENDARY, MYSTERIOUS, MYTHICAL, ITEMS AND LOCATIONS

BOWS: Gandiva (Arjuna's bow), Pinaka (Shiva's bow), Saranga (Vishnu's bow), Brahmastra (Brahma's bow), Discord (Apollo's bow), Heart (Cupid's bow), bow of Heracles

CELTIC SWORDS: Caladbolg, Caledfwlch, Ceard-nan Gallan, Claiomh Solais, Cruadh-Chosgarach, Cosgarach Mhor, Dyrnwyn, Fragarach, Mac an Luin, Moralltach, singing sword of Conaire Mor

CLOTHING: Babr-e Bayan (armored coat worn by Rostam), hide of the leviathan, hide of the Nemean lion (won by Heracles), Joseph's coat of many colors, magic girdle of Aphrodite, girdle of Hippolyta, Freyja's falcon cloak, Perseus's cap of darkness, seven-league boots, Talaria (winged sandals of Hermes), Tarnkappe (Sigurd's cloak of invisibility), Vidar's shoes

FOUR HALLOWS OF IRELAND: Ardagh Chalice, Claiomh Solais, Lia Fail, Spear Luin

HELMETS: Aegis, helmet of Rostam, helmet of Hades, Tarnhelm

MAGICAL/ICELANDIC STAVES: aegishjalmur, hulinhjalmur

JEWELRY: Agimat, Andvarinaut (ring of Andvari), Brisingamen (Freyja's necklace), Cleopatra's wheel, Draupnir (Odin's golden arm cuff), Kaustubha (Vishnu's divine jewel), necklace of Harmonia, necklace of the Lady of the Lake, Ring of Mudarra, Seal of Solomon

NORSE WEAPONS: Angurvadal, Balmung (Odin's sword), Dainsleif, Freyr's sword, Grid's Rod (Thor), Hofud (Heimdall's sword), Laevateinn, Mistilteinn, Mjolnir (hammer of Thor), Quern-biter, Skofnung, Tyrfing

OBJECTS: ambrosia, Apollo's lyre, bed of Helius, belt of Aphrodite, belt of Hippolyte, bone of Pelops, bone of Ullr, brazen castanets, brazen shield, caduceus (winged rod of Hermes), capstone of the Great Pyramid, chair of forgetfulness, cornucopia (horn of plenty), cup of Jamshid, dragon chariot of Medea, dragon chariot of Triptolemus, dragon's teeth, ephemeral fruits, Gleipnir (chain binding the Fenris wolf), Golden Apple of Discord, golden apples of Aphrodite, golden crown, Golden Fleece, golden goblet, golden maidens, Hlidskjalf (Odin's all-seeing throne), Maui fishhook, miniature aircraft from tomb at Saqquara, Palladium statue, Pandora's Box, philosopher's egg, philosopher's stone, Qarun Hoard, Sampo (Finnish magical mill), smoking mirror of Tezcatlipoca, staff of Tiresias, Thyrsus (scepter of Dionysus), Trojan horse, wings of Daedalus, wooden cow of Daedalus

REAL OBJECTS NOT FULLY UNDERSTOOD: ancient Egyptian airplane models, Antikythera device, Aztec calendar, Baghdad battery, Catalan atlas, Celtic Cross, crystal skull, iron pillar in the Quwwatul Mosque of Delhi, Dendera lamp, Djed, Flower of Life, Fuente Magna, Moai statues of Easter Island, Nazca lines, Olmec balls, Phaistos disk of Crete, Piri Reis map, Starchild Skull of Chihuahua, stone spheres of Costa Rica, Vimanas flying machine images, Voynich manuscript

SHIELDS: Achilles, Aegis (Zeus), Ancile (Mars), shield of El Cid, shield of Galahad, shield of Lancelot, Svalinn (Norse), shield of Ajax the Great

SHIPS: Argo, Bismarck, Carpathia, HMS Victory, Kon-Tiki, Mayflower, Nina, Noah's Ark, Pinta, Santa Maria, Titanic, U.S.S. Arizona, U.S.S. Constitution, U.S.S. Maine

SPEARS: Amenonuhoko, Ascalon (St. George) Gae Bolg (Cuchulainn), Gae Buide (yellow spear), Gae Derg red javelin, lance of Olyndicus, Luin (Lugh), Ogma's Whip, Gungnir (Odin), spear of Achilles, spears of the Valkyrie, Tonbogiri

UNIQUE SPEAR: Holy Lance, also called Spear of Destiny, also called Spear of Longinus, reputed to have pierced Jesus' side at the crucifixion

THIRTEEN TREASURES OF THE ISLAND OF BRITAIN: Dyrnwyn (the sword of Rhydderch Hael), hamper of Gwyddno Garanhir, horn of Brân Galed, chariot of Morgan Mwynfawr, halter of Clydno Eiddyn, knife of Llawfrodedd the Horseman, cauldron of Dyrnwch the Giant, whetstone of Tudwal Tudglyd, coat of Padarn Beisrudd, crock and dish of Rhygenydd Ysgolhaig, chessboard of Gwenddoleu ap Ceidio, mantle of Arthur in Cornwall, mantle of Tegau Gold-Breast, stone and ring of Eluned the Fortunate

CHAPTER 18 —

THREE SACRED IMPERIAL RELICS OF JAPAN: Kusanagi (sword), Yasakani no magatama (necklace), Yata no Kagami (mirror)

VEHICLES: Argo (Argonauts' oared ship), canoe of Gluskab, canoe of Maui, flying carpet of Persian Prince Housain, Chariot of Fire driven by angels, Chariot of the Sea (Poseidon), Chariot of the Sun (Helios), Chariot of Thunder (Thor), Vitthakalai (chariot of Kali), flying throne of Kai Kavus, Naglfar (ship that will sail at the time of Ragnarok), Skioblaonir (Freyr's boat), Vimana (Sanskrit)

SECRET/MYSTICAL ORGANIZATIONS

USAGE NOTE: Hundreds of secret organizations have existed throughout history. Many began as secret societies but later became public knowledge. Some are open to the public and some by invitation only. Some are religious and some are purely secular.

The definition of religious in association with secret societies varies widely, and is dependent upon the goals of the organization itself. A Christian, Satanic, or druidic group might consider itself religious, but outside observers might not.

When referencing a secret society, extreme care is advised. Research is needed to understand the origins, goals, and workings of a society. The history of a society is also important, as well as an understanding of any progression from secret to public, especially when using a secret society in historical context.

GENERAL LIST: A^A^, Ancient and Mystical Order Rosae Crucis (also called Rosicrucian Order), Bilderberg Group, Builders of the Adytum, Carbonari, Cultus Sabbati, Eastern Star, Fraternitas Rosae Crucis, Fraternitas Rosicruciana Antiqua, Fraternitas Saturni, Fraternity of the Inner Light, Freemasons, FUDOFSI, FUDOSI, Hashshashin (Order of Assassins), Hermetic Order of the Golden Dawn, Illuminates of Thanateros, Illuminati, Knights Templar, Ku Klux Klan, Men in Black, Ophite Cultus Satanas, Order of the Golden and Rosy Cross, Order of the Temple of the Rosy Cross, Ordo Aurum Solis, Ordo Templi Orientis, Rosicrucian Order Crotona Fellowship, Sangreal Sodality, Scottish Rite, Servants of the Light, Skull and Bones, Societas Rosicruciana, Society of the Horseman's Word, Solar Lodge, Temple of Set, The Black Hand, The Knights of the Golden Circle, The Sons of Liberty, The Thule Society, Thee Temple ov Psychick Youth, Theosophical Society, Typhonian Order

NOTEWORTHY EVENTS

MYSTERIOUS OCCURRENCES: aurora borealis, Paulding lights, St. Elmo's fire, Tunguska blast

LEGENDARY EVENTS: assassination of Kennedy, assassination of Lincoln, birth of Jesus, bombing of Pearl Harbor, Chicago fire of 1871, explosion of space shuttle Challenger, Green Bay Packers winning first Super Bowl in 1967, Hindenberg disaster, loss of space shuttle Columbia, lunar landing, Peshtigo fire of 1871, San Francisco earthquake of 1906, September 11, sinking of Andria Doria, sinking of Titanic, stock market crash of 1929, Woodstock

FAMOUS DISAPPEARANCES: aircraft in the Bermuda Triangle, Amelia Earhart, D. B. Cooper, Glenn Miller, Jimmy Hoffa, lost colony of Roanoke, Percy Fawcett, passengers of ship Mary Celeste

CHAPTER 19 — SYMBOLOGY & SYMBOLIC OBJECTS AND PLACES

CLASSIC HERALDRY

USAGE NOTE: The main part of the design is the escutcheon or shield.

CADENCY MARK: label, crescent, molet, martlet, annulet, fleur-de-lis, rose, cross moline, octofoil/double quatrefoil

USAGE NOTE: Cadency marks identify the birth order of the bearer; in this list, the marks are in order from the first to the ninth son.

CHARGES: beast, bird, cross, crown, chaplet, chapeaux, fish, helmet, human, insect, military item, monster, nautical, ordinary, plant, reptile, roundel, tree, weapon

USAGE NOTE: Any animal is possible as a heraldic charge, but some are historically popular and thus more "authentic." When using heraldry, consider the time period and level of historical accuracy desired.

COLORS/TINCTURES: argent (silver), azure (blue), gules (red), or (gold), purpure (purple), sable (black), vert (green)

ELEMENTS: compartment, crest, crown, ground, helm, insignia, mantle, motto, shield, supporter, torse

FUR: ermine, potent, vair

PARTITIONS: per bend, per bend sinister, per chevron, per cross, per fess, per pale, per pall, per pall reversed, per quarterly, per saltire

PARTITION DIMINUTIVES: barry, barry nebuly, bendy, chevronelly, paly

PARTITION LINES: dancette, dovetailed, embattled, engrailed, fleury-counterfleury, indented, invecked, nebuly, potente, raguly, rayonne, wavy

PATTERNS: bezants, billette, castles, crusilly, gutte, lions rampant, nails, roses, seme de lis

POSTURE

AIR CREATURES: addorsed, affronty, close, displayed, migrant, pious, prideful, rising volant, statant, striking, trussing, vigilant, volant

HEADS: cabossed, couped, couped close, erased

LAND CREATURES: couchant, dormant, passant, rampant, salient, sejant, sejant affront, sejant erect, statant

MONSTERS: bicapitated, bicorporate, sea, tricorporate, winged

MULTIPLE FIGURES: addorsed, combattant, caparisoned/barded, counter-passant, counter-salient, membered, pinioned/winged, respectant, sustaining

REPTILES: coiled erect, erect, glissant, nowed, ondoyant

SEA CREATURES: embowed, erect, haurient, naiant, urinant

SPECIAL BODY FEATURE: alerion, armed, attired, barbed, combed, crested, crined, dented, dis-

armed, double-queued, finned, flammant, gorged, habited, hooded, hoofed, horned, incensed, jelloped, langued, maned, pizzled, orbed, queued, queue-forche, sexed, tufted, unguled, vested, vorant, vulned

SPECIAL POSTURE: brandishing object, coward, guardant, maintaining object, nowed, regardant, vulning

SYMBOLIC ITEMS

ANIMALS WITH SYMBOLIC MEANING: albatross, ape, bat, bear, beaver, bee, beetle, bison, bull, butterfly, camel, cat, cicada, cougar, cow, coyote, crab, crane, cricket, crow, dog, dolphin, donkey, dove, duck, eagle, fish, fox, frog, goat, hare, hoopoe, horse, hummingbird, hyena, jaguar, kingfisher, lamb, lapwing, lion, magpie, monkey, moose, moth, mouse, ostrich, owl, panther, peacock, pig, porpoise, rabbit, rat, raven, rooster, salmon, sand dollar, scarab, scorpion, serpent, snail, sparrow, spider, stag, stork, swallow, swan, tiger, tortoise, turkey, turtle, vulture, whale, wolf, woodpecker, wren

APHRODISIACS: almond, anise, apple, asafetida, avocado, banana, champagne, cherry, chocolate, cinnamon, clove, coriander, fennel, fig, ginger, ginseng, honey, mint, oyster, raspberry, rum, strawberry, tomato, wine

USAGE NOTE: Scientists generally state that aphrodisiacs—a food or substance that increases desire or the libido—do not exist. The concept of an aphrodisiac is widely accepted, however, and may hold true in individual cases. Depending upon the setting, the mention of aphrodisiacs may seem perfectly plausible and could occur in the form of almost any food or beverage.

CHARACTERS WITH SYMBOLIC MEANING: Easter Bunny, Father Christmas, Father Time, New Year's baby, New Year's old timer, Santa Claus, Tooth Fairy

FANTASY CREATURES WITH SYMBOLIC MEANING: angel, banshee, centaur, demon, double-headed eagle, dragon, fairy, ghost, goblin, griffin, harpy, incubus, mermaid, nymph, phoenix, satyr, siren, sphinx, succubus, unicorn, vampire, werewolf, zombie

FIGURES ASSOCIATED WITH SYMBOLS: arc, arrow (branching, diagonal, down, double-ended, left, right, starburst, up), blank space, circle, cross, dot, eye, line (diagonal, horizontal, vertical, wavy), lozenge, moon, oval, segment, square, star, stick figure, sun, triangle, zigzag

PLANTS WITH SYMBOLIC MEANING: anemone, angel's trumpet, aquilegia, basil, belladonna, broom shrub, camellia, Christmas rose, chrysanthemum, clover, daisy, dandelion, Easter lily, garlic, ginseng, grape, grass, hemlock, hemp, holly, hyssop, ivy, juniper, lily, lotus, mandrake, mistletoe, nettle, orchid, pansy, parsley, passion flower, peyote, poinsettia, poppy, rose, rosemary, saffron, sage, strawberry, sunflower, tea, thyme, thorns, tobacco, tomato, wormwood

USAGE NOTE: This list is a sample of plants that have widely recognized symbolism.

SYMBOLS IN MAGIC AND RELIGION: aaskouandy, abraxas, adrinka, all-seeing eye, Asclepius, akhet, akwaba, almadel, ankh, apotrope, astrum argentums seal, atheist, awen, axis mundi, Ba, baphomet, black sun, bindhu, blazing star, caduceus, Cagliostro seal, cancellarious seal, celestial mirror, Celtic knot, chaos wheel, chi roh, chnoubis, choku rei, circle of life, cicatrix, cimaruta, Cintamani jewel, claddagh, clavicle, compass, cosmogram, crescent moon and star, cross and crown, crow's foot, crux dissimulata, cycle of life, dearinth, djed, dorje, druze star, elven star, emerald tablet, endless knot, enneagram, enso, evil eye, falun gong, farohar, feather, fire wheel, fleur-de-lis, five pillars of wisdom, flower of life, fruit of life, goat of mendes, gray wolf, Gungnir, halo, hand of Fatima, hand of glory, heavenly wheel, hex, hexagram, horned shaman, horns of Odin, Ichthys wheel, IHS, indalo, infinity, irminsul, Jain, Jizo, Kabbalah, key, khanda, knot, knot of Isis, kokopeli, kundalini serpent, labarum, labrys, labyrinth, ladder, lemniscate, lingam, lion of Judah, lingam, lotus flower, Magen David, magic circle, magic knot, magic seal, man in the maze, manaia, mandala, mandorla, mankolam, mark of the beast, mark of the bustard, maze, merkabah, Mesopotamian tree of life, Messianic seal, Metatron's cube, monad, ouroboros, pax cultura, parasparopgraho jivanam, peace sign, pen-

tacle, pentagram, question mark, quintessence, Raelian star, rangoli, rebis, ringstone symbol, roma chakra, ru, sacred heart, scales, scallop shell, Scientology symbol, scythe, seal of Shamash, Seal of Solomon, seal of the Knights Templar, seal of the truth of God, secret of Hermes, seed of life, sefer yetzirah symbol, seven-pointed star, shatkona, sheela na gig, shield knot, shou, sigil of ameth, sigil of Lucifer, smaragdina tablet, solar winged disc, Solomon's knot, spiral, star and crescent, Star of David, star of lakshmi, sufi winged heart, sun sign, swastika, talisman, tattvas, tetragrammaton, tetramorphs, theosophical society symbol, tetraktys, three jewels of Buddhism, tilaka, tiratana, tomoe, triple goddess, tripod of life, triquetra, triskele, trisula, tyet, unicursal hexagram, Unification Church symbol, uraeus, urim and thummim, valknut, vesica piscis, V.I.T.R.I.O.L. (visita interiorem terrae rectifando invenies operae lapidem), voudon veves, wheel, winged disc, wings, wisdom eyes of Buddha, world axis, yab yum, yantra, yin-yang, Y of Pythagoras, zia pueblo sun

OBJECTS IN MAGIC AND RELIGION: asson, athame, athanor, bell, bell-book-and-candle, besom, boline, book, broomstick, bull roarer, bulla, calumet, candle, cauldron, cha cha, chalice, chess pieces, corn dolly, cornicello, crucifix, crystal ball, daruma, divining rod, dreamcatcher, dreidel, drilbu, fetish, ghanta, gopura, incense, japa mala, kapala, mask, maypole, medicine wheel, menorah, mezuzah, miraculous medal, mirror, Navajo sand painting, nazar, ner tamid, New Testament, Old Testament, omamori, omphalos, onniont, palad khik, palm cross, phurba, prayer flag, prayer rug, prayer stick, prayer string (lestovka, komboloi), prayer wheel, red string, rudraksha bead, scepter, Sefer Torah, shofar, staff, tablernacle, three-pronged candelabrum, thyrsus, Torah, torii, totem, totem pole, trident, troll cross, tsa tsa, vajra, voodoo doll, wand, witch ball, wreath

CROSSES: Atlantis, Brighid's, Celtic, globus cruciger, inverted, Jerusalem, Latin, Leviathan, Lorraine, Maltese, Orthodox, rose, rosy, saltire, Scientology, serpent, St. Andrew's, St. John's, St. Peter's, sun, tau, Templar

PAPAL SYMBOLS: crossed keys, fisherman's ring, papal cross, triregnum, umbraculum

FOODS WITH RELIGIOUS OR RITUAL SIGNIFICANCE: ambrosia, bitter herbs, bread, cakes, champagne, chocolate, eggs, honey, hyssop, lamb, manna, mead, milk, nectar, oil, olives, oplatek, rice, soma, unleavened bread, water, wedding cake, wine

PENNSYLVANIA DUTCH HEX SIGNS: benevolent protection of all things great and small, blessed year, change, daddy hex, double distlefink, double-headed eagle, double trinity tulips, earth blessings, eight-pointed star, fertility, heart, inspiration, natural balance, oak leaf, paradise willkom, pointed rosette, protection from evil eye, protection from witch, rosette, single distlefink, triple star

SECULAR SYMBOLS: beckoning cat, cornucopia, cosmic egg, cowrie shell, crossroads, cube, door, doorway, double happiness, egg, fasces, fu, furka, gammadion, Great Seal of the United States, green man, horseshoe, hourglass, I Ching symbols, maneki neko, manikin, manji, mehendi, olive branch, orb, orphic egg, pa kua, paisley, scepter, skull and crossbones, smiley face, swastika, world egg, zoso

SYMBOLS OF FREEMASONRY: acacia, angle of the compass, apron, ashlar, blazing star, column, compass, 47th problem of Euclid, GAOTU, hammer and chisel, Hiram Abiff, letter G, level and plumbline, point within the circle, ruler, six-pointed star, square, temple floor, trestle board, triangle

UNITED STATES DOLLAR BILL: all-seeing eye, annuity coeptus, bald eagle, crown of thirteen stars, e pluribus unum, Great Seal of the United States, novus ordo seclorum, olive branch, pyramid, thirteen arrows, thirteen olives

HOLIDAYS

NEW YEAR: auld lang syne, baby, ball drop, champagne, clock, dance, horns, kiss, midnight, noisemakers, old man, party, party hats, Times Square, toast

VALENTINE'S DAY: arrow, candles, candy, champagne, chocolate, Cupid, diamond, dinner, engagement, engagement ring, flowers, heart, heart-shaped candy box, jewelry, pink, red, romance, roses, wedding, white

ST. PATRICK'S DAY: beer, clover, Erin go Bragh, four-leaf clover, green, green beer, Ireland, Irish dancer, leprechaun, luck, pot of gold, rainbow, St. Patrick

EASTER: basket, bonnet, bunny, candy, chick, chocolate, cross, egg dye, eggs, grass, new clothes, spring, tomb

MAY DAY: dancing, flowers, May basket, May pole, ribbon

INDEPENDENCE DAY: 1776, bunting, Continental Congress, Declaration of Independence, fireworks, founding fathers, flag, George Washington, holiday, Independence Hall, John Adams, John Hancock, July 4, Liberty bell, marching band, parade, parade float, Philadelphia, picnic, red-white-and-blue, thirteen colonies, Thomas Jefferson

HALLOWEEN: All Hallows' Eve, black cat, bobbing for apples, candy, candy corn, chocolate, cobweb, coffin, corn maze, corn stalks, costume, decorations, dry leaves, full moon, ghost, ghoul, haunted hayride, haunted house, headstone, jack-o-lantern, makeup, mask, monster, orange and black, party, pillow case, pumpkin, scarecrow, spider web, spooky noises, trick-or-treat, trick-or-treat bag, vampire, witch, witch's broom, witch's hat

THANKSGIVING: cooking, cornucopia, cranberries, dinner, dressing, flowers, football, fruit, gourds, gravy, green bean casserole, horn of plenty, Mayflower, napkins, Native Americans, Pilgrims, potatoes, prayer, pumpkin pie, relatives, relish tray, stuffing, table, tablecloth, thanks, turkey, wine, whipped cream

CHRISTMAS: Advent, Advent candle, Advent wreath, angel, animals, A Visit from St. Nicholas, bell, Bethlehem, boots, bow, box, Caesar Augustus, cake, camel, candy cane, cards, carols, census, charity, Charles Dickens, chimney, church bell, church service, Clement Moore, clothing, coal, cookies, crèche, decoration, department store, dinner, doll, donkey, Ebenezer Scrooge, eggnog, elf, Father Christmas, fireplace, frankincense, frosting, fruitcake, fudge, garland, gift, gift card, gift exchange, gift wrap, gold, holly, hooks, hot chocolate, icicle, Jesse tree, Jesus, jewelry, jingle bell, King David, King Herod, King Wenceslas, kissing ball, lights, list, little drummer boy, Magi, manger, Mary and Joseph, midnight Mass, mistletoe, mittens, movies, myrrh, Nativity, naughty or nice, Nazareth, North Pole, nutcracker, Nutcracker Suite, oplatek, ornament, ox, peppermint, pine, pipe, poinsettia, post office, prayer, present, punch, red and green, red and white, red nose, red suit, reindeer, relatives, ribbon, ribbon candy, rooftop, sack, Santa Claus, secret Santa, sheep, shepherd, shopping, shopping mall, sled, sleigh, snow, snowflake, stable, star, St. Nicholas, stocking, stollen, stress, tags, tape, teddy bear, Three Kings, tree, tree skirt, tree stand, tin horn, tinsel, Tiny Tim, toys, toy soldier, travel, vacation, velvet, visitors, wise men, wooden soldier, wrapping paper, wreath, yard decorations, Yule log

COLLECTIVE SYMBOLS

THREE THEOLOGICAL VIRTUES: faith, hope, charity

THREE WISE MEN/MAGI: Balthasar, Caspar/Gaspar, Melchior

FOUR BODILY HUMORS: black bile, blood, phlegm, yellow bile

FOUR CARDINAL VIRTUES: prudence, fortitude, justice, temperance

FOUR ELEMENTS: air, earth, fire, water

FOUR EVANGELISTS OF THE BIBLE AND THEIR SYMBOLS: Matthew (angel), Mark (lion), Luke (bull), John (eagle)

FOUR HORSEMEN OF THE APOCALYPSE: conquest (white horse), death (pale horse, sometimes translated as green), famine and/or pestilence (black horse), war (red horse)

FOUR SEASONS: autumn, spring, summer, winter

FIVE ALCHEMICAL SPIRITS: copper, mercury, silver, tin, world

FIVE WISDOMS OF BUDDHISM: all-encompassing wisdom, mirrorlike wisdom, reality wisdom, wisdom of equanimity, wisdom of individuality

SEVEN DEADLY SINS: greed, gluttony, envy, lust, pride, sloth, wrath

SEVEN HOLY VIRTUES: charity, faith, fortitude, hope, justice, prudence, temperance

SEVEN GIFTS OF THE HOLY SPIRIT: counsel, fear of the Lord, fortitude, knowledge, piety, un-

derstanding, wisdom

EIGHT ASHTAMANGALA: conch shell, dharma wheel, endless knot, lotus flower, pair of golden fish, parasol, treasure vase, victory banner

EIGHT COMPASS POINTS: east, north, northeast, northwest, south, southeast, southwest, west

TEN PERFECTIONS OF BUDDHISM: determination, diligence, generosity, insight, kindness, proper conduct, renunciation, serenity, tolerance, truthfulness

TWELVE DAYS OF CHRISTMAS: twelve drummers drumming, eleven pipers piping, ten lords a-leaping, nine ladies dancing, eight maids a-milking, seven swans a-swimming, six geese a-laying, five golden rings, four calling birds, three French hens, two turtledoves, and a partridge in a pear tree

TWELVE FRUITS OF THE HOLY SPIRIT: benignity, charity, chastity, continency, faith, goodness, joy, longanimity, mildness, modesty, peace, patience

DIVINATION AND FORTUNE TELLING

GENERAL DEVICES: animal entrails, bones, cards, crystal ball, dice, divining rod, Tarot cards, tea leaves

GENERAL TECHNIQUES: astrology, I Ching, numerology, palmistry, phrenology, séance, spirit writing

CHINESE HOROSCOPE: cock/rooster, dog, dragon, goat/sheep, horse, monkey, ox, pig, rabbit, rat, snake, tiger

ZODIAC SIGNS: Aquarius (January 20–February 18), Aries (March 21–April 19), Cancer (June 21–July 22), Capricorn (December 22–January 19), Gemini (May 21–June 20), Leo (July 23–August 22), Libra (September 23–October 22), Pisces (February 19–March 20), Sagittarius (November 22–December 21), Scorpio (October 23–November 21), Taurus (April 20–May 20), Virgo (August 23–September 22)

PALM READING

HAND SHAPES: cone-shaped, mixed, pointed, spade-shaped, square

MAJOR LINES: Fame, Fate, Head, Heart, Health, Life, Luck, Marriage, Money, Sex, Spirit, Travel

MINOR LINES: Apollo, Escape, Girdle of Venus, Influence, Intuition, Ketu, Mercury, Ominous, Opposition, Rahu, Sun, Union

MOUNTS: Jupiter, Luna, Mars negative, Mars positive, Mercury, Saturn, Sun, Venus

TAROT CARDS

MINOR ARCANA: cups, pentacles, swords, wands

MAJOR ARCANA: 0–the fool, 1–the magician, 2–the high priestess, 3–the empress, 4–the emperor, 5–the hierophant, 6–the lover, 7–the chariot, 8–justice, 9–the hermit, 10–the wheel of fortune, 11–strength, 12–the hanged man, 13–death, 14–temperance, 15–the devil, 16–the tower, 17–the star, 18–the moon, 19–the sun, 20–judgment, 21–the world

SUPERSTITIONS

USAGE NOTE: Superstitions can range from full-blown obsessions to minor rituals such as knocking on wood or throwing salt over one's shoulder. The type of superstition and the severity of reaction can become interesting personality traits.

HARBINGERS OF BAD LUCK: aces and eights/dead man's hand, adder, albatross, aurora borealis, bird droppings falling on person, black beetle, black candle, black cat, broken bird house, broken mirror, broken shoe, chop sticks left on bowl, cross-eyed persons, finding a penny tails up, Friday the 13th, horseshoe with ends pointing down, night birds seen or heard during daytime, number 13, number 666, saying the number 7 at a craps table, shrunken head, single bird enters a house, single red eye symbol, snake eyes on a pair of dice, spilled milk, spilled red wine, spilled salt, thirteenth floor in hotel, woman's apron falls off

HARBINGERS/CHARMS FOR GOOD LUCK: ankh symbol, axe image, bamboo plant, bees, blue turquoise, brass key, broken chain, bubbling fountain, cat's eye marble, chimney sweep, coal, coin in new pocket, crescent moon image, dreamcatcher netting, Egyptian scarab, finding a penny heads up, four-leaf clover, guardian angel symbol, hematite sphere, horseshoe, jade turtle carving, Japanese cat, Kachina doll, ladybug, lightning bolt image, magnet , mini dagger, North star, number 7, rabbit's foot, rainbow, red coral, sapphire, silver dime, spider on a wedding dress, stray eyelash, tiger, tiny pouch of sugar, white heather flowers, white tiger carving, wishbone, wishing well, wooden mermaid figurehead on ship

ITEMS WITH HEALING PROPERTIES: adder's tongue fern, apple, ash tree, aspen tree, betony, brambles, cobweb, cork, frog, hangman's rope, hawthorn, lettuce, mandrake, nettle, onion, peony, poplar, poppy, posthumously born child, potato, salt pork rubbed on a wart, snails, urine

USAGE NOTE: These are only superstitions; do not attempt to test any of these remedies.

OBJECTS/ACTIVITIES CONNECTED TO LORE: apple, apron, ashes, Baptism, barren ground, bat, bear, bee, beetle, Bible, birds, birthmark, birthstone, blackberries, blacksmith, blood, boasting, bones, bread, bridge, broken objects, broom, burial, butter, butterflies, calf, candle, carrot, cat, cattle, caul, celandine, chair, chalice, chicory, child's first events, childbirth, Childermas, clocks, clothing, corpse, dog, earth, eggs, eggshells, engagement ring, eyes, fern, fingernails, fingers, fish, front door, gloves, graves, hair, hearth, hen, horse, itching, lamb, laundry, moon, names, nightshade, numbers, rook, rooster, rue, salt, scissors, sex of an unborn baby, shoes, stockings, sweeping, time of birth, toad

OBJECTS THAT OFFER PROTECTION: adder stone, bay tree, birch tree, catching falling leaves, charm wand, church bells, clover, coral, hawthorn, hazel, horseshoe, juniper, mistletoe, mugwort, nail, nettle, spitting, St. John's wort, stonecrop

PRACTICES THAT ATTRACT BAD LUCK: black cat crossing one's path, break a mirror, cross a hare's path, cut down an oak tree, getting into bed on one side and getting up on the other, harming ants, bees, beetles, martins, or robins, open an umbrella in the house, telling one's age, turning a bed on Sunday or Friday, walk under a ladder

PRACTICES/OBJECTS TO ATTRACT GOOD LUCK: apple wassailing, ash tree leaves, decorate with holly and ivy, greet a chimney sweep, plant myrtle, throw confetti/rice, touch a sailor's collar; See a pin and pick it up, all the day you'll have good luck; see a pin and let it lie, bad luck you'll have all day. (Alternate: penny)

PRACTICES TO PREDICT THE FUTURE

A long apple peel thrown over the shoulder will form the shape of the first initial of a person's future spouse.

Make a dumb-cake and dream of future spouse.

Scratch the names of suitors onto onions and store away; the first to sprout will propose marriage.

Sleep with wedding cake under the pillow to dream of future spouse.

The position of a mole on the body reveals personality traits.

Throw hempseed over the shoulder at midnight to see future husband.

Monday's Child Rhyme

Monday's child is fair of face,
Tuesday's child is full of grace,
Wednesday's child is full of woe,
Thursday's child has far to go,
Friday's child is loving and giving,
Saturday's child works hard for a living,
And the child born on the Sabbath day
Is fair and wise and good and gay.

Symbolic Wedding Anniversary Gifts

Year	Traditional	Modern
1st	paper	clocks
2nd	cotton	china
3rd	leather	crystal
4th	fruit, flowers	appliances
5th	wood	silverware
6th	candy, iron	wood
7th	wool, copper	desk set
8th	bronze, pottery	linen, lace
9th	potter, willow	leather
10th	tin, aluminum	diamond jewelry
11th	steel	jewelry
12th	silk, linen	pearls
13th	lace	textiles
14th	ivory	gold
15th	crystal	watches
16th		silver holloware
17th		furniture
18th		porcelain
19th		bronze
20th	china	platinum
21st		brass, nickel
22nd		copper
23rd		silver
24th		musical instruments
25th	silver	silver
30th	pearl	diamond
35th	coral	jade
40th	ruby	ruby
45th	sapphire	sapphire
50th	gold	gold
55th	emerald	emerald
60th	yellow diamond	diamond
65th		star sapphire
70th	platinum	platinum
75th	diamond, gold	diamond, gold
80th		diamond, pearl

CHAPTER 20: DESCRIPTIVE TERMS

A thesaurus wouldn't be a thesaurus without synonyms for ordinary common words. This chapter offers alternatives to everyday adjectives, nouns, verbs, and useful categories.

ADJECTIVES

BAD: abysmal, appalling, atrocious, awful, base, calamitous, corrupt, crooked, cruel, debased, debauched, degenerate, depraved, deteriorated, dire, disastrous, dishonest, disintegrated, dismal, dissipated, dreadful, evil, fraudulent, frightful, ghastly, grave, grim, horrible, horrific, horrifying, immoral, inexcusable, malevolent, malicious, merciless, nasty, noisome, ominous, perverted, ruthless, scandalous, severe, shameless, shocking, sinful, sullied, terrible, unpleasant, unscrupulous, unspeakable, vice, wanton, wicked, worse

BEAUTIFUL: absorbing, adorable, alluring, angelic, appealing, attention grabbing, attractive, awe inspiring, awesome, babe, beguiling, breathtaking, brilliant, captivating, charismatic, charming, chic, classy, conspicuous, cute, dazzling, delectable, delicious, delightful, desirable, desired, divine, dramatic, electrifying, elegant, enthralling, enticing, entrancing, exceptional, exciting, exemplar, exhilarating, exquisite, eye catching, fabulous, fantastic, fascinating, fine, flawless, foxy, glamorous, glorious, good looking, gorgeous, handsome, heady, heavenly, hot, hunk, ideal, impressive, inspiring, intriguing, lovely, luminous, luscious, magnificent, marvelous, mesmerizing, modish, nice looking, noteworthy, outstanding, paradigm, perfect, picturesque, pleasing, pleasing to the eye, precious, pretty, prominent, radiant, remarkable, resplendent, sparkling, spectacular, spellbinding, statuesque, striking, stud, stunning, stupendous, superb, sweet, terrific, unblemished, unspoiled, wonderful, yummy

DIFFICULT: a pain, a pain in the butt, a pain in the neck, arduous, awkward, burdensome, challenging, complex, complicated, conundrum, convoluted, demanding, depraved, devious, elaborate, exigent, extended, factious, fiddly, grim, grueling, hard, hassle, incorrigible, intractable, intricate, knotty, laborious, not easy, obscure, obstinate, onerous, problematic, protracted, recalcitrant, sly, sneaky, strenuous, stubborn, testing, thorny, time-consuming, tiring, tough, tricky, trying, unmanageable, unruly, wild

EASY: a cinch, a snap, at ease, austere, basic, calm, comfortable, cool, down-to-earth, easy as one-two-three, easy as pie, effortless, laid-back, like shooting fish in a barrel, minimal, no problem, painless, piece of cake, placid, quiet, relaxed, restful, self-possessed, serene, simple, slam-dunk, soothing, still, straightforward, stress-free, tranquil, trouble-free, unadorned, uncomplicated, undemanding, unflustered, unforced, unfussy, unperturbed, unpretentious, unproblematic, unsophisticated

FAST: abrupt, accelerated, ASAP, blurring, breakneck, brief, brisk, cursory, double time, energetic, expediated, expeditious, express, fleet, flying, greased lightning, hasty, headlong, hurried, in a snap, instant, instantaneous, lickety-split, lightning fast, lightning quick, like lightning, on the double, pell-mell, peppy, posthaste, prompt, pronto, quick, quick as a jackrabbit, rapid, rushed, snappy, speedy, spirited, spry, sudden, swift, swiftly, want it done yesterday

GOOD: able, accomplished, agreeable, awesome, blameless, capable, clever, competent, consummate, decadent, decent, delightful, enjoyable, excellent, expert, fabulous, fine, first-class, first-rate, flawless, grand, great, high quality, incomparable, lovely, matchless, moral, nice, noble, obedient, pleasant, polite, premium, proficient, respectable, satisfactory, skilled, skillful, superior, superlative, talented, terrific, upright, virtuous, well brought up, well behaved, well mannered, wonderful, worthy

HEAVY: a load, arduous, bulky, burdensome, colossal, considerable, deadweight, dense, elephantine, fat, great, gross, heavyweight, immense, intense, lead-footed, loaded, mammoth, massive, onerous, severe, top-heavy, two-ton, vast, weigh a lot, weighty

LARGE: ample, big, blockbuster, boundless, broad, Brobdingnagian, bulky, capacious, chartbuster, chubby, colossal, comprehensive, considerable, copious, corpulent, enormous, epic, exorbitant, expansive, extensive, extraordinary, extravagant, far-reaching, fat, formidable, gargantuan, generous, giant, gigantic, goodly, grand, grandiose, great, heavy, hefty, herculean, heroic, high, huge, hulky, immense, imposing, jumbo, king-sized, larger than life, liberal, limitless, magnificent, majestic, major, mammoth, massive, mighty, monstrous, obese, outsized, overgrown, oversized, overweight, plump, ponderous, portly, prodigious, profuse, roomy, rotund, significant, sizeable, spacious, strapping, stupendous, substantial, superhuman, supersized, sweeping, titanic, towering, unlimited, unstinted, vast, wide

LIGHT: airy, buoyant, feathery, flimsy, fluffy, flyweight, light as air, lightweight, not heavy, thin, weightless, wispy

LOUD: bang, banging, blaring, blast, boisterous, boom, cacophony, cheer, cheering, clamorous, clanging, crack, crashing, deafening, deep, detonation, ear piercing, ear splitting, exploding, explosive, intense, loud-mouthed, noisy, piercing, raucous, roaring, rowdy, scream, screaming, shot, shrill, strident, thunderous, tumultuous, turbulent, vociferous, waking the dead, yell

NEW: advanced, avant-garde, contemporary, creative, different, extra, first of its kind, forefront, forerunner, fresh, green, ground breaking, in vogue, inexperienced, initial, innovative, latest, mint condition, modern, most recent, newborn, new-fangled, newlywed, novel, on trend, original, pioneering, pristine, prototype, recent, stylish, topical, trendy, up to date, up to the minute, vanguard

OLD: aged, ancient, antediluvian, antiquated, antique, archaic, dated, deep-rooted, defunct, distressed, elder, erstwhile, former, historic, last, long-standing, matured, obsolete, old-fashioned, outdated, out-of-date, out-of-use, passé, patinated, peaked, prehistoric, previous, primeval, primitive, primordial, redundant, ripened, seasoned, vintage, well developed; See also Elderly in the chapter Character Building

QUIET: buttoned up, can hear a pin drop, clammed up, dumb, faint, hushed, inaudible, low, low-key, muffled, muted, noiseless, peaceful, quiescent, quiet as a mouse, silent, silent as a tomb, soft, soft-spoken, soundless, speechless, still, taciturn, tight-lipped, uncommunicative, unspeaking, voiceless

SLOW: arduous, crawling, creeping, dawdling, delaying, deliberate, dozy, drawn-out, dreamy, droopy, easy, exhausted, fatigued, going backwards, gradual, half speed, imperceptible, lagging, languid, languorous, leaden, leisurely, lengthy, lethargic, lingering, listless, loitering, measured, methodical, moderate, plodding, poky, ponderous, postponing, procrastinating, prolonged, protracted, quarter speed, reluctant, sleepy, slothful, slow-moving, sluggish, snail's pace, somnolent, tardy, torpid, turtle speed, unhurried, weary

SMALL/FRAGILE: airy, atomic, dainty, delicate, diminutive, dwarf, elfin, ethereal, feeble, flimsy, frail, gossamer, inconsequential, inferior, infinitesimal, insignificant, itsy bitsy, itty bitty, junior, kid-sized, lesser, Lilliputian, little, marginal, meager, mere, microscopic, mini, miniature, minor, minuscule, minute, modest, negligible, peewee, petite, petty, pint-sized, pocket-sized, puny, scant, sheer, short, shrunken, skimpy, slight, squat, superficial, teensy, teensy weensy, teeny, teeny weeny, tiny, trifling, trivial, underdeveloped, undersized, unimportant, waiflike, wee

SMELLS: acerbic, acid, acidic, acrid, aroma, astringent, biting, bitter, bouquet, caustic, cologne, corrode, corrosion, corrosive, decay, decompose, exude, fester, film, fragrance, haze, hot, miasma, mist, molder, odor, oxidation, perfume, pungent, putrefy, putrefaction, rancid, reek, rot, scent, sharp, smog, spicy, spray, sour, spew, spurt, stale, steam, stench, stink, sweet, tang, tart, vapor, vinegary, vomit, whiff

SOUNDS: bang, bark, bawl, bay, beep, bellow, bemoan, blare, bleat, bleep, blubber, buzz, boom, cackle, call, chortle, chuckle, chirp, chirrup, clang, clank, clatter, clunk, creak, cry, drone, giggle, groan, growl, grunt, guffaw, holler, honk, hoot, howl, hum, jangle, keen, knock, laugh, moan, mutter, peep, rasp, rattle, roar, rumble, scream, screech, shriek, shout, sigh, singing, snarl, snicker, sniffle, snivel, snort, squeak, sob, swoosh, thud, toot, tweet, twitter, yell, yelp, wail, weep, whimper, whine, whisper, whoop, woof

WET: bead, bleeding, blob, blood-spattered, bloody, boggy, boil, bubble, burble, creep, damp, dampness, dewdrop, drench, dribble, drip, drool, drop, droplet, douse, emission, elixir, flood, flow, fluid, gelatinous, glob, globule, glutinous, gobbet, gooey, gore, gummy, gush, guts, exude, juice, leach, leak, leakage, liquid, liquefied, liquor, moisture, mushy, nosebleed, ooze, outflow, pus, pustule, runny, saliva, seep, seepage, slaver, slobber, squishy, soak, soft, soggy, solution, soup, spongy, spurt, stew, sticky, stream, syrupy, tacky, tear, teardrop, thick, trickle, viscous, watery, well up, wetness

UNATTRACTIVE: abhorrent, abominable, adverse, aggressive, alarming, antagonistic, atrocious, awful, bad, banged up, base, belligerent, besmirched, bleak, blemished, bloody, broken, bruised, calamitous, chilling, coarse, contaminated, contemptible, corrupted, crass, damaged, dangerous, daunting, debased, decomposed, decrepit, defiled, degraded, dented, deplorable, depraved, despicable, despoiled, deteriorating, detestable, dire, dirty, dishonored, disgusting, dismal, distasteful, distressed, dreadful, excruciating, fetid, foul, fouled, frightening, frightful, ghastly, ghoulish, grisly, gross, gruesome, harsh, hideous, homely, horrendous, horrible, horrid, hostile, ill-conceived, indecent, insufferable, intimidating, intolerable, loathsome, low, macabre, malignant, menacing, moldy, monstrous, morbid, nasty, nauseating, nerve wracking, obnox-

ious, odious, off putting, ominous, outrageous, painful, pale, pallid, poisonous, polluted, putrid, rank, repellent, repugnant, repulsive, revolting, rotten, ruined, run-down, scarred, shocking, sickening, sickly, sinister, soiled, stigma, stinking, stomach turning, sullied, tainted, threatening, ugly, unappealing, unappetizing, unattractive, unbearable, uncivilized, uncouth, unendurable, uninviting, unlikable, unpalatable, unpleasant, unsightly, unspeakable, vile, vulgar, worn, yellowed

COLORS

BLACK: charcoal, ebony, midnight black, onyx, smoky black

BROWN: beaver, bronze, burnt sienna, burnt umber, camel, chestnut, chocolate, coffee, copper, cordovan, desert sand, earth yellow, fallow, fawn, field drab, khaki, lion, liver, mahogany, ochre, raw umber, redwood, rufous, russet, rust, sand, sandy brown, seal brown, sepia, sienna, sinopia, tan, taupe, tawny, umber, wheat

BLUE: Air Force blue, Alice blue, azure, baby blue, blue cheese, blue topaz, cerulean, cobalt, cornflower, dark blue, deep sky blue, electric blue, electric indigo, federal blue, glaucous, iris, light blue, midnight blue, navy blue, periwinkle, phthalo blue, powder blue, Prussian blue, royal blue, sapphire, sky blue, steel blue, teal, true blue, turquoise, ultramarine

CYAN: aqua, aquamarine, cerulean, electric blue, mint, robin egg blue, sea green, teal, turquoise

GRAY: ash, battleship, cadet gray, cool gray, dark gray, fog, purple gray, silver, slate gray, taupe gray, wolf gray

GREEN: apple green, asparagus, bright green, chartreuse, dark olive, dark spring green, fern green, fluorescent green, forest green, grasshopper, green, green-yellow, honeydew, hunter green, jade, jungle green, kelly green, lawn green, lime, mantis, mint, mint cream, olive, olive drab, pigment green, pine green, pistachio, sea green, shamrock green, spring bud, spring green, teal, yellow-green

ORANGE: apricot, bittersweet, burnt orange, carrot orange, coral, flame, fluorescent orange, orange peel, orange-red, peach, peach-orange, peach-yellow, pumpkin, rust, safety orange, salmon, sunset, tangelo, tangerine

PINK: amaranth pink, baby pink, bubble gum pink, carnation pink, cerise, coral pink, deep pink, French rose, fuchsia, hot magenta, hot pink, lavender pink, magenta, peach, persian rose, pink, puce, rose, rose pink, salmon, shocking pink, ultra pink

PURPLE: amethyst, byzantium, cerise, eggplant, fuchsia, grape, heliotrope, indigo, lavender, lilac, orchid, pansy, plum, red-violet, thistle, violet, wisteria

RED: auburn, burgundy, cardinal, carmine, cerise, crimson, dark red, electric crimson, brick, barn red, flame, fuchsia, raspberry, red, red-violet, redwood, rose, rosewood, ruby, rust, scarlet, tomato, vermilion, wine

YELLOW: amber, antique gold, cream, daffodil, fluorescent yellow, gold, goldenrod, gold metallic, green-yellow, jonquil, lemon chiffon, lion, maize, saffron, school bus yellow, safety yellow, sunflower, sunglow, yellow ochre

WHITE: antique white, beige, blond, buff, champagne, cornsilk, cream, ecru, eggshell, floral white, ghost white, ivory, linen, magnolia, old lace, opal, pearl, seashell, snow, vanilla, white smoke

EXPLETIVES

Expletives Showing Anger or Regret: $%^&#@), *****, back off, beech/biatch/bitch, blank, blanked, blankety, blankety blank, blanking, blasted, bleep, bleeping, bloody, bloody hell, blooming, brother, crap, crud, damn, damnation, dang blasted, dang it, darn, drat, effing, farging, fecking, flipping, fluffing, frakking, freaking, fricking, frigging, fuddle duddle, funking, heck, hell, Judas Priest, mother of God, nuts, oh man, phooey, phunking, piss, poop, ruddy, shoot, shucks, son of a bitch, sons of bitches, tarnation, wretched

EXPLETIVES SHOWING DISBELIEF OR EXCITEMENT: ah, ah-ha, amazing, amen to that,

awesome, berk, blimey, Bob's your uncle, boo, boy howdy, by the dog, cool, crickey, criminy, cripes, damn fine, duck, for crying out loud, gad, gadzooks, gee, gee whiz, gee willikers, gee Wisconsin, geesh, geez, geeze, go, golly , goodness, gor (UK), gosh, great Caesar's ghost, head for the hills, hey, holy cow, holy man, holy moley, holy Moses, holy wow, hot damn, huh, jeez, Lord almighty, lordy lordy, never, no, nonsense, oh, oh my, oh my word, oh please, ouch, poppycock, really?, run, scatter, seriously?, stop, wahoo, wow, yee haw, zounds

EXPLETIVES FROM FICTION, PLAYS, OR TELEVISION: by cocke, by Saint Chicken, by the cross of the mouse foot, dren, egad, frak, frell, gadzooks, gorram, ods bodikins, shazbot, slight, struth

EMOTIONS

GENERAL EMOTIONS: abhorrence, acidity, acrimony, admire, admiration, adoration, adulation, affability, affection, aggravate, aggression, alarm, alarmed, anger, animosity, annoy, antagonism, antipathy, anxiety, anxious, apathy, appall, appreciate, apprehension, attraction, aversion, awe, belligerence, bitterness, bravery, calm, care, cherish, concern, courage, courageousness, courtesy, cowardice, crazy, daring, dedication, detestation, devotion, discourage, disgust, dislike, disparage, displease, disturb, dread, eagerness, encouraging, enrage, enthusiasm, esteem, exaltation, exasperate, fear, fearfulness, fervor, foreboding, fondness, friendliness, fright, frightened, frustrate, fury, gallantry, gentility, glorification, happiness, hate, hatred, heroism, horror, hostility, idolization, indifference, infuriate, irritation, jealousy, joy, keenness, kind, kindness, liking, loathing, love, lust, mad, madden, nerve, offend, panic, panicky, passion, phobia, piety, pleasantness, pluck, politeness, provoke, rage, rapture, resentment, respect, reverence, revulsion, repugnance, repulsion, reserve, rile, rude, scared, scorn, serenity, sharpness, shock, sorrow, sourness, spinelessness, sullenness, sweetness, terror, trepidation, upset, valor, value, vehemence, venerate, veneration, vulgar, wrath, worry, worship, zeal, zest

FORTUNATE: advantageous, auspicious, beneficial, favorable, fitting, helpful, lucky, opportune, propitious, prosperous, providential, to your advantage, well-off

HAPPY: affable, agreeable, amiable, amicable, amusing, animated, appropriate, approving, apt, assured, at ease, balanced, beside yourself, blessed, blissful, blithe, bubbly, buoyant, calm, carefree, charmed, cheerful, cheery, comfort, comfortable, complimentary, composed, confident, congenial, congruous, content, contented, contentment, cordial, cozy, delight, delighted, delightful, delirious, dynamic, ease, easy, ebullient, ecstatic, elated, enchanted, enchanting, encouraging, enjoyable, euphoric, exultant, fantastic, faultless, flattered, free from anxiety, free from care, friendly, fun-loving, genial, glad, good fun, good-humored, good-natured, gratification, gratify, gratifying, great, happy go lucky, harmonious, heartening, heavenly, high, humor, idyllic, in accord, in a state of high excitement, in good spirits, in high spirits, in rapture, in seventh heaven, jolly, jovial, joyful, jubilant, just right, just the thing, just what the doctor ordered, kind, lighthearted, likable, lively, merry, nice, not to be faulted, on cloud nine, optimistic, over the moon, overjoyed, peaceable, peaceful, picture perfect, placated, pleasant, pleased, pleasurable, positive, proud, rapturous, reassured, relaxed, relief, relieved, right, satisfied, satisfying, smiling, soothe, sparkling, spirited, suitable, sweet, thankful, thrilled, tickled pink, tranquil, triumphant, unperturbed, unspoiled, up, upbeat, uplifting, vigorous, vivacious, well balanced, wonderful

SAD: agonizing, below par, bitter, bleak, blue, brooding, bummed out, cheerless, contemptible, crestfallen, dark-minded, daunting, dejected, deplorable, depressed, depressing, desolate, despondent, difficult, dim, disappointed, disconsolate, discouraged, discouraging, disgraceful, disheartening, dismal, dismayed, dispirit, dispirited, dispiriting, distressed, distressing, doleful, dour, down in the dumps, down in the mouth, downcast, down-hearted, drab, dreary, emotional, fed up, forbidding, forlorn, forsaken, gloomy, glowering, glum, gray, grieving, grim, grim-faced, hard-faced, heartbreaking, heart-rending, hopeless, in despair, inadequate, lackluster, leaden, lethargic, lifeless, listless, low-spirited, melancholy, miserable, morose, mourn, mournful, mourning, moving, negative, ominous, painful, pathetic, pessimistic, pitiable, pitiful, poignant, regret, resentful, scowling, somber, sorrow, sorrowfulness, sour, stressful, substandard, sullen, surly, tear-jerking, touching, tragic, unbearable, unhappy, unpromising, unwelcoming, woeful, worrying, wretched

NOUNS

BEGINNING: first, first in line, front, head of the line, lead, leader, milestone, primary, scout, upfront

ENDING: conclusion, ending, final, finale, finish, last, terminal, terminate, ultimate, very last

HERO: celebrity, champ, champion, first past the post, flag-waver, fortune hunter, frontrunner, good dude, good guy, guest of honor, idol, king for a day, knight in shining armor, leading role, liberator, life saver, lord, loyalist, luminary, major player, messiah, patriot, peer of the realm, pin-up, protagonist, queen, queen for a day, redeemer, rescuer, role model, savior, stalwart, star, swashbuckler, title holder, vanquisher, victor, VIP, white hat, winner

VILLAIN: antagonist, assassin, bad guy, black hat, brute, captor, contract killer, criminal, cruel person, demolisher, destroyer, enemy, eradicator, evil doer, executioner, fiend, gangster, goon, hood, hooligan, killer, lout, mobster, murderer, Nazi, persecutor, predator, punk, ruffian, slaughterer, slayer, subjugator, thug, torturer, wicked person, witch, wrongdoer

HERO OR VILLAIN, DEPENDING UPON CIRCUMSTANCE: adversary, collaborator, competitor, conqueror, defector, deserter, double agent, hired gun, king, mole, opponent, person of interest, rival, spy, traitor, turncoat, undercover agent, unknown subject

JOURNEY: adventure, circuit, crossing, cruise, day trip, detour, excursion, expedition, exploration, flight, getaway, hike, honeymoon, jaunt, long weekend, march, mission, outing, passage, ramble, spree, stroll, tour, tramp, trek, trip, trudge, vacation, voyage, walkabout, wander

VERBS

AGREE: accept, allow, approve, authorize, bear witness, consent, endorse, okay, permit, sanction, satisfy, say aye, say yes, support, testify, tolerate

BUY: accept, achieve, acquire, add, approve, augment, attain, bargain, barter, bid, catch, collect, compensate, develop, enhance, enlarge, escalate, expand, find, fuel, gain, get, grasp, hire, improve, increase, nurture, obtain, pay, procure, purchase, raise, realize, reap, receive, remuneration, secure, seize, snatch, successfully negotiate, swell, take, take in, upgrade, win

CLEAN: bathe, brush, buff, cleanse, clear, comb, dab, declutter, decontaminate, disinfect, dry clean, dry mop, dust, filter, fluff, freshen, fumigate, iron, launder, make germ-free, make hygienic, mop, neaten, neutralize, pick up, polish, purify, organize, rake, rinse, rinse out, rub, sanitize, scour, scrub, shine, sort, spring clean, sterilize, swab, sweep, tidy, vacuum, wash, wax, weed, wipe

CLOSE/HOLD: appropriate, bar, barricade, block, bolt, bring under control, capture, chain, close up, clutch, confine, confiscate, curb, curtail, daunt, dead bolt, detain, deter, encumber, engulf, fasten, grab, grasp, hinder, hold in custody, impede, impound, imprison, incarcerate, inhibit, inter, keep, limit, lock, lock up, obstruct, overwhelm, put up the shutters, restrain, seal, secure, seize, sequester, shut, slam, snatch, stop, thwart, trap

COMMANDS: climb, come, drive, enter, exit, giddyup, go, halt, hurry, leave, move, park, stop, turn, wait, whoa

COOK: bake, blister, boil, braise, broast, brown, bubble, burn, caramelize, char, deep fry, fizz, flambé, flame, froth, fry, grill, griddle fry, gut, hard boil, harden, heat, microwave, oven roast, overheat, poach, reheat, roast, sauté, scald, scorch, simmer, singe, smolder, soft boil, steam, stew, stir fry, sweat, toast, warm up

COOKING TECHNIQUES: add, beat, blend, butcher, carve, chill, chop, combine, cool, cover, crack, cut, dice, dip, divide, drizzle, drop, dry, fold, frost, grate, ice, julienne, lace, layer, measure, mince, moisten, pack, pound, press, put through sieve, roll, salt, score, season, shape, sift, slice, spread, sprinkle, stir, strain, stuff, tie, wrap, whip

CREATE: build, coin, conceive, conjure up, construct, craft, design, devise, envisage, envision, establish, fashion, form, formulate, generate, initiate, invent, make, originate, picture, produce

EXPLORATION: See the chapter Transportation

FIX: arrange, assemble, attach, bond, build, compile, connect, construct, craft, develop, erect, fabricate, fasten, fiddle, fit, form, glue, handle, hook up, install, join, link up, make, manipulate, manufacture, mend, nail, orchestrate, organize, patch up, place, plan, position, put in, put right, put in order, raise, renovate, repair, resolve, rig, screw, secure, set up, sew, shape, staple, stick, straighten, structure, tape, tie

HARM: abuse, ache, assault, batter, beat, become rancid, blemish, blight, block, bruise, bully, bump, burn, corrode, damage, dent, destroy, deteriorate, devastate, drown, endanger, explode, hit, hurt, impair, implode, injure, kidnap, maltreat, mar, mistreat, molest, mutilate, neglect, oxidize, pillage, pinch, poison, poke, punch, rape, risk, rot, ruin, scratch, sore, spoil, starve, sting, strangle, suffocate, taint, tarnish, torture, weaken, wear, whip, withhold care, worsen, wound

KILL: abolish, annihilate, assassinate, bloodbath, bump off, butcher, contract killing, decimate, defeat, demolish, destroy, eliminate, eradicate, execute, exterminate, lay waste, mass execution, massacre, murder, obliterate, purge, put to death, ravage, raze, serial killing, slay, slaughter, snuff, stamp out, take life, waste, wipe out

LEARN: absorb, analyze, ascertain, be taught, categorize, classify, delve, detect, determine, develop, discern, discover, distinguish, experiment, expand, explore, expose, find out, gain knowledge, grow, hear, identify, investigate, perceive, pinpoint, practice, prepare, progress, realize, research, reveal, search, sense, study, uncover, understand

LOCOMOTION: See the chapter Transportation

LOVE: adore, attracted to, care for, commit, craze, dedicated, delight, desire, devoted, enjoy, fancy, faithful, feel affection, fervor, fidelity, find irresistible, fondness for, friend, infatuate, keen, kiss, like, loyal, lust, obsess, passionate, want, worship, zeal

OPEN/RELEASE: ajar, blow a hole in, boundless, breach, break down, come undone, detach, discharge, disengage, disentangle, emancipate, emit, extrude, facilitate, free, gaping, let go, let loose, liberate, open wide, pick, release, rip open, unbolt, unbound, unbutton, unchain, uncouple, undo, unfasten, unfetter, unknot, unleash, unlock, unravel, unscrew, unstitch, untangle, untie, unwrap, unyoke, work out

SOLVE: analyze, appraise, ascertain, assess, bargain, bring to light, calculate, carry out, clarify, come around, commiserate, compromise, compute, conceive, conclude, consider, decipher, decode, deduce, determine, disentangle, disprove, elucidate, estimate, evaluate, examine, experiment, explain, figure, formulate, gauge, guesstimate, hypothesize, interpret, investigate, judge, lightbulb goes on, mull over, negotiate, prove, question, reckon, reconnoiter, rendezvous, resolve, reveal, scrutinize, strategize, study, synchronize, test, theorize, think, translate, try

SPEAK: allege, answer, argue, ask, bark, bawl, bellyache, bleat, blubber, buzz, call, complain, counter, cry, declare, defy, drone, exclaim, gossip, gripe, growl, holler, howl, hum, moan, order, query, quip, reply, respond, retort, roar, shriek, screech, scream, shout, snarl, snap, snivel, sob, squeak, squeal, state, taunt, wail, weep, whimper, whisper, whine, yap, yell, yelp, yowl

USAGE NOTE: When replacing the word "said" in dialogue tags, caution is advised not to overuse alternate verbs. This can lead to slow, cluttered prose.

USAGE NOTE: In dialogue tags, care should be taken not to use verbs that do not refer to speech, such as jumped, swung, turned, or danced. Only verbs that are synonyms for speaking are appropriate in dialogue tags.

> INCORRECT: "I can't wait to go to the party!" Mary danced.
>
> CORRECT: "I can't wait to go to the party!" Mary exclaimed.

SWIMMING STROKES: See the chapter Transportation

TEACH: advance, aid, alert, assist, coach, drill, edify, educate, explain, help, instruct, lecture, mentor, school, stimulate, test, train, tutor

CHAPTER 21—STORY ELEMENTS AND TREASURE

COMMON CHARACTER ARCHETYPES: absent-minded professor, abused servant, abusive spouse, adopted child, adoptive parent, angry mob, archenemy, babysitter, blackmailed victim, blackmailer, boy next door, boy who cried wolf, bully, bumbling law enforcement, cannon fodder, caveman/woman, charlatan, child raised by wolves, child with disability, child with supernatural power, child with undiscovered magic talent, child with undiscovered skill, cleric/priest, competitor, con artist, contender, creepy child, creepy neighbor, crone, damsel in distress, dark knight, dark lady, dark lord, delicate girl with fighting prowess, divine intervention, donor, dowager, dumb athlete, dumb blond, elderly master of a craft or skill, epic hero, everyman, evil advisor, evil child, evil clown, evil law enforcement, evil robot, evil twin, fairy godmother, false hero, falsely accused person, farmer's daughter, femme fatale, folk hero, fool, forbidden friend/lover, fortuneteller, genius, gentleman thief, girl next door, grande dame, greedy person, gunfighter, hag, handsome prince, harlequin, headmaster, headmistress, healer, helpful celebrity, henchman, hermit, hero, heroine, hobo/tramp, hotshot/showoff, housebound relative, imposter, ingenue, jealous lover, jock, jungle girl/boy, kidnapped person, kind woman with lowly profession, king, knight, lady in waiting, lazy spouse/child, loner, lost soldier, lovable rogue, lovers, madman/woman, mad scientist, magical friend, masked villain, mentor, miser, mistress, monster, mysterious benefactor, nerd/geek, nice guy, noble savage, object of affection, oldest/youngest son/daughter, orphan, overbearing parent, overconfident competitor, performer, pickpocket, pirate, primitive hero, prince, princess, princess and dragon/beast, prophet, puppet, queen, religious fanatic, reluctant hero, rescuer, rogue law enforcement, romantic interest, savior, scoundrel, shaman, sidekick, slave, snake oil salesman, soldier, squire, stable boy, stepparent, stepsister/brother, stowaway, superhero, super villain, swashbuckler, toady, town drunk, tragic hero, traveling salesman, trickster, unpleasant/mean celebrity, victim, village idiot, villain, wanderer, wealthy snob, widow/widower, wise old man/woman, witch, wizard, yokel

PARANORMAL THEMES AND CONCEPTS

PARANORMAL ABILITIES: astral travel, confusion, cryokinesis, death field, de-evolution, density control, detection, domination, dual mentality, empathy, force field, genius, healing, heightened intelligence, illusion, intuition, invisibility, levitation, life leech, magnetic control, mass mind, mental blast, mental control, mental shield, mental mapping, mind blast, mind wipe, molecular disruption, out of body experience, pain transmission, phasing, photographic memory, planar travel, precognition, pyrokinesis, reflection, repulsion, telekinesis, telekinetic arm, telepathy, teleportation, temporal fugue, time manipulation, weather manipulation, will force

PARANORMAL ACTIVITY: analysis, examination, explore, exploration, ferret, haunt, haunting, hound, hunt, inquest, inquisition, inquiry, inspection, investigation, poltergeist, probe, pursuit, quest, research, scrutinize, scrutiny, séance, search, seek, stalk, study, survey, track

PARANORMAL OCCUPATIONS: ghost buster, ghost hunter, medium, paranormal researcher, psychic researcher, sensitive

PARANORMAL OCCURRENCES: apparition, bang, breeze, candles flicker, cold spot, contact, disembodied voice, door opens/closes, figure, footstep, groan, knock, levitation, missing item, moan, moving object, presence, mumble, pull, push, rattle, reflection, shadow, speck of light, spirit orb, spooked animal, tap, threat, touch, vapor, vision visit, whisper, window opens/closes

WESTERN THEMES

WESTERN PLOT DEVICES: aging gunfighter's last shootout, aliens take over western town, bad guy is secret agent, bank robbery, barbed wire blocks travel, barn dance results in fight/jealousy/marriage, barren land discovered to be valuable, bigot learns empathy for ethnic group, bison herd, cattle drive, cavalry post, Civil War begins, Civil War divides family, Civil War ends, confederate raiders attack town, crooked mayor/sheriff, dance hall girl tempts preacher, dance hall girl turns respectable, defiled Indian burial ground initiates curse, drunk becomes hero, evil railroad tries to steal land, evildoers turn good after hellish nightmare, family ranch taken by carpetbaggers, gambler cheats at cards, gold discovery, gold rush, gold/silver boom town, gun fight at the O.K. corral, gunslinger hired for task, hanging of innocent cowboy, hired gunslinger challenges duel to the death, horse race yields big loss, horse race yields big win, huge wild dog adopts fam-

ily, impoverished family receives windfall, Indian princess has romance with white man, Indian raid, Indian saves life of white man, Indians hide gold deposits, kidnapped child, marriage proposal, new gun dazzles villain, newspaper man discovers secret and fights to survive, old man becomes hero, preacher tries to convert dance hall girl, preacher turns to drink, revenge, rich land baron is villain, spoiled son commits murder and escapes consequences, stage coach robbery, starving village refused aid by rich family, stranger/angel aids desperate family, stranger/angel teaches a lesson, town is overrun by bandits/Indians/soldiers, town needs a new sheriff, train coming with goods/treasure, train coming with prisoner, train robbery, traveling preacher fakes miracles, Union and Confederate soldiers go home, white man trained by Indians, white settlers attacked by Indians, white settlers saved by Indians, wildfire, zombies rise from Boot Hill

WESTERN CLOTHING/DRESS: apron, badges, bandana, bandolier, blue jeans, bolo tie, boots, bowler hat, buckskin jacket, bustle, cape, chaps, chemise, corset, cowboy boots, cowboy hat, dance hall dress, deerskin breeches, duster, fan, floor-length skirt, fringed leather jacket, garter belt, gingham/calico dress, granny boots, great coat, gun belt, holster, homespun fabric, knee socks, knickers, large belt buckle, leather apron, neckerchief, nightshirt, ornate ladies' hat, ostrich plumes, parasol, plaid shirt, scarf, shawl, sheriff's badge, sleeve garters, sombrero, spurs, string tie, sun bonnet, Sunday dress, ten gallon hat, union suit, vest, Western shirt, white shirt with stiff collar, wool stockings

FAMOUS WESTERN LOCATIONS: Abilene, Alamo, Arizona territory, Boot Hill Graveyard, California, Carson City, Comstock Lode, Deadwood, Dodge City, Ellsworth, Fort Laramie, ghost town, Hole in the Wall, Little Bighorn, Mexican border, Oregon Trail, Rio Grande River, Salt Lake, Santa Fe Trail, Sierra Madre Mountains, Silver City, Tombstone, Virginia City

WESTERN PARAPHERNALIA/PEOPLE: Annie Oakley, bale of hay, bandit, barbed wire, Bat Masterson, Battle of the Little Bighorn, bison, Black Bart, blood brothers, boom town, bronco riding, buffalo, Buffalo Bill Cody, Buffalo Bill's Wild West Show, California Gold Rush, cattle drive, cattle herd, cattle ranch, cattlemen, Chief Crazy Horse, chuck wagon, Clanton brothers, clipper ship, Confederate States, counting coup, coup stick, covered wagon, cowboy, deputy, Doc Holliday, fort, gambler, general store, George Armstrong Custer, gold (claim, dust, mine, miner, pan, rush), gunslinger, hold-up, Hole in the Wall Gang, homestead, horse, Indian chief, Indian scout, Indian shaman, land rush, lynch mob, lynching, marshall, maverick, O.K. Corral, one-room schoolhouse, paddle wheeler, Pinkerton detective, poker, Pony Express, preacher, quick draw, range war, rifle sheath, river boat, river boat captain, rodeo, saddle, saddle blanket, saloon, saloon, saloon brawl, school marm, sharpshooter, sheep ranchers, showdown, Sitting Bull, stage coach, staking a claim, telegraph, tenderfoot, Texas Jack, tobacco, transcontinental railroad, twenty dollar gold piece, vigilante, wagon train, Wells Fargo, whisky, Wild Bill Hickok, Wyatt Earp

WESTERN WEAPONS: bow and arrow, buffalo rifle, cap and ball pistol/rifle, cavalry saber, coach gun, Colt lightning carbine, Colt peacemaker, Colt 45, derringer, French rifled cannon, Gatling gun, howitzer, knife (Bowie, clasp, flint, throwing), lance, lasso, Sharps 50 caliber rifle, shot gun, Smith & Wesson revolver, spear, tomahawk, Winchester rifle

TREASURE

COINS AND CURRENCY: clay, crown, bars, bronze, bronze shell, bullion, copper, dime, dollar, doubloon, electrum, Euro, folding money, gold, gold Doric, gold eagle, gold maple leaf, half-cent, half-dollar, iron, Krugerrand, nickel, quarter, palladium, paper money, penny, pieces of eight, platinum, silver, siglos, sovereign, steel, two bits, two-cent, twenty-cent, twenty-dollar gold piece, wooden, zinc

> **USAGE NOTE:** Coins vary widely in size, shape, and material based upon an individual culture. Currency can be designed using materials that are available or considered valuable depending on the setting. In addition to metals, currency might consist of beads, cloth, hides, iron, jade, paper, shells, silk, spices, salt, tea, wood, or other material; some of these have a historical foundation.

CHAPTER 21 —

PRECIOUS METALS: brass, bronze, copper, gold, gold leaf, gold plate, platinum, rose gold, silver, silver plate, sterling silver, titanium, white gold, yellow gold; other metals or alloys unique to a setting

GEMS AND JEWELRY

USAGE NOTE: The value of gems depends upon size, clarity, color, cut, inclusions, and rarity.

STANDARD GEMS: agate, agate geode, alexandrite, almandine garnet, amazonite, amber, amethyst, ametrine, ammolite, andalusite, andesine labradorite, apatite, aquamarine, aventurine, axinite, azotic topaz, beryl, bloodstone, boulder opal, calcite, carnelian, cassiterite, chalcedony, charoite, chocolate opal, chrome diopside, chrome tourmaline, chrysoberyl, chrysocolla, chrysoprase, citrine, clinohumite, color-change diaspore, color-change garnet, color-change sapphire, coral, danburite, demantoid garnet, dendritic agate, diamond, dumortierite quartz, emerald, epidote, fire agate, fire opal, fluorite, garnet, goshenite, grossularite garnet, hambergite, hematite, hemimorphite, hessonite garnet, howlite, idocrase, iolite, jadeite, jasper, kunzite, kyanite, labradorite, lapis lazuli, larimar, lepidolite, malachite, Mali garnet, maw-sit-sit, moonstone, morganite, mystic quartz, mystic topaz, obsidian, opal, opal doublet, orthoclase, pearl, peridot, pietersite, prehnite, pyrope garnet, quartz, quartz cat's eye, rainbow moonstone, rhodochrosite, rhodolite garnet, rose quartz, rubellite tourmaline, ruby, ruby-zoisite, rutile quartz, rutile topaz, sapphire, scapolite, seraphinite, serpentine, sillimanite cat's eye, smithsonite, smoky quartz, snowflake obsidian, sodalite, spessartite garnet, sphalerite, sphene, spinel, spodumene, strawberry quartz, sugilite, sunstone, tanzanite, tiger's eye, tiger's eye matrix, topaz, tourmaline, tsavorite garnet, turquoise, variscite, zircon

CAT'S EYE GEMS: aquamarine, andalusite, chrysoberyl, cordierite, corundum, cymophane, emerald, feldspar, fibrolite, iolite, kornerupine, quartz, rhodonite, rutile, scapolite, sillimanite, spinel, tanzanite, tourmaline, zircon

USAGE NOTE: The classic cat's eye gem is the golden brown chrysoberyl. The cat's eye effect, known as chatoyancy, is caused by parallel inclusions in the stone. Chatoyancy is possible in a number of gemstones, some of which are exceedingly rare.

STAR GEMS: aquamarine, chrysoberyl, diopside, garnet, moonstone, quartz, rose quartz, ruby, sapphire (dark blue, dark purple, gray, red), sillimanite, spinel (pink, purple), sunstone

USAGE NOTE: Star gems result from a condition that is similar to that found in cat's eye gems. Aligned needlelike inclusions create the star effect, called asterism. Value depends upon color and rarity.

GEM CUTS: baguette, bead, buff top, cabochon, cross, cross vault, cushion, emerald, French, marquise, navatte, octagon, opposed bar, oval, pear, princess, radiant, round, square, step, trapeze, triangle, trilliant, trillion

JEWELRY: accessory, adornment, anklet, armlet, badge, band, bangle, bauble, bead, bell, belt, bracelet, bracer, brooch, buckle, button, cameo, catch, chain of office, charm, chatelaine, choker, circle, circlet, clasp, clip, coat of arms, collar, collar pin, comb, corona, coronet, crest, crown, cylinder seals, cuff link, curio, decoration, device, diadem, disk, dog tags, earring, ear cuff, emblem, embroidered, great seal, keepsake, key, knickknack, knot, feather, fastener, girdle, grill, hair comb, hairpin, halo, headband, headdress, heraldic sign, honor, hook, hoop, icon, insignia, leash, locket, loop, mask, medal, medallion, memento, necklace, nimbus, nose (chain, jewel, ring, stud), orb, ornament, pendant, perfume pendant, pin, popper, ring, shell, slide, souvenir, sphere, strap, stud, symbol, talisman, tiara, tie, tie bar, tie pin, toe ring, torque, trinket, vase pin, waist chain, wreath, wristlet; See also Jewelry in the chapter Clothing

CHAPTER 22 — SCIENCE FICTION

The purpose of this chapter is not to be comprehensive, but to present a variety of concepts as reference and idea generators. Every effort has been made to present general concepts and not copyrighted material. In science fiction writing, care must be taken not to borrow proprietary terms from existing fiction, movies, or television without permission.

LITERARY CLASSIFICATIONS

SCIENCE FICTION GENRES: adventure, alternate future, alternate history, alternate universe, doomsday, erotica, graphic novel, gothic, historical, horror, humor, mystery, nanotechnology, new wave, occult, romance, science fantasy, slipstream, space opera, space supernatural, space western, superhero, weird, western

PLOT DEVICES: abnormal rate of growth, alien, alien experimentation, alien kidnapping, alien first contact, alien invasion, alternate life forms (android, cyborg, hive mind, mentally advanced/physically weak, pure mentality, replicant), anarchy, android takeover, animal control, animal swarm, animal takeover, apocalypse, artificial intelligence, bio-implants, biomedical engineering, caste system, celestial object on course for Earth, center of the earth, cloning, colonization, cross-breeding, creation of the universe, cryonics, cybernetics, dark future, discovery of God, dystopia, end of the world, eugenics, false gods, far future, futuristic weapons, galactic empire, generation ship, giant creatures/humans/insects, grandparent paradox, habitat (alien zoo, domed city, floating city, space station, underwater colony), hidden race on Earth, historical cycles repeating, horror, hostages, immortality, insect takeover, hyperspace, insatiable hunger, last person on Earth, megalomaniac, military takeover, military technology, mind interfacing, mutants, mystery, nanotechnology, natural disaster, out-of-control experiment, parallel universe, psi powers (clairvoyance, mental control, telepathy, telekinesis), predictions of the future, ransom, religion, robots, time loops, time travel, secret organizations, sex, shrinking humans, slavery, sonic weapon, space exploration, space opera, space pirates, stranded space traveler, sun burning out, terraforming, UFO, underground civilization, utopia, war monger, wormhole

GENERAL CONCEPTS

COMMON DANGERS: alien invasion, android rebellion, asteroid hitting Earth, collision, extinct bacteria/animal resurfaces, extreme cold, extreme heat, genetically altered animals turn violent, life support failure, plants take over people, radiation, robot rebellion, viral outbreak

ENERGY SOURCES/TYPES: animal powered, atomic, beta-particle, biomass, chemical, combustion, cosmic, cryogenic, electrolaser, electricity, electromagnetic, fission, fossil fuel, fusion, gamma radiation, geothermal, gravity, human powered, hydroelectric, hydrogen, ionizing, kinetic, mechanical, methane, natural gas, neutron, photon-intermediate, plasma, propane, radiation, reflected, solar, steam, tectonic, thermal, thermodynamic, ultraviolet radiation, wind

INSTALLATIONS: domed colony, floating city, Earth colony, lunar station, mining station, observation station, satellite station, solar energy collection satellite, stellar transport portal, sun station, underground city, underwater domed city, monorail mass transit

MONSTERS AND CREATURES: angel, animal with implanted weapons, android, atomic creature/human, berserk killer robot, brain-eating creatures, crazed artificial intelligence, chemically altered animal, cross-bred mad animal, demon, dimension-crossing creature, electromagnetic beast, giant human, giant bugs, intelligent animals, gelatinous animal, gene-spliced predator, giant amoeba, intelligent bacteria, intelligent slime, mind controlling creature, missing link, mutant, nano-beasts, parasites, phase creature, plasma creature, prehistoric animal, prehistoric human, radioactive creature, reptilian humanoid, robotic guardian, sentient plant, thermal creature, time traveler, wizard-like maniac, worm, zombie

OCCUPATIONS: administrator, A.I. programmer, android designer, astronaut, battle group commander, cook, drive engineer, empath, explorer, first officer, interrogator, medic, paranormal investigator, pilot, pirate, planet regulator, quantum chemist, robot technician, scientist, space station coordinator, space outpost architect, star colony planner, starship captain, starship marine, starship trooper, telepath, theorist, warp drive pilot/engineer

PHYSICAL MUTATIONS: acid secretion, ambidexterity, antennae, aromatic power, carapace, chameleon change, density control, double brain, dual organ, electrical generation, energy reflection, flight, fungicide, gas generation, gills, heat generation, heat resistance, heightened sense (agility, balance, dexterity, hearing, smell, strength, taste, touch, vision), immunity, improved metabolism, increased height, increased size, infravision, light generation, lightning rod, multiple body parts, oversized body parts, physical reflection, poison flesh, poison glands, quills, regeneration, repulsive odor, secretion, shapechanging, shortened height, sonar, sonic abilities, speech, swift movement, temperature resistance, ultravision, vampirism, webbed fingers, webbed toes, wings, X-ray vision

TRAVEL TYPES: astral, dimensional, gate, ground transportation, ley, light speed, magical, phase, portal, ship, space, spirit, stasis, teleportation, time, underwater, warp

GEAR AND VEHICLES

CLOTHING/UNIFORMS: battle armor, coveralls, diaphanous gowns, gravity boots, hazmat suit, life support suit, military dress, powered armor, radiation-proof suit, silver space suit, sun protection, space combat armor, space suit, space transport armor

DEVICES: air scrubber, artificial intelligence, artificial limb, automated medical, bioengineered medication, breathing apparatus, cloaking device, communication device, conveyor belt sidewalk/road, decoder, diagnostic medical scanner, disintegration beam, force field generator, gene repair system, holographic generator, interface, invisibility generator, regeneration technology, shrink ray, stasis pod, teleportation device, tractor beam, time travel device

ROBOTS: alien mechanical, android, animal mimic, automaton, battlebot, cleaning, clockwork mechanical, constructionbot, engineering, horticultural, humanlike, humanoid, insectoid, interpreter, maintenance, medical, nanobot, repair, security, self-reconfiguring, service, spacebot, swarmbot, telerobot, transportation, unmanned combat, warbot

VEHICLES: air board, anti-gravity sled, anti-inertia sled, asteroid miner, bathysphere, deep sea explorer, dimensional slider, fusion sleigh, hover craft, jet pack, lunar lander, lunar rover, portal scout, speeder, unmanned submarine, unmanned surface destroyer

WEAPONS: bomb (antimatter, black hole, dark matter, fusion, gamma, gauss, graviton, neutron, plasma), cannon (atomic, death ray, ion, plasma), dagger/sword (electro, energy, molecule edged, vibro), grenade (electro pulse, flash, paralysis, plasma, smart, sonic, sticky, stun), missile (antimatter, atomic, concussion, cryo, dark matter, fission, fusion, gravity, neutron, nova, planet buster, plasma, ship-killer, sun-killer, thermal), pistol or rifle (black ray, blaster, crystal, death ray, disintegration, fission, fusion, gauss, incendiary, laser, missile, needler, particle beam, plasma, protein disruptor, pulse, radiation, rail gun, slug thrower, sonic, tangier), unique (confining, cryonic, darkness generating, energy bolo, force field generator, paralyzing, stunning, torture device, vaporizing)

SPACESHIPS

SPACESHIP DRIVE SYSTEMS: antimatter, atomic, dark matter, faster-than-light, fission, fusion, gravity, hyperatomic, ion, ley, magnetic pulse, nuclear pulse propulsion, photon, plasma, psionic, quark, ramjet, reaction, rocket, solar wind, steampunk, thermal hydrogen, time, total conversion, trash conversion, uranium fueled, warp, water, wave motion

SPACESHIP SHAPES: animal, bat, bird, boat, capsule, cigar, cube, insect, irregular, oval, platform, pyramid, rocket, saucer, sphere, triangle

SPACESHIP TYPES: cargo, colony, cruise ship, deep space probe, escape pod, evacuation, explorer, generation, military (battle cruiser, battleship, carrier, cloaked scout, cruiser, destroyer, dreadnought, frigate, gunship, light cruiser, scout, shuttle, supply tender, tender, unmanned, warship), miner, private yacht, probe, space bus, spaceliner, starship, solar sail clipper, stratocruiser

CHAPTER 23: HORROR

This chapter presents a multitude of horror concepts and idea starters. Horror literature is a genre that frequently recycles common concepts and gives them a new twist; dozens of books and movies have been produced using vampires, zombies, Frankenstein's monster, aliens, deranged slashers, and so on. When writing in these genres, authors need to ask themselves what makes their material original or unique, and what new challenges face the protagonists or what clever solutions the protagonists can apply to entertain the audience.

Moments of fright can be incorporated into almost any fiction without turning the story into a horror product. Frightful moments help keep a reader's interest, build suspense, and add variety when used appropriately. Many memorable scenes have been written about the solitary damsel who hears a noise that's only the wind or a small animal, or about the concealed heroes who fear they have been discovered but a passerby fails to notice them. Often, moments of fright can provide comic relief.

True horror is different from fright. True horror challenges an audience's concept of reality or normalcy. In the real world, serial killers, monster aliens, zombies, and vampires are not supposed to exist. (We know that serial killers do exist, although they oppose our concepts of sanity and civilized society. And the jury is still out regarding the monster aliens.) To create true horror, an author must conceive a situation that challenges reality. A group of kids exploring an abandoned house can be suspenseful and frightening, but in order to achieve horror (if that's the author's intent), something bigger and deeper must be involved: the gateway to hell, a witches' coven, a mad scientist, a cannibal, and so on. Understanding the difference between fright and horror will help an author craft a plot and build appropriate scenes. An author must also have a sense of the story's purpose—whether a light, spooky, suspenseful adventure for pre-teens, or a bloodcurdling tale of a psychotic torturer for cast-iron adults.

An important horror device deserves discussion: isolation. Many books and movies use isolation to build horror. When the heroes are on a spaceship and can't expect help to arrive for several weeks, or the family is holed up in a snowbound hotel, or the explorers are on an island and the ferry won't be back until morning, the audience feels the isolation and knows that the heroes must fend for themselves. This immediately instills a degree of suspense and danger, and many authors use isolation to great advantage.

All authors hear the advice show, don't tell. It means that we don't merely describe an old house as spooky—we depict it as a house so ancient and sinister that it seemed to stare back at passersby. As an element of showing, good authors remember to make use of the five senses, and this is especially important in horror writing. Spooky or horrific sights are a good start, but what really brings a scene to life are the dripping or rustling sounds, the smells of rot or a stale tomb, the brush of a spider web or tremor of a footstep, or more rarely, the taste of bile or bitter air.

Finally, note that horror crosses paths with many other genres, including fantasy, romance, and science fiction. Horror doesn't have to be a slasher film or the genius serial killer cannibal—it can be a subtle moment to give the reader a chill, serve as a distraction, or deepen a developing mystery.

LITERARY CLASSIFICATIONS

HORROR GENRES: alien meddling, alternate Earth, alternate future, alternate history, alternate universe, ancient creature/civilization brought back to life, animal/insect swarm, demons, disaster traps people in office building/cruise ship, discovery of unknown creature/civilization, doomsday, dystopian society, erotica, escaped criminal/lunatic, exorcism, ghosts/spirits/haunting, giant creatures, gothic, graphic novel, historical, human sacrifice, humor, large scale disaster, man-made disaster, medical epidemic, medical experimentation, mystery, natural disaster, object/doll brought to life, occult, paranormal events, possession, religious prophecy comes true, romance, romantic horror, science fantasy, science fiction, serial killer, shipwreck, slasher, steampunk, teenagers trapped and stalked, undead/zombie uprising, vampires, Victorian horror, war crimes/atrocities, western, witchcraft

HORROR PLOT DEVICES: aliens, aliens regard human race as food source, ancient curse, ancient gods threaten humanity, ancient monster released during mining operation, ancient society drinks blood of virgins to remain young, ancient spell, ancient/alien technology activates and threatens destruction, android turns on creator, androids, asteroid on collision course with Earth, bad weather isolates campers/travelers/residents, beautiful

woman/man is really dead, beautiful young ghost seduces man/woman, body is switched with another person, boyfriend/girlfriend kills parents of beloved, car/tools/objects/doll animate after lightning strike, child witnesses crimes and is not believed, computer tricks users into killing, computer turns evil and murderous, conspiracy forces residents out of town, crazy recluse stalks/torments/kills neighbors, criminals steal/tamper with dangerous item, cursed item causes grief, deathtrap house kills all visitors, deranged killer stalks/attacks campground, destruction of Earth looms in seven days, dinosaurs brought back to life, disease/rot/transformation of body, Egyptian tomb, elderly persons find source of youth, evil robot, evil/insane/possessed child, experimental animals turn on scientist, explorers encounter cannibals, explorers find lost race, explorers find magical object, extinct creature emerges from isolation and causes death/destruction, factory emissions cause death/rot/wasting disease, fairy colony lures innocent victim, fake psychic assaulted by actual spirits, family curse, food supply tainted, Frankenstein monster, gateway to hell in basement of home, ghost ship, ghost wants object/body part back, ghostly army rises to fight war, ghosts of large-scale disaster rise up and wreak havoc, giant insects/vermin attack, global weather turns extremely hot/cold/wet/dry, gods require a sacrifice, gold/silver/gem discovery is guarded/haunted by evil creature, haunted hotel, haunted house lashes out at new tenants, helpful stranger turns out to be evil, homeless people preyed upon by murderer/ghouls/vampires, homeless person witnesses crimes and is ignored, hotel owner traps guests, house contains gate to hell/another place, house is intelligent/sentient, house swallows up children, house/apartment traps souls of all who live/die there, immortality, industry knowingly pollutes water/air/ground, inheritance of strange object/book, intelligent insects/creatures, kidnapping, last person on Earth, malicious fairies/fae torment country home, mind control, mind reader suffers side effects, mummy rises, mutant plants attack, mysterious invitation leads to frightening ordeal, mysterious liquid or gas, mysterious neighbor, neighbor is a vampire, nuclear disaster, object changes personality, object drains life force, old document proves person guilty of murder, ordinary tenant harbors evil secret identity, people invited to remote place, people invited to spend night in haunted house, person buried alive, person makes deal with devil, person purposely gives lovers horrible disease, person transforms into monster, person trapped without hope of rescue, person/child vanishes without a trace, pet is vampire, pets attack, pets turn to zombies, possessed scientist, possessed weapon controls wielder, problem must be solved before sunrise, property tormented by evil force after construction/renovation, psychic powers, radiation leak, relative cares for body of dead person, relatives/loved ones injured/killed/trapped, revenge, rich recluse plays deadly game, school bullies tormented by their victim, school teacher in evil plot to perform human sacrifice, science experiment makes intelligent animals, small town performs annual human sacrifice, space travelers assaulted by horrific creature, spell needed to reverse evil magic, spirits rise from graves, spoiled daughter/son tortures parents, spooky carnival ride turns deadly, stalker, stolen religious object lashes back, storm harbors evil entity, stranded after car breaks down, strange antique harbors evil force, student bitten by vampire, super-intelligent being regards humans as vermin, supernatural powers used to terrorize others, teacher is vampire, theft of body parts, threat/villain is eliminated but bigger threat/villain emerges, time traveler meddles with history, troubled student discovers evil book, trusted person turns out to be criminal, underwater monsters/giant creatures, unexpected aid from librarian/neighbor/stranger, vacation turns disastrous, vampire, victims must escape before time runs out, villain steals life force from victims, virgin sacrifice, wager creates deadly challenge, water supply imparts fatal disease, wishes are granted with dire consequences, young people suddenly age and die, zombie uprising threatens city

HORROR VOCABULARY: alarm, alert, angst-ridden, appalling, apathetic, apprehension, apprehensive, atrocious, averse, awful, bashful, blood, blooded, bloody, blurred, browbeaten, callous, canny, careful, careless, cautious, chary, cold, cold-blooded, corrupt, cowed, coy, crafty, creepy, crooked, cruel, cunning, cynical, danger, dangerous, dastardly, dead, deadly, deceitful, dejected, demoralized, depressed, derisive, devious, diffident, dire, disbelieving, discouraged, dismal, dismayed, disquiet, distasteful, distress, distrustful, doubt, doubtful, downcast, downhearted, drained, dread, dubious, eerie, evasive, exhausted, exploited, faint-hearted, fatal, fatigued, fear, fearful, fright, frightful, forbidding, foreboding, foreswear, forewarn, formless, ghastly, ghostly, gloomy, grave, grim, grisly, gorge, gouge, gouged, gruesome, guarded, guilty, halfhearted, hair-raising, harsh, hazy, heartless, horrible, horrendous, horrific, horror, humorless, iffy, incredulous, indifferent, indisposed, inhuman, intimidate, intolerable, lethal, leery, lifeless, loath, lukewarm, mean, mistrustful, mock, mocking, monstrous, mortified, nervous, nightmare, noxious, opposed, painful, panic, panic-stricken, pang, panicky, passive, perilous, petrified, pitiless, poisonous, quake, quaking, qualm, quiet, quivering, rash, raw, reckless, reclusive, reluctant, remote, restrained, reticent, ruthless, scared, scary, scheming, serious, shady, shaky, shattered, shielded, shivering, shock, shocking, shrewd, shuddering, shy, sickening, skeptical, spineless, spine-chilling, startle, subdued, subjugated, subtle, suspect, suspicious, tentative, terrible, terror, timid, timorous, tired, trembling, trepidation, toxic, undecided, underhanded, unearthly, unease, unenthusiastic, unfeeling, unresponsive, unstable, unwilling, vicious, vigilant, warn, wary, watchful, weary, withdrawn, worried

GENERAL CONCEPTS

COMMON DANGERS: aliens, army misunderstands threat, basement/cellar, bug swarm, cursed car/motorcycle, cursed object, cursed property, dinosaurs, extreme cold, extreme heat, extreme weather, Friday the 13th, full moon, giant bugs/creatures, haunted/abandoned house, idiot military commander, intelligent plants, intelligent robot, killer prom queen, midnight, not following the rules triggers horrible side effect, plant pods infect people/animals, possessed teacher, power failure, rabid animal, sea creatures, spell, splitting the group, stalker, thunderstorm, tropical plants, trusted friend goes crazy, undead, undead relative, werewolf, witch

ENERGY SOURCES/TYPES: alien technology, batteries, candle/fire, clockwork/mechanical, electricity, ghost energy, ley line, lightning, mental ability, natural gas/swamp gas, paranormal, psychic energy, pyrokinesis, solar energy cures/destoys, telekinesis, tornado, volcanic eruption, water, wind

CLASSIC ITEMS: axe, baseball bat, boat, bomb, book, bow and arrow, carpentry tools, cell phone, chain saw, clock, computer, crystal skull, cursed dagger, doll, duct tape, Egyptian artifact, fairy ring of toadstools, gallows, hammer, hangman's noose, jewelry, knife, machine gun, map, meat cleaver, monkey's paw, nail gun, pit into hell, poison, poison ring, poisoned apple, razor, robot, scroll, severed limb, silk scarf, stick of dynamite, Swiss army knife, ventriloquist dummy, wheelchair

HORROR LOCATIONS: altar, ancient mine, attic, barn, basement/cellar, bathroom, battlefield, bed and breakfast, burial ground, camp ground, car involved in deadly crash, cave/cavern, cemetery vault, church, city of Atlantis, criminal hideout, disturbed Indian burial ground, Egyptian pyramid, Egyptian tomb, fairy ring, graveyard, haunted bridge, haunted hotel, haunted house, haunted lake, haunted road, haunted ruins, historic mansion, hospital, house where murder took place, mad scientist's laboratory, remote cabin, school, shed, sphinx, Stonehenge, subway, underground catacomb, underwater city, university lab, village well, witch's house, woods

HORROR OCCUPATIONS: actress, alchemist, ambulance driver, archeologist, army officer, army private, astronaut, babysitter, banker, bishop, boyfriend, brain surgeon, butler, caretaker, campground supervisor, computer genius, cook, detective, diver, doctor, empath, exorcist, gardener, gas station attendant, girlfriend, gumshoe, gypsy fortune teller, hospital administrator, hospital orderly, hotel clerk, lab assistant, landlord, lawyer, mad scientist, maid, medic, medical examiner, model, mortuary worker, national guard officer, nurse, paranormal investigator, pilot, pirate, police officer, priest, prison warden, psychic, robot technician, scientist, tour guide, truck driver

TRAVEL MODES: alien technology , ancient portal, astral travel, camper, cruise liner, gate to other dimension, glyph portal, horse-drawn coach, jumbo jet, ley line, lots of running, motorcycle, pentagram teleportation, private plane, run-down car, spiritual doorway, submarine, time travel, train, UFO, underwater portal

SUPPORTING CAST: angry father, corrupt police officer, crazed mother, crazy person who knows the truth, creepy assistant, dumb jock, elderly sage, ghost, golem, helpful locals, kidnapped victim, know-it-all, mother who lost her baby, nosy neighbor, obnoxious preacher, practitioner of witchcraft, robot

CHAPTER 24: FANTASY

LITERARY CLASSIFICATIONS

FANTASY GENRES: adventure, allegory, alternate Earth with fantasy races/creatures, alternate history with fantasy races/creatures, fairy tale, fantastic realism, fantasy horror, fantasy romance, graphic novel, historical setting with addition of magic, magic replaces science, mystery, occult, original setting inhabited by fantasy races/creatures

FANTASY PLOT DEVICES: all citizens wield magic, animals use magic, artifact is discovered, book of magic works in nonmagical world, city of Atlantis rises, crazy woman holds secrets of magic, curse must be reversed, dragon or fantasy creature appears in nonfantasy world, fae creatures are part of society, fantasy element in historical context, fantasy element in the modern world, fictional character appears in modern world, full moon grants powers, future Earth wields magic, hidden world is revealed, imprisoned witch is released in modern world, intelligent race of animals, known artifact (such as Excalibur sword) appears in real world, lost culture is discovered, lost magical object is found, magic fights technology, magic is responsible for ancient event or object, magic serves as energy, magical object works in nonmagical world, magical powers of artifact become understood, Merlin's treasures found in modern times, people gain ability to cast spells, people gain ability to talk to animals, proof that magic is real, save the kingdom, save the princess, stolen magical item, time travel, underwater race becomes part of society, villain discovers magic, villain plans to destroy the world, villain tries to enslave population, war threatens fantasy kingdoms, wizard appears in historical period, wizard appears in modern world

GENERAL CONCEPTS

COMMON DANGERS: angry dragon, angry horde of creatures/dragons, apprentice loses control of creature, apprentice loses control over magic, crazy wizard, creatures/monsters seek revenge, curse of darkness stops sun from rising, cursed castle/tomb, cursed object, cursed scroll is read, dangerous terrain, devil makes a deal, enemy casts magic, favorite weapon is lost/destroyed, getting lost, ghosts/spirits, heroes are captured/imprisoned, hungry dragon, intelligent plants attack, intelligent sword, invisibility won't end, magic backfires, monsters, person reads magic out loud, poison, rats/insects attack town, servant rebellion, splitting the party, traps, undead/vampires/werewolves/zombies, war, warning message is ignored, witches

ENERGY SOURCES/TYPES: ancient furnace, candle/fire, clockwork/mechanical, creature power, crystals, elemental energy, geothermal, horsepower, ley energy, magic, magical explosives, magical liquid, mental powers, meteorite, solar, spiritual energy, steam, volcanic energy, water wheel, wind mill

FANTASY LOCATIONS: castle, cave, cemetery vault, cloud city, creature lair, crypt, crystal mine, domed citadel, dragon's lair, dungeon, dwarf citadel, elf village, fairy glade, floating magical island, ghostly city that appears during full moon, giants' village, guard tower, hermit's home, lost valley, lunar castle, mountain stronghold, observation turret, ogre fort, river bastion, sorcerer's palace, underground city, underground labyrinth, vampire lair, wilderness, witch queen stronghold, witch's hut, wizard tower

FANTASY OCCUPATIONS: alchemist, apothecary, archer, balloon pilot, city watchman, cleric, elf battle commander, enchanted swordsman, first officer of the kingdom, golem designer, healer, henchman, herbalist, monster army commander, monster trainer, potion maker, scroll maker, supplier of wizards' goods, telepathic assassin, wand maker, war machine engineer, war wizard, wizard's apprentice, wizard's maid

TRAVEL MODES: arcane pathway, astral, cloud transport, dimensional, elemental, enchanted animal, ground transportation, ley portal, magical flight, magical swimming, pentagram phasing, phasing, roc, teleportation, time travel, underwater entrance, water travel

SUPPORTING CAST: apprentice, barkeep, bar wench, blacksmith, bumbling servant, clockwork butler, clockwork guard, creature sidekick, doorman, elderly advisor, evil priest, ghost/spirit, golem, helpful fairy, hoard guardian, hooded stranger in a tavern, indebted dragon/powerful creature, invisible creature, jester, lady-in-waiting, lookout, man-at-arms, megalomaniac, mischievous fairy, pixie scout, seneschal, skeleton army, street urchin, village idiot, wisecracking sidekick, witch/sorcerer controlled by blackmail

VEHICLES: air ship, broomstick, chariot pulled by nightmares, coach pulled by flying creatures, elephant caravan, enchanted bathysphere, enchanted cloud, floating citadel, flying bed, flying carpet, ghost train, ghostly chariot, giant kite, giant snail ship, platform atop giant turtle, polar bear sleigh, pumpkin coach, underwater bubble vessel

APPENDIX A: COMMONLY CONFUSED WORDS

Dozens of words in the English language are frequently confused with words that have similar spelling and sound, or similar purpose and function. What follows is a guide to those easily confused words to aid in proper word choice. This list focuses on words that might trouble the fantasy, horror, science fiction, or historical author.

BREACH/BREECH

A breach is a gap, hole, or break; it can also be a violation of law or social norms.

> A breach in the castle wall allowed invaders to pour into the courtyard.
>
> Addressing the queen by her first name is a serious breach of etiquette.

In childbirth, a breech birth means the baby is born buttocks first (rather than head first).

> The baby was so large that he never turned head-down, so the breech birth was difficult.
>
> Breeches are pants or knickers.
>
> He tore his breeches while climbing over the fence.

CALLUS/CALLOUS

A callus is a thickening of the skin due to continuous rubbing or friction.

> The farmer had many calluses on his hands from working hard every day.

Callous is an adjective that means hard-hearted, emotionless, or hardened.

> Only a callous individual would not stop to help a crying child.

HARDY/HEARTY

Hardy refers to a degree of bravery or constitution.

> Hardy plants can survive the winter to grow in the spring.
>
> The soldiers were hardy enough to survive a ten-mile walk in the snow.

Hearty means exuberant or full of heart.

> His hearty laugh filled the tavern.

HOARD/HORDE

Hoard is a verb that means to collect in great quantity, and a noun that means a large quantity of stored goods.

> If you want to hoard toilet paper, you need a place to store it.
>
> Her hoard of toilet paper was ruined when the basement flooded.

A horde is a nomadic tribe, or a large number of soldiers or raiders.

> The horde of barbarians caused quite a ruckus during their annual Easter Egg hunt.

KNOCK/NOCK

A knock is a rap that causes a sound.

> Give the secret knock and the door will be opened.

To nock is to set an arrow onto a bowstring to prepare for firing.

> He can nock an arrow faster than anyone in his squad.

APPENDIX A

LECTERN/PODIUM

A lectern is a speaker's stand with a shelf for written materials that one stands behind when addressing an audience.

The speaker leaned against the lectern when she felt faint.

A podium is a platform one stands upon, often when receiving an award, such as the podium at the Olympic games for the Gold, Silver, and Bronze Medal winners.

The crowd cheered as the athletes stepped upon the podium.

PARLAY/PARLEY

Parlay refers to the use of a resource (sometimes gambling winnings) to attempt further gain.

He took a risk, but the parlay of his winnings doubled his money.

Parley means negotiation.

A parley between the two children resulted in a satisfactory division of the candy.

Note that in a popular pirate movie, the word parlay is spoken when the word parley is intended.

PENULTIMATE/ULTIMATE

Penultimate means next to last. It does not mean above or beyond ultimate.

The penultimate letter in the alphabet is Y.

Ultimate means superb, final, or something that cannot be surpassed. It can also mean fundamental.

After many detours and delays, we reached our ultimate destination, where we were treated to the ultimate luxury experience.

THERE/THEIR/THEY'RE

Use there when referring to a place

"Over there"

Also use there with the verb BE (is, am, are, was, were) to indicate the existence of something, or to mention something for the first time.

Use their to indicate possession. It is a possessive adjective and indicates that a particular noun belongs to them.

They're is a contraction of the words *they* and *are*.

TO/TOO/TWO

To is a preposition that indicates a destination or direction: We're going to the mall.

Too means "in addition" or "excessive": My sister will come, too. She is too young to drive.

Two is a number: I will buy two horses.

YOUR/YOU'RE

Your is the possessive form of you. This tends to refer to something a person has or belongs to them.

You're is the coradiction of the words *you* and *are*.

APPENDIX B: PROVERBS

Proverbs can offer numerous possibilities in fiction writing. In addition to providing characters with quotes or pearls of wisdom, they can serve as inspiration for a character's motivation, core concept, source of drive, or defining motto. The message of a proverb can also serve as a plot twist, theme, or literary device. Proverbs also make effective riddles, clues, dying words, and code elements.

A chain is only as strong as its weakest link.

A change is as good as a rest.

A dog is a man's best friend.

A drowning man will clutch at a straw.

A faint heart never won a fair lady.

A fool and his money are soon parted.

A friend in need is a friend indeed.

A good man is hard to find.

A house divided against itself cannot stand.

A house is not a home.

A job that is worth doing, is worth doing well.

A journey of a thousand miles begins with a single step.

A leopard cannot change its spots.

A little knowledge is a dangerous thing.

A man who is his own lawyer has a fool for a client.

A man's home is his castle.

A miss is as good as a mile.

A new broom sweeps clean.

A penny saved is a penny earned.

A person is known by the company he keeps.

A picture paints a thousand words.

A place for everything and everything in its place.

A poor workman blames his tools.

A problem shared is a problem halved.

A prophet is not recognized in his own land.

A rising tide lifts all boats.

A rolling stone gathers no moss.

A soft answer turns away wrath.

A stitch in time saves nine.

A thing of beauty is a joy forever.

A volunteer is worth twenty pressed men.

A watched pot never boils.

A woman's place is in the home.

Keep your powder dry.

Laugh and the world laughs with you, weep and you weep alone.

Laughter is the best medicine.

Leave well enough alone.

Let bygones be bygones.

Let sleeping dogs lie.

Let the buyer beware.

Let the punishment fit the crime.

Life is what you make it.

Lightning never strikes twice in the same place.

Little pitchers have big ears.

Little strokes fell great oaks.

Live for today, for tomorrow never comes.

Look before you leap.

Love is blind.

Love makes the world go around.

Love thy neighbor as thyself.

Love will find a way.

Make hay while the sun shines.

Make love not war.

Man does not live by bread alone.

Manners make the man.

Many a good tune is played on an old fiddle.

Many a true word is spoken in jest.

Many hands make light work.

Marry in haste, repent at leisure.

Might is right.

Mighty oaks from little acorns grow.

Misery loves company.

Moderation in all things.

Money doesn't grow on trees.

Money is the root of all evil.

Money makes the world go around.

A woman's place is in the House (and the Senate).

A woman's work is never done.

A word to the wise is enough.

Absence makes the heart grow fonder.

Absolute power corrupts absolutely.

Accidents will happen.

Actions speak louder than words.

Adversity makes strange bedfellows.

All good things must come to an end.

All publicity is good publicity.

All that glitters is not gold.

All the world loves a lover.

All things must pass.

All work and no play makes Jack a dull boy.

All's fair in love and war.

All's well that ends well.

An apple a day keeps the doctor away.

An army marches on its stomach.

An ounce of prevention is worth a pound of cure.

Any port in a storm.

April showers bring May flowers.

As you make your bed, so will you lie in it.

As you sow so shall you reap.

Ask a silly question and you'll get a silly answer.

Ask no questions and hear no lies.

Aspire to inspire.

Bad news travels fast.

Barking dogs rarely bite.

Beauty is in the eye of the beholder.

Beauty is only skin deep.

Beggars can't be choosers.

Behind every great man is a great woman.

Best to be on the safe side.

Better late than never.

Better safe than sorry.

Better the devil you know than the devil you don't.

Better to light a candle than curse the darkness.

Money talks.

Music has charms to soothe the savage breast.

Necessity is the mother of invention.

Never judge a book by its cover.

Never let the sun go down on your anger.

Never put off until tomorrow what you can do today.

Never speak ill of the dead.

Never tell tales out of school.

No man can serve two masters.

No man is an island.

No news is good news.

No one can make you feel angry without your consent.

No pain, no gain.

No rest for the wicked.

Nothing is certain but death and taxes.

Nothing ventured, nothing gained.

Oil and water don't mix.

Once a thief, always a thief.

Once bitten, twice shy.

One good turn deserves another.

One half of the world does not know how the other half lives.

One hand washes the other.

One law for the rich and another for the poor.

One man's trash is another man's treasure.

One swallow does not make a summer.

Only fools and horses work.

Opportunity never knocks twice.

Out of sight, out of mind.

Patience is a virtue.

Penny wise and pound foolish.

People who live in glass houses shouldn't throw stones.

Possession is nine-tenths of the law.

Practice makes perfect.

Practice what you preach.

Pride goes before a fall.

Procrastination is the thief of time.

Put your best foot forward.

Better to remain silent and be thought a fool than to speak and remove all doubt.

Beware of Greeks bearing gifts.

Big fish eat little fish.

Birds of a feather flock together.

Blood is thicker than water.

Boys will be boys.

Brevity is the soul of wit.

Brilliance is 1 percent inspiration and 99 percent perspiration.

Business before pleasure.

Carpe diem (seize the day).

Charity begins at home.

Children should be seen and not heard.

Cleanliness is next to godliness.

Clothes make the man.

Cold hands, warm heart.

Count your blessings.

Cowards may die many times before their death.

Cut your coat to suit your cloth.

Dead men tell no tales.

Discretion is the better part of valor.

Distance lends enchantment to the view.

Do as I say, not as I do.

Do unto others as you would have them do unto you.

Don't bite the hand that feeds you.

Don't burn your bridges behind you.

Don't change horses in midstream.

Don't count your chickens before they hatch.

Don't cross the bridge until you come to it.

Don't cut off your nose to spite your face.

Don't look a gift horse in the mouth.

Don't meet troubles half-way.

Don't put all your eggs in one basket.

Don't put the cart before the horse.

Don't rock the boat.

Don't throw the baby out with the bath water.

Don't try to walk before you can crawl.

Red sky at night, sailors delight; red sky in the morning, sailors take warning.

Rome wasn't built in a day.

Seeing is believing.

Seek and ye shall find.

Share and share alike.

Silence is golden.

Slow and steady wins the race.

Spare the rod and spoil the child.

Speak of the devil and he is bound to appear.

Speak softly and carry a big stick.

Sticks and stones may break my bones, but words will never hurt me.

Still waters run deep.

Strike while the iron is hot.

Stupid is as stupid does.

Take care of the pence and the pounds will take care of themselves.

That which does not kill us makes us stronger.

The apple never falls far from the tree.

The best defense is a good offense.

The best things in life are free.

The bigger they are, the harder they fall.

The bread always falls buttered side down.

The cobbler always wears the worst shoes.

The course of true love never did run smooth.

The customer is always right.

The darkest hour is just before the dawn.

The devil finds work for idle hands.

The devil is in the details.

The early bird catches the worm.

The end justifies the means.

The female of the species is more deadly than the male.

The grass is always greener on the other side of the fence.

The hand that rocks the cradle rules the world.

The more things change, the more they stay the same.

The pen is mightier than the sword.

The price of liberty is eternal vigilance.

The proof of the pudding is in the eating.

Don't upset the apple-cart.

Don't wash your dirty linen in public.

Doubt is the beginning, not the end, of wisdom.

Early to bed and early to rise makes a man healthy, wealthy, and wise.

East or west, home's the best.

Easy come, easy go.

Enough is as good as a feast.

Every cloud has a silver lining.

Every dog has its day.

Every Jack has his Jill.

Every man has his price.

Every picture tells a story.

Every stick has two ends.

Everyone wants to go to heaven but nobody wants to die.

Failing to plan is planning to fail.

Faith will move mountains.

Familiarity breeds contempt.

Feed a cold and starve a fever.

Fight fire with fire.

First impressions are the most lasting.

First things first.

Fish and house guests smell after three days.

Fools rush in where angels fear to tread.

Forewarned is forearmed.

Forgive and forget.

Fortune favors the brave.

Give a person enough rope and he will hang himself.

God helps those who help themselves.

Good fences make good neighbors.

Good things come to those who wait.

Great minds think alike.

Half a loaf is better than no bread.

Haste makes waste.

He who fights and runs away, lives to fight another day.

He who hesitates is lost.

He who lives by the sword shall die by the sword.

The road to hell is paved with good intentions.

The shoemaker's son always goes barefoot.

The squeaky wheel gets the grease.

The third time's the charm.

The truth will win out.

The way to a man's heart is through his stomach.

There are none so blind as those who will not see.

There are two sides to every question.

There will always be more fish in the sea.

There, but for the grace of God, go I.

There's a time and place for everything.

There's an exception to every rule.

There's honor among thieves.

There's more than one way to skin a cat.

There's no place like home.

There's no point in crying over spilled milk.

There's no point in locking the stable door after the horse has bolted.

There's no time like the present.

There's safety in numbers.

They that sow the wind, shall reap the whirlwind.

Those who do not learn from history are doomed to repeat it.

Three times a bridesmaid, never a bride.

Time and tide wait for no man.

Time flies.

Time is a great healer.

Time is money.

Time will tell.

To err is human, to forgive divine.

To everything there is a season.

To the victor go the spoils.

Tomorrow is another day.

Tomorrow never comes.

Too many cooks spoil the broth.

Truth is stranger than fiction.

Two heads are better than one.

Two wrongs don't make a right.

Hell hath no fury like a woman scorned.

Hindsight is always perfect.

Home is where the heart is.

Honesty is the best policy.

If anything can go wrong, it will.

If at first you don't succeed, try and try again.

If it isn't broken, don't fix it.

If it walks like a duck and quacks like a duck, then it's a duck.

If the mountain won't come to Mohammed, then Mohammed must go to the mountain.

If the shoe fits, wear it.

If you can't be good, be careful.

If you can't beat them, join them.

If you can't stand the heat, get out of the kitchen.

If you lie down with dogs, you will get up with fleas.

If you pay the piper, you call the tune.

If you want a thing done well, do it yourself.

Ignorance is bliss.

Imitation is the sincerest form of flattery.

In for a penny, in for a pound.

Into every life a little rain must fall.

It is better to give than to receive.

It is easy to be wise after the mistake.

It takes a thief to catch a thief.

It takes all kinds to make the world go around.

It takes one to know one.

It takes two to tango.

It's better to have loved and lost than never to have loved at all.

Jack of all trades, master of none.

Judge not, that you be not judged.

Keep your chin up.

Variety is the spice of life.

Virtue is its own reward.

Walls have ears.

Waste not, want not.

What can't be cured must be endured.

What goes up must come down.

What the eye doesn't see, the heart doesn't grieve over.

When in Rome, do as the Romans do.

When life gives you lemons, make lemonade.

When the cat's away, the mice will play.

When the going gets tough, the tough get going.

Where there's a will, there's a way.

Where there's smoke, there's fire.

While there's life, there's hope.

Wonders will never cease.

Work expands so as to fill the time allotted.

You are never too old to learn.

You are what you eat.

You can have too much of a good thing.

You can lead a horse to water, but you can't make it drink.

You can't have your cake and eat it, too.

You can't judge a book by its cover.

You can't make a silk purse from a sow's ear.

You can't make an omelette without breaking some eggs.

You can't squeeze blood from a stone.

You can't teach an old dog new tricks.

You can't turn the wind so turn the sail.

You can't win them all.

You'll catch more flies with honey than with vinegar.

Youth is wasted on the young.

ALPHABETICAL INDEX

The index that follows lists each word in this book and references the category in which it is listed followed by the number of the chapter in which it appears. Thus, the term abbot will be found in the section Religious Occupations in Chapter 1.

For further assistance in locating categories of terms, refer to the Contents at the beginning of this book.

Due to space constraints, several lengthy lists are not incorporated into the index:

PHOBIAS: Chapter 1

STAR NAMES: Chapter 11

BOOKS OF THE BIBLE: Chapter 14

MONSTER LAIRS AND LOCATIONS: Chapter 16

LIST OF POSSIBLE MAGICAL EFFECTS: Chapter 17

SYMBOLIC WEDDING ANNIVERSARY GIFTS: Chapter 19

APPENDIX A: Commonly Confused Words

APPENDIX B: Proverbs

– NUMERIC –

$%^&#@): *Expletives 20*

*******:** *Expletives 20*

0–the fool: *Major Arcana 19*

1% milk: *Dairy Beverages 6*

1%: *Milk 6*

1–the magician: *Major Arcana 19*

10–the wheel of fortune: *Major Arcana 19*

10 x sugar: *Staples 6*

11–strength: *Major Arcana 19*

12-gauge: *Shotguns General7*

12–the hanged man: *Major Arcana 19*

13–death: *Major Arcana 19*

14 temperance: *Major Arcana 19*

15–the devil: *Major Arcana 19*

16–the tower: *Major Arcana 19*

1776: *Independence Day 19*

17–the star: *Major Arcana 19*

18-inch railway howitzer: *Mortar 8*

18–the moon: *Major Arcana 19*

19–the sun: *Major Arcana 19*

2% milk: *Dairy Beverages 6*

2%: *Milk 6*

20-gauge: *Shotguns General 7*

20–judgment: *Major Arcana 19*

21–the world: *Major Arcana 19*

2S1 Gvozdika self-propelled 122mm howitzer: *Russia Military Vehicles 8*

2S1 Gvozdika self-propelled anti-aircraft 23mm gun: *Russia Military Vehicles 8*

2S3 Akatsiya self-propelled 152mm howitzer: *Russia Military Vehicles 8*

2S30 Iset self-propelled 155mm howitzer: *Russia Military Vehicles 8*

2S4 Tyulpan self-propelled 240mm mortar: *Russia Military Vehicles 8*

2S5: *Russia Military Vehicles 8*

2S7 Pion self-propelled 203mm gun: *Russia Military Vehicles 8*

2S9 Anona self-propelled 120mm mortar: *Russia Military Vehicles 8*

2–the high priestess: *Major Arcana 19*

30-cup coffee maker: *Appliances 5*

3-1/2 inch floppy disk: *Computer Equipment 5*

33-1/3 rpm record player: *Electronics 4*

3–the empress: *Major Arcana 19*

45 rpm record player: *Electronics 4*

47th problem of Euclid: *Symbols of Freemasonry 19*

4–the emperor: *Major Arcana 19*

5-1/4 inch floppy disk: *Computer Equipment 5*

52 pick-up: *Card Games 5*

5–the hierophant: *Major Arcana 19*

6–the lover: *Major Arcana 19*

78 rpm record player: *Electronics 4*

7–the chariot: *Major Arcana 19*

7TP light tank: *Poland Military Vehicles 8*

8–justice: *Major Arcana 19*

8-track tape player: *Electronics 4*

9A51 Prima 6x6 self-propelled multiple rocket launcher: *Russia Military Vehicles 8*

9P117 8x8 scud short-range ballistic missile launcher: *Russia Military Vehicles 8*

9P157 self-propelled anti-tank vehicle: *Russia Military Vehicles 8*

9S482 8x8 air defense command vehicle: *Russia Military Vehicles 8*

9–the hermit: *Major Arcana 19*

–A–

a cappella: *General Music Vocabulary 13*

a cinch: *Easy 20*

à la Seconde: *Ballet Terms 13*

a load: *Heavy 20*

a pain in the butt: *Difficult 20*

a pain in the neck: *Difficult 20*

a pain: *Difficult 20*

a posteriori: *Philosophy Basic Concepts 14*

a priori: *Philosophy Basic Concepts 14*

a snap: *Easy 20*

à Terre: *Ballet Terms 13*

A Visit from St. Nicholas: *Christmas 19*

A.I. programmer: *Occupations 22*

A^A^: *Secret/Mystical Organizations 18*

A-10 Thunderbolt II: *U.S. Air Force Aircraft 8*

A13 Cruiser Mark III medium tank: *United Kingdom Military Vehicles 8*

A27 Cromwell cruiser Mark VIII medium tank: *United Kingdom Military Vehicles 8*

A30 Challenger cruiser Mark VIII medium tank: *United Kingdom Military Vehicles 8*

A34 Comet cruiser medium tank: *United Kingdom Military Vehicles 8*

A39 Tortoise anti-tank vehicle: *United Kingdom Military Vehicles 8*

A4 AVL 4x4 armored utility vehicle: *France Military Vehicles 8*

A43 Black Prince infantry medium tank: *United Kingdom Military Vehicles 8*

A45 Caernarvon heavy tank: *United Kingdom Military Vehicles 8*

A531 armored personnel carrier: *China Military Vehicles 8*

A7SC 4x2 armored car: *United States Military Vehicles 8*

A7V Sturmpanzerwagen heavy tank: *Germany Military Vehicles 8*

A9 Cruiser Mark I medium tank: *United Kingdom Military Vehicles 8*

Aaltje: *Asteroids 11*

AAPC armored personnel carrier: *United States Military Vehicles 8*

aardvark: *Other Wild Mammals 15*

Aase: *Asteroids 11*

aatxe: *Demon 16*

AAV-7 amphibious armored vehicle: *United States Military Vehicles 8*

AAVC-7 amphibious armored personnel carrier: *United States Military Vehicles 8*

AAVC-7 amphibious command vehicle: *United States Military Vehicles 8*

AAVR-7 amphibious recovery vehicle: *United States Military Vehicles 8*

AB40 4x4 armored car: *Italy Military Vehicles 8*

AB41 4x4 armored car: *Italy Military Vehicles 8*

Abaco Island: *Boa 15*

abaddon: *Devil 16*

abalone: *Fish/Seafood Types 6*

Abarimon: *Human Races Fictional 1*

abatwa: *Demon 16*

Abatwa: *Human Races Fictional 1*

Abbadon: *Fallen Angels 14*

abbot: *Religious Occupations 1*

abdomen: *Body Parts 12*

abeam: *Boat/Ship Terminology 9*

abelia: *Shrubs 10*

Abenaki: *Native American Peoples 1*

aberration: *Monster Categories/Terms 16*

abertam: *Cheese International Varieties 6*

abhorrence: *General Emotions 20*

abhorrent: *Unattractive 20*

abigor: *Devil 16*

Abilene: *Famous Western Locations 21*

Abingdon Island giant: *Tortoises 15*

abiu: *Unusual Edible Fruits 6*

able: *Good 20*

Abnoba: *Asteroids 11*

abnormal rate of growth: *Plot Devices 22*

abode: *Residential Property 3*

aboleth: *Aquatic 16*

abolish: *Kill 20*

abominable snowman: *Mythical Creatures and Monsters 16*

abominable: *Unattractive 20*

Aboriginal Australian: *Human Ethnic Groups 1*

ALPHABETICAL INDEX

aborted entoloma: *Fungus Common Names 10*

abracadabra: *Witchcraft Vocabulary 17*

Abraham Lincoln: *Real People with Legendary Status 18*

abraxas: *Symbols in Magic and Religion 19*

abraxus: *Devil 16*

abrupt: *Fast 20*

abrus precatorius: *Poisonous Chemicals in Plants 11*

absence of blade: *Fencing Vocabulary 7*

absent without leave: *General Combat Vocabulary 7*

absent-minded professor: *Common Character Archetypes 21*

absolute dating: *Geological Vocabulary 10*

absolute entropy: *Chemistry General Vocabulary 11*

absolute humidity: *Geography General Vocabulary 10*

absolute location: *Geography General Vocabulary 10*

absolute magnitude: *Astronomy General Terms 11*

absolute zero: *Astronomy General Terms 11; Chemistry General Vocabulary 11*

absolute: *Philosophy Basic Concepts 14*

absorb: *Learn 20; Magic Vocabulary 17; Moves 7*

absorbed: *Magic Vocabulary 17*

absorbing: *Beautiful 20*

absorption spectrum: *Chemistry General Vocabulary 11*

abstinence: *Rituals 14*

Abstract expressionism: *Art Movements 13*

abstract object: *Philosophy Basic Concepts 14*

Abstract: *Art Movements 13*

abundant: *Eyebrows 1; Large/Heavy 1*

Abundantia: *Asteroids 11*

abuse: *Harm 20*

abused servant: *Common Character Archetypes 21*

abusive spouse: *Common Character Archetypes 21*

abusive: *Negative 1*

abysmal: *Bad 20*

abyss: *Afterlife/Underworld 18; Terrain Features 10*

abyssal fan: *Coastal and Oceanic 10*

abyssal plain: *Coastal and Oceanic 10; Geological Vocabulary 10*

Abyssinia: *Poker Card Games 5*

Abyssinian: *Domestic Cats 15; Horse Breeds 15*

AC-130 Spectre: *U.S. Air Force Aircraft 8*

acacia: *Symbols of Freemasonry 19*

Academia: *Asteroids 11*

academic property: *Architecture and Property 3*

Academic: *Art Movements 13*

academic: *Character Building 1; Wizard 1*

academy: *Academic Property 3*

Acadian: *Human Ethnic Groups 1*

acai: *Unusual Edible Fruits 6*

acapella: *Cheese Common Varieties 6*

accelerando: *Tempo/Mood 13*

accelerated: *Fast 20*

accent lamp: *Illumination/Light Sources 5*

accent: *Pillows 5*

accented: *Vocal/Speech Quality 1*

accept: *Agree 20; Buy 20*

access road: *Roads 9*

access tunnel: *Doors Atypical 3*

accessibility: *Geography General Vocabulary 10*

accessories: *Clothing 2*

accessory: *Jewelry 21*

acciaccatura: *General Music Vocabulary 13*

accident: *Philosophy Basic Concepts 14*

accidental: *General Music Vocabulary 13*

Accohannock: *Native American Peoples 1*

accompaniment: *General Music Vocabulary 13*

accomplice: *Spy Gear 5*

accomplished: *Good 20*

accordion: *Solitaire Card Games 5; Wind/Woodwind and Brass Musical Instruments*

accountant: *Finance 1*

accounting office: *Business Property 3*

accretion disc: *Planetary Systems 11*

accretion: *Geological Vocabulary 10*

accumulation: *Meteorology General Vocabulary 10*

Acelmese: *Human Ethnic Groups 1*

Acension: *Catholic Holy Days of Obligation 14*

acerbic: *Smells 20*

acerila: *Minerals 10*

acerola: *Unusual Edible Fruits 6*

aces and eights/dead man's hand: *Harbingers of Bad Luck 19*

aces up: *Solitaire Card Games 5*

ace-to-five lowball: *Poker Card Games 5*

acetone cyanohydrin: *Dangerous Chemicals 11*

acetone thiosemicarbazide: *Dangerous Chemicals 11*

ace-to-six lowball: *Poker Card Games 5*

ACG-1 light tank: *France Military Vehicles 8*

ACG-2 self propelled anti-tank 75mm gun: *France Military Vehicles 8*

achaierai: *Beast 16*

ache: *Harm 20*

achieve: *Buy 20*

achilles tang: *Aquarium Saltwater Fish 15*

Achilles: *Asteroids 11; Shields 18*

Achomawi: *Native American Peoples 1*

achroite: *Minerals 10*

Achzarit armored personnel carrier: *Israel Military Vehicles 8*

acid rain: *Geography General Vocabulary 10*

acid rock: *Musical Styles 13*

acid secretion: *Physical Mutations 22*

acid sulfate soil: *Soil General Vocabulary 10*

acid vial: *Spy Gear 5*

acid: *Art Media 13; Chemistry General Vocabulary 11; Smells 20; Specialty Survival Gear 5; Traps 3; Wizard's Goods 5*

acidic ooze: *Ooze 16*

acidic salt: *Chemistry General Vocabulary 11*

acidic: *Smells 20*

acidity: *General Emotions 20*

acids: *Laboratory Supplies 5*

ackee: *Unusual Edible Fruits 6*

aclis: *Missile Loads 7*

acmite: *Minerals 10*

acolyte: *Cleric 1; Religious Occupations 1*

Acoma: *Native American Peoples 1*

aconite: *Poisonous Plants 10*

aconitum: *Poisonous Chemicals in Plants 11*

acorn squash: *Vegetables 6*

acoustic guitar: *String Musical Instruments*

acoustics: *Technical Terms 13*

acquire: *Buy 20*

acrid: *Smells 20*

acrimonious: *Negative 1*

acrimony: *General Emotions 20*

acrisol: *Soil General Vocabulary 10*

acrobat: *Performing Arts 1*

acrolein: *Dangerous Chemicals 11*

Acropolis of Athens: *Unique Property 3*

acrylamide: *Dangerous Chemicals 11*

acrylic paint: *Art Materials 5; Art Media 13*

acrylonitrile: *Dangerous Chemicals 11*

acryloyl chloride: *Dangerous Chemicals 11*

actaea pachypoda: *Poisonous Chemicals in Plants 11*

actinidia: *Shrubs 10*

Actinium: *Elements 11*

action figure: *Toys 5*

action: *Games 5*

activation energy: *Chemistry General Vocabulary 11*

active cave: *Cave Anatomy 10*

active layer: *Soil General Vocabulary 10*

active metal: *Chemistry General Vocabulary 11*

active: *Mobility 1*

ACTL transport vehicle: *Italy Military Vehicles 8*

actor: *Performing Arts 1*

actress: *Horror Occupations 23; Performing Arts 1*

actual yield: *Chemistry General Vocabulary 11*

actuality: *Philosophy Basic Concepts 14*

actuary: *Finance 1*

acupressurist: *Medical Occupations 1*

acupuncturist: *Medical Occupations 1*

ACV 300 infantry fighting vehicle: *Turkey Military Vehicles 8*

ACV-S armored vehicle: *Turkey Military Vehicles 8*

ad lib: *General Music Vocabulary 13; Stage Terms 13*

ad libitum: *General Music Vocabulary 13*

Ada: *Asteroids 11*

ALPHABETICAL INDEX

adagietto: *Tempo/Mood 13*

Adagio: *Ballet Terms 13; Tempo/Mood 13*

adakite: *Igneous Rocks 10*

Adalberta: *Asteroids 11*

Adam and Eve: *Poisonous Plants 10; Wildflowers 10*

adam's apple: *Body Parts 12*

adamant: *Stubborn 1*

adamine: *Minerals 10*

add: *Buy 20*

adder stone: *Objects that Offer Protection 19*

adder: *Animals 15; Harbingers of Bad Luck 19*

adder's tongue fern: *Items with Healing Properties 19*

adder's tongue: *Garden Perennials 10*

adding machine: *Office/School Machines 5*

addition reaction: *Chemistry General Vocabulary 11*

additional Earth moons: *Hypothetical Solar System Bodies 11*

addorsed: *Air Creatures 19; Multiple Figures 19*

address book: *Office/School/Writing Supplies 5*

Adelaide: *Asteroids 11*

Adele: *Asteroids 11*

Adelgunde: *Asteroids 11*

Adelheid: *Asteroids 11*

Adelinda: *Asteroids 11*

adenoid: *Organs/Major Structures 12*

Adeona: *Asteroids 11*

adhesive forces: *Chemistry General Vocabulary 11*

adhesive: *Art Materials 5*

adiponitrile: *Dangerous Chemicals 11*

Adirondack: *Architectural Styles 3*

adjudicator: *Legal Occupations 1*

adjuster: *Legal Occupations 1*

Admete: *Asteroids 11*

administrative center: *General Buildings 3*

administrative: *Architecture and Property 3; Military Property 3*

administrator: *Occupations 22; Religious Occupations 1*

admirable bolete: *Fungus Common Names 10*

admiral: *Butterfly 15; Maritime Occupations 1; U.S. Navy Officer 8*

admiration: *General Emotions 20*

admire: *General Emotions 20*

admissions clerk: *Academic 1*

adobe: *Exterior Building Materials 3*

adolescent: *Child 1*

Adolfine: *Asteroids 11*

adopted child: *Common Character Archetypes 21*

adoptive parent: *Common Character Archetypes 21*

adorable: *Beautiful 20*

adoration: *General Emotions 20*

adore: *Love 20; Terms of Endearment 1*

Adorea: *Asteroids 11*

adornment: *Jewelry 21*

adramelech: *Devil 16*

Adrastea: *Asteroids 11; Moons 11*

adrenal gland: *Organs/Major Structures 12*

Adria: *Asteroids 11*

Adriana: *Asteroids 11*

Adriel: *Angels of Good 14*

adrift: *Boat/Ship Terminology 9*

adrinka: *Symbols in Magic and Religion 19*

adsorption: *Chemistry General Vocabulary 11*

adularia: *Minerals 10*

adulation: *General Emotions 20*

adult: *Character Building 1; Teeth 1*

advance: *Fencing Vocabulary 7; Locomotion 9; Teach 20*

advanced: *Elderly 1; Personality Other 1; New 20*

advantageous: *Fortunate 20*

Advent candle: *Christmas 19*

Advent candles: *Rituals 14*

Advent wreath: *Christmas 19; Rituals 14*

Advent: *Christmas 19*

adventure: *Fantasy Genres 24; Journey 20; Science Fiction Genres 22*

adventurer: *Barbarian 1*

adventurer's gear: *Equipment and Tools 5*

adventurers: *Character Building 1*

adversaries: *General Combat Vocabulary 7*

adversary: *Fighter 1; Hero or Villain, Depending Upon Circumstance 20*

adverse: *Unattractive 20*

advertising agent: *Publishing 1*

advisor: *Academic 1*

advisory: *Meteorology General Vocabulary 10*

advocate: *Cleric 1; Legal Occupations 1*

Adyghe: *Human Ethnic Groups 1*

adze: *Axes 7; Hand Tools 5*

adzuki bean: *Legumes 6*

Aegaeon: *Moons 11*

Aegina: *Asteroids 11*

Aegir (storms): *Norse Pantheon 14*

Aegir: *Moons 11*

Aegis: *Helmets 18; Shields 18*

aegishjalmur: *Magical/Icelandic Staves 18*

Aegle: *Asteroids 11*

Aemilia: *Asteroids 11*

Aeolia: *Asteroids 11*

aeolian landforms: *Chapter 10*

Aeria: *Asteroids 11*

aerialist: *Performing Arts 1*

aerie: *Natural Animal Homes 15*

aeronautical engineer: *Scientist 1*

aerosol can: *Improvised Weapons 7*

aerosol paint: *Art Materials 5*

aerosol: *Geography General Vocabulary 10*

aesthetician: *Personal Services 1*

Aestheticism: *Art Movements 13*

aesthetics: *Philosophy Basic Concepts 14*

Aeternitas: *Asteroids 11*

Aethra: *Asteroids 11*

Afar: *Human Ethnic Groups 1*

affability: *General Emotions 20*

affable: *Happy 20*

affected: *Vocal/Speech Quality 1*

affection: *General Emotions 20*

Affenpinscher: *Dog Breeds 15*

affettuoso: *Tempo/Mood 13*

affianced: *Relational 1*

affronty: *Air Creatures 19*

Afghan Hound: *Dog Breeds 15*

Afghan: *Imported Carpets 4*

A-Frame: *Architectural Styles 3*

African amethyst: *Minerals 10*

African cherry orange: *Unusual Edible Fruits 6*

African daisy: *Wildflowers 10*

African dwarf crocodile: *Crocodilians 15*

African dwarf: *Frogs 15*

African elephant: *Other Wild Mammals 15*

African gray: *Domesticated Pet Birds 15*

African helmeted: *Freshwater Turtles 15*

African jade: *Minerals 10*

African jewelfish: *Aquarium Freshwater Fish 15*

African keeled mud: *Freshwater Turtles 15*

African rock: *Python 15*

African sideneck: *Freshwater Turtles 15*

African sleeping sickness: *Diseases 12*

African spurred: *Tortoises 15*

African sumac: *Poisonous Plants 10*

African tent: *Tortoises 15*

African Vernacular: *Architectural Styles 3*

African wild ass: *Horses Related 15*

African: *Old World Monkeys 15; Styles of Dress 2*

African-American: *Human Ethnic Groups 1*

Africander: *Other Cows 15*

Africanized: *Bees 15*

Afrikaner: *Human Ethnic Groups 1*

Afro: *Hair Style 1*

aft: *Boat/Ship Terminology 9*

after dinner mint: *Candy General 6*

after shave lotion: *Personal Care 5*

after shave: *Personal Care 5*

afterlife: *Legendary, Mystical and Mythical Items and Locations 18; Legendary/Mythical Locations 18*

aftershock: *Geological Natural Hazards 10; Geological Vocabulary 10*

AFV: *Armored Vehicles 8*

ALPHABETICAL INDEX

agama: *Scaled Reptiles 15*

Agamemnon: *Asteroids 11*

agamid lizard: *Scaled Reptiles 15*

agar plate: *Laboratory Equipment 5*

agares: *Devil 16*

agaric mineral: *Minerals 10*

Agartha: *Fictional/Mythological Locations 18*

agate geode: *Minerals 10; Standard Gems 21*

agate jasper: *Minerals 10*

agate opal: *Minerals 10*

agate: *Minerals 10; Standard Gems 21*

Agathe: *Asteroids 11*

agatized wood: *Minerals 10*

age: *Character Building 1*

aged: *Elderly 1; Old 20*

agenda: *Laboratory Supplies 5*

agent: *General Occupations 1; Law Enforcement 1; Publishing 1*

ageratum: *Garden Annuals 10; Garden Perennials 10*

aggravate: *General Emotions 20*

aggregate: *Rock and Mineral Forms 10*

aggression: *General Emotions 20*

aggressive: *Personality Other 1; Unattractive 20*

aggressor: *Fighter 1*

agile: *Mobility 1*

agility: *Physical Mutations 22*

Agimat: *Jewelry 18*

aging gunfighter's last shootout: *Western Plot Devices 21*

agitato: *Tempo/Mood 13*

Aglaja: *Asteroids 11*

Agnes: *Asteroids 11*

Agni (fire): *Indian Pantheon 14*

Agnia: *Asteroids 11*

agonizing: *Sad 20*

agram: *Card Games 5*

Agravain: *Knights of the Round Table 18*

agree: *Verbs 20*

agreeable: *Good 20; Happy 20*

agricultural engine: *Steam Powered Farm Equipment*

agricultural occupations: *Character Building 1*

Agrippina Vaganova: *Ballet Terms 13*

Agrippina: *Asteroids 11*

agronomist: *Agricultural 1*

aground: *Boat/Ship Terminology 9*

agua nueva agate: *Minerals 10*

ague tree: *Evergreen Trees 10*

Aguntina: *Asteroids 11*

ah: *Expletives 20*

AH-6 Littlebird: *U.S. Army Helicopter 8*

AH-64 Apache: *U.S. Army Helicopter 8*

ah-ha: *Expletives 20*

ahlspiess: *Spears 7*

ahool: *Beast 16*

ahpuch: *Demon 16*

Ahrensa: *Asteroids 11*

ahriman: *Devil 16*

Ahriman: *Fallen Angels 14*

AHSVS 8×8 armored truck: *Germany Military Vehicles 8*

Ahtna: *Native American Peoples 1*

Ahto (water): *Finnish Pantheon 14*

ahuehuete: *Evergreen Trees 10*

aid: *Teach 20*

Aida: *Asteroids 11*

Aidamina: *Asteroids 11*

AIDS: *Diseases 12*

AIFV infantry fighting vehicle: *United States Military Vehicles 8*

aikuchi: *Swords One-handed 7*

Aimaq: *Human Ethnic Groups 1*

aini: *Demon 16*

air blast: *Bomb 8*

air board: *Vehicles 22*

air bus: *Air Vehicles 9*

air conditioner: *Building Systems 3*

air creatures: *Classic Heraldry 19*

air current: *Wind 10*

air filtration: *Building Systems 3*

Air Force blue: *Blue 20*

air force ranks: *Military 8*

air mass: *Geography General Vocabulary 10; Meteorology General Vocabulary 10*

air offense: *General Combat Vocabulary 7*

air pollution: *Meteorology General Vocabulary 10*

air popped popcorn: *Snacks 6*

air popper: *Appliances 5*

air potato: *Weeds 10*

air pressure: *Meteorology General Vocabulary 10*

air scrubber: *Devices 22*

air seeder: *General Farm Equipment*

air ship: *Vehicles 24*

air stream: *Wind 10*

air superiority fighter: *Military Aircraft 8*

air superiority: *General Combat Vocabulary 7*

air support: *General Combat Vocabulary 7*

air terrain warfare: *General Combat Vocabulary 7*

air vehicles: *Transportation 9*

air: *Beds 4; Composition Types 13; Elemental 16; Four Elements 19; Meteorology General Vocabulary 10*

airborne aircraft carrier: *Military Watercraft 8*

airborne command and control: *Military Aircraft 8*

airborne early warning: *Military Aircraft Pre-1962 8*

airbrush: *Art Techniques 13; Art Tools 5*

aircraft in the Bermuda Triangle: *Famous Disappearances 18*

aircraft: *Air Vehicles 9; Military 8*

airdrome: *Infrastructure Buildings 9*

Airedale Terrier: *Dog Breeds 15*

airfield: *Infrastructure Buildings 9*

airfoil: *Small Watercraft 9*

airliner: *Air Vehicles 9*

airlock: *Doors Atypical 3*

airman basic: *U.S. Air Force Enlisted 8*

airman first class: *U.S. Air Force Enlisted 8*

airman: *U.S. Air Force Enlisted 8*

airplane: *Air Vehicles 9*

airport terminal: *Infrastructure Buildings 9*

airport: *Infrastructure Buildings 9*

airship: *Air Vehicles 9*

airships: *Military 8*

airstrip: *Infrastructure Buildings 9*

air-to-air: *Air Force Missile 8*

air-to-surface: *Air Force Missile 8*

airy: *Light 20; Small/Fragile 20*

aisle: *Building Elements and Features 3; Castle Anatomy 3; Church Anatomy 3; Parts of the Theater 13*

ait: *Fluvial 10*

Aitne: *Moons 11*

ajar: *Open/Release 20*

Ak Chin: *Native American Peoples 1*

AK-47: *Semiautomatic Centerfire Rifles 7*

akadama: *Soil General Vocabulary 10*

akar saga: *Poisonous Plants 10*

Akhal Teke: *Horse Breeds 15*

akhet: *Symbols in Magic and Religion 19*

Akita: *Dog Breeds 15*

akkawi: *Cheese International Varieties 6*

aklys: *Combat, Armor, and Weapons 7*

Aksai black pied: *Pigs 15*

Akuapem: *Human Ethnic Groups 1*

akubra: *Headgear 2*

akvan: *Demon 16*

akwaba: *Symbols in Magic and Religion 19*

Akyem: *Human Ethnic Groups 1*

al: *Devil 16*

ala king: *Poultry Meals 6*

Alabama: *Native American Peoples 1*

alabaster: *Minerals 10; Minerals 10*

alacranite: *Minerals 10*

Aladdin lamp: *Illumination/Light Sources 5*

Alagasta: *Asteroids 11*

alamandine: *Minerals 10*

Alamo: *Famous Western Locations 21*

alarm clock: *Timekeeping 5*

alarm system: *Building Systems 3*

alarm: *General Emotions 20; Horror Vocabulary 23*

alarmed: *General Emotions 20*

ALPHABETICAL INDEX

alarming: *Unattractive 20*

alas: *Slope 10*

Alaska cedar: *Evergreen Trees 10*

Alaska cypress: *Evergreen Trees 10*

Alaska yellow cedar: *Evergreen Trees 10*

Alaskan brown: *Bears 15*

Alaskan larch: *Evergreen Trees 10*

Alaskan Malamute: *Dog Breeds 15*

alastor: *Devil 16*

Alauda: *Asteroids 11*

albacore tuna: *Wild Saltwater Fish 15*

Albanian: *Horse Breeds 15; Human Ethnic Groups 1*

albatross: *Animals with Symbolic Meaning 19; Harbingers of Bad Luck 19; Other Wild Birds 15*

albedo: *Astronomy General Terms 11*

albeluvisols: *Soil General Vocabulary 10*

Albères: *Other Cows 15*

Albert: *Asteroids 11*

Alberta clipper: *Snow Storms 10*

Alberta spruce: *Evergreen Trees 10*

Alberta white spruce: *Evergreen Trees 10*

albino: *Scorpion 15; Skin Types and Features 1*

Albiorix: *Moons 11*

albite-anorthite series: *Minerals 10*

album cover: *Art Genres 13*

albumin: *Blood 12*

alcalde: *Card Games 5*

Alcatraz: *Unique Property 3*

alchemical spirits: *Collective Symbols 19*

alchemist: *Fantasy Occupations 24; Horror Occupations 23*

alcohol inky cap: *Fungus Common Names 10*

alcohol: *Chemistry General Vocabulary 11; Wizard's Goods 5*

alcoholic beverages: *Food 6*

Aldabra giant: *Tortoises 15*

aldehyde: *Chemistry General Vocabulary 11*

alderman: *Government 1*

alderperson: *Government 1*

alderwoman: *Government 1*

aldicarb: *Dangerous Chemicals 11*

aldinach: *Demon 16*

aldrin: *Dangerous Chemicals 11*

ale: *Beer 6*

Alekto: *Asteroids 11*

Aleku: *Caecilians 15*

Alemannia: *Asteroids 11*

alembic: *Laboratory Equipment 5*

Alenia C27J: *U.S. Army Aircraft 8*

Alentejana: *Other Cows 15*

alerion: *Special Body Features 19*

alert: *Horror Vocabulary 23; Mobility 1; Teach 20*

Aletheia: *Asteroids 11*

Aleut: *Native American Peoples 1*

alewife: *Wild Freshwater Fish 15*

Alexander: *Garden Perennials 10*

Alexandra: *Asteroids 11*

Alexandrian laurel: *Shrubs 10*

alexandrite: *Minerals 10; Standard Gems 21*

alfalfa sprout: *Vegetables 6*

alfalfa: *Farm/Outbuilding 3*

Alfheim: *Fictional/Mythological Locations 18*

alfisol: *Soil General Vocabulary 10*

Alfred Bog Ontario: *Bogs of North America 10*

Alfred Bulltop Stormalong: *Tall Tales 18*

Algonquian: *Native American Peoples 1*

Algunde: *Asteroids 11*

Alice blue: *Blue 20*

Alice: *Asteroids 11*

alien experimentation: *Plot Devices 22*

alien first contact: *Plot Devices 22*

alien invasion: *Common Dangers 22; Plot Devices 22*

alien kidnapping: *Plot Devices 22*

alien mechanical: *Robots 22*

alien meddling: *Horror Genres 23*

alien technology : *Travel Modes 23; Energy Sources/Types 23*

alien zoo: *Plot Devices 22*

alien: *Monster Categories/Terms 16; Plot Devices 22*

aliens regard human race as food source: *Horror*

Plot Devices 23

aliens take over western town: *Western Plot Devices 21*

aliens: *Common Dangers 23; Horror Plot Devices 23; Travel Hazards 9*

Alinda: *Asteroids 11*

A-line skirt: *Ladies' Wear 2*

Aline: *Asteroids 11*

alive: *Mobility 1*

alkali metals: *Chemistry General Vocabulary 11*

alkali soil: *Soil General Vocabulary 10*

alkaline battery: *Chemistry General Vocabulary 11*

alkaline earth metals: *Chemistry General Vocabulary 11*

alkaline: *Geological Vocabulary 10*

alkaloid tomatine: *Poisonous Chemicals in Plants 11*

alkanet: *Garden Perennials 10*

Alkeste: *Asteroids 11*

Al-Khalid 2000 main battle tank: *China Military Vehicles 8*

Alkmene: *Asteroids 11*

alkonost: *Flying Creatures 16*

alkort: *Card Games 5*

alkyl group: *Chemistry General Vocabulary 11*

all citizens wield magic: *Fantasy Plot Devices 24*

all fives: *Card Games 5*

all for one and one for all: *Poker Card Games 5*

all fours: *Card Games 5*

All Hallows' Eve: *Halloween 19; Witchcraft Vocabulary 17*

all men are created equal: *Philosophy Basic Concepts 14*

All Saints: *Catholic Holy Days of Obligation 14*

allargando: *Tempo/Mood 13*

all-day sucker: *Candy General 6*

allege: *Speak 20*

Alleghenia: *Asteroids 11*

Allegheny chinkapin: *Deciduous Trees 10*

Allegheny spurge: *Garden Perennials 10*

allegory: *Fantasy Genres 24; Literary Styles 5*

allegretto: *Tempo/Mood 13*

Allégro: *Ballet Terms 13*

allegro: *Tempo/Mood 13*

allemande (Germany): *Ethnic/Folk Dances 13*

allemontite I: *Minerals 10*

allemontite II: *Minerals 10*

allemontite III: *Minerals 10*

allemontite: *Minerals 10*

Allen scythe: *General Farm Equipment*

allen wrench: *Hand Tools 5*

all-encompassing wisdom: *Five Wisdoms of Buddhism 19*

allergic reaction: *Injuries/Medical Emergencies 12*

allergies: *Anatomy and Physiology 12*

alley: *Roads 9*

alleyway: *Roads 9*

allgauer: *Cheese International Varieties 6*

alligator snapping: *Freshwater Turtles 15*

alligator-tree: *Evergreen Trees 10*

allium: *Garden Bulbs 10*

Allmogekor: *Other Cows 15*

allochthonous: *Geological Vocabulary 10*

allodapine: *Bees 15*

allosaurus: *Commonly Known Dinosaurs 15*

allotropes: *Chemistry General Vocabulary 11*

allow: *Agree 20*

alloying: *Chemistry General Vocabulary 11*

all-seeing eye: *Symbols in Magic and Religion 19; United States Dollar Bill 19*

allspice: *Spices 6*

all-terrain vehicle: *Motorized 9*

allure: *Castle Anatomy 3; Magic Vocabulary 17*

alluring: *Beautiful 20; Magic Vocabulary 17*

alluvial fan: *Fluvial 10; Geological Vocabulary 10*

alluvium: *Geological Vocabulary 10*

allyl alcohol: *Dangerous Chemicals 11*

allylamine: *Dangerous Chemicals 11*

Alma: *Asteroids 11*

Almace (Turpin): *Weapons of Legend 18*

almadel: *Symbols in Magic and Religion 19*

almandine garnet: *Standard Gems 21*

almandine spinel: *Minerals 10*

almandite: *Minerals 10*

almond milk: *Milk 6*

ALPHABETICAL INDEX

almond willow: *Deciduous Trees 10*

almond: *Aphrodisiacs 19; Nuts 6; Oils 6*

almondleaf willow: *Deciduous Trees 10*

Aloadae: *Giants of Legend 16*

aloe: *Shrubs 10*

alp horn: *Wind/Woodwind and Brass Musical Instruments*

alpaca: *Other Wild Mammals 15*

alpaca: *Transportation Animals 9*

alpha quartz: *Minerals 10*

alphabet: *Pasta 6*

Alphonsina: *Asteroids 11*

alpine fir: *Evergreen Trees 10*

alpine hemlock: *Evergreen Trees 10*

alpine larch: *Evergreen Trees 10*

alpine violet: *Garden Perennials 10*

alpine wallflower: *Garden Annuals 10*

alpine: *Butterfly 15; Newts 15; Salamanders 15*

Alsatia: *Asteroids 11*

Alstede: *Asteroids 11*

alstromeria: *Garden Bulbs 10*

Altai: *Horse Breeds 15*

altar boy/girl: *Religious Occupations 1*

altar: *Church Anatomy 3; altar: Religious Items 5; Horror Locations 23*

alternate Earth with fantasy races/creatures: *Fantasy Genres 24*

alternate Earth: *Horror Genres 23*

alternate future: *Horror Genres 23; Science Fiction Genres 22*

alternate history with fantasy races/creatures: *Fantasy Genres 24*

alternate history: *Horror Genres 23; Science Fiction Genres 22*

alternate life forms: *Plot Devices 22*

alternate universe: *Horror Genres 23; Science Fiction Genres 22*

Althaea: *Asteroids 11*

altitude: *Astronomy General Terms 11; Geography General Vocabulary 10*

alto clef: *Notation 13*

alto saxophone: *Wind/Woodwind and Brass Musical Instruments*

altocumulus: *Clouds 10*

Altona: *Asteroids 11*

altostratus: *Clouds 10*

aluette: *Card Games 5*

aluminum phosphide: *Dangerous Chemicals 11*

aluminum siding: *Exterior Building Materials 3*

Aluminum: *Elements 11*

alumroot: *Garden Perennials 10*

alurgite: *Minerals 10*

Alutiiq: *Native American Peoples 1*

alyssum: *Garden Annuals 10*

amabilis fir: *Evergreen Trees 10*

Amalasuntha: *Asteroids 11*

Amalia: *Asteroids 11*

Amalthea: *Asteroids 11; Moons 11*

Amanda: *Asteroids 11*

amaranth pink: *Pink 20*

amaranth: *Grain 6*

amaretto: *Ice Cream Flavors 6*

Amargosa: *Toads 15*

amaryllis: *Garden Bulbs 10*

Amaterasu Omikami (goddess of the sun): *Japanese Pantheon 14*

amatite: *Minerals 10*

Ama-tsu-mara (blacksmiths): *Japanese Pantheon 14*

amaze: *Magic Vocabulary 17*

amazement: *Magic Vocabulary 17*

amazing: *Expletives 20; Magic Vocabulary 17*

Amazon stone: *Minerals 10*

Amazon tree: *Boa 15*

Amazon: *Ants 15, Fighter 1; Large/Heavy 1*

Amazonian marmoset: *New World Monkeys 15*

amazonite: *Minerals 10; Standard Gems 21*

Amazonstone: *Minerals 10*

ambarella: *Unusual Edible Fruits 6*

amber opal: *Minerals 10*

amber: *Dragon 16; Eye Color 1; Wizard's Goods 5; Standard Gems 21; Yellow 20*

ambergris: *Wizard's Goods 5*

amberjack: *Wild Saltwater Fish 15*

ambidexterity: *Physical Mutations 22*

ambitious: *Personality Other 1*

amble: *Locomotion 9*

Ambriel: *Angels of Good 14*

Ambrosia: *Asteroids 11*

ambrosia: *Foods with Religious or Ritual Significance 19; Objects 18*

ambulance attendant/driver: *Medical Occupations 1*

ambulance driver: *Horror Occupations 23*

ambulance: *Military Aircraft Pre-1962 8; Military Ground Vehicles General 8; Motorized 9*

ambush: *General Combat Vocabulary 7; Traps 3*

AMC 34 light tank: *France Military Vehicles 8*

Amelia Earhart: *Famous Disappearances 18*

Amelia: *Asteroids 11*

amen to that: *Expletives 20*

Amenonuhoko: *Spears 18*

Ameraucana: *Chickens 15*

America: *Asteroids 11*

American alligator: *Crocodilians 15*

American arboreal lizard: *Scaled Reptiles 15*

American basswood: *Deciduous Trees 10*

American beech: *Deciduous Trees 10*

American black: *Bears 15*

American bobtail: *Domestic Cats 15*

American Bulldog: *Dog Breeds 15*

American cave: *Lions 15*

American Colonial: *Architectural Styles 3*

American Craftsman: *Architectural Styles 3*

American crawl: *Swimming Strokes 9*

American Cream Draft: *Horse Breeds 15*

American Creme and White: *Horse Breeds 15*

American crocodile: *Crocodilians 15*

American curl: *Domestic Cats 15*

American dream: *Garden Perennials 10*

American eel: *Wild Saltwater Fish 15*

American elm: *Deciduous Trees 10*

American Empire: *Architectural Styles 3*

American English Coonhound: *Dog Breeds 15*

American Eskimo: *Dog Breeds 15*

American feverfew: *Garden Perennials 10*

American Foursquare: *Architectural Styles 3*

American Foxhound: *Dog Breeds 15*

American fries: *Vegetables Cooked 6*

American game: *Chickens 15*

American green alder: *Deciduous Trees 10*

American hackberry: *Deciduous Trees 10*

American hogpeanut: *Wildflowers 10*

American holly: *Evergreen Trees 10*

American hop hornbeam: *Deciduous Trees 10*

American hornbeam: *Deciduous Trees 10*

American jackal: *Dogs/Canine 15*

American landrace: *Pigs 15*

American larch: *Evergreen Trees 10*

American legless lizard: *Scaled Reptiles 15*

American matsutake: *Fungus Common Names 10*

American mountain ash: *Deciduous Trees 10*

American Pit Bull Terrier: *Dog Breeds 15*

American plum: *Deciduous Trees 10*

American pokeweed: *Garden Perennials 10*

American realism: *Art Movements 13*

American ringtail: *Domestic Cats 15*

American shad: *Wild Saltwater Fish 15*

American shorthair: *Domestic Cats 15*

American sideneck river: *Freshwater Turtles 15*

American sideneck: *Freshwater Turtles 15*

American spikenard: *Garden Perennials 10*

American Staffordshire Terrier: *Dog Breeds 15*

American sycamore: *Deciduous Trees 10*

American Walking Pony: *Horse Breeds 15*

American walnut: *Deciduous Trees 10*

American Water Spaniel: *Dog Breeds 15*

American White Park: *Other Cows 15*

American willow herb: *Weeds 10*

American wirehair: *Domestic Cats 15*

American Yorkshire: *Pigs 15*

ALPHABETICAL INDEX

American: *Cheese Common Varieties 6; Coffee Bean Roasts 6; Other Cows 15*

Americium: *Elements 11*

Amerifax: *Other Cows 15*

Amesha Spenta: *Angels of Good 14*

amesite: *Minerals 10*

amethyst quartz: *Minerals 10*

amethyst: *Minerals 10; Purple 20; Standard Gems 21*

amethystine: *Python 15*

ametrine: *Minerals 10; Standard Gems 21*

Amherstia: *Asteroids 11*

amiable: *Happy 20*

amianthus: *Minerals 10*

amicable: *Happy 20*

Amicitia: *Asteroids 11*

amino acid: *Chemistry General Vocabulary 11*

aminopterin: *Dangerous Chemicals 11*

Amish: *Facial Hair Beard 1; Human Ethnic Groups 1*

amiton oxalate: *Dangerous Chemicals 11*

amiton: *Dangerous Chemicals 11*

AML 20 4×4 armored car: *France Military Vehicles 8*

AML 60 4×4 armored car: *France Military Vehicles 8*

AML 90 4×4 armored car: *France Military Vehicles 8*

ammit: *Demon 16*

ammolite: *Standard Gems 21*

ammonia: *Dangerous Chemicals 11*

ammunition storage: *Military Property 3*

Amneris: *Asteroids 11*

amoroso: *Tempo/Mood 13*

amorphous solid: *Chemistry General Vocabulary 11*

Ampella: *Asteroids 11*

ampere: *Chemistry General Vocabulary 11*

amphetamine: *Dangerous Chemicals 11*

amphibians: *Animals 15*

amphibious assault: *Military Watercraft 8*

amphibolite : *Metamorphic Rocks 10*

amphiprotism: *Chemistry General Vocabulary 11*

amphisbaena snake, Beast of Bray Road: *Mythical Creatures and Monsters 16*

amphitheater: *Academic Property 3; Entertainment Property 3*

Amphitrite: *Asteroids 11*

amphoterism: *Chemistry General Vocabulary 11*

ample: *Large 20; Large/Heavy 1*

amplifier: *Electronics 4*

ampule: *Containers and Vessels 5*

AMR 33 light tank: *France Military Vehicles 8*

Amrit Mahal: *Other Cows 15*

Amsterdam: *Architectural Styles 3*

amulet: *Typical Magical Objects 17; Witchcraft Vocabulary 17; Wizard's Goods 5*

amusement park: *Architecture and Property 3*

amusing: *Happy 20*

AMV self-propelled 81mm or 120mm mortar: *Turkey Military Vehicles 8*

AMX 30 main battle tank: *France Military Vehicles 8*

AMX 40 main battle tank: *France Military Vehicles 8*

AMX 56 main battle tank: *France Military Vehicles 8*

AMX VCI infantry fighting vehicle: *France Military Vehicles 8*

AMX-10P armored personnel carrier: *France Military Vehicles 8*

AMX-10RC 6×6 armored fighting vehicle: *France Military Vehicles 8*

AMX-13 light tank: *France Military Vehicles 8*

amygdala: *Organs/Major Structures 12*

amygdalin: *Poisonous Chemicals in Plants 11*

anabranch: *Fluvial 10*

anaconda: *General Snake Families 15*

Anacostia: *Asteroids 11*

anadama: *Bread General Varieties 6*

Anahita: *Asteroids 11*

analbite: *Minerals 10*

analysis: *Paranormal Activity 21; Philosophy Basic Concepts 14*

analyst: *Finance 1; Operations 1*

analytic: *Philosophy Basic Concepts 14*

analytical balance: *Laboratory Equipment 5*

analyze: *Learn 20; Solve 20*

Ananke: *Moons 11*

Anansi: *Insectoid 16*

anaphylactic shock: *Injuries/Medical Emergencies 12*

anarazel: *Devil 16*

anarchy: *Plot Devices 22*

anari: *Cheese International Varieties 6*

Anastasia: *Asteroids 11*

Anatolian Black: *Other Cows 15*

Anatolian Shepherd: *Dog Breeds 15*

Anatolian: *Domestic Cats 15*

anatomical foil: *Fencing Equipment 7*

anatomist: *Medical Occupations 1*

ancestor: *Relational 1*

ancestral: *Masks 2*

anchor bend: *Sailing Knots 9*

anchor chain: *Boat/Ship Anatomy 9*

anchor: *Boat/Ship Anatomy 9; Hardware 5; Media 1*

anchorage: *Marina 3; Water Terms 9*

anchovy: *Fish/Seafood Types 6; Wild Saltwater Fish 15*

Ancient and Mystical Order Rosae Crucis (also called Rosicrucian Order): *Secret/Mystical Organizations 18*

ancient creature/civilization brought back to life: *Horror Genres 23*

ancient curse: *Horror Plot Devices 23*

ancient Egyptian airplane models: *Real Objects Not Fully Understood 18*

Ancient Egyptian: *Architectural Styles 3*

ancient furnace: *Energy Sources/Types 24*

ancient gods threaten humanity: *Horror Plot Devices 23*

Ancient Greek: *Architectural Styles 3; Styles of Dress 2*

ancient mine: *Horror Locations 23*

ancient monster released during mining operation: *Horror Plot Devices 23*

ancient portal: *Travel Modes 23*

Ancient Roman: *Architectural Styles 3; Styles of Dress 2*

ancient society drinks blood of virgins to remain young: *Horror Plot Devices 23*

ancient spell: *Horror Plot Devices 23*

ancient/alien technology activates and threatens destruction: *Horror Plot Devices 23*

ancient: *Dragon 16; Elderly 1; Old 20*

Ancile: *Shields 18*

Andalusian Black: *Other Cows 15*

Andalusian Grey: *Other Cows 15*

Andalusian: *Horse Breeds 15; Human Ethnic Groups 1*

andalusite: *Cat's Eye Gems 21; Standard Gems 21*

Andamooka opal: *Minerals 10*

andante: *Tempo/Mood 13*

andantino: *Tempo/Mood 13*

andesine labradorite: *Standard Gems 21*

andesite: *Igneous Rocks 10*

andisol: *Soil General Vocabulary 10*

andoulli: *Sausage 6*

Andravida: *Horse Breeds 15*

Andrea's: *Keelback 15*

Andrew: *Twelve Apostles 14*

androgynous: *Styles of Dress 2*

android designer: *Occupations 22*

android rebellion: *Common Dangers 22*

android takeover: *Plot Devices 22*

android turns on creator: *Horror Plot Devices 23*

android: *Monsters and Creatures 22; Plot Devices 22; Robots 22*

androids: *Horror Plot Devices 23*

Andromache: *Asteroids 11*

Andromeda: *Constellations 11*

Andvarinaut: *Jewelry 18*

anemia: *Blood-Related Ailments 12*

anemometer: *Meteorology General Vocabulary 10*

anemone: *Garden Bulbs 10; Plants with Symbolic Meaning 19*

anesthesiologist: *Medical Occupations 1*

aneurysm: *Blood-Related Ailments 12; Injuries/Medical Emergencies 12*

angel food cake knife: *Kitchen Utensils 5*

angel food cake pan: *Kitchen Equipment 5*

angel food: *Cake 6*

angel hair: *Pasta 6*

angel of death: *Angels Common Terms 14*

angel of leadership: *Angels Common Terms 14*

angel wings: *Poisonous Plants 10*

angel: *Cake 6; Christmas 19; Fantasy Creatures with Symbolic Meaning 19; Monsters and Creatures 22*

ALPHABETICAL INDEX

angel's trumpet: *Plants with Symbolic Meaning 19; Poisonous Plants 10; Shrubs 10*

angelfish: *Aquarium Freshwater Fish 15; Aquarium Saltwater Fish 15*

angelic: *Beautiful 20*

Angelica tree: *Deciduous Trees 10; Shrubs 10*

Angelica: *Asteroids 11*

Angelina: *Asteroids 11*

angelite: *Minerals 10*

Angeln saddleback: *Pigs 15*

Angeln: *Other Cows 15*

angels of good: *Philosophy and Religion 14*

angels: *Philosophy and Religion 14*

angels' wings: *Fungus Common Names 10*

anger: *General Emotions 20*

Angkor Wat: *Unique Property 3*

angle grinder: *Power Tools*

angle of repose: *Soil General Vocabulary 10*

angle of the compass: *Symbols of Freemasonry 19*

angle: *Sharks 15*

Anglo-Kabarda: *Horse Breeds 15*

Anglo-Saxon: *Architectural Styles 3*

Angolan: *Python 15*

angora: *Fabric 2*

angry dragon: *Common Dangers 24*

angry father: *Supporting Cast 23*

angry horde of creatures/dragons: *Common Dangers 24*

angry large animal: *Travel Hazards 9*

angry mob: *Common Character Archetypes 21*

angry: *Character Building 1*

angst-ridden: *Horror Vocabulary 23*

angular unconformity: *Geological Vocabulary 10*

angular: *Small/Thin 1*

angulated: *Tortoises 15*

Angurvadal: *Norse Weapons 18*

Angus: *Other Cows 15*

Anhur (war): *Egyptian Pantheon 14*

Ani: *Asteroids 11*

aniline: *Dangerous Chemicals 11*

animal barns: *Amusement Park/Carnival/Circus/Fair 3*

animal bite: *Injuries/Medical Emergencies 12*

animal control: *Plot Devices 22*

animal entrails: *Fortune Telling General Devices 19*

animal fur: *Wizard's Goods 5*

animal homes: *Animals 15*

animal mimic: *Robots 22*

animal organs: *Wizard's Goods 5*

animal pen: *Farm/Outbuilding 3*

animal powered: *Energy Sources/Types 22*

animal shelter: *General Buildings 3*

animal skin: *Wizard's Goods 5*

animal stampede: *Travel Hazards 9*

animal swarm: *Plot Devices 22*

animal takeover: *Plot Devices 22*

animal transportation: *Transportation 9*

animal trap: *General Survival Gear 5*

animal with implanted weapons: *Monsters and Creatures 22*

animal/equestrian: *Character Building 1*

animal/insect swarm: *Horror Genres 23*

animal: *Art Genres 13; Masks 2; Spaceship Shapes 22*

animals use magic: *Fantasy Plot Devices 24*

animals: *Allergies 12; Christmas 19; Ten Plagues on Egypt 14*

animated items: *Magic 17*

animated: *Happy 20; Mobility 1; Monsters 16*

animato: *Tempo/Mood 13*

anime: *Art Genres 13*

animosity: *General Emotions 20*

anise bears: *Candy General 6*

anise mint: *Garden Perennials 10*

anise: *Aphrodisiacs 19; Candy General 6*

aniseed toadstool: *Fungus Common Names 10*

aniseroot: *Wildflowers 10*

anise-scented: *Fungus Common Names 10*

anisette: *Hard Liquor 6*

Anjou: *Pears 6*

ankh symbol: *Harbingers/Charms for Good Luck 19*

ankh: *Symbols in Magic and Religion 19*

ankheg: *Beast 16*

ankle straps: *Footwear/Shoes 2*

ankle: *Body Parts 12; Socks 2*

anklet: *Jewelry 2; Jewelry 21*

Ankole: *Other Cows 15*

Ankole-Watusi: *Other Cows 15*

ankylosaur: *Dinosaur Types 15*

ankylosaurus: *Commonly Known Dinosaurs 15*

Anna: *Asteroids 11*

Annefrank: *Asteroids with Unusual Names 11*

Anneliese: *Asteroids 11*

Annie Oakley: *Real People with Legendary Status 18; Western Paraphernalia/People 21*

annihilate: *Attack 7; Kill 20*

Annika: *Asteroids 11*

annite: *Minerals 10*

anniversary clock: *Timekeeping 5*

announcer: *Media 1*

annoy: *General Emotions 20*

annoyed: *Angry 1*

annuity coeptus: *United States Dollar Bill 19*

annulet: *Cadency Mark 19*

Annwn: *Afterlife/Underworld 18*

Anoghus (love): *Celtic Pantheon 14*

anoint: *Rituals 14*

Anointing of the Sick: *Sacraments 14*

anole: *Scaled Reptiles 15*

anomalous: *Sea Snake 15*

anorexic: *Small/Thin 1*

anorthose: *Minerals 10*

anorthosite: *Igneous Rocks 10*

Ansar: *Human Ethnic Groups 1*

Anschutz 1730: *Bolt Action Centerfire Rifles 7*

Anschutz model 64: *Bolt Action Rimfire Rifles 7*

Anseis: *Twelve Peers of Charlemagne 18*

Anshar (darkness): *Babylonian Pantheon 14*

answer: *Speak 20*

answering machine: *Office/School Machines 5*

ant farm: *Toys 5*

ant: *Giant Creatures 16*

Antaeus: *Giants of Legend 16*

antagonism: *General Emotions 20*

antagonist: *Fighter 1; Villain 20*

antagonistic: *Angry 1; Unattractive 20*

anteater: *Other Wild Mammals 15*

Antebellum: *Architectural Styles 3*

antechamber: *Rooms 3*

antechinus: *Other Wild Mammals 15*

antediluvian: *Old 20*

antelope bush: *Shrubs 10*

antelope: *Other Wild Mammals 15*

antennae: *Physical Mutations 22*

anterior thalamic nuclei: *Organs/Major Structures 12*

anteroom: *Rooms 3*

Anthe: *Moons 11*

anthem: *Composition Types 13*

anthias: *Aquarium Saltwater Fish 15*

anthill: *Natural Animal Homes 15*

anthodite: *Cave Anatomy 10*

anthology: *Books/Publications 5*

anthotyros: *Cheese International Varieties 6*

anthracite coal: *Metamorphic Rocks 10*

anthrax: *Diseases 12*

anthropologist: *Scientist 1*

anti-air frigate: *Military Watercraft 8*

anti-aircraft intercontinental ballistic: *Air Force Missile 8*

antibody: *Blood 12*

anticline: *Geological Vocabulary 10*

antigen: *Blood 12*

Antigo soil: *Soil General Vocabulary 10*

Antigone: *Asteroids 11*

antigorite: *Minerals 10*

anti-gravity sled: *Vehicles 22*

anti-inertia sled: *Vehicles 22*

Antikleia: *Asteroids 11*

Antikythera device: *Real Objects Not Fully Understood 18*

anti-material: *Assault Rifle 8*

antimatter: *Astronomy General Terms 11; Spaceship Drive Systems 22; Weapons 22*

antimonite: *Minerals 10*

antimony glance: *Minerals 10*

antimony pentafluoride: *Dangerous Chemicals 11*

Antimony: *Elements 11*

antimycin: *Dangerous Chemicals 11*

Antiope: *Asteroids 11*

antipasto: *Salads 6*

antipathy: *General Emotions 20*

antiperspirant: *Personal Care 5*

antipodal point: *Astronomy General Terms 11*

antiquarian: *Elderly 1*

antiquated: *Old 20*

antique dealer: *General Occupations 1*

antique gold: *Yellow 20*

antique store: *Business Property 3*

antique white: *White 20*

antique: *Old 20*

Anti-realism: *Art Movements 13*

antiserum: *Blood 12*

anti-structure weapon system: *Military Weapons General 8*

anti-submarine aircraft carrier: *Military Watercraft 8*

anti-submarine drone: *Military Aircraft Pre-1962 8*

anti-submarine frigate: *Military Watercraft 8*

anti-submarine warfare: *Helicopters 8*

anti-submarine: *Military Aircraft Pre-1962 8*

anti-tank vehicle: *Military Ground Vehicles General 8*

anti-tank weapon system: *Military Weapons General 8*

anti-tank weapon: *Military 8*

antler: *Moth 15*

Antlia: *Constellations 11*

Antonia: *Asteroids 11*

antozonite: *Minerals 10*

ants: *Animals 15*

Anu (leader of the gods): *Babylonian Pantheon 14*

Anubis (the dead): *Egyptian Pantheon 14*

anus: *Organs/Major Structures 12*

anvil/incus: *Bones 12*

anvil: *Hand Tools 5*

anxiety: *General Emotions 20*

anxious: *General Emotions 20; Vocal/Speech Quality 1*

Aoede: *Moons 11*

aorta: *Organs/Major Structures 12*

Apache pine: *Evergreen Trees 10*

Apache plume: *Garden Perennials 10; Shrubs 10*

Apache: *Native American Peoples 1*

apartment block: *Residential Property 3*

apartment house: *Residential Property 3*

apartment: *Residential Property 3*

apathetic: *Horror Vocabulary 23; Personality Other 1*

apathy: *General Emotions 20*

apatite: *Standard Gems 21*

apatosaurus: *Commonly Known Dinosaurs 15*

ape man: *Bears 15*

ape: *Animals with Symbolic Meaning 19*

apes: *Animals 15*

aphelion: *Astronomy General Terms 11*

aphrite: *Minerals 10*

Aphrodite (goddess of love): *Greek Pantheon 14*

apiarist: *Agricultural 1*

aplite: *Igneous Rocks 10*

apocalypse: *Plot Devices 22*

apogee: *Astronomy General Terms 11*

Apollo (healing, light, music, prophecy): *Roman Pantheon 14*

Apollo (the sun, truth, music, poetry, healing): *Greek Pantheon 14*

Apollo: *Minor Lines 19*

Apollo's lyre: *Objects 18*

Apollonia: *Asteroids 11*

apostle: *Cleric 1*

apothecary: *Business Property 3; Fantasy Occupations 24*

apotrope: *Symbols in Magic and Religion 19*

Appalachian English: *Pigs 15*

appall: *General Emotions 20*

appalling: *Bad 20; Horror Vocabulary 23*

Appaloosa: *Horse Breeds 15*

apparatus: *Miscellaneous Furniture 4*

apparent magnitude: *Astronomy General Terms 11*

apparent wind: *Water Terms 9*

apparition: *Magic Vocabulary 17; Paranormal Occurrences 21; Undead 16*

appassionato: *Tempo/Mood 13*

appealing: *Beautiful 20*

Appella: *Asteroids 11*

appendix: *Organs/Major Structures 12*

apperception: *Philosophy Basic Concepts 14*

apple blossom grass: *Garden Perennials 10*

apple butter: *Jam/Jelly/Preserves 6*

apple cider: *Fruit Juice 6*

apple cranberry: *Pie 6*

apple green: *Green 20*

apple peel: *Practices to Predict the Future 19*

apple streusel: *Pie 6*

apple wassailing: *Practices/Objects to Attract Good Luck 19*

apple: *Allergies 12; Aphrodisiacs 19; Cake 6; Cookie 6; Fruit Juice 6; Ice Cream Flavors 6; Muffin 6; Quick Bread 6; Items with Healing Properties 19; Objects/Activities Connected to Lore 19*

apple-cheeked: *Cheeks 1*

apples: *Food 6*

applesauce: *Cake 6*

appliances: *Equipment and Tools 5*

appliqué: *Embellishments 2*

appoggiatura: *General Music Vocabulary 13*

appraise: *Solve 20*

appraiser: *Finance 1*

appreciate: *General Emotions 20*

apprehension: *General Emotions 20; Horror Vocabulary 23*

apprehensive: *Horror Vocabulary 23*

apprentice loses control of creature: *Common Dangers 24*

apprentice loses control over magic: *Common Dangers 24*

apprentice: *General Occupations 1; Supporting Cast 24*

appropriate: *Close/Hold 20; Happy 20*

approve: *Agree 20; Buy 20*

approving: *Happy 20*

apricot jelly mushroom: *Fungus Common Names 10*

apricot: *Cookie 6; Ice Cream Flavors 6; Jam/Jelly/Preserves 6; Pit Fruits 6; Orange 20*

apricotine: *Minerals 10*

apron: *Laboratory Equipment 5; Unisex Clothing 2; Objects/Activities Connected to Lore 19; Parts of the Theater 13; Symbols of Freemasonry 19; Western Clothing/Dress 21*

apse: *Castle Anatomy 3; Church Anatomy 3*

Apshai (insects): *Egyptian Pantheon 14*

apt: *Happy 20*

Apus: *Constellations 11*

aqua aura: *Minerals 10*

aqua: *Cyan 20*

aquamarine: *Cat's Eye Gems 21; Cyan 20; Minerals 10; Standard Gems 21; Star Gems 21*

aquarium freshwater fish: *Animals 15*

aquarium saltwater fish: *Animals 15*

aquarium: *Man-Made Animal Homes 15*

Aquarius (January 20–February 18): *Zodiac Signs 19*

Aquarius: *Constellations 11*

aquatic monsters: *Monsters 16*

aquatic: *Ecosystems 10; Elf 1; Water Terms 9*

aqueduct: *Bridges 9; General Property 3*

aquifer: *Geological Vocabulary 10*

Aquila: *Constellations 11*

aquilegia: *Plants with Symbolic Meaning 19*

aquiline: *Nose 1*

Aquitania: *Asteroids 11*

Ara: *Asteroids 11; Constellations 11*

AraAppaloosa: *Horse Breeds 15*

Arab: *Human Ethnic Groups 1*

Arabella: *Asteroids 11*

Arabesque: *Ballet Terms 13*

Arabian: *Horse Breeds 15; Styles of Dress 2*

Arabica: *Coffee Varieties 6*

arable land: *Farm/Outbuilding 3*

Arachne: *Asteroids 11; Insectoid 16*

arachnids: *Animals 15*

aragonite sea: *Geological Vocabulary 10*

ALPHABETICAL INDEX

aragonite: *Cave Anatomy 10*

Aralia: *Asteroids 11*

aralia: *Shrubs 10*

Arapawa Island: *Pigs 15*

Arariel: *Angels of Good 14*

Arawn (the dead): *Celtic Pantheon 14*

araza: *Unusual Edible Fruits 6*

arbalest: *Missile Weapons 7*

arbitrator: *Legal Occupations 1*

arbor: *Landscaping 3*

arboreal: *Elf 1*

arborvitae: *Evergreen Trees 10; Shrubs 10*

arc: *Figures Associated with Symbols 19*

Arcachon Villa: *Architectural Styles 3*

arcade: *Castle Anatomy 3; Games 5; Rooms 3*

Arcadia: *Afterlife/Underworld 18*

arcane pathway: *Travel Modes 24*

arcane: *Magic Vocabulary 17*

Arce: *Deciduous Trees 10*

arch: *Body Parts 12; Bridges 9; Building Elements and Features 3; Castle Anatomy 3; Cave Anatomy 10; Coastal and Oceanic 10*

archaic: *Elderly 1; Old 20*

archangel: *Angels Common Terms 14*

archbishop: *Cleric 1; Religious Occupations 1*

archdeacon: *Cleric 1; Religious Occupations 1*

archdiocese: *Groupings 14*

archdruid: *Nature Occupations 1*

archduchess: *Royal/Noble 1*

archduke: *Royal/Noble 1*

Arche: *Moons 11*

archean eon: *Geological Vocabulary 10*

Archean Era: *Geologic Time 10*

arched: *Eyebrows 1*

archenemy: *Common Character Archetypes 21*

archeologist: *Horror Occupations 23; Scientist 1*

Archer tank destroyer: *United Kingdom Military Vehicles 8*

archer: *Castle Inhabitants and Personnel 1; Fighter 1; Fantasy Occupations 24*

archer's bonnet: *Headgear 2*

archipelago: *Coastal and Oceanic 10; Geological Vocabulary 10*

architect: *Construction 1*

architect's scale: *Architectural/Engineering Tools 5*

architectural elements: *Architecture and Property 3*

architectural structure: *Art Media 13*

architectural styles: *Architecture and Property 3*

architectural tools: *Equipment and Tools 5*

architecture paper: *Art Materials 5*

architecture: *Architecture and Property 3*

archive: *Academic Property 3*

archivist: *Academic 1*

archmage: *Wizard 1*

archpriest: *Religious Occupations 1*

archway: *Building Elements and Features 3*

arco: *Instrument Technique 13; Notation 13*

Arcology: *Architectural Styles 3*

arctic terrain warfare: *General Combat Vocabulary 7*

arctic willow: *Garden Perennials 10*

arctic: *Butterfly 15; Climatic Zones 10; Cold 10; Foxes 15*

Arcus 98DA: *Pistol Semiautomatic 7*

Ardagh Chalice: *Four Hallows of Ireland 18*

Ardennes: *Horse Breeds 15*

Arduina: *Asteroids 11*

arduous: *Difficult 20; Heavy 20; Slow 20*

Area 51: *Real Places Steeped in Legend or Mystery 18*

area air defense destroyer: *Military Watercraft 8*

area: *Terrain Features 10*

areesh: *Cheese International Varieties 6*

arena: *Entertainment Property 3*

Arend: *Comets 11*

Arend-Roland: *Comets 11*

Arequipa: *Asteroids 11*

Ares (war): *Greek Pantheon 14*

Arete: *Asteroids 11*

arête: *Glacial and Mountain 10*

Arethusa: *Asteroids 11*

Argand lamp: *Illumination/Light Sources 5*

argent (silver): *Colors/Tinctures 19*

argentiferous galena: *Minerals 10*

Argentina: *Asteroids 11*

Argentine Criollo: *Horse Breeds 15; Other Cows 15*

Argentine Dogo: *Dog Breeds 15*

Argentine: *Tortoises 15*

argentite: *Minerals 10*

argillite: *Sedimentary Rocks 10*

Argo: *Ships 18; Vehicles 18*

Argon: *Elements 11*

Argonautica fleece guardian: *Dragon 16*

Argonauts' oared ship: *Vehicles 18*

argue: *Speak 20*

argumentative: *Negative 1*

Argus Panoptes: *Giants of Legend 16*

arhat: *Unusual Edible Fruits 6*

aria: *Composition Types 13*

Ariadne: *Asteroids 11*

arid: *Climatic Zones 10; Climatic Zones Koeppen System 10; Dry 10*

aridisol: *Soil General Vocabulary 10*

Ariel: *Angels of Good 14; Moons 11*

Aries (March 21–April 19): *Zodiac Signs 19*

Aries: *Constellations 11*

aristocratic: *Personality Other 1*

Arizona 29-card pitch: *Card Games 5*

Arizona black walnut: *Deciduous Trees 10*

Arizona black: *Rattlesnake 15*

Arizona cypress: *Evergreen Trees 10*

Arizona fir: *Evergreen Trees 10*

Arizona longleaf pine: *Evergreen Trees 10*

Arizona madrone: *Deciduous Trees 10*

Arizona madrono: *Deciduous Trees 10*

Arizona oak: *Deciduous Trees 10*

Arizona rough cypress: *Evergreen Trees 10*

Arizona ruby: *Minerals 10*

Arizona territory: *Famous Western Locations 21*

Arizona walnut: *Deciduous Trees 10*

Arizona white oak: *Deciduous Trees 10*

Arizona: *Asteroids 11; Toads 15*

Ark of the Covenant: *Christian Relics 14*

Arkansas pine: *Evergreen Trees 10*

Arkansas soft pine: *Evergreen Trees 10*

arkansite: *Minerals 10*

arkose: *Sedimentary Rocks 10*

Arleigh Burke class destroyer: *U.S. Navy Vessels 8*

arm chair: *Chairs and Stools 4*

arm position high: *Fencing Vocabulary 7*

arm position inside: *Fencing Vocabulary 7*

arm position low: *Fencing Vocabulary 7*

arm position outside: *Fencing Vocabulary 7*

arm tow: *Swimming Strokes 9*

arm: *Body Parts 12*

Arma amphibious tactical wheeled armored vehicle: *Turkey Military Vehicles 8*

Armadillo wood and gravel AFV: *United Kingdom Military Vehicles 8*

armadillo: *Other Wild Mammals 15*

Armalite AR-10: *Semiautomatic Centerfire Rifles 7*

Armalite AR-25: *Pistol Semiautomatic 7*

Armalite AR30: *Bolt Action Centerfire Rifles 7*

armed merchant cruiser: *Military Watercraft 8*

armed: *Special Body Features 19*

Armenia: *Asteroids 11*

Armenian blackberry: *Weeds 10*

Armenian: *Imported Carpets 4*

armhole shirt: *Men's Wear 2*

armhook: *Squid 15*

Armida: *Asteroids 11*

arming: *Swords One-handed 7*

Arminius: *Real People with Legendary Status 18*

armistice: *General Combat Vocabulary 7*

armlet: *Jewelry 21*

armor of Achilles: *Armor of Legend 18*

armor of Beowulf: *Armor of Legend 18*

armor of Karna: *Armor of Legend 18*

armor of Thor: *Armor of Legend 18*

armor pieces: *Combat, Armor, and Weapons 7*

ALPHABETICAL INDEX

armor types: *Combat, Armor, and Weapons 7*

Armor: *Asteroids 11*

armor: *Combat, Armor, and Weapons 7; Typical Magical Objects 17*

armored car: *Armored Vehicles 8; Military Ground Vehicles General 8*

armored cruiser: *Military Watercraft 8*

armored fighting vehicle: *Armored Vehicles 8; Military Ground Vehicles General 8*

armored personnel carrier: *Military Ground Vehicles General 8*

armored security vehicle: *Military Ground Vehicles General 8*

armored vehicle: *Military Ground Vehicles General 8; SWAT Equipment 7*

armored vehicles: *Military 8*

armored vest: *Military Equipment 8*

armorer: *Castle Inhabitants and Personnel 1*

armory: *Fortification 3; Military Property 3*

armpit: *Body Parts 12*

army misunderstands threat: *Common Dangers 23*

army officer: *Horror Occupations 23*

army private: *Horror Occupations 23*

army ranks: *Military 8*

army: *Ants 15; General Combat Vocabulary 7*

Arne: *Asteroids 11*

aroma: *Smells 20*

aromatic hydrocarbons: *Chemistry General Vocabulary 11*

aromatic plant: *Wizard's Goods 5*

aromatic power: *Physical Mutations 22*

Arondight: *Arthurian Weapons 18*

arowana: *Aquarium Freshwater Fish 15*

arpeggio: *Instrument Technique 13*

arquebus. *Black Powder Weapons 7*

arrange: *Fix 20*

arrogant: *Negative 1*

arrow branching: *Figures Associated with Symbols 19*

arrow broom: *Garden Perennials 10*

arrow diagonal: *Figures Associated with Symbols 19*

arrow double-ended: *Figures Associated with Symbols 19*

arrow down: *Figures Associated with Symbols 19*

arrow left: *Figures Associated with Symbols 19*

arrow loop: *Castle Anatomy 3*

arrow right: *Figures Associated with Symbols 19*

arrow slit: *Castle Anatomy 3*

arrow starburst: *Figures Associated with Symbols 19*

arrow tooth flounder: *Wild Saltwater Fish 15*

arrow up: *Figures Associated with Symbols 19*

arrow: *Figures Associated with Symbols 19; Missile Loads 7; Traps 3; Valentine's Day 19*

arrowhawk: *Beast 16*

arrowhead: *Missile Weapons 7*

arrowsmith: *Castle Inhabitants and Personnel 1*

arroyo lupine: *Wildflowers 10*

arroyo: *Fluvial 10; Toads 15; Water Terms 9*

arsenal: *Fortification 3*

Arsenic: *Elements 11; Dangerous Chemicals 11*

arsenical pyrites: *Minerals 10*

arseniko naxou: *Cheese International Varieties 6*

arsenolamprite: *Minerals 10*

arsenous oxide: *Dangerous Chemicals 11*

arsenous trichloride: *Dangerous Chemicals 11*

arsine: *Dangerous Chemicals 11*

Arsinoe: *Asteroids 11*

Art Deco: *Architectural Styles 3; Art Movements 13*

artery: *Organs/Major Structures 12*

art gallery: *Entertainment Property 3*

art genres: *The Arts 13*

art materials: *Equipment and Tools 5*

art media: *The Arts 13*

art movements: *The Arts 13*

Art Nouveau: *Architectural Styles 3; Art Movements 13*

art principles: *The Arts 13*

art print: *Decorative Objects 4*

art school: *Academic Property 3*

art techniques: *The Arts 13*

art therapist: *Medical Occupations 1*

art tools: *Equipment and Tools 5*

Artemis (goddess of the hunt, archery, childbirth): *Greek Pantheon 14*

Artemis: *Asteroids 11*

artemisia: *Shrubs 10*

arterial highway: *Roads 9*

artery: *Roads 9*

Arthur's horses: *Arthurian Legend 18; Legendary, Mystical and Mythical Items and Locations 18*

Arthur's Round Table: *Arthurian Objects 18*

Arthurian characters: *Arthurian Legend 18; Legendary, Mystical and Mythical Items and Locations 18*

Arthurian Locations: *Arthurian Legend 18; Legendary, Mystical and Mythical Items and Locations 18*

Arthurian Objects: *Arthurian Legend 18; Legendary, Mystical and Mythical Items and Locations 18*

Arthurian Weapons: *Arthurian Legend 18; Legendary, Mystical and Mythical Items and Locations 18*

artichoke: *Vegetables 6*

articulated tractor and trailer: *Military Ground Vehicles General 8*

artifact is discovered: *Fantasy Plot Devices 24*

artifice: *Magic Vocabulary 17*

artificial color: *Allergies 12*

artificial intelligence: *Devices 22; Plot Devices 22*

artificial limb: *Devices 22*

artificial transmutation: *Chemistry General Vocabulary 11*

artificial: *Vocal/Speech Quality 1*

artillerist: *Fighter 1; Siege Engines 7*

artillery: *Cannon 7*

artisan: *Bread General Varieties 6*

artist: *Artists and Craftspeople 1; Bard 1; Castle Inhabitants and Personnel 1; Publishing 1*

artist's hat: *Headgear 2*

artiste: *Artists and Craftspeople 1; Bard 1*

artists: *Character Building 1*

Arts and Crafts: *Architectural Styles 3; Art Movements 13*

artsy: *Styles of Dress 2*

artwork: *Decorative Objects 4*

Aruba: *Rattlesnake 15*

arugula: *Vegetables 6*

asafetida: *Aphrodisiacs 19*

asag: *Demon 16*

ASAP: *Fast 20*

Asa-thor (thunder): *Norse Pantheon 14*

asbestos amphibole: *Minerals 10*

asbestos: *Minerals 10*

Ascalon: *Spears 18*

ascend: *Locomotion 9*

ascending colon: *Organs/Major Structures 12*

ascertain: *Learn 20; Solve 20*

Aschera: *Asteroids 11*

Asclepius: *Symbols in Magic and Religion 19*

ASCOD series armored vehicles: *Spain Military Vehicles 8*

ascot: *Men's Wear 2*

Asgard: *Fictional/Mythological Locations 18*

ash blond: *Hair Color 1*

ash tray: *Tableware 5*

ash tree leaves: *Practices/Objects to Attract Good Luck 19*

ash tree: *Items with Healing Properties 19*

ash: *Gray 20*

ashe juniper: *Evergreen Trees 10*

ashes: *Objects/Activities Connected to Lore 19; Rituals 14; Wizard's Goods 5*

Ashiwi: *Native American Peoples 1*

ashlar: *Symbols of Freemasonry 19*

ashleaf maple: *Deciduous Trees 10*

Ashtamangala: *Collective Symbols 19*

ashurkhana: *Religious Building 3*

ashy: *Skin Types and Features 1*

ashy-faced: *Owls 15*

Asi: *Weapons of Legend 18*

Asia: *Asteroids 11*

asiago: *Cheese Common Varieties 6*

Asian box: *Freshwater Turtles 15*

Asian elephant: *Other Wild Mammals 15*

Asian giant river terrapin: *Freshwater Turtles 15*

Asian lady: *Beetle 15*

Asian leaf: *Freshwater Turtles 15*

Asian wood: *Freshwater Turtles 15*

Asian: *Human Ethnic Groups 1; Styles of Dress 2; Keelback 15*

Asiatic black: *Bears 15*

ALPHABETICAL INDEX

Asiatic blue dayflower: *Weeds 10*

Asiatic brown: *Bears 15*

Asiatic linsang: *Other Wild Mammals 15*

Asiatic tearthumb: *Weeds 10*

Asiatic witchweed: *Weeds 10*

Asiatic: *Lions 15; Salamanders 15*

Asimov: *Asteroids with Unusual Names 11*

ask: *Speak 20*

askouandy: *Symbols in Magic and Religion 19*

ASLAV 8×8 infantry fighting vehicle: *Australia Military Vehicles 8; Canada Military Vehicles 8*

Aslog: *Asteroids 11*

asmodeus: *Devil 16*

asp: *General Snake Families 15; Viper 15*

asparagus green: *Vegetables 6*

asparagus lettuce: *Vegetables 6*

asparagus server: *Tableware 5*

asparagus white: *Vegetables 6*

asparagus: *Green 20; Soup 6*

asparagus berry: *Poisonous Plants 10;*

Aspasia: *Asteroids 11*

aspen scaber stalk: *Fungus Common Names 10*

aspen tree: *Items with Healing Properties 19*

aspen: *Deciduous Trees 10*

asphalt road: *Roads 9*

asphalt shingle: *Roofing Materials 3*

asphalt: *Geological Vocabulary 10*

aspirator: *Laboratory Equipment 5*

Asplinda: *Asteroids 11*

Asporina: *Asteroids 11*

asrai: *Water Faerie 16*

ass: *Horses Related 15; Transportation Animals 9*

assai: *Tempo/Mood 13*

assail: *General Combat Vocabulary 7*

assailant: *Fighter 1*

Assam: *Keelback 15*

assam: *Tea 6*

assamese dao: *Swords Two-handed 7*

assassin vine: *Plant 16*

assassin: *Character Building 1; Fighter 1; Villain 20*

assassinate: *Attack 7; Kill 20*

assassination of Kennedy: *Legendary Events 18*

assassination of Lincoln: *Legendary Events 18*

assassins: *Guilds 1*

assault drone: *Military Aircraft Pre-1962 8*

assault rifle: *SWAT Weapons 7*

assault: *Fencing Vocabulary 7; General Combat Vocabulary 7; Harm 20*

assegai: *Spears 7*

Assemblé: *Ballet Terms 13*

assemble: *Fix 20*

assembler: *General Occupations 1*

assembly: *Rooms 3*

assertive: *Personality Other 1*

assess: *Solve 20*

assessor: *Wizard 1*

assignment book: *Office/School/Writing Supplies 5*

assist: *Teach 20*

assistant editor: *Publishing 1*

assistant principal: *Academic 1*

associate editor: *Publishing 1*

associated state: *Political Divisions 10*

association: *Social Clubs 1*

asson: *Objects in Magic and Religion 19*

assorted: *Candy Chocolate 6*

Assumption: *Catholic Holy Days of Obligation 14*

assured: *Happy 20*

astaroth: *Devil 16*

Astarte: *Asteroids 11*

Astatine: *Elements 11*

Asteria: *Asteroids 11*

astern: *Boat/Ship Terminology 9*

asteroid hitting Earth: *Common Dangers 22*

asteroid miner: *Vehicles 22*

asteroid on collision course with Earth: *Horror Plot Devices 23*

asteroid: *Astronomy General Terms 11*

Asterope: *Asteroids 11*

asthenosphere: *Geological Vocabulary 10*

Astolpho: *Twelve Peers of Charlemagne 18*

astonishing: *Magic Vocabulary 17*

astounding: *Magic Vocabulary 17*

Astraea: *Asteroids 11*

astral travel: *Magical Transportation 17; Paranormal Abilities 21; Travel Modes 23*

astral: *Travel Modes 24; Travel Types 22*

astringent: *Smells 20*

astrolabe: *Boat/Ship Anatomy 9*

astrologer: *Cleric 1; Fortune Teller 1; Wizard 1*

astrology: *Fortune Telling General Techniques 19*

astronaut: *Horror Occupations 23; Occupations 22; Scientist 1*

astronomer: *Scientist 1*

astronomical unit: *Astronomy General Terms 11*

astrum argentums seal: *Symbols in Magic and Religion 19*

Asturian Mountain: *Other Cows 15*

Asturian Valley: *Other Cows 15*

Asturian: *Horse Breeds 15*

ASU-57 self-propelled 57mm gun: *Russia Military Vehicles 8*

ASU-85 self-propelled 85mm gun: *Russia Military Vehicles 8*

asura: *Demon 16*

Aswail: *Bears 15*

asylum: *Health Care 3*

asymmetric war: *General Combat Vocabulary 7*

at ease: *Easy 20; Happy 20*

AT105 Saxon wheeled armored personnel carrier: *United Kingdom Military Vehicles 8*

AT4: *Anti-tank 8*

Atala: *Asteroids 11*

Atalante: *Asteroids 11*

Atchisson assault shotgun: *Shotguns General 7*

Ate: *Asteroids 11*

atemoya: *Unusual Edible Fruits 6*

atgeir: *Pole Weapons 7*

Athalia: *Asteroids 11*

Athamantis: *Asteroids 11*

athame: *Daggers and Knives 7; Objects in Magic and Religion 19*

Athanasia: *Asteroids 11*

athanor: *Objects in Magic and Religion 19*

atheism: *Philosophy Basic Concepts 14*

atheist: *Symbols in Magic and Religion 19*

Athena (goddess of wisdom and combat): *Greek Pantheon 14*

Athene: *Asteroids 11*

athlete's foot: *Diseases 12*

athletic director: *Sports 1*

athletic shoes: *Clothing 2*

athletic: *Mobility 1; Socks 2; Styles of Dress 2*

Athor: *Asteroids 11*

Atira (mother goddess): *Native American Pantheon 14*

Atlantean: *Human Races Fictional 1*

Atlantic cod: *Wild Saltwater Fish 15*

Atlantic croaker: *Wild Saltwater Fish 15*

Atlantic flounder: *Wild Saltwater Fish 15*

Atlantic marmoset: *New World Monkeys 15*

Atlantic moonfish: *Wild Saltwater Fish 15*

Atlantic salmon: *Wild Saltwater Fish 15*

Atlantic spade: *Wild Saltwater Fish 15*

Atlantic thread tuna: *Wild Saltwater Fish 15*

Atlantic white cedar: *Evergreen Trees 10*

Atlantis: *Crosses 19; Sites Lost or Unproven to Exist 18*

atlas moth: *Moth 15*

atlas: *Bones 12; Books/Publications 5*

Atlas: *Moons 11*

atlatl: *Missile Weapons 7*

atmosphere: *Astronomy General Terms 11; Chemistry General Vocabulary 11; Geography General Vocabulary 10; Meteorology General Vocabulary 10*

atmospheric pressure: *Meteorology General Vocabulary 10*

atoll: *Coastal and Oceanic 10*

atom: *Chemistry General Vocabulary 11*

atomic bomb: *Spy Gear 5*

atomic creature/human: *Monsters and Creatures 22*

atomic mass unit: *Chemistry General Vocabulary 11*

atomic number: *Chemistry General Vocabulary 11*

atomic orbital: *Chemistry General Vocabulary 11*

ALPHABETICAL INDEX

atomic radius: *Chemistry General Vocabulary 11*

atomic weight: *Chemistry General Vocabulary 11*

atomic: *Energy Sources/Types 22; Small/Fragile 20; Spaceship Drive Systems 22; Weapons 22*

atonal: *General Music Vocabulary 13*

Atossa: *Asteroids 11*

AT-P tracked prime mover and artillery crew transporter: *Russia Military Vehicles 8*

atriplex: *Soil General Vocabulary 10*

atrium: *Rooms 3*

atrocious: *Bad 20; Horror Vocabulary 23; Unattractive 20*

atrocities: *General Combat Vocabulary 7*

atropine: *Poisonous Chemicals in Plants 11*

Atropos: *Asteroids 11*

ATS 56 G artillery tractor: *Russia Military Vehicles 8*

attach: *Fix 20*

attaché case: *Containers and Vessels 5; Spy Gear 5*

attached lobes: *Ears 1*

attack VTOL: *Military Aircraft 8*

attack: *Combat, Armor, and Weapons 7; Fencing Vocabulary 7; General Combat Vocabulary 7; Helicopters 8; Military Aircraft 8; Military Aircraft Pre-1962 8*

attacker: *Assassin 1; Fighter 1*

attain: *Buy 20*

attan (Afghanistan): *Ethnic/Folk Dances 13*

attendant: *General Occupations 1*

attending physician: *Medical Occupations 1*

attention grabbing: *Beautiful 20*

attic dropdown: *Doors 3*

attic: *Horror Locations 23; Rooms 3*

attired: *Special Body Features 19*

Attitude: *Ballet Terms 13*

attitude: *Dance Moves 13*

attorney: *Legal Occupations 1*

attracted to: *Love 20*

attraction: *General Emotions 20*

attractive: *Beautiful 20*

attribute: *Philosophy Basic Concepts 14*

ATV self-propelled TOW anti-tank missile: *Turkey Military Vehicles 8; United States Military Vehicles 8*

aubade: *Composition Types 13*

Aubrac: *Other Cows 15*

auburn: *Hair Color 1; Red 20*

Auckland Island: *Pigs 15*

auction: *Poker Card Games 5*

auctioneer: *General Occupations 1*

aucuba: *Shrubs 10*

audacious: *Personality Other 1*

audience chamber: *Rooms 3*

audiologist: *Medical Occupations 1*

auditor: *Finance 1*

auditorium: *Academic Property 3; Entertainment Property 3; Rooms 3*

auger: *Power Tools*

augment: *Buy 20*

augur: *Cleric 1; Illusionist 1; Wizard 1*

Augusta: *Asteroids 11*

auld lang syne: *New Year 19*

Aulie-Ata: *Other Cows 15*

aumbry: *Castle Anatomy 3*

aunt: *Female 1*

aura: *Cheese International Varieties 6*

Auravictrix: *Asteroids 11*

Aurelia: *Asteroids 11*

Auriga: *Constellations 11*

Aurora (Borealis and Australis): *Seven Wonders of the Natural World 18*

Aurora (goddess of dawn): *Roman Pantheon 14*

aurora australis: *Astronomy General Terms 11*

aurora borealis: *Astronomy General Terms 11; Harbingers of Bad Luck 19; Mysterious Occurrences 18*

Aurora: *Asteroids 11*

aurora: *Astronomy General Terms 11; Meteorology General Vocabulary 10*

auslese: *Wine White 6*

Ausonia: *Asteroids 11*

auspicious: *Fortunate 20*

austere: *Easy 20*

Austin class: *U.S. Navy Vessels 8*

Australian Braford: *Other Cows 15*

Australian Brumby: *Horse Breeds 15*

Australian Cattle Dog: *Dog Breeds 15*

Australian corroboree: *Frogs 15*

Australian crawl: *Swimming Strokes 9*

Australian freshwater crocodile: *Crocodilians 15*

Australian Friesian Sahiwal: *Other Cows 15*

Australian Lowline: *Other Cows 15*

Australian Milking Zebu: *Other Cows 15*

Australian Mist: *Domestic Cats 15*

Australian pine: *Evergreen Trees 10; Weeds 10*

Australian scrub: *Python 15*

Australian Shepherd: *Dog Breeds 15*

Australian Stock Horse: *Horse Breeds 15*

Australian swamp stonecrop: *Weeds 10*

Australian Terrier: *Dog Breeds 15*

Australian wattles: *Weeds 10*

Australian Yorkshire: *Pigs 15*

Austria: *Asteroids 11*

Austrian pine: *Evergreen Trees 10*

author: *Publishing 1*

authoritarian: *Wizard 1*

authoritative: *Personality Other 1; Vocal/Speech Quality 1*

authorize: *Agree 20*

auto car: *Railroad 9*

auto-assault gun: *Shotguns General 7*

autobiography: *Literary Styles 5*

autocannon: *Cannon 7*

autochthonous: *Geological Vocabulary 10*

autoclave: *Laboratory Equipment 5*

autocrat: *Wizard 1*

automated medical: *Devices 22*

automatic: *Doors 3*

automaton: *Construct 16; Robots 22*

automobile: *Motorized 9*

Autonoe: *Moons 11*

Auto-ordnance 1911A1: *Pistol Semiautomatic 7*

Auto-ordnance M1 Carbine: *Semiautomatic Centerfire Rifles 7*

autumn crocus: *Poisonous Plants 10*

autumn: *Four Seasons 19; Meteorology General Vocabulary 10*

autumnal crocus: *Weeds 10*

auxiliary: *Social Clubs 1*

avalanche: *Geological Natural Hazards 10*

avant-garde: *Art Genres 13; New 20*

Avenger air defense vehicle: *United States Military Vehicles 8*

Avenger class: *U.S. Navy Vessels 8*

avens: *Garden Perennials 10*

aventurine: *Minerals 10; Standard Gems 21*

avenue: *Roads 9*

averse: *Horror Vocabulary 23*

aversion: *General Emotions 20*

AVGP Cougar wheeled fire support vehicle: *Canada Military Vehicles 8*

AVGP Grizzly wheeled armored personnel carrier: *Canada Military Vehicles 8*

AVGP Husky wheeled maintenance and recovery vehicle: *Canada Military Vehicles 8*

aviation aircraft carrier: *Military Watercraft 8*

aviator cap: *Headgear 2*

avocado: *Aphrodisiacs 19; Pit Fruits 6; Vegetables 6*

Avogadro's law: *Chemistry General Vocabulary 11*

Avogadro's number: *Chemistry General Vocabulary 11*

avulsion: *Geological Natural Hazards 10*

awaruite: *Minerals 10*

awe inspiring: *Beautiful 20*

awe: *General Emotions 20; Magic Vocabulary 17*

awed: *Magic Vocabulary 17*

awen: *Symbols in Magic and Religion 19*

awesome: *Beautiful 20; Expletives 20; Good 20*

awestruck: *Magic Vocabulary 17*

awful: *Bad 20; Horror Vocabulary 23; Unattractive 20*

awkward: *Difficult 20; Mobility 1*

awl pike: *Spears 7*

awl: *Flies 15*

AWOL: *General Combat Vocabulary 7*

ax: *Hand Tools 5*

axe image: *Harbingers/Charms for Good Luck 19*

axe: *Classic Items 23*

axebeak: *Beast 16*

axe-knife: *Axes 7*

axes: *Combat, Armor, and Weapons 7*

axinite: *Standard Gems 21*

axis mundi: *Symbols in Magic and Religion 19*

axis: *Astronomy General Terms 11*

ayib: *Cheese International Varieties 6*

Aymaras: *Human Ethnic Groups 1*

ayre: *Coastal and Oceanic 10*

Ayrshire: *North American Dairy Cows 15*

azalea: *Poisonous Plants 10; Shrubs 10*

Azaouak: *Other Cows 15*

Azara's zorro: *Foxes 15*

azazel: *Devil 16*

Azazel: *Fallen Angels 14*

Azerbaijani: *Imported Carpets 4*

Azeris: *Human Ethnic Groups 1*

azi-dahaka: *Demon 16*

azimuth: *Astronomy General Terms 11*

azinphos-ethyl: *Dangerous Chemicals 11*

azinphos-methyl: *Dangerous Chemicals 11*

azotic topaz: *Standard Gems 21*

Azrael: *Angels of Good 14*

Aztec calendar: *Real Objects Not Fully Understood 18*

Aztec Indian berry: *Garden Perennials 10*

Aztec pantheon: *Philosophy and Religion 14*

Aztec: *Native American Peoples 1*

Azteca: *Horse Breeds 15*

azure (blue): *Colors/Tinctures 19*

azure copper ore: *Minerals 10*

azure damsel: *Aquarium Saltwater Fish 15*

azure: *Blue 20; Butterfly 15*

azure-malachite: *Minerals 10*

–B–

B1 Centauro 8×8 tank destroyer: *Italy Military Vehicles 8*

B-1 Lancer bomber: *U.S. Air Force Aircraft 8*

B-2 Spirit: *U.S. Air Force Aircraft 8*

B-52 Stratofortress: *U.S. Air Force Aircraft 8*

B-531 armored personnel carrier: *China Military Vehicles 8*

Ba Xuyen: *Pigs 15*

Ba: *Symbols in Magic and Religion 19*

BA-10 6×4 armored car: *Russia Military Vehicles 8*

BA-3 6×4 armored car: *Russia Military Vehicles 8*

BA-64 4×4 armored car: *Russia Military Vehicles 8*

baal: *Devil 16*

Baalbeck in Lebanon: *Real Places Steeped in Legend or Mystery 18*

babaco: *Unusual Edible Fruits 6*

Babe the Blue Ox: *Tall Tales 18*

babe: *Beautiful 20; Child 1; Female 1*

babe-in-arms: *Child 1*

Babi Kampung: *Pigs 15*

babi: *Demon 16*

babka mold: *Kitchen Equipment 5*

babka: *Bread General Varieties 6*

baboon: *Old World Monkeys 15*

Babr-e Bayan (armored coat worn by Rostam): *Clothing 18*

baby bella mushroom: *Vegetables 6*

baby blue eyes: *Garden Annuals 10; Wildflowers 10*

baby blue: *Blue 20*

baby bonnet: *Headgear 2*

baby buggy: *Human-Powered Transportation 9*

baby corn: *Vegetables 6*

baby doll nightgown: *Ladies' Wear 2*

baby doll top: *Ladies' Wear 2*

baby doll: *Toys 5*

baby peas: *Vegetables 6*

baby pink: *Pink 20*

baby rose: *Weeds 10*

baby scallop: *Fish/Seafood Types 6*

baby stroller: *Human-Powered Transportation 9*

baby Swiss: *Cheese Common Varieties 6*

baby: *Child 1; Teeth 1; New Year 19; Teeth 12*

baby's breath: *Garden Perennials 10; Wildflowers 10*

Babylonian pantheon: *Philosophy and Religion 14*

babysitter: *Common Character Archetypes 21; General Occupations 1; Horror Occupations 23*

baccarat: *Card Games 5*

Bacchus (wine): *Roman Pantheon 14*

bachata: *Dance Styles 13*

Bachaur: *Other Cows 15*

bachelor button: *Garden Annuals 10; Garden Perennials 10; Wildflowers 10*

bachelor pad: *Residential Property 3; Residential Slang 3*

bachelor: *Male 1*

bachelorette: *Female 1*

bachensteiner: *Cheese International Varieties 6*

bacinet: *Head Gear 7*

back alley: *Card Games 5*

back chair: *Chairs and Stools 4*

back float: *Swimming Strokes 9*

back off: *Expletives 20*

back street bridge: *Card Games 5*

back: *Body Parts 12*

back: *Doors 3; Garment Pieces 2; Swords One-handed 7*

backfire: *Witchcraft Vocabulary 17*

backgammon: *Games 5*

background radiation: *Chemistry General Vocabulary 11*

backhoe loader: *General Farm Equipment*

backless bench: *Seating 4*

backlight: *Technical Terms 13*

backpack: *Accessories 2; Containers and Vessels 5; General Survival Gear 5; Office/School/Writing Supplies 5*

backpacker: *Barbarian 1; Shotguns General 7*

backstage: *Parts of the Theater 13*

backstroke: *Swimming Strokes 9*

backup knot: *Sailing Knots 9*

backyard birds: *Animals 15*

bacon: *Muffin 6*

bacon-lettuce-and-tomato: *Sandwiches 6*

bacteremia: *Blood-Related Ailments 12*

bacteriologist: *Scientist 1*

bacupari: *Unusual Edible Fruits 6*

bacuri: *Unusual Edible Fruits 6*

bad food: *Travel Hazards 9*

bad guy is secret agent: *Western Plot Devices 21*

bad guy: *Villain 20*

bad luck: *Witchcraft Vocabulary 17*

bad weather isolates campers/travelers/residents: *Horror Plot Devices 23*

bad weather: *Travel Hazards 9*

bad: *Adjectives 20; Negative 1; Unattractive 20*

badge: *Jewelry 21*

badger: *Woodland Mammals 15*

badges: *Western Clothing/Dress 21*

badinerie: *Composition Types 13*

badland: *Ecosystems 10*

bad-man's oatmeal: *Poisonous Plants 10*

badminton racquet: *Sporting Goods Other 5*

badugi: *Card Games 5*

Badui: *Human Ethnic Groups 1*

bael: *Unusual Edible Fruits 6*

Baer's law: *Soil General Vocabulary 10*

baffle: *Magic Vocabulary 17; Technical Terms 13*

baffling: *Magic Vocabulary 17*

bag: *Accessories 2; Containers and Vessels 5*

bagatelle: *Composition Types 13*

Bagdemagus: *Knights of the Round Table 18*

bagel: *Bread General Varieties 6*

baggage attendant: *Hospitality 1*

bagger: *General Occupations 1*

Baghdad battery: *Real Objects Not Fully Understood 18*

bagpipe: *Wind/Woodwind and Brass Musical Instruments*

baguette bag: *Accessories 2*

baguette: *Bread General Varieties 6; Gem Cuts 21*

Baha'i Texts: *Major Religious Books 14*

bahamut: *Aquatic 16*

Bahrani: *Human Ethnic Groups 1*

bai bao: *Bears 15*

bai ze: *Beast 16*

bail bondsman: *Legal Occupations 1*

bailey: *Castle Anatomy 3*

bailiff: *Legal Occupations 1*

bailiwick: *Political Divisions 10*

bain marie: *Kitchen Equipment 5*

bait: *Fishing Gear 5; Traps 3*

Baja California slider: *Freshwater Turtles 15*

Baka: *Human Ethnic Groups 1*

bake: *Cooking Techniques 20*

baked Alaska: *Miscellaneous Dessert 6*

baked beans: *Vegetables Cooked 6*

baked: *Vegetables Cooked 6; Warm 10*

bakeneko: *Beast 16*

Baker cypress: *Evergreen Trees 10*

baker: *Food Service 1*

baker's dozen: *Solitaire Card Games 5*

baker's rack: *Storage 4*

bakers: *Cheese Common Varieties 6*

bakery: *Business Property 3*

bakewell tart: *Cake 6*

bakh-nakh: *Hand Weapons 7*

baking ammonia: *Staples 6*

baking powder: *Staples 6*

baking soda: *Staples 6*

baking: *Candy Chocolate 6*

Bakongo: *Human Ethnic Groups 1*

bala shark: *Aquarium Freshwater Fish 15*

balaclava: *Accessories 2; Headgear 2*

Baladi: *Other Cows 15*

balam: *Devil 16*

Balan: *Knights of the Round Table 18*

balance: *Art Principles 13*

Balancé: *Ballet Terms 13*

balance: *Physical Mutations 22*

balanced: *Happy 20*

balaos: *Wild Freshwater Fish 15*

balas ruby: *Minerals 10*

balbo: *Facial Hair Beard 1*

balcony: *Parts of the Theater 13; Rooms 3*

bald cypress: *Evergreen Trees 10*

bald eagle: *United States Dollar Bill 19*

bald: *Hair Style 1; Skin Types and Features 1*

Baldur (light): *Norse Pantheon 14*

bale lifter: *General Farm Equipment*

bale mover: *General Farm Equipment*

bale of hay: *Western Paraphernalia/People 21*

bale spike: *General Farm Equipment*

bale splitter: *General Farm Equipment*

bale trailer: *General Farm Equipment*

bale wrapper: *General Farm Equipment*

Balearic: *Horse Breeds 15*

baleen: *Whales 15*

baler: *General Farm Equipment*

balestra: *Fencing Vocabulary 7*

bali: *Demon 16*

Bali: *Tigers 15*

Balin: *Knights of the Round Table 18*

Balinese: *Domestic Cats 15; Human Ethnic Groups 1*

baling hook: *Hand Tools 5*

Balisarda: *Weapons of Legend 18*

Balkars: *Human Ethnic Groups 1*

ball and chain: *Bludgeons 7*

ball bearings: *Hardware 5*

ball cactus: *Garden Perennials 10*

ball drop: *New Year 19*

ball peen hammer: *Hand Tools 5*

ball: *Games 5; Toys 5; Python 15*

ballad: *Composition Types 13*

ballas: *Minerals 10*

ballast: *Boat/Ship Anatomy 9*

ballerina length skirt: *Ladies' Wear 2*

ballerina: *Ballet Terms 13; Performing Arts 1*

ballet flats: *Footwear/Shoes 2*

ballet master: *Ballet Terms 13*

ballet mistress: *Ballet Terms 13*

ballet slipper: *Dance Shoes 13*

ballet terms: *The Arts 13*

ballet: *Ballet Terms 13; Dance Styles 13*

Balletomane: *Ballet Terms 13*

ballista: *Siege Engines 7; Traps 3*

ballistic face mask: *Body Armor 7*

ballistic shield: *SWAT Equipment 7*

ballistic: *Shields Post-1900 7*

Ballon: *Ballet Terms 13*

balloon carrier: *Military Watercraft 8*

balloon flower: *Garden Perennials 10*

balloon glass: *Drinkware 5*

balloon hem skirt: *Ladies' Wear 2*

balloon pilot: *Fantasy Occupations 24*

balloon pop: *Amusement Park/Carnival/Circus/Fair 3*

balloon tender: *Military Watercraft 8*

balloon: *Air Vehicles 9; Bread General Varieties 6; Toys 5*

balloon: *Dance Moves 13*

Ballotté: *Ballet Terms 13*

ballpoint pen: *Office/School/Writing Supplies 5*

ballroom shoes: *Dance Shoes 13*

ballroom: *Rooms 3*

ballyhoo: *Wild Saltwater Fish 15*

balm: *Wizard's Goods 5*

balmoral: *Headgear 2*

Balmung: *Norse Weapons 18*

balmy: *Meteorology General Vocabulary 10*

Baloo: *Bears 15*

balsam fir: *Evergreen Trees 10*

balsam Fraser fir: *Evergreen Trees 10*

balsam poplar: *Deciduous Trees 10*

balsam: *Evergreen Trees 10; Garden Annuals 10; Wizard's Goods 5*

Baltana Romaneasca: *Other Cows 15*

Balthasar: *Three Wise Men 19*

Baltic German: *Human Ethnic Groups 1*

Baluchi: *Horse Breeds 15*

baluster: *Castle Anatomy 3*

balustrade: *Castle Anatomy 3*

Bama soil: *Soil General Vocabulary 10*

Bamar: *Human Ethnic Groups 1*

bamboo plant: *Harbingers/Charms for Good Luck 19*

bamboo shoot: *Vegetables 6*

bamboo steamer: *Kitchen Equipment 5*

bamboo: *Bats 15; Door Materials 3; Fabric 2; Pit Viper 15; Viper 15*

bamboozle: *Magic Vocabulary 17*

Bamileke: *Human Ethnic Groups 1*

Ban: *Knights of the Round Table 18*

banana chocolate chip: *Cake 6*

banana cream: *Pie 6*

banana split: *Ice Cream Desserts 6; Ice Cream Flavors 6*

banana: *Aphrodisiacs 19; Bats 15; Cake 6; Ice Cream Flavors 6; Ice Cream Toppings 6; Muffin 6; Quick Bread 6; Tropical/Exotic Fruits 6*

Banat Swabians: *Human Ethnic Groups 1*

band leader: *Musical Occupations 1*

band of holes at Pisco Valley in Chile: *Real Places Steeped in Legend or Mystery 18*

band of stability: *Chemistry General Vocabulary 11*

band saw: *Power Tools*

band theory of metals: *Chemistry General Vocabulary 11*

band: *Chemistry General Vocabulary 11; Jewelry 21*

bandana: *Western Clothing/Dress 21; Headgear 2*

band-bellied: *Owls 15*

bandeau hat: *Headgear 2*

banded chest: *Containers and Vessels 5*

banded iron formation: *Geological Vocabulary 10; Sedimentary Rocks 10*

banded mail: *Armor Types 7*

banded opal: *Minerals 10*

banded pennant: *Dragonfly 15*

banded rudderfish: *Wild Saltwater Fish 15*

banded: *Krait 15; Newts 15; Pit Viper 15*

bandel: *Cheese International Varieties 6*

bandfire opal: *Minerals 10*

bandicoot: *Other Wild Mammals 15*

bandit: *Thief 1; Western Paraphernalia/People 21*

bandolier: *Western Clothing/Dress 21*

bands: *Teeth Dental Work 1*

baneberry: *Garden Perennials 10; Wildflowers 10*

Ban-ei: *Horse Breeds 15*

bang: *Loud 20; Paranormal Occurrences 21; Sounds 20*

banged up: *Unattractive 20*

bangers and mash: *Meals 6*

banggai cardinal: *Aquarium Saltwater Fish 15*

banging: *Loud 20*

bangle bracelet: *Jewelry 2*

bangle: *Jewelry 21*

banjo: *String Musical Instruments*

bank robbery: *Western Plot Devices 21*

bank: *Business Property 3*

banker: *Finance 1; Horror Occupations 23*

Banker: *Horse Breeds 15*

Banks pine: *Evergreen Trees 10*

Banksian pine: *Evergreen Trees 10*

banneton: *Kitchen Equipment 5*

bannock: *Bread General Varieties 6*

banquet captain: *Food Service 1*

banquet hall: *Food/Drink Establishments 3*

banshee: *Fantasy Creatures with Symbolic Meaning 19; General Fae 16; Undead 16*

Bantu: *Human Ethnic Groups 1; Pigs 15*

baphomet: *Symbols in Magic and Religion 19*

Baptism: *Objects/Activities Connected to Lore 19; Sacraments 14*

bar and grill: *Food/Drink Establishments 3*

bar jack: *Wild Saltwater Fish 15*

bar line: *Notation 13*

bar mop: *Towels 5*

bar soap: *Personal Care 5*

bar stool: *Chairs and Stools 4; Improvised Weapons 7*

bar wench: *Food Service 1; Supporting Cast 24*

bar: *Close/Hold 20; Cookie 6; Food/Drink Establishments 3; Miscellaneous Furniture 4; Fluvial 10; Notation 13*

bara brith: *Bread General Varieties 6*

Barachiel: *Angels of Good 14*

Barako: *Coffee Varieties 6*

barathea: *Fabric 2*

barb: *Aquarium Freshwater Fish 15*

Barb: *Horse Breeds 15*

barbadine: *Unusual Edible Fruits 6*

barbarian: *Character Building 1; Fighter 1*

Barbary: *Lions 15*

barbecue potato chip: *Snacks 6*

barbecue sauce: *Condiments 6*

barbecue: *Property Features 3; Sandwiches 6*

barbecued chicken: *Sandwiches 6*

barbed wire blocks travel: *Western Plot Devices 21*

barbed wire: *Western Paraphernalia/People 21*

barbed: *Special Body Features 19*

barber: *Personal Services 1*

barberry: *Shrubs 10*

barbican: *Castle Anatomy 3; Fortification 3*

Barbour's map: *Freshwater Turtles 15*

Barbour's: *Pit Viper 15*

barbu: *Card Games 5*

barcarolle: *Composition Types 13*

barchan: *Aeolian 10*

bard: *Castle Inhabitants and Personnel 1; Character Building 1; Singer 1*

bardiche: *Axes 7; Pole Weapons 7*

bareboat: *Small Watercraft 9*

bare-boned: *Small/Thin 1*

bare-legged: *Owls 15*

bare-toothed russula: *Fungus Common Names 10*

bargain: *Buy 20; Solve 20; Witchcraft Vocabulary 17*

barge operator: *Maritime Occupations 1*

barghest: *Beast 16; Extraplanar 16*

baritone saxophone: *Wind/Woodwind and Brass Musical Instruments*

baritone: *Voices 13; Wind/Woodwind and Brass Musical Instruments*

Barium: *Elements 11*

bark: *Candy General 6; Sounds 20; Speak 20*

Barka: *Other Cows 15*

barkcloth: *Fabric 2*

barkeep: *Food Service 1; Supporting Cast 24*

barker's stand: *Amusement Park/Carnival/Circus/Fair 3*

barking: *Owls 15*

barley: *Grain 6; Soup 6*

barmbrack: *Bread General Varieties 6*

barn dance results in fight/jealousy/marriage: *Western Plot Devices 21*

barn lamp: *Illumination/Light Sources 5*

barn red: *Red 20*

barn: *Doors 3; Farm/Outbuilding 3; Horror Locations 23; Man-Made Animal Homes 15*

barometer: *Boat/Ship Anatomy 9; Chemistry General Vocabulary 11; Meteorology General Vocabulary 10*

barometric pressure: *Meteorology General Vocabulary 10*

baron: *Royal/Noble 1*

baroness: *Royal/Noble 1*

baronet: *Royal/Noble 1*

barong: *Swords One-handed 7*

Baroque: *Architectural Styles 3; Art Movements 13*

barracks: *Fortification 3; Hospitality 3; Military Property 3*

barracuda: *Wild Saltwater Fish 15*

barrage: *Precipitation 10*

Barre: *Ballet Terms 13; Dance Equipment 13*

barred jungle owlet: *Owls 15*

barred: *Owls 15*

barrel bag: *Accessories 2*

barrel of monkeys: *Toys 5*

barrel of sand: *Specialty Survival Gear 5*

barrel: *Containers and Vessels 5*

barren ground: *Objects/Activities Connected to Lore 19*

barren land discovered to be valuable: *Western Plot Devices 21*

barren oak: *Deciduous Trees 10*

barren strawberry: *Garden Perennials 10*

barren vegetation: *Soil General Vocabulary 10*

barretina: *Headgear 2*

barrette: *Hair Accessories 2*

barricade: *Close/Hold 20; Fortification 3*

barrier bar: *Coastal and Oceanic 10*

barrier island: *Coastal and Oceanic 10*

barrier vest: *Body Armor 7*

barrier: *Fortification 3*

barrio: *City 10*

barrista: *Food Service 1*

barrister: *Legal Occupations 1*

barroom: *Rooms 3*

barrow bolete: *Fungus Common Names 10*

barry nebuly: *Partition Diminutives 19*

barry: *Partition Diminutives 19*

bars: *Coins and Currency 21*

bartender: *Food Service 1*

barter: *Buy 20*

Bartholomew: *Twelve Apostles 14*

Bartlett: *Pears 6*

bartok: *Card Games 5*

baryte: *Minerals 10*

Barzona: *Other Cows 15*

basal ganglia: *Organs/Major Structures 12*

basalt: *Igneous Rocks 10*

basaltic trachyandesite: *Igneous Rocks 10*

basanite: *Igneous Rocks 10; Minerals 10*

base camp: *Outdoor Property 3*

base exchange (BX): *Military Property 3*

base: *Bad 20; Chemistry General Vocabulary 11; Fortification 3; Unattractive 20*

baseball bat: *Classic Items 23; Improvised Weapons 7; Sporting Goods Other 5*

baseball cap: *Headgear 2*

baseball diamond: *Entertainment Property 3*

baseball glove: *Sporting Goods Other 5*

baseball mitt: *Sporting Goods Other 5*

baseball: *Athletic Shoes 2; Poker Card Games 5; Sporting Goods Balls 5*

baseboard heater: *Building Systems 3*

baseboard: *Building Elements and Features 3*

baselard: *Swords One-handed 7*

basement rock: *Geological Vocabulary 10*

basement/cellar: *Common Dangers 23; Horror Locations 23*

basement: *Rooms 3; Windows 3*

Basenji: *Dog Breeds 15*

base-richness: *Soil General Vocabulary 10*

bash: *Attack 7*

basher hat: *Headgear 2*

bashful: *Horror Vocabulary 23*

Bashkir Curly: *Horse Breeds 15*

Bashkir: *Horse Breeds 15*

Bashkirs: *Human Ethnic Groups 1*

basic anhydride: *Chemistry General Vocabulary 11*

basic salt: *Chemistry General Vocabulary 11*

basic: *Easy 20*

basil: *Plants with Symbolic Meaning 19; Spices 6*

basilica: *Religious Building 3*

basilisk: *Beast 16; Cannon 7*

basin and range province: *Geological Vocabulary 10*

basin: *Containers and Vessels 5; Fluvial 10; Geological Vocabulary 10*

basket maker: *Artists and Craftspeople 1*

basket oak: *Deciduous Trees 10*

basket of gold: *Garden Perennials 10*

basket weave: *Fabric 2*

basket: *Cheese International Varieties 6; Containers and Vessels 5; Easter 19*

basketball court: *Entertainment Property 3; Property Features 3*

basketball toss: *Amusement Park/Carnival/Circus/Fair 3*

basketball: *Athletic Shoes 2; Sporting Goods Balls 5*

basket-hilted: *Swords One-handed 7*

basking: *Sharks 15*

basmati rice: *Grain 6*

Basotho Pony: *Horse Breeds 15*

Basque: *Human Ethnic Groups 1*

basra: *Card Games 5*

bass clarinet: *Wind/Woodwind and Brass Musical Instruments*

bass clef: *Notation 13*

bass drum: *Percussion Musical Instruments 5*

bass guitar: *String Musical Instruments*

bass saxophone: *Wind/Woodwind and Brass Musical Instruments*

bass: *Voices 13*

bass-baritone: *Voices 13*

Basset Hound: *Dog Breeds 15*

bassinet: *Beds 4*

bassist: *Musical Occupations 1*

bassoon: *Wind/Woodwind and Brass Musical Instruments*

basswood: *Deciduous Trees 10*

bastard: *Swords One-handed 7*

baste: *Sewing Techniques 2*

baster: *Kitchen Utensils 5*

Bastet (goddess of felines): *Egyptian Pantheon 14*

basting brush: *Kitchen Utensils 5*

basting syringe: *Kitchen Utensils 5*

basting: *Embroidery Stitches 2*

bastion: *Castle Anatomy 3; Fortification 3*

bastite: *Minerals 10*

Bat Masterson: *Western Paraphernalia/People 21*

bat ray: *Wild Saltwater Fish 15*

bat: *Animals with Symbolic Meaning 19; Objects/Activities Connected to Lore 19; Spaceship Shapes 22; Witchcraft Vocabulary 17*

bat-eared: *Foxes 15*

Bateleur 4×4 self-propelled multiple rocket launcher: *South Africa Military Vehicles 8*

bath house: *Outdoor Property 3*

bath oil: *Personal Care 5*

bath robe: *Unisex Clothing 2*

bath sheet: *Towels 5*

bath: *Bathrooms 3; Towels 5*

bathe: *Clean 20*

bathing suit: *Unisex Clothing 2*

batholith: *Geological Vocabulary 10*

bat house: *Man-Made Animal Homes 15*

bathroom dirty: *Travel Hazards 9*

bathroom features: *Architecture and Property 3*

bathroom fixtures: *Architecture and Property 3*

bathroom inoperative: *Travel Hazards 9*

bathroom rug: *Floor Coverings 4*

bathroom: *Horror Locations 23; Rooms 3*

bathrooms: *Architecture and Property 3*

bathtub: *Bathroom Features and Fixtures 3; Cheese Common Varieties 6*

bathysphere: *Small Watercraft 9; Vehicles 22*

batik: *Art Techniques 13; Fabric Patterns 2*

batiste: *Fabric 2*

baton Francais: *Bludgeons 7*

baton: *Bludgeons 7; Music Accessories*

bats: *Animals 15*

Batswana: *Human Ethnic Groups 1*

battalion: *General Combat Vocabulary 7*

Battement dégagé: *Ballet Terms 13*

Battement fondu développé: *Ballet Terms 13*

Battement frappé: *Ballet Terms 13*

Battement tendu: *Ballet Terms 13*

Battement: *Ballet Terms 13; Dance Moves 13*

batter bread: *Bread General Varieties 6*

batter: *Attack 7; Bread General Varieties 6; Harm 20*

batterie: *Dance Moves 13*

batteries: *Energy Sources/Types 23; General Survival Gear 5; Military Equipment 8; Office/School/Writing Supplies 5*

battering ram: *Siege Equipment 7*

Battersby's: *Caecilians 15*

battery: *Fortification 3*

batting helmet: *Headgear 2*

batting: *Fabric 2*

battle armor: *Clothing/Uniforms 22*

battle cruiser: *Military Watercraft 8; Spaceship Types 22*

battle group commander: *Occupations 22*

Battle of the Little Bighorn: *Western Paraphernalia/People 21*

battle tank: *Military Ground Vehicles General 8*

battle: *General Combat Vocabulary 7; Styles of Dress 2*

battleaxe: *Axes 7*

battlebot: *Robots 22*

battlefield: *Horror Locations 23*

battlement: *Castle Anatomy 3; Fortification 3*

battleship: *Gray 20; Military Watercraft 8; Spaceship Types 22*

Battu: *Ballet Terms 13*

batuan: *Unusual Edible Fruits 6*

batzos: *Cheese International Varieties 6*

bauble: *Jewelry 21*

Bauhaus: *Architectural Styles 3; Art Movements 13*

baupmet: *Daggers and Knives 7*

Bavaria blue: *Cheese International Varieties 6*

Bavarian pretzel: *Snacks 6*

Bavarian: *Human Ethnic Groups 1*

bawl: *Sounds 20; Speak 20*

Bay and Gable: *Architectural Styles 3*

Bay Area Regional: *Architectural Styles 3*

bay bolete: *Fungus Common Names 10*

bay laurel: *Deciduous Trees 10*

bay leaf: *Spices 6*

bay mud: *Soil General Vocabulary 10*

bay pipefish: *Aquarium Saltwater Fish 15*

bay tree: *Deciduous Trees 10; Objects that Offer Protection 19*

bay: *Castle Anatomy 3; Water Terms 9; Windows 3; Coastal and Oceanic 10; Deciduous Trees 10; Sounds 20*

bayberry: *Candles 5; Shrubs 10*

bayerite: *Minerals 10*

bayonet: *Fencing Equipment 7; Hand Weapons 7; Military Equipment 8*

bayou: *Fluvial 10; Water Features 10; Water Terms 9*

bazaar: *Business Property 3*

Bazadais: *Other Cows 15*

Bazna: *Pigs 15*

bazzite: *Minerals 10*

BB gun: *Toys 5*

bdud: *Demon 16*

be taught: *Learn 20*

beach bag: *Accessories 2*

beach cusps: *Coastal and Oceanic 10*

beach pine: *Evergreen Trees 10*

beach plum: *Pit Fruits 6*

beach ridge: *Coastal and Oceanic 10*

beach transport: *Military Watercraft 8*

beach wear: *Styles of Dress 2*

beach: *Chairs and Stools 4; Marina 3; Towels 5; Coastal and Oceanic 10*

beachhead: *General Combat Vocabulary 7*

beacon lantern: *Illumination/Light Sources 5*

bead tree: *Weeds 10*

bead: *Fishing Gear 5; Gem Cuts 21; Jewelry 21; Wet 20*

beading: *Embellishments 2*

beadwork: *Embellishments 2*

beady: *Eye Type 1*

Beagalltach (the Little Fury): *Weapons of Legend 18*

Beagle: *Dog Breeds 15*

beak willow: *Deciduous Trees 10*

beak: *Nose 1*

beaked willow: *Deciduous Trees 10*

beaked: *General Snake Families 15; Sea Snake 15; Whales 15*

beaker: *Laboratory Equipment 5*

Beal's-eyed: *Freshwater Turtles 15*

beam compass: *Architectural/Engineering Tools 5*

beam: *Boat/Ship Terminology 9; Bridges 9*

bean bag munitions: *SWAT Equipment 7*

bean bag toss: *Toys 5*

bean bag: *Chairs and Stools 4; Toys 5*

bean: *Soup 6; Vegetables 6*

beanie: *Headgear 2*

bean-nighe: *General Fae 16*

beanpole: *Small/Thin 1*

bear claw: *Donut/doughnut 6*

bear witness: *Agree 20*

bear: *Animals with Symbolic Meaning 19; Objects/Activities Connected to Lore 19; Spears 7; Traps 3; Wild Game 6*

bear's breech: *Garden Perennials 10*

bear's head: *Fungus Common Names 10*

bearberry: *Deciduous Trees 10; Shrubs 10; Unusual Edible Fruits 6*

beard: *Character Building 1*

Bearded Collie: *Dog Breeds 15*

bearded: *Axes 7; Chin 1*

beardtongue: *Garden Perennials 10*

bearing away: *Boat/Ship Terminology 9*

bearing capacity: *Soil General Vocabulary 10*

bearing: *Boat/Ship Terminology 9*

Béarnais: *Other Cows 15*

bears: *Animals 15*

bearskin: *Floor Coverings 4; Headgear 2*

beast: *Charges 19; Cheese International Varieties 6; Monsters 16*

beat cop: *Law Enforcement 1*

beat: *Attack 7; Fencing Vocabulary 7; General Music Vocabulary 13; Harm 20*

Beauceron: *Dog Breeds 15*

Beaufort wind scale: *Meteorology General Vocabulary 10*

beaujolais: *Wine Red 6*

beautician: *Personal Services 1*

beautiful woman/man is really dead: *Horror Plot Devices 23*

beautiful young ghost seduces man/woman: *Horror Plot Devices 23*

beautiful: *Adjectives 20*

beauty bush: *Shrubs 10*

beauty: *Philosophy Basic Concepts 14*

beautyberry: *Garden Perennials 10; Shrubs 10*

beaver hat: *Headgear 2*

beaver poison: *Poisonous Plants 10*

beaver tail: *Donut/doughnut 6*

beaver: *Animals with Symbolic Meaning 19; Brown 20; Facial Hair Beard 1; Woodland Mammals 15*

Beaver: *Native American Peoples 1*

beaverwood: *Deciduous Trees 10*

Bebb willow: *Deciduous Trees 10*

Bebhionn: *Moons 11*

bec de corbin: *Pole Weapons 7*

beckon: *Magic Vocabulary 17*

beckoning cat: *Secular Symbols 19*

beckoning: *Magic Vocabulary 17*

become rancid: *Harm 20*

bed and breakfast: *Hospitality 3; Horror Locations 23*

bed curtains: *Bed Linens 5*

bed linens: *Equipment and Tools 5*

bed of Helius: *Objects 18*

bed spread: *Bed Linens 5*

bed tiller: *General Farm Equipment*

bed: *Pillows 5*

bedbugs: *Travel Hazards 9*

Bedivere: *Knights of the Round Table 18*

Bedlington Terrier: *Dog Breeds 15*

Bedouin: *Human Ethnic Groups 1; Styles of Dress 2*

bedrock: *Cave Anatomy 10; Geological Vocabulary 10*

bedroll: *General Survival Gear 5*

bedroom: *Rooms 3*

bedside lamp: *Illumination/Light Sources 5*

bedsores: *Injuries/Medical Emergencies 12*

bee balm: *Garden Perennials 10*

bee fly: *Flies 15*

bee sting: *Injuries/Medical Emergencies 12*

bee: *Animals 15; Animals with Symbolic Meaning 19; Objects/Activities Connected to Lore 19*

beebalm: *Wildflowers 10*

beech nut: *Oils 6*

beech/biatch/bitch: *Expletives 20*

beech: *Deciduous Trees 10*

beechwood sickener: *Fungus Common Names 10*

beef jerky: *Snacks 6*

beef: *Food 6; Soup 6*

Beefalo: *Other Cows 15*

Beefeater's hat: *Headgear 2*

Beefmaker: *Other Cows 15*

Beefmaster: *Other Cows 15*

beefy: *Large/Heavy 1*

beehive hat: *Headgear 2*

beehive: *Hair Style 1*

beekeeper: *Agricultural 1*

beelzebub: *Devil 16*

beep: *Sounds 20*

beer garden: *Entertainment Property 3*

beer glass: *Drinkware 5*

beer peanut: *Nuts 6*

beer: *Bread General Varieties 6; Cheese Common Varieties 6; Food 6; Quick Bread 6; St. Patrick's Day 19*

beerenauslese: *Wine White 6*

bees: *Harbingers/Charms for Good Luck 19; Practices that Attract Bad Luck 19*

beeswax: *Wizard's Goods 5*

beet cleaner/loader: *General Farm Equipment*

beet green: *Vegetables 6*

beet: *Vegetable Juice 6; Vegetables 6; Pickled/Relish 6*

beetle: *Animals 15; Animals with Symbolic Meaning 19; Objects/Activities Connected to Lore 19*

beetles: *Practices that Attract Bad Luck 19*

befuddle: *Magic Vocabulary 17*

beggar my neighbor: *Card Games 5*

beggar: *General Occupations 1; Thief 1*

beginning: *Nouns 20*

begonia: *Garden Annuals 10*

beguile: *Magic Vocabulary 17; Witchcraft Vocabulary 17*

beguiling: *Beautiful 20*

behir: *Beast 16*

beige: *White 20*

beignet: *Donut/doughnut 6*

Beijing black: *Pigs 15*

being: *Philosophy Basic Concepts 14*

Belarus black pied: *Pigs 15*

Belarus Red: *Other Cows 15*

Belarusian: *Human Ethnic Groups 1*

belaying pin: *Bludgeons 7; Boat/Ship Anatomy 9*

beleaguered castle: *Solitaire Card Games 5*

belfry: *Church Anatomy 3*

Belgian Blue: *Other Cows 15*

Belgian landrace: *Pigs 15*

Belgian Malinois: *Dog Breeds 15*

Belgian Red: *Other Cows 15*

Belgian Sheepdog: *Dog Breeds 15*

Belgian Tervuren: *Dog Breeds 15*

Belgian waffle iron: *Appliances 5*

Belgian: *Horse Breeds 15*

belial: *Devil 16*

belief: *Philosophy Basic Concepts 14*

Belinda: *Moons 11*

Belize Barrier Reef: *Seven Wonders of the Underwater World 18*

Belize slider: *Freshwater Turtles 15*

belker: *Elemental 16*

bell bottom jeans: *Unisex Clothing 2*

bell pepper green: *Vegetables 6*

bell pepper orange: *Vegetables 6*

bell pepper red: *Vegetables 6*

bell pepper yellow: *Vegetables 6*

Bell Rock Lighthouse: *Seven Wonders of the Industrial World 18*

bell: *Boat/Ship Anatomy 9; Signal Devices 5; Wizard's Goods 5; Christmas 19; Jewelry 21; Objects in Magic and Religion 19*

Bell's hinge-back: *Tortoises 15*

belladonna: *Plants with Symbolic Meaning 19; Poisonous Plants 10*

bell-book-and-candle: *Objects in Magic and Religion 19*

bellflower: *Garden Perennials 10*

bellhop: *Hospitality 1*

belligerence: *General Emotions 20*

belligerent drunkard: *Travel Hazards 9*

belligerent: *Negative 1; Unattractive 20*

Bellinore: *Knights of the Round Table 18*

bellota: *Deciduous Trees 10*

bellow: *Sounds 20*

bells of Ireland: *Garden Annuals 10*

bellwort: *Garden Perennials 10*

belly dancer: *Performing Arts 1*

belly: *Body Parts 12; Dance Styles 13*

bellyache: *Speak 20*

belly-button mushroom: *Fungus Common Names 10*

Belmont Adaptaur: *Other Cows 15*

Belmont Red: *Other Cows 15*

belote: *Card Games 5*

beloved: *Terms of Endearment 1*

below par: *Sad 20*

belt of Aphrodite: *Objects 18*

belt of Hippolyte: *Objects 18*

belt pouch: *Containers and Vessels 5*

belt ranks: *Character Building 1*

belt sander: *Power Tools*

belt: *Accessories 2; Garment Pieces 2; Jewelry 21*

Belted Galloway: *Other Cows 15*

beluga: *Whales 15*

bemoan: *Sounds 20*

bemuse: *Magic Vocabulary 17*

bench scraper: *Kitchen Utensils 5*

bench: *Fluvial 10; Seating 4*

bending: *Bridges 9*

bendy: *Partition Diminutives 19*

bene elohim: *Angels Common Terms 14*

beneficial: *Fortunate 20*

Benelli M1 shotgun: *SWAT Weapons 7*

Benelli M2: *Shotguns Semiautomatic 7*

Benelli M4 shotgun: *SWAT Weapons 7*

Benelli R1: *Semiautomatic Centerfire Rifles 7*

Benelli Supernova: *Shotguns Pump 7*

Benelli Vinci: *Shotguns Semiautomatic 7*

benevolent order: *Social Clubs 1*

benevolent protection of all things great and small: *Pennsylvania Dutch Hex Signs 19*

Benfranklin: *Asteroids with Unusual Names 11*

Bengal: *Domestic Cats 15; Foxes 15; Tigers 15*

Bengali brown Shannaj: *Pigs 15*

Bengali: *Other Cows 15*

bengaline: *Fabric 2*

benignity: *Twelve Fruits of the Holy Spirit 19*

benin: *Head Gear 7*

benmoreite: *Igneous Rocks 10*

Bennett: *Comets 11*

bennu: *Flying Creatures 16*

bent: *Nose 1*

Bentheim black pied: *Pigs 15*

benthic: *Octopi 15*

bentwood rocker: *Chairs and Stools 4*

Benzaiten (goddess of the flow): *Japanese Pantheon 14*

benzenamine: *Dangerous Chemicals 11*

benzenearsonic acid: *Dangerous Chemicals 11*

benzimidazole: *Dangerous Chemicals 11*

benzotrichloride: *Dangerous Chemicals 11*

benzyl chloride: *Dangerous Chemicals 11*

benzyl cyanide: *Dangerous Chemicals 11*

Beowulf: *Fictional Characters 18*

berber carpet: *Floor Coverings 4*

berber fleece: *Fabric 2*

Berber: *Human Ethnic Groups 1*

berceuse: *Composition Types 13*

Berengier: *Twelve Peers of Charlemagne 18*

beret: *Headgear 2*

Beretta 21 bobcat: *Pistol Semiautomatic 7*

Beretta 92 semi-automatic pistol: *SWAT Weapons 7*

Beretta 92FS Type M9A1: *Pistol Semiautomatic 7*

Beretta CX4 Storm: *Semiautomatic Centerfire Rifles 7*

Beretta Onyx: *Shotguns Over/Under 7*

Beretta Stampede: *Revolver Single Action 7*

Beretta Xtrema2: *Shotguns Semiautomatic 7*

Berg: *Adder 15*

Bergelmir: *Moons 11*

bergkase: *Cheese International Varieties 6*

berk: *Expletives 20*

Berkelium: *Elements 11*

Berkshire soil: *Soil General Vocabulary 10*

Berkshire: *Pigs 15*

Berliner: *Donut/doughnut 6*

berm: *Castle Anatomy 3; Fortification 3*

Bermuda buttercup: *Weeds 10*

Bermuda chub: *Wild Saltwater Fish 15*

Bermuda grass: *Weeds 10*

Bermuda shorts: *Unisex Clothing 2*

Bermuda Triangle: *Real Places Steeped in Legend or Mystery 18*

Bernese Mountain Dog: *Dog Breeds 15*

Berrendas: *Other Cows 15*

berries: *Food 6; Wizard's Goods 5*

berry bowl: *Tableware 5*

berserk killer robot: *Monsters and Creatures 22*

berth: *Marina 3*

berunda, birds of Ares: *Flying Creatures 16*

beryl: *Standard Gems 21*

Beryllium: *Elements 11*

Bes (luck): *Egyptian Pantheon 14*

beset: *General Combat Vocabulary 7*

beside yourself: *Happy 20*

besmirched: *Unattractive 20*

besom: *Objects in Magic and Religion 19*

bespell: *Attack 7; Magic Vocabulary 17*

Bestia: *Moons 11*

beta particle: *Chemistry General Vocabulary 11*

Beta player: *Electronics 4*

Beta recorder: *Electronics 4*

beta-particle: *Energy Sources/Types 22*

betel nut palm: *Poisonous Plants 10*

betel nut: *Unusual Edible Fruits 6*

Bethlehem: *Christmas 19*

Betic midwife: *Toads 15*

betony: *Garden Perennials 10; Items with Healing Properties 19*

betrothed: *Relational 1*

Betsy Ross: *Real People with Legendary Status 18*

betta: *Aquarium Freshwater Fish 15*

better half: *Terms of Endearment 1*

bettong: *Other Wild Mammals 15*

Betty lamp: *Illumination/Light Sources 5*

between the sheets: *Card Games 5*

bevameter: *Soil General Vocabulary 10*

beverages: *Food 6*

bewegt: *Tempo/Mood 13*

bewhiskered: *Facial Hair Beard 1*

bewilder: *Magic Vocabulary 17*

bewildering: *Magic Vocabulary 17*

bewilderment: *Magic Vocabulary 17*

bewitch: *Witchcraft Vocabulary 17*

bezants: *Patterns 19*

BGM-71TOE wire guided: *Army Missile 8*

Bhagavad Gita: *Major Religious Books 14*

Bhagnari: *Other Cows 15*

bhangra (Punjab): *Ethnic/Folk Dances 13*

Bhirum Pony: *Horse Breeds 15*

Bhotia Pony: *Horse Breeds 15*

Bhotia: *Human Ethnic Groups 1*

Bhuj: *Axes 7*

Bianca: *Moons 11*

Biarmaland: *Fictional/Mythological Locations 18*

bias tape: *Notions 2*

bias: *Sewing Terms 2*

bibb lettuce: *Vegetables 6*

Bible: *Collective Symbols 19; Major Religious Books 14; Objects/Activities Connected to Lore 19*

bibliographer: *Publishing 1*

Bibliotheca (classical Greek): *Dragon 16*

bicapitated: *Monsters 19*

bich'hwa: *Hand Weapons 7*

Bichon Frise: *Dog Breeds 15*

bicolor corn: *Vegetables 6*

bicorne hat: *Headgear 2*

bicorporate: *Monsters 19*

bicuspid: *Teeth 12*

bicycle built for two: *Human-Powered Transportation 9*

bicycle: *Human-Powered Transportation 9; Locks 5*

bid: *Buy 20*

biddy: *Elderly 1*

bidet: *Bathroom Features and Fixtures 3*

Biedermeier: *Architectural Styles 3*

Biela: *Comets 11*

bifrost bridge: *Fictional/Mythological Locations 18*

big apple: *Dance Styles 13*

big bang: *Astronomy General Terms 11*

Big Bend slider: *Freshwater Turtles 15*

big bertha: *Mortar 8*

big brown: *Bats 15*

big cats: *Animals 15*

big cone Douglas fir: *Evergreen Trees 10*

big cone Douglas spruce: *Evergreen Trees 10*

big cone pine: *Evergreen Trees 10*

big cone spruce: *Evergreen Trees 10*

big drunk bean: *Deciduous Trees 10*

big ears: *Garden Perennials 10*

big eye: *Wild Saltwater Fish 15*

big eyes cad: *Wild Saltwater Fish 15*

big free-tailed: *Bats 15*

big head sea robin: *Wild Saltwater Fish 15*

big laurel: *Deciduous Trees 10*

big leaf maple: *Deciduous Trees 10*

big screen television: *Electronics 4*

big three: *Card Games 5*

big two: *Card Games 5*

big: *Large 20; Large/Heavy 1*

big-eared: *Bats 15*

bigeye tuna: *Wild Saltwater Fish 15*

big-eyed: *Bats 15*

bigfin: *Squid 15*

Bigfoot: *Mythical Creatures and Monsters 16*

biggs jasper: *Minerals 10*

bighead: *Sea Snake 15*

big-headed: *Freshwater Turtles 15*

bight: *Coastal and Oceanic 10*

bignay: *Unusual Edible Fruits 6*

bigot learns empathy for ethnic group: *Western Plot Devices 21*

bigtooth aspen: *Deciduous Trees 10*

bigtree: *Deciduous Trees 10*

bikini panties: *Ladies' Wear 2*

bikini: *Ladies' Wear 2*

bilberry: *Shrubs 10; Unusual Edible Fruits 6*

Bilbo: *Asteroids with Unusual Names 11*

bilbo: *Swords One-handed 7*

bilby: *Other Wild Mammals 15*

Bilderberg Group: *Secret/Mystical Organizations 18*

bi-level: *Residential Property 3*

bilge: *Boat/Ship Anatomy 9*

bilimbi: *Unusual Edible Fruits 6*

bilirubin: *Blood 12*

bill collector: *Finance 1*

billet: *Fortification 3*

billette: *Patterns 19*

bill-guisarme: *Pole Weapons 7*

billhook: *Pole Weapons 7*

billiards room: *Rooms 3*

billibong: *Axes 7*

Billy the Kid: *Real People with Legendary Status 18*

Biltmore ash: *Deciduous Trees 10*

Biltmore white ash: *Deciduous Trees 10*

bin: *Containers and Vessels 5*

binary acid: *Chemistry General Vocabulary 11*

binary compound: *Chemistry General Vocabulary 11*

binary: *Astronomy General Terms 11; Star Systems 11*

bind: *Fencing Vocabulary 7*

binder clip: *Office/School/Writing Supplies 5*

binder: *Office/School/Writing Supplies 5*

bindhu: *Symbols in Magic and Religion 19*

binding energy: *Chemistry General Vocabulary 11*

binding machine: *Office/School Machines 5*

bindweed: *Weeds 10*

bing cherry: *Pit Fruits 6*

binghamite: *Minerals 10*

bingo: *Card Games 5; Games 5*

binnacle: *Boat/Ship Anatomy 9*

binoculars: *Optics 5; Spy Gear 5*

biochar: *Soil General Vocabulary 10*

biochemist: *Scientist 1*

biodegradability: *Chemistry General Vocabulary 11*

bioengineered medication: *Devices 22*

bioerosion: *Geological Vocabulary 10*

biogeochemistry: *Geologic Fields of Study 10; Geological Field Work Methods 10*

biogeology: *Soil General Vocabulary 10*

biographer: *Publishing 1*

biography: *Literary Styles 5; Performance Genres 13*

bio-implants: *Plot Devices 22*

biological diversity: *Geography General Vocabulary 10*

biological war: *General Combat Vocabulary 7*

biologist: *Scientist 1*

biomass: *Energy Sources/Types 22*

biomedical engineer: *Scientist 1*

biomedical engineering: *Plot Devices 22*

biosafety cabinet: *Laboratory Equipment 5*

biosphere: *Geography General Vocabulary 10; Meteorology General Vocabulary 10*

biostratigraphy: *Geologic Fields of Study 10; Geological Vocabulary 10*

biostratinomy: *Geological Vocabulary 10*

biota: *Geography General Vocabulary 10*

bioturbation: *Geological Vocabulary 10*

birch double: *Garden Perennials 10*

birch russula: *Fungus Common Names 10*

birch tree: *Objects that Offer Protection 19*

bird bath: *Landscaping 3*

bird cage hat: *Headgear 2*

bird droppings falling on person: *Harbingers of Bad Luck 19*

bird feeder: *Landscaping 3*

bird: *Charges 19; General Snake Families 15; Spaceship Shapes 22; Venomous Arachnids 15*

bird's eye: *Notation 13*

bird's eyes: *Wildflowers 10*

bird's foot trefoil: *Garden Perennials 10; Wildflowers 10*

bird's foot: *Wizard's Goods 5*

bird's nest: *Wizard's Goods 5*

bird-brain: *Unintelligent 1*

birdcage: *Containers and Vessels 5*

bird-foot violet: *Garden Perennials 10*

birdhouse: *Man-Made Animal Homes 15*

birdie: *Sporting Goods Other 5*

birds of prey: *Animals 15*

birds: *Animals 15; Objects/Activities Connected to Lore 19*

birdwing: *Butterfly 15*

biribi: *Unusual Edible Fruits 6*

biritch: *Card Games 5*

Birman: *Domestic Cats 15*

birth of Jesus: *Legendary Events 18*

birthday cake: *Ice Cream Flavors 6*

birthday: *Cake 6; Candles 5*

birthing center: *Health Care 3*

birthmark: *Objects/Activities Connected to Lore 19; Skin Types and Features 1*

birthstone: *Objects/Activities Connected to Lore 19*

birthwort: *Garden Perennials 10*

biscuit: *Bread General Varieties 6*

Bishamonten (war): *Japanese Pantheon 14*

Bishop pine: *Evergreen Trees 10*

bishop: *Cleric 1; Religious Occupations 1; Horror Occupations 23*

bishop's flower: *Wildflowers 10*

Bishop's pine: *Evergreen Trees 10*

bishop's weed: *Garden Perennials 10*

bishop's week: *Garden Annuals 10*

Bismarck ringed: *Python 15*

bismark: *Donut/doughnut 6*

Bismarck: *Ships 18*

Bismuth: *Elements 11*

Bison 8×8 armored personnel carrier: *Canada Military Vehicles 8*

Bison concrete armored lorry: *United Kingdom Military Vehicles 8*

bison herd: *Western Plot Devices 21*

bison: *Animals with Symbolic Meaning 19; Other Wild Mammals 15; Western Paraphernalia/People 21*

bistro: *Food/Drink Establishments 3*

bit: *Transportation Animals 9*

bitch: *Dogs/Canine 15; Poker Card Games 5*

bitchy: *Grouchy 1*

bite indicator: *Fishing Gear 5*

biting insects: *Travel Hazards 9*

biting: *Smells 20*

bitoscanate: *Dangerous Chemicals 11*

bitter cherry: *Deciduous Trees 10*

bitter herbs: *Foods with Religious or Ritual Significance 19*

bitter melon: *Unusual Edible Fruits 6*

bitter root: *Garden Perennials 10*

bitter salt: *Minerals 10*

bitter: *Grouchy 1; Sad 20; Smells 20*

bitterness: *General Emotions 20*

billernut hickory: *Deciduous Trees 10*

bitternut: *Deciduous Trees 10*

bitters: *Mixers 6*

bittersweet nightshade: *Poisonous Plants 10*

bittersweet: *Orange 20*

bivalate: *Fortification 3*

bixbite: *Minerals 10*

bizarre: *Magic Vocabulary 17*

bizcochos: *Bread General Varieties 6*

BJ2020 4×4 utility vehicle: *China Military Vehicles 8*

BJ2022 Brave Warrior 4×4 utility vehicle: *China Military Vehicles 8*

BJ212 Beijing Jeep 4×4 utility vehicle: *China Military Vehicles 8*

black and gold chromis: *Aquarium Saltwater Fish 15*

Black and Tan Coonhound: *Dog Breeds 15*

black and tan: *Beer 6*

black and white television: *Electronics 4*

black and white: *Bears 15; Owls 15*

black apple: *Unusual Edible Fruits 6*

Black Bart: *Western Paraphernalia/People 21*

black bass: *Wild Freshwater Fish 15*

black bean: *Legumes 6*

black beast: *Bears 15*

black beetle: *Harbingers of Bad Luck 19*

black bile: *Four Bodily Humors 19*

black birch: *Deciduous Trees 10*

black books: *Books of Legend 18*

black bottom: *Dance Styles 13*

black caiman: *Crocodilians 15*

black Canarian: *Pigs 15*

black candle: *Harbingers of Bad Luck 19*

black cap gramma: *Aquarium Saltwater Fish 15*

black cat crossing one's path: *Practices that Attract Bad Luck 19*

black cat: *Halloween 19; Harbingers of Bad Luck 19; Witchcraft Vocabulary 17*

black chanterelle: *Fungus Common Names 10*

black cherry soda: *Soft Drinks 6*

black cherry: *Deciduous Trees 10; Ice Cream Flavors 6; Pit Fruits 6*

black clothing: *Specialty Survival Gear 5*

black cohosh: *Garden Perennials 10*

black currant: *Berries 6*

black dog: *Hangover 12*

black drum: *Wild Saltwater Fish 15*

black dwarf: *Star Types and Relatives 11*

Black Eagle main battle tank: *Russia Military Vehicles 8*

black eye: *Injuries/Medical Emergencies 12*

black fish: *Wild Saltwater Fish 15*

black fly: *Flies 15*

black forest mushroom : *Fungus Common Names 10*

Black Forest: *Cake 6; Ice Cream Flavors 6; Horse Breeds 15*

black fungus: *Fungus Common Names 10*

black hat: *Villain 20*

Black Hawk: *Real People with Legendary Status 18*

black hellebore: *Poisonous Plants 10*

black hemlock: *Evergreen Trees 10*

Black Hills spruce: *Evergreen Trees 10*

black hole: *Astronomy General Terms 11; Weapons 22*

black house: *Venomous Arachnids 15*

black howler: *New World Monkeys 15*

black ice: *Snow Events 10*

black jack oak: *Deciduous Trees 10*

black jack: *Minerals 10*

black kame: *Fungus Common Names 10*

Black Knight unmanned combat vehicle: *United States Military Vehicles 8*

black knob sawback: *Freshwater Turtles 15*

black lead: *Minerals 10*

black leopard: *Big Cats 15*

black light paint: *Art Materials 5*

black locust: *Deciduous Trees 10; Poisonous Plants 10; Weeds 10*

black lotus pollen: *Wizard's Goods 5*

black magic: *Witchcraft Vocabulary 17*

black mamba: *World's Ten Most Venomous Snakes 15*

black margate: *Wild Saltwater Fish 15*

black Maria: *Card Games 5*

black Mariah: *Poker Card Games 5*

black marlin: *Wild Saltwater Fish 15*

black marsh: *Freshwater Turtles 15*

black molly: *Aquarium Freshwater Fish 15*

black mondo grass: *Garden Perennials 10*

black myrtle: *Deciduous Trees 10*

black nightshade: *Poisonous Plants 10*

black oak: *Deciduous Trees 10*

black olive: *Vegetables 6*

black opal: *Minerals 10*

black pepper: *Spices 6*

black pine: *Evergreen Trees 10*

black plum: *Pit Fruits 6*

black powder: *Combat, Armor, and Weapons 7*

Black Pullet: *Books of Legend 18*

black raspberry: *Berries 6*

black rat: *General Snake Families 15*

black ray: *Weapons 22*

Black Russian Terrier: *Dog Breeds 15*

black saddle mushroom: *Fungus Common Names 10*

black sapote: *Unusual Edible Fruits 6*

black Slavonian: *Pigs 15*

black snakeroot: *Poisonous Plants 10*

black soy bean: *Legumes 6*

black sun: *Symbols in Magic and Religion 19*

black swallowtail: *Butterfly 15*

black tamarin: *New World Monkeys 15*

black tetra: *Aquarium Freshwater Fish 15*

black tie: *Styles of Dress 2*

black tupelo: *Deciduous Trees 10*

black walnut: *Deciduous Trees 10; Ice Cream Flavors 6*

black widow: *Female 1; Venomous Arachnids 15*

black willow: *Deciduous Trees 10*

black witch: *Moth 15*

black wood: *Freshwater Turtles 15*

black: *Ants 15; Bears 15; Bread General Varieties 6; Eye Color 1; Grapes 6; Hair Color 1; Martial Artist Belt Ranks 1; Skin Types and Features 1; Tea 6; Colors 20; Dragon 16; General Snake Families 15; Krait 15; Scorpion 15; Sea Turtles 15; Toads 15*

black-banded: *Owls 15*

Blackbeard the Pirate: *Folklore Characters 18*

black-bellied mud: *Freshwater Turtles 15*

blackberries: *Objects/Activities Connected to Lore 19*

blackberry lily: *Garden Bulbs 10; Garden Perennials 10*

blackberry: *Berries 6; Ice Cream Flavors 6; Jam/Jelly/Preserves 6*

black-breasted leaf: *Freshwater Turtles 15*

black-capped capuchin: *New World Monkeys 15*

blackening russula: *Fungus Common Names 10*

blackening waxcap: *Fungus Common Names 10*

blacker bombard: *Mortar 8*

black-eyed pea: *Legumes 6*

black-eyed Susan: *Garden Perennials 10; Wildflowers 10*

blackface minstrels: *Performance Genres 13*

blackfin tuna: *Wild Saltwater Fish 15*

Blackfoot: *Native American Peoples 1*

blackgum: *Deciduous Trees 10*

black-headed spider: *New World Monkeys 15*

black-headed: *General Snake Families 15; Python 15*

blackjack oak: *Deciduous Trees 10*

blackjack: *Card Games 5*

blacklight paint: *Art Media 13*

blackmailed victim: *Common Character Archetypes 21*

blackmailer: *Common Character Archetypes 21; Illicit Occupations 1*

black-mantled tamarin: *New World Monkeys 15*

black-necked: *Cobra 15*

blackout: *Technical Terms 13*

Blacksided Trondheim and Norland: *Other Cows 15*

blacksmith: *Artists and Craftspeople 1; Castle Inhabitants and Personnel 1; Objects/Activities Connected to Lore 19; Supporting Cast 24*

blacksmiths: *Guilds 1*

black-striped: *Keelback 15*

blacktail reef: *Sharks 15*

black-tailed horned: *Pit Viper 15*

blacktip grouper: *Aquarium Saltwater Fish 15*

blackwork: *Embellishments 2*

bladder pod: *Garden Perennials 10*

bladder senna: *Shrubs 10*

bladder: *Organs/Major Structures 12*

bladdernut: *Shrubs 10*

blade master: *Fighter 1*

blade: *Daggers and Knives 7; Fencing Equipment 7; Fishing Gear 5*

blameless: *Good 20*

Blanca Cacereña: *Other Cows 15*

blanchardite: *Minerals 10*

Blanco Orejinegro: *Other Cows 15*

Blandford soil: *Soil General Vocabulary 10*

Blanding's: *Freshwater Turtles 15*

Blanford's: *Foxes 15*

blank space: *Figures Associated with Symbols 19*

blank: *Expletives 20*

blanked: *Expletives 20*

blanket chest: *Storage 4*

blanket flower: *Garden Annuals 10; Garden Perennials 10; Wildflowers 10*

blanket: *Bed Linens 5; Door Materials 3; Embroidery Stitches 2; General Survival Gear 5; Transportation Animals 9; Bog Types 10; Octopi 15*

blankety blank: *Expletives 20*

blankety: *Expletives 20*

blanking: *Expletives 20*

blare: *Sounds 20*

blaring: *Loud 20*

blast: *Attack 7; Loud 20*

blasted: *Expletives 20*

blaster: *Weapons 22*

blazer: *Unisex Clothing 2*

blazing star: *Garden Perennials 10; Symbols in Magic and Religion 19; Symbols of Freemasonry 19*

bleak: *Sad 20; Unattractive 20*

bleary-eyed: *Eye Type 1*

bleat: *Sounds 20; Speak 20*

bleating: *Vocal/Speech Quality 1*

bleeding agaricus: *Fungus Common Names 10*

bleeding heart tetra: *Aquarium Freshwater Fish 15*

bleeding heart: *Garden Perennials 10; Poisonous Plants 10*

bleeding milky cap: *Fungus Common Names 10*

bleeding: *Injuries/Medical Emergencies 12; Wet 20*

bleep: *Expletives 20; Sounds 20*

bleeping: *Expletives 20*

blemish: *Harm 20*

blemished: *Unattractive 20*

Blemmyes: *Human Races Fictional 1*

blend: *Art Techniques 13*

blende: *Minerals 10*

blender: *Appliances 5*

blenny bicolor: *Aquarium Saltwater Fish 15*

blenny black combtooth: *Aquarium Saltwater Fish 15*

blenny black sailfin: *Aquarium Saltwater Fish 15*

blenny blackline fang: *Aquarium Saltwater Fish 15*

blenny blue and gold: *Aquarium Saltwater Fish 15*

blenny bundoon: *Aquarium Saltwater Fish 15*

blenny canary fang: *Aquarium Saltwater Fish 15*

blenny diamond: *Aquarium Saltwater Fish 15*

blenny ember: *Aquarium Saltwater Fish 15*

blessed book: *Books of Legend 18*

blessed year: *Pennsylvania Dutch Hex Signs 19*

blessed: *Happy 20*

blessing: *Rituals 14*

bleu: *Cheese Common Varieties 6*

blewit: *Fungus Common Names 10*

BLG-60 bridging vehicle: *Poland Military Vehicles 8*

blight: *Harm 20; Magic Vocabulary 17; Witchcraft Vocabulary 17*

blimey: *Expletives 20*

blimp: *Air Vehicles 9*

blind alley: *Roads 9*

blind alleys: *Solitaire Card Games 5*

blind cave tetra: *Aquarium Freshwater Fish 15*

blind Don: *Card Games 5*

blind lizard: *Scaled Reptiles 15*

blind man's buff: *Poker Card Games 5*

blind valley: *Cave Anatomy 10*

blind: *Eye Type 1; Moves 7; General Snake Families 15*

blinders: *Transportation Animals 9*

blinds: *Window Treatments 5*

blind-your-eye mangrove: *Poisonous Plants 10*

blinking: *Eye Type 1*

blissful: *Happy 20*

blister bush: *Poisonous Plants 10*

blister copper: *Minerals 10*

blister fir: *Evergreen Trees 10*

blister: *Cooking Techniques 20*

blithe: *Happy 20*

Blitz 4x4 truck: *United States Military Vehicles 8*

blitz: *Cake 6; General Combat Vocabulary 7*

blitzkrieg: *General Combat Vocabulary 7*

blizzard: *Severe Weather 10; Snow Events 10*

blob: *Ooze 16; Wet 20*

Blobitechture: *Architectural Styles 3*

block & tackle: *Hand Tools 5*

block book: *Books/Publications 5*

block: *Boat/Ship Anatomy 9; Exterior Building Materials 3; Moves 7; Sewing Techniques 2; Cave Anatomy 10; Close/Hold 20; Harm 20*

blockade: *Fortification 3; General Combat Vocabulary 7; Tactics 7*

blockbuster: *Large 20*

blockhouse: *Castle Anatomy 3; Fortification 3; Military Property 3*

blocking: *Stage Terms 13*

blocks: *Toys 5*

blond brownie: *Cookie 6*

blond: *Hair Color 1; White 20*

Blonde d'Aquitaine: *Other Cows 15*

blondie: *Cookie 6*

blood brothers: *Western Paraphernalia/People 21*

blood clot: *Injuries/Medical Emergencies 12*

blood jasper: *Minerals 10*

blood oath: *Witchcraft Vocabulary 17*

blood orange: *Citrus 6*

blood sugar drop: *Injuries/Medical Emergencies 12*

blood: *Anatomy and Physiology 12; Four Bodily Humors 19; Horror Vocabulary 23; Objects/Activities Connected to Lore 19; Python 15; Sausage 6; Ten Plagues on Egypt 14*

bloodbath: *Kill 20*

blooded: *Horror Vocabulary 23*

Bloodhound: *Dog Breeds 15*

blood-related ailments: *Anatomy and Physiology 12*

bloodroot: *Garden Perennials 10; Poisonous Plants 10*

bloodshot: *Eye Type 1*

blood-spattered: *Wet 20*

bloodstone: *Minerals 10; Standard Gems 21*

bloody crane's bill: *Garden Perennials 10*

bloody hell: *Expletives 20*

bloody Mary: *Cocktails 6*

bloody: *Expletives 20; Horror Vocabulary 23; Unattractive 20; Wet 20*

bloomers: *Undergarments 2*

blooming: *Expletives 20*

blossom: *Bats 15*

blotched emerald: *Moth 15*

blotter: *Office/School/Writing Supplies 5*

blotting paper: *Art Materials 5*

blouse: *Ladies' Wear 2*

blow a hole in: *Open/Release 20*

blow gun: *Missile Weapons 7*

blow pipe: *Missile Weapons 7*

blow to the head: *Injuries/Medical Emergencies 12*

blow torch: *Power Tools*

blow: *Flies 15*

blowhole: *Coastal and Oceanic 10*

blowing: *Wind 10*

blowout: *Aeolian 10*

BLR 4×4 armored personnel carrier: *Spain Military Vehicles 8*

blubber: *Sounds 20; Speak 20*

blubbery: *Large/Heavy 1*

bludgeons: *Combat, Armor, and Weapons 7*

blue angel: *Wild Saltwater Fish 15*

blue assessor: *Aquarium Saltwater Fish 15*

blue beech: *Deciduous Trees 10*

blue bottle fly: *Flies 15*

blue cap tourmaline: *Minerals 10*

blue cheese: *Blue 20*

blue cohosh: *Garden Perennials 10; Wildflowers 10*

blue collar: *Social Distinction 1; Styles of Dress 2*

blue devil: *Aquarium Saltwater Fish 15*

blue dwarf: *Star Types and Relatives 11*

blue fish: *Wild Saltwater Fish 15*

blue flax: *Wildflowers 10*

blue giant: *Star Types and Relatives 11*

blue gourami: *Aquarium Freshwater Fish 15*

blue gudgeon dartfish: *Aquarium Saltwater Fish 15*

blue Hawaiian: *Cocktails 6*

blue hen of Delaware: *Chickens 15*

blue indigo: *Garden Perennials 10*

blue jasper: *Minerals 10*

blue jay: *Backyard Birds 15*

blue jeans: *Unisex Clothing 2; Western Clothing/Dress 21*

blue john: *Minerals 10*

blue lace agate: *Minerals 10*

blue lagoon: *Cocktails 6*

blue marlin: *Wild Saltwater Fish 15*

blue milky cap: *Fungus Common Names 10*

blue mist spirea: *Garden Perennials 10*

blue moon: *Ice Cream Flavors 6*

blue oak: *Deciduous Trees 10*

blue paloverde: *Deciduous Trees 10*

blue parrot: *Wild Saltwater Fish 15*

blue passion flower: *Poisonous Plants 10*

blue pickerel plant: *Garden Perennials 10*

blue poplar: *Deciduous Trees 10*

blue raspberry soda: *Soft Drinks 6*

Blue Ridge command ship: *U.S. Navy Vessels 8*

blue runner: *Wild Saltwater Fish 15*

blue spiraea: *Shrubs 10*

blue spruce: *Evergreen Trees 10*

blue straggler: *Star Types and Relatives 11*

blue supergiant: *Star Types and Relatives 11*

blue swallowtail: *Butterfly 15*

blue tongue: *Unusual Edible Fruits 6*

blue topaz: *Blue 20*

blue turquoise: *Harbingers/Charms for Good Luck 19*

blue variable: *Star Types and Relatives 11*

blue vein: *Cheese Common Varieties 6*

blue vitriol: *Minerals 10*

blue: *Colors 20; Dragon 16; Eye Color 1; Martial Artist Belt Ranks 1; Krait 15; Sad 20; Scorpion 15; Sharks 15; Whales 15*

Bluebeard the Pirate: *Folklore Characters 18*

bluebell: *Garden Perennials 10*

blueberry: *Berries 6; Ice Cream Flavors 6; Jam/Jelly/Preserves 6; Muffin 6; Pie 6; Quick Bread 6; Shrubs 10*

bluebird: *Backyard Birds 15*

blue-black: *Hair Color 1*

bluebonnet: *Wildflowers 10*

blue-eyed grass: *Wildflowers 10*

bluefin tuna: *Wild Saltwater Fish 15*

bluegill: *Wild Freshwater Fish 15*

bluegrass: *Musical Styles 13*

blue-green algae: *Poisonous Plants 10*

blue gum eucalyptus: *Deciduous Trees 10*

blue gum: *Deciduous Trees 10*

blue-haired: *Elderly 1*

bluejack oak: *Deciduous Trees 10*

blues: *Musical Styles 13*

blueschist: *Metamorphic Rocks 10*

blueshift: *Astronomy General Terms 11*

bluespotted boxfish: *Aquarium Saltwater Fish 15*

bluestar : *Garden Perennials 10*

bluestreak cardinalfish: *Aquarium Saltwater Fish 15*

Bluetick Coonhound: *Dog Breeds 15*

bluff: *General Combat Vocabulary 7; Slope 10*

blunderbuss: *Black Powder Weapons 7*

blunt-nosed: *Viper 15*

Blu-ray player: *Electronics 4*

blurred: *Horror Vocabulary 23*

blurring: *Fast 20*

blush: *Makeup 5*

blusher: *Makeup 5, Fungus Common Names 10*

blushing bracket: *Fungus Common Names 10*

blushing copper: *Minerals 10*

blustery: *Wind 10*

BM-11 6×6 self-propelled multiple rocket launcher: *North Korea Military Vehicles 8*

BM-21 Grad 4×4 and 6×6 self-propelled multiple rocket launcher: *Russia Military Vehicles 8*

BMD-1 infantry fighting vehicle: *Russia Military Vehicles 8*

BMD-3 infantry fighting vehicle: *Russia Military Vehicles 8*

BMM-2 8×8 ambulance: *Russia Military Vehicles 8*

BMM-80 8×8 ambulance: *Russia Military Vehicles 8*

BMP-1 infantry fighting vehicle: *Russia Military Vehicles 8*

BMP-3 infantry fighting vehicle: *Russia Military Vehicles 8*

BMR mine clearing vehicle: *Russia Military Vehicles 8*

BMR-600 6×6 armored personnel carrier: *Spain Military Vehicles 8*

bō: *Bludgeons 7*

bo'sun: *Maritime Occupations 1*

boa: *Accessories 2; Animals 15*

boar sword: *Swords Two-handed 7*

boar: *Other Wild Mammals 15; Spears 7*

board book: *Books/Publications 5*

board game: *Toys 5*

board shorts: *Men's Wear 2*

board: *Games 5; Rooms 3*

boarding pike: *Pole Weapons 7*

boardwalk: *Roads 9*

boasting: *Objects/Activities Connected to Lore 19*

boat builder: *Maritime Occupations 1*

boat/ship anatomy: *Transportation 9*

boat/ship terminology: *Transportation 9*

boat: *Classic Items 23; Human-Powered Watercraft 9; Small Watercraft 9; Spaceship Shapes 22*

boater hat: *Headgear 2*

boathook: *Boat/Ship Anatomy 9*

boathouse: *Property Features 3*

boatswain: *Maritime Occupations 1; Navy Other Titles 8*

bob: *Hair Style 1*

Bob's your uncle: *Expletives 20*

bobber: *Fishing Gear 5*

bobbie cotton: *Socks 2*

bobbin: *Sewing Equipment 2*

bobbing for apples: *Halloween 19*

bobbins: *Poisonous Plants 10*

bobby pin: *Hair Accessories 2*

bobby: *Law Enforcement 1*

bobcat: *Big Cats 15*

bobsled: *Sporting Goods Other 5*

bobtail: *Squid 15*

bocadillo: *Bread General Varieties 6*

bocavirus: *Diseases 12*

bocce ball court: *Property Features 3*

bock: *Beer 6*

bodak: *Undead 16*

bodhisattva: *Cleric 1*

bodice: *Garment Pieces 2*

bodily humors: *Collective Symbols 19*

bodkin: *Sewing Equipment 2*

body armor: *Combat, Armor, and Weapons 7; Spy Gear 5*

body is switched with another person: *Horror Plot Devices 23*

body lice: *Diseases 12*

body moles: *Practices to Predict the Future 19*

body parts: *Anatomy and Physiology 12*

body splash: *Personal Care 5*

body spray: *Personal Care 5*

body stocking: *Ladies' Wear 2*

body suit: *Ladies' Wear 2*

body systems: *Anatomy and Physiology 12*

body type: *Character Building 1*

body wash: *Personal Care 5*

body: *Musical Instrument Parts 13*

bodyguard: *Assassin 1; Fighter 1*

Boeing C-32 passenger aircraft: *U.S. Air Force Aircraft 8*

Boeing RC-135 Reconnaissance: *U.S. Air Force Aircraft 8*

Boelen: *Python 15*

Boer: *Horse Breeds 15*

bog iron ore: *Minerals 10*

bog iron: *Minerals 10*

bog types: *Chapter 10*

bog: *Freshwater Turtles 15; Soil General Vocabulary 10; Water Features 10; Water Terms 9*

bogey man: *Folklore Characters 18*

boggart: *General Fae 16*

boggy: *Wet 20*

bogie: *General Fae 16*

bogles: *General Fae 16*

bogong: *Moth 15*

bogs of North America: *Chapter 10*

bohea: *Tea 6*

Bohemian garnet: *Minerals 10*

Bohemian: *Styles of Dress 2*

bohmite: *Minerals 10*

Boho: *Styles of Dress 2*

Bohrium: *Elements 11*

boiga: *General Snake Families 15*

boil: *Cooking Techniques 20; Injuries/Medical Emergencies 12; Wet 20; Witchcraft Vocabulary 17*

boiled leather: *Armor Types 7*

boiled sweet: *Candy General 6*

boiled wool: *Fabric 2*

boiled: *Cookie 6; Egg Styles 6; Vegetables Cooked 6*

boiler: *Building Systems 3*

boilermaker: *Cocktails 6; Construction 1*

boiling oil: *Siege Equipment 7*

boiling point: *Chemistry General Vocabulary 11*

boiling tube: *Laboratory Equipment 5*

boiling water: *Siege Equipment 7*

boils: *Ten Plagues on Egypt 14*

Bois D'arc: *Deciduous Trees 10*

boisterous: *Loud 20*

bok choy: *Vegetables 6*

bok globule: *Star Types and Relatives 11*

bokmakiri: *Cheese International Varieties 6*

bola tie: *Men's Wear 2*

bola: *Missile Weapons 7*

bold: *Personality Other 1*

bolero (Spain): *Ethnic/Folk Dances 13*

bolero coat: *Ladies' Wear 2*

bolero pants: *Ladies' Wear 2*

bolero: *Dance Styles 13*

bolide: *Astronomy General Terms 11*

bolillo: *Bread General Varieties 6*

boline: *Objects in Magic and Religion 19*

Bolivian amethyst: *Minerals 10*

Bolivian hemorrhagic fever: *Diseases 12*

boll weevil: *Beetle 15*

bolla: *Demon 16*

Bollywood: *Dance Styles 13; Styles of Dress 2*

bolo tie: *Western Clothing/Dress 21*

bologna stone: *Minerals 10*

Bolson: *Tortoises 15*

bolster: *Pillows 5*

bolt action: *Shotguns General 7*

bolt cutter: *Hand Tools 5*

bolt thrower: *Siege Engines 7*

bolt: *Close/Hold 20; Hardware 5; Locks 5; Missile Loads 7*

bolwarra: *Unusual Edible Fruits 6*

bomb glider: *Military Aircraft Pre-1962 8*

bomb suit: *Body Armor 7*

bomb: *Classic Items 23; Military 8; Weapons 22*

bombard: *Cannon 7; General Combat Vocabulary 7; Siege Engines 7*

bombardier: *Beetle 15; General Combat Vocabulary 7*

bombardment: *General Combat Vocabulary 7*

Bombay: *Domestic Cats 15*

bomber drone: *Military Aircraft Pre-1962 8*

bomber fighter: *Military Aircraft Pre-1962 8*

bomber torpedo: *Military Aircraft Pre-1962 8*

bomber: *Military Aircraft 8; Military Aircraft Pre-1962 8*

bombing of Pearl Harbor: *Legendary Events 18*

bon bon: *Candy General 6*

bon vivant: *Social Distinction 1*

bonamite: *Minerals 10*

bonbon dish: *Tableware 5*

bond energy: *Chemistry General Vocabulary 11*

bond order: *Chemistry General Vocabulary 11*

bond: *Fix 20*

bonding pair: *Chemistry General Vocabulary 11*

bondsman: *Knight 1*

bone marrow: *Blood 12*

bone of Pelops: *Objects 18*

bone of Ullr: *Objects 18*

bone opal: *Minerals 10*

bone turquoise: *Minerals 10*

bonefish: *Wild Saltwater Fish 15*

bones: *Anatomy and Physiology 12; Building Elements and Features 3; Fortune Telling General Devices 19; Objects/Activities Connected to Lore 19; Wizard's Goods 5*

bongo drum: *Percussion Musical Instruments 5*

bongrace hat: *Headgear 2*

bongrace: *Headgear 2*

bonifaz: *Cheese International Varieties 6*

boning scissors: *Kitchen Utensils 5*

boning: *Sewing Techniques 2*

boninite: *Igneous Rocks 10*

bonito tuna: *Wild Saltwater Fish 15*

bonnet: *Easter 19; Headgear 2*

bonneted: *Bats 15*

bonnet-top highboy: *Storage 4*

Bonnie and Clyde: *Real People with Legendary Status 18*

bonobo: *Apes 15*

Bonsmara: *Other Cows 15*

bony: *Small/Thin 1*

boo: *Expletives 20*

boogie board: *Sporting Goods Other 5*

boogie-woogie: *Dance Styles 13*

book cover: *Books/Publications 5; Office/School/Writing Supplies 5*

book light: *Books/Publications 5*

Book of Enoch: *Major Religious Books 14*

book of magic works in nonmagical world: *Fantasy Plot Devices 24*

Book of Mormon: *Major Religious Books 14*

Book of Moses: *Major Religious Books 14*

book of necromancy: *Books of Legend 18*

book of shadows: *Books of Legend 18*

book of summoning: *Books of Legend 18*

Book of Thoth: *Books of Legend 18*

book strap: *Office/School/Writing Supplies 5*

book: *Classic Items 23; Objects in Magic and Religion 19; Religious Items 5; Typical Magical Objects 17; Wizard's Goods 5*

bookbinder: *Artists and Craftspeople 1*

ALPHABETICAL INDEX

bookcase: *Door Materials 3; Storage 4*

bookie: *Illicit Occupations 1*

bookish: *Intelligent 1*

bookkeeper: *Finance 1*

bookmark: *Books/Publications 5*

bookplate: *Books/Publications 5*

Books of Jeu: *Major Religious Books 14*

Books of the Bible: *Philosophy and Religion 14*

books: *Equipment and Tools 5*

bookstore: *Business Property 3*

boom town: *Western Paraphernalia/People 21*

boom: *Boat/Ship Anatomy 9; Loud 20; Sounds 20; Technical Terms 13*

boombox: *Electronics 4*

boomerang: *Missile Weapons 7*

booming: *Vocal/Speech Quality 1*

boomslang: *General Snake Families 15*

boonaken: *Card Games 5*

boonie hat: *Headgear 2*

boot cut jeans: *Unisex Clothing 2*

Boot Hill Graveyard: *Famous Western Locations 21*

boot maker: *Artists and Craftspeople 1*

Bootes: *Constellations 11*

booth: *Amusement Park/Carnival/Circus/Fair 3; Building Elements and Features 3*

boots: *Christmas 19; Clothing 2; Western Clothing/Dress 21*

booty short: *Dance Clothing 13*

booty shorts: *Ladies' Wear 2*

boquila: *Unusual Edible Fruits 6*

Boran: *Other Cows 15*

Bordelais: *Other Cows 15*

Border Collie: *Dog Breeds 15*

border guard: *Law Enforcement 1*

border limber pine: *Evergreen Trees 10*

border pinyon: *Evergreen Trees 10*

Border Terrier: *Dog Breeds 15*

border white pine: *Evergreen Trees 10*

border: *Landscaping 3*

bordered white: *Moth 15*

boreal: *Owls 15; Toads 15*

bored: *Personality Other 1*

boredom: *Philosophy Basic Concepts 14*

bori: *Demon 16*

boring: *Negative 1*

Bornean orangutan: *Apes 15*

Bornean: *Pit Viper 15*

Borneo painted: *Freshwater Turtles 15*

Borneo short-tailed: *Python 15*

Born-Haber cycle: *Chemistry General Vocabulary 11*

boron hydrides: *Chemistry General Vocabulary 11*

boron trichloride: *Dangerous Chemicals 11*

boron trifluoride compound with methyl ether: *Dangerous Chemicals 11*

boron trifluoride: *Dangerous Chemicals 11*

Boron: *Elements 11*

borough: *City 10*

Borrelly: *Comets 11*

Bors: *Knights of the Round Table 18*

borscht: *Soup 6*

bort: *Minerals 10*

Borzoi: *Dog Breeds 15*

Bosc: *Pears 6*

Bosniak: *Human Ethnic Groups 1*

Bosnian Pyramid of the Sun: *Real Places Steeped in Legend or Mystery 18*

boson: *Star Types and Relatives 11*

boss: *General Occupations 1*

Boston baked beans: *Candy General 6*

Boston brown: *Bread General Varieties 6*

Boston cream: *Donut/doughnut 6*

Boston ivy: *Garden Perennials 10*

Boston lettuce: *Vegetables 6*

Boston round bottle: *Laboratory Equipment 5*

Boston Terrier: *Dog Breeds 15*

bosun's chair: *Boat/Ship Anatomy 9*

botanical: *Art Genres 13*

botanist: *Scientist 1*

botany: *Chapter 10*

boti: *Kitchen Equipment 5*

Botswana agate: *Minerals 10*

bottle maker: *Artists and Craftspeople 1*

bottle: *Containers and Vessels 5; Drinkware 5; Traps 3*

bottlebrush: *Shrubs 10*

bottled water delivery: *Public Services 3*

bottlenosed: *Dolphins 15*

bottling plant: *Business Property 3*

bottom freezer refrigerator: *Major Appliances 4*

bottom white pine: *Evergreen Trees 10*

bottomland post oak: *Deciduous Trees 10*

bottomland red oak: *Deciduous Trees 10*

botulism: *Diseases 12*

boucle: *Fabric 2*

Boudica: *Real People with Legendary Status 18*

boudin: *Geological Vocabulary 10*

boudoir: *Rooms 3*

bouffa: *Musical Styles 13*

bouffant: *Hair Style 1*

bouffe: *Musical Styles 13*

bougainvillea: *Shrubs 10*

bouillabaisse: *Fish/Seafood Meals 6*

boulder choke: *Cave Anatomy 10*

boulder opal: *Minerals 10; Standard Gems 21*

boulder: *Rock and Mineral Forms 10; Siege Equipment 7*

boule: *Bread General Varieties 6*

Boulenger's: *Caecilians 15*

boulevard: *Roads 9*

bounce: *Locomotion 9*

bouncer: *Hospitality 1*

bouncing bet: *Garden Perennials 10*

bound: *Locomotion 9*

boundary: *Geography General Vocabulary 10*

boundless: *Large 20; Open/Release 20*

bouquet: *Smells 20*

bourbon ball: *Cookie 6*

bourbon: *Hard Liquor 6*

bourguinon: *Meals 6*

bourrée (France): *Ethnic/Folk Dances 13; Dance Moves 13*

bout: *Fencing Vocabulary 7*

bouting: *Fencing Vocabulary 7*

Bouvier des Flandres: *Dog Breeds 15*

bow and arrow: *Classic Items 23; Western Weapons 21*

bow of Heracles: *Bows 18*

bow saw: *Hand Tools 5*

bow tie: *Men's Wear 2*

bow: *Boat/Ship Terminology 9; Christmas 19; Embellishments 2; Music Accessories; Windows 3*

bow-back: *Chairs and Stools 4*

bowel movement: *Excrement 12*

Bowen's reaction series: *Geological Vocabulary 10*

bowenite: *Minerals 10*

bowfront chest: *Storage 4*

bowhead: *Whales 15*

Bowie knife: *Daggers and Knives 7; Western Weapons 21*

bowl cut: *Hair Style 1*

bowl turner: *Artists and Craftspeople 1*

bowl: *Containers and Vessels 5; Kitchen Equipment 5; Typical Magical Objects 17*

bowler hat: *Western Clothing/Dress 21*

bowler: *Headgear 2*

bowline: *Sailing Knots 9*

bowling alley: *Entertainment Property 3*

bowling bag purse: *Accessories 2*

bowling: *Athletic Shoes 2*

bowman's root: *Garden Perennials 10*

bowsprit: *Boat/Ship Anatomy 9; Tortoises 15*

bowstring: *Missile Weapons 7*

bowtie: *Pasta 6*

bowyer: *Artists and Craftspeople 1; Business Property 3; Castle Inhabitants and Personnel 1*

box cutter: *Hand Tools 5*

box elder: *Deciduous Trees 10*

box office: *Parts of the Theater 13*

box purse: *Accessories 2*

box seats: *Parts of the Theater 13*

box spring: *Beds 4*

box: *Christmas 19; Containers and Vessels 5; Freshwater Turtles 15; Jellyfish 15*

boxer shorts: *Men's Wear 2*

Boxer: *Dog Breeds 15*

boxer: *Fighter 1*

boxers: *Men's Wear 2*

boxfish: *Aquarium Saltwater Fish 15*

boxthorn: *Shrubs 10*

boxwood: *Garden Perennials 10; Shrubs 10*

boxwork: *Cave Anatomy 10*

boy child: *Male 1*

boy howdy: *Expletives 20*

boy next door: *Common Character Archetypes 21*

boy who cried wolf: *Common Character Archetypes 21*

boy: *Male 1*

boyfriend/girlfriend kills parents of beloved: *Horror Plot Devices 23*

boyfriend: *Horror Occupations 23; Male 1*

Boykin Spaniel: *Dog Breeds 15*

Boyle's law: *Chemistry General Vocabulary 11*

Boynton post oak: *Deciduous Trees 10*

boysenberry: *Berries 6*

bra: *Ladies' Wear 2*

brace: *Notation 13*

bracelet cortinarius: *Fungus Common Names 10*

bracelet: *Jewelry 2; Jewelry 21*

bracer crystal ball: *Typical Magical Objects 17*

bracer: *Armor Pieces 7; Jewelry 21*

braces: *Men's Wear 2; Teeth Dental Work 1*

brachiosaurus: *Commonly Known Dinosaurs 15*

brachylophosaurus: *Commonly Known Dinosaurs 15*

bracken: *Poisonous Plants 10*

bracket: *Hardware 5*

brackish: *Geological Vocabulary 10*

bracted balsam fir: *Evergreen Trees 10*

brad: *Hardware 5*

bradawl: *Hand Tools 5*

Bradbury: *Asteroids with Unusual Names 11*

Braeburn: *Apples 6*

Braford: *Other Cows 15*

brag: *Card Games 5*

Bragi (song): *Norse Pantheon 14*

Brahma (creation god): *Indian Pantheon 14*

Brahman: *Other Cows 15*

Brahmastra: *Bows 18*

Brahmin: *Human Ethnic Groups 1*

Brahmousin: *Other Cows 15*

braid: *Hair Style 1*

braided channel: *Fluvial 10*

braided rug: *Floor Coverings 4*

braiding: *Embellishments 2*

brain stem: *Organs/Major Structures 12*

brain surgeon: *Horror Occupations 23*

brain: *Beef 6; Organs/Major Structures 12*

brain-eating creatures: *Monsters and Creatures 22*

brainiac: *Intelligent 1*

brainless: *Unintelligent 1*

brainteaser: *Magic Vocabulary 17*

brainy: *Intelligent 1*

braise: *Cooking Techniques 20*

bralet: *Ladies' Wear 2*

bramble: *Sharks 15; Shrubs 10; Weeds 10*

brambles: *Items with Healing Properties 19*

Bran: *Arthurian Characters 18*

bran: *Bread General Varieties 6; Muffin 6*

brandishing object: *Special Posture 19*

brandistock: *Spears 7*

brandy Alexander: *Ice Cream Drinks 6*

brandy: *Hard Liquor 6*

Brangus: *Other Cows 15*

Bras bas: *Ballet Terms 13*

Bras: *Ballet Terms 13*

brash: *Personality Other 1*

brass fastener: *Office/School/Writing Supplies 5*

brass key: *Harbingers/Charms for Good Luck 19*

brass knuckles: *Hand Weapons 7*

brass ore: *Minerals 10*

brass: *Beds 4; Dragon 16; Precious Metals 21*

brassiere: *Ladies' Wear 2*

Bratfest: *Asteroids with Unusual Names 11*

bratwurst: *Sausage 6*

Braunvieh: *Other Cows 15*

brave: *Personality Other 1*

bravery: *General Emotions 20*

brawny: *Large/Heavy 1*

brayer: *Art Tools 5*

brazen castanets: *Objects 18*

brazen shield: *Objects 18*

brazier: *Typical Magical Objects 17; Wizard's Goods 5*

brazil: *Nuts 6*

Brazilian amethyst: *Minerals 10*

Brazilian mud: *Viper 15*

Brazilian pepper: *Weeds 10*

Brazilian wandering: *Venomous Arachnids 15*

Brazilian waterweed: *Weeds 10*

Brazilian: *Caecilians 15*

BRDM-1 4×4 reconnaissance vehicle: *Russia Military Vehicles 8*

BRDM-3 wheeled anti-tank vehicle: *Russia Military Vehicles 8*

breach: *Open/Release 20*

bread & butter pickle: *Pickled/Relish 6*

bread and butter plate: *Tableware 5*

bread and wine: *Rituals 14*

bread basket: *Body Parts 12*

bread board: *Kitchen Equipment 5*

bread bowl: *Bread General Varieties 6*

bread flour: *Staples 6*

bread knife: *Kitchen Utensils 5*

bread maker: *Appliances 5*

bread pan: *Kitchen Equipment 5*

bread pudding: *Bread General Varieties 6; Miscellaneous Dessert 6*

bread stick: *Bread General Varieties 6*

bread: *Food 6; Foods with Religious or Ritual Significance 19; Objects/Activities Connected to Lore 19; Rituals 14*

breadbox: *Kitchen Equipment 5*

breadnut: *Unusual Edible Fruits 6*

break a leg: *Stage Terms 13*

break a mirror: *Practices that Attract Bad Luck 19*

break cedar: *Evergreen Trees 10*

break down: *Open/Release 20*

break room: *Rooms 3*

break wall: *Marina 3*

breakdance: *Dance Styles 13*

breaker bar: *Hand Tools 5*

breaker: *Water Terms 9*

breakfast nook: *Rooms 3*

breakfast: *Cheese Common Varieties 6*

breakfront china cabinet: *Storage 4*

breaking bread: *Rituals 14*

breakneck: *Fast 20*

breakout: *General Combat Vocabulary 7*

breakwall: *Water Terms 9*

breast: *Body Parts 12*

breastplate: *Armor Pieces 7*

breaststroke: *Swimming Strokes 9*

breastwork: *Castle Anatomy 3*

breathing apparatus: *Devices 22*

Breathmaker (river): *Native American Pantheon 14*

breathtaking: *Beautiful 20*

breathy: *Vocal/Speech Quality 1*

breccia: *Sedimentary Rocks 10*

breccias: *Cave Anatomy 10*

brecciated agate: *Minerals 10*

brecciated jasper: *Minerals 10*

Bredl's: *Python 15*

breechloader: *Black Powder Weapons 7; Cannon 7*

breeder reactor: *Chemistry General Vocabulary 11*

breeder: *Agricultural 1*

breeze: *Paranormal Occurrences 21; Wind 10*

Breitovo: *Pigs 15*

BREM-2 armored recovery vehicle: *Russia Military Vehicles 8*

Brer Fox: *Tall Tales 18*

Brer Rabbit: *Tall Tales 18*

Breton: *Horse Breeds 15; Human Ethnic Groups 1*

breunnerite: *Minerals 10*

Breunor: *Knights of the Round Table 18*

brew: *Witchcraft Vocabulary 17*

brewer spruce: *Evergreen Trees 10*

brewer: *Food Service 1*

brewery: *Business Property 3*

brewis: *Bread General Varieties 6*

Brian Boru: *Real People with Legendary Status 18*

Briard: *Dog Breeds 15*

bric-a-brac: *Decorative Objects 4*

Brick Gothic: *Architectural Styles 3*

brick layer: *Castle Inhabitants and Personnel 1*

brick: *Cheese Common Varieties 6; Exterior Building Materials 3; Improvised Weapons 7; Red 20*

brickearth: *Soil General Vocabulary 10*

bricklayer: *Construction 1*

bridal gown: *Ladies' Wear 2*

bridal: *Styles of Dress 2*

bride: *Special Occasion 1*

bridesmaid gown: *Ladies' Wear 2*

bridesmaid: *Special Occasion 1*

bridge mix: *Candy Chocolate 6*

bridge out: *Travel Hazards 9*

bridge pin: *Musical Instrument Parts 13*

bridge: *Boat/Ship Anatomy 9; Card Games 5; Musical Instrument Parts 13; Objects/Activities Connected to Lore 19; Teeth Dental Work 1*

bridges: *Transportation 9*

bridgework: *Teeth Dental Work 1*

bridging vehicle: *Military Ground Vehicles General 8*

Bridle of Constantine: *Relics of Jesus 14*

bridle path: *Roads 9*

bridle: *Transportation Animals 9*

bridleway: *Roads 9*

brie: *Cheese Common Varieties 6*

brief case: *Spy Gear 5*

brief panties: *Ladies' Wear 2*

brief: *Fast 20*

briefcase bomb: *Spy Gear 5*

briefcase: *Accessories 2; Containers and Vessels 5*

briefs: *Men's Wear 2*

brigadier general: *U.S. Air Force Officer 8; U.S. Army Officer 8; U.S. Marines Officer 8*

brigand: *Fighter 1; Thief 1*

brigandine: *Armor Types 7*

Brighid's: *Crosses 19*

bright green: *Green 20*

bright star: *Garden Perennials 10*

bright: *Intelligent 1; Vocal/Speech Quality 1*

Brigit (goddess of fire and poetry): *Celtic Pantheon 14*

brilliant: *Beautiful 20*

brimstone: *Minerals 10*

bring to light: *Solve 20*

bring under control: *Close/Hold 20*

brinsen: *Cheese International Varieties 6*

brio: *Tempo/Mood 13*

brioche: *Bread General Varieties 6*

Brisé volé: *Ballet Terms 13*

Brisé: *Ballet Terms 13; Dance Moves 13*

Brisingamen: *Jewelry 18*

brisk: *Fast 20; Mobility 1*

bristlecone fir: *Evergreen Trees 10*

bristled brush: *Art Tools 5*

bristly: *Facial Hair Beard 1*

Bristol Byzantine: *Architectural Styles 3*

British landrace: *Pigs 15*

British lop: *Pigs 15*

British saddleback: *Pigs 15*

British shorthair: *Domestic Cats 15*

British White: *Other Cows 15*

British Whitworth: *Bolt Action Sniper Rifles 7*

Briton: *Human Ethnic Groups 1*

Brittany: *Dog Breeds 15*

brittle: *Candy General 6; Vocal/Speech Quality 1*

broa: *Bread General Varieties 6*

broach: *Hand Tools 5*

broaching machine: *Power Tools*

broad bean: *Legumes 6*

broad: *Axes 7; Large 20; Large/Heavy 1; Swords One-handed 7; Vocal/Speech Quality 1*

broadcast seeder: *General Farm Equipment*

broadcloth: *Fabric 2*

broad-faced sac: *Venomous Arachnids 15*

broad-leaf bramble: *Unusual Edible Fruits 6*

broadleaf maple: *Deciduous Trees 10*

broadleaf plantain: *Weeds 10*

broad-leaved paper bark: *Weeds 10*

broad-nosed: *Bats 15*

broad-snouted caiman: *Crocodilians 15*

broadsword: *Fencing Equipment 7*

Broadway: *Musical Styles 13*

broast: *Cooking Techniques 20*

Brobdingnagian: *Large 20*

brocade: *Fabric 2*

broccoli rabe: *Vegetables 6*

broccoli: *Soup 6; Vegetables 6*

Broch: *Architectural Styles 3*

broderie anglaise: *Embellishments 2*

broiled: *Vegetables Cooked 6*

broiler pan: *Kitchen Equipment 5*

broken bird house: *Harbingers of Bad Luck 19*

broken bone: *Injuries/Medical Emergencies 12*

broken chain: *Harbingers/Charms for Good Luck 19*

broken engine belt: *Travel Hazards 9*

broken engine hose: *Travel Hazards 9*

broken glass: *Wizard's Goods 5*

broken mirror: *Harbingers of Bad Luck 19*

broken nose: *Injuries/Medical Emergencies 12*

broken objects: *Objects/Activities Connected to Lore 19*

broken shoe: *Harbingers of Bad Luck 19*

broken time: *Fencing Vocabulary 7*

broken: *Nose 1; Teeth 1; Unattractive 20*

bromadiolone: *Dangerous Chemicals 11*

bromine: *Dangerous Chemicals 11*

Bromine: *Elements 11*

bronchus: *Organs/Major Structures 12*

bronco riding: *Western Paraphernalia/People 21*

Brongersma's: *Pit Viper 15*

Bronsted-Lowry acid: *Chemistry General Vocabulary 11*

Bronze Age: *Styles of Dress 2*

bronze bull: *Construct 16*

bronze cory: *Aquarium Freshwater Fish 15*

bronze shell: *Coins and Currency 21*

bronze: *Brown 20; Coins and Currency 21; Dragon 16; Precious Metals 21*

bronzite: *Minerals 10*

brooch: *Jewelry 2; Jewelry 21*

brooding: *Sad 20*

brook: *Water Features 10; Water Terms 9*

Brooklyn Bridge: *Seven Wonders of the Industrial World 18*

broom bush: *Shrubs 10*

broom hickory: *Deciduous Trees 10*

broom maker: *Artists and Craftspeople 1*

broom shrub: *Plants with Symbolic Meaning 19*

broom straw: *Wizard's Goods 5*

broom: *Cleaning Supplies/Gadgets; Garden Perennials 10; Improvised Weapons 7; Magical Transportation 17; Objects/Activities Connected to Lore 19; Poisonous Plants 10; Witchcraft Vocabulary 17; Wizard's Goods 5*

broomstick: *Objects in Magic and Religion 19; Vehicles 24; Witchcraft Vocabulary 17*

Brorsen: *Comets 11*

brothel: *Entertainment Property 3*

brother: *Cleric 1; Expletives 20; Male 1*

brother-in-law: *Male 1*

brouc: *Card Games 5*

browbeaten: *Horror Vocabulary 23*

brown Bess rifle: *Black Powder Weapons 7*

brown dwarf: *Planetary Systems 11; Star Types and Relatives 11*

brown earth: *Soil General Vocabulary 10*

brown hay cap: *Fungus Common Names 10*

brown howler: *New World Monkeys 15*

brown iron ore: *Minerals 10*

brown kame: *Fungus Common Names 10*

brown mustard: *Condiments 6*

brown podzolic: *Soil General Vocabulary 10*

brown recluse: *Venomous Arachnids 15*

brown rice: *Grain 6*

brown roofed: *Freshwater Turtles 15*

brown spotted: *Pit Viper 15*

brown sugar: *Staples 6*

Brown Swiss: *North American Dairy Cows 15*

brown water: *Python 15*

brown widow: *Venomous Arachnids 15*

brown: *Bears 15; Bread General Varieties 6; Butterfly 15; Colors 20; Cooking Techniques 20; Eye Color 1; General Snake Families 15; Hair Color 1; Martial Artist Belt Ranks 1; Skin Types and Features 1; Teeth 1; Tortoises 15*

brownie: *Cookie 6; General Fae 16; Ice Cream Flavors 6; Ice Cream Mix-ins 6; Ice Cream Toppings 6; Pie 6*

Browning A-Bolt Medallion: *Bolt Action Centerfire Rifles 7*

Browning A-Bolt Stalker: *Bolt Action Centerfire Rifles 7*

Browning automatic: *Shotguns General 7*

Browning B78: *Single Shot Centerfire Rifles 7*

Browning BAR: *Semiautomatic Centerfire Rifles 7*

Browning BL-22: *Lever Action and Pump Rimfire Rifles 7*

Browning BLR Lightweight: *Lever Action and Pump Centerfire Rifles 7*

Browning BPS: *Shotguns Pump 7*

Browning BT-99: *Shotguns Single Shot 7*

Browning Buck Mark Camper: *Pistol Semiautomatic 7*

Browning Buck Mark Sporter: *Semiautomatic Rimfire Rifles 7*

Browning Buck Mark Standard URX: *Pistol Semiautomatic 7*

Browning Lightning: *Shotguns Over/Under 7*

Browning Maxus: *Shotguns Semiautomatic 7*

Browning Semiauto Grade I: *Semiautomatic Rimfire Rifles 7*

Browning T-Bolt: *Bolt Action Rimfire Rifles 7*

brown-mantled tamarin: *New World Monkeys 15*

bruang: *Bears 15*

bruin: *Bears 15*

bruise: *Harm 20; Injuries/Medical Emergencies 12*

bruised: *Unattractive 20*

Bruneau jasper: *Minerals 10*

brunette: *Hair Color 1*

bruschetta: *Bread General Varieties 6*

brush maker: *Artists and Craftspeople 1*

brush texture: *Art Media 13*

brush: *Art Tools 5; Clean 20; Cleaning Supplies/Gadgets 5; Music Accessories; Terrain Features 10; Transportation Animals 9*

brushfooted: *Butterfly 15*

brushtail possum: *Other Wild Mammals 15*

Brussels Griffon: *Dog Breeds 15*

Brussels sprouts: *Vegetables 6*

Brussels: *Cheese International Varieties 6*

Brutalist: *Architectural Styles 3*

brute: *Fighter 1; Monster Categories/Terms 16; Villain 20*

Brynhild (goddess of battle): *Norse Pantheon 14*

BT-2 light tank: *Russia Military Vehicles 8*

BT-5 light tank: *Russia Military Vehicles 8*

BTR-140 6×6 armored personnel carrier: *Russia Military Vehicles 8*

BTR-152 6×6 armored personnel carrier: *Russia Military Vehicles 8*

BTR-40 4×4 armored personnel carrier: *Russia Military Vehicles 8*

BTR-50 tracked armored personnel carrier: *Russia Military Vehicles 8*

BTR-60 8×8 armored personnel carrier: *Russia Military Vehicles 8*

BTR-90 8×8 armored personnel carrier: *Russia Military Vehicles 8*

BTR-T infantry fighting vehicle: *Russia Military Vehicles 8*

BTS-1 armored recovery vehicle: *Russia Military Vehicles 8*

BTS-3 armored recovery vehicle: *Russia Military Vehicles 8*

bubble bath: *Personal Care 5*

bubble gum pink: *Pink 20*

bubble: *Cooking Techniques 20; Magical Transportation 17; Wet 20*

bubblegum cigar: *Candy General 6*

bubblegum: *Candy General 6*

bubbling fountain: *Harbingers/Charms for Good Luck 19*

bubbly: *Happy 20*

bucatini: *Pasta 6*

buccaneer: *Barbarian 1; Thief 1*

buccellato: *Cake 6*

buche de noel: *Cake 6*

Büchner flask: *Laboratory Equipment 5*

Büchner funnel: *Laboratory Equipment 5*

buck euchre: *Card Games 5*

buck rake: *General Farm Equipment*

buckboard: *Animal-Powered Transportation 9*

bucket hat: *Headgear 2*

bucket purse: *Accessories 2*

bucket: *Boat/Ship Anatomy 9; Containers and Vessels 5*

buckeye: *Butterfly 15; Chickens 15; Deciduous Trees 10*

buckhorn parrying stick: *Hand Weapons 7*

buckle: *Jewelry 21; Miscellaneous Dessert 6*

buckler: *Shield Types 7*

buckling: *Geological Vocabulary 10*

buckram: *Fabric 2*

buckskin jacket: *Western Clothing/Dress 21*

Buckskin: *Horse Breeds 15*

buckthorn: *Shrubs 10*

buck-toothed: *Teeth 1*

buckwheat: *Grain 6*

bud vase: *Containers and Vessels 5*

Buddha's folly: *Poker Card Games 5*

Buddha's hand: *Unusual Edible Fruits 6*

Buddhism: *Collective Symbols 19*

Buddhist Texts: *Major Religious Books 14*

Buddhist: *Architectural Styles 3*

budgerigar: *Domesticated Pet Birds 15*

Budyonny: *Horse Breeds 15*

Buenos Aires tetra: *Aquarium Freshwater Fish 15*

buergerite: *Minerals 10*

buff top: *Gem Cuts 21*

buff: *Clean 20; White 20*

Buffalo 6×6 anti-mine vehicle: *United States Military Vehicles 8*

Buffalo amphibious vehicle: *United Kingdom Military Vehicles 8*

Buffalo Bill Cody: *Western Paraphernalia/People 21*

Buffalo Bill's Wild West Show: *Western Paraphernalia/People 21*

buffalo plaid: *Fabric Patterns 2*

buffalo rifle: *Western Weapons 21*

Buffalo wheeled armored personnel carrier: *France Military Vehicles 8*

buffalo: *Western Paraphernalia/People 21*

buffaloberry: *Unusual Edible Fruits 6*

Buffel 4×4 mine protected armored personnel carrier: *South Africa Military Vehicles 8*

buffer solution: *Chemistry General Vocabulary 11*

buffer: *Cleaning Supplies/Gadgets 5*

buffet: *Food/Drink Establishments 3; Storage 4*

buff-fronted: *Owls 15*

buffing cloth: *Cleaning Supplies/Gadgets 5*

buffing pad: *Cleaning Supplies/Gadgets 5*

buff-striped: *Keelback 15*

buffy flower: *Bats 15*

bug swarm: *Common Dangers 23*

bug swarms: *Travel Hazards 9*

bugbear: *Humanoid 16*

bugleweed: *Garden Perennials 10*

bugloss: *Garden Perennials 10*

bugweed: *Weeds 10*

build: *Create 20; Fix 20*

Builders of the Adytum: *Secret/Mystical Organizations 18*

building bricks: *Toys 5*

building elements: *Architecture and Property 3*

building features: *Architecture and Property 3*

building logs: *Toys 5*

building materials: *Architecture and Property 3*

building systems: *Architecture and Property 3*

built-in dishwasher: *Major Appliances 4*

built-in safe: *Building Elements and Features 3*

bulb planter: *Garden Tools*

bulette: *Beast 16*

Bulgarian white: *Pigs 15*

Bulgarian: *Imported Carpets 4*

bulging: *Forehead 1*

bulk tank: *General Farm Equipment*

bulkhead: *Boat/Ship Anatomy 9*

bulky: *Heavy 20; Large 20; Large/Heavy 1*

bull bay: *Deciduous Trees 10*

bull pine: *Evergreen Trees 10*

bull roarer: *Objects in Magic and Religion 19*

Bull Terrier: *Dog Breeds 15*

bull thistle: *Wildflowers 10*

bull: *Animals with Symbolic Meaning 19; Ants 15; General Snake Families 15*

bull's eye lantern: *Illumination/Light Sources 5*

bulla: *Objects in Magic and Religion 19*

bulldog: *Ants 15; Bats 15; Dog Breeds 15*

bullet bra: *Ladies' Wear 2*

bullet crossbow: *Missile Weapons 7*

bullet proof suit: *Spy Gear 5*

bullet proof vest: *Body Armor 7*

bullet proof: *Door Materials 3*

bullet resistant face mask: *Body Armor 7*

bullet resistant vest: *Body Armor 7*

bullet resistant: *Shields Post-1900 7*

bullet: *Missile Loads 7*

bulletin board: *Office/School/Writing Supplies 5*

bullet-proof vest: *Armor Pieces 7*

bullfrog: *Frogs 15*

bullhead: *Sharks 15; Wild Freshwater Fish 15*

bull-headed: *Stubborn 1*

bullion: *Coins and Currency 21*

Bullmastiff: *Dog Breeds 15*

bullnut: *Deciduous Trees 10*

bullock cart: *Animal-Powered Transportation 9*

bullock: *Transportation Animals 9*

bullroarer: *Wind/Woodwind and Brass Musical Instruments*

bullwhip: *Flexible 7*

bully: *Common Character Archetypes 21; Fighter 1; Harm 20; Negative 1*

bulwark: *Fortification 3*

bum: *General Occupations 1*

bumblebee: *Bees 15*

bumbling law enforcement: *Common Character Archetypes 21*

bumbling servant: *Supporting Cast 24*

bummed out: *Sad 20*

bump off: *Kill 20*

bump: *Harm 20; Injuries/Medical Emergencies 12*

bumper cars: *Amusement Park/Carnival/Circus/Fair 3*

bumpkin: *Social Distinction 1*

bun: *Bread General Varieties 6; Hair Style 1*

bundt pan: *Kitchen Equipment 5*

bundt: *Cake 6*

bune: *Devil 16*

Bungalow: *Architectural Styles 3; Residential Property 3*

bungee stick: *Pointed Weapons 7*

bungee sticks: *Traps 3*

bunion pad: *Shoe Accessories 13*

bunk bed: *Beds 4*

bunk: *Beds 4; Boat/Ship Anatomy 9*

bunker: *Fortification 3; Military Property 3*

bunnet cap: *Headgear 2*

bunny hop: *Dance Styles 13*

bunny: *Easter 19*

Bunsen burner: *Laboratory Equipment 5*

bunting: *Fabric 2; Independence Day 19*

buntline: *Sailing Knots 9*

bunyip: *Aquatic 16; Demon 16*

buoy: *Boat/Ship Anatomy 9; Marina 3*

buoyancy: *Boat/Ship Terminology 9*

buoyant: *Happy 20; Light 20*

bur oak: *Deciduous Trees 10*

Bur: *Bolt Action Sniper Rifles 7*

bura: *Card Games 5*

burble: *Wet 20*

burdensome: *Difficult 20; Heavy 20*

burdock: *Weeds 10*

bureau: *Storage 4*

buret: *Chemistry General Vocabulary 11*

burette: *Laboratory Equipment 5*

burg: *Fortification 3*

burgermeister: *Government 1*

burglar: *Thief 1*

burgundy: *Red 20; Wine Red 6*

burh: *Fortification 3*

burial chamber: *Cemetery 3*

burial ground: *Cemetery 3; Horror Locations 23*

burial shroud: *Relics of Jesus 14*

burial: *Objects/Activities Connected to Lore 19*

burka: *Headgear 2*

burlap sack: *Containers and Vessels 5*

burlap: *Fabric 2*

burlesque: *Performance Genres 13*

burly: *Large/Heavy 1*

Burmese star: *Tortoises 15*

Burmese: *Domestic Cats 15; Keelback 15; Krait 15; Python 15*

Burmilla: *Domestic Cats 15*

burn: *Cooking Techniques 20; Harm 20*

burner: *Laboratory Equipment 5*

burnish: *Art Techniques 13*

burn-out: *Sewing Terms 2; Styles of Dress 2*

Burns Bog British Columbia: *Bogs of North America 10*

burns: *Injuries/Medical Emergencies 12*

burnt orange: *Orange 20*

burnt sienna: *Brown 20*

burnt umber: *Brown 20*

burraco: *Card Games 5*

burro: *Horses Related 15*

burrow: *Locomotion 9; Natural Animal Homes 15; Terrain Features 10*

burrowing: *Owls 15; Scorpion 15; Viper 15*

burrunan: *Dolphins 15*

bursting bladder: *Traps 3*

bursting machine: *Office/School Machines 5*

bus driver: *Transportation 1*

bus shelter: *Infrastructure Buildings 9*

bus station: *Infrastructure Buildings 9*

bus stop: *Infrastructure Buildings 9*

bus terminal: *Infrastructure Buildings 9*

Bus: *Comets 11*

Busa: *Other Cows 15*

busboy/girl: *Food Service 1*

busby: *Headgear 2*

busca: *Card Games 5*

bush : *Viper 15*

bush baby: *Other Wild Mammals 15*

bush bean: *Vegetables 6*

bush bread: *Bread General Varieties 6*

bush clover: *Garden Perennials 10; Shrubs 10*

bush honeysuckle: *Shrubs 10*

bush morning glory: *Garden Perennials 10*

bush palmetto: *Garden Perennials 10*

bush pea: *Garden Perennials 10*

bush-club: *Squid 15*

Bushmaster 4×4 mine protected armored personnel carrier: *Australia Military Vehicles 8*

Bushmaster ACR Combat: *Semiautomatic Centerfire Rifles 7*

Bushmaster Carbon 15: *Semiautomatic Rimfire Rifles 7*

Bushmaster LVT-3 amphibious vehicle: *United States Military Vehicles 8*

Bushmaster Predator: *Semiautomatic Centerfire Rifles 7*

Bushmaster Varminter: *Semiautomatic Centerfire Rifles 7*

bushmaster: *General Snake Families 15*

bushy: *Eyebrows 1; Facial Hair Beard 1; Facial Hair Mustache 1; Hair Types 1*

business casual: *Styles of Dress 2*

business envelope: *Office/School/Writing Supplies 5*

business property: *Architecture and Property 3*

bust: *Card Games 5*

bustamite: *Minerals 10*

bustier: *Ladies' Wear 2*

bustle tutu: *Dance Clothing 13*

bustle: *Western Clothing/Dress 21*

busy: *Mobility 1*

butcher block: *Kitchen Equipment 5; Tables 4*

butcher knife: *Improvised Weapons 7; Kitchen Utensils 5*

butcher: *Attack 7; Castle Inhabitants and Personnel 1; Food Service 1; Kill 20*

butler: *Castle Inhabitants and Personnel 1; Horror Occupations 23*

butt: *Body Parts 12*

butte: *Erosion 10; Slope 10*

butter bean: *Legumes 6*

butter bolete: *Fungus Common Names 10*

butter brickle: *Cake 6; Ice Cream Flavors 6*

butter bur: *Garden Perennials 10*

butter dish: *Tableware 5*

butter knife: *Eating Utensils 5; Kitchen Utensils 5*

butter lettuce: *Vegetables 6*

butter milk: *Dairy Beverages 6*

butter mint: *Candy General 6*

butter mushroom: *Fungus Common Names 10*

butter pecan: *Ice Cream Flavors 6*

butter: *Cake 6; Cookie 6; Muffin 6; Objects/Activities Connected to Lore 19; Pie 6*

buttercup: *Garden Perennials 10*

butterfish: *Wild Saltwater Fish 15*

butterflies: *Objects/Activities Connected to Lore 19*

butterfly bush: *Garden Perennials 10; Shrubs 10*

butterfly milkweed: *Garden Perennials 10*

butterfly weed: *Wildflowers 10*

butterfly: *Animals 15; Animals with Symbolic Meaning 19; Bats 15; Cake 6; Chairs and Stools 4; Roof Styles 3; Sailing Knots 9; Swimming Strokes 9*

butterflyfish: *Aquarium Saltwater Fish 15*

butterfruit: *Unusual Edible Fruits 6*

butterhead lettuce: *Vegetables 6*

butternut squash: *Vegetables 6*

butternut: *Deciduous Trees 10*

butterscotch disk: *Candy General 6*

butterscotch: *Candy General 6; Cookie 6*

buttery spirit: *General Fae 16*

buttery: *Castle Anatomy 3*

butthead: *Card Games 5*

buttock: *Body Parts 12*

button bush: *Garden Perennials 10*

button hole: *Sewing Terms 2*

button man: *Thief 1*

button mangosteen: *Unusual Edible Fruits 6*

button mushroom: *Fungus Common Names 10; Vegetables 6*

button on a string: *Toys 5*

button snakeroot: *Garden Perennials 10*

button willow: *Garden Perennials 10*

button: *Embellishments 2; Fencing Equipment 7; Jewelry 21; Nose 1; Notions 2*

buttonball tree: *Deciduous Trees 10*

buttoned up: *Quiet 20*

buttonhole wheel: *Embroidery Stitches 2*

buttonhole: *Embroidery Stitches 2; Garment Pieces 2*

buttress: *Building Elements and Features 3; Castle Anatomy 3*

buy: *Verbs 20*

buyer: *Operations 1*

buzz cut: *Hair Style 1*

buzz: *Sounds 20; Speak 20*

buzzard: *Birds of Prey 15*

BWP-2000 infantry fighting vehicle: *Poland Military Vehicles 8*

BWP-40 infantry fighting vehicle: *Poland Military Vehicles 8*

by cocke: *Expletives 20*

by Saint Chicken: *Expletives 20*

by the cross of the mouse foot: *Expletives 20*

by the dog: *Expletives 20*

byaslang: *Cheese International Varieties 6*

bycoket: *Headgear 2*

bye altar: *Church Anatomy 3*

Byelorussian Harness: *Horse Breeds 15*

byssolite: *Minerals 10*

Byzantine: *Architectural Styles 3; Art Movements 13; Styles of Dress 2*

byzantium: *Purple 20*

–C–

C1 Ariete main battle tank: *Italy Military Vehicles 8*

C-12 Huron cargo: *U.S. Air Force Aircraft 8*

C-12 Huron: *U.S. Army Aircraft 8*

C13 Dardo infantry fighting vehicle: *Italy Military Vehicles 8*

C-130 Hercules: *U.S. Air Force Aircraft 8*

C-130J Super Hercules: *U.S. Air Force Aircraft 8*

C15 4×2 and 4×4 15-cwt truck: *Canada Military Vehicles 8*

C-17 Globemaster III: *U.S. Air Force Aircraft 8*

C-2 cargo transport: *U.S. Navy Aircraft 8*

C-20 Gulfstream passenger: *U.S. Air Force Aircraft 8*

C-21 Learjet: *U.S. Air Force Aircraft 8*

C-22 Boeing: *U.S. Air Force Aircraft 8*

C-23 Sherpa: *U.S. Army Aircraft 8*

C-26 Metroliner cargo: *U.S. Air Force Aircraft 8*

C-26 Metroliner: *U.S. Army Aircraft 8*

C-27J Spartan: *U.S. Air Force Aircraft 8*

C30 4×4 30-cwt truck: *Canada Military Vehicles 8*

C-37 Gulfstream: *U.S. Air Force Aircraft 8*

C-38 Gulfstream: *U.S. Air Force Aircraft 8*

C-40 Clipper: *U.S. Air Force Aircraft 8*

C-5 Galaxy cargo: *U.S. Air Force Aircraft 8*

C60 4×4 and 6×6 60-cwt truck: *Canada Military Vehicles 8*

C8 4×4 8-cwt truck: *Canada Military Vehicles 8*

C8 Quad 4x4 Tractor: *United Kingdom Military Vehicles 8*

C75 Series: *Pistol Semiautomatic 7*

CA1 light tank: *France Military Vehicles 8*

CA1091 4x25 ton truck: *China Military Vehicles 8*

cab driver: *Transportation 1*

cab stand: *Infrastructure Buildings 9*

cabana: *Residential Property 3*

cabbage palmetto: *Deciduous Trees 10*

cabbage slicer: *Kitchen Equipment 5*

cabbage: *Moth 15; Vegetables 6*

cabbie: *Transportation 1*

cabeirian horses: *Construct 16*

cabernet sauvignon: *Wine Red 6*

cabin tent: *General Survival Gear 5*

cabin: *Boat/Ship Anatomy 9; Outdoor Property 3; Residential Property 3*

cabinet member: *Government 1*

cabinet: *Bathroom Features and Fixtures 3; Building Elements and Features 3; Storage 4*

cable television provider: *Public Services 3*

cable television: *Building Systems 3*

cable: *Boat/Ship Anatomy 9; Computer Equipment 5; Fasteners 5; General Survival Gear 5; Technical Terms 13*

cable-stayed: *Bridges 9*

cabochon: *Gem Cuts 21*

cabossed: *Heads 19*

cabrerite: *Minerals 10*

Cabriole: *Ballet Terms 13*

cacciatore: *Poultry Meals 6*

cachalong opal: *Minerals 10*

cache: *Property Features 3*

Cachena: *Other Cows 15*

cackle: *Sounds 20; Witchcraft Vocabulary 17*

cacophony: *Loud 20*

cactus amethyst: *Minerals 10*

cactus citrine: *Minerals 10*

cactus quartz: *Minerals 10*

Cacus: *Giants of Legend 16*

cad: *Thief 1*

cadaverous: *Small/Thin 1*

Caddo: *Native American Peoples 1*

cadence: *General Music Vocabulary 13*

cadency mark: *Classic Heraldry 19*

cadenza: *General Music Vocabulary 13*

cadet gray: *Gray 20*

cadet: *Armed Forces Other Titles 8*

cadmium oxide: *Dangerous Chemicals 11*

cadmium smithsonite: *Minerals 10*

cadmium stearate: *Dangerous Chemicals 11*

Cadmium: *Elements 11*

Cadmus snake: *Mythical Creatures and Monsters 16*

Cador: *Knights of the Round Table 18*

caduceus: *Objects 18; Symbols in Magic and Religion 19*

caecilians: *Animals 15*

Caelum: *Constellations 11*

Caesar Augustus: *Christmas 19; Real People with Legendary Status 18*

Caesar cut: *Hair Style 1*

Caesar: *Royal/Noble 1; Salads 6*

Caesar's: *Comets 11*

café au lait: *Coffee Drinks 6*

café curtains: *Window Treatments 5*

café mocha: *Coffee Drinks 6*

café: *Food/Drink Establishments 3*

cafeteria: *Food/Drink Establishments 3*

caftan: *Unisex Clothing 2*

cage: *Containers and Vessels 5; Man-Made Animal Homes 15; Prison 3*

Cagle's map: *Freshwater Turtles 15*

Cagliostro seal: *Symbols in Magic and Religion 19*

caimito: *Unusual Edible Fruits 6*

Cairn Terrier: *Dog Breeds 15*

cairngorm: *Minerals 10*

Cairo Citadel: *Seven Wonders of the Middle Ages 18*

cajun (United States): *Ethnic/Folk Dances 13*

Cajun: *Human Ethnic Groups 1*

cake basket: *Tableware 5*

cake flour: *Staples 6*

cake plate: *Tableware 5*

cake server: *Kitchen Utensils 5*

cake stand: *Tableware 5*

cake tester: *Kitchen Utensils 5*

cake tin: *Kitchen Equipment 5*

cake yeast: *Staples 6*

cake: *Christmas 19; Food 6*

cakes: *Foods with Religious or Ritual Significance 19*

cakewalk: *Dance Styles 13*

calabar bean: *Poisonous Plants 10*

Calabar: *Python 15*

calabresella: *Card Games 5*

Caladbolg: *Celtic Swords 18*

caladium: *Garden Bulbs 10*

caladrius: *Flying Creatures 16*

calamansi: *Unusual Edible Fruits 6*

calamari: *Fish/Seafood Types 6*

calamine: *Minerals 10*

calamitous: *Bad 20; Unattractive 20*

Calamity Jane: *Real People with Legendary Status 18*

calamondin: *Unusual Edible Fruits 6*

calanque: *Coastal and Oceanic 10*

Calat Alhambra: *Unique Property 3*

calcaneous: *Bones 12*

calcareous grassland: *Soil General Vocabulary 10*

calcareous sinter: *Minerals 10*

calcareous tufa: *Minerals 10*

calcareous: *Geological Vocabulary 10*

calciocelsian: *Minerals 10*

calciorthid: *Soil General Vocabulary 10*

calciotherite: *Minerals 10*

calcisol: *Soil General Vocabulary 10*

calcite sea: *Geological Vocabulary 10*

calcite: *Cave Anatomy 10; Standard Gems 21*

calcium arsenate: *Dangerous Chemicals 11*

Calcium: *Elements 11*

calcspar: *Minerals 10*

calculate: *Solve 20*

calculated risk: *General Combat Vocabulary 7*

calculator: *Office/School/Writing Supplies 5*

caldera: *Geological Vocabulary 10; Volcanic 10*

calderite: *Minerals 10*

Caledfwlch: *Celtic Swords 18*

calf: *Body Parts 12; Objects/Activities Connected to Lore 19*

Caliban: *Moons 11*

calico bean: *Legumes 6*

calico: *Fabric Patterns 2*

California bay: *Deciduous Trees 10*

California black walnut: *Deciduous Trees 10*

California blue oak: *Deciduous Trees 10*

California bluebell: *Wildflowers 10*

California box elder: *Deciduous Trees 10*

California buckeye: *Deciduous Trees 10*

California coulter pine: *Evergreen Trees 10*

California draw: *Poker Card Games 5*

California fan palm: *Deciduous Trees 10*

California filbert: *Deciduous Trees 10*

California fuchsia: *Garden Perennials 10*

California Gold Rush: *Western Paraphernalia/People 21*

California gray: *Chickens 15*

California hazelnut: *Deciduous Trees 10*

California juniper: *Evergreen Trees 10*

California king: *Beds 4*

California laurel: *Deciduous Trees 10*

California lowball: *Poker Card Games 5*

California nutmeg: *Deciduous Trees 10*

California palm: *Deciduous Trees 10*

California poppy: *Wildflowers 10*

California red fir: *Evergreen Trees 10*

California redwood: *Deciduous Trees 10*

California spangled cat: *Domestic Cats 15*

California stud: *Poker Card Games 5*

California swamp pine: *Evergreen Trees 10*

California torreya: *Evergreen Trees 10*

California two-spot: *Octopi 15*

California walnut: *Deciduous Trees 10*

California Washington palm: *Deciduous Trees 10*

California white oak: *Deciduous Trees 10*

California: *Famous Western Locations 21; Toads 15*

californite: *Minerals 10*

Californium: *Elements 11*

caliper: *Architectural/Engineering Tools 5*

call: *Sounds 20; Speak 20*

calla: *Garden Bulbs 10*

calliopsis: *Wildflowers 10*

Callirrhoe: *Moons 11*

Callisto: *Moons 11*

callous: *Horror Vocabulary 23*

calm: *Easy 20; General Emotions 20; Happy 20; Meteorology General Vocabulary 10; Positive 1; Wind 10*

Calogrenant: *Knights of the Round Table 18*

calorie: *Chemistry General Vocabulary 11*

calorimeter: *Chemistry General Vocabulary 11; Laboratory Equipment 5*

caltrop: *Pointed Weapons 7*

calumet: *Objects in Magic and Religion 19*

Calydonian boar: *Mythical Creatures and Monsters 16*

calypso: *Card Games 5; Dance Styles 13*

Calypso: *Moons 11*

calzone: *Sandwiches 6*

Camael: *Fallen Angels 14*

Camargue: *Horse Breeds 15*

camassia: *Garden Bulbs 10*

Camazotz (bat god): *Central American Pantheon 14*

Camazotz: *Beast 16*

cambisol: *Soil General Vocabulary 10*

cambozola: *Cheese International Varieties 6*

Cambria pine: *Evergreen Trees 10*

Cambrian Period: *Geologic Time 10*

cambuk: *Bludgeons 7*

camel toes: *Footwear/Shoes 2*

camel: *Animals with Symbolic Meaning 19; Brown 20; Christmas 19; Nonvenomous Arachnids 15; Other Wild Mammals 15; Transportation Animals 9*

camellia: *Shrubs 10; Plants with Symbolic Meaning 19*

carpenteria: *Shrubs 10*

Camelopardalis: *Constellations 11*

Camelot: *Arthurian Characters 18; Arthurian Locations 18*

camembert: *Cheese Common Varieties 6*

cameo: *Jewelry 2; Jewelry 21*

camera left: *Stage Directions 13*

camera operator: *Media 1*

camera pen: *Spy Gear 5*

camera right: *Stage Directions 13*

cami: *Ladies' Wear 2*

camisole leotard: *Dance Clothing 13*

camisole: *Ladies' Wear 2*

Camlann: *Arthurian Locations 18*

camouflage: *Fabric Patterns 2; Styles of Dress 2*

camp ground: *Horror Locations 23*

camp stove: *General Survival Gear 5; Military Equipment 8*

camp: *Fortification 3; Outdoor Property 3*

campaign: *General Combat Vocabulary 7*

campanelle: *Pasta 6*

campanile: *Academic Property 3*

camper: *Motorized 9; Travel Modes 23*

campground supervisor: *Horror Occupations 23*

campground: *Outdoor Property 3*

camphechlor: *Dangerous Chemicals 11*

camphene lamp: *Illumination/Light Sources 5*

camphor laurel: *Weeds 10*

camphor tree: *Weeds 10*

campion: *Garden Perennials 10*

Campolina: *Horse Breeds 15*

campus: *Academic Property 3*

campylite: *Minerals 10*

camucamu: *Unusual Edible Fruits 6*

can hear a pin drop: *Quiet 20*

can light: *Illumination/Light Sources 5*

can opener: *Appliances 5; Kitchen Utensils 5*

can: *Containers and Vessels 5*

Canaan Dog: *Dog Breeds 15*

Canada balsam: *Evergreen Trees 10*

Canada hemlock: *Evergreen Trees 10*

Canadian amethyst: *Minerals 10*

Canadian milkvetch: *Garden Perennials 10*

Canadian pondweed: *Weeds 10*

Canadian spruce: *Evergreen Trees 10*

Canadian: *Horse Breeds 15*

Canadienne: *North American Dairy Cows 15*

canal basin: *Marina 3*

canal ray: *Chemistry General Vocabulary 11*

canal: *Water Terms 9*

canapé: *Seating 4*

Canary Island: *Other Cows 15*

canary: *Domesticated Pet Birds 15; Wild Saltwater Fish 15*

canasta: *Card Games 5*

cancellarious seal: *Symbols in Magic and Religion 19*

cancellation hearts: *Card Games 5*

Cancer (June 21–July 22): *Zodiac Signs 19*

Cancer: *Constellations 11*

cancer: *Diseases 12*

Canchim: *Other Cows 15*

candelabrum: *Candles 5*

candied fruit: *Candy General 6*

candle lamp: *Candles 5*

candle lantern: *Candles 5*

candle maker: *Artists and Craftspeople 1*

candle mold: *Candles 5*

candle stand: *Candles 5; Tables 4*

candle/fire: *Energy Sources/Types 23; Energy Sources/Types 24*

candle: *General Survival Gear 5; Objects in Magic and Religion 19; Objects/Activities Connected to Lore 19; Religious Items 5; Rituals 14; Typical Magical Objects 17; Witchcraft Vocabulary 17; Wizard's Goods 5*

candlefish: *Wild Freshwater Fish 15*

candleholder: *Candles 5*

candles flicker: *Paranormal Occurrences 21*

candles: *Equipment and Tools 5; Valentine's Day 19*

candle-snuff fungus: *Fungus Common Names 10*

candlestick lamp: *Illumination/Light Sources 5*

candlestick: *Candles 5*

candy bar: *Candy General 6*

candy buttons: *Candy General 6*

candy cane: *Candy General 6; Christmas 19*

candy cap: *Fungus Common Names 10*

candy cigarette: *Candy General 6*

candy corn: *Candy General 6; Halloween 19*

candy dish: *Tableware 5*

candy floss: *Candy General 6*

candy necklace: *Candy General 6*

candy raisin: *Candy General 6*

candy stick: *Candy General 6*

candy thermometer: *Kitchen Utensils 5*

candy: *Easter 19; Food 6; Halloween 19; Valentine's Day 19*

candylily: *Garden Perennials 10*

candytuft: *Garden Perennials 10; Wildflowers 10*

cane ash: *Deciduous Trees 10*

Cane Corso: *Dog Breeds 15*

cane: *Accessories 2; Door Materials 3; Toads 15*

canebrake: *General Snake Families 15*

caned seat: *Chairs and Stools 4*

Canes Venatiki: *Constellations 11*

Canfield: *Solitaire Card Games 5*

canine: *Teeth 12*

canines: *Animals 15*

Canis Major: *Constellations 11*

Canis Minor: *Constellations 11*

canistel: *Unusual Edible Fruits 6*

canister set: *Kitchen Equipment 5*

canister shot: *Missile Loads 7*

canisters: *Kitchen Equipment 5*

canna: *Garden Bulbs 10*

cannellini bean: *Legumes 6*

cannelloni: *Pasta 6*

canning kettle: *Kitchen Equipment 5*

cannoli: *Miscellaneous Dessert 6*

cannon ball: *Missile Loads 7*

cannon fodder: *Common Character Archetypes 21*

cannon net: *Traps 3*

cannon: *Black Powder Weapons 7; Combat, Armor, and Weapons 7; Siege Engines 7; Weapons 22*

cannonball: *Jellyfish 15*

canny: *Horror Vocabulary 23*

canoe birch: *Deciduous Trees 10*

canoe cedar: *Deciduous Trees 10*

canoe of Gluskab: *Vehicles 18*

canoe of Maui: *Vehicles 18*

canoe: *Human-Powered Watercraft 9*

canola: *Farm/Outbuilding 3; Oils 6*

canon: *Cleric 1; General Music Vocabulary 13*

canopy: *Beds 4*

cantabile: *General Music Vocabulary 13*

cantaloupe pickle: *Pickled/Relish 6*

cantaloupe: *Melons 6*

cantankerous: *Grouchy 1*

cantata: *General Music Vocabulary 13*

canteen: *Containers and Vessels 5; Drinkware 5; Food/Drink Establishments 3; General Survival Gear 5; Military Equipment 8*

Canterbury bells: *Garden Perennials 10*

cantharidin: *Dangerous Chemicals 11*

canticle: *Composition Types 13*

cantil: *General Snake Families 15*

cantilever: *Bridges 9; Building Elements and Features 3*

cantina: *Food/Drink Establishments 3*

canton: *Political Divisions 10*

Cantonese: *Human Ethnic Groups 1; Pigs 15*

cantor: *Cleric 1*

Cantor's: *Pit Viper 15*

canvas bag: *Containers and Vessels 5*

canvas texture: *Art Media 13*

canvas: *Art Materials 5; Fabric 2*

canvasser: *Wizard 1*

canyon live oak: *Deciduous Trees 10*

canyon: *Bats 15; Erosion 10*

cap and ball pistol/rifle: *Western Weapons 21*

cap pistol: *Toys 5*

cap sleeve: *Garment Pieces 2*

cap: *Headgear 2*

capable: *Good 20*

capacious: *Large 20*

capacitance probe: *Soil General Vocabulary 10*

caparisoned/barded: *Multiple Figures 19*

Cape Berkeley giant: *Tortoises 15*

Cape Cod: *Architectural Styles 3*

Cape May diamond: *Minerals 10*

cape: *Coastal and Oceanic 10; Foxes 15; Outerwear 2; Western Clothing/Dress 21; Witchcraft Vocabulary 17*

Cape: *Cobra 15; Lions 15; Tortoises 15*

capeline hat: *Headgear 2*

capellini: *Pasta 6*

caper: *Locomotion 9*

capillary action: *Chemistry General Vocabulary 11*

capillary tube: *Laboratory Equipment 5*

capillary: *Chemistry General Vocabulary 11; Organs/Major Structures 12*

capillitite: *Minerals 10*

cap-it: *Card Games 5*

capital ship: *Military Watercraft 8*

capitalism: *Philosophy Basic Concepts 14*

capitate bone: *Bones 12*

capitol police: *Law Enforcement 1*

capitol: *Administrative Property 3*

capitulate: *General Combat Vocabulary 7*

capo: *Music Accessories*

capotain: *Headgear 2*

capotasto: *Music Accessories*

capote bonnet: *Headgear 2*

cappella: *General Music Vocabulary 13*

cappuccino machine: *Appliances 5*

cappuccino: *Coffee Drinks 6; Ice Cream Flavors 6*

caprese: *Salads 6*

capri pants: *Ladies' Wear 2*

capriccioso: *Tempo/Mood 13*

caprice: *Composition Types 13*

Capricorn (December 22–January 19): *Zodiac Signs 19*

Capricornus: *Constellations 11*

capriole: *Dance Moves 13*

capris: *Ladies' Wear 2*

capsize: *Boat/Ship Terminology 9*

capstan: *Boat/Ship Anatomy 9*

capstone of the Great Pyramid: *Objects 18*

capsule: *Spaceship Shapes 22*

Captain Ahab: *Fictional Characters 18*

captain: *Maritime Occupations 1; U.S. Air Force Officer 8; U.S. Army Officer 8; U.S. Marines Officer 8; U.S. Navy Officer 8*

captivate: *Magic Vocabulary 17; Witchcraft Vocabulary 17*

captivated: *Magic Vocabulary 17*

captivating: *Beautiful 20*

captor: *Villain 20*

capture: *Close/Hold 20*

capuchin: *Headgear 2; New World Monkeys 15*

car accident: *Injuries/Medical Emergencies 12*

car carrier: *Motorized Truck 9*

car coat: *Outerwear 2*

car collision with animal: *Travel Hazards 9*

car collision: *Travel Hazards 9*

car involved in deadly crash: *Horror Locations 23*

car phone: *Spy Gear 5*

car/tools/objects/doll animate after lightning strike: *Horror Plot Devices 23*

car: *Motorized 9; Toys 5*

carabiner: *General Survival Gear 5*

caracara: *Birds of Prey 15*

Caradoc: *Knights of the Round Table 18*

carafe: *Containers and Vessels 5; Laboratory Equipment 5*

carambola: *Tropical/Exotic Fruits 6*

caramel cashew: *Ice Cream Flavors 6*

caramel popcorn: *Snacks 6*

caramel turtle: *Ice Cream Flavors 6*

caramel: *Candy General 6; Hair Color 1; Ice Cream Flavors 6; Ice Cream Toppings 6; Skin Types and Features 1*

caramelize: *Cooking Techniques 20*

carapace: *Physical Mutations 22*

caravane: *Cheese International Varieties 6*

carbachol chloride: *Dangerous Chemicals 11*

carbamic acid: *Dangerous Chemicals 11*

carbanion: *Chemistry General Vocabulary 11*

carbofuran: *Dangerous Chemicals 11*

carbon arc: *Illumination Bulb and Tube Types 5*

carbon cycle rebalancing: *Soil General Vocabulary 10*

carbon disulfide: *Dangerous Chemicals 11*

carbon dust: *Art Materials 5*

carbon film: *Geological Vocabulary 10*

carbon paper: *Office/School/Writing Supplies 5*

Carbon: *Elements 11*

carbonado: *Minerals 10*

Carbonari: *Secret/Mystical Organizations 18*

carbonate apatite: *Minerals 10*

carbonate fluorapatite: *Minerals 10*

carbonate hardgrounds: *Geological Vocabulary 10*

carbonate hydroxylapatite: *Minerals 10*

carbonate: *Geological Vocabulary 10*

carbonatecyanotrichite: *Minerals 10*

carbonate-rich apatite: *Minerals 10*

carbonate-rich fluorapatite: *Minerals 10*

carbonate-rich hydroxylapatite: *Minerals 10*

carbonatite: *Igneous Rocks 10*

Carboniferous Period: *Geologic Time 10*

carbonium ion: *Chemistry General Vocabulary 11*

carbophenothion: *Dangerous Chemicals 11*

carcharodontosaurus: *Commonly Known Dinosaurs 15*

carcinogen: *Chemistry General Vocabulary 11*

card catalog: *Office/School/Writing Supplies 5*

card games: *Equipment and Tools 5*

card reader: *Fortune Teller 1*

card shark: *Thief 1*

card sharper: *Thief 1*

card: *Art Materials 5; Art Media 13; Games 5; Tables 4*

cardamom: *Spices 6*

Carden Loyd Tankette: *United Kingdom Military Vehicles 8*

cardigan sweater: *Unisex Clothing 2*

Cardigan Welsh Corgi: *Dog Breeds 15*

cardinal flower: *Garden Perennials 10*

cardinal points: *Boat/Ship Terminology 9*

cardinal tetra: *Aquarium Freshwater Fish 15*

cardinal virtues: *Collective Symbols 19*

cardinal: *Backyard Birds 15; Cleric 1; Red 20; Religious Occupations 1*

cardinalfish: *Aquarium Saltwater Fish 15*

cardiologist: *Medical Occupations 1*

cardon: *Unusual Edible Fruits 6*

cardoon: *Garden Perennials 10*

cards: *Christmas 19; Fortune Telling General Devices 19; Toys 5*

cardstock: *Art Materials 5*

care for: *Love 20*

care: *General Emotions 20*

careen: *Boat/Ship Terminology 9*

career: *Styles of Dress 2*

carefree: *Happy 20*

careful: *Horror Vocabulary 23*

careless: *Horror Vocabulary 23*

caretaker: *Agricultural 1; Horror Occupations 23*

caretaker's home: *Cemetery 3*

cargo pants: *Dance Clothing 13*

cargo plane: *Air Vehicles 9*

cargo van: *Motorized 9*

cargo: *Helicopters 8; Large Watercraft 9; Military Aircraft 8; Spaceship Types 22*

Caribbean reef: *Sharks 15*

Caribbean: *Poker Card Games 5*

caribou: *Other Wild Mammals 15*

caricature: *Art Techniques 13*

Carina: *Constellations 11*

caring: *Positive 1*

Carinthian Blond: *Other Cows 15*

carioca: *Card Games 5*

Carme: *Moons 11*

carmine: *Red 20*

carminere: *Wine Red 6*

carnation pink: *Pink 20*

carnation: *Garden Annuals 10; Garden Perennials 10*

carnelian onyx: *Minerals 10*

carnelian: *Minerals 10; Standard Gems 21*

carnival: *Architecture and Property 3; Entertainment Property 3; Games 5; Masks 2*

Carnwennan: *Arthurian Weapons 18*

carob: *Unusual Edible Fruits 6*

Carolina beech: *Deciduous Trees 10*

Carolina hemlock: *Evergreen Trees 10*

Carolina moonseed: *Garden Perennials 10*

Carolingian: *Architectural Styles 3*

carols: *Christmas 19*

carousel: *Amusement Park/Carnival/Circus/Fair 3; Card Games 5*

carpal: *Bones 12*

Carpathia: *Ships 18*

Carpenter Gothic: *Architectural Styles 3*

carpenter plant: *Garden Perennials 10*

carpenter: *Ants 15; Artists and Craftspeople 1; Bees 15; Castle Inhabitants and Personnel 1; Construction 1*

carpentry tools: *Classic Items 23*

carpentry: *Art Techniques 13*

carpet cleaner: *Public Services 3*

carpet layer: *Construction 1*

carpet store: *Business Property 3*

carpet: *Beetle 15; Floor Coverings 4; General Snake Families 15; Interior Building Materials 3; Python 15; Sharks 15; Viper 15*

carpetbag: *Accessories 2*

carpeting: *Floor Coverings 4*

Carpo: *Moons 11*

carpool: *Motorized 9*

carport: *Property Features 3*

carrack bend: *Sailing Knots 9*

carrack: *Large Watercraft 9*

carriage clock: *Timekeeping 5*

carriage hat: *Headgear 2*

carriage: *Animal-Powered Transportation 9*

Carribean: *Styles of Dress 2*

carrier: *Containers and Vessels 5; Spaceship Types 22*

Carro Leggero tank: *Italy Military Vehicles 8*

Carro Pesante tank: *Italy Military Vehicles 8*

Carro Veloce fast tank: *Italy Military Vehicles 8*

carrot orange: *Orange 20*

carrot: *Cake 6; Objects/Activities Connected to Lore 19; Soup 6; Vegetable Juice 6; Vegetables 6*

carry out: *Solve 20*

carrying capacity: *Geography General Vocabulary 10*

Carson City: *Famous Western Locations 21*

cart: *Animal-Powered Transportation 9; Horse Drawn Farm Equipment; Human-Powered Transportation 9; Miscellaneous Furniture 4*

Carthusian: *Horse Breeds 15*

cartographer: *Geography General Vocabulary 10*

carton: *Containers and Vessels 5*

cartoon: *Art Genres 13*

cartooning: *Art Techniques 13*

cartwheel hat: *Headgear 2*

cartwright: *Artists and Craftspeople 1*

carve: *Art Techniques 13*

carving knife: *Kitchen Utensils 5*

carving materials: *Art Materials 5*

Casa Grande soil: *Soil General Vocabulary 10*

casaba: *Melons 6*

cascade: *Precipitation 10*

Cascades fir: *Evergreen Trees 10*

case: *Containers and Vessels 5; Missile Weapons 7; Music Accessories*

casemate: *Castle Anatomy 3*

casement: *Windows 3*

Casey Jones: *Real People with Legendary Status 18*

cash register: *Office/School Machines 5; Toys 5*

cashbox: *Containers and Vessels 5*

cashew apple: *Unusual Edible Fruits 6*

cashew: *Nuts 6; Oils 6*

cashier: *General Occupations 1*

cashmere: *Fabric 2*

casing: *Garment Pieces 2*

Casino hold 'em: *Poker Card Games 5*

casino: *Card Games 5; Entertainment Property 3*

cask: *Containers and Vessels 5*

casket: *Containers and Vessels 5*

Caspar/Gaspar: *Three Wise Men/Magi 19*

Caspian pond: *Freshwater Turtles 15*

Caspian: *Horse Breeds 15; Tigers 15*

casquehead lizard: *Scaled Reptiles 15*

casquetel: *Head Gear 7*

cassabanana: *Unusual Edible Fruits 6*

cassation: *Composition Types 13*

cassava: *Vegetables 6*

casserole: *Fish/Seafood Meals 6; Kitchen Equipment 5; Meals 6; Poultry Meals 6*

cassette player: *Electronics 4*

cassette recorder: *Electronics 4*

Cassiel: *Angels of Good 14*

Cassiopeia: *Constellations 11*

cassiterite: *Standard Gems 21*

Casspir mine proof wheeled APC: *South Africa Military Vehicles 8*

cast iron: *Tables 4*

cast net: *Fishing Gear 5*

caste system: *Plot Devices 22*

caste: *Social Distinction 1*

Castilian: *Human Ethnic Groups 1*

casting director: *Performing Arts 1*

casting materials: *Art Materials 5*

casting off: *Boat/Ship Terminology 9*

casting: *Geological Vocabulary 10; Stage Terms 13*

castle anatomy: *Architecture and Property 3*

castle inhabitants: *Character Building 1*

castle personnel: *Character Building 1*

Castle: *Architectural Styles 3*

castle: *Fantasy Locations 24; Fortification 3; Residential Property 3; Residential Slang 3*

castles: *Patterns 19*

castor oil plant: *Poisonous Plants 10; Weeds 10*

casual suit: *Men's Wear 2*

casual: *Styles of Dress 2*

casualty: *General Combat Vocabulary 7*

cat o' nine tails: *Flexible 7*

cat spruce: *Deciduous Trees 10*

cat: *Allergies 12; Animals with Symbolic Meaning 19; Bears 15; General Snake Families 15; Objects/Activities Connected to Lore 19; Sharks 15*

cats: *Animals 15*

cat's cradle: *Toys 5*

cat's eye marble: *Harbingers/Charms for Good Luck 19*

cat's eye: *Minerals 10*

cataclasite: *Metamorphic Rocks 10*

catacomb: *Castle Anatomy 3; Cemetery 3; Rooms 3; Terrain Features 10*

Catacombs of Korn el Shoqafa: *Seven Wonders of the Middle Ages 18*

catacombs: *Church Anatomy 3*

Catalan atlas: *Real Objects Not Fully Understood 18*

catalog: *Laboratory Supplies 5*

catalyst: *Chemistry General Vocabulary 11*

catamaran: *Small Watercraft 9*

catapult load: *Siege Equipment 7*

catapult: *Siege Engines 7*

cataracts: *Eye Type 1*

Catawba: *Native American Peoples 1*

catboat: *Small Watercraft 9*

catch: *Buy 20; Jewelry 21; Locks 5*

catcher's mitt: *Sporting Goods Other 5*

catchfly: *Garden Perennials 10; Wildflowers 10*

catching falling leaves: *Objects that Offer Protection 19*

catch-pole: *Man-Traps 7*

catch-up stroke: *Swimming Strokes 9*

categorize: *Learn 20*

category: *Philosophy Basic Concepts 14*

catenation: *Chemistry General Vocabulary 11*

caterwauling: *Vocal/Speech Quality 1*

cat-eyed: *General Snake Families 15*

catfish: *Aquarium Freshwater Fish 15; Fish/Seafood Types 6*

cathedral pyrite: *Minerals 10*

cathedral: *Religious Building 3*

cathode ray tube: *Chemistry General Vocabulary 11*

cathode: *Chemistry General Vocabulary 11*

cathodic protection: *Chemistry General Vocabulary 11*

Catholic Holy Days of Obligation: *Philosophy and Religion 14*

cation: *Chemistry General Vocabulary 11*

catmint: *Garden Perennials 10*

CATOBAR aircraft carrier: *Military Watercraft 8*

catoplepas: *Beast 16*

cat-scratch disease: *Diseases 12*

catsuit: *Ladies' Wear 2*

catsup: *Condiments 6*

cattedrale: *Religious Building 3*

cattle drive: *Western Paraphernalia/People 21; Western Plot Devices 21*

cattle herd: *Western Paraphernalia/People 21*

cattle ranch: *Western Paraphernalia/People 21*

cattle: *Farm/Outbuilding 3; Objects/Activities Connected to Lore 19*

cattlemen: *Western Paraphernalia/People 21*

catwalk: *Parts of the Theater 13; Roads 9*

caubeen: *Headgear 2*

Caucasian eagle: *Flying Creatures 16*

Caucasian shashka: *Swords One-handed 7*

Caucasian: *Other Cows 15*

caudate willow: *Deciduous Trees 10*

caul: *Objects/Activities Connected to Lore 19*

cauldron of Dyrnwch the Giant: *Thirteen Treasures of the Island of Britain 18*

cauldron: *Kitchen Equipment 5; Objects in Magic and Religion 19; Witchcraft Vocabulary 17; Wizard's Goods 5*

cauliflower fungus: *Fungus Common Names 10*

cauliflower mushroom: *Fungus Common Names 10*

cauliflower: *Nose 1; Vegetables 6*

caulk gun: *Hand Tools 5*

causality: *Philosophy Basic Concepts 14*

cause: *Philosophy Basic Concepts 14*

causeway: *Roads 9*

caustic: *Smells 20*

cautious: *Horror Vocabulary 23*

cavalier hat: *Headgear 2*

Cavalier King Charles Spaniel: *Dog Breeds 15*

Cavalier: *Ballet Terms 13*

cavalier: *Knight 1*

cavalry man: *Knight 1*

cavalry post: *Western Plot Devices 21*

cavalry saber: *Western Weapons 21*

cavalry: *Fighter 1*

cavatelli: *Pasta 6*

cave anatomy: *Chapter 10*

cave coral: *Cave Anatomy 10*

cave creek jasper: *Minerals 10*

cave mouth: *Doors Atypical 3*

cave myotis: *Bats 15*

cave pearls: *Cave Anatomy 10*

cave pool: *Cave Anatomy 10*

cave pudding: *Ooze 16*

cave system: *Cave Anatomy 10*

cave/cavern: *Horror Locations 23*

cave: *Bears 15; Chapter 10; Dwarf 1; Erosion 10; Fantasy Locations 24; Fluvial 10; Natural Animal Homes 15; Residential Slang 3*

cave-diving: *Exploration 9*

cave-in: *Geological Natural Hazards 10*

caveman/woman: *Common Character Archetypes 21*

caveman: *Styles of Dress 2*

cavern: *Dwarf 1; Natural Animal Homes 15; Terrain Features 10*

caviar spoon: *Eating Utensils 5*

cavort: *Locomotion 9*

cawesh: *Unusual Edible Fruits 6*

cay: *Water Terms 9*

Cayuse: *Horse Breeds 15; Native American Peoples 1*

Cazador tracked TOW missile carrier: *Spain Military Vehicles 8*

C-clamp: *Hardware 5; Hand Tools 5*

CD boombox: *Electronics 4*

CD player: *Electronics 4*

ceanothus: *Shrubs 10*

Ceard-nan Gallan: *Celtic Swords 18*

ceasefire: *General Combat Vocabulary 7*

Cecchetti method: *Ballet Terms 13*

Cecil soil: *Soil General Vocabulary 10*

cecropia: *Moth 15*

cecum: *Organs/Major Structures 12*

cedar chest: *Storage 4*

cedar pine: *Deciduous Trees 10*

cedar shake: *Roofing Materials 3*

cedar shingle: *Roofing Materials 3*

cedar waxwing: *Backyard Birds 15*

cedro blanco: *Deciduous Trees 10*

Cedro De La Sierra: *Deciduous Trees 10*

cedro: *Deciduous Trees 10*

Cedros Island pine: *Evergreen Trees 10*

ceffyl dwr: *Aquatic 16*

ceiling fan: *Building Systems 3*

ceiling light: *Illumination/Light Sources 5*

ceiling tile: *Building Elements and Features 3*

ceiling: *Building Elements and Features 3*

celandine: *Garden Perennials 10; Objects/Activities Connected to Lore 19*

celebrant: *Cleric 1*

celebrated: *Personality Other 1*

celebrity: *Hero 20*

celedones: *Construct 16*

celeriac: *Vegetables 6*

celery salt: *Cocktail Garnishes 6*

celery server: *Tableware 5*

celery stick: *Cocktail Garnishes 6*

celery: *Soup 6; Vegetable Juice 6; Vegetables 6*

celesta: *Percussion Musical Instruments 5*

celestial equator: *Astronomy General Terms 11*

celestial mirror: *Symbols in Magic and Religion 19*

celestial object on course for Earth: *Plot Devices 22*

celestial poles: *Astronomy General Terms 11*

celestial sphere: *Astronomy General Terms 11*

celestite: *Minerals 10*

cell block: *Prison 3*

cell phone provider: *Public Services 3*

cell phone: *Classic Items 23*

cell: *Meteorology General Vocabulary 10; Prison 3*

cellar: *Cemetery 3; Nonvenomous Arachnids 15; Rooms 3*

cellarette: *Storage 4*

cellist: *Musical Occupations 1*

cello: *String Musical Instruments*

cellophane tape: *Fasteners 5; Office/School/Writing Supplies 5*

cellular confinement: *Soil General Vocabulary 10*

cellulitis: *Diseases 12*

celosia: *Garden Annuals 10*

Celt: *Human Ethnic Groups 1*

Celtic Cross: *Real Objects Not Fully Understood 18*

Celtic knot: *Symbols in Magic and Religion 19*

Celtic pantheon: *Philosophy and Religion 14*

Celtic: *Crosses 19; Daggers and Knives 7*

cembalo: *String Musical Instruments*

cement: *Art Materials 5; Art Media 13*

cemetery vault: *Fantasy Locations 24; Horror Locations 23*

cemetery: *Architecture and Property 3; Church Anatomy 3*

cenotaph: *Cemetery 3*

Cenozoic Era: *Geologic Time 10; Geological Vocabulary 10*

census: *Christmas 19*

centaur: *Beast 16; Fantasy Creatures with Symbolic Meaning 19*

Centauro 8×8 tank destroyer: *Italy Military Vehicles 8*

Centaurus: *Constellations 11*

centenarian: *Elderly 1*

center of the Earth: *Plot Devices 22*

center pivot irrigation: *General Farm Equipment*

centerboard: *Boat/Ship Anatomy 9*

centerfire rifles: *Combat, Armor, and Weapons 7*

central air: *Building Systems 3*

Central American pantheon: *Philosophy and Religion 14*

Central American squirrel: *New World Monkeys 15*

Central American wood: *Freshwater Turtles 15*

central bearded dragon: *Scaled Reptiles 15*

central business district: *Geography General Vocabulary 10*

central chimpanzee: *Apes 15*

central incisor: *Teeth 12*

central processing unit: *Computer Equipment 5*

central vacuum: *Building Systems 3*

Centre practice: *Ballet Terms 13*

centrifuge: *Laboratory Equipment 5*

Centurion: *Tanks British 8*

Century Arms Coach: *Shotguns Side-by-Side 7*

Century International Bullpup: *Semiautomatic Centerfire Rifles 7*

cepheid variable: *Astronomy General Terms 11*

Cepheus: *Constellations 11*

ceramic beads: *Art Materials 5*

ceramic holy symbol: *Religious Items 5*

ceratopsian: *Dinosaur Types 15*

Cerberus: *Beast 16*

cereal bowl: *Containers and Vessels 5; Tableware 5*

cerebellum: *Organs/Major Structures 12*

Cereberus hound: *Twelve Labors of Hercules 16*

cerebral cortex: *Organs/Major Structures 12*

Ceres (goddess of agriculture): *Roman Pantheon 14; Planets 11*

ceriman: *Unusual Edible Fruits 6*

cerise: *Pink 20; Purple 20; Red 20*

Cerium: *Elements 11*

Cernunnus (nature): *Celtic Pantheon 14*

cerulean: *Blue 20; Cyan 20*

Ceryneian hind: *Beast 16; Twelve Labors of Hercules 16*

Cesium: *Elements 11*

Cesky Terrier: *Dog Breeds 15*

Cessna UC-35: *U.S. Army Aircraft 8*

cesspit: *Castle Anatomy 3*

cestus: *Hand Weapons 7*

cetan: *Flying Creatures 16*

Cetus: *Constellations 11*

Ceylon cedar: *Weeds 10*

Ceylon: *Krait 15*

ceylonite: *Minerals 10*

Ch'omna-ho main battle tank: *North Korea Military Vehicles 8*

CH-47 Chinook: *U.S. Army Helicopter 8*

cha cha cha: *Dance Styles 13*

cha cha: *Objects in Magic and Religion 19*

chablis: *Wine White 6*

Chaco: *Tortoises 15*

chaconne (Spain): *Ethnic/Folk Dances 13*

chafing dish: *Kitchen Equipment 5*

Chagas disease: *Diseases 12*

chain binding the Fenris wolf: *Objects 18*

chain locker: *Boat/Ship Anatomy 9*

chain mail: *Armor Types 7; Horse Barding Materials 7*

chain of office: *Jewelry 21*

chain reaction: *Chemistry General Vocabulary 11*

chain saw: *Classic Items 23; Power Tools*

chain termination step: *Chemistry General Vocabulary 11*

chain weapons: *Combat, Armor, and Weapons 7*

chain whip: *Flexible 7*

chain: *Close/Hold 20; Embroidery Stitches 2; Fasteners 5; Jewelry 2; Wizard's Goods 5*

Chaînés: *Ballet Terms 13*

chainmail coif: *Head Gear 7*

chair of forgetfulness: *Objects 18*

chair: *Improvised Weapons 7; Objects/Activities Connected to Lore 19*

chaise longue: *Seating 4*

chaise: *Animal-Powered Transportation 9*

chakram: *Missile Weapons 7*

chalcedon: *Minerals 10*

chalcedonite: *Minerals 10*

chalcedony: *Minerals 10; Standard Gems 21*

chalcedonyx: *Minerals 10*

Chalchiuhtlicue (goddess of love): *Central American Pantheon 14;*

Chalchiuhtlicue (lake goddess): *Aztec Pantheon 14*

chalcotrichite: *Minerals 10*

Chaldene: *Moons 11*

Chalet: *Architectural Styles 3*

chalet: *Residential Property 3*

Chalice of the Last Supper: *Relics of Jesus 14*

chalice: *Drinkware 5; Objects in Magic and Religion 19; Objects/Activities Connected to Lore 19; Religious Items 5*

chalk bass: *Aquarium Saltwater Fish 15*

chalk box: *Architectural/Engineering Tools 5*

chalk: *Art Materials 5; Art Media 13; Minerals 10; Office/School/Writing Supplies 5; Sedimentary Rocks 10; Wizard's Goods 5*

chalkboard: *Office/School/Writing Supplies 5*

chalk-dust flu: *Fictional Diseases 12*

challah: *Bread General Varieties 6*

challenge: *Card Games 5*

Challenger 2: *Tanks British 8*

challenger: *Fighter 1*

challenging: *Difficult 20*

challis: *Fabric 2*

chalybite: *Minerals 10*

chamber music: *Musical Styles 13*

chamber of commerce: *Guilds 1*

chamber orchestra: *Groups 13*

chamber stick: *Candles 5*

chamber: *Cave Anatomy 10; Rooms 3*

chambray: *Fabric 2*

Chamealeon: *Constellations 11*

chameleon change: *Physical Mutations 22*

chameleon: *Scaled Reptiles 15*

chamois: *Fabric 2*

chamomile: *Garden Perennials 10; Wildflowers 10*

champ: *Hero 20*

champagne blond: *Hair Color 1*

champagne glass: *Drinkware 5*

champagne: *Aphrodisiacs 19; Foods with Religious or Ritual Significance 19; New Year 19; Valentine's Day 19; White 20; Wine White 6*

champion: *Hero 20*

chamrosh: *Flying Creatures 16*

chancel: *Church Anatomy 3*

chancellor: *Religious Occupations 1*

chandelier: *Illumination/Light Sources 5*

chanfron: *Horse Barding Pieces 7*

changdao: *Swords Two-handed 7*

change of engagement: *Fencing Vocabulary 7*

change: *Pennsylvania Dutch Hex Signs 19*

changeable license plates: *Spy Gear 5*

changeling: *Human Races Fictional 1; Shapechanger 16*

Changement: *Ballet Terms 13*

changing bear maiden: *Demon 16*

channel marker: *Marina 3*

Channel Tunnel (Chunnel): *Unique Property 3*

Channel Tunnel: *Seven Wonders of the Modern World 18*

channel: *Coastal and Oceanic 10; Roads 9; Water Terms 9*

Channi: *Other Cows 15*

chanson: *Composition Types 13*

chant: *Composition Types 13; Rituals 14; Witchcraft Vocabulary 17*

Chantico (hearth goddess): *Aztec Pantheon 14*

Chantilly lace: *Fabric 2*

Chantilly/Tiffany: *Domestic Cats 15*

Chao Kung Ming (demigod of war): *Chinese Pantheon 14*

chaoite: *Minerals 10*

chaos wheel: *Symbols in Magic and Religion 19*

chaos: *Astronomy General Terms 11; Philosophy Basic Concepts 14*

chap: *Male 1*

chapati: *Bread General Varieties 6*

chapbook: *Books/Publications 5*

chapeaux: *Charges 19*

chapel: *Cemetery 3; Groups 13; Religious Building 3; Rooms 3*

chaperon hood: *Headgear 2*

chaplain: *Religious Occupations 1*

chaplet: *Charges 19*

chaps: *Special Purpose Clothing 2; Western Clothing/Dress 21*

chapter book: *Books/Publications 5*

Char 2C Alsace super-heavy tank: *France Military Vehicles 8*

Char B1 medium tank: *France Military Vehicles 8*

Char Leger Hotchkiss H-35 tank: *France Military Vehicles 8*

char: *Cooking Techniques 20*

character sketch: *Art Genres 13*

characterization of pore space in soil: *Soil General Vocabulary 10*

Charbray: *Other Cows 15*

charcoal burner: *Fungus Common Names 10*

charcoal: *Art Materials 5; Art Media 13; Black 20*

chard: *Vegetables 6*

chardonnay: *Wine White 6*

charge: *Attack 7; General Combat Vocabulary 7; Locomotion 9; Moves 7*

charger: *Tableware 5*

charges: *Classic Heraldry 19*

charichuelo: *Unusual Edible Fruits 6*

Chariot of Fire driven by angels: *Vehicles 18*

chariot of Kali: *Vehicles 18*

chariot of Morgan Mwynfawr: *Thirteen Treasures of the Island of Britain 18*

Chariot of the Sea (Poseidon): *Vehicles 18*

Chariot of the Sun: *Vehicles 18*

Chariot of Thunder: *Vehicles 18*

chariot pulled by nightmares: *Vehicles 24*

chariot: *Animal-Powered Transportation 9*

charismatic: *Beautiful 20*

charity: *Christmas 19; Seven Holy Virtues 19; Three Theological Virtues 19; Twelve Fruits of the Holy Spirit 19*

charlatan: *Common Character Archetypes 21; Thief 1; Witchcraft Vocabulary 17*

Charles Dickens: *Christmas 19*

Charles's law: *Chemistry General Vocabulary 11*

Charleston: *Dance Styles 13*

Charlie Chaplan: *Facial Hair Mustache 1*

Charlottetown soil series: *Soil General Vocabulary 10*

charm bracelet: *Jewelry 2*

charm wand: *Objects that Offer Protection 19*

charm: *Jewelry 21; Magic Vocabulary 17; Witchcraft Vocabulary 17; Wizard's Goods 5*

charmed: *Happy 20; Magic Vocabulary 17*

charmeuse: *Fabric 2*

charming: *Beautiful 20; Magic Vocabulary 17; Personality Other 1*

charnockite: *Igneous Rocks 10*

charoite: *Standard Gems 21*

Charolais: *Other Cows 15*

Charon: *Moons 11*

chart: *Boat/Ship Anatomy 9; Books/Publications 5; Laboratory Supplies 5*

chartbuster: *Large 20*

Charter Arms Bulldog: *Revolver Double Action 7*

Charter Arms Dixie Derringer: *Revolver Single Action 7*

Charter Arms Patriot: *Revolver Double Action 7*

chartreuse: *Green 20*

Chartreux: *Domestic Cats 15*

chary: *Horror Vocabulary 23*

Charybdis: *Mythical Creatures and Monsters 16*

chase the ace: *Card Games 5*

chase the pig: *Card Games 5*

chaser bin: *General Farm Equipment*

chaser: *Dragonfly 15*

chasm: *Terrain Features 10*

chasma: *Astronomy General Terms 11*

Chassé: *Ballet Terms 13*

chasse: *Dance Moves 13*

chastity: *Twelve Fruits of the Holy Spirit 19*

chasuble: *Religious Dress 2*

chateau: *Residential Property 3*

chatelaine bag: *Accessories 2*

chatelaine: *Jewelry 21*

Chatham Island giant: *Tortoises 15*

Chato Murciano: *Pigs 15*

chattering lory: *Domesticated Pet Birds 15*

chauffer: *Transportation 1*

Chausie: *Domestic Cats 15*

chauves souris: *Pole Weapons 7*

chayote: *Unusual Edible Fruits 6*

Che Guevara: *Real People with Legendary Status 18*

cheat sheet: *Technical Terms 13*

cheat: *Card Games 5*

check protector: *Office/School Machines 5*

checked: *Fabric Patterns 2*

checkerbloom: *Garden Perennials 10*

checkerboard: *Fabric Patterns 2*

checkers: *Games 5*

checkerspot: *Butterfly 15*

cheddar clothbound: *Cheese Common Varieties 6*

cheddar pink: *Garden Perennials 10*

cheddar popcorn: *Snacks 6*

cheek: *Body Parts 12*

cheekbone: *Body Parts 12*

cheeks: *Character Building 1*

cheer: *Loud 20*

cheerful: *Happy 20; Positive 1*

cheering: *Loud 20*

cheerleader: *Sports 1*

cheerless: *Sad 20*

cheery: *Happy 20*

cheese ball: *Cheese Common Varieties 6; Snacks 6*

cheese curls: *Snacks 6*

cheese dome: *Tableware 5*

cheese grater: *Kitchen Utensils 5*

cheese pizza: *Cheese Dishes 6*

cheese popcorn: *Snacks 6*

cheese potato chip: *Snacks 6*

cheese quesadilla: *Cheese Dishes 6*

cheese slicer: *Kitchen Utensils 5*

cheese spread: *Cheese Common Varieties 6*

cheese stand: *Tableware 5*

cheese: *Bread General Varieties 6; Food 6; Muffin 6; Sandwiches 6*

cheeseburger: *Meals 6; Sandwiches 6*

cheesecake: *Cake 6; Ice Cream Flavors 6; Ice Cream Mix-ins 6; Miscellaneous Dessert 6*

cheesecloth: *Fabric 2; Kitchen Equipment 5*

cheesy garlic bread: *Bread General Varieties 6*

cheetah: *Big Cats 15*

chef knife: *Kitchen Utensils 5*

chef: *Castle Inhabitants and Personnel 1; Food Service 1; Salads 6*

chef's hat: *Headgear 2*

Cheju: *Horse Breeds 15*

Chemehuevi: *Native American Peoples 1*

chemical bonds: *Chemistry General Vocabulary 11*

chemical change: *Chemistry General Vocabulary 11*

chemical equation: *Chemistry General Vocabulary 11*

chemical equilibrium: *Chemistry General Vocabulary 11*

chemical hygiene officer: *Chemistry General Vocabulary 11*

chemical hygiene plan: *Chemistry General Vocabulary 11*

chemical kinetics: *Chemistry General Vocabulary 11*

chemical periodicity: *Chemistry General Vocabulary 11*

chemical spoon: *Laboratory Equipment 5*

chemical toilet: *Bathrooms 3*

chemical war: *General Combat Vocabulary 7*

chemical: *Energy Sources/Types 22*

chemically altered animal: *Monsters and Creatures 22*

chemicals: *Cleaning Supplies/Gadgets 5*

chemise: *Ladies' Wear 2; Western Clothing/Dress 21*

chemist: *Scientist 1*

chemistry set: *Toys 5*

chemostat: *Laboratory Equipment 5*

chempedak: *Unusual Edible Fruits 6*

chenet : *Unusual Edible Fruits 6*

chenille bedspread: *Bed Linens 5*

cherimoya: *Unusual Edible Fruits 6*

cherioni: *Deciduous Trees 10*

cherish: *General Emotions 20*

cherished: *Terms of Endearment 1*

cherni vit green: *Cheese International Varieties 6*

chernozem: *Soil General Vocabulary 10*

Cherokee: *Masks 2; Native American Peoples 1*

cherrion: *Deciduous Trees 10*

cherry amaretto: *Ice Cream Flavors 6*

cherry barb: *Aquarium Freshwater Fish 15*

cherry opal: *Minerals 10*

cherry soda: *Soft Drinks 6*

cherry sour: *Candy General 6*

cherry tomato: *Vegetables 6*

cherry: *Aphrodisiacs 19; Fruit Juice 6; Ice Cream Flavors 6; Jam/Jelly/Preserves 6; Muffin 6; Pit Fruits 6; Shrubs 10;*

cherrybark oak: *Deciduous Trees 10*

chert: *Minerals 10; Sedimentary Rocks 10*

cherub: *Angels Common Terms 14*

cherubim: *Angels Common Terms 14*

cherufe: *Demon 16*

chervil: *Spices 6*

Chesapeake Bay Retriever: *Dog Breeds 15*

chess pieces: *Objects in Magic and Religion 19*

chess: *Games 5; Pie 6*

chessboard of Gwenddoleu ap Ceidio: *Thirteen Treasures of the Island of Britain 18*

chessylite: *Minerals 10*

chest freezer: *Major Appliances 4*

chest of drawers: *Storage 4*

chest on chest: *Storage 4*

chest on frame: *Storage 4*

chest pain: *Injuries/Medical Emergencies 12*

chest: *Body Parts 12; Containers and Vessels 5*

Chester white: *Pigs 15*

chesterfield: *Seating 4*

chestnut oak: *Deciduous Trees 10*

chestnut: *Brown 20; Hair Color 1*

chestnut-winged owlet: *Owls 15*

cheval mirror: *Miscellaneous Furniture 4*

chevre metsovou: *Cheese International Varieties 6*

chevron: *Facial Hair Mustache 1*

chevronelly: *Partition Diminutives 19*

chevrotain: *Other Wild Mammals 15*

chewing gum: *Candy General 6*

Cheyenne: *Native American Peoples 1*

chhena: *Cheese International Varieties 6*

chhurpi: *Cheese International Varieties 6*

chi roh: *Symbols in Magic and Religion 19*

Chianina: *Other Cows 15*

chianti: *Wine Red 6*

Chiapas giant musk: *Freshwater Turtles 15*

chic: *Beautiful 20; Personality Other 1*

Chicago bridge: *Card Games 5*

Chicago fire of 1871: *Legendary Events 18*

Chicago School: *Architectural Styles 3*

Chicago: *Poker Card Games 5*

Chichen Itza: *Real Places Steeped in Legend or Mystery 18; Unique Property 3*

chick: *Easter 19; Female 1*

chickadee: *Backyard Birds 15*

Chickasaw: *Native American Peoples 1*

chicken coop: *Farm/Outbuilding 3*

chicken foot: *Card Games 5*

chicken house: *Farm/Outbuilding 3*

chicken noodle: *Soup 6*

chicken of the woods: *Fungus Common Names 10*

chicken plates (silicon carbide): *Body Armor 7*

chicken pot pie: *Poultry Meals 6*

chicken pox: *Diseases 12*

chicken rice: *Soup 6*

chicken salad: *Sandwiches 6*

chicken: *Allergies 12; Farm/Outbuilding 3; Freshwater Turtles 15; General Snake Families 15; Poultry Types 6; Salads 6; Sandwiches 6; Soup 6*

chickens: *Animals 15*

chickpea: *Legumes 6*

chickweed: *Vegetables 6*

Chicora: *Native American Peoples 1*

chicory: *Objects/Activities Connected to Lore 19; Vegetables 6; Wildflowers 10; Wizard's Goods 5*

Chief Crazy Horse: *Western Paraphernalia/People 21*

chief financial officer: *Finance 1*

chief justice: *Legal Occupations 1*

chief master sergeant of the Air Force: *U.S. Air Force Enlisted 8*

chief master sergeant: *U.S. Air Force Enlisted 8*

chief petty officer: *U.S. Navy Enlisted 8*

chief priest: *Cleric 1*

chief warrant officer 2: *U.S. Army Warrant Officer 8; U.S. Marines Warrant Officer 8; U.S. Navy Warrant Officer 8*

chief warrant officer 3: *U.S. Army Warrant Officer 8; U.S. Marines Warrant Officer 8; U.S. Navy Warrant Officer 8*

chief warrant officer 4: *U.S. Army Warrant Officer 8; U.S. Marines Warrant Officer 8; U.S. Navy Warrant Officer 8*

chief warrant officer 5: *U.S. Army Warrant Officer 8; U.S. Marines Warrant Officer 8; U.S. Navy Warrant Officer 8*

chiefdom: *Political Divisions 10*

Chieftain MK1: *Tanks British 8*

chiffon skirt: *Dance Clothing 13*

chiffon: *Cake 6; Fabric 2*

chifforobe: *Storage 4*

chigiriki: *Chain Weapons 7*

chignon: *Hair Style 1*

Chih Sung-Tzu (storms): *Chinese Pantheon 14*

Chih-Chiang Fyu-Ya (archers): *Chinese Pantheon 14*

Chihuahua pine: *Evergreen Trees 10*

Chihuahua: *Dog Breeds 15*

Chihuahuan ridge-nosed: *Rattlesnake 15*

chilanum: *Daggers and Knives 7*

Chilcotin: *Native American Peoples 1*

child raised by wolves: *Common Character Archetypes 21*

child with disability: *Common Character Archetypes 21*

child with supernatural power: *Common Character Archetypes 21*

child with undiscovered magic talent: *Common Character Archetypes 21*

child with undiscovered skill: *Common Character Archetypes 21*

child witnesses crimes and is not believed: *Horror Plot Devices 23*

child: *Character Building 1; Relational 1*

child's first events: *Objects/Activities Connected to Lore 19*

childbirth: *Objects/Activities Connected to Lore 19*

Childermas: *Objects/Activities Connected to Lore 19*

childlike: *Small/Thin 1; Vocal/Speech Quality 1*

children's: *Performance Genres 13; Python 15; Games 5*

children's bane: *Poisonous Plants 10*

Chilean Corralero: *Horse Breeds 15*

chilean firebush: *Shrubs 10*

chili powder: *Spices 6*

chili: *Meals 6*

chilipepper: *Wild Saltwater Fish 15*

chilling: *Unattractive 20*

chilly: *Cold 10*

Chilota: *Architectural Styles 3*

chilote cap: *Headgear 2*

Chimakum: *Native American Peoples 1*

chimay: *Cheese International Varieties 6*

chime: *Percussion Musical Instruments 5*

chimera: *Beast 16; Magic Vocabulary 17*

chimney sweep: *Harbingers/Charms for Good Luck 19*

chimney: *Building Elements and Features 3; Cave Anatomy 10; Christmas 19*

chin curtain: *Facial Hair Beard 1*

chin fuzz: *Facial Hair Beard 1*

chin strip: *Facial Hair Beard 1*

chin: *Body Parts 12; Character Building 1*

china cabinet: *Storage 4*

chinaberry: *Deciduous Trees 10; Weeds 10*

Chinampo: *Other Cows 15*

chinchilla: *Fur 2; Other Wild Mammals 15*

Chincoteague Pony: *Horse Breeds 15*

Chinese alligator: *Crocodilians 15*

Chinese Black-and-White: *Other Cows 15*

Chinese cabbage: *Vegetables 6*

Chinese checkers: *Games 5*

Chinese Crested Dog: *Dog Breeds 15*

Chinese foxglove: *Garden Perennials 10*

Chinese giant: *Salamanders 15*

Chinese golden box: *Freshwater Turtles 15*

Chinese golden thread: *Freshwater Turtles 15*

Chinese ground orchid: *Garden Bulbs 10*

Chinese gunpowder: *Tea 6*

Chinese Horoscope: *Divination and Fortune Telling 19*

Chinese lantern: *Garden Perennials 10*

Chinese pantheon: *Philosophy and Religion 14*

Chinese pond: *Freshwater Turtles 15*

Chinese privet: *Weeds 10*

Chinese Shar-Pei: *Dog Breeds 15*

Chinese stripe-necked: *Freshwater Turtles 15*

Chinese tallow tree: *Weeds 10*

Chinese tearthumb: *Weeds 10*

Chinese ten: *Card Games 5*

Chinese white: *Dolphins 15*

Chinese yam: *Garden Perennials 10*

Chinese: *Art Movements 13; Cobra 15; Imported Carpets 4; Poker Card Games 5; Styles of Dress 2*

chinkapin oak: *Deciduous Trees 10*

chinkapin: *Deciduous Trees 10*

chinless: *Chin 1*

chinoise: *Kitchen Equipment 5*

chinook salmon: *Wild Saltwater Fish 15*

Chinook wind: *Wind 10*

Chinook: *Dog Breeds 15*

Chinookan: *Native American Peoples 1*

chinquapin oak: *Deciduous Trees 10*

chinquapin: *Deciduous Trees 10*

chinstrap: *Facial Hair Beard 1*

chintz: *Fabric 2*

chip board: *Interior Building Materials 3*

chip hat: *Headgear 2*

chipmunk: *Wild Game 6; Woodland Mammals 15*

chipped: *Teeth 1*

Chippendale: *Chairs and Stools 4*

Chippewa: *Native American Peoples 1*

chips: *Candy Chocolate 6*

Chiron (moon of Saturn): *Hypothetical Solar System Bodies 11*

Chiron centaur: *Mythical Creatures and Monsters 16*

Chiron: *Beast 16*

chiropractor: *Animal/Equestrian 1; Medical Occupations 1*

chirp: *Sounds 20*

chirrup: *Sounds 20*

chisel plow: *General Farm Equipment*

chisel: *Art Tools 5; Hand Tools 5*

Chitimacha: *Native American Peoples 1*

chivalrous knight: *Knight 1*

chives: *Spices 6*

chlamydia: *Diseases 12*

chlorapatite: *Minerals 10*

chlordane: *Dangerous Chemicals 11*

chlorfenvinfos: *Dangerous Chemicals 11*

chlorine: *Dangerous Chemicals 11*

Chlorine: *Elements 11*

chlormephos: *Dangerous Chemicals 11*

chlormequat chloride: *Dangerous Chemicals 11*

chloroacetic acid: *Dangerous Chemicals 11*

chloroform: *Dangerous Chemicals 11*

chloromethyl ether: *Dangerous Chemicals 11*

chloromethyl methyl ether: *Dangerous Chemicals 11*

chloropal: *Minerals 10*

chlorophacinone: *Dangerous Chemicals 11*

chlorophane: *Minerals 10*

chlorospinel: *Minerals 10*

chloroxuron: *Dangerous Chemicals 11*

chlorthiophos: *Dangerous Chemicals 11*

chnoubis: *Symbols in Magic and Religion 19*

chocolate chip: *Cake 6; Cookie 6; Ice Cream Flavors 6; Ice Cream Mix-ins 6; Muffin 6; Pie 6*

chocolate chunk: *Cookie 6; Ice Cream Mix-ins 6*

chocolate cream filled: *Donut/doughnut 6*

chocolate cream: *Pie 6*

chocolate éclair: *Miscellaneous Dessert 6*

chocolate flake: *Ice Cream Mix-ins 6*

chocolate flower: *Garden Perennials 10*

chocolate frosted: *Donut/doughnut 6*

chocolate milk: *Dairy Beverages 6*

chocolate opal: *Standard Gems 21*

chocolate sauce: *Ice Cream Toppings 6*

chocolate sundae: *Pie 6*

chocolate vine: *Garden Perennials 10*

chocolate: *Aphrodisiacs 19; Bats 15; Brown 20; Cake 6; Cookie 6; Donut/doughnut 6; Easter 19; Food 6; Foods with Religious or Ritual Significance 19; Halloween 19; Ice Cream Flavors 6; Milk 6; Muffin 6; Valentine's Day 19*

chocolate-covered caramel: *Candy Chocolate 6*

chocolate-covered cherry: *Candy Chocolate 6*

chocolate-covered peanuts: *Candy Chocolate 6*

chocolate-covered raisins: *Candy Chocolate 6*

Choctaw hog: *Pigs 15*

Choctaw: *Native American Peoples 1*

choice: *Philosophy Basic Concepts 14*

choir director: *Musical Occupations 1*

choir: *Groups 13*

choke: *Cave Anatomy 10*

chokeberry: *Shrubs 10; Unusual Edible Fruits 6*

choker: *Jewelry 21*

choking gas: *Traps 3*

choking on object: *Injuries/Medical Emergencies 12*

choku rei: *Symbols in Magic and Religion 19*

chokutō: *Swords One-handed 7*

cholera: *Diseases 12*

Cholistani: *Other Cows 15*

chondrite: *Astronomy General Terms 11*

chondrule: *Astronomy General Terms 11*

chonmage: *Hair Style 1*

Chontal: *Native American Peoples 1*

chop saw: *Power Tools*

chop sticks left on bowl: *Harbingers of Bad Luck 19*

chop: *Water Terms 9*

choppers: *Teeth 1*

chops: *Mouth 1*

chopsticks: *Kitchen Utensils 5*

chorale prelude: *Composition Types 13*

chorale: *Composition Types 13*

chord finder: *Music Accessories*

chord: *General Music Vocabulary 13*

choreographer: *Ballet Terms 13; Performing Arts 1*

choreography: *Ballet Terms 13*

chorizo: *Sausage 6*

chortle: *Sounds 20*

chorus: *Groups 13*

Chow Chow: *Dog Breeds 15*

chowder: *Soup 6*

Christ the Redeemer Statue: *Unique Property 3*

christening: *Sacraments 14*

Christian Relics: *Philosophy and Religion 14*

Christmas rose: *Plants with Symbolic Meaning 19; Poisonous Plants 10*

Christmas: *Cake 6; Candy Chocolate 6; Catholic Holy Days of Obligation 14; Holidays 19*

Christmasberry: *Weeds 10*

Christopher Columbus: *Real People with Legendary Status 18*

chromatic scale: *General Music Vocabulary 13*

chromatic: *General Music Vocabulary 13*

chromdravite: *Minerals 10*

chrome diaspore: *Minerals 10*

chrome diopside: *Standard Gems 21*

chrome garnet: *Minerals 10*

chrome tourmaline: *Minerals 10; Standard Gems 21*

chrome vesuvianite: *Minerals 10*

chrome-diopside: *Minerals 10*

chrome-enstatite: *Minerals 10*

chrome-magnetite: *Minerals 10*

chrome-spinel: *Minerals 10*

chrome-tremolite: *Minerals 10*

chromic chloride: *Dangerous Chemicals 11*

Chromium: *Elements 11*

chromohercynite: *Minerals 10*

chromosphere: *Astronomy General Terms 11*

chronicle: *Laboratory Supplies 5*

chronicler: *Bard 1; Publishing 1*

chronologically advanced: *Elderly 1*

chronometer: *Timekeeping 5*

chronostratigraphy: *Geologic Fields of Study 10*

chrysanthemum: *Plants with Symbolic Meaning 19*

chrysoberyl: *Cat's Eye Gems 21; Standard Gems 21; Star Gems 21*

chrysocolla: *Standard Gems 21*

chrysolite: *Minerals 10*

chrysomelane: *Minerals 10*

chrysopal: *Minerals 10*

chrysoprase: *Minerals 10; Standard Gems 21*

chrysotile asbestos: *Minerals 10*

chrysotile: *Minerals 10*

chu ko nu: *Missile Weapons 7*

chubby: *Cheeks 1; Large 20; Large/Heavy 1*

chuck roast: *Beef 6*

chuck steak: *Beef 6*

chuck wagon: *Western Paraphernalia/People 21*

chuckle: *Sounds 20*

chuckwalla: *Scaled Reptiles 15*

chui: *Bludgeons 7*

chukka: *Boots 2*

Chung Kuel (truth): *Chinese Pantheon 14*

chunk: *Candy Chocolate 6*

chunky peanut butter: *Staples 6*

chunky: *Large/Heavy 1*

chupa-chupa: *Unusual Edible Fruits 6*

chupalla: *Headgear 2*

chura kampo: *Cheese International Varieties 6*

chura loenpa: *Cheese International Varieties 6*

church anatomy: *Architecture and Property 3*

church bell: *Christmas 19*

church bells: *Objects that Offer Protection 19*

Church of the Holy Sepulchre: *Relics of Jesus 14*

church service: *Christmas 19*

church suit: *Men's Wear 2*

church: *Horror Locations 23; Poker Card Games 5; Religious Building 3*

Churchill: *Tanks British 8*

churchyard: *Cemetery 3*

Churrigueresque: *Architectural Styles 3*

churro: *Donut/doughnut 6*

chutney: *Condiments 6*

ciabatta: *Bread General Varieties 6*

Cicada killer: *Wasp 15*

cicada: *Animals with Symbolic Meaning 19*

cicatrix: *Symbols in Magic and Religion 19*

cichlid: *Aquarium Freshwater Fish 15*

cider: *Donut/doughnut 6*

cigar bar: *Food/Drink Establishments 3*

cigar case: *Containers and Vessels 5*

cigar: *Spaceship Shapes 22*

cigarette case: *Containers and Vessels 5*

cigarette: *Small Watercraft 9*

cilantro: *Spices 6*

Cimarron 1860 Henry: *Lever Action and Pump Centerfire Rifles 7*

Cimarron 1874 Sharps: *Single Shot Centerfire Rifles 7*

Cimarron 1885 Low Wall: *Single Shot Rimfire Rifles 7*

Cimarron Bisley SAA: *Revolver Single Action 7*

Cimarron High Wall: *Single Shot Rimfire Rifles 7*

Cimarron Lightning: *Revolver Single Action 7*

Cimarron Spencer Repeater: *Lever Action and Pump Centerfire Rifles 7*

cimaruta: *Symbols in Magic and Religion 19*

Cincinnati: *Poker Card Games 5*

cinema: *Entertainment Property 3*

cinnabarite: *Minerals 10*

cinnabar-red chanterelle: *Fungus Common Names 10*

cinnamon anemonefish: *Aquarium Saltwater Fish 15*

cinnamon bear: *Candy General 6*

cinnamon bird: *Flying Creatures 16*

cinnamon bush: *Deciduous Trees 10*

cinnamon drops: *Candy General 6*

cinnamon fern: *Wildflowers 10*

cinnamon gum: *Candy General 6*

cinnamon oak: *Deciduous Trees 10*

cinnamon roll: *Bread General Varieties 6; Donut/doughnut 6*

cinnamon stone: *Minerals 10*

cinnamon twist: *Donut/doughnut 6*

cinnamon vine: *Garden Perennials 10*

cinnamon wood: *Deciduous Trees 10*

cinnamon: *Aphrodisiacs 19; Bears 15; Bread General Varieties 6; Coffee Bean Roasts 6; Cookie 6; Ice Cream Flavors 6; Muffin 6; Quick Bread 6; Spices 6*

cinq positions des Pieds: *Ballet Terms 13*

Cinq: *Ballet Terms 13*

cinquedea: *Daggers and Knives 7; Swords One-handed 7*

cinquefoil: *Garden Perennials 10*

Cinquiéme: *Ballet Terms 13*

Cintamani jewel: *Symbols in Magic and Religion 19*

cipres: *Deciduous Trees 10*

Circinus: *Constellations 11*

circle head: *Windows 3*

circle of life: *Symbols in Magic and Religion 19*

circle skirt: *Dance Clothing 13*

circle: *Figures Associated with Symbols 19; Jewelry 21*

circlet: *Headgear 2; Jewelry 21*

circuit: *Journey 20*

circular saw: *Power Tools*

circulatory: *Body Systems 12*

circumpolar star: *Astronomy General Terms 11*

circumpolar: *Star Types and Relatives 11*

circumstellar disk: *Astronomy General Terms 11*

circus peanuts: *Candy General 6*

circus ring: *Amusement Park/Carnival/Circus/Fair 3*

circus: *Architecture and Property 3*

cirque: *Glacial and Mountain 10*

cirriform: *Clouds 10*

cirrostratus: *Clouds 10*

cirrus: *Clouds 10*

ciruela: *Deciduous Trees 10*

ciseaux: *Dance Moves 13*

cistern: *Property Features 3*

Cisuralian Age: *Geologic Time 10*

citadel: *Fortification 3; Military Property 3*

citrine: *Minerals 10; Standard Gems 21*

citron: *Citrus 6*

citrus squeezer: *Kitchen Utensils 5*

citrus swallowtail: *Butterfly 15*

citrus: *Food 6*

City Beautiful: *Architectural Styles 3*

city hall: *Administrative Property 3*

city of Atlantis rises: *Fantasy Plot Devices 24*

city of Atlantis: *Horror Locations 23*

City of Cuzco: *Real Places Steeped in Legend or Mystery 18*

City of Petra: *Unique Property 3*

city watchman: *Fantasy Occupations 24*

city: *Chapter 10; Coffee Bean Roasts 6*

cityscape: *Art Genres 13*

civet: *Other Wild Mammals 15*

civic center: *City 10*

civic virtue: *Philosophy Basic Concepts 14*

Civil War begins: *Western Plot Devices 21*

Civil War divides family: *Western Plot Devices 21*

Civil War ends: *Western Plot Devices 21*

Civil War: *General Combat Vocabulary 7*

Civil War: *Styles of Dress 2*

civilian: *General Combat Vocabulary 7*

civilians: *Character Building 1*

clabber: *Card Games 5*

claddagh: *Symbols in Magic and Religion 19*

Claiomh Solais: *Celtic Swords 18; Four Hallows of Ireland 18*

clairvoyance: *Magic Vocabulary 17; Plot Devices 22*

clairvoyant: *Cleric 1; Fortune Teller 1; Magic Vocabulary 17*

clam: *Fish/Seafood Types 6*

clamber: *Locomotion 9*

clammed up: *Quiet 20*

clamorous: *Loud 20*

clamp: *Art Tools 5; Hair Accessories 2; Hand Tools 5; Hardware 5; Laboratory Equipment 5*

clandestine: *Magic Vocabulary 17*

clang: *Sounds 20*

clanging: *Loud 20*

clank: *Sounds 20*

Clanton brothers: *Western Paraphernalia/People 21*

clapboard: *Exterior Building Materials 3*

clapper: *Bridges 9; Percussion Musical Instruments 5*

Clarent: *Arthurian Weapons 18*

claret glass: *Drinkware 5*

clarify: *Solve 20*

clarinet: *Wind/Woodwind and Brass Musical Instruments*

clarino: *Wind/Woodwind and Brass Musical Instruments*

claro opal: *Minerals 10*

clash: *General Combat Vocabulary 7*

clasp knife: *Western Weapons 21*

clasp: *Jewelry 21*

clasping coneflower: *Wildflowers 10*

class: *Philosophy Basic Concepts 14*

classic magical objects: *Magic 17*

classic: *Styles of Dress 2*

Classical ballet: *Ballet Terms 13*

classical guitar: *String Musical Instruments*

Classical realism: *Art Movements 13*

Classical: *Architectural Styles 3*

classical: *Musical Period 13; Musical Styles 13*

classify: *Learn 20*

classroom: *Academic Property 3*

classy: *Beautiful 20*

clast: *Geological Vocabulary 10*

clatter: *Sounds 20*

clavichord: *Percussion Musical Instruments 5*

clavicle: *Bones 12; Symbols in Magic and Religion 19*

claw: *Wizard's Goods 5*

clawfoot tub: *Bathroom Features and Fixtures 3*

clay bottle: *Containers and Vessels 5*

clay golem: *Construct 16*

clay guardian: *Construct 16*

clay holy symbol: *Religious Items 5*

clay ironstone: *Minerals 10*

clay tablet: *Books/Publications 5*

clay tile: *Roofing Materials 3*

clay: *Art Materials 5; Coins and Currency 21; Soil General Vocabulary 10*

claymore: *Swords One-handed 7; Swords Two-handed 7*

claypan: *Soil General Vocabulary 10*

claystone: *Sedimentary Rocks 10*

clean shaven: *Facial Hair Beard 1*

clean: *Teeth 1; Verbs 20*

cleaner: *Music Accessories*

cleaning cloth: *Music Accessories*

cleaning gadgets: *Equipment and Tools 5*

cleaning kit: *Music Accessories*

cleaning lady: *Housekeeping 1*

cleaning supplies: *Equipment and Tools 5*

cleaning woman: *Housekeeping 1*

cleaning: *Robots 22*

cleanse: *Clean 20*

clear: *Clean 20*

clearance: *Technical Terms 13*

clearwing: *Butterfly 15*

cleat hitch: *Sailing Knots 9*

cleat: *Boat/Ship Anatomy 9*

cleats: *Athletic Shoes 2*

cleavage: *Geological Vocabulary 10*

cleavelandite: *Minerals 10*

cleaver: *Daggers and Knives 7; Kitchen Utensils 5*

clef: *Notation 13*

cleft: *Cave Anatomy 10; Chin 1; Terrain Features 10*

Clegis: *Knights of the Round Table 18*

cleiophane: *Minerals 10*

Clement Moore: *Christmas 19*

clementine: *Citrus 6*

Cleopatra: *Real People with Legendary Status 18*

Cleopatra's wheel: *Jewelry 18*

clergyman: *Cleric 1*

cleric/priest: *Common Character Archetypes 21*

cleric: *Castle Inhabitants and Personnel 1; Character Building 1; Fantasy Occupations 24; Religious Occupations 1*

clerid: *Beetle 15*

clerk: *General Occupations 1*

clerodendrum: *Shrubs 10*

cleveite: *Minerals 10*

Cleveland Bay: *Horse Breeds 15*

clever: *Good 20; Intelligent 1*

clevise: *Fishing Gear 5*

click beetle: *Fungus Common Names 10*

cliff bush: *Shrubs 10*

cliff rose: *Shrubs 10*

cliff: *Coastal and Oceanic 10; Erosion 10; Fluvial 10; Geological Natural Hazards 10; Slope 10*

climate: *Geography General Vocabulary 10; Meteorology General Vocabulary 10*

climatic zones: *Chapter 10*

climatology: *Meteorology General Vocabulary 10*

climax vegetation: *Geography General Vocabulary 10*

climb: *Commands 20; Locomotion 9*

climbing gloves: *Spy Gear 5*

climbing maidenhair: *Weeds 10*

climbing rope and grappling hook: *Spy Gear 5*

climbing: *Athletic Shoes 2; Exploration 9*

cling peach: *Pit Fruits 6*

clinic: *Health Care 3*

clinocervantite: *Minerals 10*

clinochrysotile: *Minerals 10*

clinoenstatite: *Minerals 10*

clinoferrosillite: *Minerals 10*

clinohumite: *Standard Gems 21*

clinomimetite: *Minerals 10*

clinothulite: *Minerals 10*

clinozoisite: *Minerals 10*

clint: *Cave Anatomy 10*

clip: *Hair Accessories 2; Jewelry 21; Sewing Techniques 2*

clipboard: *Office/School/Writing Supplies 5*

clipper ship: *Western Paraphernalia/People 21*

clipper: *Large Watercraft 9*

clitoris: *Body Parts 12*

cloak: *Outerwear 2; Typical Magical Objects 17*

cloaked scout: *Spaceship Types 22*

cloaking device: *Devices 22; Spy Gear 5*

clobber: *Attack 7*

cloche hat: *Headgear 2*

clock: *Classic Items 23; New Year 19; Solitaire Card Games 5*

clocks: *Objects/Activities Connected to Lore 19*

clockwork butler: *Supporting Cast 24*

clockwork guard: *Supporting Cast 24*

clockwork mechanical: *Robots 22*

clockwork/mechanical: *Energy Sources/Types 23; Energy Sources/Types 24*

clog (England): *Ethnic/Folk Dances 13*

clogging shoes: *Dance Shoes 13*

clogs: *Footwear/Shoes 2*

cloister: *Church Anatomy 3; Rooms 3*

cloning: *Plot Devices 22*

cloque: *Fabric 2*

close up: *Close/Hold 20*

close: *Air Creatures 19; Verbs 20*

closed buttonhole: *Embroidery Stitches 2*

close-hauled: *Boat/Ship Terminology 9*

close-set: *Eye Type 1*

closet: *Bathroom Features and Fixtures 3; Building Elements and Features 3*

closing walls: *Traps 3*

clot: *Blood-Related Ailments 12*

cloth bag: *Containers and Vessels 5*

cloth cap: *Headgear 2*

cloth: *Art Materials 5; Art Media 13*

clothes chute: *Building Elements and Features 3*

clothing pieces: *Clothing 2*

clothing: *Christmas 19; Objects/Activities Connected to Lore 19*

cloud agate: *Minerals 10*

cloud bank: *Meteorology General Vocabulary 10*

cloud chamber: *Chemistry General Vocabulary 11*

cloud city: *Fantasy Locations 24*

cloud ear mushroom: *Fungus Common Names 10*

cloud giant: *Humanlike Groups 1*

cloud transport: *Travel Modes 24*

cloud: *Giant Humanoids 16; Meteorology General Vocabulary 10*

cloudberry: *Unusual Edible Fruits 6*

cloudburst: *Meteorology General Vocabulary 10; Precipitation 10*

clouded border: *Moth 15*

clouded leopard: *Big Cats 15*

cloud-filling: *Embroidery Stitches 2*

clouds: *Chapter 10*

cloudscape: *Art Genres 13*

cloudy: *Meteorology General Vocabulary 10*

cloudywing: *Butterfly 15*

clout: *Attack 7*

clove hitch: *Sailing Knots 9*

clove pink: *Garden Perennials 10*

clove: *Aphrodisiacs 19*

clover: *Garden Perennials 10; Objects that Offer Protection 19; Plants with Symbolic Meaning 19; St. Patrick's Day 19*

cloves: *Spices 6*

clown barb: *Aquarium Freshwater Fish 15*

clown car: *Motorized 9*

clown loach: *Aquarium Freshwater Fish 15*

clown red-eared slider: *Freshwater Turtles 15*

clown: *Bard 1*

clownfish: *Aquarium Saltwater Fish 15*

club car: *Railroad 9*

club soda: *Soft Drinks 6*

club: *Bludgeons 7; Chairs and Stools 4; Entertainment Property 3; Sandwiches 6; Social Clubs 1*

clubbing boomerang: *Bludgeons 7*

clubtail lizard: *Scaled Reptiles 15*

clueless travelers: *Travel Hazards 9*

Clumber Spaniel: *Dog Breeds 15*

clumsy: *Mobility 1*

clunk: *Sounds 20*

Cluny Abbey: *Seven Wonders of the Middle Ages 18*

cluster fig: *Unusual Edible Fruits 6*

cluster: *Bomb 8; Groupings 14*

clustered blue chanterelle: *Fungus Common Names 10*

clutch: *Accessories 2; Close/Hold 20*

Clydesdale: *Horse Breeds 15*

CN Tower: *Seven Wonders of the Modern World 18; Unique Property 3*

coach bus: *Mass Transit 9*

coach gun: *Black Powder Weapons 7; Western Weapons 21*

coach pulled by flying creatures: *Vehicles 24*

coach: *Animal-Powered Transportation 9; Sports 1; Teach 20*

coachwhip: *General Snake Families 15*

coagulation: *Blood 12*

coal bin: *Building Systems 3*

coal boat: *Large Watercraft 9*

coal chute: *Building Elements and Features 3; Building Systems 3*

coal yard: *Public Services 3*

coal: *Christmas 19; Harbingers/Charms for Good Luck 19; Sedimentary Rocks 10; Wizard's Goods 5*

coal-black: *Hair Color 1*

coarse: *Hair Types 1; Personality Other 1; Unattractive 20*

coast defense mortar: *Mortar 8*

coast Douglas fir: *Evergreen Trees 10*

Coast Guard: *Boat/Ship Terminology 9; Law Enforcement 1*

coast pignut hickory: *Evergreen Trees 10*

coast pine: *Evergreen Trees 10*

coast redwood: *Deciduous Trees 10*

coast spruce: *Evergreen Trees 10*

coast: *Coastal and Oceanic 10; Locomotion 9; Water Terms 9*

coastal defense ship: *Military Watercraft 8*

coastal landforms: *Chapter 10*

coastal laurel oak: *Deciduous Trees 10*

coastal taipan: *World's Ten Most Venomous Snakes 15*

coaster wagon: *Human-Powered Transportation 9*

coaster: *Tableware 5*

coat of arms: *Jewelry 21*

coat of Padarn Beisrudd: *Thirteen Treasures of the Island of Britain 18*

coat of plates: *Armor Types 7*

coat: *Outerwear 2; Unisex Clothing 2*

coating: *Fabric 2*

cob material: *Soil General Vocabulary 10*

cobalt bloom: *Minerals 10*

cobalt calcite: *Minerals 10*

cobalt carbonyl: *Dangerous Chemicals 11*

cobalt: *Blue 20; Dangerous Chemicals 11*

Cobalt: *Elements 11*

cobaltian adamite: *Minerals 10*

cobaltian calcite: *Minerals 10*

cobaltian dolomite: *Minerals 10*

cobaltian loellingite: *Minerals 10*

cobaltoadamite: *Minerals 10*

cobaltocalcite: *Minerals 10*

cobb: *Salads 6*

cobble: *Cave Anatomy 10*

cobbler: *Artists and Craftspeople 1; Miscellaneous Dessert 6*

cobbler's bench: *Seating 4*

cobblestone road: *Roads 9*

cobego: *Gliding Mammals 15*

cobia: *Wild Saltwater Fish 15*

coblynau: *General Fae 16*

cobra de capello: *Cobra 15*

cobra: *Animals 15*

cobrafruit: *Unusual Edible Fruits 6*

cobweb: *Halloween 19; Items with Healing Properties 19*

coccolith: *Geological Vocabulary 10*

coccolithophore: *Geological Vocabulary 10*

coccyx: *Bones 12*

Cochiti: *Native American Peoples 1*

cock/rooster: *Chinese Horoscope 19*

Cockaigne: *Fictional/Mythological Locations 18*

cockatiel: *Domesticated Pet Birds 15*

cockatoo: *Domesticated Pet Birds 15*

cockatrice: *Beast 16*

Cocker Spaniel: *Dog Breeds 15*

cockle hat: *Headgear 2*

cocklebur: *Poisonous Plants 10*

cockpit: *Boat/Ship Anatomy 9*

cockroaches: *Travel Hazards 9*

cockscomb: *Garden Annuals 10*

cocktail dress: *Ladies' Wear 2*

cocktail glass: *Drinkware 5*

cocktail hat: *Headgear 2*

cocktail mixers: *Food 6*

cocktail rye: *Bread General Varieties 6*

cocktail sauce: *Condiments 6*

cocktail: *Tables 4*

cocktails: *Food 6*

cocky apple: *Unusual Edible Fruits 6*

coconut grater: *Kitchen Utensils 5*

coconut haystacks: *Candy General 6*

coconut: *Cake 6; Cookie 6; Donut/doughnut 6; Ice Cream Flavors 6; Oils 6; Pie 6; Tropical/Exotic Fruits 6*

cod: *Fish/Seafood Types 6*

Coda: *Ballet Terms 13*

coda: *Notation 13*

code book: *Spy Gear 5*

code: *Spy Gear 5*

codex: *Books/Publications 5*

codger: *Elderly 1*

codling: *Moth 15*

coefficient of expansion: *Chemistry General Vocabulary 11*

Coeur d'Alene: *Native American Peoples 1*

coffee bar: *Food/Drink Establishments 3*

coffee bean: *Cocktail Garnishes 6*

coffee cake: *Cake 6*

coffee creamer: *Other Dairy 6*

coffee cup: *Drinkware 5*

coffee filters: *Kitchen Equipment 5*

coffee grinder: *Appliances 5*

coffee house: *Food/Drink Establishments 3*

coffee maker: *Appliances 5*

coffee mill: *Kitchen Equipment 5*

coffee pot: *Appliances 5; Tableware 5*

coffee shop: *Food/Drink Establishments 3*

coffee: *Brown 20; Candy General 6; Food 6; Ice Cream Flavors 6; Tables 4*

coffer: *Containers and Vessels 5*

coffin: *Cemetery 3; Containers and Vessels 5; Halloween 19*

cog: *Large Watercraft 9*

cognac: *Hard Liquor 6*

cogon grass: *Weeds 10*

cohesion: *Soil General Vocabulary 10*

cohesive forces: *Chemistry General Vocabulary 11*

coho salmon: *Fish/Seafood Types 6; Wild Freshwater Fish 15; Wild Saltwater Fish 15*

cohosh: *Garden Perennials 10*

Coiba Island howler: *New World Monkeys 15*

coif: *Headgear 2*

coiled erect: *Reptiles 19*

coin in new pocket: *Harbingers/Charms for Good Luck 19*

coin toss: *Amusement Park/Carnival/Circus/Fair 3*

coin: *Candy Chocolate 6; Create 20*

Cojack: *Cheese Common Varieties 6*

coke: *Chemistry General Vocabulary 11, Wizard's Goods 5*

col: *Glacial and Mountain 10*

cola: *Soft Drinks 6*

Colada (El Cid's sword): *Weapons of Legend 18*

colander: *Kitchen Equipment 5*

Colby: *Cheese Common Varieties 6*

Colby-Jack: *Cheese Common Varieties 6*

colchicine: *Dangerous Chemicals 11*

colchicum: *Garden Bulbs 10*

cold air return: *Building Systems 3*

cold finger: *Laboratory Equipment 5*

cold front: *Meteorology General Vocabulary 10*

cold pack: *Cheese Common Varieties 6*

cold room: *Rooms 3*

cold snap: *Meteorology General Vocabulary 10*

cold spot: *Paranormal Occurrences 21*

cold wave: *Meteorology General Vocabulary 10*

cold: *Chapter 10; Horror Vocabulary 23; Meteorology General Vocabulary 10; Vocal/Speech Quality 1*

cold-blooded: *Horror Vocabulary 23*

cole slaw: *Salad Dressing 6*

coleus: *Garden Annuals 10*

colichemarde: *Swords One-handed 7*

Coliseum of Rome: *Unique Property 3*

collaborator: *Hero or Villain, Depending Upon Circumstance 20*

collage: *Art Techniques 13*

collar pin: *Jewelry 21*

collar: *Garment Pieces 2; Jewelry 21*

collard greens: *Vegetables 6*

collared lizard: *Scaled Reptiles 15*

collateral damage: *General Combat Vocabulary 7*

collect: *Buy 20*

collecting cage: *Traps 3*

collection basket: *Religious Items 5*

collection plate: *Religious Items 5*

college: *Academic Property 3*

colletia: *Shrubs 10*

Collett's: *General Snake Families 15*

Collie rough: *Dog Breeds 15*

Collie smooth: *Dog Breeds 15*

colliery: *Outdoor Property 3*

colligative properties: *Chemistry General Vocabulary 11*

collision theory: *Chemistry General Vocabulary 11*

collision: *Common Dangers 22*

colloid: *Chemistry General Vocabulary 11*

collophane: *Minerals 10*

colobus: *Old World Monkeys 15*

cologne: *Personal Care 5; Smells 20*

Colombian emerald: *Minerals 10*

Colombian slider: *Freshwater Turtles 15*

colonel: *U.S. Air Force Officer 8; U.S. Army Officer 8; U.S. Marines Officer 8*

Colonial Revival: *Architectural Styles 3*

Colonial: *Architectural Styles 3; Residential Property 3; Styles of Dress 2*

colonization: *Plot Devices 22*

colony counter: *Laboratory Equipment 5*

colony: *Ants 15; City 10; Political Divisions 10; Spaceship Types 22*

color blind: *Eye Type 1*

color television: *Electronics 4*

color: *Visual Elements 13*

Colorado blue spruce: *Deciduous Trees 10*

Colorado low: *Snow Storms 10*

Colorado Ranger Horse: *Horse Breeds 15*

Colorado rubber plant: *Garden Perennials 10*

Colorado ruby: *Minerals 10*

Colorado spruce: *Deciduous Trees 10*

Colorado tick fever: *Diseases 12*

coloratura: *General Music Vocabulary 13*

color-change diaspore: *Standard Gems 21*

color-change garnet: *Standard Gems 21*

color-change sapphire: *Standard Gems 21*

colored paper: *Office/School/Writing Supplies 5*

colored pencils: *Office/School/Writing Supplies 5*

colored: *Hair Treated 1*

coloring book: *Books/Publications 5*

Colorpoint shorthair: *Domestic Cats 15*

colors: *Classic Heraldry 19*

colossal: *Heavy 20; Large 20; Large/Heavy 1*

Colosseum: *Seven Wonders of the Middle Ages 18*

colossus class aircraft carrier: *Military Watercraft 8*

Colossus of Rhodes: *Seven Wonders of the Ancient World 18; Unique Property Destroyed 3*

colossus: *Monster Categories/Terms 16*

Colt 45: *Western Weapons 21*

Colt CAR-15 carbine: *SWAT Weapons 7*

Colt lightning carbine: *Western Weapons 21*

Colt New Agent Series: *Pistol Semiautomatic 7*

Colt peacemaker: *Western Weapons 21*

Colt SAA Frontier Six Shooter: *Revolver Single Action 7*

Colt Single Action Army: *Revolver Single Action 7*

colugo: *Gliding Mammals 15; Other Wild Mammals 15*

Columbia: *Constellations 11*

Columbian spruce: *Deciduous Trees 10*

Columbian: *Caecilians 15*

columbine: *Garden Perennials 10; Poisonous Plants 10; Wildflowers 10*

Column of the Flagellation: *Relics of Jesus 14*

column: *Castle Anatomy 3; Cave Anatomy 10; General Combat Vocabulary 7; Symbols of Freemasonry 19*

columnist: *Publishing 1*

Coma Berenices: *Constellations 11*

Comanche: *Native American Peoples 1*

Comas Sola: *Comets 11*

comb binding machine: *Office/School Machines 5*

comb tooth mushroom: *Fungus Common Names 10*

comb: *Clean 20; Hair Accessories 2; Jewelry 21; Personal Care 5; Transportation Animals 9*

combat boots: *Military Equipment 8*

combat sidestroke: *Swimming Strokes 9*

combat vocabulary: *Combat, Armor, and Weapons 7*

combat: *Combat, Armor, and Weapons 7; General Combat Vocabulary 7*

combatant: *Fighter 1*

combattant: *Multiple Figures 19*

comb-back: *Chairs and Stools 4*

combed: *Special Body Features 19*

comb finned: *Squid 15*

combination reaction: *Chemistry General Vocabulary 11*

combination: *Locks 5*

combine: *Farm Transportation 9*

combined arms maneuver: *General Combat Vocabulary 7*

combover: *Hair Style 1*

combustible: *Chemistry General Vocabulary 11*

combustion: *Energy Sources/Types 22*

come around: *Solve 20*

come hither: *Styles of Dress 2*

come undone: *Open/Release 20*

come: *Commands 20*

comedian: *Bard 1*

comedy club: *Entertainment Property 3*

comedy: *Performance Genres 13*

comendite: *Igneous Rocks 10*

comet: *Astronomy General Terms 11; Moth 15*

comfit: *Donut/doughnut 6*

comfort: *Happy 20*

comfortable: *Easy 20; Happy 20*

comforter: *Bed Linens 5*

comfrey: *Garden Perennials 10*

comic: *Bard 1*

comique: *Musical Styles 13*

comma: *Butterfly 15*

command chief master sergeant: *U.S. Air Force Enlisted 8*

command sergeant major: *U.S. Army Enlisted 8*

command: *Magic Vocabulary 17*

command: *Verbs 20*

commander: *Maritime Occupations 1; U.S. Navy Officer 8*

commando aircraft carrier: *Military Watercraft 8*

commando: *Styles of Dress 2*

commentator: *Media 1*

Commerce without morality: *Philosophy 14*

commercial mushroom: *Fungus Common Names 10*

commercial: *Art Genres 13*

commiserate: *Solve 20*

commissary: *Military Property 3*

commissioner: *Law Enforcement 1*

commit: *Love 20*

committed: *Personality Other 1*

commode: *Tables 4*

commodore: *Armed Forces Other Titles 8; Navy Other Titles 8*

common barn: *Owls 15*

common broom: *Weeds 10*

common cold: *Diseases 12*

common envelope: *Star Systems 11*

common field speedwell: *Weeds 10*

common garnet: *Minerals 10*

common good: *Philosophy Basic Concepts 14*

common grass: *Owls 15*

common hackberry: *Deciduous Trees 10*

common honey locust: *Deciduous Trees 10*

common house: *Nonvenomous Arachnids 15*

common Indian: *Toads 15*

common ion effect: *Chemistry General Vocabulary 11*

common ivy: *Poisonous Plants 10; Weeds 10*

common lambsquarters: *Weeds 10*

common larch: *Deciduous Trees 10*

common map: *Freshwater Turtles 15*

common mica: *Minerals 10*

common musk: *Freshwater Turtles 15*

common opal: *Minerals 10*

common persimmon: *Deciduous Trees 10*

common red oak: *Deciduous Trees 10*

common reed: *Weeds 10*

common salt: *Minerals 10*

common sassafras: *Deciduous Trees 10*

common sense: *Philosophy Basic Concepts 14*

common store mushroom: *Fungus Common Names 10*

common toad-headed: *Freshwater Turtles 15*

common water hyacinth: *Weeds 10*

common whitetail: *Dragonfly 15*

common: *Adder 15; Caecilians 15; Cobra 15; Keelback 15; Unintelligent 1*

commoner: *Social Distinction 1*

commonly known dinosaurs: *Animals 15*

commonwealth: *Political Divisions 10*

commune: *City 10; General Property 3*

communer: *Nature Occupations 1*

communication device: *Devices 22*

communications system: *Military Equipment 8*

communion: *Religious Bread 6*

communism: *Philosophy Basic Concepts 14*

community center: *General Buildings 3*

ALPHABETICAL INDEX

community council: *Political Divisions 10*

community hall: *Church Anatomy 3; General Buildings 3*

community: *City 10*

commuter train: *Mass Transit 9*

compact fluorescent: *Illumination Bulb and Tube Types 5*

compact: *Accessories 2; Makeup 5; Motorized 9*

compact: *Star Types and Relatives 11*

compaction: *Geological Vocabulary 10*

companion animal: *Dogs/Canine 15*

companionway: *Boat/Ship Anatomy 9*

compartment: *Building Elements and Features 3; Elements 19*

compass course: *Boat/Ship Terminology 9*

compass plant: *Garden Perennials 10*

compass points: *Collective Symbols 19*

compass: *Architectural/Engineering Tools 5; Boat/Ship Anatomy 9; General Survival Gear 5; Office/School/Writing Supplies 5; Symbols in Magic and Religion 19; Symbols of Freemasonry 19*

compassionate: *Positive 1*

compensate: *Buy 20*

competent: *Good 20*

competitor: *Common Character Archetypes 21; Fighter 1; Hero or Villain, Depending Upon Circumstance 20*

compile: *Fix 20*

complain: *Speak 20*

complex ions: *Chemistry General Vocabulary 11*

complex volcano: *Volcanic 10*

complex: *Difficult 20; General Buildings 3*

complicated: *Difficult 20*

complimentary: *Happy 20*

comport: *Tableware 5*

composed: *Happy 20*

composer: *Bard 1*

composite bow: *Missile Weapons 7*

composition book: *Office/School/Writing Supplies 5*

composition stoichiometry: *Chemistry General Vocabulary 11*

composition types: *The Arts 13*

compote: *Tableware 5*

compound fracture: *Injuries/Medical Emergencies 12*

compound: *Chemistry General Vocabulary 11; Fencing Vocabulary 7; Fortification 3; General Buildings 3*

comprehensive: *Large 20*

compressed earth block: *Soil General Vocabulary 10*

compressed gas: *Chemistry General Vocabulary 11*

compression: *Bridges 9; Geological Vocabulary 10*

compromise: *Solve 20*

comptometer: *Office/School Machines 5*

compute: *Solve 20*

computer equipment: *Equipment and Tools 5*

computer generated: *Vocal/Speech Quality 1*

computer genius: *Horror Occupations 23*

computer hacker: *Spy Gear 5*

computer network: *Building Systems 3*

computer tricks users into killing: *Horror Plot Devices 23*

computer turns evil and murderous: *Horror Plot Devices 23*

computer: *Classic Items 23; Games 5; Spy Gear 5*

Comstock Lode: *Famous Western Locations 21*

con artist: *Common Character Archetypes 21*

con brio: *Tempo/Mood 13*

con man: *Travel Hazards 9*

con sordino: *Tempo/Mood 13*

con spirito: *Tempo/Mood 13*

Conandoyle: *Asteroids with Unusual Names 11*

concealed: *Moves 7*

concealer: *Makeup 5*

conceited: *Negative 1*

conceive: *Create 20; Solve 20*

concentration camp: *Prison 3*

concentration: *Card Games 5; Chemistry General Vocabulary 11; Fencing Vocabulary 7*

concept: *Philosophy Basic Concepts 14*

conceptual: *Art Genres 13*

concern: *General Emotions 20*

concerned: *Positive 1*

concert hall: *Academic Property 3; Entertainment Property 3*

concertino: *Groups 13*

concertmaster: *Musical Occupations 1*

concerto: *Composition Types 13*

conch shell: *Eight Ashtamangala 19*

Conch: *Architectural Styles 3*

concierge: *Hospitality 1*

conclude: *Solve 20*

conclusion: *Ending 20*

concoct: *Witchcraft Vocabulary 17*

concourse: *General Buildings 3; Infrastructure Buildings 9*

concrete saw: *Power Tools*

concretion: *Geological Vocabulary 10*

concubine: *Castle Inhabitants and Personnel 1*

concussion club: *Percussion Musical Instruments 5*

concussion: *Injuries/Medical Emergencies 12; Weapons 22*

condensation: *Chemistry General Vocabulary 11; Meteorology General Vocabulary 10*

condensed phases: *Chemistry General Vocabulary 11*

condensed states: *Chemistry General Vocabulary 11*

condenser: *Laboratory Equipment 5*

condescending: *Negative 1*

condiments: *Food 6*

conditioner: *General Farm Equipment; Personal Care 5*

condo: *Residential Slang 3*

condominium: *Residential Property 3*

Condor 4×4 armored personnel carrier: *Germany Military Vehicles 8*

condor agate: *Minerals 10*

condor: *Birds of Prey 15*

conduction band: *Chemistry General Vocabulary 11*

conductor: *Musical Occupations 1*

conduit: *Roads 9*

coneflower: *Garden Perennials 10*

cone-shaped: *Hand Shapes 19*

confection: *Candy General 6*

confectioner's sugar: *Staples 6*

confederate raiders attack town: *Western Plot Devices 21*

Confederate States: *Western Paraphernalia/People 21*

conference call speaker: *Office/School Machines 5*

confession: *Sacraments 14*

confetti: *Cake 6*

confidence man: *Thief 1*

confident: *Happy 20; Personality Other 1*

confine: *Close/Hold 20*

confining: *Weapons 22*

confirmation: *Sacraments 14*

confiscate: *Close/Hold 20*

conflict: *General Combat Vocabulary 7*

confluence: *Fluvial 10*

conformations: *Chemistry General Vocabulary 11*

confound: *Magic Vocabulary 17*

confrontation: *General Combat Vocabulary 7*

Confucian Texts: *Major Religious Books 14*

confuse: *Magic Vocabulary 17*

confusing cave passage: *Geological Natural Hazards 10*

confusion: *Paranormal Abilities 21*

conga drum: *Percussion Musical Instruments 5*

congenial: *Happy 20*

conglomerate: *Geological Vocabulary 10; Sedimentary Rocks 10*

Congo: *Caecilians 15; General Snake Families 15; Salamanders 15*

congregation: *Followers 14*

congress: *Government 1*

congressman: *Government 1*

congresswoman: *Government 1*

congruous: *Happy 20*

conical measure: *Laboratory Equipment 5*

conjugate acid-base pair: *Chemistry General Vocabulary 11*

conjugated double bonds: *Chemistry General Vocabulary 11*

conjunction: *Astronomy General Terms 11*

conjure up: *Create 20*

conjure: *Magic Vocabulary 17*

conjurer: *Wizard 1*

conkerberry: *Unusual Edible Fruits 6*

conman: *Illicit Occupations 1*

conn: *Special Purpose Clothing 2*

connect: *Fix 20*

Connemara Pony: *Horse Breeds 15*

conqueror: *Hero or Villain, Depending Upon Circumstance 20*

conquest (white horse): *Four Horsemen of the Apocalypse 19*

conquest: *General Combat Vocabulary 7*

conquian: *Card Games 5*

conscience: *Philosophy Basic Concepts 14*

consciousness: *Philosophy Basic Concepts 14*

consent: *Agree 20; Philosophy Basic Concepts 14*

conservation: *Art Techniques 13*

conservator: *Artists and Craftspeople 1*

conservatory: *Academic Property 3; Rooms 3*

consider: *Solve 20*

considerable: *Heavy 20; Large 20*

considerate: *Positive 1*

console television: *Electronics 4*

console: *Tableware 5*

consolidation: *Soil General Vocabulary 10*

consort: *Female 1; Groups 13*

conspicuous: *Beautiful 20*

conspiracy forces residents out of town: *Horror Plot Devices 23*

constable: *Law Enforcement 1*

constellation: *Astronomy General Terms 11*

constituency: *Political Divisions 10*

constrictor: *Boa 15; Sailing Knots 9*

construct: *Create 20; Fix 20; Monsters 16; Philosophy Basic Concepts 14*

construction paper: *Office/School/Writing Supplies 5*

construction worker: *Styles of Dress 2*

construction workers: *Guilds 1*

construction: *Character Building 1*

constructionbot: *Robots 22*

Constructivism: *Art Movements 13*

Constructivist: *Architectural Styles 3*

consulate: *Administrative Property 3*

consultant: *General Occupations 1*

consultation room: *Health Care 3*

consummate: *Good 20*

consumption: *Diseases 12*

contact binary: *Star Systems 11*

contact lenses: *Optics 5*

contact poison: *Traps 3*

contact process: *Chemistry General Vocabulary 11*

contact: *Paranormal Occurrences 21*

containers: *Equipment and Tools 5*

contaminated water: *Travel Hazards 9*

contaminated: *Unattractive 20*

conté: *Art Media 13*

Contemporary: *Architectural Styles 3*

contemporary: *Dance Styles 13; New 20*

contemptible: *Sad 20; Unattractive 20*

contemptuous: *Angry 1*

contender: *Common Character Archetypes 21; Fighter 1*

content: *Happy 20*

contented: *Happy 20*

contentment: *Happy 20*

continency: *Twelve Fruits of the Holy Spirit 19*

continent: *Geography General Vocabulary 10*

continental climate: *Geography General Vocabulary 10*

Continental Congress: *Independence Day 19*

continental crust: *Geological Vocabulary 10*

continental divide: *Geography General Vocabulary 10*

continental margin: *Geological Vocabulary 10*

continental shelf: *Coastal and Oceanic 10; Geological Vocabulary 10*

continental: *Coffee Bean Roasts 6*

continentality: *Geography General Vocabulary 10*

contingency: *Philosophy Basic Concepts 14*

continuo: *General Music Vocabulary 13*

continuous spectrum: *Chemistry General Vocabulary 11*

contouring: *Makeup 5*

contour lines: *Geography General Vocabulary 10*

contour plowing: *Soil General Vocabulary 10*

contra luz opal: *Minerals 10*

contract bridge: *Card Games 5*

contract killer: *Assassin 1; Villain 20*

contract killing: *Kill 20*

contract rummy: *Card Games 5*

contractor: *Construction 1*

contrail: *Meteorology General Vocabulary 10*

contralto: *Voices 13*

contraption: *Miscellaneous Furniture 4*

contrast: *Art Principles 13*

contre de quarte: *Fencing Vocabulary 7*

contre de sixte: *Fencing Vocabulary 7*

contre-temp: *Fencing Vocabulary 7*

control booth: *Parts of the Theater 13*

control rods: *Chemistry General Vocabulary 11*

control tower: *Infrastructure Buildings 9*

control: *Magic Vocabulary 17*

controlling: *Magic Vocabulary 17; Negative 1*

contusion: *Injuries/Medical Emergencies 12*

conundrum: *Difficult 20; Magic Vocabulary 17*

conurbation: *Geography General Vocabulary 10*

conure: *Domesticated Pet Birds 15*

convention center: *Special Purpose Structure 3*

convergence: *Meteorology General Vocabulary 10*

convergent boundary: *Geological Vocabulary 10*

conversation hearts: *Candy General 6*

convertible bra: *Ladies' Wear 2*

convertible: *Motorized 9*

conveyor analyzer: *General Farm Equipment*

conveyor belt sidewalk/road: *Devices 22*

conveyor belt: *General Farm Equipment*

convict cichlid: *Aquarium Freshwater Fish 15*

convict: *Illicit Occupations 1*

convoluted: *Difficult 20*

Coober Pedy opal: *Minerals 10*

cook: *Castle Inhabitants and Personnel 1; Food Service 1; Horror Occupations 23; Occupations 22; Verbs 20*

cookbook: *Books/Publications 5*

cookery: *Rooms 3*

cookie bowl: *Ice Cream Cones 6*

cookie cutter: *Kitchen Utensils 5*

cookie dough: *Ice Cream Flavors 6*

cookie jar: *Kitchen Equipment 5*

cookie mold: *Kitchen Equipment 5*

cookie press: *Kitchen Equipment 5*

cookie: *Food 6; Ice Cream Mix-ins 6*

cookies and cream: *Ice Cream Flavors 6*

cookies: *Christmas 19*

cooking gear: *General Survival Gear 5*

cooking techniques: *Verbs 20*

cooking: *Thanksgiving 19*

cool gray: *Gray 20*

cool summer: *Climatic Zones Koeppen System 10*

cool: *Easy 20; Expletives 20*

coolie hat: *Headgear 2*

coonskin: *Headgear 2*

coop: *Farm/Outbuilding 3; Man-Made Animal Homes 15; Residential Slang 3*

cooper: *Artists and Craftspeople 1*

Cooper's: *Caecilians 15*

coordinate covalent bond: *Chemistry General Vocabulary 11*

coordination compound: *Chemistry General Vocabulary 11*

coordination isomers: *Chemistry General Vocabulary 11*

coordination number: *Chemistry General Vocabulary 11*

coordination sphere: *Chemistry General Vocabulary 11*

coordinator: *General Occupations 1*

Coos bay laurel: *Deciduous Trees 10*

cooties: *Fictional Diseases 12*

cop: *Law Enforcement 1*

copal: *Geological Vocabulary 10*

copalm balsam: *Evergreen Trees 10*

Copernicium: *Elements 11*

copier paper: *Office/School/Writing Supplies 5*

copier: *Office/School Machines 5*

co-pilot: *Transportation 1*

coping saw: *Hand Tools 5*

copious: *Large 20*

copper adamite: *Minerals 10*

copper bowl: *Kitchen Equipment 5*

copper pyrites: *Minerals 10*

copper shot: *Wizard's Goods 5*

copper smithsonite: *Minerals 10*

copper sulfate: *Minerals 10*

copper vitriol: *Minerals 10*

copper: *Brown 20; Butterfly 15; Coins and Currency 21;*

Dragon 16; copper: Five Alchemical Spirits 19; Hair Color 1; Precious Metals 21; Wild Saltwater Fish 15

Copper: *Elements 11*

copperbanded butterflyfish: *Aquarium Saltwater Fish 15*

copperhead: *General Snake Families 15*

coppice: *Terrain Features 10*

coprolite: *Geological Vocabulary 10*

copse: *Terrain Features 10*

copy editor: *Publishing 1*

copycat: *Thief 1*

coq au vin: *Poultry Meals 6*

coquina: *Sedimentary Rocks 10*

cor anglais: *Wind/Woodwind and Brass Musical Instruments*

coral beads: *Garden Perennials 10*

coral bean: *Deciduous Trees 10*

coral bells: *Garden Perennials 10*

coral bush: *Weeds 10*

coral fungus: *Fungus Common Names 10*

coral hericium: *Fungus Common Names 10*

coral island: *Water Features 10*

coral isle: *Water Features 10*

coral pink: *Pink 20*

coral reef: *Coastal and Oceanic 10; Ecosystems 10; Water Features 10; Water Terms 9*

coral: *General Snake Families 15; Objects that Offer Protection 19; Orange 20; Standard Gems 21*

coralberry: *Weeds 10*

corbelled arch: *Castle Anatomy 3*

Corbett's: *Tigers 15*

cord: *Fasteners 5; General Survival Gear 5*

Cordel: *Moons 11*

cordial glass: *Drinkware 5*

cordial: *Happy 20*

cordierite: *Cat's Eye Gems 21*

cording: *Wizard's Goods 5*

cordon bleu: *Domesticated Pet Birds 15*

cordon: *Fortification 3; General Combat Vocabulary 7*

cordovan: *Brown 20*

corduroy: *Fabric 2*

core area: *Geography General Vocabulary 10*

core: *Geological Vocabulary 10*

coriander: *Aphrodisiacs 19; Spices 6*

cork board: *Office/School/Writing Supplies 5*

cork: *Items with Healing Properties 19*

corkbark fir: *Evergreen Trees 10*

corkscrew: *Swimming Strokes 9*

corkwood: *Shrubs 10*

cormorant: *Other Wild Birds 15*

corn chip: *Snacks 6*

corn cockle: *Poisonous Plants 10*

corn crib: *Farm/Outbuilding 3*

corn curls: *Snacks 6*

corn dog: *Amusement Park/Carnival/Circus/Fair 3; Sausage 6*

corn dolly: *Objects in Magic and Religion 19*

corn earworm: *Moth 15*

corn fritter: *Bread General Varieties 6*

corn lily: *Poisonous Plants 10*

corn maze: *Halloween 19*

corn meal: *Staples 6*

corn planter: *Horse Drawn Farm Equipment*

corn poppy: *Wildflowers 10*

corn relish: *Pickled/Relish 6*

corn spar: *Minerals 10*

corn stalks: *Halloween 19*

corn syrup: *Staples 6*

corn tortilla: *Bread General Varieties 6*

corn: *General Snake Families 15; Grain 6; Nonvenomous Arachnids 15; Oils 6; Vegetables 6*

corned beef: *Meals 6*

cornelian: *Minerals 10*

corner cupboard: *Storage 4*

corner picture: *Windows 3*

corner: *Tables 4*

cornet: *Wind/Woodwind and Brass Musical Instruments*

cornetto: *Wind/Woodwind and Brass Musical Instruments*

cornflake: *Cookie 6*

cornflower sapphire: *Minerals 10*

cornflower: *Blue 20; Wildflowers 10*

cornice: *Castle Anatomy 3*

cornicello: *Objects in Magic and Religion 19*

Cornish game: *Chickens 15*

Cornish hen: *Poultry Types 6*

Cornish Rex: *Domestic Cats 15*

Cornish: *Human Ethnic Groups 1*

cornrows: *Hair Style 1*

cornsilk: *White 20*

cornucopia: *Objects 18; Secular Symbols 19; Thanksgiving 19*

Corona Australis: *Constellations 11*

Corona Borealis: *Constellations 11*

corona: *Astronomy General Terms 11; Jewelry 21*

Coronado Island: *Rattlesnake 15*

coronet: *Headgear 2; Jewelry 21*

corporal: *U.S. Army Enlisted 8; U.S. Marines Enlisted 8*

Corporate Modern: *Architectural Styles 3*

Corps de ballet: *Ballet Terms 13*

corps de ballet: *Dance Moves 13*

Corps: *Ballet Terms 13*

corpse: *Objects/Activities Connected to Lore 19*

corpulent: *Large 20; Large/Heavy 1*

Corpus Hermeticum: *Major Religious Books 14*

corral: *Farm/Outbuilding 3; Man-Made Animal Homes 15*

correctional facility: *Military Property 3*

corridor: *Roads 9; Rooms 3*

corrie: *Glacial and Mountain 10*

Corriente: *Other Cows 15*

corrode: *Harm 20; Smells 20*

corrosion: *Chemistry General Vocabulary 11; Smells 20*

corrosive: *Smells 20*

corrugated fiberboard: *Art Materials 5*

corrupt police officer: *Supporting Cast 23*

corrupt: *Bad 20; Horror Vocabulary 23*

corrupted: *Unattractive 20*

corsac: *Foxes 15*

corset: *Ladies' Wear 2; Western Clothing/Dress 21*

Corsican pine: *Deciduous Trees 10*

Cortland: *Apples 6*

corundum: *Cat's Eye Gems 21*

corvette: *Military Watercraft 8; Small Watercraft 9*

Corvus: *Constellations 11*

corvus: *Siege Engines 7*

cory: *Aquarium Freshwater Fish 15*

corydalis: *Garden Bulbs 10*

coryphée: *Dance Moves 13*

cos lettuce: *Vegetables 6*

Cosgarach Mhor: *Celtic Swords 18*

cosmetic bag: *Accessories 2*

cosmetologist: *Personal Services 1*

cosmic egg: *Secular Symbols 19*

cosmic ray: *Astronomy General Terms 11*

cosmic: *Energy Sources/Types 22*

cosmogony: *Astronomy General Terms 11*

cosmogram: *Symbols in Magic and Religion 19*

cosmology: *Astronomy General Terms 11*

cosmos: *Garden Annuals 10; Wildflowers 10*

Cossack (Ukraine): *Ethnic/Folk Dances 13*

Cossack hat: *Headgear 2*

Cossack shashka: *Swords One-handed 7*

Cossack: *Human Ethnic Groups 1*

Costeño con Cuernos: *Other Cows 15*

costume designer: *Performing Arts 1*

costume: *Dance Clothing 13; Halloween 19; Special Purpose Clothing 2; Specialty Survival Gear 5; Styles of Dress 2*

costumer: *Artists and Craftspeople 1*

cot: *Beds 4*

cotoneaster: *Shrubs 10*

cottage fries: *Vegetables Cooked 6*

cottage loaf: *Bread General Varieties 6*

Cottage: *Architectural Styles 3*

cottage: *Cheese Moist 6; Hospitality 3; Residential Property 3*

cotton blanket: *Bed Linens 5*

cotton bollworm: *Moth 15*

cotton candy: *Amusement Park/Carnival/Circus/Fair 3; Candy General 6; Ice Cream Flavors 6*

cotton glove: *Fencing Equipment 7*

cotton gloves: *Unisex Clothing 2*

cotton picker: *General Farm Equipment*

cotton thistle: *Weeds 10*

cotton/polyester blend: *Fabric 2*

cotton: *Fabric 2; Farm/Outbuilding 3*

cottonmouth: *General Snake Families 15*

cottonseed: *Oils 6*

couatl: *Extraplanar 16*

couch: *Seating 4*

couchant: *Land Creatures 19*

couching: *Embellishments 2*

Cou-de-pied position: *Ballet Terms 13*

Cougar Gold: *Cheese Common Varieties 6*

cougar: *Animals with Symbolic Meaning 19; Big Cats 15*

couillon: *Card Games 5*

coule: *Fencing Vocabulary 7*

coulee: *Terrain Features 10*

coulomb: *Chemistry General Vocabulary 11*

coulometry: *Chemistry General Vocabulary 11*

Coulter pine: *Deciduous Trees 10*

coumaphos: *Dangerous Chemicals 11*

counsel: *Seven Gifts of the Holy Spirit 19*

counselor: *Academic 1; Cleric 1; Wizard 1*

Count Dracula: *Fictional Characters 18*

count: *Royal/Noble 1*

counter lamp: *Illumination/Light Sources 5*

counter parry: *Fencing Vocabulary 7*

counter: *Bathroom Features and Fixtures 3; Building Elements and Features 3; Speak 20*

counterattack: *Attack 7; Fencing Vocabulary 7*

counterguard: *Castle Anatomy 3*

counter-passant: *Multiple Figures 19*

counterpoint: *General Music Vocabulary 13*

counter-salient: *Multiple Figures 19*

countersink: *Hand Tools 5*

countertenor: *Voices 13*

counterweight: *Technical Terms 13*

counterweights: *Windows 3*

countess: *Royal/Noble 1*

counting coup: *Western Paraphernalia/People 21*

country & western: *Musical Styles 13*

country subdivision: *Political Divisions 10*

country: *Musical Styles 13; Political Divisions 10*

countryside: *Terrain Features 10*

county executive: *Government 1*

county seat: *Administrative Property 3*

county: *Political Divisions 10*

coup stick: *Western Paraphernalia/People 21*

Coupé jeté en tournant: *Ballet Terms 13*

coupe: *Fencing Vocabulary 7; Motorized 9*

couped close: *Heads 19*

couped: *Heads 19*

courage: *General Emotions 20; Philosophy Basic Concepts 14*

courageous: *Personality Other 1*

courageousness: *General Emotions 20*

courante (France): *Ethnic/Folk Dances 13*

course sail: *Boat/Ship Anatomy 9*

course: *Boat/Ship Terminology 9; Roads 9*

course-plotting: *Boat/Ship Terminology 9*

court piece: *Card Games 5*

court: *Administrative Property 3; Rooms 3; Royal/Noble 1*

Courtain: *Weapons of Legend 18*

courtesan: *Castle Inhabitants and Personnel 1*

courtesy: *General Emotions 20*

courthouse: *Administrative Property 3; Business Property 3*

courtier: *Castle Inhabitants and Personnel 1; Knight 1; Royal/Noble 1; Styles of Dress 2*

courtroom drama: *Performance Genres 13*

courtroom: *Art Genres 13*

courtyard: *General Buildings 3*

Couru: *Ballet Terms 13*

couscous: *Pasta 6*

cousin once removed: *Relational 1*

cousin twice removed: *Relational 1*

cousin: *Relational 1*

coutil: *Fabric 2*

covalent bond: *Chemistry General Vocabulary 11*

covalent compounds: *Chemistry General Vocabulary 11*

cove: *Coastal and Oceanic 10; Terrain Features 10; Water*

Terms 9

coven: *Witchcraft Vocabulary 17*

Covenanter Cruiser Mark V medium tank: *United Kingdom Military Vehicles 8*

cover fire: *General Combat Vocabulary 7; General Combat Vocabulary 7*

cover slip: *Laboratory Equipment 5*

cover: *General Combat Vocabulary 7; Music Accessories*

coveralls: *Clothing/Uniforms 22; Unisex Clothing 2*

covered wagon: *Western Paraphernalia/People 21*

covered: *Bridges 9*

coverlet: *Bed Linens 5*

covers: *Bed Linens 5*

covert: *Magic Vocabulary 17*

cow hitch: *Sailing Knots 9*

cow oak: *Deciduous Trees 10*

cow: *Animals with Symbolic Meaning 19; Sharks 15*

coward: *Special Posture 19*

cowardice: *General Emotions 20*

cowardly: *Personality Other 1*

cowbane: *Poisonous Plants 10*

cowbird: *Backyard Birds 15*

cowboy boots: *Western Clothing/Dress 21*

cowboy hat: *Headgear 2; Toys 5; Western Clothing/Dress 21*

cowboy pistols: *Toys 5*

cowboy: *Beetle 15; Boots 2; Cookie 6; Facial Hair Mustache 1; Western Paraphernalia/People 21*

cowcod: *Wild Saltwater Fish 15*

cowed: *Horror Vocabulary 23*

cower: *General Combat Vocabulary 7*

cowering: *Moves 7*

cowl neck: *Ladies' Wear 2*

cowpie: *Poker Card Games 5*

cowrie shell: *Secular Symbols 19*

cows and bulls: *Poisonous Plants 10*

cows: *Animals 15*

cowslip: *Garden Perennials 10*

coy: *Horror Vocabulary 23*

Coyamito agate: *Minerals 10*

Coyolxauhqui (moon goddess): *Aztec Pantheon 14*

Coyote (nature): *Native American Pantheon 14*

Coyote reconnaissance vehicle: *Canada Military Vehicles 8*

coyote: *Animals with Symbolic Meaning 19; Dogs/Canine 15; Fur 2; Other Wild Mammals 15*

cozy: *Happy 20*

CPU: *Computer Equipment 5*

CQ261 wheeled truck: *China Military Vehicles 8*

crab cake: *Fish/Seafood Meals 6*

crab cracker: *Eating Utensils 5; Kitchen Utensils 5*

crab lice: *Diseases 12*

crab: *Animals with Symbolic Meaning 19; Apples 6; Fish/Seafood Types 6; Nonvenomous Arachnids 15*

crabby: *Grouchy 1*

crab-eating: *Foxes 15*

crabmeat: *Sandwiches 6*

crab's eye: *Poisonous Plants 10*

crack: *Loud 20*

cracked wheat: *Bread General Varieties 6*

cracked: *Lips 1; Skin Types and Features 1; Teeth 1*

cracker plate: *Tableware 5*

cracker: *Butterfly 15*

cradenza: *Storage 4*

cradle: *Beds 4*

craft: *Create 20; Fix 20; Human-Powered Watercraft 9; Magic Vocabulary 17; Rooms 3; Small Watercraft 9; Witchcraft Vocabulary 17*

craftspeople: *Character Building 1*

crafty: *Horror Vocabulary 23*

crag: *Terrain Features 10*

crampons: *General Survival Gear 5*

cranberries: *Thanksgiving 19*

cranberry orange relish: *Pickled/Relish 6*

cranberry relish: *Condiments 6; Pickled/Relish 6*

cranberry: *Berries 6; Fruit Juice 6; Muffin 6; Quick Bread 6; Shrubs 10*

crane operator: *Construction 1*

crane: *Animals with Symbolic Meaning 19; Boat/Ship Anatomy 9; Flies 15; Other Wild Birds 15*

crane's bill: *Garden Perennials 10; Wildflowers 10*

cranium: *Bones 12*

cranky: *Grouchy 1*

crannog: *Fortification 3*

crap: *Excrement 12; Expletives 20*

crape myrtle: *Shrubs 10*

crappie: *Wild Freshwater Fish 15*

crapulence: *Hangover 12*

crash pad: *Residential Slang 3*

crash: *Card Games 5; Fabric 2; Locomotion 9*

crashing: *Loud 20*

crass: *Unattractive 20*

crate: *Containers and Vessels 5; Man-Made Animal Homes 15*

crater lake: *Volcanic 10*

Crater: *Constellations 11*

crater: *Astronomy General Terms 11; Terrain Features 10*

crates: *Card Games 5*

craton: *Geological Vocabulary 10*

cravat: *Men's Wear 2*

crawl: *Locomotion 9*

crawling: *Slow 20*

crayon: *Art Materials 5; Art Media 13; Office/School/Writing Supplies 5*

craze: *Love 20*

crazed artificial intelligence: *Monsters and Creatures 22*

crazed mother: *Supporting Cast 23*

crazy eights: *Card Games 5*

crazy lace agate: *Minerals 10*

crazy person who knows the truth: *Supporting Cast 23*

crazy pineapple: *Poker Card Games 5*

crazy recluse stalks/torments/kills neighbors: *Horror Plot Devices 23*

crazy wizard: *Common Dangers 24*

crazy woman holds secrets of magic: *Fantasy Plot Devices 24*

crazy: *General Emotions 20*

creak: *Sounds 20*

creaky: *Vocal/Speech Quality 1*

cream bush: *Shrubs 10*

cream cheese: *Muffin 6*

cream filled: *Donut/doughnut 6*

cream of tartar: *Staples 6*

cream puff: *Amusement Park/Carnival/Circus/Fair 3; Miscellaneous Dessert 6*

cream soup bowl: *Tableware 5*

cream: *Candy General 6; Cheese Moist 6; Mixers 6; Other Dairy 6; Pie 6; Soup 6; White 20; Yellow 20*

creamer: *Tableware 5*

creamy Italian: *Salad Dressing 6*

creamy: *Skin Types and Features 1*

creasing: *Castle Anatomy 3*

create: *Verbs 20*

creation of the universe: *Plot Devices 22*

creative: *New 20*

creativity: *Philosophy Basic Concepts 14*

creature lair: *Fantasy Locations 24*

creature of legend: *Monster Categories/Terms 16*

creature power: *Energy Sources/Types 24*

creature sidekick: *Supporting Cast 24*

creature: *Monster Categories/Terms 16*

creatures/monsters seek revenge: *Common Dangers 24*

crèche: *Christmas 19*

Cree: *Native American Peoples 1*

Creek: *Native American Peoples 1*

creek: *Water Features 10; Water Terms 9*

creel basket: *Fishing Gear 5*

creep: *Locomotion 9; Wet 20*

creeping Charlie: *Weeds 10*

creeping Jenny: *Weeds 10*

creeping phlox: *Garden Perennials 10*

creeping: *Slow 20*

creepy assistant: *Supporting Cast 23*

creepy child: *Common Character Archetypes 21*

creepy neighbor: *Common Character Archetypes 21*

creepy: *Horror Vocabulary 23; Magic Vocabulary 17*

crematorium: *Cemetery 3*

crème brulee: *Miscellaneous Dessert 6*

crème de cacao: *Hard Liquor 6*

crème de menthe: *Hard Liquor 6*

crème fraiche: *Cheese Moist 6*

crenation: *Blood 12*

crenel: *Castle Anatomy 3*

crenellation: *Castle Anatomy 3; Fortification 3*

Creole Cottage: *Architectural Styles 3*

Créole: *Human Ethnic Groups 1; Pigs 15*

crepe de chine: *Fabric 2*

crepe: *Bread General Varieties 6; Fabric 2*

crescendo: *Dynamics 13*

crescent moon and star: *Symbols in Magic and Religion 19*

crescent moon image: *Harbingers/Charms for Good Luck 19*

crescent: *Butterfly 15; Cadency Mark 19*

cresol: *Dangerous Chemicals 11*

cress: *Vegetables 6*

Cressida: *Moons 11*

crest: *Elements 19; Jewelry 21*

crested: *Newts 15; Owls 15; Special Body Features 19*

crestfallen: *Sad 20*

Cretaceous Period: *Geologic Time 10*

Cretan bull: *Twelve Labors of Hercules 16*

Cretan: *Embroidery Stitches 2*

crevasse splay: *Fluvial 10*

crevasse: *Glacial and Mountain 10; Terrain Features 10*

crevice: *Terrain Features 10*

crew cut: *Hair Style 1*

crew: *Boat/Ship Anatomy 9; Maritime Occupations 1*

crewel needle: *Sewing Equipment 2*

crewel: *Embellishments 2*

crib: *Beds 4; Residential Slang 3*

cribbage: *Card Games 5*

cricket bench: *Seating 4*

cricket cap: *Headgear 2*

cricket: *Animals with Symbolic Meaning 19; Card Games 5; Orthoptera 15*

crickey: *Expletives 20*

crime scene investigator: *Law Enforcement 1*

Crimean pine: *Deciduous Trees 10*

crimidine: *Dangerous Chemicals 11*

criminal hideout: *Horror Locations 23*

criminal property: *Architecture and Property 3*

criminal: *Illicit Occupations 1; Thief 1; Travel Hazards 9; Villain 20*

criminals steal/tamper with dangerous item: *Horror Plot Devices 23*

criminy: *Expletives 20*

crimped: *Hair Treated 1*

crimping pliers: *Hand Tools 5*

crimson clover: *Wildflowers 10*

crimson glory vine: *Garden Perennials 10*

crimson waxcap: *Fungus Common Names 10*

crimson: *Red 20*

crined: *Special Body Features 19*

crinet: *Horse Barding Pieces 7*

crinkle: *Fabric 2*

crinodendron: *Shrubs 10*

crinoline: *Fabric 2; Ladies' Wear 2*

crinum lily: *Garden Bulbs 10*

Crioulo: *Horse Breeds 15*

cripes: *Expletives 20*

crisp bread: *Bread General Varieties 6*

crisphead lettuce: *Vegetables 6*

criss cross: *Poker Card Games 5*

critic: *Publishing 1*

critical mass: *Chemistry General Vocabulary 11*

critical point: *Chemistry General Vocabulary 11*

critical pressure: *Chemistry General Vocabulary 11*

critical state soil mechanics: *Soil General Vocabulary 10*

critical temperature: *Chemistry General Vocabulary 11*

croaker: *Wild Freshwater Fish 15*

croaky: *Vocal/Speech Quality 1*

Crocea Mors (sword of Julius Caesar): *Weapons of Legend 18*

crochet: *Sewing Techniques 2*

crock and dish of Rhygenydd Ysgolhaig: *Thirteen Treasures of the Island of Britain 18*

crock: *Containers and Vessels 5; Kitchen Equipment 5*

crockery: *Kitchen Equipment 5*

crocodile agaricus: *Fungus Common Names 10*

crocodile: *Newts 15*

crocodilians: *Animals 15*

crocosmia: *Garden Bulbs 10*

crocotta: *Beast 16*

crocus: *Garden Bulbs 10*

Croisé/croisée: *Ballet Terms 13*

croissant: *Bread General Varieties 6*

cromfordite: *Minerals 10*

cromite: *Minerals 10*

crommyonian sow: *Mythical Creatures and Monsters 16*

crone: *Common Character Archetypes 21; Elderly 1; Wizard 1*

cronstedtite: *Minerals 10*

Cronus's sickle: *Weapons of Legend 18*

crook: *Illicit Occupations 1; Thief 1*

crooked mayor/sheriff: *Western Plot Devices 21*

crooked: *Bad 20; Horror Vocabulary 23; Nose 1; Teeth 1*

crooner: *Bard 1; Singer 1*

crop circles: *Real Places Steeped in Legend or Mystery 18*

crop top: *Ladies' Wear 2*

crop: *Art Techniques 13; Flexible 7; Hair Style 1*

crop-lien system: *Geography General Vocabulary 10*

croquet mallet: *Sporting Goods Other 5*

croquet: *Sporting Goods Balls 5*

croquette: *Fish/Seafood Meals 6; Meals 6; Poultry Meals 6*

cross a hare's path: *Practices that Attract Bad Luck 19*

cross and crown: *Symbols in Magic and Religion 19*

cross and orb: *Castle Anatomy 3*

cross country skis: *Sporting Goods Other 5*

cross match: *Blood 12*

cross moline: *Cadency Mark 19*

cross oak: *Deciduous Trees 10*

cross river gorilla: *Apes 15*

cross vault: *Gem Cuts 21*

cross vine: *Garden Perennials 10*

cross: *Angry 1; Charges 19; Easter 19; Embroidery Stitches 2; Fencing Vocabulary 7; Figures Associated with Symbols 19; Gem Cuts 21; Religious Items 5*

cross-bedding: *Geological Vocabulary 10*

crossbow bolt: *Missile Loads 7*

crossbowman: *Castle Inhabitants and Personnel 1; Fighter 1*

cross-bred mad animal: *Monsters and Creatures 22*

cross-breeding: *Plot Devices 22*

crossed keys: *Papal Symbols 19*

crossed: *Viper 15*

cross-eyed persons: *Harbingers of Bad Luck 19*

crossing: *Church Anatomy 3; Journey 20*

crossover: *Stage Terms 13*

crossroads: *Secular Symbols 19; Witchcraft Vocabulary 17*

cross-trainer: *Athletic Shoes 2*

crosswall: *Castle Anatomy 3*

crotchet: *Notation 13*

crotonaldehyde: *Dangerous Chemicals 11*

croucher: *Devil 16*

crouton: *Bread General Varieties 6*

crow: *Animals with Symbolic Meaning 19; Backyard Birds 15*

Crow: *Native American Peoples 1*

crow's foot: *Symbols in Magic and Religion 19*

crow's nest: *Boat/Ship Anatomy 9*

crowbar: *Hand Tools 5*

crowberry: *Shrubs 10; Unusual Edible Fruits 6*

crowbill: *Pole Weapons 7*

crowley: *Cheese Common Varieties 6*

crown braid: *Hair Style 1*

crown molding: *Building Elements and Features 3*

crown of snow: *Garden Perennials 10*

crown of thirteen stars: *United States Dollar Bill 19*

crown of thorns: *Relics of Jesus 14*

crown prince: *Royal/Noble 1*

crown princess: *Royal/Noble 1*

crown roast of pork: *Pork 6*

crown vetch: *Garden Perennials 10*

crown: *Charges 19; Coins and Currency 21; Elements 19; Headgear 2; Jewelry 2; Jewelry 21; Teeth Dental Work 1*

crowned: *General Snake Families 15*

crownwork: *Castle Anatomy 3*

crowsfoot: *Garden Perennials 10*

Cruadh-Chosgarach: *Celtic Swords 18*

crucible cover: *Laboratory Equipment 5*

crucible tongs: *Laboratory Equipment 5*

crucible: *Laboratory Equipment 5*

crucifix: *Objects in Magic and Religion 19; Religious Items 5*

crucifixion nails: *Relics of Jesus 14*

crud: *Expletives 20*

crude oil: *Geological Vocabulary 10*

cruel person: *Villain 20*

cruel: *Bad 20; Horror Vocabulary 23; Negative 1*

cruise lamp: *Illumination/Light Sources 5*

cruise liner: *Large Watercraft 9; Travel Modes 23*

cruise ship: *Large Watercraft 9; Spaceship Types 22*

cruise: *Journey 20; Locomotion 9*

cruiser killer: *Military Watercraft 8*

Cruiser Mk 1 tank: *Australia Military Vehicles 8*

cruiser: *Spaceship Types 22*

cruller: *Donut/doughnut 6*

crumb: *Bread General Varieties 6; Ice Cream Mix-ins 6*

crumpet: *Bread General Varieties 6*

crunch: *Ice Cream Mix-ins 6*

crupper: *Horse Barding Pieces 7*

crusade: *General Combat Vocabulary 7*

Crusader tank Mark VI model A15: *United Kingdom Military Vehicles 8*

crusader: *Fighter 1; Knight 1; Paladin 1*

Crusader: *Tanks British 8*

crush: *Attack 7*

crushed velvet: *Fabric 2*

crusilly: *Patterns 19*

crust: *Bread General Varieties 6; Cave Anatomy 10; Geography General Vocabulary 10; Geological Vocabulary 10*

crux dissimulata: *Symbols in Magic and Religion 19*

Crux: *Constellations 11*

cry: *Sounds 20; Speak 20*

cryo: *Weapons 22*

cryogenic: *Energy Sources/Types 22*

cryokinesis: *Paranormal Abilities 21*

cryonic: *Weapons 22*

cryonics: *Plot Devices 22*

cryosphere: *Geography General Vocabulary 10*

cryovolcano: *Volcanic 10*

crypt: *Cemetery 3; Church Anatomy 3; Fantasy Locations 24; Rooms 3*

cryptic: *Magic Vocabulary 17*

cryptozoology: *Mythical Creatures and Monsters 16*

crystal aggregates: *Snow Types 10*

crystal ball: *Fortune Telling General Devices 19; Objects in Magic and Religion 19; Witchcraft Vocabulary 17; Wizard's Goods 5*

crystal facets: *Snow Types 10*

crystal field stabilization energy: *Chemistry General Vocabulary 11*

crystal field theory: *Chemistry General Vocabulary 11*

crystal holy symbol: *Religious Items 5*

crystal lattice energy: *Chemistry General Vocabulary 11*

crystal lattice: *Chemistry General Vocabulary 11*

crystal mine: *Fantasy Locations 24*

crystal opal: *Minerals 10*

crystal pellets: *Snow Types 10*

crystal pool: *Cave Anatomy 10*

crystal reader: *Fortune Teller 1*

crystal skull: *Classic Items 23; Real Objects Not Fully Understood 18*

crystal: *Cave Anatomy 10; Rock and Mineral Forms 10; Weapons 22*

crystalline quartz: *Minerals 10*

crystalline solid: *Chemistry General Vocabulary 11*

crystalline water ice: *Snow Types 10*

crystals: *Energy Sources/Types 24; Wizard's Goods 5*

CTLS light tank: *United States Military Vehicles 8*

cu sith: *Beast 16*

cub mackerel: *Wild Saltwater Fish 15*

cub reporter: *Publishing 1*

Cuban crocodile: *Crocodilians 15*

Cuban pine: *Deciduous Trees 10*

Cuban wood: *General Snake Families 15*

Cuban: *Boa 15; Sandwiches 6*

cube steak: *Meals 6*

cube: *Secular Symbols 19; Spaceship Shapes 22*

cubicle: *Rooms 3*

Cubism: *Art Movements 13*

cuboid bone: *Bones 12*

ALPHABETICAL INDEX

Cúchulainn: *Legendary People Presumed to be Fictional 18*

cuckoo clock: *Timekeeping 5*

cuckoo owlet: *Owls 15*

cuckoo: *Bees 15; Card Games 5; Other Wild Birds 15; Wasp 15*

cuckoo-pint: *Poisonous Plants 10*

cucumber root: *Wildflowers 10*

cucumber: *Card Games 5; Vegetable Juice 6; Vegetables 6*

cudgel: *Bludgeons 7*

cudrang: *Unusual Edible Fruits 6*

cue: *Stage Terms 13*

cuello: *Horse Barding Pieces 7*

cuesta: *Erosion 10; Slope 10*

cuff bracelet: *Jewelry 2*

cuff link: *Jewelry 2; Jewelry 21*

cuff: *Attack 7; Garment Pieces 2*

cuffs: *Fasteners 5*

cuir bouillie: *Armor Types 7*

cuirass: *Armor Pieces 7*

cul-de-sac: *Roads 9*

culottes: *Ladies' Wear 2*

culpeo: *Foxes 15*

cultipacker: *General Farm Equipment*

Cultivator No. 6 trench forming machine: *United Kingdom Military Vehicles 8*

cultivator: *Agricultural 1; Garden Tools; General Farm Equipment; Horse Drawn Farm Equipment*

culture hearth: *Geography General Vocabulary 10*

culture: *Geography General Vocabulary 10*

cultured: *Personality Other 1*

Cultus Sabbati: *Secret/Mystical Organizations 18*

Culver's physic: *Garden Perennials 10*

culverin: *Cannon 7*

Culwych: *Knights of the Round Table 18*

Cuman: *Human Ethnic Groups 1*

Cumberland slider: *Freshwater Turtles 15*

Cumberland: *Pigs 15*

cumin: *Spices 6*

cumuliform: *Clouds 10*

cumulonimbus: *Clouds 10*

cumulus: *Clouds 10*

cunning: *Horror Vocabulary 23*

cup and saucer: *Garden Perennials 10*

cup of Jamshid: *Objects 18*

cup plant: *Garden Perennials 10*

cup: *Drinkware 5; Laboratory Equipment 5*

cupboard: *Building Elements and Features 3; Storage 4*

cupcake pan: *Kitchen Equipment 5*

cupcake: *Cake 6*

Cupid (love): *Roman Pantheon 14*

Cupid: *Moons 11; Valentine's Day 19*

cupid's bow: *Lips 1*

Cupid's dart: *Garden Perennials 10*

Cupik: *Native American Peoples 1*

cupola: *Castle Anatomy 3*

cuproadamite: *Minerals 10*

cupropyrite: *Minerals 10*

cups: *Minor Arcana 19*

cupuacu: *Unusual Edible Fruits 6*

curator: *Fighter 1*

curb: *Close/Hold 20*

curds: *Cheese Common Varieties 6*

Curie: *Chemistry General Vocabulary 11*

curio: *Jewelry 21*

Curium: *Elements 11*

curled dock: *Weeds 10*

curled: *Hair Treated 1*

curlew: *Other Wild Birds 15*

curly dock: *Weeds 10*

curly onion: *Garden Perennials 10*

curly: *Hair Types 1*

Curly-Coated Retriever: *Dog Breeds 15*

curly-leaf pondweed: *Weeds 10*

currant: *Shrubs 10*

current marking: *Cave Anatomy 10*

current: *Meteorology General Vocabulary 10; Water Terms 9*

curry powder: *Spices 6*

curry: *Transportation Animals 9*

curse must be reversed: *Fantasy Plot Devices 24*

curse of darkness stops sun from rising: *Common Dangers 24*

curse: *Magic Vocabulary 17; Witchcraft Vocabulary 17*

cursed car/motorcycle: *Common Dangers 23*

cursed castle/tomb: *Common Dangers 24*

cursed dagger: *Classic Items 23*

cursed item causes grief: *Horror Plot Devices 23*

cursed magic item: *Traps 3*

cursed object: *Common Dangers 23; Common Dangers 24*

cursed property: *Common Dangers 23*

cursed scroll is read: *Common Dangers 24*

cursed scroll: *Traps 3*

cursory: *Fast 20*

curtail: *Close/Hold 20*

curtain of beads: *Door Materials 3*

curtain wall: *Castle Anatomy 3*

curtain: *Cave Anatomy 10*

curtained: *Hair Style 1*

curtains: *Window Treatments 5*

Curtiss possumhaw: *Deciduous Trees 10*

curvaceous: *Large/Heavy 1*

curve square: *Sewing Equipment 2*

curved heels: *Footwear/Shoes 2*

curving: *Eyebrows 1*

curvy: *Large/Heavy 1*

cuscus: *Other Wild Mammals 15*

cushion: *Gem Cuts 21; Pillows 5*

cusk: *Wild Saltwater Fish 15*

cuspate foreland: *Coastal and Oceanic 10*

cuspid: *Teeth 12*

custard apple: *Deciduous Trees 10; Unusual Edible Fruits 6*

custard cup: *Kitchen Equipment 5*

custard filled: *Donut/doughnut 6*

custard: *Pie 6*

custodian: *Fighter 1; General Occupations 1*

cut down an oak tree: *Practices that Attract Bad Luck 19*

cut grass: *Allergies 12*

cut requiring stitches: *Injuries/Medical Emergencies 12*

cut: *Art Techniques 13; Fencing Vocabulary 7; Sewing Techniques 2*

cutbank: *Fluvial 10*

cute: *Beautiful 20*

cuteness: *Philosophy Basic Concepts 14*

cutlass fish: *Wild Saltwater Fish 15*

cutlass: *Swords One-handed 7*

cutlery: *Kitchen Utensils 5*

cutlet: *Meals 6*

cut-out: *Cookie 6*

cutpurse: *Thief 1*

cutter: *Large Watercraft 9; Small Watercraft 9*

cutting board: *Kitchen Equipment 5; Sewing Equipment 2*

cutting torch: *Art Tools 5; Power Tools*

cuttle: *Card Games 5*

cuttlefish: *Squid 15*

cuvette: *Laboratory Equipment 5*

Cuvier's dwarf caiman: *Crocodilians 15*

CV-33 light tank: *Italy Military Vehicles 8*

cwm: *Glacial and Mountain 10*

cyan: *Colors 20*

cyanide: *Poisonous Chemicals in Plants 11*

cyanogen bromide: *Dangerous Chemicals 11*

cyanogen iodide: *Dangerous Chemicals 11*

cyanogenic glycoside: *Poisonous Chemicals in Plants 11*

cyanophos: *Dangerous Chemicals 11*

cyanuric fluoride: *Dangerous Chemicals 11*

cybernetics: *Plot Devices 22*

cyborg: *Plot Devices 22*

Cyclades blunt-nosed: *Viper 15*

cycle of life: *Symbols in Magic and Religion 19*

cycle: *Composition Types 13*

cyclist's cap: *Headgear 2*

cycloheximide: *Dangerous Chemicals 11*

cyclohexylamine: *Dangerous Chemicals 11*

Cyclone class patrol boat: *U.S. Navy Vessels 8*

cyclone: *Severe Weather 10*

cyclonic flow: *Meteorology General Vocabulary 10*

cyclopean: *Eye Type 1*

Cyclops: *Human Races Fictional 1*

cyclorama: *Parts of the Theater 13*

cyclotron: *Chemistry General Vocabulary 11*

Cygnus: *Constellations 11*

cylinder seals: *Jewelry 21*

Cyllene: *Moons 11*

cymatolite: *Minerals 10*

cymbal: *Percussion Musical Instruments 5*

cymophane: *Cat's Eye Gems 21; Minerals 10*

cynical: *Horror Vocabulary 23; Negative 1*

Cypress Grove chevre: *Cheese Common Varieties 6*

cypress: *Evergreen Trees 10*

cyprine: *Minerals 10*

cyrtolite: *Minerals 10*

CZ 550 American: *Bolt Action Centerfire Rifles 7*

CZ Mallard: *Shotguns Over/Under 7*

Czech: *Human Ethnic Groups 1*

Czech: *Pigs 15*

–D–

D. B. Cooper: *Real People with Legendary Status 18; Famous Disappearances 18*

D'anjou: *Pears 6*

d'Arrest: *Comets 11*

d'Orsay pumps: *Footwear/Shoes 2*

D421 cable carrier: *China Military Vehicles 8*

da capo: *General Music Vocabulary 13*

dab: *Clean 20*

Dachshund: *Dog Breeds 15*

dacite: *Igneous Rocks 10*

dacquiri: *Cocktails 6*

dad: *Male 1*

Dada: *Art Movements 13*

dada: *Male 1*

dadao: *Swords Two-handed 7*

daddy hex: *Pennsylvania Dutch Hex Signs 19*

daddy longlegs: *Nonvenomous Arachnids 15*

daddy: *Male 1*

Dade County pine: *Evergreen Trees 10*

Dade County slash pine: *Evergreen Trees 10*

daevas: *Demon 16*

daffodil: *Garden Bulbs 10; Poisonous Plants 10; Yellow 20*

daft: *Unintelligent 1*

Dagda (leader of the gods): *Celtic Pantheon 14*

dagger/sword: *Weapons 22*

daggers: *Combat, Armor, and Weapons 7*

daggerwing: *Butterfly 15*

Dagonet: *Knights of the Round Table 18*

Dagwood: *Sandwiches 6*

Dahl: *Asteroids with Unusual Names 11*

dahlia: *Garden Bulbs 10*

Daikoku (luck): *Japanese Pantheon 14*

daikon: *Vegetables 6*

Dainsleif: *Norse Weapons 18*

dainty: *Small/Fragile 20*

dairy beverages: *Food 6*

dairy: *Farm/Outbuilding 3; Food 6*

dais: *Special Purpose Furniture 4*

daisy bush: *Shrubs 10*

Daisy Dukes: *Ladies' Wear 2*

daisy wheel typewriter: *Office/School Machines 5*

daisy: *Plants with Symbolic Meaning 19*

Dajal: *Other Cows 15*

Dakota: *Poker Card Games 5*

dale: *Slope 10*

Dales Pony: *Horse Breeds 15*

Dali: *Facial Hair Mustache 1*

Dalmatian: *Dog Breeds 15*

damage: *General Combat Vocabulary 7; Harm 20*

damaged: *Hair Types 1; Unattractive 20*

Damascus: *Other Cows 15*

damask: *Fabric 2*

dame: *Female 1; Royal/Noble 1*

dame's rocket: *Garden Perennials 10; Wildflowers 10*

Damietta: *Other Cows 15*

damn fine: *Expletives 20*

damn: *Expletives 20*

damnation: *Expletives 20*

damp: *Wet 10; Wet 20*

damper: *Bread General Varieties 6*

dampfnudel: *Bread General Varieties 6*

dampness: *Wet 20*

damsel in distress: *Common Character Archetypes 21*

damsel: *Female 1*

damselfish: *Aquarium Saltwater Fish 15*

Dan Wesson Bobtail: *Pistol Semiautomatic 7*

danaite: *Minerals 10*

danbo: *Cheese International Varieties 6*

danburite: *Standard Gems 21*

dance clothing: *The Arts 13*

dance equipment: *The Arts 13*

dance hall dress: *Western Clothing/Dress 21*

dance hall girl tempts preacher: *Western Plot Devices 21*

dance hall girl turns respectable: *Western Plot Devices 21*

dance hall: *Entertainment Property 3*

dance mat: *Dance Equipment 13*

dance moves: *The Arts 13*

dance shoes: *The Arts 13*

dance sneaker: *Dance Shoes 13*

dance studio: *Entertainment Property 3; Rooms 3*

dance styles: *The Arts 13*

dance: *Bees 15; Locomotion 9; New Year 19; Styles of Dress 2; The Arts 13; Witchcraft Vocabulary 17*

dancer: *Performing Arts 1*

dancette: *Partition Lines 19*

dancing weapon: *Typical Magical Objects 17*

dancing: *Magical Transportation 17; May Day 19*

dandelion green: *Vegetable Juice 6*

dandelion: *Plants with Symbolic Meaning 19; Weeds 10*

dander: *Allergies 12*

Dandie Dinmont Terrier: *Dog Breeds 15*

dandy: *Personality Other 1*

Dane: *Axes 7*

dang blasted: *Expletives 20*

dang it: *Expletives 20*

danger: *Horror Vocabulary 23*

dangerous terrain: *Common Dangers 24*

dangerous: *Horror Vocabulary 23; Unattractive 20*

Dangi: *Other Cows 15*

dangle earring: *Jewelry 2*

dangpa-chang: *Spears 7*

Daniel Boone: *Real People with Legendary Status 18*

Daniel Shays: *Real People with Legendary Status 18*

Daniel: *Comets 11*

Daniel's: *Caecilians 15*

danio: *Aquarium Freshwater Fish 15*

Danish blue: *Cheese International Varieties 6*

Danish Functionalism: *Architectural Styles 3*

Danish Jersey: *Other Cows 15*

Danish landrace: *Pigs 15*

Danish port-salut: *Cheese International Varieties 6*

Danish protest: *Pigs 15*

Danish Red: *Other Cows 15*

Danish tilsit: *Cheese International Varieties 6*

danish: *Donut/doughnut 6*

Danish: *Human Ethnic Groups 1*

Danse de caractère: *Ballet Terms 13*

Danse: *Ballet Terms 13*

Danu (goddess of fertility): *Celtic Pantheon 14*

Danube: *Horse Breeds 15*

dao: *Swords One-handed 7*

daoine sidhe: *Fae Related 16*

Daoist Jade Books in Heaven: *Books of Legend 18*

daphne: *Poisonous Plants 10; Shrubs 10*

Daphnis: *Moons 11*

Darcy: *Soil General Vocabulary 10*

Darcy's law: *Soil General Vocabulary 10*

Darda'il: *Angels of Good 14*

Dardo C13 infantry fighting vehicle: *Italy Military Vehicles 8*

daring: *General Emotions 20; Personality Other 1*

darjeeling: *Tea 6*

dark blue sapphire: *Star Gems 21*

dark blue: *Blue 20*

dark brown sugar: *Staples 6*

dark circles: *Eye Type 1*

dark corn syrup: *Staples 6*

dark dagger: *Moth 15*

dark earth: *Soil General Vocabulary 10*

dark future: *Plot Devices 22*

dark glasses: *Spy Gear 5*

dark gray: *Gray 20*

dark knight: *Common Character Archetypes 21*

dark lady: *Common Character Archetypes 21*

dark lord: *Common Character Archetypes 21*

dark matter star: *Star Types and Relatives 11*

dark matter: *Astronomy General Terms 11; Spaceship Drive Systems 22; Weapons 22*

dark naga: *Beast 16*

dark olive: *Green 20*

dark opal: *Minerals 10*

dark purple sapphire: *Star Gems 21*

dark red kidney bean: *Legumes 6*

dark red: *Red 20*

dark rye: *Bread General Varieties 6*

dark spring green: *Green 20*

dark zone: *Cave Anatomy 10*

dark: *Beer 6; Candy Chocolate 6; Dwarf 1; Elf 1; Vocal/Speech Quality 1*

darkmantle: *Beast 16*

dark-minded: *Sad 20*

darkness generating: *Weapons 22*

darkness: *Philosophy Basic Concepts 14; Ten Plagues on Egypt 14*

darling: *Terms of Endearment 1*

Darlington oak: *Deciduous Trees 10*

Darmstadtium: *Elements 11*

darn: *Expletives 20*

darnel: *Poisonous Plants 10*

darner: *Dragonfly 15*

darning needle: *Sewing Equipment 2*

dart throwing: *Amusement Park/Carnival/Circus/Fair 3*

dart: *Garment Pieces 2; Locomotion 9; Missile Weapons 7; Sewing Terms 2*

darter: *Dragonfly 15*

Dartmoor Pony: *Horse Breeds 15*

darts: *Traps 3*

daruma: *Objects in Magic and Religion 19*

Darwin: *Frogs 15*

Darwin's: *Foxes 15*

Dash 7: *U.S. Army Aircraft 8*

dash: *Locomotion 9*

dastardly: *Horror Vocabulary 23*

dasyus: *Demon 16*

database: *Computer Equipment 5*

date nut: *Cake 6*

date: *Cake 6; Pie 6; Tropical/Exotic Fruits 6; Unusual Edible Fruits 6*

dated: *Old 20*

datura: *Poisonous Plants 10*

Dauan Island water: *Python 15*

daughter nuclide: *Chemistry General Vocabulary 11*

daughter product: *Geological Vocabulary 10*

daughter: *Female 1*

daughter-in-law: *Female 1*

daunt: *Close/Hold 20*

daunting: *Sad 20; Unattractive 20*

dauphinite: *Minerals 10*

davenport: *Seating 4*

Davy Crockett: *Real People with Legendary Status 18; Tall Tales 18*

dawdle: *Locomotion 9*

dawdling: *Slow 20*

day care center: *Business Property 3*

daylily: *Garden Perennials 10; Wildflowers 10*

day trip: *Journey 20*

day: *Beds 4*

daydream: *Magic Vocabulary 17*

daylight hole: *Cave Anatomy 10*

dazzling: *Beautiful 20*

de Côté: *Ballet Terms 13*

de facto segregation: *Geography General Vocabulary 10*

de jure segregation: *Geography General Vocabulary 10*

De Stijl: *Art Movements 13*

deacon: *Cleric 1; Religious Occupations 1*

dead battery: *Travel Hazards 9*

dead bolt: *Close/Hold 20*

dead cave: *Cave Anatomy 10*

dead end: *Roads 9*

dead ground: *Castle Anatomy 3*

dead man's fingers: *Unusual Edible Fruits 6*

dead man's float: *Swimming Strokes 9*

dead nettle: *Garden Perennials 10*

dead reckoning: *Boat/Ship Terminology 9*

Dead Sea Scrolls: *Major Religious Books 14*

dead: *Horror Vocabulary 23; Vocal/Speech Quality 1*

deadbolt: *Hardware 5; Locks 5*

deadfall: *Traps 3*

deadly nightshade: *Poisonous Plants 10*

deadly spider: *Traps 3*

deadly: *Horror Vocabulary 23*

deadweight: *Heavy 20*

Deadwood: *Famous Western Locations 21*

deaf: *Adder 15*

deafening: *Loud 20*

dealer's choice: *Poker Card Games 5*

dean: *Academic 1*

Dean-Stark apparatus: *Laboratory Equipment 5*

dear: *Terms of Endearment 1*

dearest: *Terms of Endearment 1*

dearinth: *Symbols in Magic and Religion 19*

death (pale or green horse): *Four Horsemen of the Apocalypse 19*

death cap: *Fungus Common Names 10*

death dealer: *Fighter 1*

death field: *Paranormal Abilities 21*

death of firstborn: *Ten Plagues on Egypt 14*

death ray: *Weapons 22*

death row: *Prison 3*

death: *Adder 15; Masks 2; Philosophy Basic Concepts 14; Witchcraft Vocabulary 17*

Death's scythe: *Weapons of Legend 18*

death's-head hawkmoth: *Moth 15*

deathcamas: *Poisonous Plants 10*

death-dealer: *Assassin 1*

death-of-man: *Poisonous Plants 10*

deathstalker: *Scorpion 15*

deathtrap house kills all visitors: *Horror Plot Devices 23*

debased: *Bad 20; Unattractive 20*

debauched: *Bad 20*

debutante: *Social Distinction 1*

debye: *Chemistry General Vocabulary 11*

decaborane: *Dangerous Chemicals 11*

decadent: *Good 20*

decaf: *Coffee Drinks 6*

decaisnea: *Shrubs 10*

decanter: *Containers and Vessels 5*

decay: *Smells 20*

decayed: *Teeth 1*

deceitful: *Horror Vocabulary 23*

decent: *Good 20; Personality Other 1*

deception: *Fencing Vocabulary 7*

deciduous holly: *Deciduous Trees 10*

deciduous trees: *Chapter 10*

deciduous: *Teeth 1*

decimate: *Kill 20*

decipher: *Solve 20*

deck: *Boat/Ship Anatomy 9; Footwear/Shoes 2; Outdoor Property 3; Rooms 3*

Declaration of Independence: *Independence Day 19*

declare: *Speak 20*

decline: *Grade/Slope 10*

declutter: *Clean 20*

decode: *Solve 20*

decoder: *Devices 22*

décolletage: *Sewing Terms 2*

decompose: *Smells 20*

decomposed: *Unattractive 20*

Deconstructivism: *Art Movements 13*

Deconstructivist Modern: *Architectural Styles 3*

decontaminate: *Clean 20*

decorate with holly and ivy: *Practices/Objects to Attract Good Luck 19*

Decorated Period: *Architectural Styles 3*

decorating tips: *Kitchen Equipment 5*

decoration: *Cave Anatomy 10; Christmas 19; Jewelry 21;*

decorations: *Halloween 19*

decorative: *Art Genres 13*

decrepit: *Unattractive 20*

decrescendo: *Dynamics 13*

dedicated: *Love 20; Personality Other 1*

dedication: *General Emotions 20*

deduce: *Solve 20*

deduction: *Philosophy Basic Concepts 14*

deep dish pie pan: *Kitchen Equipment 5*

deep fry: *Cooking Techniques 20*

deep fryer: *Appliances 5*

deep or multiple cuts: *Injuries/Medical Emergencies 12*

deep pink: *Pink 20*

deep sea explorer: *Vehicles 22*

Deep Sea Vents: *Seven Wonders of the Underwater World 18*

deep sea: *Octopi 15*

deep sky blue: *Blue 20*

deep space probe: *Spaceship Types 22*

deep venous thrombosis: *Blood-Related Ailments 12*

deep: *Ears 1; Loud 20; Vocal/Speech Quality 1*

deep-rooted: *Old 20*

deep-set: *Eye Type 1*

deer horn: *Daggers and Knives 7*

deer trail: *Roads 9*

deer: *Flies 15; Other Wild Mammals 15; Wild Game 6*

deerskin breeches: *Western Clothing/Dress 21*

deerstalker hat: *Headgear 2*

de-evolution: *Paranormal Abilities 21*

defeat: *General Combat Vocabulary 7; Kill 20*

defecation: *Excrement 12*

defector: *Hero or Villain, Depending Upon Circumstance 20*

defend: *General Combat Vocabulary 7*

defender: *Fighter 1*

defense communication system: *Satellite 8*

defense in depth: *General Combat Vocabulary 7*

defense support system: *Satellite 8*

defense: *General Combat Vocabulary 7; Moves 7*

defenseless: *Moves 7*

defile: *Slope 10*

defiled Indian burial ground initiates curse: *Western Plot Devices 21*

defiled: *Unattractive 20*

defined: *Sailing Knots 9*

definition: *Philosophy Basic Concepts 14*

defunct: *Old 20*

defy: *Speak 20*

degenerate: *Bad 20; Chemistry General Vocabulary 11; Star Types and Relatives 11*

degraded: *Unattractive 20*

degree day: *Geography General Vocabulary 10*

degree: *Geography General Vocabulary 10; Meteorology General Vocabulary 10*

dehydrated: *Dry 10*

dehydration: *Injuries/Medical Emergencies 12; Travel Hazards 9*

Deimos: *Moons 11*

deinonychus: *Commonly Known Dinosaurs 15*

dejected: *Horror Vocabulary 23; Sad 20*

dekalbite: *Minerals 10*

Del Mar pine: *Evergreen Trees 10*

Delaware: *Chickens 15*

delaying: *Slow 20*

delectable: *Beautiful 20*

deli potato chip: *Snacks 6*

deliberate: *Slow 20*

Deliboz: *Horse Breeds 15*

delicate girl with fighting prowess: *Common Character Archetypes 21*

delicate: *Small/Fragile 20; Small/Thin 1*

delicious milky cap: *Fungus Common Names 10*

delicious: *Beautiful 20*

delight: *Happy 20; Love 20*

delighted: *Happy 20*

delightful: *Beautiful 20; Good 20; Happy 20*

delinquent: *Illicit Occupations 1*

delirious: *Happy 20*

delivery: *Motorized Truck 9*

dell: *Slope 10; Terrain Features 10*

delocalization: *Chemistry General Vocabulary 11*

Delphinus: *Constellations 11*

Delta post oak: *Deciduous Trees 10*

Delta Works/Zuidersee Works: *Seven Wonders of the Modern World 18*

delta: *Fluvial 10; Geological Vocabulary 10; Water Features 10*

deluge: *Precipitation 10*

delusion: *Magic Vocabulary 17*

delve: *Learn 20; Locomotion 9*

demanding: *Difficult 20*

demantoid garnet: *Standard Gems 21*

demantoid: *Minerals 10*

Demeter (goddess of fertility and agriculture): *Greek Pantheon 14*

demeton: *Dangerous Chemicals 11*

demeton-s-methyl: *Dangerous Chemicals 11*

demi bra: *Ladies' Wear 2*

demi-cannon: *Cannon 7*

demicastor hat: *Headgear 2*

demi-culvern: *Cannon 7*

Demi-plié: *Ballet Terms 13*

demisemiquaver: *Notation 13*

demitasse cup: *Drinkware 5*

Democrat: *Political Parties 1*

demography: *Geography General Vocabulary 10*

demolish: *Kill 20*

demolisher: *Assassin 1, Fighter 1; Villain 20*

demon of the lotus cave: *Demon 16*

demon patience: *Solitaire Card Games 5*

demon: *Fantasy Creatures with Symbolic Meaning 19; Monsters 16; Monsters and Creatures 22*

demonology: *Books of Legend 18*

demons: *Horror Genres 23*

demoralized: *Horror Vocabulary 23*

den: *Criminal Property 3; Natural Animal Homes 15; Rooms 3*

denaturation: *Chemistry General Vocabulary 11*

denatured: *Chemistry General Vocabulary 11*

Dendera lamp: *Real Objects Not Fully Understood 18*

dendrite: *Geological Vocabulary 10*

dendritic agate: *Minerals 10; Standard Gems 21*

dendritic crystals: *Snow Types 10*

dendrochronology: *Geologic Fields of Study 10*

dengue fever: *Diseases 12*

denim: *Fabric 2*

dense blazing star: *Wildflowers 10*

dense gentian: *Garden Perennials 10*

dense: *Heavy 20; Unintelligent 1*

density control: *Paranormal Abilities 21; Physical Mutations 22*

density: *Astronomy General Terms 11; Chemistry General Vocabulary 11*

dent: *Harm 20*

dental floss: *Personal Care 5*

dental implants: *Teeth Dental Work 1*

dental office: *Health Care 3*

dental work: *Character Building 1*

dented: *Special Body Features 19; Unattractive 20*

dentures: *Teeth Dental Work 1*

deodorant: *Personal Care 5*

Deoni: *Other Cows 15*

depart: *Locomotion 9*

department store: *Business Property 3; Christmas 19*

department: *Political Divisions 10*

dependency: *Political Divisions 10*

depilatory: *Personal Care 5*

deplorable: *Sad 20; Unattractive 20*

deposition: *Chemistry General Vocabulary 11; Geological Vocabulary 10*

depository: *Business Property 3; General Buildings 3*

depot: *Business Property 3; General Buildings 3; Infrastructure Buildings 9*

depraved: *Bad 20; Difficult 20; Unattractive 20*

depressed arch: *Castle Anatomy 3*

depressed: *Horror Vocabulary 23; Sad 20*

depressing: *Sad 20*

depression: *Meteorology General Vocabulary 10; Terrain Features 10*

deputy: *Law Enforcement 1; Western Paraphernalia/People 21*

deranged killer stalks/attacks campground: *Horror Plot Devices 23*

derby hat: *Headgear 2*

Derbyshire redcap: *Chickens 15*

derisive: *Horror Vocabulary 23; Negative 1*

derivative: *Chemistry General Vocabulary 11*

dermal toxicity: *Chemistry General Vocabulary 11*

Dermantsi pied: *Pigs 15*

dermatologist: *Medical Occupations 1*

Derrière: *Ballet Terms 13*

derringer: *Combat, Armor, and Weapons 7; Spy Gear 5; Western Weapons 21*

dervish: *Styles of Dress 2*

descant: *General Music Vocabulary 13*

descend: *Locomotion 9*

descendant: *Relational 1*

descending colon: *Organs/Major Structures 12*

Deschutes jasper: *Minerals 10*

Desdemona: *Moons 11*

desert banana: *Unusual Edible Fruits 6*

desert box: *Freshwater Turtles 15*

desert death: *Adder 15*

desert dweller: *Barbarian 1*

desert false indigo: *Weeds 10*

desert fig: *Unusual Edible Fruits 6*

desert fir: *Evergreen Trees 10*

desert palm: *Deciduous Trees 10*

desert pavement: *Aeolian 10*

desert rose: *Minerals 10*

desert sand: *Brown 20*

desert terrain warfare: *General Combat Vocabulary 7*

desert varnish: *Aeolian 10*

desert white cedar: *Evergreen Trees 10*

desert woma: *Python 15*

desert: *Climatic Zones 10; Ecosystems 10; Elf 1; Terrain Features 10; Tortoises 15*

deserter: *General Combat Vocabulary 7; Hero or Villain, Depending Upon Circumstance 20*

desertion: *General Combat Vocabulary 7*

desertlike: *Warm 10*

desert-rose: *Poisonous Plants 10*

desfontainea: *Shrubs 10*

desiccated: *Dry 10*

desiccator: *Laboratory Equipment 5*

design: *Create 20*

designated area: *Chemistry General Vocabulary 11*

designing magical objects: *Magic 17*

designing spells: *Magic 17*

desirable: *Beautiful 20*

desire: *Love 20*

desired: *Beautiful 20*

desk clerk: *Hospitality 1; Law Enforcement 1*

desk lamp: *Illumination/Light Sources 5*

desktop PC: *Computer Equipment 5*

desolate: *Sad 20*

despicable: *Unattractive 20*

Despina: *Moons 11*

despoiled: *Unattractive 20*

despondent: *Sad 20*

despot: *Wizard 1*

dessert fork: *Eating Utensils 5*

dessert plate: *Tableware 5*

dessert spoon: *Eating Utensils 5*

dessert: *Food 6*

Dessous: *Ballet Terms 13*

Dessus: *Ballet Terms 13*

destoner: *General Farm Equipment*

destroy: *Attack 7; Harm 20; Kill 20*

destroyer: *Assassin 1; Fighter 1; Spaceship Types 22; Villain 20*

destroying angel: *Fungus Common Names 10*

destruction of Earth looms in seven days: *Horror Plot Devices 23*

destructive: *Negative 1*

detach: *Open/Release 20*

detached lobes: *Ears 1*

detachment fault: *Geological Vocabulary 10*

detain: *Close/Hold 20*

detect: *Learn 20*

detection: *Paranormal Abilities 21*

detective: *Horror Occupations 23; Law Enforcement 1*

detention center: *Prison 3*

deter: *Close/Hold 20*

detergent: *Chemistry General Vocabulary 11*

deteriorate: *Harm 20*

deteriorated: *Bad 20*

deteriorating: *Unattractive 20*

determination: *Ten Perfections of Buddhism 19*

determine: *Learn 20; Solve 20*

determined: *Personality Other 1; Stubborn 1*

determinism: *Philosophy Basic Concepts 14*

deterrence: *General Combat Vocabulary 7*

detestable: *Unattractive 20*

detestation: *General Emotions 20*

detonation: *Loud 20*

detour: *Journey 20*

detox clinic: *Health Care 3*

detracting: *Personality Other 1*

deuterium arc: *Illumination Bulb and Tube Types 5*

deuterium: *Chemistry General Vocabulary 11*

deutzia: *Shrubs 10*

Deux: *Ballet Terms 13*

Deuxième: *Ballet Terms 13*

devalpa: *Devil 16*

Devant: *Ballet Terms 13*

devastate: *Attack 7; Harm 20*

develop: *Buy 20; Fix 20; Learn 20*

developed: *Personality Other 1*

development editor: *Publishing 1*

Développé: *Ballet Terms 13*

deviation: *Boat/Ship Terminology 9*

device: *Jewelry 21; Miscellaneous Furniture 4*

devil bird: *Flying Creatures 16*

devil makes a deal: *Common Dangers 24*

devil shield: *Weeds 10*

devil: *Facial Hair Mustache 1; Monsters 16; Witchcraft Vocabulary 17*

devil's carriage: *Witchcraft Vocabulary 17*

devil's paintbrush: *Garden Perennials 10*

devil's tail tearthumb: *Weeds 10*

devil's walking stick: *Deciduous Trees 10*

deviled egg plate: *Tableware 5*

devilock: *Hair Style 1*

devils and angels: *Poisonous Plants 10*

devil's cherry: *Poisonous Plants 10*

devils food: *Cake 6*

devious: *Difficult 20; Horror Vocabulary 23*

devise: *Create 20*

Devon: *Other Cows 15*

Devonian Period: *Geologic Time 10*

Devonshire Rex: *Domestic Cats 15*

devoted: *Love 20; Personality Other 1*

devotion: *General Emotions 20*

devourer: *Extraplanar 16*

dew point: *Meteorology General Vocabulary 10*

dew: *Wet 10*

dewanambo: *Demon 16*

dewberry: *Unusual Edible Fruits 6*

dewdrop: *Wet 20*

deweylite: *Minerals 10*

Dexter: *Other Cows 15*

dexterity: *Physical Mutations 22*

dexterous: *Mobility 1*

dextrorotatory: *Chemistry General Vocabulary 11*

dha: *Swords One-handed 7*

Dhanni: *Other Cows 15*

dharma wheel: *Eight Ashtamangala 19*

dhoti: *Men's Wear 2*

diabase: *Igneous Rocks 10*

diabetes: *Diseases 12*

diadem: *Headgear 2; Jewelry 21*

diagenesis: *Cave Anatomy 10; Geological Vocabulary 10*

diagnostic medical scanner: *Devices 22*

diagnostician: *Medical Occupations 1*

diagonal similarities: *Chemistry General Vocabulary 11*

diagram: *Books/Publications 5; Laboratory Supplies 5*

dialectic: *Philosophy Basic Concepts 14*

dialifor: *Dangerous Chemicals 11*

diamagnetism: *Chemistry General Vocabulary 11*

diamictite: *Sedimentary Rocks 10*

diaminopropionic acid: *Poisonous Chemicals in Plants 11*

diamond saw blade: *Power Tools*

diamond tetra: *Aquarium Freshwater Fish 15*

diamond willow: *Deciduous Trees 10*

diamond: *Face 1; Python 15; Standard Gems 21; Valentine's Day 19*

diamondback terrapin: *Freshwater Turtles 15*

diamondback: *General Snake Families 15*

diamond-leaf oak: *Deciduous Trees 10*

diamonds: *Spy Gear 5*

Diana (goddess of the hunt, moon): *Roman Pantheon 14*

Diancecht (healing): *Celtic Pantheon 14*

dianhong: *Tea 6*

dianthus: *Garden Annuals 10*

diaper service: *Public Services 3*

diaphanous gowns: *Clothing/Uniforms 22*

diaphragm: *Organs/Major Structures 12*

diapir: *Geological Vocabulary 10*

diarrhea: *Excrement 12*

diary: *Books/Publications 5*

diasporite: *Minerals 10*

diatomacious opal: *Minerals 10*

diatomite: *Minerals 10; Sedimentary Rocks 10*

diatonic scale: *General Music Vocabulary 13*

dibble: *Garden Tools*

diborane: *Dangerous Chemicals 11*

dice: *Fortune Telling General Devices 19; Games 5; General Snake Families 15; Toys 5*

dichloroethyl: *Dangerous Chemicals 11*

dichlorvos: *Dangerous Chemicals 11*

Dick Turpin: *Real People with Legendary Status 18*

dickie: *Unisex Clothing 2*

dicrotophos: *Dangerous Chemicals 11*

dictaphone machine: *Office/School Machines 5*

dictionary stand: *Special Purpose Furniture 4*

dictionary: *Office/School/Writing Supplies 5*

die grinder: *Power Tools*

diepoxybutane: *Dangerous Chemicals 11*

diesel aircraft carrier: *Military Watercraft 8*

diesel engine: *Railroad 9*

diet feeder: *General Farm Equipment*

diet: *Literary Styles 5*

diethyl chlorophosphate: *Dangerous Chemicals 11*

different: *New 20*

differential scanning calorimetry: *Chemistry General Vocabulary 11*

differential thermal analysis: *Chemistry General Vocabulary 11*

differential thermometer: *Chemistry General Vocabulary 11*

difficult: *Adjectives 20; Negative 1; Sad 20*

diffident: *Horror Vocabulary 23*

diffuse knapweed: *Weeds 10*

digest: *Books/Publications 5*

digestive: *Body Systems 12*

digger: *Bees 15; Wasp 15*

digital painting: *Art Techniques 13*

digital: *Art Media 13*

digitoxin: *Dangerous Chemicals 11*

diglycidyl ether: *Dangerous Chemicals 11*

dignified: *Personality Other 1*

digoxin: *Dangerous Chemicals 11*

digs: *Residential Slang 3*

dijerido: *Wind/Woodwind and Brass Musical Instruments*

Dijon mustard: *Condiments 6*

dike: *Cave Anatomy 10; Fortification 3; Geological Vocabulary 10*

dilettante: *Personality Other 1; Social Distinction 1*

diligence: *Ten Perfections of Buddhism 19*

dill pickle: *Pickled/Relish 6*

dill weed: *Spices 6*

dilution: *Chemistry General Vocabulary 11*

dim: *Sad 20; Unintelligent 1*

dime: *Coins and Currency 21*

dimefox: *Dangerous Chemicals 11*

dimensional portal: *Doors Atypical 3*

dimensional slider: *Vehicles 22*

dimensional travel: *Magical Transportation 17*

dimensional: *Travel Modes 24; Travel Types 22*

dimension-crossing creature: *Monsters and Creatures 22*

dimer: *Chemistry General Vocabulary 11*

dimethoate: *Dangerous Chemicals 11*

dimethyl phosphorochloridothioate: *Dangerous Chemicals 11*

dimethyldichlorosilane: *Dangerous Chemicals 11*

dimethylhydrazine: *Dangerous Chemicals 11*

dimethyl-p-phenylenediamine: *Dangerous Chemicals 11*

dimetilan: *Dangerous Chemicals 11*

diminuendo: *Dynamics 13*

diminutive: *Small/Fragile 20; Small/Thin 1*

dimmer switch: *Building Systems 3*

dimmer: *Technical Terms 13*

dimsi: *Cheese International Varieties 6*

dim-witted: *Unintelligent 1*

Dinadan: *Knights of the Round Table 18*

diner: *Food/Drink Establishments 3*

dinghy: *Human-Powered Watercraft 9; Small Watercraft 9*

Dingo 4×4 armored car: *Australia Military Vehicles 8; United Kingdom Military Vehicles 8*

dining car: *Railroad 9*

dining hall: *Food/Drink Establishments 3*

dining room: *Tables 4*

dining: *Rooms 3*

dinitrocresol: *Dangerous Chemicals 11*

dinkelbrot: *Bread General Varieties 6*

dinner fork: *Eating Utensils 5; Improvised Weapons 7*

dinner knife: *Eating Utensils 5*

dinner plate: *Tableware 5*

dinner roll: *Bread General Varieties 6*

dinner suit: *Men's Wear 2*

dinner theater: *Performance Genres 13*

dinner: *Christmas 19; Salads 6; Thanksgiving 19; Valentine's Day 19*

dino-bird: *Dinosaur Types 15*

dinosaur types: *Animals 15*

dinosaurs brought back to life: *Horror Plot Devices 23*

dinosaurs: *Common Dangers 23; Toys 5*

dinoseb: *Dangerous Chemicals 11*

dinoterb: *Dangerous Chemicals 11*

diocese: *Groupings 14*

Dione: *Moons 11*

Dionysus (wine): *Greek Pantheon 14*

diopside: *Star Gems 21*

diorama: *Art Genres 13*

diorite: *Igneous Rocks 10*

dioxathion: *Dangerous Chemicals 11*

dip slope: *Geological Vocabulary 10*

dip: *Cave Anatomy 10*

dipelta: *Shrubs 10*

diphacinone: *Dangerous Chemicals 11*

diphtheria: *Diseases 12*

diplodocus: *Commonly Known Dinosaurs 15*

dipole moment: *Chemistry General Vocabulary 11*

dipole: *Chemistry General Vocabulary 11*

dipole-dipole interactions: *Chemistry General Vocabulary 11*

dipped: *Candles 5*

dire: *Bad 20; Horror Vocabulary 23; Unattractive 20*

direct attack: *Fencing Vocabulary 7*

director: *General Occupations 1; Musical Occupations 1; Performing Arts 1*

directory: *Laboratory Supplies 5*

dirigible: *Air Vehicles 9*

dirk: *Daggers and Knives 7*

dirndl skirt: *Ladies' Wear 2*

dirt cone: *Glacial and Mountain 10*

dirt: *Improvised Weapons 7*

dirty hotel room: *Travel Hazards 9*

dirty Schultz: *Poker Card Games 5*

dirty: *Unattractive 20*

disappointed: *Sad 20*

disapproving: *Negative 1*

disarm: *Moves 7*

disarmed: *Special Body Features 19*

disaster traps people in office building/cruise ship: *Horror Genres 23*

disastrous: *Bad 20*

disbelieving: *Horror Vocabulary 23*

discern: *Learn 20*

discharge: *Attack 7; Open/Release 20*

disciple: *Cleric 1*

disco suit: *Men's Wear 2*

disco: *Dance Styles 13; Entertainment Property 3*

discolored: *Teeth 1*

disconformity: *Geological Vocabulary 10*

disconsolate: *Sad 20*

Discord: *Bows 18*

discotheque: *Entertainment Property 3*

discourage: *General Emotions 20*

discouraged: *Horror Vocabulary 23; Sad 20*

discouraging: *Sad 20*

discover: *Learn 20*

discovery of God: *Plot Devices 22*

discovery of unknown creature/civilization: *Horror Genres 23*

discus: *Aquarium Freshwater Fish 15*

disdainful: *Negative 1*

disease/rot/transformation of body: *Horror Plot Devices 23*

diseases: *Anatomy and Physiology 12*

disembodied voice: *Paranormal Occurrences 21*

disembodied: *Vocal/Speech Quality 1*

disenchant: *Magic Vocabulary 17*

disenchanted: *Magic Vocabulary 17*

disengage: *Fencing Vocabulary 7; Moves 7; Open/Release 20*

disentangle: *Open/Release 20; Solve 20*

disgraceful: *Sad 20*

disguise kit: *Specialty Survival Gear 5; Spy Gear 5*

disgust: *General Emotions 20; Philosophy Basic Concepts 14*

disgusting: *Negative 1; Unattractive 20*

dish cloth: *Towels 5*

dish rag: *Towels 5*

dish: *Towels 5*

disheartening: *Sad 20*

dishes: *Toys 5*

dishonest: *Bad 20*

dishonored: *Unattractive 20*

dishwasher: *Major Appliances 4*

dishwater blond: *Hair Color 1*

disillusion: *Magic Vocabulary 17*

disillusioned: *Personality Other 1*

disinfect: *Clean 20*

disintegrated: *Bad 20*

disintegration beam: *Devices 22*

disintegration: *Weapons 22*

disk harrow: *General Farm Equipment*

disk: *Astronomy General Terms 11; Jewelry 21*

disk-winged: *Bats 15*

dislike: *General Emotions 20*

dismal: *Bad 20; Horror Vocabulary 23; Sad 20; Unattractive 20*

dismayed: *Horror Vocabulary 23; Sad 20*

disorganized: *Personality Other 1*

disparage: *General Emotions 20*

disparaging: *Negative 1*

dispatch: *Attack 7*

dispersed phase: *Chemistry General Vocabulary 11*

dispersing medium: *Chemistry General Vocabulary 11*

dispersion: *Soil General Vocabulary 10*

dispirit: *Sad 20*

dispirited: *Sad 20*

dispiriting: *Sad 20*

displacement reactions: *Chemistry General Vocabulary 11*

displacement: *Fencing Vocabulary 7*

displayed: *Air Creatures 19*

displease: *General Emotions 20*

disposable contact lenses: *Optics 5*

disposable razor: *Personal Care 5*

disproportionation reactions: *Chemistry General Vocabulary 11*

disprove: *Solve 20*

dispute: *General Combat Vocabulary 7*

disquiet: *Horror Vocabulary 23*

disrespectful: *Negative 1*

dissected plateau: *Erosion 10*

dissecting pins: *Laboratory Equipment 5*

disseminated intravascular coagulation: *Blood-Related Ailments 12*

dissipated: *Bad 20*

dissociation constant: *Chemistry General Vocabulary 11*

dissociation: *Chemistry General Vocabulary 11*

dissonance: *General Music Vocabulary 13*

distal phalange: *Bones 12*

distasteful: *Horror Vocabulary 23; Unattractive 20*

distill: *Witchcraft Vocabulary 17*

distilland: *Chemistry General Vocabulary 11*

distillate: *Chemistry General Vocabulary 11*

distillation: *Chemistry General Vocabulary 11*

distinguish: *Learn 20*

distinguished: *Personality Other 1*

distress: *Horror Vocabulary 23*

distressed: *Old 20; Sad 20; Unattractive 20*

distressing: *Sad 20*

district: *Political Divisions 10*

distrust: *Philosophy Basic Concepts 14*

distrustful: *Horror Vocabulary 23; Negative 1*

disturb: *General Emotions 20*

disturbance: *Meteorology General Vocabulary 10*

disturbed Indian burial ground: *Horror Locations 23*

disulfoton: *Dangerous Chemicals 11*

ditch: *Fortification 3; Terrain Features 10*

dithiazanine iodide: *Dangerous Chemicals 11*

dithiobiuret: *Dangerous Chemicals 11*

dittany of Crete: *Garden Perennials 10*

ditto machine: *Office/School Machines 5*

ditto master: *Office/School/Writing Supplies 5*

div: *Devil 16*

diva: *Bard 1; Singer 1*

divan: *Seating 4*

dive: *Locomotion 9*

diver: *Horror Occupations 23; Maritime Occupations 1*

divergent plate boundary: *Geological Vocabulary 10*

divertimento: *Composition Types 13*

Divertissement: *Ballet Terms 13; Dance Moves 13*

divided bowl: *Tableware 5*

divided highway: *Roads 9*

divider: *Building Elements and Features 3*

divine intervention: *Common Character Archetypes 21*

divine: *Beautiful 20; Magic Vocabulary 17*

diviner: *Nature Occupations 1; Wizard 1*

divining rod: *Fortune Telling General Devices 19; Objects in Magic and Religion 19; Witchcraft Vocabulary 17*

divining: *Exploration 9*

divinity: *Candy General 6*

division: *Political Divisions 10*

Dixie Henry: *Lever Action and Pump Centerfire Rifles 7*

Djed: *Real Objects Not Fully Understood 18*

djed: *Symbols in Magic and Religion 19*

Djerma: *Horse Breeds 15*

djinn: *Demon 16*

djinni: *Extraplanar 16*

do ya: *Poker Card Games 5*

dobby weave: *Fabric 2*

Doberman Pinscher: *Dog Breeds 15*

Doc Holliday: *Real People with Legendary Status 18; Western Paraphernalia/People 21*

dock: *Marina 3; Water Terms 9*

docking station: *Computer Equipment 5*

dockside: *Marina 3*

dockyard: *Marina 3*

doctor: *Horror Occupations 23; Medical Occupations 1*

doctor's office: *Health Care 3*

docudrama: *Performance Genres 13*

document box: *Containers and Vessels 5*

document feeder: *Office/School Machines 5*

document shredder: *Office/School Machines 5*

document: *Books/Publications 5*

doddering: *Elderly 1*

Dodge City: *Famous Western Locations 21*

dodge: *Moves 7*

Dodinas le Savage: *Knights of the Round Table 18*

dodo: *Demon 16*

doeskin: *Fabric 2*

dog breeds: *Animals 15*

dog cart: *Animal-Powered Transportation 9*

dog catcher: *General Occupations 1*

dog collar: *Accessories 2*

dog door: *Doors Atypical 3*

dog groups: *Animals 15*

dog house: *Man-Made Animal Homes 15; Property Features 3*

dog paddle: *Swimming Strokes 9*

dog sled: *Animal-Powered Transportation 9*

dog tag silencers: *Military Equipment 8*

dog tags: *Jewelry 21; Military Equipment 8*

dog: *Allergies 12; Animals with Symbolic Meaning 19; Bears 15; Chinese Horoscope 19; Objects/Activities Connected to Lore 19*

dog's tooth violet: *Garden Bulbs 10*

dogbane: *Beetle 15*

dogberry: *Deciduous Trees 10*

dogfish: *Sharks 15*

doghobble: *Shrubs 10*

dogma: *Philosophy Basic Concepts 14*

dogs: *Animals 15*

dog-strangling vine: *Weeds 10*

dogtooth calcite: *Minerals 10*

dogtooth spar: *Minerals 10*

dog-toothed violet: *Garden Perennials 10*

Dogue de Bordeaux: *Dog Breeds 15*

dogwood: *Shrubs 10*

doily: *Miscellaneous Linens 5*

dojo: *Special Purpose Structure 3*

Dølafe: *Other Cows 15*

doldrums: *Meteorology General Vocabulary 10*

Døle: *Horse Breeds 15*

doleful: *Sad 20*

doll bed: *Toys 5*

doll buggy: *Toys 5*

doll clothes: *Toys 5*

doll stroller: *Toys 5*

doll: *Christmas 19; Classic Items 23; Female 1; Toys 5; Typical Magical Objects 17*

doll's eyes: *Garden Perennials 10*

dollar: *Coins and Currency 21; Minerals 10*

doll's eyes: *Poisonous Plants 10*

dolly: *Human-Powered Transportation 9; Technical Terms 13*

dolman sleeve: *Garment Pieces 2*

dolomite rock: *Minerals 10*

dolomite: *Sedimentary Rocks 10*

dolostone: *Minerals 10; Sedimentary Rocks 10*

dolphin crawl: *Swimming Strokes 9*

dolphin kick: *Swimming Strokes 9*

dolphin: *Animals with Symbolic Meaning 19*

dolphins: *Animals 15*

domain: *Chemistry General Vocabulary 11*

dome: *Cave Anatomy 10*

domed citadel: *Fantasy Locations 24*

domed city: *Plot Devices 22*

domed colony: *Installations 22*

domestic cats: *Animals 15*

domestic long hair: *Domestic Cats 15*

domestic medium hair: *Domestic Cats 15*

domestic shorthair: *Domestic Cats 15*

domestic: *Housekeeping 1*

domesticated farm birds: *Animals 15*

domesticated pet birds: *Animals 15*

domicile: *Residential Property 3*

dominate: *Magic Vocabulary 17*

domination: *Paranormal Abilities 21*

dominatrix: *Boots 2*

dominion: *Angels Common Terms 14*

Dominique: *Chickens 15*

domino damsel: *Aquarium Saltwater Fish 15*

dominoes: *Toys 5*

domovoi: *Demon 16*

Don hairless: *Domestic Cats 15*

Donard: *Knights of the Round Table 18*

Donati's: *Comets 11*

dong dang gui: *Garden Perennials 10*

Dongola: *Horse Breeds 15*

donjon: *Fortification 3*

donkey: *Animals with Symbolic Meaning 19; Christmas 19; Horses Related 15; Transportation Animals 9*

donor atom: *Chemistry General Vocabulary 11*

donor: *Common Character Archetypes 21*

donut cutter: *Kitchen Utensils 5*

donut hole: *Donut/doughnut 6*

donut peach: *Pit Fruits 6*

donut: *Food 6*

doo-doo: *Excrement 12*

doomsday: *Horror Genres 23; Science Fiction Genres 22*

door chime: *Building Elements and Features 3*

door jamb: *Building Elements and Features 3*

door opens/closes: *Paranormal Occurrences 21*

door: *Locks 5; Secular Symbols 19; Traps 3*

doorbell: *Building Elements and Features 3*

doorman: *Hospitality 1; Supporting Cast 24*

doors: *Architecture and Property 3*

doorway: *Building Elements and Features 3; Secular Symbols 19*

doppelganger: *Shapechanger 16*

doppelkopf: *Card Games 5*

Doppler effect: *Astronomy General Terms 11*

Dorado: *Constellations 11*

do-rag: *Headgear 2*

D-orbitals: *Chemistry General Vocabulary 11*

Dorian: *Human Ethnic Groups 1*

dorje: *Symbols in Magic and Religion 19*

Dorking: *Chickens 15*

dormant cave: *Cave Anatomy 10*

dormant: *Land Creatures 19*

dormer: *Castle Anatomy 3*

dormitory: *Residential Property 3*

Dorset gold tip: *Pigs 15*

dory: *Spears 7*

dosimeter: *Chemistry General Vocabulary 11*

dossier: *Spy Gear 5*

dot: *Figures Associated with Symbols 19*

dotage: *Elderly 1*

dōtanuki: *Swords Two-handed 7*

dotted Swiss: *Fabric Patterns 2*

dotted-stalk suillus: *Fungus Common Names 10*

doubah: *Unusual Edible Fruits 6*

double action revolver: *Combat, Armor, and Weapons 7*

double agent: *Hero or Villain, Depending Upon Circumstance 20; Law Enforcement 1*

double attack: *Fencing Vocabulary 7*

double bar line: *Notation 13*

double bass: *String Musical Instruments*

double bassoon: *Wind/Woodwind and Brass Musical Instruments*

double bird's foot trefoil: *Garden Perennials 10*

double blanket: *Embroidery Stitches 2*

double boiler: *Kitchen Equipment 5*

double bond: *Chemistry General Vocabulary 11*

double brain: *Physical Mutations 22*

double bubble mint: *Garden Perennials 10*

double Cabriole: *Ballet Terms 13*

double chain: *Embroidery Stitches 2*

double coconut: *Unusual Edible Fruits 6*

double cross: *Embroidery Stitches 2*

double crust: *Pie 6*

double daffodil: *Garden Bulbs 10*

double darning: *Embroidery Stitches 2*

double decker bus: *Mass Transit 9*

double distlefink: *Pennsylvania Dutch Hex Signs 19*

double draw: *Poker Card Games 5*

double featherstitch: *Embroidery Stitches 2*

double fisherman's: *Sailing Knots 9*

double flat: *Notation 13*

double gloriosa: *Garden Perennials 10*

double happiness: *Secular Symbols 19*

double hung: *Windows 3*

double knit: *Fabric 2*

double oven: *Major Appliances 4*

double pitch: *Roof Styles 3*

double robin white breast: *Garden Perennials 10*

double salt: *Chemistry General Vocabulary 11*

double sharp: *Notation 13*

double sink: *Bathroom Features and Fixtures 3*

double sir: *Card Games 5*

double star: *Astronomy General Terms 11*

double stop: *Instrument Technique 13*

double time: *Fast 20*

double trinity tulips: *Pennsylvania Dutch Hex Signs 19*

double trudgeon crawl: *Swimming Strokes 9*

double trudgeon: *Swimming Strokes 9*

double tulip: *Garden Bulbs 10*

double weave: *Fabric 2*

double: *Ballet Terms 13*

double: *Beds 4*

double: *Chin 1*

double: *Doors 3*

double: *Solitaire Card Games 5*

double-barreled: *Shotguns General 7*

double-breasted suit: *Men's Wear 2*

double-deck: *Bridges 9*

double-ended flail: *Chain Weapons 7*

double-headed eagle: *Fantasy Creatures with Symbolic Meaning 19; Pennsylvania Dutch Hex Signs 19*

double-headed: *Axes 7*

double-queued: *Special Body Features 19*

Doublestar Marksman: *Semiautomatic Centerfire Rifles 7*

doublet: *Armor Pieces 7; Chemistry General Vocabulary 11; Men's Wear 2*

doubloon: *Coins and Currency 21*

doubt: *Horror Vocabulary 23; Philosophy Basic Concepts 14*

doubtful: *Horror Vocabulary 23*

douc: *Old World Monkeys 15*

dough: *Bread General Varieties 6*

doughboy: *Property Features 3*

doughnut: *Food 6*

doughy: *Large/Heavy 1*

Douglas fir: *Evergreen Trees 10*

dour: *Sad 20*

douroucouli: *New World Monkeys 15*

douse: *Wet 20*

dove: *Animals with Symbolic Meaning 19; Other Wild Birds 15*

Dover sole: *Wild Saltwater Fish 15*

dovetailed: *Partition Lines 19*

dowager: *Common Character Archetypes 21; Elderly 1*

dowdy: *Styles of Dress 2*

dowel: *Fasteners 5*

down in the dumps: *Sad 20*

down in the mouth: *Sad 20*

downburst: *Meteorology General Vocabulary 10*

downcast: *Horror Vocabulary 23; Sad 20*

downdraft: *Meteorology General Vocabulary 10*

Downer soil: *Soil General Vocabulary 10*

downer: *Negative 1*

downhearted: *Horror Vocabulary 23*

down-hearted: *Sad 20*

downhill creep: *Soil General Vocabulary 10*

downhill skis: *Sporting Goods Other 5*

downlight: *Technical Terms 13*

downpour: *Precipitation 10*

Downs cell: *Chemistry General Vocabulary 11*

downspout: *Building Elements and Features 3*

downstage: *Stage Directions 13*

downstairs maid: *Housekeeping 1*

down-to-earth: *Easy 20*

downtown: *City 10*

downwind: *Boat/Ship Terminology 9; Meteorology General Vocabulary 10*

downy brome: *Weeds 10*

downy emerald: *Dragonfly 15*

downy serviceberry: *Deciduous Trees 10*

doyleite: *Minerals 10*

dozy: *Slow 20*

DP number: *Chemistry General Vocabulary 11*

DPM convoy escort vehicle: *Russia Military Vehicles 8*

DPMS Panther: *Semiautomatic Centerfire Rifles 7*

Dr. Frankenstein: *Fictional Characters 18*

Dr. John Watson: *Sir Arthur Conan Doyle 18*

drab: *Sad 20*

Draco: *Constellations 11*

draft: *Boat/Ship Terminology 9; Wind 10*

drag harrow: *General Farm Equipment; Steam Powered Farm Equipment*

drag racer: *Motorized 9*

drag: *Locomotion 9*

Dragestil: *Architectural Styles 3*

dragon (China): *Ethnic/Folk Dances 13*

dragon chariot of Medea: *Objects 18*

dragon chariot of Triptolemus: *Objects 18*

dragon or fantasy creature appears in nonfantasy world: *Fantasy Plot Devices 24*

Dragon Rouge: *Books of Legend 18*

dragon scales: *Wizard's Goods 5*

dragon skin: *Body Armor 7*

dragon tree: *Shrubs 10*

dragon: *Chinese Horoscope 19; Fantasy Creatures with Symbolic Meaning 19; Magical Transportation 17; Masks 2; Monsters 16; Witchcraft Vocabulary 17*

dragon's lair: *Fantasy Locations 24*

dragon's teeth: *Objects 18*

dragonfly: *Animals 15*

dragonfruit: *Unusual Edible Fruits 6*

dragonhead: *Garden Perennials 10*

dragonne: *Beast 16*

Dragoon 300 wheeled armored fighting vehicle: *United States Military Vehicles 8*

dragster: *Motorized 9*

drain: *Flies 15*

drainage basin: *Fluvial 10*

drainage research: *Soil General Vocabulary 10*

drained: *Horror Vocabulary 23*

drama queen: *Personality Other 1*

drama: *Literary Styles 5; Masks 2; Performance Genres 13*

dramatic: *Beautiful 20; Personality Other 1; Vocal/Speech Quality 1*

drape: *Technical Terms 13*

draperies: *Window Treatments 5*

drapery: *Cave Anatomy 10*

drapes: *Window Treatments 5*

drat: *Expletives 20*

Draupnir: *Jewelry 18*

dravite: *Minerals 10*

draw and discard bridge: *Card Games 5*

draw knife: *Hand Tools 5*

draw sheet: *Bed Linens 5*

draw: *Bridges 9; Poker Card Games 5; Slope 10*

drawbridge: *Card Games 5; Castle Anatomy 3*

drawers: *Men's Wear 2*

drawing base: *Art Materials 5*

drawing: *Art Techniques 13*

drawl: *Vocal/Speech Quality 1*

drawn-out: *Slow 20*

drawstring bag: *Accessories 2*

drawstring: *Embellishments 2; Garment Pieces 2*

dread: *General Emotions 20; Horror Vocabulary 23*

dreadful: *Bad 20; Unattractive 20*

dreadlocks: *Hair Style 1*

dreadnought: *Spaceship Types 22; Military Watercraft 8*

dream: *Art Genres 13; Magic Vocabulary 17*

dreamcatcher netting: *Harbingers/Charms for Good Luck 19*

dreamcatcher: *Objects in Magic and Religion 19*

dreamer: *Illusionist 1; Wizard 1*

dreaming: *Magic Vocabulary 17*

dreamy: *Slow 20*

dreary: *Sad 20*

dreidel: *Objects in Magic and Religion 19*

dreikanter: *Aeolian 10*

dren: *Expletives 20*

drench: *Wet 20*

drenching: *Precipitation 10*

dress gloves: *Unisex Clothing 2*

dress rehearsal: *Stage Terms 13*

dress shirt: *Men's Wear 2*

dress: *Footwear/Shoes 2; Ladies' Wear 2; Socks 2*

dressed up: *Styles of Dress 2*

dresser scarf: *Miscellaneous Linens 5*

dresser: *Storage 4*

dressing gown: *Unisex Clothing 2*

dressing room: *Parts of the Theater 13; Rooms 3*

dressing: *Bread General Varieties 6; Thanksgiving 19*

dressmaker's form: *Sewing Equipment 2*

dressy: *Styles of Dress 2*

drey: *Natural Animal Homes 15*

dribble: *Precipitation 10; Wet 20*

dried leaves: *Wizard's Goods 5*

drift: *Locomotion 9; Meteorology General Vocabulary 10*

drifter: *Barbarian 1; Thief 1*

drifting snow: *Meteorology General Vocabulary 10*

drifting: *Boat/Ship Terminology 9*

drilbu: *Objects in Magic and Religion 19*

drill bit: *Hand Tools 5*

drill core: *Geological Vocabulary 10*

drill press: *Power Tools*

drill: *Fabric 2; Hand Tools 5; Old World Monkeys 15; Teach 20*

drilosphere: *Soil General Vocabulary 10*

drink establishment: *Architecture and Property 3*

drinking hole: *Food/Drink Establishments 3*

drinkware: *Equipment and Tools 5*

drip irrigation: *General Farm Equipment*

drip: *Precipitation 10; Wet 20*

dripline: *Cave Anatomy 10*

dripstone: *Cave Anatomy 10*

drive engineer: *Occupations 22*

drive: *Commands 20; Locomotion 9; Roads 9*

drive-in: *Food/Drink Establishments 3*

driven: *Personality Other 1*

driver cap: *Headgear 2*

driver: *Ants 15; Transportation 1*

driveway: *Property Features 3*

driving gloves: *Unisex Clothing 2*

driving rain: *Precipitation 10*

driving range: *Property Features 3*

drizzle: *Precipitation 10*

dromaeosaur: *Commonly Known Dinosaurs 15*

drone: *Ants 15; Bees 15; Military Aircraft Pre-1962 8; Sounds 20; Speak 20*

drool: *Wet 20*

drooping brome: *Weeds 10*

droopy: *Personality Other 1; Slow 20*

drop anchor: *Boat/Ship Terminology 9*

drop arch: *Castle Anatomy 3*

drop: *Cookie 6; Locomotion 9; Precipitation 10; Wet 20*

drop-leaf: *Tables 4*

droplet: *Wet 20*

dropper: *Laboratory Equipment 5*

dropping funnel: *Laboratory Equipment 5*

droppings: *Excrement 12*

drought: *Meteorology General Vocabulary 10*

Droughtmaster: *Other Cows 15*

drover: *Transportation 1*

drown: *Harm 20*

drowning: *Injuries/Medical Emergencies 12*

Druaga (evil): *Babylonian Pantheon 14*

Drucker Prager yield criterion: *Soil General Vocabulary 10*

drug dealer: *Illicit Occupations 1; Travel Hazards 9*

drug mule: *Illicit Occupations 1*

drug trafficker: *Travel Hazards 9*

drug: *Demon 16*

druggist: *Medical Occupations 1*

drugstore: *Health Care 3*

druid: *Nature Occupations 1*

druid's circle: *Fantasy Property 3*

druid's grove: *Fantasy Property 3*

drum sieve: *Kitchen Utensils 5*

drum tower: *Castle Anatomy 3*

drum: *Containers and Vessels 5; Percussion Musical Instruments 5; Signal Devices 5; Typical Magical Objects 17*

drumlin field: *Glacial and Mountain 10*

drumlin: *Geological Vocabulary 10; Glacial and Mountain 10*

Drummer soil: *Soil General Vocabulary 10*

Drummond phlox: *Wildflowers 10*

Drummond post oak: *Deciduous Trees 10*

Drummond soapberry: *Deciduous Trees 10*

drumstick mushroom: *Fungus Common Names 10*

drumstick primrose: *Garden Perennials 10*

drumsticks: *Music Accessories*

drunk becomes hero: *Western Plot Devices 21*

druze star: *Symbols in Magic and Religion 19*

dry bone ore: *Minerals 10*

dry cells: *Chemistry General Vocabulary 11*

dry clean: *Clean 20*

dry cleaner: *Business Property 3*

dry erase board: *Laboratory Equipment 5; Office/School/Writing Supplies 5*

dry erase marker: *Office/School/Writing Supplies 5*

dry farming: *Geography General Vocabulary 10*

dry Jack: *Cheese Common Varieties 6*

dry lake: *Aeolian 10*

dry leaves: *Halloween 19*

dry marsala:Wine Red 6

dry mop: *Clean 20*

dry quicksand: *Soil General Vocabulary 10*

dry roasted peanut: *Nuts 6*

dry run: *Stage Terms 13*

dry snow: *Snow Types 10*

dry yeast: *Staples 6*

dry: *Chapter 10; Hair Types 1; Lips 1; Skin Types and Features 1*

dryad: *Beast 16*

dryer: *Major Appliances 4*

dryhead agate: *Minerals 10*

drying rack: *Miscellaneous Furniture 4*

dryland salinity: *Soil General Vocabulary 10*

drywall installer: *Construction 1*

drywall screw: *Hardware 5*

drywall: *Interior Building Materials 3*

DSA SA58 Carbine: *Semiautomatic Centerfire Rifles 7*

dual mentality: *Paranormal Abilities 21*

dual organ: *Physical Mutations 22*

dubbing: *Technical Terms 13*

dubious: *Horror Vocabulary 23*

Dubnium: *Elements 11*

duchess satin: *Fabric 2*

duchess: *Royal/Noble 1; Vegetables Cooked 6*

duchy: *Political Divisions 10*

duck oak: *Deciduous Trees 10*

duck: *Animals with Symbolic Meaning 19; Domesticated Farm Birds 15; Expletives 20; Fabric 2; Farm/Outbuilding 3; Other Wild Birds 15; Poultry Types 6*

ducktail: *Hair Style 1*

ducktownite: *Minerals 10*

duck-under: *Cave Anatomy 10*

duct tape: *Classic Items 23; Fasteners 5*

ductwork: *Building Systems 3*

dude ranch: *Hospitality 3*

dude: *Male 1*

Dudley willow: *Deciduous Trees 10*

dueling pistol: *Black Powder Weapons 7*

duergar: *Demon 16; Dwarf 1; General Fae 16*

duet: *Composition Types 13*

duffel purse: *Accessories 2*

dugite: *General Snake Families 15*

duke of burgundy: *Butterfly 15*

duke: *Royal/Noble 1*

duku: *Unusual Edible Fruits 6*

DUKW 6×6 amphibious utility vehicle: *United States Military Vehicles 8*

dulcet: *Vocal/Speech Quality 1*

dulcimer: *String Musical Instruments*

dull: *Hair Types 1; Negative 1; Unintelligent 1; Vocal/Speech Quality 1*

dull-witted: *Unintelligent 1*

Dülmen Pony: *Horse Breeds 15*

Dulong: *Other Cows 15*

Dumah: *Angels of Good 14*

dumb athlete: *Common Character Archetypes 21*

dumb blond: *Common Character Archetypes 21*

dumb jock: *Supporting Cast 23*

dumb: *Quiet 20; Unintelligent 1*

dumb-cake: *Practices to Predict the Future 19*

dumbcane: *Poisonous Plants 10*

Dumeril's: *Boa 15*

dumortierite quartz: *Standard Gems 21*

dump: *Residential Property 3*

dumpling: *Bread General Varieties 6; Miscellaneous Dessert 6*

dumpy: *Large/Heavy 1*

Dunatis (mountains): *Celtic Pantheon 14*

dunavia: *Cheese International Varieties 6*

dunce caps: *Garden Perennials 10*

dundrearies: *Facial Hair Beard 1*

dune holly: *Evergreen Trees 10*

dune system: *Coastal and Oceanic 10*

dune: *Aeolian 10*

dung: *Excrement 12; Witchcraft Vocabulary 17; Wizard's Goods 5*

dungeon guard: *Castle Inhabitants and Personnel 1*

dungeon: *Castle Anatomy 3; Fantasy Locations 24; Prison 3*

dunite: *Igneous Rocks 10; Minerals 10*

Dunn's: *Salamanders 15*

dunnart: *Other Wild Mammals 15*

duo: *Composition Types 13*

duodenum: *Organs/Major Structures 12*

duomo: *Religious Building 3*

dupioni: *Fabric 2*

duplex: *Residential Property 3*

duplicating fluid: *Office/School/Writing Supplies 5*

duplicating machine: *Office/School Machines 5*

durak: *Card Games 5*

Durandal (Roland's sword): *Weapons of Legend 18*

Durango rock: *Rattlesnake 15*

Durga (mother of the universe, supreme power): *Indian Pantheon 14*

durian: *Unusual Edible Fruits 6*

duricrust: *Soil General Vocabulary 10*

durisol: *Soil General Vocabulary 10*

Duroc: *Pigs 15*

dusky doglike: *Bats 15*

dusky pigmy: *Rattlesnake 15*

dusky: *Dolphins 15*

duskywing: *Butterfly 15*

dussack: *Swords One-handed 7*

dust cloth: *Cleaning Supplies/Gadgets 5*

dust devil: *Wind 10*

dust jacket: *Books/Publications 5*

dust mop: *Cleaning Supplies/Gadgets 5*

dust pan: *Cleaning Supplies/Gadgets 5*

dust ruffle: *Bed Linens 5*

dust storm: *Meteorology General Vocabulary 10*

dust: *Allergies 12; Clean 20; Wizard's Goods 5*

duster: *Western Clothing/Dress 21*

dusty miller: *Garden Annuals 10; Garden Perennials 10*

Dutch apple: *Pie 6*

Dutch Belted: *North American Dairy Cows 15*

Dutch braid: *Hair Style 1*

Dutch Colonial: *Architectural Styles 3*

Dutch Draft: *Horse Breeds 15*

Dutch Friesian: *Other Cows 15*

Dutch landrace: *Pigs 15*

Dutch Warmblood: *Horse Breeds 15*

Dutch: *Doors 3*

Dutch: *Human Ethnic Groups 1*

Dutch: *Roof Styles 3*

Dutchman's breeches: *Poisonous Plants 10; Wildflowers 10*

Dutchman's pipe: *Garden Perennials 10*

duty: *Philosophy Basic Concepts 14*

duvet cover: *Bed Linens 5*

duvet: *Bed Linens 5*

DVD player: *Electronics 4*

DVR: *Electronics 4*

dwarf blue rabbit brush: *Garden Perennials 10*

dwarf canyon live oak: *Deciduous Trees 10*

dwarf citadel: *Fantasy Locations 24*

dwarf golden: *Garden Perennials 10*

dwarf gourami: *Aquarium Freshwater Fish 15*

dwarf interior live oak: *Deciduous Trees 10*

dwarf lizard: *Scaled Reptiles 15*

dwarf marmoset: *New World Monkeys 15*

dwarf palmetto: *Garden Perennials 10*

dwarf planet: *Astronomy General Terms 11*

dwarf post oak: *Deciduous Trees 10*

dwarf red plains coreopsis: *Wildflowers 10*

dwarf red: *Garden Perennials 10*

dwarf walnut: *Deciduous Trees 10*

dwarf: *Boa 15; Character Building 1; General Fae 16; Small/Fragile 20*

dwarfish: *Small/Thin 1*

dwarfism: *Small/Thin 1*

dwelling: *Residential Property 3*

dybbuk: *Devil 16*

dyed: *Hair Treated 1*

dynamic compaction: *Soil General Vocabulary 10*

dynamic equilibrium: *Chemistry General Vocabulary 11*

dynamic: *Happy 20; Mobility 1; Vocal/Speech Quality 1*

dynamics: *The Arts 13*

Dyrnwyn: *Celtic Swords 18; Thirteen Treasures of the Island of Britain 18*

Dysnomia: *Moons 11*

Dysprosium: *Elements 11*

dystopia: *Plot Devices 22*

dystopian society: *Horror Genres 23*

DZ Durango: *Shotguns Side-by-Side 7*

Dzik armored car: *Poland Military Vehicles 8*

–E–

e pluribus unum: *United States Dollar Bill 19*

E-2 electronic warfare: *U.S. Navy Aircraft 8*

E-22 Raptor: *U.S. Air Force Aircraft 8*

E-3 Sentry airborne and command: *U.S. Air Force Aircraft 8*

E-35 Lightning II: *U.S. Air Force Aircraft 8*

E-4 Boeing : *U.S. Air Force Aircraft 8*

E-8 Joint STARS: *U.S. Air Force Aircraft 8*

E9A Widget surveillance: *U.S. Air Force Aircraft 8*

EA-18 growler electronic warfare: *U.S. Navy Aircraft 8*

EA-6 electronic warfare: *U.S. Navy Aircraft 8*

EAA Bounty Hunter: *Revolver Single Action 7*

EAA Windicator: *Revolver Double Action 7*

EAA Witness Elite Gold: *Pistol Semiautomatic 7*

EAA Witness Steel: *Pistol Semiautomatic 7*

eagerness: *General Emotions 20*

eagle: *Animals with Symbolic Meaning 19; Birds of Prey 15; Giant Creatures 16; Owls 15*

ear cuff: *Jewelry 21*

ear muffs: *Headgear 2*

ear piercing: *Loud 20*

ear plugs: *Military Equipment 8*

ear splitting: *Loud 20*

ear/eye injury: *Injuries/Medical Emergencies 12*

ear: *Body Parts 12*

Earl Grey: *Tea 6*

earl: *Royal/Noble 1*

earless monitor lizard: *Scaled Reptiles 15*

earlobe: *Body Parts 12*

early baroque: *Musical Period 13*

Early English: *Architectural Styles 3*

Early Georgian: *Architectural Styles 3*

Early Modern: *Architectural Styles 3*

Early Renaissance: *Art Movements 13*

earring: *Jewelry 2; Jewelry 21*

ears: *Character Building 1*

earth balls: *Fungus Common Names 10*

earth blessings: *Pennsylvania Dutch Hex Signs 19*

Earth colony: *Installations 22*

earth science: *Geologic Fields of Study 10*

earth yellow: *Brown 20*

earth: *Elemental 16; Four Elements 19; Objects/Activities Connected to Lore 19*

Earth: *Planets 11*

Earth's solar system: *Planetary Systems 11*

earthlight: *Meteorology General Vocabulary 10*

earthquake: *Geological Natural Hazards 10; Geological Vocabulary 10*

earthwork: *Fortification 3*

ear-to-ear smile: *Mouth 1*

ease: *Happy 20*

easel: *Art Tools 5; Toys 5*

East Anatolian Red: *Other Cows 15*

East Balkan: *Pigs 15*

East Bulgarian: *Horse Breeds 15*

East Coast diamondback terrapin: *Freshwater Turtles 15*

East Texas: *Toads 15*

east: *Eight Compass Points 19*

Easter Bunny: *Candy Chocolate 6; Characters with Symbolic Meaning 19*

Easter candle: *Candles 5; Rituals 14*

Easter egg: *Candy Chocolate 6*

Easter Island Moai: *Unique Property 3*

Easter Island: *Real Places Steeped in Legend or Mystery 18*

Easter lily: *Plants with Symbolic Meaning 19*

Easter rabbit: *Candy Chocolate 6*

Easter: *Holidays 19*

easterlies: *Meteorology General Vocabulary 10*

Eastern American: *Toads 15*

eastern arborvitae: *Evergreen Trees 10*

Eastern Australian snakeneck: *Freshwater Turtles 15*

eastern black walnut: *Deciduous Trees 10*

eastern box: *Freshwater Turtles 15*

eastern brown: *World's Ten Most Venomous Snakes 15*

eastern chicken: *Freshwater Turtles 15*

eastern chimpanzee: *Apes 15*

eastern coral: *World's Ten Most Venomous Snakes 15*

eastern diamondback: *Rattlesnake 15*

eastern fir: *Evergreen Trees 10*

eastern grass: *Owls 15*

eastern hemlock: *Evergreen Trees 10*

eastern hop hornbeam: *Deciduous Trees 10*

eastern larch: *Deciduous Trees 10*

eastern lowland gorilla: *Apes 15*

eastern mud: *Freshwater Turtles 15*

eastern painted: *Freshwater Turtles 15*

eastern persimmon: *Deciduous Trees 10*

eastern red oak: *Deciduous Trees 10*

eastern red pine: *Evergreen Trees 10*

eastern red: *Bats 15*

eastern redbud: *Deciduous Trees 10*

eastern snapping: *Freshwater Turtles 15*

eastern spiny softshell: *Freshwater Turtles 15*

eastern spruce: *Evergreen Trees 10*

Eastern Star: *Secret/Mystical Organizations 18*

eastern water: *Cobra 15*

eastern white cedar: *Evergreen Trees 10*

eastern white pine: *Evergreen Trees 10*

eastern: *Newts 15*

Eastlake: *Architectural Styles 3*

eastonite: *Minerals 10*

easy as one-two-three: *Easy 20*

easy as pie: *Easy 20*

easy chair: *Chairs and Stools 4*

easy listening: *Musical Styles 13*

easy: *Adjectives 20; Happy 20; Slow 20*

eatery: *Food/Drink Establishments 3*

eating utensils: *Equipment and Tools 5; Military Equipment 8*

eau de toilette: *Personal Care 5*

ebb tide: *Boat/Ship Terminology 9; Water Terms 9*

ebb: *Boat/Ship Terminology 9*

Ebenezer Scrooge: *Christmas 19*

ebola hemorrhagic fever: *Diseases 12*

ebony: *Black 20*

E-book: *Books/Publications 5*

EBR 8×8 reconnaissance vehicle: *France Military Vehicles 8*

ebullient: *Happy 20*

EC-130 Commando Solo electronic warfare: *U.S. Air Force Aircraft 8*

EC-130J Commando Solo: *U.S. Air Force Aircraft 8*

Écarté: *Ballet Terms 13*

écarté: *Dance Moves 13*

eccentricity: *Astronomy General Terms 11*

ecclesiastic: *Cleric 1*

Échappé sur les pointes: *Ballet Terms 13*

Échappé: *Ballet Terms 13*

echidna: *Other Wild Mammals 15*

Echidnades: *Giants of Legend 16*

echinacea: *Garden Perennials 10*

echo: *Technical Terms 13*

eclectic: *Styles of Dress 2*

eclipse: *Astronomy General Terms 11*

ecliptic: *Astronomy General Terms 11*

eclogite: *Metamorphic Rocks 10*

ecological land classification: *Soil General Vocabulary 10*

economic geology: *Geologic Fields of Study 10*

economical: *Personality Other 1*

economy of agglomeration: *Geography General Vocabulary 10*

economy of scale: *Geography General Vocabulary 10*

ecosystem ecology: *Soil General Vocabulary 10*

ecosystems: *Chapter 10*

ecru: *White 20*

ecstasy: *Philosophy Basic Concepts 14*

ecstatic: *Happy 20*

ectomorph: *Small/Thin 1*

Ector de Maris: *Knights of the Round Table 18*

Ector Ector: *Knights of the Round Table 18*

Ed Brown Classic custom: *Pistol Semiautomatic 7*

Ed Brown Damara: *Bolt Action Centerfire Rifles 7*

Ed Brown Express: *Bolt Action Centerfire Rifles 7*

Ed Brown Marine Sniper: *Bolt Action Centerfire Rifles 7*

Ed Leedskalnin's Coral Castle: *Real Places Steeped in Legend or Mystery 18*

edam: *Cheese Common Varieties 6*

edamame: *Legumes 6*

edaphic: *Soil General Vocabulary 10*

edaphology: *Soil General Vocabulary 10*

eddy: *Meteorology General Vocabulary 10*

Edelweiss: *Garden Perennials 10*

Eden Valley wood: *Minerals 10*

edging tool: *Garden Tools*

edgy: *Vocal/Speech Quality 1*

edible materials: *Art Materials 5*

edify: *Teach 20*

editor: *Publishing 1*

editor-in-chief: *Publishing 1*

educate: *Teach 20*

edulis: *Fungus Common Names 10*

Edwardian: *Styles of Dress 2*

eel: *Aquarium Saltwater Fish 15*

eelpout: *Wild Saltwater Fish 15*

Eerie Canal: *Unique Property 3*

eerie: *Horror Vocabulary 23; Magic Vocabulary 17*

Effacé/effacée: *Ballet Terms 13*

effective collisons: *Chemistry General Vocabulary 11*

effective molality: *Chemistry General Vocabulary 11*

effective nuclear charge: *Chemistry General Vocabulary 11*

effective stress: *Soil General Vocabulary 10*

effeminate: *Styles of Dress 2*

efficient: *Mobility 1*

effing: *Expletives 20*

effortless: *Easy 20*

EF-scale: *Meteorology General Vocabulary 10*

egad: *Expletives 20*

egg beater: *Kitchen Utensils 5*

egg cup: *Tableware 5*

egg drop: *Soup 6*

egg dye: *Easter 19*

egg mushroom: *Fungus Common Names 10*

egg piercer: *Kitchen Equipment 5*

egg salad: *Sandwiches 6*

egg slicer: *Kitchen Utensils 5*

egg timer: *Kitchen Utensils 5; Timekeeping 5*

egg twist: *Bread General Varieties 6*

egg: *Allergies 12; Ants 15; Dragon 16; Secular Symbols 19; Wizard's Goods 5*

eggbeater kick: *Swimming Strokes 9*

egg-eater: *General Snake Families 15*

eggfruit: *Unusual Edible Fruits 6*

eggnog: *Christmas 19; Dairy Beverages 6*

eggplant purple: *Vegetables 6*

eggplant white: *Vegetables 6*

eggplant: *Purple 20*

eggs: *Easter 19; Farm/Outbuilding 3; Food 6; Foods with Religious or Ritual Significance 19; Objects/Activities Connected to Lore 19*

eggshell: *White 20*

eggshells: *Objects/Activities Connected to Lore 19*

Egraine: *Arthurian Characters 18*

Egyptian artifact: *Classic Items 23*

Egyptian Book of the Dead: *Books of Legend 18; Major Religious Books 14*

Egyptian jasper: *Minerals 10*

Egyptian Mau: *Domestic Cats 15*

Egyptian pantheon: *Philosophy and Religion 14*

Egyptian pyramid: *Horror Locations 23*

Egyptian ratscrew: *Card Games 5*

Egyptian Revival: *Architectural Styles 3*

Egyptian scarab: *Harbingers/Charms for Good Luck 19*

Egyptian tomb: *Horror Locations 23; Horror Plot Devices 23*

Egyptian: *Art Movements 13; Cobra 15; Horse Breeds 15; Human Ethnic Groups 1; Styles of Dress 2; Tortoises 15*

EH-60 Black Hawk: *U.S. Army Helicopter 8*

eiderdown comforter: *Bed Linens 5*

Eiffel Tower: *Unique Property 3*

EIFV infantry fighting vehicle: *United States Military Vehicles 8*

eight game mix: *Poker Card Games 5*

eight maids a-milking: *Twelve Days of Christmas 19*

eight off: *Solitaire Card Games 5*

eighteen wheeler: *Motorized Truck 9*

eighth note: *Notation 13*

eight-pointed star: *Pennsylvania Dutch Hex Signs 19*

eighty-three: *Card Games 5*

Eilat stone: *Minerals 10*

Einstein: *Facial Hair Mustache 1*

Einsteinium: *Elements 11*

EJDER 6x6 armored wheeled vehicle: *Turkey Military Vehicles 8*

ejecta: *Astronomy General Terms 11*

eku: *Bludgeons 7*

el chupacabra: *Mythical Creatures and Monsters 16*

El Dorado: *Fictional/Mythological Locations 18*

El Niño: *Meteorology General Vocabulary 10*

elaborate: *Difficult 20*

elaeagnus: *Shrubs 10*

Eland 4×4 armored car: *South Africa Military Vehicles 8*

Elara: *Moons 11*

elastic: *Notions 2; Shoe Accessories 13*

elated: *Happy 20*

elbaite: *Minerals 10*

elbow pads: *Military Equipment 8*

elbow: *Body Parts 12*

elder cyclopes: *Giants of Legend 16*

elder: *Elderly 1; Garden Perennials 10; Old 20; Shrubs 10*

elderberry: *Berries 6; Poisonous Plants 10*

elderly advisor: *Supporting Cast 24*

elderly master of a craft or skill: *Common Character Archetypes 21*

elderly persons find source of youth: *Horror Plot Devices 23*

elderly sage: *Supporting Cast 23*

elderly: *Character Building 1*

electric arc: *Illumination Bulb and Tube Types 5*

electric blanket: *Bed Linens 5*

electric blue: *Blue 20; Cyan 20*

electric boogaloo: *Dance Styles 13*

electric crimson: *Red 20*

electric engine: *Railroad 9*

electric frying pan: *Appliances 5*

electric generator: *Large Tools*

electric guitar: *String Musical Instruments*

electric heating: *Building Systems 3*

electric hole punch: *Office/School Machines 5*

electric indigo: *Blue 20*

electric lamp: *Illumination/Light Sources 5*

electric roaster: *Appliances 5*

electric stapler: *Office/School Machines 5*

electric tea pot: *Appliances 5*

electric typewriter: *Office/School Machines 5*

electrical box: *Building Systems 3*

electrical conductivity: *Chemistry General Vocabulary 11*

electrical generation: *Physical Mutations 22*

electrical outlet: *Building Systems 3*

electrical plant: *Public Services 3*

electrical resistivity tomography: *Geological Field Work Methods 10*

electrical tower: *Public Services 3*

electrician: *Construction 1*

electricity: *Energy Sources/Types 22; Energy Sources/Types 23*

electrifying: *Beautiful 20*

electro pulse: *Weapons 22*

electro: *Weapons 22*

electrochemistry: *Chemistry General Vocabulary 11*

electrode potentials: *Chemistry General Vocabulary 11*

electrodes: *Chemistry General Vocabulary 11*

electrolaser: *Energy Sources/Types 22*

electrolysis: *Chemistry General Vocabulary 11*

electrolyte: *Blood 12; Chemistry General Vocabulary 11*

electrolytic cells: *Chemistry General Vocabulary 11*

electrolytic conduction: *Chemistry General Vocabulary 11*

electromagnetic beast: *Monsters and Creatures 22*

electromagnetic radiation: *Astronomy General Terms 11; Chemistry General Vocabulary 11*

electromagnetic spectrum: *Astronomy General Terms 11*

electromagnetic: *Energy Sources/Types 22*

electromotive series: *Chemistry General Vocabulary 11*

electron affinity: *Chemistry General Vocabulary 11*

electron configuration: *Chemistry General Vocabulary 11*

electron deficient compounds: *Chemistry General Vocabulary 11*

electron microscope: *Optics 5*

electron: *Chemistry General Vocabulary 11*

electronegativity: *Chemistry General Vocabulary 11*

electronic bow for guitar: *Music Accessories*

electronic game: *Toys 5*

electronic geometry: *Chemistry General Vocabulary 11*

electronic transition: *Chemistry General Vocabulary 11*

electronic warfare: *Helicopters 8; Military Aircraft 8*

electronic: *Art Media 13; Games 5*

electrophile: *Chemistry General Vocabulary 11*

electrophoresis: *Chemistry General Vocabulary 11*

electroplating: *Chemistry General Vocabulary 11*

electrum: *Coins and Currency 21; Minerals 10*

elegance: *Philosophy Basic Concepts 14*

elegant: *Beautiful 20; Personality Other 1; Pit Viper 15; Styles of Dress 2*

elegy: *Composition Types 13*

element: *Chemistry General Vocabulary 11*

elemental energy: *Energy Sources/Types 24*

elemental: *Monsters 16; Travel Modes 24*

elementary backstroke: *Swimming Strokes 9*

elementary school: *Academic Property 3*

elements: *Classic Heraldry 19; Collective Symbols 19*

elephant apple: *Unusual Edible Fruits 6*

elephant caravan: *Vehicles 24*

elephant ear: *Amusement Park/Carnival/Circus/Fair 3; Donut/doughnut 6; Garden Bulbs 10; Poisonous Plants 10*

elephant garlic: *Vegetables 6*

elephant hawk: *Moth 15*

elephant leg jeans: *Unisex Clothing 2*

elephant shrew: *Other Wild Mammals 15*

Elephant: *Tanks German 8*

elephant: *Transportation Animals 9*

elephantine: *Heavy 20*

Eleusis: *Card Games 5*

elevated train: *Mass Transit 9*

Élévation: *Ballet Terms 13*

élevation: *Dance Moves 13*

elevation: *Geography General Vocabulary 10;*

elevator: *Motorized 9; Poker Card Games 5*

eleven pipers piping: *Twelve Days of Christmas 19*

elf battle commander: *Fantasy Occupations 24*

elf village: *Fantasy Locations 24*

elf: *Character Building 1; Christmas 19; Owls 15*

elfin: *Butterfly 15; Small/Fragile 20; Small/Thin 1*

Elie ruby: *Minerals 10*

eliminate: *Attack 7; Kill 20*

elite warrior: *Knight 1*

elite: *Social Distinction 1*

elixir: *Wet 20*

Elizabethan: *Architectural Styles 3*

Elliott oak: *Deciduous Trees 10*

ellipse: *Astronomy General Terms 11*

ellipsoidal: *Technical Terms 13*

elliptical galaxy: *Astronomy General Terms 11*

Ellsworth: *Famous Western Locations 21*

eloko: *Demon 16*

elongated: *Ears 1; Tortoises 15*

elongation: *Astronomy General Terms 11*

elucidate: *Solve 20*

eluvium: *Soil General Vocabulary 10*

elven star: *Symbols in Magic and Religion 19*

Elvis: *Asteroids with Unusual Names 11*

Ely Cathedral: *Seven Wonders of the Middle Ages 18*

Elyan the White: *Knights of the Round Table 18*

Elysium: *Afterlife/Underworld 18*

emaciated: *Small/Thin 1*

emancipate: *Open/Release 20*

embalming: *Tables 4*

embankment: *Fortification 3*

embargo: *Tactics 7*

embark: *Boat/Ship Terminology 9*

embassy: *Administrative Property 3*

embattled: *Partition Lines 19*

embedded object: *Injuries/Medical Emergencies 12*

embellishments: *Clothing 2*

embezzler: *Illicit Occupations 1*

embittered: *Negative 1*

emblem: *Jewelry 21*

embossing: *Embellishments 2*

embowed: *Sea Creatures 19*

embroider: *Sewing Techniques 2*

embroidered: *Jewelry 21*

embroidery hoop: *Sewing Equipment 2*

embroidery stitches: *Clothing 2*

embroidery: *Embellishments 2*

emcee: *Media 1*

emerald serpent: *Dragon 16*

emerald tablet: *Symbols in Magic and Religion 19*

emerald tree: *Boa 15*

emerald: *Cat's Eye Gems 21; Dragon 16; Gem Cuts 21; Minerals 10; Standard Gems 21*

emergence: *Philosophy Basic Concepts 14*

emergency radio: *Meteorology General Vocabulary 10*

emergency room doctor/nurse: *Medical Occupations 1*

emergency room: *Health Care 3*

emergency: *Candles 5*

emergent coastline: *Geography General Vocabulary 10*

emery board: *Personal Care 5*

emery cloth: *Hand Tools 5*

emery: *Minerals 10*

EMF 1873 Great Western Series: *Revolver Single Action 7*

EMF 1875 Remington: *Revolver Single Action 7*

eminent: *Personality Other 1*

emirate: *Political Divisions 10*

emission spectrum: *Chemistry General Vocabulary 11*

emission: *Wet 20*

emit: *Open/Release 20*

emmer: *Grain 6*

Emo: *Styles of Dress 2*

Emory oak: *Deciduous Trees 10*

emotion: *Philosophy Basic Concepts 14*

emotional: *Sad 20*

empath: *Horror Occupations 23; Occupations 22*

empathy: *Paranormal Abilities 21*

emperor gum: *Moth 15*

Emperor tamarin: *New World Monkeys 15*

emperor: *Butterfly 15; Dragonfly 15; Royal/Noble 1*

Empire State Building: *Seven Wonders of the Modern World 18; Unique Property 3*

Empire: *Architectural Styles 3; Chairs and Stools 4*

empire: *Styles of Dress 2*

empiric generalization: *Philosophy Basic Concepts 14*

empiricism: *Philosophy Basic Concepts 14*

empress: *Royal/Noble 1*

EMT: *Medical Occupations 1*

emu apple: *Unusual Edible Fruits 6*

emu berry: *Unusual Edible Fruits 6*

emu: *Other Wild Birds 15*

emulsifying agent: *Chemistry General Vocabulary 11*

emulsion: *Chemistry General Vocabulary 11*

en Arriére: *Ballet Terms 13*

en Avant: *Ballet Terms 13*

en Cloche: *Ballet Terms 13*

en coquille: *Fish/Seafood Meals 6*

en Croix: *Ballet Terms 13*

en croute: *Fish/Seafood Meals 6*

en Dedans: *Ballet Terms 13*

en Dehors: *Ballet Terms 13*

en Diagonale: *Ballet Terms 13*

en Face: *Ballet Terms 13*

en garde: *Fencing Vocabulary 7*

en l'Air: *Ballet Terms 13*

en Tournant: *Ballet Terms 13*

enamored: *Magic Vocabulary 17*

encampment: *Outdoor Property 3*

encantado: *Aquatic 16*

enceinte: *Castle Anatomy 3*

Enceladus: *Moons 11*

enchant: *General Combat Vocabulary 7; Magic Vocabulary 17; Witchcraft Vocabulary 17*

enchanted animal: *Travel Modes 24*

enchanted bathysphere: *Vehicles 24*

enchanted boots/shoes: *Magical Transportation 17*

enchanted cloud: *Magical Transportation 17; Vehicles 24*

enchanted swordsman: *Fantasy Occupations 24*

enchanted: *Happy 20; Magic Vocabulary 17; Monster Categories/Terms 16*

enchanter: *Wizard 1*

enchanting: *Happy 20*

enchantment: *Magic Vocabulary 17; Witchcraft Vocabulary 17*

encircle: *General Combat Vocabulary 7*

Encke: *Comets 11*

enclave: *General Buildings 3; Geography General Vocabulary 10*

enclosure: *General Buildings 3; Man-Made Animal Homes 15*

encouraging: *General Emotions 20; Happy 20*

encumber: *Close/Hold 20*

encyclopedia: *Books/Publications 5*

end of the world: *Plot Devices 22*

end papers: *Books/Publications 5*

end: *Ending 20; Tables 4*

endanger: *Harm 20*

enderbite: *Igneous Rocks 10*

Enderby Island: *Other Cows 15*

ending: *Nouns 20*

endive: *Vegetables 6*

endless knot: *Eight Ashtamangala 19; Symbols in Magic and Religion 19*

endlichite: *Minerals 10*

endmill: *Power Tools*

endocannabinoid: *Body Systems 12*

endocrine: *Body Systems 12*

endocrinologist: *Medical Occupations 1*

endomorph: *Large/Heavy 1*

end-on-end: *Fabric 2*

endorheic basin: *Fluvial 10*

endorse: *Agree 20*

endosulfan: *Dangerous Chemicals 11*

endothermic: *Chemistry General Vocabulary 11*

endothermicity: *Chemistry General Vocabulary 11*

endothion: *Dangerous Chemicals 11*

endrin: *Dangerous Chemicals 11*

enebro: *Evergreen Trees 10*

enemy casts magic: *Common Dangers 24*

enemy: *Fighter 1; Villain 20*

energetic: *Fast 20; Mobility 1; Personality Other 1*

energy bolo: *Weapons 22*

energy reflection: *Physical Mutations 22*

energy: *Chemistry General Vocabulary 11; Weapons 22*

enfilade: *General Combat Vocabulary 7*

engage: *Fencing Vocabulary 7*

engagement ring: *Objects/Activities Connected to Lore 19; Valentine's Day 19*

engagement: *Fencing Vocabulary 7; Valentine's Day 19*

Engelier: *Twelve Peers of Charlemagne 18*

Engelmann spruce: *Evergreen Trees 10*

engine trouble: *Travel Hazards 9*

engine: *Miscellaneous Furniture 4*

engineer: *Castle Inhabitants and Personnel 1; Media 1; Scientist 1*

engineer's scale: *Architectural/Engineering Tools 5*

engineered lumber: *Interior Building Materials 3*

engineered secret door: *Traps 3*

engineering geology: *Geologic Fields of Study 10*
engineering tools: *Equipment and Tools 5*
engineering: *Robots 22*
Englemann daisy: *Garden Perennials 10*
English Baroque: *Architectural Styles 3*
English bow: *Missile Weapons 7*
English breakfast: *Tea 6*
English bullet crossbow: *Missile Weapons 7*
English cheddar: *Cheese Common Varieties 6*
English Cocker Spaniel: *Dog Breeds 15*
English country (England): *Ethnic/Folk Dances 13*
English daisy: *Garden Perennials 10*
English Foxhound: *Dog Breeds 15*
English horn: *Wind/Woodwind and Brass Musical Instruments*
English ivy: *Weeds 10*
English long: *Axes 7*
English Longhorn: *Other Cows 15*
English muffin: *Bread General Varieties 6*
English peas: *Vegetables 6*
English Setter: *Dog Breeds 15*
English sole: *Wild Saltwater Fish 15*
English Springer Spaniel: *Dog Breeds 15*
English stud: *Poker Card Games 5*
English Toy Spaniel: *Dog Breeds 15*
English: *Facial Hair Mustache 1*
English: *Human Ethnic Groups 1*
English: *Imported Carpets 4*
engrailed: *Partition Lines 19*
engraver: *Artists and Craftspeople 1*
engross: *Magic Vocabulary 17*
engrossed: *Magic Vocabulary 17*
engulf: *Close/Hold 20; General Combat Vocabulary 7*
enhance: *Buy 20*
enhydritic agate: *Minerals 10*
enhydro agate: *Minerals 10*
enigma: *Magic Vocabulary 17*
enigmatic: *Magic Vocabulary 17*
enjoy: *Love 20*
enjoyable: *Good 20; Happy 20*
Enki (oceans): *Sumerian Pantheon 14*
enlarge: *Buy 20*
Enlil (war): *Sumerian Pantheon 14*
enmesh: *General Combat Vocabulary 7; Magic Vocabulary 17*
enneagram: *Symbols in Magic and Religion 19*
enoki: *Fungus Common Names 10*
enormous: *Large 20; Large/Heavy 1*
enrage: *General Emotions 20*
enraged: *Angry 1*
enrapture: *Magic Vocabulary 17*
enraptured: *Magic Vocabulary 17*
Enrico Cecchetti: *Ballet Terms 13*
ensemble Greek: *Armor Types 7*
ensemble Roman: *Armor Types 7*
ensemble: *Groups 13*
ensign: *Maritime Occupations 1; U.S. Navy Officer 8*
ensnare: *General Combat Vocabulary 7; Magic Vocabulary 17*
enso: *Symbols in Magic and Religion 19*
enter: *Commands 20*
enterovirus infection: *Diseases 12*
entertainer: *Bard 1*
entertainment property: *Architecture and Property 3*
entertainment reporter: *Publishing 1*
entertainment: *Philosophy Basic Concepts 14*
enthalpy: *Chemistry General Vocabulary 11*
enthrall: *Magic Vocabulary 17; Witchcraft Vocabulary 17*
enthralled: *Magic Vocabulary 17*
enthralling: *Beautiful 20*
enthusiasm: *General Emotions 20*
enthusiastic: *Personality Other 1*
entice: *Magic Vocabulary 17; Witchcraft Vocabulary 17*
enticing: *Beautiful 20; Magic Vocabulary 17*
entisol: *Soil General Vocabulary 10*
entity: *Philosophy Basic Concepts 14*
Entlebucher Mountain: *Dog Breeds 15*
entr'acte: *Composition Types 13*
entrance hall: *Rooms 3*

entrance: *Doors 3; Magic Vocabulary 17*

entranced: *Magic Vocabulary 17*

entrancing: *Beautiful 20*

entrap: *General Combat Vocabulary 7; Magic Vocabulary 17*

entrapped: *Magic Vocabulary 17*

Entrechat six: *Ballet Terms 13*

Entrechat: *Ballet Terms 13*

entrechat: *Dance Moves 13*

entrenching tool: *Military Equipment 8*

entropy: *Chemistry General Vocabulary 11*

entry hall: *Rooms 3*

entry tools: *SWAT Equipment 7*

entry: *Doors 3; Rooms 3*

Enuma Elish: *Major Religious Books 14*

envelop: *General Combat Vocabulary 7*

envelope: *Containers and Vessels 5; Office/School/Writing Supplies 5*

envelopement: *Fencing Vocabulary 7*

environmental geology: *Geologic Fields of Study 10*

environmental: *Art Genres 13*

envisage: *Create 20*

envision: *Create 20*

envisioning: *Magic Vocabulary 17*

envy: *Seven Deadly Sins 19*

enzyme: *Chemistry General Vocabulary 11*

Eoarchean Period: *Geologic Time 10*

Eocene Age: *Geologic Time 10*

eon: *Geological Vocabulary 10*

Épaulement: *Ballet Terms 13*

epaulet: *Garment Pieces 2*

epauletted: *Bats 15*

épée: *Fencing Equipment 7; Swords One-handed 7*

epergne: *Tableware 5*

ephedra: *Shrubs 10*

ephemeral fruits: *Objects 18*

epic hero: *Common Character Archetypes 21*

epic: *Large 20*

epicenter: *Geological Vocabulary 10*

epichlorohydrin: *Dangerous Chemicals 11*

epidemic typhus: *Diseases 12*

epidote: *Minerals 10; Standard Gems 21*

Epimetheus: *Moons 11*

Epiphany: *Catholic Holy Days of Obligation 14*

epistemology: *Philosophy Basic Concepts 14*

epoch: *Geological Vocabulary 10*

epsom salt: *Minerals 10*

epsom: *Minerals 10*

EQ1108 4×2 5 ton truck: *China Military Vehicles 8*

EQ1141 4×2 8 ton truck: *China Military Vehicles 8*

EQ2050 Mengshi 4×4 utility vehicle: *China Military Vehicles 8*

EQ2058 up-armored 4×4 utility vehicle: *China Military Vehicles 8*

EQ2081 6×6 2.5 ton truck: *China Military Vehicles 8*

EQ2100 6×6 3.5 ton truck: *China Military Vehicles 8*

equalizer: *Electronics 4*

equator: *Geography General Vocabulary 10*

equilibrium constant: *Chemistry General Vocabulary 11*

equinox: *Astronomy General Terms 11*

equipment manager: *Sports 1*

equipment: *Equipment and Tools 5; Miscellaneous Furniture 4*

equivalent weight: *Chemistry General Vocabulary 11*

Equuleus: *Constellations 11*

eradicate: *Attack 7; General Combat Vocabulary 7; Kill 20*

eradicator: *Assassin 1; Villain 20*

erased: *Heads 19*

eraser: *Art Materials 5*

Erbium: *Elements 11*

ERC-20 Kriss 6×6 armored car: *France Military Vehicles 8*

ERC-60 Sagaie 6×6 armored car: *France Military Vehicles 8*

ERC-90 F1 Lynx 6×6 armored car: *France Military Vehicles 8*

ERC-90 Sagaie 2 6×6 armored car: *France Military Vehicles 8*

erect: *Fix 20; Reptiles 19; Sea Creatures 19*

Eremiel: *Angels of Good 14*

erg: *Aeolian 10; Erosion 10*

ergocalciferol: *Dangerous Chemicals 11*

ergonomic: *Chairs and Stools 4*

ergotamine tartrate: *Dangerous Chemicals 11*

Eridanus: *Constellations 11*

Erin go Bragh: *St. Patrick's Day 19*

Erinome: *Moons 11*

Eris: *Planets 11*

Eriskay Pony: *Horse Breeds 15*

Erlenmeyer flask: *Laboratory Equipment 5*

ermine: *Fur 19; Fur 2; Other Wild Mammals 15*

erosion landforms: *Chapter 10*

erosion: *Geological Vocabulary 10; Soil General Vocabulary 10*

erotic: *Art Genres 13*

erotica: *Horror Genres 23; Science Fiction Genres 22*

eroticism: *Philosophy Basic Concepts 14*

erratic: *Geological Vocabulary 10; Rock and Mineral Forms 10*

Erriapus: *Moons 11*

Errol Flynn: *Facial Hair Mustache 1*

erstwhile: *Old 20*

erubescite: *Minerals 10*

Erymanthian boar: *Twelve Labors of Hercules 16*

erythrocyte: *Blood 12*

Esaw: *Native American Peoples 1*

escalate: *Buy 20*

escallonia: *Shrubs 10*

escalloped: *Vegetables Cooked 6*

Escambia map: *Freshwater Turtles 15*

escape pod: *Spaceship Types 22*

escape velocity: *Astronomy General Terms 11*

Escape: *Minor Lines 19*

escaped criminal/lunatic: *Horror Genres 23*

escargot plate: *Tableware 5*

escarpment: *Cave Anatomy 10; Geological Vocabulary 10; Slope 10*

escort aircraft carrier: *Military Watercraft 8*

escort: *Illicit Occupations 1*

esker: *Fluvial 10; Geological Vocabulary 10; Glacial and Mountain 10*

Eskimo: *Human Ethnic Groups 1; Native American Peoples 1*

eskrima stick: *Bludgeons 7*

esophagus: *Organs/Major Structures 12*

esoteric: *Magic Vocabulary 17*

espada ropera: *Swords One-handed 7*

espadon: *Swords Two-handed 7*

espadrilles: *Footwear/Shoes 2*

espionage: *General Combat Vocabulary 7*

espresso: *Coffee Drinks 6; Ice Cream Flavors 6*

espringal: *Siege Engines 7*

esquire: *Legal Occupations 1*

esrom: *Cheese International Varieties 6*

essence: *Philosophy Basic Concepts 14*

essential oil: *Chemistry General Vocabulary 11*

Essex: *Pigs 15*

essexite: *Igneous Rocks 10*

essonite: *Minerals 10*

establish: *Create 20*

estate: *Residential Property 3*

esteem: *General Emotions 20*

Esthwaite waterweed: *Weeds 10*

estimate: *Solve 20*

estoc: *Swords One-handed 7*

Estonian bacon: *Pigs 15*

Estonian Native: *Horse Breeds 15*

Estonian Red: *Other Cows 15*

Estuarine crocodile: *Crocodilians 15*

estuary: *Coastal and Oceanic 10; Ecosystems 10; Geological Vocabulary 10*

etagere: *Storage 4*

etcher: *Artists and Craftspeople 1*

eternity: *Philosophy Basic Concepts 14*

ethanesulfonyl chloride: *Dangerous Chemicals 11*

ethanol: *Dangerous Chemicals 11*

ether: *Chemistry General Vocabulary 11; Dangerous Chemicals 11*

ethereal: *Small/Fragile 20*

etherophone: *Electronic Musical Instruments 5*

ethics: *Philosophy Basic Concepts 14*

ethion: *Dangerous Chemicals 11*

Ethiopian pegasoi: *Flying Creatures 16*

Ethiopian Texts: *Major Religious Books 14*

ethmoid bone: *Bones 12*

ethnic cleansing: *General Combat Vocabulary 7*

ethnic dances: *The Arts 13*

ethnodrama: *Books/Publications 5*

ethnotheater: *Performance Genres 13*

ethoprophos: *Dangerous Chemicals 11*

ethylene fluorohydrin: *Dangerous Chemicals 11*

ethylene oxide: *Dangerous Chemicals 11*

ethylenediamine: *Dangerous Chemicals 11*

ethyleneimine: *Dangerous Chemicals 11*

ethylthiocyanate: *Dangerous Chemicals 11*

etori: *Card Games 5*

ettercap: *Beast 16*

ettin: *Giant Humanoids 16*

etude: *Composition Types 13*

Euanthe: *Moons 11*

eucalyptus: *Weeds 10*

Eucharist: *Religious Bread 6*

Eucharistic adoration: *Rituals 14*

euchre: *Card Games 5*

eucryphia: *Shrubs 10*

eudiometer: *Laboratory Equipment 5*

Euflamm: *Dragon 16*

eugenics: *Plot Devices 22*

Eukelade: *Moons 11*

euphoric: *Happy 20*

Euporie: *Moons 11*

Eurasian cave: *Lions 15*

Eurasian water milfoil: *Weeds 10*

Euro: *Coins and Currency 21*

Europa: *Moons 11*

European black pine: *Evergreen Trees 10*

European brown: *Bears 15*

European Burmese: *Domestic Cats 15*

European cave: *Lions 15*

European elder: *Garden Perennials 10*

European larch: *Deciduous Trees 10*

European pond: *Freshwater Turtles 15*

European privet: *Weeds 10*

European shorthair: *Domestic Cats 15*

European soil bureau network: *Soil General Vocabulary 10*

European soil database: *Soil General Vocabulary 10*

European speckled alder: *Deciduous Trees 10*

european spindle: *Poisonous Plants 10*

European spruce: *Evergreen Trees 10*

European: *Human Ethnic Groups 1; Squid 15; Styles of Dress 2*

Europium: *Elements 11*

Euro-trash: *Styles of Dress 2*

Eurydome: *Moons 11*

evacuation: *Spaceship Types 22*

evade: *Moves 7*

evaluate: *Solve 20*

evaluator: *Finance 1*

evangelists: *Collective Symbols 19*

evaporate: *Geological Vocabulary 10*

evaporated: *Milk 6*

evaporating dish: *Laboratory Equipment 5*

evaporation: *Meteorology General Vocabulary 10*

evaporite: *Sedimentary Rocks 10*

evaporization: *Chemistry General Vocabulary 11*

evapotranspiration: *Geography General Vocabulary 10*

evasive: *Horror Vocabulary 23*

even: *Teeth 1*

evening bag: *Accessories 2*

evening gloves: *Spy Gear 5*

evening gown: *Ladies' Wear 2; Spy Gear 5*

evening primrose: *Garden Perennials 10; Weeds 10; Wildflowers 10*

evening stone: *Minerals 10*

evening suit: *Men's Wear 2*

evening: *Bats 15*

event horizon: *Astronomy General Terms 11*

event planner: *Special Occasion 1*

everglade: *Terrain Features 10; Water Terms 9*

evergreen: *Evergreen Trees 10*

evergreen bittersweet: *Garden Perennials 10*

evergreen coral bean: *Deciduous Trees 10*

evergreen magnolia: *Deciduous Trees 10*

evergreen trees: *Chapter 10*

everlasting: *Garden Perennials 10*

everyman: *Common Character Archetypes 21*

evil advisor: *Common Character Archetypes 21*

evil child: *Common Character Archetypes 21*

evil clown: *Common Character Archetypes 21*

evil doer: *Villain 20*

evil eye: *Symbols in Magic and Religion 19; Witchcraft Vocabulary 17*

evil law enforcement: *Common Character Archetypes 21*

evil priest: *Supporting Cast 24*

evil railroad tries to steal land: *Western Plot Devices 21*

evil robot: *Common Character Archetypes 21; Horror Plot Devices 23*

evil twin: *Common Character Archetypes 21*

evil/insane/possessed child: *Horror Plot Devices 23*

evil: *Bad 20; Negative 1; Philosophy Basic Concepts 14; Witchcraft Vocabulary 17*

evildoers turn good after hellish nightmare: *Western Plot Devices 21*

Evolène: *Other Cows 15*

evolutionalism: *Philosophy Basic Concepts 14*

ewer: *Containers and Vessels 5*

exaltation: *General Emotions 20*

examination: *Paranormal Activity 21*

examine: *Solve 20*

examiner: *Wizard 1*

examining: *Tables 4*

exasperate: *General Emotions 20*

Excalibur Lake: *Arthurian Locations 18*

Excalibur: *Arthurian Characters 18; Arthurian Weapons 18*

excavation: *Outdoor Property 3*

excellence: *Philosophy Basic Concepts 14*

excellent: *Good 20*

exceptional: *Beautiful 20*

excited state: *Chemistry General Vocabulary 11*

exciting: *Beautiful 20*

exclaim: *Speak 20*

excrement: *Anatomy and Physiology 12*

excreta: *Excrement 12*

excruciating: *Unattractive 20*

excursion: *Journey 20*

execute: *Attack 7; Kill 20*

executer: *Wizard 1*

executioner: *Assassin 1; Fighter 1; Villain 20*

executioner's: *Swords Two-handed 7*

executive chef: *Food Service 1*

executive editor: *Publishing 1*

exegetic: *Mobility 1*

exemplar: *Beautiful 20*

Exercises à la barre: *Ballet Terms 13*

exfoliation: *Geological Vocabulary 10*

exhaust fan: *Bathroom Features and Fixtures 3; Building Systems 3*

exhausted: *Horror Vocabulary 23; Slow 20*

exhibit: *Man-Made Animal Homes 15*

exhilarating: *Beautiful 20*

exhumed river channel: *Erosion 10; Fluvial 10*

exigent: *Difficult 20*

existence: *Philosophy Basic Concepts 14*

existentialism: *Philosophy Basic Concepts 14*

exit: *Commands 20; Locomotion 9*

Exmoor Pony: *Horse Breeds 15*

exodus: *Locomotion 9*

exoplanetary: *Planetary Systems 11*

exorbitant: *Large 20*

exorcism: *Horror Genres 23*

exorcist: *Horror Occupations 23*

exothermic: *Chemistry General Vocabulary 11*

exothermicity: *Chemistry General Vocabulary 11*

exotic fruits: *Food 6*

exotic shorthair: *Domestic Cats 15*

exotic: *Star Types and Relatives 11*

expand: *Buy 20; Learn 20*

expansive clay: *Soil General Vocabulary 10*

expansive: *Large 20*

expediated: *Fast 20*

expedition: *Journey 20*

expeditious: *Fast 20; Mobility 1*

experience: *Philosophy Basic Concepts 14*

experienced: *Elderly 1; Personality Other 1*

experiment: *Learn 20; Solve 20*

experimental animals turn on scientist: *Horror Plot Devices 23*

experimental: *Performance Genres 13*

expert: *Good 20*

explain: *Solve 20; Teach 20*

explode: *Attack 7; Harm 20*

exploding: *Loud 20*

exploited: *Horror Vocabulary 23*

exploration: *Journey 20; Paranormal Activity 21; Transportation 9; Verbs 20*

explore: *Learn 20; Locomotion 9; Paranormal Activity 21*

explorer: *Barbarian 1; Occupations 22; Rural Occupations 1; Spaceship Types 22*

explorers encounter cannibals: *Horror Plot Devices 23*

explorers find lost race: *Horror Plot Devices 23*

explorers find magical object: *Horror Plot Devices 23*

explosion of space shuttle Challenger: *Legendary Events 18*

explosion: *General Combat Vocabulary 7*

explosive cigar: *Spy Gear 5*

explosive golf ball: *Spy Gear 5*

explosive gum: *Spy Gear 5*

explosive item: *Spy Gear 5*

explosive jewelry: *Spy Gear 5*

explosive pen: *Spy Gear 5*

explosive ring: *Spy Gear 5*

explosive: *Chemistry General Vocabulary 11; Loud 20*

expose: *Learn 20*

exposition: *Composition Types 13*

express: *Fast 20*

Expressionism: *Art Movements 13*

Expressionist Modern: *Architectural Styles 3*

expressway: *Roads 9*

exquisite: *Beautiful 20*

extended arm tow: *Swimming Strokes 9*

extended family: *Geography General Vocabulary 10*

extended goatee: *Facial Hair Beard 1*

extended wear contact lenses: *Optics 5*

extended: *Difficult 20*

extension cord: *Office/School/Writing Supplies 5*

extension ladder: *Large Tools*

extension: *Ballet Terms 13; Geological Vocabulary 10; Philosophy Basic Concepts 14*

extensions: *Hair Style 1*

extensive: *Large 20*

exterminate: *General Combat Vocabulary 7; Kill 20*

exterminator: *General Occupations 1*

external hard drive: *Computer Equipment 5*

external speakers: *Computer Equipment 5*

extinct bacteria/animal resurfaces: *Common Dangers 22*

extinct creature emerges from isolation and causes death/destruction: *Horror Plot Devices 23*

extinction: *Astronomy General Terms 11*

extra large: *Eggs 6*

extra sharp cheddar: *Cheese Common Varieties 6*

extra: *New 20*

extraction: *General Combat Vocabulary 7; Teeth Dental Work 1*

extragalactic: *Astronomy General Terms 11*

extraordinary: *Large 20*

extraplanar: *Monsters 16*

extrapolate: *Chemistry General Vocabulary 11*

extrasensory: *Magic Vocabulary 17*

extrasolar: *Planetary Systems 11*

extraterrestrial: *Astronomy General Terms 11; Monster Categories/Terms 16*

extravagant: *Large 20*

extreme cold: *Common Dangers 22; Common Dangers 23*

extreme heat: *Common Dangers 22; Common Dangers 23*

extreme weather: *Common Dangers 23*

extricate: *General Combat Vocabulary 7*

extroverted: *Personality Other 1*

extrude: *Open/Release 20*

extrusive: *Geological Vocabulary 10*

exude: *Smells 20; Wet 20*

exultant: *Happy 20*

exurb: *Geography General Vocabulary 10*

eye agate: *Minerals 10*

eye catching: *Beautiful 20*

eye color: *Character Building 1*

eye cream: *Personal Care 5*

eye liner: *Makeup 5*

eye of newt: *Wizard's Goods 5*

eye shadow: *Makeup 5*

eye type: *Character Building 1*

eye wall: *Meteorology General Vocabulary 10*

eye: *Body Parts 12; Figures Associated with Symbols 19; Meteorology General Vocabulary 10; Organs/Major Structures 12*

eyeball: *Body Parts 12; Wizard's Goods 5*

eyebrow: *Body Parts 12*

eyebrow pencil: *Makeup 5*

eyebrows: *Character Building 1*

eyeglasses: *Optics 5*

eyelash: *Body Parts 12; Pit Viper 15; Viper 15*

eyelash curler: *Makeup 5*

eyelashes: *Wizard's Goods 5*

eyelet: *Fabric 2*

eyepiece: *Astronomy General Terms 11*

eyes: *Objects/Activities Connected to Lore 19*

eyewash: *Laboratory Equipment 5*

–F–

F15 4×2 and 4×4 15-cwt truck series: *Canada Military Vehicles 8*

F-15 Eagle fighter: *U.S. Air Force Aircraft 8*

F-15E Strike Eagle: *U.S. Air Force Aircraft 8*

F-16 Fighting Falcon: *U.S. Air Force Aircraft 8*

F30 4×4 30-cwt truck series: *Canada Military Vehicles 8*

F-5 trainer: *U.S. Navy Aircraft 8*

F60 4×4 and 6×4 60-cwt truck series: *Canada Military Vehicles 8*

FA-18 fighter: *U.S. Navy Aircraft 8*

Faassen's catnip: *Garden Perennials 10*

fabiana: *Shrubs 10*

fable: *Literary Styles 5*

fabric patterns: *Clothing 2*

fabric: *Clothing 2*

fabricate: *Fix 20*

fabulous: *Beautiful 20; Good 20; Magic Vocabulary 17*

face cloth: *Towels 5*

face paint: *Specialty Survival Gear 5*

face shield: *Masks 2*

face: *Character Building 1*

fachan: *General Fae 16*

facial features: *Character Building 1*

facial hair: *Character Building 1*

facial recognition software: *Spy Gear 5*

facilitate: *Open/Release 20*

facilities: *Bathrooms 3*

facing: *Garment Pieces 2*

fact: *Philosophy Basic Concepts 14*

factious: *Difficult 20*

factory: *Business Property 3*

factory emissions cause death/rot/wasting disease: *Horror Plot Devices 23*

faculae: *Astronomy General Terms 11*

fade: *Technical Terms 13*

faden quartz: *Minerals 10*

fae creatures are part of society: *Fantasy Plot Devices 24*

fae creatures: *Monsters 16*

fae related: *Monsters 16*

faerie glamour: *Fae Related 16*

faerie islands: *Fae Related 16*

faerie ring: *Fae Related 16*

faerie: *General Fae 16*

Faeroes Pony: *Horse Breeds 15*

Fafnir Hreidmarsson: *Dragon 16*

fagott: *Wind/Woodwind and Brass Musical Instruments*

fagotto: *Wind/Woodwind and Brass Musical Instruments*

faille: *Fabric 2*

Fail-not: *Arthurian Weapons 18*

faint: *Quiet 20*

faint-hearted: *Horror Vocabulary 23*

fainting couch: *Seating 4*

fainting: *Injuries/Medical Emergencies 12*

fair grounds: *General Property 3; Outdoor Property 3*

fair lady: *Demon 16*

fair: *Architecture and Property 3; Meteorology General Vocabulary 10; Personality Other 1*

Fairburn agate: *Minerals 10*

fairies' bonnet: *Fungus Common Names 10*

fairy candles: *Garden Perennials 10*

fairy club: *Fungus Common Names 10*

fairy colony lures innocent victim: *Horror Plot Devices 23*

fairy floss: *Candy General 6*

fairy food: *Candy General 6*

fairy glade: *Fantasy Locations 24*

fairy godmother: *Common Character Archetypes 21*

fairy lily: *Garden Perennials 10*

fairy ring of toadstools: *Classic Items 23*

fairy ring: *Fungus Common Names 10; Horror Locations 23*

fairy tale: *Fantasy Genres 24; Literary Styles 5*

fairy: *Fantasy Creatures with Symbolic Meaning 19*

fairy-ring mushroom: *Fungus Common Names 10*

faith: *Seven Holy Virtues 19; Three Theological Virtues 19; Twelve Fruits of the Holy Spirit 19*

faithful: *Followers 14; Love 20; Personality Other 1*

fake fingernails: *Makeup 5*

fake psychic assaulted by actual spirits: *Horror Plot Devices 23*

faker: *Thief 1*

fakir: *Wizard 1*

Falabella: *Horse Breeds 15*

falanouc: *Other Wild Mammals 15*

falchion: *Swords One-handed 7*

falcon: *Birds of Prey 15*

falconer: *Castle Inhabitants and Personnel 1*

falconet: *Cannon 7*

falcon's eye: *Minerals 10*

fall from height: *Injuries/Medical Emergencies 12*

fall line: *Geography General Vocabulary 10*

fall: *Locomotion 9; Meteorology General Vocabulary 10*

fallacy: *Philosophy Basic Concepts 14*

fallen angels: *Philosophy and Religion 14*

fall-front: *Desks 4*

falling snow: *Snow Events 10*

falling stalactite: *Geological Natural Hazards 10*

falling stone: *Traps 3*

fallopian tube: *Organs/Major Structures 12*

fallow land: *Farm/Outbuilding 3*

fallow: *Brown 20; Geography General Vocabulary 10*

false acacia: *Deciduous Trees 10*

false attack: *Fencing Vocabulary 7*

false banana: *Deciduous Trees 10*

false beard: *Spy Gear 5*

false cedar: *Evergreen Trees 10*

false chamomile: *Garden Perennials 10*

false cypress: *Evergreen Trees 10*

false document: *Spy Gear 5*

false dragonhead: *Garden Perennials 10*

false elm: *Deciduous Trees 10*

false eyelashes: *Makeup 5*

false fingerprints: *Spy Gear 5*

false floor: *Cave Anatomy 10; Traps 3*

false gharial: *Crocodilians 15*

false gods: *Plot Devices 22*

false hemlock: *Evergreen Trees 10*

false hero: *Common Character Archetypes 21*

false identification: *Spy Gear 5*

false indigo: *Garden Perennials 10*

false lupine: *Garden Perennials 10*

false mallow: *Garden Perennials 10*

false miterwort: *Garden Perennials 10*

false mustache: *Spy Gear 5*

false parsley: *Poisonous Plants 10*

false salvia: *Garden Perennials 10*

false shagbark: *Deciduous Trees 10*

false Solomon's seal: *Garden Perennials 10*

false strawberry: *Garden Perennials 10*

false teeth: *Teeth Dental Work 1*

false vampire: *Bats 15*

false water: *Cobra 15*

false: *Cobra 15; Personality Other 1*

falsely accused person: *Common Character Archetypes 21*

falsetto: *Vocal/Speech Quality 1; Voices 13*

falsies: *Ladies' Wear 2*

falsifier: *Thief 1*

falun gong: *Symbols in Magic and Religion 19*

Fame: *Major Lines 19*

famed: *Personality Other 1*

familiar: *Witchcraft Vocabulary 17*

family car: *Motorized 9*

family curse: *Horror Plot Devices 23*

family ranch taken by carpetbaggers: *Western Plot Devices 21*

family restaurant: *Food/Drink Establishments 3*

family: *Rooms 3*

famine and/or pestilence (black horse): *Four Horsemen of the Apocalypse 19*

famous disappearances: *Legendary, Mystical and Mythical Items and Locations 18*

famous: *Personality Other 1*

fan tan: *Card Games 5*

fan: *Accessories 2; Art Genres 13; Western Clothing/Dress 21*

fanatical: *Personality Other 1*

fancy: *Love 20; Magic Vocabulary 17; Minerals 10; Terms of Endearment 1*

fandango (Galicia): *Ethnic/Folk Dances 13*

fanfare: *Composition Types 13*

fang: *Wizard's Goods 5*

fangs: *Teeth 1*

fanning mill: *General Farm Equipment*

fanning: *Geological Vocabulary 10*

Fan-Si-Pan horned: *Pit Viper 15*

fan-tail hat: *Headgear 2*

fantasist: *Wizard 1*

fantasize: *Magic Vocabulary 17*

fantasizing: *Magic Vocabulary 17*

Fantastic realism: *Art Movements 13; Fantasy Genres 24*

fantastic: *Beautiful 20; Happy 20; Magic Vocabulary 17*

fantasy element in historical context: *Fantasy Plot Devices 24*

fantasy element in the modern world: *Fantasy Plot Devices 24*

fantasy horror: *Fantasy Genres 24*

fantasy property: *Architecture and Property 3*

fantasy romance: *Fantasy Genres 24*

fantasy: *Art Genres 13; Composition Types 13; Magic Vocabulary 17; Performance Genres 13*

fapfap: *Card Games 5*

far future: *Plot Devices 22*

Faraday constant: *Chemistry General Vocabulary 11*

Faraday's law of electrolysis: *Chemistry General Vocabulary 11*

farandole: *Historical Dances 13*

Farbauti: *Moons 11*

farce: *Performance Genres 13*

farewell-to-spring: *Wildflowers 10*

farfalle: *Pasta 6*

farging: *Expletives 20*

farm birds: *Animals 15*

farm equipment: *Equipment and Tools 5*

farm hand: *Agricultural 1*

farm market: *General Property 3; Outdoor Property 3*

farm transportation: *Transportation 9*

farm: *Architecture and Property 3; Man-Made Animal Homes 15*

farmer: *Agricultural 1; Cheese Common Varieties 6*

farmer's daughter: *Common Character Archetypes 21*

farmers: *Guilds 1*

farmers' rummy: *Card Games 5*

Farmhouse: *Architectural Styles 3*

farmhouse: *Farm/Outbuilding 3; Tables 4*

farmstead: *Farm/Outbuilding 3*

faro: *Card Games 5*

farohar: *Symbols in Magic and Religion 19*

far-reaching: *Large 20*

farrier: *Animal/Equestrian 1; Castle Inhabitants and Personnel 1*

Fars: *Human Ethnic Groups 1*

farsighted: *Eye Type 1; Magic Vocabulary 17*

fasces: *Secular Symbols 19*

fascinate: *Magic Vocabulary 17; Witchcraft Vocabulary 17*

fascinating: *Beautiful 20*

fascination: *Solitaire Card Games 5*

fascinator: *Headgear 2*

fashion doll: *Toys 5*

fashion forward: *Styles of Dress 2*

fashion model: *Styles of Dress 2*

fashion reporter: *Publishing 1*

fashion: *Create 20*

fassaite: *Minerals 10*

fast attack craft: *Military Watercraft 8*

fast food restaurant: *Food/Drink Establishments 3*

fast lane: *Roads 9*

fast movement: *Magical Transportation 17*

fast neutron: *Chemistry General Vocabulary 11*

fast track: *Card Games 5*

fast: *Adjectives 20*

fasten: *Close/Hold 20; Fix 20*

fastener: *Jewelry 21*

fasteners: *Equipment and Tools 5*

faster-than-light: *Spaceship Drive Systems 22*

fasting of the mind: *Philosophy Basic Concepts 14*

fasting: *Rituals 14*

fastness: *Fortification 3; Terrain Features 10*

fat free cottage: *Cheese Moist 6*

fat free milk: *Dairy Beverages 6*

fat free sour cream: *Other Dairy 6*

fat free: *Milk 6*

fat lamp: *Illumination/Light Sources 5*

fat lip: *Injuries/Medical Emergencies 12*

fat: *Cheeks 1; Heavy 20; Large 20; Large/Heavy 1*

fatal familial insomnia: *Diseases 12*

fatal: *Horror Vocabulary 23*

Fate: *Major Lines 19*

Father Christmas: *Characters with Symbolic Meaning 19; Christmas 19*

Father Time: *Characters with Symbolic Meaning 19*

father: *Cleric 1; Male 1*

father-in-law: *Male 1*

fathom: *Boat/Ship Terminology 9*

fatigued: *Horror Vocabulary 23; Slow 20*

Fatima: *Real Places Steeped in Legend or Mystery 18*

fatsia: *Shrubs 10*

faucet: *Bathroom Features and Fixtures 3*

fauchard: *Pole Weapons 7*

fauchard-fork: *Pole Weapons 7*

fault cave: *Cave Anatomy 10*

fault zone: *Geography General Vocabulary 10; Geological Vocabulary 10*

fault: *Cave Anatomy 10; Geography General Vocabulary 10; Geography General Vocabulary 10; Geological Vocabulary 10*

fault-block mountain: *Geography General Vocabulary 10*

faultless: *Happy 20*

faun: *Fae Related 16*

Fauvism: *Art Movements 13*

faux fur: *Fabric 2*

faux leather: *Fabric 2*

faux suede: *Fabric 2*

faux: *Fur 2*

fauxhawk: *Hair Style 1*

fava bean: *Legumes 6*

favorable: *Fortunate 20*

favorite weapon is lost/destroyed: *Common Dangers 24*

favorite: *Terms of Endearment 1*

fawn mushroom: *Fungus Common Names 10*

fawn: *Brown 20*

fax machine: *Office/School Machines 5; Spy Gear 5*

fayalite: *Minerals 10*

Faye: *Comets 11*

FCM 2C Alsace heavy tank: *France Military Vehicles 8*

FCM 36 light tank: *France Military Vehicles 8*

Fea's: *Viper 15*

fear of the Lord: *Seven Gifts of the Holy Spirit 19*

fear: *General Emotions 20; Horror Vocabulary 23*

fearful: *Horror Vocabulary 23; Owls 15*

fearfulness: *General Emotions 20*

fearless: *Personality Other 1*

feather bonnet: *Headgear 2*

feather duster: *Cleaning Supplies/Gadgets 5*

feather staff: *Spears 7*

feather: *Beds 4; Embellishments 2; Jewelry 21; Symbols in Magic and Religion 19*

feathered: *Hair Style 1*

feathers: *Wizard's Goods 5*

featherstitch: *Embroidery Stitches 2*

feathery: *Light 20*

feature reporter: *Publishing 1*

Febold Feboldson: *Tall Tales 18*

fecal matter: *Excrement 12*

feces: *Excrement 12*

fech fech: *Soil General Vocabulary 10*

fecking: *Expletives 20*

fed up: *Sad 20*

federacy: *Political Divisions 10*

federal agent: *Law Enforcement 1*

federal blue: *Blue 20*

federal building: *Administrative Property 3*

federal state: *Political Divisions 10*

Federal: *Architectural Styles 3*

Federalist: *Political Parties 1*

federated state: *Political Divisions 10*

federation: *Geography General Vocabulary 10; Political Divisions 10*

fedora: *Headgear 2*

feeble: *Small/Fragile 20*

feed grinder: *General Farm Equipment*

feed: *Technical Terms 13*

feedback: *Technical Terms 13*

feeder bands: *Meteorology General Vocabulary 10*

feel affection: *Love 20*

feelers: *Hair Style 1*

feeling: *Philosophy Basic Concepts 14*

feijoa: *Unusual Edible Fruits 6*

feint: *Fencing Vocabulary 7*

feldspar: *Cat's Eye Gems 21*

Fell Pony: *Horse Breeds 15*

fellow: *Male 1*

felon: *Illicit Occupations 1; Thief 1*

felsic: *Geological Vocabulary 10*

felt guitar pick: *Music Accessories*

felt: *Fabric 2*

female: *Character Building 1*

feminine: *Styles of Dress 2; Vocal/Speech Quality 1*

femme fatale: *Common Character Archetypes 21*

femur: *Bones 12*

fen: *Soil General Vocabulary 10; Terrain Features 10; Water Terms 9*

fenamiphos: *Dangerous Chemicals 11*

fence: *Cemetery 3; Farm/Outbuilding 3; Landscaping 3; Property Features 3; Thief 1*

fencer: *Fighter 1*

fencing equipment: *Combat, Armor, and Weapons 7*

fencing gear: *Spy Gear 5*

fencing glove: *Fencing Equipment 7*

fencing jacket: *Fencing Equipment 7*

fencing strip: *Fencing Vocabulary 7*

fencing vest: *Fencing Equipment 7*

fencing vocabulary: *Combat, Armor, and Weapons 7*

fencing: *Combat, Armor, and Weapons 7*

feng huang: *Flying Creatures 16*

Fengjing: *Pigs 15*

fenitrothion: *Dangerous Chemicals 11*

fenland: *Terrain Features 10; Water Terms 9*

fennec: *Foxes 15*

fennel: *Aphrodisiacs 19; Vegetable Juice 6; Vegetables 6*

fenrir: *Beast 16*

Fenrir: *Moons 11*

fensulfothion: *Dangerous Chemicals 11*

feral donkey: *Horses Related 15*

feral: *Monster Categories/Terms 16*

fer-de-lance: *General Snake Families 15*

Ferdinand: *Moons 11*

fermata: *Notation 13*

ferment: *Witchcraft Vocabulary 17*

Fermium: *Elements 11*

fern green: *Green 20*

fern: *Objects/Activities Connected to Lore 19*

Fernbach flask: *Laboratory Equipment 5*

fernbush: *Shrubs 10*

fern-leaf: *Garden Perennials 10*

ferrallitization: *Soil General Vocabulary 10*

Ferret FV711 armored car: *United Kingdom Military Vehicles 8*

ferret: *Paranormal Activity 21*

Ferris wheel: *Amusement Park/Carnival/Circus/Fair 3*

ferro-actinolite: *Minerals 10*

ferromagnesian mineral: *Geological Vocabulary 10*

ferro-magnesite: *Minerals 10*

ferromagnetism: *Chemistry General Vocabulary 11*

ferrosillite: *Minerals 10*

ferrotitanite: *Minerals 10*

ferrous chromite: *Minerals 10*

ferrowollastonite: *Minerals 10*

ferruginous quartz: *Minerals 10*

ferry dock: *Infrastructure Buildings 9*

ferry slip: *Infrastructure Buildings 9; Marina 3*

ferry: *Mass Transit 9; Small Watercraft 9*

fertility: *Pennsylvania Dutch Hex Signs 19*

fertilizer spreader: *Garden Tools; General Farm Equipment*

Ferumbras: *Twelve Peers of Charlemagne 18*

fervor: *General Emotions 20; Love 20*

fester: *Smells 20*

festhall: *Entertainment Property 3*

festival grounds: *General Property 3*

feta: *Cheese Common Varieties 6*

fetid shrub: *Deciduous Trees 10*

fetid: *Unattractive 20*

fetish: *Art Genres 13; Objects in Magic and Religion 19*

fetter: *Fasteners 5*

fettuccini: *Pasta 6*

feverfew: *Garden Perennials 10*

fez: *Headgear 2*

FGM-148 Javelin: *Army Missile 8*

fiancé: *Male 1*

fiancée: *Female 1*

Fiat 2000 light tank: *Italy Military Vehicles 8*

Fiat 3000 light tank: *Italy Military Vehicles 8*

Fiat 6614 wheeled armored personnel carrier: *Italy Military Vehicles 8*

Fiat 6616 heavy armored car: *Italy Military Vehicles 8*

fiberglass: *Door Materials 3*

fibrinogen: *Blood 12*

fibrolite: *Cat's Eye Gems 21*

fibula: *Bones 12*

fickle: *Personality Other 1*

fiction: *Literary Styles 5*

fictional character appears in modern world: *Fantasy Plot Devices 24*

fictional characters: *Legendary, Mystical and Mythical Items and Locations 18*

fictional diseases: *Anatomy and Physiology 12*

fictional human species: *Character Building 1*

fictional locations: *Legendary, Mystical and Mythical Items and Locations 18; Legendary/Mythical Locations 18*

fiddle: *Fix 20; String Musical Instruments*

fiddlehead: *Vegetables 6*

fiddly: *Difficult 20*

fidelity: *Love 20; Philosophy Basic Concepts 14*

field artillery: *Cannon 7; Siege Equipment 7*

field clover: *Wildflowers 10*

field corn: *Farm/Outbuilding 3*

field drab: *Brown 20*

field equipment: *Combat, Armor, and Weapons 7*

field guide: *Books/Publications 5*

field gun: *Cannon 7*

field marshal: *Armed Forces Other Titles 8*

field mouse: *Woodland Mammals 15*

field mushroom: *Fungus Common Names 10*

field pea: *Farm/Outbuilding 3*

field reporter: *Media 1*

Field Spaniel: *Dog Breeds 15*

field: *Farm/Outbuilding 3; Terrain Features 10*

fielder's mitt: *Sporting Goods Other 5*

fiend: *Monster Categories/Terms 16; Villain 20*

fiery fox: *Bears 15*

fifth planet: *Hypothetical Solar System Bodies 11*

fifty pacer: *Viper 15*

fifty-five: *Card Games 5*

fifty-six: *Card Games 5*

fig: *Aphrodisiacs 19; Tropical/Exotic Fruits 6; Wasp 15*

fig-eating: *Bats 15*

fight choreographer: *Performing Arts 1*

fighter jet: *Air Vehicles 9*

fighter VSTOL: *Military Aircraft 8*

fighter: *Character Building 1; Military Aircraft 8; Military Aircraft Pre-1962 8*

Fighting Bull: *Other Cows 15*

figurative: *Art Genres 13*

figure eight: *Sailing Knots 9*

figure skates: *Footwear/Shoes 2; Sporting Goods Other 5*

figure: *Paranormal Occurrences 21; Solve 20*

figure-eight: *Shield Types 7*

figurehead: *Boat/Ship Anatomy 9*

figurine: *Typical Magical Objects 17*

Fijolito: *Deciduous Trees 10*

filament: *Astronomy General Terms 11; Wizard's Goods 5*

Filao tree: *Weeds 10*

filbert: *Nuts 6*

file box: *Office/School/Writing Supplies 5*

file cabinet: *Storage 4*

file folder: *Office/School/Writing Supplies 5*

file: *Hand Tools 5; Laboratory Equipment 5*

filet mignon: *Beef 6*

filings: *Wizard's Goods 5*

fill dirt: *Soil General Vocabulary 10*

fill light: *Technical Terms 13*

filler paper: *Office/School/Writing Supplies 5*

fillet knife: *Kitchen Utensils 5*

fillet: *Fish/Seafood Meals 6*

filling: *Teeth Dental Work 1*

film: *Art Media 13; Smells 20*

filmstrip projector: *Office/School Machines 5*

filter funnel: *Laboratory Equipment 5*

filter paper: *Laboratory Equipment 5*

filter: *Clean 20; Laboratory Equipment 5*

FIM-92 Stinger: *Army Missile 8*

fin: *Whales 15*

finagle: *Card Games 5*

final: *Ending 20*

finale: *Ending 20*

finance: *Character Building 1*

financial advisor: *Finance 1*

find irresistible: *Love 20*

find out: *Learn 20*

find: *Buy 20*

finder: *Astronomy General Terms 11*

finding a penny heads up: *Harbingers/Charms for Good Luck 19*

finding a penny tails up: *Harbingers of Bad Luck 19*

fine spun: *Small/Thin 1*

fine: *Beautiful 20; Good 20; Hair Types 1; Personality Other 1; Small/Thin 1*

finger bowl: *Tableware 5*

finger curls: *Hair Style 1*

finger guitar pick: *Music Accessories*

finger millet: *Grain 6*

finger puppet: *Toys 5*

finger wave: *Hair Style 1*

finger: *Art Media 13; Body Parts 12; Sandwiches 6*

fingerless gloves: *Accessories 2*

fingerling potato: *Vegetables 6*

fingernail clippings: *Wizard's Goods 5*

fingernail: *Body Parts 12*

fingernails: *Objects/Activities Connected to Lore 19*

fingerprint/palmprint recognition system: *Spy Gear 5*

fingers slammed in car door: *Injuries/Medical Emergencies 12*

fingers: *Objects/Activities Connected to Lore 19*

fingertip: *Towels 5*

finish: *Ending 20*

finishing sander: *Power Tools*

finite: *Philosophy Basic Concepts 14*

Finlay: *Comets 11*

Finn: *Human Ethnic Groups 1*

finned: *Special Body Features 19*

Finnhorse: *Horse Breeds 15*

finning: *Swimming Strokes 9*

Finnish landrace: *Pigs 15*

Finnish Lapphund: *Dog Breeds 15*

Finnish magical mill: *Objects 18*

Finnish pantheon: *Philosophy and Religion 14*

Finnish Spitz: *Dog Breeds 15*

Finnish: *Other Cows 15*

Fionn mac Cumhaill: *Legendary People Presumed to be Fictional 18*

fipsen: *Card Games 5*

Fir Bolg: *Human Ethnic Groups 1*

fir darrig: *General Fae 16*

firangi: *Swords One-handed 7*

fire agate: *Minerals 10; Standard Gems 21*

fire archer: *Siege Engines 7*

fire bellied: *Toads 15*

fire birch: *Deciduous Trees 10*

fire blanket: *Laboratory Equipment 5*

fire boat: *Small Watercraft 9*

fire giant: *Humanlike Groups 1*

fire house: *Public Services 3*

fire lance barrel: *Siege Engines 7*

fire opal: *Minerals 10; Standard Gems 21*

fire pink: *Garden Perennials 10*

fire pit: *Property Features 3*

fire pot: *Siege Equipment 7*

fire ship: *Siege Engines 7*

fire station: *Public Services 3*

fire support base: *Fortification 3*

fire temple: *Religious Building 3*

fire wheel: *Symbols in Magic and Religion 19; Wildflowers 10*

fire: *Ants 15; Art Techniques 13; Elemental 16; Four Elements 19; Giant Humanoids 16; Squid 15; Witchcraft Vocabulary 17*

fireball: *Astronomy General Terms 11; Garden Perennials 10*

fire-bellied: *Frogs 15*

firebelly: *Newts 15*

firecracker plant: *Garden Annuals 10*

firecracker: *Garden Perennials 10; Wizard's Goods 5*

firefish: *Aquarium Saltwater Fish 15*

firehouse: *Chairs and Stools 4*

firemouth: *Aquarium Freshwater Fish 15*

fireplace poker: *Improvised Weapons 7*

fireplace screen: *Miscellaneous Furniture 4*

fireplace: *Building Elements and Features 3; Christmas 19*

fireside: *Building Elements and Features 3*

fire-starter: *Candles 5*

firethorn: *Shrubs 10*

firewhirl: *Meteorology General Vocabulary 10*

firewood: *Wizard's Goods 5*

fireworks: *Independence Day 19*

firm: *Personality Other 1*

first aid kit: *General Survival Gear 5; Laboratory Supplies 5; Military Equipment 8*

first alto: *Voices 13*

First Communion: *Sacraments 14*

First Eucharist: *Sacraments 14*

First Holy Communion: *Sacraments 14*

first in line: *Beginning 20*

first lady: *Government 1*

first law of thermodynamics: *Chemistry General Vocabulary 11*

first lieutenant: *U.S. Air Force Officer 8; U.S. Army Officer 8; U.S. Marines Officer 8*

first mate: *Maritime Occupations 1; Navy Other Titles 8*

first molar: *Teeth 12*

first of its kind: *New 20*

first officer of the kingdom: *Fantasy Occupations 24*

first officer: *Occupations 22*

first past the post: *Hero 20*

first sergeant: *U.S. Army Enlisted 8; U.S. Marines Enlisted 8*

first soprano: *Voices 13*

first tenor: *Voices 13*

First Transcontinental Railroad: *Seven Wonders of the Industrial World 18*

first: *Beginning 20*

first-class: *Good 20*

first-rate: *Good 20*

firth: *Coastal and Oceanic 10*

fish and chips: *Fish/Seafood Meals 6*

fish burger: *Fish/Seafood Meals 6*

fish dive: *Ballet Terms 13; Dance Moves 13*

fish knife: *Eating Utensils 5*

fish pitch: *Card Games 5*

fish pond: *Water Features 10*

fish sandwich: *Fish/Seafood Meals 6*

fish sticks: *Fish/Seafood Meals 6*

fish: *Allergies 12; Animals 15; Animals with Symbolic Meaning 19; Charges 19; Farm/Outbuilding 3; Food 6; Objects/Activities Connected to Lore 19; Owls 15*

fishbone: *Embroidery Stitches 2*

fisherman's bend: *Sailing Knots 9*

fisherman's cap: *Headgear 2*

fisherman's ring: *Papal Symbols 19*

fishing gears: *Equipment and Tools 5*

fishing: *General Snake Families 15; Owls 15; Small Watercraft 9*

fishnet tights: *Dance Clothing 13*

fishnet: *Fabric 2*

fishnets: *Ladies' Wear 2*

fishtail braid: *Hair Style 1*

fission: *Energy Sources/Types 22; Spaceship Drive Systems 22; Weapons 22*

fissure cave: *Cave Anatomy 10*

fissure: *Cave Anatomy 10; Terrain Features 10*

fist: *Body Parts 12; Hand Weapons 7*

fit: *Fix 20*

fitted sheet: *Bed Linens 5*

fitting kit: *Shoe Accessories 13*

fitting: *Fortunate 20*

five card brag: *Card Games 5*

five card draw with a bug: *Poker Card Games 5*

five card draw: *Poker Card Games 5*

five card stud high-low: *Poker Card Games 5*

five card stud: *Poker Card Games 5*

five finger: *Garden Perennials 10*

five fingers fruit: *Unusual Edible Fruits 6*

five golden rings: *Twelve Days of Christmas 19*

five hundred rummy: *Card Games 5*

five hundred: *Card Games 5*

five o'clock shadow: *Facial Hair Beard 1*

five pillars of wisdom: *Symbols in Magic and Religion 19*

five positions of the feet: *Ballet Terms 13*

five spot: *Wildflowers 10*

five wisdoms of Buddhism: *Collective Symbols 19*

five-finger: *Forehead 1*

five-leaf aralia: *Garden Perennials 10*

five-step waltz: *Historical Dances 13*

fix: *Verbs 20*

fixed bay: *Windows 3*

fixed bow: *Windows 3*

fixed wing: *Air Vehicles 9*

fixed: *Stubborn 1*

fizz: *Cooking Techniques 20*

Fjall: *Other Cows 15*

fjord: *Coastal and Oceanic 10; Glacial and Mountain 10; Water Terms 9*

flabby: *Ears 1*

flag: *Independence Day 19; Signal Devices 5*

flagon: *Containers and Vessels 5*

flagstaff: *Boat/Ship Anatomy 9*

flag-waver: *Hero 20*

flail mower: *General Farm Equipment*

flail: *Bludgeons 7; Steam Powered Farm Equipment*

flambé: *Cooking Techniques 20*

flamberge: *Pole Weapons 7*

flame opal: *Minerals 10*

flame spinel: *Minerals 10*

flame thrower: *Field Equipment 7*

flame: *Cooking Techniques 20; Orange 20; Red 20*

flame-bladed: *Swords Two-handed 7*

flamenco (Spain): *Ethnic/Folk Dances 13*

flamenco skirt: *Dance Clothing 13*

flamenco: *Dance Styles 13*

flaming catapult load: *Siege Equipment 7*

flaming rum punch: *Hot Drinks 6*

flamingo: *Other Wild Birds 15*

flammable oil: *Specialty Survival Gear 5*

flammable: *Chemistry General Vocabulary 11*

flammant: *Special Body Features 19*

flanchard: *Horse Barding Pieces 7*

Flanders poppy: *Wildflowers 10*

flange: *Hardware 5*

flank: *General Combat Vocabulary 7; Moves 7; Tactics 7*

flannel bush: *Shrubs 10*

flannel plant: *Wildflowers 10*

flannel: *Fabric 2*

flannelette: *Fabric 2*

flap: *Doors Atypical 3*

flap-footed lizard: *Scaled Reptiles 15*

flapper: *Styles of Dress 2*

flappy: *Ears 1*

flare jeans: *Unisex Clothing 2*

flare star: *Astronomy General Terms 11*

flare: *Signal Devices 5*

flash bang grenade: *SWAT Equipment 7*

flash drive: *Computer Equipment 5*

flash flood: *Meteorology General Vocabulary 10*

flash mob: *Dance Styles 13*

flash opal: *Minerals 10*

flash point: *Chemistry General Vocabulary 11*

flash powder: *Wizard's Goods 5*

flash: *Weapons 22*

flasher: *Butterfly 15*

flashfire opal: *Minerals 10*

flashlight: *General Survival Gear 5; Illumination/Light Sources 5; Military Equipment 8*

flask: *Containers and Vessels 5; Laboratory Equipment 5*

flat guitar pick: *Music Accessories*

flat head screwdriver: *Hand Tools 5*

flat screen television: *Electronics 4*

flat sheet: *Bed Linens 5*

flat tire: *Travel Hazards 9*

flat top: *Hair Style 1*

flat: *Ears 1; General Music Vocabulary 13; Nose 1; Notation 13; Residential Property 3; Roof Styles 3; Technical Terms 13; Vocal/Speech Quality 1*

flatback: *Sea Turtles 15*

flatbed: *Motorized Truck 9*

flat-bottom: *Ice Cream Cones 6*

flatbread: *Bread General Varieties 6*

Flat-Coated Retriever: *Dog Breeds 15*

flat-headed: *Bats 15*

flatiron: *Shield Types 7*

flatironed: *Hair Treated 1*

flat-nosed: *Pit Viper 15*

flats: *Footwear/Shoes 2*

flattener: *Cave Anatomy 10*

flattered: *Happy 20*

flatweave carpet: *Floor Coverings 4*

flatwood: *Soil General Vocabulary 10*

flauros: *Devil 16*

flavored cream cheese: *Cheese Moist 6*

flawless: *Beautiful 20; Good 20*

flax: *Garden Perennials 10; Seeds 6*

flaxseed: *Oils 6*

flea market: *General Property 3; Outdoor Property 3*

fleabane: *Garden Perennials 10; Wildflowers 10*

fleaker: *Laboratory Equipment 5*

fleas: *Ten Plagues on Egypt 14*

fleche: *Fencing Vocabulary 7*

flee: *Locomotion 9*

fleece flower: *Garden Perennials 10; Weeds 10*

fleece: *Fabric 2*

fleet admiral: *Maritime Occupations 1; U.S. Navy Officer 8*

fleet aircraft carrier: *Military Watercraft 8*

fleet: *Fast 20; Mobility 1*

Flemish hood: *Headgear 2*

Flemish: *Human Ethnic Groups 1*

flesh golem: *Construct 16*

flesh: *Flies 15*

fleshcrawler: *Beast 16*

fleshy: *Large/Heavy 1*

fletcher: *Business Property 3; Castle Inhabitants and Personnel 1*

fletching: *Missile Weapons 7*

fleur-de-lis: *Cadency Mark 19; Garden Perennials 10; Symbols in Magic and Religion 19*

fleury-counterfleury: *Partition Lines 19*

Fleuve: *Horse Breeds 15*

flexible curve: *Architectural/Engineering Tools 5*

flexible weapons: *Combat, Armor, and Weapons 7*

flexible: *Mobility 1*

flick: *Fencing Vocabulary 7*

flier: *Wild Freshwater Fish 15*

flies: *Animals 15; Ten Plagues on Egypt 14; Travel Hazards 9*

flight attendant: *Styles of Dress 2; Transportation 1*

flight deck cruiser: *Military Watercraft 8*

flight leader: *Armed Forces Other Titles 8*

flight: *Journey 20; Locomotion 9; Magical Transportation 17; Physical Mutations 22*

flimflam man: *Thief 1*

flimsy: *Light 20; Small/Fragile 20; Small/Thin 1*

Flinders: *Python 15*

flint and steel: *General Survival Gear 5; Illumination/Light Sources 5*

flint knife: *Western Weapons 21*

flint: *Minerals 10; Sedimentary Rocks 10*

flintlock: *Black Powder Weapons 7*

flip chart: *Office/School/Writing Supplies 5*

flip flops: *Footwear/Shoes 2*

flip: *Hair Style 1*

flipping: *Expletives 20*

flipthrough: *Hair Style 1*

float coal: *Boat/Ship Anatomy 9*

float: *Fishing Gear 5; Locomotion 9*

floating citadel: *Vehicles 24*

floating city: *Installations 22; Plot Devices 22*

floating magical island: *Fantasy Locations 24*

floating pennywort: *Weeds 10*

floating shelf: *Storage 4*

floating: *Boat/Ship Terminology 9*

flock: *Followers 14*

flocked: *Fabric 2*

flood stage: *Meteorology General Vocabulary 10*

flood: *Geological Natural Hazards 10; Severe Weather 10; Wet 20*

floodplain: *Fluvial 10*

floor buffer: *Cleaning Supplies/Gadgets 5*

floor lamp: *Illumination/Light Sources 5*

floor mat: *Floor Coverings 4*

floor wax: *Cleaning Supplies/Gadgets 5*

floor: *Building Elements and Features 3; Traps 3*

floor-length skirt: *Western Clothing/Dress 21*

flophouse: *Residential Property 3*

floppy disk: *Computer Equipment 5; Spy Gear 5*

floral white: *White 20*

floral: *Fabric Patterns 2*

Florence flask: *Laboratory Equipment 5*

Florence Nightingale: *Real People with Legendary Status 18*

Florida aspen: *Weeds 10*

Florida black: *Bears 15*

Florida box: *Freshwater Turtles 15*

Florida chicken: *Freshwater Turtles 15*

Florida cooter: *Freshwater Turtles 15*

Florida Cracker/Pineywoods: *Other Cows 15*

Florida Cracker: *Architectural Styles 3*

Florida elm: *Deciduous Trees 10*

Florida holly: *Weeds 10*

Florida Modern: *Architectural Styles 3*

Florida mud: *Freshwater Turtles 15*

Florida persimmon: *Deciduous Trees 10*

Florida red-bellied: *Freshwater Turtles 15*

Florida snapping: *Freshwater Turtles 15*

Florida softshell: *Freshwater Turtles 15*

Florida torreya: *Evergreen Trees 10*

Florida yew: *Evergreen Trees 10*

Florismart: *Twelve Peers of Charlemagne 18*

florist: *Artists and Craftspeople 1; Business Property 3; Castle Inhabitants and Personnel 1*

flos ferri: *Minerals 10*

flotation device: *Military Equipment 8*

flotation: *Chemistry General Vocabulary 11*

flour sack: *Towels 5*

flour tortilla: *Bread General Varieties 6*

flour: *Staples 6; Wizard's Goods 5*

flourless chocolate: *Cake 6*

flow of air: *Wind 10*

flow: *Wet 20*

flowage: *Water Features 10*

flower arranger: *Artists and Craftspeople 1*

flower garden: *Solitaire Card Games 5*

flower girl: *Special Occasion 1*

flower hat: *Jellyfish 15*

Flower of Life: *Real Objects Not Fully Understood 18*

flower of life: *Symbols in Magic and Religion 19*

flower of rajya: *Cheese International Varieties 6*

flower petals: *Wizard's Goods 5*

flower pot: *Improvised Weapons 7*

flower: *Wasp 15*

flower-faced: *Bats 15*

flowering rush: *Weeds 10*

flowers: *May Day 19; Thanksgiving 19; Valentine's Day 19*

flownet: *Soil General Vocabulary 10*

flowstone: *Cave Anatomy 10; Minerals 10*

fluenetil: *Dangerous Chemicals 11*

fluff: *Clean 20*

fluffing: *Expletives 20*

fluffy flakes: *Snow Types 10*

fluffy: *Light 20*

flugel horn: *Wind/Woodwind and Brass Musical Instruments*

fluid: *Wet 20*

fluids: *Chemistry General Vocabulary 11*

fluor: *Minerals 10*

fluorannite: *Minerals 10*

fluorapatite: *Minerals 10*

fluor-dravite: *Minerals 10*

fluorescence: *Chemistry General Vocabulary 11*

fluorescent green: *Green 20*

fluorescent orange: *Orange 20*

fluorescent yellow: *Yellow 20*

fluorescent: *Illumination Bulb and Tube Types 5*

fluorine: *Dangerous Chemicals 11*

Fluorine: *Elements 11*

fluorite: *Standard Gems 21*

fluoroacetamide: *Dangerous Chemicals 11*

fluoroacetic acid: *Dangerous Chemicals 11*

fluoroacetyl chloride: *Dangerous Chemicals 11*

fluorophlogopite: *Minerals 10*

fluorouracil: *Dangerous Chemicals 11*

fluorspar: *Minerals 10*

flurries: *Snow Events 10*

flush: *Card Games 5*

flushed: *Skin Types and Features 1*

flute glass: *Drinkware 5*

flute: *Wind/Woodwind and Brass Musical Instruments*

flutist: *Musical Occupations 1*

flutter back finning: *Swimming Strokes 9*

flutter kick: *Swimming Strokes 9*

flutter: *Locomotion 9*

fluvial island: *Fluvial 10*

fluvial landforms: *Chapter 10*

fluvial terrace: *Fluvial 10; Glacial and Mountain 10*

flux: *Chemistry General Vocabulary 11*

fluxweed: *Wildflowers 10*

fly loft: *Parts of the Theater 13*

fly river: *Freshwater Turtles 15*

fly: *Embroidery Stitches 2; Garment Pieces 2; Locomotion 9; Witchcraft Vocabulary 17*

flying bed: *Vehicles 24*

flying boat: *Magical Transportation 17*

flying broom: *Typical Magical Objects 17*

flying buttress: *Building Elements and Features 3*

flying carpet of Persian Prince Housain: *Vehicles 18*

flying carpet: *Magical Transportation 17; Typical Magical Objects 17; Vehicles 24*

flying claws: *Chain Weapons 7*

flying creatures: *Monsters 16*

flying disk: *Toys 5*

Flying Dutchman: *Sites Lost or Unproven to Exist 18*

flying fox: *Bats 15*

flying lemur: *Gliding Mammals 15*

flying officer: *Armed Forces Other Titles 8*

flying saucer: *Air Vehicles 9*

flying squirrel: *Gliding Mammals 15*

flying suit: *Spy Gear 5*

flying throne of Kai Kavus: *Vehicles 18*

flying: *Fast 20; General Snake Families 15; Squid 15*

flyssa: *Swords One-handed 7*

flyweight: *Light 20*

FN FAL: *Semiautomatic Centerfire Rifles 7*

FN Five-Seven USG: *Pistol Semiautomatic 7*

FN SCAR: *Assault Rifle 8; Semiautomatic Centerfire Rifles 7*

FN tactical police: *Shotguns Pump 7*

foal: *Horses 15*

foam brush: *Art Tools 5*

foam cup: *Drinkware 5*

foam: *Chemistry General Vocabulary 11*

foamflower: *Garden Perennials 10*

focaccia: *Bread General Varieties 6*

focality: *Geography General Vocabulary 10*

focus spot: *Technical Terms 13*

focus: *Technical Terms 13*

foe: *Fighter 1*

fog bank: *Wet 10*

fog horn: *Boat/Ship Anatomy 9; Signal Devices 5*

fog of war: *General Combat Vocabulary 7*

fog: *Gray 20; Water Terms 9; Wet 10*

foible blade: *Fencing Equipment 7*

foidolite: *Igneous Rocks 10*

foil mask: *Fencing Equipment 7*

foil: *Fabric 2; Swords One-handed 7*

fold buckling: *Geological Vocabulary 10*

fold: *Geological Vocabulary 10*

folder: *Containers and Vessels 5; Office/School/Writing Supplies 5*

folding money: *Coins and Currency 21*

folding screen: *Miscellaneous Furniture 4*

folding: *Chairs and Stools 4; Tables 4*

foliation: *Geological Vocabulary 10*

folk dances: *The Arts 13*

folk hero: *Common Character Archetypes 21*

folk: *Art Genres 13; Dance Styles 13; Performance Genres 13; Styles of Dress 2*

folklore: *Legendary, Mystical and Mythical Items and Locations 18*

folklorical: *Dance Shoes 13*

follow spot: *Technical Terms 13*

follow the queen: *Poker Card Games 5*

follower: *Cleric 1; Followers 14*

followers: *Philosophy and Religion 14*

follow-on cue: *Stage Terms 13*

fondness for: *Love 20*

fondness: *General Emotions 20*

Fondu/fondue: *Ballet Terms 13*

fondue fork: *Eating Utensils 5*

fonio: *Farm/Outbuilding 3*

fonofos: *Dangerous Chemicals 11*

fontange: *Hair Style 1*

fontina: *Cheese Common Varieties 6*

food car: *Railroad 9*

food court: *Food/Drink Establishments 3*

food critic: *Publishing 1*

food establishment: *Architecture and Property 3*

food mill: *Kitchen Equipment 5*

food poisoning: *Diseases 12; Injuries/Medical Emergencies 12*

food processor: *Appliances 5*

food reporter: *Publishing 1*

food service: *Character Building 1*

food supply tainted: *Horror Plot Devices 23*

food taster: *Castle Inhabitants and Personnel 1; Royal/Noble 1*

food: *Allergies 12; General Survival Gear 5*

foodborne illness: *Travel Hazards 9*

fool: *Bard 1; Common Character Archetypes 21; Miscellaneous Dessert 6*

fool's gold: *Minerals 10*

foot soldier: *Fighter 1*

foot: *Body Parts 12; Bridges 9*

football field: *Entertainment Property 3*

football: *Athletic Shoes 2; Poker Card Games 5; Sporting Goods Balls 5; Thanksgiving 19*

foothill: *Terrain Features 10*

foothills pine: *Evergreen Trees 10*

foothold: *General Combat Vocabulary 7; Traps 3*

footlight: *Technical Terms 13*

footlocker: *Storage 4*

footman: *Castle Inhabitants and Personnel 1*

footman's lance: *Pole Weapons 7*

footpad: *Thief 1*

footpath: *Roads 9*

footstep: *Paranormal Occurrences 21*

footstool: *Chairs and Stools 4*

footwear: *Clothing 2*

footwork: *Fencing Vocabulary 7*

fop: *Personality Other 1*

foppish: *Personality Other 1*

for crying out loud: *Expletives 20*

forager: *Nature Occupations 1; Rural Occupations 1*

foray: *General Combat Vocabulary 7*

Forbes cypress: *Evergreen Trees 10*

Forbes: *Comets 11*

forbidden friend/lover: *Common Character Archetypes 21*

forbidden zone: *Chemistry General Vocabulary 11*

forbidding: *Horror Vocabulary 23; Sad 20*

force field generator: *Devices 22; Weapons 22*

force field: *Paranormal Abilities 21*

force: *Attack 7*

forceful: *Personality Other 1*

ford: *Terrain Features 10*

forearm: *Body Parts 12*

forebear: *Relational 1*

foreboding: *General Emotions 20; Horror Vocabulary 23; Magic Vocabulary 17*

forebuilding: *Castle Anatomy 3*

forecart: *Horse Drawn Farm Equipment*

forecast: *Meteorology General Vocabulary 10*

forecaster: *Wizard 1*

forecastle: *Boat/Ship Anatomy 9*

forefront: *New 20*

forehead: *Body Parts 12; Character Building 1*

foreign currency: *Spy Gear 5*

foreign language dictionary: *Books/Publications 5*

foreign language: *Travel Hazards 9*

foreman: *General Occupations 1*

foremast: *Boat/Ship Anatomy 9*

forerunner: *New 20*

foresail: *Boat/Ship Anatomy 9*

foreshock: *Geological Natural Hazards 10*

foresight: *Magic Vocabulary 17*

forest dung: *Beetle 15*

forest green: *Green 20*

forest mountain: *Pigs 15*

forest owlet: *Owls 15*

forest: *Caecilians 15; Cobra 15; Ecosystems 10; Elf 1; Gnome 1; Terrain Features 10*

forestage: *Technical Terms 13*

forester: *Nature Occupations 1; Rural Occupations 1*

foreswear: *Horror Vocabulary 23*

forewarn: *Horror Vocabulary 23*

forge: *Business Property 3*

forger: *Thief 1*

forget: *Witchcraft Vocabulary 17*

forget-me-not: *Garden Annuals 10; Garden Perennials 10*

fork: *Eating Utensils 5; Garden Tools; Pole Weapons 7*

forked-leaf white oak: *Deciduous Trees 10*

forklift: *Motorized 9*

forlorn: *Sad 20*

form: *Art Techniques 13; Create 20; Fix 20; Natural Animal Homes 15; Philosophy Basic Concepts 14; Visual Elements 13*

formaela: *Cheese International Varieties 6*

formal charge: *Chemistry General Vocabulary 11*

formal dress: *Ladies' Wear 2*

formal wear: *Unisex Clothing 2*

formal: *Styles of Dress 2*

formaldehyde cyanohydrin: *Dangerous Chemicals 11*

formaldehyde: *Dangerous Chemicals 11*

formation: *Cave Anatomy 10*

former: *Old 20*

formetanate hydrochloride: *Dangerous Chemicals 11*

formidable: *Large 20*

formless: *Horror Vocabulary 23*

Formosa oolong: *Tea 6*

formosa: *Bears 15*

formothion: *Dangerous Chemicals 11*

formparanate: *Dangerous Chemicals 11*

formula: *Chemistry General Vocabulary 11*

formulate: *Create 20; Solve 20*

Fornax: *Constellations 11*

forneus: *Devil 16*

fornix: *Organs/Major Structures 12*

Fornjot: *Moons 11*

forsaken: *Sad 20*

Forseti (justice): *Norse Pantheon 14*

Forsten's: *Tortoises 15*

forsterite: *Minerals 10*

forsythia: *Shrubs 10*

Fort Laramie: *Famous Western Locations 21*

fort: *Fortification 3; Military Property 3; Western Paraphernalia/People 21*

forte blade: *Fencing Equipment 7*

forte: *Dynamics 13*

fortepiano: *Percussion Musical Instruments 5*

forthright: *Personality Other 1*

fortification agate: *Minerals 10*

fortification: *Architecture and Property 3; General Combat Vocabulary 7; Military Property 3*

fortissimo: *Dynamics 13*

fortitude: *Four Cardinal Virtues 19; Seven Gifts of the Holy Spirit 19; Seven Holy Virtues 19*

fortress: *Fortification 3*

fortunate: *Emotions 20*

fortune hunter: *Barbarian 1; Hero 20*

fortune teller: *Character Building 1, Cleric 1; Common Character Archetypes 21; Wizard 1*

fortune telling devices: *Divination and Fortune Telling 19*

fortune telling techniques: *Divination and Fortune Telling 19*

forty-one: *Card Games 5*

forum: *Entertainment Property 3*

fossa: *Other Wild Mammals 15*

fosse: *Castle Anatomy 3*

fossil agate: *Minerals 10*

fossil fuel: *Energy Sources/Types 22*

fossil fuels: *Chemistry General Vocabulary 11*

fossil opal: *Minerals 10*

fossil turquoise: *Minerals 10*

fossil: *Cave Anatomy 10; Geological Vocabulary 10*

fosthietan: *Dangerous Chemicals 11*

fothergilla: *Shrubs 10*

Fouetté en tourant: *Ballet Terms 13*

Fouetté rond de jambe en tournant: *Ballet Terms 13*

Fouetté: *Ballet Terms 13*

fouetté: *Dance Moves 13*

fougasse: *Bread General Varieties 6*

foul air: *Cave Anatomy 10*

foul: *Unattractive 20*

foulard: *Fabric 2*

fouled: *Unattractive 20*

found objects: *Art Materials 5*

found: *Art Genres 13*

foundation: *Makeup 5*

foundation garment: *Undergarments 2*

foundations: *Undergarments 2*

founding fathers: *Government 1; Independence Day 19*

foundling: *Child 1*

foundry: *Business Property 3*

fountain pen: *Office/School/Writing Supplies 5*

fountain: *Candy Chocolate 6; Property Features 3*

four calling birds: *Twelve Days of Christmas 19*

four evangelists of the Bible: *Collective Symbols 19*

Four Hallows of Ireland: *Legendary, Mystical and Mythical Items and Locations 18*

four horsemen of the apocalypse: *Collective Symbols 19*

four o'clock: *Garden Bulbs 10*

four of a kind: *Card Games 5*

four seasons: *Collective Symbols 19; Solitaire Card Games 5*

Four Square: *Architectural Styles 3*

four-card brag: *Card Games 5*

four-door: *Motorized 9*

four-leaf clover: *Harbingers/Charms for Good Luck 19; St. Patrick's Day 19*

four-needle pinyon: *Evergreen Trees 10*

four-poster: *Beds 4*

four-winged saltbush: *Garden Perennials 10*

Fouta: *Horse Breeds 15*

fowl: *Other Wild Birds 15*

fowlerite: *Minerals 10*

fowling pistol: *Black Powder Weapons 7*

fox and cubs: *Weeds 10*

Fox armored car: *United Kingdom Military Vehicles 8*

fox fairy: *Demon 16*

Fox Terrier smooth: *Dog Breeds 15*

Fox Terrier wire: *Dog Breeds 15*

fox: *Animals with Symbolic Meaning 19; Fur 2; General Snake Families 15*

Fox: *Native American Peoples 1*

foxes: *Animals 15*

foxglove: *Garden Perennials 10; Poisonous Plants 10; Wildflowers 10*

foxhole: *Fortification 3*

foxtail millet: *Grain 6*

foxtrot: *Dance Styles 13*

foxy: *Beautiful 20*

foyer: *Rooms 3*

fracas: *General Combat Vocabulary 7*

fractal in soil mechanics: *Soil General Vocabulary 10*

fractional distillation: *Chemistry General Vocabulary 11*

fracture: *Geological Vocabulary 10; Injuries/Medical Emergencies 12*

fragile: *Adjectives 20; Small/Thin 1*

fragrance: *Smells 20*

fragrant clitocybe: *Fungus Common Names 10*

Fragarach: *Celtic Swords 18*

frail: *Small/Fragile 20; Small/Thin 1*

fraipontite: *Minerals 10*

frak: *Expletives 20*

frakking: *Expletives 20*

frame: *Building Elements and Features 3; Windows 3*

framed art: *Decorative Objects 4*

framed photograph: *Decorative Objects 4*

francisca: *Axes 7*

Franciso: *Moons 11*

Francium: *Elements 11*

frangipani: *Poisonous Plants 10*

Frank: *Human Ethnic Groups 1*

Frankenstein monster: *Horror Plot Devices 23; Mythical Creatures and Monsters 16*

frankfurter: *Sausage 6*

frankincense: *Christmas 19; Wizard's Goods 5*

franklinia: *Shrubs 10*

frappe: *Dairy Beverages 6; Ice Cream Related 6*

frappuccino: *Coffee Drinks 6*

Fraser fir: *Evergreen Trees 10*

Fraternitas Rosae Crucis: *Secret/Mystical Organizations 18*

Fraternitas Rosicruciana Antiqua: *Secret/Mystical Organizations 18*

Fraternitas Saturni: *Secret/Mystical Organizations 18*

Fraternity of the Inner Light: *Secret/Mystical Organizations 18*

fraternity: *Social Clubs 1*

fraud: *Thief 1*

fraudster: *Thief 1*

fraudulent: *Bad 20*

fraxinella: *Garden Perennials 10*

fray: *General Combat Vocabulary 7*

frazil: *Minerals 10*

freaking: *Expletives 20*

Freccia VBM 8×8 infantry fighting vehicle: *Italy Military Vehicles 8*

freckles: *Skin Types and Features 1*

Frederiksborg: *Horse Breeds 15*

free from anxiety: *Happy 20*

free from care: *Happy 20*

free radical: *Chemistry General Vocabulary 11*

free will: *Philosophy Basic Concepts 14*

free: *Open/Release 20*

Freedom Arms Model 83: *Revolver Single Action 7*

Freedom class combat ship: *U.S. Navy Vessels 8*

freedom: *Philosophy Basic Concepts 14*

freefall: *Locomotion 9*

Freemasons: *Secret/Mystical Organizations 18*

freesia: *Garden Bulbs 10*

freestyle: *Swimming Strokes 9*

free-tailed: *Bats 15*

freeway: *Roads 9*

freeze: *Meteorology General Vocabulary 10*

freezing point depression: *Chemistry General Vocabulary 11*

freezing rain: *Precipitation 10*

freezing snow: *Snow Types 10*

freezing: *Cold 10; Geological Vocabulary 10*

freight car: *Railroad 9*

frell: *Expletives 20*

Fremont's crowfoot: *Garden Perennials 10*

French angel: *Wild Saltwater Fish 15*

French black truffle: *Fungus Common Names 10*

French braid: *Hair Style 1*

French Bulldog: *Dog Breeds 15*

French burnt peanuts: *Candy General 6*

French Canadian: *Human Ethnic Groups 1*

French Colonial: *Architectural Styles 3*

French cuff: *Garment Pieces 2*

French cut panties: *Ladies' Wear 2*

French foil: *Fencing Equipment 7*

French fries: *Vegetables Cooked 6, Amusement Park/Carnival/Circus/Fair 3*

French grip: *Fencing Equipment 7*

French grunt: *Wild Saltwater Fish 15*

French heels: *Footwear/Shoes 2*

French honeysuckle: *Garden Perennials 10*

French hood: *Headgear 2*

French horn: *Wind/Woodwind and Brass Musical Instruments*

French knot: *Embroidery Stitches 2*

French landrace: *Pigs 15*

French manicure: *Makeup 5*

French picture: *Windows 3*

French Provincial: *Architectural Styles 3*

French Revolution: *Styles of Dress 2*

French rifled cannon: *Western Weapons 21*

French rose: *Pink 20*

French Saddlebred: *Horse Breeds 15*

French School: *Ballet Terms 13*

French seam: *Sewing Techniques 2*

French terry: *Fabric 2*

French Trotter: *Horse Breeds 15*

French twist: *Hair Style 1*

French vanilla: *Ice Cream Flavors 6*

French: *Bread General Varieties 6; Coffee Bean Roasts 6; Gem Cuts 21; Human Ethnic Groups 1; Imported Carpets 4; Salad Dressing 6*

frequency domain sensor: *Soil General Vocabulary 10*

frequency: *Chemistry General Vocabulary 11*

fresco paint: *Art Materials 5*

fresco: *Art Media 13; Castle Anatomy 3*

fresh Jack: *Cheese Common Varieties 6*

fresh mozzarella: *Cheese Common Varieties 6*

fresh: *New 20*

freshen: *Clean 20*

freshwater fish: *Animals 15*

freshwater: *Minerals 10*

fresnel: *Technical Terms 13*

Fresno scraper: *Soil General Vocabulary 10*

fret marker: *Music Accessories*

fret saw: *Hand Tools 5*

fret: *Musical Instrument Parts13*

Freya (goddess of fertility): *Norse Pantheon 14*

Freyja's falcon cloak: *Clothing 18*

Freyja's necklace: *Jewelry 18*

Freyr's boat: *Vehicles 18*

Freyr's sword: *Norse Weapons 18*

friar: *Cleric 1*

fricking: *Expletives 20*

Friday the 13th: *Common Dangers 23; Harbingers of Bad Luck 19*

fried cheese: *Amusement Park/Carnival/Circus/Fair 3*

fried chicken: *Amusement Park/Carnival/Circus/Fair 3*

friend: *Love 20; Relational 1*

friendliness: *General Emotions 20*

friendly muttonchops: *Facial Hair Beard 1*

friendly: *Happy 20; Positive 1*

Friesian: *Horse Breeds 15*

frigate admiral: *Maritime Occupations 1*

frigate captain: *Maritime Occupations 1*

Frigate Island: *Caecilians 15*

frigate: *Spaceship Types 22*

Frigga (goddess of the air): *Norse Pantheon 14*

frigging: *Expletives 20*

fright: *General Emotions 20; Horror Vocabulary 23*

frightened: *General Emotions 20*

frightening: *Unattractive 20*

frightful: *Bad 20; Horror Vocabulary 23; Unattractive 20*

frigid: *Cold 10*

Frijolillo: *Deciduous Trees 10*

frilled lizard: *Scaled Reptiles 15*

frilled: *Sharks 15*

fringe skirt: *Dance Clothing 13*

fringe tree: *Shrubs 10*

fringe: *Fabric 2; Hair Style 1; Performance Genres 13*

fringed finger poppy mallow: *Garden Perennials 10*

fringed leather jacket: *Western Clothing/Dress 21*

fringed myotis: *Bats 15*

fringed sage: *Garden Perennials 10*

fringed tulip: *Garden Bulbs 10*

fringe-lipped: *Bats 15*

Frisian: *Human Ethnic Groups 1*

fritillaria: *Garden Bulbs 10*

fritillary: *Butterfly 15*

frittata: *Egg Styles 6*

fritter: *Donut/doughnut 6*

frock coat: *Men's Wear 2*

frog kick: *Swimming Strokes 9*

frog leg: *Other Meat 6*

frog: *Animals with Symbolic Meaning 19; Card Games 5; Giant Creatures 16; Items with Healing Properties 19; Notions 2; Witchcraft Vocabulary 17*

frogfish: *Aquarium Saltwater Fish 15*

frogs: *Animals 15; Ten Plagues on Egypt 14*

frolic: *Locomotion 9*

front crawl: *Swimming Strokes 9*

front door: *Objects/Activities Connected to Lore 19*

front end loader: *General Farm Equipment*

front man: *Musical Occupations 1*

front of house: *Parts of the Theater 13*

front room: *Rooms 3*

front woman: *Musical Occupations 1*

front: *Beginning 20; Doors 3; Garment Pieces 2; Meteorology General Vocabulary 10*

frontal bone: *Bones 12*

frontrunner: *Hero 20*

frost giant: *Humanlike Groups 1*

frost heaving: *Soil General Vocabulary 10*

frost line: *Soil General Vocabulary 10*

frost worm: *Beast 16*

frost: *Giant Humanoids 16; Minerals 10; Snow Events 10*

frostbite: *Injuries/Medical Emergencies 12*

frosted orange: *Moth 15*

frosted: *Donut/doughnut 6; Hair Treated 1*

frostiness: *Snow Events 10*

frosting: *Christmas 19*

frostwork: *Cave Anatomy 10*

frosty: *Cold 10*

froth: *Cooking Techniques 20*

froumaela: *Cheese International Varieties 6*

frozen custard: *Ice Cream Related 6*

frozen fudge pop: *Ice Cream Related 6*

frozen snow: *Snow Events 10*

frozen yogurt: *Ice Cream Related 6*

fruit cellar: *Rooms 3*

fruit cocktail: *Cake 6*

fruit drinks: *Food 6*

fruit fly: *Flies 15*

fruit hat: *Headgear 2*

fruit juice: *Food 6*

fruit market: *General Property 3; Outdoor Property 3*

fruit of life: *Symbols in Magic and Religion 19*

fruit pizza: *Miscellaneous Dessert 6*

fruit slices: *Candy General 6*

fruit: *Bats 15; Food 6; Salad Dressing 6; Thanksgiving 19*

fruitcake: *Cake 6; Christmas 19*

fruit-eating: *Bats 15*

fruity: *Vocal/Speech Quality 1*

frumpy: *Styles of Dress 2*

frustrate: *General Emotions 20*

fry bread: *Bread General Varieties 6*

fry: *Cooking Techniques 20*

frying pan: *Improvised Weapons 7; Kitchen Equipment 5*

FT-17 light tank: *France Military Vehicles 8*

FT-31 light tank: *France Military Vehicles 8*

Fu Manchu: *Facial Hair Mustache 1*

fu: *Secular Symbols 19*

fuberidazole: *Dangerous Chemicals 11*

Fuchs Transportpanzer 1: *Germany Military Vehicles 8*

fuchsia: *Garden Annuals 10; Pink 20; Purple 20; Red 20; Shrubs 10*

fuddle duddle: *Expletives 20*

fudge covered: *Donut/doughnut 6*

fudge: *Candy Chocolate 6; Christmas 19*

FUDOFSI: *Secret/Mystical Organizations 18*

FUDOSI: *Secret/Mystical Organizations 18*

fuel cells: *Chemistry General Vocabulary 11*

fuel: *Buy 20*

Fuente Magna: *Real Objects Not Fully Understood 18*

fugue: *Composition Types 13*

Fuji: *Apples 6*

Fujin (the winds): *Japanese Pantheon 14*

fujin: *Demon 16*

Fujita scale: *Meteorology General Vocabulary 10*

Fulani Sudanese: *Other Cows 15*

full chain suit: *Armor Types 7*

full city: *Coffee Bean Roasts 6*

full coverage bra: *Ladies' Wear 2*

full figure bra: *Ladies' Wear 2*

full length mirror: *Miscellaneous Furniture 4*

full moon grants powers: *Fantasy Plot Devices 24*

full moon: *Common Dangers 23; Halloween 19; Witchcraft Vocabulary 17*

full plate: *Armor Types 7*

full skirt: *Ladies' Wear 2*

full slip: *Ladies' Wear 2*

full: *Beds 4; Cheeks 1; Facial Hair Beard 1; Lips 1*

Fuller's earth: *Soil General Vocabulary 10*

full-length skirt: *Ladies' Wear 2*

fully battened sails: *Boat/Ship Terminology 9*

fulvous: *Owls 15*

fume hood: *Laboratory Equipment 5*

fumigate: *Clean 20*

fuming: *Angry 1*

fun fur: *Fabric 2*

fun house: *Amusement Park/Carnival/Circus/Fair 3*

functional diversity: *Geography General Vocabulary 10*

Functionalism: *Architectural Styles 3*

fundamental: *General Music Vocabulary 13*

funeral chapel: *Business Property 3*

funeral director: *General Occupations 1*

funeral home: *Business Property 3*

funeral parlor: *Business Property 3*

funeral suit: *Men's Wear 2*

funeral: *Masks 2; Pie 6*

funereal: *Styles of Dress 2*

fungicide: *Physical Mutations 22*

fungus common names: *Chapter 10*

fungus: *Chapter 10; Wizard's Goods 5*

funking: *Expletives 20*

fun-loving: *Happy 20*

funnel cake: *Amusement Park/Carnival/Circus/Fair 3*

funnel cloud: *Severe Weather 10*

funnel: *Kitchen Utensils 5; Laboratory Equipment 5; Severe Weather 10*

funnel-eared: *Bats 15*

funnelweb: *Venomous Arachnids 15*

funny bone: *Body Parts 12*

fur blanket: *Bed Linens 5*

fur coat: *Outerwear 2*

fur stole: *Ladies' Wear 2*

fur: *Allergies 12; Classic Heraldry 19; Clothing 2; Wizard's Goods 5*

furan: *Dangerous Chemicals 11*

furious: *Angry 1*

furka: *Secular Symbols 19*

furnace: *Building Systems 3; Property Features 3*

furniture polish: *Cleaning Supplies/Gadgets 5*

furniture store: *Business Property 3*

Furongian Age: *Geologic Time 10*

fury: *General Emotions 20*

fuschite: *Minerals 10*

fuse box: *Building Systems 3*

fusilli: *Pasta 6*

fusion sleigh: *Vehicles 22*

fusion: *Energy Sources/Types 22; Spaceship Drive Systems 22; Weapons 22*

futon: *Beds 4*

future Earth wields magic: *Fantasy Plot Devices 24*

Futurism: *Art Movements 13*

Futurist: *Architectural Styles 3*

futurist: *Wizard 1*

futuristic weapons: *Plot Devices 22*

fuzzy: *Skin Types and Features 1*

FV101 Scorpion light tank: *United Kingdom Military Vehicles 8*

FV104 Samaritan armored ambulance: *United Kingdom Military Vehicles 8*

FV105 Sultan command vehicle: *United Kingdom Military Vehicles 8*

FV106 Samson armored recovery vehicle: *United Kingdom Military Vehicles 8*

FV107 Scimitar light tank: *United Kingdom Military Vehicles 8*

FV120 Spartan self-propelled anti-tank vehicle: *United Kingdom Military Vehicles 8*

FV1601 Humber 1 ton 4×4 truck: *United Kingdom Military Vehicles 8*

FV1606 Humber 1 ton 4×4 wrecker/tow truck: *United Kingdom Military Vehicles 8*

FV1609 Humber 1 ton 4×4 armored vehicle: *United Kingdom Military Vehicles 8*

FV1620 Humber 1 ton 4×4 anti-tank vehicle: *United Kingdom Military Vehicles 8*

FV214 Conqueror main battle tank: *United Kingdom Military Vehicles 8*

FV219 armored recovery vehicle: *United Kingdom Military Vehicles 8*

FV222 Conqueror armored recovery vehicle: *United Kingdom Military Vehicles 8*

FV3804 ammunition supply vehicle: *United Kingdom Military Vehicles 8*

FV3901 bridge layer: *United Kingdom Military Vehicles 8*

FV3904 armored personnel carrier: *United Kingdom Military Vehicles 8*

FV4001 Centurion main battle tank: *United Kingdom Military Vehicles 8*

FV4002 Centurion AVLB bridging vehicle: *United Kingdom Military Vehicles 8*

FV4003 Centurion AVRE combat engineer vehicle: *United Kingdom Military Vehicles 8*

FV4005 self-propelled anti-tank gun: *United Kingdom Military Vehicles 8*

FV401 Cambridge armored personnel carrier: *United Kingdom Military Vehicles 8*

FV4010 anti-tank vehicle: *United Kingdom Military Vehicles 8*

FV4019 bulldozer: *United Kingdom Military Vehicles 8*

FV4101 self-propelled anti-tank gun: *United Kingdom Military Vehicles 8*

FV421 armored cargo carrier: *United Kingdom Military Vehicles 8*

FV424 armored engineering vehicle: *United Kingdom Military Vehicles 8*

FV426 anti-tank vehicle: *United Kingdom Military Vehicles 8*

FV4333 Stormer armored personnel carrier: *United Kingdom Military Vehicles 8*

FV435 Wavell communications vehicle: *United Kingdom Military Vehicles 8*

FV437 Pathfinder vehicle with snorkel gear: *United Kingdom Military Vehicles 8*

FV438 Wavell self-propelled anti-tank vehicle: *United Kingdom Military Vehicles 8*

FV439 signals vehicle: *United Kingdom Military Vehicles 8*

FV510 Warrior infantry fighting vehicle: *United Kingdom Military Vehicles 8*

FV511 Warrior command vehicle: *United Kingdom Military Vehicles 8*

FV512 Warrior armored repair vehicle: *United Kingdom Military Vehicles 8*

FV513 Warrior armored recovery vehicle: *United Kingdom Military Vehicles 8*

FV514 Warrior reconnaissance vehicle: *United Kingdom Military Vehicles 8*

FV515 Warrior artillery command vehicle: *United Kingdom Military Vehicles 8*

FV603 Saracen 6×6 armored personnel carrier: *United Kingdom Military Vehicles 8*

FV621 Stalwart amphibious 6×6 5 ton truck: *United Kingdom Military Vehicles 8*

FV624 Stalwart amphibious 6×6 5 ton recovery vehicle: *United Kingdom Military Vehicles 8*

FV711 Ferret 4×4 armored car: *United Kingdom Military Vehicles 8*

FV721 Fox 4×4 armored car: *United Kingdom Military Vehicles 8*

fynbo: *Cheese International Varieties 6*

–G–

gabardine: *Fabric 2*

gabbro: *Igneous Rocks 10*

gable hood: *Headgear 2*

gable: *Building Elements and Features 3; Castle Anatomy 3; Roof Styles 3*

Gabon sideneck: *Freshwater Turtles 15*

Gaboon: *Caecilians 15; Viper 15*

Gabriel: *Angels of Good 14*

gac: *Unusual Edible Fruits 6*

gad: *Expletives 20*

Gadolinium: *Elements 11*

Gadreel: *Fallen Angels 14*

gadzooks: *Expletives 20; Expletives 20*

Gae Bolg: *Spears 18*

Gae Buide: *Spears 18*

Gae Derg red javelin: *Spears 18*

Gael: *Human Ethnic Groups 1*

gaff: *Fishing Gear 5; Hand Weapons 7*

Gagiel: *Angels of Good 14*

Gaheris: *Knights of the Round Table 18*

gahnite: *Minerals 10*

gahnospinel: *Minerals 10*

gain knowledge: *Learn 20*

gain: *Buy 20*

Gainsborough hat: *Headgear 2*

gala: *Apples 6*

Galacian: *Human Ethnic Groups 1*

galactic empire: *Plot Devices 22*

galactic halo: *Astronomy General Terms 11*

galactic nucleus: *Astronomy General Terms 11*

Galahad: *Knights of the Round Table 18*

Galapagos giant: *Tortoises 15*

Galapagos Islands: *Seven Wonders of the Underwater World 18*

galatea: *Construct 16*

Galatea: *Moons 11*

Galatine: *Arthurian Weapons 18*

galaxite: *Minerals 10*

galaxy: *Astronomy General Terms 11; Star Systems 11*

Gale: *Comets 11*

gale: *Wind 10*

galenite: *Minerals 10*

galia melon: *Unusual Edible Fruits 6*

Galiceño: *Horse Breeds 15*

Galician Blond: *Other Cows 15*

Galician Pony: *Horse Breeds 15*

gall bladder: *Organs/Major Structures 12*

gall: *Wasp 15*

galla: *Demon 16*

gallant: *Personality Other 1*

gallantry: *General Emotions 20*

galleon: *Large Watercraft 9*

gallery: *Business Property 3; Castle Anatomy 3; Rooms 3*

galley: *Boat/Ship Anatomy 9; Large Watercraft 9*

galliard: *Historical Dances 13*

gallium trichloride: *Dangerous Chemicals 11*

Gallium: *Elements 11*

Galloway: *Other Cows 15*

gallows: *Classic Items 23; Witchcraft Vocabulary 17*

galop: *Historical Dances 13*

galoshes: *Boots 2*

galotyri: *Cheese International Varieties 6*

galvanizing: *Chemistry General Vocabulary 11*

gamayun: *Flying Creatures 16*

gambler cheats at cards: *Western Plot Devices 21*

gambler: *Thief 1; Western Paraphernalia/People 21*

gambling hall: *Entertainment Property 3*

gambling: *Large Watercraft 9*

gambol: *Locomotion 9*

gambooge: *Unusual Edible Fruits 6*

gambrel: *Roof Styles 3*

game: *Tables 4*

game-flip-flop: *Card Games 5*

Gamera: *Mythical Creatures and Monsters 16*

games: *Equipment and Tools 5*

gamma radiation: *Energy Sources/Types 22*

gamma ray: *Astronomy General Terms 11; Chemistry General Vocabulary 11*

gamma: *Weapons 22*

gammadion: *Secular Symbols 19*

gamygn: *Devil 16*

gandarewa: *Demon 16*

gandasa: *Axes 7*

gandharva: *Demon 16*

Gandiva: *Bows 18*

Ganelon: *Twelve Peers of Charlemagne 18*

Ganesha (education, knowledge, wisdom): *Indian Pantheon 14*

ganesha: *Demon 16*

gang: *Styles of Dress 2*

gangling: *Small/Thin 1*

gangly: *Small/Thin 1*

gangrene: *Diseases 12*

gangs: *Travel Hazards 9*

gangster: *Fighter 1; Villain 20; Styles of Dress 2*

gangue: *Chemistry General Vocabulary 11*

Ganymede: *Moons 11*

Gaolao: *Other Cows 15*

GAOTU: *Symbols of Freemasonry 19*

gaping: *Open/Release 20*

gaps: *Solitaire Card Games 5*

garage: *Doors 3; Farm/Outbuilding 3; Property Features 3*

garbage can: *Containers and Vessels 5*

garbage disposal: *Major Appliances 4*

garbage man: *General Occupations 1*

garbage: *Card Games 5; Motorized Truck 9*

garbanzo bean: *Legumes 6*

Garbo hat: *Headgear 2*

garden annuals: *Chapter 10*

garden bulbs: *Chapter 10*

garden cart: *Large Tools*

garden clogs: *Footwear/Shoes 2*

garden heliotrope: *Garden Perennials 10*

Garden of the Hesperides: *Fictional/Mythological Locations 18*

garden perennials: *Chapter 10*

garden phlox: *Garden Perennials 10*

garden shovel: *Improvised Weapons 7*

garden sorrel: *Garden Perennials 10*

garden tools: *Equipment and Tools 5*

garden: *Landscaping 3; Nonvenomous Arachnids 15; Salads 6; Windows 3*

gardener: *Castle Inhabitants and Personnel 1; Horror Occupations 23*

garderobe: *Bathrooms 3; Castle Anatomy 3*

Gareth: *Knights of the Round Table 18*

gargantuan: *Large 20; Large/Heavy 1*

gargoyle: *Humanoid 16*

Garibaldi hat: *Headgear 2*

garland: *Christmas 19*

garlic bread: *Bread General Varieties 6*

garlic marasmius: *Fungus Common Names 10*

garlic mustard: *Weeds 10*

garlic pickle: *Pickled/Relish 6*

garlic powder: *Spices 6*

garlic press: *Kitchen Utensils 5*

garlic: *Bread General Varieties 6; Plants with Symbolic Meaning 19; Vegetables 6; Wizard's Goods 5*

garment bag: *Dance Equipment 13*

garment pieces: *Clothing 2*

garnet jade: *Minerals 10*

garnet: *Standard Gems 21; Star Gems 21*

garnierite: *Minerals 10*

garnishes: *Food 6*

garret: *Rooms 3*

garrison cap: *Headgear 2*

garrison: *Fortification 3*

garrote: *Flexible 7; Spy Gear 5*

garrulous: *Personality Other 1*

garter belt: *Ladies' Wear 2; Western Clothing/Dress 21*

garter: *General Snake Families 15*

garters: *Unisex Clothing 2*

gas burner: *Laboratory Equipment 5*

gas company: *Public Services 3*

gas furnace: *Building Systems 3*

gas generation: *Physical Mutations 22*

gas mask: *Military Equipment 8*

gas permeable contact lenses: *Optics 5*

gas plant: *Garden Perennials 10*

gas station attendant: *Horror Occupations 23; Business Property 3*

gas syringe: *Laboratory Equipment 5*

gas: *Traps 3; Wizard's Goods 5*

Gascon: *Other Cows 15; Pigs 15*

Gaspar/Caspar: *Three Wise Men/Magi 19*

gastric juice: *Wizard's Goods 5*

gastroenterologist: *Medical Occupations 1*

gastrolith: *Geological Vocabulary 10*

gastrophetes: *Siege Engines 7*

gate house: *Castle Anatomy 3*

gate to other dimension: *Travel Modes 23*

gate: *Building Elements and Features 3; Doors Atypical 3; Landscaping 3; Property Features 3; Travel Types 22*

gatecrasher: *Thief 1*

gated community: *Residential Property 3*

gatehouse: *Fortification 3*

gate-leg: *Tables 4*

gates: *Amusement Park/Carnival/Circus/Fair 3*

gateway to hell in basement of home: *Horror Plot Devices 23*

Gateway: *Ballet Terms 13*

gateway: *Doors Atypical 3*

gathering: *Embellishments 2*

Gatling gun: *Western Weapons 21*

Gato: *Domestic Cats 15*

gauchos: *Ladies' Wear 2*

gauge: *Solve 20*

gaunt: *Small/Thin 1*

gauntlet: *Armor Pieces 7; Hand Weapons 7*

gauss: *Weapons 22; Weapons 22*

gauze: *Fabric 2*

Gawain: *Knights of the Round Table 18*

gawky: *Small/Thin 1*

gay: *Styles of Dress 2*

gayfeather: *Garden Perennials 10*

GAZ 46 4×4 utility vehicle: *Russia Military Vehicles 8*

GAZ-5903 8×8 armored personnel carrier: *Russia Military Vehicles 8*

gazar: *Fabric 2*

gazebo: *Outdoor Property 3; Property Features 3*

gazpacho. gumbo: *Soup 6*

gbejna: *Cheese International Varieties 6*

GCT self-propelled 155mm artillery: *France Military Vehicles 8*

gear shaper: *Power Tools*

gear: *Equipment and Tools 5*

Geb (the earth): *Egyptian Pantheon 14*

gecko: *Scaled Reptiles 15*

gee whiz: *Expletives 20*

gee willikers: *Expletives 20*

gee Wisconsin: *Expletives 20*

gee: *Expletives 20*

geeky: *Styles of Dress 2*

geesh: *Expletives 20*

geez: *Expletives 20*

geeze: *Expletives 20*

Gegenees: *Giants of Legend 16*

Geiger counter: *Chemistry General Vocabulary 11*

gel: *Chemistry General Vocabulary 11*

gelada: *Old World Monkeys 15*

gelatin mold: *Kitchen Equipment 5*

gelatin: *Salads 6*

gelatinous animal: *Monsters and Creatures 22*

gelatinous: *Octopi 15; Wet 20*

gelato: *Ice Cream Related 6*

Gelbray: *Other Cows 15*

Gelbvieh: *Other Cows 15*

Gelderlander: *Horse Breeds 15*

gelding: *Horses 15*

gelisol: *Soil General Vocabulary 10*

gelite: *Minerals 10*

gelundener kase: *Cheese International Varieties 6*

gem stones: *Art Materials 5*

gemelli: *Pasta 6*

Gemini (May 21–June 20): *Zodiac Signs 19*

Gemini: *Constellations 11*

gemologist: *Artists and Craftspeople 1*

gems: *Wizard's Goods 5*

gender: *Character Building 1*

gene repair system: *Devices 22*

general Air Force chief of staff: *U.S. Air Force Officer 8*

general building: *Architecture and Property 3*

general fae: *Monsters 16*

general occupations: *Character Building 1*

general of the Air Force: *U.S. Air Force Officer 8*

general of the Army: *U.S. Army Officer 8*

general practitioner: *Medical Occupations 1*

general property: *Architecture and Property 3*

general purpose: *Bomb 8*

general store: *Western Paraphernalia/People 21*

general: *Fighter 1; U.S. Army Officer 8; U.S. Marines Officer 8*

generate: *Create 20*

generation ship: *Plot Devices 22*

generation: *Spaceship Types 22*

generosity: *Ten Perfections of Buddhism 19*

generous: *Large 20; Positive 1*

gene-spliced predator: *Monsters and Creatures 22*

genetically altered animals turn violent: *Common Dangers 22*

genial: *Happy 20*

genie bottle: *Typical Magical Objects 17*

genie: *Extraplanar 16; Humanoid 16*

genip: *Unusual Edible Fruits 6*

genius: *Common Character Archetypes 21; Intelligent 1; Paranormal Abilities 21*

genocide: *General Combat Vocabulary 7*

genoise: *Cake 6*

gent: *Male 1*

genthite: *Minerals 10*

gentian: *Garden Perennials 10*

gentility: *General Emotions 20*

gentle: *Grade/Slope 10; Positive 1*

gentleman thief: *Common Character Archetypes 21*

gentleman: *Male 1*

gentleman's club: *Entertainment Property 3*

genuflect: *Rituals 14*

genuine: *Personality Other 1*

geo: *Coastal and Oceanic 10*

geoarchaeology: *Geologic Fields of Study 10*

geocaching: *Exploration 9*

geochemistry: *Geologic Fields of Study 10*

geochronology: *Geologic Fields of Study 10*

geode: *Geological Vocabulary 10*

geodetics: *Geologic Fields of Study 10*

Geoffrey's spider : *New World Monkeys 15*

Geoffrey's tamarin: *New World Monkeys 15*

geographical zones: *Chapter 10*

geography vocabulary: *Chapter 10*

geography: *Chapter 10*

geologic concepts: *Chapter 10*

geologic fields of study: *Chapter 10*

geologic map: *Geological Vocabulary 10*

geologic time: *Chapter 10*

geological field work methods: *Chapter 10*

geological mapping: *Geological Field Work Methods 10*

geological modeling: *Geologic Fields of Study 10*

geological natural hazards: *Chapter 10*

geological vocabulary: *Chapter 10*

geologist: *Scientist 1*

geology: *Chapter 10*

geomancer: *Scientist 1*

geometallurgy: *Geologic Fields of Study 10*

geometric: *Tortoises 15*

geometrical isomers: *Chemistry General Vocabulary 11*

geomicrobiology: *Geologic Fields of Study 10; Geological Field Work Methods 10*

geomorphology: *Geography General Vocabulary 10; Geologic Fields of Study 10*

geomythology: *Geologic Fields of Study 10*

geophysics: *Geologic Fields of Study 10*

George Armstrong Custer: *Western Paraphernalia/People 21*

George Washington: *Independence Day 19*

georgette: *Fabric 2*

Georgia Guidestones: *Real Places Steeped in Legend or Mystery 18*

Georgian: *Architectural Styles 3; Human Ethnic Groups 1*

geosmin: *Soil General Vocabulary 10*

geosphere: *Geography General Vocabulary 10*

geosynchronous orbit: *Astronomy General Terms 11*

geotechnical engineering: *Geologic Fields of Study 10*

geotechnical investigation: *Soil General Vocabulary 10*

geothermal: *Energy Sources/Types 22; Energy Sources/Types 24*

Geraint: *Knights of the Round Table 18*

geranium: *Garden Annuals 10*

gerasene: *Devil 16*

Gerbera daisy: *Garden Annuals 10*

gerbil: *Pocket Pets 15*

geriatric: *Elderly 1*

Gerier: *Twelve Peers of Charlemagne 18*

Gerin: *Twelve Peers of Charlemagne 18*

German Angus: *Other Cows 15*

German chocolate: *Cake 6; Ice Cream Flavors 6*

German dance: *Ethnic/Folk Dances 13*

German garlic: *Garden Perennials 10*

German landrace: *Pigs 15*

German Pinscher: *Dog Breeds 15*

German Red Pied: *Other Cows 15*

German rye: *Bread General Varieties 6*

German Shepherd: *Dog Breeds 15*

German Shorthaired Pointer: *Dog Breeds 15*

German solo: *Card Games 5*

German statice : *Garden Perennials 10*

German stone crossbow: *Missile Weapons 7*

German whist: *Card Games 5*

German Wirehaired Pointer: *Dog Breeds 15*

German: *Human Ethnic Groups 1*

German: *Wasp 15*

germander: *Garden Perennials 10*

Germanium: *Elements 11*

germicidal: *Illumination Bulb and Tube Types 5*

Geronimo: *Real People with Legendary Status 18*

Gershwin: *Asteroids with Unusual Names 11*

Geryon: *Giants of Legend 16; Twelve Labors of Hercules 16*

gesso paint: *Art Materials 5*

gesso: *Art Media 13*

get: *Buy 20*

getaway car: *Spy Gear 5*

getaway: *Journey 20*

getting into bed on one side and getting up on the other: *Practices that Attract Bad Luck 19*

getting lost: *Common Dangers 24; Travel Hazards 9*

gewürztraminer: *Wine White 6*

geyser eruption: *Geological Natural Hazards 10*

geyser: *Volcanic 10*

geyserite: *Minerals 10*

ghanta: *Objects in Magic and Religion 19*

ghast: *Undead 16*

ghastly: *Bad 20; Horror Vocabulary 23; Unattractive 20*

Ghengis Khan: *Real People with Legendary Status 18*

Ghenna: *Sites Lost or Unproven to Exist 18*

ghetto: *City 10; Geography General Vocabulary 10; Styles of Dress 2*

ghost buster: *Paranormal Occupations 21*

ghost energy: *Energy Sources/Types 23*

ghost hunter: *Paranormal Occupations 21*

ghost naga: *Extraplanar 16*

ghost ship: *Horror Plot Devices 23*

ghost town: *Famous Western Locations 21*

ghost train: *Vehicles 24*

ghost wants object/body part back: *Horror Plot Devices 23*

ghost white: *White 20*

ghost/spirit: *Supporting Cast 24*

ghost: *Fantasy Creatures with Symbolic Meaning 19; Halloween 19; Nonvenomous Arachnids 15; Supporting Cast 23; Undead 16*

ghost-faced: *Bats 15*

ghostlight: *Technical Terms 13*

ghostly army rises to fight war: *Horror Plot Devices 23*

ghostly chariot: *Vehicles 24*

ghostly city that appears during full moon: *Fantasy Locations 24*

ghostly: *Horror Vocabulary 23*

ghosts of large-scale disaster rise up and wreak havoc: *Horror Plot Devices 23*

ghosts/spirits/haunting: *Horror Genres 23*

ghosts/spirits: *Common Dangers 24*

ghoul: *Halloween 19; Undead 16*

ghoula: *Demon 16*

ghoulish: *Unattractive 20*

giant amoeba: *Monsters and Creatures 22*

giant arborvitae: *Evergreen Trees 10*

giant axon: *Squid 15*

giant bugs/creatures: *Common Dangers 23*

giant bugs: *Monsters and Creatures 22*

giant burnet: *Garden Perennials 10*

giant cat: *Bears 15*

giant chinkapin: *Deciduous Trees 10*

giant chinquapin: *Deciduous Trees 10*

giant cow parsley: *Weeds 10*

giant creatures/humans/insects: *Plot Devices 22*

giant creatures: *Horror Genres 23; Magical Transportation 17; Monsters 16*

giant evergreen chinquapin: *Deciduous Trees 10*

giant flowered salvia: *Garden Perennials 10*

giant granadilla: *Unusual Edible Fruits 6*

giant hogweed: *Poisonous Plants 10; Weeds 10*

giant human: *Monsters and Creatures 22*

giant humanoids: *Monsters 16*

giant insects/vermin attack: *Horror Plot Devices 23*

giant kite: *Vehicles 24*

giant Pacific: *Octopi 15*

giant panda: *Bears 15; Other Wild Mammals 15*

giant red cedar: *Evergreen Trees 10*

giant reed: *Weeds 10*

giant salvinia: *Weeds 10*

Giant Schnauzer: *Dog Breeds 15*

giant sequoia: *Deciduous Trees 10*

giant slide: *Amusement Park/Carnival/Circus/Fair 3*

giant snail ship: *Vehicles 24*

giant spider webs: *Traps 3*

giant steps: *Magical Transportation 17*

giant wooly: *Bats 15*

giant: *Humanlike Groups 1; Large 20; Large/Heavy 1; Salamanders 15; Squid 15*

giantlike: *Large/Heavy 1*

giants of legend: *Monsters 16*

giants: *Monsters 16*

giants' village: *Fantasy Locations 24*

gibbon: *Apes 15*

giddee giddee: *Poisonous Plants 10*

giddyup: *Commands 20*

Gidran: *Horse Breeds 15*

gifblaar: *Poisonous Plants 10*

gift card: *Christmas 19*

gift exchange: *Christmas 19*

gift wrap: *Christmas 19*

gift: *Christmas 19*

Gifts of the Magi: *Relics of Jesus 14*

gig bag: *Music Accessories*

giganotosaurus: *Commonly Known Dinosaurs 15*

gigantic: *Large 20; Large/Heavy 1*

gigantism: *Large/Heavy 1*

giggle: *Sounds 20*

gigue: *Historical Dances 13*

Gila monster: *Scaled Reptiles 15*

gilled antelope: *Beast 16*

gill-man: *Mythical Creatures and Monsters 16*

gills: *Physical Mutations 22*

gin rummy: *Card Games 5*

gin: *Hard Liquor 6*

ging: *Card Games 5*

ginger : *Garden Perennials 10*

ginger ale: *Soft Drinks 6*

ginger bread: *Cake 6; Cookie 6*

ginger jar lamp: *Illumination/Light Sources 5*

ginger pine: *Evergreen Trees 10*

ginger snap: *Cookie 6*

ginger: *Aphrodisiacs 19; Beer 6; Hair Color 1; Spices 6; Vegetables 6*

gingham/calico dress: *Western Clothing/Dress 21*

gingham: *Fabric Patterns 2*

ginseng: *Aphrodisiacs 19; Plants with Symbolic Meaning 19*

giocoso: *Tempo/Mood 13*

Gir: *Other Cows 15*

giraffe: *Other Wild Mammals 15*

girandole mirror: *Miscellaneous Furniture 4*

Girard: *Twelve Peers of Charlemagne 18*

girasol: *Minerals 10*

girder: *Bridges 9*

girdle of Hippolyta: *Clothing 18*

girdle of might: *Armor of Legend 18*

Girdle of Venus: *Minor Lines 19*

girdle: *Jewelry 21; Ladies' Wear 2*

girl next door: *Common Character Archetypes 21*

girl: *Female 1*

girlfriend: *Female 1; Horror Occupations 23*

girly-girl: *Styles of Dress 2*

Girru (fire): *Babylonian Pantheon 14*

girth hitch: *Sailing Knots 9*

giusto: *Tempo/Mood 13*

give ground: *General Combat Vocabulary 7*

glacial cave: *Cave Anatomy 10*

glacial horn: *Glacial and Mountain 10*

glacial landforms: *Chapter 10*

glacial till: *Geography General Vocabulary 10*

glacial: *Squid 15*

glaciated snow: *Snow Events 10*

glaciation: *Geography General Vocabulary 10*

glacier cave: *Glacial and Mountain 10*

glacier foreland: *Glacial and Mountain 10*

glacier: *Bears 15; Geography General Vocabulary 10; Glacial and Mountain 10; Minerals 10; Terrain Features 10*

glaciology: *Geologic Fields of Study 10; Geological Field Work Methods 10*

glacis: *Castle Anatomy 3*

glad: *Happy 20*

glade: *Ecosystems 10*

glade: *Terrain Features 10*

gladiator: *Fighter 1*

gladiolus: *Garden Bulbs 10*

gladius: *Swords One-handed 7*

glaive: *Daggers and Knives 7; Pole Weapons 7*

glaive-guisarme: *Pole Weapons 7*

glamorous: *Beautiful 20*

glamour: *Magic Vocabulary 17*

Glan: *Other Cows 15*

glass beads: *Art Materials 5*

glass block: *Windows 3*

glass bottle: *Containers and Vessels 5*

glass bottom: *Small Watercraft 9*

glass catfish: *Aquarium Freshwater Fish 15*

glass cutter: *Hand Tools 5*

glass golem: *Construct 16*

glass holy symbol: *Religious Items 5*

glass lizard: *Scaled Reptiles 15*

glass mirror: *Personal Care 5*

glass opal: *Minerals 10*

glass rod: *Laboratory Equipment 5*

glass: *Art Genres 13; Art Materials 5; Art Media 13; Door*

Materials 3; Drinkware 5; Geological Vocabulary 10; Octopi 15; Roofing Materials 3

glassblower: *Artists and Craftspeople 1; Business Property 3*

glasses: *Optics 5*

glastig: *Water Faerie 16*

glaucous willow: *Deciduous Trees 10*

glaucous: *Blue 20*

glaze paint: *Art Materials 5*

glaze: *Art Media 13; Art Techniques 13; Minerals 10*

glaze: *Precipitation 10*

glazed nuts: *Candy General 6*

glazed: *Donut/doughnut 6*

gleaner: *General Farm Equipment*

gleek: *Card Games 5*

Gleipnir: *Objects 18*

Glen of Imaal Terrier: *Dog Breeds 15*

glen: *Slope 10; Terrain Features 10*

Glengarry bonnet: *Headgear 2*

Glenn Miller: *Famous Disappearances 18*

gley soil: *Soil General Vocabulary 10*

gleysols: *Soil General Vocabulary 10*

glide: *Fencing Vocabulary 7; Locomotion 9*

glider: *Air Vehicles 9; Military Aircraft Pre-1962 8; Toys 5*

gliding mammals: *Animals 15*

gliding possum: *Gliding Mammals 15*

gliding: *Swimming Strokes 9*

Glissade: *Ballet Terms 13*

glissade: *Dance Moves 13*

glissando: *Instrument Technique 13*

glissant: *Reptiles 19*

glob: *Wet 20*

global positioning system: *Boat/Ship Anatomy 9; Satellite 8*

global warming: *Meteorology General Vocabulary 10*

global weather turns extremely hot/cold/wet/dry: *Horror Plot Devices 23*

globe amaranth: *Garden Annuals 10*

globe mallow: *Garden Perennials 10*

globe thistle: *Garden Perennials 10*

globe: *Geography General Vocabulary 10*

globeflower: *Garden Perennials 10*

globular cluster: *Astronomy General Terms 11*

globule: *Wet 20*

globus cruciger: *Crosses 19*

Glock 17: *Pistol Semiautomatic 7*

Glock semi-automatic pistol : *SWAT Weapons 7*

glockenspiel: *Percussion Musical Instruments 5*

gloomy: *Horror Vocabulary 23; Sad 20*

glorification: *General Emotions 20*

Gloriosa daisy: *Garden Perennials 10*

gloriosa lily: *Garden Bulbs 10*

glorious: *Beautiful 20*

glory of the snow: *Garden Bulbs 10*

glory pea: *Shrubs 10*

glossy: *General Snake Families 15*

Gloucester: *Other Cows 15*

Gloucestershire old spots: *Pigs 15*

glove box: *Laboratory Equipment 5*

gloves: *Laboratory Equipment 5; Military Equipment 8; Objects/Activities Connected to Lore 19; Spy Gear 5; Unisex Clothing 2*

glowering: *Sad 20*

glowlight tetra: *Aquarium Freshwater Fish 15*

glowstick: *Illumination/Light Sources 5*

glucose: *Blood 12*

glue gun: *Power Tools*

glue stick: *Art Materials 5; Office/School/Writing Supplies 5*

glue: *Art Materials 5; Fix 20; Office/School/Writing Supplies 5; Shoe Accessories 13*

glum: *Sad 20*

gluten: *Allergies 12*

glutinous: *Wet 20*

gluttony: *Seven Deadly Sins 19*

glycerin: *Wizard's Goods 5*

glycoalkaloid: *Poisonous Chemicals in Plants 11*

glyph portal: *Travel Modes 23*

gnat: *Flies 15*

gnats: *Ten Plagues on Egypt 14*

gneiss: *Metamorphic Rocks 10*

gnome: *Character Building 1*

Gnostic Texts: *Major Religious Books 14*

go fish: *Card Games 5*

go stop: *Card Games 5*

go: *Commands 20; Expletives 20; Locomotion 9*

goat of mendes: *Symbols in Magic and Religion 19*

goat/sheep: *Chinese Horoscope 19*

goat: *Animals with Symbolic Meaning 19; Other Wild Mammals 15*

goat's: *Milk 6*

goatee: *Facial Hair Beard 1*

goatsbeard: *Garden Perennials 10; Wildflowers 10*

gobbet: *Wet 20*

Göbekli Tepe: *Real Places Steeped in Legend or Mystery 18*

goblet: *Drinkware 5*

goblin: *Fantasy Creatures with Symbolic Meaning 19; General Fae 16; Humanlike Groups 1; Humanoid 16; Sharks 15*

gobo: *Vegetables 6*

Gobra: *Other Cows 15*

goby: *Aquarium Saltwater Fish 15*

God: *Philosophy Basic Concepts 14*

godfather: *Cocktails 6*

Godman's: *Pit Viper 15*

godmother: *Cocktails 6*

gods require a sacrifice: *Horror Plot Devices 23*

godwit: *Other Wild Birds 15*

Godzilla: *Mythical Creatures and Monsters 16*

goggles: *Military Equipment 8*

Goibhne (blacksmiths): *Celtic Pantheon 14*

going backwards: *Slow 20*

gokudo: *Thief 1*

gold claim: *Western Paraphernalia/People 21*

gold crown: *Garden Perennials 10*

gold discovery: *Western Plot Devices 21*

gold Doric: *Coins and Currency 21*

gold dust: *Garden Perennials 10; Western Paraphernalia/People 21*

gold eagle: *Coins and Currency 21*

gold finch: *Backyard Birds 15*

gold holy symbol: *Religious Items 5*

gold leaf: *Art Materials 5; Precious Metals 21*

gold maple leaf: *Coins and Currency 21*

gold metallic: *Yellow 20*

gold mine: *Western Paraphernalia/People 21*

gold miner: *Western Paraphernalia/People 21*

gold net: *Garden Perennials 10*

gold opal: *Minerals 10*

gold pan: *Specialty Survival Gear 5; Western Paraphernalia/People 21*

gold plate: *Precious Metals 21*

gold rush: *Western Paraphernalia/People 21; Western Plot Devices 21*

gold yarrow: *Wildflowers 10*

gold/silver boom town: *Western Plot Devices 21*

gold/silver/gem discovery is guarded/haunted by evil creature: *Horror Plot Devices 23*

gold: *Cake 6; Christmas 19; Coins and Currency 21; Dragon 16; Precious Metals 21; Yellow 20*

Gold: *Elements 11*

Gold's tree: *Cobra 15*

goldball: *Garden Perennials 10*

golden Alexander: *Garden Perennials 10*

Golden American Saddlebred: *Horse Breeds 15*

Golden Apple of Discord: *Objects 18*

golden apples of Aphrodite: *Objects 18*

golden bells: *Garden Perennials 10*

golden beryl: *Minerals 10*

golden blond: *Hair Color 1*

golden brown: *Hair Color 1*

golden chanterelle: *Fungus Common Names 10*

golden chinkapin: *Deciduous Trees 10*

golden citrine: *Minerals 10*

golden crown: *Objects 18*

golden fir: *Evergreen Trees 10*

Golden Fleece: *Objects 18*

Golden Gate Bridge: *Seven Wonders of the Modern World 18; Unique Property 3*

golden goblet: *Objects 18*

golden maidens: *Construct 16; Objects 18*

Golden Monkey: *Tea 6*

golden needle: *Fungus Common Names 10*

Golden Plates: *Books of Legend 18*

golden poppy: *Garden Perennials 10*

golden puffer: *Aquarium Saltwater Fish 15*

Golden Retriever: *Dog Breeds 15*

golden silk: *Nonvenomous Arachnids 15*

golden stag: *Beetle 15*

golden star: *Garden Perennials 10*

golden strawberry: *Garden Perennials 10*

golden stripe soapfish: *Aquarium Saltwater Fish 15*

golden tabby: *Tigers 15*

golden thread: *Freshwater Turtles 15*

golden willow: *Deciduous Trees 10*

golden: *Toads 15*

golden-bloomed: *Beetle 15*

golden-headed lion tamarin: *New World Monkeys 15*

goldenleaf chestnut: *Deciduous Trees 10*

golden-mantled tamarin: *New World Monkeys 15*

goldenrod: *Garden Perennials 10; Weeds 10; Yellow 20*

goldenseal: *Wildflowers 10*

goldfish: *Aquarium Freshwater Fish 15*

gold-flecked: *Eye Color 1*

goldhorn: *Beast 16*

Goldilocks: *Fictional Characters 18*

golem designer: *Fantasy Occupations 24*

golem: *Supporting Cast 23; Supporting Cast 24*

golf cap: *Headgear 2*

golf club rifle: *Spy Gear 5*

golf club: *Improvised Weapons 7*

golf course: *Property Features 3*

golf: *Athletic Shoes 2; Card Games 5; Solitaire Card Games 5*

Goliath: *Frogs 15*

golly : *Expletives 20*

gondola: *Human-Powered Watercraft 9*

Gondwanaland: *Geological Vocabulary 10*

gong gong: *Demon 16*

gong: *Percussion Musical Instruments 5*

gonorrhea: *Diseases 12*

good dude: *Hero 20*

good fun: *Happy 20*

good guy: *Hero 20*

good looking: *Beautiful 20*

good luck charm: *Witchcraft Vocabulary 17*

good measure: *Solitaire Card Games 5*

good: *Adjectives 20; Philosophy Basic Concepts 14; Positive 1; Witchcraft Vocabulary 17*

Goodding willow: *Deciduous Trees 10*

good-humored: *Happy 20*

goodly: *Large 20*

good-natured: *Happy 20; Positive 1*

goodness: *Expletives 20; Twelve Fruits of the Holy Spirit 19*

gooey: *Wet 20*

Googie: *Architectural Styles 3*

goon: *Fighter 1; Villain 20*

goose head: *Wild Saltwater Fish 15*

goose: *Domesticated Farm Birds 15; Other Wild Birds 15; Poultry Types 6*

gooseberry leafed globe mallow: *Garden Perennials 10*

gooseberry: *Berries 6*

goosefoot maple: *Deciduous Trees 10*

gooseneck loosestrife: *Garden Perennials 10*

gooseneck: *Tableware 5*

Goosewhite: *Arthurian Objects 18*

gopher: *General Snake Families 15; Tortoises 15; Woodland Mammals 15*

gopherwood: *Evergreen Trees 10*

gopura: *Objects in Magic and Religion 19*

gor (UK): *Expletives 20*

Gordon Setter: *Dog Breeds 15*

gordonia: *Evergreen Trees 10*

gore: *Garment Pieces 2; Wet 20*

gorge and canyon: *Fluvial 10*

gorge: *Horror Vocabulary 23; Terrain Features 10*

gorged: *Special Body Features 19*

gorgeous: *Beautiful 20*

gorget: *Armor Pieces 7*

gorgon: *Beast 16; Humanoid 16*

gorgonzola: *Cheese Common Varieties 6*

gorram: *Expletives 20*

gorse: *Shrubs 10*

gosh: *Expletives 20*

goshenite: *Minerals 10; Standard Gems 21*

goslarite: *Minerals 10*

gospel: *Musical Styles 13*

gossamer wing: *Butterfly 15*

gossamer: *Fabric 2; Small/Fragile 20*

gossan: *Metamorphic Rocks 10*

gossip: *Speak 20*

Goth: *Styles of Dress 2*

Gothic Revival: *Architectural Styles 3*

Gothic: *Architectural Styles 3*

gothic: *Horror Genres 23; Moth 15; Science Fiction Genres 22*

Gotland: *Horse Breeds 15*

gouache paint: *Art Materials 5*

gouache: *Art Media 13*

gouda: *Cheese Common Varieties 6; Cheese International Varieties 6*

gouge: *Attack 7; Horror Vocabulary 23*

gouged: *Horror Vocabulary 23*

goulash: *Meals 6*

goumi: *Unusual Edible Fruits 6*

gour: *Cave Anatomy 10*

gourami: *Aquarium Freshwater Fish 15*

gourds: *Thanksgiving 19*

goutweed: *Garden Perennials 10*

government: *Character Building 1*

governor: *Government 1*

Gowen cypress: *Evergreen Trees 10*

gown: *Ladies' Wear 2*

GPS: *Boat/Ship Anatomy 9; Spy Gear 5*

grab: *Close/Hold 20*

grace note: *General Music Vocabulary 13*

grace: *Rituals 14*

graceful: *Mobility 1; Personality Other 1*

gracious: *Personality Other 1*

grackle: *Backyard Birds 15*

grade school: *Academic Property 3*

grade: *Cave Anatomy 10; Chapter 10*

gradual: *Slow 20*

graduate: *Special Occasion 1*

graduated cylinder: *Laboratory Equipment 5*

graduation gown: *Special Purpose Clothing 2*

graffiti: *Art Genres 13*

grafito: *Minerals 10*

graham cracker: *Cake 6; Cookie 6*

Graham's law: *Chemistry General Vocabulary 11*

Grail Sword: *Arthurian Weapons 18*

grain auger: *General Farm Equipment*

grain cart: *General Farm Equipment*

grain cleaner: *General Farm Equipment*

grain dryer: *General Farm Equipment*

grain seeder: *Horse Drawn Farm Equipment*

grain: *Farm/Outbuilding 3; Food 6*

gramophone: *Electronics 4*

granadilla: *Unusual Edible Fruits 6*

granary: *Bread General Varieties 6; Farm/Outbuilding 3*

grand Assemblé en tournant: *Ballet Terms 13*

grand Battement en cloche: *Ballet Terms 13*

grand Battement: *Ballet Terms 13*

grand boubou: *Men's Wear 2*

Grand Canyon: *Rattlesnake 15; Seven Wonders of the Natural World 18*

grand duchess: *Royal/Noble 1*

grand duke: *Royal/Noble 1*

Grand Grimoire: *Books of Legend 18*

grand in attitude Jeté: *Ballet Terms 13*

grand Jeté: *Ballet Terms 13*

Grand Oracle of Heaven: *Books of Legend 18*

grand Pas de deux: *Ballet Terms 13*

grand prince: *Royal/Noble 1*

grand princess: *Royal/Noble 1*

grand Sissonne ouverte: *Ballet Terms 13*

Grand/grande: *Ballet Terms 13*

grand: *Good 20; Large 20*

grandchild: *Relational 1*

granddad: *Male 1*

granddaughter: *Female 1*

grande dame: *Common Character Archetypes 21*

grande Pirouette à la second: *Ballet Terms 13*

grandfather clock: *Timekeeping 5*

grandfather: *Male 1*

grandiose: *Large 20*

grandma: *Female 1*

grandmaster: *Martial Artist/Monk 1*

grandmother clock: *Timekeeping 5*

grandmother: *Female 1*

grandpa: *Male 1*

grandparent paradox: *Plot Devices 22*

grandparent: *Relational 1*

grandson: *Male 1*

grandstand: *Amusement Park/Carnival/Circus/Fair 3*

granita: *Ice Cream Related 6*

granite: *Art Materials 5; Igneous Rocks 10*

granny boots: *Western Clothing/Dress 21*

granny panties: *Ladies' Wear 2*

Granny Smith: *Apples 6*

granny: *Boots 2; Sailing Knots 9*

granodiorite: *Igneous Rocks 10*

granophyre: *Igneous Rocks 10*

granular ice material: *Snow Types 10*

granular snow: *Snow Types 10*

granulated sugar: *Staples 6*

granulation: *Astronomy General Terms 11*

granulite: *Metamorphic Rocks 10*

granulocyte: *Blood 12*

grape caulerpa: *Weeds 10*

grape hyacinth: *Garden Bulbs 10*

grape soda: *Soft Drinks 6*

grape tomato: *Vegetables 6*

grape: *Fruit Juice 6; Garden Perennials 10; Jam/Jelly/Preserves 6; Plants with Symbolic Meaning 19; Purple 20*

grapefruit knife: *Kitchen Utensils 5*

grapefruit spoon: *Eating Utensils 5*

grapefruit: *Fruit Juice 6*

grapes: *Food 6*

grapeseed: *Oils 6*

graph: *Laboratory Supplies 5*

graphic designer: *Publishing 1*

graphic equalizer: *Electronics 4*

graphic novel: *Fantasy Genres 24; Horror Genres 23; Science Fiction Genres 22*

graphite: *Art Materials 5; Art Media 13*

grapnel: *Boat/Ship Anatomy 9*

grappling hook: *General Survival Gear 5*

grasp: *Buy 20; Close/Hold 20*

grass pollen: *Allergies 12*

grass rush: *Weeds 10*

grass shears: *Garden Tools*

grass: *Easter 19; General Snake Families 15; Plants with Symbolic Meaning 19; Roofing Materials 3; Squid 15; Venomous Arachnids 15*

grasshopper: *Green 20; Ice Cream Drinks 6; Orthoptera 15; Pie 6*

grassland: *Ecosystems 10; Terrain Features 10*

grater: *Kitchen Utensils 5*

gratification: *Happy 20*

gratify: *Happy 20*

gratifying: *Happy 20*

grating: *Vocal/Speech Quality 1*

graupel: *Meteorology General Vocabulary 10; Snow Types 10*

grave digger: *General Occupations 1*

grave diggers: *Guilds 1*

grave dust: *Wizard's Goods 5*

grave: *Bad 20; Cemetery 3; Horror Vocabulary 23; Tempo/Mood 13*

gravel pit: *Outdoor Property 3*

gravel: *Cave Anatomy 10; Rock and Mineral Forms 10*

gravelly: *Vocal/Speech Quality 1*

graves: *Objects/Activities Connected to Lore 19*

graveyard earth: *Wizard's Goods 5*

graveyard tree: *Poisonous Plants 10*

graveyard: *Cemetery 3; Horror Locations 23*

graviera: *Cheese International Varieties 6*

gravitational erosion: *Soil General Vocabulary 10*

gravitational lens: *Astronomy General Terms 11*

graviton: *Weapons 22*

gravity boots: *Clothing/Uniforms 22*

gravity wagon: *General Farm Equipment*

gravity: *Astronomy General Terms 11; Energy Sources/Types 22; Spaceship Drive Systems 22; Weapons 22*

gravy boat: *Tableware 5*

gravy: *Thanksgiving 19*

gray alder: *Deciduous Trees 10*

gray beech: *Deciduous Trees 10*

gray birch: *Deciduous Trees 10*

gray dogwood: *Deciduous Trees 10*

gray elm: *Deciduous Trees 10*

gray king fish: *Wild Saltwater Fish 15*

gray langur: *Old World Monkeys 15*

gray myotis: *Bats 15*

gray oak: *Deciduous Trees 10*

gray pine: *Evergreen Trees 10*

gray popcorn tree: *Weeds 10*

gray reef: *Sharks 15*

gray sapphire: *Star Gems 21*

gray sole: *Wild Saltwater Fish 15*

gray squirrel: *Woodland Mammals 15*

gray triggerfish: *Wild Saltwater Fish 15*

gray willow: *Deciduous Trees 10*

gray wolf: *Symbols in Magic and Religion 19*

gray: *Colors 20; Dragon 16; Elf 1; Eye Color 1; Foxes 15; Hair Color 1; Sad 20*

grayleaf willow: *Deciduous Trees 10*

gray-leaved willow: *Deciduous Trees 10*

gray-stemmed dogwood: *Deciduous Trees 10*

grazed seam allowance: *Sewing Techniques 2; Sewing Terms 2*

grazing land: *Farm/Outbuilding 3*

grazioso: *Tempo/Mood 13*

grease gun: *Hand Tools 5*

grease: *Moth 15*

greased lightning: *Fast 20*

greasepaint: *Technical Terms 13*

greaser: *Styles of Dress 2*

great aunt: *Female 1*

Great Barrier Reef: *Seven Wonders of the Natural World 18; Seven Wonders of the Underwater World 18*

Great Basin: *Rattlesnake 15*

great Caesar's ghost: *Expletives 20*

great chamber: *Castle Anatomy 3*

great circle route: *Geography General Vocabulary 10*

great coat: *Western Clothing/Dress 21*

Great Dane: *Dog Breeds 15*

great granddaughter: *Female 1*

great grandfather: *Male 1*

great grandmother: *Female 1*

great grandson: *Male 1*

great gray: *Owls 15*

great hall: *Castle Anatomy 3; Rooms 3*

great hawk: *Owls 15*

great helm: *Head Gear 7*

great horned: *Owls 15*

great merrybells: *Garden Perennials 10*

great northern bean: *Legumes 6*

Great Plains: *Toads 15*

great pondhawk: *Dragonfly 15*

Great Pyramid at Giza: *Real Places Steeped in Legend or Mystery 18; Unique Property 3; Seven Wonders of the Ancient World 18*

Great Pyrennes: *Dog Breeds 15*

great room: *Rooms 3*

Great Seal of the United States: *Secular Symbols 19; United States Dollar Bill 19*

great seal: *Jewelry 21*

great uncle: *Male 1*

Great Wall of China: *Seven Wonders of the Middle Ages 18; Unique Property 3*

great white: *Sharks 15*

great: *Good 20; Happy 20; Heavy 20; Large 20; Large/Heavy 1; Personality Other 1; Swords Two-handed 7*

greater blue-ringed: *Octopi 15*

greater celandine: *Garden Perennials 10; Poisonous Plants 10*

greater siren: *Salamanders 15*

greater sooty: *Owls 15*

Greater Swiss Mountain Dog: *Dog Breeds 15*

greave: *Armor Pieces 7*

grebe hat: *Headgear 2*

grebe: *Other Wild Birds 15*

Grecian couch: *Seating 4*

greed: *Seven Deadly Sins 19*

greedy person: *Common Character Archetypes 21*

greedy: *Negative 1*

Greek drama: *Performance Genres 13*

Greek fire: *Illumination/Light Sources 5; Siege Equipment 7*

Greek pantheon: *Philosophy and Religion 14*

Greek Revival: *Architectural Styles 3*

Greek Shorthorn: *Other Cows 15*

Greek Steppe: *Other Cows 15*

Greek valerian: *Garden Perennials 10*

Greek yogurt: *Other Dairy 6*

Greek: *Art Movements 13; Human Ethnic Groups 1; Tortoises 15*

green alder: *Deciduous Trees 10*

Green Bay Packers winning first Super Bowl in 1967: *Legendary Events 18*

green bean casserole: *Thanksgiving 19; Vegetables Cooked 6*

green bean: *Vegetables 6*

green beer: *St. Patrick's Day 19*

green beryl: *Minerals 10*

green cabbage: *Vegetables 6*

green chromis: *Aquarium Saltwater Fish 15*

green goddess: *Salad Dressing 6*

green hag: *Humanoid 16*

green jasper: *Minerals 10*

Green Knight: *Arthurian Characters 18*

green knight: *Knight 1*

green lead ore: *Minerals 10*

green leaf lettuce: *Vegetables 6*

green locust: *Deciduous Trees 10*

green lynx: *Nonvenomous Arachnids 15*

Green Man: *Folklore Characters 18*

green man: *Secular Symbols 19*

green market: *General Property 3; Outdoor Property 3*

green moray: *Wild Saltwater Fish 15*

green olive: *Vegetables 6*

green onion: *Vegetables 6*

green onyx: *Minerals 10*

green split pea: *Legumes 6*

green spotted: *Wild Saltwater Fish 15*

green spurge: *Weeds 10*

green sturgeon: *Wild Saltwater Fish 15*

green tree: *Frogs 15; Pit Viper 15; Python 15*

green: *Colors 20; Dragon 16; Eye Color 1; General Snake Families 15; Grapes 6; Green 20; Martial Artist Belt Ranks 1; New 20; Pears 6; Political Parties 1; Roofing Materials 3; Salads 6; Sea Turtles 15; St. Patrick's Day 19; Tea 6*

green-and-gold: *Garden Perennials 10*

greengage: *Unusual Edible Fruits 6*

greenhouse effect: *Astronomy General Terms 11; Chemistry General Vocabulary 11; Meteorology General Vocabulary 10*

greenhouse: *Business Property 3; Farm/Outbuilding 3; Property Features 3*

greenschist: *Metamorphic Rocks 10*

green-spored parasol: *Fungus Common Names 10*

greenstick fracture: *Injuries/Medical Emergencies 12*

greenstreak: *Butterfly 15*

greenthreads: *Garden Perennials 10*

green-yellow: *Green 20; Yellow 20*

greet a chimney sweep: *Practices/Objects to Attract Good Luck 19*

greeter: *General Occupations 1*

Gregale: *Winds of the Mediterranean 10*

Gregorian chant: *Composition Types 13*

Gregorio Cortez: *Real People with Legendary Status 18*

Greip: *Moons 11*

grenade launcher: *Spy Gear 5*

grenade machine gun: *Military Weapons General 8*

grenade: *Black Powder Weapons 7; Military Weapons General 8; Siege Equipment 7; Spy Gear 5; Weapons 22*

grenadine: *Mixers 6*

Grendl: *Fictional Characters 18*

grevenbroeker: *Cheese International Varieties 6*

grevillea: *Shrubs 10*

grey birch: *Deciduous Trees 10*

grey dogwood: *Deciduous Trees 10*

grey oak: *Deciduous Trees 10*

grey she-oak: *Deciduous Trees 10*

grey zorro: *Foxes 15*

Grey's: *Sea Snake 15*

Greyhound: *Dog Breeds 15*

greywacke: *Sedimentary Rocks 10*

Grice: *Pigs 15*

grid: *Geography General Vocabulary 10*

Grid's Rod: *Norse Weapons 18*

griddle cake: *Bread General Varieties 6*

griddle fry: *Cooking Techniques 20*

griddle: *Appliances 5; Kitchen Equipment 5*

gridiron: *Kitchen Equipment 5*

grieving: *Sad 20*

griffin: *Fantasy Creatures with Symbolic Meaning 19; Flying Creatures 16; Beast 16; Magical Transportation 17*

Griflet le Fise de Dieu: *Knights of the Round Table 18*

grifter: *Illicit Occupations 1; Thief 1*

grig: *General Fae 16*

grigori: *Angels Common Terms 14*

grike: *Cave Anatomy 10*

grill pan: *Kitchen Equipment 5*

grill plate: *Tableware 5*

grill: *Appliances 5; Cooking Techniques 20; Jewelry 21*

grilled cheese: *Sandwiches 6*

grilled halloumi: *Cheese International Varieties 6*

grim reaper: *Beast 16*

grim: *Bad 20; Difficult 20; Horror Vocabulary 23; Sad 20*

Grimaldi scaled: *Squid 15*

grim-faced: *Sad 20*

grimoire: *Typical Magical Objects 17*

Grimoirium Verum: *Books of Legend 18*

grinding machine: *Power Tools*

grinding wheel: *Power Tools*

grinding: *Dance Styles 13*

grindstone: *Large Tools*

grip: *Magic Vocabulary 17*

gripe: *Speak 20*

gripped: *Magic Vocabulary 17*

griselinia: *Shrubs 10*

grisly: *Horror Vocabulary 23; Unattractive 20*

grissini: *Bread General Varieties 6*

gritstone: *Sedimentary Rocks 10*

grivet: *Old World Monkeys 15*

grizzly: *Bears 15*

groan: *Paranormal Occurrences 21; Sounds 20*

grocery store dots: *Poker Card Games 5*

grocery store: *Business Property 3*

groin: *Body Parts 12*

Groningen Whiteheaded: *Other Cows 15*

Groningen: *Horse Breeds 15*

groom: *Animal/Equestrian 1; Special Occasion 1*

groom's: *Cake 6*

groomsman: *Special Occasion 1*

grooved diving: *Beetle 15*

groove-toothed: *Bats 15*

gross: *Heavy 20; Unattractive 20*

grossularite garnet: *Standard Gems 21*

grossularite: *Minerals 10*

grotesque: *Art Genres 13; Masks 2; Performance Genres 13*

grot-hole: *Cave Anatomy 10*

grotto: *Cave Anatomy 10; Terrain Features 10*

grouchy hotel employee: *Travel Hazards 9*

grouchy officials: *Travel Hazards 9*

grouchy waiter/waitress: *Travel Hazards 9*

grouchy: *Character Building 1*

ground bass: *General Music Vocabulary 13*

ground beef: *Beef 6*

ground breaking: *New 20*

ground cedar: *Wildflowers 10*

ground chuck: *Beef 6*

ground cloth: *General Survival Gear 5*

ground elder: *Garden Perennials 10*

ground fog: *Wet 10*

ground glass: *Wizard's Goods 5*

ground offense: *General Combat Vocabulary 7*

ground plum: *Garden Perennials 10*

ground pork: *Pork 6*

ground sirloin: *Beef 6*

ground superiority: *General Combat Vocabulary 7*

ground support: *General Combat Vocabulary 7*

ground transportation: *Travel Modes 24; Travel Types 22*

ground: *Beetle 15; Elements 19; General Snake Families 15; Nonvenomous Arachnids 15; Sharks 15*

ground-penetrating radar: *Geological Field Work Methods 10*

grounds: *Amusement Park/Carnival/Circus/Fair 3*

groundskeeper: *Castle Inhabitants and Personnel 1*

groundstreak: *Butterfly 15*

ground-trog: *Cave Anatomy 10*

groundwater detection: *Geological Field Work Methods 10*

groundwater: *Cave Anatomy 10*

groundwater-related subsidence: *Soil General Vocabulary 10*

group captain: *Armed Forces Other Titles 8*

grouper: *Aquarium Saltwater Fish 15; Fish/Seafood Types 6; Wild Saltwater Fish 15*

groupings: *Philosophy and Religion 14*

groups: *The Arts 13*

grouse: *Poultry Types 6*

grove: *Ecosystems 10; Terrain Features 10*

grow light: *Illumination Bulb and Tube Types 5*

grow: *Learn 20*

grower: *Agricultural 1*

growing season: *Geography General Vocabulary 10*

growl: *Sounds 20; Speak 20*

grown: *Adult 1*

grown-up: *Adult 1*

grueling: *Difficult 20*

gruesome: *Horror Vocabulary 23; Unattractive 20*

gruff: *Vocal/Speech Quality 1*

grumichama: *Unusual Edible Fruits 6*

grumpy: *Grouchy 1*

grunge: *Styles of Dress 2*

grunt: *Sounds 20*

Grus: *Constellations 11*

gruyere: *Cheese Common Varieties 6*

G-string: *Unisex Clothing 2*

Guadalupe Island pine: *Evergreen Trees 10*

Guadalupe spiny softshell: *Freshwater Turtles 15*

Guadalupian Age: *Geologic Time 10*

guanabana: *Unusual Edible Fruits 6*

Guangxi: *Horse Breeds 15*

guard position: *Fencing Vocabulary 7*

guard tower: *Castle Anatomy 3; Fantasy Locations 24*

guard: *Castle Inhabitants and Personnel 1; Fencing Equipment 7; Fighter 1; General Combat Vocabulary 7*

guardant: *Special Posture 19*

guarded: *Horror Vocabulary 23*

guardhouse: *Fortification 3*

guardian ad litem: *Legal Occupations 1*

guardian angel symbol: *Harbingers/Charms for Good Luck 19*

guardian angel: *Angels Common Terms 14*

guardian naga: *Beast 16*

guardian: *Fighter 1*

Guatemalan black howler: *New World Monkeys 15*

guava: *Tropical/Exotic Fruits 6*

guavaberry: *Unusual Edible Fruits 6*

Gudali: *Other Cows 15*

gudmundite: *Minerals 10*

guelph soil: *Soil General Vocabulary 10*

guenon: *Old World Monkeys 15*

guereza: *Old World Monkeys 15*

guerilla: *Tactics 7*

Guernsey fleabane: *Weeds 10*

Guernsey: *North American Dairy Cows 15*

guerrilla war: *General Combat Vocabulary 7*

guerrilla: *Fighter 1*

guesstimate: *Solve 20*

guess-your-weight: *Amusement Park/Carnival/Circus/Fair 3*

guest of honor: *Hero 20; Special Occasion 1*

guffaw: *Sounds 20*

guide: *Barbarian 1; General Occupations 1*

guided missile cruiser: *Military Watercraft 8*

guided missile destroyer: *Military Watercraft 8*

guided missile frigate: *Military Watercraft 8*

guild: *Business Property 3; General Buildings 3; Social Clubs 1*

guilds: *Character Building 1*

guilty: *Horror Vocabulary 23*

Guinae: *Caecilians 15*

guinea hen: *Domesticated Farm Birds 15*

Guinea hog: *Pigs 15*

guinea pig: *Pocket Pets 15*

Guinevere: *Arthurian Characters 18*

guisarme: *Pole Weapons 7*

guisarme-voulge: *Pole Weapons 7*

guitar pick: *Music Accessories*

guitar: *String Musical Instruments*

gulag: *Prison 3*

gulch: *Erosion 10*

gules (red): *Colors/Tinctures 19*

gulf black willow: *Deciduous Trees 10*

Gulf coast box: *Freshwater Turtles 15*

Gulf Coast: *Toads 15*

gulf cypress: *Evergreen Trees 10*

gulf flounder: *Wild Saltwater Fish 15*

Gulf low: *Snow Storms 10*

gulf toad fish: *Wild Saltwater Fish 15*

gulf: *Coastal and Oceanic 10; Terrain Features 10; Water Terms 9*

gull: *Other Wild Birds 15*

gullible: *Personality Other 1*

gully washer: *Meteorology General Vocabulary 10*

gully: *Erosion 10; Fluvial 10; Slope 10*

gum arabic: *Wizard's Goods 5*

gum tree: *Weeds 10*

gum: *Boots 2*

gumball: *Candy General 6*

gumbo file: *Deciduous Trees 10*

gumbo lily: *Garden Perennials 10*

gumdrop: *Candy General 6*

gummi bears: *Candy General 6*

gummi fish: *Candy General 6*

gummi worms: *Candy General 6*

gummy: *Wet 20*

gumshoe: *Horror Occupations 23*

gumwood: *Deciduous Trees 10*

gun belt: *Western Clothing/Dress 21*

gun crew: *Siege Engines 7*

gun down: *Attack 7*

gun fight at the O.K. corral: *Western Plot Devices 21*

gun holster: *Toys 5*

gun: *Spy Gear 5*

gunboat: *Military Watercraft 8*

gunfighter: *Common Character Archetypes 21*

Gungnir: *Spears 18; Symbols in Magic and Religion 19*

Gunn: *Comets 11*

gunner sergeant: *U.S. Marines Enlisted 8*

gunship: *Military Aircraft 8; Spaceship Types 22*

gunslinger hired for task: *Western Plot Devices 21*

gunslinger: *Western Paraphernalia/People 21*

gunwale: *Boat/Ship Anatomy 9*

guppy: *Aquarium Freshwater Fish 15*

gurdwara: *Religious Building 3*

Gurkha: *Assassin 1*

guru: *Wizard 1*

gurz: *Bludgeons 7*

gush: *Wet 20*

gusset: *Garment Pieces 2*

gust: *Wind 10*

gut: *Body Parts 12; Cooking Techniques 20*

guta: *Demon 16*

guts: *Card Games 5; Wet 20*

gutte: *Patterns 19*

gutter: *Building Elements and Features 3*

guttural: *Vocal/Speech Quality 1*

Guy de Bourgogne: *Twelve Peers of Charlemagne 18*

Guy Fawkes: *Real People with Legendary Status 18*

guy: *Male 1*

guyot: *Volcanic 10*

Guzerat: *Other Cows 15*

gwyllion: *Demon 16*

gym mat: *Dance Equipment 13*

gym: *Athletic Shoes 2; Socks 2*

gymnasium: *Academic Property 3; Entertainment Property 3*

gymnast: *Performing Arts 1*

gymnite: *Minerals 10*

gynecologist: *Medical Occupations 1*

gypcrust: *Soil General Vocabulary 10*

gypsisol: *Soil General Vocabulary 10*

gypsite: *Minerals 10*

gypsum board: *Interior Building Materials 3*

gypsum flower: *Cave Anatomy 10; Minerals 10*

gypsum rock: *Minerals 10*

gypsum: *Cave Anatomy 10*

gypsy bonnet: *Headgear 2*

gypsy fortune teller: *Horror Occupations 23*

gypsy hat: *Headgear 2*

gypsy mushroom: *Fungus Common Names 10*

gypsy: *Fortune Teller 1; Moth 15; Styles of Dress 2; Thief 1; Wanderer 1*

gyrate: *Locomotion 9*

gyro: *Sandwiches 6*

gyroscope: *Toys 5*

–H–

H&K semi-automatic pistol: *SWAT Weapons 7*

H&R Buffalo Classic: *Single Shot Centerfire Rifles 7*

H&R CR Carbine: *Single Shot Centerfire Rifles 7*

H&R Hunter: *Single Shot Centerfire Rifles 7*

H&R Tamer: *Shotguns Single Shot 7*

H&R ultra slug: *Shotguns Single Shot 7*

H&R Ultra Varmint: *Single Shot Rimfire Rifles 7*

H35 light tank: *France Military Vehicles 8*

habanera (Cuba): *Ethnic/Folk Dances 13*

Haber process: *Chemistry General Vocabulary 11*

haberdasher: *Artists and Craftspeople 1*

habitable zone: *Planetary Systems 11*

habitat: *Man-Made Animal Homes 15; Plot Devices 22; Residential Property 3*

habitation: *Residential Property 3*

habited: *Special Body Features 19*

haboob: *Meteorology General Vocabulary 10*

Habu: *General Snake Families 15; Pit Viper 15*

habutai: *Fabric 2*

Hachiman (divine protection): *Japanese Pantheon 14*

hackberry: *Deciduous Trees 10; Unusual Edible Fruits 6*

hackmanite: *Minerals 10*

hackmatack: *Deciduous Trees 10*

Hackney: *Horse Breeds 15*

haddock: *Fish/Seafood Types 6; Wild Saltwater Fish 15*

Hadean Era: *Geologic Time 10*

Hades (underworld): *Greek Pantheon 14*

Hades: *Afterlife/Underworld 18*

Hadraniel: *Angels of Good 14*

hadrosaur: *Dinosaur Types 15*

Haflinger: *Horse Breeds 15*

hafnium zircon: *Minerals 10*

Hafnium: *Elements 11*

hag: *Common Character Archetypes 21; General Fae 16; Humanoid 16; Wizard 1*

Hagen's: *Pit Viper 15*

Hagia Sophia: *Seven Wonders of the Middle Ages 18; Unique Property 3*

Haidi: *Native American Peoples 1*

hail stones: *Snow Types 10*

hail: *Severe Weather 10; Ten Plagues on Egypt 14*

hailstone: *Minerals 10*

hair accessories: *Clothing 2*

hair brush: *Personal Care 5*

hair color: *Character Building 1*

hair comb: *Jewelry 21*

hair gel: *Personal Care 5*

hair mousse: *Personal Care 5*

hair net: *Hair Accessories 2*

hair pick: *Personal Care 5*

hair spray: *Personal Care 5*

hair style: *Character Building 1*

hair stylist: *Personal Services 1*

hair treated: *Character Building 1*

hair type: *Character Building 1*

hair: *Body Parts 12; Character Building 1; Objects/Activities Connected to Lore 19; Wizard's Goods 5*

hairless: *Skin Types and Features 1*

hairpiece: *Headgear 2*

hairpin: *Jewelry 21*

hair-raising: *Horror Vocabulary 23*

hairstreak: *Butterfly 15*

hairy stereum: *Fungus Common Names 10*

hairy: *Skin Types and Features 1*

hairy-footed: *Bats 15*

hairy-nosed: *Bats 15*

Haitian Creole: *Human Ethnic Groups 1*

hakea: *Shrubs 10*

haladie: *Daggers and Knives 7*

halberd: *Pole Weapons 7*

Hale-Bopp: *Comets 11*

half and half: *Beer 6; Other Dairy 6*

half blind valley: *Cave Anatomy 10*

half hitch: *Sailing Knots 9*

half moon: *Pole Weapons 7*

half note: *Notation 13*

half pike: *Spears 7*

half speed: *Slow 20*

half: *Elf 1*

halfbreed: *Minerals 10*

half-brother: *Male 1*

half-caf: *Coffee Drinks 6*

half-cell: *Chemistry General Vocabulary 11*

half-cent: *Coins and Currency 21*

half-city: *Coffee Bean Roasts 6*

half-dollar: *Coins and Currency 21*

halfhearted: *Horror Vocabulary 23*

half-life: *Chemistry General Vocabulary 11; Geological Vocabulary 10*

half-mask: *Masks 2*

half-moon purse: *Accessories 2*

half-pint: *Small/Thin 1*

half-reaction: *Chemistry General Vocabulary 11*

half-sheet: *Cake 6*

half-sister: *Female 1*

half-slip: *Ladies' Wear 2*

half-timber: *Castle Anatomy 3; Exterior Building Materials 3*

half-truth: *Philosophy Basic Concepts 14*

Halimede: *Moons 11*

hall tree: *Miscellaneous Furniture 4*

hall: *Castle Anatomy 3; Cave Anatomy 10; Rooms 3*

Hall's honeysuckle: *Garden Perennials 10*

Halley: *Comets 11*

Hallikar: *Other Cows 15*

Halloween: *Candy General 6; Holidays 19; Masks 2; Styles of Dress 2; Witchcraft Vocabulary 17*

hallucination: *Magic Vocabulary 17*

hallulla: *Bread General Varieties 6*

hallway: *Castle Anatomy 3; Rooms 3*

Halmahera: *Python 15*

halo: *Jewelry 21; Meteorology General Vocabulary 10; Symbols in Magic and Religion 19*

halo-brim hat: *Headgear 2*

halogen: *Illumination Bulb and Tube Types 5*

halogens: *Chemistry General Vocabulary 11*

halt: *Commands 20*

halter bra: *Ladies' Wear 2*

halter leotard: *Dance Clothing 13*

halter of Clydno Eiddyn: *Thirteen Treasures of the Island of Britain 18*

halter top: *Ladies' Wear 2*

halyard: *Boat/Ship Anatomy 9*

ham patty: *Meals 6*

ham salad: *Sandwiches 6*

ham: *Pork 6; Sandwiches 6*

hamalat al-arsh: *Angels Common Terms 14*

hamate bone: *Bones 12*

hambergite: *Standard Gems 21*

hamburger patty: *Meals 6*

hamburger: *Amusement Park/Carnival/Circus/Fair 3; Beef 6; Meals 6; Sandwiches 6*

hamlet: *City 10*

hammer and chisel: *Symbols of Freemasonry 19*

hammer drill: *Power Tools*

hammer of Thor: *Norse Weapons 18*

hammer/malleus: *Bones 12*

hammer: *Art Tools 5; Attack 7; Bludgeons 7; Classic Items 23; Hand Tools 5; Musical Instrument Parts 13; Pole Weapons 7; Tools 7*

hammerhead: *Sharks 15*

hammock: *Beds 4; Boat/Ship Anatomy 9*

hamper of Gwyddno Garanhir: *Thirteen Treasures of the Island of Britain 18*

Hampshire: *Pigs 15*

hamster: *Pocket Pets 15*

Han: *Human Ethnic Groups 1*

hanbō: *Bludgeons 7*

hanbok dress: *Ladies' Wear 2*

hanbok: *Men's Wear 2*

hancockite: *Minerals 10*

hand and foot: *Card Games 5*

hand cannon: *Cannon 7*

hand crossbow: *Missile Weapons 7*

hand foot and mouth disease: *Diseases 12*

hand jive: *Dance Styles 13*

hand lens: *Laboratory Equipment 5*

hand mixer: *Appliances 5*

hand of Fatima: *Symbols in Magic and Religion 19*

hand of glory: *Symbols in Magic and Religion 19*

hand packed: *Ice Cream 6*

hand saw: *Hand Tools 5*

hand shapes: *Palm Reading 19*

hand shears: *Garden Tools*

hand tools 5: *Equipment and Tools 5*

hand truck: *Garden Tools; Human-Powered Transportation 9*

hand weapons: *Combat, Armor, and Weapons 7*

hand: *Axes 7; Body Parts 12; Sharks 15; Towels 5*

hand-and-a-half: *Swords Two-handed 7*

handcar: *Human-Powered Transportation 9*

handcuffs: *Fasteners 5*

handgun: *Cannon 7*

handguns: *Combat, Armor, and Weapons 7*

handkase: *Cheese International Varieties 6*

handkerchief: *Accessories 2*

handle: *Fix 20*

handlebar: *Facial Hair Mustache 1*

handmaid: *Housekeeping 1*

handmaiden: *Housekeeping 1*

handsome prince: *Common Character Archetypes 21*

handsome: *Beautiful 20*

hang glider: *Air Vehicles 9*

hangar: *Infrastructure Buildings 9*

hanging folder: *Office/School/Writing Supplies 5*

Hanging Gardens of Babylon: *Seven Wonders of the Ancient World 18; Unique Property Destroyed 3*

hanging of innocent cowboy: *Western Plot Devices 21*

hanging valley: *Glacial and Mountain 10*

hanging: *Witchcraft Vocabulary 17*

hangman's noose: *Classic Items 23*

hangman's rope: *Items with Healing Properties 19*

hangout: *Criminal Property 3; Residential Slang 3*

hangover: *Anatomy and Physiology 12*

Haniel: *Angels of Good 14*

Hanoverian: *Horse Breeds 15*

Hansel and Gretel: *Fictional Characters 18*

hansom cab: *Animal-Powered Transportation 9*

hantavirus pulmonary syndrome: *Diseases 12*

Hante: *Pigs 15*

happiness: *General Emotions 20; Philosophy Basic Concepts 14*

happy go lucky: *Happy 20*

Happy Hunting Grounds: *Afterlife/Underworld 18*

happy: *Emotions 20; Positive 1*

Harajuku: *Styles of Dress 2*

harass: *General Combat Vocabulary 7*

Harbor of Rio de Janeiro: *Seven Wonders of the Natural World 18*

harbor patrol: *Boat/Ship Terminology 9; Law Enforcement 1*

harbor: *Marina 3; Water Terms 9*

hard boil: *Cooking Techniques 20*

hard boiled: *Egg Styles 6*

hard cider: *Beer 6*

hard contact lenses: *Optics 5*

hard hat: *Headgear 2*

hard head catfish: *Wild Saltwater Fish 15*

hard lemonade: *Beer 6*

hard liquor: *Food 6*

hard maple: *Deciduous Trees 10*

hard rock: *Musical Styles 13*

hard squash: *Vegetables 6*

hard water: *Chemistry General Vocabulary 11*

hard: *Bread General Varieties 6; Candy General 6; Difficult 20; Vocal/Speech Quality 1*

hardanger: *Embellishments 2*

hardbound: *Books/Publications 5*

hardcover: *Books/Publications 5*

harden: *Cooking Techniques 20*

hard-faced: *Sad 20*

hardpan: *Soil General Vocabulary 10*

hardtack: *Bread General Varieties 6*

hardware: *Equipment and Tools 5*

hardwood: *Interior Building Materials 3*

hardy ice plant: *Garden Perennials 10*

hardy plumbago: *Shrubs 10*

hare: *Animals with Symbolic Meaning 19; Wild Game 6; Woodland Mammals 15*

harebell: *Garden Perennials 10*

harem girl: *Styles of Dress 2*

Hariana: *Other Cows 15*

Harlem Renaissance: *Art Movements 13*

harlequin opal: *Minerals 10*

harlequin: *Bats 15; Common Character Archetypes 21; General Snake Families 15; Masks 2*

harm: *Verbs 20*

harming ants: *Practices that Attract Bad Luck 19*

harmonic tremor: *Geography General Vocabulary 10*

harmonica: *Wind/Woodwind and Brass Musical Instruments*

harmoniemusik: *Composition Types 13*

harmonious: *Happy 20*

harmonium: *Wind/Woodwind and Brass Musical Instruments*

harmony: *Art Principles 13; General Music Vocabulary 13; Philosophy Basic Concepts 14*

harness: *Transportation Animals 9*

harp: *String Musical Instruments*

Harpalyke: *Moons 11*

Harpers Ferry class: *U.S. Navy Vessels 8*

harpoon: *Fishing Gear 5; Missile Weapons 7; Spears 7*

harpsichord: *String Musical Instruments*

harpy: *Fantasy Creatures with Symbolic Meaning 19; Flying Creatures 16; Humanoid 16*

harrier: *Birds of Prey 15*

Harrier: *Dog Breeds 15*

harrow: *General Farm Equipment*

Harry le Fise Lake: *Knights of the Round Table 18*

harsh: *Horror Vocabulary 23; Unattractive 20; Vocal/Speech Quality 1*

Hartón: *Other Cows 15*

Harut: *Angels of Good 14*

harvest: *Tables 4*

harvester: *General Farm Equipment*

harzburgite: *Igneous Rocks 10*

harzer: *Cheese International Varieties 6*

hash brown: *Vegetables Cooked 6*

hash: *Meals 6*

Hashshashin (Order of Assassins): *Secret/Mystical Organizations 18*

Hassium: *Elements 11*

hassle: *Difficult 20*

hassock: *Seating 4*

hasta: *Spears 7*

Hastselts (red lord): *Native American Pantheon 14*

Hastsezini (black lord): *Native American Pantheon 14*

hasty: *Fast 20; Mobility 1*

hat: *Headgear 2; Spy Gear 5*

hatch: *Boat/Ship Anatomy 9; Doors Atypical 3*

hatchback: *Motorized 9*

hatchet marlin swordfish: *Wild Saltwater Fish 15*

hatchet: *Axes 7; Hand Tools 5*

hatchetfish: *Aquarium Freshwater Fish 15*

hatchling: *Dragon 16*

hatchway: *Doors Atypical 3*

hate: *General Emotions 20*

Hathor (dancing): *Egyptian Pantheon 14*

Hati: *Moons 11*

hatred: *General Emotions 20*

hauberk: *Armor Pieces 7*

haulm topper: *General Farm Equipment*

haulout transporter: *General Farm Equipment*

Haumea: *Planets 11*

haunt: *Cemetery 3; Criminal Property 3; Paranormal Activity 21*

haunted bridge: *Horror Locations 23*

haunted hayride: *Halloween 19*

haunted hotel: *Horror Locations 23; Horror Plot Devices 23*

haunted house lashes out at new tenants: *Horror Plot Devices 23*

haunted house: *Halloween 19; Horror Locations 23*

haunted lake: *Horror Locations 23*

haunted road: *Horror Locations 23*

haunted ruins: *Horror Locations 23*

haunted/abandoned house: *Common Dangers 23*

haunting: *Paranormal Activity 21*

haurient: *Sea Creatures 19*

Hausa: *Human Ethnic Groups 1*

haute couture: *Styles of Dress 2*

Hauteclaire: *Weapons of Legend 18*

Havana Brown: *Domestic Cats 15*

havanaise (Cuba): *Ethnic/Folk Dances 13*

Havanese: *Dog Breeds 15*

havarti: *Cheese Common Varieties 6*

have a heart: *Poker Card Games 5*

haven: *General Buildings 3; Water Terms 9*

Hawaiian shirt: *Unisex Clothing 2*

Hawaiian: *Human Ethnic Groups 1*

hawaiite: *Igneous Rocks 10*

hawk: *Birds of Prey 15;*

hawk's eye: *Minerals 10*

hawker: *Dragonfly 15*

hawkfish: *Aquarium Saltwater Fish 15*

hawksbill: *Sea Turtles 15*

hawkweed: *Garden Perennials 10*

Hawthorn jewel: *Beetle 15*

hawthorn: *Items with Healing Properties 19; Objects that Offer Protection 19; Shrubs 10*

hay chopper: *Horse Drawn Farm Equipment*

hay fork: *Tools 7*

hay rake: *General Farm Equipment*

hay tedder: *General Farm Equipment; Horse Drawn Farm Equipment*

hay wagon: *Farm Transportation 9*

hay: *Farm/Outbuilding 3*

hayloft: *Farm/Outbuilding 3*

Hays Converter: *Other Cows 15*

hayseed: *Social Distinction 1*

haytorite: *Minerals 10*

hazardous waste: *Geography General Vocabulary 10*

haze: *Meteorology General Vocabulary 10; Smells 20*

hazel alder: *Deciduous Trees 10*

hazel: *Eye Color 1; Objects that Offer Protection 19*

hazelnut: *Candy General 6; Nuts 6; Oils 6*

hazmat suit: *Clothing/Uniforms 22*

hazy: *Horror Vocabulary 23*

HC-30 search and rescue: *U.S. Air Force Aircraft 8*

HD DVD: *Electronics 4*

head and taillight tetra: *Aquarium Freshwater Fish 15*

head cheese: *Meals 6*

head chef: *Food Service 1*

head for the hills: *Expletives 20*

head gear: *Combat, Armor, and Weapons 7; Teeth Dental Work 1*

head lettuce: *Vegetables 6*

head lice: *Diseases 12*

head of the line: *Beginning 20*

head: *Axes 7; Bathrooms 3; Boat/Ship Anatomy 9; Body Parts 12*

Head: *Major Lines 19*

headband: *Headgear 2; Jewelry 21*

headdress: *Headgear 2; Jewelry 21*

headgear: *Clothing 2*

heading: *Swords Two-handed 7*

headland: *Coastal and Oceanic 10; Soil General Vocabulary 10; Terrain Features 10*

ALPHABETICAL INDEX

Headless Horseman: *Fictional Characters 18*

headlong: *Fast 20*

headmaster: *Academic 1; Common Character Archetypes 21*

headmistress: *Academic 1; Common Character Archetypes 21*

headquarters: *General Buildings 3*

heads: *Classic Heraldry 19*

headset: *Technical Terms 13*

headstone: *Halloween 19*

headstrong: *Stubborn 1*

heady: *Beautiful 20*

healer: *Common Character Archetypes 21; Fantasy Occupations 24; Medical Occupations 1*

healing: *Paranormal Abilities 21*

health care property: *Architecture and Property 3*

health center: *Health Care 3*

health resort: *Health Care 3*

health spa: *Health Care 3*

Health: *Major Lines 19*

hear: *Learn 20*

hearing: *Physical Mutations 22*

hearse: *Motorized 9*

heart attack: *Injuries/Medical Emergencies 12*

heart of Jesus: *Poisonous Plants 10*

Heart: *Bows 18; Major Lines 19*

heart: *Beef 6; Organs/Major Structures 12; Pennsylvania Dutch Hex Signs 19; Valentine's Day 19*

heartbreaking: *Sad 20*

heartening: *Happy 20*

hearth broom: *Cleaning Supplies/Gadgets 5*

hearth stool: *Chairs and Stools 4*

hearth: *Building Elements and Features 3; Geography General Vocabulary 10; Objects/Activities Connected to Lore 19; Rooms 3*

heartleaf Alexander: *Garden Perennials 10*

heartless: *Horror Vocabulary 23*

heart-nosed: *Bats 15*

heart-rending: *Sad 20*

hearts: *Candy Chocolate 6; Card Games 5*

heart-shaped box: *Candy Chocolate 6*

heart-shaped candy box: *Valentine's Day 19*

heart-shaped: *Beds 4; Face 1*

heat capacity: *Chemistry General Vocabulary 11*

heat exhaustion/stroke: *Injuries/Medical Emergencies 12; Travel Hazards 9*

heat generation: *Physical Mutations 22*

heat gun: *Power Tools*

heat index: *Meteorology General Vocabulary 10*

heat of condensation: *Chemistry General Vocabulary 11*

heat of crystallization: *Chemistry General Vocabulary 11*

heat of fusion: *Chemistry General Vocabulary 11*

heat of solution: *Chemistry General Vocabulary 11*

heat of vaporization: *Chemistry General Vocabulary 11*

heat proof suit: *Spy Gear 5*

heat resistance: *Physical Mutations 22*

heat wave: *Meteorology General Vocabulary 10*

heat: *Chemistry General Vocabulary 11; Cooking Techniques 20; Meteorology General Vocabulary 10*

heated: *Angry 1*

heater: *Shield Types 7*

heath: *Ecosystems 10; Shrubs 10*

heather: *Sewing Terms 2; Shrubs 10*

heating duct: *Building Systems 3*

heating oil delivery: *Public Services 3*

heaven: *Afterlife/Underworld 18*

Heaven's Will (sword of Thuan Thien): *Weapons of Legend 18*

heavenly wheel: *Symbols in Magic and Religion 19*

heavenly: *Beautiful 20; Happy 20*

heaving line: *Sailing Knots 9*

heavy air: *Boat/Ship Terminology 9*

heavy battleship: *Military Watercraft 8*

heavy body armor: *SWAT Equipment 7*

heavy cavalry blade: *Swords One-handed 7*

heavy cavalry man: *Knight 1*

heavy chain: *Fasteners 5*

heavy cream: *Other Dairy 6*

heavy cruiser: *Military Watercraft 8*

heavy industry: *Geography General Vocabulary 10*

heavy metal: *Musical Styles 13*

heavy mortar: *Mortar 8*

heavy rain: *Precipitation 10*

heavy rifle: *Military Weapons General 8*

heavy rope: *General Survival Gear 5*

heavy set: *Large/Heavy 1*

heavy spar: *Minerals 10*

heavy string: *Fasteners 5*

heavy water: *Chemistry General Vocabulary 11*

heavy: *Adjectives 20; Character Building 1; Large 20; Mobility 1*

heavyweight: *Heavy 20*

he-balsam: *Evergreen Trees 10*

hebe: *Shrubs 10*

Hecate (goddess of magic): *Greek Pantheon 14*

heck: *Expletives 20*

Heckler & Koch G36 carbine: *SWAT Weapons 7*

Heckler & Koch MP5 submachine gun: *SWAT Weapons 7*

Heckler & Koch UMP submachine gun: *SWAT Weapons 7*

Hector de Maris: *Knights of the Round Table 18*

Hector's: *Dolphins 15*

hedge apple: *Deciduous Trees 10*

hedge garlic: *Weeds 10*

hedge trimmer: *Power Tools*

hedge: *Landscaping 3*

hedgehog mushroom: *Fungus Common Names 10*

hedgehog: *Mortar 8; Woodland Mammals 15*

Hediger's: *Sea Snake 15*

hedonism: *Philosophy Basic Concepts 14*

heel gripper: *Shoe Accessories 13*

heel: *Body Parts 12; Bread General Varieties 6*

heels: *Footwear/Shoes 2*

hefty: *Large 20; Large/Heavy 1*

Hegemone: *Moons 11*

heightened intelligence: *Paranormal Abilities 21*

heightened sense: *Physical Mutations 22*

Heimdall (the white god): *Norse Pantheon 14*

Heimdall's sword: *Norse Weapons 18*

Heinz 57: *Dogs/Canine 15*

Heisenberg uncertainty principle: *Chemistry General Vocabulary 11*

Hekatonkheires: *Giants of Legend 16*

Hel (goddess of death): *Norse Pantheon 14*

Hel: *Afterlife/Underworld 18*

held: *Magic Vocabulary 17*

heldentenor: *Voices 13*

Helen's flower: *Garden Perennials 10*

Helene: *Moons 11*

helicopter carrier: *Military Watercraft 8*

helicopter: *Air Vehicles 9*

helicopters: *Military 8*

Helike: *Moons 11*

heliodor: *Minerals 10*

heliodorite: *Minerals 10*

heliopause: *Astronomy General Terms 11*

Heliopolis: *Architectural Styles 3*

heliosphere: *Astronomy General Terms 11*

heliotrope: *Garden Annuals 10; Garden Perennials 10; Minerals 10; Purple 20*

helium planet: *Star Types and Relatives 11*

Helium: *Elements 11*

hell: *Afterlife/Underworld 18; Expletives 20; Witchcraft Vocabulary 17*

hellbender: *Salamanders 15*

Hellenistic: *Art Movements 13*

hellhound: *Beast 16*

hellim: *Cheese International Varieties 6*

helm: *Boat/Ship Anatomy 9; Elements 19; Head Gear 7*

helmet flower: *Garden Perennials 10*

helmet lizard: *Scaled Reptiles 15*

helmet of Hades: *Helmets 18*

helmet of Rostam: *Helmets 18*

helmet: *Charges 19; Head Gear 7; Military Equipment 8*

helmsman: *Boat/Ship Anatomy 9*

help: *Teach 20*

helpful celebrity: *Common Character Archetypes 21*

helpful fairy: *Supporting Cast 24*

helpful locals: *Supporting Cast 23*

helpful stranger turns out to be evil: *Horror Plot Devices 23*

helpful: *Fortunate 20; Positive 1*

hem: *Embroidery Stitches 2; Garment Pieces 2; Sewing Techniques 2*

hematite sphere: *Harbingers/Charms for Good Luck 19*

hematite: *Standard Gems 21*

hematocrit: *Blood 12*

hematologic: *Blood 12*

hematologist: *Blood 12*

hematoma: *Blood-Related Ailments 12*

hemimorphite: *Standard Gems 21*

hemisphere: *Geography General Vocabulary 10*

hemlock spruce: *Evergreen Trees 10*

hemlock: *Evergreen Trees 10; Plants with Symbolic Meaning 19; Poisonous Plants 10*

hemochromatosis: *Blood-Related Ailments 12*

hemoglobin: *Blood 12*

hemolysis: *Blood 12*

hemophilia: *Blood-Related Ailments 12*

hemorrhage: *Blood-Related Ailments 12*

hemostasis: *Blood 12*

hemp: *Fabric 2; Farm/Outbuilding 3; Plants with Symbolic Meaning 19*

hempseed: *Practices to Predict the Future 19*

hen and chicks: *Garden Perennials 10*

hen of the woods: *Fungus Common Names 10*

hen: *Objects/Activities Connected to Lore 19*

henbane: *Poisonous Plants 10*

henchman: *Common Character Archetypes 21; Fantasy Occupations 24; Fighter 1*

Heng (thunder spirit): *Native American Pantheon 14*

Hengroen: *Arthur's Horses 18*

henhouse: *Natural Animal Homes 15*

henley: *Unisex Clothing 2*

Henry ACU-Bolt: *Bolt Action Rimfire Rifles 7*

Henry lever action: *Lever Action and Pump Rimfire Rifles 7*

Henry pump action: *Lever Action and Pump Rimfire Rifles 7*

henway: *Poker Card Games 5*

hepatica: *Wildflowers 10*

hepatitis: *Diseases 12*

Hephaestus (blacksmiths, fire): *Greek Pantheon 14*

Hepplewhite: *Chairs and Stools 4*

Hequ: *Horse Breeds 15*

Hera (goddess of marriage and family): *Greek Pantheon 14*

Heracles (demigod of strength): *Greek Pantheon 14*

heraldic sign: *Jewelry 21*

heraldic thistle: *Weeds 10*

herb twopence: *Weeds 10*

herbaceous plants: *Chapter 10*

herbal: *Tea 6*

herbalist: *Fantasy Occupations 24; Nature Occupations 1*

herbs: *Wizard's Goods 5*

herculean: *Large 20*

Hercules' club: *Deciduous Trees 10; Shrubs 10*

Hercules: *Constellations 11*

hercynite: *Minerals 10*

herding: *Dog Groups 15*

Hereford: *Other Cows 15; Pigs 15*

Herens: *Other Cows 15*

herensugue: *Demon 16*

Heritage Rough rider Large Bore: *Revolver Single Action 7*

Heritage Rough Rider Smallbore: *Revolver Single Action 7*

Herkimer diamond: *Minerals 10*

Herman's: *Tortoises 15*

hermeneutics: *Philosophy Basic Concepts 14*

Hermes (travel, business, sports, messenger of the gods): *Greek Pantheon 14*

Hermetic Order of the Golden Dawn: *Secret/Mystical Organizations 18*

hermetic order: *Social Clubs 1*

Hermippe: *Moons 11*

hermit: *Common Character Archetypes 21; Rural Occupations 1*

hermit's home: *Fantasy Locations 24*

hero or villain depending upon circumstance: *Nouns 20*

hero: *Common Character Archetypes 21; Nouns 20*

heroes are captured/imprisoned: *Common Dangers 24*

heroic proportions: *Large/Heavy 1*

heroic: *Large 20; Large/Heavy 1; Personality Other 1*

heroine: *Common Character Archetypes 21*

heroism: *General Emotions 20*

heron: *Other Wild Birds 15*

heron's-bill: *Garden Perennials 10*

herpes simplex: *Diseases 12*

herring: *Fish/Seafood Types 6; Wild Saltwater Fish 15*

herringbone braid: *Hair Style 1*

herringbone: *Embroidery Stitches 2; Fabric Patterns 2*

Herse: *Moons 11*

herve: *Cheese International Varieties 6*

Hervis de Revel: *Knights of the Round Table 18*

HESCO bastion: *Soil General Vocabulary 10*

Hesediel: *Angels of Good 14*

Hesperides: *Twelve Labors of Hercules 16*

hessonite garnet: *Standard Gems 21*

hessonite: *Minerals 10*

Hester Prynne: *Fictional Characters 18*

Hestia (goddess of the hearth): *Greek Pantheon 14*

heterogeneous catalyst: *Chemistry General Vocabulary 11*

heterogeneous equilibria: *Chemistry General Vocabulary 11*

hex: *Magic Vocabulary 17; Symbols in Magic and Religion 19; Witchcraft Vocabulary 17*

hexagonite: *Minerals 10*

hexagram: *Symbols in Magic and Religion 19*

hexamethylenediamine: *Dangerous Chemicals 11*

hey: *Expletives 20*

Heylan: *Knights of the Round Table 18*

Hezuo: *Pigs 15*

HH-60 Search and Rescue: *Rotary Wing Aircraft 8*

Hi'iaka: *Moons 11*

Hiawatha: *Fictional Characters 18*

hibiscus: *Garden Annuals 10; Shrubs 10*

hibschite: *Minerals 10*

hickory pine: *Evergreen Trees 10*

hidden race on Earth: *Plot Devices 22*

hidden world is revealed: *Fantasy Plot Devices 24*

hidden: *Magic Vocabulary 17*

hiddenite: *Minerals 10*

hide of the leviathan: *Clothing 18*

hide of the Nemean lion (won by Heracles): *Clothing 18*

hide: *Armor Types 7; Door Materials 3*

hideaway: *Beds 4; Criminal Property 3*

hideous: *Unattractive 20*

hideout: *Criminal Property 3; Residential Property 3*

hiding: *Magic Vocabulary 17*

Hieroglyphic river cooter: *Freshwater Turtles 15*

hi-fi: *Electronics 4*

high and tight: *Hair Style 1*

high card pool: *Card Games 5*

high chair: *Chairs and Stools 4*

high cheekbones: *Cheeks 1*

high chest: *Storage 4*

high Chicago: *Poker Card Games 5*

high class: *Social Distinction 1*

high priest: *Cleric 1*

high quality: *Good 20*

High Renaissance: *Art Movements 13*

high school: *Academic Property 3*

high society: *Social Distinction 1*

high speed rail: *Mass Transit 9*

high: *Elf 1; Forehead 1; Happy 20; Large 20; Meteorology General Vocabulary 10*

highball glass: *Drinkware 5*

highboy: *Storage 4*

high-cut panties: *Ladies' Wear 2*

highland live oak: *Deciduous Trees 10*

Highland Pony: *Horse Breeds 15*

Highland: *Other Cows 15*

highland: *Swords Two-handed 7*

Highlander: *Domestic Cats 15*

highlands: *Climatic Zones Koeppen System 10*

highlight: *Makeup 5*

highlighted: *Hair Treated 1*

highlighter: *Office/School/Writing Supplies 5*

high-low: *Poker Card Games 5*

high-pitched: *Vocal/Speech Quality 1*

high-resolution stratigraphy: *Geological Field Work Methods 10*

high-rise: *Residential Property 3*

highway: *Roads 9*

highwayman: *Thief 1*

Hiisi (evil): *Finnish Pantheon 14*

hike: *Journey 20; Locomotion 9*

hiking: *Boots 2; Exploration 9; Socks 2*

hill giant: *Humanlike Groups 1*

hill: *Dwarf 1; Giant Humanoids 16; Glacial and Mountain 10; Gnome 1; Keelback 15; Slope 10*

Hill's oak: *Deciduous Trees 10*

hillfort: *Castle Anatomy 3*

hillock: *Terrain Features 10*

Hilo soil: *Soil General Vocabulary 10*

hilt: *Fencing Equipment 7*

Himalayan balsam: *Weeds 10*

Himalayan blackberry: *Weeds 10*

Himalayan snow: *Bears 15*

Himalayan: *Domestic Cats 15; Keelback 15*

Himalia: *Moons 11*

HIMARS: *Multiple Rocket Launcher 8*

hime cut: *Hair Style 1*

Hindenberg disaster: *Legendary Events 18*

hinder: *Close/Hold 20*

Hindi: *Human Ethnic Groups 1*

Hindu Texts: *Major Religious Books 14*

Hindu: *Architectural Styles 3*

hinge line: *Geological Vocabulary 10*

hinge: *Geological Vocabulary 10; Hardware 5*

Hino (storm): *Native American Pantheon 14*

hinterland: *Geography General Vocabulary 10*

Hinterwald: *Other Cows 15*

hip hugger jeans: *Unisex Clothing 2*

hip: *Body Parts 12; Boots 2; Roof Styles 3*

hipflask: *Containers and Vessels 5*

hiphop: *Dance Shoes 13*

hiphop: *Dance Styles 13*

hippalektryon: *Flying Creatures 16*

hippie: *Styles of Dress 2*

hippo tang: *Aquarium Saltwater Fish 15*

hippocamp: *Beast 16*

hippocampus: *Aquatic 16; Organs/Major Structures 12*

hippogriff: *Beast 16; Magical Transportation 17*

hippopotamus: *Other Wild Mammals 15*

hipster panties: *Ladies' Wear 2*

Hiram Abiff: *Symbols of Freemasonry 19*

hiranyakashipu: *Demon 16*

hire: *Buy 20*

hired gun: *Assassin 1; Fighter 1; Hero or Villain, Depending Upon Circumstance 20*

hired gunslinger challenges duel to the death: *Western Plot Devices 21*

hirtenkase: *Cheese International Varieties 6*

Hispanic: *Human Ethnic Groups 1*

histoplasmosis: *Diseases 12*

historic mansion: *Horror Locations 23*

historic: *Old 20*

historical cycles repeating: *Plot Devices 22*

historical dances: *The Arts 13*

historical geology: *Geologic Fields of Study 10*

historical setting with addition of magic: *Fantasy Genres 24*

historical: *Art Genres 13; Horror Genres 23; Performance Genres 13; Science Fiction Genres 22*

histosol: *Soil General Vocabulary 10*

hit man: *Assassin 1*

hit: *Attack 7; Harm 20*

hit-and-run: *Tactics 7*

Hitchcock: *Asteroids with Unusual Names 11; Chairs and Stools 4*

Hitler: *Facial Hair Mustache 1*

hitter: *Assassin 1*

hive mind: *Plot Devices 22*

hive: *Bees 15; Natural Animal Homes 15*

HK Mark 23: *Pistol Semiautomatic 7*

HK416 carbine: *SWAT Weapons 7*

Hlidskjalf: *Objects 18*

Hmong: *Human Ethnic Groups 1*

HMS Victory: *Ships 18*

ho'ok: *Demon 16*

hoar frost: *Snow Events 10*

hoard guardian: *Supporting Cast 24*

hoarding: *Castle Anatomy 3*

hoarse: *Vocal/Speech Quality 1*

hoary alder: *Deciduous Trees 10*

hoary skullcap: *Garden Perennials 10*

hoary zorro: *Foxes 15*

hoary: *Bats 15; Elderly 1*

hoatzin: *Other Wild Birds 15*

hoax: *Magic Vocabulary 17*

hobbing machine: *Power Tools*

hobgoblin: *Humanlike Groups 1*

hobo bag: *Accessories 2*

hobo/tramp: *Common Character Archetypes 21*

hobo: *Styles of Dress 2; Thief 1; Venomous Arachnids 15; Wanderer 1*

Ho-Chunk: *Native American Peoples 1*

hockey pads: *Sporting Goods Other 5*

hockey puck: *Sporting Goods Other 5*

hockey skates: *Footwear/Shoes 2; Sporting Goods Other 5*

hockey stick: *Sporting Goods Other 5*

hockey: *Masks 2*

hocks: *Pork 6*

hocus pocus: *Witchcraft Vocabulary 17*

hoe: *Garden Tools; Tools 7*

hoecake: *Bread General Varieties 6*

hoeroa bone: *Missile Weapons 7*

hofoingi: *Cheese International Varieties 6*

Hofud: *Norse Weapons 18*

hog fish: *Wild Saltwater Fish 15*

hog oiler: *Steam Powered Farm Equipment*

hog scraper: *Candles 5*

hog: *Farm/Outbuilding 3*

hogback: *Erosion 10*

Hogg Island: *Boa 15*

hognose: *General Snake Families 15*

hog-nosed: *Bats 15; Viper 15*

hognut: *Deciduous Trees 10*

hog-toothed spar: *Minerals 10*

hoi polloi: *Social Distinction 1*

hoist: *Boat/Ship Terminology 9*

hoisting sail: *Boat/Ship Terminology 9*

hojalito: *Deciduous Trees 10*

Hokkaido: *Horse Breeds 15*

hokm: *Card Games 5*

hoko yari: *Spears 7*

hola: *Card Games 5*

Holando-Argentino: *Other Cows 15*

Holbein: *Embroidery Stitches 2*

hold in custody: *Close/Hold 20*

hold: *Boat/Ship Anatomy 9; Residential Property 3; Verbs 20*

holdbacks: *Window Treatments 5*

holder: *Containers and Vessels 5*

holding: *Residential Property 3*

hold-up: *Western Paraphernalia/People 21*

Hole in the Wall Gang: *Western Paraphernalia/People 21*

hole in the wall: *Doors Atypical 3; Residential Slang 3*

Hole in the Wall: *Famous Western Locations 21*

hole punch: *Office/School/Writing Supplies 5*

hole: *Criminal Property 3; Natural Animal Homes 15; Residential Slang 3*

holiday: *Independence Day 19; Styles of Dress 2*

Holland: *Chickens 15*

holler: *Sounds 20; Speak 20*

hollow log: *Natural Animal Homes 15*

hollow tree: *Natural Animal Homes 15*

hollow: *Cheeks 1; Terrain Features 10*

holly bay: *Evergreen Trees 10*

holly blue: *Minerals 10*

holly: *Christmas 19; Plants with Symbolic Meaning 19; Poisonous Plants 10; Shrubs 10*

hollyhock: *Garden Perennials 10*

Hollywood garbage: *Card Games 5*

Hollywood: *Beds 4; Styles of Dress 2*

Holmes: *Comets 11*

Holmium: *Elements 11*

Holocene Age: *Geologic Time 10*

holographic generator: *Devices 22*

Holstein: *North American Dairy Cows 15*

Holsteiner: *Horse Breeds 15*

holster: *Western Clothing/Dress 21*

holt: *Natural Animal Homes 15*

Holy Body and Blood of Christ: *Catholic Holy Days of Obligation 14*

holy book: *Religious Items 5*

Holy Coat: *Relics of Jesus 14*

holy communion: *Religious Bread 6*

holy cow: *Expletives 20*

holy knight: *Paladin 1*

Holy Lance/Spear of Destiny/Spear of Longinus: *Relics of Jesus 14*

Holy Lance: *Unique Spear 18*

holy man: *Cleric 1; Expletives 20*

holy moley: *Expletives 20*

holy Moses: *Expletives 20*

holy orders: *Sacraments 14*

Holy Spirit: *Collective Symbols 19*

Holy Sponge: *Relics of Jesus 14*

holy symbol: *Religious Items 5*

holy war: *General Combat Vocabulary 7*

holy warrior: *Paladin 1*

holy water sprinkler: *Bludgeons 7*

holy water: *Religious Items 5; Rituals 14*

holy woman: *Cleric 1*

holy wow: *Expletives 20*

holystone: *Boat/Ship Anatomy 9*

homburg: *Headgear 2*

home office: *General Buildings 3*

home: *Residential Property 3*

Home's hinge-back: *Tortoises 15*

homeless people preyed upon by murderer/ghouls/vampires: *Horror Plot Devices 23*

homeless person witnesses crimes and is ignored: *Horror Plot Devices 23*

homeless: *Social Distinction 1*

homely: *Unattractive 20*

homeopath: *Medical Occupations 1*

homespun fabric: *Western Clothing/Dress 21*

homestead: *Residential Property 3; Western Paraphernalia/People 21*

homogeneous catalyst: *Chemistry General Vocabulary 11*

homogeneous equilibria: *Chemistry General Vocabulary 11*

homogeneous mixture: *Chemistry General Vocabulary 11*

homogenizer: *Laboratory Equipment 5*

homologous series: *Chemistry General Vocabulary 11*

homonuclear: *Chemistry General Vocabulary 11*

Honduran wood: *Freshwater Turtles 15*

honest: *Personality Other 1*

honey bells: *Garden Perennials 10*

honey fungus bootlace: *Fungus Common Names 10*

honey locust: *Deciduous Trees 10; Weeds 10*

honey mushroom: *Fungus Common Names 10*

honey mustard: *Condiments 6*

honey opal: *Minerals 10*

honey roasted peanut: *Nuts 6*

honey server: *Kitchen Utensils 5*

honey shucks locust: *Deciduous Trees 10*

honey: *Aphrodisiacs 19; Bears 15; Bees 15; Foods with Religious or Ritual Significance 19; Staples 6; Terms of Endearment 1*

honeycomb: *Bees 15*

honeydew: *Green 20; Melons 6*

honeyed: *Vocal/Speech Quality 1*

honeymoon bridge: *Card Games 5*

honeymoon: *Journey 20*

honeysuckle: *Garden Perennials 10; Shrubs 10*

honk: *Sounds 20*

honor: *Jewelry 21*

hoochie mama: *Styles of Dress 2*

hood: *Fighter 1; Garment Pieces 2; Headgear 2; Villain 20*

hooded lantern: *Illumination/Light Sources 5*

hooded stranger in a tavern: *Supporting Cast 24*

hooded: *Special Body Features 19*

hoodoo: *Erosion 10*

hoof fungus: *Fungus Common Names 10*

hoofed: *Special Body Features 19*

hook and eye: *Notions 2*

hook and loop fastener: *Notions 2*

hook up: *Fix 20*

hook: *Fishing Gear 5; Jewelry 21; Locks 5; Swords One-handed 7*

hooked carpet: *Floor Coverings 4*

hooked: *Nose 1; Squid 15*

hook-fauchard: *Pole Weapons 7*

hooks: *Christmas 19*

hookworm: *Diseases 12*

hoola: *Card Games 5*

hooligan: *Fighter 1; Villain 20*

hoop earring: *Jewelry 2*

hoop skirt: *Ladies' Wear 2*

hoop: *General Snake Families 15; Jewelry 21*

hoopoe: *Animals with Symbolic Meaning 19*

Hoosier: *Storage 4*

hoot: *Owls 15; Sounds 20*

hooter: *Nose 1*

Hoover Dam: *Seven Wonders of the Industrial World 18; Unique Property 3*

hop hornbeam: *Deciduous Trees 10*

hop: *Locomotion 9*

hope chest: *Storage 4*

hope: *Seven Holy Virtues 19; Three Theological Virtues 19*

hopeful: *Personality Other 1; Positive 1*

hopeless: *Sad 20*

hopflower oregano: *Garden Perennials 10*

Hopi: *Native American Peoples 1; Rattlesnake 15*

hopper car: *Railroad 9*

hops: *Farm/Outbuilding 3; Garden Perennials 10*

hopsack: *Fabric 2*

hora (Israel): *Ethnic/Folk Dances 13*

hora: *Hand Weapons 7*

horehound: *Garden Perennials 10*

horizon: *Geography General Vocabulary 10*

horn lead: *Minerals 10*

horn of Brân Galed: *Thirteen Treasures of the Island of Britain 18*

horn of plenty: *Fungus Common Names 10; Objects 18; Thanksgiving 19*

horn: *Boat/Ship Anatomy 9; Sharks 15; Wind/Woodwind and Brass Musical Instruments*

hornblendite: *Igneous Rocks 10*

hornbook: *Books/Publications 5*

horned desert: *Viper 15*

horned lizard: *Scaled Reptiles 15*

horned melon: *Unusual Edible Fruits 6*

horned shaman: *Symbols in Magic and Religion 19*

horned: *Adder 15; Sea Snake 15; Special Body Features 19; Viper 15*

hornet: *Wasp 15*

hornfaced: *Bees 15*

hornfels: *Metamorphic Rocks 10*

hornpipe (England): *Ethnic/Folk Dances 13*

hornpipe: *Composition Types 13*

horns of Odin: *Symbols in Magic and Religion 19*

horns: *New Year 19*

horn-skinned: *Bats 15*

hornstone: *Minerals 10*

Horologium: *Constellations 11*

horrendous: *Horror Vocabulary 23; Unattractive 20*

horrible: *Bad 20; Horror Vocabulary 23; Personality Other 1; Unattractive 20*

horrid: *Unattractive 20*

horrific: *Bad 20; Horror Vocabulary 23*

horrifying: *Bad 20*

Horro: *Other Cows 15*

horror: *General Emotions 20; Horror Vocabulary 23; Monster Categories/Terms 16; Performance Genres 13; Plot Devices 22; Science Fiction Genres 22*

horse barding materials: *Combat, Armor, and Weapons 7*

horse barding pieces: *Combat, Armor, and Weapons 7*

horse bow: *Missile Weapons 7*

horse breeds: *Animals 15*

horse chestnut: *Deciduous Trees 10; Poisonous Plants 10*

horse drawn farm equipment: *Equipment and Tools 5*

horse eye jack: *Wild Saltwater Fish 15*

horse mushroom: *Fungus Common Names 10*

horse race yields big loss: *Western Plot Devices 21*

horse race yields big win: *Western Plot Devices 21*

horse trail: *Roads 9*

horse trailer: *Farm Transportation 9*

horse: *Animals with Symbolic Meaning 19; Art Genres 13; Chinese Horoscope 19; Flies 15; Objects/Activities Connected to Lore 19; Transportation Animals 9; Western Paraphernalia/People 21*

HORSE: *Poker Card Games 5*

horsecar: *Animal-Powered Transportation 9*

horse-drawn barge/boat: *Animal-Powered Transportation 9*

horse-drawn coach: *Travel Modes 23*

horse-drawn tram: *Animal-Powered Transportation 9*

horseman: *Knight 1*

horseman's lance: *Pole Weapons 7*

horseman's pick: *Pointed Weapons 7*

horsemint: *Garden Perennials 10*

horsepower: *Energy Sources/Types 24*

horseradish: *Condiments 6; Vegetables 6*

horses: *Animals 15*

horseshoe nail: *Transportation Animals 9*

horseshoe with ends pointing down: *Harbingers of Bad Luck 19*

horseshoe: *Bats 15; Facial Hair Mustache 1; Harbingers/Charms for Good Luck 19; Objects that Offer Protection 19; Pit Viper 15; Secular Symbols 19; Transportation Animals 9*

horsetail Casuarina: *Evergreen Trees 10*

horsey: *Teeth 1*

horticultural: *Robots 22*

horticulturalist: *Agricultural 1*

Horus (demigod of revenge): *Egyptian Pantheon 14*

hose clamp: *Laboratory Equipment 5*

hose: *Garden Tools*

HOSE: *Poker Card Games 5*

hosiery: *Accessories 2*

hoskin: *Card Games 5*

hospice: *Health Care 3*

hospital administrator: *Horror Occupations 23*

hospital gown: *Special Purpose Clothing 2*

hospital orderly: *Horror Occupations 23*

hospital: *Beds 4; Health Care 3; Horror Locations 23; Military Aircraft Pre-1962 8; Military Property 3*

hospitality: *Architecture and Property 3; Character Building 1*

host/hostess: *Food Service 1; Media 1*

host: *Angels Common Terms 14; Religious Bread 6; Special Occasion 1*

hosta: *Garden Perennials 10*

hostages: *Plot Devices 22*

hostel: *Hospitality 3*

hostelry: *Hospitality 3*

hostess: *Special Occasion 1*

hostile hippies: *Travel Hazards 9*

hostile locals: *Travel Hazards 9*

hostile: *Angry 1; Unattractive 20*

hostility: *General Emotions 20*

hot air oven: *Laboratory Equipment 5*

hot and sour: *Soup 6*

hot bacon: *Salad Dressing 6*

hot beverage: *Improvised Weapons 7*

hot buttered rum: *Hot Drinks 6*

hot chocolate pot: *Tableware 5*

hot chocolate: *Christmas 19*

hot cider: *Fruit Drinks 6*

hot damn: *Expletives 20*

hot dish: *Fish/Seafood Meals 6; Poultry Meals 6*

hot dog roller: *Appliances 5*

hot dog: *Amusement Park/Carnival/Circus/Fair 3; Sausage 6*

hot drinks: *Food 6*

hot fudge: *Ice Cream Toppings 6*

hot magenta: *Pink 20*

hot milk: *Cake 6*

hot pants: *Ladies' Wear 2*

hot pink: *Pink 20*

hot pitch: *Siege Equipment 7*

hot plate: *Appliances 5; Laboratory Equipment 5*

hot pot: *Appliances 5*

hot rod: *Motorized 9*

hot spot: *Geography General Vocabulary 10*

hot spring: *Geological Vocabulary 10*

hot tub: *Property Features 3*

hot: *Beautiful 20; Smells 20; Warm 10*

hotel clerk: *Horror Occupations 23*

hotel manager: *Hospitality 1*

hotel owner traps guests: *Horror Plot Devices 23*

hotel: *Hospitality 3*

hothouse: *Farm/Outbuilding 3*

Hotoru (wind): *Native American Pantheon 14*

hotshot/showoff: *Common Character Archetypes 21*

Hottentot fig: *Weeds 10*

Houdek soil: *Soil General Vocabulary 10*

hound fish: *Wild Saltwater Fish 15*

hound: *Dog Groups 15; Paranormal Activity 21; Sharks 15*

houndmaster: *Castle Inhabitants and Personnel 1*

houndstooth: *Fabric Patterns 2*

hourglass: *Dolphins 15; Secular Symbols 19; Timekeeping 5; Witchcraft Vocabulary 17*

house contains gate to hell/another place: *Horror Plot Devices 23*

house finch: *Backyard Birds 15*

house is intelligent/sentient: *Horror Plot Devices 23*

house left: *Stage Directions 13*

house of worship: *Religious Building 3*

house right: *Stage Directions 13*

house swallows up children: *Horror Plot Devices 23*

house where murder took place: *Horror Locations 23*

house/apartment traps souls of all who live/die there: *Horror Plot Devices 23*

house: *Bats 15; Flies 15; Parts of the Theater 13; Residential Property 3*

houseboat: *Small Watercraft 9*

housebound relative: *Common Character Archetypes 21*

housebreaker: *Thief 1*

housekeeper: *Housekeeping 1*

housekeeping: *Character Building 1*

house-to-house terrain warfare: *General Combat Vocabulary 7*

housewife: *General Occupations 1*

housing: *Military Property 3*

Houston: *Toads 15*

Hovawart: *Dog Breeds 15*

hovel: *Residential Property 3*

hover craft: *Vehicles 22*

hover: *Locomotion 9*

howdah: *Animal-Powered Transportation 9*

howitzer: *Cannon 7; Military 8; Western Weapons 21*

howl: *Sounds 20; Speak 20*

howler: *New World Monkeys 15*

howlite: *Standard Gems 21*

how-to book: *Books/Publications 5*

Hrunting (Beowulf): *Weapons of Legend 18*

Hua Mulan: *Legendary People Presumed to be Fictional 18*

Huail: *Arthurian Characters 18*

Huan-Ti (war): *Chinese Pantheon 14*

huaraches: *Footwear/Shoes 2*

hubbard squash: *Vegetables 6*

Hubbardston blue cow: *Cheese Common Varieties 6*

Hubble's law: *Astronomy General Terms 11*

hubby: *Male 1*

huckleberry: *Berries 6; Shrubs 10*

huckster booth: *Amusement Park/Carnival/Circus/Fair 3*

huckster: *Thief 1*

Hucul: *Horse Breeds 15*

Hudson bay pine: *Evergreen Trees 10*

Hudson River school: *Art Movements 13*

hudsonia: *Shrubs 10*

Huehueteotl (war): *Aztec Pantheon 14*

huge wild dog adopts family: *Western Plot Devices 21*

huge: *Large 20; Large/Heavy 1*

huh: *Expletives 20*

Huhueteotl (fire): *Central American Pantheon 14*

Hui Chinese: *Human Ethnic Groups 1*

huito: *Unusual Edible Fruits 6*

Huitzilopochtli (father of all gods): *Aztec Pantheon 14*

Huitzilopochtli (war): *Central American Pantheon 14*

hula (United States): *Ethnic/Folk Dances 13*

huldrefolk: *Devil 16*

hulinhjalmur: *Magical/Icelandic Staves 18*

hulky: *Large 20; Large/Heavy 1*

hull: *Boat/Ship Anatomy 9*

hum: *Sounds 20; Speak 20*

human body: *Art Media 13*

human ethnic groups: *Character Building 1*

human groups: *Character Building 1*

human papillomavirus (HPV): *Diseases 12*

human powered: *Energy Sources/Types 22*

human rights: *Philosophy Basic Concepts 14*

human sacrifice: *Horror Genres 23*

human stroke: *Swimming Strokes 9*

human: *Apes 15; Character Building 1; Charges 19*

humanism: *Philosophy Basic Concepts 14*

humanlike: *Character Building 1; Robots 22*

humanoid: *Monsters 16; Robots 22*

human-powered transportation: *Transportation 9*

humble plant: *Weeds 10*

Humboldt: *Squid 15*

humbug: *Card Games 5*

Hume soil: *Soil General Vocabulary 10*

Hume's: *Owls 15*

humerus: *Bones 12*

humid subtropical: *Climatic Zones Koeppen System 10*

humid: *Meteorology General Vocabulary 10; Wet 10*

humidifier: *Building Systems 3*

humidity: *Meteorology General Vocabulary 10*

humidor: *Containers and Vessels 5*

humin: *Soil General Vocabulary 10*

Hummel: *Tanks German 8*

hummingbird hawkmoth: *Moth 15*

hummingbird: *Animals with Symbolic Meaning 19; Backyard Birds 15; Garden Perennials 10*

hummock holly: *Evergreen Trees 10*

hummock: *Terrain Features 10*

humor: *Happy 20; Horror Genres 23; Science Fiction Genres 22*

humoresque: *Composition Types 13*

humorist: *Bard 1*

humorless: *Horror Vocabulary 23*

humpback: *Whales 15*

humus: *Geography General Vocabulary 10; Soil General Vocabulary 10*

Hun: *Human Ethnic Groups 1*

hunchback: *Flies 15*

Hund's rule: *Chemistry General Vocabulary 11*

hundred and ten: *Card Games 5*

hundred pacer: *General Snake Families 15*

hundred-handed-ones: *Giant Humanoids 16*

Hungarian Grey: *Other Cows 15*

hungarian opal: *Minerals 10*

Hungarian Warmblood: *Horse Breeds 15*

Hungarian: *Human Ethnic Groups 1; Sausage 6*

hungry dragon: *Common Dangers 24*

hunk: *Beautiful 20*

hunt gun: *Black Powder Weapons 7*

hunt: *Paranormal Activity 21*

hunter green: *Green 20*

hunting hat: *Headgear 2*

hunting: *Styles of Dress 2; Swords One-handed 7*

huntmaster: *Castle Inhabitants and Personnel 1*

huntsman: *Venomous Arachnids 15*

Hupa: *Native American Peoples 1*

hurdle: *Locomotion 9*

hurlbat: *Axes 7*

Huron: *Native American Peoples 1*

hurricane force: *Wind 10*

hurricane lamp: *Illumination/Light Sources 5*

hurricane lantern: *Illumination/Light Sources 5*

hurricane season: *Meteorology General Vocabulary 10*

hurricane: *Severe Weather 10*

hurried: *Fast 20; Mobility 1*

hurry: *Commands 20*

hurt: *Harm 20*

hurtle: *Locomotion 9*

husband: *Male 1*

hushed: *Quiet 20*

hushpuppy: *Bread General Varieties 6*

husky: *Large/Heavy 1; Vocal/Speech Quality 1*

hussainia: *Religious Building 3*

hut: *Residential Property 3*

hutch: *Storage 4*

Hutterite: *Human Ethnic Groups 1*

Hutu: *Human Ethnic Groups 1*

huwawa: *Demon 16*

HVAC: *Building Systems 3*

hwandudaedo: *Swords One-handed 7*

HY472 6×6 truck tractor and trailer: *China Military Vehicles 8*

hyacinth opal: *Minerals 10*

hyacinth: *Garden Bulbs 10; Minerals 10; Poisonous Plants 10*

Hyakutake: *Comets 11*

hyalite: *Minerals 10*

hyaloclastite: *Igneous Rocks 10*

hyalophane: *Minerals 10*

hybrid: *Art Genres 13; Monster Categories/Terms 16*

hybridization: *Chemistry General Vocabulary 11*

hydra: *Beast 16; Dragon 16*

Hydra: *Constellations 11; Moons 11*

hydrangea: *Shrubs 10*

hydrargillite: *Minerals 10*

hydrargyllite: *Minerals 10*

hydrargyrum: *Minerals 10*

hydrate isomers: *Chemistry General Vocabulary 11*

hydrate: *Chemistry General Vocabulary 11*

hydration energy: *Chemistry General Vocabulary 11*

hydration: *Chemistry General Vocabulary 11*

hydraulic conductivity: *Soil General Vocabulary 10*

hydraulic torque wrench: *Power Tools*

hydrazine: *Dangerous Chemicals 11*

hydric soil: *Soil General Vocabulary 10*

hydride: *Chemistry General Vocabulary 11*

hydro axe mulching: *Soil General Vocabulary 10*

hydrocarbon exploration: *Geological Field Work Methods 10*

hydrocarbons: *Chemistry General Vocabulary 11*

hydrocyanic acid: *Dangerous Chemicals 11*

hydroelectric: *Energy Sources/Types 22*

hydrogarnet: *Minerals 10*

hydrogen bond: *Chemistry General Vocabulary 11*

hydrogen chloride: *Dangerous Chemicals 11*

hydrogen cyanide: *Poisonous Chemicals in Plants 11*

hydrogen dioxide: *Minerals 10*

hydrogen fluoride: *Dangerous Chemicals 11*

hydrogen peroxide: *Dangerous Chemicals 11*

hydrogen selenide: *Dangerous Chemicals 11*

hydrogen sulfide: *Dangerous Chemicals 11*

hydrogen: *Astronomy General Terms 11; Energy Sources/Types 22*

Hydrogen: *Elements 11*

hydrogenation: *Chemistry General Vocabulary 11*

hydrogen-oxygen fuel cell: *Chemistry General Vocabulary 11*

hydrogeology: *Geologic Fields of Study 10*

hydrogrossular: *Minerals 10*

hydrohalite: *Minerals 10*

hydrologic cycle: *Meteorology General Vocabulary 10*

hydrological transport model: *Soil General Vocabulary 10*

hydrology: *Meteorology General Vocabulary 10*

hydrolysis constant: *Chemistry General Vocabulary 11*

hydrolysis: *Chemistry General Vocabulary 11*

hydromedusa: *Jellyfish 15*

hydrometer: *Chemistry General Vocabulary 11; Meteorology General Vocabulary 10*

hydropedology: *Soil General Vocabulary 10*

hydrophane opal: *Minerals 10*

hydrophilic colloids: *Chemistry General Vocabulary 11*

hydrophobic soil: *Soil General Vocabulary 10*

hydroponics: *General Farm Equipment; Geography General Vocabulary 10*

hydroquinone: *Dangerous Chemicals 11*

hydrosphere: *Geography General Vocabulary 10; Meteorology General Vocabulary 10*

hydrostatic equilibrium: *Astronomy General Terms 11*

hydrothermal vent: *Geological Vocabulary 10*

hydroxyl-apatite: *Minerals 10*

Hydrus: *Constellations 11*

hyena: *Animals with Symbolic Meaning 19; Other Wild Mammals 15*

hygrometer: *Meteorology General Vocabulary 10*

hymn: *Composition Types 13*

hymnal: *Printed Music 13; Religious Items 5*

hyoid bone: *Bones 12*

hyper: *Personality Other 1*

hyperatomic: *Spaceship Drive Systems 22*

Hyperborea: *Fictional/Mythological Locations 18*

hypercinnabar: *Minerals 10*

hypergalaxy: *Astronomy General Terms 11*

hypergiant: *Star Types and Relatives 11*

Hyperion: *Moons 11*

hypermarket: *Business Property 3*

Hypermodernism: *Art Movements 13*

hypernova: *Star Types and Relatives 11*

Hyperrealism: *Art Movements 13*

hypersaline: *Geological Vocabulary 10*

hyperspace: *Plot Devices 22*

hypersthene: *Minerals 10*

hyperthermia: *Injuries/Medical Emergencies 12*

hypnotist: *Illusionist 1*

hypnotize: *Magic Vocabulary 17*

hypocrite: *Thief 1*

hypothalamus: *Organs/Major Structures 12*

hypothermia: *Injuries/Medical Emergencies 12*

hypothesize: *Solve 20*

hyrax: *Other Wild Mammals 15*

Hyrrokkin: *Moons 11*

hyssop skullcap: *Garden Perennials 10*

hyssop: *Foods with Religious or Ritual Significance 19; Garden Perennials 10; Plants with Symbolic Meaning 19; Shrubs 10*

–I–

I Ching symbols: *Secular Symbols 19*

I Ching: *Fortune Telling General Techniques 19*

I doubt it: *Card Games 5*

Iapetus: *Moons 11*

I-beam: *Building Elements and Features 3*

Iberian: *Pigs 15*

Ibizan Hound: *Dog Breeds 15*

iblis: *Devil 16*

IC-135 Open Skies observation system: *U.S. Air Force Aircraft 8*

Icabod Crane: *Fictional Characters 18*

ice age: *Geography General Vocabulary 10*

ice aggregate: *Snow Types 10*

ice box: *Major Appliances 4*

ice bucket: *Tableware 5*

ice cave: *Cave Anatomy 10*

ice cream cake roll: *Ice Cream Desserts 6*

ice cream cake: *Ice Cream Desserts 6*

ice cream drinks: *Food 6*

ice cream flavors: *Food 6*

ice cream parlor: *Chairs and Stools 4*

ice cream roll: *Cake 6*

ice cream sandwich: *Ice Cream Desserts 6*

ice cream scoop: *Kitchen Utensils 5*

ice cream toppings: *Food 6*

ice cream: *Cake 6; Food 6; Mixers 6; Motorized Truck 9*

ice crystals: *Meteorology General Vocabulary 10*

ice lattice: *Snow Types 10*

ice man: *Food Service 1*

ice nucleus: *Snow Types 10*

ice pack: *Snow Events 10*

ice particles: *Snow Types 10*

ice pellets: *Snow Types 10*

ice pick: *Kitchen Utensils 5*

ice pop: *Ice Cream Related 6*

ice skates: *Footwear/Shoes 2; Sporting Goods Other 5*

ice snow: *Snow Types 10*

ice storm: *Severe Weather 10*

ice: *Art Materials 5; Astronomy General Terms 11; Bears 15; Climatic Zones Koeppen System 10; Snow Events 10; Terrain Features 10*

iceberg lettuce: *Vegetables 6*

iceberg: *Minerals 10; Terrain Features 10*

iceboat: *Small Watercraft 9*

iced oatmeal: *Cookie 6*

iced tea glass: *Drinkware 5*

iced tea spoon: *Eating Utensils 5*

iced: *Coffee Drinks 6*

Iceland poppy: *Wildflowers 10*

Iceland spar magnesite: *Minerals 10*

Iceland spar: *Minerals 10*

Icelander: *Human Ethnic Groups 1*

Icelandic Sheepdog: *Dog Breeds 15*

Icelandic staves: *Legendary, Mystical and Mythical Items*

and Locations 18

Icelandic: *Horse Breeds 15; Other Cows 15*

icelandite: *Igneous Rocks 10*

ichnology: *Geological Vocabulary 10*

Ichthys wheel: *Symbols in Magic and Religion 19*

icicle: *Christmas 19; Meteorology General Vocabulary 10; Minerals 10*

iciness: *Snow Events 10*

icon: *Jewelry 21*

icy: *Cold 10*

Ida red: *Apples 6*

ida: *Swords One-handed 7*

Idaho white pine: *Evergreen Trees 10*

idea: *Philosophy Basic Concepts 14*

ideal gas law: *Chemistry General Vocabulary 11*

ideal gas: *Chemistry General Vocabulary 11*

ideal solution: *Chemistry General Vocabulary 11*

ideal: *Beautiful 20*

idealism: *Philosophy Basic Concepts 14*

identify: *Learn 20*

identity thief: *Illicit Occupations 1*

identity: *Philosophy Basic Concepts 14*

ideology: *Philosophy Basic Concepts 14*

idiot military commander: *Common Dangers 23*

idocrase: *Minerals 10; Standard Gems 21*

idol: *Hero 20*

idolization: *General Emotions 20*

Idun (goddess of the spring): *Norse Pantheon 14*

idyllic: *Happy 20*

iffy: *Horror Vocabulary 23*

ifrit: *Demon 16*

igloo: *Residential Property 3*

igneous rock: *Geological Vocabulary 10*

igneous rocks: *Chapter 10*

ignimbrite: *Igneous Rocks 10*

ignition tube: *Laboratory Equipment 5*

ignorance: *Philosophy Basic Concepts 14*

iguanas: *Scaled Reptiles 15*

iguanid: *Scaled Reptiles 15*

iguanodon: *Commonly Known Dinosaurs 15*

IHS: *Symbols in Magic and Religion 19*

Ijiraq: *Moons 11*

ijolite: *Igneous Rocks 10*

ikat: *Fabric 2*

Ikeya-Seki: *Comets 11*

ileum: *Organs/Major Structures 12*

ilium: *Bones 12*

Illawarra: *Other Cows 15*

ill-conceived: *Unattractive 20*

illicit occupations: *Character Building 1*

Illinois nut: *Deciduous Trees 10*

Illuminates of Thanateros: *Secret/Mystical Organizations 18*

Illuminati: *Secret/Mystical Organizations 18*

illumination: *Equipment and Tools 5*

illusion: *Fabric 2; Magic Vocabulary 17; Paranormal Abilities 21; Traps 3*

illusionary: *Magic Vocabulary 17*

illusionist: *Character Building 1*

illustrator: *Publishing 1*

illustrious: *Personality Other 1*

Ilmatar (goddess of mothers): *Finnish Pantheon 14*

ilmenorutile: *Minerals 10*

Image of Edessa: *Relics of Jesus 14*

imam: *Cleric 1*

imambargah: *Religious Building 3*

imbe: *Unusual Edible Fruits 6*

imdugud: *Demon 16*

imitator: *Thief 1*

Immaculate Conception: *Catholic Holy Days of Obligation 14*

immense: *Heavy 20; Large 20; Large/Heavy 1*

immerse: *Magic Vocabulary 17*

immersion: *Rituals 14*

immobilization: *Soil General Vocabulary 10*

immoral: *Bad 20*

immortality: *Horror Plot Devices 23; Plot Devices 22*

immune: *Body Systems 12*

immunity: *Physical Mutations 22*

imp: *Extraplanar 16*

impact driver: *Power Tools*

impact wrench: *Power Tools*

impair: *Harm 20*

impaled object: *Injuries/Medical Emergencies 12*

impasse: *General Combat Vocabulary 7*

impatiens: *Garden Annuals 10*

impede: *Close/Hold 20*

impenetrable: *Magic Vocabulary 17*

imperceptible: *Slow 20*

imperial topaz: *Minerals 10*

imperial: *Facial Hair Beard 1; Facial Hair Mustache 1; Moth 15*

implants: *Teeth Dental Work 1*

implode: *Harm 20*

imposing: *Large 20; Large/Heavy 1*

imposter: *Common Character Archetypes 21; Thief 1*

impound: *Close/Hold 20*

impoverished family receives windfall: *Western Plot Devices 21*

impressed: *Tortoises 15*

Impressionism: *Art Movements 13*

impressionism: *Musical Styles 13*

impressionist: *Thief 1*

impressive: *Beautiful 20*

imprison: *Close/Hold 20*

imprisoned witch is released in modern world: *Fantasy Plot Devices 24*

impromptu: *Composition Types 13*

improve: *Buy 20*

improved metabolism: *Physical Mutations 22*

improved white: *Pigs 15*

improvisation: *General Music Vocabulary 13*

improvised weapons: *Combat, Armor, and Weapons 7*

imsil: *Cheese International Varieties 6*

in a snap: *Fast 20*

in a state of high excitement: *Happy 20*

in accord: *Happy 20*

in between: *Card Games 5*

in despair: *Sad 20*

in good spirits: *Happy 20*

in harm's way: *Boat/Ship Terminology 9*

in high spirits: *Happy 20*

in rapture: *Happy 20*

in seventh heaven: *Happy 20*

in vogue: *New 20*

inactive: *Mobility 1*

inadequate: *Sad 20*

Inanna (goddess of war): *Sumerian Pantheon 14*

inaudible: *Quiet 20*

Inca rose: *Minerals 10*

Inca: *Human Ethnic Groups 1*

incandescent: *Illumination Bulb and Tube Types 5*

incantation: *Witchcraft Vocabulary 17*

incarcerate: *Close/Hold 20*

incendiary: *Weapons 22*

incense cedar: *Evergreen Trees 10*

incense: *Objects in Magic and Religion 19; Rituals 14; Wizard's Goods 5*

incensed: *Angry 1; Special Body Features 19*

inceptisol: *Soil General Vocabulary 10*

incisor: *Teeth 12*

inclination: *Astronomy General Terms 11*

incline: *Grade/Slope 10*

incomparable: *Good 20*

inconsequential: *Small/Fragile 20*

incorrigible: *Difficult 20*

increase: *Buy 20*

increased height: *Physical Mutations 22*

increased size: *Physical Mutations 22*

incredible: *Magic Vocabulary 17*

incredulous: *Horror Vocabulary 23*

incubator: *Laboratory Equipment 5*

incubus: *Demon 16; Fantasy Creatures with Symbolic Meaning 19*

incursion: *General Combat Vocabulary 7*

indalo: *Symbols in Magic and Religion 19*

indebted dragon/powerful creature: *Supporting Cast 24*

indecent: *Unattractive 20*

Indefatigable Island giant: *Tortoises 15*

indefatiguable: *Mobility 1*

indented: *Partition Lines 19*

indentured labor: *Geography General Vocabulary 10*

Independence class combat ship: *U.S. Navy Vessels 8*

Independence Day: *Holidays 19*

Independence Hall: *Independence Day 19*

index card: *Office/School/Writing Supplies 5*

index: *Laboratory Supplies 5*

Indian banana: *Deciduous Trees 10*

Indian blanket: *Wildflowers 10*

Indian chief: *Western Paraphernalia/People 21*

Indian gharial: *Crocodilians 15*

Indian licorice: *Poisonous Plants 10*

Indian pantheon: *Philosophy and Religion 14*

Indian physic: *Garden Perennials 10*

Indian princess has romance with white man: *Western Plot Devices 21*

Indian raid: *Western Plot Devices 21*

Indian saves life of white man: *Western Plot Devices 21*

Indian scout: *Western Paraphernalia/People 21*

Indian shaman: *Western Paraphernalia/People 21*

Indian soap plant: *Deciduous Trees 10*

Indian star: *Tortoises 15*

Indian strawberry: *Garden Perennials 10*

Indian turnip: *Garden Perennials 10*

Indian: *Art Movements 13; Barbarian 1; Bread General Varieties 6; Cobra 15; Human Ethnic Groups 1; Imported Carpets 4; Krait 15; Lions 15; Python 15*

Indianmeal: *Moth 15*

Indians hide gold deposits: *Western Plot Devices 21*

indicators: *Chemistry General Vocabulary 11*

indicolite: *Minerals 10*

indifference: *General Emotions 20*

indifferent: *Horror Vocabulary 23; Personality Other 1*

indignant: *Negative 1*

indigo: *Garden Perennials 10; General Snake Families 15; Purple 20; Shrubs 10*

indisposed: *Horror Vocabulary 23*

Indium: *Elements 11*

Indo-Brazilian: *Other Cows 15*

Indochinese: *Tigers 15*

indolent: *Mobility 1*

Indonesian water: *Python 15*

Indra (leader of the gods): *Indian Pantheon 14*

inducement: *Magic Vocabulary 17*

induction: *Philosophy Basic Concepts 14*

Indus: *Constellations 11*

industrial complex: *Special Purpose Structure 3*

industrial laser: *Spy Gear 5*

industrial park: *General Property 3*

industry knowingly pollutes water/air/ground: *Horror Plot Devices 23*

inert S-pair effect: *Chemistry General Vocabulary 11*

inexcusable: *Bad 20*

inexperienced: *New 20*

inexplicable: *Magic Vocabulary 17*

infallibility: *Philosophy Basic Concepts 14*

infamous: *Personality Other 1*

infant: *Child 1*

infantry fighting vehicle: *Armored Vehicles 8*

infantry fighting vehicle: *Military Ground Vehicles General 8*

infantry: *Fighter 1*

infatuate: *Love 20*

inference: *Philosophy Basic Concepts 14*

inferior conjunction: *Astronomy General Terms 11*

inferior nasal conchae: *Bones 12*

inferior planet: *Astronomy General Terms 11*

inferior: *Small/Fragile 20*

inferno: *Afterlife/Underworld 18*

infiltration: *General Combat Vocabulary 7*

infinite: *Philosophy Basic Concepts 14*

infinitesimal: *Small/Fragile 20*

infinity: *Symbols in Magic and Religion 19*

infirmary: *Health Care 3; Military Property 3*

inflatable raft: *Human-Powered Watercraft 9*

inflexible: *Stubborn 1*

inflow cave: *Cave Anatomy 10*

influence: *Magic Vocabulary 17*

Influence: *Minor Lines 19*

influenza: *Diseases 12*

infrastructure buildings: *Transportation 9*

infravision: *Physical Mutations 22*

infuriate: *General Emotions 20*

infuriated: *Angry 1*

infuse: *Witchcraft Vocabulary 17*

ingenue: *Common Character Archetypes 21*

inglenook: *Rooms 3*

ingot: *Wizard's Goods 5*

inheritance of strange object/book: *Horror Plot Devices 23*

inhibit: *Close/Hold 20*

inhibitory catalyst: *Chemistry General Vocabulary 11*

inhuman: *Horror Vocabulary 23*

initial: *New 20*

initiate: *Attack 7; Create 20*

injera: *Bread General Varieties 6*

injure: *Attack 7; Harm 20*

injures: *Anatomy and Physiology 12*

injustice: *Philosophy Basic Concepts 14*

ink bottle: *Office/School/Writing Supplies 5*

ink cartridge: *Office/School/Writing Supplies 5*

ink paint: *Art Materials 5*

ink: *Art Materials 5; Art Media 13; Office/School/Writing Supplies 5; Wizard's Goods 5*

inky cap: *Fungus Common Names 10*

inland box elder: *Deciduous Trees 10*

inland taipan: *World's Ten Most Venomous Snakes 15*

inland waterway: *Water Terms 9*

inlet: *Coastal and Oceanic 10; Water Terms 9*

inline skates: *Human-Powered Transportation 9; Sporting Goods Other 5*

inmate: *Illicit Occupations 1*

inn: *Food/Drink Establishments 3; Hospitality 3*

inner curtain: *Castle Anatomy 3*

inner orbital complex: *Chemistry General Vocabulary 11*

inner ward: *Castle Anatomy 3*

innocence: *Philosophy Basic Concepts 14*

innovative: *New 20*

Inokinki: *Native American Peoples 1*

inquest: *Paranormal Activity 21*

inquiry: *Paranormal Activity 21*

inquisition: *General Combat Vocabulary 7; Paranormal Activity 21*

insatiable hunger: *Plot Devices 22*

inscrutable: *Magic Vocabulary 17*

insect bites: *Injuries/Medical Emergencies 12*

insect takeover: *Plot Devices 22*

insect: *Charges 19; Spaceship Shapes 22*

insectoid: *Monsters 16; Robots 22*

insects: *Wizard's Goods 5*

insertion: *General Combat Vocabulary 7*

inset pocket: *Garment Pieces 2*

inshore lizard: *Wild Saltwater Fish 15*

insight: *Ten Perfections of Buddhism 19*

insignia: *Elements 19; Jewelry 21*

insignificant: *Small/Fragile 20*

Insignis pine: *Evergreen Trees 10*

insistent: *Stubborn 1*

insoluble compound: *Chemistry General Vocabulary 11*

inspection: *Paranormal Activity 21*

Inspector LeStrade: *Sir Arthur Conan Doyle 18*

inspiration: *Pennsylvania Dutch Hex Signs 19*

inspiring: *Beautiful 20*

install: *Fix 20*

instant rice: *Grain 6*

instant: *Fast 20*

instantaneous: *Fast 20*

instant-read thermometer: *Kitchen Utensils 5*

instep: *Body Parts 12*

instigate: *Attack 7*

instruct: *Teach 20*

instructor: *Academic 1; Animal/Equestrian 1*

instrument stand: *Music Accessories*

instrument technique: *The Arts 13*

instrument: *Miscellaneous Furniture 4*

instrumentation: *General Music Vocabulary 13*

insubstantial: *Small/Thin 1*

insufferable: *Unattractive 20*

insufficient: *Small/Thin 1*

insular: *Geography General Vocabulary 10*

insulated gloves: *Spy Gear 5*

insulator: *Chemistry General Vocabulary 11*

insurance agency: *Business Property 3*

insurgency: *General Combat Vocabulary 7*

insurgent: *Fighter 1*

insurrectionary: *Fighter 1*

integrated rate equation: *Chemistry General Vocabulary 11*

integumentary: *Body Systems 12*

intellect: *Philosophy Basic Concepts 14*

intellectual intuition: *Philosophy Basic Concepts 14*

intellectual: *Academic 1; Intelligent 1*

intelligent animals: *Monsters and Creatures 22*

intelligent bacteria: *Monsters and Creatures 22*

intelligent insects/creatures: *Horror Plot Devices 23*

intelligent item: *Typical Magical Objects 17*

intelligent plants attack: *Common Dangers 24*

intelligent plants: *Common Dangers 23*

intelligent race of animals: *Fantasy Plot Devices 24*

intelligent robot: *Common Dangers 23*

intelligent slime: *Monsters and Creatures 22*

intelligent sword: *Common Dangers 24*

intelligent: *Character Building 1*

intense: *Heavy 20; Loud 20*

intention: *Philosophy Basic Concepts 14*

intentionality: *Philosophy Basic Concepts 14*

inter: *Close/Hold 20*

Interactive: *Architectural Styles 3*

interbedded: *Geological Vocabulary 10*

interception: *Fencing Vocabulary 7*

intercity rail: *Mass Transit 9*

intercom: *Office/School Machines 5*

interface: *Devices 22*

interfacing: *Garment Pieces 2*

interfluve: *Slope 10*

interior decorator: *Construction 1*

interior designer: *Construction 1*

interior live oak: *Deciduous Trees 10*

interlaced running: *Embroidery Stitches 2*

interlining: *Garment Pieces 2*

interloper: *Thief 1*

interlude: *Composition Types 13*

intermediate combination: *Windows 3*

intermediate cuneiform bone: *Bones 12*

intermediate phalange: *Bones 12*

intermezzo: *Composition Types 13*

intermolecular forces: *Chemistry General Vocabulary 11*

intern: *Medical Occupations 1*

international astronomical union: *Astronomy General Terms 11*

international date line: *Geography General Vocabulary 10*

International gothic: *Art Movements 13*

International Humic Substances Society: *Soil General Vocabulary 10*

International Soil Reference and Information Center: *Soil General Vocabulary 10*

International Union of Soil Sciences: *Soil General Vocabulary 10*

International: *Architectural Styles 3*

internet connection: *Computer Equipment 5*

interoffice envelope: *Office/School/Writing Supplies 5*

interplanetary magnetic field: *Astronomy General Terms 11*

interpret: *Solve 20*

interpreter: *Robots 22*

interrogator: *Occupations 22*

interstate: *Roads 9*

interstellar medium: *Astronomy General Terms 11*

inter-tidal: *Ecosystems 10*

interval: *General Music Vocabulary 13; Notation 13*

intervening opportunity: *Geography General Vocabulary 10*

intimate apparel: *Undergarments 2*

intimates: *Undergarments 2*

intimidate: *Horror Vocabulary 23*

intimidating: *Unattractive 20*

intimidator: *Fighter 1*

intolerable: *Horror Vocabulary 23; Unattractive 20*

intonation: *General Music Vocabulary 13*

intracoastal waterway: *Geography General Vocabulary 10*

intractable: *Difficult 20*

intrepid: *Personality Other 1*

intricate: *Difficult 20*

intriguing: *Beautiful 20*

introverted: *Personality Other 1*

intruder: *Thief 1*

intrusion: *Geological Vocabulary 10*

Intuition: *Minor Lines 19*

intuition: *Paranormal Abilities 21; Philosophy Basic Concepts 14*

Inuit: *Native American Peoples 1*

inundation: *Precipitation 10*

invade: *General Combat Vocabulary 7*

invader: *Fighter 1; General Combat Vocabulary 7*

invasion: *General Combat Vocabulary 7*

invecked: *Partition Lines 19*

invent: *Create 20*

inventory: *Laboratory Supplies 5*

inversion: *Meteorology General Vocabulary 10*

inverted breaststroke: *Swimming Strokes 9*

inverted butterfly: *Swimming Strokes 9*

inverted relief: *Erosion 10*

inverted triangle: *Face 1*

inverted: *Crosses 19*

investigate: *Learn 20; Solve 20*

investigation: *Paranormal Activity 21*

investigative reporter: *Media 1*

invisibility generator: *Devices 22*

invisibility won't end: *Common Dangers 24*

invisibility: *Paranormal Abilities 21*

invisible creature: *Supporting Cast 24*

invisible: *Moves 7*

invitation: *Fencing Vocabulary 7*

invoke: *Magic Vocabulary 17*

invoker: *Wizard 1*

Io: *Moons 11*

Iocaste: *Moons 11*

iodide: *Illumination Bulb and Tube Types 5*

Iodine: *Elements 11*

iolite: *Cat's Eye Gems 21; Standard Gems 21*

Iomud: *Horse Breeds 15*

ion product for water: *Chemistry General Vocabulary 11*

ion: *Chemistry General Vocabulary 11; Spaceship Drive Systems 22; Weapons 22*

ionic bonding: *Chemistry General Vocabulary 11*

ionic compunds: *Chemistry General Vocabulary 11*

ionic geometry: *Chemistry General Vocabulary 11*

ionization constant: *Chemistry General Vocabulary 11*

ionization energy: *Chemistry General Vocabulary 11*

ionization isomers: *Chemistry General Vocabulary 11*

ionization: *Chemistry General Vocabulary 11*

ionizing: *Energy Sources/Types 22*

ionosphere: *Astronomy General Terms 11*

Iowa blue: *Chickens 15*

Ipanema: *Bats 15*

Irani: *Human Ethnic Groups 1*

Iranian: *Human Ethnic Groups 1*

irate: *Angry 1*

Ireland: *St. Patrick's Day 19*

Irene Adler: *Sir Arthur Conan Doyle 18*

Iridium: *Elements 11*

iridot: *Minerals 10*

iris agate: *Minerals 10*

iris quartz: *Minerals 10*

iris: *Blue 20; Doors Atypical 3; Garden Bulbs 10*

Irish (Ireland): *Ethnic/Folk Dances 13*

Irish breakfast: *Tea 6*

Irish coffee: *Hot Drinks 6*

Irish dancer: *St. Patrick's Day 19*

Irish Draught: *Horse Breeds 15*

Irish Moiled: *Other Cows 15*

Irish moss: *Garden Perennials 10*

Irish Red & White Setter: *Dog Breeds 15*

Irish Setter: *Dog Breeds 15*

Irish stepdance: *Dance Shoes 13*

Irish Terrier: *Dog Breeds 15*

Irish Water Spaniel: *Dog Breeds 15*

Irish Wolfhound: *Dog Breeds 15*

Irish: *Human Ethnic Groups 1*

irminsul: *Symbols in Magic and Religion 19*

iron cross: *Poker Card Games 5*

Iron Crown of Lombardy: *Relics of Jesus 14*

iron gloves: *Armor of Legend 18*

iron golem: *Construct 16*

iron meteorite: *Astronomy General Terms 11*

iron mica: *Minerals 10*

iron oak: *Deciduous Trees 10*

iron pillar in the Quwwatul Mosque of Delhi: *Real Objects Not Fully Understood 18*

iron rose: *Minerals 10*

iron star: *Star Types and Relatives 11*

iron: *Beds 4; Clean 20; Coins and Currency 21; Dangerous Chemicals 11; Elements 11; Improvised Weapons 7; Minerals 10; Sewing Equipment 2; Sewing Techniques 2*

ironclad warship: *Military Watercraft 8*

ironed: *Hair Treated 1*

ironing board: *Improvised Weapons 7; Sewing Equipment 2*

irons: *Fasteners 5*

ironweed: *Garden Perennials 10; Wildflowers 10*

ironwood: *Deciduous Trees 10*

Iroquois: *Native American Peoples 1*

irregular galaxy: *Astronomy General Terms 11*

irregular satellite: *Astronomy General Terms 11*

irregular: *Spaceship Shapes 22*

irritable: *Negative 1*

irritated: *Negative 1*

irritation: *General Emotions 20*

irukandji: *Jellyfish 15*

Isaac Newton: *Asteroids with Unusual Names 11*

Isabela Island giant: *Tortoises 15*

Isabelline: *Architectural Styles 3*

ischium: *Bones 12*

iserine: *Minerals 10*

Ishikawa Goemon: *Real People with Legendary Status 18*

Ishtar (goddess of love and war): *Babylonian Pantheon 14*

isinglass: *Minerals 10*

Isis (goddess of magic): *Egyptian Pantheon 14*

isitwalangcengce: *Demon 16*

Islamic Texts: *Major Religious Books 14*

Islamic: *Architectural Styles 3; Art Movements 13*

island arc: *Geological Vocabulary 10*

island council: *Political Divisions 10*

island gray: *Foxes 15*

island: *Coastal and Oceanic 10*

Islands of the Blessed: *Afterlife/Underworld 18*

Isle of Avalon: *Arthurian Locations 18*

islet: *Coastal and Oceanic 10*

isobar: *Meteorology General Vocabulary 10*

isobenzan: *Dangerous Chemicals 11*

isocyanic acid: *Dangerous Chemicals 11*

isodrin: *Dangerous Chemicals 11*

isoelectric: *Chemistry General Vocabulary 11*

isohyet: *Geography General Vocabulary 10*

isolation cell: *Prison 3*

isomers: *Chemistry General Vocabulary 11*

Isonoe: *Moons 11*

isophorone diisocyanate: *Dangerous Chemicals 11*

isopropylmethylpyrazolyl dimethylcarbamate: *Dangerous Chemicals 11*

isopyre: *Minerals 10*

isotherm: *Meteorology General Vocabulary 10*

isotope geochemistry: *Geologic Fields of Study 10*

isotope geology: *Geologic Fields of Study 10*

isotope: *Geological Vocabulary 10*

isotopes: *Chemistry General Vocabulary 11*

Israeli Holstein: *Other Cows 15*

Israeli Red: *Other Cows 15*

Israfel: *Angels of Good 14*

istesso: *Tempo/Mood 13*

isthmus: *Coastal and Oceanic 10*

Istoben: *Other Cows 15*

itacolumite: *Sedimentary Rocks 10*

Itaipu Dam: *Seven Wonders of the Modern World 18*

Italian bean: *Legumes 6*

Italian bugloss: *Garden Perennials 10*

Italian foil: *Fencing Equipment 7*

Italian Greyhound: *Dog Breeds 15*

Italian grip: *Fencing Equipment 7*

Italian ice: *Ice Cream Related 6*

Italian landrace: *Pigs 15*

Italian plum: *Pit Fruits 6*

Italian School: *Ballet Terms 13*

Italian white truffle: *Fungus Common Names 10*

Italian: *Bread General Varieties 6; Coffee Bean Roasts 6; Human Ethnic Groups 1; Poker Card Games 5; Sausage 6*

Italianate: *Architectural Styles 3*

itching: *Objects/Activities Connected to Lore 19*

itinerant: *Barbarian 1; Wanderer 1*

itsy bitsy: *Small/Fragile 20*

itty bitty: *Small/Fragile 20*

Itzamna (medicine): *Central American Pantheon 14*

Ivoire: *Twelve Peers of Charlemagne 18*

Ivon: *Twelve Peers of Charlemagne 18*

ivory horn: *Wind/Woodwind and Brass Musical Instruments 10; Poisonous Plants 10*

ivory: *Art Materials 5; Skin Types and Features 1; White 20*

ivy geranium: *Garden Annuals 10*

ivy: *Garden Perennials 10; Plants with Symbolic Meaning 19; Shrubs 10*

Ixtlilton (healing and gaming): *Aztec Pantheon 14*

Ixworth: *Chickens 15*

iya: *Demon 16*

–J–

jab: *Attack 7*

Jabberwock: *Asteroids with Unusual Names 11*

jabberwock: *Dragon 16*

jaboncillo: *Deciduous Trees 10*

jabuticaba: *Unusual Edible Fruits 6*

Jacare caiman: *Crocodilians 15*

jacinth: *Minerals 10*

Jack Dempsey: *Aquarium Freshwater Fish 15*

jack hammer: *Power Tools*

jack in the pulpit: *Garden Bulbs 10; Garden Perennials*

Jack London: *Asteroids with Unusual Names 11*

jack oak: *Deciduous Trees 10*

jack pine: *Evergreen Trees 10*

Jack the Giant Killer: *Fictional Characters 18*

Jack the Ripper: *Real People with Legendary Status 18*

jack the shifter: *Poker Card Games 5*

jack: *Horses Related 15*

jackal: *Other Wild Mammals 15*

jackalope: *Mythical Creatures and Monsters 16*

jacket: *Outerwear 2; Unisex Clothing 2*

jackfruit: *Unusual Edible Fruits 6*

jackhammer: *Large Tools*

jackknife: *General Survival Gear 5*

jack-o-lantern: *Halloween 19*

jacks back: *Poker Card Games 5*

jacks or better: *Poker Card Games 5*

jacks: *Toys 5*

Jacob's ladder: *Garden Perennials 10*

Jacobean: *Architectural Styles 3*

Jacquard: *Fabric 2*

jaculus: *Beast 16*

jade turtle carving: *Harbingers/Charms for Good Luck 19*

jade: *Green 20; Minerals 10*

jadeite: *Standard Gems 21*

Jagdpanther: *Tanks German 8*

Jagdpanzer Jaguar 1 self-propelled HOT missile vehicle: *Germany Military Vehicles 8*

Jagdpanzer Jaguar 2 self-propelled TOW missile vehicle: *Germany Military Vehicles 8*

Jagdpanzer Kanone tank destroyer: *Germany Military Vehicles 8*

Jagdpanzer Rakete self-propelled SS.11 missile vehicle: *Germany Military Vehicles 8*

Jaguar main battle tank: *Germany Military Vehicles 8*

jaguar: *Animals with Symbolic Meaning 19; Big Cats 15*

jail: *Prison 3*

jailbird: *Illicit Occupations 1*

jailhouse: *Prison 3*

jailor: *Castle Inhabitants and Personnel 1*

Jain Texts: *Major Religious Books 14*

Jain: *Symbols in Magic and Religion 19*

Jakaltek: *Human Ethnic Groups 1*

jalousie: *Windows 3*

jam: *Food 6*

Jamaica Black: *Other Cows 15*

Jamaica Hope: *Other Cows 15*

Jamaica Red: *Other Cows 15*

Jamaican: *Boa 15; Human Ethnic Groups 1*

Jambe: *Ballet Terms 13*

jambul: *Unusual Edible Fruits 6*

jameed: *Cheese International Varieties 6*

James Bond: *Asteroids with Unusual Names 11*

James Island giant: *Tortoises 15*

James the Greater: *Twelve Apostles 14*

James the Lesser: *Twelve Apostles 14*

Jamestown weed: *Poisonous Plants 10*

Jane Eyre: *Fictional Characters 18*

jangle: *Sounds 20*

janitor caddy: *Cleaning Supplies/Gadgets 5*

janitor: *General Occupations 1*

jansky: *Astronomy General Terms 11*

Janus (gates): *Roman Pantheon 14*

Janus: *Moons 11*

japa mala: *Objects in Magic and Religion 19*

Japanese barberry: *Weeds 10*

Japanese bobtail: *Domestic Cats 15*

Japanese cat: *Harbingers/Charms for Good Luck 19*

Japanese Chin: *Dog Breeds 15*

Japanese climbing fern: *Weeds 10*

Japanese darning: *Embroidery Stitches 2*

Japanese honeysuckle: *Weeds 10*

Japanese knotweed: *Weeds 10*

Japanese landrace: *Pigs 15*

Japanese millet: *Grain 6*

Japanese pantheon: *Philosophy and Religion 14*

Japanese parsley: *Garden Perennials 10*

Japanese quince: *Shrubs 10*

Japanese stiltgrass: *Weeds 10*

Japanese wineberry: *Weeds 10*

Japanese wood: *Freshwater Turtles 15*

Japanese: *Art Movements 13; Beetle 15; Human Ethnic Groups 1; Styles of Dress 2*

jar: *Candles 5; Containers and Vessels 5*

jargon: *Minerals 10*

jargoon: *Minerals 10*

jarhead: *Hair Style 1*

Jarlsberg: *Cheese Common Varieties 6*

Jarnsaxa: *Moons 11*

jasmine rice: *Grain 6*

jasmine: *Shrubs 10*

jasp agate: *Minerals 10*

jaspe: *Minerals 10*

jasper opal: *Minerals 10*

jasper: *Minerals 10; Standard Gems 21*

jaspillite: *Sedimentary Rocks 10*

jasponyx: *Minerals 10*

Jassic: *Human Ethnic Groups 1*

jata: *Demon 16*

jatoba: *Unusual Edible Fruits 6*

Jaulan: *Other Cows 15*

jaunt: *Journey 20; Locomotion 9*

Java: *Chickens 15*

Javan: *Tigers 15*

Javanese: *Domestic Cats 15; Human Ethnic Groups 1*

javelin: *Missile Weapons 7*

jaw harp: *Percussion Musical Instruments 5*

jaw: *Body Parts 12*

jawbreaker: *Candy General 6*

jawfish: *Aquarium Saltwater Fish 15*

jaws: *Mouth 1*

jazz ballet: *Dance Styles 13*

jazz pants: *Dance Clothing 13*

jazz: *Dance Shoes 13; Dance Styles 13*

jazz: *Musical Styles 13*

jealous lover: *Common Character Archetypes 21*

jealousy: *General Emotions 20*

jeans: *Unisex Clothing 2*

jeep: *Motorized 9*

jeez: *Expletives 20*

Jeffersonian: *Architectural Styles 3*

jeffersonite: *Minerals 10*

Jeffrey pine: *Evergreen Trees 10*

jeggings: *Ladies' Wear 2*

Jegudiel: *Angels of Good 14*

Jehoel: *Angels of Good 14*

Jeju black: *Pigs 15*

jejunum: *Organs/Major Structures 12*

jelloped: *Special Body Features 19*

jelly baby: *Fungus Common Names 10*

jelly bean: *Candy General 6*

jelly cabinet: *Storage 4*

jelly filled: *Donut/doughnut 6*

jelly nougat: *Candy General 6*

jelly opal: *Minerals 10*

jelly palm: *Unusual Edible Fruits 6*

jelly roll pan: *Kitchen Equipment 5*

jelly roll: *Cake 6*

jelly sieve: *Kitchen Equipment 5*

jelly: *Food 6; Ooze 16; Wizard's Goods 5*

jellyfish float: *Swimming Strokes 9*

jellyfish: *Animals 15*

Jengki: *Architectural Styles 3*

Jenny Lind: *Beds 4*

jenny: *Horses Related 15*

jequirity: *Poisonous Plants 10*

Jequn: *Angels of Good 14*

Jerahmeel: *Angels of Good 14*

Jerdon's jumping: *Ants 15*

Jerdon's: *Pit Viper 15; Sea Snake 15*

jerry hat: *Headgear 2*

Jersey Devil: *Mythical Creatures and Monsters 16*

Jersey giant: *Chickens 15*

Jersey pine: *Evergreen Trees 10*

Jersey red: *Pigs 15*

jersey: *Fabric 2*

Jersey: *North American Dairy Cows 15*

Jerusalem artichoke: *Vegetables 6*

Jerusalem cherry: *Poisonous Plants 10*

Jerusalem sage: *Shrubs 10*

Jerusalem: *Crosses 19*

Jesse James: *Real People with Legendary Status 18*

Jesse tree: *Christmas 19*

jester: *Bard 1; Castle Inhabitants and Personnel 1; Masks 2; Performing Arts 1; Royal/Noble 1; Supporting Cast 24*

Jesus: *Christmas 19*

jet pack: *Air Vehicles 9; Vehicles 22*

jet stream: *Meteorology General Vocabulary 10; Water Terms 9; Wind 10*

jet: *Astronomy General Terms 11*

jet-black: *Hair Color 1*

Jeté battu: *Ballet Terms 13*

Jeté entrelacé: *Ballet Terms 13*

Jeté: *Ballet Terms 13*

jeté: *Dance Moves 13*

jetty: *Marina 3; Water Terms 9*

jewel case: *Containers and Vessels 5*

jewel: *Squid 15*

jeweler: *Artists and Craftspeople 1*

jewelfish: *Aquarium Freshwater Fish 15*

jewelry: *Christmas 19; Classic Items 23; Clothing 2; Typical Magical Objects 17; Valentine's Day 19*

jewelweed: *Weeds 10*

Jewish: *Human Ethnic Groups 1*

Jewish rye: *Bread General Varieties 6*

jezebel: *Butterfly 15*

jian: *Swords One-handed 7*

jib: *Boat/Ship Anatomy 9*

jibe: *Boat/Ship Terminology 9*

jibing: *Boat/Ship Terminology 9*

jibneh arabieh: *Cheese International Varieties 6*

jicama: *Vegetables 6*

jig borer: *Power Tools*

jig saw: *Power Tools*

jig: *Architectural/Engineering Tools 5; Historical Dances 13*

jigsaw puzzle: *Toys 5*

jihad: *General Combat Vocabulary 7*

Jimmy Hoffa: *Famous Disappearances 18*

jimson weed: *Poisonous Plants 10*

jingle bell: *Christmas 19*

Jinhua: *Pigs 15*

Jinzhou: *Horse Breeds 15*

jitterbug: *Dance Styles 13*

jittery: *Vocal/Speech Quality 1*

jive: *Dance Styles 13*

Jizo: *Symbols in Magic and Religion 19*

jo: *Bludgeons 7*

Joan of Arc: *Real People with Legendary Status 18*

jock itch: *Diseases 12*

jock: *Common Character Archetypes 21; Styles of Dress 2*

jockey: *Animal/Equestrian 1; Transportation 1; Transportation Animals 9*

jocote: *Unusual Edible Fruits 6*

Joe Magarac: *Tall Tales 18*

Joe-Pye weed: *Garden Perennials 10*

jogging stroller: *Human-Powered Transportation 9*

jogging: *Athletic Shoes 2*

Johannesberg riesling: *Wine White 6*

John (eagle): *Four Evangelists of the Bible and Their Symbols 19*

John Adams: *Independence Day 19*

John Brown: *Real People with Legendary Status 18*

John Crow bead: *Poisonous Plants 10*

John dory: *Wild Saltwater Fish 15*

John Hancock: *Independence Day 19*

John Henry: *Legendary People Presumed to be Fictional 18*

john: *Bathrooms 3; Illicit Occupations 1*

John: *Twelve Apostles 14*

Johnny Appleseed: *Real People with Legendary Status 18*

Johnny cake: *Bread General Varieties 6*

Johnny jump-up: *Garden Annuals 10; Wildflowers 10*

Johnville Bog Quebec: *Bogs of North America 10*

join: *Fix 20*

joint fir: *Garden Perennials 10*

joint operations: *General Combat Vocabulary 7*

joint: *Cave Anatomy 10; Food/Drink Establishments 3; Geological Vocabulary 10; Residential Slang 3*

jointer planer: *Power Tools*

jointer: *Power Tools*

joist: *Building Elements and Features 3; Castle Anatomy 3; General Combat Vocabulary 7*

jojoba: *Shrubs 10*

joker: *Bard 1*

jokester: *Bard 1*

jolly: *Happy 20*

Jonagold: *Apples 6*

jonquil: *Garden Bulbs 10; Yellow 20*

Jophiel: *Angels of Good 14*

jory soil: *Soil General Vocabulary 10*

Josef Stalin heavy tank: *Russia Military Vehicles 8*

Joseph Cinqué: *Real People with Legendary Status 18*

Joseph Pines Bog Virginia: *Bogs of North America 10*

Joseph's coat of many colors: *Clothing 18*

josephinite: *Minerals 10*

Joshua tree: *Shrubs 10*

jota (Spain): *Ethnic/Folk Dances 13*

Jotunheim: *Fictional/Mythological Locations 18*

joule: *Chemistry General Vocabulary 11*

journal: *Books/Publications 5*

journalist: *Publishing 1*

journey cake: *Bread General Varieties 6*

journey: *Locomotion 9; Nouns 20*

jousting lance: *Pole Weapons 7*

jovial: *Happy 20*

joy: *General Emotions 20; Twelve Fruits of the Holy Spirit 19*

Joyeuse (Charlemagne's sword): *Weapons of Legend 18*

joyful: *Happy 20*

Juan Bautista Cabral: *Legendary People Presumed to be Fictional 18*

Juan Santamaria: *Real People with Legendary Status 18*

jubilant: *Happy 20*

Judas Priest: *Expletives 20*

Judas tree: *Deciduous Trees 10*

Judas: *Twelve Apostles 14*

Judas's ear: *Fungus Common Names 10*

Jude: *Twelve Apostles 14*

judge: *Legal Occupations 1; Solve 20*

judge's robe: *Special Purpose Clothing 2*

judgment: *Philosophy Basic Concepts 14*

jug: *Containers and Vessels 5*

Jugendstil: *Architectural Styles 3*

juggler: *Castle Inhabitants and Personnel 1*

juggling balls: *Specialty Survival Gear 5; Toys 5*

juggling clubs: *Specialty Survival Gear 5*

juice glass: *Drinkware 5*

juice: *Wet 20*

juicer: *Appliances 5*

jujube: *Unusual Edible Fruits 6*

jukjangchangbo: *Spears 7*

Juliet cap: *Headgear 2*

Juliet: *Moons 11*

juliette sleeve: *Garment Pieces 2*

Julius Caesar: *Real People with Legendary Status 18*

July 4: *Independence Day 19*

jumbie bead: *Poisonous Plants 10*

jumbo jet: *Air Vehicles 9; Travel Modes 23*

jumbo shrimp: *Fish/Seafood Types 6*

jumbo: *Eggs 6; Large 20*

jump rope: *Toys 5*

jump up: *Dance Styles 13*

jump: *Locomotion 9*

jumping: *Nonvenomous Arachnids 15; Viper 15*

junco: *Backyard Birds 15*

June: *Beetle 15*

juneberry: *Deciduous Trees 10*

jungle girl/boy: *Common Character Archetypes 21*

jungle green: *Green 20*

Jungle joker: *Bears 15*

jungle terrain warfare: *General Combat Vocabulary 7*

jungle: *Climatic Zones 10; Ecosystems 10; Elf 1; Gnome 1; Terrain Features 10*

junior high school: *Academic Property 3*

junior: *Beds 4; Child 1; Small/Fragile 20*

juniper berry: *Unusual Edible Fruits 6*

juniper: *Evergreen Trees 10; Objects that Offer Protection 19; Plants with Symbolic Meaning 19; Shrubs 10*

junk: *Large Watercraft 9*

Juno (goddess of women, marriage): *Roman Pantheon 14*

Jupiter (leader of the gods): *Roman Pantheon 14*

Jupiter: *Mounts 19; Planets 11*

Jurassic Period: *Geologic Time 10*

jurisdiction: *Geography General Vocabulary 10*

jury-rig: *Boat/Ship Terminology 9*

just right: *Happy 20*

just the thing: *Happy 20*

just what the doctor ordered: *Happy 20*

justice: *Four Cardinal Virtues 19; Legal Occupations 1; Philosophy Basic Concepts 14; Seven Holy Virtues 19*

Justitia (goddess of law): *Roman Pantheon 14*

Jutland: *Horse Breeds 15*

jutte: *Bludgeons 7*

jutting stalactite: *Geological Natural Hazards 10*

juvenile: *Child 1*

–K–

K capture: *Chemistry General Vocabulary 11*

K1 main battle tank: *North Korea Military Vehicles 8*

K2 Black Panther main battle tank: *North Korea Military Vehicles 8*

K9 unit: *SWAT Equipment 7*

Kabarda: *Horse Breeds 15*

Kabbalah: *Symbols in Magic and Religion 19*

kabinett: *Wine White 6*

kabob: *Fish/Seafood Meals 6*

kabosu: *Unusual Edible Fruits 6*

Kachina doll: *Harbingers/Charms for Good Luck 19*

Kachina: *Masks 2*

kaemmererite: *Minerals 10*

kahikatea: *Unusual Edible Fruits 6*

KAHR K9: *Pistol Semiautomatic 7*

kaia: *Demon 16*

Kailasa Temple in India: *Real Places Steeped in Legend or Mystery 18*

kaiser: *Card Games 5*

Kakhetian: *Pigs 15*

kalathaki: *Cheese International Varieties 6*

kalathotos: *Cheese International Varieties 6*

Kale: *Moons 11*

kale: *Vegetable Juice 6; Vegetables 6*

kaleidoscope: *Optics 5*

kalevanpojat: *Demon 16*

Kali (goddess of death): *Indian Pantheon 14*

kalinka (Russia): *Ethnic/Folk Dances 13*

kalkaska sand: *Soil General Vocabulary 10*

Kallichore: *Moons 11*

kalookie: *Card Games 5*

kalter schlag: *Card Games 5*

Kalyke: *Moons 11*

kamacite: *Minerals 10*

kame delta: *Glacial and Mountain 10*

kame: *Geological Vocabulary 10; Glacial and Mountain 10*

kammererite: *Minerals 10*

kampilan: *Swords One-handed 7*

kanabō: *Bludgeons 7*

Kanburian: *Pit Viper 15*

kane: *Terrain Features 10*

kangaroo: *Other Wild Mammals 15*

Kangayam: *Other Cows 15*

Kankrej: *Other Cows 15*

Kansas City lowball: *Poker Card Games 5*

kapala: *Objects in Magic and Religion 19*

kapellmeister: *Musical Occupations 1*

kapok: *Unusual Edible Fruits 6*

kappa: *Aquatic 16; Demon 16*

Karabair: *Horse Breeds 15*

Karabakh: *Horse Breeds 15*

karabela: *Swords One-handed 7*

karakul: *Headgear 2*

Karan Fries: *Other Cows 15*

Karan Swiss: *Other Cows 15*

Karelian: *Human Ethnic Groups 1*

Kari: *Moons 11*

kariba weed: *Weeds 10*

karikeftos: *Cheese International Varieties 6*

karina: *Demon 16*

karkalla: *Unusual Edible Fruits 6*

karner blue: *Butterfly 15*

karonda: *Unusual Edible Fruits 6*

karren: *Cave Anatomy 10*

Karst topography: *Terrain Features 10*

karst: *Geography General Vocabulary 10; Geological Vocabulary 10*

Karttikeya (demigod of war): *Indian Pantheon 14*

Kasdeja: *Angels of Good 14*

kaseri: *Cheese International Varieties 6*

kashkaval: *Cheese International Varieties 6*

kashkawan: *Cheese International Varieties 6*

kashta: *Cheese International Varieties 6*

kaskara: *Swords One-handed 7*

kasoite: *Minerals 10*

katana: *Swords Two-handed 7*

Katanga: *Lions 15*

katar: *Swords One-handed 7*

katara: *Daggers and Knives 7*

katiki: *Cheese International Varieties 6*

katoite: *Minerals 10*

katydid: *Orthoptera 15*

katzbalger: *Swords One-handed 7*

Kaulback's lance-headed: *Pit Viper 15*

Kaustubha: *Jewelry 18*

Kawasaki disease: *Diseases 12*

Kay: *Knights of the Round Table 18*

kayak: *Human-Powered Watercraft 9*

kayeri: *Demon 16*

Kazakh: *Horse Breeds 15; Other Cows 15*

Kaznakov's: *Viper 15*

kazoo: *Wind/Woodwind and Brass Musical Instruments*

KC-10 Extender tanker: *U.S. Air Force Aircraft 8*

KC-135 Stratotanker: *U.S. Air Force Aircraft 8*

ke'lets: *Demon 16*

keel: *Boat/Ship Anatomy 9*

keelback: *Animals 15*

keelboat: *Small Watercraft 9*

keelhaul: *Boat/Ship Terminology 9*

keeling: *Boat/Ship Terminology 9*

keemun: *Tea 6*

keen: *Love 20; Personality Other 1; Sounds 20*

keenness: *General Emotions 20*

keep: *Close/Hold 20; Fortification 3*

keepsake: *Jewelry 21*

Keeshond: *Dog Breeds 15*

kefalograviera: *Cheese International Varieties 6*

kefalotyri: *Cheese International Varieties 6*

kei apple: *Unusual Edible Fruits 6*

Kele: *Pigs 15*

kelly green: *Green 20*

kelpie: *Aquatic 16; Beast 16; Demon 16; General Fae 16*

Kelvin: *Astronomy General Terms 11; Meteorology General Vocabulary 10*

Kemerovo: *Pigs 15*

Kemp's ridley: *Sea Turtles 15*

kennel: *Man-Made Animal Homes 15*

Kentucky long rifle: *Black Powder Weapons 7*

Kenwariya: *Other Cows 15*

kepi: *Headgear 2*

Kepler's first law: *Astronomy General Terms 11*

Kepler's second law: *Astronomy General Terms 11*

Kepler's third law: *Astronomy General Terms 11*

keratitis: *Diseases 12*

Kermode: *Bears 15*

kerogen: *Soil General Vocabulary 10*

kerosene lamp: *Illumination/Light Sources 5*

kerosene: *Illumination/Light Sources 5*

kerria: *Shrubs 10*

Kerry Blue Terrier: *Dog Breeds 15*

Kerry Bog Pony: *Horse Breeds 15*

Kerry: *North American Dairy Cows 15*

kesong: *Cheese International Varieties 6*

kestrel: *Birds of Prey 15*

Ket: *Human Ethnic Groups 1*

ketch: *Small Watercraft 9*

ketchup: *Condiments 6*

ketone: *Chemistry General Vocabulary 11*

kettle cooked potato chip: *Snacks 6*

kettle corn: *Snacks 6*

kettle drum: *Percussion Musical Instruments 5*

kettle hat: *Head Gear 7*

kettle: *Geological Vocabulary 10; Glacial and Mountain 10; Kitchen Equipment 5; Terrain Features 10; Witchcraft Vocabulary 17*

Ketu: *Minor Lines 19*

keule: *Unusual Edible Fruits 6*

kevenhuller hat: *Headgear 2*

Kevlar vest: *Body Armor 7*

key apple: *Unusual Edible Fruits 6*

key light: *Technical Terms 13*

key lime: *Citrus 6; Ice Cream Flavors 6; Pie 6*

Key of Solomon: *Books of Legend 18*

key punch machine: *Office/School Machines 5*

key signature: *Notation 13*

key: *Jewelry 21; Musical Instrument Parts 13; Notation 13; Symbols in Magic and Religion 19; Wizard's Goods 5*

keyboard: *Computer Equipment 5; Musical Instrument Parts 13*

keyhole: *Cave Anatomy 10; Sewing Terms 2*

keyliner: *Publishing 1*

keypad: *Building Systems 3*

keys: *Laboratory Equipment 5*

keystone: *Building Elements and Features 3; Castle Anatomy 3*

khabhanda: *Demon 16*

Khajuraho Monuments in India: *Real Places Steeped in Legend or Mystery 18*

khaki: *Brown 20*

khakis: *Unisex Clothing 2*

Kham Plateau: *Pit Viper 15*

khanda: *Swords One-handed 7; Symbols in Magic and Religion 19*

Khao Manee: *Domestic Cats 15*

Khasi Hills: *Keelback 15*

Khepri: *Insectoid 16*

Kherigarh: *Other Cows 15*

Khillari: *Other Cows 15*

khoa: *Cheese International Varieties 6*

Kholmogory: *Other Cows 15*

khopesh: *Swords One-handed 7*

Khufi: *Human Ethnic Groups 1*

Ki (goddess of nature): *Sumerian Pantheon 14*

kiang: *Horses Related 15*

kick scooter: *Human-Powered Transportation 9*

kick sled: *Human-Powered Transportation 9*

Kickapoo: *Native American Peoples 1*

kid: *Child 1*

kidnap: *Harm 20*

kidnapped child: *Western Plot Devices 21*

kidnapped person: *Common Character Archetypes 21*

kidnapped victim: *Supporting Cast 23*

kidnapping: *Horror Plot Devices 23*

kidney ore: *Minerals 10*

kidney: *Daggers and Knives 7; Organs/Major Structures 12*

kid-sized: *Small/Fragile 20*

kielbasa: *Sausage 6*

Kiger Mustang: *Horse Breeds 15*

kiliakai: *Demon 16*

kilij: *Swords One-handed 7*

Kilis: *Other Cows 15*

kill zone: *Fortification 3*

kill: *Attack 7; Technical Terms 13; Verbs 20*

"killer algae": *Weeds 10*

killer prom queen: *Common Dangers 23*

killer: *Assassin 1; Bees 15; Fighter 1; Villain 20; Whales 15*

killie: *Wild Saltwater Fish 15*

Kilment Voroshilov heavy tank: *Russia Military Vehicles 8*

kiln: *Art Tools 5; Business Property 3*

kiloparsec: *Astronomy General Terms 11*

kilt: *Unisex Clothing 2*

kiltie loafers: *Footwear/Shoes 2*

Kimber 84M: *Bolt Action Centerfire Rifles 7*

Kimber Crimson Carry: *Pistol Semiautomatic 7*

Kimber Montana: *Bolt Action Centerfire Rifles 7*

kimberlite: *Igneous Rocks 10; Minerals 10*

kimchee: *Vegetables 6*

kimono: *Ladies' Wear 2*

kin: *Relational 1*

kind woman with lowly profession: *Common Character Archetypes 21*

kind: *General Emotions 20; Happy 20; Positive 1*

kindergartener: *Child 1*

kindness: *General Emotions 20; Ten Perfections of Buddhism 19*

kinetic energy: *Chemistry General Vocabulary 11*

kinetic: *Energy Sources/Types 22*

kinetic-molecular theory: *Chemistry General Vocabulary 11*

King Arthur: *Arthurian Characters 18*

king bolete: *Fungus Common Names 10*

king brown: *General Snake Families 15*

King David: *Christmas 19*

king for a day: *Hero 20*

King Herod: *Christmas 19; Real People with Legendary Status 18*

king salmon: *Fish/Seafood Types 6; Wild Freshwater Fish 15*

King Solomon's mines: *Sites Lost or Unproven to Exist 18*

king topaz: *Minerals 10*

King Wenceslas: *Christmas 19*

king: *Beds 4; Card Games 5; Cobra 15; Common Character Archetypes 21; General Snake Families 15; Hero or Villain, Depending Upon Circumstance 20; Royal/Noble 1*

king's corners: *Card Games 5*

kingfisher: *Animals with Symbolic Meaning 19; Other Wild Birds 15*

king-sized: *Large 20*

kingu: *Demon 16*

kink band: *Geological Vocabulary 10*

kink: *Geological Vocabulary 10*

kinky: *Hair Types 1*

kinradite: *Minerals 10*

kinsman: *Relational 1*

Kiowa: *Native American Peoples 1*

kippah: *Headgear 2*

kipunji: *Old World Monkeys 15*

Kiputytto (goddess of sickness): *Finnish Pantheon 14*

Kiraman Katibin: *Angels of Good 14*

Kirdi Pony: *Horse Breeds 15*

kirin: *Beast 16*

Kirkwood gap: *Astronomy General Terms 11*

Kisber Felver: *Horse Breeds 15*

kishi: *Demon 16*

Kishijoten (goddess of luck): *Japanese Pantheon 14*

Kiso: *Horse Breeds 15*

kiss: *Love 20; New Year 19; Rituals 14*

kissing ball: *Christmas 19*

kissing gourami: *Aquarium Freshwater Fish 15*

kiss-me-quick hat: *Headgear 2*

kit: *Foxes 15; Technical Terms 13*

kitchen curtains: *Window Treatments 5*

kitchen equipment: *Equipment and Tools 5*

kitchen fairies: *Demon 16*

kitchen scissors: *Kitchen Utensils 5*

kitchen set: *Toys 5*

kitchen stool: *Chairs and Stools 4*

kitchen string: *Fasteners 5*

kitchen utensils: *Equipment and Tools 5*

kitchen: *Rooms 3; Tables 4; Towels 5*

kite: *Birds of Prey 15; Shield Types 7*

kitembilla: *Unusual Edible Fruits 6*

kith: *Relational 1*

kitsune: *Demon 16*

kitsune-tsuki: *Demon 16*

kitten heel: *Footwear/Shoes 2*

kittlite: *Minerals 10*

Kiviuq: *Moons 11*

kiwano: *Unusual Edible Fruits 6*

kiwi: *Other Wild Birds 15; Tropical/Exotic Fruits 6*

kiwiberry: *Berries 6*

Kiyomizu-dera: *Unique Property 3*

Kladenets (Russian magic sword): *Weapons of Legend 18*

Kladruby: *Horse Breeds 15*

klastos: *Geological Vocabulary 10*

Kleiner Panzerbefehlwagen I command Panzer I tank: *Germany Military Vehicles 8*

klewang: *Swords One-handed 7*

Klondike: *Solitaire Card Games 5*

Knabstrup: *Horse Breeds 15*

knapsack: *Containers and Vessels 5*

knapweed: *Garden Perennials 10*

knaves: *Card Games 5*

knee pads: *Military Equipment 8*

knee socks: *Western Clothing/Dress 21*

knee: *Body Parts 12; Socks 2*

kneecap (patella): *Bones 12*

knee-highs: *Socks 2*

kneel: *Rituals 14*

kneeling: *Chairs and Stools 4*

knickers: *Men's Wear 2; Undergarments 2; Western Clothing/Dress 21*

knickknack: *Decorative Objects 4; Jewelry 21*

knife of Llawfrodedd the Horseman: *Thirteen Treasures of the Island of Britain 18*

knife sharpener: *Kitchen Equipment 5*

knife: *Art Tools 5; Classic Items 23; Daggers and Knives 7; Eating Utensils 5; Hand Tools 5; Kitchen Utensils 5; Military Equipment 8; Western Weapons 21*

knight grand commander: *Knight 1*

knight in shining armor: *Hero 20*

knight of the cross: *Paladin 1*

Knight SR-15: *Semiautomatic Centerfire Rifles 7*

knight: *Castle Inhabitants and Personnel 1; Character Building 1; Common Character Archetypes 21; Fighter 1; Knight 1; Royal/Noble 1*

knight-errant: *Knight 1*

knights hospitaller: *Knight 1*

knights of Bath: *Knight 1*

Knights of the Round Table: *Arthurian Characters 18; Arthurian Legend 18; Legendary, Mystical and Mythical Items and Locations 18*

Knights Templar: *Secret/Mystical Organizations 18*

knit cap: *Headgear 2*

knit hat: *Headgear 2*

knit: *Fabric 2; Sewing Techniques 2*

knives: *Combat, Armor, and Weapons 7*

knob: *Terrain Features 10*

knobcone pine: *Deciduous Trees 10*

knobkierrie: *Bludgeons 7*

knob-scaled lizard: *Scaled Reptiles 15*

knock: *Paranormal Occurrences 21; Sounds 20*

knocker: *General Fae 16*

knock-out drops: *Spy Gear 5*

knock-out whist: *Card Games 5*

knoll: *Slope 10; Terrain Features 10*

knot of Isis: *Symbols in Magic and Religion 19*

knot: *Boat/Ship Anatomy 9; Hair Style 1; Jewelry 21; Meteorology General Vocabulary 10; Symbols in Magic and Religion 19*

knotted blanket: *Embroidery Stitches 2*

knotted carpet: *Floor Coverings 4*

knotty: *Difficult 20*

knout: *Flexible 7*

know-it-all: *Supporting Cast 23*

Knowledge without character: *Philosophy 14*

knowledge: *Philosophy Basic Concepts 14; Seven Gifts of the Holy Spirit 19*

Knowlton hop hornbeam: *Deciduous Trees 10*

known artifact (such as Excalibur sword) appears in real world: *Fantasy Plot Devices 24*

known: *Personality Other 1*

koala: *Other Wild Mammals 15*

Koba: *Tall Tales 18*

kobold: *General Fae 16; Humanoid 16*

kodachi: *Swords One-handed 7*

Kodiak: *Bears 15*

kodo millet: *Grain 6*

kofia: *Headgear 2*

kohlrabi: *Vegetables 6*

Kojime: *Comets 11*

kokopeli: *Symbols in Magic and Religion 19*

kolache: *Donut/doughnut 6*

komatiite: *Igneous Rocks 10*

komboloi prayer string: *Objects in Magic and Religion 19*

komodo dragon: *Scaled Reptiles 15*

Komondor: *Dog Breeds 15*

komyati: *Cheese International Varieties 6*

Kongō (trident): *Weapons of Legend 18*

Kongo: *Human Ethnic Groups 1*

Kon-Tiki: *Ships 18*

konzertmeister: *Musical Occupations 1*

kopanisti: *Cheese International Varieties 6*

Kopff: *Comets 11*

Koran: *Major Religious Books 14*

Korat: *Domestic Cats 15*

Kore: *Moons 11*

Korean boxwood: *Garden Perennials 10*

Korean fan: *Hand Weapons 7*

Korean hand plow: *Garden Tools*

Korean native: *Pigs 15*

Korean: *Human Ethnic Groups 1*

korlan: *Unusual Edible Fruits 6*

kornerupine: *Cat's Eye Gems 21*

korozott: *Cheese International Varieties 6*

koschei: *Demon 16*

kosher pickle: *Pickled/Relish 6*

kosk: *Devil 16*

kowhai: *Shrubs 10*

kozel: *Card Games 5*

krabi: *Swords One-handed 7*

kraft envelope: *Office/School/Writing Supplies 5*

krait: *Animals 15*

kraken: *Aquatic 16; Card Games 5; Mythical Creatures and Monsters 16*

krasotyri: *Cheese International Varieties 6*

krema: *Cheese International Varieties 6*

kribensis: *Aquarium Freshwater Fish 15*

Kris Empu Gadring (kris of Ken Arok): *Weapons of Legend 18*

kris knife: *Daggers and Knives 7*

Krishna Valley: *Other Cows 15*

Krskopolje: *Pigs 15*

Krugerrand: *Coins and Currency 21*

krumping: *Dance Styles 13*

Krypton: *Elements 11*

Kryptos sculpture at the CIA in Langley Virginia: *Real Places Steeped in Legend or Mystery 18*

Ku Klux Klan: *Secret/Mystical Organizations 18*

Kuan Yin (goddess of mercy): *Chinese Pantheon 14*

Kubelwagen 4-wheeler: *Germany Military Vehicles 8*

Kublai Khan: *Real People with Legendary Status 18*

kudu: *Poisonous Plants 10*

kudzu: *Weeds 10*

kufi: *Headgear 2*

kuhli loach: *Aquarium Freshwater Fish 15*

Kuiper belt: *Astronomy General Terms 11*

kukri: *Swords One-handed 7*

kulshedra: *Demon 16*

kumbhakarna: *Demon 16*

kumquat: *Citrus 6*

Kuna: *Native American Peoples 1*

kundalini serpent: *Symbols in Magic and Religion 19*

Kunekune. Lacombe: *Pigs 15*

kung fu master: *Martial Artist/Monk 1*

kunzite: *Minerals 10; Standard Gems 21*

Kurd: *Human Ethnic Groups 1*

Kurdi: *Other Cows 15*

Kuri: *Other Cows 15*

kuru: *Diseases 12*

kurunthadi: *Bludgeons 7*

kuru-pira: *Demon 16*

Kusanagi (sword): *Three Sacred Imperial Relics of Japan 18*

Kusanagi-no-tsurugi (sword of Susanoo): *Weapons of Legend 18*

Kushiel: *Angels of Good 14*

Kushum: *Horse Breeds 15*

Kustanai: *Horse Breeds 15*

kutjera: *Unusual Edible Fruits 6*

kutnohorite: *Minerals 10*

Kuvasz: *Dog Breeds 15*

Kvenland: *Fictional/Mythological Locations 18*

kwai muk: *Unusual Edible Fruits 6*

kwaito: *Cheese International Varieties 6*

kyanite: *Standard Gems 21*

–L–

l'istesso: *Tempo/Mood 13*

L3/35 Carro Veloce light tank: *Italy Military Vehicles 8*

La Belle Lucie: *Solitaire Card Games 5*

la canne: *Bludgeons 7*

la Cote Mal Taile: *Knights of the Round Table 18*

la follia: *Composition Types 13*

lab assistant: *Horror Occupations 23*

lab coat: *Special Purpose Clothing 2*

lab: *Academic Property 3; Rooms 3*

Labanotation: *Ballet Terms 13*

labarum: *Symbols in Magic and Religion 19*

label: *Cadency Mark 19*

labia: *Body Parts 12*

labneh: *Cheese International Varieties 6*

labor camp: *Outdoor Property 3; Prison 3*

laboratory equipment: *Equipment and Tools 5*

laboratory supplies: *Equipment and Tools 5*

laboratory: *Academic Property 3; Business Property 3; Rooms 3; Tables 4*

labored: *Mobility 1*

laborer: *General Occupations 1*

laborious: *Difficult 20*

Labrador Retriever: *Dog Breeds 15*

labradorite: *Standard Gems 21*

labrys: *Symbols in Magic and Religion 19*

labyrinth of Daedalus: *Fictional/Mythological Locations 18*

labyrinth: *Cave Anatomy 10; General Buildings 3; Symbols in Magic and Religion 19; Terrain Features 10*

lace: *Cookie 6; Fabric 2*

lacebark: *Shrubs 10*

Lacerta: *Constellations 11*

lacertid: *Scaled Reptiles 15*

lace-ups: *Footwear/Shoes 2*

lack of cell phone service: *Travel Hazards 9*

lack of radio/TV reception: *Travel Hazards 9*

lack of toilet paper: *Travel Hazards 9*

lackluster: *Sad 20*

lacrimal bone: *Bones 12*

lactonitrile: *Dangerous Chemicals 11*

lacustrine plain: *Geography General Vocabulary 10*

lacy phacelia: *Wildflowers 10*

lacy veil: *Garden Perennials 10*

lad: *Male 1*

ladder: *Boat/Ship Anatomy 9; Large Tools; Siege Equipment 7; Symbols in Magic and Religion 19; Technical Terms 13*

ladderback: *Chairs and Stools 4*

ladenios: *Cheese International Varieties 6*

ladies' gun: *Derringer 7*

ladies' room: *Bathrooms 3*

ladies' tresses: *Garden Perennials 10*

ladies' wear: *Clothing 2*

ladle: *Kitchen Utensils 5*

ladotyri: *Cheese International Varieties 6*

lady apple: *Unusual Edible Fruits 6*

lady bug: *Beetle 15*

lady finger: *Cake 6*

Lady Godiva: *Real People with Legendary Status 18*

lady-in-waiting: *Castle Inhabitants and Personnel 1; Common Character Archetypes 21; Royal/Noble 1, Supporting Cast 24*

lady love: *Female 1*

Lady of Shalot: *Arthurian Characters 18*

lady of the evening: *Illicit Occupations 1*

Lady of the Lake: *Arthurian Characters 18*

lady: *Female 1; Royal/Noble 1*

lady's leek: *Garden Perennials 10*

lady's leg : *Deciduous Trees 10*

lady's maid: *Housekeeping 1*

lady's mantle: *Garden Perennials 10*

lady's: *Desks 4*

ladybells: *Garden Perennials 10*

ladybug: *Harbingers/Charms for Good Luck 19*

ladyfish: *Wild Saltwater Fish 15*

Laestrygonians: *Giants of Legend 16*

Laevateinn: *Norse Weapons 18*

lager: *Beer 6*

lagging: *Slow 20*

lagoon: *Coastal and Oceanic 10*

Lagrange point: *Astronomy General Terms 11*

Laguna agate: *Minerals 10*

Laguna: *Native American Peoples 1*

lahar: *Soil General Vocabulary 10*

laid-back: *Easy 20; Personality Other 1*

laimosphere: *Soil General Vocabulary 10*

lair: *Criminal Property 3; Natural Animal Homes 15; Terrain Features 10*

lairs: *Monsters 16*

Lake Baikal: *Seven Wonders of the Underwater World 18*

lake effect: *Meteorology General Vocabulary 10*

lake perch: *Fish/Seafood Types 6*

Lake Superior agate: *Minerals 10*

lake trout: *Fish/Seafood Types 6; Wild Freshwater Fish 15*

lake: *Water Features 10*

lake-effect precipitation: *Snow Events 10*

lake-effect snow: *Snow Events 10*

Lakeland Terrier: *Dog Breeds 15*

Lakota: *Native American Peoples 1*

Lakshmi (goddess of fortune): *Indian Pantheon 14*

lama: *Cleric 1*

lamassu: *Beast 16*

lamb chops: *Other Meat 6*

lamb: *Animals with Symbolic Meaning 19; Foods with Religious or Ritual Significance 19; Objects/Activities Connected to Lore 19; Other Meat 6*

lamb's ear: *Garden Perennials 10*

Lambert's locoweed: *Garden Perennials 10*

lambs wool: *Shoe Accessories 13*

lame brain Pete: *Poker Card Games 5*

lamé: *Fabric 2; Fencing Equipment 7*

lame: *Kitchen Utensils 5*

lament: *Composition Types 13*

lamentations: *Composition Types 13*

lamia: *Beast 16; Demon 16; Shapechanger 16*

laminar flow cabinet: *Laboratory Equipment 5*

laminar leather: *Armor Types 7*

laminator: *Office/School Machines 5*

Lamona: *Chickens 15*

Lamorak de Gales: *Knights of the Round Table 18*

lamp: *Illumination/Light Sources; Tables 4*

lamproite: *Igneous Rocks 10*

lamprophyre: *Igneous Rocks 10*

lampshade: *Facial Hair Mustache 1*

lance corporal: *U.S. Marines Enlisted 8*

lance of Olyndicus: *Spears 18*

lance rest: *Armor Pieces 7*

lance: *Spears 7; Western Weapons 21*

lancehead: *General Snake Families 15*

lance-headed: *Rattlesnake 15*

lance-leaved coreopsis: *Wildflowers 10*

Lancelot: *Knights of the Round Table 18*

lancet arch: *Castle Anatomy 3*

lancet: *Castle Anatomy 3; Laboratory Equipment 5*

land breeze: *Wind 10*

land creatures: *Classic Heraldry 19*

land improvement: *Soil General Vocabulary 10*

land mine: *Field Equipment 7*

land rush: *Western Paraphernalia/People 21*

landfall: *Meteorology General Vocabulary 10*

landing field: *Infrastructure Buildings 9*

landing net: *Fishing Gear 5*

landing: *Marina 3*

landler (Austria): *Ethnic/Folk Dances 13*

landlord: *Horror Occupations 23*

landscape agate: *Minerals 10*

landscape: *Art Genres 13*

landscaping: *Architecture and Property 3*

landslide: *Geological Natural Hazards 10*

landspout: *Meteorology General Vocabulary 10*

lane: *Roads 9*

langsat: *Unusual Edible Fruits 6*

langued: *Special Body Features 19*

languid: *Slow 20*

languorous: *Slow 20*

langur: *Old World Monkeys 15*

lanky: *Small/Thin 1*

lantana: *Garden Annuals 10; Shrubs 10*

lantern oil: *General Survival Gear 5*

lantern plant: *Garden Perennials 10*

lantern: *Castle Anatomy 3; Chin 1; General Survival Gear 5; Illumination/Light Sources 5; Signal Devices 5*

Lanthanide contraction: *Chemistry General Vocabulary 11*

Lanthanides: *Chemistry General Vocabulary 11*

Lanthanum: *Elements 11*

lanzones: *Unusual Edible Fruits 6*

Laomedeia: *Moons 11*

lap: *Desks 4*

lapel: *Garment Pieces 2*

LaPerm: *Domestic Cats 15*

lapis lazuli: *Minerals 10; Standard Gems 21*

lapis: *Minerals 10*

lappi: *Cheese International Varieties 6*

lapsang souchong: *Tea 6*

lapsi: *Unusual Edible Fruits 6*

laptop computer: *Spy Gear 5*

laptop: *Computer Equipment 5*

lapwing: *Animals with Symbolic Meaning 19*

larch ladybird: *Beetle 15*

larch: *Deciduous Trees 10*

lardizabala: *Unusual Edible Fruits 6*

large barrel: *Containers and Vessels 5*

large belt buckle: *Western Clothing/Dress 21*

large black: *Pigs 15*

large black-white: *Pigs 15*

large chest: *Containers and Vessels 5*

large forest: *Bats 15*

large intestine: *Organs/Major Structures 12*

large light: *Adjectives 20*

large sack: *Containers and Vessels 5*

large scale disaster: *Horror Genres 23*

large shield: *General Snake Families 15*

large shrimp: *Fish/Seafood Types 6*

large tools: *Equipment and Tools 5*

large white: *Pigs 15*

large: *Character Building 1*

large: *Ears 1; Eggs 6; Face 1; Shield Types 7; Teeth 1*

large-eyed: *Pit Viper 15*

large-flower magnolia: *Deciduous Trees 10*

large-flowered waterweed: *Weeds 10*

larger than life: *Large 20*

large-tooth aspen: *Deciduous Trees 10*

larghetto: *Tempo/Mood 13*

largo: *Tempo/Mood 13*

Larim wrist knife: *Hand Weapons 7*

larimar: *Minerals 10; Standard Gems 21*

Larissa: *Moons 11*

larkspur: *Garden Annuals 10; Poisonous Plants 10*

larva: *Ants 15*

larynx: *Organs/Major Structures 12*

Las Vegas: *Styles of Dress 2*

lasagna: *Meals 6; Pasta 6*

laser beam: *Spy Gear 5*

laser guided: *Bomb 8*

laser level: *Architectural/Engineering Tools 5*

laser line level: *Architectural/Engineering Tools 5*

laser measuring tool: *Architectural/Engineering Tools 5*

laser pointer: *Office/School Machines 5*

laser: *Weapons 22*

lass: *Female 1*

lassa fever: *Diseases 12*

lassie: *Female 1*

lasso: *Flexible 7; Western Weapons 21*

last one: *Card Games 5*

last person on Earth: *Horror Plot Devices 23; Plot Devices 22*

last rites: *Sacraments 14*

last: *Ending 20; Old 20*

late baroque: *Musical Period 13*

late harvest riesling: *Wine White 6*

late: *Personality Other 1*

lateral cuneiform bone: *Bones 12*

lateral earth pressure: *Soil General Vocabulary 10*

lateral file cabinet: *Storage 4*

lateral incisor: *Teeth 12*

lateral parry: *Fencing Vocabulary 7*

laterite: *Sedimentary Rocks 10*

latest: *New 20*

latex gloves: *Spy Gear 5*

latex paint: *Art Materials 5; Art Media 13*

latex: *Allergies 12*

lathe: *Hand Tools 5*

lathi: *Bludgeons 7*

Latin: *Crosses 19*

latite: *Igneous Rocks 10*

latitude: *Boat/Ship Terminology 9; Geography General Vocabulary 10*

latrine: *Bathrooms 3*

latte: *Coffee Drinks 6*

lattice: *Pie 6*

Latvian Brown: *Other Cows 15*

Latvian white: *Pigs 15*

Latvian: *Horse Breeds 15; Human Ethnic Groups 1*

latvijas: *Cheese International Varieties 6*

laugh and lie down: *Card Games 5*

laugh: *Sounds 20*

laughing: *Owls 15*

launch: *Attack 7; Boat/Ship Terminology 9; Locomotion 9; Marina 3*

launder: *Clean 20*

laundry: *Objects/Activities Connected to Lore 19; Rooms 3*

laurel leaf oak: *Deciduous Trees 10*

laurel magnolia: *Deciduous Trees 10*

laurel oak: *Deciduous Trees 10*

laurel: *Deciduous Trees 10*

laus: *Card Games 5*

lava cave: *Cave Anatomy 10*

lava dome: *Volcanic 10*

lava flow: *Volcanic 10*

lava lake: *Volcanic 10*

lava lamp: *Illumination/Light Sources 5*

lava plain: *Volcanic 10*

lava spine: *Volcanic 10*

lava tube: *Volcanic 10*

lava: *Cake 6; Elemental 16; Geography General Vocabulary 10; Geological Natural Hazards 10; Geological Vocabulary 10*

lavaka: *Erosion 10*

lavalier microphone: *Technical Terms 13*

lavash: *Bread General Varieties 6*

lavatory: *Bathrooms 3; Rooms 3*

lavender amethyst: *Minerals 10*

lavender cotton: *Garden Perennials 10; Shrubs 10*

lavender monkey flower: *Garden Perennials 10*

lavender pink: *Pink 20*

lavender: *Eye Color 1; Purple 20; Shrubs 10*

law enforcement: *Character Building 1*

law of combining volumes: *Chemistry General Vocabulary 11*

law of conservation of energy: *Chemistry General Vocabulary 11*

law of conservation of matter and energy: *Chemistry General Vocabulary 11*

law of conservation of matter: *Chemistry General Vocabulary 11*

law of definite proportions: *Chemistry General Vocabulary 11*

law of partial pressures: *Chemistry General Vocabulary 11*

law of superposition: *Geologic Concepts 10*

lawbreaker: *Illicit Occupations 1*

lawman: *Law Enforcement 1*

lawn aerator: *Power Tools*

lawn edger: *Power Tools*

lawn green: *Green 20*

lawn mower: *Power Tools*

lawn roller: *Large Tools*

lawn sweeper: *Large Tools*

lawn: *Fabric 2; Landscaping 3*

Lawrencium: *Elements 11*

Lawson cypress: *Evergreen Trees 10*

Lawson false cypress: *Evergreen Trees 10*

lawyer: *Horror Occupations 23; Legal Occupations 1*

lawyer's wig: *Fungus Common Names 10*

lay out: *Sewing Techniques 2*

lay waste: *Kill 20*

layer: *Cake 6*

layered: *Hair Style 1; Salads 6*

laying on of hands: *Rituals 14*

lazy daisy: *Embroidery Stitches 2*

lazy spouse/child: *Common Character Archetypes 21*

lazy: *Negative 1; Personality Other 1*

le seur peas: *Vegetables 6*

le wavreumont: *Cheese International Varieties 6*

leach: *Wet 20*

leaching model: *Soil General Vocabulary 10*

leaching: *Geography General Vocabulary 10; Soil General Vocabulary 10*

lead glance: *Minerals 10*

lead pipe: *Improvised Weapons 7*

lead plant: *Garden Perennials 10*

lead spar: *Minerals 10*

lead storage battery: *Chemistry General Vocabulary 11*

lead: *Beginning 20*

Lead: *Elements 11*

leaded glass: *Building Elements and Features 3*

leaden: *Sad 20; Slow 20*

leader: *Beginning 20; Fighter 1; Musical Occupations 1*

lead-footed: *Heavy 20*

leading role: *Hero 20*

leading seaman: *Navy Other Titles 8*

leading staff: *Pole Weapons 7*

leading-light: *Wizard 1*

leadplant: *Wildflowers 10*

leadwort: *Garden Annuals 10; Garden Perennials 10; Shrubs 10*

leaf blower: *Power Tools*

leaf insect: *Phasmid 15*

leaf lettuce: *Vegetables 6*

leaf monkey: *Old World Monkeys 15*

leaf: *Viper 15*

leaf-chinned: *Bats 15*

leafcutter: *Ants 15*

leafcutting: *Bees 15*

leaf-nosed: *Bats 15; Viper 15*

leaf-shaped: *Daggers and Knives 7*

leafwing: *Butterfly 15*

leafy spurge: *Weeds 10*

leak: *Wet 20*

leakage: *Wet 20*

lean: *Small/Thin 1*

Leaning Tower of Pisa: *Seven Wonders of the Middle Ages 18; Unique Property 3*

lean-to: *Outdoor Property 3; Residential Property 3; Roof Styles 3*

leap: *Locomotion 9*

learn: *Verbs 20*

leash: *Jewelry 21*

least duckweed: *Weeds 10*

leather apron: *Western Clothing/Dress 21*

leather cap: *Head Gear 7*

leather coat: *Armor Pieces 7*

leather coif: *Head Gear 7*

leather glove: *Fencing Equipment 7*

leather gloves: *Unisex Clothing 2*

leather jack: *Wild Saltwater Fish 15*

leather rope: *General Survival Gear 5*

leather sack: *Containers and Vessels 5*

leather: *Armor Types 7; Chairs and Stools 4; Door Materials 3; Fabric 2; Horse Barding Materials 7*

leatherback: *Sea Turtles 15*

leatherleaf: *Shrubs 10*

leatherwood: *Shrubs 10*

leave: *Commands 20; Locomotion 9*

Lebanese: *Human Ethnic Groups 1*

lechosos opal: *Minerals 10*

Leclanché cell: *Chemistry General Vocabulary 11*

Leçon: *Ballet Terms 13*

lectern: *Special Purpose Furniture 4*

lecture hall: *Academic Property 3*

lecture room: *Academic Property 3*

lecture: *Teach 20*

LED: *Illumination Bulb and Tube Types 5*

Leda: *Moons 11*

ledge: *Building Elements and Features 3; Cave Anatomy 10*

ledum: *Shrubs 10*

leech: *Giant Creatures 16*

Lee-Enfield SMLE: *Bolt Action Centerfire Rifles 7*

leek: *Vegetables 6*

leery: *Horror Vocabulary 23*

leeward: *Boat/Ship Terminology 9; Geography General Vocabulary 10; Meteorology General Vocabulary 10*

leeway: *Boat/Ship Terminology 9*

lefse: *Bread General Varieties 6*

left-hand dagger: *Daggers and Knives 7*

left-handed grip: *Fencing Vocabulary 7*

leg o'mutton sleeve: *Garment Pieces 2*

leg warmers: *Accessories 2; Dance Clothing 13*

leg: *Body Parts 12; Cave Anatomy 10*

Legacy Escort: *Shotguns Semiautomatic 7*

Legacy Howa: *Bolt Action Centerfire Rifles 7*

Legacy Puma M92: *Lever Action and Pump Centerfire Rifles 7*

legal aide: *Legal Occupations 1*

legal assistant: *Legal Occupations 1*

legal pad: *Office/School/Writing Supplies 5*

legal secretary: *Legal Occupations 1*

legal: *Character Building 1*

legally blind: *Eye Type 1*

legato: *Tempo/Mood 13*

legend: *Geography General Vocabulary 10; Literary Styles 5*

legendary events: *Legendary, Mystical and Mythical Items and Locations 18*

legendary people presumed to be fictional: *Legendary, Mystical and Mythical Items and Locations 18*

legendary: *Personality Other 1*

leggero: *Tempo/Mood 13*

leggings: *Dance Clothing 13; Ladies' Wear 2*

leghold: *Traps 3*

leghorn bonnet: *Headgear 2*

Legionnaires' disease: *Diseases 12*

legless lizard: *Scaled Reptiles 15*

legno: *Instrument Technique 13*

legs: *Technical Terms 13*

legumes: *Food 6*

Leicoma: *Pigs 15*

leipajuusto: *Cheese International Varieties 6*

leisure suit: *Men's Wear 2*

leisurely: *Slow 20*

leitmotif: *General Music Vocabulary 13*

Leliel: *Angels of Good 14*

lemmy: *Facial Hair Beard 1*

lemniscate: *Symbols in Magic and Religion 19*

lemon chiffon: *Yellow 20*

lemon cream: *Pie 6*

lemon lace vine: *Garden Perennials 10*

lemon lily: *Garden Perennials 10*

lemon meringue: *Pie 6*

lemon mint: *Wildflowers 10*

lemon opal: *Minerals 10*

lemon poppyseed: *Muffin 6*

lemon quartz: *Minerals 10*

lemon tetra: *Aquarium Freshwater Fish 15*

lemon twist: *Cocktail Garnishes 6*

lemon wheel: *Cocktail Garnishes 6*

lemon: *Ants 15; Cake 6; Citrus 6; Ice Cream Flavors 6; Oils 6*

lemonade: *Amusement Park/Carnival/Circus/Fair 3; Fruit Drinks 6*

lemon-lime soda: *Soft Drinks 6*

lemur: *Other Wild Mammals 15*

Lemuria: *Fictional/Mythological Locations 18*

Lenape: *Native American Peoples 1*

lengthy: *Slow 20*

lens: *Wizard's Goods 5*

Lenten rose: *Garden Perennials 10*

lentic freshwater: *Ecosystems 10*

lenticular galaxy: *Astronomy General Terms 11*

lentil: *Legumes 6; Soup 6*

lento: *Tempo/Mood 13*

Leo (July 23–August 22): *Zodiac Signs 19*

Leo Minor: *Constellations 11*

Leo: *Constellations 11*

Leodegrance: *Knights of the Round Table 18*

Leonberger: *Dog Breeds 15*

Leonese: *Human Ethnic Groups 1*

Leopard I tank: *Germany Military Vehicles 8*

leopard jasper: *Minerals 10*

leopard lizard: *Scaled Reptiles 15*

leopard plant: *Garden Perennials 10*

leopard stone: *Minerals 10*

leopard: *Butterfly 15; Fur 2; Tortoises 15*

Leopard: *Tanks German 8*

leopard's bane: *Garden Perennials 10*

leotard: *Dance Clothing 13; Ladies' Wear 2*

lepidolite: *Standard Gems 21*

lepidomelane: *Minerals 10*

leprechaun: *General Fae 16; St. Patrick's Day 19*

Leprechaun: *Human Races Fictional 1*

leprosy: *Diseases 12*

leptophos: *Dangerous Chemicals 11*

leptosol: *Soil General Vocabulary 10*

Lepus: *Constellations 11*

Lernaean hydra: *Twelve Labors of Hercules 16*

Les Baer Custom Police Special: *Semiautomatic Centerfire Rifles 7*

Les Baer Custom Ultimate AR: *Semiautomatic Centerfire Rifles 7*

Les Baer H.C. 40: *Pistol Semiautomatic 7*

leshii: *Devil 16*

lesser black: *Krait 15*

lesser brown: *Scorpion 15*

Lesser Key of Solomon: *Books of Legend 18*

lesser masked: *Owls 15*

lesser sooty: *Owls 15*

lesser yellow underwing: *Moth 15*

lesser: *Small/Fragile 20*

lessivage: *Soil General Vocabulary 10*

lestovka prayer string: *Objects in Magic and Religion 19*

let go: *Open/Release 20*

let it ride: *Card Games 5*

let loose: *Open/Release 20*

lethal webcaps: *Fungus Common Names 10*

lethal: *Horror Vocabulary 23*

lethargic: *Mobility 1; Personality Other 1; Sad 20; Slow 20*

Let-Tec PF9: *Pistol Semiautomatic 7*

letter G: *Symbols of Freemasonry 19*

Letterism: *Art Movements 13*

letterpress: *Art Media 13*

lettsomite: *Minerals 10*

lettuce edge: *Embellishments 2*

lettuce: *Items with Healing Properties 19*

leuco-garnet: *Minerals 10*

leucoxene: *Minerals 10*

leukemia: *Blood-Related Ailments 12*

leukocyte: *Blood 12*

levant: *Viper 15*

Levante: *Winds of the Mediterranean 10*

level and plumbline: *Symbols of Freemasonry 19*

leveling effect: *Chemistry General Vocabulary 11*

lever action: *Shotguns General 7*

leviathan: *Aquatic 16*

Leviathan: *Crosses 19*

levin opal: *Minerals 10*

levitate: *Locomotion 9*

levitation: *Magical Transportation 17; Paranormal Abilities 21; Paranormal Occurrences 21*

lewisite: *Dangerous Chemicals 11*

ley energy: *Energy Sources/Types 24*

ley line: *Energy Sources/Types 23; Travel Modes 23; Witchcraft Vocabulary 17*

ley portal: *Travel Modes 24*

ley: *Spaceship Drive Systems 22; Travel Types 22*

leyak: *Demon 16*

leycesteria: *Shrubs 10*

Leyden: *Card Games 5*

Lhasa Apso: *Dog Breeds 15*

lherzolite: *Igneous Rocks 10*

Lia Fail: *Four Hallows of Ireland 18*

liaison: *Law Enforcement 1*

liar: *Thief 1*

Libeccio: *Winds of the Mediterranean 10*

liberal: *Large 20*

liberate: *Open/Release 20*

liberator: *Hero 20*

Liberian black mud: *Freshwater Turtles 15*

Liberica: *Coffee Varieties 6*

Libertarian Republican: *Political Parties 1*

Liberty bell: *Independence Day 19*

Liberty spikes: *Hair Style 1*

Libra (September 23–October 22): *Zodiac Signs 19*

Libra: *Constellations 11*

libram: *Witchcraft Vocabulary 17*

librarian: *Academic 1*

library lamp: *Illumination/Light Sources 5*

Library of Alexandria: *Unique Property Destroyed 3*

library: *Academic Property 3; Rooms 3*

libration: *Astronomy General Terms 11*

libretto: *Printed Music 13*

lice: *Ten Plagues on Egypt 14*

lich: *Undead 16*

lickety-split: *Fast 20*

licorice pastel: *Candy General 6*

licorice wheel: *Candy General 6*

licorice: *Candy General 6*

liddicoatite: *Minerals 10*

liderc: *Demon 16*

liebfraumilch: *Wine White 6*

Liechtenstein: *Human Ethnic Groups 1*

lied: *General Music Vocabulary 13*

lieutenant colonel: *U.S. Air Force Officer 8; U.S. Army Officer 8; U.S. Marines Officer 8*

lieutenant commander: *U.S. Navy Officer 8*

lieutenant general: *U.S. Air Force Officer 8; U.S. Army Officer 8; U.S. Marines Officer 8*

lieutenant junior grade: *U.S. Navy Officer 8*

lieutenant: *Fighter 1; Maritime Occupations 1; U.S. Navy Officer 8*

life boat: *Human-Powered Watercraft 9*

life cycle: *Geography General Vocabulary 10*

life imitating art: *Philosophy Basic Concepts 14*

life jacket: *Boat/Ship Anatomy 9*

life leech: *Paranormal Abilities 21*

life line: *Boat/Ship Anatomy 9*

life raft: *Human-Powered Watercraft 9*

life saver: *Hero 20*

life support failure: *Common Dangers 22*

life support suit: *Clothing/Uniforms 22*

Life: *Major Lines 19*

lifeguard: *General Occupations 1*

lifeless: *Horror Vocabulary 23; Sad 20*

lifeline: *Military Equipment 8*

lifesaving stroke: *Swimming Strokes 9*

ligament: *Organs/Major Structures 12*

ligature: *General Music Vocabulary 13*

liger: *Tigers 15*

light as air: *Light 20*

light battleship: *Military Watercraft 8*

light blue: *Blue 20*

light brown apple: *Moth 15*

light brown sugar: *Staples 6*

light bulbs: *Equipment and Tools 5*

light capital ship: *Military Watercraft 8*

light chain: *Fasteners 5*

light corn syrup: *Staples 6*

light cream: *Other Dairy 6*

light cruiser: *Military Watercraft 8; Spaceship Types 22*

light destroyer: *Military Watercraft 8*

light fixture: *Building Systems 3; Illumination/Light Sources 5*

light fleet aircraft carrier: *Military Watercraft 8*

light generation: *Physical Mutations 22*

light industry: *Geography General Vocabulary 10*

light mortar: *Mortar 8*

light opal: *Minerals 10*

light rain: *Precipitation 10*

light reconnaissance vehicle: *Military Ground Vehicles General 8*

light red kidney bean: *Legumes 6*

light rope: *General Survival Gear 5*

light rye: *Bread General Varieties 6*

light sources: *Equipment and Tools 5*

light speed: *Travel Types 22*

light string: *Fasteners 5*

light support weapon: *Military Weapons General 8*

light switch: *Building Systems 3*

light tank: *Military Ground Vehicles General 8*

light tubes: *Equipment and Tools 5*

light wind: *Wind 10*

light year: *Astronomy General Terms 11*

light yogurt: *Other Dairy 6*

light: *Art Media 13; Beer 6; Candy Chocolate 6; Philosophy Basic Concepts 14; Vocal/Speech Quality 1*

lightbulb goes on: *Solve 20*

lighter: *Illumination/Light Sources 5*

lighthearted: *Happy 20; Personality Other 1*

Lighthouse at Alexandria: *Seven Wonders of the Ancient World 18; Unique Property Destroyed 3*

lighthouse: *Marina 3; Signal Devices 5*

lighting designer: *Performing Arts 1*

lighting magnifier: *Illumination/Light Sources 5*

lighting plan: *Technical Terms 13*

lightning bolt image: *Harbingers/Charms for Good Luck 19*

lightning fast: *Fast 20*

lightning quick: *Fast 20*

lightning ridge opal: *Minerals 10*

lightning rod: *Physical Mutations 22*

lightning strike: *General Combat Vocabulary 7*

lightning: *Energy Sources/Types 23; Severe Weather 10; Traps 3*

lights: *Christmas 19*

lightweight: *Light 20*

lighvan: *Cheese International Varieties 6*

Ligne: *Ballet Terms 13*

lignite: *Sedimentary Rocks 10*

likable: *Happy 20*

like a foghorn: *Vocal/Speech Quality 1*

like fingernails on a chalkboard: *Vocal/Speech Quality 1*

like lightning: *Fast 20*

like shooting fish in a barrel: *Easy 20*

like: *Love 20*

liking: *General Emotions 20*

lilac: *Purple 20; Shrubs 10*

Lilith: *Devil 16*

Lilliputian: *Small/Fragile 20*

lillypilly: *Unusual Edible Fruits 6*

lily of the valley: *Garden Bulbs 10; Garden Perennials 10; Poisonous Plants 10*

lily: *Garden Bulbs 10; Garden Perennials 10; Plants with Symbolic Meaning 19*

lily-of-the-valley tree: *Deciduous Trees 10*

lilyturf: *Garden Perennials 10*

lima bean: *Legumes 6*

limb: *Astronomy General Terms 11; Body Parts 12*

limber: *Mobility 1*

limbic cortex: *Organs/Major Structures 12*

limbic: *Beer 6; Body Systems 12*

limbo: *Afterlife/Underworld 18*

limburger: *Cheese International Varieties 6*

lime juice: *Mixers 6*

lime wedge: *Cocktail Garnishes 6*

lime wheel: *Cocktail Garnishes 6*

lime: *Butterfly 15; Citrus 6; Green 20*

limeade: *Fruit Drinks 6*

limeberry: *Unusual Edible Fruits 6*

limelight: *Illumination/Light Sources 5; Technical Terms 13*

limequat: *Unusual Edible Fruits 6*

lime-soda feldspar: *Minerals 10*

limestone cave: *Cave Anatomy 10*

limestone onyx: *Minerals 10*

limestone pavement: *Erosion 10*

limestone: *Cave Anatomy 10; Minerals 10; Sedimentary Rocks 10*

Liming soil: *Soil General Vocabulary 10*

limit: *Close/Hold 20*

limited-access highway: *Roads 9*

limitless: *Large 20*

Limousin: *Other Cows 15*

limousine: *Motorized 9*

limping: *Mobility 1*

Limpurger: *Other Cows 15*

linamarase: *Poisonous Chemicals in Plants 11*

linamarin: *Poisonous Chemicals in Plants 11*

Lincoln Red: *Other Cows 15*

Lincolnshire curly-coated: *Pigs 15*

lindane: *Dangerous Chemicals 11*

linden: *Deciduous Trees 10*

lindy hop: *Dance Styles 13*

line dancing: *Dance Styles 13*

line diagonal: *Figures Associated with Symbols 19*

line horizontal: *Figures Associated with Symbols 19*

line of defense: *General Combat Vocabulary 7*

line vertical: *Figures Associated with Symbols 19*

line wavy: *Figures Associated with Symbols 19*

line: *Boat/Ship Anatomy 9; Fasteners 5; Fencing Vocabulary 7; Figures Associated with Symbols 19; Fishing Gear 5; Roads 9; Sewing Techniques 2; Visual Elements 13*

linear accelerator: *Chemistry General Vocabulary 11*

linear aeration: *Soil General Vocabulary 10*

linen service: *Public Services 3*

linen: *Fabric 2; White 20*

linens: *Equipment and Tools 5*

liner plate: *Tableware 5*

liner: *Large Watercraft 9*

ling cod: *Wild Saltwater Fish 15*

lingam: *Symbols in Magic and Religion 19*

lingerie: *Ladies' Wear 2*

lingering: *Slow 20*

lingonberry: *Berries 6*

linguine: *Pasta 6*

linguistics: *Philosophy Basic Concepts 14*

lining: *Fabric 2; Garment Pieces 2*

link up: *Fix 20*

linsey-woolsey: *Fabric 2*

lint brush: *Cleaning Supplies/Gadgets 5*

lint: *Wizard's Goods 5*

lintel: *Building Elements and Features 3; Castle Anatomy 3*

lion (China): *Ethnic/Folk Dances 13*

lion of Judah: *Symbols in Magic and Religion 19*

lion tamarin: *New World Monkeys 15*

lion: *Animals with Symbolic Meaning 19; Big Cats 15; Brown 20; Yellow 20*

lion's mane: *Jellyfish 15*

Lionel: *Knights of the Round Table 18*

lioness: *Big Cats 15*

lionfish: *Aquarium Saltwater Fish 15*

lions rampant: *Patterns 19*

lions: *Animals 15*

lioumere: *Demon 16*

lip: *Bears 15; Body Parts 12*

lip gloss: *Makeup 5*

lip liner: *Makeup 5*

Lipizzan: *Horse Breeds 15*

lips: *Character Building 1*

lipstick: *Candy General 6; Makeup 5*

liptauer: *Cheese International Varieties 6*

liquefaction: *Geological Natural Hazards 10; Geological Vocabulary 10*

liquefied: *Wet 20*

liquid leaks in luggage: *Travel Hazards 9*

liquid manure spreader: *General Farm Equipment*

liquid silver: *Minerals 10*

liquid: *Wet 20*

liquor: *Wet 20*

liripipe: *Headgear 2*

lisp: *Vocal/Speech Quality 1*

lissome: *Mobility 1*

list of possible magical effects: *Magic 17*

list: *Christmas 19; Laboratory Supplies 5*

listening device: *Spy Gear 5*

listeriosis: *Diseases 12*

listless: *Personality Other 1; Sad 20; Slow 20*

litany: *Rituals 14*

literary styles: *Equipment and Tools 5*

literature: *Card Games 5*

lithe: *Mobility 1*

lithium hydride: *Dangerous Chemicals 11*

lithium mica: *Minerals 10*

Lithium: *Elements 11*

lithosphere: *Geography General Vocabulary 10*

lithostratigraphy: *Geologic Fields of Study 10*

lithoxyl opal: *Minerals 10*

Lithuanian Heavy Draft: *Horse Breeds 15*

Lithuanian native: *Pigs 15*

Lithuanian Red: *Other Cows 15*

Lithuanian white: *Pigs 15*

Lithuanian: *Human Ethnic Groups 1*

litmus paper: *Laboratory Supplies 5*

litter: *Animal-Powered Transportation 9; Dogs/Canine 15; Human-Powered Transportation 9*

Little Bighorn: *Famous Western Locations 21*

Little Bo Peep: *Fictional Characters 18*

little boys' room: *Bathrooms 3*

little David: *Mortar 8*

little drummer boy: *Christmas 19*

little fruit: *Bats 15*

little girls' room: *Bathrooms 3*

little lady: *Female 1*

little pickles: *Garden Perennials 10*

Little Red Riding Hood: *Fictional Characters 18*

little walnut: *Deciduous Trees 10*

little: *Bats 15; Owls 15; Small/Fragile 20; Small/Thin 1*

littleleaf mock orange: *Garden Perennials 10*

littoral terrain warfare: *General Combat Vocabulary 7*

liuyedao: *Swords One-handed 7*

live cave: *Cave Anatomy 10*

live oak: *Deciduous Trees 10*

livebearer: *Aquarium Freshwater Fish 15*

lively: *Happy 20; Mobility 1*

liver opal: *Minerals 10*

liver: *Beef 6; Brown 20; Organs/Major Structures 12*

liverleaf: *Garden Perennials 10*

Liverpool rummy: *Card Games 5*

livestock trailer: *Farm Transportation 9*

livid: *Angry 1*

living room: *Rooms 3*

livno: *Cheese International Varieties 6*

Livny: *Pigs 15*

lixisol: *Soil General Vocabulary 10*

liza: *Wild Saltwater Fish 15*

lizard fish: *Wild Saltwater Fish 15*

lizard folk: *Humanoid 16*

lizard tail: *Garden Perennials 10*

lizard: *Giant Creatures 16*

lizardite: *Minerals 10*

lizardman: *Humanoid 16*

llama: *Other Wild Mammals 15; Transportation Animals 9*

Llamrei: *Arthur's Horses 18*

Llandovery Age: *Geologic Time 10*

LMT Defender: *Semiautomatic Centerfire Rifles 7*

loach: *Aquarium Freshwater Fish 15*

loaded: *Heavy 20*

loader: *General Farm Equipment*

loaf: *Bread General Varieties 6*

loafers: *Footwear/Shoes 2*

loam: *Soil General Vocabulary 10*

loan shark: *Illicit Occupations 1*

loath: *Horror Vocabulary 23*

loathing: *General Emotions 20*

loathsome: *Unattractive 20*

loba: *Card Games 5*

Lobatse hinge-back: *Tortoises 15*

lobby: *Parts of the Theater 13; Rooms 3*

lobbyist: *Legal Occupations 1*

lobelia: *Garden Annuals 10*

Lobera: *Weapons of Legend 18*

loblolly bay: *Deciduous Trees 10; Shrubs 10*

loblolly pine: *Evergreen Trees 10*

lobster fork: *Eating Utensils 5*

lobster pick: *Eating Utensils 5*

lobster: *Fish/Seafood Types 6*

locathah: *Humanoid 16*

Loch Ness monster: *Mythical Creatures and Monsters 16*

Loch Ness: *Real Places Steeped in Legend or Mystery 18*

lock picks: *Specialty Survival Gear 5; Spy Gear 5*

lock up: *Close/Hold 20*

lock: *Close/Hold 20; Office/School/Writing Supplies 5; Traps 3; Water Terms 9; Windows 3; Wizard's Goods 5*

locker: *Boat/Ship Anatomy 9; Office/School/Writing Supplies 5; Storage 4*

locket: *Jewelry 21*

locking pliers: *Hand Tools 5*

locks: *Equipment and Tools 5*

lockup: *Prison 3*

locomotion: *Transportation 9; Verbs 20*

locomotive: *Railroad 9*

locust: *Deciduous Trees 10; Orthoptera 15*

locusts: *Ten Plagues on Egypt 14*

loden: *Fabric 2*

lodestone: *Minerals 10; Specialty Survival Gear 5; Wizard's Goods 5*

lodge: *Hospitality 3; Natural Animal Homes 15; Outdoor Property 3; Residential Property 3*

lodgepole pine: *Evergreen Trees 10*

loess: *Aeolian 10; Geological Vocabulary 10; Soil General Vocabulary 10*

loft: *Beds 4; Rooms 3*

log cabin: *Residential Property 3*

log: *Boat/Ship Anatomy 9; Bridges 9; Exterior Building Materials 3; Improvised Weapons 7; Laboratory Supplies 5*

loganberry: *Berries 6*

logbook: *Laboratory Supplies 5*

Loge: *Moons 11*

loge: *Parts of the Theater 13*

logger: *Rural Occupations 1*

loggerhead: *Sea Turtles 15*

logic: *Philosophy Basic Concepts 14*

logician: *Wizard 1*

logistics: *General Combat Vocabulary 7; Operations 1*

logos: *Philosophy Basic Concepts 14*

Lohani: *Other Cows 15*

Lohot: *Knights of the Round Table 18*

loin chop: *Pork 6*

loin guard: *Armor Pieces 7*

loin roast: *Pork 6*

loitering: *Slow 20*

Lokai: *Horse Breeds 15*

Loki (god of evil): *Norse Pantheon 14*

löllingite: *Minerals 10*

lollipop: *Candy General 6*

London Eye: *Unique Property 3*

London lowball: *Poker Card Games 5*

London Sewerage System: *Seven Wonders of the Industrial World 18*

loner: *Common Character Archetypes 21*

long bow: *Missile Weapons 7*

long gloves: *Unisex Clothing 2*

long in the tooth: *Elderly 1*

long John: *Donut/doughnut 6*

long johns: *Unisex Clothing 2*

long skirt: *Ladies' Wear 2*

long sleeve leotard: *Dance Clothing 13*

long sleeve t-shirt: *Unisex Clothing 2*

long sleeve: *Garment Pieces 2*

long sword (England): *Ethnic/Folk Dances 13*

long underwear: *Unisex Clothing 2*

long weekend: *Journey 20*

long: *Ears 1; Facial Hair Beard 1; Hair Style 1; Swords One-handed 7; Teeth 1*

longan: *Unusual Edible Fruits 6*

longanimity: *Twelve Fruits of the Holy Spirit 19*

long-beaked willow: *Deciduous Trees 10*

long-beaked: *Dolphins 15*

longbill spearfish: *Wild Saltwater Fish 15*

longboard: *Human-Powered Transportation 9*

long-eared myotis: *Bats 15*

long-eared: *Owls 15*

longevity fruit: *Unusual Edible Fruits 6*

long-fin swordtail: *Aquarium Freshwater Fish 15*

longfin: *Sharks 15*

longhorn cheddar: *Cheese Common Varieties 6*

longhorned cowfish: *Aquarium Saltwater Fish 15*

longitude: *Boat/Ship Terminology 9; Geography General Vocabulary 10*

longkong: *Unusual Edible Fruits 6*

longleaf Casuarina: *Evergreen Trees 10*

long-legged: *Bats 15; Flies 15*

long-limbed: *Large/Heavy 1*

long-line bra: *Ladies' Wear 2*

long-nosed: *Adder 15; Bats 15; Viper 15*

longship: *Human-Powered Watercraft 9*

long-snouted: *Bats 15*

long-standing: *Old 20*

long-suffering: *Negative 1*

longtail: *Butterfly 15*

long-tailed: *Bats 15; Rattlesnake 15*

long-tongued: *Bats 15*

long-whiskered owlet: *Owls 15*

lonsdaleite: *Minerals 10*

loo: *Bathrooms 3; Card Games 5*

looking glass: *Wizard's Goods 5*

lookout: *Fighter 1; Maritime Occupations 1; Supporting Cast 24*

loon: *Other Wild Birds 15*

loop: *Jewelry 21; Traps 3*

loophole: *Castle Anatomy 3*

loose leaf paper: *Office/School/Writing Supplies 5*

loose powder: *Makeup 5*

loose rock: *Geological Natural Hazards 10*

loosestrife: *Garden Perennials 10*

looter: *Thief 1*

looting: *General Combat Vocabulary 7*

Lopingian Age: *Geologic Time 10*

lopping shears: *Garden Tools*

loquacious: *Personality Other 1*

loquat: *Shrubs 10; Unusual Edible Fruits 6*

lora: *General Snake Families 15*

Lord almighty: *Expletives 20*

Lord Howe Island stick: *Phasmid 15*

lord: *Hero 20*

lords and ladies: *Poisonous Plants 10*

lordy lordy: *Expletives 20*

lore master: *Bard 1; Nature Occupations 1*

lorelei: *Water Faerie 16*

lori: *Cheese International Varieties 6*

lorikeet: *Domesticated Pet Birds 15*

Lorraine: *Crosses 19*

Los Angeles class attack submarine: *U.S. Navy Vessels 8*

losing lodam: *Card Games 5*

Losino: *Horse Breeds 15*

loss of space shuttle Columbia: *Legendary Events 18*

lost colony of Roanoke: *Famous Disappearances 18*

lost culture is discovered: *Fantasy Plot Devices 24*

lost luggage: *Travel Hazards 9*

lost magical object is found: *Fantasy Plot Devices 24*

lost reservations: *Travel Hazards 9*

lost sites: *Legendary, Mystical and Mythical Items and Locations 18; Legendary/Mythical Locations 18*

lost soldier: *Common Character Archetypes 21*

lost valley: *Fantasy Locations 24*

lost: *Gnome 1*

lotaustralin: *Poisonous Chemicals in Plants 11*

lotic freshwater: *Ecosystems 10*

lots of running: *Travel Modes 23*

lotus flower: *Eight Ashtamangala 19; Symbols in Magic and Religion 19*

lotus: *Plants with Symbolic Meaning 19*

loud: *Adjectives 20; Personality Other 1; Vocal/Speech Quality 1*

loud-mouthed: *Loud 20*

Louis heels: *Footwear/Shoes 2*

lounge chair: *Chairs and Stools 4*

lounge pants: *Unisex Clothing 2*

loungewear: *Styles of Dress 2*

loup garou: *Lycanthrope 16*

loupe: *Laboratory Equipment 5*

Lourdais: *Other Cows 15*

loure (France): *Ethnic/Folk Dances 13*

lout: *Villain 20*

louvre: *Castle Anatomy 3*

lovable rogue: *Common Character Archetypes 21*

love in a mist: *Garden Annuals 10*

love: *General Emotions 20; Philosophy Basic Concepts 14; Terms of Endearment 1; Verbs 20*

lovebird: *Domesticated Pet Birds 15*

Lovejoy: *Comets 11*

lovely fir: *Evergreen Trees 10*

lovely: *Beautiful 20; Good 20; Personality Other 1*

lover: *Terms of Endearment 1*

lovers: *Common Character Archetypes 21*

loveseat: *Seating 4*

Loviatar (goddess of pain): *Finnish Pantheon 14*

loving: *Positive 1*

low chest: *Storage 4*

low Chicago: *Poker Card Games 5*

low clouds: *Meteorology General Vocabulary 10*

low fat cottage: *Cheese Moist 6*

low fat milk: *Dairy Beverages 6*

low fat sour cream: *Other Dairy 6*

low fat: *Milk 6*

low line attack: *Fencing Vocabulary 7*

low line counterattack: *Fencing Vocabulary 7*

low line parry: *Fencing Vocabulary 7*

low pressure system: *Meteorology General Vocabulary 10*

low rise jeans: *Unisex Clothing 2*

low spin complex: *Chemistry General Vocabulary 11*

low: *Boots 2; Forehead 1; Meteorology General Vocabulary 10; Poker Card Games 5; Quiet 20; Unattractive 20; Vocal/Speech Quality 1*

Low's Japanese creeper: *Garden Perennials 10*

lowball: *Poker Card Games 5*

lowboy: *Storage 4*

Lowbrow: *Art Movements 13*

Löwchen: *Dog Breeds 15*

low class: *Personality Other 1*

lower class: *Social Distinction 1*

lowfat: *Ice Cream 6*

low-key: *Quiet 20*

lowland hackberry: *Deciduous Trees 10*

lowland: *Geological Vocabulary 10; Swords Two-handed 7; Terrain Features 10*

lowly: *Personality Other 1*

low-spirited: *Sad 20*

loyal: *Love 20; Personality Other 1*

loyalist: *Hero 20*

loyalty: *Philosophy Basic Concepts 14*

lozenge: *Figures Associated with Symbols 19*

LSVW 4x4 utility vehicle: *Italy Military Vehicles 8*

Lu Yueh (epidemics): *Chinese Pantheon 14*

Lucan: *Knights of the Round Table 18*

Lucerne hammer: *Bludgeons 7; Pole Weapons 7*

Lucifer: *Devil 16*

Luck: *Major Lines 19*

luck: *St. Patrick's Day 19*

lucky charm: *Witchcraft Vocabulary 17*

lucky: *Fortunate 20*

Ludlow Age: *Geologic Time 10*

luff: *Boat/Ship Terminology 9*

lug wrench: *Hand Tools 5*

luggage: *Containers and Vessels 5*

Lugh (generalities): *Celtic Pantheon 14*

Luhya: *Human Ethnic Groups 1*

Luin: *Spears 18*

Luing: *Other Cows 15*

Luke (bull): *Four Evangelists of the Bible and Their Symbols 19*

lukewarm: *Horror Vocabulary 23*

Lumbee: *Native American Peoples 1*

lumber yard: *Business Property 3*

lumber: *Interior Building Materials 3*

luminary: *Hero 20*

luminosity: *Astronomy General Terms 11*

luminous: *Beautiful 20*

Lummi: *Native American Peoples 1*

lumpy: *Large/Heavy 1*

luna: *Moth 15*

Luna: *Mounts 19*

lunar castle: *Fantasy Locations 24*

lunar eclipse: *Astronomy General Terms 11*

lunar lander: *Vehicles 22*

lunar landing: *Legendary Events 18*

lunar month: *Astronomy General Terms 11*

lunar rover: *Vehicles 22*

lunar soil: *Soil General Vocabulary 10*

lunar station: *Installations 22*

lunate bone: *Bones 12*

lunatic: *Personality Other 1*

lunation: *Astronomy General Terms 11*

lunch lady: *Food Service 1*

luncheon plate: *Tableware 5*

luneberg: *Cheese International Varieties 6*

lung: *Organs/Major Structures 12*

lunge: *Attack 7; Fencing Vocabulary 7; Locomotion 9*

lungwort: *Garden Perennials 10*

lupine: *Garden Perennials 10*

lupinine: *Poisonous Chemicals in Plants 11*

Lupus: *Constellations 11*

lurch: *Locomotion 9*

lure: *Fishing Gear 5; Magic Vocabulary 17*

luscious: *Beautiful 20; Lips 1*

Lusitano: *Horse Breeds 15*

lussatine: *Minerals 10*

lussatite: *Minerals 10*

lust: *General Emotions 20; Love 20; Seven Deadly Sins 19*

lusty: *Personality Other 1*

lute: *String Musical Instruments*

Lutetium: *Elements 11*

lutung: *Old World Monkeys 15*

luxury suit: *Men's Wear 2*

luxury: *Motorized 9*

LVTE-5 amphibious mine clearing vehicle: *United States Military Vehicles 8*

Lyall's larch: *Deciduous Trees 10*

lycanthrope: *Monsters 16*

lycanthropy: *Fictional Diseases 12*

lychee: *Unusual Edible Fruits 6*

Lydian: *Dragon 16*

Lyme disease: *Diseases 12*

lymphatic: *Body Systems 12*

lymphocyte: *Blood 12*

lymphoma: *Blood-Related Ailments 12*

lynch mob: *Western Paraphernalia/People 21*

lynching: *Western Paraphernalia/People 21*

lynx: *Big Cats 15; Giant Creatures 16*

Lynx: *Constellations 11*

Lyonesse: *Arthurian Locations 18*

Lyra: *Constellations 11*

lyre: *General Snake Families 15; String Musical Instruments*

lyre-back: *Chairs and Stools 4*

lyretail anthias: *Aquarium Saltwater Fish 15*

Lyrical abstraction: *Art Movements 13*

lyrical: *Dance Shoes 13*

lyricist: *Bard 1*

Lysithea: *Moons 11*

–M–

M'Bayar: *Horse Breeds 15*

M1 6×4 armored vehicle: *United States Military Vehicles 8*

M1 Abrams main battle tank: *United States Military Vehicles 8*

M1 Abrams: *Tanks American 8*

M1 Garand: *Semiautomatic Centerfire Rifles 7*

M1 Isherman medium tank: *Israel Military Vehicles 8*

M10 Wolverine tank destroyer: *United States Military Vehicles 8*

M1015 electronic warfare systems carrier: *United States Military Vehicles 8*

M1042 HMMWV 4x4 shelter carrier: *United States Military Vehicles 8*

M109: *Howitzer 8*

M11 pistol: *Small Arms 8*

M110 semiautomatic: *Sniper Rifle 8*

M113 armored personnel carrier: *United States Military Vehicles 8*

M117 Guardian 4x4 armored security vehicle: *United States Military Vehicles 8*

M119: *Howitzer 8*

M120: *Mortar 8*

M133 6x6 canteen vehicle: *United States Military Vehicles 8*

M133 armored flamethrower: *United States Military Vehicles 8*

M139 6x6 bridge layer: *United States Military Vehicles 8*

M14 sniper rifle: *SWAT Weapons 7*

M14: *Assault Rifle 8; Semiautomatic Centerfire Rifles 7*

M152 4×4 radio and command utility vehicle: *Canada Military Vehicles 8*

M16 MGMC anti-aircraft vehicle: *United States Military Vehicles 8*

M16 rifle: *Small Arms 8*

M16: *Assault Rifle 8; Semiautomatic Centerfire Rifles 7*

M162 Vulcan air defense system: *United States Military Vehicles 8*

M18 Hellcat self-propelled 76mm anti-tank gun: *United States Military Vehicles 8*

M1911 semi-automatic pistol: *SWAT Weapons 7*

M198: *Howitzer 8*

M2 Bradley infantry fighting vehicle: *United States Military Vehicles 8*

M2 Bradley: *Tanks American 8*

M2 heavy: *Machine Gun 8*

M2 machine gun: *Small Arms 8*

M2: *Vehicle-Mounted Weapon System 8*

M203 grenade launcher: *Rifle Attachment 8*

M22: *Assault Rifle 8*

M224: *Mortar 8*

M230 autocannon: *Vehicle-Mounted Weapon System 8*

M231 FPW: *Assault Rifle 8*

M24 Chaffee light tank: *United States Military Vehicles 8*

M24 medium belt-fed: *Machine Gun 8*

M24: *Bolt Action Sniper Rifles 7; Sniper Rifle 8*

M240 Storm 4×4 utility vehicle: *Israel Military Vehicles 8*

M240: *Vehicle-Mounted Weapon System 8*

M242 autocannon: *Vehicle-Mounted Weapon System 8*

M249: *Machine Gun 8*

M25 Dragon Wagon tank transporter: *United States Military Vehicles 8*

M252: *Mortar 8*

M26 Pershing tank: *United States Military Vehicles 8*

M26 Pershing: *Tanks American 8*

M268 6×6 propellant tanker: *United States Military Vehicles 8*

M270: *Multiple Rocket Launcher 8*

M289 wheeled missile launcher truck: *United States Military Vehicles 8*

M29 Weasel cargo carrier: *United States Military Vehicles 8*

M3 Bradley armored reconnaissance vehicle: *United States Military Vehicles 8*

M3 Grant: *Tanks American 8*

M3 Lee medium tank: *United States Military Vehicles 8*

M31 Honest John rocket carrier: *United States Military Vehicles 8*

M35 6x6 armored truck: *United States Military Vehicles 8*

M36 Nike-Hercules launcher-loader: *United States Military Vehicles 8*

M36 self-propelled 90mm anti-tank gun: *United States Military Vehicles 8*

M3A1 Stuart III: *Tanks American 8*

M4 carbine: *Assault Rifle 8; SWAT Weapons 7*

M4 mortar halftrack carrier: *United States Military Vehicles 8*

M4 rifle: *Small Arms 8*

M40: *Bolt Action Sniper Rifles 7*

M41 Walker Bulldog light tank: *United States Military Vehicles 8*

M45 armored serving and refueling vehicle: *United States Military Vehicles 8*

M46 Patton medium tank: *United States Military Vehicles 8*

M46 Patton: *Tanks American 8*

M47 6x6 dump truck: *United States Military Vehicles 8*

M48 Chaparral tracked surface-to-air missile carrier: *United States Military Vehicles 8*

M50 6x6 water tanker: *United States Military Vehicles 8*

M50 super Sherman medium tank: *United States Military Vehicles 8*

M551 Sheridan: *Tanks American 8*

M56 anti-tank vehicle: *United States Military Vehicles 8*

M561 Gama 6×6 articulated truck: *United States Military Vehicles 8*

M58 smoke generator vehicle: *United States Military Vehicles 8*

M6 4×4 1.5 ton bomb disposal truck: *United States Military Vehicles 8*

M6 Linebacker self-propelled anti-aircraft vehicle: *United States Military Vehicles 8*

M60 belt-fed: *Machine Gun 8*

M60 MBT: *Tanks American 8*

M60 Patton main battle tank: *United States Military Vehicles 8*

M601 4x4 power generator carrier: *United States Military Vehicles 8*

M624 6x6 dump truck: *United States Military Vehicles 8*

M656 8×8 5 ton air-transportable and floatable truck: *United States Military Vehicles 8*

M67 medium flamethrower tank: *United States Military Vehicles 8*

M7 snow tractor: *United States Military Vehicles 8*

M756 6x6 pipeline maintenance vehicle: *United States Military Vehicles 8*

M763 6x6 telephone maintenance vehicle: *United States Military Vehicles 8*

M764 6x6 earth boring maintenance vehicle: *United States Military Vehicles 8*

M777: *Howitzer 8*

M82A1 SASR: *Bolt Action Sniper Rifles 7*

M9 bayonet: *Rifle Attachment 8*

M9 pistol: *Small Arms 8*

M9: *Semiautomatic Pistol 8*

M901 ITV self-propelled TOW missile launcher: *United States Military Vehicles 8*

M992 FAASV ammunition vehicle: *United States Military Vehicles 8*

ma: *Female 1*

Maalik: *Angels of Good 14*

maar: *Volcanic 10*

Mab: *Moons 11*

mabolo: *Unusual Edible Fruits 6*

Mac an Luin: *Celtic Swords 18*

macabre: *Unattractive 20*

macadamia: *Nuts 6; Oils 6*

macana: *Bludgeons 7*

macaque: *Old World Monkeys 15*

macaroni and cheese: *Cheese Dishes 6*

macaroni: *Pasta 6*

macaroon: *Cookie 6*

macaw: *Domesticated Pet Birds 15*

mace: *Bludgeons 7; Spices 6*

Macedonian: *Human Ethnic Groups 1*

machair: *Coastal and Oceanic 10*

machete: *Garden Tools; Swords One-handed 7; Tools 7*

machicolations: *Castle Anatomy 3*

machine gun: *Classic Items 23; Military 8; Military Weapons General 8*

machine operator: *General Occupations 1*

machine shop: *Farm/Outbuilding 3*

machine: *Miscellaneous Furniture 4*

Machu Picchu: *Real Places Steeped in Legend or Mystery 18; Unique Property 3*

mackerel: *Sharks 15; Wild Saltwater Fish 15*

mackintosh: *Apples 6; Outerwear 2; Unisex Clothing 2*

mackintoshite: *Minerals 10*

Macklot's: *Python 15*

MacLeay river: *Freshwater Turtles 15*

Macnab cypress: *Evergreen Trees 10*

macroburst: *Meteorology General Vocabulary 10*

macrocyte: *Blood 12*

mad scientist: *Common Character Archetypes 21; Horror Occupations 23*

mad scientist's laboratory: *Horror Locations 23*

mad: *Angry 1; General Emotions 20; Negative 1*

Madagascan flat-tailed: *Tortoises 15*

Madagascan spider: *Tortoises 15*

Madagascan sunset: *Moth 15*

Madagascar big-headed sideneck: *Freshwater Turtles 15*

Madagascar ground: *Boa 15*

Madagascar iguanid: *Scaled Reptiles 15*

Madagascar tree: *Boa 15*

Madagascar Zebu: *Other Cows 15*

madame white: *Demon 16*

madden: *General Emotions 20*

made man: *Thief 1*

Madeira citrine: *Minerals 10*

madeira: *Cake 6*

Madeiran: *Human Ethnic Groups 1*

madeline: *Cookie 6*

Madiera winter cherry: *Poisonous Plants 10*

madman/woman: *Common Character Archetypes 21*

Madras plaid shorts: *Men's Wear 2*

Madras plaid: *Fabric Patterns 2*

madrigal: *Composition Types 13*

madroña: *Deciduous Trees 10*

madrone: *Deciduous Trees 10*

madroño: *Deciduous Trees 10*

madrono: *Unusual Edible Fruits 6*

maestoso: *Tempo/Mood 13*

maestro: *Musical Occupations 1*

mafic: *Geological Vocabulary 10*

Mag Mell: *Afterlife/Underworld 18*

Magach main battle tank: *Israel Military Vehicles 8*

magazine rack: *Miscellaneous Furniture 4*

magazine: *Books/Publications 5; Fortification 3*

Magellanic clouds: *Astronomy General Terms 11*

Magen David: *Symbols in Magic and Religion 19*

magenta: *Pink 20*

Magi: *Christmas 19*

Magia Naturalus: *Books of Legend 18*

magic backfires: *Common Dangers 24*

magic belt: *Armor of Legend 18*

magic circle: *Symbols in Magic and Religion 19; Witchcraft Vocabulary 17*

magic effects: *Magic 17*

magic fights technology: *Fantasy Plot Devices 24*

magic girdle of Aphrodite: *Clothing 18*

magic is responsible for ancient event or object: *Fantasy Plot Devices 24*

magic knot: *Symbols in Magic and Religion 19*

Magic realism: *Art Movements 13*

magic replaces science: *Fantasy Genres 24*

magic seal: *Symbols in Magic and Religion 19*

magic serves as energy: *Fantasy Plot Devices 24*

magic synonyms: *Magic 17*

magic types: *Magic 17*

magic vocabulary: *Magic 17*

magic wand: *Wizard's Goods 5*

magic: *Energy Sources/Types 24; Magic Vocabulary 17*

magical explosives: *Energy Sources/Types 24*

magical flight: *Travel Modes 24*

magical friend: *Common Character Archetypes 21*

magical gate: *Magical Transportation 17*

magical hole: *Magical Transportation 17*

magical liquid: *Energy Sources/Types 24*

magical map: *Magical Transportation 17*

magical object works in nonmagical world: *Fantasy Plot Devices 24*

magical objects: *Magic 17*

magical powers of artifact become understood: *Fantasy Plot Devices 24*

magical spells: *Magic 17*

magical swimming: *Travel Modes 24*

magical transportation creatures: *Magic 17*

magical transportation devices: *Magic 17*

magical transportation effects: *Magic 17*

magical transportation: *Magic 17*

magical: *Magic Vocabulary 17; Traps 3; Travel Types 22*

magician: *Illusionist 1; Witchcraft Vocabulary 17; Wizard 1*

magistrate: *Legal Occupations 1*

magma: *Geography General Vocabulary 10; Geological Vocabulary 10*

magna paint: *Art Materials 5; Art Media 13*

magnesiochromite: *Minerals 10*

Magnesium: *Elements 11*

magnet : *Harbingers/Charms for Good Luck 19; Specialty Survival Gear 5*

magnetar: *Star Types and Relatives 11*

magnetic control: *Paranormal Abilities 21*

magnetic east: *Boat/Ship Terminology 9*

magnetic field: *Astronomy General Terms 11*

magnetic north: *Boat/Ship Terminology 9*

magnetic pole: *Astronomy General Terms 11*

magnetic pulse: *Spaceship Drive Systems 22*

magnetic quantum number: *Chemistry General Vocabulary 11*

magnetic south: *Boat/Ship Terminology 9*

magnetic stirrer: *Laboratory Equipment 5*

magnetic tape recorder: *Electronics 4*

magnetic west: *Boat/Ship Terminology 9*

magnetosphere: *Astronomy General Terms 11*

Magni (strength): *Norse Pantheon 14*

magnificat: *Composition Types 13*

magnificence: *Philosophy Basic Concepts 14*

magnificent: *Beautiful 20; Large 20*

magnifying glass: *Laboratory Equipment 5; Optics 5; Wizard's Goods 5*

magnitude: *Astronomy General Terms 11*

magnolia vine: *Garden Perennials 10*

magnolia: *Shrubs 10; White 20*

magpie: *Animals with Symbolic Meaning 19*

Magyar: *Human Ethnic Groups 1*

maharishi: *Cleric 1; Wizard 1*

mahi mahi: *Fish/Seafood Types 6*

mahisha-asura: *Demon 16*

mahogany plant: *Garden Perennials 10*

mahogany: *Brown 20*

mahonia: *Shrubs 10*

mahr: *Demon 16*

mai tai: *Cocktails 6*

maiasaura peeblesorum: *Commonly Known Dinosaurs 15*

maid/matron of honor: *Special Occasion 1*

maid: *Castle Inhabitants and Personnel 1; Female 1; Horror Occupations 23; Housekeeping 1*

maiden: *Female 1*

maidenhair tree: *Garden Perennials 10*

maid-of-all-work: *Housekeeping 1*

maid-servant: *Housekeeping 1*

mail hauberk: *Armor Pieces 7*

mail piercer: *Pole Weapons 7*

mail shirt: *Armor Pieces 7*

mail slot: *Building Elements and Features 3*

mailbox: *Building Elements and Features 3*

main battle tank: *Military Ground Vehicles General 8*

main belt: *Astronomy General Terms 11*

main gauche: *Daggers and Knives 7*

main line: *Roads 9*

main road: *Roads 9*

main sequence: *Planetary Systems 11*

Maine Anjou: *Other Cows 15*

Maine coon: *Domestic Cats 15*

mainframe: *Computer Equipment 5*

mainsail: *Boat/Ship Anatomy 9*

maintaining object: *Special Posture 19*

maintenance vehicle: *Military Ground Vehicles General 8*

maintenance worker: *General Occupations 1*

maintenance: *Robots 22*

maish krej: *Cheese International Varieties 6*

maitre d': *Food Service 1*

maitre d'hotel: *Food Service 1*

maize: *Grain 6; Yellow 20*

majdoule: *Cheese International Varieties 6*

majestic: *Large 20*

major arcana: *Tarot Cards 19*

major domo: *Castle Inhabitants and Personnel 1*

major general: *U.S. Air Force Officer 8; U.S. Army Officer 8; U.S. Marines Officer 8*

major lines: *Palm Reading 19*

major planet: *Astronomy General Terms 11*

major player: *Hero 20*

major religious books: *Philosophy and Religion 14*

major road: *Roads 9*

major: *Large 20; Notation 13; U.S. Air Force Officer 8; U.S. Army Officer 8; U.S. Marines Officer 8*

make germ-free: *Clean 20*

make hygienic: *Clean 20*

make: *Create 20; Fix 20*

Makemake: *Planets 11*

makeup artist: *Personal Services 1*

makeup bag: *Accessories 2*

makeup brush: *Makeup 5*

makeup kit: *Specialty Survival Gear 5*

makeup mirror: *Miscellaneous Furniture 4*

makeup remover: *Makeup 5*

makeup: *Halloween 19; Technical Terms 13*

Makumuno Assumbo: *Caecilians 15*

Malabar rock: *Pit Viper 15*

malachite: *Standard Gems 21*

malacolite: *Minerals 10*

Malagasy iguana: *Scaled Reptiles 15*

Malagigi: *Twelve Peers of Charlemagne 18*

malagueña (Spain): *Ethnic/Folk Dances 13*

malaia garnet: *Minerals 10*

malaka: *Cheese International Varieties 6*

malaria: *Blood-Related Ailments 12; Diseases 12*

malaya garnet: *Minerals 10*

Malayan flat-shelled: *Freshwater Turtles 15*

Malayan: *Krait 15; Pit Viper 15; Tigers 15*

malbrouck: *Old World Monkeys 15*

male: *Character Building 1*

malevolent: *Bad 20; Personality Other 1*

Mali garnet: *Minerals 10; Standard Gems 21*

malibar: *Swords One-handed 7*

malicious fairies/fae torment country home: *Horror Plot Devices 23*

malicious: *Bad 20; Personality Other 1*

malignant: *Unattractive 20*

Malik: *Angels of Good 14*

mall cop: *Law Enforcement 1*

mallet: *Art Tools 5; Hand Tools 5*

mallow: *Garden Annuals 10; Garden Perennials 10*

malononitrile: *Dangerous Chemicals 11*

Malopolski: *Horse Breeds 15*

malpais: *Erosion 10; Volcanic 10*

malphas: *Devil 16*

malt liquor: *Beer 6*

malt: *Ice Cream Related 6*

malted milk: *Dairy Beverages 6*

Maltese cross: *Garden Perennials 10*

Maltese: *Crosses 19; Dog Breeds 15; Human Ethnic Groups 1*

maltreat: *Harm 20*

malva: *Garden Perennials 10*

Malvi: *Other Cows 15*

mama: *Female 1*

mamba: *General Snake Families 15*

mambo: *Dance Styles 13*

mamelon: *Volcanic 10*

mameluke: *Swords One-handed 7*

mamey: *Unusual Edible Fruits 6*

mammals: *Animals 15*

mammary gland: *Organs/Major Structures 12*

mammatus cloud: *Clouds 10*

mammee apple: *Unusual Edible Fruits 6*

mammon: *Devil 16*

mammoth: *Heavy 20; Large 20; Magical Transportation 17; Other Wild Mammals 15*

mamoncillo: *Unusual Edible Fruits 6*

mamu: *Demon 16*

man in the maze: *Symbols in Magic and Religion 19*

man of the earth: *Garden Perennials 10*

man on horseback: *Fungus Common Names 10*

man: *Male 1*

man's best friend: *Dogs/Canine 15*

manacles: *Fasteners 5*

manager: *General Occupations 1; Sports 1*

managing editor: *Publishing 1*

manaia: *Symbols in Magic and Religion 19*

Manannan mac lir (the sea): *Celtic Pantheon 14*

man-at-arms: *Fighter 1; Supporting Cast 24*

manatee: *Other Wild Mammals 15*

man-catcher: *Man-Traps 7*

Manchester Terrier: *Dog Breeds 15*

manchineel tree: *Poisonous Plants 10*

manchineel: *Poisonous Plants 10*

Manchu: *Human Ethnic Groups 1*

mandala: *Symbols in Magic and Religion 19*

Mandalong: *Other Cows 15*

mandarin hat: *Headgear 2*

mandarin orange: *Citrus 6*

mandible: *Bones 12*

mandolin: *Kitchen Equipment 5; String Musical Instruments*

mandorla: *Symbols in Magic and Religion 19*

mandrake: *Items with Healing Properties 19; Plants with Symbolic Meaning 19*

mandrill: *Old World Monkeys 15*

Mandylion: *Relics of Jesus 14*

maned: *Owls 15; Special Body Features 19*

Manèges: *Ballet Terms 13*

maneki neko: *Secular Symbols 19*

mangabey: *Old World Monkeys 15*

Mangalarga: *Horse Breeds 15*

Mangalitsa: *Pigs 15*

mangan diaspore: *Minerals 10*

manganapatite: *Minerals 10*

manganbabingtonite: *Minerals 10*

manganese: *Dangerous Chemicals 11*

Manganese: *Elements 11*

manganophyllite: *Minerals 10*

manganowollastonite: *Minerals 10*

mangansiderite: *Minerals 10*

manganvesuvianite: *Minerals 10*

manger: *Christmas 19; Relics of Jesus 14*

mango: *Fruit Juice 6; Tropical/Exotic Fruits 6*

mangonel: *Siege Engines 7*

mangrove: *General Snake Families 15; Pit Viper 15; Sea Snake 15*

Mangshan: *Pit Viper 15*

manhattan: *Cocktails 6*

manicotti: *Pasta 6*

manicure: *Makeup 5*

manicure set: *Makeup 5*

manicurist: *Personal Services 1*

manikin: *Secular Symbols 19*

manila folder: *Office/School/Writing Supplies 5*

manipulate: *Fix 20; Magic Vocabulary 17*

manipulation rummy: *Card Games 5*

Manitoba maple: *Deciduous Trees 10*

manji: *Secular Symbols 19*

mankolam: *Symbols in Magic and Religion 19*

man-made animal homes: *Animals 15*

man-made boundaries: *Chapter 10*

man-made disaster: *Horror Genres 23*

manna: *Foods with Religious or Ritual Significance 19*

mannequin: *Sewing Equipment 2*

Mannerism: *Art Movements 13*

manni: *Card Games 5*

manoao: *Unusual Edible Fruits 6*

manometer: *Chemistry General Vocabulary 11*

manor: *Residential Property 3*

manouri: *Cheese International Varieties 6*

mansard: *Roof Styles 3*

mansion: *Residential Property 3*

manticore: *Beast 16*

mantilla: *Headgear 2*

mantis: *Green 20*

mantle of Arthur in Cornwall: *Thirteen Treasures of the Island of Britain 18*

mantle of Tegau Gold-Breast: *Thirteen Treasures of the Island of Britain 18*

mantle scarf: *Miscellaneous Linens 5*

mantle: *Building Elements and Features 3; Elements 19; Geography General Vocabulary 10; Geological Vocabulary 10; Outerwear 2*

mantled howler: *New World Monkeys 15*

mantlet: *Castle Anatomy 3*

mantou: *Bread General Varieties 6*

man-traps: *Combat, Armor, and Weapons 7*

manual awning: *Windows 3*

manual typewriter: *Office/School Machines 5*

manuane: *Demon 16*

manubrium: *Bones 12*

Manueline: *Architectural Styles 3*

manufacture: *Fix 20*

manuka: *Shrubs 10*

manure: *Excrement 12*

manuscript: *Books/Publications 5*

manx: *Domestic Cats 15*

Manx: *Human Ethnic Groups 1*

many-banded krait: *World's Ten Most Venomous Snakes 15*

many-banded: *Krait 15*

many-horned: *Adder 15*

Manzanita scaber stalk: *Fungus Common Names 10*

manzanita: *Evergreen Trees 10; Shrubs 10*

Maori: *Human Ethnic Groups 1*

map case: *Books/Publications 5*

map: *Boat/Ship Anatomy 9; Books/Publications 5; Classic Items 23; General Survival Gear 5; Geography General Vocabulary 10*

maple: *Candy General 6; Ice Cream Flavors 6*

ma-praang: *Unusual Edible Fruits 6*

maps: *Equipment and Tools 5*

maqui: *Unusual Edible Fruits 6*

MAR 290 self-propelled multiple rocket launcher: *Israel Military Vehicles 8*

mar: *Harm 20*

mara: *Demon 16*

marabou: *Embellishments 2; Fabric 2*

maraging (steel): *Fencing Equipment 7*

marang: *Unusual Edible Fruits 6*

maraschino cherry: *Cocktail Garnishes 6; Ice Cream Toppings 6*

marauder: *Fighter 1; Thief 1*

marble top: *Tables 4*

marble: *Art Materials 5; Cake 6; Cave Anatomy 10; Metamorphic Rocks 10; Minerals 10*

marbled beauty: *Moth 15*

marbled cheddar: *Cheese Common Varieties 6*

marbled hatchetfish: *Aquarium Freshwater Fish 15*

marbled rye: *Bread General Varieties 6*

marbled: *Salamanders 15*

marbleize: *Art Techniques 13*

marbles: *Toys 5; Wizard's Goods 5*

march: *Journey 20; Locomotion 9*

Marchigiana: *Other Cows 15*

marching band: *Independence Day 19*

marchioness: *Royal/Noble 1*

marchocias: *Devil 16*

Marco Polo: *Real People with Legendary Status 18*

Marder II self-propelled 75mm antitank gun: *Germany Military Vehicles 8*

Mardi Gras: *Masks 2*

Marduk (the city): *Babylonian Pantheon 14*

mare: *Astronomy General Terms 11; Demon 16; Horses 15*

maredsous: *Cheese International Varieties 6*

Maremmana: *Other Cows 15*

Mares of Diomedes: *Twelve Labors of Hercules 16*

Margaret: *Moons 11*

margarita glass: *Drinkware 5*

margate: *Wild Saltwater Fish 15*

marginal: *Small/Fragile 20*

marginated: *Tortoises 15*

margrave: *Royal/Noble 1*

margravine: *Royal/Noble 1*

Marhuas: *Knights of the Round Table 18*

marigold: *Garden Annuals 10*

marimba: *Percussion Musical Instruments 5*

marina: *Architecture and Property 3; Water Terms 9*

marine camp: *Fortification 3*

marine comet: *Aquarium Saltwater Fish 15*

marine expeditionary: *Military Aircraft Pre-1962 8*

marine geology: *Geologic Fields of Study 10*

marine ranks: *Military 8*

marine terrace: *Coastal and Oceanic 10; Geological Vocabulary 10*

marine west coast: *Climatic Zones Koeppen System 10*

marine: *Art Genres 13; Ecosystems 10*

mariner: *Maritime Occupations 1*

mariners: *Guilds 1*

mariposite: *Minerals 10*

maritime climate: *Geography General Vocabulary 10*

maritime patrol: *Military Aircraft 8*

maritime: *Character Building 1; Water Terms 9*

marjoram: *Spices 6*

Mark (lion): *Four Evangelists of the Bible and Their Symbols 19*

mark of the beast: *Symbols in Magic and Religion 19*

mark of the bustard: *Symbols in Magic and Religion 19*

marker points: *Fencing Equipment 7*

marker: *Art Materials 5; Art Media 13; Office/School/Writing Supplies 5*

market square: *Outdoor Property 3*

market stall: *Outdoor Property 3*

market: *Business Property 3; General Property 3; Outdoor Property 3*

marketplace: *General Property 3; Outdoor Property 3*

marking out: *Stage Terms 13*

marl: *Sedimentary Rocks 10*

Marlin 39A: *Lever Action and Pump Rimfire Rifles 7*

Marlin model 336: *Lever Action and Pump Centerfire Rifles 7*

Marlin model 60: *Semiautomatic Rimfire Rifles 7*

Marlin model 915Y: *Bolt Action Rimfire Rifles 7*

Marlin XL7: *Bolt Action Centerfire Rifles 7*

marmalade jar: *Tableware 5*

marmatite: *Minerals 10*

marmolite: *Minerals 10*

marmoset: *New World Monkeys 15*

marocain: *Fabric 2*

maroon clown: *Aquarium Saltwater Fish 15*

marquess: *Royal/Noble 1*

marquis hat: *Headgear 2*

marquis: *Royal/Noble 1*

marquise: *Gem Cuts 21*

marriage proposal: *Western Plot Devices 21*

marriage rummy: *Card Games 5*

marriage: *Beds 4*

Marriage: *Major Lines 19; Sacraments 14*

Mars (war): *Roman Pantheon 14*

Mars colony: *Fictional/Mythological Locations 18*

Mars negative: *Mounts 19*

Mars positive: *Mounts 19*

Mars: *Planets 11*

marsala: *Wine Red 6*

marsh click: *Beetle 15*

Marsh daisy: *Chickens 15*

marsh marigold: *Garden Perennials 10; Wildflowers 10*

marsh: *Fluvial 10; Water Features 10; Water Terms 9*

marshal: *Armed Forces Other Titles 8*

marshall: *Western Paraphernalia/People 21*

marshland: *Water Features 10; Water Terms 9*

marshmallow ice cream cone: *Candy General 6*

marshmallow: *Candy General 6; Ice Cream Flavors 6; Ice Cream Mix-ins 6; Ice Cream Toppings 6*

marsupial mole: *Other Wild Mammals 15*

marsupial: *Other Wild Mammals 15*

Martha Washington's plume: *Garden Perennials 10*

martial artist: *Character Building 1*

martial arts belt ranks: *Character Building 1*

martial arts: *Styles of Dress 2*

martin: *Backyard Birds 15*

martingale: *Fencing Equipment 7*

martini glass: *Drinkware 5*

martini: *Cocktails 6*

martins: *Practices that Attract Bad Luck 19*

martite: *Minerals 10*

martlet: *Cadency Mark 19*

martyrium: *Religious Building 3*

marula: *Unusual Edible Fruits 6*

Marut: *Angels of Good 14*

maruta: *Demon 16*

marvelous: *Beautiful 20*

Marwari: *Horse Breeds 15*

Mary and Joseph: *Christmas 19*

Mary Janes: *Footwear/Shoes 2*

Mary—Mother of God: *Catholic Holy Days of Obligation 14*

marzipan: *Candy General 6*

Masai: *Other Cows 15*

masakari: *Axes 7*

mascara: *Makeup 5*

mascarpone: *Cheese Moist 6*

mascot: *Sports 1*

masculine: *Styles of Dress 2; Vocal/Speech Quality 1*

mashed: *Vegetables Cooked 6*

Mashona: *Other Cows 15*

mask: *Halloween 19; Jewelry 21; Objects in Magic and Religion 19*

masked villain: *Common Character Archetypes 21*

masked: *Owls 15*

masking fire: *General Combat Vocabulary 7*

masking tape: *Fasteners 5; Office/School/Writing Supplies 5*

masks: *Clothing 2*

mason: *Bees 15; Castle Inhabitants and Personnel 1; Construction 1*

masonry saw: *Hand Tools 5*

masonry screw: *Hardware 5*

masque: *Styles of Dress 2*

masquerade: *Masks 2; Styles of Dress 2*

mass (also missa): *Composition Types 13*

mass action expression: *Chemistry General Vocabulary 11*

mass deficiency: *Chemistry General Vocabulary 11*

mass execution: *Kill 20*

mass mind: *Paranormal Abilities 21*

mass number: *Chemistry General Vocabulary 11*

mass spectrometer: *Chemistry General Vocabulary 11*

mass transit: *Transportation 9*

mass: *Astronomy General Terms 11; Chemistry General Vocabulary 11*

massacre: *Attack 7; Kill 20*

massage parlor: *Entertainment Property 3*

massage therapist: *Animal/Equestrian 1*

massage: *Chairs and Stools 4; Tables 4*

Massai: *Human Ethnic Groups 1; Lions 15*

Massasauga: *Rattlesnake 15*

massive: *Heavy 20; Large 20; Large/Heavy 1*

Massurrealism: *Art Movements 13*

mast: *Boat/Ship Anatomy 9*

mastelo: *Cheese International Varieties 6*

master chief petty officer of the navy: *U.S. Navy Enlisted 8*

master chief petty officer: *U.S. Navy Enlisted 8*

master gunnery sergeant: *U.S. Marines Enlisted 8*

master of illusion: *Illusionist 1*

master sergeant: *U.S. Air Force Enlisted 8; U.S. Army Enlisted 8; U.S. Marines Enlisted 8*

master/mistress of ceremonies: *Media 1*

master: *Male 1*

masterwort: *Garden Perennials 10*

mastiff: *Bats 15*

Mastiff: *Dog Breeds 15*

mastodon: *Other Wild Mammals 15*

match safe: *Illumination/Light Sources 5*

match: *Fencing Vocabulary 7*

matchbox: *Illumination/Light Sources 5*

matches: *Illumination/Light Sources 5; Military Equipment 8*

matchless: *Good 20*

mate: *Navy Other Titles 8*

mated colander pot: *Kitchen Equipment 5*

matelassé: *Fabric 2*

maternity bra: *Ladies' Wear 2*

maternity panties: *Ladies' Wear 2*

maternity: *Ladies' Wear 2*

math: *Games 5*

matinee hat: *Headgear 2*

matka: *Fabric 2*

matriarch: *Cleric 1; Female 1*

matricaria: *Garden Perennials 10*

matrix opal: *Minerals 10*

matron: *Female 1*

matsutake: *Fungus Common Names 10*

matte jersey: *Fabric 2*

matter: *Astronomy General Terms 11; Chemistry General Vocabulary 11; Philosophy Basic Concepts 14*

matter-of-fact: *Vocal/Speech Quality 1*

Matthew (angel): *Four Evangelists of the Bible and Their Symbols 19*

Matthew: *Twelve Apostles 14*

Matthias: *Twelve Apostles 14*

mattress pad: *Bed Linens 5*

mattress: *Beds 4*

mature: *Adult 1*

matured: *Old 20*

matzo ball: *Bread General Varieties 6*

matzo cracker: *Bread General Varieties 6*

matzo meal: *Bread General Varieties 6*

Maui fishhook: *Objects 18*

maul oak: *Deciduous Trees 10*

maul: *Bludgeons 7*

Maure: *Other Cows 15*

Mauritius thorn: *Weeds 10*

Mauser K98k carbine: *Bolt Action Centerfire Rifles 7*

Mausoleum of Halicarnassus: *Seven Wonders of the Ancient World 18; Unique Property Destroyed 3*

mausoleum: *Cemetery 3*

maverick: *Western Paraphernalia/People 21*

maw: *Mouth 1*

maw-sit-sit: *Standard Gems 21*

maxi skirt: *Ladies' Wear 2*

maxilla: *Bones 12*

Maximilian sunflower: *Wildflowers 10*

maxixe: *Dance Styles 13*

May basket: *May Day 19*

May Day: *Holidays 19*

May highflyer: *Moth 15*

May pole: *May Day 19*

Maya: *Native American Peoples 1*

mayapple: *Garden Perennials 10; Poisonous Plants 10; Wildflowers 10*

Mayflower: *Ships 18; Thanksgiving 19*

mayhaw: *Unusual Edible Fruits 6*

Maylay: *Bears 15*

mayonnaise server: *Tableware 5*

mayonnaise: *Condiments 6; Salad Dressing 6*

mayor: *Government 1*

maypole (England): *Ethnic/Folk Dances 13*

maypole: *Objects in Magic and Religion 19*

Mazandarani: *Other Cows 15*

maze: *Cave Anatomy 10; Property Features 3; Symbols in Magic and Religion 19; Terrain Features 10; Traps 3*

mazurka (Polish): *Ethnic/Folk Dances 13*

Mazurka/mazurek: *Ballet Terms 13*

Mbochi: *Human Ethnic Groups 1*

mbulu: *Demon 16*

MC-130 Combat Talon: *U.S. Air Force Aircraft 8*

McMahon's: *Viper 15*

McNaught: *Comets 11*

mead: *Foods with Religious or Ritual Significance 19; Wine White 6*

meadow mushroom: *Fungus Common Names 10*

meadow parsley: *Garden Perennials 10*

meadow rue: *Garden Perennials 10*

meadow saffron: *Poisonous Plants 10*

meadow: *Ecosystems 10; Gnome 1; Terrain Features 10*

meadowsweet: *Garden Perennials 10*

meager: *Small/Fragile 20*

meal prayer: *Rituals 14*

meals: *Food 6*

meals-ready-to-eat: *Military Equipment 8*

mealy blue sage: *Wildflowers 10*

mean: *Horror Vocabulary 23; Negative 1*

meander: *Fluvial 10; Locomotion 9*

meaning of life: *Philosophy Basic Concepts 14*

meaning: *Philosophy Basic Concepts 14*

measles: *Diseases 12*

measure: *Fencing Vocabulary 7; Notation 13*

measured: *Slow 20*

measuring cups: *Kitchen Equipment 5*

measuring spoon: *Kitchen Utensils 5*

meat board: *Kitchen Equipment 5*

meat cleaver: *Classic Items 23*

meat pies: *Food 6*

meat saw: *Kitchen Equipment 5*

meat tenderizer: *Kitchen Utensils 5*

meat thermometer: *Kitchen Utensils 5*

meat: *Ants 15*

meatball: *Meals 6*

meatloaf: *Meals 6*

mechanic: *General Occupations 1; Thief 1*

mechanical: *Energy Sources/Types 22*

mechanism: *Chemistry General Vocabulary 11; Miscellaneous Furniture 4*

mechlorethamine: *Dangerous Chemicals 11*

meconium: *Excrement 12*

medal: *Jewelry 21*

medallion: *Jewelry 21*

media: *Character Building 1; Rooms 3*

medial cuneiform bone: *Bones 12*

medic: *Horror Occupations 23; Medical Occupations 1; Occupations 22*

medical assistant: *Medical Occupations 1*

medical emergencies: *Anatomy and Physiology 12*

medical emergency: *Travel Hazards 9*

medical epidemic: *Horror Genres 23*

medical examiner: *Horror Occupations 23*

medical experimentation: *Horror Genres 23*

medical occupations: *Character Building 1*

medical office: *Business Property 3*

medical personnel: *Styles of Dress 2*

medical: *Literary Styles 5; Robots 22*

medication: *Allergies 12*

medicine cabinet: *Bathroom Features and Fixtures 3*

medicine wheel: *Objects in Magic and Religion 19*

medieval hood: *Headgear 2*

Medieval: *Architectural Styles 3*

medieval: *Styles of Dress 2*

meditation: *Rituals 14*

Mediterranaean: *Climatic Zones Koeppen System 10; Climatic Zones 10*

Mediterranean climate: *Geography General Vocabulary 10*

Mediterranean Revival: *Architectural Styles 3*

medium chain: *Fasteners 5*

medium cheddar: *Cheese Common Varieties 6*

medium peas: *Vegetables 6*

medium sack: *Containers and Vessels 5*

medium shrimp: *Fish/Seafood Types 6*

medium: *Eggs 6; Fortune Teller 1; Paranormal Occupations 21; Wizard 1*

Medjugorje in Bosnia-Herzegovina: *Real Places Steeped in Legend or Mystery 18*

medlar: *Unusual Edible Fruits 6*

medley: *Swimming Strokes 9*

medulla: *Organs/Major Structures 12*

Medusa: *Humanoid 16*

meeting: *Rooms 3*

Megaclite: *Moons 11*

Megaliths of Carnac: *Real Places Steeped in Legend or Mystery 18*

megalomaniac: *Plot Devices 22; Supporting Cast 24*

megamouth: *Sharks 15*

mehendi: *Secular Symbols 19*

Meishan: *Pigs 15*

Meitnerium: *Elements 11*

Meker-Fisher burner: *Laboratory Equipment 5*

mekkerbek: *Cheese International Varieties 6*

melancholy: *Negative 1; Sad 20*

mélange: *Geological Vocabulary 10*

melanite: *Minerals 10*

Melba toast: *Bread General Varieties 6*

Melchior: *Three Wise Men/Magi 19*

Meleagant: *Knights of the Round Table 18*

melee: *General Combat Vocabulary 7; Moves 7*

melichlora: *Cheese International Varieties 6*

melinjo: *Unusual Edible Fruits 6*

melisma: *General Music Vocabulary 13*

mellow: *Personality Other 1; Vocal/Speech Quality 1*

mélodie: *Composition Types 13*

melodrama: *Performance Genres 13*

melodramatic: *Vocal/Speech Quality 1*

melon baller: *Kitchen Utensils 5*

melon pear: *Unusual Edible Fruits 6*

melon: *Allergies 12*

melon-headed: *Dolphins 15*

melons: *Food 6*

melting point: *Chemistry General Vocabulary 11*

melton: *Fabric 2*

Melusine: *Dragon 16*

member: *Followers 14*

membered: *Multiple Figures 19*

memento: *Decorative Objects 4; Jewelry 21*

Memon: *Human Ethnic Groups 1*

memorial park: *Cemetery 3*

memorial: *Cemetery 3; Church Anatomy 3*

memory board: *Technical Terms 13*

memory bridge: *Card Games 5*

memory: *Solitaire Card Games 5*

Men in Black: *Secret/Mystical Organizations 18*

men's club: *Social Clubs 1*

men's room: *Bathrooms 3*

men's wear: *Clothing 2*

menaccanite: *Minerals 10*

menacing: *Unattractive 20*

menaulion: *Spears 7*

mend: *Fix 20*

Mendelevium: *Elements 11*

mendikot: *Card Games 5*

menilite: *Minerals 10*

meningitis: *Diseases 12*

meniscus: *Chemistry General Vocabulary 11*

Mennonite: *Human Ethnic Groups 1*

Menominee: *Native American Peoples 1*

menorah: *Objects in Magic and Religion 19; Rituals 14*

Mensa: *Constellations 11*

mental ability: *Energy Sources/Types 23*

mental blast: *Paranormal Abilities 21*

mental control: *Paranormal Abilities 21; Plot Devices 22*

mental mapping: *Paranormal Abilities 21*

mental powers: *Energy Sources/Types 24*

mental shield: *Paranormal Abilities 21*

mental: *Philosophy Basic Concepts 14*

mentally advanced/physically weak: *Plot Devices 22*

mentally ill: *Personality Other 1*

mentor: *Common Character Archetypes 21; General Occupations 1; Teach 20*

Menzies' spruce: *Evergreen Trees 10*

menziesia: *Shrubs 10*

Mephistopheles: *Fallen Angels 14*

Mer Bleue Bog Ontario : *Bogs of North America 10*

mercenary: *Assassin 1; Fighter 1*

mercerized cotton: *Fabric 2*

merchant aircraft carrier: *Military Watercraft 8*

merchant: *Castle Inhabitants and Personnel 1; General Occupations 1*

merchant's scale: *Large Tools*

merchantman: *Large Watercraft 9; Military Watercraft 8*

merchants: *Guilds 1*

merciless: *Bad 20*

mercuric acetate: *Dangerous Chemicals 11*

mercuric chloride: *Dangerous Chemicals 11*

mercuric oxide: *Dangerous Chemicals 11*

Mercury (messenger of the gods): *Roman Pantheon 14*

Mercury moon: *Hypothetical Solar System Bodies 11*

mercury vapor: *Illumination Bulb and Tube Types 5*

Mercury: *Elements 11; Minor Lines 19; Mounts 19; Planets 11*

mercury: *Five Alchemical Spirits 19*

mercy: *Philosophy Basic Concepts 14*

mere: *Bludgeons 7; Small/Fragile 20*

merengue: *Dance Styles 13*

Mérens Pony: *Horse Breeds 15*

merfolk: *Aquatic 16; Humanlike Groups 1*

meridian: *Astronomy General Terms 11*

meringue: *Pie 6*

merino wool: *Fabric 2*

merkabah: *Symbols in Magic and Religion 19*

Merlin: *Arthurian Characters 18*

Merlin's spellbook: *Arthurian Objects 18*

Merlin's treasures found in modern times: *Fantasy Plot Devices 24*

merlon: *Castle Anatomy 3*

merlot: *Wine Red 6*

Mermaid/Merfolk: *Human Races Fictional 1*

mermaid: *Fantasy Creatures with Symbolic Meaning 19; Water Faerie 16*

merman/mermaid: *Aquatic 16*

Merovingian: *Architectural Styles 3*

merrow: *Demon 16; Water Faerie 16*

merry widow hat: *Headgear 2*

merry widow: *Ladies' Wear 2*

merry: *Happy 20*

merry-go-round: *Amusement Park/Carnival/Circus/Fair 3*

mesa: *Erosion 10; Slope 10*

mescal bean sophora: *Evergreen Trees 10*

mescal bean: *Evergreen Trees 10; Shrubs 10*

mesh: *Cheese International Varieties 6; Fabric 2*

mesmerist: *Illusionist 1*

mesmerize: *Magic Vocabulary 17*

mesmerized: *Magic Vocabulary 17*

mesmerizing: *Beautiful 20*

Mesoarchean Period: *Geologic Time 10*

mesomorph: *Large/Heavy 1*

Mesopotamian Tablets of Destiny: *Books of Legend 18*

Mesopotamian tree of life: *Symbols in Magic and Religion 19*

Mesopotamian: *Art Movements 13*

Mesoproterozoic Period: *Geologic Time 10*

Mesozoic Era: *Geologic Time 10*

mesquite: *Weeds 10*

mess hall: *Military Property 3*

mess kit: *General Survival Gear 5*

Messara: *Horse Breeds 15*

messenger bag: *Accessories 2*

messenger of God: *Angels Common Terms 14*

messenger: *Angels Common Terms 14*

messer: *Swords One-handed 7*

messiah: *Hero 20*

Messianic seal: *Symbols in Magic and Religion 19*

Mestizo: *Human Ethnic Groups 1*

mesto: *Tempo/Mood 13*

metacarpal: *Bones 12*

metacinnabarite: *Minerals 10*

metal beads: *Art Materials 5*

metal bottle: *Containers and Vessels 5*

metal crafter: *Artists and Craftspeople 1*

metal dust: *Wizard's Goods 5*

metal guitar pick: *Music Accessories*

metal halide: *Illumination Bulb and Tube Types 5*

metal ladder: *Large Tools*

metal mirror: *Personal Care 5*

metal polish: *Cleaning Supplies/Gadgets 5*

metal saw: *Hand Tools 5*

metal: *Art Materials 5; Art Media 13; Astronomy General Terms 11; Chemistry General Vocabulary 11; Roofing Materials 3*

metallic bonding: *Chemistry General Vocabulary 11*

metallic dog: *Construct 16*

metallophone: *Percussion Musical Instruments 5*

metallurgy: *Chemistry General Vocabulary 11*

metalmark: *Butterfly 15*

metals or alloys unique to a setting: *Precious Metals 21*

metalworking lathe: *Power Tools*

metamorphic petrology: *Geologic Fields of Study 10*

metamorphic rock: *Geological Vocabulary 10*

metamorphic rocks: *Chapter 10*

metamorphism: *Geological Vocabulary 10*

metamorphosis: *General Music Vocabulary 13*

Metaphysical painting: *Art Movements 13*

metaphysics: *Philosophy Basic Concepts 14*

metatarsal: *Bones 12*

Metatron: *Angels of Good 14*

Metatron's cube: *Symbols in Magic and Religion 19*

meteor hammer: *Chain Weapons 7; Flexible 7*

meteor shower: *Astronomy General Terms 11*

meteor: *Astronomy General Terms 11*

meteoric iron: *Minerals 10*

meteorite: *Astronomy General Terms 11; Energy Sources/Types 24*

meteoroid: *Astronomy General Terms 11*

meteorologist: *Media 1; Meteorology General Vocabulary 10*

meteorology vocabulary: *Chapter 10*

meteorology: *Chapter 10; Meteorology General Vocabulary 10*

metes and bounds: *Geography General Vocabulary 10*

methacrolein diacetate: *Dangerous Chemicals 11*

methacrylic anhydride: *Dangerous Chemicals 11*

methacrylonitrile: *Dangerous Chemicals 11*

methacryloyl chloride: *Dangerous Chemicals 11*

methacryloyloxyethyl isocyanate: *Dangerous Chemicals 11*

methamidophos: *Dangerous Chemicals 11*

methane: *Energy Sources/Types 22*

methanesulfonyl fluoride: *Dangerous Chemicals 11*

methidathion: *Dangerous Chemicals 11*

methiocarb: *Dangerous Chemicals 11*

method: *Philosophy Basic Concepts 14*

methodical: *Slow 20*

methodology: *Philosophy Basic Concepts 14*

methods: *Ballet Terms 13*

methomyl: *Dangerous Chemicals 11*

Methone: *Moons 11*

Methuselah: *Elderly 1*

methyl bromide: *Dangerous Chemicals 11*

methyl chloroformate: *Dangerous Chemicals 11*

methyl hydrazine: *Dangerous Chemicals 11*

methyl isocyanate: *Dangerous Chemicals 11*

methyl isothiocyanate: *Dangerous Chemicals 11*

methyl phenkapton: *Dangerous Chemicals 11*

methyl phosphonic dichloride: *Dangerous Chemicals 11*

methyl thiocyanate: *Dangerous Chemicals 11*

methyl vinyl ketone: *Dangerous Chemicals 11*

methyl: *Dangerous Chemicals 11*

methylmercuric dicyanamide: *Dangerous Chemicals 11*

Metis: *Moons 11*

metolcarb: *Dangerous Chemicals 11*

metro: *Mass Transit 9*

metronome: *Music Accessories*

metropolis: *City 10*

metropolitan: *Cleric 1*

metsovella: *Cheese International Varieties 6*

metsovone: *Cheese International Varieties 6*

metzo forte: *Dynamics 13*

meurtriere: *Castle Anatomy 3*

Meuse-Rhine-Yssel: *Other Cows 15*

mevinphos: *Dangerous Chemicals 11*

Mewati: *Other Cows 15*

mexacarbate: *Dangerous Chemicals 11*

Mexican blue oak: *Deciduous Trees 10*

Mexican border: *Famous Western Locations 21*

Mexican buckeye: *Shrubs 10*

Mexican fire opal: *Minerals 10*

Mexican giant musk: *Freshwater Turtles 15*

Mexican green: *Rattlesnake 15*

Mexican hat: *Garden Perennials 10; Wildflowers 10*

Mexican heather: *Garden Annuals 10*

Mexican juniper: *Evergreen Trees 10*

Mexican lace agate: *Minerals 10*

Mexican onyx: *Minerals 10*

Mexican orange blossom: *Shrubs 10*

Mexican ornate slider: *Freshwater Turtles 15*

Mexican persimmon: *Deciduous Trees 10*

Mexican pinyon: *Evergreen Trees 10*

Mexican poppy: *Weeds 10*

Mexican soapberry: *Deciduous Trees 10*

Mexican stud: *Poker Card Games 5*

Mexican sweat: *Poker Card Games 5*

Mexican walnut: *Deciduous Trees 10*

Mexican wedding cake: *Cookie 6*

Mexican west coast: *Rattlesnake 15*

Mexican white pine: *Evergreen Trees 10*

Mexican: *Caecilians 15; Human Ethnic Groups 1; Salamanders 15*

Meyers parrot: *Domesticated Pet Birds 15*

mezuzah: *Objects in Magic and Religion 19*

mezzo: *General Music Vocabulary 13*

mezzosoprano: *Voices 13*

MH-47 Chinook: *U.S. Army Helicopter 8*

MH-53 Sea Dragon: *Rotary Wing Aircraft 8*

MH-60 Black Hawk: *U.S. Army Helicopter 8*

MH-60: *Rotary Wing Aircraft 8*

MIA: *General Combat Vocabulary 7*

Miami soil: *Soil General Vocabulary 10*

miao dao: *Swords Two-handed 7*

miasma: *Smells 20*

mica cap: *Fungus Common Names 10*

mica: *Minerals 10*

Michael: *Angels of Good 14*

Michigan rummy: *Card Games 5*

Michigan: *Card Games 5*

micro camera: *Spy Gear 5*

microbrew: *Beer 6*

microburst: *Meteorology General Vocabulary 10*

microcachrys: *Shrubs 10*

microchip: *Spy Gear 5*

microcline and sanidine: *Minerals 10*

microcrystalline quartz: *Minerals 10*

microfiber: *Fabric 2*

microfilm: *Spy Gear 5*

micrometer: *Architectural/Engineering Tools 5*

micropaleontology: *Geologic Fields of Study 10; Geological Vocabulary 10*

microphone: *Computer Equipment 5; Spy Gear 5; Technical Terms 13*

microplane grater: *Kitchen Utensils 5*

microscope: *Laboratory Equipment 5; Optics 5*

microscopic: *Small/Fragile 20*

Microscopium: *Constellations 11*

microtiter plate: *Laboratory Equipment 5*

microwave oven: *Appliances 5; Major Appliances 4*

microwave popcorn: *Snacks 6*

microwave: *Cooking Techniques 20*

Mictlantecuhtle (the dead): *Aztec Pantheon 14*

Mictlantecuhtli (death): *Central American Pantheon 14*

Midas tamarin: *New World Monkeys 15*

midbrain: *Organs/Major Structures 12*

Mid-Century Modern: *Architectural Styles 3*

Middle Ages: *Art Movements 13*

middle baroque: *Musical Period 13*

middle blade: *Fencing Equipment 7*

middle class: *Social Distinction 1*

Middle Eastern: *Styles of Dress 2*

Middle white: *Pigs 15*

middle-aged: *Adult 1*

midge: *Flies 15*

midget faded: *Rattlesnake 15*

midget pickle: *Pickled/Relish 6*

midget: *Small/Thin 1*

midi skirt: *Ladies' Wear 2*

Midland painted: *Freshwater Turtles 15*

midnight baseball: *Poker Card Games 5*

midnight black: *Black 20*

midnight blue: *Blue 20*

midnight Mass: *Christmas 19*

midnight: *Common Dangers 23; New Year 19; Witchcraft Vocabulary 17*

mid-ocean ridge: *Coastal and Oceanic 10; Volcanic 10*

mid-oceanic ridge: *Geological Vocabulary 10*

Midrash: *Major Religious Books 14*

midshipman: *Maritime Occupations 1; Navy Other Titles 8*

midsummer's eve: *Fae Related 16; Witchcraft Vocabulary 17*

midwife: *Medical Occupations 1*

midyim: *Unusual Edible Fruits 6*

Mielikki (goddess of nature): *Finnish Pantheon 14*

mighty: *Card Games 5; Large 20; Large/Heavy 1*

migmatite: *Metamorphic Rocks 10*

migrant: *Air Creatures 19; Barbarian 1*

mihrab: *Church Anatomy 3*

Mike Fink: *Real People with Legendary Status 18*

milbenkase: *Cheese International Varieties 6*

mild cheddar: *Cheese Common Varieties 6*

mildness: *Twelve Fruits of the Holy Spirit 19*

mile-a-minute weed: *Weeds 10*

mile-a-minute: *Garden Perennials 10*

milestone: *Beginning 20*

milfoil: *Garden Perennials 10*

militant: *Personality Other 1*

military academy: *Academic Property 3*

military base: *Fortification 3*

military college: *Fortification 3*

military dress: *Clothing/Uniforms 22*

military equipment: *Military 8*

military fork: *Spears 7*

military hat: *Headgear 2*

military institute: *Fortification 3*

military intelligence facility: *Military Property 3*

military item: *Charges 19*

military outpost: *Fortification 3*

military property: *Architecture and Property 3*

military ranks: *Military 8*

military school: *Academic Property 3*

military station: *Fortification 3*

military takeover: *Plot Devices 22*

military technology: *Plot Devices 22*

military transportation: *Transportation 9*

military uniform: *Styles of Dress 2*

military vehicles: *Military 8*

military weapons: *Military 8*

military: *Art Genres 13; Spaceship Types 22*

military industrial complex: *General Combat Vocabulary 7*

milk chute: *Building Elements and Features 3*

milk opal: *Minerals 10*

milk shake: *Dairy Beverages 6*

milk tanker: *Farm Transportation 9*

milk teeth: *Teeth 1*

milk thistle: *Weeds 10*

milk: *Allergies 12; Candy Chocolate 6; Dairy Beverages 6; Food 6; Foods with Religious or Ritual Significance 19; General Snake Families 15; Motorized Truck 9; Teeth 12; Wizard's Goods 5*

Milking Devon: *North American Dairy Cows 15*

milking house: *Farm/Outbuilding 3*

milking machine: *General Farm Equipment*

milking parlor: *Farm/Outbuilding 3*

milking pipeline: *General Farm Equipment*

Milking Shorthorn: *North American Dairy Cows 15*

milking stool: *Chairs and Stools 4*

milkshake machine: *Appliances 5*

milkshake: *Ice Cream Related 6*

milkvetch: *Garden Perennials 10*

milkweed: *Garden Annuals 10; Garden Perennials 10*

milkwort: *Shrubs 10*

milky quartz: *Minerals 10*

mill pond: *Water Features 10*

mill: *Business Property 3; Special Purpose Structure 3*

mille: *Card Games 5*

millet: *Grain 6*

millibar: *Astronomy General Terms 11*

milling cutter: *Power Tools*

million bells: *Garden Annuals 10*

Mimas: *Moons 11*

mime: *Ballet Terms 13; Performing Arts 1*

mimeograph machine: *Office/School Machines 5*

mimi: *Demon 16*

mimic: *Octopi 15*

Mimung (Wudga): *Weapons of Legend 18*

mincemeat: *Pie 6*

mind blast: *Paranormal Abilities 21*

mind control: *Horror Plot Devices 23*

mind controlling creature: *Monsters and Creatures 22*

mind interfacing: *Plot Devices 22*

mind reader suffers side effects: *Horror Plot Devices 23*

mind wipe: *Paranormal Abilities 21*

mind: *Philosophy Basic Concepts 14*

mind reader: *Wizard 1*

mindreading: *Magic Vocabulary 17*

mine field: *Fortification 3*

mine shaft: *Outdoor Property 3*

mine: *Outdoor Property 3*

miner: *Rural Occupations 1; Spaceship Types 22*

miner's: *Axes 7*

mineral salt: *Minerals 10*

mineral: *Geological Vocabulary 10; Rock and Mineral Forms 10*

mineralization: *Geological Vocabulary 10; Soil General Vocabulary 10*

mineralogist: *Scientist 1*

mineralogy: *Geologic Fields of Study 10*

minerals: *Chapter 10*

Minerva (goddess of magic): *Roman Pantheon 14*

minestrone: *Soup 6*

minesweeper : *U.S. Navy Vessels 8*

mini blinds: *Window Treatments 5*

mini mall: *Business Property 3*

mini market: *General Property 3*

mini skirt: *Ladies' Wear 2*

mini: *Donut/doughnut 6; Motorized 9; Small/Fragile 20; Small/Thin 1*

miniature aircraft from tomb at Saqquara: *Objects 18*

Miniature Bull Terrier: *Dog Breeds 15*

miniature explosive: *Spy Gear 5*

miniature hen and chicks: *Garden Perennials 10*

miniature painting: *Art Genres 13*

Miniature Pinscher: *Dog Breeds 15*

Miniature Poodle: *Dog Breeds 15*

Miniature Schnauzer: *Dog Breeds 15*

miniature submarine: *Spy Gear 5*

miniature: *Dragon 16; Horses 15; Pigs 15; Small/Fragile 20; Small/Thin 1*

Miniature: *Horse Breeds 15*

minibike: *Motorized 9*

minibridge: *Card Games 5*

mini dagger: *Harbingers/Charms for Good Luck 19*

minidisc player: *Electronics 4*

minim: *Notation 13*

minimal: *Easy 20*

Minimalism: *Art Movements 13*

minimizer bra: *Ladies' Wear 2*

mining geology: *Geologic Fields of Study 10*

mining station: *Installations 22*

minion: *Witchcraft Vocabulary 17; Wizard's Goods 5*

minister: *Cleric 1*

minivan: *Motorized 9*

mink: *Fur 2; Other Wild Mammals 15*

minke: *Whales 15*

minnow: *Wild Freshwater Fish 15; Wild Saltwater Fish 15*

Minokawa Buta: *Pigs 15*

minon: *Cannon 7*

minor arcana: *Tarot Cards 19*

minor lines: *Palm Reading 19*

minor planet: *Astronomy General Terms 11*

minor: *Child 1; Notation 13; Small/Fragile 20*

minority: *Philosophy Basic Concepts 14*

minotaur: *Beast 16; Beetle 15; Giant Humanoids 16*

Minskin: *Domestic Cats 15*

minstrel: *Bard 1; Castle Inhabitants and Personnel 1; Musical Occupations 1; Singer 1*

mint chocolate chip: *Ice Cream Flavors 6*

mint condition: *New 20*

mint cream: *Green 20*

mint meltaway: *Candy Chocolate 6*

mint shrub: *Garden Perennials 10*

mint: *Aphrodisiacs 19; Candy General 6; Cyan 20; Green 20; Ice Cream Flavors 6*

minuet (France): *Ethnic/Folk Dances 13*

minuet: *Historical Dances 13*

minuscule: *Small/Fragile 20*

minute: *Small/Fragile 20*

minx: *Female 1*

Minzhu: *Pigs 15*

Miocene Age: *Geologic Time 10*

Mira variable: *Star Types and Relatives 11*

miracle fruit: *Unusual Edible Fruits 6*

miracle: *Magic Vocabulary 17*

miracles: *Magic Vocabulary 17*

miraculous medal: *Objects in Magic and Religion 19*

miraculous: *Magic Vocabulary 17*

mirage: *Magic Vocabulary 17*

Miranda: *Moons 11*

Mirandesa: *Other Cows 15*

mire: *Terrain Features 10*

mirror ball: *Technical Terms 13*

mirror: *Bathroom Features and Fixtures 3; Building Elements and Features 3; Dance Equipment 13; Magical Transportation 17; Miscellaneous Furniture 4; Objects in Magic and Religion 19; Personal Care 5; Signal Devices 5; Wizard's Goods 5*

mirrorlike wisdom: *Five Wisdoms of Buddhism 19*

Misaki: *Horse Breeds 15*

miscellaneous: *Dog Groups 15*

mischievous fairy: *Supporting Cast 24*

miscibility: *Chemistry General Vocabulary 11*

miser: *Common Character Archetypes 21*

miserable: *Sad 20*

misericorde: *Swords One-handed 7*

misleading: *Personality Other 1*

mispickel: *Minerals 10*

miss: *Female 1*

missey-mossey: *Deciduous Trees 10*

missile cruiser: *Military Watercraft 8*

missile loads: *Combat, Armor, and Weapons 7*

missile mortar: *Military 8*

missile silo: *Fortification 3*

missile weapons: *Combat, Armor, and Weapons 7*

missile: *Weapons 22*

missing in action: *General Combat Vocabulary 7*

missing item: *Paranormal Occurrences 21*

missing link: *Monsters and Creatures 22*

missing: *Teeth 1*

Mission: *Architectural Styles 3*

mission: *Journey 20*

missionary: *Cleric 1*

Mississippi mud: *Poker Card Games 5; Freshwater Turtles 15*

Mississippi valley oak: *Deciduous Trees 10*

Mississippian Age: *Geologic Time 10*

Missouri Fox Trotting Horse: *Horse Breeds 15*

Missouri primrose: *Garden Perennials 10; Wildflowers 10*

missy: *Female 1*

mist flower: *Garden Perennials 10*

mist: *Magical Transportation 17; Precipitation 10; Smells 20*

mister: *Male 1*

Misterrogers: *Asteroids with Unusual Names 11*

Mistilteinn: *Norse Weapons 18*

mistletoe: *Christmas 19; Objects that Offer Protection 19; Plants with Symbolic Meaning 19; Poisonous Plants 10; Shrubs 10*

mistral wind: *Wind 10*

Mistral: *Winds of the Mediterranean 10*

mistreat: *Harm 20*

mistress: *Common Character Archetypes 21; Female 1*

mistrustful: *Horror Vocabulary 23*

miter box: *Hand Tools 5; Large Tools*

miter saw: *Power Tools*

miter: *Religious Dress 2; Sewing Techniques 2*

mithraeum: *Religious Building 3*

mitomycin c: *Dangerous Chemicals 11*

mittens: *Accessories 2; Christmas 19*

mixed peas: *Vegetables 6*

mixed: *Hand Shapes 19*

mixer: *Technical Terms 13*

mixing bowl: *Containers and Vessels 5; Kitchen Equipment 5*

mixing spoon: *Kitchen Utensils 5*

mixture: *Chemistry General Vocabulary 11*

Miyako: *Horse Breeds 15*

mizzen mast: *Boat/Ship Anatomy 9*

mizzen: *Boat/Ship Anatomy 9*

mizzle: *Precipitation 10*

Mjolnir: *Norse Weapons 18*

MK 19: *Vehicle-Mounted Weapon System 8*

MK19 belt fed grenade machine gun: *Machine Gun 8*

Mneme: *Moons 11*

moab hat: *Headgear 2*

Moai statues of Easter Island: *Real Objects Not Fully Understood 18*

moan: *Paranormal Occurrences 21; Sounds 20; Speak 20*

moat: *Castle Anatomy 3; Fortification 3*

mob boss: *Illicit Occupations 1*

mobile phone: *Spy Gear 5*

mobility: *Character Building 1*

mobster: *Fighter 1; Thief 1; Villain 20*

moccasin: *General Snake Families 15*

moccasins: *Footwear/Shoes 2*

mocha: *Ice Cream Flavors 6*

mock orange: *Garden Perennials 10; Shrubs 10*

mock: *Horror Vocabulary 23*

mockernut hickory: *Deciduous Trees 10*

mockernut: *Deciduous Trees 10*

mocking: *Horror Vocabulary 23; Negative 1*

mockingbird: *Backyard Birds 15*

Moctezuma agate: *Minerals 10*

mode: *General Music Vocabulary 13*

model airplane: *Toys 5*

model car: *Toys 5*

model rocket: *Toys 5*

model: *Horror Occupations 23*

modeling materials: *Art Materials 5*

modem: *Computer Equipment 5*

moderate: *Slow 20*

moderato: *Tempo/Mood 13*

moderator: *Media 1*

Modern American: *Architectural Styles 3*

modern game: *Chickens 15*

Modern: *Architectural Styles 3*

modern: *Dance Styles 13; Musical Period 13; New 20*

Modernism: *Art Movements 13*

modest: *Keelback 15; Small/Fragile 20*

modesty: *Twelve Fruits of the Holy Spirit 19*

Modicana: *Other Cows 15*

modish: *Beautiful 20*

Modoc cypress: *Evergreen Trees 10*

Modoc: *Native American Peoples 1*

modular tactical vest: *Body Armor 7*

modulated: *Vocal/Speech Quality 1*

Mohandas Gandhi: *Real People with Legendary Status 18; Philosophy 14*

Mohave: *Native American Peoples 1*

Mohawk: *Hair Style 1; Native American Peoples 1*

Mohican: *Native American Peoples 1*

Mohs scale of hardness: *Geological Vocabulary 10*

moiré: *Fabric 2*

moist: *Lips 1; Wet 10*

moisture: *Wet 10; Wet 20*

Mojave blue agate: *Minerals 10*

Mojave: *Rattlesnake 15*

molality: *Chemistry General Vocabulary 11*

molar: *Teeth 12*

molasses: *Cookie 6; Staples 6; Wizard's Goods 5*

molbo: *Cheese International Varieties 6*

mold: *Allergies 12; Wizard's Goods 5*

molder: *Smells 20*

molding: *Geological Vocabulary 10*

moldy: *Unattractive 20*

mole fraction: *Chemistry General Vocabulary 11*

mole: *Hero or Villain, Depending Upon Circumstance 20; Salamanders 15; Skin Types and Features 1; Thief 1; Viper 15; Woodland Mammals 15*

molecular cloud: *Astronomy General Terms 11; Star Types and Relatives 11*

molecular disruption: *Paranormal Abilities 21*

molecular equation: *Chemistry General Vocabulary 11*

molecular formula: *Chemistry General Vocabulary 11*

molecular weight: *Chemistry General Vocabulary 11*

molecule edged: *Weapons 22*

molecule: *Chemistry General Vocabulary 11*

molest: *Harm 20*

molet: *Cadency Mark 19*

mollisol: *Soil General Vocabulary 10*

Mollucan: *Python 15*

Molly Pitcher: *Legendary People Presumed to be Fictional 18*

molly: *Aquarium Freshwater Fish 15*

molten chocolate: *Cake 6*

molto: *Tempo/Mood 13*

Molybdenum: *Elements 11*

mom jeans: *Ladies' Wear 2*

mom: *Female 1*

mombin: *Unusual Edible Fruits 6*

mommy: *Female 1*

Mon: *Human Ethnic Groups 1*

mona monkey: *Old World Monkeys 15*

monad: *Symbols in Magic and Religion 19*

monadnock: *Erosion 10; Glacial and Mountain 10*

monarch: *Butterfly 15*

monastery: *Cheese Common Varieties 6; Religious Building 3*

monastic warrior: *Paladin 1*

Monday's Child Rhyme: *Superstitions 19*

mondo grass: *Garden Perennials 10*

mondseer: *Cheese International Varieties 6*

money belt: *Specialty Survival Gear 5*

money changer: *Finance 1*

money changers: *Guilds 1*

money lender: *Finance 1*

money plant: *Garden Annuals 10*

money/supplies stolen: *Travel Hazards 9*

Money: *Major Lines 19*

moneywort: *Garden Perennials 10; Weeds 10*

Mong Cai: *Pigs 15*

Mongol: *Human Ethnic Groups 1*

Mongolian: *Horse Breeds 15; Other Cows 15*

mongoose: *Other Wild Mammals 15*

monitor del monte: *Other Wild Mammals 15*

monitor lizard: *Scaled Reptiles 15*

monitor: *Computer Equipment 5; Military Watercraft 8; Technical Terms 13*

monk: *Character Building 1; Cleric 1; Religious Occupations 1; Styles of Dress 2*

monk's cloth: *Fabric 2*

monk's hood vine: *Garden Perennials 10*

monkey flower: *Garden Perennials 10*

monkey head: *Fungus Common Names 10*

monkey wrench: *Hand Tools 5*

monkey: *Animals with Symbolic Meaning 19; Bread General Varieties 6; Chinese Horoscope 19*

monkey's fist: *Sailing Knots 9*

monkey's paw: *Classic Items 23; Sailing Knots 9*

monkey-faced: *Bats 15*

monkeys: *Animals 15*

monkshood: *Garden Perennials 10; Poisonous Plants 10*

Monoceros: *Constellations 11*

monocle: *Optics 5*

monocled: *Cobra 15*

monocrotophos: *Dangerous Chemicals 11*

monody: *Composition Types 13*

monogram: *Embellishments 2*

mononucleosis: *Diseases 12*

monophony: *Composition Types 13*

monorail mass transit: *Installations 22*

monorail: *Mass Transit 9; Railroad 9*

monoscope: *Optics 5*

monotone: *Vocal/Speech Quality 1*

monotonous: *Vocal/Speech Quality 1*

mons meg: *Siege Engines 7*

monsignor: *Religious Occupations 1*

monsoon: *Precipitation 10*

monster army commander: *Fantasy Occupations 24*

monster categories: *Monsters 16*

monster lairs and locations: *Monsters 16*

monster lairs: *Monsters 16*

monster mortar: *Mortar 8*

monster terms: *Monsters 16*

monster trainer: *Fantasy Occupations 24*

monster: *Charges 19; Common Character Archetypes 21; Halloween 19; Motorized Truck 9*

monsters: *Classic Heraldry 19; Common Dangers 24*

monstrance: *Religious Items 5*

monstrous: *Horror Vocabulary 23; Large 20; Large/Heavy 1; Unattractive 20*

montafoner sauerkase: *Cheese International Varieties 6*

Montbéliard: *Other Cows 15*

Monte Carlo: *Solitaire Card Games 5*

Monte Cristo: *Sandwiches 6*

Montenegrin: *Human Ethnic Groups 1*

Monterey cypress: *Evergreen Trees 10*

Monterey Jack dry: *Cheese Common Varieties 6*

Monterey Jack: *Cheese Common Varieties 6*

Monterey pine: *Evergreen Trees 10*

Montezuma bald cypress: *Evergreen Trees 10*

Montezuma swordtail: *Aquarium Freshwater Fish 15*

Montezuma's revenge: *Travel Hazards 9*

Montpellier: *General Snake Families 15*

monument: *Cemetery 3*

monzogranite: *Igneous Rocks 10*

monzonite: *Igneous Rocks 10*

moocher: *Thief 1*

mood: *The Arts 13*

moon carrot: *Garden Perennials 10*

moon colony: *Fictional/Mythological Locations 18*

moon: *Bridges 9; Cake 6; Figures Associated with Symbols 19; Jellyfish 15; Objects/Activities Connected to Lore 19; Witchcraft Vocabulary 17*

Moon: *Moons 11*

moonflower: *Garden Annuals 10*

moonlight: *Witchcraft Vocabulary 17*

moonmilk: *Cave Anatomy 10*

moonraker: *Boat/Ship Anatomy 9*

moonseed: *Poisonous Plants 10; Shrubs 10*

moonstone: *Minerals 10; Standard Gems 21; Star Gems 21*

moor: *Ecosystems 10*

Moor: *Human Ethnic Groups 1*

Moor's Head tourmaline: *Minerals 10*

mooring hitch: *Sailing Knots 9*

mooring: *Boat/Ship Anatomy 9*

mooring-under-sail: *Boat/Ship Terminology 9*

moose: *Animals with Symbolic Meaning 19; Other Wild Mammals 15*

moosewood: *Deciduous Trees 10*

mop bucket: *Cleaning Supplies/Gadgets 5*

mop: *Clean 20; Cleaning Supplies/Gadgets 5; Hair Style 1*

Mora Romagnola: *Pigs 15*

Morab: *Horse Breeds 15*

moraine: *Geological Vocabulary 10; Glacial and Mountain 10*

moral: *Good 20*

morality play: *Performance Genres 13*

Moralltach: *Celtic Swords 18*

morass: *Terrain Features 10*

Moravian: *Human Ethnic Groups 1*

morbid: *Unattractive 20*

Mordred: *Arthurian Characters 18*

morel mushroom: *Vegetables 6*

morel: *Fungus Common Names 10*

Morelet's crocodile: *Crocodilians 15*

morenosite: *Minerals 10*

Morgan Hill jasper: *Minerals 10*

Morgan LeFay: *Arthurian Characters 18*

Morgan: *Horse Breeds 15*

Morgana: *Arthurian Characters 18*

Morganeuse: *Arthurian Characters 18*

morganite: *Minerals 10; Standard Gems 21*

morinda: *Unusual Edible Fruits 6*

morion: *Minerals 10*

Moriori: *Human Ethnic Groups 1*

Mormon Texts: *Major Religious Books 14*

morning coat: *Men's Wear 2*

morning fog: *Hangover 12*

morning glory: *Garden Annuals 10*

morning star: *Bludgeons 7*

Moro: *Human Ethnic Groups 1*

moron: *Unintelligent 1*

moronic: *Unintelligent 1*

morose: *Sad 20*

Morrigan (goddess of war): *Celtic Pantheon 14*

morris (Britain): *Ethnic/Folk Dances 13*

morrisonite: *Minerals 10*

Morrow's honeysuckle: *Weeds 10*

Morse code: *Signal Devices 5*

mortar and pestle: *Kitchen Utensils 5; Laboratory Equipment 5*

mortar: *Cannon 7; Military Weapons General 8*

mortarboard: *Headgear 2*

mortician: *Medical Occupations 1*

mortified: *Horror Vocabulary 23*

mortino: *Unusual Edible Fruits 6*

mortuary worker: *Horror Occupations 23; Medical Occupations 1*

Morucha: *Other Cows 15*

mosaic: *Art Techniques 13*

mosey: *Locomotion 9*

Mosin-Nagant: *Bolt Action Sniper Rifles 7*

mosque: *Religious Building 3*

mosquito: *Flies 15*

moss agate: *Minerals 10*

moss campion: *Garden Perennials 10*

moss crepe: *Fabric 2*

moss heather: *Shrubs 10*

moss jasper: *Minerals 10*

moss opal: *Minerals 10*

moss rose: *Garden Annuals 10*

moss verbena: *Wildflowers 10*

Mossberg 464: *Lever Action and Pump Centerfire Rifles 7; Lever Action and Pump Rimfire Rifles 7*

Mossberg 4X4: *Bolt Action Centerfire Rifles 7*

Mossberg 500 shotgun: *SWAT Weapons 7*

Mossberg Magnum: *Shotguns Semiautomatic 7*

Mossberg model 500: *Shotguns Pump 7*

Mossberg model 802 Plinkster: *Bolt Action Rimfire Rifles 7*

Mossberg Silver Reserve: *Shotguns Side-by-Side 7*

mosso: *Tempo/Mood 13*

mossottite: *Minerals 10*

mossycup oak: *Deciduous Trees 10*

mossy overcup oak: *Deciduous Trees 10*

most recent: *New 20*

mostaccioli: *Pasta 6*

motel: *Hospitality 3*

motet: *Composition Types 13*

moth fly: *Flies 15*

moth stroke: *Swimming Strokes 9*

moth: *Animals 15; Animals with Symbolic Meaning 19*

Mother Nature: *Folklore Characters 18*

mother nuclide: *Chemistry General Vocabulary 11*

mother of God: *Expletives 20*

mother of millions: *Poisonous Plants 10*

mother of opal: *Minerals 10*

mother of pearl opal: *Minerals 10*

mother of thyme: *Garden Perennials 10*

mother who lost her baby: *Supporting Cast 23*

mother: *Cleric 1; Female 1*

mother-in-law: *Female 1*

Mothman: *Folklore Characters 18*

Mothra: *Mythical Creatures and Monsters 16*

motif: *General Music Vocabulary 13*

motion detector: *Building Systems 3; SWAT Equipment 7*

motion sensor: *Building Systems 3*

motion sickness: *Injuries/Medical Emergencies 12; Travel Hazards 9*

motion: *Philosophy Basic Concepts 14*

motivated: *Personality Other 1*

moto: *Tempo/Mood 13*

motor coach: *Mass Transit 9*

motor pool: *Military Property 3*

motor vehicle: *Motorized 9*

motorcycle: *Motorized 9; Spy Gear 5; Travel Modes 23*

motorized truck: *Transportation 9*

motorized: *Transportation 9*

motte: *Castle Anatomy 3*

motte-and-bailey: *Fortification 3*

mottled: *Owls 15; Skin Types and Features 1*

motto: *Elements 19*

Motuo bamboo: *Pit Viper 15*

moulin: *Glacial and Mountain 10*

mound: *Natural Animal Homes 15; Terrain Features 10*

Mount Calvary: *Relics of Jesus 14*

Mount Everest: *Seven Wonders of the Natural World 18*

Mount Olympus: *Fictional/Mythological Locations 18*

Mount Rushmore: *Unique Property 3*

mount: *Terrain Features 10*

mountain alder: *Deciduous Trees 10*

mountain ash: *Deciduous Trees 10*

mountain avens: *Shrubs 10*

mountain birch: *Deciduous Trees 10*

mountain black cherry: *Deciduous Trees 10*

mountain bluet: *Garden Perennials 10*

mountain cedar: *Evergreen Trees 10*

mountain climbing: *Exploration 9*

mountain cork: *Minerals 10*

mountain cove: *Glacial and Mountain 10*

mountain cypress: *Evergreen Trees 10*

mountain fairy: *Demon 16*

mountain fringe: *Garden Perennials 10*

mountain giant: *Humanlike Groups 1*

mountain goat: *Other Wild Mammals 15*

mountain gold: *Garden Perennials 10*

mountain gorilla: *Apes 15*

mountain hemlock: *Evergreen Trees 10*

mountain lady's mantle: *Garden Perennials 10*

mountain landforms: *Chapter 10*

mountain laurel: *Deciduous Trees 10; Poisonous Plants 10; Shrubs 10*

mountain leather: *Minerals 10*

mountain lion: *Big Cats 15*

mountain mahogany: *Deciduous Trees 10; Shrubs 10*

mountain man: *Barbarian 1*

mountain mint: *Garden Perennials 10*

mountain oak: *Deciduous Trees 10*

mountain opal: *Minerals 10*

mountain pass: *Glacial and Mountain 10; Slope 10*

mountain pine: *Evergreen Trees 10*

mountain range: *Glacial and Mountain 10*

mountain red oak: *Deciduous Trees 10*

mountain spruce: *Evergreen Trees 10*

mountain stronghold: *Fantasy Locations 24*

mountain war: *General Combat Vocabulary 7*

mountain white oak: *Deciduous Trees 10*

mountain white pine: *Evergreen Trees 10*

mountain: *Adder 15; Climatic Zones 10; Dwarf 1; Ecosystems 10; Giant Humanoids 16; Glacial and Mountain 10; Gnome 1*

mountaineering: *Exploration 9*

mountaintop: *Terrain Features 10*

mounted warrior: *Knight 1*

Mountie: *Law Enforcement 1*

mounts: *Palm Reading 19*

Moura: *Pigs 15*

mourn: *Sad 20*

mournful: *Sad 20*

mourning bonnet: *Headgear 2*

mourning cloak: *Butterfly 15*

mourning dove: *Backyard Birds 15*

mourning hat: *Headgear 2*

mourning hood: *Headgear 2*

mourning: *Sad 20*

mourning: *Styles of Dress 2*

mouse ears: *Wildflowers 10*

mouse pad: *Computer Equipment 5*

mouse: *Animals with Symbolic Meaning 19; Computer Equipment 5; Traps 3; Venomous Arachnids 15; Woodland Mammals 15*

mousebird: *Other Wild Birds 15*

mouse-tailed: *Bats 15*

mousseline: *Fabric 2*

mousy: *Personality Other 1*

mouth harp: *Percussion Musical Instruments 5*

mouth: *Body Parts 12; Character Building 1*

mouthpiece: *Musical Instrument Parts 13*

mouthwash: *Personal Care 5*

move: *Commands 20; Locomotion 9*

moveable: *Bridges 9*

movement: *Art Principles 13; General Music Vocabulary 13*

moves: *Combat, Armor, and Weapons 7*

movie critic: *Publishing 1*

movie popcorn: *Snacks 6*

movie projector: *Office/School Machines 5*

movie screen: *Office/School Machines 5*

movie theater: *Entertainment Property 3*

movies: *Christmas 19*

moving object: *Paranormal Occurrences 21*

moving: *Sad 20*

mower: *General Farm Equipment; Horse Drawn Farm Equipment*

Moyle: *Horse Breeds 15*

Mozambique spitting: *Cobra 15*

mozzarella: *Cheese Common Varieties 6*

MP5 submachine gun: *Small Arms 8*

MQ-1 Predator unmanned system: *U.S. Air Force Aircraft 8*

MQ-1C Grey Eagle unmanned: *U.S. Navy Aircraft 8*

MQ-1C Warrior: *U.S. Army Helicopter 8*

MQ-9 Reaper: *U.S. Air Force Aircraft 8*

mqundu: *Cheese International Varieties 6*

Mr. Spock: *Asteroids with Unusual Names 11*

MRE: *Military Equipment 8*

MRI BFR: *Revolver Single Action 7*

MRI Desert Eagle Series: *Pistol Semiautomatic 7*

MRI Magnum Lite Eagle: *Bolt Action Centerfire Rifles 7*

Mrs. Hudson: *Sir Arthur Conan Doyle 18*

Mrs.: *Female 1*

M-style: *Roof Styles 3*

Mt. Atlas daisy: *Garden Perennials 10*

MTK-2 mine clearing vehicle: *Russia Military Vehicles 8*

Mu: *Fictional/Mythological Locations 18*

Mu'aqqibat: *Angels of Good 14*

Muck soil: *Soil General Vocabulary 10*

Muckleshoot: *Native American Peoples 1*

mud daubers: *Wasp 15*

mud volcano: *Volcanic 10*

mud: *Adder 15; Elemental 16; Exterior Building Materials 3; Freshwater Turtles 15; General Snake Families 15; Soil General Vocabulary 10; Wasp 15*

mudslide: *Geological Natural Hazards 10*

mudsnake: *Sea Snake 15*

mudstone: *Sedimentary Rocks 10*

Muenster: *Cheese Common Varieties 6*

muff pistol: *Derringer 7*

muff: *Accessories 2*

muff-box hat: *Headgear 2*

muffed old English game: *Chickens 15*

muffin pan: *Kitchen Equipment 5*

muffin tin: *Kitchen Equipment 5*

muffin: *Food 6*

muffled: *Quiet 20*

muffler: *Accessories 2*

muffuletta: *Sandwiches 6*

mufti: *Cleric 1*

mug: *Drinkware 5*

mugearite: *Igneous Rocks 10*

mugger: *Crocodilians 15; Fighter 1; Illicit Occupations 1*

muggy: *Wet 10*

mugwort: *Objects that Offer Protection 19*

muir cap: *Headgear 2*

mukluks: *Boots 2*

Mukota: *Pigs 15*

mulberry: *Berries 6; Deciduous Trees 10*

mulch tiller: *General Farm Equipment*

mule: *Horses Related 15; Transportation Animals 9*

Mulefoot: *Pigs 15*

mules: *Footwear/Shoes 2*

mulish: *Stubborn 1*

mull over: *Solve 20*

mullein: *Garden Perennials 10; Wildflowers 10*

mullet: *Hair Style 1; Wild Saltwater Fish 15*

mullicite: *Minerals 10*

mulligatawny: *Soup 6*

mullion: *Geological Vocabulary 10*

multiflora rose: *Weeds 10*

multi-mission VTOL: *Military Aircraft 8*

multi-mission: *Helicopters 8; Military Aircraft 8*

multiplanetary: *Planetary Systems 11*

multiple body parts: *Physical Mutations 22*

multiple figures: *Classic Heraldry 19*

multiple myeloma: *Blood-Related Ailments 12*

multiple rocket launcher: *Military 8*

multiple: *Star Systems 11*

multiple-eyed: *Eye Type 1*

Multiscale European Soil Information System: *Soil General Vocabulary 10*

Multiscale Soil Information Systems: *Soil General Vocabulary 10*

multi-star: *Planetary Systems 11*

mumble: *Paranormal Occurrences 21*

mummified: *Dry 10*

mummy powder: *Wizard's Goods 5*

mummy rises: *Horror Plot Devices 23*

mummy wrapping: *Wizard's Goods 5*

mummy: *Mythical Creatures and Monsters 16; Undead 16*

mumps: *Diseases 12*

munchkin: *Child 1*

Munchkin: *Domestic Cats 15*

Mundilfari: *Moons 11*

mundu: *Unusual Edible Fruits 6*

mung bean: *Legumes 6*

municipal district: *Political Divisions 10*

municipality: *City 10; Political Divisions 10*

munitions storage: *Fortification 3*

Munkar: *Angels of Good 14*

muntries: *Unusual Edible Fruits 6*

Murboden: *Other Cows 15*

murder hole: *Castle Anatomy 3*

murder: *Attack 7; Kill 20*

murderer: *Assassin 1; Fighter 1; Illicit Occupations 1; Villain 20*

Murgese: *Horse Breeds 15*

Murgleis: *Weapons of Legend 18*

Muriel: *Angels of Good 14*

muriqui: *New World Monkeys 15*

Murphy: *Beds 4*

Murray Grey: *Other Cows 15*

Murray river: *Freshwater Turtles 15*

Musca: *Constellations 11*

muscadine: *Unusual Edible Fruits 6*

muscimol: *Dangerous Chemicals 11*

muscle car: *Motorized 9*

muscle cramps: *Injuries/Medical Emergencies 12*

muscle memory: *Fencing Vocabulary 7*

muscle pull: *Injuries/Medical Emergencies 12*

muscle shirt: *Men's Wear 2*

muscle-bound: *Large/Heavy 1*

musclewood: *Deciduous Trees 10*

muscular: *Large/Heavy 1*

musculoskeletal: *Body Systems 12*

museum: *Academic Property 3; Beetle 15; Entertainment Property 3; Military Property 3*

mushroom hat: *Headgear 2*

mushroom tourmaline: *Minerals 10*

mushroom: *Pickled/Relish 6; Soup 6; Vegetables 6; Wizard's Goods 5*

mushy: *Wet 20*

music room: *Rooms 3*

music stand: *Music Accessories*

music therapist: *Medical Occupations 1*

music vocabulary: *The Arts 13*

music: *The Arts 13*

musical director: *Musical Occupations 1; Performing Arts 1*

musical instrument: *Specialty Survival Gear 5; Typical Magical Objects 17*

musical instruments: *Equipment and Tools 5*

musical occupations: *Character Building 1*

musical period: *The Arts 13*

musical styles: *The Arts 13*

musical: *Performance Genres 13*

musician: *Bard 1; Musical Occupations 1*

musk deer: *Other Wild Mammals 15*

musk ox: *Other Wild Mammals 15*

musk thistle: *Weeds 10*

musk: *Beetle 15; Melons 6*

muskeg: *Soil General Vocabulary 10*

musket: *Black Powder Weapons 7*

musketeer: *Fighter 1*

muslin: *Fabric 2*

Muspelheim: *Fictional/Mythological Locations 18*

mustache: *Character Building 1*

mustached: *Bats 15*

Mustang: *Horse Breeds 15*

mustard gas: *Dangerous Chemicals 11*

mustard greens: *Vegetables 6*

mustard: *Seeds 6; Spices 6*

mutant plants attack: *Horror Plot Devices 23*

mutant: *Monster Categories/Terms 16; Monsters and Creatures 22*

mutants: *Plot Devices 22*

mute: *Music Accessories*

muted: *Quiet 20*

mutilate: *Harm 20*

mutineer: *Fighter 1*

mutiny: *General Combat Vocabulary 7*

mutt: *Dogs/Canine 15*

mutter: *Sounds 20*

mutton: *Other Meat 6*

muttonchops: *Facial Hair Beard 1*

Muturu: *Other Cows 15*

muzzle loader: *Cannon 7*

muzzle: *Nose 1*

Myakka soil: *Soil General Vocabulary 10*

mybock: *Beer 6*

Mycroft Holmes: *Sir Arthur Conan Doyle 18*

mylonite: *Metamorphic Rocks 10*

mynah: *Domesticated Pet Birds 15*

myocardial infarction: *Blood-Related Ailments 12*

myotis: *Bats 15*

Myrhorod: *Pigs 15*

myricaria: *Shrubs 10*

myrickite: *Minerals 10*

myristicin: *Poisonous Chemicals in Plants 11*

myrmecoleon: *Insectoid 16*

myrmekite: *Minerals 10*

myrmidon: *Insectoid 16*

myrrh: *Christmas 19; Wizard's Goods 5*

myrtle: *Deciduous Trees 10; Garden Perennials 10; Shrubs 10*

myrtlewood: *Deciduous Trees 10*

mysteries: *Magic Vocabulary 17*

mysterious benefactor: *Common Character Archetypes 21*

mysterious invitation leads to frightening ordeal: *Horror Plot Devices 23*

mysterious liquid or gas: *Horror Plot Devices 23*

mysterious neighbor: *Horror Plot Devices 23*

mysterious occurrences: *Legendary, Mystical and Mythical Items and Locations 18*

mysterious: *Magic Vocabulary 17*

mystery: *Fantasy Genres 24; Horror Genres 23; Magic Vocabulary 17; Performance Genres 13; Plot Devices 22; Science Fiction Genres 22*

mystic quartz: *Standard Gems 21*

mystic topaz: *Standard Gems 21*

mystic: *Fortune Teller 1; Illusionist 1; Magic Vocabulary 17; Wizard 1*

mystical organizations: *Legendary, Mystical and Mythical Items and Locations 18*

mystical: *Magic Vocabulary 17*

myth: *Magic Vocabulary 17; Philosophy Basic Concepts 14*

mythic: *Magic Vocabulary 17*

mythical creatures: *Monsters 16*

mythical monsters: *Monsters 16*

mythical: *Magic Vocabulary 17*

mythological locations: *Legendary, Mystical and Mythical Items and Locations 18; Legendary/Mythical Locations 18*

mythology: *Literary Styles 5*

mythos: *Philosophy Basic Concepts 14*

myzithra: *Cheese International Varieties 6*

–N–

naan: *Bread General Varieties 6*

naartjie: *Unusual Edible Fruits 6*

nabulsi: *Cheese International Varieties 6*

nachtmusik: *Composition Types 13*

nadir: *Astronomy General Terms 11*

Naegling (Beowulf): *Weapons of Legend 18*

Nag Hammadi Texts: *Major Religious Books 14*

naga: *Beast 16*

Naga: *Human Ethnic Groups 1*

nageia: *Unusual Edible Fruits 6*

Nagelring: *Weapons of Legend 18*

naginata: *Pole Weapons 7*

Naglfar: *Vehicles 18*

Nagori: *Other Cows 15*

Nagraj King of Snakes: *Mythical Creatures and Monsters 16*

nagual: *Shapechanger 16*

naiad: *Aquatic 16; Water Faerie 16*

Naiad: *Moons 11*

naiant: *Sea Creatures 19*

nail clipper: *Personal Care 5*

nail file: *Personal Care 5*

nail gun: *Classic Items 23; Improvised Weapons 7; Power Tools*

nail head spar: *Minerals 10*

nail polish: *Makeup 5*

nail: *Fix 20; Hardware 5; Objects that Offer Protection 19*

nails: *Patterns 19*

naïve: *Art Genres 13; Personality Other 1*

Naked Indian: *Deciduous Trees 10*

naked-backed: *Bats 15*

Nakir: *Angels of Good 14*

Namaka: *Moons 11*

Namaqua dwarf: *Adder 15*

namarrgon: *Demon 16*

namboca: *Deciduous Trees 10*

name: *Philosophy Basic Concepts 14*

nameko: *Fungus Common Names 10*

names: *Objects/Activities Connected to Lore 19*

Namo: *Twelve Peers of Charlemagne 18*

nana: *Female 1*

nance: *Unusual Edible Fruits 6*

nandao: *Swords Two-handed 7*

nangka: *Unusual Edible Fruits 6*

Nanna-Sin (moon): *Sumerian Pantheon 14*

nannyberry: *Unusual Edible Fruits 6*

nano-beasts: *Monsters and Creatures 22*

nanobot: *Robots 22*

Nanook: *Bears 15*

nanotechnology: *Plot Devices 22; Science Fiction Genres 22*

Nanyang: *Other Cows 15*

nap: *Card Games 5; Sewing Terms 2*

napa cabbage: *Vegetables 6*

napalm: *Card Games 5*

nape: *Body Parts 12*

napkin: *Table Linens 5*

napkins: *Thanksgiving 19*

Naples onion: *Garden Perennials 10*

Napolean: *Cake 6*

nappy dish: *Tableware 5*

naranjilla: *Unusual Edible Fruits 6*

Narborough Island giant: *Tortoises 15*

Narragansett soil: *Soil General Vocabulary 10*

Narragansett: *Native American Peoples 1*

narrative: *Art Genres 13; Literary Styles 5*

narrator: *Academic 1*

narrow dock: *Weeds 10*

narrow road: *Roads 9*

narrow: *Eyebrows 1; Lips 1; Mouth 1; Small/Thin 1*

narrow-mouthed: *Toads 15*

narrows: *Roads 9*

narthex: *Church Anatomy 3*

Narvi: *Moons 11*

nasal bone: *Bones 12*

nasal: *Vocal/Speech Quality 1*

Naskapi: *Native American Peoples 1*

naso tang: *Aquarium Saltwater Fish 15*

nasturtium: *Garden Annuals 10*

nasty: *Bad 20; Negative 1; Unattractive 20*

Nat Turner: *Real People with Legendary Status 18*

natal grass: *Weeds 10*

Natal hinge-back: *Tortoises 15*

natal redtop: *Weeds 10*

Natchez silt loam: *Soil General Vocabulary 10*

Nathan Hale: *Real People with Legendary Status 18*

nation: *Philosophy Basic Concepts 14*

national guard officer: *Horror Occupations 23*

National Guard Post: *Special Purpose Structure 3*

National Hurricane Center (NHC): *Meteorology General Vocabulary 10*

National Show Horse: *Horse Breeds 15*

National Society of Consulting Soil Scientists: *Soil General Vocabulary 10*

National Weather Service (NWC): *Meteorology General Vocabulary 10*

national: *Art Genres 13*

nation-state: *Political Divisions 10*

Native American pantheon: *Philosophy and Religion 14*

Native American peoples: *Character Building 1*

Native Americans: *Thanksgiving 19*

native antimony: *Minerals 10*

native arsenic: *Minerals 10*

native bismuth: *Minerals 10*

native copper: *Minerals 10*

native gold: *Minerals 10*

native iron: *Minerals 10*

native lead: *Minerals 10*

native mercury: *Minerals 10*

native nickel: *Minerals 10*

native platinum: *Minerals 10*

native silver: *Minerals 10*

native state: *Chemistry General Vocabulary 11*

native sulfur: *Minerals 10*

native tellurium: *Minerals 10*

native: *Barbarian 1; Styles of Dress 2*

Nativity: *Christmas 19*

natural animal homes: *Animals 15*

natural arch: *Cave Anatomy 10; Erosion 10*

natural balance: *Pennsylvania Dutch Hex Signs 19*

natural bridge: *Cave Anatomy 10*

natural disaster: *Horror Genres 23; Plot Devices 22*

natural gas/swamp gas: *Energy Sources/Types 23*

natural gas: *Energy Sources/Types 22*

natural levee: *Fluvial 10*

natural organic matter: *Soil General Vocabulary 10*

natural pool: *Fluvial 10*

natural radioactivity: *Chemistry General Vocabulary 11*

natural salt: *Minerals 10*

natural selection: *Philosophy Basic Concepts 14*

natural: *General Music Vocabulary 13; Notation 13*

naturalist: *Nature Occupations 1*

nature magic: *Witchcraft Vocabulary 17*

nature occupations: *Character Building 1*

nature: *Philosophy Basic Concepts 14*

naughty or nice: *Christmas 19*

nauseating: *Unattractive 20*

nautical: *Charges 19*

Navajo sand painting: *Objects in Magic and Religion 19*

Navajo: *Masks 2; Native American Peoples 1*

naval offense: *General Combat Vocabulary 7*

naval orange: *Citrus 6*

naval superiority: *General Combat Vocabulary 7*

naval support: *General Combat Vocabulary 7*

naval terrain warfare: *General Combat Vocabulary 7*

navatte: *Gem Cuts 21*

nave: *Church Anatomy 3*

navel: *Body Parts 12*

navicular bone: *Bones 12*

navigation: *Boat/Ship Terminology 9*

navigator: *Transportation 1*

Navy Arms 1873: *Revolver Single Action 7; Single Shot Centerfire Rifles 7*

Navy Arms 1885 High Wall: *Single Shot Centerfire Rifles 7*

Navy Arms Henry: *Lever Action and Pump Centerfire Rifles 7*

navy bean: *Legumes 6*

navy blue: *Blue 20*

navy ranks (rates): *Military 8*

navy vessels: *Military 8*

naxos: *Cheese International Varieties 6*

nazar: *Objects in Magic and Religion 19*

Nazareth: *Christmas 19*

Nazca lines: *Real Objects Not Fully Understood 18*

Nazi: *Architectural Styles 3; Villain 20*

N'dama: *Other Cows 15*

nealite: *Minerals 10*

Neanderthal: *Forehead 1*

Neapolitan Mastiff: *Dog Breeds 15*

near: *Beer 6*

near-sighted: *Eye Type 1*

neat: *Personality Other 1*

neaten: *Clean 20*

Nebelung: *Domestic Cats 15*

nebula: *Astronomy General Terms 11*

nebuly: *Partition Lines 19*

necessary room: *Bathrooms 3*

necessity: *Philosophy Basic Concepts 14*

neck support: *Pillows 5*

neck tie: *Men's Wear 2*

neck: *Body Parts 12; Musical Instrument Parts 13*

neckbeard: *Facial Hair Beard 1*

neckerchief: *Western Clothing/Dress 21*

necklace of Harmonia: *Jewelry 18*

necklace of the Lady of the Lake: *Jewelry 18*

necklace: *Jewelry 2; Jewelry 21*

neckline: *Garment Pieces 2*

necromancer: *Wizard 1*

necromancy: *Magic Vocabulary 17*

Necronomicon: *Books of Legend 18*

necropolis: *Cemetery 3*

nectar: *Bats 15; Foods with Religious or Ritual Significance 19*

nectarine: *Pie 6; Pit Fruits 6*

Ned Kelly: *Real People with Legendary Status 18*

needle fish: *Wild Saltwater Fish 15*

needle tin: *Minerals 10*

needle: *Sewing Equipment 2; Wizard's Goods 5*

needlefelt carpet: *Floor Coverings 4*

needlepoint carpet: *Floor Coverings 4*

needler: *Weapons 22*

neem: *Unusual Edible Fruits 6*

negative: *Character Building 1; Sad 20*

neglect: *Harm 20*

negligee: *Ladies' Wear 2*

negligible: *Small/Fragile 20*

negotiate: *Solve 20*

Negrito: *Human Ethnic Groups 1*

Nehru collar: *Garment Pieces 2*

neighbor is a vampire: *Horror Plot Devices 23*

neighborhood association: *Guilds 1*

neighborhood: *City 10*

Neijiang: *Pigs 15*

neillia: *Shrubs 10*

Neith: *Hypothetical Solar System Bodies 11; Moons 11*

Nelore: *Other Cows 15*

Nemean lion: *Twelve Labors of Hercules 16*

Nemesis: *Hypothetical Solar System Bodies 11*

Neoarchean Period: *Geologic Time 10*

Neoclassical: *Architectural Styles 3; Art Movements 13; Musical Styles 13*

Neodymium: *Elements 11*

Neogene Period: *Geologic Time 10*

Neo-Greek: *Architectural Styles 3*

Neoism: *Art Movements 13*

Neolithic: *Architectural Styles 3*

neon message board: *Office/School/Writing Supplies 5*

neon tetra: *Aquarium Freshwater Fish 15*

Neon: *Elements 11*

neon: *Illumination Bulb and Tube Types 5*

neopolitan: *Ice Cream Flavors 6*

Neoproterozoic Period: *Geologic Time 10*

neotropical ground lizard: *Scaled Reptiles 15*

Neo-Vernacular: *Architectural Styles 3*

Nepal: *Tea 6*

Nepalese browntop: *Weeds 10*

nepheline syenite: *Igneous Rocks 10*

nephelinite: *Igneous Rocks 10*

nephew: *Male 1*

Nephilim: *Human Races Fictional 1*

nephrite: *Minerals 10*

Nephthys (goddess of wealth): *Egyptian Pantheon 14*

nepouite: *Minerals 10*

Neptune (oceans): *Roman Pantheon 14*

Neptune: *Planets 11*

Neptunium: *Elements 11*

ner tamid: *Objects in Magic and Religion 19*

nerd/geek: *Common Character Archetypes 21*

nerdy: *Styles of Dress 2*

Nereid: *Moons 11*

Nergal (the dead): *Babylonian Pantheon 14*

Nernst Equation: *Chemistry General Vocabulary 11*

nerve wracking: *Unattractive 20*

nerve: *General Emotions 20*

nerves: *Organs/Major Structures 12*

nervous: *Body Systems 12; Horror Vocabulary 23; Personality Other 1*

nervy: *Personality Other 1*

neslite: *Minerals 10*

Neso: *Moons 11*

Nessie: *Mythical Creatures and Monsters 16*

nest: *Natural Animal Homes 15*

net: *Fabric 2; Fishing Gear 5; Flexible 7; Traps 3*

netherworld: *Afterlife/Underworld 18*

netleaf hackberry: *Deciduous Trees 10*

netting: *Fabric 2*

nettle : *Garden Perennials 10; Items with Healing Properties 19; Objects that Offer Protection 19; Plants with Symbolic Meaning 19; Wildflowers 10*

nettletree: *Deciduous Trees 10*

Neuf: *Ballet Terms 13*

Neufchatel: *Cheese Moist 6*

neurotoxic amino acid: *Poisonous Chemicals in Plants 11*

Neuschwanstein: *Unique Property 3*

neutralization: *Chemistry General Vocabulary 11*

neutralize: *Clean 20; General Combat Vocabulary 7*

neutrino: *Astronomy General Terms 11*

neutron star: *Astronomy General Terms 11*

neutron: *Chemistry General Vocabulary 11; Energy Sources/Types 22; Star Types and Relatives 11; Weapons 22*

Nevada opal: *Minerals 10*

never: *Expletives 20*

new canasta: *Card Games 5*

new clothes: *Easter 19*

New England aster: *Wildflowers 10*

New England: *Architectural Styles 3; Coffee Bean Roasts 6*

New Forest Pony: *Horse Breeds 15*

New Guinea crocodile: *Crocodilians 15*

New Guinea impatiens: *Garden Annuals 10*

New Guinea snapping: *Freshwater Turtles 15*

new gun dazzles villain: *Western Plot Devices 21*

New Hampshire: *Chickens 15*

New Jersey tea: *Garden Perennials 10*

New Kirgiz: *Horse Breeds 15*

New Mexico locust: *Deciduous Trees 10*

new potato: *Vegetables 6*

New Testament Apocrypha: *Major Religious Books 14*

New Testament: *Major Religious Books 14; Objects in Magic and Religion 19; Philosophy and Religion 14*

new wave: *Musical Styles 13; Science Fiction Genres 22*

New World monkeys: *Animals 15*

New Year: *Holidays 19*

New Year's baby: *Characters with Symbolic Meaning 19*

New Year's old timer: *Characters with Symbolic Meaning 19*

New York strip: *Beef 6*

new: *Adjectives 20*

newborn: *Child 1; New 20*

Newburg: *Fish/Seafood Meals 6*

newel: *Building Elements and Features 3; Castle Anatomy 3*

new-fangled: *New 20*

Newfoundland Pony: *Horse Breeds 15*

Newfoundland: *Dog Breeds 15*

newlywed: *New 20*

Newmark's influence chart: *Soil General Vocabulary 10*

news reporter: *Publishing 1*

newsboy cap: *Headgear 2*

newspaper man discovers secret and fights to survive: *Western Plot Devices 21*

newspaper with hole cut out: *Spy Gear 5*

newspaper: *Books/Publications 5*

newspaperman: *Publishing 1*

Newton's first law of motion: *Astronomy General Terms 11*

Newton's second law of motion: *Astronomy General Terms 11*

Newton's third law of motion: *Astronomy General Terms 11*

newts: *Animals 15*

NEXRAD: *Meteorology General Vocabulary 10*

Nez Percé: *Native American Peoples 1*

ngarara: *Demon 16*

Nguni: *Other Cows 15*

nguri: *Cheese International Varieties 6*

nib/pen: *Art Media 13*

Nicaraguan slider: *Freshwater Turtles 15*

niccolo: *Minerals 10*

nice guy: *Common Character Archetypes 21*

nice looking: *Beautiful 20*

nice: *Good 20; Happy 20*

niche: *Church Anatomy 3*

nicholsonite: *Minerals 10*

nickel bloom: *Minerals 10*

nickel carbonyl: *Dangerous Chemicals 11*

nickel: *Coins and Currency 21; Minerals 10*

Nickel: *Elements 11*

nickel-cadmium cell: *Chemistry General Vocabulary 11*

nickelian loellingite: *Minerals 10*

nickel-iron: *Minerals 10*

Nicobar bamboo: *Pit Viper 15*

Nicobar Island: *Keelback 15*

nicotiana: *Garden Annuals 10*

nicotine sulfate: *Dangerous Chemicals 11*

nicotine: *Dangerous Chemicals 11*

niece: *Female 1*

nigella: *Garden Annuals 10*

Nigerian black mud: *Freshwater Turtles 15*

Nigerian chimpanzee: *Apes 15*

night baseball: *Poker Card Games 5*

night birds seen or heard during daytime: *Harbingers of Bad Luck 19*

night cap: *Headgear 2*

night club: *Entertainment Property 3; Styles of Dress 2*

night cream: *Personal Care 5*

night hag: *Extraplanar 16*

night light: *Illumination/Light Sources 5*

night lizard: *Scaled Reptiles 15*

night monkey: *New World Monkeys 15*

night stand: *Tables 4*

night vision optics: *SWAT Equipment 7*

night vision system: *Military Equipment 8*

night watchman: *Horror Occupations 23; Law Enforcement 1*

night witch: *Demon 16*

night: *Adder 15; General Snake Families 15*

nightgown: *Ladies' Wear 2*

Nighthawk Custom 10-8 Dominator: *Pistol Semiautomatic 7*

nighthawk: *Backyard Birds 15*

nightingale: *Domesticated Pet Birds 15*

nightjar: *Other Wild Birds 15*

nightmare: *Beast 16; Extraplanar 16; Horror Vocabulary 23; Masks 2*

nightshade: *Garden Perennials 10; Objects/Activities Connected to Lore 19*

nightshirt: *Unisex Clothing 2; Western Clothing/Dress 21*

nightstick: *Bludgeons 7*

nightwear: *Unisex Clothing 2*

nihilism: *Philosophy Basic Concepts 14*

niigataite: *Minerals 10*

Nike (goddess of victory): *Greek Pantheon 14*

Nile crocodile: *Crocodilians 15*

Nilgiri: *Keelback 15*

nilgiri: *Tea 6*

Nimari: *Other Cows 15*

nimble: *Mobility 1*

nimbostratus: *Clouds 10*

nimbus: *Clouds 10; Jewelry 21*

nimcha: *Swords One-handed 7*

Nimitz class aircraft carrier: *U.S. Navy Vessels 8*

Nina: *Ships 18*

nine card Don: *Card Games 5*

nine five two: *Card Games 5*

nine ladies dancing: *Twelve Days of Christmas 19*

nine ring: *Swords One-handed 7*

ninebark: *Shrubs 10*

nine-card brag: *Card Games 5*

ninety-eight: *Card Games 5*

ninety-nine: *Card Games 5*

Ningxiang: *Pigs 15*

Nin-Hursag (goddess of the earth): *Sumerian Pantheon 14*

ninimini: *Demon 16*

ninja: *Assassin 1; Fighter 1; Martial Artist/Monk 1*

ninjato: *Swords One-handed 7*

Niobium: *Elements 11*

nip in the air: *Cold 10*

Nipomo agate: *Minerals 10*

nipper: *Child 1*

nippy: *Cold 10*

nisse: *Demon 16*

nitric oxide: *Dangerous Chemicals 11*

nitrobenzene: *Dangerous Chemicals 11*

nitrocyclohexane: *Dangerous Chemicals 11*

nitrogen cycle: *Chemistry General Vocabulary 11*

nitrogen dioxide: *Dangerous Chemicals 11*

Nitrogen: *Elements 11*

nitrosodimethylamine: *Dangerous Chemicals 11*

Ni-Vanuatu: *Human Ethnic Groups 1*

Nix: *Moons 11*

nixie: *Aquatic 16; Demon 16; General Fae 16; Water Faerie 16*

NMR tube: *Laboratory Equipment 5*

no air conditioning : *Travel Hazards 9*

No Cha (demigod of thieves): *Chinese Pantheon 14*

no heat: *Travel Hazards 9*

no peek: *Poker Card Games 5*

no problem: *Easy 20*

no: *Expletives 20*

Noah's Ark: *Ships 18*

Nobelium: *Elements 11*

noble fir: *Evergreen Trees 10*

Noble gases: *Chemistry General Vocabulary 11*

noble orthoclase: *Minerals 10*

noble savage: *Common Character Archetypes 21*

noble: *Character Building 1; Good 20; Knight 1; Personality Other 1; Styles of Dress 2*

noctule: *Bats 15*

nocturne: *Composition Types 13*

nodal region: *Geography General Vocabulary 10*

nodding thistle: *Weeds 10*

noddy: *Card Games 5*

no-fly zone: *General Combat Vocabulary 7*

nogal: *Deciduous Trees 10*

nogalillo: *Deciduous Trees 10*

nogalito: *Deciduous Trees 10*

noil: *Fabric 2*

noiseless: *Quiet 20*

noisemakers: *New Year 19*

noisome: *Bad 20*

noisy: *Loud 20*

Noma: *Horse Breeds 15*

nomad: *Barbarian 1*

nominalism: *Philosophy Basic Concepts 14*

nonagenarian: *Elderly 1*

nonbonding orbital: *Chemistry General Vocabulary 11*

nondairy: *Milk 6*

nonelectrolyte: *Chemistry General Vocabulary 11*

nonet: *Composition Types 13*

nonfiction: *Literary Styles 5*

noni: *Unusual Edible Fruits 6*

nonpareil: *Candy Chocolate 6*

nonpolar bond: *Chemistry General Vocabulary 11*

nonsense: *Expletives 20*

nonsporting: *Dog Groups 15*

Nooitgedacht Pony: *Horse Breeds 15*

Nootka cypress: *Evergreen Trees 10*

Nootka false cypress: *Evergreen Trees 10*

nor'easter: *Meteorology General Vocabulary 10; Snow Storms 10*

norbormide: *Dangerous Chemicals 11*

Nordic dragonhead: *Garden Perennials 10*

Nordland: *Horse Breeds 15*

Norfold grey: *Chickens 15*

Norfolk Terrier: *Dog Breeds 15*

Noric: *Horse Breeds 15*

norite : *Igneous Rocks 10*

norm: *Philosophy Basic Concepts 14*

Norma: *Constellations 11*

normal fault: *Geological Vocabulary 10*

normal: *Meteorology General Vocabulary 10*

Norman: *Architectural Styles 3*

Normande: *Other Cows 15*

Norse pantheon: *Philosophy and Religion 14*

Norse weapons: *Legendary, Mystical and Mythical Items and Locations 18*

North African helmeted: *Freshwater Turtles 15*

North American Arms Guardian: *Pistol Semiautomatic 7*

North American dairy cows: *Animals 15*

North American spotted: *Freshwater Turtles 15*

North American wood: *Freshwater Turtles 15*

North Carolina pine: *Evergreen Trees 10*

north caucasian: *Pigs 15*

north frigid zone: *Geographical Zones 10*

North Pole: *Christmas 19*

north Siberian: *Pigs 15*

North star: *Harbingers/Charms for Good Luck 19*

North Swedish Horse: *Horse Breeds 15*

north temperate zone: *Geographical Zones 10*

north: *Eight Compass Points 19*

Northeast Congo: *Lions 15*

northeast: *Eight Compass Points 19*

northeastern hill: *Krait 15*

Northeastern: *Horse Breeds 15*

northern black-knobbed map: *Freshwater Turtles 15*

northern black-tailed: *Rattlesnake 15*

northern crepe myrtle: *Garden Perennials 10*

northern hackberry: *Deciduous Trees 10*

northern hawk: *Owls 15*

northern king fish: *Wild Saltwater Fish 15*

northern maidenhair fern: *Wildflowers 10*

northern pike: *Fish/Seafood Types 6; Wild Freshwater Fish 15*

northern pin oak: *Deciduous Trees 10*

northern pine: *Evergreen Trees 10*

northern red oak: *Deciduous Trees 10*

Northern Red Sea: *Seven Wonders of the Underwater World 18*

northern red-bellied: *Freshwater Turtles 15*

northern red-faced: *Freshwater Turtles 15*

Northern Renaissance: *Art Movements 13*

northern rightwhale: *Dolphins 15*

northern scrub pine: *Evergreen Trees 10*

northern snakeneck: *Freshwater Turtles 15*

northern white cedar: *Evergreen Trees 10*

northern white pine: *Evergreen Trees 10*

northern yellow: *Bats 15*

northern: *Bats 15*

northwest: *Eight Compass Points 19*

Norway pine: *Evergreen Trees 10*

Norway spruce: *Evergreen Trees 10*

Norwegian Buhund: *Dog Breeds 15*

Norwegian Elkhound: *Dog Breeds 15*

Norwegian Fjord: *Horse Breeds 15*

Norwegian forest cat: *Domestic Cats 15*

Norwegian landrace: *Pigs 15*

Norwegian Lundehund: *Dog Breeds 15*

Norwegian red: *North American Dairy Cows 15*

Norwegian Yorkshire: *Pigs 15*

Norwegian: *Human Ethnic Groups 1*

Norwich Terrier: *Dog Breeds 15*

no-sail-zone: *Boat/Ship Terminology 9*

nose chain: *Jewelry 21*

nose jewel: *Jewelry 21*

nose ring: *Jewelry 21*

nose stud: *Jewelry 21*

nose: *Body Parts 12; Character Building 1*

nosebleed: *Injuries/Medical Emergencies 12; Wet 20*

nosed: *Bats 15*

nose-horned: *Viper 15*

Nostradamus: *Real People with Legendary Status 18*

nostrandite: *Minerals 10*

nostril: *Body Parts 12*

nosy neighbor: *Supporting Cast 23*

not breathing: *Injuries/Medical Emergencies 12*

not easy: *Difficult 20*

not following the rules triggers horrible side effect: *Common Dangers 23*

not heavy: *Light 20*

not to be faulted: *Happy 20*

notable: *Personality Other 1*

notation: *Ballet Terms 13; The Arts 13*

note: *Notation 13*

notebook computer: *Computer Equipment 5*

notebook: *Office/School/Writing Supplies 5*

notepad: *Military Equipment 8; Office/School/Writing Supplies 5*

noteworthy: *Beautiful 20*

nothingness: *Philosophy Basic Concepts 14*

Nothung (Siegfried): *Weapons of Legend 18*

no-till method: *Soil General Vocabulary 10*

notion: *Philosophy Basic Concepts 14*

notions: *Clothing 2*

notorious: *Personality Other 1*

nougat: *Candy General 6*

noumenon: *Philosophy Basic Concepts 14*

Nova Scotia Duck Tolling Retriever: *Dog Breeds 15*

nova: *Astronomy General Terms 11; Weapons 22*

novel: *Books/Publications 5; New 20*

novelist: *Publishing 1*

novelty: *Undergarments 2*

novus ordo seclorum: *United States Dollar Bill 19*

nowed: *Reptiles 19; Special Posture 19*

noxious: *Horror Vocabulary 23*

Nuada (war): *Celtic Pantheon 14*

Nubian: *Human Ethnic Groups 1*

nuckelavee: *Beast 16; Demon 16*

nuclear aircraft carrier: *Military Watercraft 8*

nuclear binding energy: *Chemistry General Vocabulary 11*

nuclear cruiser: *Military Watercraft 8*

nuclear disaster: *Horror Plot Devices 23*

nuclear fission: *Chemistry General Vocabulary 11*

nuclear fusion: *Astronomy General Terms 11*

nuclear powered frigate: *Military Watercraft 8*

nuclear pulse propulsion: *Spaceship Drive Systems 22*

nuclear reaction: *Chemistry General Vocabulary 11*

nuclear reactor: *Chemistry General Vocabulary 11*

nuclear submarine: *Military Watercraft 8*

nuclear war: *General Combat Vocabulary 7*

nucleons: *Chemistry General Vocabulary 11*

nucleus: *Chemistry General Vocabulary 11*

nuclides: *Chemistry General Vocabulary 11*

nude: *Art Genres 13*

numbat: *Other Wild Mammals 15*

number 13: *Harbingers of Bad Luck 19*

number 666: *Harbingers of Bad Luck 19*

number 7: *Harbingers/Charms for Good Luck 19*

numbers: *Objects/Activities Connected to Lore 19*

numerologist: *Fortune Teller 1*

numerology: *Fortune Telling General Techniques 19*

numinous: *Magic Vocabulary 17*

nun: *Cleric 1; Styles of Dress 2*

nunatak: *Glacial and Mountain 10*

nunchaku: *Bludgeons 7*

nungu: *Unusual Edible Fruits 6*

Nuriel: *Angels of Good 14*

nurse: *Academic 1; Horror Occupations 23; Medical Occupations 1; Sharks 15*

nurse's cap: *Headgear 2*

nursery: *Business Property 3*

nursing bra: *Ladies' Wear 2*

nursing home: *Residential Property 3*

nurture: *Buy 20*

nut bark: *Candy General 6*

nut brittle: *Candy General 6*

nut cluster: *Candy Chocolate 6*

nut driver: *Hand Tools 5*

nut grinder: *Kitchen Utensils 5*

nut pine: *Evergreen Trees 10*

nut: *Cake 6; Hardware 5*

Nutcracker Suite: *Christmas 19*

nutcracker: *Christmas 19; Kitchen Utensils 5*

nutmeg grater: *Kitchen Utensils 5*

nutmeg: *Cocktail Garnishes 6; Moth 15; Spices 6*

nutritionist: *Animal/Equestrian 1*

nuts & bolts: *Snacks 6*

nuts: *Expletives 20; Food 6; Ice Cream Toppings 6*

nuzu-ndu: *Deciduous Trees 10*

nylon rope: *General Survival Gear 5*

nylons: *Ladies' Wear 2*

nymph: *Fantasy Creatures with Symbolic Meaning 19; General Fae 16*

nymphalidae: *Butterfly 15*

Nysa: *Fictional/Mythological Locations 18*

–O–

oak barrel: *Containers and Vessels 5*

oak leaf: *Pennsylvania Dutch Hex Signs 19*

oak mushroom: *Fungus Common Names 10*

oak: *Shrubs 10*

oak-knower: *Nature Occupations 1*

oak-prophet: *Nature Occupations 1*

oak-seer: *Nature Occupations 1*

oar maker: *Maritime Occupations 1*

oar: *Boat/Ship Anatomy 9*

oarlock: *Boat/Ship Anatomy 9*

oarstroke: *Swimming Strokes 9*

oasis: *Water Features 10*

oat: *Grain 6*

oath: *Witchcraft Vocabulary 17*

oatmeal chocolate chip: *Cookie 6*

oatmeal date: *Cookie 6*

oatmeal raisin: *Cookie 6*

oatmeal: *Bread General Varieties 6; Cake 6*

Oaxacan small-headed: *Rattlesnake 15*

oazis: *Cheese International Varieties 6*

Ob: *Horse Breeds 15*

obbligato: *General Music Vocabulary 13*

obedience plant: *Garden Perennials 10*

obedient: *Good 20*

Oberon: *Moons 11*

obese: *Large 20; Large/Heavy 1*

obituary writer: *Publishing 1*

object changes personality: *Horror Plot Devices 23*

object drains life force: *Horror Plot Devices 23*

object of affection: *Common Character Archetypes 21*

object/doll brought to life: *Horror Genres 23*

object: *Philosophy Basic Concepts 14*

objective: *General Combat Vocabulary 7*

objectivity: *Philosophy Basic Concepts 14*

oblateness: *Astronomy General Terms 11*

obligation: *Philosophy Basic Concepts 14*

obliquity: *Astronomy General Terms 11*

obliterate: *Attack 7; Kill 20*

oblong: *Face 1*

obnoxious preacher: *Supporting Cast 23*

obnoxious travelers: *Travel Hazards 9*

obnoxious: *Negative 1; Unattractive 20*

oboe: *Wind/Woodwind and Brass Musical Instruments*

obscure: *Difficult 20; Magic Vocabulary 17*

obscurity: *Magic Vocabulary 17*

observation scout: *Military Aircraft Pre-1962 8*

observation station: *Installations 22*

observation turret: *Fantasy Locations 24*

observation: *Helicopters 8; Military Aircraft 8; Military Aircraft Pre-1962 8*

obsess: *Love 20*

obsessed: *Personality Other 1*

obsidian: *Daggers and Knives 7; Igneous Rocks 10; Standard Gems 21*

obsolete: *Old 20*

obstetrician: *Medical Occupations 1*

obstinate: *Difficult 20; Stubborn 1*

obstruct: *Close/Hold 20*

obtain: *Buy 20*

obtusa oak: *Deciduous Trees 10*

Ocasta (magic): *Native American Pantheon 14*

occasional: *Chairs and Stools 4; Tables 4*

occidental turquoise: *Minerals 10*

occipital bone: *Bones 12*

occult: *Fantasy Genres 24; Horror Genres 23; Science Fiction Genres 22*

occultation: *Astronomy General Terms 11*

occupation: *General Combat Vocabulary 7*

occupational therapist: *Medical Occupations 1*

occupations: *Character Building 1*

ocean escort frigate: *Military Watercraft 8*

ocean jasper: *Minerals 10*

ocean liner: *Large Watercraft 9*

ocean perch: *Fish/Seafood Types 6*

ocean trigger: *Wild Saltwater Fish 15*

ocean: *Coastal and Oceanic 10; Water Terms 9*

oceanic basin: *Coastal and Oceanic 10*

oceanic landforms: *Chapter 10*

oceanic plateau: *Coastal and Oceanic 10*

oceanic trench: *Coastal and Oceanic 10; Volcanic 10*

oceanic: *Dolphins 15; Ecosystems 10; Water Terms 9*

ochre: *Brown 20*

Ocicat: *Domestic Cats 15*

octagon: *Gem Cuts 21*

octagonal: *Windows 3*

octahedral: *Chemistry General Vocabulary 11*

octahedrite: *Minerals 10*

octane number: *Chemistry General Vocabulary 11*

Octans: *Constellations 11*

octave: *General Music Vocabulary 13*

octet: *Composition Types 13*

October daphne: *Garden Perennials 10*

octofoil/double quatrefoil: *Cadency Mark 19*

octogenarian: *Elderly 1*

octopi: *Animals 15*

octopus: *Fish/Seafood Types 6; Giant Creatures 16*

odango: *Hair Style 1*

odd: *Magic Vocabulary 17*

odd-nosed: *Old World Monkeys 15*

Odin (ruler of all gods): *Norse Pantheon 14*

Odin's all-seeing throne: *Objects 18*

Odin's golden arm cuff: *Jewelry 18*

Odin's raven: *Flying Creatures 16*

Odin's sword: *Norse Weapons 18*

odious: *Unattractive 20*

odontolite: *Minerals 10*

odor: *Smells 20*

ods bodikins: *Expletives 20*

Oenpelli: *Python 15*

Of Occult Philosophy or Of Magical Ceremonies: *The Fourth Book: Books of Legend 18*

Of the Supreme Mysteries of Nature: *Books of Legend 18*

OF-120 main battle tank: *Italy Military Vehicles 8*

OF-40 main battle tank: *Italy Military Vehicles 8*

off putting: *Unattractive 20*

offal: *Body Parts 12*

offend: *General Emotions 20*

offender: *Illicit Occupations 1; Thief 1*

offensive: *General Combat Vocabulary 7*

offering: *Rituals 14*

offertory: *Rituals 14*

office building: *Business Property 3*

office equipment store: *Business Property 3*

office furniture store: *Business Property 3*

office machines: *Equipment and Tools 5*

office park: *Business Property 3*

office supplies: *Equipment and Tools 5*

office: *Business Property 3; Cemetery 3; Chairs and Stools 4; Rooms 3*

officer cadet: *Armed Forces Other Titles 8*

officer: *Fighter 1*

off-key: *Vocal/Speech Quality 1*

offset spatuala: *Kitchen Utensils 5*

offshore patrol vessel: *Military Watercraft 8*

offspring: *Relational 1*

offstage: *Stage Terms 13*

ogee arch: *Castle Anatomy 3*

ogee frame mirror: *Miscellaneous Furniture 4*

Oghma (knowledge): *Celtic Pantheon 14*

Ogier the Dane: *Twelve Peers of Charlemagne 18*

Oglala: *Native American Peoples 1*

Ogma's Whip: *Spears 18*

ogopogo: *Aquatic 16; Mythical Creatures and Monsters 16*

ogre fort: *Fantasy Locations 24*

ogre mage: *Giant Humanoids 16*

ogre: *Giant Humanoids 16; Humanlike Groups 1*

oh hell!: *Card Games 5*

oh man: *Expletives 20*

oh my word: *Expletives 20*

oh my: *Expletives 20*

oh please: *Expletives 20*

oh: *Expletives 20*

OH-58 Kiowa: *U.S. Army Helicopter 8*

Ohio class missile submarine: *U.S. Navy Vessels 8*

oil and vinegar Italian: *Salad Dressing 6*

oil and vinegar: *Salad Dressing 6*

oil cloth: *Fabric 2; General Survival Gear 5*

oil fish: *Wild Saltwater Fish 15*

oil lamp: *Illumination/Light Sources 5*

oil lantern: *Illumination/Light Sources 5*

oil paint: *Art Materials 5; Art Media 13*

oil painting: *Decorative Objects 4*

oil rig: *Outdoor Property 3*

oil shale: *Sedimentary Rocks 10*

oil spritzer: *Kitchen Equipment 5*

oil tank: *Building Systems 3*

oil: *Chemistry General Vocabulary 11; Foods with Religious or Ritual Significance 19; Illumination/Light Sources 5; Wizard's Goods 5*

oilette: *Castle Anatomy 3*

oilnut: *Deciduous Trees 10*

oils: *Food 6*

oily: *Hair Types 1*

oisanite: *Minerals 10*

Ojibwa: *Native American Peoples 1*

O.K. Corral: *Western Paraphernalia/People 21*

okapi: *Other Wild Mammals 15*

okay: *Agree 20*

oke hat: *Headgear 2*

Okinawan: *Human Ethnic Groups 1*

Oklahoma 10-point pitch: *Card Games 5*

okra: *Vegetables 6*

Oktoberfest: *Beer 6*

olallieberry: *Unusual Edible Fruits 6*

Olbers: *Comets 11*

old as the hills: *Elderly 1*

old coot: *Elderly 1*

old document proves person guilty of murder: *Horror Plot Devices 23*

Old English game: *Chickens 15*

Old English pheasant fowl: *Chickens 15*

Old English Sheepdog: *Dog Breeds 15*

old fart: *Elderly 1*

old fashioned bleeding heart: *Garden Perennials 10*

old fashioned: *Cocktails 6*

old folks' home: *Residential Property 3*

old lace: *White 20*

old maid: *Card Games 5*

old man becomes hero: *Western Plot Devices 21*

old man of the mountain: *Garden Perennials 10*

old man of the prairie: *Garden Perennials 10*

old man of the woods: *Fungus Common Names 10*

old man: *New Year 19*

old man's beard: *Weeds 10*

old master: *Art Genres 13*

Old Testament Apocrypha: *Major Religious Books 14*

Old Testament Pseudepigrapha: *Major Religious Books 14*

Old Testament: *Major Religious Books 14; Objects in Magic and Religion 19; Philosophy and Religion 14*

old woman: *Garden Perennials 10*

Old World climbing fern: *Weeds 10*

Old World monkeys: *Animals 15*

old: *Adjectives 20; Elderly 1*

Oldenburg: *Horse Breeds 15*

older than dirt: *Elderly 1*

oldest/youngest son/daughter: *Common Character Archetypes 21*

old-fashioned: *Old 20; Styles of Dress 2*

Oldfield birch: *Deciduous Trees 10*

Oldfield pine: *Evergreen Trees 10*

oldster: *Elderly 1*

old-timer: *Elderly 1*

oleander: *Poisonous Plants 10; Shrubs 10*

Oligocene Age: *Geologic Time 10*

oligonite: *Minerals 10*

olive branch: *United States Dollar Bill 19; Secular Symbols 19*

olive dish: *Tableware 5*

olive drab: *Green 20*

olive ridley: *Sea Turtles 15*

olive: *Cocktail Garnishes 6; Green 20; Oils 6; Python 15; Sea Snake 15; Vegetables 6; Wild Saltwater Fish 15*

Oliver Hazard Perry class frigate: *U.S. Navy Vessels 8*

Oliver Twist: *Fictional Characters 18 Baba Yaga: Folklore Characters 18*

Oliver: *Twelve Peers of Charlemagne 18*

olives: *Foods with Religious or Ritual Significance 19*

olivinoid: *Minerals 10*

Ollantaytambo in Peru: *Real Places Steeped in Legend or Mystery 18*

olm: *Salamanders 15*

Olmec balls: *Real Objects Not Fully Understood 18*

olomoucke syrecky: *Cheese International Varieties 6*

oltermanni: *Cheese International Varieties 6*

Olympic Arms Cohort: *Pistol Semiautomatic 7*

Olympic Arms K4B: *Semiautomatic Centerfire Rifles 7*

Omaha high: *Poker Card Games 5*

Omaha: *Poker Card Games 5*

omamori: *Objects in Magic and Religion 19*

ombre: *Footwear/Shoes 2; Hair Treated 1; Sewing Terms 2*

omelet: *Egg Styles 6*

omi: *Card Games 5*

ominous: *Bad 20; Sad 20; Unattractive 20*

Ominous: *Minor Lines 19*

Omoikane (thought): *Japanese Pantheon 14*

omphalos: *Objects in Magic and Religion 19*

on cloud nine: *Happy 20*

on guard: *Fencing Vocabulary 7*

on the double: *Fast 20*

on trend: *New 20*

onager: *Horses Related 15; Siege Engines 7*

ondoyant: *Reptiles 19*

one foot in the grave: *Elderly 1*

one hundred: *Card Games 5*

one-arm Joe: *Card Games 5*

one-button suit: *Men's Wear 2*

one-day flu: *Hangover 12*

one-eyed: *Eye Type 1*

onegite: *Minerals 10*

Oneida: *Native American Peoples 1*

one room schoolhouse: *Western Paraphernalia/People 21*

onerous: *Difficult 20; Heavy 20*

one-step: *Dance Styles 13*

ongaonga: *Poisonous Plants 10*

Ongole: *Other Cows 15*

on-grade mat foundation for expansive soils: *Soil General Vocabulary 10*

oni: *Demon 16*

onice: *Minerals 10*

onion: *Garden Perennials 10; Items with Healing Properties 19; Pickled/Relish 6; Vegetables 6*

onions: *Practices to Predict the Future 19*

online: *Games 5*

onniont: *Objects in Magic and Religion 19*

ono: *Axes 7*

onofrite: *Minerals 10*

Onondaga: *Native American Peoples 1*

onslaught: *General Combat Vocabulary 7*

onstage: *Stage Terms 13*

on-the-go: *Mobility 1*

ontology: *Philosophy Basic Concepts 14*

onyx marble: *Minerals 10*

onyx opal: *Minerals 10*

onyx: *Black 20; Minerals 10*

oolite: *Sedimentary Rocks 10*

oolitic: *Geological Vocabulary 10*

oolong: *Tea 6*

Oort cloud: *Astronomy General Terms 11*

ooze: *Monsters 16; Wet 20*

opal doublet: *Standard Gems 21*

opal jasper: *Minerals 10*

opal matrix: *Minerals 10*

OPAL Soil Center: *Soil General Vocabulary 10*

opal: *Standard Gems 21; White 20*

opaline: *Minerals 10*

opalite: *Minerals 10*

opalized bone: *Minerals 10*

opalized fossil: *Minerals 10*

opalized shell: *Minerals 10*

opalized wood: *Minerals 10*

opaque projector: *Office/School Machines 5*

open an umbrella in the house: *Practices that Attract Bad Luck 19*

open cluster: *Astronomy General Terms 11*

open market: *General Property 3; Outdoor Property 3*

open range: *Geography General Vocabulary 10*

open sextet: *Chemistry General Vocabulary 11*

open wide: *Open/Release 20*

open: *Verbs 20*

open-top cupboard: *Storage 4*

opera glasses: *Optics 5*

opera gloves: *Ladies' Wear 2*

opera house: *Entertainment Property 3*

opera singer: *Singer 1*

opera: *Musical Styles 13; Performance Genres 13*

operatic: *Vocal/Speech Quality 1*

operating theater: *Health Care 3*

operation: *General Combat Vocabulary 7*

operational goal: *General Combat Vocabulary 7*

operations: *Character Building 1*

operetta: *Musical Styles 13; Performance Genres 13*

Ophan: *Angels of Good 14*

Ophelia: *Moons 11*

ophiolite: *Minerals 10*

Ophite Cultus Satanas: *Secret/Mystical Organizations 18*

Ophiuchus: *Constellations 11*

ophthalmologist: *Medical Occupations 1*

oplatek (Christmas wafer): *Bread General Varieties 6; Christmas 19; Foods with Religious or Ritual Significance 19*

opossum tree: *Deciduous Trees 10*

opossum: *Wild Game 6; Woodland Mammals 15*

opponent: *Fighter 1; Hero or Villain, Depending Upon Circumstance 20*

opportune: *Fortunate 20*

opportunist: *Barbarian 1*

oppose: *General Combat Vocabulary 7*

opposed bar: *Gem Cuts 21*

opposed: *Horror Vocabulary 23*

opposition: *Astronomy General Terms 11; Fencing Vocabulary 7*

Opposition: *Minor Lines 19*

oppress: *Magic Vocabulary 17*

oppressor: *Wizard 1*

optical activity: *Chemistry General Vocabulary 11*

optical calcite: *Minerals 10*

optical sight: *Military Equipment 8*

optician: *Medical Occupations 1*

optics: *Equipment and Tools 5*

optimistic: *Happy 20; Personality Other 1*

optometrist: *Medical Occupations 1*

opus: *General Music Vocabulary 13*

or (gold): *Colors/Tinctures 19*

or robins: *Practices that Attract Bad Luck 19*

oracle: *Cleric 1; Wizard 1*

orange and black: *Halloween 19*

orange coconut: *Cake 6*

orange hawkweed: *Weeds 10*

orange jelly: *Fungus Common Names 10*

orange marmalade: *Jam/Jelly/Preserves 6*

orange oak: *Deciduous Trees 10*

orange peel: *Orange 20*

orange pekoe: *Tea 6*

orange roughy: *Wild Saltwater Fish 15*

orange slice: *Cocktail Garnishes 6*

orange slices: *Candy General 6*

orange: *Cake 6; Citrus 6; Colors 20; Fruit Juice 6; Ice Cream Flavors 6; Martial Artist Belt Ranks 1; Oils 6*

orangeade: *Fruit Drinks 6*

orange-capped scaber stalk: *Fungus Common Names 10*

orange-collared: *Keelback 15*

orange-finned loach: *Aquarium Freshwater Fish 15*

orange-red: *Orange 20*

orangetip: *Butterfly 15*

orangite: *Minerals 10*

orator: *Bard 1*

oratorio: *Composition Types 13*

oratory: *Castle Anatomy 3; Religious Building 3*

orb weaver: *Venomous Arachnids 15*

orb: *Jewelry 21; Secular Symbols 19*

orbed: *Special Body Features 19*

orbicular jasper: *Minerals 10*

orbiculate batfish: *Aquarium Saltwater Fish 15*

orbiculated jasper: *Minerals 10*

orbit: *Astronomy General Terms 11*

orbital sander: *Power Tools*

orc: *Humanlike Groups 1; Humanoid 16*

orchard: *Farm/Outbuilding 3*

orchestra pit: *Parts of the Theater 13*

orchestra seating: *Parts of the Theater 13*

orchestra: *Groups 13*

orchestrate: *Fix 20*

orchestration: *General Music Vocabulary 13*

orchid: *Bees 15; Plants with Symbolic Meaning 19; Purple 20*

orda: *Cheese International Varieties 6*

ordeal beans: *Poisonous Plants 10*

order knight: *Knight 1*

Order of the Golden and Rosy Cross: *Secret/Mystical Organizations 18*

Order of the Temple of the Rosy Cross: *Secret/Mystical Organizations 18*

order: *Speak 20*

ordering rock strata: *Geologic Concepts 10*

ordinary tenant harbors evil secret identity: *Horror Plot Devices 23*

ordinary: *Charges 19*

Ordo Aurum Solis: *Secret/Mystical Organizations 18*

Ordo Templi Orientis: *Secret/Mystical Organizations 18*

Ordovician Period: *Geologic Time 10*

ore: *Chemistry General Vocabulary 11*

oregano: *Spices 6*

Oregon alder: *Deciduous Trees 10*

Oregon cedar: *Evergreen Trees 10*

Oregon Douglas fir: *Evergreen Trees 10*

Oregon maple: *Deciduous Trees 10*

Oregon myrtle: *Deciduous Trees 10*

Oregon snakeskin agate: *Minerals 10*

Oregon Trail: *Famous Western Locations 21*

Oregon white truffle: *Fungus Common Names 10*

organ gun: *Cannon 7*

organ: *Electronic Musical Instruments 5*

organdy: *Fabric 2*

organic chemistry: *Chemistry General Vocabulary 11*

organist: *Musical Occupations 1*

organizations: *Character Building 1; Legendary, Mystical and Mythical Items and Locations 18*

organize: *Clean 20; Fix 20*

organized: *Personality Other 1*

organorhodium complex: *Dangerous Chemicals 11*

organs/major structures: *Anatomy and Physiology 12*

organza: *Fabric 2*

oriel: *Castle Anatomy 3*

oriental alabaster: *Minerals 10*

oriental garnet: *Minerals 10*

Oriental rug: *Floor Coverings 4*

Oriental: *Domestic Cats 15; Imported Carpets 4*

Orifiel: *Angels of Good 14*

original setting inhabited by fantasy races/creatures: *Fantasy Genres 24*

original: *New 20*

originate: *Create 20*

Orinoco crocodile: *Crocodilians 15*

oriole: *Backyard Birds 15*

Orion: *Constellations 11; Giants of Legend 16*

Orlando: *Twelve Peers of Charlemagne 18*

Orlov Trotter: *Horse Breeds 15*

Orma Boran: *Other Cows 15*

ornament: *Christmas 19; Jewelry 21*

ornamental kale: *Garden Annuals 10*

ornamental Swiss chard: *Garden Annuals 10*

ornate box: *Freshwater Turtles 15*

ornate ladies' hat: *Western Clothing/Dress 21*

ornate wood: *Freshwater Turtles 15*

ornery: *Grouchy 1*

ornithomimid: *Dinosaur Types 15*

ornithopod: *Dinosaur Types 15*

orogenesis: *Geological Vocabulary 10*

orographic cloud: *Clouds 10*

orographic rainfall: *Geography General Vocabulary 10*

Oropa: *Other Cows 15*

orotund: *Vocal/Speech Quality 1*

Orovada soil: *Soil General Vocabulary 10*

orphan: *Child 1; Common Character Archetypes 21*

orphic egg: *Secular Symbols 19*

Orphism: *Art Movements 13*

orphrey: *Embellishments 2*

Orpington: *Chickens 15*

orris root: *Garden Perennials 10*

orthent: *Soil General Vocabulary 10*

orthoantigorite: *Minerals 10*

orthochamosite: *Minerals 10*

orthochrysotile: *Minerals 10*

orthoclase: *Standard Gems 21*

orthodontic office: *Health Care 3*

Orthodox: *Crosses 19*

orthoptera: *Animals 15*

Orthosie: *Moons 11*

orzo: *Pasta 6*

os coxae: *Bones 12*

Osage orange: *Deciduous Trees 10*

Osage: *Native American Peoples 1*

oscar: *Aquarium Freshwater Fish 15*

Osiris (nature): *Egyptian Pantheon 14*

osmanthus: *Shrubs 10*

Osmium: *Elements 11*

osmosis: *Chemistry General Vocabulary 11*

osmotic pressure: *Chemistry General Vocabulary 11*

osnaburg: *Fabric 2*

osprey: *Birds of Prey 15*

Ossabaw Island: *Pigs 15*

osteopath: *Medical Occupations 1*

ostinato: *General Music Vocabulary 13*

ostrich plume: *Garden Perennials 10*

ostrich plumes: *Western Clothing/Dress 21*

ostrich: *Animals with Symbolic Meaning 19; Other Wild Birds 15*

Ostro: *Winds of the Mediterranean 10*

Ostwald process: *Chemistry General Vocabulary 11*

Oterma: *Comets 11*

other cows: *Animals 15*

other personality: *Character Building 1*

other wild birds: *Animals 15*

Otie: *Native American Peoples 1*

otocinclus: *Aquarium Freshwater Fish 15*

ōtsuchi: *Bludgeons 7*

otter: *Giant Creatures 16; Other Wild Mammals 15*

Otterhound: *Dog Breeds 15*

ottoman: *Fabric 2; Seating 4*

Otton: *Twelve Peers of Charlemagne 18*

Ottonian: *Architectural Styles 3*

Otuel: *Twelve Peers of Charlemagne 18*

ouabain: *Dangerous Chemicals 11*

oubliette: *Castle Anatomy 3*

ouch: *Expletives 20*

ought: *Philosophy Basic Concepts 14*

our lady's bedstraw: *Garden Perennials 10*

ouroboros: *Symbols in Magic and Religion 19*

out of body experience: *Paranormal Abilities 21*

out of distance: *Fencing Vocabulary 7*

out of gas: *Travel Hazards 9*

out of style: *Styles of Dress 2*

out of tune: *Vocal/Speech Quality 1*

outbuilding: *Architecture and Property 3*

outcropping: *Terrain Features 10*

outdated: *Old 20*

outdoor property: *Architecture and Property 3*

outer curtain: *Castle Anatomy 3*

outer orbital complex: *Chemistry General Vocabulary 11*

outer tactical vest: *Body Armor 7*

outer ward: *Castle Anatomy 3*

outerwear: *Clothing 2*

outflow cave: *Cave Anatomy 10*

outflow: *Meteorology General Vocabulary 10; Wet 20*

outgoing tide: *Boat/Ship Terminology 9*

outgoing: *Personality Other 1*

outhouse: *Bathrooms 3; Farm/Outbuilding 3; Residential Property 3; Travel Hazards 9*

outing: *Journey 20*

outlaw: *Illicit Occupations 1*

outline: *Embroidery Stitches 2*

outlook: *Meteorology General Vocabulary 10*

out-of-control experiment: *Plot Devices 22*

out-of-date: *Old 20*

out-of-use: *Old 20*

outpost: *Fortification 3*

outraged: *Angry 1*

outrageous: *Unattractive 20*

outrigger: *Human-Powered Watercraft 9*

outsized: *Large 20*

outstanding: *Beautiful 20*

outwash fan: *Glacial and Mountain 10*

outwash plain: *Glacial and Mountain 10*

outwash: *Geography General Vocabulary 10*

Ouvert/ouverte: *Ballet Terms 13*

oval: *Face 1; Figures Associated with Symbols 19; Gem Cuts 21; Shield Types 7; Spaceship Shapes 22*

Ovambo: *Other Cows 15*

ovary: *Organs/Major Structures 12*

oven mitt: *Kitchen Equipment 5*

oven roast: *Cooking Techniques 20*

oven: *Major Appliances 4*

over coat: *Outerwear 2; Unisex Clothing 2*

over easy: *Egg Styles 6*

over hard: *Egg Styles 6*

over medium: *Egg Styles 6*

over the moon: *Happy 20*

over the rainbow: *Fictional/Mythological Locations 18*

overalls: *Unisex Clothing 2*

overbearing parent: *Common Character Archetypes 21*

overboard: *Boat/Ship Terminology 9*

overboots: *Boots 2*

overburden pressure: *Soil General Vocabulary 10*

overburden: *Geography General Vocabulary 10*

overcast: *Meteorology General Vocabulary 10*

overcome: *Attack 7*

overconfident competitor: *Common Character Archetypes 21*

overcup oak: *Deciduous Trees 10*

overgrown: *Large 20*

overhang: *Cave Anatomy 10; Terrain Features 10*

overhead lamp: *Illumination/Light Sources 5*

overhead projector: *Office/School Machines 5*

overhead: *Doors 3*

overheat: *Cooking Techniques 20*

overjoyed: *Happy 20*

overpass: *Roads 9*

overshoes: *Boots 2*

oversized body parts: *Physical Mutations 22*

oversized: *Large 20*

overstuffed: *Chairs and Stools 4*

over-the-knee: *Socks 2*

overthrow: *General Combat Vocabulary 7*

overture: *Composition Types 13*

overweight: *Large 20; Large/Heavy 1*

overwhelm: *Attack 7; Close/Hold 20; General Combat Vocabulary 7*

oviraptor philoceratops: *Commonly Known Dinosaurs 15*

Owain: *Knights of the Round Table 18*

Owen: *Knights of the Round Table 18*

owl monkey: *New World Monkeys 15*

owl: *Animals with Symbolic Meaning 19; Birds of Prey 15*

owlbear: *Beast 16*

owlet: *Owls 15*

owlman: *Flying Creatures 16*

owls: *Animals 15*

Owyhee jasper: *Minerals 10*

ox: *Chinese Horoscope 19; Christmas 19; Other Wild Mammals 15; Transportation Animals 9*

oxalic acid: *Poisonous Chemicals in Plants 11*

oxalis: *Garden Bulbs 10*

oxamyl: *Dangerous Chemicals 11*

oxbow lake: *Fluvial 10; Water Features 10*

ox-demon: *Demon 16*

oxetane: *Dangerous Chemicals 11*

oxeye daisy: *Garden Perennials 10; Wildflowers 10*

Oxford ragwort: *Weeds 10*

Oxford sandy and black: *Pigs 15*

oxford: *Fabric 2; Footwear/Shoes 2*

oxidation numbers: *Chemistry General Vocabulary 11*

oxidation: *Chemistry General Vocabulary 11; Smells 20*

oxidation-reduction reactions: *Chemistry General Vocabulary 11*

oxide: *Chemistry General Vocabulary 11*

oxidize: *Harm 20*

oxidizing agent: *Chemistry General Vocabulary 11*

oxisol: *Soil General Vocabulary 10*

oxtail: *Soup 6*

oxydisulfoton: *Dangerous Chemicals 11*

Oxygen: *Elements 11*

oyster mushroom: *Fungus Common Names 10*

oyster plate: *Tableware 5*

oyster: *Aphrodisiacs 19; Fish/Seafood Types 6*

Ozanna le Cure Hardy: *Knights of the Round Table 18*

Ozark chinkapin: *Deciduous Trees 10*

Ozark white cedar: *Evergreen Trees 10*

ozone: *Meteorology General Vocabulary 10*

–P–

P-240 8×8 switchboard vehicle: *Russia Military Vehicles 8*

P-3 maritime patrol: *U.S. Navy Aircraft 8*

P4: *Moons 11*

pa kua: *Secular Symbols 19*

pa: *Male 1*

Paaliaq: *Moons 11*

pace: *Locomotion 9*

pachycephalosaur: *Dinosaur Types 15*

pachyderm: *Other Wild Mammals 15*

pachysandra: *Shrubs 10*

Pacific Coast alder: *Deciduous Trees 10*

Pacific halibut: *Wild Saltwater Fish 15*

Pacific hemlock: *Evergreen Trees 10*

Pacific Islander: *Human Ethnic Groups 1*

Pacific madrone: *Deciduous Trees 10*

Pacific moonfish: *Wild Saltwater Fish 15*

Pacific myrtle: *Deciduous Trees 10*

Pacific pond: *Freshwater Turtles 15*

Pacific Ponderosa pine: *Evergreen Trees 10*

Pacific red cedar: *Evergreen Trees 10*

Pacific silver fir: *Evergreen Trees 10*

Pacific willow: *Deciduous Trees 10*

Pacific yew: *Evergreen Trees 10*

Pacific: *Newts 15*

pack mule: *Transportation Animals 9*

pack: *Containers and Vessels 5; Military Equipment 8*

package: *Containers and Vessels 5*

packaged: *Bread General Varieties 6*

packet: *Containers and Vessels 5*

pact: *Witchcraft Vocabulary 17*

paczki: *Donut/doughnut 6*

pad: *Residential Slang 3*

padded bra: *Ladies' Wear 2*

padded: *Armor Types 7; Horse Barding Materials 7*

paddle boat: *Human-Powered Watercraft 9*

paddle wheeler: *Western Paraphernalia/People 21*

paddle-tail: *Newts 15*

paddlewheel: *Large Watercraft 9*

paddock: *Farm/Outbuilding 3*

paddy straw mushroom: *Fungus Common Names 10*

paddy wagon: *Motorized Truck 9*

padlock with key: *Locks 5*

padparadschah: *Minerals 10*

pads: *Sporting Goods Other 5*

pagan: *Nature Occupations 1*

page one: *Card Games 5*

page: *Castle Inhabitants and Personnel 1*

pageant dress: *Ladies' Wear 2*

pageboy: *Hair Style 1*

pagoda bush: *Shrubs 10*

pagoda: *Religious Building 3*

Pahaliah: *Angels of Good 14*

pail: *Cleaning Supplies/Gadgets 5; Containers and Vessels 5*

pain au levain: *Bread General Varieties 6*

pain transmission: *Paranormal Abilities 21*

painful: *Horror Vocabulary 23; Sad 20; Unattractive 20*

painless: *Easy 20*

paint brush: *Hand Tools 5*

paint ore: *Minerals 10*

paint roller: *Hand Tools 5*

paint: *Art Materials 5; Art Media 13; Art Techniques 13; Sewing Techniques 2*

Paint: *Horse Breeds 15*

painted boulder: *Minerals 10*

painted comber: *Aquarium Saltwater Fish 15*

painted lady: *Butterfly 15*

painted river terrapin: *Freshwater Turtles 15*

painted suillus: *Fungus Common Names 10*

painted wood: *Freshwater Turtles 15*

painter: *Construction 1*

painter's brush: *Facial Hair Mustache 1*

painters' tape: *Fasteners 5*

painting: *Decorative Objects 4*

pair of golden fish: *Eight Ashtamangala 19*

pairing energy: *Chemistry General Vocabulary 11*

pairing: *Chemistry General Vocabulary 11*

paisley: *Fabric Patterns 2; Secular Symbols 19*

pajama cardinal: *Aquarium Saltwater Fish 15*

pajamas: *Unisex Clothing 2*

pajsbergite: *Minerals 10*

Pakistani: *Imported Carpets 4*

pakol: *Headgear 2*

palace: *Card Games 5; Residential Property 3*

palad khik: *Objects in Magic and Religion 19*

paladin: *Character Building 1; Fighter 1*

Palamedes/Palomides: *Knights of the Round Table 18*

palate: *Body Parts 12*

palatine bone: *Bones 12*

Palau: *Owls 15; Seven Wonders of the Underwater World 18*

pale beauty: *Moth 15*

pale: *Foxes 15; Unattractive 20*

Paleoarchean Period: *Geologic Time 10*

paleoart: *Art Genres 13*

Paleocene Age : *Geologic Time 10*

paleoclimatology: *Geologic Fields of Study 10*

Paleogene Period: *Geologic Time 10*

paleontology: *Geologic Fields of Study 10; Geological Field Work Methods 10*

Paleoproterozoic Period: *Geologic Time 10*

paleosol: *Soil General Vocabulary 10*

Paleozoic Era: *Geologic Time 10*

Palestinian: *Human Ethnic Groups 1; Viper 15*

palette knife: *Art Tools 5*

palette: *Art Tools 5*

palis: *Demon 16*

palisade: *Castle Anatomy 3; Fortification 3; Geography General Vocabulary 10*

Palladian: *Architectural Styles 3*

Palladium statue: *Objects 18*

palladium: *Coins and Currency 21*

Palladium: *Elements 11*

Pallas': *Viper 15*

pallasite: *Minerals 10*

pallet jack: *Human-Powered Transportation 9*

pallet: *Beds 4; Containers and Vessels 5*

pallid: *Bats 15; Unattractive 20*

palm: *Body Parts 12; Oils 6; Viper 15*

palm cross: *Objects in Magic and Religion 19*

palm reader: *Fortune Teller 1*

palma Christi: *Poisonous Plants 10*

Palmeria citrine: *Minerals 10*

palmistry: *Fortune Telling General Techniques 19*

palms: *Rituals 14*

Palo blanco: *Deciduous Trees 10*

palometa: *Wild Saltwater Fish 15*

Palomino: *Horse Breeds 15*

palpusztai: *Cheese International Varieties 6*

paly: *Partition Diminutives 19*

pampas grass: *Weeds 10*

Pampas: *Foxes 15*

pampas: *Terrain Features 10*

Pan (nature): *Greek Pantheon 14*

pan bread: *Bread General Varieties 6*

pan de piso: *Bread General Varieties 6*

pan dulce: *Bread General Varieties 6*

pan pipes: *Wind/Woodwind and Brass Musical Instruments*

pan serrano: *Bread General Varieties 6*

pan: *Containers and Vessels 5; Kitchen Equipment 5; Card Games 5*

Pan: *Moons 11*

panabas: *Swords Two-handed 7*

Panama Canal: *Seven Wonders of the Industrial World 18; Seven Wonders of the Modern World 18; Unique Property 3*

Panamanian night monkey: *New World Monkeys 15*

pancake turner: *Kitchen Utensils 5*

pancake: *Bread General Varieties 6; Tortoises 15; Vegetables Cooked 6*

pancreas: *Organs/Major Structures 12*

pandesal: *Bread General Varieties 6*

pandoeren: *Card Games 5*

Pandora: *Moons 11*

Pandora's Box: *Objects 18*

pandoro: *Bread General Varieties 6*

pane: *Windows 3*

paneer: *Cheese International Varieties 6*

panel: *Motorized Truck 9*

paneling: *Building Elements and Features 3*

panettone: *Bread General Varieties 6*

pang: *Horror Vocabulary 23*

Pangea: *Geological Vocabulary 10*

pangolin: *Other Wild Mammals 15*

panhandle hook: *Snow Storms 10*

panhandle: *Geography General Vocabulary 10*

panic: *General Emotions 20; Horror Vocabulary 23*

panicky: *General Emotions 20; Horror Vocabulary 23*

panicled dogwood: *Deciduous Trees 10*

panic-stricken: *Horror Vocabulary 23*

panini: *Sandwiches 6*

panné: *Fabric 2*

pansy: *Garden Annuals 10; Garden Perennials 10; Plants with Symbolic Meaning 19; Purple 20*

pant suit: *Ladies' Wear 2*

Pantaneiro: *Horse Breeds 15*

pantellerite: *Igneous Rocks 10*

pantheism: *Philosophy Basic Concepts 14*

panther: *Animals with Symbolic Meaning 19*

panties: *Ladies' Wear 2*

pantomime: *General Music Vocabulary 13; Performance Genres 13*

pantry: *Rooms 3*

pants: *Unisex Clothing 2*

pantyhose: *Ladies' Wear 2*

Panzer VI Tiger heavy tank: *Germany Military Vehicles 8*

papa: *Male 1*

papal cross: *Papal Symbols 19*

papaya: *Tropical/Exotic Fruits 6; Unusual Edible Fruits 6*

paper bag: *Containers and Vessels 5*

paper bark tea tree: *Weeds 10*

paper birch: *Deciduous Trees 10*

paper bush: *Shrubs 10*

paper clip: *Office/School/Writing Supplies 5*

paper cup: *Drinkware 5*

paper cutter: *Office/School/Writing Supplies 5*

paper dolls: *Toys 5*

paper folding tool: *Office/School/Writing Supplies 5*

paper money: *Coins and Currency 21*

paper umbrella: *Cocktail Garnishes 6*

paper: *Art Materials 5; Art Media 13; Door Materials 3; Office/School/Writing Supplies 5; Wasp 15*

paperback: *Books/Publications 5*

paperboard: *Art Materials 5*

papershell pinyon: *Evergreen Trees 10*

papier-mâché: *Art Materials 5*

papilionidae: *Butterfly 15*

Papillon: *Dog Breeds 15*

papionini: *Old World Monkeys 15*

paprika: *Spices 6*

paprikash: *Meals 6*

Papuan: *Python 15*

papyrus: *Office/School/Writing Supplies 5*

Para PXT 1911: *Pistol Semiautomatic 7*

Para Tactical Target: *Semiautomatic Centerfire Rifles 7*

parable: *Literary Styles 5*

parabolic reflector: *Illumination Bulb and Tube Types 5*

paracelsian: *Minerals 10*

parachrysotile: *Minerals 10*

parachute: *Air Vehicles 9;Fabric 2; Military Equipment 8; Spy Gear 5*

parade float: *Independence Day 19*

parade ground: *Fortification 3*

parade grounds: *Military Property 3*

parade torch: *Illumination/Light Sources 5*

parade: *Independence Day 19; Locomotion 9*

paradigm: *Beautiful 20*

paradise willkom: *Pennsylvania Dutch Hex Signs 19*

paradise: *Afterlife/Underworld 18*

paradisefish: *Aquarium Freshwater Fish 15*

parados: *Castle Anatomy 3*

paradox: *Philosophy Basic Concepts 14*

paraffin: *Illumination/Light Sources 5*

Paraiba tourmaline: *Minerals 10*

parakeet: *Domesticated Pet Birds 15*

parallax: *Astronomy General Terms 11*

parallel bars: *Sporting Goods Other 5*

parallel universe: *Plot Devices 22*

paralysis: *Weapons 22*

paralyze: *Attack 7*

paralyzing: *Weapons 22*

paramagnetism: *Chemistry General Vocabulary 11*

paramedic: *Medical Occupations 1*

paramo donkey: *Horses Related 15*

paramour: *Female 1*

paranormal events: *Horror Genres 23*

paranormal investigator: *Horror Occupations 23; Occupations 22*

paranormal researcher: *Paranormal Occupations 21*

paranormal: *Energy Sources/Types 23; Magic Vocabulary 17; Monster Categories/Terms 16*

parapet: *Castle Anatomy 3; Fortification 3; Roof Styles 3*

parapsychologist: *Wizard 1*

paraquat methosulfate: *Dangerous Chemicals 11*

paraquat: *Dangerous Chemicals 11*

parasites: *Monsters and Creatures 22*

parasol mushroom: *Fungus Common Names 10*

parasol: *Accessories 2; Eight Ashtamangala 19; Western Clothing/Dress 21*

parasparopgraho jivanam: *Symbols in Magic and Religión 19*

paratha: *Bread General Varieties 6*

parathion: *Dangerous Chemicals 11*

parathion-methyl: *Dangerous Chemicals 11*

parathyroid gland: *Organs/Major Structures 12*

parchment: *Art Materials 5; Books/Publications 5; Office/School/Writing Supplies 5; Wizard's Goods 5*

parent: *Relational 1*

parfait glass: *Tableware 5*

parfait: *Ice Cream Desserts 6*

parhelion: *Meteorology General Vocabulary 10*

Paricutin volcano: *Seven Wonders of the Natural World 18*

parietal bone: *Bones 12*

paring knife: *Kitchen Utensils 5*

Paris green: *Dangerous Chemicals 11*

parish center: *Church Anatomy 3*

parish: *City 10; Groupings 14*

parishioner: *Followers 14*

park: *Commands 20; General Property 3;*

parka: *Outerwear 2; Unisex Clothing 2*

parker house roll: *Bread General Varieties 6*

parking lot: *General Property 3*

parking structure: *General Property 3*

parkway: *Roads 9*

Parliament: *Administrative Property 3*

parmesan: *Cheese Common Varieties 6*

parmigiano reggiano: *Cheese International Varieties 6*

Parnassian: *Butterfly 15*

parrot feather: *Weeds 10*

parrot tulip: *Garden Bulbs 10*

parrot: *Domesticated Pet Birds 15; General Snake Families 15*

parrotlet: *Domesticated Pet Birds 15*

parry octave: *Fencing Vocabulary 7*

Parry pinyon: *Evergreen Trees 10*

parry prime: *Fencing Vocabulary 7*

parry quatre: *Fencing Vocabulary 7*

parry quinte: *Fencing Vocabulary 7*

parry seconde: *Fencing Vocabulary 7*

parry septime: *Fencing Vocabulary 7*

parry sixte: *Fencing Vocabulary 7*

parry tierce: *Fencing Vocabulary 7*

parrying: *Daggers and Knives 7*

parsec: *Astronomy General Terms 11*

Parsi: *Human Ethnic Groups 1*

parsley: *Plants with Symbolic Meaning 19; Spices 6; Veg-*

etable Juice 6

parsnip: *Vegetables 6; Weeds 10*

Parson Russell Terrier: *Dog Breeds 15*

parson: *Cleric 1*

part: *General Music Vocabulary 13*

parted: *Hair Style 1*

Parthenais: *Other Cows 15*

partial plate: *Teeth Dental Work 1*

partial pressure: *Chemistry General Vocabulary 11*

particle beam: *Weapons 22*

particle board: *Interior Building Materials 3*

particle size: *Soil General Vocabulary 10*

particular: *Philosophy Basic Concepts 14*

particulate matter: *Chemistry General Vocabulary 11*

partisan: *Pole Weapons 7*

partita: *Composition Types 13*

partition diminutives: *Classic Heraldry 19*

partition lines: *Classic Heraldry 19*

partition: *Building Elements and Features 3*

partitions: *Classic Heraldry 19*

partly cloudy: *Meteorology General Vocabulary 10*

partners: *Desks 4*

partridge in a pear tree: *Twelve Days of Christmas 19*

partridge pea: *Wildflowers 10*

partridge: *Poultry Types 6*

parts of the theater: *The Arts 13*

party hats: *New Year 19*

party mint: *Candy General 6*

party: *Halloween 19; New Year 19*

pas Ballonné: *Ballet Terms 13*

Pas de bourrée couru: *Ballet Terms 13*

Pas de bourrée: *Ballet Terms 13*

Pas de chat: *Ballet Terms 13*

Pas de deux: *Ballet Terms 13*

pas de deux: *Dance Moves 13*

Pas de quatre: *Ballet Terms 13*

pas de seul: *Dance Moves 13*

Pas de trois: *Ballet Terms 13*

Pas de valse: *Ballet Terms 13*

Pas marché: *Ballet Terms 13*

Pas: *Ballet Terms 13*

PASGT helmet: *Body Armor 7*

PASGT vest: *Body Armor 7*

Pashtun: *Human Ethnic Groups 1*

Pasiphae: *Moons 11*

Pasithee: *Moons 11*

paskahousu: *Card Games 5*

paski sir: *Cheese International Varieties 6*

paso doble: *Dance Styles 13*

Paso Fino: *Horse Breeds 15*

pasque flower: *Garden Perennials 10*

pass the trash: *Poker Card Games 5*

pass: *Fencing Vocabulary 7; Locomotion 9*

passage: *Cave Anatomy 10; Journey 20; Roads 9; Rooms 3*

passageway: *Roads 9; Rooms 3*

Passamaquoddy: *Native American Peoples 1*

passant: *Land Creatures 19*

passé: *Fencing Vocabulary 7; Old 20*

Passelande: *Arthur's Horses 18*

passendale: *Cheese International Varieties 6*

passenger car: *Railroad 9*

passenger jet: *Air Vehicles 9*

passenger liner: *Small Watercraft 9*

passenger terminal: *Infrastructure Buildings 9*

passenger: *Military Aircraft 8*

passengers of ship Mary Celeste: *Famous Disappearances 18*

passerine: *Other Wild Birds 15*

passing lane: *Roads 9*

passion flower: *Plants with Symbolic Meaning 19*

passion fruit: *Tropical/Exotic Fruits 6*

passion play: *Performance Genres 13*

passion: *Composition Types 13; General Emotions 20; Philosophy Basic Concepts 14*

passionate: *Love 20*

passionfruit: *Fruit Juice 6*

passive: *Horror Vocabulary 23*

passport: *Spy Gear 5*

pasta sauce: *Meals 6*

pasta: *Food 6; Salads 6*

paste: *Wizard's Goods 5*

pastel mint: *Candy General 6*

pastel: *Art Media 13*

pastels: *Art Materials 5*

pasteurized processed: *Cheese Common Varieties 6*

paston: *Card Games 5*

pastor: *Cleric 1; Religious Occupations 1*

pastoral associate: *Religious Occupations 1*

pastoral: *Art Genres 13*

pastorale: *Composition Types 13*

pastry bag: *Kitchen Utensils 5*

pastry blender: *Kitchen Utensils 5*

pastry brush: *Kitchen Utensils 5*

pastry chef: *Food Service 1*

pastry flour: *Staples 6*

pasture: *Farm/Outbuilding 3*

pasty: *Sandwiches 6*

Patagonian: *Squid 15*

patch pocket: *Garment Pieces 2*

patch up: *Fix 20*

patch: *Terrain Features 10*

patchnose: *General Snake Families 15*

patella: *Bones 12*

patera: *Astronomy General Terms 11*

path: *Roads 9*

pathetic: *Sad 20*

pathway: *Roads 9*

patience: *Twelve Fruits of the Holy Spirit 19*

patinated: *Old 20*

patio: *Doors 3; Property Features 3; Tables 4*

patriarch: *Cleric 1; Male 1; Religious Occupations 1*

patrician: *Personality Other 1; Styles of Dress 2*

patriot: *Army Missile 8; Hero 20*

patrol bomber: *Military Aircraft Pre-1962 8*

patrol cap: *Headgear 2*

patrol torpedo bomber: *Military Aircraft Pre-1962 8*

patrol: *Military Aircraft Pre-1962 8*

pattern/rhythm: *Art Principles 13*

pattern: *Philosophy Basic Concepts 14; Sewing Equipment 2*

patterns: *Classic Heraldry 19*

patty: *Meals 6*

patu: *Bludgeons 7*

patupairehe: *Demon 16*

Paul Bunyan: *Tall Tales 18*

Paul Revere lantern: *Illumination/Light Sources 5*

Paul Revere: *Real People with Legendary Status 18*

Paulding lights: *Mysterious Occurrences 18*

pauldron: *Armor Pieces 7*

paunchy: *Large/Heavy 1*

pavan: *Historical Dances 13*

pavement: *Ants 15; Roads 9*

pavilion tent: *General Survival Gear 5*

pavilion: *Outdoor Property 3*

pavis: *Shield Types 7*

pavlova: *Cake 6*

Pavo: *Constellations 11*

Pawnee: *Native American Peoples 1*

pawpaw apple: *Deciduous Trees 10*

pawpaw: *Deciduous Trees 10; Unusual Edible Fruits 6*

pax cultura: *Symbols in Magic and Religion 19*

Paxton soil: *Soil General Vocabulary 10*

pay: *Buy 20*

pazuzu: *Demon 16*

PC: *Computer Equipment 5*

pea coat: *Outerwear 2; Unisex Clothing 2*

pea tree: *Shrubs 10*

pea: *Beetle 15*

peace keeping force: *General Combat Vocabulary 7*

peace sign: *Symbols in Magic and Religion 19*

peace: *Philosophy Basic Concepts 14; Twelve Fruits of the Holy Spirit 19*

peaceable: *Happy 20*

peaceful: *Happy 20; Quiet 20*

peach anthias: *Aquarium Saltwater Fish 15*

peach bells: *Garden Perennials 10*

peach beryl: *Minerals 10*

peach fuzz: *Facial Hair Beard 1*

peach oak: *Deciduous Trees 10*

peach soda: *Soft Drinks 6*

peach willow: *Deciduous Trees 10*

peach: *Ice Cream Flavors 6; Jam/Jelly/Preserves 6; Muffin 6; Orange 20; Pie 6; Pink 20; Pit Fruits 6; Skin Types and Features 1*

peaches-and-cream: *Skin Types and Features 1*

peachleaf willow: *Deciduous Trees 10*

peach-orange: *Orange 20*

peach-yellow: *Orange 20*

peacock copper: *Minerals 10*

peacock flower: *Garden Bulbs 10*

peacock ore: *Minerals 10*

peacock: *Animals with Symbolic Meaning 19; Butterfly 15*

peak: *Terrain Features 10*

peaked: *Old 20*

peanut brittle: *Candy General 6*

peanut bunker: *Wild Saltwater Fish 15*

peanut butter and banana: *Sandwiches 6*

peanut butter and jelly: *Sandwiches 6*

peanut butter cup: *Candy Chocolate 6*

peanut butter fudge: *Candy General 6*

peanut butter: *Cookie 6; Ice Cream Flavors 6; Staples 6*

peanut: *Allergies 12; Legumes 6; Oils 6*

pear: *Gem Cuts 21; Jam/Jelly/Preserves 6; Pie 6*

pearl bush: *Shrubs 10*

pearl gourami: *Aquarium Freshwater Fish 15*

pearl millet: *Grain 6*

pearl opal: *Minerals 10*

pearl spar: *Minerals 10*

pearl: *Standard Gems 21; White 20*

pearlwort: *Garden Perennials 10*

pearly everlasting: *Garden Perennials 10*

pearly whites: *Teeth 1*

pearly: *Teeth 1*

pearly-eye: *Butterfly 15*

pears: *Food 6*

peas: *Vegetables 6*

peasant: *Styles of Dress 2*

peat: *Bog Types 10; Soil General Vocabulary 10*

pebble: *Cave Anatomy 10; Rock and Mineral Forms 10*

pecan finger: *Cookie 6*

pecan hickory: *Deciduous Trees 10*

pecan: *Deciduous Trees 10; Nuts 6; Oils 6; Pie 6*

peccary: *Other Wild Mammals 15*

pecorino: *Cheese Common Varieties 6*

Pecos Bill: *Tall Tales 18*

pedal car: *Toys 5*

pedalfer: *Soil General Vocabulary 10*

pedestal sink: *Bathroom Features and Fixtures 3*

pedestal: *Special Purpose Furniture 4*

pedestal-base: *Tables 4*

pediatrician: *Medical Occupations 1*

pedicure: *Makeup 5*

pediment: *Castle Anatomy 3; Erosion 10*

pediplain: *Erosion 10*

pedocal: *Soil General Vocabulary 10*

pedodiversity: *Soil General Vocabulary 10*

pedology: *Geologic Fields of Study 10; Soil General Vocabulary 10*

pedophile: *Illicit Occupations 1*

Pedro: *Card Games 5*

peek-a-boo bra: *Ladies' Wear 2*

peel: *Fortification 3*

peeler: *Kitchen Utensils 5*

peep toe pumps: *Footwear/Shoes 2*

peep: *Sounds 20*

peer of the realm: *Hero 20*

peeved: *Angry 1*

peewee: *Small/Fragile 20*

peg: *Hardware 5*

pegasus: *Beast 16; Magical Transportation 17*

Pegasus: *Constellations 11*

pegmatite: *Igneous Rocks 10*

pegs and jokers: *Card Games 5*

peignoir set: *Ladies' Wear 2*

peignoir: *Ladies' Wear 2*

Pekingese: *Dog Breeds 15*

pekoe: *Tea 6*

pelican: *Other Wild Birds 15*

Pelinore Pellinor: *Knights of the Round Table 18*

pelite: *Geological Vocabulary 10; Metamorphic Rocks 10*

Pelleas: *Knights of the Round Table 18*

Pellene: *Moons 11*

pell-mell: *Fast 20*

pelmanism: *Card Games 5*

pelvic girdle: *Bones 12*

pelvic inflammatory disease (PIV): *Diseases 12*

pelvis: *Body Parts 12*

Pembroke Welsh Corgi: *Dog Breeds 15*

pen and ink: *Art Media 13*

pen holder: *Art Tools 5*

pen: *Art Tools 5; Farm/Outbuilding 3; Office/School/Writing Supplies 5*

penal colony: *Prison 3*

penal complex: *Prison 3*

Penance: *Sacraments 14*

Penché/penchée: *Ballet Terms 13*

pencil case: *Office/School/Writing Supplies 5*

pencil grip: *Office/School/Writing Supplies 5*

pencil ore: *Minerals 10*

pencil post: *Beds 4*

pencil pouch: *Office/School/Writing Supplies 5*

pencil sharpener: *Office/School Machines 5; Office/School/Writing Supplies 5*

pencil skirt: *Ladies' Wear 2*

pencil: *Art Materials 5; Art Media 13; Facial Hair Mustache 1; Military Equipment 8*

penciled: *Eyebrows 1*

pendant: *Cave Anatomy 10; Jewelry 2; Jewelry 21*

Pendragon family: *Arthurian Characters 18*

Penemue: *Angels of Good 14*

peneplain: *Erosion 10*

penetrating: *Vocal/Speech Quality 1*

penetration: *General Combat Vocabulary 7*

penguin: *Other Wild Birds 15; Solitaire Card Games 5*

peninsula cooter: *Freshwater Turtles 15*

peninsula tiger: *World's Ten Most Venomous Snakes 15*

peninsula: *Coastal and Oceanic 10*

penis: *Body Parts 12; Organs/Major Structures 12*

penitentiary: *Prison 3*

penne rigate: *Pasta 6*

penne: *Pasta 6*

penneech: *Card Games 5*

pennies from heaven: *Card Games 5*

pennine: *Minerals 10*

penninite: *Minerals 10*

Pennsylvania Dutch: *Human Ethnic Groups 1*

Pennsylvania German: *Human Ethnic Groups 1*

Pennsylvanian Age: *Geologic Time 10*

penny loafers: *Footwear/Shoes 2*

penny: *Coins and Currency 21*

pennywort: *Garden Perennials 10*

Penobscot: *Native American Peoples 1*

pentaborane: *Dangerous Chemicals 11*

pentacarbonyl: *Dangerous Chemicals 11*

pentacle: *Symbols in Magic and Religion 19; Typical Magical Objects 17; Witchcraft Vocabulary 17; Wizard's Goods 5*

pentacles: *Minor Arcana 19*

pentadecylamine: *Dangerous Chemicals 11*

Pentagon: *Special Purpose Structure 3*

pentagram phasing: *Travel Modes 24*

pentagram teleportation: *Travel Modes 23*

pentagram: *Symbols in Magic and Religion 19; Typical Magical Objects 17; Witchcraft Vocabulary 17*

pentas: *Garden Annuals 10*

pentatonic: *General Music Vocabulary 13*

penumbra: *Astronomy General Terms 11*

peony: *Garden Perennials 10; Items with Healing Properties 19*

people gain ability to cast spells: *Fantasy Plot Devices 24*

people gain ability to talk to animals: *Fantasy Plot Devices 24*

people invited to remote place: *Horror Plot Devices 23*

people invited to spend night in haunted house: *Horror Plot Devices 23*

peplum: *Garment Pieces 2*

pepper gun: *Shotguns General 7*

pepper jack: *Cheese Common Varieties 6*

pepper mill: *Kitchen Equipment 5*

pepper relish: *Pickled/Relish 6*

pepper spray: *SWAT Equipment 7*

pepper: *Pickled/Relish 6; Spices 6*

pepperball pistol: *SWAT Weapons 7*

pepperbush: *Shrubs 10*

peppered cory: *Aquarium Freshwater Fish 15*

peppered: *Moth 15*

pepperidge: *Deciduous Trees 10*

peppering: *Precipitation 10*

peppermint bark: *Candy General 6*

peppermint disk: *Candy General 6*

peppermint stick: *Candy General 6*

peppermint: *Candy General 6; Christmas 19; Tea 6*

pepperoncini: *Pickled/Relish 6*

pepperwood: *Deciduous Trees 10*

peppy: *Fast 20*

per bend sinister: *Partitions 19*

per bend: *Partitions 19*

per chevron: *Partitions 19*

per cross: *Partitions 19*

per fess: *Partitions 19*

per pale: *Partitions 19*

per pall reversed: *Partitions 19*

per pall: *Partitions 19*

per quarterly: *Partitions 19*

per saltire: *Partitions 19*

peracetic acid: *Dangerous Chemicals 11*

perambulator: *Human-Powered Transportation 9*

percale: *Fabric 2*

perceive: *Learn 20*

percent by mass: *Chemistry General Vocabulary 11*

percent composition: *Chemistry General Vocabulary 11*

percent purity: *Chemistry General Vocabulary 11*

percentage ionization: *Chemistry General Vocabulary 11*

perception: *Philosophy Basic Concepts 14*

perceptive: *Magic Vocabulary 17*

perceptual: *Art Genres 13*

perch: *Wild Freshwater Fish 15*

Percheron: *Horse Breeds 15*

Percival: *Knights of the Round Table 18*

percolation: *Cave Anatomy 10*

percolator: *Appliances 5*

percula clown: *Aquarium Saltwater Fish 15*

percussionist: *Musical Occupations 1*

Percy Fawcett: *Famous Disappearances 18*

Perdita: *Moons 11*

perennial lupine: *Wildflowers 10*

perfect: *Beautiful 20*

performance art: *Performance Genres 13*

performance genres: *The Arts 13*

performance practice: *General Music Vocabulary 13*

performer: *Common Character Archetypes 21; Wizard 1*

performing arts: *Character Building 1*

perfume pendant: *Jewelry 21*

perfume: *Personal Care 5; Smells 20; Spy Gear 5*

pergola: *Landscaping 3*

pericline: *Minerals 10*

peridot: *Minerals 10; Standard Gems 21*

peridotite: *Igneous Rocks 10*

perigee: *Astronomy General Terms 11*

perihelion: *Astronomy General Terms 11*

perilous: *Horror Vocabulary 23*

Peringuey's: *Adder 15*

period: *Chemistry General Vocabulary 11*

periodic law: *Chemistry General Vocabulary 11*

periodic table: *Chemistry General Vocabulary 11*

periodicity: *Chemistry General Vocabulary 11*

peristerite: *Minerals 10*

periwinkle: *Blue 20; Garden Perennials 10; Shrubs 10*

permafrost: *Geography General Vocabulary 10; Meteorology General Vocabulary 10*

permanent marker: *Office/School/Writing Supplies 5*

permanent wave: *Hair Treated 1*

permanent: *Hair Treated 1; Teeth 1; Teeth 12*

permeability: *Soil General Vocabulary 10*

permeable: *Cave Anatomy 10*

permed: *Hair Treated 1*

Permian Period: *Geologic Time 10*

permit: *Agree 20*

peroxide: *Chemistry General Vocabulary 11*

Perpendicular: *Architectural Styles 3*

Perron-Mrkos: *Comets 11*

persecutor: *Fighter 1; Villain 20; Wizard 1*

Perseus: *Constellations 11*

Perseus's cap of darkness: *Clothing 18*

pershing: *Donut/doughnut 6*

Persian lilac: *Weeds 10*

persian rose: *Pink 20*

Persian rug: *Floor Coverings 4*

Persian silk tree: *Weeds 10*

Persian stonecrest: *Garden Perennials 10*

Persian violet: *Garden Perennials 10*

Persian: *Domestic Cats 15; Human Ethnic Groups 1; Imported Carpets 4; Lions 15*

persimmon (sometimes 'simmon): *Deciduous Trees 10*

persimmon: *Tropical/Exotic Fruits 6*

persistent: *Stubborn 1*

person buried alive: *Horror Plot Devices 23*

person makes deal with devil: *Horror Plot Devices 23*

person of interest: *Hero or Villain, Depending Upon Circumstance 20*

person purposely gives lovers horrible disease: *Horror Plot Devices 23*

person reads magic out loud: *Common Dangers 24*

person transforms into monster: *Horror Plot Devices 23*

person trapped without hope of rescue: *Horror Plot Devices 23*

person/child vanishes without a trace: *Horror Plot Devices 23*

persona: *Masks 2*

personal care: *Equipment and Tools 5*

personal communications radio: *Military Equipment 8*

personal computer: *Computer Equipment 5*

personal floatation device: *Boat/Ship Anatomy 9*

personal jet pack: *Spy Gear 5*

personal music player: *Electronics 4*

personal services: *Character Building 1*

personality: *Character Building 1*

personnel carrier: *Armored Vehicles 8*

persuasion: *Magic Vocabulary 17*

perthite: *Minerals 10*

perturb: *Astronomy General Terms 11*

Peruvian Paso: *Horse Breeds 15*

perverted: *Bad 20*

Peshtigo fire of 1871: *Legendary Events 18*

pessimistic: *Negative 1; Personality Other 1; Sad 20*

pestilence: *Ten Plagues on Egypt 14*

pet birds: *Animals 15*

pet carrier: *Containers and Vessels 5*

pet is vampire: *Horror Plot Devices 23*

pet: *Terms of Endearment 1; Witchcraft Vocabulary 17*

petard: *Siege Equipment 7*

Peter Pan collar: *Garment Pieces 2*

Peter: *Twelve Apostles 14*

Peterbald: *Domestic Cats 15*

Petit Albert: *Books of Legend 18*

Petit Basset Griffon Vendeen: *Dog Breeds 15*

petit Battement sur le cou-de-pied: *Ballet Terms 13*

petit handlebar: *Facial Hair Mustache 1*

petit Jeté: *Ballet Terms 13*

Petit/petite: *Ballet Terms 13*

petite: *Small/Fragile 20; Small/Thin 1*

petition: *Rituals 14*

petits fours: *Cake 6*

petrale sole: *Wild Saltwater Fish 15*

petrel: *Other Wild Birds 15*

Petri dish: *Laboratory Equipment 5*

petrichor: *Soil General Vocabulary 10*

petrified wood: *Minerals 10*

petrified: *Horror Vocabulary 23*

petro physics: *Geologic Fields of Study 10*

petroleum geology: *Geologic Fields of Study 10*

petroleum: *Wizard's Goods 5*

petrology: *Geologic Fields of Study 10*

petroti: *Cheese International Varieties 6*

pets attack: *Horror Plot Devices 23*

pets turn to zombies: *Horror Plot Devices 23*

petticoat tail: *Cookie 6*

petticoat: *Ladies' Wear 2*

petty officer 1st class: *U.S. Navy Enlisted 8*

petty officer 2nd class: *U.S. Navy Enlisted 8*

petty officer 3rd class: *U.S. Navy Enlisted 8*

petty: *Small/Fragile 20*

petunia: *Garden Annuals 10*

peumo: *Unusual Edible Fruits 6*

pew: *Seating 4*

pewter cupboard: *Storage 4*

pewtersmith: *Artists and Craftspeople 1*

pey: *Demon 16*

peyote: *Plants with Symbolic Meaning 19*

pezzottaite: *Minerals 10*

Phaistos disk of Crete: *Real Objects Not Fully Understood 18*

phalange: *Bones 12*

phallus: *Fungus Common Names 10*

phalsa: *Unusual Edible Fruits 6*

Phanerozoic Eon: *Geologic Time 10*

phantasm: *Magic Vocabulary 17; Undead 16*

phantom quartz: *Minerals 10*

phantom: *Undead 16*

Pharaoh Hound: *Dog Breeds 15*

pharaoh: *Ants 15; Masks 2*

pharmacist: *Medical Occupations 1*

pharmacy: *Business Property 3; Health Care 3*

pharynx: *Organs/Major Structures 12*

phase creature: *Monsters and Creatures 22*

phase diagram: *Chemistry General Vocabulary 11*

phase spider: *Beast 16*

phase: *Astronomy General Terms 11; Travel Types 22*

phasing: *Paranormal Abilities 21; Travel Modes 24*

phasma: *Undead 16*

phasmid: *Animals 15*

phat: *Card Games 5*

pheasant: *Poultry Types 6*

phenol: *Chemistry General Vocabulary 11; Dangerous Chemicals 11*

phenomenological reduction: *Philosophy Basic Concepts 14*

phenomenology: *Philosophy Basic Concepts 14*

phenomenon: *Philosophy Basic Concepts 14*

phenoxarsine: *Dangerous Chemicals 11*

phenyl dichloroarsine: *Dangerous Chemicals 11*

phenylhydrazine hydrochloride: *Dangerous Chemicals 11*

phenylmercury acetate: *Dangerous Chemicals 11*

phenylsilatrane: *Dangerous Chemicals 11*

phenylthiourea: *Dangerous Chemicals 11*

Philadelphia Deringer: *Derringer 7*

Philadelphia: *Independence Day 19*

philharmonia: *Groups 13*

philharmonic: *Groups 13*

Philip: *Twelve Apostles 14*

Philippine cobra: *World's Ten Most Venomous Snakes 15*

Philippine crocodile: *Crocodilians 15*

Philippine native: *Other Cows 15; Pigs 15*

Philippine: *Cobra 15; Pit Viper 15*

Phillips screwdriver: *Hand Tools 5*

philosopher: *Wizard 1*

philosopher's egg: *Objects 18*

philosopher's stone: *Objects 18*

philosophy concepts: *Philosophy and Religion 14*

philosophy: *Philosophy and Religion 14; Philosophy Basic Concepts 14*

phlebotomy: *Blood 12*

phlegm: *Four Bodily Humors 19*

phlox: *Garden Annuals 10*

phobia: *General Emotions 20*

phobias: *Character Building 1*

Phobos: *Moons 11*

Phoebe: *Moons 11*

phoebe: *Other Wild Birds 15*

Phoenician: *Human Ethnic Groups 1*

Phoenix: *Constellations 11*

phoenix: *Fantasy Creatures with Symbolic Meaning 19;*

Flying Creatures 16

phonograph cylinder: *Electronics 4*

phonograph: *Electronics 4*

phonolite: *Igneous Rocks 10*

phony: *Personality Other 1*

phooey: *Expletives 20*

phooka: *General Fae 16*

phosacetim: *Dangerous Chemicals 11*

phosfolan: *Dangerous Chemicals 11*

phosgene: *Dangerous Chemicals 11*

phosmet: *Dangerous Chemicals 11*

phosphamidon: *Dangerous Chemicals 11*

phosphine: *Dangerous Chemicals 11*

phosphonothioic acid: *Dangerous Chemicals 11*

phosphorescence: *Cave Anatomy 10*

phosphoric acid: *Dangerous Chemicals 11*

phosphorothioic acid: *Dangerous Chemicals 11*

phosphorus oxychloride: *Dangerous Chemicals 11*

phosphorus pentachloride: *Dangerous Chemicals 11*

phosphorus pentoxide: *Dangerous Chemicals 11*

phosphorus trichloride: *Dangerous Chemicals 11*

phosphorus: *Dangerous Chemicals 11*

Phosphorus: *Elements 11*

photinia: *Shrubs 10*

photoelectric effect: *Chemistry General Vocabulary 11*

photograph: *Decorative Objects 4*

photographer: *Publishing 1*

photographic memory: *Paranormal Abilities 21*

photography: *Art Media 13*

photon: *Astronomy General Terms 11; Chemistry General Vocabulary 11; Spaceship Drive Systems 22*

photon-intermediate: *Energy Sources/Types 22*

Photorealism: *Art Movements 13*

photosphere: *Astronomy General Terms 11*

phrase book: *Books/Publications 5*

phrase: *General Music Vocabulary 13*

phreatic development: *Cave Anatomy 10*

phrenologist: *Fortune Teller 1*

phrenology: *Fortune Telling General Techniques 19*

phthalo blue: *Blue 20*

phunking: *Expletives 20*

phurba: *Objects in Magic and Religion 19*

phylactery: *Typical Magical Objects 17*

phyllite: *Metamorphic Rocks 10*

physical attributes: *Character Building 1*

physical body: *Philosophy Basic Concepts 14*

physical reflection: *Physical Mutations 22*

physical therapist: *Medical Occupations 1*

physician's assistant: *Medical Occupations 1*

physicist: *Scientist 1*

physiographic region: *Geography General Vocabulary 10*

physostigmine: *Dangerous Chemicals 11*

phytohaemagglutinin: *Poisonous Chemicals in Plants 11*

piandao: *Swords One-handed 7*

pianissimo: *Dynamics 13*

pianist: *Musical Occupations 1*

piano quartet: *Groups 13*

piano quintet: *Groups 13*

piano trio: *Groups 13*

piano: *Dynamics 13; Electronic Musical Instruments 5; Percussion Musical Instruments 5*

pianoforte: *Percussion Musical Instruments 5*

piazza: *Outdoor Property 3*

piccolo: *Wind/Woodwind and Brass Musical Instruments*

pichtogalo chanion: *Cheese International Varieties 6*

pick a partner: *Poker Card Games 5*

pick holder: *Music Accessories*

pick up: *Clean 20*

pick: *Axes 7; Garden Tools; Open/Release 20, Pointed Weapons 7; Pole Weapons 7*

pickaxe: *Garden Tools*

picket: *Fighter 1; Fortification 3; General Combat Vocabulary 7*

pickle relish: *Condiments 6; Pickled/Relish 6*

pickle: *Cocktail Garnishes 6; Pickled/Relish 6*

pickled onion: *Cocktail Garnishes 6*

pickles: *Food 6*

pickpocket: *Common Character Archetypes 21; Illicit Occupations 1; Thief 1*

pickup sticks: *Toys 5*

pickup: *Motorized Truck 9; Music Accessories*

picnic boat: *Small Watercraft 9*

picnic: *Independence Day 19; Tables 4*

piconite: *Minerals 10*

picotite: *Minerals 10*

picotiter plate: *Laboratory Equipment 5*

picrite: *Igneous Rocks 10*

picrochromite: *Minerals 10*

picroilmenite: *Minerals 10*

picrolite: *Minerals 10*

picrotoxin: *Dangerous Chemicals 11*

Pict: *Human Ethnic Groups 1*

Pictor: *Constellations 11*

picture book: *Books/Publications 5*

picture jasper: *Minerals 10*

picture perfect: *Happy 20*

picture rock: *Minerals 10*

picture: *Create 20; Decorative Objects 4; Windows 3*

picturesque: *Beautiful 20*

pie bird: *Kitchen Utensils 5*

pie crust: *Ice Cream Mix-ins 6*

pie hole: *Mouth 1*

pie pan: *Kitchen Equipment 5*

pie plant: *Garden Perennials 10*

pie safe: *Storage 4*

pie: *Fish/Seafood Meals 6; Food 6*

piece of cake: *Easy 20*

pieces of eight: *Coins and Currency 21*

piedmont: *Geography General Vocabulary 10*

Piedmontese: *Other Cows 15*

pier: *Castle Anatomy 3; Marina 3; Water Terms 9*

pierced: *Ears 1*

piercing: *Axes 7; Loud 20*

pieris: *Shrubs 10*

pietersite: *Standard Gems 21*

Piétrain: *Pigs 15*

piety: *General Emotions 20; Seven Gifts of the Holy Spirit 19*

pig pen: *Farm/Outbuilding 3*

pig roast: *Pork 6*

pig: *Animals with Symbolic Meaning 19; Card Games 5; Chinese Horoscope 19*

pig's ear: *Fungus Common Names 10*

pigeon pea: *Farm/Outbuilding 3*

pigeon: *Backyard Birds 15; Domesticated Pet Birds 15*

pigfish: *Wild Saltwater Fish 15*

pigheaded: *Stubborn 1*

pigment green: *Green 20*

Pigmy weed: *Weeds 10*

pig-nosed: *Freshwater Turtles 15*

pignut hickory: *Deciduous Trees 10*

pignut: *Deciduous Trees 10*

pigs: *Animals 15*

pig-tailed monkey: *Old World Monkeys 15*

pigtails: *Hair Style 1*

pika: *Woodland Mammals 15*

pike line: *Tactics 7*

pike: *Fish/Seafood Types 6; Pointed Weapons 7; Spears 7*

pilaster: *Castle Anatomy 3*

pile carpet: *Floor Coverings 4*

pile hitch: *Sailing Knots 9*

pile of 28: *Solitaire Card Games 5*

pile: *Sewing Terms 2*

pileus cloud: *Clouds 10*

pilferer: *Thief 1*

Pilgrim chest: *Storage 4*

Pilgrims: *Thanksgiving 19*

piling: *Boat/Ship Anatomy 9*

pillage: *General Combat Vocabulary 7; Harm 20*

pillaging: *General Combat Vocabulary 7*

pillar: *Candles 5; Cave Anatomy 10*

pillbox hat: *Headgear 2*

pillbox: *Fortification 3*

pillow case: *Bed Linens 5; Halloween 19*

pillow protector: *Bed Linens 5*

pillow slip: *Bed Linens 5*

pillow: *Shoe Accessories 13*

pillows: *Equipment and Tools 5*

pillowtop mattress: *Beds 4*

pilot fish jack: *Wild Saltwater Fish 15*

pilot officer: *Armed Forces Other Titles 8*

pilot: *Dolphins 15; Horror Occupations 23; Occupations 22; Transportation 1; Whales 15*

pilotta: *Card Games 5*

pilsner: *Beer 6*

pilum: *Missile Weapons 7*

Pima: *Native American Peoples 1*

pimiento: *Vegetables 6*

pimp: *Illicit Occupations 1; Styles of Dress 2*

pin blanc: *Evergreen Trees 10*

pin curls: *Hair Style 1*

pin cushion: *Sewing Equipment 2*

pin oak: *Deciduous Trees 10*

pin: *Hardware 5; Jewelry 2; Jewelry 21*

piña colada: *Cocktails 6; Ice Cream Flavors 6*

pinabete: *Evergreen Trees 10*

pinafore: *Ladies' Wear 2*

Pinaka: *Bows 18*

pinball game: *Toys 5*

pincer maneuver: *Tactics 7*

pinch: *Harm 20*

Pinconning: *Cheese Common Varieties 6*

pincushion cactus: *Garden Perennials 10*

pincushion flower: *Garden Annuals 10; Garden Perennials 10*

Pindos Pony: *Horse Breeds 15*

pine cone: *Wizard's Goods 5*

pine green: *Green 20*

pine mushroom: *Fungus Common Names 10*

pine needles: *Wizard's Goods 5*

pine nut: *Oils 6*

pine: *Christmas 19; General Snake Families 15*

pineal gland: *Organs/Major Structures 12*

pineapple lily: *Garden Bulbs 10*

pineapple opal: *Minerals 10*

pineapple upside-down: *Cake 6*

pineapple wedge: *Cocktail Garnishes 6*

pineapple: *Cake 6; Jam/Jelly/Preserves 6; Poker Card Games 5; Tropical/Exotic Fruits 6*

pinfire opal: *Minerals 10*

pingo: *Glacial and Mountain 10*

pingpong ball toss: *Amusement Park/Carnival/Circus/Fair 3*

pingpong: *Sporting Goods Balls 5*

Pinhook Bog Indiana: *Bogs of North America 10*

Pinia: *Horse Breeds 15*

pinioned/winged: *Multiple Figures 19*

pink bean: *Legumes 6*

pink belly snapper: *Freshwater Turtles 15*

pink belly: *Freshwater Turtles 15*

pink fleece flower: *Garden Perennials 10*

Pink Floyd: *Asteroids with Unusual Names 11*

pink grapefruit: *Citrus 6*

pink lady's thumb: *Weeds 10*

pink ladyslipper: *Wildflowers 10*

pink prairie onion: *Garden Perennials 10*

pink salmon: *Wild Saltwater Fish 15*

pink siris: *Weeds 10*

pink spinel: *Star Gems 21*

pink squirrel: *Ice Cream Drinks 6*

pink: *Colors 20; Eye Color 1; Pink 20; Valentine's Day 19*

Pinkerton detective: *Western Paraphernalia/People 21*

pinks: *Garden Annuals 10; Garden Perennials 10*

pinnacle: *Castle Anatomy 3; Terrain Features 10*

pinned down: *General Combat Vocabulary 7*

pinochle: *Card Games 5*

pinot grigio: *Wine White 6*

pinot noir: *Wine Red 6*

pinpoint opal: *Minerals 10*

pinpoint: *Learn 20*

pins: *Sewing Equipment 2*

pinstripe: *Fabric Patterns 2*

Pinta Island giant: *Tortoises 15*

Pinta: *Ships 18*

Pintabian: *Horse Breeds 15*

pinto bean: *Legumes 6*

Pinto: *Horse Breeds 15*

pint-sized: *Small/Fragile 20*

pinup girl: *Styles of Dress 2*

pin-up: *Hero 20*

pinuti: *Swords One-handed 7*

pinwheel: *Cookie 6; Toys 5*

pinyang: *Poisonous Plants 10*

Pinzgauer: *Other Cows 15*

pioneer: *Barbarian 1; Styles of Dress 2*

pioneering: *New 20*

pious: *Air Creatures 19*

pipe cleaners: *Cleaning Supplies/Gadgets 5*

pipe cutter: *Hand Tools 5*

pipe opal: *Minerals 10*

pipe wrench: *Hand Tools 5*

pipe: *Cave Anatomy 10; Christmas 19; General Snake Families 15; Hardware 5*

piperidine pirimifos-ethyl: *Dangerous Chemicals 11*

pipes: *Building Systems 3*

pipette: *Laboratory Equipment 5*

piping: *Embellishments 2*

pipistrelle: *Bats 15*

pip-pip: *Card Games 5*

Piqué: *Ballet Terms 13*

piqué: *Fabric 2*

piquet: *Card Games 5*

pirate ship: *Large Watercraft 9*

pirate: *Common Character Archetypes 21; Fighter 1; Horror Occupations 23; Maritime Occupations 1; Occupations 22; Styles of Dress 2; Thief 1*

Piri Reis map: *Real Objects Not Fully Understood 18*

pirouette piquée: *Ballet Terms 13*

pirouette: *Ballet Terms 13; Dance Moves 13*

Pisces (February 19–March 20): *Zodiac Signs 19*

Pisces Austrinus: *Constellations 11*

Pisces: *Constellations 11*

piscina: *Castle Anatomy 3*

pishacha: *Demon 16*

pishe pasha: *Card Games 5*

pisiform bone: *Bones 12*

pisolite: *Cave Anatomy 10*

piss: *Expletives 20*

pissed off: *Angry 1*

pistachio: *Green 20; Ice Cream Flavors 6; Nuts 6; Oils 6; Shrubs 10*

pistacite: *Minerals 10*

piste: *Fencing Vocabulary 7*

pisti: *Card Games 5*

Pistis Sophia: *Major Religious Books 14*

pistol crossbow: *Missile Weapons 7*

pistol grip: *Fencing Equipment 7*

pistol or rifle: *Weapons 22*

pistol: *Black Powder Weapons 7; Combat, Armor, and Weapons 7; Military Weapons General 8; Spy Gear 5*

pistoleer: *Fighter 1*

pistols: *Combat, Armor, and Weapons 7*

pit : *Viper 15*

pit crater: *Volcanic 10*

pit fruits: *Food 6*

pit into hell: *Classic Items 23*

pit toilet: *Bathrooms 3*

pit viper: *Animals 15*

pit: *Cave Anatomy 10; Property Features 3; Technical Terms 13; Terrain Features 10; Traps 3*

pita: *Bread General Varieties 6*

pitanga: *Unusual Edible Fruits 6*

pitaya: *Unusual Edible Fruits 6*

pitch fork: *Tools 7*

pitch opal: *Minerals 10*

pitch pine: *Evergreen Trees 10*

pitch pipe: *Music Accessories*

pitch with fives: *Card Games 5*

pitch: *Card Games 5; Cave Anatomy 10; Entertainment Property 3; General Music Vocabulary 13; Stage Terms 13*

pitchblende: *Minerals 10*

pitcher: *Containers and Vessels 5; Improvised Weapons 7; Tableware 5*

pitchfork: *Garden Tools*

pitching: *Castle Anatomy 3*

pitchy: *Vocal/Speech Quality 1*

pith helmet: *Headgear 2*

pitiable: *Sad 20*

pitiful: *Sad 20*

pitiless: *Horror Vocabulary 23*

pitomba: *Unusual Edible Fruits 6*

piton: *General Survival Gear 5*

pittosporum: *Shrubs 10*

pitty pat: *Card Games 5*

pituitary gland: *Organs/Major Structures 12*

più: *General Music Vocabulary 13*

pivoting floor: *Traps 3*

Pixel art: *Art Movements 13*

pixie scout: *Supporting Cast 24*

pixie: *General Fae 16; Hair Style 1; Small/Thin 1*

Pixie-Bob: *Domestic Cats 15*

pizelle: *Cookie 6*

pizza crust: *Bread General Varieties 6*

pizza cutter: *Kitchen Utensils 5*

pizza oven: *Appliances 5*

pizza pan: *Kitchen Equipment 5*

pizza peel: *Kitchen Equipment 5*

pizza popcorn: *Snacks 6*

pizza: *Meals 6*

pizzeria: *Food/Drink Establishments 3*

pizzicato: *Instrument Technique 13*

pizzled: *Special Body Features 19*

pjs: *Unisex Clothing 2*

placated: *Happy 20*

place: *Fix 20*

placemat: *Table Linens 5*

placid: *Easy 20*

placket: *Garment Pieces 2*

plaggen soil: *Soil General Vocabulary 10*

plagioclase feldspar: *Minerals 10*

plague: *Diseases 12*

plaid shirt: *Western Clothing/Dress 21*

plaid: *Fabric Patterns 2*

plain potato chip: *Snacks 6*

plain: *Donut/doughnut 6; Slope 10; Terrain Features 10*

plainchant: *Composition Types 13*

plains coreopsis: *Wildflowers 10*

plait: *Hair Style 1*

plan: *Fix 20*

planar crystals: *Snow Types 10*

planar travel: *Paranormal Abilities 21; Magical Transportation 17*

plançon a picot: *Bludgeons 7*

plane tree: *Deciduous Trees 10*

plane: *Hand Tools 5*

planemo: *Astronomy General Terms 11*

planer: *Power Tools*

planes rider: *Barbarian 1*

planet buster: *Weapons 22*

planet regulator: *Occupations 22*

Planet V: *Hypothetical Solar System Bodies 11*

Planet X: *Hypothetical Solar System Bodies 11*

planet: *Astronomy General Terms 11*

planetary geology: *Geologic Fields of Study 10*

planetary mass object: *Astronomy General Terms 11*

planetary nebula: *Astronomy General Terms 11; Star Types and Relatives 11*

planetesimal: *Astronomy General Terms 11*

planitia: *Astronomy General Terms 11*

planked fish: *Fish/Seafood Meals 6*

planks: *Door Materials 3*

planosol: *Soil General Vocabulary 10*

plant myrtle: *Practices/Objects to Attract Good Luck 19*

plant pods infect people/animals: *Common Dangers 23*

plant stand: *Tables 4*

plant: *Business Property 3; Charges 19; Monsters 16; Thief 1*

plantain: *Tropical/Exotic Fruits 6*

plantation owner: *Agricultural 1*

plantation: *Farm/Outbuilding 3*

planter: *Agricultural 1; General Farm Equipment; Tables 4*

plants take over people: *Common Dangers 22*

planum: *Astronomy General Terms 11*

plaqué: *Fencing Vocabulary 7*

plasma creature: *Monsters and Creatures 22*

plasma cutter: *Power Tools*

plasma television: *Electronics 4*

plasma: *Astronomy General Terms 11; Blood 12; Chemistry General Vocabulary 11; Energy Sources/Types 22; Minerals 10; Spaceship Drive Systems 22; Weapons 22*

plaster: *Art Materials 5; Art Media 13; Interior Building Materials 3*

plasterer: *Construction 1*

plastic animals: *Toys 5*

plastic army men: *Toys 5*

plastic bag: *Containers and Vessels 5*

plastic beads: *Art Materials 5*

plastic bottle: *Containers and Vessels 5*

plastic containers: *Kitchen Equipment 5*

plastic cup: *Drinkware 5*

plastic explosives: *Spy Gear 5*

plastic guitar pick: *Music Accessories*

plastic sack: *Containers and Vessels 5*

plastic: *Art Materials 5; General Survival Gear 5*

plastron: *Fencing Equipment 7*

plate crystals: *Snow Types 10*

plate harness: *Armor Pieces 7*

plate mail: *Armor Types 7*

plate reader: *Laboratory Equipment 5*

plate tectonic theory: *Geologic Concepts 10*

plate tectonics: *Geologic Fields of Study 10; Geological Vocabulary 10*

plate: *Horse Barding Materials 7; Tableware 5; Teeth Dental Work 1*

plateau: *Slope 10*

plated lizard: *Scaled Reptiles 15*

platelet: *Blood 12*

platform atop giant turtle: *Vehicles 24*

platform pumps: *Footwear/Shoes 2*

platform rocker: *Chairs and Stools 4*

platform: *Beds 4; Building Elements and Features 3; Computer Equipment 5; Spaceship Shapes 22*

platforms: *Footwear/Shoes 2*

platinum: *Coins and Currency 21; Hair Color 1; Precious Metals 21*

Platinum: *Elements 11*

platted land: *Geography General Vocabulary 10*

platter: *Tableware 5*

platy: *Aquarium Freshwater Fish 15*

platypus: *Other Wild Mammals 15*

play: *Rooms 3*

playback: *Technical Terms 13*

player: *Musical Occupations 1; Sports 1*

playground: *Games 5; General Property 3*

playing field: *Entertainment Property 3*

playpen: *Miscellaneous Furniture 4*

playwright: *Publishing 1*

plaza: *General Property 3; Outdoor Property 3*

Plazan Sand Cat light armored vehicle: *Israel Military Vehicles 8*

pleasant: *Good 20; Happy 20*

pleasantness: *General Emotions 20*

pleased: *Happy 20*

pleasing to the eye: *Beautiful 20*

pleasing: *Beautiful 20*

pleasurable: *Happy 20*

Pleasure without conscience: *Philosophy 14*

pleat: *Sewing Techniques 2*

plecostomus: *Aquarium Freshwater Fish 15*

Plein Air: *Art Movements 13*

Pleistocene Age: *Geologic Time 10*

pleonast: *Minerals 10*

pleonaste: *Minerals 10*

plethodontid: *Salamanders 15*

pleura: *Organs/Major Structures 12*

plié: *Ballet Terms 13; Dance Moves 13*

pliers: *Art Tools 5; Hand Tools 5*

plinth: *Building Elements and Features 3; Castle Anatomy 3*

Pliocene Age: *Geologic Time 10*

plissé: *Fabric 2*

plod: *Locomotion 9*

plodding: *Mobility 1; Slow 20*

Plott: *Dog Breeds 15*

plover: *Other Wild Birds 15*

plow: *General Farm Equipment*

plowing engine: *Steam Powered Farm Equipment*

pluck: *General Emotions 20*

plucked: *Eyebrows 1*

plucky: *Personality Other 1*

plugged: *Ears 1*

plum pudding: *Miscellaneous Dessert 6*

plum: *Jam/Jelly/Preserves 6; Pie 6; Pit Fruits 6; Purple 20*

plumbago: *Garden Perennials 10; Minerals 10*

plumb-bob: *Architectural/Engineering Tools 5*

plumber: *Construction 1*

plumber's snake: *Hand Tools 5*

plumber's: *Motorized Truck 9*

plumbers: *Guilds 1*

plumbing: *Building Systems 3*

plume agate: *Minerals 10*

plume poppy: *Garden Perennials 10*

plume: *Head Gear 7; Headgear 2*

plummet: *Locomotion 9*

plummy: *Vocal/Speech Quality 1*

plumose: *Geological Vocabulary 10*

plump: *Large 20; Large/Heavy 1*

plunder: *General Combat Vocabulary 7*

plunge pool: *Cave Anatomy 10; Fluvial 10*

plunge: *Attack 7; Locomotion 9*

plunger: *Hand Tools 5*

pluot: *Pit Fruits 6*

plural society: *Geography General Vocabulary 10*

plush carpet: *Floor Coverings 4*

plush: *Fabric 2*

plus-minus: *Card Games 5*

Pluto (underworld): *Roman Pantheon 14*

Pluto: *Planets 11*

plutonium: *Dangerous Chemicals 11*

Plutonium: *Elements 11*

Plymouth Rock: *Chickens 15*

Plymouth: *Cheese Common Varieties 6*

plywood: *Interior Building Materials 3*

pneumatic torque wrench: *Power Tools*

pneumococcal infection: *Diseases 12*

pneumonia: *Diseases 12*

poach: *Cooking Techniques 20*

poached: *Egg Styles 6*

poacher's spade: *Garden Tools*

Pocahontas: *Asteroids with Unusual Names 11*

poch: *Card Games 5*

pocket battleship: *Military Watercraft 8*

pocket dictionary: *Books/Publications 5*

pocket flap: *Garment Pieces 2*

pocket knife: *Hand Tools 5*

pocket mirror: *Personal Care 5*

pocket pets: *Animals 15*

pocket protector: *Accessories 2*

pocket ship: *Magical Transportation 17*

pocket square: *Accessories 2*

pocket watch: *Jewelry 2; Timekeeping 5*

pocket: *Containers and Vessels 5; Doors 3; Garment Pieces 2*

pocketbook: *Accessories 2*

pocketed free-tailed: *Bats 15*

pocket-sized: *Small/Fragile 20*

pockmarked: *Skin Types and Features 1*

poco: *General Music Vocabulary 13*

pod: *Chairs and Stools 4*

podiatrist: *Medical Occupations 1*

podium: *Special Purpose Furniture 4*

podsol: *Soil General Vocabulary 10*

poet: *Bard 1; Castle Inhabitants and Personnel 1; Publishing 1*

poetry: *Books/Publications 5*

pogacha: *Bread General Varieties 6*

pogo stick: *Toys 5*

pogo: *Dance Styles 13*

poignant: *Sad 20*

poinsettia: *Christmas 19; Plants with Symbolic Meaning 19; Poisonous Plants 10*

point bar: *Fluvial 10*

point d'esprit: *Fabric 2*

point in line: *Fencing Vocabulary 7*

point within the circle: *Symbols of Freemasonry 19*

point: *Fencing Vocabulary 7; Terrain Features 10*

pointe shoe cover: *Shoe Accessories 13*

pointe shoes: *Ballet Terms 13*

pointe: *Dance Moves 13; Dance Shoes 13*

pointed arch: *Castle Anatomy 3*

pointed collar: *Garment Pieces 2*

pointed hat: *Witchcraft Vocabulary 17*

pointed rosette: *Pennsylvania Dutch Hex Signs 19*

pointed shoes: *Witchcraft Vocabulary 17*

pointed weapons: *Combat, Armor, and Weapons 7*

pointed: *Chin 1; Ears 1; Eyebrows 1; Hand Shapes 19*

pointelle: *Fabric 2*

Pointer: *Dog Breeds 15*

pointer: *Office/School/Writing Supplies 5*

Pointillism: *Art Movements 13*

pointy: *Nose 1; Teeth 1*

poised: *Personality Other 1*

poison coated spike: *Traps 3*

poison dart: *Frogs 15*

poison flesh: *Physical Mutations 22*

poison glands: *Physical Mutations 22*

poison hemlock: *Weeds 10*

poison ivy/oak/sumac: *Travel Hazards 9*

poison ivy: *Poisonous Plants 10; Weeds 10*

poison needle: *Traps 3*

poison oak: *Poisonous Plants 10*

poison pie: *Fungus Common Names 10*

poison powder: *Spy Gear 5*

poison ring: *Classic Items 23; Spy Gear 5*

poison ryegrass: *Poisonous Plants 10*

poison sumac: *Poisonous Plants 10*

poison thorns: *Traps 3*

poison: *Classic Items 23; Common Dangers 24; Harm 20; Specialty Survival Gear 5; Wizard's Goods 5*

poisoned apple: *Classic Items 23*

poisoned lipstick: *Spy Gear 5*

poisoning: *Injuries/Medical Emergencies 12*

poisonous insects: *Travel Hazards 9*

poisonous plants: *Chapter 10; Travel Hazards 9*

poisonous: *Horror Vocabulary 23; Negative 1; Unattractive 20*

Poisson: *Ballet Terms 13*

Poitou donkey: *Horses Related 15*

poitrel: *Horse Barding Pieces 7*

poke bonnet: *Headgear 2*

poke: *Attack 7; Farm/Outbuilding 3; Harm 20*

poker bull: *Poker Card Games 5*

poker games: *Equipment and Tools 5*

poker menteur: *Poker Card Games 5*

poker plant: *Garden Perennials 10*

poker: *Solitaire Card Games 5; Western Paraphernalia/People 21*

pokeweed: *Poisonous Plants 10*

poky: *Prison 3; Slow 20*

polacca: *General Music Vocabulary 13*

Poland China: *Pigs 15*

polar bear sleigh: *Vehicles 24*

polar bond: *Chemistry General Vocabulary 11*

polar front: *Meteorology General Vocabulary 10*

polar: *Bears 15; Climatic Zones 10; Meteorology General Vocabulary 10*

polarimeter: *Chemistry General Vocabulary 11*

polarization: *Chemistry General Vocabulary 11*

pole bean: *Vegetables 6*

pole star: *Star Types and Relatives 11*

pole weapons: *Combat, Armor, and Weapons 7*

pole: *Axes 7; Fishing Gear 5*

poleaxe: *Pole Weapons 7*

polecat wood: *Evergreen Trees 10*

polenta: *Grain 6*

police action: *General Combat Vocabulary 7*

police officer: *Horror Occupations 23; Law Enforcement 1*

police station: *Business Property 3; Public Services 3*

policeman's cap: *Headgear 2*

polignac: *Card Games 5*

polio: *Diseases 12*

Polish Cathedral: *Architectural Styles 3*

Polish Hussar: *Armor Types 7*

Polish Konik: *Horse Breeds 15*

Polish Lowland Sheepdog: *Dog Breeds 15*

Polish poker: *Poker Card Games 5*

Polish red dog: *Card Games 5*

Polish Red: *Other Cows 15*

polish: *Clean 20*

Polish: *Human Ethnic Groups 1; Sausage 6*

polished cotton: *Fabric 2*

polished: *Personality Other 1*

Polite: *Architectural Styles 3*

polite: *Good 20*

politeness: *General Emotions 20*

political consciousness: *Philosophy Basic Concepts 14*

political divisions: *Chapter 10*

political parties: *Character Building 1*

political: *Art Genres 13*

Politics without principle: *Philosophy 14*

polka dot: *Fabric Patterns 2; Garden Annuals 10*

polka: *Historical Dances 13; Musical Styles 13*

poll worker: *Government 1*

pollack: *Fish/Seafood Types 6*

Polled Hereford: *Other Cows 15*

pollen: *Allergies 12; Travel Hazards 9; Wasp 15*

pollock: *Wild Saltwater Fish 15*

pollutant: *Meteorology General Vocabulary 10*

polluted: *Unattractive 20*

Pollyanna: *Hair Style 1; Personality Other 1*

polo mallet: *Sporting Goods Other 5*

polo shirt: *Unisex Clothing 2*

polo: *Sporting Goods Balls 5*

polonaise (Polish): *Ethnic/Folk Dances 13*

polonaise: *Ballet Terms 13*

Polonium: *Elements 11*

polonium-210: *Dangerous Chemicals 11*

polophony: *Composition Types 13*

poltergeist: *Paranormal Activity 21*

polycythemia: *Blood-Related Ailments 12*

polydentate: *Chemistry General Vocabulary 11*

Polydeuces: *Moons 11*

polyene: *Chemistry General Vocabulary 11*

polyester: *Fabric 2*

polymer clay: *Art Materials 5*

polymer: *Chemistry General Vocabulary 11*

polymerization: *Chemistry General Vocabulary 11*

polymorphous: *Chemistry General Vocabulary 11*

Polynesian: *Human Ethnic Groups 1*

polyphemus: *Moth 15*

polyprotic acid: *Chemistry General Vocabulary 11*

pomcite: *Unusual Edible Fruits 6*

pomegranate: *Fruit Juice 6; Tropical/Exotic Fruits 6*

pomelo: *Unusual Edible Fruits 6*

Pomeranian: *Dog Breeds 15*

pommel horse: *Sporting Goods Other 5*

pommel: *Fencing Equipment 7*

pommerac: *Unusual Edible Fruits 6*

pompadour bag: *Accessories 2*

pompadour heels: *Footwear/Shoes 2*

pompadour: *Hair Style 1*

pompano: *Wild Saltwater Fish 15*

pom-pom: *Fungus Common Names 10*

ponaturi: *Demon 16*

poncho: *Military Equipment 8*

pond cypress: *Evergreen Trees 10*

pond: *Bats 15; Freshwater Turtles 15; Landscaping 3; Water Features 10*

pond-apple: *Unusual Edible Fruits 6*

Ponderosa pine: *Evergreen Trees 10*

ponderous: *Large 20; Large/Heavy 1; Mobility 1; Slow 20*

Ponente: *Winds of the Mediterranean 10*

pongee: *Fabric 2*

poniard: *Daggers and Knives 7*

pons: *Organs/Major Structures 12*

Pons-Brooks: *Comets 11*

Pons-Winnecke: *Comets 11*

ponte di roma: *Fabric 2*

pontoon boat: *Small Watercraft 9*

pontoon: *Bridges 9; Card Games 5*

Ponwar: *Other Cows 15*

Pony Express: *Western Paraphernalia/People 21*

Pony of the Americas: *Horse Breeds 15*

pony: *Horses 15; Transportation Animals 9*

ponytail holder: *Hair Accessories 2*

ponytail: *Hair Style 1*

poo: *Excrement 12*

pooka: *Beast 16*

pool balls: *Improvised Weapons 7*

pool cue: *Improvised Weapons 7*

pool: *Property Features 3*

poop deck: *Boat/Ship Anatomy 9*

poop: *Excrement 12; Expletives 20*

poor road conditions: *Travel Hazards 9*

Pop art: *Art Movements 13*

pop gun: *Toys 5*

pop singer: *Singer 1*

pop: *Male 1; Musical Styles 13; Soft Drinks 6*

popcorn ball: *Candy General 6; Snacks 6*

popcorn popper: *Appliances 5*

popcorn: *Snacks 6*

Pope Joan: *Card Games 5*

pope: *Religious Occupations 1*

poplar gray: *Moth 15*

poplar: *Items with Healing Properties 19*

poplin: *Fabric 2*

popover: *Bread General Varieties 6*

popper: *Jewelry 21*

popping: *Dance Styles 13*

poppy jasper: *Minerals 10*

poppy mallow: *Garden Perennials 10*

poppy: *Garden Perennials 10; Items with Healing Properties 19; Plants with Symbolic Meaning 19; Seeds 6*

poppycock: *Expletives 20*

poppyseed: *Cake 6; Spices 6*

populated place: *Geography General Vocabulary 10*

Porcelain Tower of Nanjing: *Seven Wonders of the Middle Ages 18; Unique Property Destroyed 3*

porcelain vine: *Garden Perennials 10*

porcelain: *Skin Types and Features 1*

porch: *Outdoor Property 3; Rooms 3*

porcini: *Fungus Common Names 10*

porcupine meatball: *Meals 6*

porcupine puffer: *Aquarium Saltwater Fish 15*

porcupine: *Woodland Mammals 15*

pore water pressure: *Soil General Vocabulary 10*

porgy: *Wild Saltwater Fish 15*

pork fish: *Wild Saltwater Fish 15*

pork: *Food 6*

porkpie hat: *Headgear 2*

porosity: *Soil General Vocabulary 10*

porphyry: *Geological Vocabulary 10; Igneous Rocks 10*

porpoise: *Animals with Symbolic Meaning 19*

porsild spruce: *Evergreen Trees 10*

Port Darwin: *Sea Snake 15*

Port de bras: *Ballet Terms 13*

Port Orford cedar: *Evergreen Trees 10*

Port Orford white cedar: *Evergreen Trees 10*

port silt loam: *Soil General Vocabulary 10*

port tack: *Boat/Ship Terminology 9*

port wine stain: *Skin Types and Features 1*

port: *Boat/Ship Terminology 9; Marina 3; Water Terms 9*

portabella mushroom: *Vegetables 6*

portable CD player: *Electronics 4*

portable dishwasher: *Major Appliances 4*

portable engine: *Steam Powered Farm Equipment*

portable radar unit: *Spy Gear 5*

portable television: *Electronics 4*

portal scout: *Vehicles 22*

portal: *Doors 3; Magical Transportation 17; Travel Types 22*

portamento: *General Music Vocabulary 13*

portcullis: *Castle Anatomy 3*

Porté/portée: *Ballet Terms 13*

porter: *Beer 6; Hospitality 1*

porterhouse: *Beef 6*

portfolio: *Containers and Vessels 5*

Portia: *Moons 11*

portico: *Doors 3*

portly: *Large 20; Large/Heavy 1*

port-of-call: *Water Terms 9*

ALPHABETICAL INDEX

portrait: *Art Genres 13; Decorative Objects 4*

Portuguese Water Dog: *Dog Breeds 15*

Portuguese: *Human Ethnic Groups 1; Viper 15*

Poseidon (the seas): *Greek Pantheon 14*

Poseidon's Trident: *Weapons of Legend 18*

poser: *Magic Vocabulary 17*

position: *Fix 20*

positions des Bras: *Ballet Terms 13*

positive: *Character Building 1; Happy 20*

positron: *Chemistry General Vocabulary 11*

possessed scientist: *Horror Plot Devices 23*

possessed teacher: *Common Dangers 23*

possessed weapon controls wielder: *Horror Plot Devices 23*

possession: *Horror Genres 23; Political Divisions 10*

possibility: *Philosophy Basic Concepts 14*

possum oak: *Deciduous Trees 10*

possum pine: *Evergreen Trees 10*

possumhaw: *Deciduous Trees 10*

possumwood: *Deciduous Trees 10*

post cedar: *Evergreen Trees 10*

post driver: *General Farm Equipment*

post earring: *Jewelry 2*

post exchange (PX): *Military Property 3*

post horn: *Wind/Woodwind and Brass Musical Instruments*

post locust: *Deciduous Trees 10*

post oak: *Deciduous Trees 10*

post office: *Christmas 19; Public Services 3*

post ship: *Military Watercraft 8*

post traumatic stress: *General Combat Vocabulary 7*

post: *Building Elements and Features 3; Fortification 3*

postage meter: *Office/School Machines 5*

postage scale: *Office/School Machines 5*

poster board: *Office/School/Writing Supplies 5*

postern gate: *Castle Anatomy 3*

posthaste: *Fast 20*

posthole digger: *Garden Tools*

posthumously born child: *Items with Healing Properties 19*

Post-impressionism: *Art Movements 13*

post-industrial: *Geography General Vocabulary 10*

postlude: *Composition Types 13*

Postmodern: *Architectural Styles 3*

Post-modernism: *Art Movements 13*

postponing: *Slow 20*

posture: *Classic Heraldry 19*

pot bellied: *Large/Heavy 1*

pot of gold: *St. Patrick's Day 19*

pot pie: *Meals 6*

pot roast: *Meals 6*

pot watcher: *Kitchen Equipment 5*

pot: *Containers and Vessels 5*

potash mica: *Minerals 10*

potassium arsenite: *Dangerous Chemicals 11*

potassium cyanide: *Dangerous Chemicals 11*

potassium feldspar: *Minerals 10*

potassium silver cyanide: *Dangerous Chemicals 11*

Potassium: *Elements 11*

potato chip: *Cookie 6; Snacks 6*

potato masher: *Kitchen Utensils 5*

potato planter: *General Farm Equipment*

potato plow: *Horse Drawn Farm Equipment*

potato spinner: *General Farm Equipment; Horse Drawn Farm Equipment*

potato: *Bread General Varieties 6; Donut/doughnut 6; Items with Healing Properties 19; Vegetables 6*

potatoes au gratin: *Vegetables Cooked 6*

potatoes: *Thanksgiving 19*

Potawatomi: *Native American Peoples 1*

Potawatomi plum: *Deciduous Trees 10*

potch: *Minerals 10*

potency: *Philosophy Basic Concepts 14*

potent: *Fur 19*

potentate: *Angels Common Terms 14*

potente: *Partition Lines 19*

potential energy: *Chemistry General Vocabulary 11*

potholder: *Kitchen Equipment 5*

pothole: *Cave Anatomy 10*

potion maker: *Fantasy Occupations 24*

potion: *Typical Magical Objects 17; Witchcraft Vocabulary 17; Wizard's Goods 5*

potoroo: *Other Wild Mammals 15*

potrero: *Erosion 10*

potter: *Artists and Craftspeople 1; Wasp 15*

potter's wheel: *Art Tools 5*

potting bench: *Tables 4*

potting shed: *Property Features 3*

Pottok: *Horse Breeds 15*

potty: *Bathrooms 3; Chairs and Stools 4*

pouch: *Accessories 2; Containers and Vessels 5; Missile Weapons 7*

pouched: *Bats 15*

poultry seasoning: *Spices 6*

poultry: *Food 6*

pounce: *Attack 7; Locomotion 9*

pound: *Attack 7; Cake 6*

pouring pitchforks: *Precipitation 10*

pouring: *Precipitation 10*

Poveglia Island in Italy: *Real Places Steeped in Legend or Mystery 18*

poverty pine: *Evergreen Trees 10*

poverty: *Rituals 14*

POW: *General Combat Vocabulary 7*

powder blue tang: *Aquarium Saltwater Fish 15*

powder blue: *Blue 20*

powder: *Makeup 5, Personal Care 5; Snow Types 10*

powdered sugar: *Donut/doughnut 6; Staples 6*

powderpost: *Beetle 15*

power cord: *Computer Equipment 5*

power drill: *Power Tools*

power failure: *Common Dangers 23*

power lathe: *Power Tools*

power link box: *General Farm Equipment*

power plant: *Public Services 3*

power strip: *Office/School/Writing Supplies 5*

power tiller: *General Farm Equipment*

power tool: *Art Tools 5; Improvised Weapons 7*

power tools: *Equipment and Tools 5*

power trowel: *Power Tools*

power: *Angels Common Terms 14; Witchcraft Vocabulary 17*

powered armor: *Clothing/Uniforms 22*

powerful: *Large/Heavy 1; Owls 15*

Powhatan: *Native American Peoples 1*

pox: *Witchcraft Vocabulary 17*

practice yard: *Fortification 3*

practice: *Learn 20*

practitioner of witchcraft: *Supporting Cast 23*

practitioner: *Wizard 1*

prairie aster: *Wildflowers 10*

prairie baptisia: *Garden Perennials 10*

prairie clover: *Garden Perennials 10*

prairie coneflower : *Garden Perennials 10*

prairie groundsel: *Garden Perennials 10*

prairie mallow: *Garden Perennials 10*

prairie smoke: *Garden Perennials 10*

prairie spiderwort : *Garden Perennials 10*

prairie wolf: *Dogs/Canine 15*

Prairie: *Architectural Styles 3*

prairie: *Ecosystems 10; Terrain Features 10*

praline: *Candy General 6; Ice Cream Flavors 6*

pram: *Human-Powered Transportation 9*

prance: *Locomotion 9*

prase opal: *Minerals 10*

prase: *Minerals 10*

praseme: *Minerals 10*

Praseodymium: *Elements 11*

prasiolite: *Minerals 10*

prawn: *Fish/Seafood Types 6*

Praxidike: *Moons 11*

prayer beads: *Religious Items 5*

prayer book: *Religious Items 5*

prayer flag: *Objects in Magic and Religion 19*

prayer rug: *Floor Coverings 4; Objects in Magic and Religion 19; Religious Items 5*

prayer shawl: *Religious Items 5*

prayer stick: *Objects in Magic and Religion 19*

prayer string: *Objects in Magic and Religion 19*

prayer wheel: *Objects in Magic and Religion 19*

prayer: *Christmas 19; Rituals 14; Thanksgiving 19*

praying hands: *Rituals 14*

praziolite: *Minerals 10*

preacher tries to convert dance hall girl: *Western Plot Devices 21*

preacher turns to drink: *Western Plot Devices 21*

preacher: *Cleric 1; Religious Occupations 1; Western Paraphernalia/People 21*

Precambrian Eon: *Geologic Time 10*

precanine: *Teeth 12*

precatory bean: *Poisonous Plants 10*

preceptor: *Medical Occupations 1*

precession: *Astronomy General Terms 11*

Precieuse: *Weapons of Legend 18*

precious beryl: *Minerals 10*

precious cat's eye: *Minerals 10*

precious fire opal: *Minerals 10*

precious opal: *Minerals 10*

precious: *Beautiful 20; Terms of Endearment 1*

precipice: *Terrain Features 10*

precipitate: *Chemistry General Vocabulary 11*

precipitation: *Chapter 10; Meteorology General Vocabulary 10*

precision drill: *General Farm Equipment*

precognition: *Paranormal Abilities 21*

predator: *Assassin 1; Villain 20*

pre-dawn: *General Combat Vocabulary 7*

predecessor: *Relational 1*

prediction: *Magic Vocabulary 17*

predictions of the future: *Plot Devices 22*

predictor: *Wizard 1*

preemptive strike: *General Combat Vocabulary 7*

prefecture: *Political Divisions 10*

preferans: *Card Games 5*

preference: *Card Games 5*

prehistoric animal: *Monsters and Creatures 22*

prehistoric human: *Monsters and Creatures 22*

prehistoric: *Old 20*

prehnite: *Standard Gems 21*

prelate: *Religious Occupations 1*

prelude: *Composition Types 13*

Premier/première: *Ballet Terms 13*

premium: *Good 20*

premolar: *Teeth 12*

preparation: *Fencing Vocabulary 7*

prepare: *Learn 20*

preppie: *Styles of Dress 2*

preschool: *Academic Property 3*

preschooler: *Child 1*

presence: *Paranormal Occurrences 21*

present: *Christmas 19*

presentation: *Fencing Vocabulary 7*

preservatives: *Allergies 12*

preserves: *Food 6*

president: *Card Games 5; Government 1*

press: *Fencing Vocabulary 7; Sewing Techniques 2*

pressed back: *Chairs and Stools 4*

pressed powder: *Makeup 5*

pressure washer: *Cleaning Supplies/Gadgets 5; Large Tools*

pressure: *Meteorology General Vocabulary 10*

prestidigitator: *Illusionist 1; Wizard 1*

prestissimo: *Tempo/Mood 13*

presto: *Tempo/Mood 13*

pretty: *Beautiful 20*

pretzel nugget: *Snacks 6*

pretzel rod: *Snacks 6*

pretzel stick: *Snacks 6*

pretzel twist: *Snacks 6*

pretzel: *Bread General Varieties 6; Snacks 6*

prevailing wind: *Meteorology General Vocabulary 10; Wind 10*

prevailing winds: *Geography General Vocabulary 10*

previous: *Old 20*

prickle-cone pine: *Evergreen Trees 10*

prickly ash: *Deciduous Trees 10*

prickly elder: *Deciduous Trees 10*

prickly pear: *Unusual Edible Fruits 6; Weeds 10*

prickly pine: *Evergreen Trees 10*

prickly: *Sharks 15*

pride: *Seven Deadly Sins 19*

prideful: *Air Creatures 19; Personality Other 1*

Pridoli Age: *Geologic Time 10*

Pridwen: *Arthurian Objects 18*

priest: *Castle Inhabitants and Personnel 1; Cleric 1; Horror Occupations 23; Religious Occupations 1*

primary standard: *Chemistry General Vocabulary 11*

primary voltaic cells: *Chemistry General Vocabulary 11*

primary: *Beginning 20*

prime farmland: *Soil General Vocabulary 10*

Prime Meridian: *Geography General Vocabulary 10*

prime rib: *Beef 6*

primer paint: *Art Materials 5*

primer: *Art Media 13*

primeval: *Old 20*

primitive hero: *Common Character Archetypes 21*

primitive: *Art Genres 13; Elf 1; Old 20; Styles of Dress 2*

Primitivism: *Art Movements 13*

primordial: *Old 20*

primrose: *Garden Perennials 10*

prince: *Common Character Archetypes 21; Royal/Noble 1*

prince's plume: *Garden Perennials 10*

princess and dragon/beast: *Common Character Archetypes 21*

princess pine: *Evergreen Trees 10*

princess tree: *Weeds 10*

princess: *Common Character Archetypes 21; Gem Cuts 21; Royal/Noble 1*

principal dancer: *Performing Arts 1*

principal: *Academic 1*

principality: *Angels Common Terms 14*

principle of cross-cutting relationships: *Geologic Concepts 10*

principle of faunal succession: *Geologic Concepts 10*

principle of inclusions and components: *Geologic Concepts 10*

principle of intrusive relationships: *Geologic Concepts 10*

principle of lateral continuity: *Geologic Concepts 10*

principle of original horizontality: *Geologic Concepts 10*

principle of superposition: *Geologic Concepts 10*

principle: *Philosophy Basic Concepts 14*

print: *Decorative Objects 4*

printed music: *The Arts 13*

printed: *Fabric Patterns 2*

printer: *Computer Equipment 5; Office/School Machines 5*

printing press: *Office/School Machines 5*

printmaking: *Art Techniques 13*

prison bars: *Doors 3*

prison guard: *Law Enforcement 1*

prison matron: *Law Enforcement 1*

prison ship: *Prison 3*

prison warden: *Horror Occupations 23*

prison: *Architecture and Property 3*

prisoner of war: *General Combat Vocabulary 7*

prisoner: *General Combat Vocabulary 7; Illicit Occupations 1*

pristine: *New 20*

private 2: *U.S. Army Enlisted 8*

private clinic: *Health Care 3*

private first class: *U.S. Army Enlisted 8; U.S. Marines Enlisted 8*

private plane: *Travel Modes 23*

private yacht: *Spaceship Types 22*

private: *U.S. Army Enlisted 8; U.S. Marines Enlisted 8*

privateer: *Maritime Occupations 1; Military Watercraft 8*

privet: *Poisonous Plants 10; Shrubs 10*

privy: *Bathrooms 3; Rooms 3*

prized: *Terms of Endearment 1*

probe: *Paranormal Activity 21; Spaceship Types 22*

problem must be solved before sunrise: *Horror Plot Devices 23*

problematic: *Difficult 20*

proboscis monkey: *Old World Monkeys 15*

proceed: *Locomotion 9*

Process art: *Art Movements 13*

processed cheddar: *Cheese Common Varieties 6*

procession: *Rituals 14*

processor: *Computer Equipment 5*

procrastinating: *Slow 20*

procure: *Buy 20*

prod: *Attack 7*

prodigious: *Large 20*

prodigy: *Child 1*

produce sorter: *General Farm Equipment*

produce: *Create 20*

Professor James Moriarty: *Sir Arthur Conan Doyle 18*

professor: *Academic 1*

proficient: *Good 20*

profiler: *Law Enforcement 1*

profuse: *Large 20*

progeny: *Relational 1*

proglacial lake: *Glacial and Mountain 10*

prognathous: *Chin 1*

prograde orbit: *Astronomy General Terms 11*

programme music: *Composition Types 13*

progress: *Learn 20; Philosophy Basic Concepts 14*

proja: *Bread General Varieties 6*

projected intermediate: *Windows 3*

projected: *Vocal/Speech Quality 1*

projection: *Stage Terms 13*

projector television: *Electronics 4*

projector: *Office/School Machines*

prolonged: *Slow 20*

Prom dress: *Ladies' Wear 2*

Prom: *Styles of Dress 2*

promecarb: *Dangerous Chemicals 11*

promenade: *Locomotion 9*

Prometheus: *Moons 11*

Promethium: *Elements 11*

prominence: *Astronomy General Terms 11; Terrain Features 10*

prominent: *Beautiful 20; Chin 1; Forehead 1; Nose 1; Personality Other 1*

promontory: *Terrain Features 10*

prompt book: *Technical Terms 13*

prompt: *Fast 20*

prone: *General Combat Vocabulary 7; Moves 7*

pronghorn: *Other Wild Mammals 15*

pronto: *Fast 20*

proof that magic is real: *Fantasy Plot Devices 24*

proofreader: *Publishing 1*

prop: *Boat/Ship Anatomy 9*

propaganda: *Art Genres 13*

propane lantern: *Illumination/Light Sources 5*

propane: *Energy Sources/Types 22; General Survival Gear 5*

propargyl bromide: *Dangerous Chemicals 11*

proper conduct: *Ten Perfections of Buddhism 19*

proper motion: *Astronomy General Terms 11*

properties: *Technical Terms 13*

property features: *Architecture and Property 3*

property tormented by evil force after construction/renovation: *Horror Plot Devices 23*

property types: *Architecture and Property 3*

property: *Philosophy Basic Concepts 14*

prophecy: *Magic Vocabulary 17*

prophet: *Cleric 1; Common Character Archetypes 21; Wizard 1*

propionitrile: *Dangerous Chemicals 11*

propiophenone: *Dangerous Chemicals 11*

propitious: *Fortunate 20*

proportion: *Art Principles 13*

proposition: *Philosophy Basic Concepts 14*

props: *Technical Terms 13*

propyleneimine: *Dangerous Chemicals 11*

prosauopod: *Dinosaur Types 15*

proscenium: *Parts of the Theater 13*

proso millet: *Grain 6*

prospecting: *Exploration 9*

prospector: *Facial Hair Mustache 1*

Prospero: *Moons 11*

prosperous: *Fortunate 20*

prostate: *Organs/Major Structures 12*

prostitute: *Illicit Occupations 1; Travel Hazards 9*

Protactinium: *Elements 11*

protagonist: *Hero 20*

protected cruiser: *Military Watercraft 8*

protection from evil eye: *Pennsylvania Dutch Hex Signs 19*

protection from witch: *Pennsylvania Dutch Hex Signs 19*

protector: *Fighter 1*

protein disruptor: *Weapons 22*

Proterozoic Era: *Geologic Time 10*

protest: *Art Genres 13*

Proteus: *Moons 11*

prothoate: *Dangerous Chemicals 11*

protoceratops andrewsi: *Commonly Known Dinosaurs 15*

proton: *Chemistry General Vocabulary 11*

protoplanetary disk: *Astronomy General Terms 11*

protostar: *Astronomy General Terms 11*

prototype: *New 20*

protracted: *Difficult 20; Slow 20*

protractor: *Architectural/Engineering Tools 5; Office/School/Writing Supplies 5*

proud: *Happy 20; Personality Other 1*

prove: *Solve 20*

provel: *Cheese Common Varieties 6*

proven: *Personality Other 1*

providential: *Fortunate 20*

province: *Political Divisions 10*

provoke: *General Emotions 20*

provoker: *Fighter 1*

provolone: *Cheese Common Varieties 6*

prowler: *Thief 1*

proximal phalange: *Bones 12*

PRP-4 Deyterij artillery reconnaissance vehicle: *Poland Military Vehicles 8; Russia Military Vehicles 8*

prudence: *Four Cardinal Virtues 19; Seven Holy Virtues 19*

prune: *Pie 6; Pit Fruits 6*

pruning shears: *Garden Tools*

Prusik: *Sailing Knots 9*

Prussian blue: *Blue 20*

pry bar: *Hand Tools 5*

Przewalski: *Horse Breeds 15*

psalm: *Composition Types 13*

Psamathe: *Moons 11*

psamment: *Soil General Vocabulary 10*

psammite: *Geological Vocabulary 10; Metamorphic Rocks 10*

pseudobinary ionic compounds: *Chemistry General Vocabulary 11*

pseudocrater: *Volcanic 10*

pseudodragon: *Dragon 16*

Pseudomonarchia Daemonum: *Books of Legend 18*

pseudotachylite: *Metamorphic Rocks 10*

psezpolnica: *Demon 16*

psi powers: *Plot Devices 22*

psionic: *Spaceship Drive Systems 22*

psoriasis: *Skin Types and Features 1*

psychedelic: *Art Genres 13*

psychiatrist: *Medical Occupations 1*

psychic energy: *Energy Sources/Types 23*

psychic powers: *Horror Plot Devices 23*

psychic researcher: *Paranormal Occupations 21*

psychic: *Fortune Teller 1; Horror Occupations 23; Magic Vocabulary 17; Wizard 1*

psycho: *Poker Card Games 5*

psychological drama: *Performance Genres 13*

psychologist: *Academic 1; Medical Occupations 1*

psychology: *Literary Styles 5*

psychotherapist: *Medical Occupations 1*

Ptah (the stars): *Egyptian Pantheon 14*

ptarmigan: *Other Wild Birds 15*

pub: *Food/Drink Establishments 3*

pubic lice: *Diseases 12*

pubis: *Bones 12*

public address system: *Technical Terms 13*

public house: *Food/Drink Establishments 3; Hospitality 3*

public market: *General Property 3; Outdoor Property 3*

public pool: *General Property 3; Outdoor Property 3*

public services: *Architecture and Property 3*

public way: *Roads 9*

public: *Art Genres 13*

publications: *Equipment and Tools 5*

publicity: *Stage Terms 13*

publisher: *Publishing 1*

publishing: *Character Building 1*

puce: *Pink 20*

puck: *Demon 16*

Puck: *Moons 11*

pucker: *Sewing Terms 2*

pudding wife: *Wild Saltwater Fish 15*

pudding: *Miscellaneous Dessert 6*

puddle: *Water Features 10*

pudgy: *Large/Heavy 1*

Pueblo: *Architectural Styles 3; Native American Peoples 1*

Puerto Rican: *Boa 15; Human Ethnic Groups 1*

puff of air: *Wind 10*

puff: *Adder 15; Wind 10*

puffball: *Fungus Common Names 10*

pufferfish: *Aquarium Saltwater Fish 15*

puffin: *Other Wild Birds 15*

puffy sleeve: *Garment Pieces 2*

Pug: *Dog Breeds 15*

pug: *Nose 1*

pugilist: *Fighter 1*

pulasan: *Unusual Edible Fruits 6*

Puli: *Dog Breeds 15*

pull: *Paranormal Occurrences 21*

pull-apart: *Bread General Varieties 6*

pullback: *Hair Style 1*

pulled pork: *Meals 6; Sandwiches 6*

pulley: *Boat/Ship Anatomy 9; Hand Tools 5*

pulling rescue stroke: *Swimming Strokes 9*

Pullman car: *Railroad 9*

pullover sweater: *Unisex Clothing 2*

pulpit: *Special Purpose Furniture 4*

pulsar: *Astronomy General Terms 11; Planetary Systems 11; Star Types and Relatives 11*

pulse: *Weapons 22*

pulwar: *Swords One-handed 7*

Puma Punku in Bolivia: *Real Places Steeped in Legend or Mystery 18*

puma: *Big Cats 15*

pumice: *Igneous Rocks 10*

pummel: *Attack 7*

pummelo: *Unusual Edible Fruits 6*

pump action: *Shotguns General 7*

pumpernickel: *Bread General Varieties 6*

pumpkin bar: *Cookie 6*

pumpkin coach: *Vehicles 24*

pumpkin pie: *Thanksgiving 19*

pumpkin: *Cookie 6; Halloween 19; Ice Cream Flavors 6; Muffin 6; Orange 20; Pie 6; Quick Bread 6; Vegetable Juice 6; Vegetables 6*

pumpkinseed: *Wild Freshwater Fish 15*

pumps: *Footwear/Shoes 2*

punch bowl: *Tableware 5*

punch cup: *Drinkware 5*

punch: *Attack 7; Christmas 19; Fruit Drinks 6; Hand Tools 5; Harm 20*

punching ball: *Toys 5*

punctual: *Personality Other 1*

pungent: *Smells 20*

Punjabi: *Human Ethnic Groups 1*

punk oak: *Deciduous Trees 10*

punk: *Art Genres 13; Styles of Dress 2; Villain 20*

punt: *Human-Powered Watercraft 9*

puny: *Small/Fragile 20*

pup tent: *General Survival Gear 5*

pup: *Dogs/Canine 15*

puppet: *Common Character Archetypes 21; Toys 5*

puppeteer: *Performing Arts 1*

puppetry: *Performance Genres 13*

Puppis: *Constellations 11*

puppy: *Dogs/Canine 15*

pupunha: *Unusual Edible Fruits 6*

purchase: *Buy 20*

purchasing manager: *Operations 1*

pure mentality: *Plot Devices 22*

purebred: *Dogs/Canine 15*

puree sieve: *Kitchen Equipment 5*

purgatory: *Afterlife/Underworld 18*

purge: *Attack 7, Kill 20*

puri: *Bread General Varieties 6*

Puriel: *Angels of Good 14*

purify: *Clean 20*

Purism: *Art Movements 13*

purl: *Sewing Techniques 2*

purple apple-berry: *Unusual Edible Fruits 6*

purple cabbage: *Vegetables 6*

purple coneflower: *Garden Perennials 10; Wildflowers 10*

purple copper ore: *Minerals 10*

purple dewplant: *Weeds 10*

purple fountain grass: *Garden Annuals 10*

purple gray: *Gray 20*

purple horse mint: *Wildflowers 10*

purple leaf Japanese parsley: *Garden Perennials 10*

purple loosestrife: *Weeds 10*

purple lythrum: *Weeds 10*

purple pitcher: *Weeds 10*

purple prairie clover: *Wildflowers 10*

purple rockcress: *Garden Perennials 10*

purple spinel: *Star Gems 21*

purple tansy: *Wildflowers 10*

purple worm: *Beast 16*

purple: *Colors 20; Dragon 16; Martial Artist Belt Ranks 1*

purple-leaf wintercreeper: *Garden Perennials 10*

purple-striped: *Jellyfish 15*

purplewing: *Butterfly 15*

purpura: *Blood 12*

purpure (purple): *Colors/Tinctures 19*

purse gun: *Derringer 7*

purse: *Accessories 2*

pursed: *Lips 1*

purslane: *Garden Annuals 10; Vegetables 6*

pursue: *General Combat Vocabulary 7*

pursuit: *Military Aircraft Pre-1962 8; Paranormal Activity 21*

pus: *Wet 20*

push broom: *Cleaning Supplies/Gadgets 5*

push pins: *Office/School/Writing Supplies 5*

push: *Paranormal Occurrences 21; Poker Card Games 5*

push-up bra: *Ladies' Wear 2*

push-up candlestick: *Candles 5*

pushy: *Negative 1; Personality Other 1*

pustule: *Wet 20*

put in order: *Fix 20*

put in: *Fix 20*

put right: *Fix 20*

put to death: *Kill 20*

put up the shutters: *Close/Hold 20*

putlog hole: *Castle Anatomy 3*

putlog: *Castle Anatomy 3*

putrefaction: *Smells 20*

putrefy: *Smells 20*

putrid: *Unattractive 20*

putting green: *Property Features 3*

putty knife: *Hand Tools 5*

puzzle: *Magic Vocabulary 17*

puzzlement: *Magic Vocabulary 17*

puzzling: *Magic Vocabulary 17*

pycnite: *Minerals 10*

pycnometer: *Laboratory Equipment 5*

pygmy forest: *Soil General Vocabulary 10*

pygmy marmoset: *New World Monkeys 15*

pygmy: *Owls 15; Python 15; Small/Thin 1; Whales 15*

pyralspite: *Minerals 10*

pyramid: *Cemetery 3; Facial Hair Mustache 1; Poker Card Games 5; Religious Building 3; Roof Styles 3; Solitaire Card Games 5; Spaceship Shapes 22; United States Dollar Bill 19*

Pyrenean Shepherd: *Dog Breeds 15*

Pyrenean Tarpan: *Horse Breeds 15*

Pyrenees pine: *Evergreen Trees 10*

pyridine: *Dangerous Chemicals 11*

pyriminil: *Dangerous Chemicals 11*

pyrite cube: *Minerals 10*

pyrite sun: *Minerals 10*

pyritohedron: *Minerals 10*

pyro-hydra: *Beast 16*

pyrokinesis: *Energy Sources/Types 23; Paranormal Abilities 21*

pyrope garnet: *Standard Gems 21*

pyrophane: *Minerals 10*

pyroxenite: *Igneous Rocks 10*

python: *Animals 15*

Pyxis: *Constellations 11*

PzKw Tiger: *Tanks German 8*

PzKw V Panther G: *Tanks German 8*

–Q–

Qaphsiel: *Angels of Good 14*

Qarun Hoard: *Objects 18*

Qatgani: *Horse Breeds 15*

Qinchuan: *Other Cows 15*

quadrangle: *Castle Anatomy 3*

quadraphonic stereo: *Electronics 4*

quadrature: *Astronomy General Terms 11*

quadrille: *Card Games 5; Historical Dances 13*

quadruple: *Star Systems 11*

quagmire: *Terrain Features 10; Water Terms 9*

quail: *Poultry Types 6*

quake: *Horror Vocabulary 23*

quaking aspen: *Deciduous Trees 10*

quaking: *Horror Vocabulary 23*

quality: *Philosophy Basic Concepts 14*

qualm: *Horror Vocabulary 23*

quama: *Swords One-handed 7*

quantity: *Philosophy Basic Concepts 14*

quantum chemist: *Occupations 22*

quantum mechanics: *Chemistry General Vocabulary 11*

quantum numbers: *Chemistry General Vocabulary 11*

Quarab: *Horse Breeds 15*

quark: *Spaceship Drive Systems 22*

quarrel: *Missile Loads 7*

quarry: *Outdoor Property 3*

Quarter Horse: *Horse Breeds 15*

quarter note: *Notation 13*

Quarter Pony: *Horse Breeds 15*

quarter speed: *Slow 20*

quarter vine: *Garden Perennials 10*

quarter: *Coins and Currency 21*

quarterdeck: *Boat/Ship Anatomy 9*

quarters: *Rooms 3*

quarterstaff: *Bludgeons 7*

quarter-tone: *General Music Vocabulary 13*

quartet: *Groups 13*

quartz cat's eye: *Standard Gems 21*

quartz diorite: *Igneous Rocks 10*

quartz monzonite: *Igneous Rocks 10*

quartz: *Cat's Eye Gems 21; Standard Gems 21; Star Gems 21*

quartzite: *Metamorphic Rocks 10*

quasar: *Astronomy General Terms 11*

quasistar: *Star Types and Relatives 11*

quasi-stellar object: *Astronomy General Terms 11*

quasit: *Beast 16*

quassia: *Shrubs 10*

Quaternary Period: *Geologic Time 10*

quaternary: *Geological Vocabulary 10*

Quatre: *Ballet Terms 13*

Quatrième: *Ballet Terms 13*

quaver: *Notation 13*

quavering: *Vocal/Speech Quality 1*

quay: *Marina 3; Water Terms 9*

quayside: *Marina 3*

Quechuas: *Human Ethnic Groups 1*

queen angel: *Wild Saltwater Fish 15*

Queen Anne: *Architectural Styles 3; Chairs and Stools 4*

Queen Anne's lace: *Garden Perennials 10; Wildflowers 10*

queen for a day: *Hero 20*

queen of the meadow: *Garden Perennials 10*

queen of the night cactus: *Weeds 10*

queen parrot: *Wild Saltwater Fish 15*

queen trigger: *Wild Saltwater Fish 15*

queen: *Ants 15; Beds 4; Bees 15; Common Character Archetypes 21; General Snake Families 15; Hero 20; Royal/Noble 1*

queen's: *Cake 6*

Queensland agate: *Minerals 10*

Queensland opal: *Minerals 10*

Queenslander: *Architectural Styles 3*

quercitron oak: *Deciduous Trees 10*

quercitron: *Deciduous Trees 10*

Quern-biter: *Norse Weapons 18*

query: *Speak 20*

queso: *Cheese Common Varieties 6*

quesong puti: *Cheese International Varieties 6*

quest: *Paranormal Activity 21*

Questing Beast: *Mythical Creatures and Monsters 16*

question mark: *Symbols in Magic and Religion 19*

question: *Solve 20*

Quetzalcoatl (leader of the gods): *Central American Pantheon 14*

queued: *Special Body Features 19*

queue-forche: *Special Body Features 19*

quiche: *Egg Styles 6*

quick as a jackrabbit: *Fast 20*

quick bread: *Food 6*

quick change room: *Parts of the Theater 13*

quick clay: *Soil General Vocabulary 10*

quick draw: *Western Paraphernalia/People 21*

quick sand: *Traps 3*

quick: *Fast 20; Mobility 1*

quick-rise yeast

quicksand: *Geological Natural Hazards 10; Soil General Vocabulary 10; Terrain Features 10*

quicksilver: *Minerals 10*

quiescent: *Quiet 20*

quiet as a mouse: *Quiet 20*

quiet: *Adjectives 20; Easy 20; Horror Vocabulary 23; Personality Other 1; Vocal/Speech Quality 1*

quill and ink: *Art Media 13*

quill pen: *Art Tools 5*

quill: *Office/School/Writing Supplies 5; Wizard's Goods 5*

quillay: *Shrubs 10*

quills: *Physical Mutations 22*

quilt rack: *Miscellaneous Furniture 4*

quilt: *Bed Linens 5*

quilted nylon vest: *Body Armor 7*

quilted: *Fabric 2*

quilter's quarter: *Sewing Equipment 2*

quilting needle: *Sewing Equipment 2*

quilting: *Embellishments 2; Embroidery Stitches 2*

quince: *Unusual Edible Fruits 6*

quinoa: *Grain 6*

quintessence: *Symbols in Magic and Religion 19*

quintet: *Groups 13*

quintuple: *Star Systems 11*

quinzite opal: *Minerals 10*

quip: *Speak 20*

quiver: *Containers and Vessels 5; Missile Weapons 7*

quivering: *Horror Vocabulary 23*

quodlibet: *Composition Types 13*

quoin: *Castle Anatomy 3*

quoll: *Other Wild Mammals 15*

–R–

Ra (leader of the gods): *Egyptian Pantheon 14*

rabbi: *Cleric 1; Religious Occupations 1*

rabbit: *Animals with Symbolic Meaning 19; Chinese Horoscope 19; Wild Game 6; Woodland Mammals 15*

rabbit's foot: *Harbingers/Charms for Good Luck 19*

rabbitfish: *Aquarium Saltwater Fish 15*

rabble: *Social Distinction 1*

rabid animal: *Common Dangers 23*

rabies: *Diseases 12*

raccoon: *Woodland Mammals 15*

race horse: *Card Games 5*

race track: *Toys 5*

race: *Motorized 9*

racer: *General Snake Families 15; Military Aircraft Pre-1962 8*

racerback bra: *Ladies' Wear 2*

racetrack: *Transportation Animals 9*

racing demon: *Card Games 5*

Racking Horse: *Horse Breeds 15*

radar: *Meteorology General Vocabulary 10*

radial arm saw: *Power Tools*

radial velocity: *Astronomy General Terms 11*

radiant floor heating: *Building Systems 3*

radiant: *Astronomy General Terms 11; Beautiful 20; Gem Cuts 21*

radiata pine: *Evergreen Trees 10*

radiated: *Tortoises 15*

radiation belt: *Astronomy General Terms 11*

radiation burns: *Injuries/Medical Emergencies 12*

radiation leak: *Horror Plot Devices 23*

radiation: *Astronomy General Terms 11; Chemistry General Vocabulary 11; Common Dangers 22; Energy Sources/Types 22; Meteorology General Vocabulary 10; Weapons 22*

radiation-proof suit: *Clothing/Uniforms 22*

radiator: *Building Systems 3; Pasta 6*

radical: *Chemistry General Vocabulary 11*

radicchio: *Vegetables 6*

radio and command utility vehicle: *Military Ground Vehicles General 8*

radio cabinet: *Electronics 4*

radio controlled car: *Toys 5*

radio drama: *Performance Genres 13*

radio: *Electronics 4*

radioactive creature: *Monsters and Creatures 22*

radioactive dating: *Chemistry General Vocabulary 11*

radioactive tracer: *Chemistry General Vocabulary 11*

radioactivity: *Chemistry General Vocabulary 11*

radiolite opal: *Minerals 10*

radish: *Vegetables 6*

Radium: *Elements 11*

radius: *Bones 12*

Radon: *Elements 11*

raejuusto: *Cheese International Varieties 6*

Raelian star: *Symbols in Magic and Religion 19*

raft: *Human-Powered Watercraft 9*

rag curls: *Hair Style 1*

rag rug: *Floor Coverings 4*

rag: *Cleaning Supplies/Gadgets 5*

ragamuffin: *Child 1*

Ragamuffin: *Domestic Cats 15*

Ragdoll: *Domestic Cats 15*

ragdoll: *Toys 5*

rage: *General Emotions 20*

raglan sleeve: *Garment Pieces 2*

ragtop: *Motorized 9*

Raguel: *Angels of Good 14*

raguly: *Partition Lines 19*

ragweed: *Allergies 12; Weeds 10*

ragwort: *Poisonous Plants 10*

rahu: *Demon 16*

Rahu: *Minor Lines 19*

raid: *General Combat Vocabulary 7*

raider: *Fighter 1; Thief 1*

Raijin (storms): *Japanese Pantheon 14*

rail gun: *Weapons 22*

rail station: *Infrastructure Buildings 9*

rail terminal: *Infrastructure Buildings 9*

rail yard: *Infrastructure Buildings 9*

rail: *Boat/Ship Anatomy 9; Mass Transit 9; Railroad 9*

railing: *Boat/Ship Anatomy 9*

railroad canasta: *Card Games 5*

railroad lantern: *Illumination/Light Sources 5*

railroad: *Bridges 9; Transportation 9*

rain bands: *Precipitation 10*

rain coat: *Outerwear 2; Unisex Clothing 2*

rain forest: *Terrain Features 10*

rain gauge: *Meteorology General Vocabulary 10*

rain lily: *Garden Bulbs 10; Garden Perennials 10*

rain shadow: *Meteorology General Vocabulary 10*

rain shower: *Precipitation 10*

rain: *Boots 2; Precipitation 10*

rainbow agate: *Minerals 10*

rainbow aura quartz: *Minerals 10*

rainbow bridge: *Fictional/Mythological Locations 18*

rainbow garnet: *Minerals 10*

rainbow hematite: *Minerals 10*

rainbow moonstone: *Standard Gems 21*

rainbow opal: *Minerals 10*

rainbow parrot: *Wild Saltwater Fish 15*

rainbow quartz: *Minerals 10*

rainbow runner: *Wild Saltwater Fish 15*

rainbow trout: *Fish/Seafood Types 6; Wild Freshwater Fish 15*

rainbow: *Boa 15; Frogs 15; Garden Perennials 10*

rainbow: *Harbingers/Charms for Good Luck 19; Precipitation 10; St. Patrick's Day 19*

rainbowfish: *Aquarium Freshwater Fish 15*

raincoat: *Outerwear 2*

raindrop: *Precipitation 10*

rainfall: *Precipitation 10*

rainforest rocket: *Frogs 15*

rainforest: *Ecosystems 10*

raining cats and dogs: *Precipitation 10*

raining frogs: *Precipitation 10*

rainshadow: *Geography General Vocabulary 10*

rainwater: *Precipitation 10*

raise: *Buy 20; Fix 20*

raised beach: *Coastal and Oceanic 10*

raised: *Bog Types 10*

raisin: *Bread General Varieties 6; Cake 6; Grapes 6; Quick Bread 6*

rake: *Clean 20; Garden Tools; Improvised Weapons 7; Thief 1; Tools 7*

rakshasa: *Demon 16; Humanlike Groups 1; Humanoid 16*

rallentando: *Tempo/Mood 13*

ram: *Aquarium Freshwater Fish 15; Locomotion 9*

ram's horn: *Squid 15*

ramble: *Journey 20; Locomotion 9*

rambler rose: *Weeds 10*

rambler: *Barbarian 1*

rambutan: *Unusual Edible Fruits 6*

ramchi: *Card Games 5*

ramekin: *Tableware 5*

ramen noodle: *Soup 6*

ramjet: *Spaceship Drive Systems 22*

Ramman (storms): *Babylonian Pantheon 14*

ramming speed: *Boat/Ship Terminology 9*

ramp: *Vegetables 6*

rampant: *Land Creatures 19*

rampart: *Castle Anatomy 3; Fortification 3*

ranch hand: *Agricultural 1*

Ranch: *Architectural Styles 3*

ranch: *Farm/Outbuilding 3; Residential Property 3; Salad Dressing 6*

rancher: *Agricultural 1*

rancid: *Smells 20*

random orbital sander: *Power Tools*

range war: *Western Paraphernalia/People 21*

range: *Major Appliances 4*

ranged combat: *General Combat Vocabulary 7; Moves 7*

ranger body armor: *Body Armor 7*

ranger: *Cookie 6; Fighter 1; Nature Occupations 1; Rural Occupations 1*

rangoli: *Symbols in Magic and Religion 19*

rangy: *Large/Heavy 1*

rank: *Unattractive 20*

rankers: *Soil General Vocabulary 10*

ransack: *General Combat Vocabulary 7*

ranseur: *Spears 7*

ransom: *Plot Devices 22*

Raoult's law: *Chemistry General Vocabulary 11*

rape: *Harm 20*

rapeseed: *Farm/Outbuilding 3; Oils 6*

Raphael: *Angels of Good 14*

rapid: *Fast 20; Fluvial 10; Mobility 1*

rapier: *Fencing Equipment 7; Swords One-handed 7*

rapist: *Fighter 1; Illicit Occupations 1*

rapscallion: *Thief 1*

rapt: *Magic Vocabulary 17*

raptor: *Birds of Prey 15; Dinosaur Types 15*

rapture: *General Emotions 20*

rapturous: *Happy 20*

Raqib: *Angels of Good 14*

raschel: *Fabric 2*

rash: *Horror Vocabulary 23*

rasorite: *Minerals 10*

rasp: *Hand Tools 5; Sounds 20*

raspberries: *Ice Cream Toppings 6*

raspberry beryl: *Minerals 10*

raspberry garnet: *Minerals 10*

raspberry spar: *Minerals 10*

raspberry: *Aphrodisiacs 19; Ice Cream Flavors 6; Jam/Jelly/Preserves 6; Muffin 6; Pie 6; Red 20*

raspberyl: *Minerals 10*

Rasputin: *Real People with Legendary Status 18*

raspy: *Vocal/Speech Quality 1*

rat kangaroo: *Other Wild Mammals 15*

Rat Terrier: *Dog Breeds 15*

rat: *Animals with Symbolic Meaning 19; Chinese Horoscope 19; General Snake Families 15; Giant Creatures 16; Other Wild Mammals 15; Pocket Pets 15*

ratchet: *Hand Tools 5*

rate of reaction: *Chemistry General Vocabulary 11*

rate-determining step: *Chemistry General Vocabulary 11*

rate-law expression: *Chemistry General Vocabulary 11*

Rath: *Other Cows 15*

Rathi: *Other Cows 15*

Rätien Gray: *Other Cows 15*

rationality: *Philosophy Basic Concepts 14*

rations: *Military Equipment 8*

Ratri (goddess of thieves and the night): *Indian Pantheon 14*

rats/insects attack town: *Common Dangers 24*

rattail: *Hair Style 1*

rattan fruit: *Unusual Edible Fruits 6*

rattan: *Door Materials 3*

rattle: *Paranormal Occurrences 21; Percussion Musical Instruments 5; Sounds 20*

rattler: *Rattlesnake 15*

rattlesnake master: *Garden Perennials 10*

rattlesnake: *Animals 15*

rauchkase: *Cheese International Varieties 6*

raucous: *Loud 20; Vocal/Speech Quality 1*

ravage: *Attack 7; Kill 20*

ravana: *Demon 16*

Raven (nature): *Native American Pantheon 14*

raven: *Animals with Symbolic Meaning 19; Other Wild Birds 15*

ravine: *Slope 10*

ravioli: *Pasta 6*

raw umber: *Brown 20*

raw: *Horror Vocabulary 23*

rayon: *Fabric 2*

rayonne: *Partition Lines 19*

raze: *Kill 20*

Raziel: *Angels of Good 14*

razor blade: *Hand Tools 5; Personal Care 5*

razor cut: *Hair Style 1*

razor: *Classic Items 23; Personal Care 5*

razz: *Card Games 5*

RC-12 Huron: *U.S. Army Aircraft 8*

reactants: *Chemistry General Vocabulary 11*

reaction quotient: *Chemistry General Vocabulary 11*

reaction ratio: *Chemistry General Vocabulary 11*

reaction stoichiometry: *Chemistry General Vocabulary 11*

reaction: *Spaceship Drive Systems 22*

reading lamp: *Illumination/Light Sources 5*

read-through: *Stage Terms 13*

real people with legendary status: *Legendary, Mystical and Mythical Items and Locations 18*

real places steeped in legend or mystery: *Legendary, Mystical and Mythical Items and Locations 18*

Realism: *Art Movements 13*

realism: *Philosophy Basic Concepts 14*

reality wisdom: *Five Wisdoms of Buddhism 19*

reality: *Philosophy Basic Concepts 14*

realize: *Buy 20; Learn 20*

really?: *Expletives 20*

reamer: *Hand Tools 5; Kitchen Utensils 5*

reap: *Buy 20*

reaper: *Horse Drawn Farm Equipment; Steam Powered Farm Equipment*

reaper-binder: *Horse Drawn Farm Equipment; Steam Powered Farm Equipment*

rear admiral (lower): *U.S. Navy Officer 8*

rear admiral (upper): *U.S. Navy Officer 8*

rear admiral: *Maritime Occupations 1*

rear arch: *Castle Anatomy 3*

rear: *Doors 3; Moves 7*

reason: *Philosophy Basic Concepts 14*

reassured: *Happy 20*

rebel: *Fighter 1; Styles of Dress 2*

rebellion: *General Combat Vocabulary 7*

rebis: *Symbols in Magic and Religion 19*

rebound: *Locomotion 9*

rec room: *Rooms 3*

recalcitrant: *Difficult 20*

receding hairline: *Forehead 1*

receive: *Buy 20*

receiver: *Electronics 4*

recent: *New 20*

receptacle: *Containers and Vessels 5*

reception area: *Rooms 3*

reception: *Desks 4*

receptionist: *Operations 1*

recessed lighting: *Building Systems 3*

reciprocating saw: *Power Tools*

reciprocity: *Philosophy Basic Concepts 14*

recitative: *Composition Types 13*

reckless: *Horror Vocabulary 23*

reckon: *Solve 20*

recliner: *Chairs and Stools 4*

reclusive: *Horror Vocabulary 23*

recognized: *Personality Other 1*

recoil: *General Combat Vocabulary 7; Locomotion 9*

Reconciliation: *Sacraments 14*

reconnaissance vehicle: *Military Ground Vehicles General 8*

reconnoiter: *Solve 20*

record player: *Electronics 4; Office/School Machines 5*

record: *Laboratory Supplies 5*

recorder: *Wind/Woodwind and Brass Musical Instruments*

recording studio: *Business Property 3*

recovery: *Fencing Vocabulary 7*

recreation center: *Military Property 3*

recreation room: *Rooms 3*

recreational vehicle: *Motorized 9*

rectangular: *Face 1; Shield Types 7*

rector: *Cleric 1*

rectory: *Church Anatomy 3*

rectum: *Organs/Major Structures 12*

red alder: *Deciduous Trees 10*

red and green: *Christmas 19*

red and white: *Christmas 19*

Red Angus: *Other Cows 15*

red apion weevil: *Beetle 15*

red bean: *Deciduous Trees 10; Legumes 6*

red beech: *Deciduous Trees 10*

red beryl: *Minerals 10*

red birch: *Deciduous Trees 10*

red black: *Salamanders 15*

red blood: *Python 15*

Red Brangus: *Other Cows 15*

red cabbage: *Vegetables 6*

red carpet: *Styles of Dress 2*

red cell: *Blood 12*

red chard: *Vegetables 6*

red cherry: *Pit Fruits 6*

red child: *Demon 16*

red claw: *Scorpion 15*

red cobalt: *Minerals 10*

red coral: *Harbingers/Charms for Good Luck 19*

red corn poppy: *Wildflowers 10*

red currant: *Berries 6*

red cypress: *Evergreen Trees 10*

red delicious: *Apples 6*

red diamond: *Rattlesnake 15*

red dog: *Card Games 5*

red drum: *Wild Saltwater Fish 15*

red dwarf: *Planetary Systems 11; Star Types and Relatives 11*

red ear sunfish: *Wild Freshwater Fish 15*

red elm: *Deciduous Trees 10*

red false mallow: *Garden Perennials 10*

red fir: *Evergreen Trees 10*

red flash opal: *Minerals 10*

red frog black frog: *Card Games 5*

Red Fulani: *Other Cows 15*

red giant: *Astronomy General Terms 11; Star Types and Relatives 11*

red grapefruit: *Citrus 6*

red hake: *Wild Saltwater Fish 15*

red hickory: *Deciduous Trees 10*

red hot poker: *Garden Perennials 10*

red hots: *Candy General 6*

red iron ore: *Minerals 10*

red lead ore: *Minerals 10*

red leaf lettuce: *Vegetables 6*

red licorice: *Candy General 6*

red maple: *Deciduous Trees 10*

red Mediterranean soil: *Soil General Vocabulary 10*

red mulberry: *Deciduous Trees 10*

red nose: *Christmas 19*

red nova: *Star Types and Relatives 11*

red oak: *Deciduous Trees 10*

red onion: *Vegetables 6*

red panda: *Other Wild Mammals 15*

red pepper: *Spices 6*

Red Pied Friesian: *Other Cows 15*

red pierrot: *Butterfly 15*

red pine: *Evergreen Trees 10*

red plum: *Deciduous Trees 10; Pit Fruits 6*

Red Poll: *Other Cows 15*

Red Polled Østland: *Other Cows 15*

red potato: *Vegetables 6*

red puccoon: *Garden Perennials 10*

Red Pyramid at Dashur: *Real Places Steeped in Legend or Mystery 18*

red sapphire: *Star Gems 21*

Red Sindhi: *Other Cows 15*

red spitting: *Cobra 15*

red spruce: *Evergreen Trees 10*

Red Square: *Unique Property 3*

red squirrel: *Woodland Mammals 15*

Red Steppe: *Other Cows 15*

red string: *Objects in Magic and Religion 19*

red suit: *Christmas 19*

red supergiant: *Star Types and Relatives 11*

red tails cad: *Wild Saltwater Fish 15*

red tomato: *Vegetables 6*

red valerian: *Garden Perennials 10*

red velvet: *Cake 6*

red wattle: *Pigs 15*

red willow: *Deciduous Trees 10*

red wine glass: *Drinkware 5*

red: *Ants 15; Colors 20 Dragon 16; Foxes 15; Grapes 6; Hair Color 1; Martial Artist Belt Ranks 1; Red 20; Scorpion 15; Valentine's Day 19*

redback: *Venomous Arachnids 15*

redbay: *Deciduous Trees 10*

redberry juniper: *Evergreen Trees 10*

Redbone Coonhound: *Dog Breeds 15*

red-brown skipjack: *Beetle 15*

redbud: *Deciduous Trees 10*

redcap: *General Fae 16*

red-cheeked mud: *Freshwater Turtles 15*

red-chested owlet: *Owls 15*

reddish brown: *Hair Color 1*

red-eared slider: *Freshwater Turtles 15*

redeemer: *Hero 20*

red-footed: *Tortoises 15*

redgum: *Deciduous Trees 10*

red-headed: *Krait 15*

red-hot test: *Witchcraft Vocabulary 17*

redneck: *Social Distinction 1; Styles of Dress 2*

red-necked: *Keelback 15*

redoublement: *Fencing Vocabulary 7*

redoubt: *Fortification 3*

redoul: *Poisonous Plants 10*

redshift: *Astronomy General Terms 11*

red-spotted: *Toads 15*

redtail botia: *Aquarium Freshwater Fish 15*

red-tailed bamboo: *Pit Viper 15*

red-tailed monkey: *Old World Monkeys 15*

red-tailed shark: *Aquarium Freshwater Fish 15*

red-tailed: *Boa 15*

red-tipped coral mushroom: *Fungus Common Names 10*

reducing agent: *Chemistry General Vocabulary 11*

redundant: *Old 20*

red-violet: *Purple 20; Red 20*

red-white-and-blue: *Independence Day 19*

red-winged blackbird: *Backyard Birds 15*

redwood: *Brown 20; Deciduous Trees 10; Red 20*

reed: *Exterior Building Materials 3; Musical Instrument Parts13*

reedy: *Vocal/Speech Quality 1*

reef: *Sailing Knots 9; Water Terms 9*

reefing: *Boat/Ship Terminology 9*

reek: *Smells 20*

reel: *Fishing Gear 5; Historical Dances 13; Locomotion 9*

reel-to-reel tape recorder: *Electronics 4*

Reeves turtle: *Freshwater Turtles 15*

refectory: *Castle Anatomy 3; Food/Drink Establishments 3; Tables 4*

reference guide: *Books/Publications 5*

reference: *Books/Publications 5*

references: *Art Principles 13*

refined: *Personality Other 1*

refinery: *Special Purpose Structure 3*

reflected: *Energy Sources/Types 22*

reflection: *Paranormal Abilities 21; Paranormal Occurrences 21*

reflector: *Candles 5*

reform: *Philosophy Basic Concepts 14*

reformatory: *Prison 3*

refrigerated drawer: *Major Appliances 4*

refrigerated: *Motorized Truck 9*

refrigerator car: *Railroad 9*

refrigerator pickle: *Pickled/Relish 6*

refrigerator/freezer: *Major Appliances 4*

refrigerator: *Cookie 6; Major Appliances 4*

refuge: *Criminal Property 3*

regal bolete: *Fungus Common Names 10*

regal: *Personality Other 1*

regardant: *Special Posture 19*

regatta: *Boat/Ship Terminology 9*

Regency: *Architectural Styles 3*

regeneration technology: *Devices 22*

regeneration: *Physical Mutations 22*

Reggiana: *Other Cows 15*

region: *Geography General Vocabulary 10; Political Divisions 10*

régisseur: *Dance Moves 13*

register: *General Music Vocabulary 13; Laboratory Supplies 5*

regosol: *Soil General Vocabulary 10*

regret: *Sad 20*

regular satellite: *Astronomy General Terms 11*

regular: *Coffee Drinks 6*

rehab: *Health Care 3*

rehabilitation hospital: *Health Care 3*

rehearsal room: *Rooms 3*

rehearsal skirt: *Dance Clothing 13*

reheat: *Cooking Techniques 20*

reindeer: *Christmas 19; Transportation Animals 9*

relational: *Character Building 1*

relative cares for body of dead person: *Horror Plot Devices 23*

relative humidity: *Meteorology General Vocabulary 10*

relative: *Relational 1*

relatives/loved ones injured/killed/trapped: *Horror Plot Devices 23*

relatives: *Christmas 19; Thanksgiving 19*

relaxed: *Easy 20; Happy 20*

relay: *Swimming Strokes 9*

release: *Open/Release 20; Verbs 20*

Relevé: *Ballet Terms 13*

relic: *Witchcraft Vocabulary 17*

Relics of Jesus: *Philosophy and Religion 14*

relief: *Happy 20*

relieved: *Happy 20*

religion: *Plot Devices 22*

religious bread: *Food 6*

religious dress: *Clothing 2*

religious fanatic: *Common Character Archetypes 21*

religious institution: *Religious Building 3*

religious items: *Equipment and Tools 5*

religious occupations: *Character Building 1*

religious property: *Architecture and Property 3*

religious prophecy comes true: *Horror Genres 23*

religious: *Art Genres 13*

relish tray: *Tableware 5; Thanksgiving 19*

relish: *Food 6*

reluctant dragon: *Dragon 16*

reluctant hero: *Common Character Archetypes 21*

reluctant: *Horror Vocabulary 23; Slow 20*

remarkable: *Beautiful 20*

remi: *Card Games 5*

Remiel: *Angels of Good 14*

Remington 1911 R1: *Pistol Semiautomatic 7*

Remington 700P sniper rifle: *SWAT Weapons 7*

Remington 870 shotgun: *SWAT Weapons 7*

Remington Marine Magnum: *Shotguns Pump 7*

Remington model 572: *Lever Action and Pump Rimfire Rifles 7*

Remington model 700: *Bolt Action Centerfire Rifles 7*

Remington model SP-10: *Shotguns Semiautomatic 7*

Remington R-15: *Semiautomatic Centerfire Rifles 7*

Remington synthetic: *Lever Action and Pump Centerfire Rifles 7*

remise: *Fencing Vocabulary 7*

Remodernism: *Art Movements 13*

remorhaz: *Beast 16*

remote cabin: *Horror Locations 23*

remote: *Horror Vocabulary 23*

remoudou: *Cheese International Varieties 6*

remuneration: *Buy 20*

Renaissance: *Architectural Styles 3; Styles of Dress 2*

rendezvous: *Solve 20*

rendzina: *Soil General Vocabulary 10*

renovate: *Fix 20*

renowned: *Personality Other 1*

renunciation: *Ten Perfections of Buddhism 19*

repair: *Fix 20; Robots 22*

repairman: *General Occupations 1*

repeating action: *Shotguns General 7*

repeating crossbow: *Missile Weapons 7*

repellent: *Negative 1; Unattractive 20*

repertoire: *Stage Terms 13*

répétiteur: *Dance Moves 13*

replicant: *Plot Devices 22*

reply: *Speak 20*

report cover: *Office/School/Writing Supplies 5*

reporter: *Publishing 1*

repository: *General Buildings 3*

reprehensible: *Personality Other 1*

representation: *Philosophy Basic Concepts 14*

representative: *Government 1*

reprise: *General Music Vocabulary 13*

reprised attack: *Fencing Vocabulary 7*

reproachful: *Negative 1*

reproductive: *Body Systems 12*

reptile: *Charges 19; Monster Categories/Terms 16*

reptiles: *Animals 15; Classic Heraldry 19*

reptilian humanoid: *Monsters and Creatures 22*

republic: *Political Divisions 10*

repugnance: *General Emotions 20*

repugnant: *Unattractive 20*

repulsion: *General Emotions 20; Paranormal Abilities 21*

repulsive odor: *Physical Mutations 22*

repulsive: *Unattractive 20*

requiem mass: *Composition Types 13*

requiem: *Sharks 15*

resale shop: *Business Property 3*

rescuer: *Common Character Archetypes 21; Hero 20*

research facility: *Military Property 3*

research: *Learn 20; Military Aircraft Pre-1962 8; Paranormal Activity 21*

researcher: *Academic 1; General Occupations 1; Wizard 1*

resentful: *Negative 1; Sad 20*

resentment: *General Emotions 20*

reserve: *General Emotions 20*

reservoir: *Special Purpose Structure 3*

residence: *Residential Property 3*

resident: *Medical Occupations 1*

residential property: *Architecture and Property 3*

residential slang: *Architecture and Property 3*

resistance: *General Combat Vocabulary 7*

resolve: *Fix 20; Solve 20*

resonance: *Astronomy General Terms 11; Chemistry General Vocabulary 11*

resonant: *Vocal/Speech Quality 1*

resort: *Hospitality 3*

resource: *Geography General Vocabulary 10*

respect: *General Emotions 20*

respectable: *Good 20*

respectant: *Multiple Figures 19*

respectful: *Personality Other 1*

respiratory: *Body Systems 12*

resplendent: *Beautiful 20*

respond: *Speak 20*

responsible: *Personality Other 1*

rest home: *Health Care 3*

rest: *Notation 13*

restaurant: *Food/Drink Establishments 3*

restful: *Easy 20*

resting place: *Cemetery 3*

restoration comedy: *Performance Genres 13*

restrain: *Close/Hold 20*

restrained: *Horror Vocabulary 23*

rest room: *Bathrooms 3; Rooms 3*

retail store: *Business Property 3*

retainer: *Teeth Dental Work 1*

reticent: *Horror Vocabulary 23*

reticulated: *Python 15*

reticule handbag: *Accessories 2*

Reticulum: *Constellations 11*

retina scanner: *Spy Gear 5*

retinalite: *Minerals 10*

Retinta: *Other Cows 15*

Retiré: *Ballet Terms 13*

retiree: *Special Occasion 1*

retort stand: *Laboratory Equipment 5*

retort: *Laboratory Equipment 5; Speak 20*

retreat in force: *General Combat Vocabulary 7*

retreat: *Fencing Vocabulary 7; General Buildings 3; General Combat Vocabulary 7; Locomotion 9*

retriever: *Dog Groups 15*

retro: *Styles of Dress 2*

retrograde motion: *Astronomy General Terms 11*

retrograde orbit: *Astronomy General Terms 11*

reuben: *Sandwiches 6*

reveal: *Learn 20; Solve 20; Stage Terms 13*

revenge: *Horror Plot Devices 23; Western Plot Devices 21*

revered: *Elderly 1*

reverence: *General Emotions 20*

reverend: *Cleric 1; Religious Occupations 1*

reverent: *Personality Other 1*

reverse fault: *Geological Vocabulary 10*

reverse osmosis: *Chemistry General Vocabulary 11*

reversible reaction: *Chemistry General Vocabulary 11*

reversible: *Fabric 2*

reversis: *Card Games 5*

revetment: *Castle Anatomy 3*

reviewer: *Publishing 1*

revolt: *General Combat Vocabulary 7*

revolting: *Unattractive 20*

revolution: *General Combat Vocabulary 7*

revolver: *Combat, Armor, and Weapons 7*

revulsion: *General Emotions 20*

rex sole: *Wild Saltwater Fish 15*

Reynolds dilatancy: *Soil General Vocabulary 10*

rghifa: *Bread General Varieties 6*

Rh factor: *Blood 12*

Rh negative: *Blood 12*

Rh positive: *Blood 12*

rhapsody: *Composition Types 13*

Rhea: *Moons 11*

Rhenium: *Elements 11*

Rhine Center Bog Wisconsin: *Bogs of North America 10*

rhine: *Wine White 6*

rhinestone: *Embellishments 2*

rhinoceros: *Beetle 15; Other Wild Mammals 15; Viper 15*

Rhode Island red: *Chickens 15*

Rhode Island white: *Chickens 15*

Rhodesian Ridgeback: *Dog Breeds 15*

Rhodium: *Elements 11*

rhodochrosite onyx: *Minerals 10*

rhodochrosite: *Standard Gems 21*

rhododendron: *Shrubs 10; Weeds 10*

rhodolite garnet: *Standard Gems 21*

rhodolite: *Minerals 10*

rhodonite: *Cat's Eye Gems 21*

rhombic night: *Adder 15*

rhomboid: *Squid 15*

rhombus: *Wind/Woodwind and Brass Musical Instruments*

Rhongomiant/Ron: *Arthurian Weapons 18*

rhubarb: *Cake 6; Garden Perennials 10; Jam/Jelly/Preserves 6; Pie 6; Poisonous Plants 10; Vegetables 6*

rhyacolite: *Minerals 10*

rhyodacite : *Igneous Rocks 10*

rhyolite: *Igneous Rocks 10*

rhythm & blues (R&B): *Musical Styles 13*

rhythm: *General Music Vocabulary 13*

ria: *Coastal and Oceanic 10*

rib chop: *Pork 6*

rib knit: *Fabric 2*

rib: *Bones 12*

riband jasper: *Minerals 10*

ribbed moraine: *Glacial and Mountain 10*

ribbed: *Newts 15*

ribbon braid: *Hair Style 1*

ribbon candy: *Christmas 19*

ribbon: *Candy General 6; Christmas 19; General Snake Families 15; Ice Cream Mix-ins 6; May Day 19; Shoe Accessories 13; Wizard's Goods 5*

ribbon-back: *Chairs and Stools 4*

riberry: *Unusual Edible Fruits 6*

ribs: *Beef 6*

rice flour: *Staples 6*

rice grain spar: *Minerals 10*

rice huller: *General Farm Equipment*

rice pudding: *Miscellaneous Dessert 6*

rice steamer: *Appliances 5*

rice: *Bread General Varieties 6; Foods with Religious or Ritual Significance 19; Grain 6*

riced: *Vegetables Cooked 6*

ricer: *Kitchen Utensils 5*

rich land baron is villain: *Western Plot Devices 21*

rich recluse plays deadly game: *Horror Plot Devices 23*

rich: *Vocal/Speech Quality 1*

Richardsonian: *Architectural Styles 3*

ricin: *Dangerous Chemicals 11*

rickrack: *Embellishments 2*

rickshaw: *Human-Powered Transportation 9*

ricotta: *Cheese Moist 6*

Riddell's goldenrod: *Garden Perennials 10*

riddle: *Magic Vocabulary 17*

riddling: *Magic Vocabulary 17*

ride the bus: *Card Games 5*

ride: *Locomotion 9*

rider: *Animal/Equestrian 1*

ridge beech: *Deciduous Trees 10*

ridge white oak: *Deciduous Trees 10*

ridge: *Erosion 10; Meteorology General Vocabulary 10; Slope 10*

ridger: *General Farm Equipment*

riding crop: *Improvised Weapons 7*

riding hood: *Headgear 2*

riding: *Boots 2; Shotguns General 7*

Ridwan: *Angels of Good 14*

riesling: *Wine White 6*

riffle: *Fluvial 10*

riff-raff: *Social Distinction 1*

rifle attachment: *Military 8*

rifle sheath: *Western Paraphernalia/People 21*

rifle: *Military Weapons General 8; Spy Gear 5*

rift valley: *Glacial and Mountain 10*

rift: *Cave Anatomy 10; Terrain Features 10*

rig: *Boat/Ship Anatomy 9; Fix 20*

rigatoni: *Pasta 6*

rigaudon (France): *Ethnic/Folk Dances 13*

rigger: *Construction 1*

rigging: *Boat/Ship Anatomy 9; Technical Terms 13*

right ascension: *Astronomy General Terms 11*

right to exist: *Philosophy Basic Concepts 14*

right: *Happy 20; Philosophy Basic Concepts 14*

righteous: *Personality Other 1*

right-handed grip: *Fencing Vocabulary 7*

right-of-way: *Fencing Vocabulary 7*

rile: *General Emotions 20*

rill: *Cave Anatomy 10; Soil General Vocabulary 10*

rime: *Snow Events 10*

rimfire rifles: *Combat, Armor, and Weapons 7*

rimstone dam: *Cave Anatomy 10*

rimstone: *Cave Anatomy 10*

rimu: *Unusual Edible Fruits 6*

Rinaldo: *Twelve Peers of Charlemagne 18*

ring bearer: *Special Occasion 1*

ring binder: *Office/School/Writing Supplies 5*

ring bologna: *Sausage 6*

ring dragon: *Dragon 16*

ring galaxy: *Astronomy General Terms 11*

ring mail: *Armor Types 7*

ring of Andvari: *Jewelry 18*

Ring of Mudarra: *Jewelry 18*

ring toss: *Amusement Park/Carnival/Circus/Fair 3*

ring: *Cake 6; Embellishments 2; Farm/Outbuilding 3; Jewelry 21; Typical Magical Objects 17; Witchcraft Vocabulary 17; Wizard's Goods 5*

ringed: *Caecilians 15*

ringing: *Vocal/Speech Quality 1*

ringlet: *Butterfly 15*

ringlets: *Hair Style 1*

ringstone symbol: *Symbols in Magic and Religion 19*

ringwoodite: *Minerals 10*

ringwork: *Castle Anatomy 3; Fortification 3*

ringworm: *Diseases 12*

Rinkhals: *Cobra 15*

rinse out: *Clean 20*

rinse: *Clean 20*

Rio Grande River: *Famous Western Locations 21*

riot control agent: *SWAT Equipment 7*

riot gun: *Shotguns General 7*

riot: *Shields Post-1900 7*

rip open: *Open/Release 20*

rip tide: *Water Terms 9*

rip: *Sewing Techniques 2*

riparian rights: *Geography General Vocabulary 10*

ripe olive: *Vegetables 6*

ripened: *Old 20*

ripidolite: *Minerals 10*

riposte: *Fencing Vocabulary 7*

ripple: *Ice Cream Mix-ins 6*

rise: *Ballet Terms 13; Locomotion 9*

rising volant: *Air Creatures 19*

risk: *Harm 20*

ritardando: *Tempo/Mood 13*

ritenuto: *Tempo/Mood 13*

ritornello: *General Music Vocabulary 13*

Ritter: *Knight 1*

rituals: *Philosophy and Religion 14*

rival: *Hero or Villain, Depending Upon Circumstance 20*

river : *Freshwater Turtles 15*

river alder: *Deciduous Trees 10*

river bastion: *Fantasy Locations 24*

river birch: *Deciduous Trees 10*

river boat captain: *Western Paraphernalia/People 21*

river boat: *Western Paraphernalia/People 21*

river channel migration: *Geological Natural Hazards 10*

river delta: *Coastal and Oceanic 10*

river island: *Fluvial 10*

river jack: *General Snake Families 15;Viper 15*

river oak: *Deciduous Trees 10*

river plum: *Deciduous Trees 10*

river poison tree: *Poisonous Plants 10*

river rock: *Rock and Mineral Forms 10*

river she-oak: *Deciduous Trees 10*

river walnut: *Deciduous Trees 10*

river: *Fluvial 10; Gnome 1; Water Features 10; Water Terms 9*

riverbank: *Natural Animal Homes 15; Water Features 10; Water Terms 9*

riverside: *Marina 3; Water Terms 9*

rivet gun: *Power Tools*

rivet: *Embellishments 2; Magic Vocabulary 17*

riveted: *Magic Vocabulary 17*

rivulet: *Water Features 10; Water Terms 9*

rize: *Tea 6*

road rage: *Travel Hazards 9*

road washed out: *Travel Hazards 9*

roadblock: *Travel Hazards 9*

roads: *Transportation 9*

roadway: *Roads 9*

roam: *Locomotion 9*

roar: *Sounds 20; Speak 20*

roaring: *Loud 20*

roast beef: *Sandwiches 6*

roast: *Beef 6; Cooking Techniques 20*

roasted corn: *Amusement Park/Carnival/Circus/Fair 3*

roasting rack: *Kitchen Utensils 5*

Rob Roy: *Real People with Legendary Status 18*

robber: *Flies 15; Thief 1*

robbers' rummy: *Card Games 5*

robe: *Religious Dress 2; Unisex Clothing 2*

robin egg blue: *Cyan 20*

Robin Hood: *Legendary People Presumed to be Fictional 18*

robin white breast: *Garden Perennials 10*

robin: *Backyard Birds 15*

roble: *Deciduous Trees 10*

robot rebellion: *Common Dangers 22*

robot system: *Military Equipment 8*

robot technician: *Horror Occupations 23; Occupations 22*

robot: *Classic Items 23; Construct 16; Dance Styles 13; Supporting Cast 23*

robotic guardian: *Monsters and Creatures 22*

robotic: *Vocal/Speech Quality 1*

robots: *Plot Devices 22*

robust: *Large/Heavy 1*

Robusto: *Coffee Varieties 6*

roc: *Flying Creatures 16; Giant Humanoids 16; Magical Transportation 17; Travel Modes 24*

Roche limit: *Astronomy General Terms 11*

roche moutonnée: *Erosion 10; Glacial and Mountain 10*

rock 'n' roll star: *Singer 1*

rock 'n' roll: *Musical Styles 13*

rock bass: *Wild Freshwater Fish 15*

rock candy: *Candy General 6*

rock cedar: *Evergreen Trees 10*

rock chestnut oak: *Deciduous Trees 10*

rock climbing: *Exploration 9*

rock cress: *Garden Perennials 10*

rock crystal: *Minerals 10*

rock face: *Terrain Features 10*

rock fall: *Geological Natural Hazards 10; Traps 3*

rock flour: *Soil General Vocabulary 10*

rock formations: *Erosion 10*

rock forms: *Chapter 10*

rock garden statice: *Garden Perennials 10*

rock hammer: *Hand Tools 5*

rock maple: *Deciduous Trees 10*

rock oak: *Deciduous Trees 10*

rock pick: *Hand Tools 5*

rock pile: *Cave Anatomy 10*

Rock River Government Model: *Semiautomatic Centerfire Rifles 7*

rock rose: *Garden Perennials 10*

rock salt: *Minerals 10*

rock shelter: *Cave Anatomy 10; Slope 10*

rock star: *Styles of Dress 2*

rock windrower: *General Farm Equipment*

rock: *Geological Vocabulary 10; Missile Loads 7*

rock-cut basin: *Fluvial 10*

rocker: *Chairs and Stools 4*

rocket larkspur: *Wildflowers 10*

rocket launcher: *Spy Gear 5*

rocket ship: *Air Vehicles 9*

rocket: *Air Vehicles 9; Locomotion 9; Spaceship Drive Systems 22; Spaceship Shapes 22*

rockfoil: *Garden Perennials 10*

rocking chair: *Chairs and Stools 4*

rock-loving: *Scorpion 15*

rockrose: *Shrubs 10*

rocks glass: *Drinkware 5*

rocks: *Chapter 10; Improvised Weapons 7*

Rocky Mountain birch: *Deciduous Trees 10*

Rocky Mountain fir: *Evergreen Trees 10*

Rocky Mountain Horse: *Horse Breeds 15*

Rocky Mountain penstemon: *Wildflowers 10*

Rocky mountain spotted fever: *Diseases 12*

Rocky Mountain: *Toads 15*

rocky road: *Ice Cream Flavors 6*

Rococo: *Architectural Styles 3; Art Movements 13*

rod: *Bludgeons 7; Fishing Gear 5; Typical Magical Objects 17*

rod-back: *Chairs and Stools 4*

Roddenberry: *Asteroids with Unusual Names 11*

rodent: *Other Wild Mammals 15*

rodeo: *Western Paraphernalia/People 21*

rodoric: *Cheese International Varieties 6*

ROE: *Poker Card Games 5*

Roentgenium: *Elements 11*

rogatywka: *Headgear 2*

rogue law enforcement: *Common Character Archetypes 21*

rogue: *Thief 1*

rogueite: *Minerals 10*

Rojhan: *Other Cows 15*

Roland: *Twelve Peers of Charlemagne 18*

role model: *Hero 20*

role-playing: *Games 5*

roll your own: *Poker Card Games 5*

rollaway: *Beds 4*

rolled beeswax: *Candles 5*

rolled: *Cookie 6; Hair Style 1*

roller coaster: *Amusement Park/Carnival/Circus/Fair 3*

roller pin: *Hair Accessories 2*

roller skates: *Footwear/Shoes 2; Human-Powered Transportation 9; Sporting Goods Other 5*

roller: *General Farm Equipment; Hair Accessories 2*

rolling hitch: *Sailing Knots 9*

rolling pin sock: *Kitchen Utensils 5*

rolling pin: *Kitchen Utensils 5*

rolling stock: *Railroad 9*

rolling: *Ballet Terms 13*

rollinia: *Unusual Edible Fruits 6*

rolltop: *Desks 4*

roma chakra: *Symbols in Magic and Religion 19*

Roma: *Human Ethnic Groups 1*

romadur: *Cheese International Varieties 6*

Romagnola: *Other Cows 15*

romaine lettuce: *Vegetables 6*

Roman collar: *Religious Dress 2*

Roman pantheon: *Philosophy and Religion 14*

Roman scissor: *Hand Weapons 7*

Roman shade: *Window Treatments 5*

Roman: *Architectural Styles 3; Art Movements 13; Nose 1*

romance: *Horror Genres 23; Science Fiction Genres 22; Valentine's Day 19*

Romanesque: *Architectural Styles 3; Art Movements 13*

Romanian: *Human Ethnic Groups 1*

romano: *Cheese Common Varieties 6*

romantic ballet: *Ballet Terms 13*

romantic horror: *Horror Genres 23*

romantic interest: *Common Character Archetypes 21*

Romantic: *Architectural Styles 3*

romantic: *Musical Period 13; Styles of Dress 2*

Romanticism: *Art Movements 13*

Rome beauty: *Apples 6*

Romosinuano: *Other Cows 15*

romp: *Locomotion 9*

Rond de jambe à terre: *Ballet Terms 13*

Rond de jambe en l'air: *Ballet Terms 13*

Rond de jambe: *Ballet Terms 13*

ronda: *Card Games 5*

rondel: *Armor Pieces 7*

rondo: *Composition Types 13*

ronin: *Fighter 1*

roof crust: *Cave Anatomy 10*

roof styles: *Architecture and Property 3*

roof vent: *Building Elements and Features 3*

roof: *Building Elements and Features 3*

roofer: *Construction 1*

roofing materials: *Architecture and Property 3*

roofridge: *Castle Anatomy 3*

rooftop: *Christmas 19*

rooibos: *Tea 6*

rook: *Objects/Activities Connected to Lore 19; Other Wild Birds 15*

rooms: *Architecture and Property 3*

roomy: *Cheese International Varieties 6; Large 20*

rooster: *Animals with Symbolic Meaning 19; Objects/Activities Connected to Lore 19*

root beel barrel: *Candy General 6*

root beer: *Soft Drinks 6*

root canal: *Teeth Dental Work 1*

root cellar: *Farm/Outbuilding 3; Rooms 3*

roots: *Wizard's Goods 5*

rootsicle: *Cave Anatomy 10*

rope braid: *Hair Style 1*

rope dart: *Flexible 7*

rope tornado: *Meteorology General Vocabulary 10*

rope: *Beds 4; Boat/Ship Anatomy 9; Bridges 9; Fasteners 5; General Survival Gear 5; Spy Gear 5*

roper: *Beast 16*

roquefort: *Cheese Common Varieties 6*

Rosalind: *Moons 11*

rosary pea: *Poisonous Plants 10*

rosary: *Rituals 14*

rose angel: *Wildflowers 10*

rose garden: *Landscaping 3*

rose gold: *Precious Metals 21*

rose grower: *Agricultural 1*

rose hip: *Tea 6; Unusual Edible Fruits 6*

rose mallow: *Garden Perennials 10; Wildflowers 10*

rose natal grass: *Weeds 10*

rose of Sharon: *Garden Perennials 10; Shrubs 10*

rose of the rockery: *Garden Perennials 10*

rose pepper: *Weeds 10*

rose pink: *Pink 20*

rose quartz: *Minerals 10; Standard Gems 21; Star Gems 21*

rose sage: *Garden Perennials 10*

rose: *Beetle 15; Cadency Mark 19; Crosses 19; Pink 20; Plants with Symbolic Meaning 19; Red 20; Shrubs 10*

rosecomb: *Chickens 15*

rose-fruited juniper: *Evergreen Trees 10*

rosella: *Domesticated Pet Birds 15*

rosemaling: *Art Genres 13*

rosemary: *Plants with Symbolic Meaning 19; Shrubs 10; Spices 6*

roses: *Patterns 19; Valentine's Day 19*

rosette: *Musical Instrument Parts 13; Pennsylvania Dutch Hex Signs 19*

rosewood: *Red 20*

rosickyite: *Minerals 10*

Rosicrucian Order Crotona Fellowship: *Secret/Mystical Organizations 18*

rosin box: *Dance Equipment 13*

rosinca: *Minerals 10*

rosolite: *Minerals 10*

Rossi model 17: *Single Shot Rimfire Rifles 7*

Rossi model 351: *Revolver Double Action 7*

Rossi Rio Grande: *Lever Action and Pump Centerfire Rifles 7*

Rossi slug: *Shotguns Single Shot 7*

rostrum: *Building Elements and Features 3*

rosy barb: *Aquarium Freshwater Fish 15*

rosy: *Boa 15; Crosses 19*

rot: *Harm 20; Smells 20*

rotary card storage: *Office/School/Writing Supplies 5*

rotary side delivery rake: *Horse Drawn Farm Equipment*

rotary tiller: *General Farm Equipment*

rotary tool: *Power Tools*

rotary wing aircraft: *Military 8*

rotation: *Astronomy General Terms 11*

rotavirus: *Diseases 12*

rotelle: *Pasta 6*

roti: *Bread General Varieties 6*

rotini: *Pasta 6*

rotorcycle: *Military Aircraft Pre-1962 8*

rototiller: *Power Tools*

rotten: *Teeth 1; Unattractive 20*

Rottweiler: *Dog Breeds 15*

rotund: *Large 20; Large/Heavy 1*

roué: *Thief 1*

rouge: *Makeup 5*

rough bark cypress: *Evergreen Trees 10*

rough: *Sharks 15; Vocal/Speech Quality 1*

rough-scaled: *Python 15*

rough-toothed: *Dolphins 15*

roulade needle: *Kitchen Equipment 5*

rouladen: *Meals 6*

round cake pan: *Kitchen Equipment 5*

round leaf: *Bats 15*

round ray: *Wild Saltwater Fish 15*

round the world: *Poker Card Games 5*

round: *Cake 6; Cheeks 1; Ears 1; Face 1; Gem Cuts 21; Mouth 1; Nose 1; Shield Types 7; Vocal/Speech Quality 1; Windows 3*

round-bottom flask: *Laboratory Equipment 5*

round-eared: *Bats 15*

rounded arch: *Castle Anatomy 3*

rounded: *Cheeks 1; Chin 1*

roundel: *Charges 19*

roundhead: *Bludgeons 7*

roundwood: *Deciduous Trees 10*

rousette: *Bats 15*

rout: *General Combat Vocabulary 7; Locomotion 9; Moves 7*

route: *Roads 9*

router table: *Large Tools*

router: *Computer Equipment 5; Power Tools*

rove: *Beetle 15; Locomotion 9*

rover: *Barbarian 1; Wanderer 1*

rowan: *Deciduous Trees 10; Unusual Edible Fruits 6*

rowboat: *Human-Powered Watercraft 9*

rowdy: *Loud 20*

royal blue: *Blue 20*

royal casino: *Card Games 5*

royal gala: *Apples 6*

royal gramma: *Aquarium Saltwater Fish 15*

royal sail: *Boat/Ship Anatomy 9*

royal: *Character Building 1; Python 15*

Royale: *Ballet Terms 13*

royale: *Facial Hair Beard 1*

royalty: *Styles of Dress 2*

RQ-11 Raven unmanned: *U.S. Navy Aircraft 8*

RQ-170 Sentinel: *U.S. Air Force Aircraft 8*

RQ-4 Global Hawk: *U.S. Air Force Aircraft 8*

RQ-5 Hunter unmanned: *U.S. Navy Aircraft 8*

RQ-7 Shadow unmanned: *U.S. Navy Aircraft 8*

ru: *Symbols in Magic and Religion 19*

rub: *Art Techniques 13; Clean 20*

rubato: *Tempo/Mood 13*

rubber bands: *Teeth Dental Work 1*

rubber bridge: *Card Games 5*

rubber cement: *Office/School/Writing Supplies 5*

rubber guitar pick: *Music Accessories*

rubber raft: *Human-Powered Watercraft 9*

rubber scraper: *Kitchen Utensils 5*

rubber: *Boa 15; Roofing Materials 3; Wizard's Goods 5*

rubbers: *Boots 2*

rubble: *Castle Anatomy 3*

rubella: *Diseases 12*

rubellite tourmaline: *Standard Gems 21*

rubellite: *Minerals 10*

rubicelle: *Minerals 10*

Rubidium: *Elements 11*

rubing: *Cheese International Varieties 6*

ruby fuschite: *Minerals 10*

ruby jack: *Minerals 10*

ruby red: *Lips 1*

ruby spinel: *Minerals 10*

ruby sulfur: *Minerals 10*

ruby zoisite: *Minerals 10*

ruby: *Dragon 16; Minerals 10; Red 20; Standard Gems 21; Star Gems 21*

ruby-zoisite: *Standard Gems 21*

rucksack: *Accessories 2; Containers and Vessels 5*

rudder fish: *Wild Saltwater Fish 15*

rudder: *Boat/Ship Anatomy 9*

ruddy: *Expletives 20; Skin Types and Features 1*

rude: *General Emotions 20; Negative 1*

Rudra (goddess of dead): *Indian Pantheon 14*

rudraksha bead: *Objects in Magic and Religion 19*

rue anemone: *Garden Perennials 10; Wildflowers 10*

rue: *Garden Perennials 10; Objects/Activities Connected to Lore 19; Shrubs 10*

ruff and honours: *Card Games 5*

ruffian: *Fighter 1; Villain 20*

ruffle: *Garment Pieces 2*

rufous: *Brown 20; Owls 15*

rufous-banded: *Owls 15*

rufous-legged: *Owls 15*

rug rat: *Child 1*

rug: *Floor Coverings 4*

rugby: *Sporting Goods Balls 5*

Ruger Hawkeye: *Bolt Action Centerfire Rifles 7*

Ruger LCP: *Pistol Semiautomatic 7*

Ruger LCR: *Revolver Double Action 7*

Ruger Light Sporter: *Single Shot Centerfire Rifles 7*

Ruger Mark III: *Pistol Semiautomatic 7*

Ruger Mini-14: *Semiautomatic Centerfire Rifles 7*

Ruger model 77 Target: *Bolt Action Centerfire Rifles 7*

Ruger New Bearcat: *Revolver Single Action 7*

Ruger New Model Blackhawk Bisley: *Revolver Single Action 7*

Ruger New Vaquero: *Revolver Single Action 7*

Ruger Ranch: *Semiautomatic Centerfire Rifles 7*

Ruger Red Label: *Shotguns Over/Under 7*

Ruger Redhawk: *Revolver Double Action 7*

ruin: *Harm 20*

ruined: *Unattractive 20*

ruler: *Architectural/Engineering Tools 5; Office/School/Writing Supplies 5; Sewing Equipment 2; Symbols of Freemasonry 19*

rum cherry: *Deciduous Trees 10*

rum dark: *Hard Liquor 6*

rum light: *Hard Liquor 6*

rum: *Aphrodisiacs 19; Cake 6; Ice Cream Flavors 6*

rumali roti: *Bread General Varieties 6*

rumanite: *Minerals 10*

rumba: *Dance Styles 13*

rumberry: *Unusual Edible Fruits 6*

rumble: *Sounds 20*

rummy 500: *Card Games 5*

rummy: *Card Games 5*

rummynose tetra: *Aquarium Freshwater Fish 15*

rump roast: *Beef 6*

run: *Expletives 20; Locomotion 9*

run-down car: *Travel Modes 23*

run-down: *Unattractive 20*

rune tree: *Deciduous Trees 10*

rungu: *Bludgeons 7*

runner bean: *Vegetables 6*

runner oak: *Deciduous Trees 10*

runner: *Floor Coverings 4; Table Linens 5*

running attack: *Fencing Vocabulary 7*

running bowline: *Sailing Knots 9*

running: *Athletic Shoes 2; Embroidery Stitches 2*

runny: *Wet 20*

runway: *Infrastructure Buildings 9*

Ruppell's: *Foxes 15*

rupturewort: *Garden Perennials 10*

rural district: *Political Divisions 10*

rural occupations: *Character Building 1*

rusalka: *Devil 16*

ruse: *Magic Vocabulary 17*

rush light: *Illumination/Light Sources 5*

rush seat: *Chairs and Stools 4*

rush: *Locomotion 9*

rushan: *Cheese International Varieties 6*

rushed: *Fast 20*

Russell Terrier: *Dog Breeds 15*

Russell's: *Viper 15*

russet potato: *Vegetables 6*

russet: *Brown 20*

Russian bank: *Card Games 5*

Russian Black Pied: *Other Cows 15*

Russian Blue: *Domestic Cats 15*

Russian Don: *Horse Breeds 15*

Russian Heavy Draft: *Horse Breeds 15*

Russian hibiscus: *Garden Perennials 10*

Russian jasper: *Minerals 10*

Russian knapweed: *Weeds 10*

Russian Revival: *Architectural Styles 3*

Russian sage: *Garden Perennials 10; Shrubs 10*

Russian School: *Ballet Terms 13*

Russian Trotter: *Horse Breeds 15*

Russian tutu: *Dance Clothing 13*

Russian vine: *Weeds 10*

Russian: *Human Ethnic Groups 1; Tortoises 15*

russula-like waxy cap: *Fungus Common Names 10*

rust: *Brown 20; Orange 20; Red 20*

Rustic: *Architectural Styles 3*

rutabaga: *Vegetables 6*

Ruthenium: *Elements 11*

Rutherfordium: *Elements 11*

ruthless: *Bad 20; Horror Vocabulary 23*

ruti: *Poisonous Plants 10*

rutilated quartz: *Minerals 10*

rutile quartz: *Standard Gems 21*

rutile topaz: *Standard Gems 21*

rutile: *Cat's Eye Gems 21*

Ruyi Jingu Bang staff: *Weapons of Legend 18*

RV: *Motorized 9*

rye: *Grain 6; Hard Liquor 6*

Ryujin (the sea): *Japanese Pantheon 14*

–S–

S orbital: *Chemistry General Vocabulary 11*

S.S. Great Eastern: *Seven Wonders of the Industrial World 18*

S/2000 J 11: *Hypothetical Solar System Bodies 11*

Sabal palmetto: *Deciduous Trees 10*

saber cut: *Fencing Vocabulary 7*

saber mask: *Fencing Equipment 7*

saber parry: *Fencing Vocabulary 7*

saber thrust: *Fencing Vocabulary 7*

saber: *Fencing Equipment 7; Swords One-handed 7*

saber-toothed: *Tigers 15*

sabi star: *Poisonous Plants 10*

sabia: *Shrubs 10*

sabino: *Evergreen Trees 10*

sable (black): *Colors/Tinctures 19*

sabotage: *General Combat Vocabulary 7*

Sabra main battle tank: *Israel Military Vehicles 8*

sacher torte: *Cake 6*

sachet: *Containers and Vessels 5*

Sachiel: *Angels of Good 14*

sack suit: *Men's Wear 2*

sack: *Christmas 19; Containers and Vessels 5*

sackbut: *Wind/Woodwind and Brass Musical Instruments*

Saco Heath Bog Maine: *Bogs of North America 10*

sacramental bread: *Religious Bread 6*

Sacraments: *Philosophy and Religion 14*

sacred heart: *Symbols in Magic and Religion 19*

sacred: *Magic Vocabulary 17*

sacristy: *Church Anatomy 3*

sacrum: *Bones 12*

sac-winged: *Bats 15*

sad: *Emotions 20; Negative 1*

saddle: *Footwear/Shoes 2; Transportation Animals 9; Western Paraphernalia/People 21*

saddlebag: *Accessories 2; Containers and Vessels 5; Transportation Animals 9*

saddle blanket: *Transportation Animals 9; Western Paraphernalia/People 21*

Saddlebred: *Horse Breeds 15*

sadhu: *Cleric 1*

safe room: *Rooms 3*

safe: *Containers and Vessels 5*

safecracking tools: *Spy Gear 5*

safehouse: *Criminal Property 3; Spy Gear 5*

safety curtain: *Technical Terms 13*

safety goggles: *Laboratory Equipment 5*

safety orange: *Orange 20*

safety shower: *Laboratory Equipment 5*

safety sucker: *Candy General 6*

safety vest: *Special Purpose Clothing 2*

safety yellow: *Yellow 20*

safflower: *Oils 6; Seeds 6*

saffron milkcap: *Fungus Common Names 10*

saffron: *Plants with Symbolic Meaning 19; Spices 6; Yellow 20*

Safir: *Knights of the Round Table 18*

safou: *Unusual Edible Fruits 6*

saga: *Cheese International Varieties 6; Literary Styles 5*

sage: *Bard 1; Garden Annuals 10; Garden Perennials 10; Plants with Symbolic Meaning 19; Shrubs 10; Spices 6; Wizard 1*

sagebrush: *Shrubs 10*

sagenite agate: *Minerals 10*

sagenite: *Minerals 10*

sageretia: *Unusual Edible Fruits 6*

Sagitta: *Constellations 11*

Sagittarius (November 22–December 21): *Zodiac Signs 19*

Sagittarius: *Constellations 11*

Sagramore: *Knights of the Round Table 18*

saguaro: *Unusual Edible Fruits 6*

Sahara desert: *Ants 15*

Sahiwal: *Other Cows 15*

sahuagin: *Beast 16*

SahysMod: *Soil General Vocabulary 10*

sail frigate: *Military Watercraft 8*

sail maker: *Maritime Occupations 1*

sail zone: *Boat/Ship Terminology 9*

sail: *Boat/Ship Anatomy 9; Locomotion 9*

sailboard: *Human-Powered Watercraft 9*

sailboat: *Small Watercraft 9*

sailcloth: *Fabric 2*

sailfin molly: *Aquarium Freshwater Fish 15*

sailfish: *Wild Saltwater Fish 15*

sailing knots: *Transportation 9*

sailor cap: *Headgear 2*

sailor: *Maritime Occupations 1; Navy Other Titles 8*

Saint Bernard: *Dog Breeds 15*

Saint Nicholas: *Real People with Legendary Status 18*

saintie: *Spears 7*

saker: *Cannon 7*

saki cup: *Drinkware 5*

saki monkey: *New World Monkeys 15*

saki server: *Drinkware 5*

Sako 85: *Bolt Action Centerfire Rifles 7*

Sako Quad Hunter: *Bolt Action Rimfire Rifles 7*

sakura: *Cheese International Varieties 6*

salad bowl: *Containers and Vessels 5; Tableware 5*

salad crisper: *Kitchen Equipment 5*

salad dressing: *Food 6*

salad fork: *Eating Utensils 5*

salad girl: *Food Service 1*

salad plate: *Tableware 5*

salad potato: *Vegetables 6*

salad: *Food 6*

salaite: *Minerals 10*

salak: *Unusual Edible Fruits 6*

salakot: *Headgear 2*

salal: *Shrubs 10; Unusual Edible Fruits 6*

salamander: *Elemental 16; Extraplanar 16*

salamanders: *Animals 15*

salami: *Sandwiches 6*

salcomine: *Dangerous Chemicals 11*

Salers: *Other Cows 15*

sales girl/lady/man/woman: *General Occupations 1*

salesman: *Personality Other 1*

salient: *Land Creatures 19*

saline seep: *Soil General Vocabulary 10*

salite: *Minerals 10*

saliva: *Wet 20*

salivary gland: *Organs/Major Structures 12*

salle: *Fencing Vocabulary 7*

sallow: *Skin Types and Features 1*

Sally Ann Thunder Ann Whirlwind Crockett: *Tall Tales 18*

sally forth: *Locomotion 9*

sally-port: *Castle Anatomy 3*

salmon calcite: *Minerals 10*

salmon: *Animals with Symbolic Meaning 19; Fish/Seafood Types 6; Orange 20; Pink 20*

salmonberry: *Unusual Edible Fruits 6*

salon: *Rooms 3*

saloon brawl: *Western Paraphernalia/People 21*

saloon: *Food/Drink Establishments 3; Western Paraphernalia/People 21*

saloop: *Deciduous Trees 10*

Salorn: *Other Cows 15*

salsa: *Dance Styles 13*

salsify: *Vegetables 6*

salt and pepper shakers: *Tableware 5*

salt bridge: *Chemistry General Vocabulary 11*

salt cellar: *Tableware 5*

Salt Lake: *Famous Western Locations 21*

salt marsh: *Coastal and Oceanic 10; Ecosystems 10; Soil General Vocabulary 10*

salt pork rubbed on a wart: *Items with Healing Properties 19*

salt shaker: *Kitchen Utensils 5*

salt: *Minerals 10; Objects/Activities Connected to Lore 19*

salt-and-pepper: *Hair Color 1*

saltarello (Italian): *Ethnic/Folk Dances 13*

Saltbox: *Architectural Styles 3*

saltcedar: *Weeds 10*

salting the earth: *Soil General Vocabulary 10*

saltire: *Crosses 19*

saltmarsh cordgrass: *Weeds 10*

SaltMod: *Soil General Vocabulary 10*

saltwater: *Minerals 10*

saltwater taffy: *Candy General 6*

Saluki: *Dog Breeds 15*

salute: *Fencing Vocabulary 7*

salver: *Tableware 5*

salvia: *Garden Annuals 10*

salvo: *General Combat Vocabulary 7*

sam jeet kwun: *Bludgeons 7*

samael: *Devil 16*

Samael: *Fallen Angels 14*

Samarium: *Elements 11*

samba: *Card Games 5; Dance Styles 13*

Sami: *Human Ethnic Groups 1*

sammite: *Minerals 10*

Samoan: *Human Ethnic Groups 1*

samovar: *Tableware 5*

Samoyed: *Dog Breeds 15*

sample collection: *Geological Field Work Methods 10*

Sampo: *Objects 18*

samso: *Cheese International Varieties 6*

Samson: *Twelve Peers of Charlemagne 18*

Samuel Steele: *Real People with Legendary Status 18*

samurai: *Fighter 1; Swords One-handed 7*

San Antonio class: *U.S. Navy Vessels 8*

San Francisco earthquake of 1906: *Legendary Events 18*

San Francisco: *Poker Card Games 5*

San Joaquin soil: *Soil General Vocabulary 10*

San Martinero: *Other Cows 15*

san michali: *Cheese International Varieties 6*

sanction: *Agree 20*

sanctuary: *Church Anatomy 3; General Buildings 3*

sanctum: *General Buildings 3*

sand boil: *Soil General Vocabulary 10*

sand calcite: *Minerals 10*

sand celestine: *Minerals 10*

sand dab: *Wild Saltwater Fish 15*

sand dollar: *Animals with Symbolic Meaning 19*

sand gypsum: *Minerals 10*

sand launces: *Wild Freshwater Fish 15*

sand perch: *Wild Saltwater Fish 15*

sand pine: *Evergreen Trees 10*

sand pit: *Terrain Features 10*

sand post oak: *Deciduous Trees 10*

sand roller: *Wild Freshwater Fish 15*

sand seatrout: *Wild Saltwater Fish 15*

sand volcano: *Volcanic 10*

sand: *Art Materials 5; Art Techniques 13; Boa 15; Brown 20; Cave Anatomy 10; Flies 15; Improvised Weapons 7; Scorpion 15; Soil General Vocabulary 10; Traps 3; Viper 15; Wasp 15; Wizard's Goods 5*

Sandalphon: *Angels of Good 14*

sandals: *Footwear/Shoes 2*

sandbag: *Soil General Vocabulary 10; Technical Terms 13*

sandbank: *Terrain Features 10*

sandbar: *Water Terms 9*

sander: *Power Tools*

sandgrouse: *Other Wild Birds 15*

sandhill post oak: *Deciduous Trees 10*

sandhill: *Aeolian 10*

sandjack oak: *Deciduous Trees 10*

sand-loving: *Scorpion 15*

Sandman: *Folklore Characters 18*

sandpaper oak: *Deciduous Trees 10*

sandpaper: *Hand Tools 5*

sandstone: *Sedimentary Rocks 10*

sandstorm: *Meteorology General Vocabulary 10*

sandtile: *Wild Saltwater Fish 15*

sandur: *Glacial and Mountain 10*

sandwich loaf: *Sandwiches 6*

sandwich server: *Tableware 5*

sandwich: *Cookie 6; Food 6*

sandwort: *Garden Perennials 10*

sandy brown: *Brown 20*

sangha: *Cleric 1*

sangiovese: *Wine Red 6*

Sangreal Sodality: *Secret/Mystical Organizations 18*

sangria: *Wine Red 6*

sanguine: *Skin Types and Features 1*

Sanhe: *Horse Breeds 15; Other Cows 15*

sanitarium: *Health Care 3*

sanitation worker: *General Occupations 1*

sanitize: *Clean 20*

Santa Ana wind: *Wind 10*

Santa Claus cap: *Headgear 2*

Santa Claus: *Characters with Symbolic Meaning 19; Christmas 19; Facial Hair Beard 1; Melons 6*

Santa Cruz: *Other Cows 15*

Santa Fe Trail: *Famous Western Locations 21*

Santa Gertrudis: *Other Cows 15*

Santa Lucia fir: *Evergreen Trees 10*

Santa Maria: *Ships 18*

Santa Rosa Island torrey pine: *Evergreen Trees 10*

Santa's village at the North Pole: *Sites Lost or Unproven to Exist 18*

santol: *Unusual Edible Fruits 6*

Sao Paulo: *Caecilians 15*

Sao: *Moons 11*

sap: *Bludgeons 7; Hand Weapons 7; Wizard's Goods 5*

sapgum: *Deciduous Trees 10*

saponification: *Chemistry General Vocabulary 11*

sapphire quartz: *Minerals 10*

sapphire: *Blue 20; Dragon 16; Harbingers/Charms for Good Luck 19; Minerals 10; Standard Gems 21*

sapsucker: *Backyard Birds 15*

sarabande: *Historical Dances 13*

Sarabi: *Other Cows 15*

Saranga: *Bows 18*

sarcastic: *Personality Other 1*

sarcophagus: *Cemetery 3; Containers and Vessels 5*

sard: *Minerals 10*

Sardinian: *Human Ethnic Groups 1*

sardonic: *Personality Other 1*

sardonyx: *Minerals 10*

sargasso sea: *Sites Lost or Unproven to Exist 18*

Sargent cypress: *Evergreen Trees 10*

sari: *Ladies' Wear 2*

Sariel: *Angels of Good 14*

sarin: *Dangerous Chemicals 11*

sarissa: *Spears 7*

sarma: *Meals 6*

sarong skirt: *Ladies' Wear 2*

SARS: *Diseases 12*

sash: *Garment Pieces 2*

sashay: *Locomotion 9*

saskatoonberry: *Unusual Edible Fruits 6*

Sasquatch: *Mythical Creatures and Monsters 16*

sassafras: *Deciduous Trees 10*

Satan: *Fallen Angels 14*

satanchia: *Devil 16*

satchel: *Accessories 2; Containers and Vessels 5*

sateen: *Fabric 2*

satellite linkup: *Spy Gear 5*

satellite station: *Installations 22*

satellite: *Astronomy General Terms 11; Military 8*

satin spar: *Minerals 10*

satin walnut: *Deciduous Trees 10*

satin: *Embroidery Stitches 2;Fabric 2*

satire: *Performance Genres 13*

satirist: *Bard 1*

satisfactory: *Good 20*

satisfied: *Happy 20*

satisfy: *Agree 20*

satisfying: *Happy 20*

saturate: *Precipitation 10*

saturated hydrocarbons: *Chemistry General Vocabulary 11*

saturated solution: *Chemistry General Vocabulary 11*

saturated: *Cave Anatomy 10*

saturation bombing: *General Combat Vocabulary 7*

Saturn (harvest): *Roman Pantheon 14*

Saturn: *Mounts 19; Planets 11*

satyr: *Butterfly 15; Fae Related 16; Fantasy Creatures with Symbolic Meaning 19; General Fae 16; Mythical Creatures and Monsters 16*

sauce boat: *Tableware 5*

saucer: *Spaceship Shapes 22; Tableware 5*

sauerbraten: *Meals 6*

sauerkraut: *Vegetables 6*

Sauk: *Native American Peoples 1*

sauna: *Rooms 3*

saunter: *Locomotion 9*

sauropod: *Dinosaur Types 15*

sausage: *Food 6; Pork 6*

Saut de basque: *Ballet Terms 13*

sauté pan: *Kitchen Equipment 5*

Sauté/sautée: *Ballet Terms 13*

sauté: *Cooking Techniques 20*

sauterne: *Wine White 6*

Sauvagine: *Weapons of Legend 18*

sauvignon blanc: *Wine White 6*

Savage Cub: *Bolt Action Rimfire Rifles 7*

Savage Mark I: *Bolt Action Rimfire Rifles 7*

savage: *Barbarian 1*

Savannah: *Domestic Cats 15*

savannah: *Ecosystems 10*

save the kingdom: *Fantasy Plot Devices 24*

save the princess: *Fantasy Plot Devices 24*

savin: *Deciduous Trees 10*

savior: *Common Character Archetypes 21; Hero 20*

savory: *Spices 6*

Savoy cabbage: *Vegetables 6*

Savu: *Python 15*

saw fish: *Wild Saltwater Fish 15*

saw: *Art Tools 5; Hand Tools 5*

sawbuck: *Tables 4*

sawed-off: *Shotguns General 7*

saw-scaled viper: *World's Ten Most Venomous Snakes 15*

saw-scaled: *Viper 15*

sawshark: *Sharks 15*

saw-shelled snapping: *Freshwater Turtles 15*

sawtooth: *Roof Styles 3*

saw-whet: *Owls 15*

Saxon: *Human Ethnic Groups 1*

saxony: *Fabric 2*

saxophone: *Wind/Woodwind and Brass Musical Instruments*

say aye: *Agree 20*

say yes: *Agree 20*

saying the number 7 at a craps table: *Harbingers of Bad Luck 19*

scaber stalk: *Fungus Common Names 10*

scabies: *Diseases 12*

scaffolding: *Castle Anatomy 3*

scald: *Cooking Techniques 20*

scale mail: *Armor Types 7*

scale: *Architectural/Engineering Tools 5; General Music Vocabulary 13; Geography General Vocabulary 10; Horse Barding Materials 7; Kitchen Equipment 5; Laboratory Equipment 5; Locomotion 9*

scaled reptiles: *Animals 15*

scaled sardine: *Wild Saltwater Fish 15*

scales: *Symbols in Magic and Religion 19*

scali: *Bread General Varieties 6*

scallion: *Vegetables 6*

scallop shell: *Symbols in Magic and Religion 19*

scallop: *Embellishments 2*

scalloped oak: *Moth 15*

scalloped: *Shield Types 7*

scallopwing: *Butterfly 15*

scalp: *Body Parts 12*

scalpel: *Laboratory Equipment 5*

scaly: *Lips 1; Skin Types and Features 1*

scalybark hickory: *Deciduous Trees 10*

scam artist: *Thief 1*

scampi-style: *Fish/Seafood Meals 6*

scandalous: *Bad 20*

Scandium: *Elements 11*

scanner: *Computer Equipment 5; Office/School Machines 5*

scant: *Small/Fragile 20*

scaphoid bone: *Bones 12*

scapolite: *Cat's Eye Gems 21; Standard Gems 21*

scapula: *Bones 12*

scapular: *Religious Dress 2*

scarab: *Animals with Symbolic Meaning 19*

scarecrow: *Halloween 19*

scared: *General Emotions 20; Horror Vocabulary 23*

scarf: *Accessories 2; Hair Accessories 2; Headgear 2; Western Clothing/Dress 21*

scarified: *Skin Types and Features 1*

scarlet flax: *Wildflowers 10*

scarlet hood: *Fungus Common Names 10*

scarlet lobelia: *Wildflowers 10*

scarlet maple: *Deciduous Trees 10*

scarlet oak: *Deciduous Trees 10*

scarlet rocket: *Garden Perennials 10*

scarlet sage: *Wildflowers 10*

scarlet: *Red 20*

scarp: *Astronomy General Terms 11; Castle Anatomy 3*

scarred: *Skin Types and Features 1; Unattractive 20*

scary: *Horror Vocabulary 23*

scat: *Card Games 5; Excrement 12*

scatter gun: *Shotguns General 7*

scatter pin: *Jewelry 2*

scatter: *Expletives 20*

scattered: *Meteorology General Vocabulary 10*

scenic agate: *Minerals 10*

scenic designer: *Performing Arts 1*

scenic painting: *Art Genres 13*

scent: *Smells 20*

scented: *Candles 5*

scepter of Dionysus: *Objects 18*

scepter quartz: *Minerals 10*

scepter: *Bludgeons 7; Objects in Magic and Religion 19; Secular Symbols 19*

schalenblende: *Minerals 10*

schaum torte: *Miscellaneous Dessert 6*

schedule: *Laboratory Supplies 5*

schefferite: *Minerals 10*

schema: *Laboratory Supplies 5*

schematic: *Books/Publications 5*

schemer: *Bard 1*

scheming: *Horror Vocabulary 23*

scherbencobalt: *Minerals 10*

schernikite: *Minerals 10*

scherzo: *Composition Types 13*

Schipperke: *Dog Breeds 15*

schist: *Metamorphic Rocks 10*

schistosomiasis: *Diseases 12*

Schlegel's: *Viper 15*

Schlenk flask: *Laboratory Equipment 5*

Schleswiger Heavy Draft: *Horse Breeds 15*

schnapps and hot chocolate: *Hot Drinks 6*

schnapps peach: *Hard Liquor 6*

schnapps peppermint: *Hard Liquor 6*

schnapps root beer: *Hard Liquor 6*

schnapsen: *Card Games 5*

Schnauzer Standard: *Dog Breeds 15*

Schneck oak: *Deciduous Trees 10*

Schneider's dwarf caiman: *Crocodilians 15*

schnitzel: *Meals 6*

schnoz: *Nose 1*

schnozzle: *Nose 1*

scholar: *Academic 1; Wizard 1*

school bag: *Containers and Vessels 5; Office/School/Writing Supplies 5*

school board member: *Academic 1*

school bullies tormented by their victim: *Horror Plot Devices 23*

school bus yellow: *Yellow 20*

school glue: *Office/School/Writing Supplies 5*

school machines: *Equipment and Tools 5*

school marm: *Styles of Dress 2; Western Paraphernalia/People 21*

school supplies: *Equipment and Tools 5*

school teacher in evil plot to perform human sacrifice: *Horror Plot Devices 23*

school uniform: *Special Purpose Clothing 2; Styles of Dress 2*

school: *Academic Property 3; Church Anatomy 3; Desks 4; Horror Locations 23; Mass Transit 9; Teach 20*

schoolgirl: *Female 1*

schoolmaster's: *Desks 4*

schooner glass: *Drinkware 5*

schooner: *Large Watercraft 9*

schorl: *Minerals 10*

schorlomite: *Minerals 10*

schottische: *Historical Dances 13*

schuhplattler (Austria, Germany): *Ethnic/Folk Dances 13*

Schultze's: *Pit Viper 15*

Schwarzwälder Fuchs: *Horse Breeds 15*

schweitersäbel: *Swords One-handed 7*

schwimmen: *Card Games 5*

science experiment makes intelligent animals: *Horror Plot Devices 23*

science fantasy: *Horror Genres 23; Science Fiction Genres 22*

science fiction: *Horror Genres 23; Literary Styles 5; Performance Genres 13*

Science without humanity: *Philosophy 14*

science: *Philosophy Basic Concepts 14*

scientist: *Character Building 1; Horror Occupations 23; Occupations 22*

Scientology symbol: *Symbols in Magic and Religion 19*

Scientology: *Crosses 19*

scimitar: *Swords One-handed 7*

scion: *Relational 1; Thief 1*

scissors kick: *Swimming Strokes 9*

scissors: *Hand Tools 5; Objects/Activities Connected to Lore 19; Sewing Equipment 2*

Scobey soil: *Soil General Vocabulary 10*

scoliid: *Wasp 15*

sconce: *Candles 5*

scone: *Bread General Varieties 6*

scoop: *Ice Cream 6; Kitchen Equipment 5*

scoopula: *Laboratory Equipment 5*

scooter: *Human-Powered Transportation 9; Toys 5*

scops: *Owls 15*

scorch: *Cooking Techniques 20*

scorched earth: *Tactics 7*

score: *Printed Music 13*

scoria: *Igneous Rocks 10*

scorn: *General Emotions 20*

scornful: *Negative 1*

Scorpio (October 23–November 21): *Zodiac Signs 19*

scorpion man: *Insectoid 16*

scorpion mud: *Freshwater Turtles 15*

scorpion rockfish: *Wild Saltwater Fish 15*

scorpion: *Animals 15; Animals with Symbolic Meaning 19; Siege Engines 7; Solitaire Card Games 5*

Scorpius: *Constellations 11*

Scotch bluebells: *Garden Perennials 10*

Scotch broom: *Weeds 10*

scotch: *Hard Liquor 6*

Scots dumpy: *Chickens 15*

Scots grey: *Chickens 15*

Scots pine: *Evergreen Trees 10*

Scots thistle: *Weeds 10*

Scottish Deerhound: *Dog Breeds 15*

Scottish Fold: *Domestic Cats 15*

Scottish Rite: *Secret/Mystical Organizations 18*

Scottish Terrier: *Dog Breeds 15*

Scottish thistle: *Weeds 10*

Scottish: *Human Ethnic Groups 1*

scoundrel: *Common Character Archetypes 21; Thief 1*

scour: *Clean 20*

scourge: *Hand Weapons 7*

scout bomber: *Military Aircraft Pre-1962 8*

scout observation: *Military Aircraft Pre-1962 8*

scout trainer: *Military Aircraft Pre-1962 8*

scout: *Barbarian 1; Beginning 20*

scout: *Military Aircraft Pre-1962 8; Spaceship Types 22*

scowling: *Sad 20*

scraggly: *Facial Hair Beard 1*

scramble: *Locomotion 9*

scrambled: *Egg Styles 6*

scrape: *Injuries/Medical Emergencies 12*

scraper: *Art Tools 5; Hand Tools 5; Horse Drawn Farm Equipment; Kitchen Utensils 5*

scratch awl: *Hand Tools 5*

scratch board: *Art Materials 5*

scratch: *Harm 20*

scrawled cowfish: *Wild Saltwater Fish 15*

scrawny: *Small/Thin 1*

scream: *Loud 20; Sounds 20; Speak 20*

screaming: *Loud 20; Vocal/Speech Quality 1*

scree: *Rock and Mineral Forms 10; Slope 10*

screech: *Owls 15; Sounds 20; Speak 20*

screen: *Doors 3; Windows 3*

screw gun: *Power Tools*

screw machine: *Power Tools*

screw your neighbor: *Card Games 5*

screw: *Fix 20; Hardware 5*

screwdriver: *Hand Tools 5*

scribbled boxfish: *Aquarium Saltwater Fish 15*

scribe: *Academic 1; Castle Inhabitants and Personnel 1*

scrim: *Parts of the Theater 13*

script: *Technical Terms 13*

scroll maker: *Fantasy Occupations 24*

scroll saw: *Power Tools*

scroll tube: *Specialty Survival Gear 5*

scroll: *Books/Publications 5; Classic Items 23; Religious Items 5; Typical Magical Objects 17; Wizard's Goods 5*

scrotum: *Body Parts 12*

scrub bay: *Deciduous Trees 10*

scrub brush: *Cleaning Supplies/Gadgets 5*

scrub holly: *Evergreen Trees 10*

scrub interior live oak: *Deciduous Trees 10*

scrub live oak: *Deciduous Trees 10*

scrub oak: *Deciduous Trees 10*

scrub pine: *Evergreen Trees 10*

scrub: *Clean 20*

scrubby post oak: *Deciduous Trees 10*

scrunchie: *Hair Accessories 2*

scrutinize: *Paranormal Activity 21; Solve 20*

scrutiny: *Paranormal Activity 21*

scryer: *Fortune Teller 1*

scuba gear: *Spy Gear 5*

scuba rebreather: *Spy Gear 5*

scuffs: *Footwear/Shoes 2*

scullery maid: *Castle Inhabitants and Personnel 1; Housekeeping 1*

scullery: *Rooms 3*

sculling: *Swimming Strokes 9*

sculpin: *Wild Saltwater Fish 15*

sculpt: *Art Techniques 13*

sculpted carpet: *Floor Coverings 4*

sculptor: *Castle Inhabitants and Personnel 1*

Sculptor: *Constellations 11*

scuppernong: *Unusual Edible Fruits 6*

scurry: *Locomotion 9*

scuttle: *Locomotion 9*

Scutum: *Constellations 11*

Scylla: *Mythical Creatures and Monsters 16*

scythe: *Garden Tools; Symbols in Magic and Religion 19; Tools 7*

scythe-leaved willow: *Deciduous Trees 10*

sea bass: *Wild Saltwater Fish 15*

sea breeze: *Wind 10*

sea buckthorn: *Shrubs 10*

sea cave: *Cave Anatomy 10; Coastal and Oceanic 10*

sea creature: *Monster Categories/Terms 16*

sea creatures: *Classic Heraldry 19; Common Dangers 23*

sea fire: *Siege Equipment 7*

sea green: *Cyan 20; Green 20*

sea holly: *Garden Perennials 10*

sea kayak: *Human-Powered Watercraft 9*

sea lavender: *Garden Perennials 10*

sea level: *Geography General Vocabulary 10*

sea lion: *Other Wild Mammals 15*

sea nettle: *Jellyfish 15*

sea pink: *Garden Perennials 10*

sea plane: *Air Vehicles 9*

sea robin: *Wild Saltwater Fish 15*

sea scallop: *Fish/Seafood Types 6*

sea snake: *Animals 15*

sea: *Bears 15; Coastal and Oceanic 10; Monsters 19; Water Terms 9*

seabag: *Military Equipment 8*

Seaborgium: *Elements 11*

seacraft aircraft carrier: *Military Watercraft 8*

seadog: *Maritime Occupations 1*

seafoam: *Candy General 6*

seafood newburg: *Fish/Seafood Meals 6*

seafood: *Food 6; Salads 6*

seahorse: *Aquarium Saltwater Fish 15*

seal brown: *Brown 20*

seal of Shamash: *Symbols in Magic and Religion 19*

Seal of Solomon: *Jewelry 18; Symbols in Magic and Religion 19*

seal of the Knights Templar: *Symbols in Magic and Religion 19*

seal of the truth of God: *Symbols in Magic and Religion 19*

seal: *Close/Hold 20; Other Wild Mammals 15*

sealing wax: *Specialty Survival Gear 5*

sealskin: *Fur 2*

Sealyham Terrier: *Dog Breeds 15*

seam allowance: *Garment Pieces 2; Sewing Terms 2*

seam binding: *Notions 2*

seam gauge: *Sewing Equipment 2*

seam opal: *Minerals 10*

seam ripper: *Sewing Equipment 2*

seaman apprentice: *U.S. Navy Enlisted 8*

seaman recruit: *U.S. Navy Enlisted 8*

seaman: *Maritime Occupations 1; U.S. Navy Enlisted 8*

seamount: *Coastal and Oceanic 10*

seamstress: *Artists and Craftspeople 1; Castle Inhabitants and Personnel 1*

séance: *Fortune Telling General Techniques 19; Paranormal Activity 21*

seaplane carrier: *Military Watercraft 8*

seaplane tender: *Military Watercraft 8*

seaport: *Marina 3*

search and rescue: *Helicopters 8; Military Aircraft 8*

search: *Learn 20; Paranormal Activity 21*

Sears Tower: *Unique Property 3*

seashell: *White 20*

seashells: *Wizard's Goods 5*

seashore: *Water Terms 9*

seasick: *Boat/Ship Terminology 9*

seaside daisy: *Garden Perennials 10*

seaside: *Water Terms 9*

seasoned: *Old 20*

seasons: *Collective Symbols 19*

seat: *Seating 4*

seats: *Parts of the Theater 13*

seawater: *Minerals 10*

Seawolf class attack submarine: *U.S. Navy Vessels 8*

seaworthy: *Boat/Ship Terminology 9*

Sebastapol: *Card Games 5*

sebettu: *Demon 16*

Sebright: *Chickens 15*

Sechuran zorro: *Foxes 15*

second alto: *Voices 13*

second cousin: *Relational 1*

second hand high: *Poker Card Games 5*

second law of thermodynamics: *Chemistry General Vocabulary 11*

second lieutenant: *U.S. Air Force Officer 8; U.S. Army Officer 8; U.S. Marines Officer 8*

second mate: *Navy Other Titles 8*

second molar: *Teeth 12*

second soprano: *Voices 13*

second tenor: *Voices 13*

secondary lighting: *Technical Terms 13*

second-sighted: *Magic Vocabulary 17*

secret agent: *General Occupations 1; Law Enforcement 1*

secret entrance: *Doors Atypical 3*

Secret Grimoire of Turiel: *Books of Legend 18*

secret identity: *Spy Gear 5*

secret of Hermes: *Symbols in Magic and Religion 19*

secret organizations: *Legendary, Mystical and Mythical*

Items and Locations 18; Plot Devices 22

secret room: *Rooms 3*

secret Santa: *Christmas 19*

secret service: *Law Enforcement 1*

secret: *Magic Vocabulary 17*

secretary bird: *Birds of Prey 15*

secretary: *Academic 1; Desks 4; Operations 1*

secretion: *Physical Mutations 22*

section: *Political Divisions 10*

secure: *Buy 20; Close/Hold 20; Fix 20*

security guard: *Law Enforcement 1*

security system: *Building Systems 3; Locks 5*

security: *Doors 3; General Combat Vocabulary 7; Robots 22; Rooms 3*

sedan chair: *Human-Powered Transportation 9*

sedan: *Motorized 9*

sedentary: *Mobility 1*

sedge: *Viper 15*

sediment strap: *Geological Vocabulary 10*

sediment: *Cave Anatomy 10*

sedimentary rock: *Geological Vocabulary 10*

sedimentary rocks: *Chapter 10*

sedimentology: *Geologic Fields of Study 10*

see a penny and pick it up: *Practices/Objects to Attract Good Luck 19*

see a pin and pick it up: *Practices/Objects to Attract Good Luck 19*

seed cake: *Bread General Varieties 6*

seed drill: *General Farm Equipment; Horse Drawn Farm Equipment*

seed of life: *Symbols in Magic and Religion 19*

seeds: *Allergies 12; Food 6; Wizard's Goods 5*

seeing eye dog: *Dogs/Canine 15*

seeing red: *Angry 1*

seek: *Paranormal Activity 21*

seelie court: *Fae Related 16*

seep: *Card Games 5; Wet 20*

seepage water: *Cave Anatomy 10*

seepage: *Wet 20*

seer: *Nature Occupations 1; Wizard 1*

seersucker: *Fabric 2*

Sefer Torah: *Objects in Magic and Religion 19*

sefer yetzirah symbol: *Symbols in Magic and Religion 19*

segment: *Figures Associated with Symbols 19*

segue: *Stage Terms 13*

seguidilla (Spain): *Ethnic/Folk Dances 13*

Segwarides: *Knights of the Round Table 18*

Seiland zircon: *Minerals 10*

seismologist: *Scientist 1*

seismology: *Geologic Fields of Study 10*

Seitz soil: *Soil General Vocabulary 10*

seize: *Buy 20; Close/Hold 20; General Combat Vocabulary 7; Magic Vocabulary 17*

sejant affront: *Land Creatures 19*

sejant erect: *Land Creatures 19*

sejant: *Land Creatures 19*

Seker (light): *Egyptian Pantheon 14*

Sekhmet (goddess of destruction): *Egyptian Pantheon 14*

Seki-Lines: *Comets 11*

Selaphiel: *Angels of Good 14*

selection/rejection: *Poker Card Games 5*

selenious acid: *Dangerous Chemicals 11*

selenite: *Minerals 10*

Selenium: *Elements 11*

self heal: *Garden Perennials 10*

self: *Philosophy Basic Concepts 14*

self-assured: *Personality Other 1*

self-centered: *Negative 1*

self-help: *Literary Styles 5*

selfish: *Negative 1*

self-loading wagon: *General Farm Equipment*

self-portrait: *Art Genres 13*

self-possessed: *Easy 20*

self-propelled artillery: *Armored Vehicles 8*

self-propelled rocket launcher: *Military Ground Vehicles General 8*

self-reconfiguring: *Robots 22*

self-sacrificing: *Personality Other 1*

self-stick notes: *Office/School/Writing Supplies 5*

self-taught: *Art Genres 13*

selkie: *Aquatic 16; Water Faerie 16*

Selkie: *Human Races Fictional 1*

Selkirk Rex: *Domestic Cats 15*

Selkup: *Human Ethnic Groups 1*

Selle Francais: *Horse Breeds 15*

selles-sur-cher: *Cheese International Varieties 6*

seltzer: *Soft Drinks 6*

selvage: *Sewing Terms 2*

semantics: *Philosophy Basic Concepts 14*

seme de lis: *Patterns 19*

semi: *Motorized Truck 9*

semiarid: *Climatic Zones Koeppen System 10*

semiautomatic pistol: *Military 8*

semi-automatic rifle: *Military Weapons General 8*

semibreve: *Notation 13*

semicarbazide hydrochloride: *Dangerous Chemicals 11*

semi-circular: *Roof Styles 3*

semiconductor: *Chemistry General Vocabulary 11*

semi-formal: *Styles of Dress 2*

seminal vesicle: *Organs/Major Structures 12*

seminarian: *Cleric 1*

seminary: *Academic Property 3; Religious Building 3*

Seminole: *Bats 15; Native American Peoples 1*

semiopal: *Minerals 10*

semi-opera: *Composition Types 13*

semipermeable membrane: *Chemistry General Vocabulary 11*

semiquaver: *Notation 13*

Semirechye: *Pigs 15*

Semovente 47 self-propelled 47mm gun: *Italy Military Vehicles 8*

sempre: *General Music Vocabulary 13*

senator: *Government 1*

Seneca: *Native American Peoples 1*

senecio: *Shrubs 10*

Senegal flapshell: *Freshwater Turtles 15*

Senegal: *Domesticated Pet Birds 15*

Senegalese: *Human Ethnic Groups 1*

Senepol: *Other Cows 15*

seneschal: *Supporting Cast 24*

senior airman: *U.S. Air Force Enlisted 8*

senior chief petty officer: *U.S. Navy Enlisted 8*

senior citizen: *Elderly 1*

senior master sergeant: *U.S. Air Force Enlisted 8*

senior: *Elderly 1*

sensation: *Philosophy Basic Concepts 14*

sense: *Learn 20; Philosophy Basic Concepts 14*

sensei: *Martial Artist/Monk 1*

sensitive plant: *Weeds 10*

sensitive: *Paranormal Occupations 21*

sensory: *Philosophy Basic Concepts 14*

sentient plant: *Monsters and Creatures 22*

sentinel: *Fighter 1*

sentry: *Fighter 1*

senza: *General Music Vocabulary 13*

separatory funnel: *Laboratory Equipment 5*

Sepher Yetzirah: *Major Religious Books 14*

sepia: *Brown 20*

sepsis: *Blood 12; Diseases 12*

Sept: *Ballet Terms 13*

September 11: *Legendary Events 18*

septet: *Groups 13*

septuagenarian: *Elderly 1*

septum: *Organs/Major Structures 12*

septuple: *Star Systems 11*

sepulcher: *Cemetery 3; Church Anatomy 3*

sequence: *Poker Card Games 5*

sequencing: *Technical Terms 13*

sequester: *Close/Hold 20; Magic Vocabulary 17*

sequin: *Embellishments 2*

seraph: *Angels Common Terms 14*

Seraphiel: *Angels of Good 14*

seraphim: *Angels Common Terms 14*

seraphinite: *Minerals 10; Standard Gems 21*

Serb: *Human Ethnic Groups 1*

serenade: *Composition Types 13*

serene: *Easy 20*

serenity: *General Emotions 20; Ten Perfections of Buddhism 19*

serf: *Castle Inhabitants and Personnel 1*

serge: *Fabric 2; Sewing Techniques 2*

sergeant first class: *U.S. Army Enlisted 8*

sergeant major of the army: *U.S. Army Enlisted 8*

sergeant major of the Marine Corps: *U.S. Marines Enlisted 8*

sergeant major: *Aquarium Saltwater Fish 15; Card Games 5; U.S. Army Enlisted 8; U.S. Marines Enlisted 8*

sergeant: *U.S. Army Enlisted 8; U.S. Marines Enlisted 8*

seria: *Musical Styles 13*

serial killer: *Fighter 1; Horror Genres 23; Illicit Occupations 1*

serial killing: *Kill 20*

serialism: *General Music Vocabulary 13*

sericite: *Minerals 10*

Series 2 Age: *Geologic Time 10*

Series 3 Age: *Geologic Time 10*

serious: *Horror Vocabulary 23; Personality Other 1*

seriously?: *Expletives 20*

serotine: *Bats 15*

serpae tetra: *Aquarium Freshwater Fish 15*

Serpens: *Constellations 11*

serpent: *Animals with Symbolic Meaning 19; Crosses 19*

serpentine marble: *Minerals 10*

serpentine rock: *Minerals 10*

serpentine soil: *Soil General Vocabulary 10*

serpentine: *Standard Gems 21*

serpentinite: *Metamorphic Rocks 10; Minerals 10*

serrated hinge-back: *Tortoises 15*

serrated star: *Tortoises 15*

serum: *Blood 12*

servant rebellion: *Common Dangers 24*

servant: *Housekeeping 1*

Servants of the Light: *Secret/Mystical Organizations 18*

server: *Computer Equipment 5; Food Service 1*

service club: *Social Clubs 1*

service: *Robots 22*

serviceberry: *Unusual Edible Fruits 6*

serving bowl: *Tableware 5*

serving girl: *Food Service 1*

serving spoon: *Eating Utensils 5; Kitchen Utensils 5*

sesame: *Oils 6; Seeds 6*

Set (evil): *Egyptian Pantheon 14*

set up: *Fix 20*

Setebos: *Moons 11*

set-in sleeve: *Garment Pieces 2*

sett: *Natural Animal Homes 15*

settee: *Seating 4*

settlement: *City 10; Political Divisions 10*

seven and a half: *Card Games 5*

Seven Blunders of the World: *Philosophy 14*

seven bridge: *Card Games 5*

seven card stud: *Poker Card Games 5*

seven deadly sins: *Collective Symbols 19*

seven gifts of the Holy Spirit: *Collective Symbols 19*

seven holy virtues: *Collective Symbols 19*

seven rocks: *Card Games 5*

seven son flower: *Garden Perennials 10*

seven swans a-swimming: *Twelve Days of Christmas 19*

seven wonders of the world: *Legendary, Mystical and Mythical Items and Locations 18*

seven-armed: *Octopi 15*

seven-league boots: *Clothing 18*

seven-pointed star: *Symbols in Magic and Religion 19*

severe weather: *Chapter 10*

severe: *Bad 20; Heavy 20*

severed limb: *Classic Items 23*

sew: *Fix 20; Sewing Techniques 2*

sewage: *Excrement 12*

sewermen: *Guilds 1*

sewing basket: *Sewing Equipment 2*

sewing cabinet: *Storage 4*

sewing equipment: *Clothing 2*

sewing kit: *Sewing Equipment 2*

sewing line: *Sewing Terms 2*

sewing machine: *Sewing Equipment 2*

sewing needle: *Sewing Equipment 2*

sewing techniques: *Clothing 2*

sewing terms: *Clothing 2*

sewing: *Rooms 3*

sex of an unborn baby: *Objects/Activities Connected to Lore 19*

Sex: *Major Lines 19*

sex: *Plot Devices 22*

sexed: *Special Body Features 19*

Sextans: *Constellations 11*

sextant: *Boat/Ship Anatomy 9*

sextet: *Groups 13*

sextuple: *Star Systems 11*

sexy: *Styles of Dress 2; Vocal/Speech Quality 1*

Seychelles: *Caecilians 15*

Seyfert galaxy: *Astronomy General Terms 11*

sfela: *Cheese International Varieties 6*

SH-60 antisubmarine: *Rotary Wing Aircraft 8*

shack: *Farm/Outbuilding 3; Residential Property 3*

shackles: *Fasteners 5*

shadblow: *Deciduous Trees 10*

shadbush: *Deciduous Trees 10*

shade: *Art Techniques 13; Undead 16; Window Treatments 5*

shades: *Accessories 2*

shadow mastiff: *Extraplanar 16*

shadow puppet: *Toys 5*

shadow: *Dragon 16; Dwarf 1; Elf 1; Paranormal Occurrences 21; Undead 16*

shadowy: *Magic Vocabulary 17*

shady: *Horror Vocabulary 23*

shaft: *Castle Anatomy 3; Cave Anatomy 10*

shag carpet: *Floor Coverings 4*

shag: *Dance Styles 13; Hair Style 1*

shagbark hickory: *Deciduous Trees 10*

shaggy mane: *Fungus Common Names 10*

shaggy parasol mushroom: *Fungus Common Names 10*

shaggy: *Bats 15; Eyebrows 1*

Shagya: *Horse Breeds 15*

shah: *Royal/Noble 1*

shaitan: *Devil 16*

Shakak (winter spirit): *Native American Pantheon 14*

Shaker: *Chairs and Stools 4*

Shakespeare: *Performance Genres 13*

Shakespearean: *Styles of Dress 2*

shaky: *Horror Vocabulary 23; Vocal/Speech Quality 1*

shale: *Sedimentary Rocks 10*

shallot: *Vegetables 6*

shallow seismic surveys: *Geological Field Work Methods 10*

shaman: *Cleric 1; Common Character Archetypes 21; Masks 2; Religious Occupations 1; Wizard 1*

Shambhala: *Fictional/Mythological Locations 18*

shambling mound: *Plant 16*

shameful plant: *Weeds 10*

shameless: *Bad 20*

shampoo: *Personal Care 5*

shamrock green: *Green 20*

shamshir: *Swords One-handed 7*

Shamshir-e-Zomorrodnegar: *Weapons of Legend 18*

Shamsiel: *Fallen Angels 14*

Shan Hai Ching (the sea): *Chinese Pantheon 14*

Shanghai: *Card Games 5*

Shangri-la: *Fictional/Mythological Locations 18*

Shang-Ti (leader of the gods): *Chinese Pantheon 14*

shanklish: *Cheese International Varieties 6*

shantung: *Fabric 2*

shanty: *Residential Property 3*

shape: *Art Techniques 13; Fix 20; Visual Elements 13*

shapechanger: *Monsters 16; Nature Occupations 1*

shapechanging: *Physical Mutations 22*

shaper: *Power Tools*

shapeshift: *Witchcraft Vocabulary 17*

Sharabi: *Other Cows 15*

sharecropping: *Geography General Vocabulary 10*

shareeravadi: *Bludgeons 7*

shark: *Fish/Seafood Types 6;*

sharks: *Animals 15*

sharkskin suit: *Men's Wear 2*

sharkskin: *Fabric 2*

sharp cheddar: *Cheese Common Varieties 6*

sharp: *General Music Vocabulary 13; Intelligent 1; Notation 13; Smells 20; Vocal/Speech Quality 1*

sharpening stone: *Hand Tools 5*

sharpening wheel: *Large Tools*

sharper: *Thief 1*

sharpness: *General Emotions 20*

sharp-nosed: *Viper 15*

Sharps 50 caliber rifle: *Western Weapons 21*

sharpshooter: *General Combat Vocabulary 7; Law Enforcement 1; Western Paraphernalia/People 21*

Shasta daisy: *Garden Perennials 10; Wildflowers 10*

Shasta fir: *Evergreen Trees 10*

Shasta red fir: *Evergreen Trees 10*

shatkona: *Symbols in Magic and Religion 19*

shattered: *Horror Vocabulary 23*

shaved: *Hair Style 1*

shaver: *Child 1; Personal Care 5*

shaving brush: *Personal Care 5*

shaving cream: *Personal Care 5*

shaving mug: *Personal Care 5*

shaving soap: *Personal Care 5*

shavings: *Wizard's Goods 5*

Shaw's: *Sea Snake 15*

shawl skirt: *Ladies' Wear 2*

shawl: *Cave Anatomy 10; Western Clothing/Dress 21*

Shawnee: *Native American Peoples 1*

shazbot: *Expletives 20*

shear grab: *General Farm Equipment*

shear strength test: *Soil General Vocabulary 10*

shear strength: *Soil General Vocabulary 10*

shear zone: *Geological Vocabulary 10*

shear: *Bridges 9*

shears: *Sewing Equipment 2*

sheath dress: *Ladies' Wear 2*

sheath-tailed: *Bats 15*

she-balsam: *Evergreen Trees 10*

shed: *Farm/Outbuilding 3; Horror Locations 23; Property Features 3*

shedim: *Devil 16*

sheela na gig: *Symbols in Magic and Religion 19*

sheep ranchers: *Western Paraphernalia/People 21*

sheep: *Christmas 19; Farm/Outbuilding 3; Other Wild Mammals 15*

sheep's: *Milk 6*

sheepshank: *Sailing Knots 9*

sheepshead: *Card Games 5*

sheer: *Fabric 2; Small/Fragile 20*

sheers: *Window Treatments 5*

sheet bend: *Sailing Knots 9*

sheet pan: *Kitchen Equipment 5*

sheet protector: *Office/School/Writing Supplies 5*

sheet: *Boat/Ship Anatomy 9; Cake 6; Printed Music 13*

sheeting: *Fabric 2*

shelf bra: *Ladies' Wear 2*

shelf: *Building Elements and Features 3*

shell keep: *Castle Anatomy 3*

shell opal: *Minerals 10*

shell star: *Astronomy General Terms 11*

shell trumpet: *Wind/Woodwind and Brass Musical Instruments*

shell: *Jewelry 21; Ladies' Wear 2; Natural Animal Homes 15; Pasta 6*

shellbark hickory: *Deciduous Trees 10*

shellfish: *Allergies 12*

shellfish-scented russula: *Fungus Common Names 10*

shelter: *Fortification 3; Outdoor Property 3*

shen: *Shapechanger 16*

Shenandoah: *Facial Hair Beard 1*

sheng: *Wind/Woodwind and Brass Musical Instruments*

she-oak: *Deciduous Trees 10*

shepherd satellite: *Astronomy General Terms 11*

shepherd: *Castle Inhabitants and Personnel 1; Christmas 19*

shepherd's crook: *Bludgeons 7*

shepherd's: *Axes 7*

shepherdess: *Castle Inhabitants and Personnel 1*

Sheraton: *Chairs and Stools 4*

sherbet dish: *Tableware 5*

sherbet glass: *Drinkware 5*

sherbet: *Ice Cream Related 6*

sheriff: *Law Enforcement 1*

sheriff's badge: *Western Clothing/Dress 21*

Sherlock Holmes: *Sir Arthur Conan Doyle 18*

Sherman Firefly medium tank: *United Kingdom Mili-*

tary Vehicles 8

sherpa: *Fabric 2*

Sherpa: *Human Ethnic Groups 1*

sherry topaz: *Minerals 10*

sherry: *Wine Red 6*

shetan: *Demon 16*

Shetland Pony: *Horse Breeds 15*

Shetland Sheepdog: *Dog Breeds 15*

shetland: *Fabric 2*

Shetland: *Other Cows 15*

shi ti shou: *Bears 15*

Shiba Inu: *Dog Breeds 15*

shield bearer: *Fighter 1*

shield knot: *Symbols in Magic and Religion 19*

shield maiden: *Fighter 1*

shield of Ajax the Great: *Shields 18*

shield of El Cid: *Shields 18*

shield of Galahad: *Shields 18*

shield of Lancelot: *Shields 18*

shield types: *Combat, Armor, and Weapons 7*

shield volcano: *Volcanic 10*

shield: *Cave Anatomy 10; Elements 19*

shielded: *Horror Vocabulary 23*

shielding effect: *Chemistry General Vocabulary 11*

shield-nosed: *Cobra 15*

shields: *Combat, Armor, and Weapons 7*

shield-tailed: *General Snake Families 15*

shifty: *Eye Type 1*

Shih Tzu: *Dog Breeds 15*

shiitake: *Fungus Common Names 10*

shikomizue: *Swords One-handed 7*

shillelagh: *Bludgeons 7*

Shiloh Sharps Long Range Express: *Single Shot Centerfire Rifles 7*

Shiloh Sharps: *Single Shot Centerfire Rifles 7*

shimmy: *Ladies' Wear 2*

shin guards: *Sporting Goods Other 5*

shin oak: *Deciduous Trees 10*

shin: *Body Parts 12*

shine: *Clean 20*

shiner: *Injuries/Medical Emergencies 12*

shingle: *Roofing Materials 3*

shingles: *Diseases 12*

shinglewood: *Evergreen Trees 10*

shining bluestar: *Garden Perennials 10*

shining cat: *Bears 15*

shining one: *Angels Common Terms 14*

Shinto Texts: *Major Religious Books 14*

shiny: *Hair Types 1; Teeth 1*

ship of the line: *Military Watercraft 8*

ship that will sail at the time of Ragnarok: *Vehicles 18*

ship: *Small Watercraft 9; Travel Types 22*

ship's biscuit: *Bread General Varieties 6*

ship-killer: *Weapons 22*

shipmast locust: *Deciduous Trees 10*

shipova: *Unusual Edible Fruits 6*

shipwreck: *Horror Genres 23*

shiraz: *Wine Red 6*

shire: *City 10*

Shire: *Horse Breeds 15*

Shirley poppy: *Wildflowers 10*

Shirley Temple: *Hair Style 1*

shirozulite: *Minerals 10*

shirred: *Egg Styles 6*

shirring: *Embellishments 2*

shirt: *Unisex Clothing 2*

shitake mushroom: *Vegetables 6*

Shiva (destruction): *Indian Pantheon 14*

shivering: *Horror Vocabulary 23*

shoal: *Coastal and Oceanic 10; Fluvial 10; Water Terms 9*

Shock Art: *Art Movements 13*

shock: *General Emotions 20; Horror Vocabulary 23; Injuries/Medical Emergencies 12*

shocking pink: *Pink 20*

shocking: *Bad 20; Horror Vocabulary 23; Unattractive 20*

shoe accessories: *The Arts 13*

shoe device: *Spy Gear 5*

shoe lace: *Accessories 2*

shoe string: *Accessories 2*

shoe: *Transportation Animals 9*

shoelace licorice: *Candy General 6*

Shoemaker-Levy: *Comets 11*

shoes: *Clothing 2; Objects/Activities Connected to Lore 19*

shoestring: *Vegetables Cooked 6*

shofar: *Objects in Magic and Religion 19*

shoo-fly: *Pie 6*

shoot: *Attack 7; Card Games 5; Expletives 20*

Shooters Arms Military Pistol: *Pistol Semiautomatic 7*

shooting gallery: *Amusement Park/Carnival/Circus/Fair 3*

shooting star: *Garden Perennials 10*

shop: *Business Property 3*

shopkeeper: *General Occupations 1*

shoplifter: *Illicit Occupations 1; Thief 1*

shopping bag: *Accessories 2; Containers and Vessels 5*

shopping cart: *Human-Powered Transportation 9*

shopping mall: *Business Property 3; Christmas 19*

shopping tote: *Accessories 2*

shopping: *Christmas 19*

shore bay: *Deciduous Trees 10*

shore pine: *Evergreen Trees 10*

shore: *Coastal and Oceanic 10; Water Terms 9*

shoreline: *Water Terms 9*

short bow: *Missile Weapons 7*

short gloves: *Unisex Clothing 2*

short rib: *Beef 6*

short shorts: *Ladies' Wear 2*

short skirt: *Ladies' Wear 2*

short sleeve t-shirt: *Unisex Clothing 2*

short sleeve: *Garment Pieces 2*

short straw pine: *Evergreen Trees 10*

short: *Ears 1; Facial Hair Beard 1; Nose 1; Small/Fragile 20; Small/Thin 1; Swords One-handed 7*

short-beaked: *Dolphins 15*

short-browed: *Owls 15*

short-eared: *Owls 15*

shortened height: *Physical Mutations 22*

short-faced: *Bears 15*

shortfin: *Sharks 15*

shorthead worm lizard: *Scaled Reptiles 15*

short-headed: *Bats 15*

Shorthorn: *Other Cows 15*

shortleaf pine: *Evergreen Trees 10*

shortleaf yellow pine: *Evergreen Trees 10*

short-nosed: *Bats 15*

shorts: *Undergarments 2; Unisex Clothing 2*

short-stalked slippery cap: *Fungus Common Names 10*

short-stem russula: *Fungus Common Names 10*

short-tailed: *Bats 15*

Shoshone: *Native American Peoples 1*

shoshonite: *Igneous Rocks 10*

shot glass: *Drinkware 5*

shot gun: *Western Weapons 21*

shot: *Loud 20*

shotbush: *Deciduous Trees 10*

Shotgun: *Architectural Styles 3*

shotgun: *Military Weapons General 8*

shotguns: *Combat, Armor, and Weapons 7*

shou: *Symbols in Magic and Religion 19*

shoulder bag: *Accessories 2; Containers and Vessels 5*

shoulder length: *Hair Style 1*

shoulder: *Body Parts 12*

shout: *Sounds 20; Speak 20*

shouting: *Vocal/Speech Quality 1*

shovel: *Garden Tools*

show house: *Entertainment Property 3*

show judge: *Animal/Equestrian 1*

showboat: *Large Watercraft 9*

showdown: *Western Paraphernalia/People 21*

shower cap: *Headgear 2*

shower doors: *Bathroom Features and Fixtures 3*

shower over tub: *Bathroom Features and Fixtures 3*

shower stall: *Bathroom Features and Fixtures 3*

shower: *Bathroom Features and Fixtures 3; Precipitation 10*

showgirl: *Styles of Dress 2*

showroom: *Rooms 3*

showy primrose: *Wildflowers 10*

shredded pork: *Pork 6*

shrew opossum: *Other Wild Mammals 15*

shrew: *Woodland Mammals 15*

shrewd: *Horror Vocabulary 23*

shriek: *Sounds 20; Speak 20*

shrill: *Loud 20; Vocal/Speech Quality 1*

shrimp boat: *Small Watercraft 9*

shrimp: *Farm/Outbuilding 3; Fish/Seafood Types 6; Salads 6; Small/Thin 1*

shrimpy: *Small/Thin 1*

shrine: *Religious Building 3*

shrink ray: *Devices 22*

shrink: *Medical Occupations 1*

shrinking humans: *Plot Devices 22*

Shroud of Turin: *Relics of Jesus 14*

shroud: *Boat/Ship Anatomy 9; Rituals 14*

shrub ice plant: *Garden Perennials 10*

shrub swamp: *Soil General Vocabulary 10*

shrubby cinquefoil: *Shrubs 10*

shrubs: *Chapter 10*

shrunken head: *Harbingers of Bad Luck 19*

shrunken: *Small/Fragile 20*

Shu (the sky): *Egyptian Pantheon 14*

shucks: *Expletives 20*

shuddering: *Horror Vocabulary 23*

shuffle: *Locomotion 9*

shuffling: *Mobility 1*

Shumard oak: *Deciduous Trees 10*

Shumard red oak: *Deciduous Trees 10*

shuriken: *Missile Weapons 7*

shut: *Close/Hold 20*

shut-in: *Fluvial 10*

shutter: *Building Elements and Features 3; Windows 3*

shutters: *Window Treatments 5*

shuttle: *Mass Transit 9; Spaceship Types 22*

shuttlecock: *Sporting Goods Other 5*

shy: *Horror Vocabulary 23; Personality Other 1*

siamang: *Apes 15*

Siamese crocodile: *Crocodilians 15*

Siamese fighting fish: *Aquarium Freshwater Fish 15*

Siamese: *Domestic Cats 15*

Siarnaq: *Moons 11*

sibat: *Spears 7*

Siberian amethyst blue quartz: *Minerals 10*

Siberian black pied: *Pigs 15*

Siberian Husky: *Dog Breeds 15*

Siberian: *Domestic Cats 15; Tigers 15*

siberite: *Minerals 10*

sibling: *Relational 1*

Siboney: *Other Cows 15*

sibyl: *Wizard 1*

Sibylline Books: *Books of Legend 18*

sica: *Swords One-handed 7*

Sicilian Baroque: *Architectural Styles 3*

Sicilian: *Human Ethnic Groups 1*

siciliana: *Composition Types 13*

sickbay: *Fortification 3; Health Care 3*

sickening: *Horror Vocabulary 23; Unattractive 20*

sickle cell disease: *Blood-Related Ailments 12*

sickle mower: *Horse Drawn Farm Equipment*

sickle: *Garden Tools; General Farm Equipment; Tools 7*

sickle-sword: *Swords One-handed 7*

sicklewing: *Butterfly 15*

Sickling: *Ballet Terms 13*

sickly: *Unattractive 20*

sickroom: *Health Care 3*

side altar: *Church Anatomy 3*

side by side refrigerator: *Major Appliances 4*

side chapel: *Church Anatomy 3*

side drum: *Percussion Musical Instruments 5*

side road: *Roads 9*

side stroke: *Swimming Strokes 9*

side valley: *Glacial and Mountain 10*

side: *Chairs and Stools 4; Doors 3; Salads 6; Swords One-handed 7; Tables 4*

sideboard: *Storage 4*

sideboards: *Facial Hair Beard 1*

sideburns: *Facial Hair Beard 1*

sidecar: *Cocktails 6; Motorized 9*

sidekick: *Common Character Archetypes 21*

sidelight: *Windows 3*

sidereal month: *Astronomy General Terms 11*

sidereal period: *Astronomy General Terms 11*

sidereal: *Astronomy General Terms 11*

siderophyllite: *Minerals 10*

sideroplesite: *Minerals 10*

sideshow: *Amusement Park/Carnival/Circus/Fair 3*

sidewalk: *Property Features 3*

sidewinder: *General Snake Families 15*

siege crew: *Combat, Armor, and Weapons 7; Siege Engines 7*

siege crossbow: *Siege Engines 7*

siege engines: *Combat, Armor, and Weapons 7*

siege equipment: *Combat, Armor, and Weapons 7*

siege mortar: *Mortar 8*

siege tower: *Siege Engines 7*

siege: *Tactics 7*

Siegfried: *Legendary People Presumed to be Fictional 18*

sienna: *Brown 20*

Sierra alder: *Deciduous Trees 10*

Sierra live oak: *Deciduous Trees 10*

Sierra lodgepole pine: *Evergreen Trees 10*

Sierra Madre Mountains: *Famous Western Locations 21*

Sierra-Cascade lodgepole pine: *Evergreen Trees 10*

sieve: *Kitchen Equipment 5*

Sif (goddess of battle skill): *Norse Pantheon 14*

sifter: *Kitchen Utensils 5*

SIG 556: *Semiautomatic Centerfire Rifles 7*

Sig Sauer P250: *Pistol Semiautomatic 7*

Sig Sauer semi-automatic pistol: *SWAT Weapons 7*

sigh: *Sounds 20*

sightline: *Stage Terms 13*

sightseeing bus: *Mass Transit 9*

sigil of ameth: *Symbols in Magic and Religion 19*

sigil of Lucifer: *Symbols in Magic and Religion 19*

siglos: *Coins and Currency 21*

sigma bonds: *Chemistry General Vocabulary 11*

sigma orbital: *Chemistry General Vocabulary 11*

sign of the Cross: *Rituals 14*

signal devices: *Equipment and Tools 5*

signal fire: *Signal Devices 5*

signet ring: *Jewelry 2*

significant other: *Relational 1*

significant: *Large 20; Large/Heavy 1*

Sikh Texts: *Major Religious Books 14*

Sikkim: *Keelback 15*

silage trailer: *Farm Transportation 9*

silane: *Dangerous Chemicals 11*

silence: *Rituals 14*

silent as a tomb: *Quiet 20*

silent: *Quiet 20*

silica: *Minerals 10*

silicafied wood: *Minerals 10*

Silicon: *Elements 11*

silicones: *Chemistry General Vocabulary 11*

silk bay: *Deciduous Trees 10*

silk rope: *General Survival Gear 5*

silk sack: *Containers and Vessels 5*

silk scarf: *Classic Items 23*

silk string: *Fasteners 5*

silk tassel: *Shrubs 10*

silk: *Fabric 2*

silk-knit: *Fabric 2*

silkweed: *Garden Perennials 10*

silkworm: *Moth 15*

Silky Terrier: *Dog Breeds 15*

sill: *Castle Anatomy 3; Windows 3*

sillimanite cat's eye: *Standard Gems 21*

sillimanite: *Cat's Eye Gems 21; Star Gems 21*

silo: *Farm/Outbuilding 3*

silt: *Cave Anatomy 10; Soil General Vocabulary 10*

siltstone: *Sedimentary Rocks 10*

Silurian Period: *Geologic Time 10*

Silvanus (nature): *Celtic Pantheon 14*

silver arowana: *Aquarium Freshwater Fish 15*

silver birch: *Deciduous Trees 10*

silver butterfly bush: *Garden Perennials 10*

Silver City: *Famous Western Locations 21*

silver dime: *Harbingers/Charms for Good Luck 19*

silver dollar: *Aquarium Freshwater Fish 15*

silver ear mushroom: *Fungus Common Names 10*

silver fir: *Evergreen Trees 10*

silver glance: *Minerals 10*

silver holy symbol: *Religious Items 5*

silver lace vine: *Garden Perennials 10*

silver maple: *Deciduous Trees 10*

silver mirror: *Personal Care 5*

Silver Needle: *Tea 6*

silver perch: *Wild Saltwater Fish 15*

silver pine: *Evergreen Trees 10*

silver plate: *Precious Metals 21*

silver polish: *Cleaning Supplies/Gadgets 5*

silver seatrout: *Wild Saltwater Fish 15*

silver space suit: *Clothing/Uniforms 22*

silver spruce: *Evergreen Trees 10*

silver vine: *Garden Perennials 10*

silver: *Coins and Currency 21; Dragon 16; Five Alchemical Spirits 19; Gray 20; Hair Color 1; Masks 2; Moth 15; Precious Metals 21*

Silver: *Elements 11*

silverbell: *Shrubs 10*

silvered: *Bats 15*

silver-haired: *Bats 15; Elderly 1*

silver-leafed nettle: *Garden Perennials 10*

silversmith: *Artists and Craftspeople 1*

silvertip fir: *Evergreen Trees 10*

silvervein creeper: *Garden Perennials 10*

silvery: *Vocal/Speech Quality 1*

Simbrah: *Other Cows 15*

Simiel: *Angels of Good 14*

Simmental: *Other Cows 15*

simmer: *Cooking Techniques 20*

simnel: *Cake 6*

Simon: *Twelve Apostles 14*

simple fracture: *Injuries/Medical Emergencies 12*

simple syrup: *Mixers 6*

simple: *Easy 20*

Sind: *Krait 15*

sinfonia concertante: *Composition Types 13*

sinfonia: *Composition Types 13*

sinfonietta: *Composition Types 13*

sinful: *Bad 20*

Singapore sling: *Cocktails 6*

Singapura: *Domestic Cats 15*

singe: *Cooking Techniques 20*

singer: *Bard 1; Character Building 1*

singing item: *Typical Magical Objects 17*

singing sword of Conaire Mor: *Celtic Swords 18*

singing: *Rituals 14; Sounds 20; Vocal/Speech Quality 1*

single action revolver: *Combat, Armor, and Weapons 7*

single bird enters a house: *Harbingers of Bad Luck 19*

single bond: *Chemistry General Vocabulary 11*

single distlefink: *Pennsylvania Dutch Hex Signs 19*

single dummy bridge: *Card Games 5*

single leaf: *Bats 15*

single pitch: *Roof Styles 3*

single red eye symbol: *Harbingers of Bad Luck 19*

single: *Beds 4*

Single-Footing Horse: *Horse Breeds 15*

single-minded: *Personality Other 1*

singlet: *Special Purpose Clothing 2*

singsong: *Vocal/Speech Quality 1*

singspiel: *Composition Types 13*

singularity: *Astronomy General Terms 11*

sinister: *Unattractive 20*

sink wrench: *Hand Tools 5*

sink: *Bathroom Features and Fixtures 3; Locomotion 9*

sinker: *Fishing Gear 5*

sinkhole: *Cave Anatomy 10; Geography General Vocabulary 10; Geological Natural Hazards 10; Terrain Features 10*

sinking of Andria Doria: *Legendary Events 18*

sinking of Titanic: *Legendary Events 18*

Sinope: *Moons 11*

sinopia: *Brown 20*

Sinti: *Human Ethnic Groups 1*

Sioux: *Native American Peoples 1*

siphon: *Cave Anatomy 10; Siege Equipment 7*

sippet: *Bread General Varieties 6*

Sir Arthur Conan Doyle: *Legendary, Mystical and Mythical Items and Locations 18*

sire: *Dogs/Canine 15*

siren: *Fantasy Creatures with Symbolic Meaning 19; Mythical Creatures and Monsters 16*

sirene: *Cheese International Varieties 6*

sirenje: *Cheese International Varieties 6*

Siri: *Other Cows 15*

sirloin tip roast: *Beef 6*

sirloin: *Beef 6*

Sirocco: *Winds of the Mediterranean 10*

Siskiyou cypress: *Evergreen Trees 10*

Sissonne fermée: *Ballet Terms 13*

Sissonne: *Ballet Terms 13*

sister: *Cleric 1; Female 1*

sister-in-law: *Female 1*

site: *Geography General Vocabulary 10*

sites unproven to exist: *Legendary, Mystical and Mythical Items and Locations 18; Legendary/Mythical Locations 18*

Sitka alder: *Deciduous Trees 10*

Sitka cypress: *Evergreen Trees 10*

Sitka spruce: *Evergreen Trees 10*

Sitting Bull: *Real People with Legendary Status 18; Western Paraphernalia/People 21*

situation: *Geography General Vocabulary 10*

six geese a-laying: *Twelve Days of Christmas 19*

Six: *Ballet Terms 13*

six-board chest: *Storage 4*

six-card brag: *Card Games 5*

six-pointed star: *Symbols of Freemasonry 19*

sixteenth note: *Notation 13*

sixty-three: *Card Games 5*

size: *Character Building 1*

sizeable: *Large 20; Large/Heavy 1*

ska: *Musical Styles 13; Styles of Dress 2*

skald: *Bard 1*

skanking: *Dance Styles 13*

skarn: *Metamorphic Rocks 10*

skate: *Wild Saltwater Fish 15*

skateboard: *Human-Powered Transportation 9; Sporting Goods Other 5*

skater: *Styles of Dress 2*

Skathi: *Moons 11*

skating rink: *Entertainment Property 3*

skeletal: *Small/Thin 1*

skeleton army: *Supporting Cast 24*

skeleton key: *Locks 5*

skeleton: *Dragon 16; Undead 16*

skeptical: *Horror Vocabulary 23; Personality Other 1*

sketch artist: *Law Enforcement 1*

sketch pad: *Art Materials 5*

ski cap: *Headgear 2*

ski jacket: *Outerwear 2*

ski vest: *Outerwear 2*

ski: *Boots 2; Masks 2*

skid: *Locomotion 9*

skidder: *Horse Drawn Farm Equipment*

skid-steer loader: *General Farm Equipment*

skiff: *Human-Powered Watercraft 9; Small Watercraft 9*

skill: *Games 5*

skilled: *Good 20*

skillet: *Kitchen Equipment 5*

skillful: *Good 20*

skim milk: *Dairy Beverages 6*

skim: *Milk 6*

skimmer hat: *Headgear 2*

skimmer: *Dragonfly 15; Kitchen Utensils 5*

skimmia: *Shrubs 10*

skimpy: *Small/Fragile 20*

skin and bones: *Small/Thin 1*

skin features: *Character Building 1*

skin type: *Character Building 1*

skin: *Organs/Major Structures 12*

skinchanger: *Nature Occupations 1*

skinks: *Scaled Reptiles 15*

skinning knife: *Hand Tools 5*

skinny jeans: *Unisex Clothing 2*

skinny: *Small/Thin 1*

skinwalker: *Shapechanger 16*

Skioblaonir: *Vehicles 18*

skip: *Locomotion 9*

skipjack tuna: *Wild Saltwater Fish 15*

skipper: *Butterfly 15*

skipperling: *Butterfly 15*

skirmish: *General Combat Vocabulary 7*

skirt: *Ladies' Wear 2*

skitgubbe: *Card Games 5*

skivvies: *Undergarments 2*

Skjellerup-Maristany: *Comets 11*

Skofnung: *Norse Weapons 18*

skoggra: *Demon 16*

Skoll: *Moons 11*

skort: *Ladies' Wear 2*

skripavac: *Cheese International Varieties 6*

skulk: *Locomotion 9*

Skull and Bones: *Secret/Mystical Organizations 18*

skull and crossbones: *Secular Symbols 19*

skullcap: *Garden Perennials 10; Headgear 2; Religious Dress 2*

skully: *Headgear 2*

skunk cory: *Aquarium Freshwater Fish 15*

skunk spruce: *Evergreen Trees 10*

skunk vine: *Weeds 10*

skunk: *Woodland Mammals 15*

skunks: *Travel Hazards 9*

sky blue: *Blue 20*

sky giant: *Humanlike Groups 1*

sky: *Meteorology General Vocabulary 10*

Skye Terrier: *Dog Breeds 15*

skyr: *Cheese International Varieties 6*

Skyros Pony: *Horse Breeds 15*

skysail: *Boat/Ship Anatomy 9*

skyscape: *Art Genres 13*

skyscraper: *General Buildings 3*

skywalk: *Bridges 9; Roads 9*

slack: *Vocal/Speech Quality 1*

slacks: *Unisex Clothing 2*

slam: *Close/Hold 20*

slam-dunk: *Easy 20*

slammer: *Prison 3*

slanted: *Eye Type 1; Eyebrows 1*

slap: *Attack 7*

slapjack: *Card Games 5*

slash and burn: *General Combat Vocabulary 7*

slash pine: *Evergreen Trees 10*

slasher: *Horror Genres 23*

slat-back: *Chairs and Stools 4*

slate gray: *Gray 20*

slate pencil: *Office/School/Writing Supplies 5*

slate: *Interior Building Materials 3; Metamorphic Rocks 10; Office/School/Writing Supplies 5; Roofing Materials 3*

slaughter: *Attack 7; Kill 20*

slaughterer: *Assassin 1; Villain 20*

Slav: *Human Ethnic Groups 1*

slave ship: *Large Watercraft 9*

slave: *Common Character Archetypes 21*

slaver: *Wet 20*

slavery: *Plot Devices 22*

slay: *Attack 7; Kill 20*

slayer: *Assassin 1; Fighter 1; Villain 20*

sled: *Animal-Powered Transportation 9; Christmas 19; Sporting Goods Other 5; Toys 5*

sledgehammer: *Hand Tools 5; Improvised Weapons 7; Tools 7*

sledge: *Animal-Powered Transportation 9*

sleep gas: *Spy Gear 5*

sleep: *Witchcraft Vocabulary 17*

sleeper car: *Railroad 9*

sleeper sofa: *Beds 4*

sleeping bag: *Military Equipment 8*

sleeping grass: *Weeds 10*

sleeping mat: *Beds 4*

sleeping plant: *Wildflowers 10*

sleepwear: *Styles of Dress 2*

sleepy: *Eye Type 1; Slow 20*

sleet: *Precipitation 10; Snow Types 10*

sleeve garters: *Western Clothing/Dress 21*

sleeve: *Garment Pieces 2*

sleigh: *Beds 4; Christmas 19*

slender: *Small/Thin 1*

slender-snouted crocodile: *Crocodilians 15*

slicked: *Hair Style 1*

slickenside: *Geological Vocabulary 10*

slide projection: *Art Techniques 13*

slide projector: *Office/School Machines 5*

slide: *Jewelry 21; Laboratory Equipment 5; Music Accessories*

slides: *Footwear/Shoes 2*

sliding stone: *Traps 3*

sliding T-bevel: *Architectural/Engineering Tools 5*

sliding: *Doors 3; Windows 3*

slight: *Expletives 20; Small/Fragile 20; Small/Thin 1*

slim: *Small/Thin 1*

slime: *Ooze 16*

sling stone: *Missile Loads 7*

sling: *Fishing Gear 5; Missile Weapons 7*

slingback: *Footwear/Shoes 2*

slingshot: *Toys 5*

slink: *Locomotion 9*

slip and fall: *Injuries/Medical Emergencies 12*

slip knot: *Sailing Knots 9*

slip: *Ladies' Wear 2; Marina 3; Water Terms 9*

slip-on: *Footwear/Shoes 2*

slipped buntline: *Sailing Knots 9*

slippers: *Footwear/Shoes 2*

slippery customer: *Thief 1*

slippery elm: *Deciduous Trees 10*

slippery rock: *Geological Natural Hazards 10*

slippery Sam: *Card Games 5*

slipstream: *Science Fiction Genres 22*

slit drum: *Percussion Musical Instruments 5*

slit-faced: *Bats 15*

slither: *Locomotion 9*

sliver/splinter: *Injuries/Medical Emergencies 12*

slobber: *Wet 20*

sloe gin: *Hard Liquor 6*

slog: *Locomotion 9*

sloop: *Large Watercraft 9; Military Watercraft 8*

slope landforms: *Chapter 10*

slope stability: *Soil General Vocabulary 10*

slope: *Chapter 10*

sloppy joe: *Sandwiches 6*

slosh: *Card Games 5*

slot cars: *Toys 5*

sloth: *Bears 15; Seven Deadly Sins 19*

slothful: *Slow 20*

slotted spoon: *Kitchen Utensils 5*

slouch cap: *Headgear 2*

slouch: *Boots 2*

slough: *Terrain Features 10*

Slovak: *Human Ethnic Groups 1*

Slovene: *Human Ethnic Groups 1*

Slovenian Cika: *Other Cows 15*

slow butterfly: *Swimming Strokes 9*

slow cooker: *Appliances 5*

slow: *Adjectives 20; Mobility 1; Unintelligent 1*

slow-moving: *Slow 20*

slug thrower: *Weapons 22*

sluggish: *Mobility 1; Slow 20*

slumber cap: *Hair Accessories 2*

slump: *Miscellaneous Dessert 6; Soil General Vocabulary 10*

slungshot: *Chain Weapons 7*

slurry agitator: *General Farm Equipment*

slush: *Fruit Drinks 6; Snow Types 10*

slushie: *Fruit Drinks 6*

slutty: *Styles of Dress 2*

sly: *Difficult 20*

smack: *Attack 7*

small arms: *Military 8*

small barrel: *Containers and Vessels 5*

small black: *Pigs 15*

small bodied: *Newts 15*

small chest: *Containers and Vessels 5*

small intestine: *Organs/Major Structures 12*

small sack: *Containers and Vessels 5*

small shrimp: *Fish/Seafood Types 6*

small solar system body: *Astronomy General Terms 11*

small sword: *Fencing Equipment 7*

small town performs annual human sacrifice: *Horror Plot Devices 23*

small whip: *Flexible 7*

small white: *Butterfly 15; Pigs 15*

small: *Adjectives 20; Character Building 1; Ears 1; Eggs 6; Face 1; Mouth 1; Shield Types 7; Swords One-handed 7; Teeth 1; Vocal/Speech Quality 1*

smallclothes: *Undergarments 2*

small-eared zorro: *Foxes 15*

small-eyed: *General Snake Families 15*

small-footed myotis: *Bats 15*

small-fruited mountain ash: *Deciduous Trees 10*

small-headed: *Flies 15*

smallpox: *Diseases 12*

smalls: *Undergarments 2*

small-seed white ash: *Deciduous Trees 10*

smaragdina tablet: *Symbols in Magic and Religion 19*

smarmy: *Personality Other 1*

smart board: *Office/School Machines 5*

smart: *Intelligent 1; Weapons 22*

smear: *Card Games 5*

smell: *Physical Mutations 22*

smelling stick: *Deciduous Trees 10*

smells: *Adjectives 20*

smelt: *Fish/Seafood Types 6*

smilax: *Shrubs 10*

smiley face: *Secular Symbols 19*

smiling: *Happy 20*

Smith & Wesson Bodyguard: *Revolver Double Action 7*

Smith & Wesson Elite Gold: *Shotguns Side-by-Side 7*

Smith & Wesson Elite Silver: *Shotguns Over/Under 7*

Smith & Wesson Hunter: *Revolver Double Action 7*

Smith & Wesson I-bolt: *Bolt Action Centerfire Rifles 7*

Smith & Wesson M&P 15-22: *Semiautomatic Rimfire Rifles 7*

Smith & Wesson M&P15: *Semiautomatic Centerfire Rifles 7*

Smith & Wesson model 10: *Revolver Double Action 7*

Smith & Wesson model 2000: *Shotguns Semiautomatic 7*

Smith & Wesson Night Guard: *Revolver Double Action 7*

Smith & Wesson revolver: *Western Weapons 21*

Smith & Wesson: *Pistol Semiautomatic 7*

smithsonite: *Standard Gems 21*

smithy: *Business Property 3*

smocking: *Embellishments 2*

smog: *Meteorology General Vocabulary 10; Smells 20*

smoke bomb: *Spy Gear 5*

smoke bush: *Garden Perennials 10*

smoke grenade: *Military Weapons General 8*

smoke machine: *Technical Terms 13*

smoke: *Magical Transportation 17; Meteorology General Vocabulary 10; Signal Devices 5*

smoked: *Cheese Common Varieties 6*

smokescreen: *Tactics 7*

smoketree: *Shrubs 10*

smoking cap: *Headgear 2*

smoking jacket: *Men's Wear 2*

smoking mirror of Tezcatlipoca: *Objects 18*

smoking stand: *Tables 4*

smoky black: *Black 20*

smoky quartz: *Minerals 10; Standard Gems 21*

smoky: *Bats 15; Vocal/Speech Quality 1*

smolder: *Cooking Techniques 20*

smooth bark cypress: *Evergreen Trees 10*

smooth bark hickory: *Deciduous Trees 10*

smooth bark oak: *Deciduous Trees 10*

smooth bebb willow: *Deciduous Trees 10*

smooth chanterelle: *Fungus Common Names 10*

smooth cordgrass: *Weeds 10*

smooth horsetail: *Wildflowers 10*

smooth peanut butter: *Staples 6*

smooth puffer: *Wild Saltwater Fish 15*

smooth scouring rush: *Wildflowers 10*

smooth shaven: *Facial Hair Beard 1*

smooth: *Chin 1; General Snake Families 15; Hair Types 1; Lips 1; Skin Types and Features 1; Vocal/Speech Quality 1*

smoothie: *Fruit Drinks 6*

snack mix: *Snacks 6*

snack plate: *Tableware 5*

snacks: *Food 6*

snail: *Animals with Symbolic Meaning 19*

snail's pace: *Slow 20*

snails: *Items with Healing Properties 19*

snail-seed: *Garden Perennials 10*

snake bite: *Injuries/Medical Emergencies 12*

snake eyes on a pair of dice: *Harbingers of Bad Luck 19*

snake families: *Animals 15*

Snake man (war): *Native American Pantheon 14*

snake oil salesman: *Common Character Archetypes 21; Thief 1*

snake: *Chinese Horoscope 19*

snake-foot: *Tables 4*

snakefruit: *Unusual Edible Fruits 6*

snakehead: *Garden Perennials 10*

snakeroot: *Garden Perennials 10*

snakes: *Animals 15; Travel Hazards 9*

snakeskin agate: *Minerals 10*

snakeskin: *Wizard's Goods 5*

snakeweed: *Poisonous Plants 10*

snap peas: *Vegetables 6*

snap: *Fishing Gear 5; Notions 2; Speak 20*

snapdragon: *Garden Annuals 10; Garden Perennials 10*

snapper: *Wild Saltwater Fish 15*

snapping: *Freshwater Turtles 15*

snappy: *Fast 20*

snare drum: *Percussion Musical Instruments 5*

snare: *Traps 3*

snarl: *Sounds 20; Speak 20*

snatch: *Buy 20; Close/Hold 20*

sneak: *Locomotion 9*

sneakers: *Footwear/Shoes 2*

sneaky: *Difficult 20*

sneering: *Negative 1*

sneezeweed: *Garden Perennials 10; Wildflowers 10*

snicker: *Sounds 20*

snickerdoodle: *Cookie 6*

sniffle: *Sounds 20*

snifter: *Drinkware 5*

snipe fly: *Flies 15*

sniper rifle: *Military 8; Military Weapons General 8; Spy Gear 5*

sniper rifles: *Combat, Armor, and Weapons 7*

sniper: *Assassin 1; Fighter 1; General Combat Vocabulary 7; Law Enforcement 1*

sniping: *General Combat Vocabulary 7*

snips: *Art Tools 5*

snivel: *Sounds 20; Speak 20*

snobbish: *Personality Other 1*

snood: *Headgear 2*

snook: *Wild Saltwater Fish 15*

snoot: *Nose 1*

snorkel: *Viper 15*

snorkeling: *Swimming Strokes 9*

snort: *Sounds 20*

snout: *Nose 1*

snow aggregate: *Snow Types 10*

snow angel: *Snow Events 10*

snow ball: *Cookie 6*

snow band: *Snow Events 10*

snow belt: *Snow Events 10*

snow berry: *Unusual Edible Fruits 6*

snow blower: *Power Tools*

snow cave: *Snow Events 10*

snow cover: *Snow Events 10*

snow crystals: *Snow Types 10*

snow day: *Snow Events 10*

snow drift: *Snow Events 10*

snow events: *Chapter 10*

snow fort: *Snow Events 10*

snow grains: *Snow Types 10*

snow ice: *Snow Types 10*

snow leopard: *Big Cats 15*

snow level: *Meteorology General Vocabulary 10*

snow line: *Meteorology General Vocabulary 10*

snow mushroom: *Fungus Common Names 10*

snow on the mountain: *Garden Annuals 10*

snow pack: *Snow Events 10*

snow pants: *Outerwear 2*

snow peas: *Vegetables 6*

snow pellets: *Snow Types 10*

snow plow: *Motorized Truck 9; Power Tools; Snow Events 10*

snow saucer: *Sporting Goods Other 5*

snow shoeing: *Snow Events 10*

snow shoes: *Footwear/Shoes 2*

snow shovel: *Improvised Weapons 7*

snow shower: *Snow Events 10*

snow skiing: *Snow Events 10*

snow skis: *Sporting Goods Other 5*

snow slab: *Snow Events 10*

snow sledding: *Snow Events 10*

snow squall: *Snow Events 10*

snow types: *Chapter 10*

snow: *Boots 2; Christmas 19; Minerals 10; Precipitation 10; White 20*

snowball: *Snow Events 10*

snowbank false morel: *Fungus Common Names 10*

snowberry: *Shrubs 10*

snowboard: *Sporting Goods Other 5*

snowboarding: *Snow Events 10*

snowdrop: *Garden Bulbs 10; Garden Perennials 10*

snowfall: *Snow Events 10*

snowflake obsidian: *Standard Gems 21*

snowflake: *Christmas 19; Minerals 10; Snow Events 10*

snowflakes: *Snow Types 10*

snow-in-summer: *Garden Perennials 10*

snowline: *Geography General Vocabulary 10*

snowman: *Snow Events 10*

snowmelt: *Snow Events 10*

snowmobile suit: *Outerwear 2*

snowmobile: *Snow Events 10*

Snowshoe: *Domestic Cats 15*

snowstorm: *Severe Weather 10; Snow Events 10*

snowstorms: *Chapter 10*

snowy tansy: *Garden Perennials 10*

snowy: *Owls 15*

snub-nosed monkey: *Old World Monkeys 15*

snuff: *Kill 20*

snuffbox: *Containers and Vessels 5*

snuffer: *Candles 5*

soak: *Wet 20*

soaking tub: *Bathroom Features and Fixtures 3*

soaking: *Precipitation 10*

soap: *Personal Care 5*

soapberry: *Deciduous Trees 10; Shrubs 10*

soapbox racer: *Toys 5*

soaprock: *Minerals 10*

soapstone: *Metamorphic Rocks 10; Minerals 10*

soapweed: *Garden Perennials 10*

soapwort: *Garden Perennials 10*

soar: *Locomotion 9*

sob: *Sounds 20; Speak 20*

soca: *Dance Styles 13*

soccer field: *Entertainment Property 3*

soccer: *Athletic Shoes 2; Sporting Goods Balls 5*

sociable couch: *Seating 4*

social climber: *Social Distinction 1*

social clubs: *Character Building 1*

social commentary: *Performance Genres 13*

social contract: *Philosophy Basic Concepts 14*

social distinction: *Character Building 1*

socialism: *Philosophy Basic Concepts 14*

Socialist realism: *Art Movements 13*

Societas Rosicruciana: *Secret/Mystical Organizations 18*

society garlic: *Garden Bulbs 10; Garden Perennials 10*

society girl: *Social Distinction 1*

Society of the Horseman's Word: *Secret/Mystical Organizations 18*

society: *Philosophy Basic Concepts 14*

sock cap: *Headgear 2*

sock monkey: *Toys 5*

socket wrench: *Hand Tools 5*

socks: *Clothing 2*

sod cutter: *Garden Tools*

sod: *Exterior Building Materials 3*

soda bottle: *Improvised Weapons 7*

soda bread: *Bread General Varieties 6*

soda feldspar: *Minerals 10*

soda straw: *Cave Anatomy 10*

soda water: *Soft Drinks 6*

soda: *Soft Drinks 6*

sodaclase: *Minerals 10*

soda-lime feldspar: *Minerals 10*

sodalite: *Standard Gems 21*

sodality: *Social Clubs 1*

sodium arsenate: *Dangerous Chemicals 11*

sodium azide: *Dangerous Chemicals 11*

sodium cacodylate: *Dangerous Chemicals 11*

sodium cyanide: *Dangerous Chemicals 11*

sodium fluoroacetate: *Dangerous Chemicals 11*

sodium pentachlorophenate: *Dangerous Chemicals 11*

sodium selenate: *Dangerous Chemicals 11*

sodium selenite: *Dangerous Chemicals 11*

sodium vapor: *Illumination Bulb and Tube Types 5*

Sodium: *Elements 11*

sofa bed: *Beds 4*

sofa: *Seating 4*

soffit: *Building Elements and Features 3; Castle Anatomy 3*

soft boil: *Cooking Techniques 20*

soft boiled: *Egg Styles 6*

soft bread stick: *Bread General Varieties 6*

Soft Coated Wheaten Terrier: *Dog Breeds 15*

soft contact lenses: *Optics 5*

soft drinks: *Food 6*

soft elm: *Deciduous Trees 10*

soft maple: *Deciduous Trees 10*

soft pine: *Evergreen Trees 10*

soft pretzel: *Snacks 6*

soft rock: *Musical Styles 13*

soft serve: *Ice Cream 6*

soft shoe: *Dance Styles 13*

soft: *Quiet 20; Vocal/Speech Quality 1; Wet 20*

softball: *Sporting Goods Balls 5*

softcover: *Books/Publications 5*

softshell: *Freshwater Turtles 15*

soft-shelled hickory: *Deciduous Trees 10*

soft-spoken: *Quiet 20;Vocal/Speech Quality 1*

soggy: *Wet 20*

soil alkalinity: *Soil General Vocabulary 10*

soil amendment: *Soil General Vocabulary 10*

soil and water assessment tool: *Soil General Vocabulary 10*

Soil Association: *Soil General Vocabulary 10*

soil biodiversity: *Soil General Vocabulary 10*

soil biology: *Soil General Vocabulary 10*

soil carbon: *Soil General Vocabulary 10*

soil cement: *Soil General Vocabulary 10*

soil chemistry: *Soil General Vocabulary 10*

soil classification: *Soil General Vocabulary 10*

soil compaction: *Soil General Vocabulary 10*

soil conditioner: *Soil General Vocabulary 10*

Soil Conservation and Domestic Allotment Act: *Soil General Vocabulary 10*

soil conservation: *Soil General Vocabulary 10*

soil contamination: *Soil General Vocabulary 10*

soil crust: *Soil General Vocabulary 10*

soil depletion: *Soil General Vocabulary 10*

soil ecology: *Soil General Vocabulary 10*

soil erosion: *Soil General Vocabulary 10*

soil fertility: *Soil General Vocabulary 10*

soil food web: *Soil General Vocabulary 10*

soil functions: *Soil General Vocabulary 10*

soil gradation: *Soil General Vocabulary 10*

soil guideline value: *Soil General Vocabulary 10*

soil health: *Soil General Vocabulary 10*

soil horizon: *Soil General Vocabulary 10*

soil inoculant: *Soil General Vocabulary 10*

soil life: *Soil General Vocabulary 10*

soil liquefaction: *Geological Vocabulary 10; Soil General Vocabulary 10*

soil management: *Soil General Vocabulary 10*

soil mechanics: *Geologic Fields of Study 10; Soil General Vocabulary 10*

soil moisture sensors: *Soil General Vocabulary 10*

soil moisture: *Soil General Vocabulary 10*

soil nailing: *Soil General Vocabulary 10*

soil organic matter: *Soil General Vocabulary 10*

soil pH: *Soil General Vocabulary 10*

soil physics: *Soil General Vocabulary 10*

soil policy: *Soil General Vocabulary 10*

soil profile: *Soil General Vocabulary 10*

soil resilience: *Soil General Vocabulary 10*

soil respiration: *Soil General Vocabulary 10*

soil salinity control: *Soil General Vocabulary 10*

soil salinity: *Soil General Vocabulary 10*

Soil Science Society of America: *Soil General Vocabulary 10*

soil science: *Geologic Fields of Study 10; Soil General Vocabulary 10*

soil series: *Soil General Vocabulary 10*

soil solarization: *Soil General Vocabulary 10*

soil steam sterilization: *Soil General Vocabulary 10*

soil structure: *Soil General Vocabulary 10*

soil survey: *Soil General Vocabulary 10*

soil test: *Soil General Vocabulary 10*

soil texture: *Soil General Vocabulary 10*

soil type: *Soil General Vocabulary 10*

soil vocabulary: *Chapter 10*

soil water retention: *Soil General Vocabulary 10*

soil: *Chapter 10; Soil General Vocabulary 10*

soiled: *Unattractive 20*

soils retrogression and degradation: *Soil General Vocabulary 10*

Sokoke: *Domestic Cats 15*

solar cycle: *Astronomy General Terms 11*

solar eclipse: *Astronomy General Terms 11*

solar energy collection satellite: *Installations 22*

solar energy cures/destoys: *Energy Sources/Types 23*

solar flare: *Astronomy General Terms 11*

Solar Lodge: *Secret/Mystical Organizations 18*

solar nebula: *Astronomy General Terms 11*

solar sail clipper: *Spaceship Types 22*

solar wind: *Astronomy General Terms 11; Spaceship Drive Systems 22*

solar winged disc: *Symbols in Magic and Religion 19*

solar: *Castle Anatomy 3; Energy Sources/Types 22; Energy Sources/Types 24*

solder: *Art Techniques 13*

soldering iron: *Power Tools*

soldier course brick: *Building Elements and Features 3*

soldier: *Armed Forces Other Titles 8; Beetle 15; Common Character Archetypes 21; Fighter 1; Flies 15*

soldierfish: *Aquarium Saltwater Fish 15*

sole: *Body Parts 12*

Soledad pine: *Evergreen Trees 10*

solid: *Large/Heavy 1*

solitaire 13: *Solitaire Card Games 5*

solitaire games: *Equipment and Tools 5*

solitary confinement: *Prison 3*

solo whist: *Card Games 5*

solo: *Card Games 5*

soloist: *Singer 1*

Solomon's knot: *Symbols in Magic and Religion 19*

Solomon's seal: *Garden Perennials 10*

solonchak: *Soil General Vocabulary 10*

solonetz: *Soil General Vocabulary 10*

solstice: *Astronomy General Terms 11; Witchcraft Vocabulary 17*

solubility product constant: *Chemistry General Vocabulary 11*

solubility product principle: *Chemistry General Vocabulary 11*

solute: *Chemistry General Vocabulary 11*

solution flute: *Cave Anatomy 10*

solution: *Chemistry General Vocabulary 11; Wet 20*

solvation: *Chemistry General Vocabulary 11*

solve: *Verbs 20*

solvent: *Chemistry General Vocabulary 11*

solvolysis: *Chemistry General Vocabulary 11*

soma: *Foods with Religious or Ritual Significance 19*

Somali Pony: *Horse Breeds 15*

Somali: *Domestic Cats 15; Human Ethnic Groups 1*

somber: *Sad 20*

sombrero: *Headgear 2; Western Clothing/Dress 21*

sommelier: *Castle Inhabitants and Personnel 1; Food Service 1*

somnolent: *Slow 20*

son of a bitch: *Expletives 20*

son: *Male 1*

sonar: *Physical Mutations 22*

sonata: *Composition Types 13*

sonata-form: *Composition Types 13*

sonatina: *Composition Types 13*

soncoya: *Unusual Edible Fruits 6*

songbook: *Printed Music 13*

songstress: *Bard 1; Singer 1*

sonic abilities: *Physical Mutations 22*

sonic weapon: *Plot Devices 22*

sonic: *Weapons 22*

son-in-law: *Male 1*

Sonoma jack: *Cheese Common Varieties 6*

Sonoran desert: *Tortoises 15*

Sonoran green: *Toads 15*

Sonoran mud: *Freshwater Turtles 15*

Sonoran: *General Snake Families 15*

sons of bitches: *Expletives 20*

soot: *Wizard's Goods 5*

soothe: *Happy 20*

soothing: *Easy 20; Vocal/Speech Quality 1*

soothsayer: *Cleric 1; Wizard 1*

sootiest: *Fighter 1*

sootywing: *Butterfly 15*

sop: *Bread General Varieties 6*

sopaipilla: *Bread General Varieties 6; Donut/doughnut 6*

sophisticated: *Personality Other 1*

sophomoric: *Child 1*

soprano saxophone: *Wind/Woodwind and Brass Musical Instruments*

sorb: *Unusual Edible Fruits 6*

sorbaria: *Shrubs 10*

sorbet: *Ice Cream Related 6*

sorcerer: *Nature Occupations 1; Witchcraft Vocabulary 17; Wizard 1*

sorcerer's palace: *Fantasy Locations 24*

sorceress: *Witchcraft Vocabulary 17*

sorcery: *Witchcraft Vocabulary 17*

sore: *Harm 20*

sorghum: *Staples 6*

sorority: *Social Clubs 1*

Sorraia: *Horse Breeds 15*

sorrel tree: *Deciduous Trees 10*

sorrel: *Vegetables 6; Weeds 10*

sorrow: *General Emotions 20; Sad 20*

sorrowfulness: *Sad 20*

sort: *Clean 20*

sortie: *General Combat Vocabulary 7*

sostenuto: *General Music Vocabulary 13*

sotto voce: *General Music Vocabulary 13*

sotto: *Vocal/Speech Quality 1*

souesite: *Minerals 10*

soufflé: *Cake 6*

souk: *Followers 14; Outdoor Property 3*

soul patch: *Facial Hair Beard 1*

soul: *Philosophy Basic Concepts 14*

sound check: *Technical Terms 13*

sound designer: *Performing Arts 1*

sound: *Coastal and Oceanic 10; Traps 3; Water Terms 9*

soundless: *Quiet 20*

sounds: *Adjectives 20*

soup cup: *Tableware 5*

soup plate: *Tableware 5*

soup pot: *Kitchen Equipment 5*

soup spoon: *Eating Utensils 5*

soup: *Food 6; Wet 20*

sour cherry: *Pit Fruits 6*

sour cream & onion potato chip: *Snacks 6*

sour cream apple: *Pie 6*

sour cream raisin: *Pie 6*

sour cream: *Donut/doughnut 6; Other Dairy 6; Salad Dressing 6*

sour dock: *Weeds 10*

sour orange: *Citrus 6*

sour: *Candy General 6; Negative 1; Sad 20; Smells 20*

sourdough: *Bread General Varieties 6*

sourgum: *Deciduous Trees 10*

sourness: *General Emotions 20*

soursop: *Unusual Edible Fruits 6*

sourwood: *Deciduous Trees 10*

sous chef: *Food Service 1*

Sousaphone: *Wind/Woodwind and Brass Musical Instruments*

South African casino: *Card Games 5*

South African ghost: *Frogs 15*

South African jade: *Minerals 10*

South American: *Caecilians 15*

South Andaman: *Krait 15*

South China: *Tigers 15*

South Devon: *Other Cows 15*

South Florida slash pine: *Evergreen Trees 10*

south frigid zone: *Geographical Zones 10*

south temperate zone: *Geographical Zones 10*

south: *Eight Compass Points 19*

Southeast African: *Lions 15*

southeast: *Eight Compass Points 19*

southern balsam fir: *Evergreen Trees 10*

southern belle: *Styles of Dress 2*

southern blue gum: *Weeds 10*

Southern California black walnut: *Deciduous Trees 10*

Southern California walnut: *Deciduous Trees 10*

Southern Colonial: *Architectural Styles 3*

southern crabapple: *Unusual Edible Fruits 6*

southern cypress: *Evergreen Trees 10*

southern fir: *Evergreen Trees 10*

southern hackberry: *Deciduous Trees 10*

southern king fish: *Wild Saltwater Fish 15*

southern magnolia: *Deciduous Trees 10*

Southern Pacific: *Rattlesnake 15*

southern puffer: *Wild Saltwater Fish 15*

southern red oak: *Deciduous Trees 10*

southern rightwhale: *Dolphins 15*

southern sting ray: *Wild Saltwater Fish 15*

southern sweetbay: *Deciduous Trees 10*

southern white cedar: *Evergreen Trees 10*

southern yellow pine: *Evergreen Trees 10*

southern yellow: *Bats 15*

southern: *Toads 15*

Southwest African: *Lions 15*

southwest: *Eight Compass Points 19*

southwestern black willow: *Deciduous Trees 10*

southwestern locust: *Deciduous Trees 10*

southwestern peach willow: *Deciduous Trees 10*

southwestern speckled: *Rattlesnake 15*

southwestern white pine: *Evergreen Trees 10*

southwestern Woodhouse's: *Toads 15*

southwestern: *Styles of Dress 2*

souvenir: *Decorative Objects 4; Jewelry 21*

sovereign state: *Political Divisions 10*

sovereign: *Coins and Currency 21*

Soviet Heavy Draft: *Horse Breeds 15*

sovite: *Igneous Rocks 10*

Soxhlet extractor: *Laboratory Equipment 5*

soy milk: *Milk 6*

soy: *Allergies 12*

soybean: *Legumes 6; Oils 6*

soybeans: *Farm/Outbuilding 3*

spa: *Rooms 3*

space bus: *Spaceship Types 22*

space combat armor: *Clothing/Uniforms 22*

space exploration: *Plot Devices 22*

space invader: *Monster Categories/Terms 16*

Space Needle: *Unique Property 3*

space opera: *Plot Devices 22; Science Fiction Genres 22*

space outpost architect: *Occupations 22*

space pirates: *Plot Devices 22*

space ship: *Air Vehicles 9*

space shuttle: *Air Vehicles 9*

space station coordinator: *Occupations 22*

space station: *Plot Devices 22*

space suit: *Clothing/Uniforms 22; Spy Gear 5*

space supernatural: *Science Fiction Genres 22*

space transport armor: *Clothing/Uniforms 22*

space travelers assaulted by horrific creature: *Horror Plot Devices 23*

space war: *General Combat Vocabulary 7*

space western: *Science Fiction Genres 22*

space: *Art Genres 13; Philosophy Basic Concepts 14; Travel Types 22; Visual Elements 13*

spacebot: *Robots 22*

spaceliner: *Spaceship Types 22*

spacers: *Teeth Dental Work 1*

spacious: *Large 20*

spade: *Garden Tools*

spades: *Card Games 5*

spade-shaped: *Hand Shapes 19*

spadiced owlet: *Owls 15*

spading machine: *General Farm Equipment*

spadrone: *Swords One-handed 7*

spadroon: *Swords One-handed 7*

spaetzel: *Bread General Varieties 6*

spaghetti: *Pasta 6*

Spanish bluebell: *Garden Bulbs 10*

Spanish brook: *Newts 15*

Spanish broom: *Shrubs 10*

Spanish cane: *Weeds 10*

Spanish Colonial Revival: *Architectural Styles 3*

Spanish Mustang: *Horse Breeds 15*

Spanish oak: *Deciduous Trees 10*

Spanish onion: *Vegetables 6*

Spanish snapdragon: *Garden Perennials 10*

spanish tamarind: *Unusual Edible Fruits 6*

Spanish: *Coffee Bean Roasts 6*

Spanish: *Human Ethnic Groups 1*

Spanish: *Imported Carpets 4*

Spanish-Barb: *Horse Breeds 15*

Spanish-Norman: *Horse Breeds 15*

spar: *Boat/Ship Anatomy 9; Card Games 5*

spare: *Small/Thin 1*

sparkling water: *Soft Drinks 6*

sparkling wine: *Wine White 6*

sparkling: *Beautiful 20; Happy 20*

sparrow: *Animals with Symbolic Meaning 19; Backyard Birds 15*

sparse: *Eyebrows 1*

Spartacus: *Real People with Legendary Status 18*

sparteine: *Poisonous Chemicals in Plants 11*

sparth: *Axes 7*

spatha: *Swords One-handed 7*

spats: *Footwear/Shoes 2; Men's Wear 2*

spatula: *Kitchen Utensils 5; Laboratory Equipment 5*

speak: *Verbs 20*

speaker phone: *Office/School Machines 5*

speaker: *Electronics 4*

speakers: *Office/School Machines 5*

Spear Luin: *Four Hallows of Ireland 18*

spear of Achilles: *Spears 18*

Spear of Destiny: *Unique Spear 18*

Spear of Longinus: *Unique Spear 18*

spear thrower: *Missile Weapons 7*

spear: *Fishing Gear 5; Traps 3; Western Weapons 21*

speargun: *Fishing Gear 5*

spearmint leaves: *Candy General 6*

spear-nosed: *Bats 15*

spears of the Valkyrie: *Spears 18*

spears: *Combat, Armor, and Weapons 7*

special agent: *Law Enforcement 1*

special body feature: *Classic Heraldry 19*

special education teacher: *Academic 1*

special occasion: *Character Building 1*

special ops operative: *Assassin 1*

special ops: *Fighter 1*

special posture: *Classic Heraldry 19*

special purpose clothing: *Clothing 2*

special purpose property: *Architecture and Property 3*

specialist: *Academic 1; U.S. Army Enlisted 8*

specialized suit: *Spy Gear 5*

species: *Character Building 1*

specific gravity bottle: *Laboratory Equipment 5*

specific gravity: *Chemistry General Vocabulary 11*

specific heat: *Chemistry General Vocabulary 11*

specific rate constant: *Chemistry General Vocabulary 11*

specific storage: *Soil General Vocabulary 10*

specific weight: *Soil General Vocabulary 10*

speck of light: *Paranormal Occurrences 21*

speckle-bellied: *Keelback 15*

speckled alder: *Deciduous Trees 10*

spectacled caiman: *Crocodilians 15*

spectacled lizard: *Scaled Reptiles 15*

spectacled: *Bears 15; Cobra 15; Owls 15*

spectacles: *Optics 5*

spectacular: *Beautiful 20*

spectator ions: *Chemistry General Vocabulary 11*

spectator pumps: *Footwear/Shoes 2*

specter: *Masks 2; Undead 16*

spectrolite: *Minerals 10*

spectrometer: *Astronomy General Terms 11*

spectrophotometer: *Laboratory Equipment 5*

spectroscopy: *Astronomy General Terms 11*

spectrum: *Astronomy General Terms 11; Chemistry General Vocabulary 11*

specularite: *Minerals 10*

speculation: *Card Games 5*

speculative: *Philosophy Basic Concepts 14*

speech quality: *Character Building 1*

speech: *Physical Mutations 22*

speechless: *Quiet 20*

speed skates: *Footwear/Shoes 2; Sporting Goods Other 5*

speed: *Card Games 5; Small Watercraft 9*

speeder: *Vehicles 22*

speedwell: *Garden Perennials 10; Wildflowers 10*

speedy: *Fast 20; Mobility 1*

Speke's hinge-back: *Tortoises 15*

speleology: *Geologic Fields of Study 10*

speleotherm: *Cave Anatomy 10*

spell needed to reverse evil magic: *Horror Plot Devices 23*

spell: *Common Dangers 23; Magic Vocabulary 17; Witchcraft Vocabulary 17*

spellbinding: *Beautiful 20*

spellbook: *Witchcraft Vocabulary 17; Wizard's Goods 5*

spellbound: *Magic Vocabulary 17*

spellcaster: *Wizard 1*

spellcasting: *Witchcraft Vocabulary 17*

spelt: *Grain 6*

spelunking: *Exploration 9*

sperm: *Whales 15*

spessartite garnet: *Standard Gems 21*

spessartite: *Minerals 10*

spetum: *Spears 7*

spew: *Smells 20*

sphaerosiderite: *Minerals 10*

sphalerite: *Standard Gems 21*

sphene: *Standard Gems 21*

sphenoid bone: *Bones 12*

sphere: *Jewelry 21; Spaceship Shapes 22*

spherocobaltite: *Minerals 10*

sphinx: *Beast 16; Fantasy Creatures with Symbolic Meaning 19; Horror Locations 23; Magical Transportation 17; Mythical Creatures and Monsters 16*

Sphinx: *Real Places Steeped in Legend or Mystery 18; Unique Property 3*

sphinx-andro: *Beast 16*

sphinx-crio: *Beast 16*

sphinx-gyno: *Beast 16*

sphinx-hiera: *Beast 16*

sphinxlike: *Magic Vocabulary 17*

Sphynx: *Domestic Cats 15*

spice chest: *Containers and Vessels 5*

spice grinder: *Appliances 5; Kitchen Equipment 5*

spice tree: *Deciduous Trees 10*

spice: *Allergies 12; Cake 6*

spicebush: *Shrubs 10*

spiced apples: *Pickled/Relish 6*

spices: *Food 6; Wizard's Goods 5*

spicules: *Astronomy General Terms 11*

spicy: *Smells 20*

spider lily: *Garden Bulbs 10*

spider on a wedding dress: *Harbingers/Charms for Good Luck 19*

spider web: *Halloween 19; Wizard's Goods 5*

spider: *Animals with Symbolic Meaning 19; Giant Creatures 16; Kitchen Equipment 5; New World Monkeys 15; Solitaire Card Games 5; Wizard's Goods 5*

spiders: *Animals 15; Travel Hazards 9*

spiderwort: *Garden Perennials 10*

spigot mortar: *Mortar 8*

spike harrow: *General Farm Equipment*

spike maul: *Hand Tools 5*

spike: *Fasteners 5; Garden Annuals 10; Hand Tools 5; Hardware 5; Pointed Weapons 7; Traps 3*

spiked buckler: *Shield Types 7*

spiked club: *Bludgeons 7*

spiked gauntlet: *Hand Weapons 7*

spiked loosestrife: *Weeds 10*

spiked mace: *Bludgeons 7*

spiked water milfoil: *Weeds 10*

spiked: *Hair Style 1*

spikes: *General Survival Gear 5*

spilled milk: *Harbingers of Bad Luck 19*

spilled red wine: *Harbingers of Bad Luck 19*

spilled salt: *Harbingers of Bad Luck 19*

spin: *Locomotion 9*

spinach soufflé: *Vegetables Cooked 6*

spinach: *Salads 6; Vegetables 6*

spinal cord: *Organs/Major Structures 12*

spindle: *Shrubs 10*

spindly: *Small/Thin 1*

spine: *Body Parts 12*

spine-bellied: *Sea Snake 15*

spine-chilling: *Horror Vocabulary 23*

spinel: *Cat's Eye Gems 21; Minerals 10; Standard Gems 21*

spineless: *Horror Vocabulary 23*

spinelessness: *General Emotions 20*

spinet: *String Musical Instruments*

spinnaker: *Boat/Ship Anatomy 9*

spinner: *Dolphins 15; Fishing Gear 5*

Spinone Italiano: *Dog Breeds 15*

spinosaurus: *Commonly Known Dinosaurs 15*

spiny monkey-orange: *Unusual Edible Fruits 6*

spiny: *Freshwater Turtles 15; Newts 15*

spiny-headed: *Sea Snake 15*

spinytail lizard: *Scaled Reptiles 15*

spiraea: *Shrubs 10*

spiral galaxy: *Astronomy General Terms 11*

spiral notebook: *Office/School/Writing Supplies 5*

spiral: *Pasta 6; Symbols in Magic and Religion 19*

spirea: *Garden Perennials 10*

spirit level: *Architectural/Engineering Tools 5*

spirit naga: *Beast 16*

spirit of motion: *Angels Common Terms 14*

spirit orb: *Paranormal Occurrences 21*

spirit writing: *Fortune Telling General Techniques 19*

Spirit: *Major Lines 19*

spirit: *Philosophy Basic Concepts 14; Travel Types 22; Undead 16*

spirited: *Fast 20; Happy 20*

spirits rise from graves: *Horror Plot Devices 23*

spiritual doorway: *Travel Modes 23*

spiritual energy: *Energy Sources/Types 24*

spiritual: *Magic Vocabulary 17*

spiritual guide: *Wizard 1*

spiritualism: *Philosophy Basic Concepts 14*

spiritualist: *Cleric 1; Fortune Teller 1; Wizard 1*

spit in the ocean: *Poker Card Games 5*

spit: *Card Games 5; Coastal and Oceanic 10*

Spitaler: *Comets 11*

spite and malice: *Card Games 5*

spiteful: *Negative 1*

spitting: *Cobra 15; Objects that Offer Protection 19; Precipitation 10*

spitzer: *Card Games 5*

splash cup: *Cave Anatomy 10*

spleen: *Organs/Major Structures 12*

splendid: *Positive 1*

splint mail: *Armor Types 7*

split ends: *Hair Types 1*

Split Level: *Architectural Styles 3*

split ring and wire: *Fishing Gear 5*

split sole jazz: *Dance Shoes 13*

splits: *Dance Moves 13*

splitting maul: *Hand Tools 5*

splitting the group: *Common Dangers 23*

splitting the party: *Common Dangers 24*

splitting wedge: *Hand Tools 5*

spodic soil: *Soil General Vocabulary 10*

spodumene: *Standard Gems 21*

spoil: *Harm 20*

spoiled daughter/son tortures parents: *Horror Plot Devices 23*

spoiled food: *Travel Hazards 9*

spoiled son commits murder and escapes consequences: *Western Plot Devices 21*

Sponde: *Moons 11*

sponge roller: *Hair Accessories 2*

sponge: *Cake 6; Cleaning Supplies/Gadgets 5; Fungus Common Names 10*

spongework: *Cave Anatomy 10*

spongy: *Wet 20*

spontoon: *Spears 7*

spooked animal: *Paranormal Occurrences 21*

spooky carnival ride turns deadly: *Horror Plot Devices 23*

spooky noises: *Halloween 19*

spool-turned: *Tables 4*

spoon rest: *Kitchen Equipment 5*

spoon: *Eating Utensils 5; Fishing Gear 5; Kitchen Utensils 5*

spoonbread: *Bread General Varieties 6*

spoons: *Card Games 5*

spork: *Eating Utensils 5*

sport coat: *Men's Wear 2*

sporting goods: *Equipment and Tools 5*

sporting: *Dog Groups 15; Personality Other 1*

sports bra: *Ladies' Wear 2*

sports car: *Motorized 9; Spy Gear 5*

sports center: *Entertainment Property 3*

sports club: *Entertainment Property 3*

sports occupations: *Character Building 1*

sports reporter: *Publishing 1*

sportscaster: *Media 1*

sportswear: *Styles of Dress 2*

sporty: *Styles of Dress 2*

spot fish: *Wild Saltwater Fish 15*

spot hearts: *Card Games 5*

spotfin croaker: *Wild Saltwater Fish 15*

spotlight: *Technical Terms 13*

spot-nosed monkey: *Old World Monkeys 15*

spots: *Pigs 15*

spotted knapweed: *Weeds 10*

spotted little: *Owls 15*

spotted mandarin: *Aquarium Saltwater Fish 15*

spotted moray: *Wild Saltwater Fish 15*

spotted oak: *Deciduous Trees 10*

spotted owlet: *Owls 15*

spotted parsley: *Poisonous Plants 10*

spotted pond: *Freshwater Turtles 15*

spotted scorpion: *Wild Saltwater Fish 15*

spotted seatrout: *Wild Saltwater Fish 15*

spotted: *Bats 15; Dolphins 15; Newts 15; Owls 15; Python 15; Salamanders 15*

spouse: *Relational 1*

SPR-2 8×8 electronic warfare vehicle: *Russia Military Vehicles 8*

sprain: *Injuries/Medical Emergencies 12*

spray cheese in a can: *Cheese Common Varieties 6*

spray: *Precipitation 10; Smells 20*

sprayer: *General Farm Equipment*

spreader: *Kitchen Utensils 5*

spreading ridges: *Geography General Vocabulary 10*

spreadsheet: *Laboratory Supplies 5*

spree: *Journey 20*

spriggan: *General Fae 16; Shapechanger 16*

sprightly: *Mobility 1*

spring agaricus: *Fungus Common Names 10*

spring birch: *Deciduous Trees 10*

spring bud: *Green 20*

spring clean: *Clean 20*

spring green: *Green 20*

spring tine harrow: *Horse Drawn Farm Equipment*

spring: *Cave Anatomy 10; Easter 19; Fluvial 10; Four Seasons 19; Locomotion 9; Meteorology General Vocabulary 10*

spring-blade: *Traps 3*

Springfield 1903: *Bolt Action Centerfire Rifles 7*

Springfield 1911A-1: *Pistol Semiautomatic 7*

Springfield M1A: *Semiautomatic Centerfire Rifles 7*

spring-loaded: *Traps 3*

sprinkler: *Garden Tools*

sprint: *Locomotion 9*

Spruance class: *U.S. Navy Vessels 8*

Spruce Hole Bog New Hampshire: *Bogs of North America 10*

spruce pine: *Evergreen Trees 10*

sprung floor: *Dance Equipment 13*

spry: *Fast 20; Mobility 1*

spurge: *Garden Perennials 10*

spurred snapdragon: *Wildflowers 10*

spurs: *Western Clothing/Dress 21*

spurt: *Smells 20; Wet 20*

spy camera: *Spy Gear 5*

spy gear: *Equipment and Tools 5*

spy: *Castle Inhabitants and Personnel 1; General Combat Vocabulary 7; General Occupations 1; Hero or Villain, Depending Upon Circumstance 20*

spyglass: *Optics 5*

spying: *General Combat Vocabulary 7*

squab: *Poultry Types 6*

squad: *General Combat Vocabulary 7*

squadron leader: *Armed Forces Other Titles 8*

squadron: *General Combat Vocabulary 7*

squall line: *Meteorology General Vocabulary 10*

squall: *Severe Weather 10; Water Terms 9; Wind 10*

square cake pan: *Kitchen Equipment 5*

square chain: *Embroidery Stitches 2*

square dance (United States): *Ethnic/Folk Dances 13*

square knot: *Sailing Knots 9*

square: *Architectural/Engineering Tools 5; Cake 6; Chin 1; Face 1; Figures Associated with Symbols 19; Gem Cuts 21; Hand Shapes 19; Shield Types 7; Symbols of Freemasonry 19*

squarespot anthias: *Aquarium Saltwater Fish 15*

squash blossom: *Vegetables 6*

squat: *Small/Fragile 20; Small/Thin 1*

squeak: *Sounds 20; Speak 20*

squeaky: *Vocal/Speech Quality 1*

squeal: *Speak 20*

squeegee: *Cleaning Supplies/Gadgets 5*

squeeze: *Cave Anatomy 10*

squid: *Animals 15; Giant Creatures 16*

squill: *Garden Bulbs 10*

squint: *Castle Anatomy 3*

squinty: *Eye Type 1*

squire fish: *Wild Saltwater Fish 15*

squire: *Castle Inhabitants and Personnel 1; Common Character Archetypes 21; Fighter 1; Knight 1*

squirl: *Wild Saltwater Fish 15*

squirrel: *New World Monkeys 15; Wild Game 6*

squirrelfish: *Aquarium Saltwater Fish 15*

squishy: *Wet 20*

Sri Lankan: *Pit Viper 15*

S-shaped: *Seating 4*

St. Andrew's Cross: *Venomous Arachnids 15*

St. Andrew's: *Crosses 19*

St. Elmo's fire: *Boat/Ship Terminology 9; Meteorology General Vocabulary 10; Mysterious Occurrences 18*

St. John's wort: *Garden Perennials 10; Objects that Offer Protection 19; Weeds 10*

St. John's: *Crosses 19*

St. Nicholas: *Christmas 19*

St. Patrick: *St. Patrick's Day 19*

St. Patrick's Day: *Holidays 19*

St. Peter's: *Crosses 19*

staazer: *Cheese International Varieties 6*

stab: *Attack 7*

stable boy: *Animal/Equestrian 1; Common Character Archetypes 21*

stable footing: *Moves 7*

stable manager: *Animal/Equestrian 1*

stable master: *Animal/Equestrian 1*

stable: *Christmas 19; Farm/Outbuilding 3; Flies 15; Man-Made Animal Homes 15; Property Features 3*

stablehand: *Castle Inhabitants and Personnel 1*

stack: *Cake 6; Coastal and Oceanic 10*

stacked heels: *Footwear/Shoes 2*

stadium: *Entertainment Property 3*

Staff of Moses: *Christian Relics 14*

staff of Tiresias: *Objects 18*

staff sergeant: *U.S. Air Force Enlisted 8; U.S. Army Enlisted 8; U.S. Marines Enlisted 8*

staff sling: *Missile Weapons 7*

staff vine: *Shrubs 10*

staff: *Bludgeons 7; Notation 13; Objects in Magic and Religion 19; Typical Magical Objects 17*

staffelite: *Minerals 10*

Staffordshire Bull Terrier: *Dog Breeds 15*

stag: *Animals with Symbolic Meaning 19*

stage coach robbery: *Western Plot Devices 21*

stage coach: *Animal-Powered Transportation 9; Western Paraphernalia/People 21*

stage directions: *The Arts 13*

stage left: *Stage Directions 13*

stage manager: *Performing Arts 1*

stage right: *Stage Directions 13*

stage terms: *The Arts 13*

stage: *Amusement Park/Carnival/Circus/Fair 3; Building Elements and Features 3; Parts of the Theater 13*

stagger: *Locomotion 9*

staghorn sumac: *Deciduous Trees 10*

stagnosol: *Soil General Vocabulary 10*

stained glass: *Building Elements and Features 3; Windows 3*

stained: *Teeth 1*

staircase: *Building Elements and Features 3; Traps 3*

stairway: *Building Elements and Features 3*

stairwell: *Building Elements and Features 3*

staking a claim: *Western Paraphernalia/People 21*

stalactite: *Cave Anatomy 10; Minerals 10*

stalagmite: *Cave Anatomy 10; Minerals 10*

stale: *Smells 20*

stalemate: *General Combat Vocabulary 7*

stalk: *General Combat Vocabulary 7; Paranormal Activity 21*

stalker: *Common Dangers 23; Horror Plot Devices 23; Thief 1*

stall market: *General Property 3*

stall: *Farm/Outbuilding 3; Rooms 3*

stallion: *Horses 15*

stalwart: *Hero 20; Personality Other 1*

stamatini: *Cheese International Varieties 6*

stamp out: *Kill 20*

stampede: *Locomotion 9*

stand mixer: *Appliances 5*

stand: *Special Purpose Furniture 4*

standard electrode potential: *Chemistry General Vocabulary 11*

standard electrodes: *Chemistry General Vocabulary 11*

standard entropy: *Chemistry General Vocabulary 11*

standard molar enthalphy of formation: *Chemistry General Vocabulary 11*

Standard Poodle: *Dog Breeds 15*

standard reaction: *Chemistry General Vocabulary 11*

Standardbred: *Horse Breeds 15*

stand-by: *Stage Terms 13*

standing cupboard: *Storage 4*

standing cypress: *Wildflowers 10*

standing rib roast: *Beef 6*

standing rigging: *Boat/Ship Anatomy 9*

standing wine cups: *Garden Perennials 10*

standup collar: *Garment Pieces 2*

stand-up comedian: *Bard 1*

stannane: *Dangerous Chemicals 11*

staple gun: *Hand Tools 5*

staple product: *Geography General Vocabulary 10*

staple puller: *Office/School/Writing Supplies 5*

staple: *Fix 20*

stapler: *Office/School/Writing Supplies 5*

staples: *Food 6; Hand Tools 5; Office/School/Writing Supplies 5*

star and crescent: *Symbols in Magic and Religion 19*

star anise: *Shrubs 10; Spices 6*

star apple: *Unusual Edible Fruits 6*

star cluster: *Astronomy General Terms 11; Star Systems 11*

star colony planner: *Occupations 22*

star fortification: *Fortification 3*

star fruit: *Tropical/Exotic Fruits 6*

star muscovite: *Minerals 10*

Star of David: *Religious Items 5; Symbols in Magic and Religion 19*

star of lakshmi: *Symbols in Magic and Religion 19*

star quartz: *Minerals 10*

star ruby: *Minerals 10*

star sapphire: *Minerals 10*

star: *Astronomy General Terms 11; Christmas 19; Elf 1; Figures Associated with Symbols 19; Hero 20*

starboard: *Boat/Ship Terminology 9*

starburst ice plant: *Garden Perennials 10*

Starchild Skull of Chihuahua: *Real Objects Not Fully Understood 18*

starch-root: *Poisonous Plants 10*

stargazer: *Wild Saltwater Fish 15*

starleaf gum: *Deciduous Trees 10*

starlite: *Minerals 10*

starry flounder: *Wild Saltwater Fish 15*

starry: *Wild Saltwater Fish 15*

starship captain: *Occupations 22*

starship marine: *Occupations 22*

starship trooper: *Occupations 22*

starship: *Spaceship Types 22*

startle: *Horror Vocabulary 23*

starve: *Harm 20*

starving village refused aid by rich family: *Western Plot Devices 21*

stashburns: *Facial Hair Beard 1*

stasis pod: *Devices 22*

stasis: *Travel Types 22*

statant: *Air Creatures 19; Land Creatures 19*

state: *Political Divisions 10; Speak 20*

statement: *Philosophy Basic Concepts 14*

static mixer: *Laboratory Equipment 5*

statice: *Garden Annuals 10; Garden Perennials 10*

station wagon: *Motorized 9*

stationary front: *Meteorology General Vocabulary 10*

stationary steam engine: *Steam Powered Farm Equipment*

stationery: *Office/School/Writing Supplies 5*

Stations of the Cross: *Rituals 14*

Statue of Liberty: *Unique Property 3*

Statue of Zeus at Olympia: *Seven Wonders of the Ancient World 18; Unique Property Destroyed 3*

statue: *Decorative Objects 4*

statuesque: *Beautiful 20*

statuette: *Decorative Objects 4*

stave oak: *Deciduous Trees 10*

stays: *Men's Wear 2*

steady state theory: *Astronomy General Terms 11*

steak knife: *Eating Utensils 5; Improvised Weapons 7; Kitchen Utensils 5*

steak: *Beef 6*

steal war: *Card Games 5*

stealer: *Thief 1*

stealth bomber: *Military Aircraft 8*

stealth fighter: *Military Aircraft 8*

steam blast: *Traps 3*

steam box: *Power Tools*

steam cleaner: *Cleaning Supplies/Gadgets 5*

steam engine: *Railroad 9*

steam frigate: *Military Watercraft 8*

steam powered farm equipment: *Equipment and Tools 5*

steam tractor: *Steam Powered Farm Equipment*

steam: *Cooking Techniques 20; Elemental 16; Energy Sources/Types 22; Energy Sources/Types 24; Sewing Techniques 2; Smells 20; Wet 10*

steamer trunk: *Storage 4*

steamer: *Sewing Equipment 2*

steampunk: *Horror Genres 23; Spaceship Drive Systems 22*

steamship round: *Beef 6*

steamy: *Wet 10*

steatite: *Minerals 10*

steel blue: *Blue 20*

steel guitar: *String Musical Instruments*

steel horn: *Wind/Woodwind and Brass Musical Instruments*

steel wool: *Hand Tools 5*

steel worker: *Construction 1*

steel: *Coins and Currency 21; Door Materials 3; Shield Types 7*

steel-jawed: *Traps 3*

steel-string guitar: *String Musical Instruments*

steep: *Grade/Slope 10*

steeple: *Church Anatomy 3*

steer: *Boat/Ship Terminology 9*

steering: *Boat/Ship Terminology 9*

stegosaur: *Dinosaur Types 15*

stegosaurus: *Commonly Known Dinosaurs 15*

steirerkase: *Cheese International Varieties 6*

Stejneger's bamboo: *Pit Viper 15*

stellar black hole: *Star Types and Relatives 11*

stellar nursery: *Star Types and Relatives 11*

stellar transport portal: *Installations 22*

stellar wind: *Astronomy General Terms 11*

stem lettuce: *Vegetables 6*

stench: *Smells 20*

stencil machine: *Office/School Machines 5*

stencil: *Art Tools 5*

stencils: *Office/School/Writing Supplies 5*

steno pad: *Office/School/Writing Supplies 5*

stenographer pad: *Office/School/Writing Supplies 5*

stenotype: *Office/School Machines 5*

stentorian: *Vocal/Speech Quality 1*

step ladder: *Large Tools*

step: *Gem Cuts 21; Locomotion 9*

stepbrother: *Male 1*

stepdaughter: *Female 1*

stepfather: *Male 1*

stephanandra: *Shrubs 10*

Stephano: *Moons 11*

stepmother: *Female 1*

stepparent: *Common Character Archetypes 21*

stepped: *Castle Anatomy 3*

stepping stones: *Landscaping 3*

stepping: *Dance Styles 13*

steps: *Building Elements and Features 3*

stepsister/brother: *Common Character Archetypes 21*

stepsister: *Female 1*

stepson: *Male 1*

stereo: *Electronics 4*

stereoscope: *Optics 5*

sterilize: *Clean 20*

sterling silver: *Precious Metals 21*

stern castle: *Boat/Ship Anatomy 9*

stern: *Boat/Ship Terminology 9*

sternum: *Bones 12*

Stetson hat: *Headgear 2*

Stevens Cadet: *Bolt Action Rimfire Rifles 7*

Stevens model 30: *Single Shot Rimfire Rifles 7*

Stevens model 512: *Shotguns Over/Under 7*

stew: *Cooking Techniques 20; Meals 6; Wet 20*

steward: *Fighter 1; General Occupations 1*

stewardess: *Transportation 1*

steyned: *Castle Anatomy 3*

Steyr AUG: *Semiautomatic Centerfire Rifles 7*

STI Spartan Lawman: *Pistol Semiautomatic 7*

STI Texican: *Revolver Single Action 7*

stick figure: *Figures Associated with Symbols 19*

stick of dynamite: *Classic Items 23*

Stick: *Architectural Styles 3*

stick: *Fix 20*

sticky notes: *Office/School/Writing Supplies 5*

sticky: *Traps 3; Weapons 22; Wet 20*

stiff vervain: *Wildflowers 10*

stiff: *Mobility 1; Vocal/Speech Quality 1*

stigma: *Unattractive 20*

stiletto: *Daggers and Knives 7; Flies 15; General Snake Families 15*

stilettos: *Footwear/Shoes 2*

still life: *Art Genres 13*

still: *Easy 20; Quiet 20*

stilton: *Cheese Common Varieties 6*

stilts: *Footwear/Shoes 2*

Stimson's: *Python 15*

stimulate: *Teach 20*

sting: *Harm 20*

stinger grenade: *SWAT Equipment 7*

stinger: *Cocktails 6; Injuries/Medical Emergencies 12*

stink horn with face fly: *Fungus Common Names 10*

stink: *Smells 20*

stinking cedar: *Evergreen Trees 10*

stinking nutmeg: *Deciduous Trees 10*

stinking yew: *Evergreen Trees 10*

stinking: *Unattractive 20*

stinkpot musk: *Freshwater Turtles 15*

stinkweed: *Poisonous Plants 10*

stir bar: *Laboratory Equipment 5*

stir fry: *Cooking Techniques 20*

stirge: *Beast 16*

stirring rod: *Laboratory Equipment 5*

stirrup/stapes: *Bones 12*

stitch kit: *Shoe Accessories 13*

stitch: *Card Games 5*

STOBAR aircraft carrier: *Military Watercraft 8*

stock broker: *Finance 1*

stock exchange: *Special Purpose Structure 3*

stock market crash of 1929: *Legendary Events 18*

stock ticker: *Office/School Machines 5*

stockade: *Castle Anatomy 3; Fortification 3; Prison 3*

stocking cap: *Headgear 2*

stocking gun: *Derringer 7*

stocking: *Christmas 19*

stockings: *Ladies' Wear 2; Objects/Activities Connected to Lore 19*

stockpot: *Kitchen Equipment 5*

stockroom: *Business Property 3; Rooms 3*

stockyard: *Business Property 3*

Stoeger Coach: *Shotguns Side-by-Side 7*

Stoeger Cougar 8000: *Pistol Semiautomatic 7*

stoicism: *Philosophy Basic Concepts 14*

Stoke's aster: *Garden Perennials 10*

Stokes's: *Sea Snake 15*

stole: *Religious Dress 2*

stolen luggage: *Travel Hazards 9*

stolen magical item: *Fantasy Plot Devices 24*

stolen religious object lashes back: *Horror Plot Devices 23*

stollen: *Bread General Varieties 6; Christmas 19*

stomach turning: *Unattractive 20*

stomach: *Organs/Major Structures 12*

Stone Age: *Art Movements 13; Styles of Dress 2*

stone and ring of Eluned the Fortunate: *Thirteen Treasures of the Island of Britain 18*

Stone Canyon jasper: *Minerals 10*

stone giant: *Humanlike Groups 1*

stone golem: *Construct 16*

stone holy symbol: *Religious Items 5*

stone jug: *Kitchen Equipment 5*

stone meteorite: *Astronomy General Terms 11*

stone picker: *General Farm Equipment*

stone spheres of Costa Rica: *Real Objects Not Fully Understood 18*

stone: *Art Materials 5; Art Media 13; Axes 7; Door Materials 3; Elemental 16; Exterior Building Materials 3; Giant Humanoids 16; Interior Building Materials 3; Missile Loads 7*

stonecrop sedum: *Garden Perennials 10*

stonecrop: *Objects that Offer Protection 19*

Stonehenge: *Horror Locations 23; Real Places Steeped in Legend or Mystery 18; Seven Wonders of the Middle Ages 18; Unique Property 3*

stool pigeon: *General Occupations 1*

stool: *Excrement 12*

stop thrust: *Fencing Vocabulary 7*

stop: *Close/Hold 20; Commands 20; Expletives 20*

stopper knot: *Sailing Knots 9*

stopper: *Laboratory Equipment 5*

stops: *Card Games 5*

stopwatch: *Timekeeping 5*

storage box: *Office/School/Writing Supplies 5*

storage shed: *Farm/Outbuilding 3*

storage: *Military Property 3*

store: *Business Property 3*

storehouse: *Business Property 3*

storeroom: *Business Property 3*

stork: *Animals with Symbolic Meaning 19; Other Wild Birds 15*

stork's bill: *Garden Perennials 10*

storm cellar: *Farm/Outbuilding 3*

storm giant: *Humanlike Groups 1*

storm harbors evil entity: *Horror Plot Devices 23*

storm lamp: *Illumination/Light Sources 5*

storm surge: *Severe Weather 10*

storm tracks: *Meteorology General Vocabulary 10*

storm: *Doors 3; Giant Humanoids 16; Moves 7; Severe Weather 10; Windows 3*

Storybook: *Architectural Styles 3*

storybook: *Books/Publications 5*

storyteller: *Academic 1*

stout: *Beer 6; Large/Heavy 1*

stove: *Major Appliances 4*

stovepipe: *Building Elements and Features 3*

stovepipe hat: *Headgear 2*

STOVL aircraft carrier: *Military Watercraft 8*

stowaway: *Common Character Archetypes 21*

straight jacket: *Special Purpose Clothing 2*

straight razor: *Personal Care 5*

straight skirt: *Ladies' Wear 2*

straight: *Eyebrows 1; Hair Types 1*

straightedge: *Architectural/Engineering Tools 5*

straighten: *Fix 20*

straightened: *Hair Treated 1*

straightforward: *Easy 20*

strainer: *Kitchen Equipment 5*

strait: *Coastal and Oceanic 10*

stranded after car breaks down: *Horror Plot Devices 23*

stranded space traveler: *Plot Devices 22*

strange antique harbors evil force: *Horror Plot Devices 23*

strange big-eared brown: *Bats 15*

stranger/angel aids desperate family: *Western Plot Devices 21*

stranger/angel teaches a lesson: *Western Plot Devices 21*

strangle: *Harm 20*

strangled: *Vocal/Speech Quality 1*

strangling vine: *Plant 16*

Strangmoor Bog Michigan: *Bogs of North America 10*

strap: *Garment Pieces 2; Jewelry 21; Music Accessories*

strapless bra: *Ladies' Wear 2*

strapping: *Large 20; Large/Heavy 1*

strategic goal: *General Combat Vocabulary 7*

strategic offensive: *General Combat Vocabulary 7*

strategize: *Solve 20*

strath: *Slope 10*

stratigraphic mapping: *Geological Field Work Methods 10*

stratigraphy: *Geologic Fields of Study 10*

stratocruiser: *Spaceship Types 22*

stratocumulus: *Clouds 10*

stratosphere: *Meteorology General Vocabulary 10*

stratovolcano: *Volcanic 10*

stratus: *Clouds 10*

straw hat: *Headgear 2*

straw mushroom: *Fungus Common Names 10*

straw: *Cave Anatomy 10; Eating Utensils 5; Hair Color 1*

strawberries: *Ice Cream Toppings 6*

strawberry blond: *Hair Color 1*

strawberry blossom weevil: *Beetle 15*

strawberry pear: *Unusual Edible Fruits 6*

strawberry quartz: *Standard Gems 21*

strawberry shortcake: *Miscellaneous Dessert 6*

strawberry: *Aphrodisiacs 19; Berries 6; Garden Perennials 10; Ice Cream Flavors 6; Jam/Jelly/Preserves 6; Pie 6; Plants with Symbolic Meaning 19*

strawflower: *Garden Annuals 10*

stray eyelash: *Harbingers/Charms for Good Luck 19*

stream pool: *Fluvial 10*

stream sink: *Cave Anatomy 10*

stream tin: *Minerals 10*

stream: *Fluvial 10; Water Features 10; Water Terms 9; Wet 20*

streambed: *Cave Anatomy 10*

streaming: *Precipitation 10*

streamlet: *Water Features 10*

street painting: *Art Genres 13*

street poster: *Art Genres 13*

street urchin: *Supporting Cast 24*

street: *Art Genres 13; Roads 9*

streetcar: *Animal-Powered Transportation 9*

streetwalker: *Styles of Dress 2*

strength: *Physical Mutations 22*

strenuous: *Difficult 20*

streptococcal infection: *Diseases 12*

stress: *Christmas 19*

stress-free: *Easy 20*

stressful: *Sad 20*

stretch: *Fabric 2*

stretcher: *Human-Powered Transportation 9*

stretto: *General Music Vocabulary 13*

streusel: *Cake 6; Ice Cream Mix-ins 6; Muffin 6; Pie 6*

stride: *Locomotion 9*

strident: *Loud 20; Vocal/Speech Quality 1*

strigae: *Demon 16*

strike: *Attack 7; Cave Anatomy 10; General Combat Vocabulary 7*

striker: *Laboratory Equipment 5*

striking: *Air Creatures 19; Beautiful 20*

string bass: *String Musical Instruments*

string tie: *Western Clothing/Dress 21*

string trimmer: *Power Tools*

string: *Bog Types 10; Cheese Common Varieties 6; Fasteners 5; Kitchen Equipment 5; Musical Instrument Parts 13; Wizard's Goods 5*

stringbean: *Small/Thin 1*

stringendo: *Tempo/Mood 13*

strip binding supplies: *Office/School/Writing Supplies 5*

strip club: *Entertainment Property 3*

strip farming: *Soil General Vocabulary 10*

strip mall: *Business Property 3*

strip: *Poker Card Games 5; Roads 9*

stripe: *Fabric Patterns 2*

striped bass: *Wild Saltwater Fish 15*

striped burrfish: *Aquarium Saltwater Fish 15*

striped maple: *Deciduous Trees 10*

striped marlin: *Wild Saltwater Fish 15*

striped minnow: *Wild Saltwater Fish 15*

striped oak: *Deciduous Trees 10*

striped: *Bats 15; Dolphins 15; Owls 15*

stripe-faced: *Bats 15*

stripling: *Male 1*

stroganoff: *Meals 6*

stroke: *Injuries/Medical Emergencies 12*

stroll: *Journey 20; Locomotion 9*

strong electrolyte: *Chemistry General Vocabulary 11*

strong: *Chin 1; Large/Heavy 1; Personality Other 1*

strongbox: *Containers and Vessels 5*

stronghold: *Fortification 3*

strongpoint: *Fortification 3*

strontian: *Minerals 10*

Strontium: *Elements 11*

struck by falling object: *Injuries/Medical Emergencies 12*

structural bench: *Erosion 10*

structural geology: *Geologic Fields of Study 10*

structural isomers: *Chemistry General Vocabulary 11*

structural mapping: *Geological Field Work Methods 10*

structural terrace: *Erosion 10*

Structuralism: *Architectural Styles 3*

structure: *Fix 20*

strut: *Locomotion 9*

struth: *Expletives 20*

strüverite: *Minerals 10*

strychnine sulfate: *Dangerous Chemicals 11*

strychnine tree: *Poisonous Plants 10*

strychnine: *Dangerous Chemicals 11*

stubble: *Facial Hair Beard 1*

stubborn: *Character Building 1; Difficult 20*

stubby: *Nose 1; Small/Thin 1*

stucco: *Exterior Building Materials 3*

stud earring: *Jewelry 2*

stud: *Beautiful 20; Embellishments 2; Jewelry 21; Poker Card Games 5*

studded leather: *Armor Types 7; Horse Barding Materials 7*

student bitten by vampire: *Horror Plot Devices 23*

student union: *Academic Property 3*

student: *Academic 1; Styles of Dress 2*

studio: *Art Genres 13; Business Property 3, Rooms 3*

study: *Composition Types 13; Learn 20; Paranormal Activity 21; Rooms 3; Solve 20*

stuffed animal: *Toys 5*

stuffed pepper: *Meals 6*

stuffed pork chop: *Meals 6*

stuffing: *Bread General Varieties 6; Thanksgiving 19*

stulchak: *Dance Moves 13*

stumble: *Locomotion 9*

stump puffball: *Fungus Common Names 10*

stump: *Coastal and Oceanic 10*

stun grenade: *SWAT Equipment 7*

stun: *Attack 7; Moves 7; Weapons 22*

stunning: *Beautiful 20; Weapons 22*

stupa: *Religious Building 3*

stupefy: *Magic Vocabulary 17*

stupendous: *Beautiful 20; Large 20*

stupid: *Unintelligent 1*

Sturmgewehr 44: *Semiautomatic Centerfire Rifles 7*

Stuttgart soil: *Soil General Vocabulary 10*

sty: *Farm/Outbuilding 3; Man-Made Animal Homes 15*

stygian: *Owls 15*

style: *Philosophy Basic Concepts 14*

styles of dress: *Clothing 2*

stylish: *New 20; Personality Other 1*

stylolite: *Geological Vocabulary 10*

stylus: *Art Tools 5; Office/School/Writing Supplies 5*

Stymphalian birds: *Flying Creatures 16; Twelve Labors of Hercules 16*

styrax: *Shrubs 10*

subalpine fir: *Evergreen Trees 10*

subalpine larch: *Deciduous Trees 10*

subaqueous soil: *Soil General Vocabulary 10*

subarctic: *Climatic Zones 10; Climatic Zones Koeppen System 10*

subcompact: *Motorized 9*

subdivision: *Residential Property 3*

subdue: *Attack 7*

subdued: *Horror Vocabulary 23*

subdwarf: *Star Types and Relatives 11*

subgiant: *Star Types and Relatives 11*

subglacial mound: *Volcanic 10*

subject: *General Music Vocabulary 13; Philosophy Basic Concepts 14*

subjugated: *Horror Vocabulary 23*

subjugator: *Villain 20*

sublieutenant: *Navy Other Titles 8*

sublimation: *Chemistry General Vocabulary 11*

sublime: *Philosophy Basic Concepts 14*

submarine canyon: *Coastal and Oceanic 10*

submarine volcano: *Volcanic 10*

submarine: *Military Watercraft 8; Sandwiches 6; Travel Modes 23*

submariner: *Maritime Occupations 1*

submerge: *Locomotion 9*

submit: *General Combat Vocabulary 7*

subsidence: *Soil General Vocabulary 10*

subsoil: *Soil General Vocabulary 10*

subsoiler: *General Farm Equipment*

substance: *Chemistry General Vocabulary 11; Philosophy Basic Concepts 14*

substandard: *Sad 20*

substantial: *Large 20; Large/Heavy 1*

substitution: *Philosophy Basic Concepts 14; Poker Card Games 5*

subterranean vault: *Cemetery 3*

subtle: *Horror Vocabulary 23*

subtropical: *Climatic Zones 10; Meteorology General Vocabulary 10*

suburbs: *City 10*

subway: *Horror Locations 23; Mass Transit 9*

successfully negotiate: *Buy 20*

successor: *Relational 1*

succubus: *Demon 16; Fantasy Creatures with Symbolic Meaning 19*

succulent lupine: *Wildflowers 10*

sucker: *Candy General 6*

sucker-footed: *Bats 15*

suckiaug: *Soil General Vocabulary 10*

Sudan Country-Bred: *Horse Breeds 15*

Sudanese: *Human Ethnic Groups 1*

Sudarium of Oviedo: *Relics of Jesus 14*

Sudarshana Chakra: *Weapons of Legend 18*

sudden: *Fast 20*

suede cloth: *Fabric 2*

suevite: *Metamorphic Rocks 10*

suffering: *Philosophy Basic Concepts 14*

suffocate: *Harm 20*

Suffolk: *Horse Breeds 15*

sufi winged heart: *Symbols in Magic and Religion 19*

sugar apple: *Unusual Edible Fruits 6*

sugar bowl: *Containers and Vessels 5; Tableware 5*

sugar cane: *Farm/Outbuilding 3*

sugar cone: *Ice Cream Cones 6*

sugar glider: *Gliding Mammals 15*

sugar hackberry: *Deciduous Trees 10*

sugar loaf hat: *Headgear 2*

sugar maple: *Deciduous Trees 10*

sugar pine: *Evergreen Trees 10*

sugar snap peas: *Vegetables 6*

sugar spoon: *Eating Utensils 5*

sugar: *Ants 15; Cookie 6; Donut/doughnut 6; Mixers 6; Staples 6; Wizard's Goods 5*

sugarberry: *Deciduous Trees 10*

sugar-free: *Candy General 6; Ice Cream 6*

sugarplum: *Deciduous Trees 10*

sugilite: *Standard Gems 21*

suicide tree: *Poisonous Plants 10*

suisan marble: *Minerals 10*

suit: *Men's Wear 2; Unisex Clothing 2*

suitable: *Happy 20*

suitcase: *Containers and Vessels 5*

suite: *Composition Types 13*

sul ponticello: *Instrument Technique 13*

sulfotep: *Dangerous Chemicals 11*

sulfoxide: *Dangerous Chemicals 11*

sulfur cosmos: *Weeds 10*

sulfur dioxide: *Dangerous Chemicals 11*

sulfur tetrafluoride: *Dangerous Chemicals 11*

sulfur thrower: *Siege Engines 7*

sulfur trioxide: *Dangerous Chemicals 11*

Sulfur: *Elements 11*

sulfur: *Illumination Bulb and Tube Types 5; Minerals 10; Wizard's Goods 5*

sulfuric acid: *Dangerous Chemicals 11*

sulky: *Negative 1*

sullen: *Sad 20*

sullenness: *General Emotions 20*

sullied: *Bad 20; Unattractive 20*

sulphur flower: *Garden Perennials 10*

sulphur: *Butterfly 15*

sultana: *Unusual Edible Fruits 6*

sultanate: *Political Divisions 10*

sultry: *Warm 10*

suluguni: *Cheese International Varieties 6*

sulz: *Meals 6*

sumac: *Shrubs 10; Weeds 10*

Sumatran orangutan: *Apes 15*

Sumatran short-tailed: *Python 15*

Sumatran: *Tigers 15*

Sumerian pantheon: *Philosophy and Religion 14*

Sumerian: *Architectural Styles 3*

sumi paint: *Art Materials 5*

sumi-e: *Art Media 13*

summer kitchen: *Rooms 3*

summer snowflake: *Garden Bulbs 10*

summer solstice: *Garden Perennials 10; Witchcraft Vocabulary 17*

summer squash yellow: *Vegetables 6*

summer truffle: *Fungus Common Names 10*

summer: *Four Seasons 19; Meteorology General Vocabulary 10*

summery: *Warm 10*

summit: *Glacial and Mountain 10; Slope 10; Terrain Features 10*

summon: *Magic Vocabulary 17*

sump pump: *Building Systems 3*

sump: *Cave Anatomy 10*

sun bonnet: *Headgear 2; Western Clothing/Dress 21*

sun burning out: *Plot Devices 22*

sun catfish: *Aquarium Freshwater Fish 15*

sun daisy: *Garden Perennials 10*

sun dial fish: *Wild Saltwater Fish 15*

sun dog: *Meteorology General Vocabulary 10*

sun dress: *Ladies' Wear 2*

sun hat: *Headgear 2*

sun opal: *Minerals 10*

sun pillar: *Meteorology General Vocabulary 10*

sun protection: *Clothing/Uniforms 22*

sun rose: *Garden Perennials 10*

sun sign: *Symbols in Magic and Religion 19*

sun station: *Installations 22*

sun: *Bears 15; Beetle 15; Cake 6; Crosses 19; sun: Figures Associated with Symbols 19*

Sun: *Minor Lines 19; Mounts 19*

sunbeam: *General Snake Families 15*

sunbittern: *Other Wild Birds 15*

sunburn: *Injuries/Medical Emergencies 12; Travel Hazards 9*

sundae: *Ice Cream Desserts 6*

Sunday best: *Styles of Dress 2*

Sunday dress: *Western Clothing/Dress 21*

sundial: *Timekeeping 5*

sundrop: *Garden Perennials 10*

sunflower: *Garden Annuals 10; Garden Perennials 10; Oils 6; Plants with Symbolic Meaning 19; Seeds 6; Yellow 20*

sunglasses: *Accessories 2; Military Equipment 8*

sunglow: *Yellow 20*

sunken room: *Building Elements and Features 3*

sunken: *Cheeks 1*

sun-killer: *Weapons 22*

sunny side up: *Egg Styles 6*

sunray flower: *Garden Perennials 10*

sunrise: *Meteorology General Vocabulary 10*

sunset hyssop: *Garden Perennials 10*

sunset: *Meteorology General Vocabulary 10; Orange 20*

sunspot: *Astronomy General Terms 11*

sunstone: *Minerals 10; Standard Gems 21; Star Gems 21*

sunstroke: *Injuries/Medical Emergencies 12*

super highway: *Roads 9*

super villain: *Common Character Archetypes 21*

superb: *Beautiful 20*

supercarrier: *Military Watercraft 8*

supercell: *Meteorology General Vocabulary 10*

supercomputer: *Computer Equipment 5*

supercooled cloud droplets: *Snow Types 10*

supercooled liquids: *Chemistry General Vocabulary 11*

supercritical fluid: *Chemistry General Vocabulary 11*

superdreadnaught: *Military Watercraft 8*

superficial: *Small/Fragile 20*

superfine sugar: *Staples 6*

supergiant: *Astronomy General Terms 11; Star Types and Relatives 11*

superhero: *Common Character Archetypes 21; Science Fiction Genres 22*

superhuman: *Large 20*

superimpose: *Art Techniques 13*

super-intelligent being regards humans as vermin: *Horror Plot Devices 23*

superintendant: *Academic 1*

superior conjunction: *Astronomy General Terms 11*

superior planet: *Astronomy General Terms 11*

superior: *Good 20; Personality Other 1*

superlative: *Good 20*

supermarket: *Business Property 3*

supermax: *Prison 3*

supernatural powers used to terrorize others: *Horror Plot Devices 23*

supernatural: *Magic Vocabulary 17*

supernova remnant: *Astronomy General Terms 11*

supernova: *Astronomy General Terms 11; Star Types and Relatives 11*

supersaturated: *Cave Anatomy 10*

supersized: *Large 20*

superstore: *Business Property 3*

supervolcano: *Volcanic 10*

supper club: *Food/Drink Establishments 3*

supple: *Mobility 1*

supplier of wizards' goods: *Fantasy Occupations 24*

supply tender: *Spaceship Types 22*

support ring: *Laboratory Equipment 5*

support: *Agree 20*

supporter: *Elements 19*

supporting leg: *Ballet Terms 13*

supremacy: *General Combat Vocabulary 7*

Suprematívism: *Art Movements 13*

supreme court justice: *Legal Occupations 1*

sur les Demi-pointes: *Ballet Terms 13*

sur les Pointes: *Ballet Terms 13*

Surabaya Babi: *Pigs 15*

surah: *Fabric 2*

surem: *Demon 16*

surf: *Water Terms 9*

surface-to-air missile: *Spy Gear 5*

surface-to-air: *Air Force Missile 8*

surfboard: *Human-Powered Watercraft 9*

surficial mapping: *Geological Field Work Methods 10*

surge channel: *Coastal and Oceanic 10*

surge: *Meteorology General Vocabulary 10*

surgeon: *Medical Occupations 1*

surgeonfish: *Aquarium Saltwater Fish 15*

surgical center: *Health Care 3*

surgical scrubs: *Special Purpose Clothing 2*

surgical strike: *General Combat Vocabulary 7*

surgical: *Tables 4*

surili: *Old World Monkeys 15*

Surinam: *Toads 15*

surly: *Negative 1; Sad 20*

Surma (demigod of death): *Finnish Pantheon 14*

surprise attack: *General Combat Vocabulary 7*

surprise: *Attack 7; General Combat Vocabulary 7*

Surrealism: *Art Movements 13*

surrender: *General Combat Vocabulary 7; Moves 7*

surreptitious: *Magic Vocabulary 17*

surrey: *Animal-Powered Transportation 9*

surround sound system: *Electronics 4*

surround: *General Combat Vocabulary 7; Tactics 7*

Surtur: *Moons 11*

surveillance: *Art Genres 13; General Combat Vocabulary 7; Military Aircraft 8*

survey: *Paranormal Activity 21*

surveying of topographic features: *Geological Field Work Methods 10*

survival float: *Swimming Strokes 9*

survival gear: *Equipment and Tools 5*

survival travel stroke: *Swimming Strokes 9*

Surya (sun): *Indian Pantheon 14*

Susanoo-no-mikoto (water): *Japanese Pantheon 14*

sushi: *Fish/Seafood Meals 6*

suspect: *Horror Vocabulary 23*

suspenders: *Accessories 2*

suspense: *Performance Genres 13*

suspension: *Bridges 9; Chemistry General Vocabulary 11*

suspicious: *Horror Vocabulary 23; Personality Other 1*

Sussex Spaniel: *Dog Breeds 15*

Sussex: *Chickens 15; Other Cows 15*

sustainable yield: *Geography General Vocabulary 10*

sustaining: *Multiple Figures 19*

Suttungr: *Moons 11*

SUV: *Motorized 9*

suzette: *Vegetables Cooked 6*

Svalinn: *Shields 18*

swab: *Clean 20*

Swabian-Hall: *Pigs 15*

swaddling clothes: *Relics of Jesus 14*

swagger: *Locomotion 9*

Swahili: *Human Ethnic Groups 1*

swallow: *Animals with Symbolic Meaning 19; Backyard Birds 15*

swallowwort: *Weeds 10*

swamp bay: *Deciduous Trees 10*

swamp birch: *Deciduous Trees 10*

swamp blackgum: *Deciduous Trees 10*

swamp boat: *Small Watercraft 9*

swamp cedar: *Evergreen Trees 10*

swamp chestnut oak: *Deciduous Trees 10*

swamp cypress: *Evergreen Trees 10*

swamp heater: *Building Systems 3*

swamp hickory: *Deciduous Trees 10*

swamp holly: *Evergreen Trees 10*

swamp laurel oak: *Deciduous Trees 10*

swamp magnolia: *Deciduous Trees 10*

swamp milkweed: *Garden Perennials 10*

swamp monster: *Aquatic 16*

swamp oak: *Deciduous Trees 10*

swamp pine: *Evergreen Trees 10*

swamp post oak: *Deciduous Trees 10*

swamp red oak: *Deciduous Trees 10*

swamp Spanish oak: *Deciduous Trees 10*

swamp tupelo: *Deciduous Trees 10*

swamp water: *Cocktails 6; Wizard's Goods 5*

swamp white oak: *Deciduous Trees 10*

swamp willow oak: *Deciduous Trees 10*

swamp willow: *Deciduous Trees 10*

swamp: *Fluvial 10; Water Features 10; Water Terms 9*

swamping: *Boat/Ship Terminology 9*

swampland: *Water Features 10*

swan: *Animals with Symbolic Meaning 19; Other Wild Birds 15*

swarm: *Monster Categories/Terms 16*

swarmbot: *Robots 22*

swashbuckler: *Barbarian 1; Common Character Archetypes 21; Hero 20*

swastika: *Secular Symbols 19; Symbols in Magic and Religion 19*

SWAT equipment: *Combat, Armor, and Weapons 7*

SWAT team: *Law Enforcement 1*

SWAT weapons: *Combat, Armor, and Weapons 7*

swather: *General Farm Equipment*

sway: *Locomotion 9*

swazi casino: *Card Games 5*

Swazi: *Human Ethnic Groups 1*

sweat clothes: *Styles of Dress 2*

sweat pants: *Unisex Clothing 2*

sweat: *Bees 15; Cooking Techniques 20; Socks 2*

sweatband: *Headgear 2; Military Equipment 8*

sweater coat: *Ladies' Wear 2*

sweater dress: *Ladies' Wear 2*

sweater set: *Ladies' Wear 2*

sweater vest: *Unisex Clothing 2*

sweater: *Unisex Clothing 2*

sweatshirt: *Unisex Clothing 2*

Swede: *Human Ethnic Groups 1*

Swedish fish: *Candy General 6*

Swedish Friesian: *Other Cows 15*

Swedish landrace: *Pigs 15*

Swedish Red Polled: *Other Cows 15*

Swedish Red-and-White: *Other Cows 15*

Swedish Vallhund: *Dog Breeds 15*

Swedish Warmblood: *Horse Breeds 15*

sweep: *Clean 20*

sweeping compound: *Hardware 5*

sweeping: *Large 20; Objects/Activities Connected to Lore 19*

sweet Alyssum: *Wildflowers 10*

sweet apple-berry: *Unusual Edible Fruits 6*

sweet autumn clematis: *Garden Perennials 10*

sweet bay: *Deciduous Trees 10*

sweet bean locust: *Deciduous Trees 10*

sweet coneflower: *Garden Perennials 10*

sweet corn: *Vegetables 6*

sweet flag: *Garden Perennials 10*

sweet granadilla: *Unusual Edible Fruits 6*

sweet gum: *Deciduous Trees 10*

sweet lemon: *Unusual Edible Fruits 6*

sweet magnolia: *Deciduous Trees 10*

sweet marsala: *Wine Red 6*

sweet pea: *Garden Annuals 10; Garden Perennials 10*

sweet pecan: *Deciduous Trees 10*

sweet pepper: *Unusual Edible Fruits 6*

sweet pickle: *Pickled/Relish 6*

sweet pignut hickory: *Deciduous Trees 10*

sweet potato: *Vegetables 6*

sweet roll: *Bread General Varieties 6*

sweet tooth: *Fungus Common Names 10*

sweet William: *Garden Annuals 10; Garden Perennials 10; Wildflowers 10*

sweet woodruff: *Garden Perennials 10*

sweet: *Beautiful 20; Happy 20; Smells 20; Terms of Endearment 1*

sweetbread mushroom: *Fungus Common Names 10*

sweetbread: *Beef 6*

sweetfern: *Shrubs 10*

sweetheart: *Terms of Endearment 1*

sweetie pie: *Terms of Endearment 1*

sweetie: *Terms of Endearment 1*

sweetness: *General Emotions 20*

sweetshrub: *Shrubs 10*

sweetsop: *Unusual Edible Fruits 6*

sweet-sour: *Pickled/Relish 6*

sweetspire: *Shrubs 10*

sweetwater agate: *Minerals 10*

swell: *Buy 20; Meteorology General Vocabulary 10; Water Terms 9*

swellfront chest: *Storage 4*

swift movement: *Physical Mutations 22*

swift: *Backyard Birds 15; Fast 20; Foxes 15; Mobility 1*

swiftly: *Fast 20*

swim cap: *Headgear 2*

swim cover-up: *Ladies' Wear 2*

swim fins: *Footwear/Shoes 2*

swim suit: *Unisex Clothing 2*

swim trunks: *Men's Wear 2*

swim: *Locomotion 9*

swimming pool: *Property Features 3*

swimming strokes: *Transportation 9; Verbs 20*

swing: *Attack 7; Dance Styles 13*

swinging: *Doors 3*

swing-leg: *Tables 4*

swipe: *Attack 7*

swirl hole: *Cave Anatomy 10*

Swiss army knife: *Classic Items 23*

Swiss Chalet: *Architectural Styles 3*

Swiss chard: *Vegetables 6*

Swiss jass: *Card Games 5*

Swiss roll: *Cake 6*

Swiss steak: *Meals 6*

Swiss: *Cheese Common Varieties 6; Human Ethnic Groups 1*

switchback: *Grade/Slope 10*

switchblade: *Daggers and Knives 7*

switchboard: *Office/School Machines 5*

swivel: *Doors 3; Fishing Gear 5*

swivel-base: *Chairs and Stools 4*

swoosh: *Sounds 20*

sword arm: *Fencing Vocabulary 7*

sword cane: *Accessories 2; Spy Gear 5; Swords One-handed 7*

sword fighting: *Fencing Vocabulary 7*

sword hand: *Fencing Vocabulary 7*

sword in the stone: *Arthurian Objects 18*

sword of Atilla: *Weapons of Legend 18*

sword of Peleus: *Weapons of Legend 18*

sword of Rhydderch Hael: *Thirteen Treasures of the Island of Britain 18*

sword stick: *Swords One-handed 7*

swordfish: *Wild Saltwater Fish 15*

sword-nosed: *Bats 15*

swords: *Combat, Armor, and Weapons 7; Minor Arcana 19*

swordstaff: *Spears 7*

swordtail: *Aquarium Freshwater Fish 15*

Sworn Book of Honorius: *Books of Legend 18*

Sycamore fig: *Unusual Edible Fruits 6*

sycamore: *Deciduous Trees 10*

sycophant: *Followers 14*

Sycorax: *Moons 11*

Sydney Opera House: *Unique Property 3*

syenite: *Igneous Rocks 10*

symbol: *Jewelry 21; Philosophy Basic Concepts 14*

Symbolic Wedding Anniversary Gifts: *Superstitions 19*

Symbolism: *Art Movements 13*

symphonic poem: *Composition Types 13*

symphony: *Composition Types 13*

synagogue: *Religious Building 3*

synchronize: *Solve 20*

synchronized swimming: *Swimming Strokes 9*

synchronous rotation: *Astronomy General Terms 11*

synod: *Groupings 14*

synodic period: *Astronomy General Terms 11*

syntax: *Philosophy Basic Concepts 14*

synthesizer: *Electronic Musical Instruments 5*

synthetic resin: *Art Materials 5*

synthetic: *Philosophy Basic Concepts 14*

syphilis: *Diseases 12*

syrah: *Wine Red 6*

Syrian garnet: *Minerals 10*

Syrian: *Bears 15*

syrian: *Cheese International Varieties 6*

syrupy: *Wet 20*

szabla: *Swords One-handed 7*

–T–

T-1 Jayhawk trainer: *U.S. Air Force Aircraft 8*

T-34 trainer: *U.S. Navy Aircraft 8*

T-34: *Tanks Russian 8*

T-38 Talon: *U.S. Air Force Aircraft 8*

T-41 Mescalero: *U.S. Air Force Aircraft 8*

T-44 trainer: *U.S. Navy Aircraft 8*

T-45 trainer: *U.S. Navy Aircraft 8*

T-51 Cessna: *U.S. Air Force Aircraft 8*

T-55 main battle tank: *Russia Military Vehicles 8*

T-6 Texan II: *U.S. Air Force Aircraft 8*

T-6 trainer: *U.S. Navy Aircraft 8*

T-64: *Tanks Russian 8*

T-80: *Tanks Russian 8*

tabard: *Special Purpose Clothing 2*

tabarzin: *Axes 7*

tabasheer: *Minerals 10*

table lamp: *Illumination/Light Sources 5*

table linens: *Equipment and Tools 5*

table mountain pine: *Evergreen Trees 10*

table saw: *Power Tools*

table tennis: *Sporting Goods Balls 5*

table: *Thanksgiving 19*

tablecloth: *Table Linens 5; Thanksgiving 19*

tablernacle: *Objects in Magic and Religion 19*

tablet: *Computer Equipment 5; Wizard's Goods 5*

Tablets of the Ten Commandments: *Christian Relics 14*

tableware: *Equipment and Tools 5*

tabun: *Dangerous Chemicals 11*

tachi: *Swords Two-handed 7*

tachylyte: *Igneous Rocks 10*

taciturn: *Quiet 20*

tack hammer: *Hand Tools 5*

tack: *Boat/Ship Anatomy 9; Hardware 5; Sewing Techniques 2; Transportation Animals 9*

tackcloth: *Hardware 5*

tacking: *Boat/Ship Terminology 9*

tackle box: *Fishing Gear 5*

tackle: *Boat/Ship Anatomy 9; Fishing Gear 5*

tacks: *Wizard's Goods 5*

tacky green russula: *Fungus Common Names 10*

tacky: *Wet 20*

taco shell: *Bread General Varieties 6*

tactical goal: *General Combat Vocabulary 7*

tactical vest: *Military Equipment 8*

tactical: *Shields Post-1900 7*

tactics: *Combat, Armor, and Weapons 7; General Combat Vocabulary 7*

taenite: *Minerals 10*

tafelmusik: *Composition Types 13*

taffeta: *Fabric 2*

taffy: *Candy General 6*

tag alder: *Deciduous Trees 10*

tag board: *Office/School/Writing Supplies 5*

Tagalog: *Human Ethnic Groups 1*

tagliatelle: *Pasta 6*

tags: *Christmas 19*

Tahitian apple: *Unusual Edible Fruits 6*

Tahoka daisy: *Wildflowers 10*

taiaha: *Bludgeons 7*

taiga: *Ecosystems 10*

Taihu: *Pigs 15*

tail: *Hair Style 1*

tailcoat: *Men's Wear 2*

tailed tailless: *Bats 15*

tailless leaf-nosed: *Bats 15*

tailless whip: *Scorpion 15*

tailless: *Bats 15*

tailor: *Artists and Craftspeople 1; Castle Inhabitants and Personnel 1*

tailor's chalk: *Sewing Equipment 2*

tailored: *Styles of Dress 2*

tailors: *Guilds 1*

taint: *Harm 20*

tainted: *Unattractive 20*

taipan: *General Snake Families 15*

Taishuh: *Horse Breeds 15*

Taiwan: *Human Ethnic Groups 1*

Taj Mahal: *Seven Wonders of the Middle Ages 18; Unique Property 3*

take in: *Buy 20*

take life: *Kill 20*

take: *Buy 20*

taker: *Thief 1*

taking the blade: *Fencing Vocabulary 7*

takoba: *Swords One-handed 7*

talapoin: *Old World Monkeys 15*

Talaria (winged sandals of Hermes): *Clothing 18*

talc carbonate: *Metamorphic Rocks 10*

talented: *Good 20*

talik: *Soil General Vocabulary 10*

talisman: *Jewelry 21; Symbols in Magic and Religion 19; Witchcraft Vocabulary 17*

talkative: *Personality Other 1*

talking item: *Typical Magical Objects 17*

tall tales: *Legendary, Mystical and Mythical Items and Locations 18*

tall: *Large/Heavy 1*

tallow: *Illumination/Light Sources 5*

Talmud: *Major Religious Books 14*

Talos: *Construct 16*

talus: *Bones 12*

talwar: *Swords One-handed 7*

tam o'shanter: *Headgear 2*

tam: *Headgear 2*

tamandua: *Other Wild Mammals 15*

tamarack larch: *Deciduous Trees 10*

tamarack pine: *Evergreen Trees 10*

tamarack: *Deciduous Trees 10*

tamarillo: *Unusual Edible Fruits 6*

tamarin: *New World Monkeys 15*

tamarind: *Unusual Edible Fruits 6*

tamarisk: *Weeds 10*

tamarix: *Shrubs 10*

tambo: *Bludgeons 7*

tambour: *Sewing Equipment 2*

tambourine: *Percussion Musical Instruments 5*

tami: *Kitchen Equipment 5*

Tamil: *Human Ethnic Groups 1*

Taming Sari (kriss of Hang Tuah): *Weapons of Legend 18*

tam-tam: *Percussion Musical Instruments 5*

Tamworth: *Pigs 15*

tan oak: *Deciduous Trees 10*

tan: *Brown 20*

Tanana soil: *Soil General Vocabulary 10*

tanbark oak: *Deciduous Trees 10*

tanbark: *Beetle 15*

Tancitaran dusky: *Rattlesnake 15*

tandem bicycle: *Human-Powered Transportation 9*

tang: *Aquarium Saltwater Fish 15; Smells 20*

tanga: *Ladies' Wear 2*

tangelo: *Citrus 6; Orange 20*

tangerine: *Citrus 6; Orange 20*

tangier: *Weapons 22*

tangle: *Magic Vocabulary 17; Terrain Features 10*

tango: *Dance Styles 13*

Tanimbar: *Python 15*

tanjong: *Unusual Edible Fruits 6*

tank leotard: *Dance Clothing 13*

tank top: *Dance Clothing 13; Ladies' Wear 2; Unisex Clothing 2*

tank: *Armored Vehicles 8*

tankard: *Drinkware 5*

tanker car: *Railroad 9*

tanker: *Large Watercraft 9; Military Aircraft 8; Military Aircraft Pre-1962 8; Motorized Truck 9*

tankini: *Ladies' Wear 2*

tanks: *Military 8*

tanner: *Castle Inhabitants and Personnel 1*

Tannersville Cranberry Bog Pennsylvania: *Bogs of North America 10*

tanning lamp: *Illumination Bulb and Tube Types 5*

tanoak: *Deciduous Trees 10*

Tantalum: *Elements 11*

tanto: *Tempo/Mood 13*

tanuki: *Shapechanger 16*

tanzanite: *Cat's Eye Gems 21; Minerals 10; Standard Gems 21*

Taoist Texts: *Major Religious Books 14*

tap and die: *Power Tools*

tap pants: *Ladies' Wear 2*

tap: *Dance Shoes 13; Dance Styles 13; Food/Drink Establishments 3; Paranormal Occurrences 21*

tape gun: *Office/School/Writing Supplies 5*

tape measure: *Architectural/Engineering Tools 5; Sewing Equipment 2*

tape: *Christmas 19; Fasteners 5; Fix 20; Office/School/Writing Supplies 5; Shoe Accessories 13*

taper: *Candles 5*

taper-bearer: *Cleric 1*

tapestry weave carpet: *Floor Coverings 4*

tapestry: *Art Media 13; Fabric 2*

tapioca pudding: *Miscellaneous Dessert 6*

tapir: *Other Wild Mammals 15*

taqiya: *Headgear 2*

tar and gravel: *Roofing Materials 3*

tarantella (Italy): *Ethnic/Folk Dances 13*

tarantula: *Venomous Arachnids 15*

Tarawa class amphibious assault ship: *U.S. Navy Vessels 8*

tardy: *Slow 20*

Tarentaise: *Other Cows 15*

targ: *Shield Types 7*

target drone: *Military Aircraft Pre-1962 8*

target: *General Combat Vocabulary 7*

targeting: *General Combat Vocabulary 7*

tarn: *Terrain Features 10*

tarnation: *Expletives 20*

Tarnhelm: *Helmets 18*

tarnish: *Harm 20*

Tarnkappe (Sigurd's cloak of invisibility): *Clothing 18*

tarnowitzite: *Minerals 10*

taro: *Garden Bulbs 10; Vegetables 6*

tarok: *Card Games 5*

Tarot cards: *Fortune Telling General Devices 19*

tarp: *General Survival Gear 5*

Tarpan: *Horse Breeds 15*

tarpaulin: *General Survival Gear 5; Military Equipment 8*

tarpon: *Wild Saltwater Fish 15*

Tarqeq: *Moons 11*

tarsal: *Bones 12*

tarsier: *Other Wild Mammals 15*

tart cherry: *Pit Fruits 6*

tart pan: *Kitchen Equipment 5*

tart: *Candy General 6; Cookie 6; Miscellaneous Dessert 6; Smells 20*

tartan: *Fabric 2*

tartar sauce: *Condiments 6*

Tartarian honeysuckle: *Weeds 10*

Tartarus: *Afterlife/Underworld 18*

Tarus 738 TCP: *Pistol Semiautomatic 7*

Tarvos: *Moons 11*

tascate: *Evergreen Trees 10*

taser: *SWAT Weapons 7*

Tasmanian blue gum: *Weeds 10; Deciduous Trees 10*

Tasmanian devil: *Other Wild Mammals 15*

Tasmanian tiger: *Other Wild Mammals 15*

Tasmanian wolf: *Other Wild Mammals 15*

taste: *Philosophy Basic Concepts 14; Physical Mutations 22*

tattoo artist: *Personal Services 1*

tattvas: *Symbols in Magic and Religion 19*

tau: *Crosses 19*

taunt: *Speak 20*

taupe gray: *Gray 20*

taupe: *Brown 20*

Taurus (April 20–May 20): *Zodiac Signs 19*

Taurus 4510: *Revolver Double Action 7*

Taurus Judge Public Defender Polymer: *Revolver Double Action 7*

Taurus Model 85 Protector Polymer: *Revolver Double Action 7*

Taurus Raging Bull Series: *Revolver Double Action 7*

Taurus Tracker: *Revolver Double Action 7*

Taurus: *Constellations 11*

tausendeins: *Card Games 5*

taut: *Vocal/Speech Quality 1*

tautline hitch: *Sailing Knots 9*

tavern: *Food/Drink Establishments 3; Tables 4*

tavis wyrm: *Extraplanar 16*

tawiskaron: *Demon 16*

Tawleed: *Horse Breeds 15*

tawny hawkweed: *Weeds 10*

tawny: *Brown 20; Owls 15*

tawny-browed: *Owls 15*

tax collector: *Castle Inhabitants and Personnel 1; Finance 1*

taxes: *Card Games 5*

taxi stand: *Infrastructure Buildings 9*

taxi: *Motorized 9*

tayberry: *Unusual Edible Fruits 6*

Taygete: *Moons 11*

Taylor: *Comets 11*

Taylor's & CO. 1873 Cattleman Bird's Head: *Revolver Single Action 7*

Taylor's & CO. 1873: *Revolver Single Action 7*

Taylor's Lightning: *Lever Action and Pump Centerfire Rifles 7*

Taylor's model 1885: *Single Shot Rimfire Rifles 7*

te deum: *Composition Types 13*

tea bowl: *Drinkware 5*

tea cart: *Miscellaneous Furniture 4*

tea chest: *Containers and Vessels 5*

tea cup: *Drinkware 5*

tea glass: *Drinkware 5*

tea kettle: *Kitchen Equipment 5*

tea leaves: *Fortune Telling General Devices 19; Wizard's Goods 5*

tea length skirt: *Ladies' Wear 2*

tea pot: *Tableware 5*

tea set: *Toys 5*

tea table: *Erosion 10*

tea: *Food 6; Plants with Symbolic Meaning 19; Tables 4; Towels 5*

teacake: *Cake 6*

teach: *Verbs 20*

teacher is vampire: *Horror Plot Devices 23*

teacher: *Academic 1*

teal: *Blue 20; Cyan 20; Green 20*

tealight: *Candles 5*

team doctor: *Sports 1*

tear gas grenade: *SWAT Equipment 7*

tear: *Wet 20*

teardrop: *Wet 20*

tear-jerking: *Sad 20*

teased: *Hair Style 1*

teaspoon: *Eating Utensils 5*

Tecate cypress: *Evergreen Trees 10*

Tecciztecatl (oceans): *Aztec Pantheon 14*

Technetium: *Elements 11*

technical rehearsal: *Stage Terms 13*

technical sergeant: *U.S. Air Force Enlisted 8*

technical terms: *The Arts 13*

technical writer: *Publishing 1*

technician: *General Occupations 1*

technology reporter: *Publishing 1*

technosol: *Soil General Vocabulary 10*

Teclu burner: *Laboratory Equipment 5*

tectonic plates: *Geography General Vocabulary 10*

tectonic: *Energy Sources/Types 22*

teddy bear: *Christmas 19; Toys 5*

teddy: *Ladies' Wear 2*

teen pathi: *Card Games 5*

teen: *Child 1*

teenager: *Child 1*

teenagers trapped and stalked: *Horror Genres 23*

teensy weensy: *Small/Fragile 20*

teensy: *Small/Fragile 20; Small/Thin 1*

teeny weeny: *Small/Fragile 20*

teeny: *Small/Fragile 20*

teeth: *Anatomy and Physiology 12; Character Building 1; Wizard's Goods 5*

teff: *Grain 6*

Tefnut (goddess of storms): *Egyptian Pantheon 14*

tegu: *Scaled Reptiles 15*

tektite: *Astronomy General Terms 11*

Telchines: *Mythical Creatures and Monsters 16*

telefunken: *Card Games 5*

telegraph: *Signal Devices 5; Western Paraphernalia/People 21*

telekinesis: *Energy Sources/Types 23; Paranormal Abilities 21; Plot Devices 22*

telekinetic arm: *Paranormal Abilities 21*

telekinetic: *Magic Vocabulary 17*

Telemark: *Other Cows 15*

telemetry suit: *Spy Gear 5*

telepath: *Occupations 22; Wizard 1*

telepathic assassin: *Fantasy Occupations 24*

telepathic: *Magic Vocabulary 17*

telepathist: *Wizard 1*

telepathy: *Paranormal Abilities 21; Plot Devices 22*

telephone company: *Public Services 3*

telephone lines: *Building Systems 3*

telephone wiring: *Building Systems 3*

telephone: *Office/School Machines 5; Tables 4*

teleportation device: *Devices 22*

teleportation: *Magical Transportation 17; Paranormal Abilities 21; Traps 3; Travel Modes 24; Travel Types 22*

telerobot: *Robots 22*

telescope: *Astronomy General Terms 11; Octopi 15; Optics 5*

Telescopium: *Constellations 11*

telesina: *Card Games 5*

Telesto: *Moons 11*

teletype: *Office/School Machines 5*

television rock: *Minerals 10*

television stone: *Minerals 10*

television: *Electronics 4*

Tellem: *Human Races Fictional 1*

telling one's age: *Practices that Attract Bad Luck 19*

tellurium hexafluoride: *Dangerous Chemicals 11*

tellurium: *Dangerous Chemicals 11*

Tellurium: *Elements 11*

Tempel: *Comets 11*

tempera paint: *Art Materials 5*

tempera: *Art Media 13*

temperament: *General Music Vocabulary 13*

temperance: *Four Cardinal Virtues 19; Philosophy Basic Concepts 14; Seven Holy Virtues 19*

temperate deciduous: *Ecosystems 10*

temperate evergreen: *Ecosystems 10*

temperate: *Climatic Zones 10; Meteorology General Vocabulary 10*

temperature resistance: *Physical Mutations 22*

temperature: *Chemistry General Vocabulary 11; Meteorology General Vocabulary 10*

tempest: *Wind 10*

Templar: *Crosses 19; Styles of Dress 2*

templar: *Fighter 1; Knight 1; Paladin 1*

template: *Architectural/Engineering Tools 5*

temple floor: *Symbols of Freemasonry 19*

Temple of Artemis at Ephesus: *Seven Wonders of the Ancient World 18*

Temple of Artemis: *Unique Property Destroyed 3*

Temple of Set: *Secret/Mystical Organizations 18*

temple: *Body Parts 12; Pit Viper 15; Religious Building 3; Viper 15*

tempo rubato: *Tempo/Mood 13*

tempo: *The Arts 13*

temporal bone: *Bones 12*

temporal fugue: *Paranormal Abilities 21*

Temps lié sur les pointes: *Ballet Terms 13*

tempt: *Magic Vocabulary 17*

temptation: *Magic Vocabulary 17*

ten gallon hat: *Western Clothing/Dress 21*

ten lords a-leaping: *Twelve Days of Christmas 19*

ten perfections of Buddhism: *Collective Symbols 19*

ten-card regrets: *Poker Card Games 5*

tench: *Wild Freshwater Fish 15*

tender destroyer: *Military Watercraft 8*

tender: *Spaceship Types 22*

tenderfoot: *Western Paraphernalia/People 21*

tenderloin: *Pork 6*

tendon: *Organs/Major Structures 12*

ten-gallon hat: *Headgear 2*

tengu: *Demon 16; Flying Creatures 16; Shapechanger 16*

Tennessee Walking Horse: *Horse Breeds 15*

Tennin: *Angels of Good 14*

tennis court: *Entertainment Property 3; Property Features 3*

tennis racquet: *Sporting Goods Other 5*

tennis: *Athletic Shoes 2; Sporting Goods Balls 5*

tenor saxophone: *Wind/Woodwind and Brass Musical Instruments*

tense: *Vocal/Speech Quality 1*

tension: *Bridges 9*

tent: *Amusement Park/Carnival/Circus/Fair 3; Military Equipment 8; Outdoor Property 3; Residential Property 3*

tentacled: *General Snake Families 15*

tentative: *Horror Vocabulary 23*

tent-making: *Bats 15*

tepetate: *Soil General Vocabulary 10*

Tepeyollotl (mountains): *Aztec Pantheon 14*

tephrite: *Igneous Rocks 10*

TEPP: *Dangerous Chemicals 11*

tepui: *Erosion 10*

Terbium: *Elements 11*

terbufos: *Dangerous Chemicals 11*

terminal tackle: *Fishing Gear 5*

terminal: *Computer Equipment 5; Ending 20; Infrastructure Buildings 9*

terminate: *Ending 20*

terminator: *Astronomy General Terms 11*

terminus: *Infrastructure Buildings 9*

terms of endearment: *Character Building 1*

ternary acid: *Chemistry General Vocabulary 11*

ternary form: *General Music Vocabulary 13*

terra preta: *Soil General Vocabulary 10*

Terra rosa soil: *Soil General Vocabulary 10*

terrace farming: *Soil General Vocabulary 10*

terrace: *Cave Anatomy 10; Outdoor Property 3; Property Features 3; Slope 10*

terraced: *Grade/Slope 10*

terracette: *Soil General Vocabulary 10*

terracettes: *Slope 10*

terraforming: *Plot Devices 22*

terragator: *General Farm Equipment*

terrain features: *Chapter 10*

terramechanics: *Soil General Vocabulary 10*

terrarium: *Man-Made Animal Homes 15*

Terreneuvian Age: *Geologic Time 10*

terrestrial iron: *Minerals 10*

terrestrial planet: *Astronomy General Terms 11*

terrestrial: *Astronomy General Terms 11*

terrible: *Bad 20; Horror Vocabulary 23*

terrier: *Dog Groups 15*

terrific: *Beautiful 20; Good 20*

territory: *Geography General Vocabulary 10; Political Divisions 10*

terror: *General Emotions 20; Horror Vocabulary 23*

terrorist: *Fighter 1*

terrorists: *Travel Hazards 9*

terry cloth: *Fabric 2*

terry velour: *Fabric 2*

Tersk: *Horse Breeds 15*

Terzaghi's Principle: *Soil General Vocabulary 10*

Tesla coil: *Laboratory Equipment 5*

tessen: *Hand Weapons 7*

test tube holder: *Laboratory Equipment 5*

test tube rack: *Laboratory Equipment 5*

test tube: *Laboratory Equipment 5*

test: *Solve 20; Teach 20*

Testament of Solomon: *Books of Legend 18*

testicle: *Body Parts 12; Organs/Major Structures 12*

testify: *Agree 20*

testing: *Difficult 20*

tetanus: *Diseases 12*

tetchy: *Negative 1*

Tethys ocean: *Geological Vocabulary 10*

Tethys: *Moons 11*

tetra: *Aquarium Freshwater Fish 15*

tetraethyllead: *Dangerous Chemicals 11*

tetraethyltin: *Dangerous Chemicals 11*

tetraferriannite: *Minerals 10*

tetraferriphlogopite: *Minerals 10*

tetragrammaton: *Symbols in Magic and Religion 19*

tetrahedral: *Chemistry General Vocabulary 11*

tetraktys: *Symbols in Magic and Religion 19*

tetramorphs: *Symbols in Magic and Religion 19*

tetranitromethane: *Dangerous Chemicals 11*

tetrataenite: *Minerals 10*

Teutonic knight: *Knight 1*

Texan: *Styles of Dress 2*

Texas 42: *Card Games 5*

Texas arbutus: *Deciduous Trees 10*

Texas black walnut: *Deciduous Trees 10*

Texas bluebonnet: *Wildflowers 10*

Texas cedar: *Evergreen Trees 10*

Texas cooter: *Freshwater Turtles 15*

Texas emerald: *Dragonfly 15*

Texas goat cheese: *Cheese Common Varieties 6*

Texas hold'em: *Poker Card Games 5*

Texas Jack: *Western Paraphernalia/People 21*

Texas Longhorn: *Other Cows 15*

Texas madrone: *Deciduous Trees 10*

Texas madroño: *Deciduous Trees 10*

Texas map: *Freshwater Turtles 15*

Texas mountain laurel: *Deciduous Trees 10*

Texas oak: *Deciduous Trees 10*

Texas paintbrush: *Wildflowers 10*

Texas persimmon: *Deciduous Trees 10*

Texas Ranger: *Law Enforcement 1*

Texas red oak: *Deciduous Trees 10*

Texas rose: *Garden Perennials 10*

Texas spiny softshell: *Freshwater Turtles 15*

Texas sugarberry: *Deciduous Trees 10*

Texas toast: *Bread General Varieties 6*

Texas walnut: *Deciduous Trees 10*

Texas white truffle: *Fungus Common Names 10*

Texas: *Toads 15; Tortoises 15*

Texate: *Deciduous Trees 10*

Texon: *Other Cows 15*

textbook: *Books/Publications 5*

textile: *Art Genres 13*

textiles: *Art Materials 5*

texting gloves: *Accessories 2*

texture: *Visual Elements 13*

texturize: *Art Techniques 13*

Tezcatlipoca (illusion and war): *Aztec Pantheon 14*

Tezcatlipoca (sun): *Central American Pantheon 14*

TH-57 Training: *Rotary Wing Aircraft 8*

TH-67 Creek: *U.S. Army Helicopter 8*

Thai: *Domestic Cats 15; Human Ethnic Groups 1*

thalamus: *Organs/Major Structures 12*

Thalassa: *Moons 11*

thallium sulfate: *Dangerous Chemicals 11*

Thallium: *Elements 11*

thallous carbonate: *Dangerous Chemicals 11*

thallous chloride: *Dangerous Chemicals 11*

thallous malonate: *Dangerous Chemicals 11*

thallous sulfate: *Dangerous Chemicals 11*

thalweg: *Fluvial 10*

thankful: *Happy 20*

thanks: *Thanksgiving 19*

Thanksgiving: *Holidays 19*

Tharparkar: *Other Cows 15*

thatch: *Door Materials 3; Roofing Materials 3*

thaw depth: *Soil General Vocabulary 10*

thaw: *Meteorology General Vocabulary 10*

The Art of Divine Magic: *Books of Legend 18*

The Black Hand: *Secret/Mystical Organizations 18*

The Fourth Book of Occult Philosophy: *Books of Legend 18*

the Golden Rule: *Philosophy Basic Concepts 14*

the good the bad and the ugly: *Poker Card Games 5*

The Knights of the Golden Circle: *Secret/Mystical Organizations 18*

The Magus: *Books of Legend 18*

The Philosophical Merlin: *Books of Legend 18*

The Picatrix: *Books of Legend 18*

the prince: *Fungus Common Names 10*

The Sixth and Seventh Books of Moses: *Books of Legend 18*

The Smith of Kochel: *Real People with Legendary Status 18*

The Sons of Liberty: *Secret/Mystical Organizations 18*

The Thule Society: *Secret/Mystical Organizations 18*

theater of the absurd: *Performance Genres 13*

theater of war: *General Combat Vocabulary 7*

theater technician: *Performing Arts 1*

theater: *Academic Property 3; Entertainment Property 3; Rooms 3; The Arts 13; The Arts 13*

Theban: *Dragon 16*

Thebe: *Moons 11*

Thee Temple ov Psychick Youth: *Secret/Mystical Organizations 18*

theena shee: *Fae Related 16*

theft of body parts: *Horror Plot Devices 23*

Theia: *Hypothetical Solar System Bodies 11*

Thelxinoe: *Moons 11*

theme: *General Music Vocabulary 13*

Themis: *Hypothetical Solar System Bodies 11*

Themisto: *Moons 11*

theological virtues: *Collective Symbols 19*

theoretical yield: *Chemistry General Vocabulary 11*

theorist: *Occupations 22; Wizard 1*

theorize: *Solve 20*

theosophical society symbol: *Symbols in Magic and Religion 19*

Theosophical Society: *Secret/Mystical Organizations 18*

therapist: *Medical Occupations 1*

theremin: *Electronic Musical Instruments 5*

therizinosaur: *Dinosaur Types 15*

thermal cracking: *Chemistry General Vocabulary 11*

thermal creature: *Monsters and Creatures 22*

thermal hydrogen: *Spaceship Drive Systems 22*

thermal imaging system: *Military Equipment 8*

thermal underwear: *Unisex Clothing 2*

thermal: *Energy Sources/Types 22; Fabric 2; Meteorology General Vocabulary 10; Weapons 22*

thermodynamic: *Energy Sources/Types 22*

thermodynamics: *Chemistry General Vocabulary 11*

thermometer: *Kitchen Utensils 5; Laboratory Equipment 5; Meteorology General Vocabulary 10*

thermonuclear energy: *Chemistry General Vocabulary 11*

thermonuclear: *Bomb 8*

thermostat: *Building Systems 3*

theropod: *Dinosaur Types 15*

thesaurus: *Books/Publications 5; Office/School/Writing Supplies 5*

Thessalian: *Horse Breeds 15*

thick: *Eyebrows 1; Hair Types 1; Unintelligent 1; Vocal/Speech Quality 1; Wet 20*

thick-eared: *Bats 15*

thicket: *Terrain Features 10*

thick-headed: *Flies 15*

thickness planer: *Power Tools*

thickset: *Large/Heavy 1*

thick-thumbed: *Bats 15*

thief: *Character Building 1; Thief 1*

thief's tools: *Specialty Survival Gear 5*

thief's: *Masks 2*

Thiele tube: *Laboratory Equipment 5*

thieves: *Guilds 1*

thigh: *Body Parts 12*

thigh-high stockings: *Ladies' Wear 2*

thigh-high: *Boots 2*

thimbleberry: *Unusual Edible Fruits 6; Wildflowers 10*

thin spaghetti: *Pasta 6*

thin: *Character Building 1; Eyebrows 1; Facial Hair Beard 1; Hair Types 1; Light 20; Lips 1; Small/Thin 1; Vocal/Speech Quality 1*

thing in itself: *Philosophy Basic Concepts 14*

think: *Solve 20*

thinker: *Wizard 1*

thinking: *Philosophy Basic Concepts 14*

thinleaf alder: *Deciduous Trees 10*

thin-lipped: *Lips 1*

thiocarbazide: *Dangerous Chemicals 11*

thiofanox: *Dangerous Chemicals 11*

thionazin: *Dangerous Chemicals 11*

thiophenol: *Dangerous Chemicals 11*

thiosemicarbazide: *Dangerous Chemicals 11*

thiourea: *Dangerous Chemicals 11*

third cousin: *Relational 1*

third law of thermodynamics: *Chemistry General Vocabulary 11*

third molar: *Teeth 12*

thirteen arrows: *United States Dollar Bill 19*

thirteen colonies: *Independence Day 19*

thirteen olives: *United States Dollar Bill 19*

thirteen treasures of the Island of Britain: *Legendary, Mystical and Mythical Items and Locations 18*

thirteenth floor in hotel: *Harbingers of Bad Luck 19*

thirty-second note: *Notation 13*

thistle tube: *Laboratory Equipment 5*

thistle: *Garden Annuals 10; Purple 20*

thixotropy: *Soil General Vocabulary 10*

Thomas Jefferson: *Independence Day 19*

Thomas: *Twelve Apostles 14*

Thompson 1927A1: *Semiautomatic Centerfire Rifles 7*

Thompson Center Encore: *Pistol Single Shot 7*

Thompson Center Encore: *Single Shot Centerfire Rifles 7*

Thompson Center G2 Contender: *Pistol Single Shot 7*

Thompson Center R55: *Semiautomatic Rimfire Rifles 7*

Thompson Contender: *Shotguns Single Shot 7*

Thompson Pro Hunter: *Pistol Single Shot 7*

thong panties: *Ladies' Wear 2*

thongs: *Footwear/Shoes 2*

thoracic surgeon: *Medical Occupations 1*

thorax: *Body Parts 12*

Thorium: *Elements 11*

thorn apple: *Poisonous Plants 10*

thorns: *Plants with Symbolic Meaning 19; Travel Hazards 9*

thorny devil: *Scaled Reptiles 15*

thorny: *Difficult 20*

thorogummite: *Minerals 10*

Thoroughbred: *Horse Breeds 15*

thoroughfare: *Roads 9*

Thoth (knowledge): *Egyptian Pantheon 14*

thought: *Philosophy Basic Concepts 14*

thoughtful: *Positive 1*

thousand island: *Salad Dressing 6*

thrash: *Attack 7*

thread restorer: *Power Tools*

thread: *Fasteners 5; Notions 2; Wizard's Goods 5*

threaded chain: *Embroidery Stitches 2*

threaded herringbone: *Embroidery Stitches 2*

threadfin anthias: *Aquarium Saltwater Fish 15*

threadleaf bluestar: *Garden Perennials 10*

threat/villain is eliminated but bigger threat/villain emerges: *Horror Plot Devices 23*

threat: *Paranormal Occurrences 21*

threatening: *Unattractive 20*

three bean: *Pickled/Relish 6*

three card brag: *Card Games 5*

three card: *Poker Card Games 5*

three five seven: *Poker Card Games 5*

three French hens: *Twelve Days of Christmas 19*

three jewels of Buddhism: *Symbols in Magic and Religion 19*

Three Kings: *Christmas 19*

three sacred imperial relics of Japan: *Legendary, Mystical and Mythical Items and Locations 18*

Three Tomes of Occult Philosophy: *Books of Legend 18*

three witches (from Macbeth): *Witchcraft Vocabulary 17*

Threebear soil: *Soil General Vocabulary 10*

three-button suit: *Men's Wear 2*

three-card Monte: *Card Games 5*

three-hole punch: *Office/School/Writing Supplies 5*

three-legged stool: *Chairs and Stools 4*

three-piece suit: *Men's Wear 2*

three-point plow: *Horse Drawn Farm Equipment*

three-prong: *Fencing Equipment 7*

three-pronged candelabrum: *Objects in Magic and Religion 19*

three-quarter length sleeve: *Garment Pieces 2*

three-section staff: *Bludgeons 7*

three-spined stickleback: *Wild Freshwater Fish 15*

three-spot gourami: *Aquarium Freshwater Fish 15*

three-striped night monkey: *New World Monkeys 15*

three-toed sloth: *Other Wild Mammals 15*

three-weapon mask: *Fencing Equipment 7*

thresher: *Sharks 15*

threshing machine: *Horse Drawn Farm Equipment; Steam Powered Farm Equipment*

threshold: *Building Elements and Features 3; Doors 3; Geography General Vocabulary 10*

thrift shop: *Styles of Dress 2*

thrift: *Garden Perennials 10*

thrilled: *Happy 20*

thriller: *Garden Perennials 10*

throat spray: *Music Accessories*

throat: *Body Parts 12*

throaty: *Vocal/Speech Quality 1*

throne: *Angels Common Terms 14; Chairs and Stools 4; Rooms 3*

through cave: *Cave Anatomy 10*

through street: *Roads 9*

throughflow: *Soil General Vocabulary 10*

throw confetti/rice: *Practices/Objects to Attract Good Luck 19*

throw rug: *Floor Coverings 4*

throw: *Bed Linens 5; Pillows 5*

throwing blade: *Missile Weapons 7*

throwing hachet: *Missile Weapons 7*

throwing knife: *Daggers and Knives 7; Western Weapons 21*

throwing star: *Missile Weapons 7*

throwing: *Axes 7*

thrust: *Attack 7; Fencing Vocabulary 7*

thruway: *Roads 9*

Thrymr: *Moons 11*

thud: *Sounds 20*

thug: *Fighter 1; Illicit Occupations 1; Thief 1; Villain 20*

thulite: *Minerals 10*

Thulium: *Elements 11*

thumb drive: *Computer Equipment 5*

thumb guitar pick: *Music Accessories*

thumb tacks: *Office/School/Writing Supplies 5*

thumb: *Body Parts 12*

thumb-back: *Chairs and Stools 4*

thumbless: *Bats 15*

thumbnail: *Body Parts 12*

thumbprint: *Cookie 6*

thump: *Attack 7*

Thunberg's barberry: *Weeds 10*

thunder egg: *Minerals 10*

thunder: *Severe Weather 10*

thunderbird: *Flying Creatures 16*

thunderhead: *Severe Weather 10*

thunderous: *Loud 20*

thundersnow: *Snow Events 10*

thunderstorm: *Common Dangers 23; Severe Weather 10*

Thuoc Nhieu: *Pigs 15*

thuringite: *Minerals 10*

thwart: *Close/Hold 20*

thyme: *Garden Perennials 10; Plants with Symbolic Meaning 19; Shrubs 10; Spices 6*

thymus gland: *Organs/Major Structures 12*

Thyone: *Moons 11*

thyroid gland: *Organs/Major Structures 12*

Thyrsus: *Objects 18*

thyrsus: *Objects in Magic and Religion 19*

tiamat: *Demon 16*

Tiamat: *Dragon 16*

tiara: *Headgear 2; Jewelry 2; Jewelry 21*

Tibetan bamboo: *Pit Viper 15*

Tibetan Book of the Dead: *Major Religious Books 14*

Tibetan Mastiff: *Dog Breeds 15*

Tibetan Spaniel: *Dog Breeds 15*

Tibetan Terrier: *Dog Breeds 15*

Tibetan: *Foxes 15; Human Ethnic Groups 1; Pigs 15*

Tibeti: *Tea 6*

tibia: *Bones 12*

tic polonga: *General Snake Families 15*

tick: *Giant Creatures 16*

ticked off: *Angry 1*

ticker tape: *Office/School/Writing Supplies 5*

ticket booth: *Amusement Park/Carnival/Circus/Fair 3; Infrastructure Buildings 9*

ticket seller: *General Occupations 1*

ticket taker: *General Occupations 1*

ticking: *Fabric 2*

tickled pink: *Happy 20*

ticks: *Injuries/Medical Emergencies 12*

tickseed: *Garden Perennials 10; Wildflowers 10*

Ticonderoga class cruiser: *U.S. Navy Vessels 8*

tic-tac-toe: *Poker Card Games 5*

tidal force: *Astronomy General Terms 11*

tidal heating: *Astronomy General Terms 11*

tidbit plate: *Tableware 5*

tiddly-wink: *Card Games 5*

tide mill: *Special Purpose Structure 3*

tide pool: *Natural Animal Homes 15*

tide: *Water Terms 9*

tideland spruce: *Evergreen Trees 10*

tides: *Geological Natural Hazards 10*

Tidewater: *Architectural Styles 3*

tidy tips: *Wildflowers 10*

tidy: *Clean 20*

tie back: *Garment Pieces 2*

tie bar: *Jewelry 2;Jewelry 21*

tie pin: *Jewelry 2; Jewelry 21*

tie: *Fix 20; Jewelry 21; Men's Wear 2*

tiebacks: *Window Treatments 5*

tie-dye: *Embellishments 2*

tiered server: *Tableware 5*

tiered skirt: *Ladies' Wear 2*

tiered: *Cake 6*

tiers: *Window Treatments 5*

tie-up: *Marina 3*

Tiffanie: *Domestic Cats 15*

Tiffany lamp: *Illumination/Light Sources 5*

Tifton soil: *Soil General Vocabulary 10*

tiger barb: *Aquarium Freshwater Fish 15*

tiger: *Animals with Symbolic Meaning 19; Beetle 15; Big Cats 15; Bread General Varieties 6; Chinese Horoscope 19; General Snake Families 15; Harbingers/Charms for Good Luck 19; Keelback 15; Pit Viper 15; Rattlesnake 15; Sharks 15*

tiger's eye matrix: *Standard Gems 21*

tiger's eye: *Minerals 10; Standard Gems 21*

tiger's jaws: *Garden Perennials 10*

tiger-banded peckoltia: *Aquarium Freshwater Fish 15*

tigers: *Animals 15*

tight rope walker: *Performing Arts 1*

tight: *Vocal/Speech Quality 1*

tight-lipped: *Lips 1; Quiet 20*

tights: *Dance Clothing 13; Ladies' Wear 2*

tighty-whiteys: *Men's Wear 2*

tilaka: *Symbols in Magic and Religion 19*

tilapia: *Fish/Seafood Types 6*

tile cutter: *Power Tools*

tile fish: *Wild Saltwater Fish 15*

tile nipper: *Hand Tools 5*

tile setter: *Construction 1*

tile: *Art Materials 5; Building Elements and Features 3; Interior Building Materials 3; Roofing Materials 3*

Till Eulenspiegel: *Legendary People Presumed to be Fictional 18*

tillage: *Soil General Vocabulary 10*

Tillamook cheddar: *Cheese Common Varieties 6*

tiller: *Boat/Ship Anatomy 9; Farm Transportation 9*

tilsit: *Cheese International Varieties 6*

tilt-a-whirl: *Amusement Park/Carnival/Circus/Fair 3*

tilt-top: *Tables 4*

timber: *Door Materials 3; Rattlesnake 15*

timberland: *Terrain Features 10*

timberline larch: *Deciduous Trees 10*

Timbuktu: *Real Places Steeped in Legend or Mystery 18*

time distance: *Geography General Vocabulary 10*

time loops: *Plot Devices 22*

time manipulation: *Paranormal Abilities 21*

time of birth: *Objects/Activities Connected to Lore 19*

time signature: *Notation 13*

time travel device: *Devices 22*

time travel: *Fantasy Plot Devices 24; Plot Devices 22; Travel Modes 23; Travel Modes 24*

time traveler meddles with history: *Horror Plot Devices 23*

time traveler: *Monsters and Creatures 22*

time: *General Music Vocabulary 13; Philosophy Basic Concepts 14; Spaceship Drive Systems 22; Travel Types 22*

time-consuming: *Difficult 20*

timed thrust: *Fencing Vocabulary 7*

timekeeping: *Equipment and Tools 5*

timer: *Kitchen Utensils 5; Timekeeping 5*

Times Square: *New Year 19*

timetable: *Laboratory Supplies 5*

timid: *Horror Vocabulary 23; Personality Other 1*

timing: *Fencing Vocabulary 7*

Timor: *Python 15*

timorous: *Horror Vocabulary 23*

timpani: *Percussion Musical Instruments 5*

tin cup: *Drinkware 5*

tin horn: *Christmas 19*

tin stone: *Minerals 10*

Tin: *Elements 11*

tin: *Five Alchemical Spirits 19*

tincal: *Minerals 10*

tinctures: *Classic Heraldry 19*

tinder: *General Survival Gear 5*

tinderbox: *Illumination/Light Sources 5*

tinker: *Castle Inhabitants and Personnel 1*

tinsel: *Christmas 19*

tinsmith: *Artists and Craftspeople 1*

tinted: *Hair Treated 1*

tiny peas: *Vegetables 6*

tiny pouch of sugar: *Harbingers/Charms for Good Luck 19*

tiny shrimp: *Fish/Seafood Types 6*

Tiny Tim: *Christmas 19*

tiny twist pretzel: *Snacks 6*

tiny: *Caecilians 15; Small/Fragile 20; Small/Thin 1*

tiptoe: *Locomotion 9*

Tir na Nog: *Afterlife/Underworld 18*

tiramisu: *Cake 6*

tiratana: *Symbols in Magic and Religion 19*

tire iron: *Hand Tools 5; Improvised Weapons 7*

tired: *Horror Vocabulary 23*

tiring: *Difficult 20*

tirodite: *Minerals 10*

tiroler graukase: *Cheese International Varieties 6*

titan stick: *Phasmid 15*

titan: *Giant Humanoids 16*

Titan: *Moons 11*

Titania: *Moons 11*

titanic: *Large 20*

Titanic: *Ships 18*

titanium tetrachloride: *Dangerous Chemicals 11*

Titanium: *Elements 11*

titanium: *Precious Metals 21*

titanoferrite: *Minerals 10*

titano-hematite: *Minerals 10*

titano-magnetite: *Minerals 10*

titanosaur: *Dinosaur Types 15*

tithe: *Rituals 14*

tithing plate: *Religious Items 5*

titi monkey: *New World Monkeys 15*

titian: *Hair Color 1*

Titicaca water: *Frogs 15*

title holder: *Hero 20*

titled: *Personality Other 1*

titration: *Chemistry General Vocabulary 11*

Tiwanaku: *Real Places Steeped in Legend or Mystery 18*

Tizona (El Cid's sword): *Weapons of Legend 18*

Tlaloc (rain god): *Central American Pantheon 14*

Tlazolteotl (goddess of vice): *Central American Pantheon 14*

to windward: *Boat/Ship Terminology 9*

to your advantage: *Fortunate 20*

toad lily: *Garden Perennials 10*

toad: *Giant Creatures 16; Objects/Activities Connected to Lore 19; Witchcraft Vocabulary 17*

toadflax: *Garden Annuals 10; Garden Perennials 10; Wildflowers 10*

toads: *Animals 15*

toadstool: *Wizard's Goods 5*

toady: *Common Character Archetypes 21*

toast point: *Bread General Varieties 6*

toast: *Bread General Varieties 6; Cooking Techniques 20; New Year 19*

toaster oven: *Appliances 5*

toaster: *Appliances 5*

tobacco: *Farm/Outbuilding 3; Plants with Symbolic Meaning 19; Western Paraphernalia/People 21*

Tobadzistsini (war spirit): *Native American Pantheon 14*

toboggan cap: *Headgear 2*

toccata: *Composition Types 13*

toddle: *Locomotion 9*

toddler: *Beds 4; Child 1*

toe pad: *Shoe Accessories 13*

toe ring: *Jewelry 21*

toe spacer: *Shoe Accessories 13*

toe wrap: *Shoe Accessories 13 arabesque: Dance Moves 13*

toe: *Body Parts 12; Dance Shoes 13*

toenail: *Body Parts 12*

toffee: *Candy General 6; Ice Cream Flavors 6; Pie 6*

Tohono: *Native American Peoples 1*

toilet brush: *Cleaning Supplies/Gadgets 5*

toilet cleaner: *Cleaning Supplies/Gadgets 5*

toilet paper holder: *Bathroom Features and Fixtures 3*

toilet paper: *General Survival Gear 5; Military Equipment 8*

toilet water: *Personal Care 5*

toilet: *Bathroom Features and Fixtures 3; Bathrooms 3; Rooms 3*

Tokara: *Horse Breeds 15*

Tokyo-X: *Pigs 15*

tolerance: *Ten Perfections of Buddhism 19*

tolerate: *Agree 20*

Tolkien: *Asteroids with Unusual Names 11*

toll road: *Roads 9*

Toltec: *Human Ethnic Groups 1*

toluene 2: *Dangerous Chemicals 11*

Tom & Jerry: *Dairy Beverages 6*

Tom Collins: *Cocktails 6*

Tom S. Cooperrider-Kent Bog Ohio: *Bogs of North America 10*

tomahawk: *Axes 7; Western Weapons 21*

tomatillo: *Vegetables 6*

tomato cage: *Garden Tools*

tomato knife: *Kitchen Utensils 5*

tomato soup: *Cake 6*

tomato: *Aphrodisiacs 19; Plants with Symbolic Meaning 19; Poisonous Plants 10; Red 20; Soup 6; Vegetable Juice 6; Vegetables 6*

tomb: *Bats 15; Cemetery 3; Easter 19; Rooms 3*

tombeau: *Composition Types 13*

tombolo: *Coastal and Oceanic 10*

tomboy: *Styles of Dress 2*

Tombstone: *Famous Western Locations 21*

tome: *Books/Publications 5; Typical Magical Objects 17*

Tommy Knockers: *Folklore Characters 18*

tommy-knockers: *Demon 16*

Tomoe Gozen: *Real People with Legendary Status 18*

tomoe: *Symbols in Magic and Religion 19*

tonalite: *Igneous Rocks 10*

Tonbogiri: *Spears 18*

tone poem: *Composition Types 13*

tone: *General Music Vocabulary 13; Visual Elements 13*

toneless: *Vocal/Speech Quality 1*

toner cartridge: *Office/School/Writing Supplies 5*

toner: *Office/School/Writing Supplies 5*

tonfa: *Bludgeons 7*

Tonga: *Human Ethnic Groups 1*

Tongans: *Human Ethnic Groups 1*

tongs: *Hand Tools 5; Kitchen Utensils 5; Laboratory Equipment 5*

tongue and groove pliers: *Hand Tools 5*

tongue: *Beef 6; Body Parts 12*

tonic water: *Soft Drinks 6*

Tonkinese: *Domestic Cats 15*

tonsil: *Body Parts 12; Organs/Major Structures 12*

tonsured: *Hair Style 1*

tool bit: *Power Tools*

tool chest: *Containers and Vessels 5*

tools: *Combat, Armor, and Weapons 7; Equipment and Tools 5*

toot: *Sounds 20*

Tooth Fairy: *Characters with Symbolic Meaning 19*

tooth powder: *Personal Care 5*

tooth: *Body Parts 12*

toothache tree: *Deciduous Trees 10*

toothbrush: *Facial Hair Mustache 1; Personal Care 5*

toothpaste: *Personal Care 5*

top freezer refrigerator: *Major Appliances 4*

top handle purse: *Accessories 2*

top hat: *Headgear 2*

top knot: *Hair Style 1*

top: *Ladies' Wear 2; Toys 5*

topaz: *Standard Gems 21*

topazolite: *Minerals 10*

topgallant: *Boat/Ship Anatomy 9*

top-heavy: *Heavy 20*

topi: *Headgear 2*

topical: *New 20*

topographic map: *Geography General Vocabulary 10*

topography: *Geography General Vocabulary 10*

topper: *General Farm Equipment*

topple: *Locomotion 9*

topsail: *Boat/Ship Anatomy 9*

top-security center: *Prison 3*

topsoil: *Soil General Vocabulary 10*

topstitching: *Embellishments 2*

tor: *Erosion 10*

Tor: *Knights of the Round Table 18*

Torah: *Major Religious Books 14; Objects in Magic and Religion 19*

torch lily: *Garden Perennials 10*

torch singer: *Singer 1*

torch: *General Survival Gear 5; Illumination/Light Sources 5*

torenia: *Garden Annuals 10*

Tori: *Horse Breeds 15*

torii: *Objects in Magic and Religion 19*

torite: *Minerals 10*

tormenter: *Wizard 1*

tornado alley: *Meteorology General Vocabulary 10*

tornado: *Energy Sources/Types 23; Magical Transportation 17; Severe Weather 10*

torpedo boat destroyer: *Military Watercraft 8*

torpedo boat: *Military Watercraft 8*

torpedo bomber: *Military Aircraft Pre-1962 8*

torpedo grass: *Weeds 10*

torpedo scout: *Military Aircraft Pre-1962 8*

torpedo: *Military Aircraft Pre-1962 8*

torpid: *Mobility 1; Slow 20*

torque wrench: *Hand Tools 5; Power Tools*

torque: *Jewelry 21*

torrent: *Precipitation 10*

torrential rain: *Precipitation 10*

torrey pine: *Evergreen Trees 10*

torrid zone: *Geographical Zones 10*

torse: *Elements 19*

torsion: *Bridges 9*

torso: *Body Parts 12*

tortellini: *Pasta 6*

tortilla: *Bread General Varieties 6*

tortilla chip: *Bread General Varieties 6; Snacks 6*

tortoise: *Animals with Symbolic Meaning 19; Beetle 15; Siege Engines 7*

tortoises: *Animals 15*

tortoiseshell: *Butterfly 15*

torture device: *Weapons 22*

torture: *Harm 20*

torturer: *Illicit Occupations 1; Villain 20*

Tosa: *Dog Breeds 15*

tossed: *Salads 6*

tot: *Child 1*

total conversion: *Spaceship Drive Systems 22*

total ionic equation: *Chemistry General Vocabulary 11*

tote: *Accessories 2*

totem pole: *Objects in Magic and Religion 19*

totem: *Objects in Magic and Religion 19*

Totsuka no Tsurugi (sword of Yamata no Orochi): *Weapons of Legend 18*

Tou Mu (goddess of the north star): *Chinese Pantheon 14*

toucan: *Domesticated Pet Birds 15*

touch a sailor's collar: *Practices/Objects to Attract Good Luck 19*

touch: *Fencing Vocabulary 7; Paranormal Occurrences 21; Physical Mutations 22*

touché: *Fencing Vocabulary 7*

touching: *Sad 20*

touch-me-not: *Weeds 10*

tough guy: *Fighter 1*

tough: *Difficult 20; Fighter 1*

touloumisio: *Cheese International Varieties 6*

tounjski sir: *Cheese International Varieties 6*

toupee: *Headgear 2*

Tour de force: *Ballet Terms 13*

tour de Promenade: *Ballet Terms 13*

Tour en l'air: *Ballet Terms 13*

tour guide: *General Occupations 1; Horror Occupations 23*

Tour jeté: *Ballet Terms 13*

tour: *Journey 20; Locomotion 9*

tourists: *Travel Hazards 9*

tourmalinated quartz: *Minerals 10*

tourmaline: *Cat's Eye Gems 21; Standard Gems 21*

tournament blackjack: *Card Games 5*

tow: *Motorized Truck 9*

towel bar: *Bathroom Features and Fixtures 3*

towel rack: *Bathroom Features and Fixtures 3*

towels: *Equipment and Tools 5*

tower grater: *Kitchen Utensils 5*

Tower of Babel: *Sites Lost or Unproven to Exist 18*

tower: *Building Elements and Features 3; Castle Anatomy 3; Fortification 3; Shield Types 7*

towering: *Large 20; Large/Heavy 1*

towerkarst: *Cave Anatomy 10*

towhead: *Fluvial 10*

towheaded: *Hair Color 1*

towing: *Boat/Ship Terminology 9*

town drunk: *Common Character Archetypes 21*

Town House: *Architectural Styles 3*

town is overrun by bandits/Indians/soldiers: *Western Plot Devices 21*

town needs a new sheriff: *Western Plot Devices 21*

town square: *Outdoor Property 3*

town: *City 10*

township and range: *Geography General Vocabulary 10*

township: *City 10*

toxic pool: *Traps 3*

toxic shock syndrome: *Diseases 12*

toxic: *Horror Vocabulary 23*

toxoplasmosis: *Diseases 12*

toy chest: *Containers and Vessels 5; Storage 4*

Toy Fox Terrier: *Dog Breeds 15*

Toy Manchester Terrier: *Dog Breeds 15*

Toy Poodle: *Dog Breeds 15*

toy soldier: *Christmas 19*

toy: *Dog Groups 15*

Toyger: *Domestic Cats 15*

Toyism: *Art Movements 13*

toyon: *Unusual Edible Fruits 6*

toys: *Christmas 19; Equipment and Tools 5*

trace: *Meteorology General Vocabulary 10*

trachea: *Organs/Major Structures 12*

trachyandesite: *Igneous Rocks 10*

trachyte: *Igneous Rocks 10*

tracing paper: *Art Materials 5; Sewing Equipment 2*

track: *Athletic Shoes 2; Paranormal Activity 21; Railroad 9; Roads 9*

tracked tank destroyer: *Military Ground Vehicles General 8*

tracking device: *Spy Gear 5*

tractor beam: *Devices 22*

tractor mounted forklift: *General Farm Equipment*

tractor trailer: *Motorized Truck 9*

tractor: *Card Games 5; Farm Transportation 9*

trade union: *Guilds 1*

trade wind: *Water Terms 9*

traders: *Guilds 1*

Traditional Japanese: *Architectural Styles 3*

traditional: *Roof Styles 3*

Traditions 1874 Sharps: *Single Shot Centerfire Rifles 7*

traffic lane: *Roads 9*

traffic reporter: *Media 1*

tragedy: *Performance Genres 13*

tragic hero: *Common Character Archetypes 21*

tragic: *Sad 20*

trail: *Roads 9*

trailblazer: *Barbarian 1*

trailer trash: *Social Distinction 1; Styles of Dress 2*

trailer: *Farm Transportation 9*

trailing arbutus: *Shrubs 10*

train car: *Armored Vehicles 8*

train coming with goods/treasure: *Western Plot Devices 21*

train coming with prisoner: *Western Plot Devices 21*

train robbery: *Western Plot Devices 21*

train set: *Toys 5*

train station: *Infrastructure Buildings 9*

train: *Mass Transit 9; Railroad 9; Teach 20; Travel Modes 23*

trainer glider: *Military Aircraft Pre-1962 8*

trainer: *Animal/Equestrian 1; Military Aircraft 8; Military Aircraft Pre-1962 8; Sports 1; Transportation Animals 9*

training facility: *Military Property 3*

training VTOL: *Military Aircraft 8*

training: *Helicopters 8; Military Airships Pre-1962 8*

trains: *Card Games 5*

traipse: *Locomotion 9*

traitor: *Hero or Villain, Depending Upon Circumstance 20*

Trakehner: *Horse Breeds 15*

tram: *Animal-Powered Transportation 9; Mass Transit 9*

tramaran: *Small Watercraft 9*

Tramontane: *Winds of the Mediterranean 10*

tramp: *Journey 20; Locomotion 9; Styles of Dress 2; Thief 1; Wanderer 1*

trance: *Magic Vocabulary 17*

tranquil: *Easy 20; Happy 20*

trans-1: *Dangerous Chemicals 11*

transcendental: *Philosophy Basic Concepts 14*

transcontinental railroad: *Western Paraphernalia/People 21*

transcription: *General Music Vocabulary 13*

transept: *Church Anatomy 3*

transfusion: *Blood 12*

Transgressive art: *Art Movements 13*

transhumance: *Geography General Vocabulary 10*

transistor radio: *Electronics 4*

transit: *Astronomy General Terms 11*

transiting: *Planetary Systems 11*

transition state theory: *Chemistry General Vocabulary 11*

transitional mirror: *Miscellaneous Furniture 4*

translate: *Solve 20*

translator: *Academic 1*

transmitter: *Electronics 4*

trans-neptunian object: *Astronomy General Terms 11*

transom: *Castle Anatomy 3; Technical Terms 13; Windows 3*

transplanter: *General Farm Equipment*

transport box: *General Farm Equipment*

transport glider: *Military Aircraft Pre-1962 8*

transport single engine: *Military Aircraft Pre-1962 8*

transport truck: *Military Ground Vehicles General 8*

transport: *Military Aircraft Pre-1962 8; Military Watercraft 8*

transportation occupations: *Character Building 1*

transportation: *Robots 22; Transportation 9*

transposition: *General Music Vocabulary 13*

Transvaal jade: *Minerals 10*

Transvaal: *Lions 15*

transverse colon: *Organs/Major Structures 12*

transverse flute: *Wind/Woodwind and Brass Musical Instruments*

Transylvanian: *Human Ethnic Groups 1*

trap door: *Traps 3*

trap: *Attack 7; Cave Anatomy 10; Close/Hold 20; Fishing Gear 5; General Combat Vocabulary 7; Mouth 1; Technical Terms 13; Travel Hazards 9*

trap-door: *Venomous Arachnids 15*

trapeze: *Gem Cuts 21*

trapezium: *Bones 12*

trapezoid bone: *Bones 12*

trapiche emerald: *Minerals 10*

trapper: *Agricultural 1; Rural Occupations 1*

trappista: *Cheese International Varieties 6*

traps: *Architecture and Property 3; Common Dangers 24*

trapunto: *Embellishments 2*

trash bags: *Cleaning Supplies/Gadgets 5*

trash can lid: *Improvised Weapons 7*

trash can: *Containers and Vessels 5*

trash collector: *General Occupations 1*

trash compactor: *Major Appliances 4*

trash conversion: *Spaceship Drive Systems 22*

Travancore: *Tortoises 15*

travel clock: *Timekeeping 5*

travel hazards: *Transportation 9*

travel: *Christmas 19; Locomotion 9; Styles of Dress 2*

Travel: *Major Lines 19*

traveler: *Barbarian 1*

traveler's diarrhea: *Injuries/Medical Emergencies 12; Travel Hazards 9*

traveling case: *Containers and Vessels 5*

traveling chest: *Storage 4*

traveling preacher fakes miracles: *Western Plot Devices 21*

traveling salesman: *Common Character Archetypes 21*

traverse: *Windows 3*

travertine: *Minerals 10; Sedimentary Rocks 10*

travois: *Animal-Powered Transportation 9*

tray: *Tableware 5*

treading water: *Swimming Strokes 9*

treant: *Plant 16*

treasure chest: *Containers and Vessels 5*

treasure flower: *Garden Annuals 10*

treasure vase: *Eight Ashtamangala 19*

treasure: *Terms of Endearment 1*

treasurer: *Academic 1*

treasury: *Castle Anatomy 3*

treaty: *General Combat Vocabulary 7*

treble clef: *Notation 13*

treble: *Voices 13*

trebuchet: *Siege Engines 7*

tree : *Viper 15*

tree ear: *Fungus Common Names 10*

tree house: *Residential Property 3*

tree hugger: *Nature Occupations 1*

tree line: *Geography General Vocabulary 10*

tree lupin: *Shrubs 10*

tree mallow: *Garden Annuals 10; Garden Perennials 10; Shrubs 10*

tree nut: *Allergies 12*

tree of heaven: *Weeds 10*

tree peony: *Shrubs 10*

tree poppy: *Shrubs 10*

tree shrew: *Other Wild Mammals 15*

tree skirt: *Christmas 19*

tree stand: *Christmas 19*

tree trimmer: *General Farm Equipment*

tree: *Allergies 12; Bats 15; Boa 15; Charges 19; Christmas 19; Elf 1; General Snake Families 15; Natural Animal Homes 15*

Treeing Walker Coonhound: *Dog Breeds 15*

trees: *Chapter 10; Poker Card Games 5*

trek: *Journey 20; Locomotion 9*

trekker: *Barbarian 1*

trembling aspen: *Deciduous Trees 10*

trembling: *Horror Vocabulary 23*

tremolo: *Instrument Technique 13*

tremor: *Vocal/Speech Quality 1*

tremulous: *Vocal/Speech Quality 1*

trench coat: *Outerwear 2; Spy Gear 5; Unisex Clothing 2*

trench terrain warfare: *General Combat Vocabulary 7*

trench: *Fortification 3*

trencher: *Tableware 5*

trendsetter: *Wizard 1*

trendy: *New 20*

trepidation: *General Emotions 20; Horror Vocabulary 23*

tres leches: *Cake 6*

trespasser: *Thief 1*

trestle board: *Symbols of Freemasonry 19*

trestle: *Bridges 9*

triamiphos: *Dangerous Chemicals 11*

triangle: *Architectural/Engineering Tools 5; Face 1; Figures Associated with Symbols 19; Gem Cuts 21; Percussion Musical Instruments 5; Spaceship Shapes 22; Symbols of Freemasonry 19*

triangular: *Shield Types 7*

Triangulum Austraulis: *Constellations 11*

Triangulum: *Constellations 11*

Triassic Period: *Geologic Time 10*

triazofos: *Dangerous Chemicals 11*

tribal: *Art Genres 13; Styles of Dress 2*

tribesman: *Barbarian 1*

tributary: *Water Features 10; Water Terms 9*

tricarbonyl methylcyclopentadienyl: *Dangerous Chemicals 11*

triceratops: *Commonly Known Dinosaurs 15*

trichinellosis: *Diseases 12*

trichloroacetyl chloride: *Dangerous Chemicals 11*

trichloroethylsilane: *Dangerous Chemicals 11*

trichloronate: *Dangerous Chemicals 11*

trichlorophenylsilane: *Dangerous Chemicals 11*

trick or treat: *Masks 2*

trick: *Magic Vocabulary 17*

trickery: *Magic Vocabulary 17*

trickle: *Precipitation 10; Wet 20*

trick-or-treat bag: *Halloween 19*

trick-or-treat: *Halloween 19*

trickster: *Common Character Archetypes 21; Thief 1*

tricky: *Difficult 20*

tri-colored: *Bats 15*

tricorn hat: *Headgear 2*

tricorporate: *Monsters 19*

tricot: *Fabric 2*

tricycle: *Human-Powered Transportation 9*

trident: *Bats 15; Fishing Gear 5; Objects in Magic and Religion 19; Spears 7; Tools 7*

triethoxysilane: *Dangerous Chemicals 11*

triffid weed: *Weeds 10*

trifle bowl: *Tableware 5*

trifle: *Miscellaneous Dessert 6*

trifling: *Small/Fragile 20*

triggerfish: *Wild Saltwater Fish 15; Aquarium Saltwater Fish 15*

trigger: *Attack 7*

trilby: *Headgear 2*

tri-level: *Residential Property 3*

trill: *General Music Vocabulary 13*

trilliant: *Gem Cuts 21*

trillion: *Gem Cuts 21*

trilogy: *Books/Publications 5*

trim line: *Glacial and Mountain 10*

trim: *Building Elements and Features 3; Sewing Techniques 2; Small/Thin 1*

trimethylchlorosilane: *Dangerous Chemicals 11*

trimethyltin chloride: *Dangerous Chemicals 11*

Trinculo: *Moons 11*

trinket: *Jewelry 21*

trio sonata: *Composition Types 13*

trio: *Groups 13*

trip wire: *Traps 3*

trip: *Journey 20*

triphane: *Minerals 10*

triphenyltin chloride: *Dangerous Chemicals 11*

triple draw: *Poker Card Games 5*

triple goddess: *Symbols in Magic and Religion 19*

triple point: *Meteorology General Vocabulary 10*

triple star: *Pennsylvania Dutch Hex Signs 19*

triple tail: *Wild Saltwater Fish 15*

triple: *Chin 1; Star Systems 11*

tripod of life: *Symbols in Magic and Religion 19*

tripod stool: *Chairs and Stools 4*

Tripoli: *Card Games 5*

trips to win: *Poker Card Games 5*

triquestrum bone: *Bones 12*

triquetra: *Symbols in Magic and Religion 19*

triregnum: *Papal Symbols 19*

Trishula (trident of Shiva): *Weapons of Legend 18*

trishula: *Spears 7*

triskele: *Symbols in Magic and Religion 19*

Tristan: *Knights of the Round Table 18*

trisula: *Symbols in Magic and Religion 19*

triticale: *Grain 6*

tritoma: *Garden Perennials 10*

Triton: *Moons 11*

triumphal arch: *Special Purpose Structure 3*

triumphant: *Happy 20*

trivial: *Small/Fragile 20*

trochodendron: *Shrubs 10*

troglodyte: *Humanoid 16*

trogon: *Other Wild Birds 15*

Trois: *Ballet Terms 13*

Troisiéme: *Ballet Terms 13*

Trojan horse: *Objects 18*

trojan: *Astronomy General Terms 11*

troll cross: *Objects in Magic and Religion 19*

troll: *Giant Humanoids 16; Humanlike Groups 1; Humanoid 16*

trolley: *Animal-Powered Transportation 9*

trombone: *Wind/Woodwind and Brass Musical Instruments*

trondhjemite: *Igneous Rocks 10*

troodon formosus: *Commonly Known Dinosaurs 15*

troop transport destroyer: *Military Watercraft 8*

troop: *Armed Forces Other Titles 8; General Combat Vocabulary 7*

trooper: *Castle Inhabitants and Personnel 1; Fighter 1*

tropane alkaloids: *Poisonous Chemicals in Plants 11*

tropheus moorii: *Aquarium Freshwater Fish 15*

Tropic of Cancer: *Geography General Vocabulary 10*

Tropic of Capricorn: *Geography General Vocabulary 10*

tropical deciduous: *Ecosystems 10*

tropical depression: *Meteorology General Vocabulary 10*

tropical disturbance: *Meteorology General Vocabulary 10*

tropical dry: *Climatic Zones Koeppen System 10*

tropical evergreen: *Ecosystems 10*

tropical forest: *Terrain Features 10*

tropical fruits: *Food 6*

tropical peat: *Soil General Vocabulary 10*

tropical plants: *Common Dangers 23*

tropical rain forest: *Terrain Features 10*

tropical soda apple: *Weeds 10*

tropical storm: *Severe Weather 10*

tropical wave: *Meteorology General Vocabulary 10*

tropical wet: *Climatic Zones Koeppen System 10*

tropical: *Bats 15; Climatic Zones 10; Meteorology General Vocabulary 10; Rattlesnake 15; Warm 10*

tropics: *Geography General Vocabulary 10*

tropidurid lizard: *Scaled Reptiles 15*

troposphere: *Meteorology General Vocabulary 10*

troppo: *Tempo/Mood 13*

trotto: *Historical Dances 13*

troubadour: *Bard 1; Singer 1*

troubled student discovers evil book: *Horror Plot Devices 23*

trouble-free: *Easy 20*

trough: *Meteorology General Vocabulary 10*

trounce: *Attack 7*

trouser leg jeans: *Unisex Clothing 2*

trouser: *Socks 2*

trousers: *Men's Wear 2*

trout lily: *Garden Perennials 10*

trow: *General Fae 16*

trowel: *Garden Tools*

truce: *General Combat Vocabulary 7*

truck driver: *Horror Occupations 23*

truck: *Technical Terms 13; Toys 5*

trucker's hitch: *Sailing Knots 9*

trudge: *Journey 20; Locomotion 9*

trudgeon crawl: *Swimming Strokes 9*

trudgeon: *Swimming Strokes 9*

true blue: *Blue 20*

true daisy: *Garden Annuals 10*

true wind: *Water Terms 9*

truffle: *Oils 6*

trumpet chanterelle: *Fungus Common Names 10*

trumpet creeper: *Garden Perennials 10*

trumpet flower: *Garden Annuals 10*

trumpet of death: *Fungus Common Names 10*

trumpet: *Wind/Woodwind and Brass Musical Instruments*

trumpet-eared: *Bats 15*

trumps: *Card Games 5*

truncheon: *Bludgeons 7*

trundle: *Beds 4*

trunk: *Containers and Vessels 5; Storage 4*

trunks: *Men's Wear 2*

truss: *Bridges 9; Castle Anatomy 3; Technical Terms 13*

trussing: *Air Creatures 19*

trust: *Philosophy Basic Concepts 14*

trusted friend goes crazy: *Common Dangers 23*

trusted person turns out to be criminal: *Horror Plot Devices 23*

truth: *Philosophy Basic Concepts 14*

truthfulness: *Ten Perfections of Buddhism 19*

truth-seeker: *Wizard 1*

try: *Solve 20*

trying: *Difficult 20*

tsa tsa: *Objects in Magic and Religion 19*

Tsavo: *Lions 15*

tsavorite garnet: *Standard Gems 21*

tsavorite: *Minerals 10*

t-shirt: *Unisex Clothing 2*

Tsivilsk: *Pigs 15*

T-square: *Office/School/Writing Supplies 5*

T-straps: *Footwear/Shoes 2*

Tsukiyomi (moon): *Japanese Pantheon 14*

tsunami: *Geological Natural Hazards 10*

Tswana: *Other Cows 15*

Tuatha-de-danann: *Fae Related 16*

tub: *Containers and Vessels 5*

tuba: *Wind/Woodwind and Brass Musical Instruments*

tube agate: *Minerals 10*

tube pan: *Kitchen Equipment 5*

tube top: *Ladies' Wear 2*

tube: *Cave Anatomy 10; Laboratory Equipment 5; Socks 2*

tube-nosed: *Bats 15*

tuber vervain: *Wildflowers 10*

tuberculosis: *Diseases 12*

tuberous begonia: *Garden Annuals 10; Garden Bulbs 10*

tubeteika: *Headgear 2*

tubing: *Laboratory Equipment 5*

tubular bells: *Percussion Musical Instruments 5*

Tucana: *Constellations 11*

tuck: *Sewing Techniques 2*

Tudor Revival: *Architectural Styles 3*

Tudor: *Architectural Styles 3*

tufa: *Cave Anatomy 10; Minerals 10*

tuff: *Igneous Rocks 10*

tufted carpet: *Floor Coverings 4*

tufted ice plant: *Garden Perennials 10*

tufted: *Bats 15; Special Body Features 19*

Tuli: *Other Cows 15*

tulip poplar: *Deciduous Trees 10*

tulip skirt: *Dance Clothing 13*

tulip tree: *Deciduous Trees 10*

tulip: *Garden Bulbs 10*

tulle: *Fabric 2*

tumble: *Locomotion 9*

tumbler: *Drinkware 5; Performing Arts 1*

tummy shaper: *Ladies' Wear 2*

tumultuous: *Loud 20*

tun: *Containers and Vessels 5*

tuna patty: *Fish/Seafood Meals 6*

tuna salad: *Sandwiches 6*

tuna: *Fish/Seafood Types 6; Salads 6; Wild Saltwater Fish 15*

tundra: *Climatic Zones Koeppen System 10; Ecosystems 10*

tuner: *Music Accessories*

Tungsten: *Elements 11*

Tunguska blast: *Mysterious Occurrences 18*

Tunguska-M1 2S9M air-defense vehicle: *Russia Military Vehicles 8*

Tunguska-M1 self-propelled twin 30mm anti-aircraft guns and missiles: *Russia Military Vehicles 8*

tuning fork: *Music Accessories*

tuning peg: *Musical Instrument Parts 13*

tunnel of love: *Amusement Park/Carnival/Circus/Fair 3*

tunnel valley: *Glacial and Mountain 10*

tunnel: *Cave Anatomy 10; Natural Animal Homes 15; Outdoor Property 3; Roads 9*

Tuonetar (goddess of the underworld): *Finnish Pantheon 14*

Tuoni (underworld): *Finnish Pantheon 14*

tupelo gum: *Deciduous Trees 10*

tupelo: *Deciduous Trees 10*

tuque: *Headgear 2*

turaco: *Other Wild Birds 15*

turban: *Headgear 2*

turbidite: *Sedimentary Rocks 10*

turbulence: *Meteorology General Vocabulary 10*

turbulent: *Loud 20*

turca: *General Music Vocabulary 13*

turd: *Excrement 12*

tureen: *Tableware 5*

turgite: *Minerals 10*

Turk: *Human Ethnic Groups 1*

Turk's cap: *Garden Perennials 10*

Turk's head: *Sailing Knots 9*

turkey fat ore: *Minerals 10*

turkey jerky: *Snacks 6*

turkey vulture: *Other Wild Birds 15*

turkey: *Animals with Symbolic Meaning 19; Domesticated Farm Birds 15; Other Wild Birds 15; Poultry Types 6; Sandwiches 6; Thanksgiving 19*

Turkish Angora: *Domestic Cats 15*

Turkish coffee: *Coffee Drinks 6*

Turkish delight: *Candy General 6*

Turkish Grey Steppe: *Other Cows 15*

Turkish taffy: *Candy General 6*

Turkish towel: *Towels 5*

Turkish Van: *Domestic Cats 15*

Turkish: *Imported Carpets 4; Poker Card Games 5*

Turkmen: *Imported Carpets 4*

turmeric: *Spices 6*

turn: *Commands 20; Locomotion 9; Stage Terms 13*

turncoat: *Hero or Villain, Depending Upon Circumstance 20*

turndun: *Wind/Woodwind and Brass Musical Instruments*

turning a bed on Sunday or Friday: *Practices that Attract Bad Luck 19*

turning bridge: *Castle Anatomy 3*

turnip green: *Vegetables 6*

turnip: *Moth 15; Vegetable Juice 6; Vegetables 6*

turn-out: *Ballet Terms 13*

turntable: *Electronics 4*

Turopolje: *Pigs 15*

turquoise odontolite: *Minerals 10*

turquoise: *Blue 20; Cyan 20; Standard Gems 21*

turret lathe: *Power Tools*

turret: *Building Elements and Features 3; Castle Anatomy 3; Fortification 3*

turtle float: *Swimming Strokes 9*

turtle speed: *Slow 20*

turtle stroke: *Swimming Strokes 9*

turtle: *Animals with Symbolic Meaning 19*

turtlehead: *Garden Perennials 10; Sea Snake 15*

turtleneck: *Unisex Clothing 2*

turtles: *Animals 15*

tussah: *Fabric 2*

Tutankhamun: *Real People with Legendary Status 18*

tutor: *Teach 20*

Tutsi: *Human Ethnic Groups 1*

tutti frutti: *Ice Cream Flavors 6*

tutti: *General Music Vocabulary 13*

Tuttle: *Comets 11*

tutu: *Ballet Terms 13; Dance Clothing 13; Ladies' Wear 2*

tuxedo shirt: *Men's Wear 2*

tuxedo: *Men's Wear 2; Spy Gear 5*

tuya: *Volcanic 10*

tv stone: *Minerals 10*

TV table: *Tables 4*

TV tray: *Tables 4*

Tvashtri (demigod of science): *Indian Pantheon 14*

twang: *Vocal/Speech Quality 1*

tweed: *Fabric 2*

tweet: *Sounds 20*

tweezers: *Personal Care 5*

Twelve Apostles: *Philosophy and Religion 14*

twelve days of Christmas: *Collective Symbols 19*

twelve drummers drumming: *Twelve Days of Christmas 19*

twelve fruits of the Holy Spirit: *Collective Symbols 19*

twelve labors of Hercules: *Monsters 16*

twelve peers of Charlemagne: *Legendary, Mystical and Mythical Items and Locations 18*

twelve-note composition: *General Music Vocabulary 13*

twelve-string guitar: *String Musical Instruments*

twenty dollar gold piece: *Western Paraphernalia/People 21*

twenty-cent: *Coins and Currency 21*

twenty-dollar gold piece: *Coins and Currency 21*

twenty-one: *Card Games 5*

twice-baked: *Vegetables Cooked 6*

twig: *General Snake Families 15*

twilight: *Meteorology General Vocabulary 10*

twill: *Fabric 2*

twin set: *Ladies' Wear 2*

twin: *Beds 4*

twine: *Fasteners 5; General Survival Gear 5*

twinflower: *Shrubs 10*

twin-spotted: *Rattlesnake 15*

twinspur: *Garden Annuals 10; Garden Perennials 10*

twist: *Hair Style 1*

twisted ankle: *Injuries/Medical Emergencies 12*

twisted chain: *Embroidery Stitches 2*

twister: *Severe Weather 10*

twitter: *Sounds 20*

two bits: *Coins and Currency 21*

two half hitches: *Sailing Knots 9*

two hundred: *Card Games 5*

two penny grass: *Weeds 10*

two turtledoves: *Twelve Days of Christmas 19*

two-button suit: *Men's Wear 2*

two-cent: *Coins and Currency 21*

two-centered arch: *Castle Anatomy 3*

two-colored bolete: *Fungus Common Names 10*

two-eyed: *Eye Type 1*

two-handed hammer: *Bludgeons 7*

two-handed: *Axes 7*

two-legged worm lizard: *Scaled Reptiles 15*

two-piece suit: *Men's Wear 2*

two-prong: *Fencing Equipment 7*

two-spot ladybird: *Beetle 15*

two-step: *Dance Styles 13; Historical Dances 13*

two-striped walking stick: *Phasmid 15*

two-toed sloth: *Other Wild Mammals 15*

two-ton: *Heavy 20*

two-way radio: *Spy Gear 5*

two-wheel tractor: *Farm Transportation 9*

tybo: *Cheese International Varieties 6*

Tyche (goddess of good fortune): *Greek Pantheon 14*

Tyche: *Hypothetical Solar System Bodies 11*

tyet: *Symbols in Magic and Religion 19*

tyke: *Child 1*

Tyndall effect: *Chemistry General Vocabulary 11*

Type 86 Kubelwagen 4×4 utility vehicle: *Germany Military Vehicles 8*

Type 87 Kommandeurwagen 4×4 command vehicle: *Germany Military Vehicles 8*

type: *Philosophy Basic Concepts 14*

typesetter: *Publishing 1*

typesetting machine: *Office/School Machines 5*

typewriter: *Office/School Machines 5*

Typhon: *Giants of Legend 16*

Typhonian Order: *Secret/Mystical Organizations 18*

typhoon: *Severe Weather 10*

typical magical objects: *Magic 17*

Tyr (victory): *Norse Pantheon 14*

tyrannosaur: *Dinosaur Types 15*

tyrannosaurus: *Commonly Known Dinosaurs 15*

tyrant: *Fighter 1; Wizard 1*

Tyrfing: *Norse Weapons 18*

Tyrolean grey: *Cheese International Varieties 6*

Tzaphqiel: *Angels of Good 14*

–U–

U.S. Fire Arms .22 Plinker: *Revolver Single Action 7*

U.S. Fire Arms Bisley: *Revolver Single Action 7*

U.S. Fire Arms Double Eagle: *Revolver Single Action 7*

U.S. Fire Arms Gunslinger: *Revolver Single Action 7*

U.S. Fire Arms Rodeo: *Revolver Single Action 7*

U.S.S. Arizona: *Ships 18*

U.S.S. Constitution: *Ships 18*

U.S.S. Maine: *Ships 18*

uakari monkey: *New World Monkeys 15*

Uberti Lightning: *Lever Action and Pump Centerfire Rifles 7*

Uberti Model 1873 Buntline: *Revolver Single Action 7*

Uberti Rolling Block: *Single Shot Rimfire Rifles 7*

Uberti Top-Break Schofield: *Revolver Single Action 7*

uchigatana: *Swords Two-handed 7*

udu: *Demon 16*

UFO: *Plot Devices 22; Travel Modes 23*

uglifruit: *Citrus 6*

ugly milkcap: *Fungus Common Names 10*

ugly: *Card Games 5; Unattractive 20*

ugni: *Unusual Edible Fruits 6*

ugrandite: *Minerals 10*

UH-1 Iroquois: *U.S. Army Helicopter 8*

UH-60 Black Hawk: *U.S. Army Helicopter 8*

UH-72 Lakota: *U.S. Army Helicopter 8*

Ukko (leader of the gods): *Finnish Pantheon 14*

Ukrainian Beef: *Other Cows 15*

Ukrainian Grey: *Other Cows 15*

Ukrainian Saddle: *Horse Breeds 15*

Ukrainian spotted steppe: *Pigs 15*

Ukrainian white steppe: *Pigs 15*

Ukrainian Whitehead: *Other Cows 15*

Ukrainian: *Human Ethnic Groups 1*

Ulama ball court at Nahuatl: *Real Places Steeped in Legend or Mystery 18*

Uller (magic): *Norse Pantheon 14*

ulna: *Bones 12*

ultimate: *Ending 20*

ultisol: *Soil General Vocabulary 10*

ultra pink: *Pink 20*

ultralite: *Minerals 10*

ultramarine: *Blue 20*

ultraviolet radiation: *Energy Sources/Types 22*

ultraviolet: *Astronomy General Terms 11*

ultravision: *Physical Mutations 22*

umbalite: *Minerals 10*

umber: *Brown 20*

Umblachery: *Other Cows 15*

umbra: *Astronomy General Terms 11*

umbraculum: *Papal Symbols 19*

umbrella polypore : *Fungus Common Names 10*

umbrella stand: *Miscellaneous Furniture 4*

umbrella: *Accessories 2*

umbric horizon: *Soil General Vocabulary 10*

Umbriel: *Moons 11*

umbrisol: *Soil General Vocabulary 10*

Una de Gato: *Deciduous Trees 10*

unabridged dictionary: *Books/Publications 5*

unadorned: *Easy 20*

unafraid: *Personality Other 1*

unakite: *Minerals 10*

unappealing: *Unattractive 20*

unappetizing: *Unattractive 20*

unattractive: *Adjectives 20; Unattractive 20*

unbearable: *Sad 20; Unattractive 20*

unbleached flour: *Staples 6*

unblemished: *Beautiful 20*

unbolt: *Open/Release 20*

unbound: *Open/Release 20*

unbreakable mirror: *Personal Care 5*

unbutton: *Open/Release 20*

uncanny: *Magic Vocabulary 17*

uncaring: *Negative 1*

unchain: *Open/Release 20*

uncivilized: *Unattractive 20*

uncle: *Male 1*

uncomfortable bed: *Travel Hazards 9*

uncommitted: *Personality Other 1*

uncommunicative: *Quiet 20*

uncomplicated: *Easy 20*

uncompromising: *Stubborn 1*

unconcerned: *Personality Other 1*

unconstructed: *Styles of Dress 2*

unconventional war: *General Combat Vocabulary 7*

uncouple: *Open/Release 20*

uncouth:*Unattractive 20*

uncover: *Learn 20*

undead relative: *Common Dangers 23*

undead/vampires/werewolves/zombies: *Common Dangers 24*

undead/zombie uprising: *Horror Genres 23*

undead: *Common Dangers 23; Dragon 16; Monsters 16*

undecided: *Horror Vocabulary 23*

undemanding: *Easy 20*

under slung grenade launcher: *Military Weapons General 8*

underage: *Child 1*

underarm: *Body Parts 12*

underclothes: *Undergarments 2*

undercover agent: *Hero or Villain, Depending Upon Circumstance 20*

undercurrent: *Water Terms 9*

undercut: *Hair Style 1*

underdeveloped: *Small/Fragile 20*

undergarments: *Clothing 2*

undergraduate: *Academic 1*

underground catacomb: *Horror Locations 23*

underground city: *Fantasy Locations 24; Installations 22*

underground civilization:*Plot Devices 22*

underground labyrinth: *Fantasy Locations 24*

underground: *Art Genres 13; Terrain Features 10*

undergrowth: *Terrain Features 10*

underhanded: *Horror Vocabulary 23*

undernourished: *Small/Thin 1*

underpants: *Undergarments 2*

undershirt: *Men's Wear 2*

undersize: *Small/Thin 1*

undersized: *Small/Fragile 20*

understand: *Learn 20*

understanding: *Philosophy Basic Concepts 14; Seven Gifts of the Holy Spirit 19*

undertone: *Vocal/Speech Quality 1*

underwater bubble vessel: *Vehicles 24*

underwater car: *Spy Gear 5*

underwater city: *Horror Locations 23*

underwater colony: *Plot Devices 22*

underwater domed city: *Installations 22*

underwater entrance: *Travel Modes 24*

underwater monsters/giant creatures: *Horror Plot Devices 23*

underwater portal: *Travel Modes 23*

underwater race becomes part of society: *Fantasy Plot Devices 24*

underwater: *Swimming Strokes 9; Travel Types 22*

underway: *Boat/Ship Terminology 9*

underwear: *Undergarments 2*

underweight: *Small/Thin 1*

underwire bra: *Ladies' Wear 2*

underworld: *Legendary, Mystical and Mythical Items and Locations 18; Legendary/Mythical Locations 18*

underwriter: *Finance 1*

undine: *Water Faerie 16*

undistinguished: *Personality Other 1*

undo: *Open/Release 20*

undulated: *Pit Viper 15*

unearthly: *Horror Vocabulary 23*

unease: *Horror Vocabulary 23*

unemployed: *Social Distinction 1*

unendurable: *Unattractive 20*

unenthusiastic:*Horror Vocabulary 23*

uneven parallel bars:*Sporting Goods Other 5*

uneven:*Chin 1*

unexpected aid from librarian/neighbor/stranger: *Horror Plot Devices 23*

unexpected death: *Travel Hazards 9*

unexplained: *Magic Vocabulary 17*

unfasten: *Open/Release 20*

unfathomable: *Magic Vocabulary 17*

unfeeling: *Horror Vocabulary 23*

unfetter: *Open/Release 20*

unflustered: *Easy 20*

unforced: *Easy 20*

unfussy: *Easy 20*

unguent: *Wizard's Goods 5*

unguled: *Special Body Features 19*

unhappy: *Sad 20*

unhurried: *Slow 20*

unibrow: *Eyebrows 1*

unicorn: *Beast 16; Fantasy Creatures with Symbolic Meaning 19; Magical Transportation 17*

unicursal hexagram: *Symbols in Magic and Religion 19*

unicycle: *Human-Powered Transportation 9*

Unification Church symbol: *Symbols in Magic and Religion 19*

unified sequence drone: *Military Aircraft Pre-1962 8*

Unified Soil Classification System: *Soil General Vocabulary 10*

uniform service: *Public Services 3*

uniform: *Styles of Dress 2*

uniformitarianism: *Geologic Concepts 10*

unimportant: *Small/Fragile 20*

unincorporated: *City 10*

unintelligent: *Character Building 1*

uninterested: *Personality Other 1*

uninviting: *Unattractive 20*

Union and Confederate soldiers go home: *Western Plot Devices 21*

union cloth: *Fabric 2*

union suit: *Unisex Clothing 2; Western Clothing/Dress 21*

Union: *Minor Lines 19*

unique occupations: *Character Building 1*

unique property destroyed: *Architecture and Property 3*

unique property: *Architecture and Property 3*

unique: *Weapons 22*

unisex clothing: *Clothing 2*

unisex: *Styles of Dress 2*

unison: *General Music Vocabulary 13*

unitard: *Dance Clothing 13*

unity: *Art Principles 13; Philosophy Basic Concepts 14; Philosophy Basic Concepts 14*

universal time: *Astronomy General Terms 11*

universal: *Philosophy Basic Concepts 14*

universality: *Philosophy Basic Concepts 14*

university lab: *Horror Locations 23*

university: *Academic Property 3*

unkempt: *Eyebrows 1*

unknot: *Open/Release 20*

unknowable: *Magic Vocabulary 17*

unknown subject: *Hero or Villain, Depending Upon Circumstance 20*

unknown: *Magic Vocabulary 17; Personality Other 1*

unleash: *Attack 7; Open/Release 20*

unleavened bread: *Foods with Religious or Ritual Significance 19*

unleavened: *Bread General Varieties 6*

unlikable: *Unattractive 20*

unlimited: *Large 20*

unlock: *Open/Release 20*

unmanageable: *Difficult 20*

unmanned aerial vehicle: *Military Aircraft 8*

unmanned combat: *Robots 22*

unmanned submarine: *Vehicles 22*

unmanned surface destroyer: *Vehicles 22*

unmanned: *Spaceship Types 22*

unmentionables: *Undergarments 2*

unmovable: *Stubborn 1*

unmoving: *Stubborn 1*

unnatural: *Magic Vocabulary 17*

unobservable: *Philosophy Basic Concepts 14*

unpalatable: *Unattractive 20*

unperturbed: *Easy 20; Happy 20*

unpiloted drone: *Military Aircraft Pre-1962 8*

unpleasant/mean celebrity: *Common Character Archetypes 21*

unpleasant: *Bad 20; Unattractive 20*

unpretentious: *Easy 20*

unproblematic: *Easy 20*

unpromising: *Sad 20*

unravel: *Open/Release 20*

unreasonable: *Negative 1*

unresponsive: *Horror Vocabulary 23*

unruly: *Difficult 20*

unsaturated hydrocarbons: *Chemistry General Vocabulary 11*

unscrew: *Open/Release 20*

unscrupulous: *Bad 20*

unseelie court: *Fae Related 16*

unshaven: *Facial Hair Beard 1*

unsightly: *Unattractive 20*

unsophisticated: *Easy 20*

unspeakable: *Bad 20; Unattractive 20*

unspeaking: *Quiet 20*

unspoiled: *Beautiful 20; Happy 20*

unstable footing: *Moves 7*

unstable: *Horror Vocabulary 23; Meteorology General Vocabulary 10*

unstinted: *Large 20*

unstitch: *Open/Release 20*

Untamo (dreams): *Finnish Pantheon 14*

untangle: *Open/Release 20*

untie: *Open/Release 20*

Ununnilium: *Elements 11*

unusual edible fruits: *Food 6*

unusual: *Magic Vocabulary 17*

unwelcoming: *Sad 20*

unwilling: *Horror Vocabulary 23*

unwise: *Unintelligent 1*

unworldly: *Magic Vocabulary 17*

unwrap: *Open/Release 20*

unyoke: *Open/Release 20*

ALPHABETICAL INDEX

up the river: *Prison 3*

up to date: *New 20*

up to the minute: *New 20*

up: *Happy 20*

upbeat: *Happy 20*

updo: *Hair Style 1*

updraft: *Meteorology General Vocabulary 10*

upfront: *Beginning 20*

upgrade: *Buy 20*

upheaval: *General Combat Vocabulary 7; Geological Vocabulary 10*

upholstery hammer: *Hand Tools 5*

upland willow oak: *Deciduous Trees 10*

uplands: *Climatic Zones Koeppen System 10*

uplifting: *Happy 20*

upper arm: *Body Parts 12*

upper class: *Social Distinction 1; Personality Other 1*

upper echelon: *Social Distinction 1*

upright freezer: *Major Appliances 4*

upright: *Good 20*

uprising: *General Combat Vocabulary 7*

upset stomach: *Injuries/Medical Emergencies 12*

upset: *General Emotions 20*

upside-down catfish: *Aquarium Freshwater Fish 15*

upside-down: *Cake 6*

upstage: *Stage Directions 13*

upstairs maid: *Housekeeping 1*

upwelling: *Meteorology General Vocabulary 10*

upwind: *Meteorology General Vocabulary 10*

Ur: *Sites Lost or Unproven to Exist 18*

Uracoan: *Rattlesnake 15*

uraeus: *Symbols in Magic and Religion 19*

Ural Black Pied: *Other Cows 15*

uralite: *Minerals 10*

uranium fueled: *Spaceship Drive Systems 22*

Uranium: *Elements 11*

uranothorite: *Minerals 10*

Urantia Book: *Major Religious Books 14*

Uranus (sky): *Roman Pantheon 14*

Uranus: *Planets 11*

urban terrain warfare: *General Combat Vocabulary 7*

urban: *Art Genres 13*

urchin: *Child 1; Geological Vocabulary 10*

urda: *Cheese International Varieties 6*

ureter: *Organs/Major Structures 12*

urethra: *Organs/Major Structures 12*

urgent care center: *Health Care 3*

Urgonian: *Geological Vocabulary 10*

Uriel: *Angels of Good 14*

Uriens: *Knights of the Round Table 18*

urim and thummim: *Symbols in Magic and Religion 19*

urinant: *Sea Creatures 19*

urinary: *Body Systems 12*

urine: *Excrement 12; Items with Healing Properties 19*

urn: *Containers and Vessels 5*

Ursa Major: *Constellations 11*

Ursa Minor: *Constellations 11*

Ursini's:*Viper 15*

Urutu: *General Snake Families 15*

Urzhum: *Pigs 15*

USB connector: *Computer Equipment 5*

USDA soil taxonomy: *Soil General Vocabulary 10*

USFA-sanctioned: *Fencing Vocabulary 7*

ushabti: *Construct 16*

ushanka: *Headgear 2*

u-shaped valley: *Glacial and Mountain 10*

Ushas (goddess of the dawn): *Indian Pantheon 14*

usher: *Special Occasion 1*

ustochrept: *Soil General Vocabulary 10*

Ustym Karmaliuk: *Real People with Legendary Status 18*

utahite: *Minerals 10*

uterus: *Organs/Major Structures 12*

Uther Pendragon: *Arthurian Characters 18*

utility knife: *Hand Tools 5; Kitchen Utensils 5*

utility transport: *Military Aircraft Pre-1962 8*

utility: *Helicopters 8; Military Aircraft 8; Military Aircraft*

Pre-1962 8

Utopia: *Fictional/Mythological Locations 18*

utopia: *Plot Devices 22*

Utu (sun): *Sumerian Pantheon 14*

UV lamp: *Illumination Bulb and Tube Types 5*

uvite: *Minerals 10*

uvula: *Body Parts 12*

Uzziel: *Angels of Good 14*

–V–

V-242 Storm Mark III 4×4 utility vehicle: *Israel Military Vehicles 8*

vacation turns disastrous: *Horror Plot Devices 23*

vacation wear: *Styles of Dress 2*

vacation: *Christmas 19; Journey 20*

vacuum bottle: *Containers and Vessels 5*

vacuum cleaner: *Cleaning Supplies/Gadgets 5*

vacuum dry box: *Laboratory Equipment 5*

vacuum: *Clean 20*

vadose development: *Cave Anatomy 10*

vagabond: *Thief 1; Wanderer 1*

vagina: *Body Parts 12; Organs/Major Structures 12*

vagrant: *Barbarian 1; Wanderer 1*

vair: *Fur 19*

Vajra (staff of Indra): *Weapons of Legend 18*

vajra: *Objects in Magic and Religion 19*

Valadon: *Knights of the Round Table 18*

valance: *Window Treatments 5*

vale: *Fluvial 10; Gnome 1; Slope 10*

valence bond theory: *Chemistry General Vocabulary 11*

valence electrons: *Chemistry General Vocabulary 11*

valence shell electron pair repulsion theory: *Chemistry General Vocabulary 11*

Valencian: *Human Ethnic Groups 1*

Valentine's Day: *Holidays 19*

valerian: *Garden Perennials 10*

Valhalla: *Afterlife/Underworld 18*

valiant: *Personality Other 1*

validity: *Philosophy Basic Concepts 14*

valinomycin: *Dangerous Chemicals 11*

valknut: *Symbols in Magic and Religion 19*

valley oak: *Deciduous Trees 10*

valley shoulder: *Slope 10*

valley white oak: *Deciduous Trees 10*

valley willow: *Deciduous Trees 10*

valley: *Erosion 10; Fluvial 10; Glacial and Mountain 10; Slope 10*

valor: *General Emotions 20*

value: *General Emotions 20; Philosophy Basic Concepts 14; Visual Elements 13*

vambrace: *Armor Pieces 7*

vampire bat: *Beast 16*

vampire lair: *Fantasy Locations 24*

vampire: *Bats 15; Fantasy Creatures with Symbolic Meaning 19; Halloween 19; Horror Plot Devices 23; Squid 15; Undead 16*

vampires: *Horror Genres 23*

vampirism: *Physical Mutations 22*

Van Allen belts: *Astronomy General Terms 11*

van de Graff generator: *Laboratory Equipment 5*

van dyke: *Facial Hair Beard 1*

van: *Motorized 9*

Vanadium: *Elements 11*

vanadiumdravite: *Minerals 10*

Vandal: *Human Ethnic Groups 1*

Vandyke: *Embroidery Stitches 2*

vanguard: *New 20*

vanilla bean: *Ice Cream Flavors 6*

vanilla: *Ice Cream Flavors 6; Unusual Edible Fruits 6; White 20*

vanity: *Bathroom Features and Fixtures 3; Tables 4*

vanquisher: *Hero 20*

vapor pressure: *Chemistry General Vocabulary 11*

vapor trail: *Meteorology General Vocabulary 10*

vapor: *Chemistry General Vocabulary 11; Meteorology General Vocabulary 10; Paranormal Occurrences 21; Smells 20*

vaporizing: *Weapons 22*

vapors: *Diseases 12*

variable star: *Astronomy General Terms 11*

variable: *Star Types and Relatives 11*

variation: *Ballet Terms 13; General Music Vocabulary 13*

variegated copper: *Minerals 10*

variegated ground ivy: *Garden Perennials 10*

variegated sweet marjoram: *Garden Perennials 10*

variegated yellow rocket: *Garden Perennials 10*

variety show: *Performance Genres 13*

variety store: *Business Property 3*

variety: *Art Principles 13*

Variscan orogeny: *Geological Vocabulary 10*

variscite: *Standard Gems 21*

varnish: *Art Materials 5*

Varuna (law and order): *Indian Pantheon 14*

vas deferens: *Organs/Major Structures 12*

vase pin: *Jewelry 21*

vase: *Containers and Vessels 5; Improvised Weapons 7; Tableware 5*

Vasey shin oak: *Deciduous Trees 10*

vast: *Heavy 20; Large 20; Large/Heavy 1*

vat: *Containers and Vessels 5*

Vatican: *Unique Property 3*

Vatikan: *Card Games 5*

vaudeville: *Performance Genres 13*

vault: *Building Elements and Features 3; Castle Anatomy 3; Cemetery 3; Locomotion 9; Rooms 3*

Vayu (sky): *Indian Pantheon 14*

VCR: *Electronics 4*

veal: *Farm/Outbuilding 3*

vegetable bowl: *Tableware 5*

vegetable juice: *Food 6*

vegetable knife: *Kitchen Utensils 5*

vegetable: *Oils 6; Salads 6; Soup 6*

vegetables: *Food 6*

vegetation and slope stability: *Soil General Vocabulary 10*

vehemence: *General Emotions 20*

vehicle-mounted weapon system: *Military 8*

vehicles: *Transportation 9*

veil of lace: *Garden Perennials 10*

Veil of Veronica: *Relics of Jesus 14*

veil: *Headgear 2*

veiled hat: *Headgear 2*

veiled: *Magic Vocabulary 17*

veiling: *Magic Vocabulary 17*

vein: *Geological Vocabulary 10; Organs/Major Structures 12*

Vela: *Constellations 11*

veldt: *Ecosystems 10*

vellum: *Art Materials 5; Office/School/Writing Supplies 5; Wizard's Goods 5*

velociraptor mongoliensis: *Commonly Known Dinosaurs 15*

velour: *Fabric 2*

velvet copper ore: *Minerals 10*

velvet foot: *Fungus Common Names 10*

velvet mesquite: *Deciduous Trees 10*

velvet sumac: *Deciduous Trees 10*

velvet tourmaline: *Minerals 10*

velvet: *Art Genres 13; Christmas 19; Fabric 2*

velveteen: *Fabric 2*

velvety: *Vocal/Speech Quality 1*

Venda: *Human Ethnic Groups 1*

veneer: *Interior Building Materials 3*

veneers: *Teeth Dental Work 1*

venerable: *Elderly 1*

venerate: *General Emotions 20*

veneration of the Cross: *Rituals 14*

veneration: *General Emotions 20*

Venetian blinds: *Window Treatments 5*

Venetian Renaissance: *Art Movements 13*

Venetian sumac: *Garden Perennials 10*

Venetian: *Human Ethnic Groups 1*

venison: *Other Meat 6*

venom: *Wizard's Goods 5*

venomous: *Negative 1*

vent: *Building Systems 3; Geography General Vocabulary 10; Volcanic 10*

ventifact: *Aeolian 10*

ventilation: *Building Systems 3*

ventriloquism: *Performance Genres 13*

ventriloquist dummy: *Classic Items 23*

ventriloquist: *Performing Arts 1*

venture: *Locomotion 9*

Venus (goddess of love): *Roman Pantheon 14*

Venus fly trap: *Plant 16*

Venus hair quartz: *Minerals 10*

Venus hair stone: *Minerals 10*

Venus slipper: *Wildflowers 10*

Venus: *Mounts 19; Planets 11*

Veracruz amethyst: *Minerals 10*

veranda: *Outdoor Property 3; Rooms 3*

verbena: *Garden Annuals 10; Shrubs 10*

Vercingetorix: *Real People with Legendary Status 18*

verde antique: *Minerals 10*

verdelite: *Minerals 10*

Verdi: *Facial Hair Beard 1*

verging: *Geological Vocabulary 10*

verismo: *General Music Vocabulary 13*

vermarine: *Minerals 10*

vermicelli: *Pasta 6*

vermilion bird: *Flying Creatures 16*

vermilion: *Red 20; Wild Saltwater Fish 15*

vermouth dry: *Hard Liquor 6*

vermouth sweet: *Hard Liquor 6*

Vernacular: *Architectural Styles 3*

vert (green): *Colors/Tinctures 19*

vertebra: *Bones 12*

vertisol: *Soil General Vocabulary 10*

vervain: *Garden Perennials 10; Shrubs 10*

vervet: *Old World Monkeys 15*

very last: *Ending 20*

vesica piscis: *Symbols in Magic and Religion 19*

vesper iris: *Garden Perennials 10*

vesper: *Bats 15*

vespers: *Composition Types 13; Rituals 14*

vessel: *Small Watercraft 9*

vessels: *Equipment and Tools 5*

vest: *Unisex Clothing 2; Western Clothing/Dress 21*

Vesta (goddess of hearth): *Roman Pantheon 14*

vested: *Special Body Features 19*

vestibular: *Body Systems 12*

vestibule: *Church Anatomy 3; Rooms 3*

Vestland Fjord: *Other Cows 15*

Vestland Red Polled: *Other Cows 15*

vestment: *Religious Dress 2; Religious Items 5*

veterinarian: *Animal/Equestrian 1*

veterinary assistant: *Animal/Equestrian 1*

VHS player: *Electronics 4*

VHS recorder: *Electronics 4*

viaduct: *Bridges 9; Roads 9*

vial: *Containers and Vessels 5; Wizard's Goods 5*

vibrant: *Vocal/Speech Quality 1*

vibraphone: *Percussion Musical Instruments 5*

vibrating: *Beds 4*

vibrato: *General Music Vocabulary 13; Vocal/Speech Quality 1*

vibro stone column: *Soil General Vocabulary 10*

vibro: *Weapons 22*

viburnum: *Shrubs 10*

vicar general: *Religious Occupations 1*

vicar: *Cleric 1; Religious Occupations 1*

vice admiral: *Maritime Occupations 1; U.S. Navy Officer 8*

vice president: *Government 1*

vice: *Bad 20*

vicereine: *Royal/Noble 1*

viceroy: *Butterfly 15; Royal/Noble 1*

viceroyalty: *Political Divisions 10*

vichysoisse: *Soup 6*

vicious: *Horror Vocabulary 23; Negative 1*

victim: *Common Character Archetypes 21*

victims must escape before time runs out: *Horror Plot Devices 23*

victor: *Hero 20*

Victoria Falls: *Seven Wonders of the Natural World 18*

Victorian horror: *Horror Genres 23*

Victorian: *Architectural Styles 3; Chairs and Stools 4; Residential Property 3; Roof Styles 3; Styles of Dress 2*

victory banner: *Eight Ashtamangala 19*

Victrola: *Electronics 4*

Vidalia onion: *Vegetables 6*

Vidar's shoes: *Clothing 18*

video camera: *Spy Gear 5*

video cassette recorder: *Electronics 4*

video projector: *Office/School Machines 5*

Vienna: *Bread General Varieties 6; Coffee Bean Roasts 6*

Vienna coffee: *Coffee Drinks 6*

Vietnamese potbelly: *Pigs 15*

Vietnamese: *Human Ethnic Groups 1; Tea 6*

vigil: *Candles 5*

vigilant: *Air Creatures 19; Horror Vocabulary 23*

vigilante: *Western Paraphernalia/People 21*

vigoroso: *Tempo/Mood 13*

vigorous: *Happy 20; Mobility 1*

Viking: *Axes 7; Fighter 1*

vile: *Unattractive 20*

Villa: *Architectural Styles 3*

villa: *Residential Property 3*

village administrator: *Government 1*

village idiot: *Common Character Archetypes 21; General Occupations 1; Social Distinction 1; Supporting Cast 24*

village square: *Outdoor Property 3*

village well: *Horror Locations 23*

village: *City 10*

villain discovers magic: *Fantasy Plot Devices 24*

villain plans to destroy the world: *Fantasy Plot Devices 24*

villain steals life force from victims: *Horror Plot Devices 23*

villain tries to enslave population: *Fantasy Plot Devices 24*

villain: *Common Character Archetypes 21; Illicit Occupations 1; Nouns 20*

Vimana: *Vehicles 18*

Vimanas flying machine images: *Real Objects Not Fully Understood 18*

vinaigrette: *Salad Dressing 6*

vinca vine: *Garden Annuals 10*

vinca: *Garden Annuals 10; Shrubs 10*

vine: *General Snake Families 15*

vinegar tree: *Deciduous Trees 10*

vinegary: *Smells 20*

vintage: *Elderly 1; Motorized 9; Old 20; Styles of Dress 2*

vintner: *Castle Inhabitants and Personnel 1; Food Service 1*

vinyl acetate monomer: *Dangerous Chemicals 11*

vinyl paint: *Art Materials 5*

vinyl siding: *Exterior Building Materials 3*

vinyl: *Art Media 13*

viol: *String Musical Instruments*

viola d'amore: *String Musical Instruments*

viola: *Garden Annuals 10; String Musical Instruments*

violane: *Minerals 10*

viole da gamba: *String Musical Instruments*

violet: *Dragon 16; Eye Color 1; Garden Perennials 10; Purple 20*

violin: *String Musical Instruments*

violinist: *Musical Occupations 1*

violist: *Musical Occupations 1*

violone: *String Musical Instruments*

VIP transport: *Military Aircraft 8*

VIP/passenger transport: *Military Aircraft 8*

VIP: *Hero 20*

viper: *Animals 15*

viral outbreak: *Common Dangers 22*

virgin sacrifice: *Horror Plot Devices 23*

Virgin Valley opal: *Minerals 10*

virgin's bower: *Garden Perennials 10*

virginal: *String Musical Instruments*

Virginia bluebells: *Wildflowers 10*

Virginia City: *Famous Western Locations 21*

Virginia class attack submarine: *U.S. Navy Vessels 8*

Virginia creeper: *Garden Perennials 10*

Virginia live oak: *Deciduous Trees 10*

Virginia pine: *Evergreen Trees 10*

Virgo (August 23–September 22): *Zodiac Signs 19*

Virgo cluster: *Astronomy General Terms 11*

Virgo: *Constellations 11*

virtual: *Philosophy Basic Concepts 14*

virtue: *Angels Common Terms 14; Philosophy Basic Concepts 14*

virtuoso: *Ballet Terms 13*

virtuous: *Good 20*

vis-à-vis: *Seating 4*

Visayan: *Human Ethnic Groups 1*

viscount: *Royal/Noble 1*

viscountess: *Royal/Noble 1*

viscous: *Wet 20*

Vishnu (mercy): *Indian Pantheon 14*

Vishnu's divine jewel: *Jewelry 18*

visibility: *Meteorology General Vocabulary 10*

visible light: *Astronomy General Terms 11*

vision system: *Military Equipment 8*

vision visit: *Paranormal Occurrences 21*

vision: *Magic Vocabulary 17; Physical Mutations 22*

visionary: *Wizard 1*

visitation: *Rituals 14*

visitors: *Christmas 19*

visor: *Headgear 2*

visored: *Bats 15*

visual art: *The Arts 13*

visual cue: *Stage Terms 13*

visual elements: *The Arts 13*

visual magnitude: *Astronomy General Terms 11*

vital: *Large/Heavy 1*

V.I.T.R.I.O.L. (visita interiorem terrae rectifando invenies operae lapidem): *Symbols in Magic and Religion 19*

vitreous enamel paint: *Art Materials 5*

vitreous enamel: *Art Media 13*

vitrinite: *Geological Vocabulary 10*

Vitthakalai: *Vehicles 18*

vivace: *Tempo/Mood 13*

vivacious: *Happy 20*

Vivien: *Arthurian Characters 18*

Vizsla: *Dog Breeds 15*

Vlaamperd: *Horse Breeds 15*

Vlad the Impaler: *Real People with Legendary Status 18*

Vladimir Heavy Draft: *Horse Breeds 15*

V-neck t-shirt: *Unisex Clothing 2*

vocal quality: *Character Building 1*

vocalise: *Composition Types 13*

vociferous: *Loud 20*

vodka: *Hard Liquor 6*

vodyanoi: *Demon 16*

vogue: *Dance Styles 13*

voice coach: *Musical Occupations 1*

voice recorder: *Spy Gear 5*

voice: *Character Building 1*

voiceless: *Quiet 20*

voices: *The Arts 13*

void ratio: *Soil General Vocabulary 10*

void: *Philosophy Basic Concepts 14*

voile: *Fabric 2*

voivodeship: *Political Divisions 10*

Volans: *Constellations 11*

volant: *Air Creatures 19*

Volcan wolf giant: *Tortoises 15*

volcanic arc: *Coastal and Oceanic 10*

volcanic cone: *Volcanic 10*

volcanic craters: *Volcanic 10*

volcanic dam: *Volcanic 10*

volcanic energy: *Energy Sources/Types 24*

volcanic eruption: *Energy Sources/Types 23; Geological Natural Hazards 10*

volcanic field: *Volcanic 10*

volcanic group: *Volcanic 10*

volcanic island: *Volcanic 10*

volcanic landforms: *Chapter 10*

volcanic plateau: *Volcanic 10*

volcanic plug: *Volcanic 10*

volcanism: *Geologic Concepts 10*

volcano: *Volcanic 10*

volcanology: *Geologic Fields of Study 10*

vole: *Woodland Mammals 15*

Volga blue: *Minerals 10*

Volga German: *Human Ethnic Groups 1*

volley fire: *General Combat Vocabulary 7*

Volo Bog Illinois: *Bogs of North America 10*

Völsunga Saga: *Dragon 16*

voltage: *Chemistry General Vocabulary 11*

voltaic cells: *Chemistry General Vocabulary 11*

volume: *Visual Elements 13*

volumetric flask: *Laboratory Equipment 5*

voluntary: *Composition Types 13*

volunteer: *General Occupations 1*

voluptuous: *Lips 1*

vomer: *Bones 12*

vomit: *Smells 20*

voodoo doll: *Objects in Magic and Religion 19*

voodoo priest: *Unique 1*

voodoo priestess: *Unique 1*

vorant: *Special Body Features 19*

vorpal blade: *Typical Magical Objects 17*

vortex mixer: *Laboratory Equipment 5*

vortex: *Meteorology General Vocabulary 10*

Vorticism: *Art Movements 13*

Vosges: *Other Cows 15*

votive: *Candles 5*

voudon veves: *Symbols in Magic and Religion 19*

voulge: *Pole Weapons 7; Swords One-handed 7*

voyage: *Journey 20; Locomotion 9*

voyager: *Barbarian 1*

Voynich manuscript: *Real Objects Not Fully Understood 18*

vucub-caquix: *Demon 16*

vug: *Geological Vocabulary 10*

Vulcan (craftsmanship): *Roman Pantheon 14*

Vulcan: *Hypothetical Solar System Bodies 11*

Vulcanoids: *Hypothetical Solar System Bodies 11*

vulgar: *General Emotions 20; Unattractive 20*

vulkodlak: *Beast 16*

vulned: *Special Body Features 19*

vulning: *Special Posture 19*

Vulpecula: *Constellations 11*

vulture: *Animals with Symbolic Meaning 19; Bees 15; Other Wild Birds 15*

vulva: *Body Parts 12*

Vyatka: *Horse Breeds 15*

–W–

wackestone: *Sedimentary Rocks 10*

waddy: *Bludgeons 7*

waders: *Boots 2*

waders: *Fishing Gear 5*

wadi: *Fluvial 10*

wadsleyite: *Minerals 10*

wafer cone: *Ice Cream Cones 6*

wafer: *Bread General Varieties 6; Candy General 6; Religious Bread 6*

waffle bowl: *Ice Cream Cones 6*

waffle cone: *Ice Cream Cones 6*

waffle fries: *Vegetables Cooked 6*

waffle iron: *Appliances 5*

waffle: *Bread General Varieties 6; Fabric 2*

waft: *Wind 10*

wag: *Bard 1*

wager creates deadly challenge: *Horror Plot Devices 23*

Wagler's: *Pit Viper 15*

wagon loader: *General Farm Equipment*

wagon plow: *Horse Drawn Farm Equipment*

wagon train: *Animal-Powered Transportation 9; Western Paraphernalia/People 21*

wagon wheel: *Pasta 6*

wagon: *Animal-Powered Transportation 9; Farm Transportation 9; Garden Tools; Toys 5*

Wagyu: *Other Cows 15*

wahoo: *Expletives 20; Wild Saltwater Fish 15*

waif: *Child 1*

waiflike: *Small/Fragile 20*

wail: *Sounds 20; Speak 20*

Wailing Wall: *Unique Property 3*

wainwright: *Artists and Craftspeople 1*

waist chain: *Jewelry 21*

waist cincher: *Ladies' Wear 2*

waist: *Body Parts 12*

waistband: *Garment Pieces 2*

waistcoat: *Men's Wear 2*

wait: *Commands 20*

waiter/waitress: *Food Service 1*

waiting room: *Health Care 3*

waiting: *Rooms 3*

Wakan-tanka (sun and wind): *Native American Pantheon 14*

wake robin: *Poisonous Plants 10*

wake: *Boat/Ship Terminology 9*

waking the dead: *Loud 20*

wakizashi: *Swords One-handed 7*

wale: *Sewing Terms 2*

walk under a ladder: *Practices that Attract Bad Luck 19*

walk: *Locomotion 9; Roads 9*

walkabout: *Journey 20*

walkie-talkie: *Spy Gear 5; Toys 5*

walk-in closet: *Rooms 3*

walking dead: *Fictional Diseases 12*

walking plow: *Horse Drawn Farm Equipment*

walking stick: *Accessories 2; General Survival Gear 5; Phasmid 15*

walking: *Athletic Shoes 2; Bears 15*

walk-through: *Cave Anatomy 10*

walkway: *Property Features 3; Roads 9*

wall chaser: *Power Tools*

wall cloud: *Meteorology General Vocabulary 10*

wall eye pollock: *Wild Saltwater Fish 15*

wall gun: *Black Powder Weapons 7*

wall mirror: *Miscellaneous Furniture 4*

wall oven: *Major Appliances 4*

wall shelf: *Storage 4*

wall stair: *Castle Anatomy 3*

Wall Street: *Poker Card Games 5*

wall walk: *Castle Anatomy 3*

wall: *Art Materials 5; Art Media 13; Building Elements and Features 3; Fortification 3*

Wall's: *Keelback 15*

wallaby: *Other Wild Mammals 15*

wallet: *Accessories 2*

walleye pike: *Fish/Seafood Types 6; Wild Freshwater Fish 15*

wallflower: *Garden Annuals 10; Wildflowers 10*

wallop: *Attack 7*

wall-to-wall carpet: *Floor Coverings 4*

walnut: *Deciduous Trees 10; Nuts 6; Oils 6*

walpurti: *Other Wild Mammals 15*

walrus: *Facial Hair Mustache 1; Other Wild Mammals 15*

Walter's pine: *Evergreen Trees 10*

Walther G22: *Semiautomatic Rimfire Rifles 7*

Walther P22: *Pistol Semiautomatic 7*

Walther PPS: *Pistol Semiautomatic 7*

waltz: *Dance Styles 13; Historical Dances 13*

wampee: *Unusual Edible Fruits 6*

wand bloom: *Garden Perennials 10*

wand maker: *Fantasy Occupations 24*

wand: *Objects in Magic and Religion 19; Typical Magical Objects 17; Witchcraft Vocabulary 17*

wander: *Journey 20; Locomotion 9*

wanderer: *Barbarian 1; Common Character Archetypes 21*

wanderers: *Character Building 1*

wandering: *Scorpion 15*

wands: *Minor Arcana 19*

want it done yesterday: *Fast 20*

want: *Love 20*

wanton: *Bad 20*

war (red horse): *Four Horsemen of the Apocalypse 19*

war bonnet: *Head Gear 7*

war council: *General Combat Vocabulary 7*

war crimes/atrocities: *Horror Genres 23*

war cry: *Moves 7*

war dart: *Missile Loads 7*

war fan: *Hand Weapons 7*

war hammer: *Bludgeons 7*

war hat: *Head Gear 7*

war machine engineer: *Fantasy Occupations 24*

war monger: *Plot Devices 22*

war of attrition: *General Combat Vocabulary 7*

war plane: *Air Vehicles 9*

war threatens fantasy kingdoms: *Fantasy Plot Devices 24*

war tribunal: *General Combat Vocabulary 7*

war wizard: *Fantasy Occupations 24*

war: *Art Genres 13; Card Games 5; Common Dangers 24*

wara: *Cheese International Varieties 6*

waratah: *Shrubs 10*

warbler: *Other Wild Birds 15*

warbot: *Robots 22*

ward: *Political Divisions 10*

warden: *Fighter 1; Law Enforcement 1*

wardrobe: *Storage 4*

wardroom: *Boat/Ship Anatomy 9*

warehouse: *Business Property 3*

warfare: *General Combat Vocabulary 7*

warfarin: *Dangerous Chemicals 11*

warlock: *Witchcraft Vocabulary 17; Wizard 1*

warm summer: *Climatic Zones Koeppen System 10*

warm up: *Cooking Techniques 20*

warm: *Chapter 10; Meteorology General Vocabulary 10; Positive 1; Vocal/Speech Quality 1*

warmouth: *Wild Freshwater Fish 15*

warn: *Horror Vocabulary 23*

warning message is ignored: *Common Dangers 24*

warning: *Meteorology General Vocabulary 10*

warp drive pilot/engineer: *Occupations 22*

warp: *Sewing Terms 2; Spaceship Drive Systems 22; Travel Types 22*

warrant officer: *U.S. Army Warrant Officer 8; U.S. Marines Warrant Officer 8; U.S. Navy Warrant Officer 8*

warren: *General Buildings 3; Natural Animal Homes 15; Terrain Features 10*

warrior angel: *Angels Common Terms 14*

warrior: *Ants 15; Fighter 1*

warship: *Military Watercraft 8; Spaceship Types 22*

wart: *General Snake Families 15; Witchcraft Vocabulary 17*

warty: *Newts 15; Skin Types and Features 1*

wary: *Horror Vocabulary 23*

wascoite: *Minerals 10*

wash basin: *Containers and Vessels 5*

wash bottle: *Laboratory Equipment 5*

wash cloth: *Towels 5*

wash opal: *Minerals 10*

wash rag: *Towels 5*

wash: *Art Techniques 13; Clean 20; Fluvial 10*

washable marker: *Office/School/Writing Supplies 5*

washer: *Hardware 5; Major Appliances 4*

washerwoman: *Housekeeping 1*

washing machine front load: *Major Appliances 4*

washing machine top load: *Major Appliances 4*

Washington palm: *Deciduous Trees 10*

washingtonite: *Minerals 10*

Washo: *Native American Peoples 1*

Washoe pine: *Evergreen Trees 10*

washstand: *Tables 4*

Wasp class: *U.S. Navy Vessels 8*

wasp: *Animals 15*

waste basket: *Containers and Vessels 5*

waste: *Excrement 12; Kill 20*

wasteful: *Personality Other 1*

wasteland: *Ecosystems 10; Terrain Features 10*

wastrel: *General Occupations 1*

watch cap: *Headgear 2*

watch chain: *Jewelry 2*

watch fob: *Jewelry 2*

watch glass: *Laboratory Equipment 5*

watch tower: *Fortification 3; Military Property 3*

watch: *Fighter 1; Jewelry 2; Law Enforcement 1; Meteorology General Vocabulary 10; Timekeeping 5*

watchful: *Horror Vocabulary 23*

watchman: *Fighter 1; Law Enforcement 1*

watchman's cap: *Headgear 2*

water apple: *Unusual Edible Fruits 6*

water beech: *Deciduous Trees 10*

water birch: *Deciduous Trees 10*

water bottle: *Drinkware 5; Military Equipment 8*

water buffalo: *Other Wild Mammals 15; Transportation Animals 9*

water bus: *Small Watercraft 9*

water caltrop: *Weeds 10*

water chestnut: *Vegetables 6; Weeds 10*

water clock: *Timekeeping 5*

water closet: *Bathrooms 3*

water container: *General Survival Gear 5*

water content: *Soil General Vocabulary 10*

water craft: *Military 8*

water cycle: *Meteorology General Vocabulary 10*

water elm: *Deciduous Trees 10*

water equivalent: *Chemistry General Vocabulary 11*

water faerie: *Monsters 16*

water feature: *Landscaping 3*

water features: *Chapter 10*

water fern: *Weeds 10*

water glass: *Drinkware 5*

water gourd: *Containers and Vessels 5*

water hemlock: *Poisonous Plants 10*

water hyacinth: *Weeds 10*

water knot: *Sailing Knots 9*

water lily: *Wildflowers 10*

water moccasin: *General Snake Families 15*

water oak: *Deciduous Trees 10*

water opal: *Minerals 10*

water pistol: *Amusement Park/Carnival/Circus/Fair 3*

water polo stroke: *Swimming Strokes 9*

water proof suit: *Spy Gear 5*

water purification system: *Military Equipment 8*

water shoes: *Footwear/Shoes 2*

water sink: *Cave Anatomy 10*

water skis: *Sporting Goods Other 5*

water snipe fly: *Flies 15*

water spout: *Water Terms 9*

water supply imparts fatal disease: *Horror Plot Devices 23*

water table: *Geography General Vocabulary 10*

water taxi: *Small Watercraft 9*

water terms: *Transportation 9*

water test: *Witchcraft Vocabulary 17*

water tower: *Military Property 3*

water travel: *Travel Modes 24*

water treatment plant: *Public Services 3*

water wheel: *Energy Sources/Types 24*

water white oak: *Deciduous Trees 10*

water works: *Public Services 3*

water: *Adder 15; Beds 4; Beetle 15; Elemental 16; Energy Sources/Types 23; Foods with Religious or Ritual Significance 19; Four Elements 19; General Snake Families 15; Meteorology General Vocabulary 10; Rituals 14; Spaceship Drive Systems 22; Traps 3; Wizard's Goods 5*

waterborne illness: *Travel Hazards 9*

watercolor paint: *Art Materials 5*

watercolor: *Art Media 13*

watercourse: *Water Features 10; Water Terms 9*

watercraft: *Transportation 9*

watercress: *Sandwiches 6*

water-dropwort: *Poisonous Plants 10*

waterfall: *Doors Atypical 3; Fluvial 10; Geological Natural Hazards 10; Landscaping 3*

waterfowl: *Other Wild Birds 15*

waterfront: *Marina 3; Water Terms 9*

watering can: *Garden Tools*

watering hole: *Food/Drink Establishments 3*

waterlily tulip: *Garden Bulbs 10*

watermelon pickle: *Pickled/Relish 6*

watermelon tourmaline: *Minerals 10*

watermelon: *Ice Cream Flavors 6; Melons 6*

watermill: *Farm/Outbuilding 3*

watershed: *Fluvial 10*

waterside: *Marina 3*

waterskin: *Containers and Vessels 5*

waterspout: *Severe Weather 10*

waterway: *Water Terms 9*

watery milkcap: *Fungus Common Names 10*

watery: *Eye Type 1; Wet 20*

wattle: *Castle Anatomy 3*

wattled: *Bats 15*

wave cut platform: *Coastal and Oceanic 10*

wave motion: *Spaceship Drive Systems 22*

wave: *Embroidery Stitches 2; Meteorology General Vocabulary 10; Water Terms 9*

wavelength: *Astronomy General Terms 11*

wavy: *Hair Types 1; Partition Lines 19*

wavyleaf alder: *Deciduous Trees 10*

wax applicator: *Cleaning Supplies/Gadgets 5*

wax bean: *Vegetables 6*

wax begonia: *Garden Annuals 10*

wax bottles: *Candy General 6*

wax lips: *Candy General 6*

wax opal: *Minerals 10*

wax: *Art Materials 5; Clean 20; Cleaning Supplies/Gadgets 5; Moth 15; Specialty Survival Gear 5; Wizard's Goods 5*

waxbill: *Domesticated Pet Birds 15*

waxed string: *Fasteners 5*

waxed wings: *Magical Transportation 17*

way: *Roads 9*

wayfarer: *Barbarian 1*

waylay: *General Combat Vocabulary 7*

waypoint: *Water Terms 9*

Wea: *Native American Peoples 1*

weak electrolyte: *Chemistry General Vocabulary 11*

weak field ligand: *Chemistry General Vocabulary 11*

weak: *Small/Thin 1; Vocal/Speech Quality 1*

weaken: *Harm 20*

weakfish: *Wild Saltwater Fish 15*

weakling: *Small/Thin 1*

Wealth without work: *Philosophy 14*

wealthy snob: *Common Character Archetypes 21*

weapon black: *Specialty Survival Gear 5*

weapon master: *Siege Engines 7*

weapon oil: *Specialty Survival Gear 5*

weapon: *Charges 19; General Survival Gear 5; Spy Gear 5; Typical Magical Objects 17*

weapons of mass destruction: *General Combat Vocabulary 7*

weapons storage: *Fortification 3*

weapons: *Combat, Armor, and Weapons 7*

weaponsmith: *Artists and Craftspeople 1; Castle Inhabitants and Personnel 1*

wear: *Harm 20*

wearable: *Art Genres 13*

weary: *Horror Vocabulary 23; Personality Other 1; Slow 20*

weasel: *Woodland Mammals 15*

weather balloon: *Meteorology General Vocabulary 10*

weather gauge: *Boat/Ship Anatomy 9*

weather girl/man: *Media 1*

weather manipulation: *Paranormal Abilities 21*

weather map: *Meteorology General Vocabulary 10*

weather plant: *Poisonous Plants 10*

weather reconnaissance: *Military Aircraft 8*

weather satellite: *Meteorology General Vocabulary 10*

weather: *Meteorology General Vocabulary 10*

Weatherby Model XXII: *Bolt Action Rimfire Rifles 7*

Weatherby Orion: *Shotguns Side-by-Side 7*

Weatherby PA-08: *Shotguns Pump 7*

weathering: *Castle Anatomy 3; Cave Anatomy 10; Meteorology General Vocabulary 10; Soil General Vocabulary 10*

weathervane: *Meteorology General Vocabulary 10*

weave: *Hair Style 1; Sewing Techniques 2*

weaver: *Ants 15; Artists and Craftspeople 1; Other Wild Birds 15*

weaving needle: *Sewing Equipment 2*

weaving: *Embroidery Stitches 2*

web: *Natural Animal Homes 15*

webbed fingers: *Physical Mutations 22*

webbed toes: *Physical Mutations 22*

websterite: *Igneous Rocks 10*

wedding cake: *Foods with Religious or Ritual Significance 19; Practices to Predict the Future 19*

wedding chapel: *Business Property 3*

wedding gown: *Ladies' Wear 2*

wedding planner: *Special Occasion 1*

wedding veil: *Headgear 2*

wedding: *Cake 6; Valentine's Day 19*

wedge: *Footwear/Shoes 2; Hair Style 1; Hand Tools 5; Meteorology General Vocabulary 10*

wee folk: *General Fae 16*

wee: *Small/Fragile 20*

weed: *Clean 20*

weeds: *Chapter 10*

weep: *Sounds 20; Speak 20*

weeping oak: *Deciduous Trees 10*

weeping spruce: *Evergreen Trees 10*

wehrlite: *Igneous Rocks 10*

weigela: *Shrubs 10*

weigh a lot: *Heavy 20*

weigh anchor: *Boat/Ship Terminology 9*

weightless: *Light 20*

weighty: *Heavy 20*

Weimaraner: *Dog Breeds 15*

weird: *Magic Vocabulary 17; Science Fiction Genres 22*

weiss: *Beer 6*

weisslacker: *Cheese International Varieties 6*

Welara Pony: *Horse Breeds 15*

welcome mat: *Floor Coverings 4*

welcoming: *Positive 1*

weld: *Art Techniques 13*

welder: *Power Tools*

well balanced: *Happy 20*

well behaved: *Good 20*

well brought up: *Good 20*

well developed: *Old 20*

well fed: *Large/Heavy 1*

well house: *Farm/Outbuilding 3*

well mannered: *Good 20*

well padded: *Large/Heavy 1*

well up: *Wet 20*

well: *Property Features 3*

well-bred: *Personality Other 1*

Wellies: *Boots 2*

Wellington: *Boots 2*

well-known: *Personality Other 1*

well-off: *Fortunate 20*

Wells Fargo: *Western Paraphernalia/People 21*

Welsh Black: *Other Cows 15*

Welsh Cob: *Horse Breeds 15*

Welsh Pony: *Horse Breeds 15*

Welsh Springer Spaniel: *Dog Breeds 15*

Welsh Terrier: *Dog Breeds 15*

Welsh water faerie: *Water Faerie 16*

Welsh: *Cake 6; Human Ethnic Groups 1; Pigs 15*

wench: *Female 1*

Wendat: *Native American Peoples 1*

wendigo: *Beast 16*

Wenlock Age: *Geologic Time 10*

werebear: *Lycanthrope 16*

wereboar: *Lycanthrope 16*

werepanther: *Lycanthrope 16*

werepython: *Lycanthrope 16*

wererat: *Lycanthrope 16*

wereraven: *Lycanthrope 16*

weretiger: *Lycanthrope 16*

werewolf: *Common Dangers 23; Fantasy Creatures with Symbolic Meaning 19; Lycanthrope 16*

Wessex saddleback: *Pigs 15*

West African Barb: *Horse Breeds 15*

West African: *Caecilians 15*

West African: *Lions 15*

West Coast hemlock: *Evergreen Trees 10*

West French white: *Pigs 15*

West Highland White Terrier: *Dog Breeds 15*

West Nile fever: *Diseases 12*

West Texas live oak: *Deciduous Trees 10*

West Virginia spruce: *Evergreen Trees 10*

West: *Comets 11*

west: *Eight Compass Points 19*

westerly: *Meteorology General Vocabulary 10; Water Terms 9*

western alder: *Deciduous Trees 10*

western balsam fir: *Evergreen Trees 10*

western black willow: *Deciduous Trees 10*

western box elder: *Deciduous Trees 10*

western chimpanzee: *Apes 15*

western chinkapin: *Deciduous Trees 10*

western diamondback: *Rattlesnake 15*

western grape: *Beetle 15*

western green: *Toads 15*

western hackberry: *Deciduous Trees 10*

western hemlock: *Evergreen Trees 10*

western hog-nosed: *Viper 15*

western hop hornbeam: *Deciduous Trees 10*

western lowland gorilla: *Apes 15*

western painted: *Freshwater Turtles 15*

western pond: *Freshwater Turtles 15*

western red cedar: *Evergreen Trees 10*

western red: *Bats 15*

Western shirt: *Western Clothing/Dress 21*

western soapberry: *Deciduous Trees 10*

western spruce: *Evergreen Trees 10*

Western Sudan Pony: *Horse Breeds 15*

western tiger: *World's Ten Most Venomous Snakes 15*

western white pine: *Evergreen Trees 10*

western white spruce: *Evergreen Trees 10*

western yellow pine: *Evergreen Trees 10*

western yellow: *Bats 15*

western yew: *Evergreen Trees 10*

western: *Art Genres 13; Horror Genres 23; Performance Genres 13; Science Fiction Genres 22*

Western: *Styles of Dress 2*

Westfall: *Comets 11*

wet cave: *Cave Anatomy 10*

wet erase marker: *Office/School/Writing Supplies 5*

wet forest: *Caecilians 15*

wet market: *General Property 3*

wet snow: *Snow Types 10*

wet/dry vacuum: *Power Tools*

wet: *Adjectives 20; Chapter 10*

weta: *Orthoptera 15*

Wetar Island: *Python 15*

wetland: *Ecosystems 10; Water Terms 9*

wetness: *Wet 20*

Weymouth pine: *Evergreen Trees 10*

Weywot (sky): *Native American Pantheon 14*

whack: *Attack 7*

whale: *Animals with Symbolic Meaning 19; Sharks 15*

whale oil: *Illumination/Light Sources 5*

whales: *Animals 15*

whammy bar: *Music Accessories*

wharf: *Marina 3; Water Terms 9*

wheat: *Allergies 12; Beer 6; Bread General Varieties 6; Brown 20; Grain 6*

wheel lock: *Black Powder Weapons 7*

wheel: *Boat/Ship Anatomy 9; Symbols in Magic and Religion 19*

wheelbarrow: *Human-Powered Transportation 9; Large Tools*

wheelchair: *Classic Items 23; Human-Powered Transportation 9*

wheelwright: *Artists and Craftspeople 1*

wheezy: *Vocal/Speech Quality 1*

whetstone of Tudwal Tudglyd: *Thirteen Treasures of the Island of Britain 18*

whetstone: *Hand Tools 5*

Whidbey Island class: *U.S. Navy Vessels 8*

whiff: *Smells 20*

Whig: *Political Parties 1*

whimper: *Sounds 20; Speak 20*

whimsy: *Magic Vocabulary 17*

whine: *Sounds 20; Speak 20*

whining: *Vocal/Speech Quality 1*

whip: *Flexible 7; General Snake Families 15; Harm 20; Scorpion 15*

whipcord: *Fabric 2*

whiplash willow: *Deciduous Trees 10*

whiplash: *Squid 15*

whipped cream: *Ice Cream Toppings 6; Other Dairy 6; Thanksgiving 19*

whipped running: *Embroidery Stitches 2*

whipped web: *Embroidery Stitches 2*

Whippet Mk A medium tank: *United Kingdom Military Vehicles 8*

Whippet: *Dog Breeds 15*

whipping cream: *Other Dairy 6*

Whipple: *Comets 11*

whiptail: *Scaled Reptiles 15*

whirl: *Locomotion 9*

whirlwind: *Severe Weather 10*

whisk broom: *Cleaning Supplies/Gadgets 5*

whisk: *Kitchen Utensils 5*

whiskered: *Bats 15*

whiskers: *Facial Hair Beard 1*

whisky: *Western Paraphernalia/People 21; Hard Liquor 6; Poker Card Games 5*

whisky sour: *Cocktails 6*

whisper: *Paranormal Occurrences 21; Sounds 20; Speak 20*

whispery: *Vocal/Speech Quality 1*

whist: *Card Games 5*

whistle knot: *Sailing Knots 9*

whistle: *Signal Devices 5*

whistlewood: *Deciduous Trees 10*

whistling pine: *Evergreen Trees 10*

white alder: *Deciduous Trees 10*

white antelope: *Beast 16*

white ash: *Deciduous Trees 10*

white balsam: *Evergreen Trees 10*

white baneberry: *Poisonous Plants 10*

white bay: *Deciduous Trees 10*

white bean: *Legumes 6*

white beech: *Deciduous Trees 10*

white birch: *Deciduous Trees 10*

white board: *Office/School/Writing Supplies 5*

white bouquet: *Garden Perennials 10*

White Cáceres: *Other Cows 15*

white cedar: *Evergreen Trees 10; Weeds 10*

white cell: *Blood 12*

white chanterelle: *Fungus Common Names 10*

white chard: *Vegetables 6*

White Cliffs opal: *Minerals 10*

white cloud: *Aquarium Freshwater Fish 15*

white clover: *Weeds 10*

white collar: *Social Distinction 1; Styles of Dress 2*

white corn: *Vegetables 6*

white croaker: *Wild Saltwater Fish 15*

white currant: *Berries 6*

white cypress: *Evergreen Trees 10*

white dwarf: *Astronomy General Terms 11; Star Types and Relatives 11*

white elm: *Deciduous Trees 10*

white feldspar: *Minerals 10*

white fir: *Evergreen Trees 10*

white flesh peach: *Pit Fruits 6*

white flour: *Staples 6*

white gold: *Precious Metals 21*

white grapefruit: *Citrus 6*

white grunt: *Wild Saltwater Fish 15*

white gum: *Deciduous Trees 10*

white hat: *Hero 20*

white heather flowers: *Harbingers/Charms for Good Luck 19*

white hickory: *Deciduous Trees 10*

white jelly fungus: *Fungus Common Names 10*

white knapweed: *Weeds 10*

white knight: *Knight 1*

white laurel: *Deciduous Trees 10*

white lead ore: *Minerals 10*

white locust: *Deciduous Trees 10*

white magic: *Witchcraft Vocabulary 17*

white man trained by Indians: *Western Plot Devices 21*

white marlin: *Wild Saltwater Fish 15*

white merlot: *Wine White 6*

white monkey: *Demon 16*

white myrtle: *Deciduous Trees 10*

white oak: *Deciduous Trees 10*

white onion: *Vegetables 6*

white opal: *Minerals 10*

White Park: *Other Cows 15*

white pepper: *Spices 6*

white pine: *Evergreen Trees 10*

white popcorn: *Snacks 6*

white potato: *Vegetables 6*

white rice: *Grain 6*

white sassafras: *Deciduous Trees 10*

white settlers attacked by Indians: *Western Plot Devices 21*

white settlers saved by Indians: *Western Plot Devices 21*

white shirt with stiff collar: *Western Clothing/Dress 21*

white smoke: *White 20*

white snakeroot: *Poisonous Plants 10*

white soda: *Soft Drinks 6*

white spruce: *Evergreen Trees 10*

white stag: *Beast 16*

white sturgeon: *Wild Saltwater Fish 15*

white sugar: *Staples 6*

white tie: *Styles of Dress 2*

white tiger carving: *Harbingers/Charms for Good Luck 19*

white topaz: *Minerals 10*

white trash: *Social Distinction 1; Styles of Dress 2*

white walnut: *Deciduous Trees 10*

white willow: *Deciduous Trees 10*

white wine glass: *Drinkware 5*

white witch: *Moth 15*

white zinfandel: *Wine White 6*

white: *Bats 15; Bears 15; Cake 6; Colors 20; Dragon 16; Hair Color 1; Martial Artist Belt Ranks 1; Skin Types and Features 1;*

Tea 6; Teeth 1; Tigers 15; Valentine's Day 19

whitecap: *Water Terms 9*

white-chinned: *Owls 15*

white-faced: *Owls 15*

whitefish: *Fish/Seafood Types 6; Wild Freshwater Fish 15*

white-fronted capuchin: *New World Monkeys 15*

white-headed capuchin: *New World Monkeys 15*

whiteheart hickory: *Deciduous Trees 10*

white-lipped: *Cobra 15; Keelback 15; Python 15*

white-mantled tamarin: *New World Monkeys 15*

whiteness: *Snow Events 10*

whiteout: *Meteorology General Vocabulary 10; Snow Events 10*

whites (clothing): *Fencing Equipment 7*

whiteschist: *Metamorphic Rocks 10*

white-shouldered: *Bats 15*

white-sided: *Dolphins 15*

white-spotted: *Jellyfish 15*

white-tail: *Venomous Arachnids 15*

whitetip reef: *Sharks 15*

white-winged dog: *Bats 15*

whiting: *Wild Saltwater Fish 15*

whittle: *Art Techniques 13*

whoa: *Commands 20*

whole blood: *Blood 12*

whole house fan: *Building Systems 3*

whole milk: *Dairy Beverages 6*

whole note: *Notation 13*

whole wheat flour: *Staples 6*

whole wheat tortilla: *Bread General Varieties 6*

whole wheat: *Bread General Varieties 6*

whole: *Milk 6*

whoop: *Sounds 20*

whoopie pie: *Cookie 6*

whooping cough (pertussis): *Diseases 12*

whore: *Illicit Occupations 1*

whorled milkweed: *Wildflowers 10*

whorled water milfoil: *Weeds 10*

whortleberry: *Unusual Edible Fruits 6*

Wicca: *Witchcraft Vocabulary 17*

Wiccan: *Witchcraft Vocabulary 17*

wichtlein: *General Fae 16*

wicked person: *Villain 20*

wicked: *Bad 20; Negative 1*

wicker: *Chairs and Stools 4; Door Materials 3; Tables 4*

wicket: *Castle Anatomy 3*

wicking: *Wizard's Goods 5*

wide: *Large 20; Large/Heavy 1; Mouth 1*

wide-man: *Wizard 1*

widow/widower: *Common Character Archetypes 21*

widow: *Female 1; Wild Saltwater Fish 15*

widow's frill: *Wildflowers 10*

widow's peak: *Forehead 1; Hair Style 1*

widower: *Male 1*

Wielkopolski: *Horse Breeds 15*

wiener: *Sausage 6*

wife beater: *Men's Wear 2*

wife: *Female 1*

wig: *Headgear 2*

Wigar: *Arthurian Objects 18*

wiggle trace: *Geological Vocabulary 10*

wight: *Undead 16*

wiglet: *Headgear 2*

wild arum: *Poisonous Plants 10*

wild bergamot: *Wildflowers 10*

Wild Bill Hickok: *Facial Hair Beard 1; Real People with Legendary Status 18; Western Paraphernalia/People 21*

wild birds: *Animals 15*

wild black cherry: *Deciduous Trees 10*

wild carrot: *Poisonous Plants 10; Weeds 10*

wild cherry: *Deciduous Trees 10*

wild china tree: *Deciduous Trees 10*

wild chinaberry: *Deciduous Trees 10*

wild comfrey: *Wildflowers 10*

wild fish: *Animals 15*

wild freshwater fish: *Animals 15*

wild game: *Food 6*

wild garlic: *Wildflowers 10*

wild geranium: *Wildflowers 10*

wild ginger: *Garden Perennials 10; Wildflowers 10*

wild lettuce: *Wildflowers 10*

wild mammals: *Animals 15*

wild oats: *Garden Perennials 10; Wildflowers 10*

wild onion: *Garden Perennials 10*

wild parsnip: *Poisonous Plants 10*

wild petunia: *Garden Perennials 10*

wild plum: *Deciduous Trees 10*

wild privet: *Weeds 10*

wild rice: *Grain 6*

wild saltwater fish: *Animals 15*

wild snowball: *Garden Perennials 10*

wild strawberry: *Wildflowers 10*

wild taro: *Weeds 10*

Wild: *Comets 11*

wild: *Difficult 20; Elf 1; Eyebrows 1; Hair Types 1; Magic Vocabulary 17*

wildebeest: *Other Wild Mammals 15*

wilderness: *Fantasy Locations 24; Terrain Features 10*

wildfire: *Western Plot Devices 21*

wildflowers: *Chapter 10*

wildlife: *Art Genres 13*

will force: *Paranormal Abilities 21*

will o' the wisp: *General Fae 16*

will: *Philosophy Basic Concepts 14*

willful: *Personality Other 1*

William Tell: *Legendary People Presumed to be Fictional 18*

William Wallace: *Real People with Legendary Status 18*

williamsite: *Minerals 10*

will-o'-wisp: *Beast 16*

willow beauty: *Moth 15*

willow fomes: *Fungus Common Names 10*

willow oak: *Deciduous Trees 10*

willow: *Garden Perennials 10; Shrubs 10*

Wils quinine: *Garden Perennials 10*

Wilson Combat standard: *Shotguns Pump 7*

Wilson Comp: *Pistol Semiautomatic 7*

Wilson Professional: *Pistol Semiautomatic 7*

Wilson Protector: *Pistol Semiautomatic 7*

Wilson Sentinel: *Pistol Semiautomatic 7*

Wilson Tactical Elite: *Pistol Semiautomatic 7*

wiluite: *Minerals 10*

wimp: *Small/Thin 1*

wimple: *Headgear 2*

win: *Buy 20*

winch: *Boat/Ship Anatomy 9*

Winchester Black Powder: *Single Shot Centerfire Rifles 7*

Winchester Extra Light Grade: *Lever Action and Pump Centerfire Rifles 7*

Winchester model 101: *Shotguns Over/Under 7*

Winchester rifle: *Western Weapons 21*

Winchester Safari: *Lever Action and Pump Centerfire Rifles 7*

Winchester Super X3: *Shotguns Semiautomatic 7*

Winchester Ultimate Shadow: *Bolt Action Centerfire Rifles 7*

Winchester Wildcat: *Bolt Action Rimfire Rifles 7*

wind advisory: *Wind 10*

wind chill factor: *Meteorology General Vocabulary 10*

wind chill: *Cold 10; Meteorology General Vocabulary 10*

wind flower: *Garden Bulbs 10*

wind mill: *Energy Sources/Types 24; Farm/Outbuilding 3*

wind shear: *Meteorology General Vocabulary 10*

wind turbine: *Special Purpose Structure 3*

wind vane: *Meteorology General Vocabulary 10*

wind: *Chapter 10; Energy Sources/Types 22; Energy Sources/Types 23*

windburn: *Injuries/Medical Emergencies 12*

windigo: *Demon 16*

window cleaner: *Cleaning Supplies/Gadgets 5*

window envelope: *Office/School/Writing Supplies 5*

window opens/closes: *Paranormal Occurrences 21*

window treatments: *Equipment and Tools 5*

window washer: *Housekeeping 1*

window: *Cave Anatomy 10; Flies 15*

windowpane plaid: *Fabric Patterns 2*

windows: *Architecture and Property 3*

winds of the Mediterranean: *Chapter 10*

Windsnyer: *Pigs 15*

windsock: *Meteorology General Vocabulary 10*

Windsor cap: *Headgear 2*

Windsor Castle: *Unique Property 3*

Windsor soil: *Soil General Vocabulary 10*

Windsor: *Chairs and Stools 4*

windstorm: *Wind 10*

windward: *Geography General Vocabulary 10*

wine barrel: *Containers and Vessels 5*

wine bottle: *Improvised Weapons 7*

wine cellar: *Rooms 3*

wine cup: *Garden Perennials 10; Wildflowers 10*

wine raspberry: *Weeds 10*

wine refrigerator: *Major Appliances 4*

wine: *Aphrodisiacs 19; Food 6; Foods with Religious or Ritual Significance 19; Red 20; Rituals 14; Thanksgiving 19*

wineberry: *Unusual Edible Fruits 6; Weeds 10*

wine-cap strophoria: *Fungus Common Names 10*

winemaker: *Food Service 1*

wineskin: *Containers and Vessels 5*

wing commander: *Armed Forces Other Titles 8*

wing of bat: *Wizard's Goods 5*

wing wall: *Castle Anatomy 3*

wing: *Chairs and Stools 4*

winged disc: *Symbols in Magic and Religion 19*

winged rod of Hermes: *Objects 18*

winged: *Monsters 19; Spears 7*

winging: *Swimming Strokes 9*

wings of Daedalus: *Objects 18*

wings: *Hair Style 1; Magical Transportation 17; Parts of the Theater 13; Physical Mutations 22; Symbols in Magic and Religion 19*

wingtips: *Footwear/Shoes 2*

winking: *Owls 15*

Winnebago: *Chickens 15*

winner: *Hero 20*

winnowing fan: *Steam Powered Farm Equipment*

winnowing machine: *Steam Powered Farm Equipment*

winter aconite: *Garden Bulbs 10*

winter blanket: *Bed Linens 5*

winter coat: *Unisex Clothing 2*

winter creeper vine: *Weeds 10*

winter fat: *Garden Perennials 10*

winter flounder: *Wild Saltwater Fish 15*

winter hazel: *Shrubs 10*

winter jacket: *Outerwear 2*

winter kitchen: *Rooms 3*

winter mushroom: *Fungus Common Names 10*

winter solstice: *Witchcraft Vocabulary 17*

winter squash: *Vegetables 6*

winter wolf: *Beast 16*

winter: *Four Seasons 19; Meteorology General Vocabulary 10; Moth 15; Socks 2*

winter's bark: *Shrubs 10*

winterberry: *Deciduous Trees 10*

wintercreeper: *Garden Perennials 10*

wintersweet: *Shrubs 10*

Winto: *Native American Peoples 1*

wintry: *Cold 10*

wipe out: *Kill 20*

wipe: *Clean 20*

wire birch: *Deciduous Trees 10*

wire brush: *Hand Tools 5*

wire cutter: *Art Tools 5; Hand Tools 5; Spy Gear 5*

wire gauze: *Laboratory Equipment 5*

wire stripper: *Hand Tools 5*

wire: *Art Materials 5; Computer Equipment 5; Teeth Dental Work 1; Traps 3*

Wirehaired Pointing Griffon: *Dog Breeds 15*

wireless internet: *Building Systems 3*

wireless telephone: *Building Systems 3*

wiring: *Building Systems 3*

Wirot's: *Pit Viper 15*

Wirtanen: *Comets 11*

wisdom eyes of Buddha: *Symbols in Magic and Religion 19*

wisdom of equanimity: *Five Wisdoms of Buddhism 19*

wisdom of individuality: *Five Wisdoms of Buddhism 19*

wisdom: *Philosophy Basic Concepts 14; Seven Gifts of the Holy Spirit 19; Teeth 12*

wise man: *Cleric 1; Nature Occupations 1*

wise men/magi: *Collective Symbols 19*

wise men: *Christmas 19*

wise old man/woman: *Common Character Archetypes 21*

wisecracking sidekick: *Supporting Cast 24*

wish: *Magic Vocabulary 17*

wishbone: *Harbingers/Charms for Good Luck 19*

wishes are granted with dire consequences: *Horror Plot Devices 23*

wishing well: *Harbingers/Charms for Good Luck 19*

wispy: *Hair Types 1; Light 20*

wisteria: *Purple 20*

wit: *Bard 1*

witch ball: *Objects in Magic and Religion 19*

witch hazel: *Deciduous Trees 10; Shrubs 10*

witch queen stronghold: *Fantasy Locations 24*

witch/sorcerer controlled by blackmail: *Supporting Cast 24*

witch: *Common Character Archetypes 21; Common Dangers 23; Halloween 19; Villain 20; Wizard 1*

witch's broom: *Halloween 19*

witch's hat: *Halloween 19*

witch's house: *Horror Locations 23*

witch's hut: *Fantasy Locations 24*

witchcraft vocabulary: *Magic 17*

witchcraft: *Horror Genres 23; Magic 17*

witches butter: *Fungus Common Names 10*

witches: *Common Dangers 24*

witches' Sabbath: *Witchcraft Vocabulary 17*

witchy: *Grouchy 1*

withdraw: *General Combat Vocabulary 7; Locomotion 9*

withdrawal: *General Combat Vocabulary 7*

withdrawn: *Horror Vocabulary 23*

withering: *Personality Other 1*

withhold care: *Harm 20*

wizard appears in historical period: *Fantasy Plot Devices 24*

wizard appears in modern world: *Fantasy Plot Devices 24*

wizard tower: *Fantasy Locations 24*

wizard: *Character Building 1; Common Character Archetypes 21*

wizard's apprentice: *Fantasy Occupations 24*

wizard's goods: *Equipment and Tools 5*

wizard's maid: *Fantasy Occupations 24*

wizard's tower: *Fantasy Property 3*

wizard-like maniac: *Monsters and Creatures 22*

wizened: *Elderly 1*

wobbegong: *Sharks 15*

wobbly: *Vocal/Speech Quality 1*

woeful: *Sad 20*

Woermann's: *Bats 15*

wolf fish: *Wild Saltwater Fish 15*

wolf gray: *Gray 20*

wolf hop hornbeam: *Deciduous Trees 10*

Wolf: *Comets 11*

wolf: *Animals with Symbolic Meaning 19; General Snake Families 15; Other Wild Mammals 15; Spears 7; Venomous Arachnids 15*

wolf's milk: *Fungus Common Names 10*

wolfberry: *Unusual Edible Fruits 6*

wolfman: *Humanoid 16*

wolfsbane: *Poisonous Plants 10; Wizard's Goods 5*

wolverine: *Woodland Mammals 15*

woma: *Python 15*

woman: *Female 1*

woman's apron falls off: *Harbingers of Bad Luck 19*

womanizer: *Negative 1*

wombat: *Other Wild Mammals 15*

women's club: *Social Clubs 1*

wonder hedge: *Shrubs 10*

wonder: *Magic Vocabulary 17; Philosophy Basic Concepts 14*

wonderful: *Beautiful 20; Good 20; Happy 20; Magic Vocabulary 17*

Wonders of the World: *Legendary/Mythical Locations 18*

wongi: *Unusual Edible Fruits 6*

wonton wrapper: *Bread General Varieties 6*

wonton: *Bread General Varieties 6*

wood apple: *Unusual Edible Fruits 6*

wood betony: *Wildflowers 10*

wood chips: *Wizard's Goods 5*

wood cut: *Art Techniques 13*

wood dor: *Beetle 15*

wood ear mushroom: *Fungus Common Names 10*

wood horn: *Wind/Woodwind and Brass Musical Instruments*

wood lizard: *Scaled Reptiles 15*

wood of the True Cross: *Relics of Jesus 14*

wood opal: *Minerals 10*

wood poppy: *Garden Perennials 10*

wood saw: *Hand Tools 5*

wood screw: *Hardware 5*

wood shaper: *Power Tools*

wood soldier: *Flies 15*

wood sorrel: *Weeds 10*

wood sunflower: *Garden Perennials 10*

wood tin: *Minerals 10*

wood violet: *Wildflowers 10*

wood wives: *Demon 16*

wood working: *Art Techniques 13*

wood: *Art Materials 5; Art Media 13; Door Materials 3; Elf 1; Exterior Building Materials 3; Interior Building Materials 3; Owls 15; Terrain Features 10*

woodbine: *Garden Perennials 10*

woodcutter: *Rural Occupations 1*

wooden blinds: *Window Treatments 5*

wooden cow of Daedalus: *Objects 18*

wooden holy symbol: *Religious Items 5*

wooden ladder: *Large Tools*

wooden mermaid figurehead on ship: *Harbingers/Charms for Good Luck 19*

wooden soldier: *Christmas 19*

wooden spoon: *Kitchen Utensils 5*

wooden: *Coins and Currency 21; Shield Types 7*

woodland mammals: *Animals 15*

woodland: *Terrain Features 10*

wood-nymph: *Butterfly 15*

woodpecker: *Animals with Symbolic Meaning 19; Backyard Birds 15*

woods: *Ecosystems 10; Horror Locations 23; Terrain Features 10*

woodshed: *Property Features 3*

Woodstock: *Legendary Events 18*

woodwaxen: *Garden Perennials 10*

woody plants: *Chapter 10*

woody: *Motorized 9*

woof: *Sounds 20*

wool blanket: *Bed Linens 5*

wool stockings: *Western Clothing/Dress 21*

wool: *Fabric 2; Socks 2*

woolly hop hornbeam: *Deciduous Trees 10*

woolly larch: *Deciduous Trees 10*

woolly thistle: *Weeds 10*

Woolworth: *Poker Card Games 5*

wooly milkcap: *Fungus Common Names 10*

wooly monkey: *New World Monkeys 15*

wooly spider: *New World Monkeys 15*

wooly thyme: *Garden Perennials 10*

Wooton: *Desks 4*

Worcestershire sauce: *Mixers 6*

word: *Games 5*

worg: *Beast 16*

work gloves: *Unisex Clothing 2*

work of art: *Philosophy Basic Concepts 14*

work of fiction: *Books/Publications 5*

work out: *Open/Release 20*

work: *Boots 2; Rooms 3; Tables 4*

worker: *Ants 15; Bees 15*

working class: *Social Distinction 1*

working girl: *Illicit Occupations 1*

working leg: *Ballet Terms 13*

working poor: *Social Distinction 1*

working: *Dog Groups 15*

workplace: *Business Property 3*

workshop: *Business Property 3; Rooms 3*

workspace: *Rooms 3*

workstation: *Building Elements and Features 3*

world axis: *Symbols in Magic and Religion 19*

World Congress Of Soil Science: *Soil General Vocabulary 10*

world egg: *Secular Symbols 19*

World Trade Center: *Unique Property Destroyed 3*

world: *Five Alchemical Spirits 19*

world's ten most venomous snakes: *Animals 15*

worm lizard: *Scaled Reptiles 15*

worm patterned: *Caecilians 15*

worm: *General Snake Families 15; Monsters and Creatures 22*

wormhole: *Plot Devices 22*

wormwood: *Garden Perennials 10; Plants with Symbolic Meaning 19*

worn: *Unattractive 20*

worried: *Horror Vocabulary 23*

worry: *General Emotions 20*

worrying: *Sad 20*

worse: *Bad 20*

worsen: *Harm 20*

Worship without sacrifice: *Philosophy 14*

worship: *General Emotions 20; Love 20*

worshiper: *Followers 14*

worsted: *Fabric 2*

worthy: *Good 20*

wound: *Attack 7; Harm 20*

woundwort: *Garden Perennials 10*

woven carpet: *Floor Coverings 4*

woven web: *Embroidery Stitches 2*

wow: *Expletives 20*

wraith: *Undead 16*

wrap skirt: *Dance Clothing 13*

wrapping paper: *Christmas 19*

wrasse: *Aquarium Saltwater Fish 15*

wrath: *General Emotions 20; Seven Deadly Sins 19*

wreath: *Christmas 19; Headgear 2; Jewelry 21; Objects in Magic and Religion 19*

wren: *Animals with Symbolic Meaning 19*

wrench: *Hand Tools 5*

wrestle: *Attack 7*

wrestler: *Fighter 1*

wrestling: *Athletic Shoes 2*

wretched: *Expletives 20; Sad 20*

Wright willow: *Deciduous Trees 10*

wringer: *Cleaning Supplies/Gadgets 5*

wrinkle-faced: *Bats 15*

wrist watch: *Jewelry 2*

wrist: *Body Parts 12*

wristband: *Accessories 2*

wristlet: *Accessories 2; Jewelry 21*

wristwatch: *Timekeeping 5*

writer: *Publishing 1*

writing materials: *General Survival Gear 5*

writing supplies: *Equipment and Tools 5*

writing: *Desks 4; Tables 4*

wrongdoer: *Villain 20*

Wu: *Human Ethnic Groups 1*

wunderkind: *Child 1*

wutu: *General Snake Families 15*

Wuzishan: *Pigs 15*

Wyandotte: *Chickens 15*

Wyatt Earp: *Real People with Legendary Status 18; Western Paraphernalia/People 21*

Wynaad: *Keelback 15*

wyvern: *Beast 16; Magical Transportation 17*

WZ302 self-propelled 122mm mortar/gun: *China Military Vehicles 8*

WZ501 infantry fighting vehicle: *China Military Vehicles 8*

WZ504 self-propelled anti-tank vehicle: *China Military Vehicles 8*

WZ91 4×4 self-propelled HJ-8 anti-tank missile carrier: *China Military Vehicles 8*

–X–

X chromosome: *Female 1*

Xanadu: *Real Places Steeped in Legend or Mystery 18*

xanthitane: *Minerals 10*

xanthite: *Minerals 10*

xanthoceras: *Shrubs 10*

Xenon: *Elements 11*

xerces blue: *Butterfly 15*

Xilingol: *Horse Breeds 15*

Xinjiang Brown: *Other Cows 15*

xiphoid process: *Bones 12*

xiphos: *Swords One-handed 7*

XM2010 Enhanced: *Sniper Rifle 8*

Xoloitzcuintli: *Dog Breeds 15*

X-ray astronomy: *Astronomy General Terms 11*

x-ray diffraction: *Geological Vocabulary 10*

x-ray fluorescence: *Geological Vocabulary 10*

x-ray glasses: *Spy Gear 5*

X-ray star: *Astronomy General Terms 11*

X-ray vision: *Physical Mutations 22*

X-ray: *Astronomy General Terms 11*

xygalo: *Cheese International Varieties 6*

xylophone: *Percussion Musical Instruments 5*

xylosma: *Shrubs 10*

xylylene dichloride: *Dangerous Chemicals 11*

xynomizithra: *Cheese International Varieties 6*

xynotyro: *Cheese International Varieties 6*

–Y–

Y chromosome: *Male 1*

Y of Pythagoras: *Symbols in Magic and Religion 19*

yab yum: *Symbols in Magic and Religion 19*

yacht club: *Marina 3*

yacht water craft: *Small Watercraft 9*

yacht: *Small Watercraft 9*

yak: *Other Wild Mammals 15; Transportation Animals 9*

yakirai: *Demon 16*

yaksas: *Demon 16*

Yakut: *Horse Breeds 15*

Yakuts: *Human Ethnic Groups 1*

yakuza: *Thief 1*

yam: *Vegetables 6*

Yama *(demigod of death)*: *Indian Pantheon 14*

yamantaka: *Demon 16*

Yanan: *Pigs 15*

Yanbian: *Other Cows 15*

yanmaodao: *Swords One-handed 7*

Yanomami: *Human Ethnic Groups 1*

Yanqi: *Horse Breeds 15*

yantok: *Unusual Edible Fruits 6*

yantra: *Symbols in Magic and Religion 19*

yap: *Mouth 1; Speak 20*

Yaqui: *Native American Peoples 1*

yarara: *General Snake Families 15*

yard decorations: *Christmas 19*

yard scraper: *General Farm Equipment*

yard stick: *Office/School/Writing Supplies 5*

yard: *Boat/Ship Anatomy 9; Church Anatomy 3*

yardang: *Aeolian 10*

yari: *Spears 7*

yarmulke: *Headgear 2*

yarn: *Literary Styles 5; Notions 2*

yarrow: *Garden Perennials 10; Wildflowers 10*

Yasakani no magatama (necklace): *Three Sacred Imperial Relics of Japan 18*

Yata no Kagami (mirror): *Three Sacred Imperial Relics of Japan 18*

yawara: *Bludgeons 7*

yawl: *Small Watercraft 9*

yawning: *Vocal/Speech Quality 1*

yeast: *Staples 6*

yedoma: *Soil General Vocabulary 10*

yee haw: *Expletives 20*

yell: *Loud 20; Sounds 20; Speak 20*

yellow archangel: *Garden Perennials 10*

yellow bass: *Wild Freshwater Fish 15*

yellow bean: *Vegetables 6*

yellow bellied: *Sea Snake 15*

yellow bile: *Four Bodily Humors 19*

yellow birch: *Deciduous Trees 10*

yellow brain fungus: *Fungus Common Names 10*

yellow butt oak: *Deciduous Trees 10*

yellow cedar: *Evergreen Trees 10*

yellow chard: *Vegetables 6*

yellow chestnut oak: *Deciduous Trees 10*

yellow citrine: *Minerals 10*

yellow cockspur: *Weeds 10*

yellow copper: *Minerals 10*

yellow corn: *Vegetables 6*

yellow cosmos: *Weeds 10; Wildflowers 10*

yellow cypress: *Evergreen Trees 10*

yellow delicious: *Apples 6*

yellow dock: *Weeds 10*

yellow dwarf: *Astronomy General Terms 11*

yellow fin: *Wild Saltwater Fish 15*

yellow flag: *Garden Perennials 10*

yellow gold: *Precious Metals 21*

yellow gum: *Deciduous Trees 10*

yellow horned poppy: *Garden Perennials 10*

yellow jack: *Wild Saltwater Fish 15*

yellow jacket: *Wasp 15*

yellow Jessamine: *Poisonous Plants 10*

yellow locust: *Deciduous Trees 10*

yellow mombin: *Unusual Edible Fruits 6*

yellow mud: *Freshwater Turtles 15*

yellow mustard: *Condiments 6*

yellow myrtle: *Deciduous Trees 10*

yellow nutsedge: *Weeds 10*

yellow oak: *Deciduous Trees 10*
yellow ochre: *Yellow 20*
yellow onion: *Vegetables 6*
yellow perch: *Wild Freshwater Fish 15*
yellow pine: *Evergreen Trees 10*
yellow plum: *Deciduous Trees 10*
yellow popcorn: *Snacks 6*
yellow poplar: *Deciduous Trees 10*
yellow sac: *Venomous Arachnids 15*
yellow sapote: *Unusual Edible Fruits 6*
yellow slash pine: *Evergreen Trees 10*
yellow split pea: *Legumes 6*
yellow spruce: *Evergreen Trees 10*
yellow starthistle: *Weeds 10*
yellow storksbill: *Garden Perennials 10*
yellow stripe shad: *Wild Saltwater Fish 15*
yellow supergiant: *Star Types and Relatives 11*
yellow swallowtail: *Butterfly 15*
yellow tail flounder: *Wild Saltwater Fish 15*
yellow tang: *Aquarium Saltwater Fish 15*
yellow tomato: *Vegetables 6*
yellow willow: *Deciduous Trees 10*
yellow: *Bats 15; Cake 6; Cobra 15; Colors 20; Martial Artist Belt Ranks 1; Pears 6*
yellow-bark oak: *Deciduous Trees 10*
yellow-bellied slider: *Freshwater Turtles 15*
yellow-eared: *Bats 15*
yellowed: *Teeth 1; Unattractive 20*
yellowfin tuna: *Wild Saltwater Fish 15*
yellow-footed: *Tortoises 15*
yellow-green: *Green 20*
yellow-lipped: *Bats 15*
yellowroot: *Shrubs 10*
yellowtail damsel: *Aquarium Saltwater Fish 15*
yellowtail: *Moth 15; Wild Saltwater Fish 15*
yellow-throated big: *Bats 15*
yellowwood: *Deciduous Trees 10*
yelp: *Sounds 20; Speak 20*
yerba mate: *Tea 6*
yeti: *Mythical Creatures and Monsters 16*
yett: *Castle Anatomy 3*
yew brush: *Evergreen Trees 10*
yew: *Evergreen Trees 10; Shrubs 10*
yezerha-ra: *Demon 16*
Yggdrasil: *Fictional/Mythological Locations 18*
yield: *General Combat Vocabulary 7*
Yili: *Horse Breeds 15*
Yingdehong: *Tea 6*
yin-yang: *Symbols in Magic and Religion 19*
Ymir: *Moons 11*
yoga pants: *Ladies' Wear 2*
yogi: *Cleric 1*
yogurt: *Other Dairy 6*
yokel: *Common Character Archetypes 21*
Yonaguni: *Horse Breeds 15*
Yorkshire blue and white: *Pigs 15*
Yorkshire Terrier: *Dog Breeds 15*
Yosemite: *Toads 15*
young lady: *Female 1*
young man: *Male 1*
young people suddenly age and die: *Horror Plot Devices 23*
young stellar object: *Star Types and Relatives 11*
young: *Dragon 16*
Young's modulus: *Geological Vocabulary 10*
youngberry: *Unusual Edible Fruits 6*
youngster: *Child 1*
youth: *Beds 4; Child 1*
Yowah nut: *Minerals 10*
yowl: *Speak 20*
yoyo: *Toys 5*
Ytterbium: *Elements 11*
Yttrium: *Elements 11*
yttrocerite: *Minerals 10*
yttrofluorite: *Minerals 10*
yuan-ti: *Beast 16*
yucca: *Shrubs 10*
Yugoslav: *Human Ethnic Groups 1*
Yukon gold potato: *Vegetables 6*
Yukon hold'em: *Poker Card Games 5*
Yukon: *Card Games 5; Solitaire Card Games 5*
Yule log: *Christmas 19*

Yuma: *Bats 15; Native American Peoples 1*

yummy: *Beautiful 20*

Yunnan: *Keelback 15*

yunwi-djunsti: *Demon 16*

Yupik: *Native American Peoples 1*

Yvain: *Knights of the Round Table 18*

Ywain the Bastard: *Knights of the Round Table 18*

Ywain: *Knights of the Round Table 18*

–Z–

Zabaniyah: *Angels of Good 14*

Zachariel: *Angels of Good 14*

Zadkiel: *Angels of Good 14*

Zambo: *Human Ethnic Groups 1*

Zaniskari Pony: *Horse Breeds 15*

zanthoxylum: *Shrubs 10*

Zapotec: *Human Ethnic Groups 1*

zauschneria: *Shrubs 10*

zeal: *General Emotions 20; Love 20*

zebra danio: *Aquarium Freshwater Fish 15*

zebra finch: *Domesticated Pet Birds 15*

zebra jasper: *Minerals 10*

zebra swallowtail: *Butterfly 15*

zebra: *Horses Related 15; Sharks 15*

Zellers bolete: *Fungus Common Names 10*

Zen Texts: *Major Religious Books 14*

zenith: *Astronomy General Terms 11*

zenobia: *Shrubs 10*

zeolite: *Geological Vocabulary 10*

Zephon: *Angels of Good 14*

zephyr: *Wind 10*

zeppelin: *Air Vehicles 9*

zest: *General Emotions 20*

zester: *Kitchen Utensils 5*

Zeus *(weather, leader of the gods)***:** *Greek Pantheon 14*

Zeus's eagle: *Flying Creatures 16*

Zeus's thunderbolts: *Weapons of Legend 18*

Zhemaichu: *Horse Breeds 15*

zia pueblo sun: *Symbols in Magic and Religion 19*

zig zag vine: *Unusual Edible Fruits 6*

zigzag chain: *Embroidery Stitches 2*

zigzag: *Figures Associated with Symbols 19; Sewing Techniques 2*

zinc blende: *Minerals 10*

zinc phosphide: *Dangerous Chemicals 11*

zinc: *Coins and Currency 21*

Zinc: *Elements 11*

zinfandel: *Wine Red 6*

zinnia: *Garden Annuals 10*

zip drive: *Computer Equipment 5*

zipper bag: *Containers and Vessels 5*

zipper: *Notions 2*

zircon: *Cat's Eye Gems 21; Standard Gems 21*

Zirconium: *Elements 11*

zither: *String Musical Instruments*

ziziphus: *Shrubs 10*

Zochipilli (gambling): *Central American Pantheon 14*

Zodiac signs: *Divination and Fortune Telling 19*

zodiac: *Astronomy General Terms 11; Solitaire Card Games 5*

zodiacal light: *Astronomy General Terms 11*

zombie uprising threatens city: *Horror Plot Devices 23*

zombie: *Cocktails 6; Dragon 16; Fantasy Creatures with Symbolic Meaning 19; Monsters and Creatures 22; Undead 16*

zombies rise from Boot Hill: *Western Plot Devices 21*

zone refining: *Chemistry General Vocabulary 11*

zone: *Meteorology General Vocabulary 10*

zoning: *Geography General Vocabulary 10*

zoo: *General Property 3; Man-Made Animal Homes 15*

zoot suit: *Men's Wear 2*

zopf: *Bread General Varieties 6*

Zophiel: *Angels of Good 14*

Zoroastrian Texts: *Major Religious Books 14*

zoso: *Secular Symbols 19*

zounds: *Expletives 20*

zucchetto: *Headgear 2*

zucchini: *Cake 6; Quick Bread 6; Vegetables 6*

Zulfiqar *(sword of Ali)***:** *Weapons of Legend 18*

zultanite: *Minerals 10*

Zuni: *Native American Peoples 1*

zweihänder: *Swords Two-handed 7*

zwieback: *Bread General Varieties 6*

zydeco *(United States)***:** *Ethnic/Folk Dances 13*

zygomatic bone: *Bones 12*